THE EUROPEAN DEFENCE UNION

European Union Law Series

This series brings together major works in the field of European Union Law. It features a diverse range of publications, including comprehensive handbooks designed to teach European Union Law, treaties for legal practitioners and academics, monographs on specialised topics and some of the best doctoral dissertations from across Europe. Additionally, it includes publications detailing conference proceedings on topical issues, as well as commentaries on major judgments and decisions handed down by the Court of Justice of the European Union.

P. Durand and A. Gilbert-d'Halluin (eds.), *Directive (EU) 2022/2464 as regards Corporate Sustainability Reporting (CSRD)*, 2024.

G. Marti (ed.), *European Citizenship through the Lens of EU Values*, 2025.

A. Gridel, *Financial Markets and Instruments in Private International Law*, 2025.

A. Bensoussan, J. Bensoussan and V. Bensoussan-Brulé, *The European AI Act. Summary, Key Points and Article-by-Article Analysis*, 2025.

G. Cavalier, *European R&D Tax Incentives. Contribution to the Emergence of a Concept*, 2025.

P. Pailler, *How to Best Regulate Crypto-Assets? The EU and UAE Perspectives*, 2025.

V. Davio, *EU Fundamental Rights as a Special Source for the European Court of Human Rights*, 2026.

THE EUROPEAN DEFENCE UNION

AN ARTICLE-BY-ARTICLE COMMENTARY

Elsa Bernard, Quentin Loïez
and Stéphane Rodrigues (eds.)

INTERSENTIA
LEFEBVRE GROUP

Intersentia
Lefebvre Belgium SA
Avenue Jean Monnet, 4
1348 Louvain-la-Neuve
Belgium
Email: contact@larcier-intersentia.com

Distribution for the UK, Ireland and
Rest of the World (excl. France, Belgium and Luxembourg)
Ingram Publisher Services UK
1 Deltic Avenue, Rooksley
Milton Keynes MK13 8LD
United Kingdom
Tel: +44 1752 202 301 | Fax: +44 1752 202 331
Email: ipsuk.customercare@ingramcontent.com

Distribution for France and Other Countries (excl. Ireland and the UK)
Interforum Editis
92 avenue de France
75013 Paris
France

Distribution for Belgium and Luxembourg (excl. France, Ireland and the UK)
Larcier-Intersentia
Avenue Jean Monnet, 4
1348 Louvain-la-Neuve
Belgium

The European Defence Union. An Article-by-Article Commentary

ISBN : 978-1-83970-575-5
D/2026/06040/0219
NUR 828

British Library Cataloguing in Publication Data. A catalogue record for this book is available from the British Library

LIST OF CONTRIBUTORS

Frédéric Allemand is a researcher in EU law at the Faculty of Law, Economics and Finance of the University of Luxembourg, where he co-directs the Robert Schuman Initiative – a Jean Monnet Centre of Excellence. He is also Lecturer on EMU law, Public Finances, and European Policies at INALCO, Paris 1 Panthéon-Sorbonne University, SciencesPo Rennes & University of Lille. His research focuses primarily on European economic governance, European public finances, currency, and the European institutional system.

Fabrice Andreone has a PhD in law, is accredited to direct research (French HDR) and has a PhD in legal sciences. He is currently an Adviser/Senior Expert at DG RTD.02 (Science policy, advice and ethics), having previously been Director of the Brussels office of Airbus Helicopter (Eurocopter) and responsible for European affairs in the President's Private Office. His publications focus on European administration and civil service issues, the EU institutions and European defence and R&I policies. He chairs the Association of French Officials of the European Union in Brussels (AFFCE).

Renaud Bellais holds a PhD in economics and has been MBDA's Group Chief Defence Economist since 2023. He is a research associate at ENSTA Bretagne (Brest) and CESICE, Grenoble Alpes University. He is also co-director of the Observatoire de la Défense at the Fondation Jean Jaurès, Paris.

Elsa Bernard is a professor of public law at the University of Lille and at the College of Europe. She is also Lecturer on EU defence at Sciences Po Paris. She is co-director of the European Union Law Master's programme of the University of Lille, and Dean's Assessor for Research at the FSJPS (Faculty of Law, Political Science and Social Sciences). A member of the CRDP (ULR 4487), she held the Jean Monnet Chair on 'Belonging to the EU' (2019–2024). Her research focuses on EU law and in particular on European defence, a subject to which she has devoted several studies. During the production of this book, Elsa Bernard was hosted at the College of Europe (Bruges), where she enjoyed the status of visiting researcher.

Anne-Hélène Bertana is a postdoctoral researcher in public law at the University of Bordeaux, specialising in public international and european law. She is associated to the Centre de recherche et de documentation en droit international et européen (CRDEI) and the Institut de recherche Montesquieu (IRM). Her thesis, defended in 2024, focuses on the evolution of defence cooperation in Europe.

Yves Buchet de Neuilly is a professor of political science at the Université Paris 1 Panthéon-Sorbonne and a member of the Centre Européen de Sociologie et de Science Politique (CESSP). His research focuses mainly on foreign policy decision-making processes, multilateral crisis management instruments and relations between international collective security organisations.

Nicolas Clinchamps is professor of public law at the Université Sorbonne Paris Nord. He is a member of the Institut de droit public Sciences politiques et sociales. His work focuses on European security and defence. His publications include *Paxa Europa. L'Union européenne, espace de paix en sursis ?* (co-edited with Pierre-Yves Monjal, Bruylant, 2025), *Asile et migrations. Quelles solidarités? Quelles responsabilités* (co-edited with

Jean-Jacques Menuret, Mare et Martin, 2023); *Sécurité et environnement* (co-edited with Christel Cournil, Catherine Fabregoule and Geetha Ganapathy-Doré, Bruylant, 2016); *L'autonomie stratégique de l'Union européenne, Perspectives, responsabilité, ambitions et limites de la défense européenne* (co-edited with Pierre-Yves Monjal, Larcier, 2015); and *Parlement européen et droit parlementaire. Essai sur la naissance du droit parlementaire de l'Union européenne* (LGDJ, Bibliothèque constitutionnelle et de science politique, volume 124, 2006).

Élise Daniel has a PhD in public law and is currently a civil servant at the French Ministry of Economy and Finance (Minefi), after spending several years at the European Law Office of the Legal Affairs Directorate of the Ministry of Defence.

Stéphane De La Rosa is professor of public law at the Université Paris-Est Créteil. Holder of a Jean Monnet Chair and director of the MIL (Markets, Institutions, Liberties) research laboratory, his research focuses on contemporary changes in EU economic law, in the areas of public procurement law, competition law, regulated markets, financing instruments and economic and social cohesion. He is the author of numerous articles in these fields and of a cross-disciplinary textbook on 'Droit européen de la commande publique' (Bruylant-Larcier).

Alain De Neve is a research associate at the Centre for Security and Defence Studies (CESD) at the Royal Military Academy (Brussels). His research interests include military technological innovation, nuclear deterrence, the arms industry and aerospace.

Angelo Ferrazzoli is currently a legal analyst and project manager at the European Commission. He has worked in various units of DG R&I, then the Research Executive Agency (REA), on the design and implementation of the Horizon 2020 and Horizon Europe programmes, with a focus on research stakeholders within the European Research Area (ERA) and the issue of researcher mobility. He holds degrees in law, European studies and management, including a Masters in Industrial and Technological Management from Solvay Business School, and is also Deputy Secretary General of AFFCE (Association des françaises et français des institutions communautaires et européennes).

Daniel Fiott is Professor of Political Science at the Centre for Security, Diplomacy and Strategy (CSDS) at the Vrije Universiteit Brussel. He is a non-resident senior fellow at the Real Instituto Elcano in Madrid. His research focuses on European defence industry policy.

Nicolas Gros-Verheyde is a journalist specialising in European and defence issues. A graduate in law and political science from the Université Paris 1 Panthéon-Sorbonne and the IHEDN (Institut des hautes études de la défense nationale), he has worked for over twenty years with European institutions and NATO. Editor-in-chief of *B2 Bruxelles2*, the daily newspaper for geopolitical Europe, he has also been a correspondent for *Ouest-France* and *Sud-Ouest*. He is the author of *La Défense européenne à l'heure de la guerre en Ukraine. Des tabous tombent* (Éditions du Villard, June 2024).

Anne Hamonic is a senior lecturer in public law at the University of Rennes, a member of the Institut de l'Ouest: Droit et Europe (IODE – CNRS UM 6262) and co-director of the Master's degree in European Law at the University of Rennes. Her research focuses on the law of the European Union, in particular its external action, including the CFSP and CSDP. She edited the book *La spécificité de la défense en droit de l'Union européenne* (Presses universitaires de Rennes, April 2025).

Maeve Kieffer has a PhD in public law and is currently a civil servant at the Ministry of Ecological transition, having previously worked for several years at the European Law Office of the Legal Affairs Directorate of the Ministry of Defence.

Fabio Liberti has been a policy advisor at the European Commission since 2021, working for the Directorate-General for Defence Industry and Space (DG DEFIS). He works in the unit responsible for industrial policy in defence. Between 2013 and 2021 he worked at the European Defence Agency, in the Directorate working on industrial issues. Previously, he was Director of Research at the Institut des Relations Internationales et Stratégiques (IRIS) in Paris.

Quentin Loïez has held the position of Legal and Policy Affairs Officer at the European Commission since November 2020. Before joining the Directorate-General for Defence Industry and Space (DG DEFIS), he worked in the Directorate-General for Economic and Financial Affairs and the Directorate-General for Migration and Home Affairs. Quentin Loïez holds a Master's degree in International and European Law from the University of Lille.

Jean-Christophe Martin is Professor of Public Law at the Université Côte d'Azur. He heads the Institute for Peace and Development and holds the UNESCO Chair in 'Peace and Development through Law'. He is a member of the Research Centre on International and European Law (LADIE – UPR 7414) and works mainly on issues relating to the use of force, the maintenance of international peace and security, the European Union's external relations, and the law of the sea.

Anne Millet-Devalle is a Professor of Public Law at the Université Côte d'Azur, where she directed the Research Centre on International and European Law (LADIE UPR 7414) from 2017 to 2024. From 2019 to 2024, she held a Jean Monnet Chair on 'The European Union and Crisis Management', and is also responsible for a Master 2 degree in International Security and a university degree (DU) in International Humanitarian Law. Her research interests include international and European security law, disarmament law, non-proliferation and export controls on arms and dual-use goods, humanitarian law and the law of humanitarian action.

Athanase Popov holds a PhD in EU law. Employed as a European official since November 2010, he is also an associate member of IREDIES and a regular contributor to legal journals in several languages, specialising in nuclear law, procedural and lately also EEA law. In 2024, he was a candidate in the European elections in Luxembourg on a citizens' initiative list. In 2025, he spent a few months at the EFTA Court while on leave on personal grounds from the European Commission and also published his first monograph for Larcier-Bruylant.

Aymeric Potteau is Professor of Public Law at the University of Lille and Dean of the Faculty of Legal, Political and Social Sciences (FSJPS). A member of the CRDP (ULR 4487) and its public law research team, he specialises in general European Union law and, more specifically, European public finance, European human rights law and the external action of sub-state authorities. He is also head of the Master's programme in International and European Law (DIDE) at the University of Lille.

Sabrina Robert is a professor of law at Nantes University. She is a member of the Law and Social Change Research Centre (Laboratoire Droit & Changement Social) and an associate member of IREDIES (Université Paris 1). She specialises in international economic law. She works on the EU's external trade policy and is particularly interested in European foreign investment law. She has published several studies on the framework for screening direct investment in Europe, focusing on the security dimension of this system.

Stéphane Rodrigues is a Senior lecturer and is qualified to direct research (HDR) in public law at the Université Paris 1 Panthéon-Sorbonne. He is a member of the Institut d'études et de recherche en droit international et européen de la Sorbonne (IREDIES) and is director of the Master 2 degree 'Stratégies industrielles et politiques publiques de défense'. He is also Lecturer on EU defence at Sciences Po Paris. His publications focus in particular on the European public services regime (*see* his doctoral thesis on this subject, published in 2000) and, for the past ten years, on the European internal market in defence. In 2018, he co-founded the *Entretiens annuels de la défense européenne* (EDE). He is a member of the editorial board of *Cahiers de droit européen* (Larcier, Brussels). He is also a member of the Brussels Bar and a partner at Lallemand, Legros & Joyn.

Edouard Simon has held the position of Legal and Policy Affairs Officer at the European Commission since 2022 within the Directorate-General for Defence Industry and Space (DG DEFIS). He was previously Research Director at IRIS from 2020 to 2022, specialising in European security and defence issues, as well as industrial and armaments policy. He also headed the Brussels office of the *think tank Confrontations Europe* from 2017 to 2020, and previously spent four years in the legal department of Airbus. Edouard Simon holds a PhD in European Union law from the Université Paris 1 Panthéon-Sorbonne, and an MBA from ESSEC Business School. His thesis, defended in 2017, focuses on the role of EU law in the integration of arms procurement policies.

Catherine Schneider is a qualified law professor (1985), Professor Emeritus at the University of Grenoble-Alpes (2017), Doctor *honoris causa* of the University of Nijni Novgorod (2002), J. Monnet Chair in European Law (1998), coordinator of the J. Monnet Centre of Excellence (CEJM) in Grenoble (1999–2017), Director (2002–2009) and member of the Centre for Studies on International Defence and Security and European Cooperation (CESICE EA-2420) and in charge of the CFSP column in the ADUE since 2012.

Fabien Terpan is a senior lecturer in public law at Sciences Po Grenoble-UGA, a member of CESICE (Centre d'études sur la sécurité internationale et les coopérations européennes) and the holder of a Jean Monnet Chair. His research activities cover the European Union's external action, its defence policy, soft law and the relationship between law and politics within the EU.

Bertrand Warusfel is Professor of Public Law at the University of Paris 8. He is Vice-Chairman of the French Association of Security and Defence Law (AFDSD) and a member of the Paris Bar. He co-edited (with Prof. Sébastien-Yves Laurent) the book *Transformations et réformes de la sécurité et du renseignement en Europe*, PUB, 2016, and published, among others: 'L'entrée de l'Union européenne dans les champs de la défense et de la sécurité' (*Cahiers de la sécurité et de la justice*, 1st semester 2014, nos. 27-28) and 'Conservation des données et sécurité nationale au regard du droit de l'Union européenne' (*Annuaire 2022 du droit de la sécurité et de la défense*, 2022).

FOREWORD: TOWARDS A EUROPEAN DEFENCE UNION

Elsa Bernard
Professor of Public Law at the University of Lille
Jean Monnet Chair
Member of the Rights and Perspectives of Law Research Centre (CRDP, ULR 4487),

Quentin Loïez[1]
Legal and Policy Officer at the European Commission (DG DEFIS)

and

Stéphane Rodrigues
Senior lecturer (HDR) in public law at the Université Paris 1 Panthéon-Sorbonne
Member of the Sorbonne Institute for Research in International and European Law (IREDIES-EA 4536)
Member of the Brussels Bar

On 4 March 2025, Ursula von der Leyen, the President of the European Commission presented an unprecedented initiative – the ReArm Europe plan[2] – having noted that:

> We are living in the most momentous and dangerous of times. I do not need to describe the grave nature of the threats that we face. Or the devastating consequences that we will have to endure if those threats would come to pass. Because the question is no longer whether Europe's security is threatened in a very real way. Or whether

[1] This analysis, which is provided in a personal capacity, reflects the views only of the author, and can in no way be regarded as the official position of the European Commission.

[2] See E. Bernard's commentary on the Preamble in this publication.

> Europe should shoulder more of the responsibility for its own security. In truth, we have long known the answers to those questions. The real question in front of us is whether Europe is prepared to act as decisively as the situation dictates. And whether Europe is ready and able to act with the speed and the ambition that is needed.[3]

This announcement was made more than three years after the beginning of Russia's war of aggression against Ukraine, and a few days after US Vice President J.D. Vance announced in Munich that the threat he worries the most about for Europe 'is not Russia, it's not China, it's not any other external actor', but it is 'the retreat of Europe from some of its most fundamental values, values shared with the United States of America'.[4]

Indeed, the security context of the European Union (EU) deteriorated between the publication of the French version of this book in 2024 and this English version drafted in 2025, not just because of Russia's ongoing threat and rapid move toward a wartime economy, or because the new US administration has 'directly and unambiguously express[ed] that stark strategic realities prevent the United States of America from being primarily focused on the security of Europe'.[5] But the deterioration also follows 'uncertainties stemming from the advent of a geopolitical situation in which the Union has to markedly step up its efforts to ensure its defence autonomously'.[6]

As Andrius Kubilius, the Commissioner for Defence and Space, noted in June 2025, '[w]hile Americans are preparing to move out from Europe, and Russians are growing stronger, we need to start to discuss […] how the true European Defence Union with the responsibility to defend Europe independently, will be created'.[7]

This emerging European Defence Union is examined here in an Article-by-Article Commentary.

---

3 Press statement by President von der Leyen on the defence package, 4 March 2025, https://ec.europa.eu/commission/presscorner/detail/et/statement_25_673.

4 https://securityconference.org/assets/02_Dokumente/01_Publikationen/2025/Selected_Key_Speeches_Vol._II/MSC_Speeches_2025_Vol2_Ansicht_gekürzt.pdf.

5 Opening Remarks by Secretary of Defense Pete Hegseth at Ukraine Defense Contact Group (As Delivered), U.S. Department of Defense > Speech, available at: https://www.defense.gov/News/Speeches/Speech/article/4064113/opening-remarks-by-secretary-of-defense-pete-hegseth-at-ukraine-defense-contact/.

6 Council Regulation (EU) 2025/1106 of 27 May 2025 establishing the Security Action for Europe (SAFE) through the Reinforcement of the European Defence Industry Instrument, [2025] *OJ* L2025/1106, Recital 8.

7 A. Kubilius, Keynote Speech, European Defence and Security Summit, Brussels, 10 June 2025.

The notion of a 'European Defence Union', which neither the European Commission[8] nor the European Parliament[9] hesitate to use, has never been used by the European Council. This is hardly surprising given that the term, as we understand it and as the Commission and Parliament understand it, covers both the traditional defence pillar of the European Union (i.e. the Common Foreign and Security Policy (CFSP) branch, as well as the Common Security and Defence Policy (CSDP)), and, for some years now, its former 'Community' pillar, from which defence originally seemed to be excluded. While the CSDP is the prerogative of the European Council, which, according to the Treaties, is responsible for deciding on the transition from 'the progressive framing of a common defence policy for the Union' to a 'common defence policy',[10] the Member States do not have the same pre-eminence in supranational areas covered by the Treaty on the Functioning of the European Union (TFEU). Here, the Commission, the European Parliament and the Court of Justice, in particular, exercise their prerogatives. It is therefore understandable that Member States are cautious about the idea of a European Defence Union, implying a degree of integration in an area of sovereignty embodied, within the EU, by the highly intergovernmental CSDP.

Thus, the European Defence Union transcends the distinction between the supranational and intergovernmental spheres, and so should be viewed not only from the angle of the Treaty on European Union (TEU), which governs CSDP, but also from the angle of the TFEU as well as the Treaty establishing the European Atomic Energy Community (TEAEC, also known as the Euratom Treaty). Each of these is covered in the three parts of this publication.

Defence 'has as its object to ensure at all times and in all circumstances and against all forms of aggression, the security and integrity of the territory and the life of the population'.[11] A glance at the table of contents here shows that, in a profoundly deteriorating security environment, defence is now being incorporated into ever more numerous and varied areas of European Union law. As reiterated by the European Council in its conclusions of 26 June 2025, the European Union 'must become more sovereign, more responsible for its own defence and better equipped to act and deal autonomously and in a

---

8 See President Jean-Claude Juncker's State of the Union address on 13 September 2017 and President Ursula Von der Leyen's State of the Union address in September 2021.

9 European Parliament resolution of 17 February 2022 on the implementation of the common security and defence policy – annual report 2021 (2021/2183(INI)). More recently, Mrs von der Leyen stated that 'it is time to build a genuine European Defence Union', in the context of the political guidelines for her new term of office (2024-2029): see speech of 18 July 2024 to the European Parliament in Strasbourg, Statement No. 24/3871).

10 See the preamble to the Treaty on European Union (TEU) and Article 42(2) thereof.

11 In the absence of a definition of this concept in the European treaties, we refer to French Ordinance No. 59-147 of 7 January 1959 on the general organisation of defence, as amended by Ordinance No. 2004-1374 of 20 December 2004 in the legislative part of France's Defence Code (authors' translation).

coordinated way with immediate and future challenges and threats, with a 360° approach' (see also conclusions of the European Council of 18 December 2025). Against this background, and although it was not designed for this purpose, the legal framework of the TFEU is therefore conducive to the development of the European Defence Union, and many of its articles now serve as the legal bases for secondary legislation that characterises a form of European integration in this area.

Yet this phenomenon is the source of two methodological difficulties encountered in the design of this article-by-article commentary.

The first of these difficulties consists in the delicate demarcation of the provisions to be commented on, due to the evolving and sometimes vague nature of the contours of the European Defence Union.

For example, when the structure of the book was first discussed, there was no intention of commenting on Article 212 TFEU, which had never been used for European defence. However, that provision was taken as one of the legal bases for the proposal for a European Defence Industry Programme (EDIP), presented by the European Commission in March 2024,[12] and it therefore seemed necessary to reserve a place for it here. The same goes for Article 122 TFEU, which is not commented on in the French version of this publication, but which had to be commented on in the English version, since it serves as the legal basis of the SAFE Regulation, adopted on 27 May 2025.[13]

Other provisions of the Treaties may well prove conducive to consolidating the European Defence Union in the future.

In preparing this publication, various editorial choices had to be made. One was to comment only on binding legal acts, despite the importance of the various 'Strategies' and 'European Action Plans' or other 'roadmaps' in this area, some of which have been adopted in the form of joint communications from the Commission and the High Representative.[14] These are nevertheless often analysed in the context of commentaries on articles of the Treaties or secondary legislation. Another choice has been to focus on acts in which

---

12 Proposal for a Regulation of the European Parliament and of the Council concerning the establishment of the European Defence Industrial Programme and of a framework of measures to ensure the availability and timely supply of defence products, COM/2024/150 final. On 29 December 2025, the Regulation (EU) 2025/2643 of 16 December 2025 establishing the European Defence Industry Programme and a framework of measures to ensure the timely availability and supply of defence products ('EDIP Regulation') has been published (OJ L/2025/2643).

13 Council Regulation (EU) 2025/1106 of 27 May 2025 establishing the Security Action for Europe (SAFE) through the Reinforcement of the European Defence Industry Instrument, [2025] *OJ* L2025/1106.

14 Such as the *Global Strategy* for the CFSP of 2016, the *Strategic Compass* of 2022, the *Space Strategy* of 2023, the *EU Maritime Security Strategy* revised in 2023 and its *Action Plan*, the new *European Defence Industrial Strategy* (EDIS) of 2024 or the most recent *Defence Readiness Roadmap 2030* of October 2025.

defence issues are central rather than marginal, even if it is not always easy to establish limits between the two.[15]

This publication cannot therefore claim to be exhaustive.

The second methodological difficulty concerns the structure of the publication, since, on the one hand, an article of primary law (serving as the basis for a main entry) may serve as the legal basis for several acts of secondary law (this is the case, for example, of Article 173 TFEU). On the other hand, an act of secondary law may have several legal bases (this is the case, for example, of the Regulation establishing the European Defence Fund,[16] the legal bases of which are Articles 173 and 182 TFEU). Here again, choices had to be made for organisational reasons. In principle, when an act of secondary legislation has several legal bases, it is commented on under the article of the Treaty cited first in the citations of this act, which indicate its legal bases (for example, for the European Defence Fund, this is Article 173 TFEU). However, where the first legal basis cited is not substantially the main one, the secondary act is commented on under the entry for another article that also serves as its main legal basis: as, for example, with the ASAP Regulation,[17] which is based on Articles 114 TFEU and 173 TFEU but which falls mainly within the scope of Article 173 TFEU and is therefore commented on under this entry.

This article-by-article approach, including both primary and secondary legislation, is not without its flaws. However, it does have the merit of presenting the European Defence Union through the legal rules that make up the EU legal order. To do this, we have called on academics as well as practitioners specialising in the defence sector, some of whom were directly involved in drafting the acts analysed. Where appropriate, their analyses are

[15] Examples of secondary legislation contributing to the EU's cyber-defence policy include Regulation (EU) 2019/881 on the European Union Agency for Cybersecurity (ENISA) and on cybersecurity certification of information and communication technologies, known as the 'Cybersecurity Regulation', [2019] *OJ* L151/15, and the Joint Communication from the Commission and the High Representative of 10 November 2022 on the EU's cyber-defence policy (document JOIN (2022) 49 final). Similarly, defence issues are interfering in the policy to combat climate change: see the Joint Communication from the Commission and the High Representative of 28 June 2023 entitled 'A new outlook to the climate and security nexus: addressing the impact of climate change and environmental degradation on peace, security and defence' (document JOIN (2023) 19 final), which follows on from the European External Action Service (EEAS) Climate Change and Defence Roadmap of 6 November 2020 (document EEAS(2020)1251).

[16] Regulation (EU) 2021/697 of the European Parliament and of the Council of 29 April 2021 establishing the European Defence Fund and repealing Regulation (EU) 2018/1092, [2021] *OJ* L170/149.

[17] Regulation (EU) 2023/1525 of the European Parliament and of the Council of 20 July 2023 on supporting ammunition production ASAP), [2023] *OJ* L185/7.

accompanied by an academic commentary to combine undeniable technical expertise with the hindsight required for a critical study.[18]

Putting the European Defence Union into perspective in this way invites us to question the scope and limits of European integration in defence matters. How can we reconcile the Union's respect for 'essential State functions, including ensuring the territorial integrity of the State, maintaining law and order and safeguarding national security'[19] with the desire regularly expressed by the European Council[20] and the Council to see the Union 'further increase its defence readiness and enhance its sovereignty through additional efforts [...] in accordance with Member States' competences'?[21]

Through their analyses of EU law, the authors who contributed to this publication have highlighted the obstacles on the road to a European Defence Union, but also the progress made, in a worrying geopolitical context requiring the Member States to do 'more, better, together and European', to quote a well-known leitmotif in European defence. Our sincere thanks go to them.

---

18 This is the case, for example, with Article 173 TFEU, discussed by Daniel Fiott and, from the perspective of the new European Defence Industrial Strategy (EDIS), by Fabio Liberti, who worked on the drafting of this text within the European Commission's DEFIS Directorate-General.

19 Art. 4(2) TEU.

20 See Chapter III of the recent European Council conclusions of 23 October 2025.

21 Council conclusions on EU security and defence, 27 May 2024.

PREFACE

The history of the European Union (EU) is unfolding in an unpredictable international environment that is becoming increasingly dangerous by the day. The future had already been darkened by threats from clearly identified adversaries. Now, a new shadow has been cast over the EU's outlook: the sudden and brutal confirmation – long anticipated and feared – that the Atlantic Alliance no longer truly binds anyone, apart from those who still claim its protection.

Within a year of taking office in January 2025, the Trump II administration has tilted the axes of global geopolitics and left Europe alone to face its destiny. Confronted with a Russian military threat and the risk of economic subordination driven by the power politics now openly embraced by both China and the United States, the European Union is not yet on the brink of the abyss. It does, however, have its back against the wall.

In this context, the notion of a 'European Defence Union' takes on its full meaning. The European Union faces a historic choice. It can raise itself to the status of an autonomous power, capable of existing and asserting itself within the balance of power, in the name of values that are now distinctly its own. Or it can resign itself to losing control of its future, as the 'real' sovereignty of the nation-states that compose it dissolves into the de facto submission to external empires.

This is no longer merely a perception confined to the socio-economic sphere or even to the realm of hybrid confrontation: from Greenland and Denmark to the Baltic States and Poland, fears of direct or indirect infringements on European territorial sovereignty are now well founded.

A European Defence Union is a project that would offer Member States the opportunity to move forward together. It would allow them to assert collective military power, potentially emancipating them from the Atlantic Alliance, by creating a form of collective – but also national – sovereignty, which is currently slipping away. By further integrating their 'national defence' policies, the Union could draw on a considerable market, enabling the necessary shift in scale to establish a more competitive defence industry that is economically more efficient and capable of reclaiming markets that have largely been lost to third-country industries. This transformation is nevertheless still hindered by a dual fragmentation of supply and demand, the legacies of industrial strategies that were historically centred on nation-states.

Yet creating a European Defence Union presupposes a clear understanding of what the idea actually encompasses, the dynamics that drive it, the obstacles it faces, and above all, the means of overcoming them.

While the political nature of these obstacles has already been widely analysed, particularly since the outbreak of the war in Ukraine, the same cannot be said of the legal obstacles. Yet the European Union is a legal order founded upon treaties, of which the Member States are the authors and the 'masters', to use the established expression.[1] These treaties confer competences on European institutions, which are entrusted with adopting secondary legislation. Both the treaties and these acts of secondary law warrant close attention. The former determine the scope of the Union's powers to act in the field of defence, and therefore also define their limits. The latter are increasingly extending into the domain of defence through policies and instruments that were not originally designed for that purpose: industrial policy, certainly, but also research, transport, competition and, more broadly, the internal market. No examination of a European Defence Union can therefore do without a thorough legal analysis. This is indispensable, though admittedly complex, owing to its technical nature and novelty.

The interest and merit of this innovative publication lie precisely here: to engage directly with such a legal approach. It enables the reader to assess the steps already taken by the EU, to understand the acts adopted and the instruments developed which, in practice, are bringing us closer to a European Defence Union.

* * *

One of the great paradoxes of the European Union is that its most operational concepts and mechanisms are often also the least precisely defined, particularly with regard to their ultimate purpose or final form. Thus, Article 1 of the Treaty on European Union (TEU) describes the Union as 'the process of creating an ever-closer union among the peoples of Europe', while carefully refraining from specifying any definitive point of culmination. The same holds true for the many processes of 'integration', which were meant to contribute to the realisation of this Union. Today, it would be difficult indeed to define the ultimate endpoint of the 'internal market', as the question of whether it does – or does not – tend toward a 'single market' remains the subject of intense debate.

Defence is no exception, as Article 42(2) of the TEU provides that the Common Security and Defence Policy (CSDP) encompasses the 'gradual development' of a common defence policy for the Union. Yet the authors of the Treaty appear to have succumbed to the temptation of envisaging a

[1] According to the expression used by the German Federal Constitutional Court in its so-called Maastricht judgment (BVerfG, decision of 12 October 1993, 2 BvR 2134/92 and 2 BvR 2159/92).

'fully realised' form of a European Defence Union, stating that this gradual evolution 'will lead to a common defence, when the European Council, acting unanimously, so decides'.

Despite the Treaty's determination to bring it to fruition, the ultimate form of a European Defence Union remains open. Paradoxically, this is also its strength. It remains a horizon that recedes as one approaches it, while simultaneously generating a powerful and irreversible dynamic. Although the distance to be covered may still seem great, the progress already made is considerable. In today's geopolitical turbulence, this horizon offers a reference point for the peoples of Europe in their pursuit of security, even if the relevance of a European Defence Union is as intuitive as its realisation remains hypothetical.

It is hardly surprising that this concept is the cause of tension and apparent contradictions. For it is, in effect, a kind of oxymoron – a union of opposites. How, indeed, can one conceive of 'defence readiness' as a genuinely European objective when defence has always embodied the 'ultimate' form of sovereign power? Since the drafters of the Treaties could not envision the Union's purpose as a dead end, they have effectively invited us to transcend this contradiction by adopting a new paradigm. But how?

First, it should be noted that at no point did the drafters of the Treaties contemplate what might, in theory, seem self-evident: that the European Union should also function as a military alliance. European integration took place in the shadow of NATO and under an American umbrella, for a variety of reasons. Yet the self-evidence of the past seventy years now poses two problems.

First, *the Russian aggression in Ukraine has reminded us that a high intensity 'conventional' conflict is, above all, a war of attrition, whose outcome is determined on industrial and economic grounds.* While NATO, as a military alliance, is poorly equipped to organise an economy sufficiently prepared for war to serve as a credible deterrent, the European Union, by contrast, is relatively well positioned, thanks to its economic, regulatory and financial capacity. Pooling resources and optimising them at the Union level could enable each Member State to defend itself more effectively, and to defend the EU as a geographical and political bloc that is now indivisible. This is a shared asset that has become vital.

Secondly, *the credibility of NATO's European security guarantee is now seriously eroded*, as the alliance's military power rests overwhelmingly on the United States. Europe must therefore urgently rethink the governance of its defence to ensure its effectiveness in the event of American disengagement. It must devise or reinforce mechanisms of solidarity and mutual assistance among Member States, both within NATO's European pillar and beyond the alliance. At the same time, the Union must substantially strengthen its defence industrial base to be commensurate with its security requirements.

After a long period of modest progress – particularly in diplomacy and the CSDP – driven primarily by a concern for external projection in an expeditionary mode, a sharp acceleration occurred on the industrial front from 2015 onwards, prompted by the invasion of Crimea, Brexit and Donald Trump's first election. In early 2022, the Strategic Compass confirmed a shift in the CSDP, placing greater emphasis on investment in defensive capabilities to deter aggression. The European Defence Fund (EDF), adopted in 2021, marked a major turning point by mobilising the European budget for the first time to support a transnational, cooperative defence R&D effort of €7 billion.

Another pivotal moment was, of course, Russia's brutal invasion of Ukraine in February 2022. Within days, the European Peace Facility (EPF) had been transformed into a major instrument of military support for Ukraine.[2] The reaction was equally quick in the industrial sphere. Within a few months, the Commission proposed emergency programmes to establish new frameworks for intervention, building on the stark assessment set out in its Joint Communication on the Defence Investment Gaps Analysis and Way Forward, published just weeks after the attack.

The European Defence Industry Reinforcement through Common Procurement Act (EDIRPA) has provided Member States with financial incentives for joint acquisitions, transforming €310 million of European investment into over €11 billion for urgently needed equipment, ranging from 155 mm shells to armoured vehicles and missiles. Meanwhile, the Act in Support of Ammunition Production (ASAP), proposed and adopted with unprecedented speed, mobilised €500 million from the EU budget to generate €1.35 billion in investment in production facilities, quadrupling ammunition output within the Union in just 18 months.

This surge marked the beginning of a paradigm shift. In 2025, it was reflected first in the adoption of the Security Action for Europe (SAFE) instrument, which provided €150 billion in loans to Member States (guaranteed by the EU budget) to support the joint acquisition of capabilities required by the 'Defence Readiness 2030' objective. In the same year, the European Defence Industry Programme (EDIP) expanded the range of incentives available for European defence industrial cooperation, including with Ukraine. Finally, in early 2026, the European Commission proposed a new instrument for substantial support to Ukraine, including in terms of capabilities, through the Ukraine Support Loan.

The European Defence Union is therefore underway in practical terms, if not by design, then at least by necessity. Yet it still faces three major obstacles, spanning both the political and economic spheres.

---

2 At the end of 2025, the EU had provided approximately €170 billion of support to Ukraine, including more than €60 billion in specific support for its war effort.

First, *on the political front, decision-making mechanisms and the principles that guide them remain essentially national.* The absence of a common vision and centralised decision-making capacity confines European countries to the role of spectators in international affairs, as decisions are fundamentally national and anchored in the sacrosanct principle of unanimity that governs the intergovernmental framework. While the Union's adversaries aim at its disintegration, Europeans have yet to fully acknowledge the reality of their interdependence. Even the most Eurosceptic should concede that the military aggression of a single Member State would have devastating consequences for all 26 others, and that a weak response would undermine the Union's ability to shape its own destiny. This deficiency prevents the EU from equipping itself with the resolve, tools and procedures necessary to act decisively and swiftly in defence of its interests, thereby ensuring both its credibility and resilience.

Secondly, *the decision-making and industrial fragmentation of the 27-member bloc limits its effectiveness in addressing Europe's capability gaps.* The Union remains economically inefficient, being too often a patchwork of narrowly national markets, whose interdependence is frequently overlooked as value chains extend beyond borders without sufficient attention to their overall resilience. Lacking visibility on limited national orders that often disregard interoperability, Europe's current defence industries prioritise large export orders at the expense of Europe's defence, in order to recoup investments. Moreover, these interdependencies render the industrial base vulnerable to any significant shock within the internal market. It was only in 2025, and with some reluctance, that the EU finally established, through EDIP, a system for monitoring value chains and supporting the security of supply.

By failing to effectively integrate their defence markets, Member States have denied their industries the efficiency gains that could reinforce the EU's geopolitical weight. Intra-EU trade in defence products remains constrained and is growing more slowly than defence trade with third countries, perpetuating worrying capability dependencies.

Finally, a third obstacle combines the first two: *the inability of the EU's intergovernmental and Community pillars to communicate effectively and thereby give real shape to a European Defence Union.* It is as if these two components were irreconcilable, undermining any effort to align European power postures with the reality of industrial capacity. To date, it remains impossible to convene the High Representative, the EEAS, the Member States, the EDA, and the Commission to identify the 'super-priorities' on which the EU budget should be decisively focused, from among the Member States' common capabilities. The persistence of national visions – each shielding its own priorities from marginalisation, even if secondary – continues to place narrow national interests above the common good, effectively guaranteeing inaction.

* * *

However, the pressure of events and the rapid, massive deterioration of the security environment are opening pathways that must be seized to overcome these obstacles.

First, it is urgent *to make transnational cooperation the norm in defence, both among Member States and among industry actors.* This cooperation must be conceived not only at the European level but also in diplomatic and operational terms. Only an effective industrial organisation at Union level, combined with the sustained pooling of substantial investments, can bridge the remaining capability gaps.

The already tangible results of the European Defence Fund (EDF) illustrate this dynamic: by the end of 2027, the development of around forty prototypes should have been initiated or completed – in a remarkable continuity of effort – with a view to their acquisition by the armed forces of the Member States. Even more decisive, however, are the secondary effects generated by this process.

On the one hand, by working with the Commission on the Fund's programming, Member States commit to agreeing on collective priorities beyond the unanimity requirement. On the other hand, the industry receives subsidies only through transnational partnerships, opening opportunities across borders. Finally, the short, non-negotiable deadlines create a binding requirement to deliver results. This is the major innovation and a true turning point.

Consequently, the EDF not only promotes the maturation of new technologies and the development of new products or systems, free from ITAR-type restrictions and intended for joint acquisition but also fosters the emergence of a shared culture of European cooperation that, gradually, is driving a paradigm shift.

Secondly, it is necessary *to devise more effective collective decision-making mechanisms, grounded in the security interdependence of Member States, and to enshrine European solidarity as a cardinal principle of the Union.* When asserted, this constitutes the most effective deterrent. European solidarity with Ukraine has, to date, been remarkable, with few exceptions. These exceptions have compelled the EU to work around the principle of unanimity, in a sometimes-creative process. Indeed, the principle of unanimity is now geopolitically untenable, promoting a shift toward qualified majority voting that still needs to be embedded in new decision-making mechanisms.

Finally, the adoption of a security-of-supply regime under EDIP opens the way to *true collective economic governance of defence preparedness.* European monitoring of value chains, combined with, where necessary, the use of priority-rated orders, embodies the emergence of industrial European solidarity for defence purposes. The same applies to the recent major initiative in *military mobility*, an essential condition for European operational credibility. A package of measures is expected to be adopted by the co-legislators by the end of 2026.

The Union's ability to mobilise forces and equipment rapidly will provide a concrete test of Europeans' capacity to translate political commitments into effective capabilities.

* * *

Ultimately, the realisation of the European Defence Union could demonstrate that the apparent weaknesses of geopolitical and economic interdependence can be transformed into strengths, provided that a process of hybridisation between the two ecosystems – the CSDP and the policies conducted under the TFEU – is undertaken without hesitation. Even under the current Treaties, it is urgently necessary to establish, first, a clear link between the defence of the Union as a bloc and that of its 27 Member States. Second, the demands of European security must be immediately translated into the economic and industrial decisions they require, with the support of the European budget.

The concept of a European Defence Union, although somewhat precarious, straddling two treaties and two modes of governance, is therefore fully operational, insofar as the industrial and economic dimensions of the new challenges are drawn into the defence domain within the material scope of the TFEU. The concept can generate a powerful leverage effect. Resolving the tension between these two poles requires a twofold transcendence: a 'Union', certainly, but *sui generis*, one that cannot be reduced to being a mere legal-economic union governed by technical rules; and a 'defence' European Union that dispels the illusion of being confined to the political-military sphere, now encompassing the full spectrum of activities covered by the TFEU, in the industrial, economic, and societal fields.

It is precisely this 'intersectionality' of the concept that gives it full relevance today, while simultaneously revealing its incompleteness. It focuses attention on the need to invent new governance, that spans political decision-making and industrial and economic action. The aim is indeed to build a solid bridge between the two treaties. By consulting this publication, readers will find not only the keys to understanding what is currently at stake, but also the conceptual and legal tools to think independently about what the future of European defence could and should be.

François Arbault[3]
Director Defence Industrial Programmes
at the European Commission (DG DEFIS)

[3] This analysis, which is provided in a personal capacity, reflects the views only of the author, and can in no way be regarded as the official position of the European Commission.

LIST OF ABBREVIATIONS

AFET	Committee on Foreign Affairs of the European Parliament
AG	Advocate General
ASAP	Act in Support of Ammunition Production
BEPGs	Broad economic policy guidelines
CapTechs	Capability and Technology Groups
CARD	Coordinated Annual Review of Defence
CCP	Common Commercial Policy
CDP	Capability Development Plan
CE	Common Era (in place of AD, Anno Domini)
CEF	Connecting Europe Facility
CETA	Comprehensive Economic and Trade Agreement
CFIUS	Committee on Foreign Investment in the US
CFREU	Charter of Fundamental Rights of the European Union
CivOpsHQ	Civilian Operations Headquarters
CFSP	Common Foreign and Security Policy
CJEU	Court of Justice of the European Union
CJTF	Combined Joint Task Force
CMC	Crisis Management Concept
CMO	Crisis Management Operation
CMP	Coordinated Maritime Presences
COARM	Conventional Arms Export Subgroup of the EU Working Party on Non-Proliferation and Arms Exports
CONOPS	Concept of Operations
COREPER	Committee of Permanent Representatives
COREU	*CORespondance EUropéenne*
CPCC	Civilian Planning and Conduct Capability
CPPNM	Convention on the Physical Protection of Nuclear Material
CRT	Civilian Response Teams

CPME	Union Civil Protection Mechanism
CSDP	Common Security and Defence Policy
DEF	Defence Equity Facility
DG DEFIS	Directorate-General for Defence Industry and Space (European Commission)
DGA	Directorate-General for Armaments
DIANA	Defence Innovation Accelerator for the North Atlantic
DPO	Department of Peacekeeping Operations
DSACEUR	Deputy Supreme Allied Commander Europe
DTD or (Defence) Transfer Directive	Directive 2009/43/EC simplifying terms and conditions of transfers of defence-related products within the Community
DUI	Dual-Use Item
EAA	Export Administration Act
EAEC	European Atomic Energy Community or Euratom Community
EAGGF	European Agricultural Guidance and Guarantee Fund
EAR	Export Administration Regulations
EASA	European Aviation Safety Agency
ECN	European Competition Network
ECRA	Export Control Reform Act
ECSC	European Coal and Steel Community
ECtHR	European Court of Human Rights
EDA	European Defence Agency
EDC	European Defence Community
EDF	European Defence Fund
EDIDP	European Defence Industrial Development Programme
EDIP	European Defence Industry Programme
EDIRPA	European Defence Industry Reinforcement Through Common Procurement Act
EDIS	European Defence Industrial Strategy
EDTIB	European Defence Technological and Industrial Base
EEA	European Economic Area
EEAS	European External Action Service
EEC	European Economic Community

EEC Treaty	Treaty establishing the European Economic Community
ERA	European Research Area
EFSI	European Fund for Strategic Investments
EFTA	European Free Trade Association
EGF	European Globalisation Adjustment Fund for Displaced Workers
EIB	European Investment Bank
EICACS	European Initiative for Collaborative Air Combat Standardisation
EIF	European Investment Fund
ELDO	European Launcher Development Organisation
EMU	Economic and Monetary Union
EPC	European political cooperation
EPF	European Peace Facility
ERCC	Emergency Response Coordination Centre
ERDF	European Regional Development Fund
ERIC	European Research Infrastructure Consortium
ESA	European Space Agency
ESDC	European Security and Defence College
ESDI	European Security and Defence Identity
ESDP	European Security and Defence Policy
ESF	European Social Fund
ESRO	European Space Research Organisation
ESS	European Security Strategy
EU	European Union
EU INTCEN	EU Intelligence and Situation Centre
Eu-LISA	European Agency for the Operational Management of Large-scale IT Systems
EU SOFA	EU Status of Forces Agreement
EUAM	EU Assistance Mission or EU Advisory Mission
EUAVSEC	European Union Aviation Security Mission
EUBAM	EU Border Assistance Mission
EUBG	European Battlegroup
EUCAP	European Capacity Building Mission
EUCST	European Union Civil Service Tribunal

EUDIS	EU Defence Innovation Scheme
EUFOR	EU Forces
EUGS	EU Global Strategy
EUISS	European Union Institute for Security Studies
EUJUST LEX	European Union Integrated Rule of Law Mission
EULEX	EU Rule of Law Mission
EUMAM	EU Military Assistance Mission OR EU Military Advisory Mission
EUMC	European Union Military Committee
EUMM	EU Monitoring Mission
EUMPM	EU Military Partnership Mission
EUMS	European Union Military Staff
EUNAVFOR	EU Naval Force
EUPAT	EU Police Advisory Team Mission
EUPM	EU Partnership Mission
EUPM	European Union Police Mission
EUPOL	EU Police Mission
Eurocorps	European Rapid Reaction Corps
Eurogendfor	European Gendarmerie Force
EUSDI	EU Security and Defence Initiative in support of West African countries in the Gulf of Guinea
EUSEC	EU Security Sector Reform Mission
EUSPA	European Union Agency for the Space Programme
EUSR	EU Special Representative
EUSTAMS	EU Stabilisation Action in Mopti and Ségou
EUTM	EU Training Mission
FAST	Fund to Accelerate Defence Supply Chains Transformation
FMS	Foreign Military Sales
FDI	Foreign Direct Investment
FPRD	Framework Programme for Research and Development
FPRTD	Framework Programmes for Research and Technological Development
FRS	Foundation for Strategic Research
FTC	Fixed-term Contract
GBER	General Block Exemption Regulation

GDPR	General Data Protection Regulation
GOVSATCOM	Governmental Satellite Communications
GPA	Agreement on Government Procurement
HCOC	Hague Code of Conduct against Ballistic Missile Proliferation
HEDI	Hub for EU Defence Innovation
HR/VP	EU High Representative of the Union for Foreign Affairs and Security Policy/Vice- President for the European Commission
Hybrid CoE	European Centre of Excellence for Countering Hybrid Threats
IAEA	International Atomic Energy Agency
IHL	International Humanitarian Law
IPCR	Integrated Political Crisis Response
ISTAR	Intelligence, Surveillance, Target Acquisition And Recognition
ITRE	Committee on Industry, Research and Energy (European Parliament)
JSCC	Joint Support Coordination Cell
JSSAG	Joint Space Strategy Advisory Group
KEDO	Korean Peninsula Energy Development Organisation
KSA	Key Strategic Activities
LOI	Letter of Intent
MFF	Multiannual Financial Framework
MIPS	Maintenance of International Peace and Security
MPCC	Military Planning and Conduct Capability
MPSO	Military Peace Support Operation
MTCR	Missile Technology Control Regime
NATO	North Atlantic Treaty Organisation
NCI Agency	NATO Communications and Information Agency
NEA	Nuclear Energy Agency
NIF	NATO Innovation Fund
NPT	Treaty on the Non-Proliferation of Nuclear Weapons
NRF	NATO Response Force
NSG	Nuclear Suppliers Group
NSO	NATO Standardisation Office

NSPA	NATO Support and Procurement Agency
NTM-A	NATO Training Mission-Afghanistan
OCCAR	Organisation for Joint Armament Cooperation
OECD	Organisation for Economic Co-operation and Development
OHQ	Operational Headquarters
OMC	Open Method of Coordination
OPLAN	Operation Plan
PADR	Preparatory Action for Defence Research
PESCO	Permanent Structured Cooperation
POCO	Political Committee
PPP	Public-Private Partnership
PSC	Political and Security Committee
R&D	Research and Development
RDC	Rapid Deployment Capacity
RoE	Rules of Engagement
RTC	Research Tax Credit
SAFE	Security Action for Europe
SatCen	European Union Satellite Centre
SBA	Single Basic Act
SEAP	Structure for European Armaments Programmes
SEDE	Subcommittee on Security and Defence of the European Parliament
SESI	Strategic European Security Initiative
SGEI	Services of General Economic Interest
SHAPE	Supreme Headquarters Allied Powers Europe
SIAé	*Service industriel de l'aéronautique*/Aeronautic industrial service
SMA	*Service militaire adapté*/Adapted military service
SMEs	Small and Medium-Sized Enterprises
SNA	*Service de navigation aérienne*/Air Navigation Service
SOFA	Status of Force Agreement
SOMA	Status of Mission Agreement
SSA	Space Situational Awareness
STEP	Strategic Technologies for Europe Platform

STM	Space Traffic Management
SURE	Support to mitigate Unemployment Risks in an Emergency
TEAEC/Euratom Treaty	Treaty on the European Atomic Energy Community
TEC	Treaty Establishing the European Community
TECE	Treaty Establishing a Constitution for Europe
TEU	Treaty on European Union
TFEU	Treaty on the Functioning of the European Union
UN	United Nations
WEU	Western European Union
WMD	Weapons of Mass Destruction
WTO	World Trade Organization
WU	Western Union

ACKNOWLEDGEMENTS

The co-editors of this publication would like to thank Ms Moya Jones and Mr Nicholas Sowels for translating, post-editing and formatting this updated English version of the French edition entitled *L'Union européenne de la défense. Commentaire article par article*, published by Larcier-Intersentia in November 2024. They are also grateful to Léa Hesdin and Sébastien Pechberty for their contributions.

Finally, their thanks go to GIS Euro-Lab, the *Centre de recherche Droits et Perspectives du droit* (CRDP – University of Lille), and the *Institut de recherche en droit international et européen de la Sorbonne* (IREDIES – Paris 1 Panthéon-Sorbonne University), without which this publication would not have been possible.

Funding and support for the R-CDP-24-006-DePERU project were provided by the France-2030 programme, funded by France's central government, and the Initiative of Excellence of the University of Lille.

EURO-Lab
GIS | Groupement d'intérêt scientifique

CRDP
Centre de Recherche Droits et Perspectives du Droit
ULR n°4487

Université de Lille

PANTHÉON SORBONNE
UNIVERSITÉ PARIS 1
INSTITUT DE RECHERCHE EN DROIT INTERNATIONAL ET EUROPÉEN DE LA SORBONNE EA 4536

PANTHÉON SORBONNE
UNIVERSITÉ PARIS 1
ÉCOLE DE DROIT DE LA SORBONNE

Cross Disciplinary Projects Lille

Elsa BERNARD Quentin LOÏEZ Stéphane RODRIGUES

TABLE OF CONTENTS

> **Editor's note:** derivative acts are in principle commented on under the first article of the Treaty set out in the citations as the legal basis for the act in question, except in the rare cases where this first legal basis is not the main one in terms of substance.

PART I

THE TREATY ON EUROPEAN UNION (TEU)

PART III

NUCLEAR LAW WITHIN THE SCOPE OF THE COMMON SECURITY AND DEFENCE POLICY

PART I

The Treaty on European Union (TEU)

PREAMBLE TO THE TREATY ON EUROPEAN UNION: PARAGRAPH 11

Elsa BERNARD
Professor of Public Law at the University of Lille
Jean Monnet Chair
Member of the Rights and Perspectives of Law Research Centre (CRDP, ULR 4487)

Preamble to the Treaty on European Union, paragraph 11

The Heads of State of the Member States of the European Union, [...]

Resolved to implement a common foreign and security policy including the progressive framing of a common defence policy, which might lead to a common defence in accordance with the provisions of Article 42, thereby reinforcing the European identity and its independence in order to promote peace, security and progress in Europe and in the world, [...]

In view of the further steps to be taken to advance European integration;

Have decided to establish a European Union [...]

The preamble to the Treaty on European Union (TEU) sets out the inspiration, desires, resolutions and objectives of the Member States – the authors of the Treaties – by formulating considerations which go far beyond the scope of the law and appear to fall more within the scope of politics, philosophy, psychology or even incantation. All this is drafted in often imprecise terms, as is perfectly illustrated by the paragraph under comment here. It declares that Member States are 'resolved to implement a common foreign and security policy including the progressive framing of a common defence policy'. This 'might' (conditional, therefore) lead to a 'common defence', with great advantages, since it would reinforce nothing less than 'the European identity and its independence in order to promote peace, security and progress in Europe and in the world'.

Although the preamble does not have the legal scope of the Articles of the Treaty, such as, for example, Article 42 TEU, to which the paragraph on European defence expressly refers, its value is not merely declaratory, since it may be taken into account by the courts when interpreting EU law, in accordance with the teleological method of interpretation.[1] It is, however, doubtful whether the wording commented on here will one day be used for this purpose, first of all because of the immunity from jurisdiction which applies largely to the Common Security and Defence Policy (CSDP);[2] second, because the wording in question is essentially reproduced – with more detail – in Article 42 (1) and (2) TEU; and finally, because its terms are particularly abstruse.

From the outset of the TEU, its preamble referred to European defence. This is not surprising in so far as the European Union established by the Maastricht Treaty in 1992 included a pillar dedicated to a Common Foreign and Security Policy (CFSP), the original version stating that it included the definition of 'the eventual framing' of a common defence policy, which 'might in time lead' to a common defence, 'thereby reinforcing the European identity and its independence in order to promote peace, security and progress in Europe and in the world'.[3] Thus, with the institution of the European Union in the early 1990s, the then twelve Member States decided to define a common defence policy[4] and, with a view to advancing European integration, to explore the possibility of a 'common defence'. This step was considered to be 'with the single currency, the most striking testimony of the qualitative leap that the Maastricht Treaty can represent'.[5] Indeed, until then, and since the failure of the European Defence Community (EDC) in 1954, just the idea of European integration in defence seemed to be taboo: the defence of Europe, which was excluded from Community construction, was a matter for the North Atlantic Treaty Organisation (NATO), or to a lesser extent, for the Western European Union (WEU), which succeeded the Western Union (WU).

From the WU to the WEU

A brief historical reminder is needed in order to explain both the context in which the paragraph under comment was adopted and its convoluted

---

1 See, for example, the judgment of the Court of Justice (Full Court) of 10 December 2018, Case C-621/18, *Wightman* and Others, ECLI:EU:C:2018:999, paras. 61 and 62.

2 See the commentaries by N. Gros-Verheyde and C. Schneider in this publication.

3 The words 'eventual framing' and 'in time', which were also found in Article J.4 (1) TEU, were deleted by the Treaty of Amsterdam (1997), both in the preamble and in the new Article 17 TEU (formerly Article J.4 TEU). Since the Amsterdam revision, the formula has remained the same.

4 In the body of the Treaty, that policy was then expressly referred to as the 'European Security and Defence Policy' (ESDP). It became the Common Security and Defence Policy (CSDP) with the Lisbon Treaty (2007).

5 E. Zoller, in V. Constantinesco, R. Kovar and D. Simon (dir.), *Traité sur l'Union européenne – Commentaire article par article*, Paris, Economica, 1995, p. 800; Y. Gautier and D. Simon, 'Maastricht: progrès quantitatifs ou sauts qualitatifs', *Europe*, January 1992, pp. 1–5, [author's translation].

wording. To this end, it is necessary to go back to the establishment of the 'Western Union' (WU) by the five States which signed the Treaty of Brussels on 17 March 1948, namely the United Kingdom, France and the three Benelux countries (Belgium, the Netherlands and Luxembourg). Designed primarily to counter the expansionist tendencies of the Soviet Union,[6] the WU imposed an obligation on its members to provide automatic military assistance.[7] It was the first form of military integration after the Second World War, with *ad hoc* multilateral military structures, namely a Permanent Military Committee with its own Military Staff[8] and an Inter-allied Commanders-in-Chief Committee composed of the five Member States. The latter retained control over pre-identified forces which had to be made available to the organisation on request.[9]

One year later, on 4 April 1949, the WU Member States signed the North Atlantic Treaty with the United States and Canada, but also with Denmark, Iceland, Italy, Norway and Portugal, leading to the creation of NATO. However, as early as 1951, the military organisation carried out under the Brussels Treaty was integrated into NATO, which was already indicative of Europe's renunciation of its own military structures in favour of the Atlantic Alliance. It was only in October 1954, after this absorption, that the WU Member States signed the Protocol amending and supplementing the 1948 Treaty of Brussels with Italy and the Federal Republic of Germany (FRG). The so-called Paris Agreements allowed the Federal Republic of Germany and Italy to integrate a new international organisation replacing the WU: the Western European Union (WEU).[10] The North Atlantic Council then 'agreed with the terms of the Agreement on Forces of the Western European Union', while deciding, on the eve of the signing of the Paris Agreements, that 'all forces of member nations stationed in the area of the Allied Command, Europe, shall be placed under the authority of the Supreme Allied Commander, Europe, or other appropriate

---

6 The negotiations of that treaty were ongoing at the time of the 'Prague coup' in February 1948. This contributed to a substantial change in the terms of the obligation of mutual assistance which, in the Dunkirk Treaty, concluded one year earlier by the United Kingdom and France, was limited to the event that one of the parties was again engaged in a conflict with Germany (Article 3 of the Dunkirk Treaty of 4 March 1947).

7 Article 4 of the Treaty of Brussels states that 'If any of the High Contracting Parties should be the object of an armed attack in Europe, the other High Contracting Parties will, in accordance with the provisions of Article 51 of the Charter of the United Nations, afford the Party so attacked all the military and other aid and assistance in their power'.

8 It is made up of three major commands for each armed service: land, sea and air.

9 These were nine divisions, including four British, four French and one Belgian.

10 As a result, Germany's occupation status was terminated. However, its rearmament was subject to limitations relating to weapons of mass destruction (atomic, chemical and bacteriological) and certain conventional weapons, the list of which could be revised by a two-thirds majority by the WEU Council. These limitations would be abolished by the WEU Council in 1984.

NATO Command and under the direction of the NATO military authorities'.[11] The WEU's dependence on NATO also stemmed from the new version of the Brussels Treaty, which recognised 'the undesirability of duplicating the military staffs of NATO' and stated that the Council and the Arms Control Agency,[12] two WEU bodies, 'will rely on the appropriate military authorities of NATO for information and advice on military matters'.[13]

From the 1950s, European defence was therefore conceived as a prerogative of the Atlantic Alliance, the WEU being relegated, until the 1980s, to a forum for consultation and cooperation for the reconstruction of the European economy, arms control and the resolution of certain specific problems such as that of Saarland.[14]

Failure of the EDC

In the meantime, Community construction had started. The Treaty of Paris established the European Coal and Steel Community (ECSC), and was signed by France, Germany, Italy, Belgium, the Netherlands and Luxembourg in April 1951. It was shortly followed by the drafting, on a French proposal, of a treaty to extend the ECSC's experience to the field of defence. The idea dated back to 1950, when Jean Monnet and his staff designed a plan for a European Defence Community (EDC). Proposed by the President of the French Council of Ministers, René Pleven, in October 1950, the plan envisaged the creation of a European army involving Germany, which would thus be rearmed without rebuilding a national army. According to Robert Schuman, this was part of the construction of 'a whole and complete Europe'.[15]

The French Government's plan for a European Defence Community which was studied at the Paris Conference on 15 February 1951 by the future ECSC

11 '[W]ith the exception of those forces intended for the defence of overseas territories and other forces which the North Atlantic Treaty Organisation has recognised or will recognise as suitable to remain under national command', Resolution of the North Atlantic Council for the Implementation of Section IV of the Final Act of the London Conference, 22 October 1954, available at www.CVCE.eu.

12 The Arms Control Agency was set up under the WEU to lay down provisions on the control of nuclear, biological and chemical weapons, on the one hand, and to prohibit the manufacture of certain categories of so-called conventional weapons, on the other. It also supervised the Federal Republic of Germany (see footnote 11 above). It ceased its activities in 1985.

13 Art. 4(2) of the Treaty of Brussels.

14 This territory was received by France in 1919 as part of the post-war reparations, and returned to Germany in 1935 before being included in the French occupation zone after the Second World War. The Paris Agreements resulted in the Saarland being given a European status under the authority of the WEU in 1954. A referendum held on 23 October 1955 allowed a majority of Saarlanders to express their refusal to retain this status, so that after WEU elections, Saarland returned to the Federal Republic of Germany.

15 Speech by Robert Schuman on 24 November 1950; 'Notre plan de défense européenne n'est ni une manœuvre ni un subterfuge', *Le Monde*, Archives, 25 November 1950.

Member States, in the presence of British and American representatives and members of the Supreme Headquarters Allied Powers Europe (SHAPE), was particularly ambitious.[16] It aimed in particular at the integration of all the air and land forces of the Member States, the non-autonomy of national units, the establishment of a common budget and an armaments programme which would be administered by an 'Executive Board of Commissioners' independent of the Member States.[17] The European defence forces had to remain under the Supreme Allied Command in Europe/SHAPE command and, in times of war, would be under its operational control. The main idea, as set out by Robert Schuman, was 'to create an army common to the six participating States: not a coalition army, bringing together the various national armies under a single command, but a homogeneous army, where the national, human and material elements of which it is composed will be merged to a large extent'.[18] This European army was to intervene in the event of aggression against one of the Member States.[19] After various experiences, including developments in British feelings towards this project,[20] the Treaty establishing a European Defence Community and the Protocols on reciprocal safeguards between the EDC and NATO were signed on 27 May 1952.

This treaty differs greatly from the Pleven plan. The EDC institutions were not those devised by Jean Monnet: decisions were not taken by a body independent of States, like the High Authority under the ECSC, but by the Council of Ministers, which had to decide unanimously on important issues. Moreover, the prerogatives of these institutions were largely subordinate to NATO.[21] Although the Treaty did provide for the creation of 'European

---

16 For a very comprehensive analysis of the negotiation of the Treaty establishing the EDC, see C.S. Anderson, *L'impossible alliance?*, Paris, Éditions de la Sorbonne, 2020, and more specifically Chapter VII, 'La Communauté européenne de défense', pp. 265-328. See also C. Franc, 'Histoire militaire – L'échec de la Communauté européenne de défense (1951-1954) ou l'impossible Europe de la défense ', *Revue Défense Nationale*, 2015/9, No. 784, pp. 121-123.

17 'This Executive Board of the Community does not receive or request any government instructions and will therefore have supranational character and power. It will also control the production, import and export of war material, as well as the training, administration and recruitment of European defence forces', [author's translation] C. Sanderson, *L'impossible alliance?*, Paris, Éditions de la Sorbonne, 2020, para. 8.

18 Speech to the National Assembly, 11 January 1952, quoted by C.S. Anderson, *L'impossible alliance?*, Paris, Éditions de la Sorbonne, 2020, para. 36, [author's translation].

19 'In the name of solidarity enshrined not only in texts making mutual assistance compulsory, but in practice, and in particular in the geographical reality. Thus, the common army guarantees common security' [author's translation], Robert Schuman's speech to the National Assembly on 11 January 1952, *ibid.*

20 See C.S. Sanderson, *L'impossible alliance?*, Paris, Éditions de la Sorbonne, 2020.

21 According to General de Gaulle, 'the Treaty attributes quasi-discretionary rights to the Commander-in-Chief, Atlantic in respect of France's destiny, such as, in any event, at no time, in any country, any government ever granted to any of its generals' [author's translation], Charles de Gaulle Press Conference (Paris, 25 February 1953), www.CVCE.eu.

Defence Forces', they were composed of 'contingents placed at the disposal of the Community by Member States with a view to their fusion under the conditions provided for in the present Treaty'[22] and the national armed forces were not to disappear. They were simply capped so as not to compromise 'the participation of each Member State in the European Defence Forces',[23] in a way that differed from one Member State to another.

The Treaty had been ratified by Germany, Belgium, the Netherlands and Luxembourg, but at a time when Italy was preparing to do the same, the French Assembly voted against its ratification on 30 August 1954, thereby putting an end to the draft EDC and, for several decades, to any attempt to draw up a common defence policy within the Community.

In the early 1960s, the failure of the political union project proposed by the 'Fouchet Plans'[24] highlighted the differences between Member States, in particular as regards the modalities of their cooperation on foreign policy and, more specifically, in the field of security and defence, as regards the arrangements for linking a common defence policy with NATO.[25]

From European political cooperation to the Maastricht Treaty

A new step was taken at the beginning of the 1970s with the European Political Cooperation (EPC), which, set up outside the Community framework, was finally incorporated into it by the Single European Act in 1986. Intergovernmental in nature and exclusively devoted to foreign policy, the EPC was the result of a gentlemen's agreement between the Member States.[26] It provided a framework for the adoption by foreign ministers of various reports, which, at least initially, did not show any willingness to commit to a European defence policy. Thus, in their 'Declaration on European Identity', made in Copenhagen on 14 December 1973 – a few months after the United Kingdom's accession to the European Community, which was of course not trivial – the Heads of State and Government recalled that 'those of them who are members of the Atlantic Alliance consider that in the present circumstances there is no alternative to the security provided by the nuclear weapons of the United

22 Art. 9 of the Treaty establishing the European Defence Community.

23 Art. 10(5) of the Treaty establishing the European Defence Community.

24 Named after Christian Fouchet, a French diplomat and former Gaullist Member of Parliament, who presented two draft treaties in 1961 and 1962 establishing a Union of states based on intergovernmental cooperation in foreign and defence policy, science, culture and the protection of human rights.

25 According to Article 2 of the first draft Treaty, the Union's aim is, inter alia, 'to strengthen, in cooperation with the other free nations, the security of Member States against any aggression by adopting of a common defence policy'. Article 2 of the second draft states that 'It shall be the aim of the Union to reconcile, co-ordinate and unify the policy of Member states in spheres of common interest: foreign policy, economics, cultural affairs and defence'.

26 On 27 October 1970, the Foreign Ministers meeting in Luxembourg adopted the Davignon Report, named after the Belgian diplomat who drafted it.

States and by the presence of North American forces in Europe'. The positions taken by the European Council in the early 1980s were therefore limited to the purely economic aspects of European security and attempts to extend the EPC's competences to defence issues were bound to fail.[27]

Once again, it was in the margins of Community construction that European security and defence issues were dealt with, and more specifically in the framework of the WEU, which was 'relaunched' in 1984. In the Rome Declaration of 27 October 1984, the Ministers of Foreign Affairs and Defence of the seven WEU Member States called for 'continued efforts to preserve peace, strengthen deterrence and defence' and stated 'their determination to make better use of the WEU framework'.[28] The declaration also recalls that, in accordance with the amended Brussels Treaty, the WEU Council may examine the 'implications for Europe of crises in other regions of the world'.[29] These statements would be consolidated in the 'Platform on European Security Interests' adopted in The Hague in 1987: the Ministers of Foreign Affairs and Defence of the WEU Member States recalled the commitment of the States 'to build a European Union in accordance with the Single European Act, which we all signed as members of the European Community' and said they were 'convinced that the construction of an integrated Europe will remain incomplete as long as it does not include security and defence'.[30] This reference to the Single European Act adopted a year earlier is a manifestation of the rapprochement between the WEU and the Community's legal framework, which continued with the Maastricht Treaty.

The WEU would prove to be conducive to closer cooperation when its competences were extended to peace management and crisis management operations established following the Petersberg Declaration, which was adopted at the end of the WEU Ministerial Council of June 1992.[31] With the ad hoc

[27] This is true of the Genscher-Colombo Plan, named after the German and Italian foreign ministers who presented proposals to the Member States and the European Parliament in 1981 to strengthen the coordination of the European common foreign policy. A draft European Act was presented to the London European Council of 26 and 27 November 1981 and, on the basis of the work of an intergovernmental working group, the Stuttgart European Council of 17–19 June, 1983 adopted a solemn declaration on the European Union which called for the strengthening of common policies, involved the Commission and Parliament in the work of European political cooperation, and suggested in particular the general application of majority voting in the Council of Ministers. However, the concrete effects of this statement would be limited.

[28] Statement of the WEU Foreign Affairs and Defence Ministers (Rome, 27 October 1984), www.CVCE.eu, para. 3.

[29] Statement cited above, para. 8.

[30] Preamble to the Platform on European Security Interests (The Hague, 27 October 1987), para. 2.

[31] Petersberg Declaration by the WEU Council of Ministers, 19 June 1992, www.CVCE.eu. On this statement, see A. Hamonic's commentary on Article 43 TEU in this publication.

military structures needed to carry out these missions and operations,[32] the WEU effectively conducted several missions and operations between 1993 and 2001, in particular in the context of conflicts and crises in the Balkans.[33]

A few months before the Petersberg Declaration, the Maastricht Treaty had been signed, which considered the WEU to be an 'integral part of the development of the European Union'.[34]

While in 1986, when the Single European Act was signed, the conditions for discussing the prospect of a common defence between the Member States were not yet met, they were in 1991, when the Intergovernmental Conference on Political Union began, under the successive presidencies of Luxembourg and the Netherlands. At that time, the dislocation of the Soviet Union and the resulting de-escalation of tensions – which, moreover,[35] is recalled in the preamble to the TEU – led to fears[36] that Europe would be less protected by the United States and made it possible to envisage that Europeans would take greater responsibility for their own defence. Moreover, the strictly economic dimension of Community construction was in the process of being supplemented by a political dimension, the defence of which could hardly be completely overlooked.

In the context of this construction of the Community, the aim was to 'attempt to go beyond the mechanisms of classical political cooperation as defined by the Single Act, in order to bring them closer to more Community-oriented treatment, without, however, moving towards a genuine communitarisation of foreign policy'.[37] This led to the pillar structure, which was preferred to

---

32 These were the Planning Cell (1993), the Torrejon Satellite Observation Centre (1993), the Military Committee (1998) and the Situation Centre (1996), which had been grouped together in 1998 with the Planning Cell to create a WEU Military Staff. These structures were transferred to the European Union in 2000. See C. Schneider's comment in this publication.

33 See A. Hamonic's commentary on Article 43 TEU in this publication.

34 Article J. 4(2) states that 'The Union requests the Western European Union (WEU), which is an integral part of the development of the Union, to elaborate and implement decisions and actions of the Union which have defence implications. The Council shall, in agreement with the institutions of the WEU, adopt the necessary practical arrangements'. Then, in paragraph 5 of that article, it 'shall not prevent the development of closer cooperation between two or more Member States on a bilateral level, in the framework of the WEU and the Atlantic Alliance, provided such cooperation does not run counter to or impede that provided for in this Title'. A declaration (No 30) on the WEU was also annexed to the Treaty on European Union. See our commentary on Article 42 TEU in this publication.

35 The importance of the Washington Treaty on the abolition of intermediate nuclear forces signed by US President Ronald Reagan and Secretary General of the Communist Party of the Soviet Union Mikhail Gorbatchev on 8 December 1987 should be stressed.

36 In the Preamble of the Maastricht Treaty, the Member States recall 'the historic importance of the ending of the division of the European continent and the need to create firm basis for the construction of the future Europe'.

37 J. Cloos, G. Reinnesch, D. Vignes and J. Weyland, *Le traité de Maastricht – Genèse, analyse et commentaires*, Brussels, Bruylant, 1993, p. 466, [author's translation].

the unitary structure for moving from cooperation to common action on the CFSP, which included, as we know, in its preamble, 'the eventual framing of a common defence policy, which might in time lead to a common defence'. This also explains the ambiguity of the wording used and the particularly obscure distinction between the concepts of 'common defence policy' and 'common defence'.[38]

Each of these terms reflects a different approach on the part of the Member States. The negotiations at the Intergovernmental Conference clearly show that 'the term common defence involved the creation of an integrated command with common armed forces structures, that is to say integrated armed units which can be placed under a single equally integrated command'.[39] Although there was no intention to compete with NATO structures but rather to create a European intervention force operating outside the NATO area, the British refused to commit to such an undertaking. The term 'common defence policy' was an acceptable compromise. The wording in the preamble stating that this policy could lead to a 'common defence' is the result of these various national approaches.

The fact remains that a 'common defence' is still mentioned in the preamble to the TEU in the form of a process, an ongoing integration, which consists first and foremost of the 'progressive framing of a common defence policy', which has actually been done since the Maastricht Treaty (I). On the other hand, the 'common defence', which could result from this 'common defence policy', still appears utopian in 2025 (II). While it is not clear what this common defence would be, its ability to strengthen the 'European identity and its independence in order to promote peace, security and progress in Europe and the world' deserves to be analysed (III).

I. THE 'PROGRESSIVE FRAMING OF A COMMON DEFENCE POLICY'

As provided for by the Maastricht Treaty, the common defence policy experienced a sluggish start in a relatively calm security environment (Section A). However, the deterioration of this environment and the growth of threats from the mid-2010s would contribute to its development (Section B).

---

38 The meticulous analysis of the Maastricht Treaty negotiations by the then twelve Member States by J. Cloos, G. Reinnesch, D. Vignes and J. Weyland sheds light on this semantic choice; *ibid.*, pp. 463 et seq., spec. p. 471.

39 J. Cloos, G. Reinnesch, D. Vignes and J. Weyland, *Le traité de Maastricht – Genèse, analyse et commentaires*, Brussels, Bruylant, 1993, pp. 471–472, [author's translation].

A. SLUGGISH BEGINNINGS

By referring to the 'progressive framing of a common defence policy', the Member States which drafted the Treaties put European defence in a process, a dynamic which is not specific to this field but which, more generally, is the mark of this 'integration law',[40] first of the European Community, and now of the European Union. That definition 'to be built' of the common defence policy thus appears logically in the preamble to the TEU,[41] alongside other objectives, other dimensions of the integrative process, such as that of creating 'an ever closer union among the peoples of Europe'.[42] However, while the latter resolution is also mentioned in the preamble to the Treaty on the Functioning of the European Union (TFEU),[43] this is not the case with the progressive definition of common defence, which was then conceived as falling exclusively within the CFSP, and thus the Treaty on European Union, and not within the Community or supranational area governed by the TFEU. On the other hand, the terms chosen to refer to this 'work in progress' in the field of defence demonstrate the great caution – or even a certain reluctance – of the Member States.

However, the momentum announced in the preamble to the Maastricht Treaty was effective: the definition of a common defence policy has evolved since 1992 and the fact that the name of this policy changed with the Lisbon revision is no longer a mere formality: there is undoubtedly more in 'common' between yesterday's 'European Security and Defence Policy' and today's 'Common Security and Defence Policy'.

From the Maastricht Treaty onwards, however, the process took several years to get started.

The fact that the WEU was originally the EU's 'sword arm' explains the immobility of the first years.[44] While the Union has been designed and aims to

---

40 According to the expression already used in 1960, by P. Reuter, *Organisations européennes*, 2nd ed., Thémis, Paris, PUF. See also P. Pescatore, *Le Droit de l'intégration. Emergence d'un phénomène nouveau dans les relations Internationales selon l'expérience des Communautés Européennes*, Brussels, Bruylant, 1972, republished in 2005; finally, see L.-J Constantinesco, for whom 'European integration is not an act but a future; it is not an established situation but a process; it is not a result, but the action to lead to that result', La nature juridique des Communautés européennes, Lecture given at the University of Liège, 23 November 1978.

41 The reference to this progressivity can be found in Article 2(4) TFEU and Article 42(2)(1) TEU.

42 Preamble to the TEU, para. 13.

43 Para. 1.

44 Article J.4(2) stated that 'the Union requests the Western European Union (WEU), which is an integral part of the development of the Union, to elaborate and implement decisions and actions of the Union which have defence implications'. See my commentary on Article 42 TEU in this publication.

'promote peace, its values and the well-being of its peoples',[45] defence is not in its DNA.[46] Moreover, European defence has always been pursued by national defences and NATO for most EU Member States.[47] Finally, the differences between these States, and in particular between France and the United Kingdom as regards the role of NATO, for a long time paralysed any development of the common defence policy, the revival of which is precisely seen as dating back to the bilateral meeting in Saint Malo between British Prime Minister Tony Blair and French President Jacques Chirac in December 1998. The declaration resulting from this meeting could be seen as the demonstration of the end of the British reluctance regarding any development of ESDP for fear of duplication with NATO.[48] It states that 'the Union must have the capacity for autonomous action, backed up by credible military forces, the means to decide to use them, and a readiness to do so, in order to respond to international crises,'[49] in strong terms which already refer to European strategic autonomy, and which were adopted by the Cologne European Council in June 1999.

The first outlines of the definition of a common defence policy were thus carried out, with preparations for the measures necessary to achieve those objectives and the detailed rules for including the functions of the WEU 'necessary for the EU to fulfil its new responsibilities in the area of the Petersberg tasks'.[50] The implementation of these decisions took place six months later, at the Helsinki Summit,[51] with the adoption by the European Council of a number of measures, in particular those enabling the transfer to the European Union of the military powers which had hitherto belonged to the WEU.[52] Capability objectives, i.e. the number and type of capabilities that Member States should be able to allocate to Union crisis management missions and operations, were

45 Art. 3 TEU, ex Art. 2 TEU.

46 Moreover, it is still 'in order to promote peace, security and progress in Europe and the world' that the Common Defence Policy is mentioned in the preamble.

47 See below, Section I.B, and the commentary on Article 42 TEU, in this publication.

48 This development, initiated by a very Europhile Prime Minister, was also the result of awareness of Member States' dependence on the United States in the context of the Bosnian crisis, and of their inability to act autonomously, especially when the US refuses to engage in a conflict.

49 See https://www.vie-publique.fr/discours/148017-declaration-conjointe-franco-britannique-sur-la-defense-europeenne-dans.

50 Presidency Conclusions, Cologne European Council, 3–4 June, 1999.

51 Presidency Conclusions, Helsinki European Council, 10–11 December 1999. www.consilium.europa.eu/media/21045/helsinki-conseil-europeen-conclusions-de-la-presidence.pdf.

52 It was then envisaged that Member States, 'cooperating voluntarily in EU-led operations', would be able to deploy, by 2003, 'within 60 days' and 'sustain for at least 1 year military forces of up to 50,000–60,000 persons capable of the full range of Petersberg tasks'. At the institutional level, a Political and Security Committee, a Military Committee and a Military Staff were planned within the Council, as well as the establishment of a committee coordinating civilian crisis management tools, see C. Schneider's comment in this publication.

then set out swiftly.[53] At the end of 2001, the observation was made that 'the Union is now capable of conducting some crisis-management operations',[54] which indeed was confirmed, as from 2003, when the first civilian and/or military missions and operations in the Union's neighbourhood were carried out.[55] Two years later, the European Council adopted the 'European Security Strategy' presented by Javier Solana, who was then the EU High Representative for the CFSP.[56] The document, subtitled 'A secure Europe in a better world', identified the main threats to the EU's security in a 'post-11 September 2001' context and proposed measures to address them.

As regards primary law, the Treaty of Nice first, and then the Lisbon Treaty (following the Treaty establishing a Constitution for Europe),[57] endorsed the successive developments brought about by the European Council.[58] However, the definition of the common defence policy did not progress in the decade 2003–2013.

B. PROGRESS FOSTERED BY INCREASED THREATS

In view of the deteriorating security environment in the Union, the weakness of national defence budgets and the fragmentation of European defence markets, in December 2013 the European Council required Heads of State or Government to identify 'priority actions for stronger cooperation'.[59] This included addressing underinvestment in defence research and technology. However, the measures requested from the Council, the High Representative, the European Defence Agency, the Member States and even the European Commission on account of its internal market and industrial competences were not be proposed, with priority being given to other areas of concern, such as the migration crisis.

Defence issues were thus removed from the European agenda for a few years, until Federica Mogherini, the High Representative of the Union for

---

53 At the Santa Maria da Feira European Council on 19–20 June 2000.

54 Presidency Conclusions, Laeken European Council, 14–15 December 2001, Annex 2, www.consilium.europa.eu/media/20946/68779.pdf.

55 Javier Solana in 2003, when he presented the European Security Strategy.

56 European Council, *A secure Europe in a better world. European Security Strategy*, Brussels, 12 December 2003.

57 A reading of the work of Working Group VIII on Defence, chaired by Michel Barnier, is particularly informative on the challenges and plans for a common defence policy, see the report by the Chair of Working Group VIII on Defence to the Members of the Convention, CONV 461/02 – WG VIII 22, Brussels, 16 October 2002.

58 For the details of this development, see E. Bernard, 'Le Conseil européen: le monopole de la défense européenne?', in D. Blanc (dir.), *Le Conseil européen, le politique des politiques de l'UE*, Brussels, Larcier, 2023, pp. 337–350.

59 Conclusions of 20 December 2013, p. 1, para. 1.

Foreign Affairs and Security Policy, responding to an invitation from the European Council,[60] presented her 'Global Strategy for the EU's Foreign and Security Policy', which 'nurtures the ambition of strategic autonomy for the European Union',[61] so that Europe can 'promote peace and security within and beyond its borders'.[62] It was a real step forward in the definition of a common defence policy within the EU that the High Representative then proposed, for the first time, establishing a link between this autonomy and a prerogative considered to fall exclusively within NATO: the defence of the territory. The Global Strategy states that 'while NATO exists to defend its members – most of which are European – from external attack, Europeans must be better equipped, trained and organised to contribute decisively to such collective efforts, as well as to act autonomously if and when necessary'.[63] The subject was probably too sensitive for the European Council, which merely 'welcomed' the Strategy in June 2016,[64] before approving its implementation by the Council,[65] and then 'welcomed' the Commission's proposals for a European Defence Action Plan.[66]

This plan was presented at the end of 2016, in a worrying geopolitical context for the European Union: the announcement of Brexit following the UK referendum in 2016,[67] an increasingly threatening security context with wars in the EU neighbourhood and Russia's invasion of Crimea, terrorist attacks in EU Member States and finally the election of Donald Trump as US President, who questioned the reliability of US allies (and thus that of NATO). The fact that the plan was presented to the Commission, a supranational institution which does not have powers under the CSDP, is explained by the proposal to set up a European Defence Fund (EDF) financed by the budget of the European Union, to encourage collaborative defence industry and research projects,[68] two

---

60 At the June 2015 European Council, the High Representative was asked to continue 'the process of strategic reflection with a view to developing, in close cooperation with the Member States, an EU Global Strategy on foreign and security policy issues', para. 10(b) of the Conclusions of 25–26 June, 2015.

61 European Union, 'Shared Vision, Common Action: A stronger Europe. A Global Strategy for the European Union's Foreign and Security Policy', 2016, p. 3.

62 Ibid., p. 14.

63 Ibid., p. 16.

64 European Council meeting of 28 June 2016 – Conclusions, para. 20.

65 European Council conclusions of 15 December 2016, paras. 11 and 12.

66 Communication from the Commission to the European Parliament, the European Council, the Council, the European Economic and Social Committee and the Committee of the Regions, European Defence Action Plan, COM(2016) 950 Final, 30 November 2016.

67 See E. Bernard, 'L'impact du Brexit sur la politique européenne de sécurité et de défense', *Annuaire Français de Droit International 2019*, 2020, pp. 355–364.

68 Regulation (EU) 2021/697 of the European Parliament and of the Council of 29 April 2021 establishing the European Defence Fund and repealing Regulation (EU) 2018/1092, [2021] *OJ* L170/149. See the comments of D. Fiott (Article 173 TFEU), F. Liberti (new strategy for the European defence industry) and S. Rodrigues (European Defence Fund), in this publication.

supranational policy areas, which therefore fall within the remit not only of the Commission, but also of the European Parliament and of the Court of Justice.

Other measures were also proposed to support Member States in their efforts to increase the efficiency of their spending in common defence capabilities. The progressive definition of the common defence referred to in the preamble to the TEU then also falls within the legal framework of the TFEU.

While various actions were then taken by the Council in the context of CFSP/CSDP, such as the Coordinated Annual Review on Defence (CARD),[69] the Permanent Structured Cooperation (PESCO),[70] the Military Conduct and Planning Capability (MPCC)[71] in 2017, or, a few years later, the European Peace Facility (EPF),[72] a common defence policy was being developed gradually in the so-called 'Community' area, in particular through the development of the European Defence Technological and Industrial Base (EDTIB).[73]

Since 2019, the Commission has had a Directorate-General for Defence Industry and Space (DG DEFIS), and so has initiated significant actions 'to contribute to European defence, boost innovation and address strategic dependencies'.[74]

The war in Ukraine has of course further contributed to this development, both in the intergovernmental CSDP and supranational domains.[75] The Strategic Compass endorsed by the European Council in March 2022,[76] a few

---

69 See the presentation of this mechanism on the website of the European Defence Agency, //eda. europa.eu/what-we-do/EU-defence-initiatives/coordinated-annual-review-on-defence- (card).

70 Council Decision (CFSP) 2017/2315 of 11 December 2017 establishing permanent structured cooperation (PESCO) and determining the list of participating Member States, [2017] *OJ* L331/57. See Q. Loïez's comment in this publication.

71 Council Decision (EU) 2017/971 of 8 June 2017 determining the planning and conduct arrangements for EU non-executive military CSDP missions, [2017] *OJ* L146/133.

72 Council Decision (CFSP) 2021/509 of 22 March 2021 establishing a European Peace Facility, and repealing Decision (CFSP) 2015/528, [2021] *OJ* L102/14.

73 This 'communitarisation' began in 2009 with Directive 2009/43/EC of 6 May 2009 simplifying terms and conditions of transfers of defence-related products within the Community, [2009] *OJ* L146/1, p. 1 (see the commentary by E. Daniel and M. Kieffer, in this publication) and Directive 2009/81/EC of 13 July 2009 on the coordination of procedures for the award of certain works contracts, supply contracts and service contracts by contracting authorities or entities in the fields of defence and security [2009] *OJ* L 216/76 (see the commentary by S. Rodrigues, in this publication). For a genearal approach to this phenomenon, see E. Bernard, 'La communautarisation de la défense européenne dans le contexte de la guerre en Ukraine', *Revue Trimestrielle de Droit Européen (RTDE)*, 2023/4, pp. 325–350.

74 See 'Defence: Commission unveils significant actions to contribute to European defence, boost innovation and address strategic dependencies', European Commission press release, 15 February 2022, ec.europa.eu/commission/presscorner/detail/fr/IP_22_924.

75 See in particular the comments on the ASAP and EDIRPA regulations (by E. Bernard) and the commentary on the EDIP regulation (by E. Simon) and the commentary on the new strategy for the European defence industry (by F. Liberti) in this publication.

76 European Council meeting – Conclusions, 24–25 March, 2022; 'A Strategic Compass for Security and Defence – For a European Union that protects its citizens, values and interests, and contributes to international peace and security', Council of the European Union, 21 March 2022, 7371/22.

weeks after the start of the war, showed the scale and variety of short-term measures to be taken to address the threats and challenges facing the Union.[77]

In 2025, Trump's second term as President of the United States and his erratic positions, particularly in the context of the war in Ukraine, sharply conveyed to Europeans that American disengagement from European security was no longer a mere possibility but an undeniable reality. This realisation highlighted the imperative for Europe to bolster its defence capabilities and to increasingly assume responsibility for the continent's security in a more autonomous manner.

In March 2025, the President of the European Commission presented a plan called 'ReArm Europe Plan/Readiness 2030'. This defence package, which was approved by the European Council,[78] provides financial levers to the Member States to strengthen European defence capabilities with new financial means. According to the Commission, it could mobilise €800 billion for European security and defence through five sets of measures.

First, on 19 March 2025, The Commission proposed a new regulation 'establishing the Security Action for Europe (SAFE) through the reinforcement of the European defence industry Instrument'.[79] This regulation, based on Article 122 of the TFEU,[80] is designed to create the temporary, emergency instrument 'SAFE' that 'will provide up to EUR 150 billion in loans to Member States for defence investment, which allows procurement of defence capabilities in priority areas identified by the European Council'.[81] The funds raised on capital markets is disbursed to Member States upon demand and on the condition that they plan to carry out activities, expenditures and measures through common procurement with the aim of supporting the adaptation of the European Defence Technological and Industrial Base (EDTIB) to the structural changes.

Second, the National Escape Clause of the Stability and Growth Pact has been activated to allow national defence spending to increase without being counted towards the 3% public deficit threshold. Based on an initial estimate of an average 1.5% increase in GDP over the next four years, the Commission puts the volume of military expenditure at €650 billion until 2030. But this is

---

77 E. Bernard, 'La "boussole stratégique", nouveau plan d'action pour la sécurité et la défense de l'Union européenne', in J.-C. Martin (dir.), 'Union européenne et droit international', *AFDI*, 2022, pp. 570–583.

78 European Council conclusions on European defence, 6 March 2025, EUCO 6/25.

79 Proposal for a Council Regulation establishing the Security Action for Europe (SAFE) through the reinforcement of European defence industry Instrument, COM(2025) 122 final, 19 March 2025. See the commentary by D. Fiott in this publication.

80 See the commentary by F. Allemand in this publication.

81 These priority areas are air and missile defence, artillery systems, missiles and ammunition, drones and anti-drone systems, strategic enablers and critical infrastructure protection, including in relation to space, cyber, artificial intelligence and electronic warfare, and military mobility.

mere speculation, since firstly, all Member States are not in a position to take on more debt, and secondly, the EU has no authority to force their hand on military budgets.

Third, the Commission is looking for the mid-term review of the Cohesion Policy to provide additional possibilities and incentives for Member States to increase funding to the defence sector in cohesion policy programmes.

Fourth, the European Investment Bank Group should widen the scope of its lending to defence and security projects.[82]

Lastly, the ReArm Europe Plan/Readiness 2030 aims at mobilising private capital by accelerating the Savings and Investments Union, which should make it easier to mobilise private savings and to channel investments into defence.

A few days after the presentation of this plan, the Commission unveiled the White Paper for European Defence Readiness 2030,[83] which acknowledges that 'the moment has come for Europe to re-arm'.[84]

If the White Paper covers all areas for improving European defence readiness, the document, considered as a 'road map' by Ursula von der Leyen,[85] does not add any groundbreaking ideas to the ones presented in the ReArm Europe Plan. After providing an updated threat perspective for the EU, the White Paper mentions various actions to close critical capability gaps in the priority areas identified in the 'ReArm Europe' plan. Another preoccupation is to increase military support for Ukraine, with a view to integrating its defence industry into the EU's internal market. Non surprisingly, the White Paper acknowledges the need to work towards a strong and innovative European defence industry, which is based on six strategic orientations: a) supporting, strengthening and promoting industrial capabilities across the EU; b) securing the supply of critical industry inputs and reducing dependencies; c) building a genuine EU-wide market for defence equipment; d) simplifying existing rules and cutting red tape; e) stimulating research and development to foster innovation; and f) retaining, attracting and developing talent, improving skills and expertise in the defence sector.

Regarding the surge in defence spending, the options set out in the ReArm Europe plan are confirmed in the White Paper 'to address the most immediate

---

[82] See S. Rodrigues, comments on Articles 308 and 309 TFEU in this publication.

[83] Joint White Paper for European Defence Readiness 2030, Brussels, 19 March 2025, JOIN(2025) 120 Final.

[84] See also Joint Communication to the European Parliament, the European Council and the Council – Preserving Peace – Defence Readiness Roadmap 2030, 16 October 2025, JOIN(2025) 27 final.

[85] Speech by President von der Leyen on European defence at the Royal Danish Military Academy, 18 March 2025, https://ec.europa.eu/commission/presscorner/detail/nl/speech_25_814.

needs and help mitigate the consequences of past-investment'.[86] The following are thus mentioned 1) the new loan facility previously mentioned as the Security Action for Europe (SAFE) instrument; 2) the coordinated activation of the National Escape Clause of the Stability and Growth Pact; 3) using existing EU financial instruments for defence and making them more flexible to allow more defence investment; 4) a greater role for the European Investment Bank (EIB); and 5) the mobilisation of more private capital.

Finally, the White Paper acknowledges the importance of strengthening security partnerships with NATO and with certain key third countries, in particular the United States, the United Kingdom, Norway, Canada, Turkey and Indo-Pacific partners as well as Australia and New Zealand.

One week after the publication of the White Paper, the security emergency that gripped the European Union at the start of 2025 was also starkly underscored by the Commission and the High Representative launching the 'Preparedness Union Strategy', to provide a unified framework to prevent, detect and respond effectively to security threats.[87]

Against this background and following Donald Trump's return to the White House in January 2025, there is no doubt that the European Union sent an important political signal regarding its growing role in defence and its willingness to establish itself as a genuine actor of the defence of Europe, as independently as possible from the United States. But at this stage, the plan, proposal and papers delivered must be followed by practical measures to ensure impact and notably to build a more integrated European defence industrial base.

Thus, significant progress has been made in recent years in the 'progressive framing of a common defence policy'. However, this progress has not yet resulted in a 'common defence', as envisaged in the preamble to the TEU.

II. ARE THE PROSPECTS OF A 'COMMON DEFENCE' UTOPIAN?

The characteristics of a potential 'common defence', towards which the European Council could decide to shift, have never been clarified (Section A), as proof that the issue is not and has never been formally relevant, since there are many obstacles still facing such a project (Section B).

---

86 Joint White Paper for European Defence Readiness 2030, Brussels, 19 March 2025, JOIN(2025) 120 Final. 16.

87 Joint Communication to the European Parliament, the European Council, The Council, The European Economic and Social Committee and the Committee of the regions on the European Preparedness Union Strategy, JOIN(2025) 130 Final.

A. BLURRED FEATURES

On the basis that the concept of 'common defence' implies, as was feared in the Maastricht Treaty negotiations,[88] the formation of integrated armed units under an equally integrated command, that is to say, the establishment of a European army and the defence of the territory of the Union, it is clear that the 'progressive framing of a common defence policy' has still not been reached at this stage of integration, which would somehow be its paroxysm. This is also how common defence seems to be viewed by European citizens, who, in the context of the Conference on the Future of Europe, advocated 'common armed forces, used for self-defence purposes and to preclude aggressive military action of any kind, with the capacity to provide support in times of crisis'.[89]

In any event, it can be inferred from the Treaty that common defence differs not only from the 'common defence policy' but also from a collective self-defence alliance, since the latter has been provided for since the Treaty of Lisbon[90] without it being considered that a common defence exists within the EU. Academic writers have pointed out that the relevant criterion of demarcation between the common defence policy and common defence is in the organisation of military security. It is the transfer of sovereignty in this area that would make it possible to switch from common defence policy to common defence. That would be the case '1. in the transition to majority rule in decisions about military operations of the Union, 2. with an obligation on Member States to participate in joint missions, 3. in creating integrated command structures in the Union and especially, 4. in the formation of integrated armed forces'.[91]

The conditions for achieving this level of political and military unification within the Union are set out in Article 42 TEU, to which the preamble expressly refers, and Paragraph 2 of which largely reproduces the wording under comment here, but adds further details. It states that the Union's common defence policy will lead to a common defence, 'when the European Council, acting unanimously, so decides'. If the use of a future tense in this provision replaces the use of the conditional in the preamble, a decision of the European Council to that effect would not be sufficient since, where appropriate, it would still have to recommend the Member States to adopt 'such a decision in accordance with their respective constitutional requirements'. It is true that this procedure avoids the cumbersome process of Treaty revision.[92] However, so many precautions on the part of the Member States prove, if any proof

88 See above, introduction.

89 Conference on the Future of Europe, Report on the Final Outcome, May 2022, online.

90 Art. 42(7) TEU. See the commentary by J.-C. Martin in this publication.

91 H.-J. Blanke and S. Mangiameli (eds.), *The Treaty on European Union – A Commentary*, Berlin, Springer, 2013, p. 1214.

92 As provided for in Art. 48 TEU.

were needed, the extent to which they 'are ontologically required to act with sovereignty in the military sphere'.[93] Unsurprisingly, the very ambiguous shift from 'common defence policy' to 'common defence' has not taken place so far. The heads of state or government meeting within the European Council have never demonstrated any political will to this end. On the contrary, the 'Protocol on the concerns of the Irish people on the Treaty of Lisbon' states that that treaty 'does not provide for the creation of a European army or for conscription to any military formation'.[94] This is a clear reminder, the sole purpose of which is to reassure a State wishing to maintain its neutrality, but which once again expressly emphasises the absence of State intentions to that effect.

Moreover, as stated in Article 42(3) TEU, it is the Member States which 'shall make civilian and military capabilities available to the Union for the implementation of the common security policy, to contribute to the objectives defined by the Council'. As the Union does not have its own forces and its capabilities are only those made available by the Member States, it is difficult to envisage the existence of a truly integrated defence within the EU.

The practice of states' capability contributions to CSDP missions and operations – contributions that remain free and are therefore often very modest, when they are not inexistent – is also an indication of the low willingness of the Member States to move towards a common defence.[95] To this end, the Strategic Compass adopted in March 2022 provides for the establishment of an EU Rapid Deployment Capacity (EU RDC), which was declared operational in May 2025. It will 'swiftly deploy a modular force of up to 5,000 troops, including land, air and maritime components, as well as the required strategic enablers'.[96] Composed of both former Battlegroups and/or Member States' pre-identified military forces and capabilities, the RDC aims to substantially modify the existing Battlegroups.[97] The latter, which had to be able to be deployed for crisis management beyond the EU's borders within 10 days, for a period of 30 to 120 days, have been operational since 2007. However, they have never been deployed, as their volume (1,500 to 2,000 soldiers), their temporary

93 R. Le Gleut and H. Conway-Mouret, 'Quelle boussole stratégique pour l'Union européenne?' Information Report No. 753 (2020–2021) drawn up on behalf of the Committee on Foreign Affairs, Defence and the Armed Forces, 7 July 2021, p. 12, [author's translation].

94 Art. 3(9) of the Protocol of 13 June 2012. It should be recalled that protocols have the same legal value as the Treaty, to which they are assimilated (Art. 51 TEU).

95 See A. Hamonic's commentary on Article 43 TEU in this publication.

96 European Council meeting – Conclusions, 24–25 March, 2022; 'A Strategic Compass for Security and Defence – For a European Union that protects its citizens, values and interests, and contributes to international peace and security', Council of the European Union, 21 March 2022, 7371/22, p. 25.

97 The EU Battlegroup Concept was adopted by the Military Committee and endorsed by the Ministers of Defence of the European Union on 14 June 2004.

nature (bi-annual rotation), their inadaptability to the crises that arise and their insufficient funding, do not promote their effective use. The Strategic Compass therefore plans to reform them in order to lead to 'a more robust and flexible instrument', for instance through 'different levels of operational readiness', based on 'tailored force packages including land, maritime and air components', with longer stand-by period. While, with the EU RDC, Member States commit to increasing the preparedness and availability of the armed forces, these could only be used for crisis management and not for collective defence, which remains the responsibility of NATO for most Member States. The EU RDC therefore does not contribute to the shift towards a genuine common defence, especially as many outstanding issues remain regarding its establishment, in particular its funding, which the Strategic Compass does not regulate.[98]

The full operational capability of the Military Planning and Conduct Capability (MPCC), which is integrated into the EU Military Staff, would also be likely to move towards a common defence. Its competences are now limited to so-called 'non-executive' operations (e.g. training, advising or observation missions). But the Strategic Compass plans to extend them to executive operations.[99] For the Council, this includes strengthening MPCC's secure communication and information systems and providing MPCC with 'the necessary personnel and funding' to enable it 'to plan and conduct complex multi-domain operations, including in non-permissive environments'.[100] Again, for the Council, 'once the MPCC is fully operational, it should be seen as the preferred command and control structure for military missions, operations and exercises and the EU RDC'.[101] These competences, combined with the prospect of joint exercises, should bring the MPCC even closer to being the headquarters of the EU armed forces. However, it is precisely to avoid mentioning a 'European army' which some States do not want to see, that the concept of 'European headquarters' was carefully avoided in the Strategic Compass.

As if it was still necessary to reassure the Member States in 2025, the Joint White Paper for European Defence Readiness 2030 states that 'Member

98 In its conclusions of 27 May 2024, the Council on EU Security and Defence 'recalls the commitment to expand and extend the scope of common costs for EU military missions and operations, exercises, and the EU RDC, and looks forward to its operationalisation as soon as possible'.

99 In addition to non-executive military missions, the Military Planning and Conduct Capability will be able to take over, initially (by 2025), 'two small-scale or one medium-scale executive operation/s', European Council meeting – Conclusions, 24–25 March, 2022; 'A Strategic Compass for Security and Defence – For a European Union that protects its citizens, values and interests, and contributes to international peace and security', Council of the European Union, 21 March 2022, 7371/22, p. 30.

100 Council conclusions on EU security and defence; 27 May 2024.

101 Ibid.

States will always retain responsibility for their own troops, from doctrine to deployment, and for the definition needs of their armed forces'.[102]

The fact remains that the possibility of a European army was raised both by French President Emmanuel Macron[103] and then Chancellor Angela Merkel,[104] and before them, by then Commission President Jean-Claude Juncker.[105]

However, the idea has never flourished among the members of the European Council and neither the war in Ukraine, nor the weakening of confidence in American protection since 2025 seem to have revived it in the speeches of its promoters. Thus, while there is no doubt today that a common defence policy has been progressively defined within the EU, the attributes of which go beyond the CSDP alone,[106] there are still a number of obstacles to the design of a common defence.

B. VARIOUS BARRIERS

Speaking in favour of a European army, German Chancellor Angela Merkel was eager to add in 2018: 'that would not be an army in competition with NATO – don't misunderstand me – but it could be an effective complement to NATO. Nobody wants to call traditional alliances into question'.[107] That clarification highlights the existence of a first possible obstacle to the design of a common defence within the Union.

Under the second sub-paragraph of Article 42(2) TEU, the policy of the Union 'shall respect the obligations of certain Member States, which see their common defence realised in the North Atlantic Treaty Organisation (NATO), under the North Atlantic Treaty and be compatible with the common security

---

[102] Joint White Paper for European Defence Readiness 2030, Brussels, 19 March 2025, JOIN(2025) 120 final, p. 5.

[103] For example, in an interview of 6 November 2018, Emmanuel Macron stated: 'Europeans will not be protected if we do not decide to have a true European army', www.publicsenat.fr/actualites/non-classe/macron-propose-une-vraie-armee-europeenne-135122, [author's translation].

[104] Angela Merkel, commenting a few days after Emmanuel Macron's words quoted above, 'In the light of the evolution of recent years, we should develop a vision that allows us one day to create a genuine European army', Speech to the European Parliament, 13 November 2018, www.bundesregierung.de/breg-fr/service/archives/discours-prononcé-par-madame-angela-merkel-chancelière-de-la-république-fédérale-d-allemagne-devant-le-parlement-européen-le-13-novembre-2018-à-strasbourg-1550690 [author's translation].

[105] In an interview with Welt am Sonntag in 2015, President Juncker said: 'With its own army, Europe could respond more credibly to the threat to peace in a Member State or in a neighbouring state. One wouldn't have a European army to deploy it immediately. But a common European army would convey a clear message to Russia that we are serious about defending our European values', Jean-Claude Juncker wants a European army, Euractiv, 9 March 2015.

[106] In this sense, see the foreword of this book.

[107] Angela Merkel, Speech to the European Parliament, 13 November 2018.

and defence policy established within that framework'. However, the existence of NATO and the fact that 23 EU Member States belong to this organisation still raises concerns for some governments – particularly the most Atlanticist of them – about the risks of duplication.[108] The prospect that a European defence might displease and disengage non-EU allies, in particular the United States, is also not an incentive to bring such a project to fruition, especially in the circumstances that Europe has been experiencing since 2022.

Indeed, the first years of the war in Ukraine have shown that the defence of Europe is largely ensured by the United States. The countries of Central and Eastern Europe, for which the Russian threat is particularly acute, but also the historically Atlanticist Member States, therefore did not see the value of engaging in European defence, at least until Donald Trump's second mandate.[109] European defence could, however, be designed to complement and reinforce defence provided by NATO, as Angela Merkel stated. Although the two approaches to defence are not, as a matter of principle, incompatible, they have long been perceived as such.

Moreover, a European defence would require more convergence between the 27 concepts of defence that prevail in the EU. The diversity of situations in this sovereign and highly sensitive area does not support 'common' or 'European' thinking and policy in this area. Firstly, as regards the status of these States, some are, as we have seen, members of NATO, but not others; some are neutral; some non-aligned; one of them, Denmark, had a CSDP opt-out clause until 2022, while being a NATO member.[110] Diversity also characterises the situation of Member States as regards their budgetary efforts and the structuring of their defence budgets (e.g. the share allocated to research and development (R&D) or equipment), their capabilities to deploy forces, their type of army (professional or conscripts), the existence or otherwise of nuclear capabilities, and of course their defence industry. The latter, which is powerful in some countries, has for a long time remained virtually non-existent in others. This great diversity is explained by the heterogeneity that characterises the Member States as regards their relationship to the use of force, threat identification and relations with third countries (in particular the

---

108 The four non-allied Member States are Austria, Ireland, Cyprus and Malta.

109 See for instance and among many declarations, the Opening Remarks delivered on 12 February 2025 by US Defence Secretary Pete Hegseth at the 26th Iteration of the Ukraine Defense Contact Group Meeting in Nato: 'the United States does not believe that NATO membership for Ukraine is a realistic outcome of a negotiated settlement. Instead, any security guarantee must be backed by capable European and non-European troops. If these troops are deployed as peacekeepers to Ukraine at any point, they should be deployed as part of a non-NATO mission. And they should not be covered under Article 5. There also must be robust international oversight of the line of contact. To be clear, as part of any security guarantee, there will not be U.S. troops deployed to Ukraine'.

110 Denmark terminated this 30-year exemption following a referendum in June 2022.

powers of the United States, Türkiye, Russia, China, etc.), all of which vary according to the history and geographical location of each state.

Such heterogeneity could only fuel state resistance to European defence,[111] especially since Article 42(2)(2) TEU, to which the preamble to the TEU refers, states that the CSDP 'shall not prejudice the specific character of the security and defence policy of certain Member States', which is intended in particular to be neutral.[112] But how far could a common defence go without affecting this 'specific character'?

The question raised by another provision of the TEU – Article 4(2)[113] – is of the same nature since it follows that the Union shall respect the Member States' 'essential State functions, ensuring the territorial integrity of the State, maintaining law and order and safeguarding national security'. It is then clarified that national security – which includes national defence – 'remains the sole responsibility of each Member State'.[114] Again, it is legitimate to question the compatibility of common defence with such a provision. How can genuine European defence be conceived so as not to limit, at least to a certain extent, both the specific character of the Member States' defence policies, their 'essential functions' and their responsibility for defence?

The question arises of course in the field of CSDP, but it now also arises in the supranational field, in the light of the Commission's proposals concerning, in particular, the internal market and the European defence industry.[115] The fact that the European Council calls on the Commission to propose particularly

---

[111] See E. Bernard, 'Les résistances des États membres à la mise en place d'une Union européenne de la défense', in E. Cartier, R. de Bellescize and M. Ubeda-Saillard (dir.), *Résistance du droit et droit de la résistance*, Brussels, Larcier, 2024, pp. 319–331.

[112] Testifying to the distrust of Member States in this regard is the fact that Declarations 13 and 14 annexed to the Treaty on European Union at the time of the Lisbon revision reiterated twice that the provisions governing the common security and defence policy are without 'prejudice to the specific character of the security and defence policy of the Member States'. See also the Joint White Paper for European Defence Readiness 2030, which states that 'the EU will always act in a way that is without prejudice to the specific character of the security and defence policy of certain Member States and taking into consideration the security and defence interests of all Member States', Joint White Paper for European Defence Readiness 2030, Brussels, 19 March 2025, JOIN(2025) 120 Final p. 5.

[113] See B. Warusfel's commentary on that provision in this publication.

[114] Declarations 13 and 14 annexed to the Treaty on European Union also recall that the provisions governing the CFSP 'will not affect the existing legal basis, responsibilities, and powers of each Member State in relation to the formulation and conduct of its foreign policy, its national diplomatic service, relations with third countries and participation in international organisations, including a Member State's membership of the Security Council of the United Nations'.

[115] In this publication, see the comments: on Article 114 TFEU by S. Rodrigues; on Article 173 TFEU by D. Fiott; on the New European Defence Industrial Strategy (EDIS) by F. Liberti; on the European Defence Industry Programme (EDIP) by E. Simon; and on the ASAP and EDIRPA regulations by E. Bernard.

ambitious measures 'quickly',[116] while regularly recalling the need to respect the competences of the Member States,[117] does not provide any clarification. Quite the contrary. This schizophrenia demonstrates the difficult reconciliation between, on the one hand, the stated objectives of moving towards a European defence that is undoubtedly more effective than 27 national defences and, on the other hand, the protection of national sovereignty in this area.

In these circumstances, 'common defence' within the EU remains utopian, even though the return of war to Europe and the deterioration of the EU's security environment have contributed to commendable efforts to increase the collective dimension of European defence policy. According to the preamble, such a common defence would, however, reinforce 'European identity and its independence in order to promote peace, security and progress in Europe and in the world', which is not irrelevant in the current geopolitical context.

III. STRENGTHENING 'EUROPEAN IDENTITY AND ITS INDEPENDENCE IN ORDER TO PROMOTE PEACE, SECURITY AND PROGRESS IN EUROPE AND IN THE WORLD THROUGH COMMON DEFENCE

The preamble to the TEU establishes a causal link which it is necessary to clarify between a possible common defence and, on the one hand, the identity of Europe (Section A) and, on the other hand, its independence (Section B), with the aim of promoting peace, security and progress, not only in Europe but also in the world.

---

[116] See, for example, the invitation to the Commission by the Heads of State and Government meeting in Versailles in March 2022 to propose 'any further initiative necessary to strengthen the European defence industrial and technological base'. See also the conclusions of the European Council of 21–22 March 2024, in which it 'invites the Council, the High Representative and the Commission to swiftly advance work on the Joint Communication on a European Defense Industrial Strategy (EDIS)'.

[117] See, for example, the conclusions of the European Council of 21–22 March 2024: 'increasing and enhancing the Union' sovereignty will require additional efforts, in accordance Member States' competences', just after the announcement of the Union's commitment 'to increasing its overall defence readiness and capabilities to match its needs and ambition in the context of rising security challenges' and its resolution in 'reducing its strategic dependencies and scaling up its capabilities', para. 15. More recently, in its conclusions of 6 March 2025, the European Council stressed 'the need to continue to substantially increase expenditure on Europe's security and defence', 'in line with the respective competences conferred by the Treaties, and in light of the recent letter by the President of the Commission', para. 3.

A. THE LINK BETWEEN COMMON DEFENCE AND THE EUROPEAN IDENTITY

It is particularly difficult to determine what exactly is meant by the 'European identity' that a common defence would strengthen, as the authors of the preamble have pointed out since the Maastricht Treaty. Indeed, identity as a 'permanent and fundamental character of someone, of a group, which makes their individuality, their singularity'[118] is an ungraspable concept which is understood by its function rather than its substance.[119]

According to the preamble, a common defence would be likely to strengthen an identity, which is so difficult to perceive at EU level[120] when it is essential to it. Indeed, only an identity of Europe, an identity of the Union, or a European identity – whatever the name chosen[121] would truly make the Union a political project, based on a European *demos*, united by the same sense of belonging.[122] At a time when the European ideal is evaporating and when we see the return of nationalisms and a crisis of values, the question of a European identity, which could be the continuation of this 'identity of Europe' mentioned in the preamble, appears more important than ever.

Could a common defence contribute to this?

It is still necessary to determine how this European identity could be built up. It would involve, on the one hand, an 'awareness of sameness and therefore a sense of belonging to the community',[123] which Paul Ricoeur calls

---

118 As defined by the Larousse dictionary, with author's translation.

119 See M. Kieffer, for whom 'the existence of an identity can be seen in the existence of an identity discourse, rather than defined by an agreed set of immutable values' [author's translation], *Recherches sur l'identité de l'Union européenne*, PhD Thesis, University of Strasbourg, 2015. French. NNT: 2015STRAA032. tel-01371619, p. 23.

120 As L. Van Midelaar states, 'in European history, the glory of one nation is often the disaster of another', 'Why forge a European narrative? Identity policy in Europe. Needs and constraints of a common narrative' [author's translation], in A. Arjakovsky (dir.), *Histoire de la conscience européenne*, Paris, Salvator, 2016, p. 44.

121 The distinction between identity *of Europe* and a *European identity* does not seem to have been taken into account in the Treaty, the different language versions of which refer to one or other of these identities indiscriminately. For example, reference is made to *'l'identité de l'Europe'*, *'la identidad y la independencia europeas'*, *'l'identità dell'Europa e la sua indipendenza'*, *'a identidade europeia e a sua Independência'* or *'die Identität und Unabhängigkeit Europas'*.

122 In the 'Declaration on European Identity' of 1973, the Heads of State or Government referred to ' the diversity of cultures within the framework of a common European civilization, the attachment to common values and principles, the increasing convergence of attitudes to life, the awareness of having specific interests in common and the determination to take part in the construction of a United Europe,' which 'give the European Identity its originality and its own dynamism', 'Declaration on European Identity', Copenhagen, 14–15 December 1973.

123 R. Mehdi, 'L'identité de l'Union européenne ', in M. Fatin-Rouge Stéfanini, A. Levade, V. Michel and R. Mehdi (dir.), *L'identité à la croisée des États et de l'Europe. Quel sens? Quelles fonctions?*, Brussels, Bruylant, 2015, pp. 143–160.

the identity-*idem* (identity sameness or similitude),[124] and, on the other hand, attributes of differentiation, distinguished from 'the other', that is to say, in the same author's words, an identity-*ipse* (identity selfhood).[125] In any event, this European identity is evolving and, if it is not possible to rely on a common heritage, it must be built towards the future, towards the awareness of a common destiny.[126] However, in the current geopolitical context of the return of war to the European continent, the development of a common defence could indeed be the catalyst for citizens' sense of belonging to the Union and thus of European identity.

Indeed, identity is built 'in adversity'.[127] Moreover, the *common* dimension of this defence could be a project shared both between the States and among European citizens to ensure their security, beyond their differences and divergences: 'what makes a nation', Ernest Renan said, is to 'have done great things together' and to 'want to do more' in the future.[128]

The above-mentioned work of the Citizens' Convention demonstrates such a desire. Even though the European Union is not a nation, at the end of 2022, a survey showed that the Russian invasion of Ukraine had increased participants' interest in European politics, and strengthened their commitment to the EU.[129] The war thus caused, at least in its early stages, a 'rally around the European flag' effect.[130] The European Parliament 2025 survey shows that Europeans have high expectations from the EU in its role protecting them against global challenges and security risks.[131] This statement should be verified over time, but security and defence issues seem to be more conducive to the development of a sense of belonging than the market, standards and bureaucracy, to which the EU is too often reduced.

This identity-*idem* also seems particularly important at a time when the community of values advocated by the Treaties is cracking within the Union

---

124 P. Ricoeur, *Soi-même comme un autre*, Paris, Seuil, 1990.

125 Ibid.

126 E. Morin, *Penser l'Europe*, Folio, Paris, Gallimard, 1990, p. 197. See also J.L. Quermonne, *L'Union européenne dans le temps long*, Paris, Presses de Sciences Po, 2008, p. 20 and M. Castillo, 'Identité nationale et identité européenne. Un destin commun?', *Studies*, 2014/12, pp. 53–61.

127 According to economist and philosopher A. Sen, *Identités et violence*, Odile Jacob, 2007, p. 23. See also the words of E. Renan, who considered that 'common suffering unites more than joy'; *Qu'est-ce qu'une nation?*, Conference at the Sorbonne, 11 March 1882, [author's translation].

128 E. Renan, ibid., [author's translation].

129 N.D. Steiner, R. Berlinschi, E. Farvaque, J. Fidrmuc, P. Harms, A. Mihailov, M. Neugart and P. Stanek, 'Rallying around the EU flag: Russia's invasion of Ukraine and attitudes towards European integration', *JCMS*, 13 December 2022.

130 The *Zeitenwende* was evoked by Chancellor O. Scholz, for whom 'the Union is our future', Speech at Charles University in Prague, 29 August 2022.

131 https://europa.eu/eurobarometer/surveys/detail/3492.

itself,[132] and where divergences between Member States are undermining European identity, be it the identity of the Union as an organisation or the sense of belonging of its citizens. While these common values define, as stated by the Court of Justice, 'the very identity of the European Union as a common legal order',[133] the systemic attacks perpetrated by some Member States against these values make it less and less easy to have faith in their 'common' dimension and in their ability to create the sense of belonging necessary for European identity.

Beyond this *identity-idem*, the *identity-ipse* – as a source of differentiation from 'the other' – could be reinforced through the development of a common defence, which would send a 'signal of existence to the outside'.[134] It would affirm, as the preamble seems to suggest, the presence of 'Europe' or 'the Union' in relation to other powers, including allied powers such as the United States. Indeed, the preamble's reference to Europe's independence also appears to allude to its relationship with these other powers, particularly its allies.

B. THE LINK BETWEEN A COMMON DEFENCE AND EUROPE'S INDEPENDENCE

The reference in the preamble to the 'independence of Europe', which a common defence would strengthen, is understood in the light of the historical context in which it was decided to place the European security and defence policy in the TEU.[135] The US presence in this project, whether via NATO or independently thereof, has always been very strong, highlighting their interest in the issue of security in Europe, in line with what the Europeans themselves had requested. However, the US did not always expect to be called upon to interfere in discussions on the definition of the common defence policy within the EU. For example, during the Maastricht Treaty negotiations, US Secretary of State James Baker sent Member States a document outlining the United States' position on the future CFSP/CSDP. While expressing support for the project, including its defence dimension, the document made that support conditional: NATO needed to be strengthened, it needed to remain an integrated defence structure and to maintain leadership over all other forums to provide collective

132 Art. 2 of the Treaty on the EU.

133 Case C-156/21, *Hungary v. European Parliament and Council*, ECLI:EU:2022:97, para. 127, and Case C-157/21, *Poland v. European Parliament and Council*, ECLI:EU:C:2022:98, para. 135.

134 M. Catala, 'La Communauté à la recherche de son identité. De l'Europe des citoyens à la citoyenneté européenne [1957-1992]', *Relations internationales*, 2009, No. 3, p. 87, [author's translation].

135 See the introduction above.

defence. The Americans also called for European defence deliberations to be open to all NATO members.[136]

In this context, the link drawn in the preamble between common defence and Europe's independence reflects the drafters' apparent desire to assert a measure of autonomy for Europe – or, today, for the Union, following the disappearance of the WEU. This autonomy is asserted both internally, with respect to the Member States, which, while not stripped of their competences under the CFSP/CSDP, exercise them within limits defined by the Treaties;[137] and externally, with regard to third countries—particularly allied powers—whose protection is coupled, in some cases, with a high degree of interference.[138]

Thus, the possible existence of this 'common defence' would obviously raise the question of the EU's independence from NATO in ensuring its security and defence. Although this preoccupation became more focused in 2025 with Donald Trump's second mandate as President of the United States, it seems unrealistic, in a context of globalisation and multilateralism, to envisage the complete independence of a group of states from the rest of the world. That's why the concepts of *autonomy*, even *strategic autonomy* and *sovereignty*, are nowadays preferred, in European speeches and texts, to that of *independence*. As these concepts are also sources of tension and divergence between Member States,[139] we may agree with the words of then Council President Charles Michel, for whom 'sovereignty, independence, empowerment… whichever word you use, it's the substance that counts. Less dependence, more influence'.[140] Although the preamble refers to Europe's independence in a conditional and highly evasive manner, this objective, transformed into the quest for European strategic autonomy, has become essential in recent years.

---

136 J. Cloos, G. Reinnesch, D. Vignes and J. Weyland, *Le traité de Maastricht - Genèse, analyse et commentaires*, Brussels, Bruylant, 1993, p. 470.

137 See E. Neframi, 'La politique étrangère et de sécurité commune et l'identité de l'Union européenne ', *AFDI*, Vol. 50, 2004, pp. 826–860, spec. pp. 842–845. On the question of competences, see C. Schneider's commentary on Articles 23 to 40 TEU, in this publication.

138 As Max Bergman has noted, 'top officials may believe that the United States is being clear that it wants Europe to do more to handle its security. But the diplomats and officials who develop U.S. policy on Europe enjoy European dependence and the influence it provides: the United States gets to call the shots', 'Europe on Its Own. Why the United States Should Want a Better-Armed EU', Foreign Affairs, 22 August 2022, [https//www.foreignaffairs.com/europe/europe-its-own].

139 See E. Bernard, 'L'autonomie stratégique de l'Union européenne à l'épreuve d'une double crise: entre confiance et méfiance', in E. Bernard and F. Grabias (eds.), *La confiance en temps de crise*, Brussels, Larcier, 2021, pp. 307–326.

140 C. Michel, 'Strategic autonomy for Europe – the aim of our generation' – speech by President Charles Michel to the Bruegel think tank, 28 September 2020. On the differences between these different concepts, see D. Fiott, 'Strategic autonomy: towards "European sovereignty" in defence?', *EUISS*, November 2018, and by the same author, 'European sovereignty, Strategy and interdependence', *EUISS*, 23 July 2021.

Strategic autonomy was referred to by High Representative Federica Mogherini in 2016,[141] the aim being that the EU should be able to take decisions without being prevented from doing so by other powers (political component), conducting military operations autonomously (operational component) and producing the military equipment needed to carry out operations (industrial component).[142] Thus, the concept had its origin in the field of defence,[143] but it has untethered itself from it since. While remaining largely undetermined, it now refers to the Union's ability to equip itself, in terms of defence, access to the internal market, energy, cybersecurity, hybrid threats and digital sovereignty, in particular, with 'the tools needed to assert itself in defending its interests and values'.[144] This independence is naturally sought from threatening powers, but also, as European countries have recently realised, from the US, despite the fact that the US is allied with most Member States via NATO. Indeed, the United States' main security concern has been focused on the Indo-Pacific since the 'pivot to Asia' under the Obama presidency.[145] Whether it is because of the need for the United States to prioritise engagement in the Indo-Pacific or for other political reasons (as the reelection of Donald Trump in November 2024 has proven), the US disengagement in Europe has shifted from a simple risk to a brutal reality.

It is therefore necessary to strengthen the Union's autonomy in defence matters. This was certainly the objective of the Strategic Compass,[146] even though it is only very discreetly set out.[147] By providing a *common* strategic

---

141 European Union, 'Shared Vision, Common Action: A stronger Europe. A Global Strategy for the European Union's Foreign and Security Policy', 2016.

142 See F. Mauro, 'Autonomie stratégique: le nouveau graal de la défense européenne ', *Les rapports du GRIP*, 2018, pp. 14 et seq., and 'L'autonomie stratégique, cet obscur objet du désir', *Les rapports du GRIP*, 2021.

143 Its first mention by the European Council on the need to strengthen the European defence industry dates back to 2013.

144 T. Breton, 'Repenser notre sécurité: vers l'autonomie stratégique de l'Europe', Speech at the European Parliament, 25 June 2020.

145 The national security strategy approved by the Biden administration on 12 October 2022 recognises that China 'presents America's most consequential geopolitical challenge' because of its overall capabilities; The White House, 'National Security Strategy', 12 October 2022, p. 11.

146 European Council meeting – Conclusions, 24–25 March, 2022; 'A Strategic Compass for Security and Defence – For a European Union that protects its citizens, values and interests, and contributes to international peace and security', Council of the European Union, 21 March 2022, 7371/22.

147 The reference to the 'EU's strategic autonomy' appears only once in the document, even though it is towards the direction of that autonomy that the Compass points: see E. Bernard, 'La "Boussole stratégique", nouveau plan d'action pour la sécurité et la défense de l'Union européenne', *Annuaire français de droit international* (AFDI), 2023, December 2023. See also, D. Fiott and J. Mazarr, according to whom 'a more subterranean approach to EU strategic autonomy can arguably be seen in the Strategic Compass', 'Solid Foundation, Rocky Future? Assessing Transatlantic Defence and Security Ties After NATO's Madrid Summit, *CEPS Policy Insights*, No. 2022/26, July 2022, p. 7.

direction for defence policy and proposing the adoption of concrete European measures, in the short term, on all aspects of this policy – industrial, financial, capability and operational – the Compass calls on the Member States to move towards the common defence referred to in the conditional terms of the preamble to the TEU and thus towards the Union's strategic autonomy.

Great progress has been made in less than ten years, and even more so since the outbreak of the war in Ukraine, in the progressive framing of a common defence policy. The shift towards a genuine common defence, as referred to in the Preamble, with its consequences for Europe's identity and independence, now depends on the political will of the Member States, which is still too hard to perceive.

ARTICLE 4(2) TEU: THE EUROPEAN UNION'S RESPECT FOR NATIONAL IDENTITY AND SECURITY

Bertrand WARUSFEL
Professor at the University of Paris 8
Member of the Paris Bar
Vice-Chairman of the French Association of Security and Defence Law (AFDSD)

> **Article 4(2) TEU**
>
> The Union shall respect the equality of Member States before the Treaties as well as their national identities, inherent in their fundamental structures, political and constitutional, inclusive regional and local self-government. It shall respect the essential State functions, including ensuring the territorial integrity of the State, maintaining law and order and safeguarding national security. In particular, national security remains the sole responsibility of each Member State.

The provisions on the national identity of the Member States, their essential functions, and particularly their national security are totally absent from the Treaty of Rome. They are the result of subsequent texts which have sought to strengthen the political dimension of European integration and to organise the relationship between the national and European legal orders. Thus, it was in the Maastricht Treaty that, for the first time, an article was introduced which stated that 'the Union shall respect the national identities of its Member States, whose systems of government are founded on the principles of democracy'.

[1] But it was in the draft European Constitutional Treaty of 2004 that an Article, 1-5, was included on relations between the Union and the Member

[1] This subsequently became Article 6 of the Treaty of Amsterdam.

States, which ended by stating that the Union 'shall respect [...] [the Member States'] essential State functions, including ensuring the territorial integrity of the State, maintaining law and order and safeguarding national security'. This logic is understandable: since the 2004 draft constitution intended to give EU law an autonomous constitutional basis, it was necessary for the new Treaty to specify that the essential functions of the Member States (and therefore their internal constitutional orders) were taken into account and respected by the Union.

Article 4 TEU is therefore first and foremost an article devoted to the sharing out of competences between the Union and the Member States, as is Article 5 TEU, to which it explicitly refers and which subjects the exercise of these competences to the principles of subsidiarity and proportionality. There is also the question of relations between the Union and the Member States, in the third paragraph, which highlights the principle of 'loyal cooperation' for the proper fulfilment of the objectives and tasks set out in the Treaty.

The second paragraph of Article 4 TEU is therefore a provision that affects the relationship between the systems of national (and particularly constitutional) legal orders and the European legal order.

It is thus on the basis of taking into account the national identities and essential functions of the Member States that their respective national security systems are explicitly recognised in EU law, with legal consequences that the Court of Justice and national courts have only partially clarified.

The concept of national identity in Union law echoes the concept of 'constitutional identity', which each Member State has a duty to protect, including where it has consented to certain limitations on sovereignty.[2] According to the Court and in application of the Treaties, 'the preservation of the Member States' national identities is a legitimate aim respected by the Community legal order (as is indeed acknowledged in Article F(1) of the Treaty on European Union)'.[3] However, it reserves the right to assess whether such a motive can justify a derogation from Union law. For example, it has held that 'the protection of national identity cannot justify exclusion of nationals of other Member States from all the posts in an area such as education, with the exception of those involving direct or indirect participation in the exercise of powers conferred by public law and duties designed to safeguard the general interests of the State or of other public authorities'.[4] More recently, the Court has been even clearer in stating that 'even though, as is apparent from Article 4(2) TEU, the European Union respects the national identities

2 On how EU law takes account of the constitutional identity of the Member States, see in particular F.-X. Millet, *L'Union européenne et l'identité constitutionnelle des États membres*, Paris, LGDJ, 2013.

3 Case C-473/93, *Commission v Luxembourg*, ECLI:EU:C:1996:263, para. 35.

4 Ibid., para. 36.

of the Member States, inherent in their fundamental structures, political and constitutional, such that those States enjoy a certain degree of discretion in implementing the principles of the rule of law, it in no way follows that that obligation as to the result to be achieved may vary from one Member State to another' and that consequently 'whilst they have separate national identities, inherent in their fundamental structures, political and constitutional, which the European Union respects, the Member States adhere to a concept of 'the rule of law' which they share, as a value common to their own constitutional traditions, and which they have undertaken to respect at all times'.[5]

This conditional respect for the identity of each Member State is based on the list in the second paragraph of Article 4 TEU, which refers to several complementary elements. First, the Union shall respect the 'political and constitutional structures' of the Member States, including their local and regional organisation. In this way, the Treaty leaves the Member States entirely free to adopt the constitutional and administrative organisation they wish, whether federal or simply decentralised. However, this apparent neutrality of EU law is also an indirect means of subjecting sub-State bodies to comply with EU law, since the Member States 'may not invoke the principles of their internal administrative organisation in order to avoid the obligations arising out of EU law. Far from being synonymous with indifference, Article 4(2) makes it possible, on the contrary, to recognise the existence of sub-State bodies, which is not without consequence'.[6]

To give more operational content to this delicate provision of the Treaty, Article 4 also refers to the Union's respect for the 'essential State functions'. Here again, the text gives no positive definition of this concept, but illustrates it by listing three non-exhaustive functions: ensuring territorial integrity, maintaining law and order and safeguarding national security. All these functions clearly relate to the 'security' aspect of State action, in the sense that Paul Leroy-Beaulieu already stated (in 1890) that 'the primary function of the State is to guarantee security: the collective security of the nation, the specific security of the individual and his rights'.[7]

This recognition of the Member States' functions in the area of security is also the result of Article 72 TFEU, which confirms the autonomy of State responsibilities in relation to the common provisions establishing the European area of freedom, security and justice: '[T]his Title shall not affect the exercise of the responsibilities incumbent upon Member States with regard to

---

[5] Case C-157/21, *Poland v European Parliament and Council*, ECLI:EU:C:2022:98, paras. 265 and 266 (*idem* Case C-156).

[6] V. Donier, 'L'incidence du droit de l'Union européenne sur le traitement jurisprudentiel de la décentralisation', *Titre VII*, no. 9, October 2022.

[7] P. Leroy-Beaulieu, *L'État moderne et ses fonctions*, 3rd ed., Paris, Guillaumin & cie, 1890, p. 98.

the maintenance of law and order and the safeguarding of internal security'. Similarly, Article 73 TFEU gives Member States exclusively the prerogative 'to organise between themselves and under their responsibility such forms of cooperation and coordination as they deem appropriate between the competent departments of their administrations responsible for safeguarding national security'. The Court of Justice has not hesitated to recognise that 'Member States [...] retain exclusive competence as regards the maintenance of public order and the safeguarding of internal security'.[8]

Some of these concerns for the security of States, explicitly recognised by the current Treaties and the case law of the Court, have been present since 1957. One such is Article 223 of the Treaty of Rome (now Article 346 TFEU), which recognised that the 'essential interests of security' of a Member State authorise it to keep information secret or to adopt derogatory measures 'connected with the production of or trade in arms, munitions and war material',[9] or Article 36 (now Article 36 TFEU), which allows restrictions on freedom of movement on grounds of public policy or public security. But the Court of Justice has always interpreted this restrictively, seeing it as 'a detailed and conditional derogation'.[10]

By contrast, the reference to 'national security' as one of the essential State functions is a more recent innovation, dating back only to the Draft Treaty establishing a Constitution for Europe, before finding its place in Article 4(2) TEU (Section I) and giving rise to a body case law that clarifies the scope of this concept as it is understood in EU law (Section II), as well as the scope of the derogations that it may justify in secondary law (Section III).

I. NATIONAL SECURITY AS ONE OF THE ESSENTIAL FUNCTIONS OF EACH MEMBER STATE

Departing from the example of the European Court of Human Rights which, although applying the provisions of the Convention and its numerous references to the national security of Member States, did not really seek to define precisely the content of this concept, the Court of Luxembourg was finally led in 2020 to specify how EU law takes account of the national security of Member States.

To do so, the Court's case law can rely on the two references to 'national security' in Article 4(2) TEU: firstly, as one of the 'essential State functions',

---

8 Case C-265/95, *Commission v France*, ECLI:EU:C:1997:595 and Case C-394/97, *Heinonen*, ECLI:EU:C:1999:308.

9 See the commentary on Article 346 TFEU by S. Rodrigues in this publication.

10 See in particular S. Trombettta, 'La protection des intérêts nationaux de la défense quand la défense devient européenne', *Revue du marché commun et de l'Union européenne*, 2005, pp. 441 et seq.

but also by interpreting the last sentence of paragraph 2, which states that 'national security remains the sole responsibility of each Member State'.

Firstly, concerning the Union's obligation to respect the essential State function, it has been said that this is one of the 'many provisions introduced by the Member States as "masters of the Treaties" to protect their national competences considered essential against unlimited erosion by European integration'.[11] The national security of each Member State logically finds its place alongside two other essential functions: ensuring 'its territorial integrity' and 'maintaining law and order'.

It should be noted, however, that this enumeration lacks a certain rigour. The protection of the territorial integrity of the State is generally considered to be an integral part of national security and not a collateral and separate function.[12] Thus, for example, the French definition of 'national security' in Article L. 1111-1 of the Defence Code makes 'territorial integrity' one of the primary objectives of France's national security strategy.

Conversely, 'maintaining law and order' seems, in its generality, to cover a conceptual perimeter that goes beyond what can be understood by the 'national security' of a Member State. This is undoubtedly what the Court of Justice sought to rectify when, in October 2020, it adopted a definition of national security that makes no reference to the concept of public order.[13]

But having made these two reservations about the wording of Article 4(2) TEU, the central assertion that national security is part of the essential functions of the State is consistent both with the national security assertions of the main Member States[14] and with the approach to national security taken by the Court of Justice.

Indeed, one of the remarkable aspects of the application of Article 4 TEU is that in recent years the Court of Justice has agreed to draw conclusions from it and to define the concept of national security in terms of EU law.

---

11 J. Monar, 'L'Union européenne et les fonctions essentielles de l'État: le cas de la sécurité intérieure', *Annuaire de droit de l'Union européenne*, 2022, p. 76.

12 For example, the document setting out Germany's national security strategy logically states that 'the overarching guiding principle for the Federal Government's actions is to protect our country, its free democratic order and our values' (Integrated Security for Germany – National Security Strategy, June 2023, p. 11).

13 See below.

14 The above-mentioned French definition gives as an example (not exhaustive) of a national security objective 'the protection of the population, the integrity of the territory and the permanence of the institutions of the Republic'.

II. A POSITIVE DEFINITION OF NATIONAL SECURITY BY THE COURT OF JUSTICE OF THE EUROPEAN UNION

Traditionally, the judges of the Court of Justice used to provide few definitions of the security grounds that might affect the application of EU law.[15] Thus, with regard to the concept of 'public security' as referred to in Article 36 of the EC Treaty, the Court merely stated that it 'covers both a Member State's internal security and its external security'.[16] In so doing, the Court in Luxembourg also followed the practice of the Court in Strasbourg, which does not give a precise definition of national security (although the concept is widely used in the Convention), leaving the Member States a wide margin of discretion.[17]

In 2020, however, the Court of Justice of the European Union broke with this practice by providing for the first time a detailed substantive definition of this 'national security', which appears not only in numerous texts of secondary legislation but also in Article 4(2) TEU. In its two judgments of 6 October 2020,[18] the supreme court of EU law held that the national security of Member States includes 'protecting the essential functions of the State and the fundamental interests of society' and that this includes in particular 'the prevention and punishment of activities capable of seriously destabilising the fundamental constitutional, political, economic or social structures of a country and, in particular, of directly threatening society, the population or the State itself, such as terrorist activities.'[19]

On reading the case law definition of 'national security', the link with Article 4(2) TEU is quite clear: national security covers all the special protective measures that a State shall be able to take to preserve the core of its sovereignty. In particular, there is real consistency between the protection of the 'fundamental structures of a country' and the respect due to the national identity of the Member States. More indirectly, the 'fundamental interests of

---

15 In 2014, the G29 Working Party was able to write that 'there is, however, no clear definition of what is to be understood as 'national security' in EU legislation' (Article 29 Data Protection Working Party, *Discussion paper on the surveillance of electronic communications for intelligence and national security purposes*, 5 December 2014, p. 23).

16 Case C-367/89, *Richardt*, ECLI:EU:C:1991:376, para. 22.

17 See in particular, *National Security and the Case Law of the European Court of Human Rights*, European Court of Human Rights – Research Division, 2013 p. 49.

18 Joined Cases C-511/18, C-512/18 and C-520/18, *La Quadrature du N18*, ECLI:EU:C:2020:791:20, Case C-623/17, *Privacy Interna*, ECLI:EU:C:2020:790.

19 *La Quadrature du Net/French Data Network* judgment, ibid., para. 135. The same definition was used in its subsequent judgment: Case C-140/20, *Commissioner of An Garda Síochána and Others*, ECLI:EU:C:2022:258, para. 61. See Case C-601/21, *Commission v Poland*, ECLI:EU:C:2023:629, para. 79, with reference to Article 346 TFEU and Case C-470/21, *La Quadrature du Net*, ECLI:EU:C:2024:370, para. 66.

society' protected here echo the 'essential interests of [the] security' of each Member State, which are also protected in Article 346 TEU.[20]

Finally, the material content of national security as it results from the examples proposed remains fairly consistent with some of the national formulations of the concept of national security. For example, the German strategy refers to the protection of 'the people, sovereignty and territorial integrity of our country, the European Union and our allies;.[21] And if we take as a reference the aforementioned article L. 1111-1 of the French Defence Code, it explicitly mentions as an objective of national security 'the protection of the population, the integrity of the territory and the permanence of the institutions of the Republic'.

As for the special mention of 'terrorist activities', this may seem more topical than the other threats mentioned, but it reflects the importance of the fight against terrorism as a priority security concern for European States for almost twenty years,[22] and also for the European institutions, which have themselves adopted their own strategy for preventing and mobilising against terrorism.[23]

There remains, however, one aspect that the definition given by the Court of Justice does not cover: the fight against 'serious crime'. In the two aforementioned judgments of 6 October 2020, this area is clearly distinguished from the various aspects of national security: '[T]he importance of the objective of safeguarding national security, read in the light of Article 4(2) TEU, goes beyond that of the other objectives referred to in Article 15(1) of Directive 2002/58, inter alia the objectives of combating crime in general, even serious crime, and of safeguarding public security'.[24] As a result, the fight against serious crime has been denied the possibility of requesting the mass storage of the data of subscribers to electronic communication services, even though such prior mass storage has been authorised by the CJEU on grounds of national

20 See the commentary on this provision by S. Rodrigues in this work.

21 Integrated Security for Germany – National Security Strategy, June 2023 p. 21. As for Germany's law on the protection of the Constitution, it punishes the actions of those 'who aim to significantly undermine the functioning of the federal government, the States or their institutions' (*Bundesverfassungsschutzgesetz*, Art. 4(1)(b)).

22 In France, the 'prevention of terrorism' is one of the fundamental interests of the nation covered by Article L. 811-3 of the *Code de la sécurité intérieure* (which defines the areas of competence of the State's intelligence services).

23 In the Union's Strategic Compass, terrorism and violent extremism are mentioned as representing 'a serious threat to peace and security, within the EU and beyond' ('A Strategic Compass for Security and Defence', doc. no. 7371/22, 4 May 2022, p. 11). See also Europol's annual report: Report 2023 on the terrorism situation and trends in the European Union – TE-SAT Report, Europol, 2023. Finally, Article 75 TFEU refers directly to the taking of common measures to prevent and combat the financing of terrorism.

24 Joined Cases C-511/18, C-512/18 and C-520/18, *La Quadrature du Net*, ECLI:EU:C:2020:791, para. 136 and Case C-623/17, *Privacy International*, ECLI:EU:C:2020:790, para. 75.

security.[25] This exclusion of issues relating to the fight against organised crime from the scope of national security therefore prevents judicial investigations in this sensitive area from benefiting from the same technical facilities as the intelligence services in their national security missions. However, this strict position has been reiterated and reinforced by two more recent judgments of 2022, which state that '[w]here those data have exceptionally been retained in a general and indiscriminate way for the purpose of the safeguarding of national security [...], the national authorities competent to undertake criminal investigations cannot access those data in the context of criminal proceedings, without depriving of any effectiveness the prohibition on such retention for the purpose of combating serious crime'.[26]

But Article 4(2) TEU does more than simply introduce national security into the text of the Treaty and, in return, requires a common definition. It also affirms the specific competence of States in this area, which again calls for interpretation by the Court of Justice.

III. THE CONSIDERATION OF THE EXCLUSIVITY OF NATIONAL SECURITY SYSTEMS IN EU LAW

Although Articles 1-5 of the draft Constitutional Treaty of 2006 already referred to national security as one of the essential functions of the State that the Union had to respect, it was only when the Treaty of Lisbon was concluded that a final sentence was added to the second paragraph of the current Article 4 TEU to state that 'national security remains the sole responsibility of each Member State'. Although new to the Treaties, this concept was not absent from secondary law, as can be seen, for example, from Recital 1 of Directive 2009/81 on defence and security procurement, which already stated in 2009 that 'national security remains the sole responsibility of each Member State, both in the field of both defence and security'.[27]

This enshrinement in the Treaty could have led to the assumption that the formula was no longer to be interpreted restrictively, like the other safeguarding

---

[25] On the reconciliation between the retention of connection data and the protection of privacy and fundamental rights, see in particular B. Warusfel, 'Conservation des données et sécurité nationale au regard du droit de l'Union européenne', in *Annuaire 2022 du droit de la sécurité et de la défense*, 2022, pp. 161–173.

[26] Case C-140/20, *Commissioner of An Garda Síochána and Others*, ECLI:EU:C:2022:258, para. 100 and Joined Case C-793/19 and C-794/19, *Space Net*, ECLI:EU:C:2022:702, para. 130.

[27] Directive 2009/81 of 13 July 2009 on the coordination of procedures for the award of certain works contracts, supply contracts and service contracts by contracting authorities or entities in the fields of defence. See the commentary on this directive by S. Rodrigues in this publication.

clauses, but as giving each Member State complete exclusivity, going so far as to leave it free to assess alone the derogations justified under EU law by its national security imperatives.[28] In its aforementioned 2014 document, the G29 Group also stated that 'the EU is not allowed to legislate on issues related to the national security of the Member States'.[29]

This was the argument put forward by France and several other Member States when preliminary questions were referred to the CJEU concerning the prerogatives conferred on their security and intelligence services by the various national laws.[30] According to the La *Quadrature du Net/* judgment, 'the Czech and Estonian Governments, Ireland, and the French, Cypriot, Hungarian, Polish, Swedish and United Kingdom Governments submit, in essence, that Directive 2002/58 does not apply to national legislation such as that at issue in the main proceedings, since the purpose of that legislation is to safeguard national security. The intelligence services' activities, in so far as they relate to the maintenance of public order and to the safeguarding of internal security and territorial integrity, are part of the essential functions of the Member States and, consequently, are within their exclusive competence, as evidenced, in particular, by the third sentence of Article 4(2) TEU'.[31] However, the Court of Justice rejected this argument and, in these two judgments, explicitly refused to accept the reasoning of the intervening States, which would have resulted in the Court recognising its lack of competence to assess the relevance and proportionality of the security measures relied on by the Member States: 'according to the Court's settled case-law, although it is for the Member States to define their essential security interests and to adopt appropriate measures to ensure their internal and external security, the mere fact that a national measure has been taken for the purpose of protecting national security cannot render EU law inapplicable and exempt the Member States from their obligation to comply with that law'.[32]

In asserting its jurisdiction and rejecting the broad interpretation of the national security exception put forward by certain Member States, the Court

---

28 For an interpretation along these lines, see A. Puttler, 'Le renforcement de la notion d'identité nationale dans l'Union européenne', in *Quel avenir pour l'intégration européenne?* [online], Presses universitaires François-Rabelais, 2010, pp. 19–186 (which refers to Article 4 as 'a barrier that the Union must never cross' and considers that its paragraph 2 'becomes an enforceable provision').

29 Document G29, 2014, p. 23.

30 In France, these include the provisions of the Electronic Communications Code requiring electronic communications operators to retain connection data, and in particular those of Book 8 of the Internal Security Code providing for the use of such data by intelligence services for national security purposes.

31 Joined Cases C-511/18, C-512/18 and C-520/18, *La Quadrature du Net*, ECLI:EU:C:2020:791, para. 89.

32 Ibid., para. 99. In the same vein: Case C-623/17, *Privacy International*, ECLI:EU:C:2020:790, para. 49.

of Justice relied on several earlier judgments, including those adopting a restrictive interpretation of the various safeguarding clauses deriving from the Treaty of Rome (and in particular those in Articles 36 and 223).[33] It also referred to a third, more recent judgment, which has the advantage of directly concerning the application of Article 4(2) TEU. This case involved several Member States (Poland, Hungary and the Czech Republic) which had explicitly used Article 4(2) to justify their refusal to implement certain provisions of EU law (relating to the readmission of foreign nationals). Faced with the joint invocation of Articles 4(2) TEU and 72 TFEU, the Court rejected the argument, stating that 'there is nothing to indicate that effectively safeguarding the essential State functions to which the latter provision refers, such as that of protecting national security, could not be carried out other than by not applying Decisions 2015/1523 and 2015/1601'.[34] In January 2024, the judges in Luxembourg took the view that the activities of a committee of enquiry into the police did not fall within the scope of national security.[35] In a more recent judgement, the CJEU also rejected Slovakia's argument (also supported by the Estonian and French governments) that Article 4(2) allowed States to retain their own national jurisdiction to assess alone the margin of appreciation they deem necessary to preserve their national security.[36]

It is clear from these rulings that, far from leaving the Member States completely free to invoke their national security as a reason for derogating from EU law, the Court of Justice is claiming that it should be able to verify whether the national security grounds invoked by a Member State appear to be justified by a risk of serious interference with essential State functions that can only be avoided by the derogation requested.

Defined in this way, the condition that must be met for a Member State to be able to invoke a national security reservation seems rather difficult to fulfil and does not take much account of the fact that – unlike the other safeguard clauses – Article 4(2) TEU does not merely authorise a State to take a few derogating measures in case of need, but more broadly limits the Union's competence in areas relating to the national security of the various Member States.

It may therefore be considered that other decisions concerning security issues (anti-terrorism, intelligence, protection against foreign interference, violent extremism, etc.) should allow the Court of Justice to clarify how and

---

33 Case C-300/11, *ZZ*, ECLI:EU:C:2013:363, para. 38 and Case C-187/16, *Commission v Austria (State Printing Office)*, ECLI:EU:C:2018:194, para. 76.

34 Joined Cases C-715/17, C-718/17 and C-719/17, *Commission v Poland, Hungary & Czech Republic*, ECLI:EU:C:2020:257, para. 170.

35 Case C-33/22, *Österreichische Datenschutzbehörde*, ECLI:EU:C:2024:46.

36 Case C-185/23, *Protectus*, ECLI:EU:C:2024:657, para. 62

to what extent the assertion of the national security of each Member State should be taken into consideration by secondary legislation and its case law.

As far as France is concerned, the subtle decision of the French *Conseil d'État* (Council of State)[37] in the *French Data Network Case* in 2021 (ruling on the consequences in French law of the *La Quadrature du Net* ruling of 2020) put the debate in its proper place. It mentioned (without, however, carrying out its threat) the fact that, if EU law did not seem to provide sufficient protection for the fundamental interests of the nation and the prevention of breaches of public order, the *Conseil d'État* would reserve the right to give precedence to these constitutional requirements to oppose, if necessary, the application in France of a European standard that conflicted with its national security.[38] Like any relatively new text, Article 4(2) of the Treaty on the European Union has not yet fully found its place in the legal architecture of the European Union or its relationship with the parallel development of a European internal and external security policy. However, recent rulings by the Court of Justice give an initial indication of the need to clarify the scope of this article and to give it a useful effect with regard to relations between the European Union and its Member States in the perilous area of defence and national security issues.

---

[37] The Council of State is the highest administrative jurisdiction in the French legal system.

[38] See in particular. L. Azoulai and D. Ritleng, 'L'État, c'est moi – Le Conseil d'État, la sécurité et la conservation des données', *RTDE*, April–June 2021, pp. 349–373.

ARTICLES 23 TO 40 TEU: COMMON PROVISIONS ON THE CFSP/CSDP

Catherine SCHNEIDER
Emeritus Professor at the University of Grenoble Alpes

Article 23

The Union's action on the international scene, pursuant to this Chapter, shall be guided by the principles, shall pursue the objectives of, and be conducted in accordance with, the general provisions laid down in Chapter 1.

Article 24

1. The Union's competence in matters of common foreign and security policy shall cover all areas of foreign policy and all questions relating to the Union's security, including the progressive framing of a common defence policy that might lead to a common defence.

The common foreign and security policy is subject to specific rules and procedures. It shall be defined and implemented by the European Council and the Council acting unanimously, except where the Treaties provide otherwise. The adoption of legislative acts shall be excluded. The common foreign and security policy shall be put into effect by the High Representative of the Union for Foreign Affairs and Security Policy and by Member States, in accordance with the Treaties. The specific role of the European Parliament and of the Commission in this area is defined by the Treaties. The Court of Justice of the European Union shall not have jurisdiction with respect to these provisions, with the exception of its jurisdiction to monitor compliance with Article 40 of this Treaty and to review the legality of certain decisions as provided for by the second paragraph of Article 275 of the Treaty on the Functioning of the European Union.

2. Within the framework of the principles and objectives of its external action, the Union shall conduct, define and implement a common foreign and security policy, based on the development of mutual political solidarity among Member States, the identification of questions of general interest and the achievement of an ever-increasing degree of convergence of Member States' actions.

3. The Member States shall support the Union's external and security policy actively and unreservedly in a spirit of loyalty and mutual solidarity and shall comply with the Union's action in this area.

The Member States shall work together to enhance and develop their mutual political solidarity. They shall refrain from any action which is contrary to the interests of the Union or likely to impair its effectiveness as a cohesive force in international relations.

The Council and the High Representative shall ensure compliance with these principles.

Article 25

The Union shall conduct the common foreign and security policy by:

a) defining general guidelines;

b) adopting decisions defining:

i) actions to be undertaken by the Union;

ii) positions to be taken by the Union;

iii) the arrangements for the implementation of the decisions referred to in points i) and ii);

and by

c) strengthening systematic cooperation between Member States in the conduct of policy.

Article 26

1. The European Council shall identify the Union's strategic interests, determine the objectives of and define general guidelines for the common foreign and security policy, including for matters with defence implications. It shall adopt the necessary decisions.

If international developments so require, the President of the European Council shall convene an extraordinary meeting of the European Council in order to define the strategic lines of the Union's policy in the face of such developments.

2. The Council shall frame the common foreign and security policy and take the decisions necessary for defining and implementing it on the basis of the general guidelines and strategic lines defined by the European Council.

The Council and the High Representative of the Union for Foreign Affairs and Security Policy shall ensure the unity, consistency and effectiveness of action by the Union.

The Council and the High Representative of the Union for Foreign Affairs and Security Policy shall ensure the unity, consistency and effectiveness of action by the Union.

3. The common foreign and security policy shall be put into effect by the High Representative and by the Member States, using national and Union resources.

Article 27

1. The High Representative of the Union for Foreign Affairs and Security Policy, who shall chair the Foreign Affairs Council, shall contribute through his proposals to the development of the common foreign and security policy and shall ensure implementation of the decisions adopted by the European Council and the Council.

2. The High Representative shall represent the Union for matters relating to the common foreign and security policy. He shall conduct political dialogue with third parties on the Union's behalf and shall express the Union's position in international organisations and at international conferences

3. In fulfilling his mandate, the High Representative shall be assisted by a European External Action Service. This service shall work in cooperation with the diplomatic services of the Member States and shall comprise officials from relevant departments of the General Secretariat of the Council and of the Commission as well as staff seconded from national diplomatic services of the Member States. The organisation and functioning of the European External Action Service shall be established by a decision of the Council. The Council shall act on a proposal from the High Representative after consulting the European Parliament and after obtaining the consent of the Commission.

Article 28

1. Where the international situation requires operational action by the Union, the Council shall adopt the necessary decisions. They shall lay down their objectives, scope, the means to be made available to the Union, if necessary their duration, and the conditions for their implementation.

If there is a change in circumstances having a substantial effect on a question subject to such a decision, the Council shall review the principles and objectives of that decision and take the necessary decisions.

2. Decisions referred to in paragraph 1 shall commit the Member States in the positions they adopt and in the conduct of their activity.

3. Whenever there is any plan to adopt a national position or take national action pursuant to a decision as referred to in paragraph 1, information shall be provided by the Member State concerned in time to allow, if necessary, for prior consultations within the Council. The obligation to provide prior information shall not apply to measures which are merely a national transposition of Council decisions.

4. In cases of imperative need arising from changes in the situation and failing a review of the Council decision as referred to in paragraph 1, Member States may take the necessary measures as a matter of urgency having regard to the general objectives of that decision. The Member State concerned shall inform the Council immediately of any such measures.

5. Should there be any major difficulties in implementing a decision as referred to in this Article, a Member State shall refer them to the Council which shall discuss them and seek appropriate solutions. Such solutions shall not run counter to the objectives of the decision referred to in paragraph 1 or impair its effectiveness.

Article 29

The Council shall adopt decisions which shall define the approach of the Union to a particular matter of a geographical or thematic nature. Member States shall ensure that their national policies conform to the Union positions.

Article 30

1. Any Member State, the High Representative of the Union for Foreign Affairs and Security Policy, or the High Representative with the Commission's support, may refer any question relating to the common foreign and security policy to the Council and may submit to it, respectively, initiatives or proposals.

2. In cases requiring a rapid decision, the High Representative, of his own motion, or at the request of a Member State, shall convene an extraordinary Council meeting within 48 hours or, in an emergency, within a shorter period.

Article 31

1. Decisions under this Chapter shall be taken by the European Council and the Council acting unanimously, except where this Chapter provides otherwise. The adoption of legislative acts shall be excluded.

When abstaining in a vote, any member of the Council may qualify its abstention by making a formal declaration under the present subparagraph. In that case, it shall not be obliged to apply the decision, but shall accept that the decision commits the Union. In a spirit of mutual solidarity, the Member State concerned shall refrain from any action likely to conflict with or impede Union action based on that decision and the other Member States shall respect its position. If the members of the Council qualifying their abstention in this way represent at least one third of the Member States comprising at least one third of the population of the Union, the decision shall not be adopted.

2. By derogation from the provisions of paragraph 1, the Council shall act by a qualified majority:

– when adopting a decision defining a Union action or position on the basis of a decision of the European Council relating to the Union's strategic interests and objectives, as referred to in Article 22(1),

– when adopting a decision defining a Union action or position, on a proposal which the High Representative of the Union for Foreign Affairs and Security Policy has presented following a specific request from the European Council, made on its own initiative or that of the High Representative,

– when adopting any decision implementing a decision defining a Union action or position,

– when appointing a special representative in accordance with Article 33.

If a member of the Council declares that, for vital and stated reasons of national policy, it intends to oppose the adoption of a decision to be taken by qualified majority, a vote shall not be taken. The High Representative will, in close consultation with the Member State involved, search for a solution acceptable to it. If he does not succeed, the Council may, acting by a qualified majority, request that the matter be referred to the European Council for a decision by unanimity.

3. The European Council may unanimously adopt a decision stipulating that the Council shall act by a qualified majority in cases other than those referred to in paragraph 2.

4. Paragraphs 2 and 3 shall not apply to decisions having military or defence implications.

5. For procedural questions, the Council shall act by a majority of its members.

Article 32

Member States shall consult one another within the European Council and the Council on any matter of foreign and security policy of general interest in order to determine a common approach. Before undertaking any action on the international scene or entering into any commitment which could affect the Union's interests, each Member State shall consult the others within the European Council or the Council. Member States shall ensure, through the convergence of their actions, that the Union is able to assert its interests and values on the international scene. Member States shall show mutual solidarity.

When the European Council or the Council has defined a common approach of the Union within the meaning of the first paragraph, the High Representative of the Union for Foreign Affairs and Security Policy and the Ministers for Foreign Affairs of the Member States shall coordinate their activities within the Council.

The diplomatic missions of the Member States and the Union delegations in third countries and at international organisations shall cooperate and shall contribute to formulating and implementing the common approach.

Article 33

The Council may, on a proposal from the High Representative of the Union for Foreign Affairs and Security Policy, appoint a special representative with a mandate in relation to particular policy issues. The special representative shall carry out his mandate under the authority of the High Representative.

Article 34

1. Member States shall coordinate their action in international organisations and at international conferences. They shall uphold the Union's positions in such forums. The High Representative of the Union for Foreign Affairs and Security Policy shall organise this coordination.

In international organisations and at international conferences where not all the Member States participate, those which do take part shall uphold the Union's positions.

2. In accordance with Article 24(3), Member States represented in international organisations or international conferences where not all the Member States participate shall keep the other Member States and the High Representative informed of any matter of common interest.

Member States which are also members of the United Nations Security Council will concert and keep the other Member States and the High Representative fully informed. Member States which are members of the Security Council will, in the execution of their functions, defend the positions and the interests of the Union, without prejudice to their responsibilities under the provisions of the United Nations Charter.

When the Union has defined a position on a subject which is on the United Nations Security Council agenda, those Member States which sit on the Security Council shall request that the High Representative be invited to present the Union's position.

Article 35

The diplomatic and consular missions of the Member States and the Union delegations in third countries and international conferences, and their representations to international organisations, shall cooperate in ensuring that decisions defining Union positions and actions adopted pursuant to this Chapter are complied with and implemented.

They shall step up cooperation by exchanging information and carrying out joint assessments.

They shall contribute to the implementation of the right of citizens of the Union to protection in the territory of third countries as referred to in Article 20(2)(c) of the Treaty on the Functioning of the European Union and of the measures adopted pursuant to Article 23 of that Treaty.

Article 36

The High Representative of the Union for Foreign Affairs and Security Policy shall regularly consult the European Parliament on the main aspects and the basic choices of the common foreign and security policy and the common security and defence policy and inform it of how those policies evolve. He shall ensure that the views of the European Parliament are duly taken into consideration. Special representatives may be involved in briefing the European Parliament.

The European Parliament may address questions or make recommendations to the Council or the High Representative. Twice a year it shall hold a debate on progress in implementing the common foreign and security policy, including the common security and defence policy.

Article 37

The Union may conclude agreements with one or more States or international organisations in the areas covered by this Chapter.

Article 38

Without prejudice to Article 240 of the Treaty on the Functioning of the European Union, a Political and Security Committee shall monitor the international situation in the areas covered by the common foreign and security policy and contribute to the definition of policies by delivering opinions to the Council at the request of the Council or of the High Representative of the Union for Foreign Affairs and Security Policy or on its own initiative. It shall also monitor the implementation of agreed policies, without prejudice to the powers of the High Representative.

Within the scope of this Chapter, the Political and Security Committee shall exercise, under the responsibility of the Council and of the High Representative, the political control and strategic direction of the crisis management operations referred to in Article 43.

The Council may authorise the Committee, for the purpose and for the duration of a crisis management operation, as determined by the Council, to take the relevant decisions concerning the political control and strategic direction of the operation.

Article 39

In accordance with Article 16 of the Treaty on the Functioning of the European Union and by way of derogation from paragraph 2 thereof, the Council shall adopt a decision laying down the rules relating to the protection of individuals with regard to the processing of personal data by the Member States when carrying out activities which fall within the scope of this Chapter, and the rules relating to the free movement of such data. Compliance with these rules shall be subject to the control of independent authorities.

Article 40

The implementation of the common foreign and security policy shall not affect the application of the procedures and the extent of the powers of the institutions laid down by the Treaties for the exercise of the Union competences referred to in Articles 3 to 6 of the Treaty on the Functioning of the European Union.

Similarly, the implementation of the policies listed in those Articles shall not affect the application of the procedures and the extent of the powers of the institutions laid down by the Treaties for the exercise of the Union competences under this Chapter.

Article 23 of the Treaty on European Union (TEU) introduces the chapter on the specific provisions of the Common Foreign and Security Policy (CFSP), and more specifically the section on 'common provisions'. This article rather tersely refers to the principles and objectives, as defined in the general provisions on the Union's external action, regarding the action developed by the Union under the CFSP, including the Common Security and Defence Policy (CSDP), (Section I). The first paragraph of the following provision, Article 24, states that the Union's competence in this area 'shall cover all areas of foreign policy and all questions relating to the Union's security, including the progressive framing of a common defence policy that might lead to a common defence'. However, the CFSP/CSDP and the specific law governing it are the subject of controversy in the literature and in case law, either because of the imprecision of its scope and field of application, the questioning of the out-of-system dimension of its powers, or the singularity of its acts (Section II). Furthermore, these actions rely on *ad hoc* bodies, progressively created for external action in general or more specifically dedicated to the CFSP and its defence component (Section III).

I. THE VALUES, PRINCIPLES AND OBJECTIVES OF THE CFSP/CSDP

We are well aware of the importance of principles, objectives and values in EU law, which are all markers of the Union's history, its specific identity and, in the field of external relations, its desire to assert itself on the international stage, over and above the defence of its interests, the defence and promotion of its values. We will not dwell on the semantic shifts and conceptual ambiguities that govern the distinction between principles, objectives and values in EU law, which have often and rightly been emphasised by legal writers.[1]

On a more political level, it is well known that their sometimes uncertain or even 'lax' definition or qualification owes much to the compromises resulting from negotiations on the Treaties. Nonetheless, it is true that values, principles and objectives are at the heart of the European project and serve both internal purposes, in relations between the Union and its Member States, and external purposes, in the Union's international projection: values, principles and objectives essentially fulfil three functions: i) interpreting Union law, ii) delimiting the Union's competences, but also iii) providing a framework for those of the Member States.

With regard more specifically to external action, the method of bringing together in the first general provision of Article 21 TEU (Chapter 1 of Title V),

---

1 See in particular C. Blumann, 'Objectifs et principes en droit communautaire' and C. Flaesch-Mougin, 'Typologie des principes de l'Union', in *Liber amicorum en l'honneur de Jean Raux: le droit de l'Union européenne en principes*, Rennes, Apogée, Publications du CEJM de Rennes, 2006.

to which Article 23 TEU refers, the principles, objectives and values applicable to all areas of external action (both in the TFEU and the CFSP), reflects a specific willingness which has been unanimously welcomed. The aim is to strengthen the Union's image on the international stage, making it a more visible but also a more global stakeholder, while respecting the diversity of its conferred competences. These are different in nature and scope, and are 'fragmented' between the two treaties on the Union and the functioning of the EU. Thus the CFSP and its common security and defence component are the only policies included in the TEU, in Sections 1 and II respectively of Chapter 2 of Title IV of this Treaty. It should be emphasised that, behind these displays of its unique international identity, the Union claims to be rooted in the values, principles and objectives that presided over its creation and development (Section A). Although there are indeed, values, principles and objectives common to all external action, to which the CFSP and its common defence and security component contribute, the specific nature of the rules and procedures of the CFSP/CSDP is also very concrete (Section B).

A. COMMON VALUES, PRINCIPLES AND OBJECTIVES FOR EXTERNAL ACTION THAT DO NOT EXCLUDE SPECIFIC VARIATIONS FOR THE CFSP/CSDP

Article 21(1) TEU,[2] to which Article 23 TEU implicitly refers, lists democracy, the rule of law, the universality and indivisibility of human rights and fundamental freedoms, human dignity, equality and solidarity and respect for the principles of the United Nations Charter and international law among the values and principles of the Union's external action. This corpus, which is in a way consubstantial with the Union's own creation, development and enlargement, is also the basis of its external action (including its security and defence action), by demonstrating not only the Union's desire to respect them but also to promote them in the rest of the world. The values thus undergo a form of mutation so that, beyond the display of the Union's identity, they are transformed into objectives whose promotion is intended to cover all external action. Compared with Article 2 TEU, the provisions of Article 21(1) TEU reveal both material and formal differences, which have not escaped the notice of legal writers. Human rights are thus given additional characteristics – universality and indivisibility – which are evidence of a strong vision that is so

---

2 'The Union's action on the international scene is based on the principles which governed its creation, development and enlargement, and which it aims to promote in the rest of the world: democracy, the rule of law, the universality and indivisibility of human rights and fundamental freedoms, respect for human dignity, the principles of equality and solidarity, and respect for the principles of the United Nations Charter and international law'.

widely shared by the Member States that, for a long time, they did not feel the need to state it expressly in their domestic sphere. But this vision is sometimes challenged in the rest of the world, in the name of cultural specificities and opposition to 'Western hegemony'. Furthermore, in terms of terminology, there have been several 'semantic shifts' from values (Art. 2 TEU) to principles, which affect numerous concepts and illustrate the conceptual blurring between values and principles that has been commented on repeatedly. The fact remains that the choice made by Article 21 TEU of the term 'principle' has the merit of densifying the legal reality of the concepts listed and ultimately of making a distinction between the existential dimension of the Union's values, through which it affirms its identity to the rest of the world, and the operationality of its principles[3] which guide its action. Certain principles and values are common to all of the Union's external action, while not excluding, in some cases, a specific application to the CFSP, and therefore to the common security and defence policy (Section 1). The specific nature of the CFSP rules and procedures set out in the second subparagraph of Article 24(1) is undoubtedly one of the most fundamental principles of this policy, including its security and defence dimension, and is part of the protection of the intergovernmental nature of the CFSP (Section 2).

1. Setting Out the Union's Values and Principles and Displaying Its Unique International Identity

We know that it is up to the Council and the Commission, assisted by the High Representative, to ensure consistency between the different areas of external action on the one hand, and between these and other EU policies on the other.[4] This requirement for consistency seems all the more justified given the extraordinary fragmentation of the mosaic of external action policies, which are 'scattered' between the two treaties and their fundamentally different ambiences of integration or intergovernmentalism. In the specific area of the CFSP, and therefore of the common security and defence policy, this responsibility for ensuring consistency falls solely to the Council and the High Representative, under the second subparagraph of Article 26(2). Moreover, the TEU brings together in a single mechanism the principles of unity, consistency and effectiveness, which are closely linked in addition to

---

3 See I. Bosse Platière, *L'article 3 du traité UE: recherche sur une exigence de cohérence de l'action extérieure de l'UE*, Brussels, Bruylant, 2009, p. 143.

4 Under the terms of the second subparagraph of Article 21(3), 'The Union shall ensure consistency between the different areas of its external action and between these and its other policies. The Council and the Commission, assisted by the High Representative of the Union for Foreign Affairs and Security Policy, shall ensure that consistency and shall cooperate to that effect'. On the need for consistency in the EU's external action, see I. Bosse Platiere, ibid.

their specific functions (Section a). As for the spirit of loyalty and mutual solidarity recalled in Article 24(2) and (3) of the TEU, these are undoubtedly a CFSP-specific variation of the general principle of loyal cooperation as it now appears in Article 4(3) of the TEU and which, as we know, was reconfigured by the Treaty of Lisbon.[5] This singular variation of loyal cooperation in the CFSP is justified by the *sui generis* nature of the competences held by the Union in this policy, including defence, and which is not without consequences for their articulation with those of the Member States (Section b).

a. – Unity and Consistency

i. *The Principle of Unity*

The principle of unity refers to the idea that the Union must appear on the international stage as a single player, despite the obligatory coexistence of its external actions with those of its Member States. The latter are particularly attentive to any limitation of their sovereignty in the sensitive areas of their external action and *a fortiori* their foreign policy and their security and defence. The area of defence and security is certainly the one that most challenges the differences between Member States, whether in terms of their budgetary and human capacities, their strategic and economic interests, or their perception of the issues and alliances involved. The Franco-German partnership has often borne the brunt of these differences, including recently in the handling of support for Ukraine. The unity of the Union is a factor in the effectiveness of its diplomatic and security action and its ability to present a united and solid front in asserting its identity, anchored in the specific values it intends to defend and promote in a composite world where the interests of States are often divergent or even competing.

At the interinstitutional level, unity involves the Union's international representation, which is particularly complex,[6] and closely dependent on exogenous factors (including especially the status of a wide range of international organisations) but also endogenous factors, and which is shared between the President of the European Council and the High Representative in the specific area of the CFSP. According to the second subparagraph of Article 15(6) TEU, the President of the European Council 'shall, at his level and in that capacity, ensure the external representation of the Union on issues

[5] The essence of this reconfiguration results from the fact that Article 4(3) TEU 're-establishes', as it were, the balance of loyal cooperation between the Union and the Member States, which respect and assist each other, and thus puts an end to the 'unilateral nature' of the positive and negative obligations of the Member States towards the Union that characterised the former provisions of ex-Article 10 TFEU.

[6] See D. Bouvier, *La représentation internationale de l'Union européenne*, Brussels, Bruylant, 2020.

concerning its common foreign and security policy, without prejudice to the powers of the High Representative', who, it should be remembered, is at least theoretically omnipresent in the specific area of the CSDP.[7] The level of representation of the President of the European Council is therefore that of the Heads of State and Government and their capacity is that of being President of the highest body of the Union. However, unlike the High Representative, this representative function in the context of the CFSP is limited by the absence of any real power of proposal conferred on the President of the European Council in this area and by their rather secondary role in CFSP matters, and even more so in security and defence matters. The main responsibility of the President of the European Council is rather more internal, and is to ensure the smooth running of the European Council. The role of the High Representative in representing the EU in matters relating to the CFSP, established by Article 27(2) of the TEU, is of a completely different significance: it is reinforced by the powers conferred on them by the Treaty of Lisbon in the areas of common foreign and security policy, including defence: the conduct of political dialogue with third countries (previously exercised by the rotating Presidency of the Union), the expression of the Union's positions within international organisations, and finally, in accordance with the second and third subparagraphs of Article 34(2) TEU the presentation, at the request of Member States which sit on the UN Security Council, of the Union's position on a question on the Security Council's agenda. The many formal expressions of the High Representative's representative function have thus developed in a significant way,[8] helping to make the Union's positions clearer and more effective, including in the field of defence and international security.

The principle of unity, which calls for multiple expressions of varying normative nature and density, is closely linked to the nature of the external competences held by the European Union. It cannot be developed in the same way depending on whether the Union has exclusive, shared or, as in the case of the CFSP, simply parallel competences with those of its Member States, *especially* when they are very circumscribed, as in the field of the CSDP, which is in no way comparable to that of *defence*, as it is usually understood in the sphere of a state. It should be remembered that the CSDP, in its current form, simply aims to provide the Union with civil and military operational capabilities that the Member States make available for its crisis management

[7] It is true that the 'dual role of foreign policy/common security and defence policy' remains fairly dependent on the personality of the holder of the office and his or her interest in defence issues. During her term of office, Baroness Ashton gave priority to her diplomatic activities to the detriment of defence and security.

[8] Communications following bilateral meetings and multilateral summits, comments on topical issues, remarks on specific themes, speeches, etc.

missions and which they simply undertake to improve progressively.[9] It does not confer any competence on the Union in matters of collective defence, beyond the deceptive mutual defence clause in Article 42(7) TEU.[10] It must not affect the specific character of the policies of certain Member States. A genuine common defence policy, which would be defined progressively and lead to a common defence, is certainly envisaged in the Treaty, but its creation is subject to a decision of the European Council adopted by unanimity.[11]

Unity will therefore not really be implemented based on integration in these particular areas of foreign policy and its defence component, but rather based on cooperation or coordination, especially when its implementation concerns diplomatic or security activities, without necessarily taking the form of highly normative acts. Unity is sometimes achieved by means other than legally binding acts, such as the use of solemn declarations by the European Council or the Council. The declaration adopted at the end of the informal meeting held in Versailles (11 March 2022), days after Russia invaded Ukraine on 24 February 2022, is an excellent example.

Finally, unity can also be implemented through non-normative, specific and targeted channels, including in the field of defence and security. One thinks of the new powers conferred on the High Representative by the Treaty of Lisbon: the first concerns the organisation of coordination between Member States within international organisations or conferences;[12] the second, more specific to security and defence, concerns the power conferred on the High Representative to present the common position of the Union to the Security Council.[13] All these legislative and non-legislative channels are an illustration of the obvious proximity between unity on the one hand and consistency and loyal cooperation on the other.

ii. *The Need for Consistency*[14]

The need for consistency is also reiterated and even specified in the TFEU first and foremost in a general and comprehensive manner by the 'standardised' provisions of the Treaty on European Union relating to the Union's external action. It is expressed through several cross-cutting objectives which permeate each of its policies and actions.[15]

---

9 See Art. 42 TEU.

10 See the commentary by J.-C. Martin in this publication.

11 See E. Bernard's commentary on the Preamble in this publication.

12 Art. 34(1) TEU.

13 Third subparagraph of Art. 34(2) TEU.

14 See Art. 131, as well as the second subparagraphs of Arts. 21(3) and 26(2) TEU.

15 For trade policy, see Art. 207(1) TFEU; for development cooperation policy, see Art. 208(1) TFEU; for economic and financial cooperation, see Art. 212(1) TFEU.

At institutional level, as at material level, consistency is both vertical between actions on the international stage of the institutions of the Union itself and that of its Member States. But it is also 'doubly horizontal', because it is necessary to articulate all the Union's external policies and actions in a coherent way, but also to promote convergence between the actions of the Member States, which is even more necessary but also more complex in the field of security and defence, given the divergent approaches of the Member States in this area.

Vertical consistency between the Union's external action and that of the Member States is closely conditioned by the nature of the competences held by the Union, which naturally calls for a specific form of consistency for the CFSP/CSDP. At the institutional level, the CFSP/CSDP is thus assigned 'guardians' who are different to those for external action. Indeed, the Council and the High Representative alone, to the exclusion of the Commission, are responsible for ensuring the consistency of the CFSP and its unity and effectiveness,[16] a task made all the more complex by the fact that, as in the specific framework of the CSDP, the Union may hold 'truncated competences',[17] and that the Member States wish to protect their sovereignty in these matters, which is also guaranteed by certain specific provisions. One example is the second subparagraph of Article 42(2), which clearly states that the defence aspect of the CFSP shall not affect the specific character of the security policy of certain Member States, nor shall it affect the wish of others to include their common defence within the framework of NATO.[18] It is therefore easier to understand that the exercise by the Union of its competence in these intensely sovereign functions of foreign policy, defence and security does not entail any real obligation but rather a simple 'duty of loyalty' which should not be confused with the principle of loyal cooperation (see below, Section 2).

In addition to the institutional and substantive consistency between all the Union's external policies and within the CFSP itself, consistency must also be assessed in the light of the values of the Union enshrined in Article 21(1)

---

16 Second subparagraph of Art. 26(2) TEU.

17 In the specific area of the CSDP and of Section 2 of Chapter 2 of the specific provisions of the Common Foreign and Security Policy, the Union's competences are, as the law currently stands, limited solely to crisis management missions and cannot affect the specific actions of its Member States. Although it includes the progressive definition of a common defence policy, the creation of common defence is subject to a unanimous decision by the European Council and to the adoption of a decision by each Member State in accordance with its constitutional rules (see the commentary by Elsa Bernard in this publication). Furthermore, the Union's competences do not cover the defence of the territorial integrity of its Member States, which remains their reserved domain and which they have agreed to implement under the mutual assistance clause (see the commentary on Article 42(7) TEU by Jean-Christophe Martin in this publication).

18 See the respective comments by Elsa Bernard (first subparagraph of Art. 42(2)) and Yves Buchet de Neuilly (second subparagraph of Art. 42(2) in this publication).

TEU. It results not only from the fact that the external action of the Union in all its components (TEU and TFEU) *shall respect* these values, but also from the fact that it intends to *defend and promote them* on the international stage. One of the most emblematic expressions of this common link between external policies and values is undoubtedly that of political conditionality,[19] whereby the Union makes its economic and trade relations with third parties subject to compliance with political conditions, in particular respect for democracy, the rule of law and human rights. Better known in the context of its treaty-based activity, which is also governed by the *pacta sunt servanda* principle and the *non adimpleti contractus* exception, political conditionality has seen a significant expansion in the practice of the Union's external action, whether treaty-based or not. This is undoubtedly one of the 'hallmarks' of the Union's external action, which goes beyond the search for the necessary conciliation inherent in the fragmentation of its external action, but transcends it to some extent, to participate in the particular identity that the Union intends to display to the rest of the world. Over and above the different ways in which political conditionality has been asserted, which has developed a great deal, particularly – but not exclusively – in the conventional practice of the Union, including the CFSP,[20] it is naturally the conditionality based on the triptych of democracy, the rule of law and human rights that constitutes the hard core of this synergy between external action and the defence of the Union's values. The CFSP,[21] but also its CSDP defence component, make a significant contribution to this.[22] In fact, the CFSP is behind the densification of a network of rules in favour of defence, the promotion of this triptych and the strengthening of the Union's toolbox, including the creation in 2012 of an EU Special Representative for Human Rights.[23] This body was created in the name of consistency, particularly between all the EU's external policies on defending and promoting human rights on the international stage.

It is true that the consistency of external action still suffers, beyond its semantic evolutions, from a limited justiciability which has generally led

---

19 See C. Schneider, 'Au cœur de la coopération internationale de l'Union européenne: quelle stratégie à venir pour la conditionnalité politique', in *Mélanges en l'honneur du professeur Jean Touscoz*, Nice, France Europe, 2007, pp. 750 et seq.

20 See, in particular, for the CFSP's conventional activity, J. Auvret-Finck, 'La conditionnalité des droits de l'homme dans les accords de l'Union européenne relatifs à la lutte contre la piraterie maritime', in C. Chevallier-Govers and C. Schneider, *L'Europe et la lutte contre la piraterie maritime*, Paris, Pedone, 2015, pp. 245 et seq.

21 C. Schneider, 'Les droits fondamentaux, frein ou moteur de la PESC: atouts et faiblesses de la diplomatie européenne en matière de droits de l'homme', in J. Andriantsimbazovina (ed.), *Droits fondamentaux et intégration européenne*, Paris, Mare & Martin, 2021, pp. 117 et s.

22 One need only recall, for example, the extensive training in human rights and humanitarian law provided as part of CSDP military and civilian missions. See Anne Hamonic's commentary in this publication.

23 See Decision 2012/440/CFSP of 25 July 2012.

doctrine to prefer the qualification of requirement or imperative of consistency rather than that of principle. One of the main difficulties arises from the difficulty of retaining consistency as an autonomous basis for determining that a Member State has infringed a position of the Union.[24]

In the final analysis, we can only emphasise the particular and complex interweaving of unity, consistency and loyal cooperation, or the duty of loyalty, even if the doctrine has sometimes attempted to theorise on this subject. For some authors, consistency relates to the relationship between actions and policies, while loyal cooperation concerns the relationship between stakeholders. Other authors have sought to differentiate between the two based on their justiciability, emphasising, in contrast to loyal cooperation, the minimalist justiciability of consistency, which is limited solely to the review of the legal basis carried out especially in the context of the case between the Commission and the Council on the proliferation of small arms and light weapons.[25] Thus at best consistency would only have a confirmatory or interpretative value in relation to existing norms.[26]

b. – Loyal Cooperation, Spirit of Loyalty and Mutual Solidarity[27]

The principle of loyal cooperation is a major principle of Community integration, and is inherent in a particularly complex system for distributing competences between the organisation and its Member States, while being rooted in a logic of integration. It was redefined with the Treaty of Lisbon, and has not failed to affect the Union's external relations.[28]

While the principle of loyal cooperation is applicable to all external action according to a now-classic reading grid that seeks to decipher its vertical dimension in relations between the Union and its Member States, as well as its dual horizontal dimension in inter-institutional relations within the Union and in relations between Member States, the principle of loyal cooperation is nevertheless subject to variations that are specific to the CFSP, and therefore to the EU's common security and defence policy.

---

24 See e.g. Case C-620/16, *Commission v Germany*, ECLI:EU:C:2019:256. In this case, the Court abandoned consistency after having nevertheless generally noted that when a Member State departs from a Council decision, there may be repercussions for the unity and the consistency of the Union's action within COTIF: it chose instead to rely on the requirement of unity arising from the duty of loyal cooperation in Article 4(3) TEU, which it found to have been breached in this case.

25 Cf. Case 91/05, *Commission v Council*, ECLI:EU:C:2008:288.

26 See C. Blumann, *Droit institutionnel de l'Union européenne*, Paris, LexisNexis, 2023, pp. 161 et seq.

27 Art. 24(3) TEU.

28 See M. Fartunova-Michel and J.-F. Delile, *La coopération loyale dans les relations extérieures de l'Union européenne*, Brussels, Bruylant, 2023.

The first of these vertical variations is to be found in Article 24(3) TEU,[29] which has somewhat enriched the former provisions of ex-Article 11 TEU: States are not only asked to support the Union's foreign and security policy actively and unreservedly, *but also to respect it.* It should be emphasised that Article 24(3) TEU has substituted *'loyal cooperation'* with *'the spirit of loyalty'* in relations between the Member States and the Union. Meanwhile, the obligation incumbent upon them, as set out in the second subparagraph of Article 24(3), is simply to refrain from any action against the Union which is contrary to its interests or likely to impair its effectiveness as a cohesive force in international relations.

In addition, a second approach stems from the idea of *'mutual solidarity'* and complements *'the spirit of loyalty'* in two ways. The first results from the provisions of Article 31 TEU, which defines the 'obligations' of a Member State which formally abstains from a CFSP decision taken unanimously. These obligations appear to be less binding. In addition to the fact that its formal abstention releases the State from its obligation to apply the decision, its duties with regard to the spirit of loyalty towards the Union are also attenuated. It is in fact simply asked to refrain from any action likely 'to conflict' with that of the Union or *'to impede it'.* It is reasonable to think that there is a difference in degree of obligation between the national position which is asked not to be *'contrary to'* the action of the Union and that which *'would conflict'* with it. The abstaining State clearly has a greater margin of action for its national position, which could undoubtedly be contrary to the Union's action without coming into conflict with it. Finally, it should be emphasised that the position of the abstaining State must be respected by the other Member States, which covers the horizontal dimension of mutual solidarity in terms of relations between Member States.

The second subparagraph of Article 24(3) TEU thus refers in general terms to this idea of mutual political solidarity between Member States, which they 'shall *work together*' to strengthen. More specifically, the Member States, whose sovereign competences in the area of foreign and security policy are subject to the principle of reservation, must work to achieve synergy between their national positions and actions. However, in addition to the very general definition of mutual political solidarity proposed by Article 24(3) TEU, CFSP/CSDP law offers more precise variations by imposing specific requirements on

[29] 'The Member States shall support the Union's external and security policy actively and unreservedly in a spirit of loyalty and mutual solidarity and shall comply with the Union's action in this area.
The Member States shall work together to enhance and develop their mutual political solidarity. They shall refrain from any action which is contrary to the interests of the Union or likely to impair its effectiveness as a cohesive force in international relations.
The Council and the High Representative shall ensure compliance with these principles'.

Member States in their mutual relations, in terms of information, consultation, prior consultation and coordination.

The *information* requirements imposed on Member States are the result of several provisions. Under Article 28(3) TEU, a Member State is obliged to inform its partners of 'any plan to adopt a national position or take national action pursuant to a decision' of the European Union involving operational action. This does not refer to 'measures which are merely a national transposition of Council decisions', but to other measures. It must do so 'in time to allow, if necessary, for prior consultations within the Council'. In addition, Member States which are parties to an international organisation or conference in which not all Member States participate must keep the latter informed, as well as the High Representative in accordance with Article 34(2) TEU, which makes explicit reference to Article 24(3) TEU and to the spirit of loyalty and mutual solidarity. Finally, as regards the Security Council in particular, there is the same requirement for those represented there to provide information to the other Member States and to the High Representative.

Other requirements concern *the consultation of Member States* within the European Council and the Security Council on any issue of general interest, following Article 32 TEU, requirements which the Treaty of Lisbon has strengthened by adding the objective of 'determining a common approach'.

In addition to the requirement for consultation, *the requirement for coordination* between Member States is a stronger expression of mutual solidarity than consultation, and is expressed in several ways. Firstly, when a common approach has been defined by the European Council or the Security Council based on Article 32 TEU, Member States are required to coordinate their activities within the Council. This coordination is carried out both by their respective ministers and by the High Representative.[30] In addition to this situation where the Union has a common approach to a foreign and security policy issue of general interest, the Member States are also called upon to coordinate their activities within international organisations and conferences,[31] where they will be called upon to defend the Union's interests, which justifies the responsibility given to the High Representative to ensure this coordination.

Lastly, under Article 32(1) TEU, each Member State is required to *consult* its partners *before* taking any action on the international stage or entering into any commitment which could affect the Union's interests. This consultation is carried out by the Member States within the European Council to ensure that they enable the Union to assert its interests and values on the international stage, through the convergence of their actions.

---

30 Art. 32(2) TEU.

31 Art. 34(1) TEU.

These various arrangements show how closely the unity, spirit of loyalty and mutual solidarity implemented within the framework of the two major CFSP institutions, the European Council and the Council, are interwoven. However, it is also true that there is a form of 'decentralised acceptance' of these requirements through the organisation of cooperation between, on the one hand, the EU delegations and, on the other, the diplomatic and consular missions of the Member States for their respective contributions to the formulation of the CFSP/CSDP and its implementation. The third subparagrah of Article 32 TEU states that, through their cooperation, the delegations and the diplomatic and consular missions shall contribute to both the development and the implementation of the Union's 'common approache[s]'. Furthermore, Article 35 TEU calls for their respective cooperation to ensure that CFSP 'decisions' involving operational action or a common position are complied with and implemented. Lastly, it should be emphasised that certain practical ways of stepping up their cooperation are expressly identified, such as the exchange of information or the preparation of joint assessments.

Both the idea of 'the spirit of loyalty' *and* that of 'mutual political solidarity' are new expressions of the specific nature of the CFSP, and therefore of the EU's common security and defence policy, which obviously find their basis in the particular nature of the competences held by the Union in this area and in the distribution of its competences with those of the Member States. The system of distributing competences specific to the CFSP is based on the 'coexistence of parallel competences' by the Union on the one hand, and by the Member States on the other. In this respect, it cannot be ignored that the singularity of this system is largely unrelated to the objective of integration in which loyal cooperation is rooted. The general spirit of intergovernmentalism that governs cooperation in the field of the CFSP and its defence component, the CSDP, which does not exclude their Europeanisation, particularly in the form of cooperation consequently calls for specific modes of articulation which are just variations on the borrowings from the principles, requirements or imperatives of integration.

2. *The Breakdown of Objectives and the Need for a Global Approach to External Action*

The unified system for external action, which we owe to Article 21 TEU as revised by the Treaty of Lisbon, seeks to present the Union as a global stakeholder, capable of mobilising a range of levers, policies and actions to achieve several objectives. These are listed in Article 21(2) TEU, which is a synthesis of those set out in the previous versions of the Treaties.

a. – The 'Cross-Cutting' but also Specific Dimension of CFSP/CSDP Objectives

As far as the CFSP is concerned, its diplomatic aspect (foreign policy) can be considered to 'cut across', as it were, all the objectives of external action. But it is also true that its CSDP strand is more specifically concerned with certain objectives: in particular those of safeguarding the security, independence and integrity of the Union,[32] which were introduced in the Treaties of Amsterdam and Nice and have already given rise to several commentaries. Indeed, it may be asked what exactly the 'integrity of the Union' means in terms of the usual interpretations, such as territorial integrity, for an entity that does not, strictly speaking, have any territory other than that of its Member States, even if it does have external borders.[33] And it is true that the reference to the principles of the United Nations and international law had already created ambiguity. On this point, the Treaty of Lisbon has not helped to clarify matters by introducing the mutual assistance clause in Article 42(7) TEU, a variation on the right to legitimate self-defence that is specific to the unidentified political object.[34]

Moreover, the objectives listed in Article 21(2)(c) TEU undoubtedly refer to the CFSP and its CSDP component, both for diplomatic action and for crisis management: 'preserve peace, prevent conflicts and strengthen international security, in accordance with the purposes and principles of the United Nations Charter, with the principles of the Helsinki Final Act and with the aims of the Charter of Paris, including those relating to external borders'. It is nevertheless true that 'external borders' in EU law, transcending the usual acceptance that internationalists might have had of them, are of as much, if not more, interest in the area of freedom and justice (AFSJ) than the CFSP itself. This is the polymorphism of the concept of security specific to EU law, which combines international security and internal security, at times not without difficulty, given the complexity of its system of distributive competence.

b. – Is the Pooling of External Action Objectives Conducive to Extending the Scope of the CFSP?

Does enshrining the objectives of the Union's external action in a standardised and synthesised formal presentation encourage porosity between all its external policies strictly speaking, and the external aspects of sectoral policies? Above

32 Art. 21(2)(a) TEU.

33 See J.-C. Martin (ed.), *La gestion des frontières extérieures de l'UE: défis et perspectives en matière de sécurité et de sureté*, Paris, Pedone, 2011 and more particularly the contributions by J.-C. Martin, 'Quelle gestion pour quelles frontières', pp. 9 et seq. and by C. Schneider, 'La gestion intégrée par l'Union de ses frontières extérieures et de leurs enjeux sécuritaires ou l'art du paradoxe', pp. 281 et seq.

34 See the commentary on this provision by J.-C. Martin in this publication.

all, does it benefit the CFSP/CSDP, given the indeterminacy of its field of competence (any foreign policy issue), and the extension of this field of application to other policies?

These are all questions that deserve to be asked and that call for nuanced answers. For example, in 2012,[35] the Court held that the absence of an express reference to the fight against terrorism in the system of targeted CFSP sanctions laid down in Article 215(2) TFEU did not exclude from its scope those relating to the fight against international terrorism: the latter could indeed fall within one of the objectives of Article 21(2) TEU, namely preserving peace, preventing conflict and strengthening international security. Similarly, and still in the area of restrictive measures, the contribution of the 2022 *RT France v Council* case[36] should be noted, which saw the General Court of the European Union accept that a measure that aimed at banning the broadcasting of Russian media on the territory of the Union was covered by the CFSP, based on a broad interpretation of the CFSP covering all aspects of foreign policy and all issues affecting the security of the Union, as well as the decisions of Article 29 TEU including the Common Position.[37] But it is not only in the field of unilateral acts that the 'attractiveness of the CFSP' and its capacity to extend its field of application to the detriment of other policies, and in particular the AFSJ, are displayed. This is clearly demonstrated by the case law relating to the EU agreements concluded with Mauritius[38] and Tanzania[39] concerning the transfer by operation EUNAVFOR Atalanta of persons suspected of acts of piracy.[40]

B. CFSP/CSDP 'SUBJECT TO SPECIFIC RULES AND PROCEDURES'[41]

The specific nature of the rules and procedures applicable to the CFSP, referred to in the second subparagraph of Article 24(1) TEU, must be assessed from the dual perspective of the other external policies of the TFEU (Section 1) and the 'derogations from common/case law by the CFSP' enjoyed by the defence component of the CSDP (Section 2).

---

35 Case C-130/10, *Parliament v Council*, ECLI:EU:C:2012:472.

36 See Case T-125/22, *RT France v Council*, ECLI:EU:T:2022:483.

37 See Section II below.

38 See Case C-658/11, *Parliament v Council*, ECLI:EU:C:2014:2025.

39 Case C-663/14, *Parliament v Council*, ECLI:EU:T:2017:480.

40 See below, Section II, as well as the commentary on Article 43 TEU by A. Hamonic in this publication.

41 Second subparagraph of Article 24(1) TEU. See also Article 39 TEU on the adoption by the Council of specific rules on the protection of individuals with regard to the processing of personal data by the Member States when carrying out activities which fall within the scope of the CFSP, and on the free circulation of such data, in accordance with the requirement of Article 16 TFEU (see the commentary on this article by S. Rodrigues in this publication).

1. *The Specific Institutional and Procedural Features of the CFSP*

In addition to the impact of the principle of specificity that permeates this policy, both concerning the competences held by the Union (see footnote) and the acts that it adopts (see footnote), it is worth highlighting its specific institutional implications (second subparagraph of Article 24(1) TEU) and, above all, the more procedural implication arising from the requirement of unanimity for its decision-making process (Article 31 TEU).

a. – The 'Institutional Imbalance' Specific to the CFSP (Second Subparagraph of Article 24(1))

The institutional balance which governs the organisation and operation of the CFSP, including its CSDP component, is largely at variance with the 'integration law' which governs the construction of the Community and which, within the framework of the TFEU, governs the other areas of external action. Indeed, the respective status assigned to the institutions contrasts quite radically with their status under the TFEU.

i. *The European Council and the Council of the European Union*

These two institutions form the 'hard core' of a policy firmly rooted in an intergovernmentalism that is 'protected' by the unanimity rule.[42] As we know, since the Treaty of Lisbon, the European Council has, in addition to its power to give impetus to the CFSP, a genuine power of *decision* (Article 28(1) TEU), which contrasts with its lack of legislative function in the areas covered by the TFEU (Article 15(1)). Yet this power cannot be compared with the power conferred on the European Council by the Treaty of Amsterdam to adopt *common strategies,* the normativity of which was rightly questioned. Moreover, in the specific area of the CSDP, the European Council has the particular power to decide unanimously on the 'transition' from a *defence policy* to a *common defence,* the absence of a definition of the latter raising highly complex questions.[43] It is nonetheless true that the question of the European Council's monopoly on European defence matters can legitimately be raised.[44]

---

42 Second subparagraph of Article 21(1) TEU and Article 31 TEU.

43 This role of the European Council derives from Article 42(2), which states that '[t]he common security and defence policy shall include the progressive framing of a common Union defence policy. This will lead to a common defence, when the European Council, acting unanimously, so decides'. See Elsa Bernard's commentary on the preamble and Article 42 in this publication.

44 See also E. Bernard, 'Le Conseil européen: le monopole de la défense européenne?', in D. Blanc (ed.), *Le Conseil européen, le politique des politiques de l'UE*, Brussels, Larcier, 2023, pp. 337–350.

We also know that the Council plays a central role, both in terms of standard-setting[45] through its involvement at 'all ends of the standard-setting chain' (definition and implementation), and in terms of its non-standard-setting activities, which are particularly developed in the area of foreign and security policy.

ii. *CFSP Resistance to the Democratisation of the EU*[46]

• Exclusion of normative acts

The resistance of the CFSP and therefore of the CSDP to democratisation stems first and foremost from the exclusion of the European Parliament from the adoption of normative acts. The latter is not involved in the decisions relating to this policy, for which it has been given no place, even under the reduced angle of a cooperation procedure, though some of these acts could involve the Parliament. This is the case, for example, of the restrictive measures set out in Articles 29 TEU and 215 TFEU, about which the European Parliament regularly makes demands, given their risks to freedom and the legitimacy it claims in the defence of fundamental rights. However, although the Treaty of Lisbon has somewhat opened up certain avenues for this type of decision, its focus is bringing them under the jurisdiction of the Parliament,[47] rather

45 See for example: Council Decision (CFSP) 2017/809 of 11 May 2017 in support of the implementation of United Nations Security Council Resolution 1540 (2004) on the non-proliferation of weapons of mass destruction and their means of delivery, [2017] *OJ* L121/39; Council Decision (CFSP) 2015/2309 of 10 December 2015 on the promotion of effective arms export controls, [2015] *OJ* L326/56; Council Decision (CFSP) 2015/2215 of 30 November 2015 in support of UNSCR 2235 (2015), establishing an OPCW-UN joint investigative mechanism to identify the perpetrators of chemical attacks in the Syrian Arab Republic, [2015] *OJ* L314/51; Council Decision (CFSP) 2015/1908 of 22 October 2015 in support of a global reporting mechanism on illicit small arms and light weapons and other illicit conventional weapons and ammunition to reduce the risk of their illicit trade ('iTrace II'), [2015] *OJ* L278/15; Council Decision (CFSP) 2015/528 of 27 March 2015 establishing a mechanism to administer the financing of the common costs of European Union operations having military or defence implications (Athena) and repealing Decision 2011/871/CFSP, [2015] *OJ* L84/39. Council Decision 2014/42/CFSP of 28 January 2014 amending Decision 2012/281/CFSP in the framework of the European Security Strategy in support of the Union proposal for an international Code of Conduct on outer-space activities, [2014] *OJ* L26/42.

46 C. Schneider, 'Brèves réflexions iconoclastes sur la déconstitutionnalisation de la PESC et de la PESD', in E. Brosset, C. Chevallier-Govers, V. Edjaharian and C. Schneider (eds.), *Le Traité de Lisbonne reconfiguration ou déconstitutionnalisation de l'UE*, Brussels, Bruylant, 2009, pp. 287 et seq.; C. Schneider, 'Le contrôle démocratique de la PESC', in J. Auvret-Finck (ed.), *Le Parlement européen après l'entrée en vigueur du Traité de Lisbonne*, Brussels, Larcier, 2013, pp. 109 et seq. L. Balmond, 'Le Parlement européen et la PSDC', in J. Auvret-Finck (ed.), *Le Parlement européen après l'entrée en vigueur du Traité de Lisbonne*, Brussels, Larcier, 2013. C. Schneider, 'Le renforcement de la légitimité de la PESC', in J. Auvret-Finck (ed.), *Vers une relance de la politique de sécurité et de défense commune?*, Brussels, Larcier, 2014, pp. 69 et seq.

47 See Articles 24(1) TEU and 275 TFEU, as well as the commentary by N. Gros-Verheyde and C. Schneider in this publication.

than democratising them through Parliamentary involvement. Similarly, and this time with regard to the EU's conventional activity, the approval of the European Parliament is not required for agreements relating exclusively or mainly to the CFSP, unlike many of those concluded in the context of its external action under the TFEU. Here again, the CFSP remains a bastion of resistance to the efforts made throughout the construction of the Community to democratise the Union and increase the legitimacy of its actions. The status of the European Parliament in CFSP matters is thus largely reduced to political control, via consultation or information.

- Reduced information and consultation rights

The European Parliament's 'right to information' relates first of all to certain normative acts: this is the case for restrictive measures under Article 215(1) TFEU involving the reduction or interruption of economic and financial relations with third countries, which have been the subject of information from the Council to the European Parliament since the Treaty of Lisbon. The same applies to agreements concluded under the CFSP, which, following Article 218(10) TFEU, require the Parliament to be informed, a requirement which has been strengthened in relation to the previous Treaties. Information is in fact immediate, full and complete at all stages of the procedure and the Court monitors compliance with it, refusing to accept, as the Council maintained, differences in degree, as regards this information, with non-CFSP agreements and affirming that 'Parliament's involvement in the decision-making process is the reflection, at EU level, of a fundamental democratic principle'.[48]

However, in addition to information on the CFSP's standard-setting activities, the information provided to Parliament also concerns the policy's non-standard-setting activities, as specified in Articles 15(6)(d) TEU[49] and 36(1) TEU,[50] which are all innovations resulting from the Treaty of Lisbon. The first provision is not specific to the CFSP, but covers it nonetheless. For example, the President of the European Council is required to submit a report to the Parliament after each European Council, which covers all the issues addressed and therefore does not exclude those relating to the CFSP. Article 36(1) TEU

48 See the cases relating to the agreements concluded by the Union in the context of the fight against maritime piracy with Mauritius and with Tanzania: Case C-658/11 (EU-Mauritius Agreement), *Parliament v Council*, ECLI:EU:C:2014:2025; Case C-263/14 (EU-Tanzania Agreement), *Parliament v Council*, ECLI:EU:C:2016:435. On these cases, see the commentary in this publication by A. Hamonic.

49 Under the terms of this provision, the European Council 'shall present a report to the European Parliament after each of the meetings of the European Council'.

50 Under the terms of this provision, '[t]he High Representative of the Union for Foreign Affairs and Security Policy shall regularly consult the European Parliament on the main aspects and the basic choices of the common foreign and security policy and the common security and defence policy and inform it of how those policies evolve. He shall ensure that the views of the European Parliament are duly taken into consideration. Special representatives may be involved in briefing the European Parliament'.

establishes an obligation for the High Representative to inform the Parliament on the development of the CFSP, *including its CSDP component*, this precision being a new feature of the Treaty of Lisbon. The transfer to the High Representative of this responsibility to inform the Parliament is also new.[51] This can be explained by the significant strengthening of the latter's status under the Treaty of Lisbon. A final new feature is that special representatives may be involved in informing the Parliament. In practice, the information provided to the Parliament is based on regular dialogue between the High Representative and their EEAS departments with the Parliament's Foreign Affairs Committee (AFAT) and its two sub-committees, including the Defence Committee (SEDE).

Consultation of the Parliament in the field of the CFSP was first provided for in Article 36(1) TEU, which established the principle of regular consultation of the Parliament by the High Representative on the main aspects and basic choices of the common foreign and security policy, including the CSDP. The Lisbon Treaty proposes a definition *ratione materiae* of consultation that has not really changed, with the exception of the express addition of its applicability to the CSDP. The criterion of 'the main aspects and basic choices' is sufficiently broad to leave room for the margin of appreciation of the new holder of this obligation, namely the High Representative, who also has the same margin of appreciation to 'ensure that the views of the Parliament are duly taken into account'. In any event, the question arises as to what exactly is covered by the notions of 'main aspects' and 'fundamental choices' of a foreign and security policy: does this preferably concern broad, even abstract, strategic options or rather 'practical management' and actions on the ground?

The Parliament has tended to emphasise the second option, in the many demands it has made in its various resolutions and recommendations, and during the discussion on the creation of the EEAS.[52] For example, it has demanded to be consulted on the definition of the role and mandates of the special representatives, and even regarding the interview for their appointment. Similarly, in the more specific context of the CSDP, the Parliament has demanded to be consulted at least on the missions and operations set out in Article 43 TEU, in particular the crisis management concept (CMC). This may be considered a 'reasonable demand' insofar as the CMC relates only to the Union's general political approach in response to a particular crisis and not to the strategic and military aspects of the operations or missions themselves.[53]

The transfer of responsibility from the rotating Presidency of the Council for informing and consulting the Parliament on the CFSP and its defence

---

51 Before the Treaty of Lisbon, it had an influence on the Presidency of the Council and the Commission.

52 See below.

53 See the commentary in this publication by A. Hamonic.

aspects to the High Representative undoubtedly represents progress in the democratisation of dialogue in this area, thanks to the Treaty of Lisbon. The highly targeted competences of the High Representative, including in the field of CSDP, make them a highly specialised interlocutor, who is more available and more legitimate than the rotating Council Presidency. This is consistent with the new role assigned to the High Representative/Vice President (HR/VP) by the Treaty of Lisbon, namely the Presidency of the Foreign Affairs Council and which, at least *de facto,* covers a number of meetings of defence ministers. These, it should be remembered, are not Council meetings as such, but simply informal meetings excluding any adoption of CFSP-type decisions.

This transfer has led to an undeniable form of sharing of foreign policy issues between the apparatuses of the EEAS and the European Parliament, in particular its Foreign Affairs Committee (AFAT) and its Defence Subcommittee (SEDE). It is thus on the basis of its rights to information and consultation that the European Parliament exercises its political control over the CFSP and CSDP through the traditional parliamentary instruments of debates and questions, resolutions accompanied by reports and recommendations. The Treaty of Lisbon strengthened these rights with Article 36(2) TEU.[54] The European Parliament now debates the progress made in implementing the CFSP and CSDP twice a year rather than just once. Lastly, since the Treaty of Lisbon, the European Parliament's powers to make recommendations or put questions are no longer limited to the Council alone, but also include the High Representative, who is now the European Parliament's main interlocutor, at least for matters relating to the CFSP and its defence aspects.

The European Parliament's general power of consultation on CFSP and CSDP matters based on Article 36 TEU is not its only prerogative. Mention should also be made of the existence of a specific and *ad hoc* consultative power conferred on it by Article 27(3) TEU and concerning the European External Action Service (EEAS), the founding act relating to its organisation and operation being a Council decision that was adopted on 10 July 2010.[55] While Article 27(3) reserves the initiative for this decision to the High Representative, it also provides not only for the approval of the Commission but also for consultation of the Parliament, which has developed a very dynamic approach to the matter.[56]

---

[54] 'The European Parliament may address questions or make recommendations to the Council or the High Representative. Twice a year it shall hold a debate on progress in implementing the common foreign and security policy, including the common security and defence policy.'

[55] See Decision 2010/427/EU of 26 July 2020 establishing the organisation and functioning of the European External Action Service (EEAS).

[56] See below.

iii. *The Marginalisation of the European Commission*

This marginalisation of the Commission from the CSDP, which should not be confused with defence issues related to the internal market, industrial policy or research policy questions, has rightly been highlighted by the doctrine.[57] There have been many examples of this affecting the various functions of the Commission.

It applies firstly to its international representation function, which the Commission had been able to develop in particular by exercising *de facto* the right of active legation of the Communities through its delegations to third countries. This had already been reduced by the creation of the CFSP under the Maastricht Treaty, with the 'Commission delegations' performing no Union representation function in this area.

Incontrovertible because of the emergence and development of the CFSP and its CSDP component, the Commission's setbacks in terms of representing the Union have been aggravated by the Treaty of Lisbon and the 'changes' it has brought about for the Union delegations.[58] Now placed under the authority of the High Representative and attached to the EEAS, their remit, previously limited to 'Community affairs', has been extended to include the CFSP and its defence aspects, to which they make a significant contribution.

The Commission has also seen significant reductions in its usual standard-setting powers. Its exclusion from the adoption of CFSP/CSDP decisions was already firmly rooted in the history of foreign policy cooperation between Member States. Initially sidelined in the context of European Political Cooperation (EPC) and then 'associated' with this cooperation by the Single European Act of 1986, the Maastricht Treaty and the CFSP gave the Commission a power of initiative which it shares with the Member States.[59] However, the Lisbon Treaty took this away from the Commission, by giving it only the possibility of 'supporting' a proposal from the High Representative[60] or on the basis of joint proposals with the HR/VP in the field of restrictive measures under Article 215 TFEU. Unlike in the case of the other external policies of the TEU, the Commission is also not the negotiator of agreements relating exclusively or mainly to the CFSP, this function again being assigned to the High Representative by the Treaty of Lisbon.[61] In this area, the HR/VP

57 F. Terpan, 'La place de la Commission dans la PESC-PSDC: marginalisation ou nouvelles opportunités', in J. Auvret-Finck (ed.), *La Commission en voie de redynamisation*, Paris, Pedone, 2017. E. Bernard, 'La communautarisation de la défense européenne dans le contexte de la guerre en Ukraine', *RTDE*, 2023/4, pp. 325–350.

58 See Art. 221 TFEU.

59 Art. J(8)(3).

60 Art. 30.1 TEU.

61 Art. 218(3), TFEU.

succeeds the Presidency of the Council which, until then, could 'be assisted the Commission as appropriate'.[62]

Another illustration of the Commission's marginalisation with regard to the CFSP/CSDP is its exclusion from the functions of implementing and executing this policy. These functions are entrusted respectively to the Council,[63] the High Representative and the Member States.[64] The exception is for economic and financial restrictive measures, which require a large number of regulations for their implementation.

This marginalisation is also the result of the fact that, in practice, the Commission has not really tried to take advantage of the few opportunities offered to it by the Treaties, either institutionally (duplication of the High Representative's functions) or functionally (autonomous and shared initiative between the Maastricht and Lisbon Treaties), to remedy this marginalisation.

Nonetheless, over and above this marginalisation in both institutional and functional terms, the EU does have certain opportunities to 'interfere' in the CFSP/CSDP.[65] The first of these is the responsibility entrusted to it to ensure the consistency of the various areas of external action of the Union. Since the Treaty of Lisbon, the Commission shares this responsibility with the Council and the High Representative.[66] This responsibility, which is justified by its powers of initiative and implementation in the external policies of the TFEU, is all the more important in view of the global approaches that the Union is tending to develop more and more to compensate, as best it can, for the 'schizophrenia' of its external action.

The Commission's powers in budgetary matters constitute 'another gateway' for interfering in the field of CFSP and therefore CSDP. The budget allocated to these policies, although modest, does not escape the Commission's powers of initiative and execution.[67]

The same applies to the supervision it retains over the EU delegations for the implementation of programmes financed by the various and numerous financial instruments for external action under the Community pillar, which makes their organisation and operation particularly complex.[68]

---

62 Ex-Art. 24(1) TEU.

63 Art. 26(2) TEU.

64 Art. 26(3) TEU.

65 See F. Terpan, 'La place de la Commission dans la PESC-PSDC: marginalisation ou nouvelles opportunités?', in J. Auvret-Finck (dir.), *La Commission en voie de redynamisation*, Paris, Pedone, 2017. E. Bernard, 'La communautarisation de la défense européenne dans le contexte de la guerre en Ukraine', *RTDE*, 2023/4, pp. 325–350.

66 Second subparagraph of Art. 21(3) TEU.

67 See the commentary on Article 41 TEU by A. Potteau in this publication.

68 See C. Schneider, 'Le Service d'action extérieure (SEAE) de l'Union, évolutionnisme ou illusionnisme du système d'action extérieure de l'UE?', in *L'identité du droit de l'Union européenne. Mélanges en l'honneur de Claude Blumann*, Brussels, Bruylant, 2015, pp. 783 et seq.

Finally, the Commission's powers as guardian of the Treaties give it a degree of power to interfere in the CFSP/CSDP field, for example when it pleads the erroneous legal basis of a CFSP/CSDP decision or the infringement of Article 40 TEU. In conclusion, it should come as no surprise that the Commission has sought other entry points in the Treaty on the Functioning of the European Union for interfering more specifically in defence matters: these are the internal market and the security reserves of Articles 346 to 348 TEU, industrial policy and, of course, research and development policy. But such 'communitarisation', which is amply discussed in this publication, should not be confused with the communitarisation of the CFSP and its CSDP.

iv. *The Court of Justice's Lack of Jurisdiction Concerning the CFSP/CSDP*

The immunity from jurisdiction of the CFSP/CSDP has a long history. It dates back to the very creation of the CFSP, but in terms that are specific to the Maastricht Treaty, which established it 'in a negative manner' by listing the Community institutional provisions applicable to the CFSP, relating to the Parliament, the Council and the Commission, while none of those concerning the Court of Justice appeared.[69] The immunity from jurisdiction of the CFSP/CSDP was maintained by the Treaty of Lisbon, albeit with a new, apparently clearer provision, which can now be found in the current second subparagraph of Articles 24(1) TEU[70] and Article 275 TFEU.[71] Article 24(1) TEU provides that the Court 'shall not have jurisdiction with respect to these provisions'. These are the specific CFSP provisions contained in Chapter 2 of Title V of the TEU,[72] including Article 24 TEU. Immunity applies only to these provisions and to acts adopted on their basis. Article 275(1) TFEU, for its part, establishes immunity by making an initial, fairly general reference to the fact that the Court 'shall not have jurisdiction with respect to the provisions relating to CFSP'. However, such a reference goes well beyond the specific provisions of the CFSP Chapter referred to in Article 24(1) TEU and could have opened the way to a broader interpretation of jurisdictional immunity, in particular to acts which, without having been taken within the framework of this Chapter, could have benefited from immunity because they *related to the CFSP*. Finally, Article 275(1) TFEU sets out a second criterion of immunity for acts adopted

---

[69] Art. J.11 and L. TEU.

[70] 'The Court of Justice of the European Union shall not have jurisdiction with respect to these provisions, with the exception of its jurisdiction to monitor compliance with Article 40 of this Treaty and to review the legality of certain decisions as provided for by the second paragraph of Article 275 of the Treaty on the Functioning of the European Union'.

[71] See the commentary on this provision by N. Gros-Verheyde and C. Schneider in this publication.

[72] Art. 23–46 TEU.

on a CFSP legal basis. The question will soon arise as to whether the CFSP legal basis of an act is sufficient in itself to prevent the Court from reviewing it.

However, the Treaties provide for exceptions to the Court's lack of jurisdiction over the CFSP, including its CSDP component. As stated in the second subparagraph of Article 24(1) TEU, the Court has jurisdiction 'to monitor compliance with Article 40 of this Treaty and to review the legality of certain decisions referred to in the second paragraph of Article 275 of the Treaty on the Functioning of the European Union'.

Article 40 TEU,[73] to which the second subparagraph of Article 24(1) TEU refers, has its origins in Article M of the Maastricht Treaty, which already provided that 'nothing in this Treaty shall affect the Treaties establishing the European Communities or the subsequent Treaties and Acts modifying or supplementing them'. Such a provision was understandable given the particular and new architecture of the Union system based on three pillars: the Community pillar and the two new pillars constituted by the CFSP on the one hand, and JHA on the other. As the latter two pillars were created based on intergovernmental logic, it was important to protect what was already established for the Community and its supranational logic from possible 'contamination' by intergovernmental logic. This protection of the Community Treaties was taken up by subsequent amendments to the TEU.

The absorption of the Community realised by the Treaty of Lisbon has not, however, reduced 'inter-pillar tensions'. In fact, the formal unification of external action brought about by the Treaty may even be said to have served to reinforce them. The main areas affected by this interference with the CFSP are development cooperation policies, trade policy and exports of dual-use goods, and the area of freedom, security and justice, which since the Lisbon Treaty has had its own sanctions mechanism independent of that of the CFSP. It is up to the courts to 'arbitrate' these interferences, either based on a breach of Article 40 TEU or as part of the review of the legal basis of acts and agreements. In the area of sanctions in particular, the duality of legal regimes,[74] introduced by the Treaty of Lisbon and a source of major power issues, gave rise to an

---

73 'The implementation of the common foreign and security policy shall not affect the application of the procedures and the extent of the powers of the institutions laid down by the Treaties for the exercise of the Union competences referred to in Articles 3 to 6 of the Treaty on the Functioning of the European Union.
Similarly, the implementation of the policies listed in those Articles shall not affect the application of the procedures and the extent of the powers of the institutions laid down by the Treaties for the exercise of the Union competences under this Chapter'.

74 See C. Schneider, 'Economic sanctions imposed by the European Union', *JDE*, vol. 221, September 2015.

initial major dispute concerning the choice of the legal basis for a regulation on sanctions in the context of the fight against terrorism.[75]

Article 40 TEU, which was introduced by the Treaty of Lisbon and replaces former Article 47 TEU, breaks new ground. By surviving the disappearance of the pillars and fitting into the new context of the attribution of a single legal personality to the Union, it maintains the specific nature of the CFSP and perhaps even strengthens it. It puts an end to the 'asymmetry' that characterised the ex-Article 47 mechanism. The latter established a form of hierarchy based on the priority given to the protection of Community treaties by a prohibition on the CFSP alone affecting them. Article 40 TEU 'restores the balance' by also prohibiting the implementation of the policies referred to in the TFEU[76] from affecting the application of the procedures, and the extent of the respective powers of the institutions for the exercise of their competences in the field of the CFSP. At the same time, the explicit reference which Article 40 TEU makes to the competences of Articles 3 to 6 TFEU should be emphasised, as it definitively closes the door to certain interpretations which had been developed by the Council in a case opposing it to the Commission, which contested the legal basis of a CFSP joint action granting assistance to the ECOWAS to limit small arms and light weapons transfers.[77] Nonetheless, the fact remains that the judicialisation of Article 40 TEU has undoubtedly been neutralised to some extent by the rebalancing introduced by the Lisbon Treaty.

The other exception to the Court's jurisdiction concerns the review of the legality of restrictive measures, also known as 'sanctions', against third countries, non-State entities or individuals. It is provided for in Article 275(2) TFEU, and is therefore the subject of a commentary under that provision.[78]

The CSDP is no exception to the Court's activism in pushing back its incompetence.

Thus, despite their eminently political, including military, dimension, actions taken in the context of crisis management missions do not escape the Court's control, and many crisis management missions have already been

---

75 Case C-130/10, *Parliament v Council*, ECLI:EU:C:2012:472, concerns the Parliament's challenge to the choice of the legal basis of the CFSP rather than that of Article 75 TFEU for a regulation on sanctions in the context of the fight against terrorism. Having accepted that the fight against terrorism could also fall within the scope of the CFSP, the Court, on the basis of its classic reasoning on the search for the appropriate legal basis (search for the centre of gravity of the act based on the objective criteria of its aims and content), concluded in favour of the CFSP's legal basis.

76 Art. 3 to 6 TFEU.

77 Case C-91/05, *Commission v Council*, ECLI:EU:C:2008:288. On this occasion, the Council attempted to reduce the scope of the CFSP non-affection clause by arguing that it would only apply where there was exclusive Community competence, which of course was not the case in this instance, which concerned 'competition between the CFSP and development cooperation' (in this case the Cotonou Agreement between the EU and the ACP).

78 See the commentary by C. Schneider in this publication.

subjected to tough controls by the Court.[79] The legal reasoning is reminiscent of that of acts of government, in that it separates the 'management acts' of these missions and field operations from the political dimension of their implementation. Their 'CFSP context' is not sufficient to exclude the Court's jurisdiction under Article 270 TFEU on the settlement of disputes between the Union and its servants[80] and under the Financial Regulation on the award of public contracts.[81] In 2024, for example, the Court did not hesitate to admit a reference for a preliminary ruling on the interpretation of the founding joint action of the EULEX Kosovo mission relating to the determination of the employer of that mission.[82] Finally, and still concerning the EULEX Kosovo mission, the contribution of the cases *KD* and *KS* C-29/22 P and C-44/22 P of 10 September 2024 concerning an action for non-contractual liability brought by the immediate family of two persons killed or missing in 1999 in Kosovo must be emphasised. The Court relied on its previous case law on the interpretation of the CFSP's jurisdictional immunity under Article 24 TEU, in which it established its jurisdiction to rule on certain acts and omissions falling within the scope of CSDP missions, insofar as they were not directly connected with its political and strategic choices (paragraph 118). This is clearly the situation in the present case concerning the mission's decisions on the choice of its staff (paragraph 128), the absence of provisions providing for legal aid in proceedings before a review board (paragraph 130), and lastly the decisions on whether or not to subject the mission's acts and omissions to a judicial review mechanism (paragraph 132). On the other hand, according to the Court, the decision to revoke the executive mandate of a CSDP mission is a political and strategic choice that cannot be reviewed by the courts (paragraph 136).

In addition, and beyond the question of the exact scope of the exception to the jurisdictional immunity of the CFSP in Articles 24(1) TEU and 275(2)

---

79 This is the case of the European Union Police Mission (EUPM) in Bosnia and Herzegovina with the numerous *H v Council* cases, including the Grand Chamber decision of 19 July 2016; the EULEX Kosovo mission (Case C-439/13 P, *Elitaliana SpA v Eulex Kosovo*, ECLI:EU:C:2015:753, Case C-730/18 P, Opinion of AG Tanchev of 5 Mach 2020, in Case C-730/18 P, *SC v Eulex Kosovo*, ECLI:EU:C:2020:176 and Joined Cases C-29/22 P and C-44/22, *KS, KD v European Commission*, ECLI:EU:C:2024:725); the EUCAP Sahel Niger mission, which has twice been reviewed by the Court of First Instance in connection with complaints of psychological harassment (Case T-763/16, *PY v EUCAP Sahel*, ECLI:EU:T:2018:181 and Case T-692/18, *M. Montanari v SEAE*, ECLI:EU:T:2019:850. On this issue see C. Schneider, 'Les dynamiques ambivalentes de la gestion de crise', in A. Hamonic, *Quelle spécificité pour l'Europe de la défense*, forthcoming. See also A. Hamonic's commentary on Article 43 TEU in this publication.

80 See the commentary by N. Gros-Verheyde in this publication.

81 See the commentary on Directive 2009/81/EC of the European Parliament and of the Council of 13 July 2009 by S. Rodrigues in this publication.

82 Case C-283/20, *CO and Others v MJ and Others*, ECLI:EU:C:2022:126. According to the Court's interpretation, it is not the Commission, the EEAS or the Council, but EULEX Kosovo itself.

TFEU, there are other indirect 'outbreaks of jurisdictional control' affecting the CSDP that are worth noting. Firstly, in the area of the Union's contractual activities relating to crisis management operations, the Court reviews the legal basis, relating to CFSP or otherwise, for agreements such as the transfer of persons suspected of piracy,[83] or respect for the Parliament's right to be fully informed in accordance with Article 218(10) TFEU and which covers all agreements of the Union including those of the CFSP.[84] Taking an even broader view of the legal issues relating to the 'proximity of the CFSP' to judicial review, it should be emphasised that the Court has held that jurisdictional immunity does not preclude its review of documents relating to CFSP.[85]

b. – The Procedural Expression of CFSP Specificity: The Unanimity Decision-Making Process[86]

Unanimity is an essential feature of the CFSP, of its intergovernmental nature and of the decision-making process within the European Council (in place of consensus) and the Council.[87] It is intimately linked to the history of cooperation between Member States in the field of foreign policy, including the CSDP, where unanimity is essential for decision-making. Indeed, the principle of unanimity governing the CFSP/CSDP, a veritable red line for many States for very different reasons, has never been called into question, but only gradually and very cautiously 'toned down' through various legal techniques.

i. *Unanimous with Constructive Abstentions*[88]

A first 'mitigation' of unanimity concerns its very definition, which does not necessarily require the approval of all the States: the abstention of one or more States does not have the effect of preventing the adoption of the decision that will be binding on the Union and its Member States, except in exceptional cases.[89] This is the famous mechanism of constructive abstention introduced by the Treaty of Amsterdam and set out in the second subparagraph of Article 31(1)

---

83 See C. Rapoport, 'Le rattachement à la PESC des accords de transfert de l'Union européenne en matière de piraterie maritime', in C. Chevallier-Govers and C. Schneider (eds.), *L'Europe et la lutte contre la piraterie maritime*, Paris, Pedone, 2015, pp. 163 et seq.

84 Case C-658/11, *European Parliament v Council*, ECLI:EU:C:2014:2025; Case C-263/14, *European Parliament v Council*, ECLI:EU:C:2016:435.

85 Case T-14/98 *Hautala v Council*, ECLI:EU:T:1999:157; Case C-353/99 P, *Council v Hautala*, ECLI:EU:C:2001:661.

86 Art. 24(1) and 31 TEU.

87 Art. 31 TEU.

88 Second subparagraph of Art. 31(1) TEU.

89 The decision may not be adopted if the Member States abstaining and accompanying their abstention with the formal declaration provided for in the second subparagraph of Article 31(1) TEU represent at least one third of the Member States comprising at least one third of the population.

TEU. There are two distinct ways in which this works, with different effects for the State concerned: either it remains bound by the decision taken by the Union, or, on the contrary, and because it has accompanied its abstention with a formal declaration to this effect, it will not be bound to apply it, on the understanding that, in accordance with its duty of loyalty, it will refrain from any action likely to conflict with that of the Union implied by the said decision, or simply to obstruct it. Although this mechanism was hailed in legal terms as a welcome unlocking of the unanimity requirement, giving the CFSP/CSDP greater flexibility and responsiveness, hopes were largely disappointed because this mechanism has scarcely been used. In its communication of 18 September 2018,[90] the Commission pointed out that it had only been used once (in 2008 in connection with the Kosovo crisis), and that the emergency brake offered to States, allowing them not to be obliged to apply the decision in the event of a formal declaration to that effect, had not produced the expected effects. Since that report, however, there has been a slight increase in the use of constructive abstention, thanks in particular to Hungary. For example, it invoked Article 31 TEU when the framework decision creating the EUMAM Ukraine military assistance mission was adopted in October 2022. Similarly, Hungary was behind the insertion of a special provision in the CFSP Decision of 18 March 2024,[91] the purpose of which was to increase the financial ceiling of the European Peace Facility by €5 billion, through a *specific assistance measure* earmarked for Ukraine. This decision exceptionally provides for the right of a Member State which has abstained in accordance with Article 31(1) TEU not to contribute to an assistance measure to be financed by this specific amount, even if it means making an additional contribution to other assistance measures. This mechanism is distinct from that contained in Article 5(3) of the founding decision of the EFF, which introduces a limited *ad hoc* abstention mechanism for the particular benefit of a State that does not wish to contribute to an assistance measure relating to the supply of lethal weapons.

ii. *Exceptions to the Unanimity Requirement*[92] *and Their Limitation by the 'Appeal Clause'*[93]

A second legal technique for mitigating the unanimity requirement is the use of derogations permitted expressly by the Treaty. Some of these are of a general

90 See COM(2018) 647 final, 'A stronger global actor: a more efficient decision-making for EU Common Foreign and Security Policy', 19 September 2018.

91 See Decision CFSP 2024/890, amending Decision CFSP 2021/509 establishing a European Peace Facility.

92 Art. 31(2) TEU.

93 Second subparagraph of Art. 31(2) TEU.

nature,[94] and are listed in Article 31(2) TEU, being inherited from previous law. Firstly, there is the case referred to in the first subparagraph of Article 31(2) TEU, which 'takes over' the provision introduced by the Treaty of Amsterdam whereby Council decisions taken on the basis of a common strategy of the European Council are taken by a majority: this provision has been 'cleaned up' to take account of the consequences of the abandonment of the old common strategies and the emergence of European Council decisions on the Union's strategic interests and objectives. The same applies to the adoption of *implementing decisions* defining a common action or position.[95] Finally, the third legacy of previous law is the appointment of special representatives under Article 33 TEU.[96] However, the Treaty of Lisbon has introduced a new derogation from unanimity. This concerns Council decisions adopted on a proposal from the High Representative *submitted at the specific request of the European Council:*[97] this specific request may result either from the European Council's own initiative or from an initiative from the High Representative in person. The scope of this derogation should not be overestimated. It does not apply to every Council decision taken on the basis of an initiative by the High Representative, but only to certain, very specific decisions. Had it been otherwise, and because the High Representative now has the power of initiative, the principle of unanimity governing the CFSP/CSDP would have been profoundly affected.

With very limited *ratione materiae*, the scope of qualified majority voting is further reduced by the provisions of the second subparagraph of Article 31(2) TEU, which confers special rights on a Member State wishing to oppose the adoption of a CFSP decision subject to qualified majority voting. This mechanism is certainly not new in principle, but the Treaty of Lisbon brought about a relative revision of the arrangements. The State invoking it must no longer rely on *important* and stated reasons of national policy,[98] but on *vital and stated reasons of* national policy, which would *a priori* restrict its right. The fact remains that such a mechanism gives a minority State a 'right of veto' with suspensive effect, which prevents the decision from being adopted: since the Treaty of Lisbon, the way has been open for the High Representative to seek, in

---

94 There are also very specific cases where the principle of unanimity is waived. See the European Council decision appointing the High Representative and putting an end to their functions, which requires the agreement of the President of the Commission (Art. 18(1) TEU); the Council decision on the status and operating procedures of the European Defence Agency (Art. 45(2) TEU); the Council decision establishing permanent structured cooperation (Art. 46(2) TEU) and the Council decision welcoming a new Member State to permanent structured cooperation (Art. 46(3)).

95 Third subparagraph of Art. 31(2) TEU.

96 Fourth subparagraph of Art. 31(2) TEU.

97 Second subparagraph of Art. 31(2) TEU.

98 Ex-Art. 23 TEU.

consultation with the State concerned, a solution acceptable to the latter, which in the event of failure opens up yet another alternative. This is the purpose of the third technique, the *appeal clause,* which is intended to replace the failure of the High Representative to find a solution. The Council is thus empowered, but not obliged (insofar as *it is able*), to refer the matter by qualified majority to the European Council for a unanimous decision.

iii. *The Passerelle Clause*[99]

This so-called passerelle or simplified revision clause, which appears in Article 31(3) TEU, is a final technique for reducing the unanimity requirement for the adoption of CFSP acts. It gives the European Council the right to extend the cases of qualified majority voting listed in paragraph 2 of the same article. It still needs to adopt the decision that will give effect to this unanimous extension.

It is clear that every precaution is being taken rightly to protect the principle of unanimity in the CFSP. Nevertheless, the existence of such a mechanism, which avoids the need to revise the Treaties, is fuelling hopes that this policy will be opened up further to qualified majority voting. It helps to reinvigorate the recurring controversy between the advocates of unanimity and their opponents, particularly since the Treaty of Amsterdam. The passerelle clause undoubtedly explains the current frequency of proposals to extend qualified majority voting under the CFSP, since these could now be put into practice in a simplified manner thanks to Article 31(3) TEU.

iv. *Extending Qualified Majority Voting under the CFSP: A Real or False Debate?*

Indeed, there is no need to point out that even when qualified majority voting is applicable under the Treaty on the Functioning of the European Union (TFEU), it is rarely used in reality, with the Member States generally substituting it with consensus. It is nonetheless true that in the specific area of foreign and security policy, unanimity is often denounced as preventing the Union from adapting to changing realities and reacting rapidly to urgent situations. Based on this recurrent criticism, various avenues have been explored in an attempt to 'improve the CFSP' through this particular channel of its decision-making process.

One of them, which Federica Mogherini advocated when she took office as High Representative, would be to ensure that qualified majority voting, when provided for in the Treaty, is actually applied, and not replaced by consensus. Of course, she was thinking of certain cases rather than others, the most

[99] Art. 31(3) TEU.

'common' and the most likely ones to bring about a real change in the way the CFSP operates, such as decisions to implement a common action or position. But on this point, the High Representative was unsuccessful, a failure that is fairly predictable given the history of the 'Community method' and the bad uses of qualified majority voting.

Another technique, which has occasionally been mentioned, would involve opening the appeal clause under Article 31(2) TEU to one Member State (a scenario that is difficult to envisage) or to several Member States (the precise number of which would need to be determined). One of the most frequently discussed options would be to use the passerelle clause in Article 31(3) TEU to introduce new cases of qualified majority voting. For example, the Commission put forward specific proposals in its communication of 19 September 2018 in three specific cases: i) the adoption of EU positions on human rights in international forums; ii) the adoption and amendment of sanctions regimes; and lastly iii) decisions relating to CSDP civilian missions.[100] The Member States are also making their voices heard in this recurring debate on opening up the CFSP more to qualified majority voting, as shown by the joint statement which brought together several of them on 14 June 2023 and which takes up some of the proposals made by the Commission.[101] In any case, here the question remains as to whether these new cases of qualified majority voting can escape the syndrome of consensus substitution.

2. *The Specific Features of the CSDP Concerning the CFSP*

a. – Is the CSDP Becoming Autonomous from the CFSP?

Under current positive law, the CSDP remains a simple component of the CFSP, which has consequences at the institutional level, the most well-known of which is certainly the absence of a specific 'Defence' configuration of the Council or, in the Parliament, of a specialised committee that would no longer be reduced to the status of a sub-committee of the Foreign Affairs Committee (FAC). The debates on the lack of autonomy of the CSDP have indeed intensified considerably, as a result of developments in defence, through specific channels that owe nothing to the 'truncated CSDP' of the TEU. These

---

[100] See 'A stronger global actor: a more efficient decision-making for EU Common Foreign and Security Policy', COM(2018) 647, 19 September 2018, and more particularly paras. 5.1, 5.2 and 5.3.

[101] See the joint statement by the foreign ministers of Germany, Belgium, Luxembourg, the Netherlands, Romania, Slovenia and Spain, which includes the proposal to use the passerelle clause for decisions on the operationalisation of civilian crisis management missions (the founding decision still requires unanimity), and the adoption of common positions on human rights within international organisations, https://allemagneenfrance.diplo.de/fr-fr/actualites-nouvelles-d-allemagne/02-Europe/-/2601824.

include, of course, the 'Community channels' of the internal market, research and development (R&D) policy and industrial policy. It is therefore easy to imagine the potential avenues to be explored from an institutional point of view (including the creation of a commissioner for defence industries, which was mooted for the Commission that took office in the autumn of 2024), as a result of significant advances in integration in the defence sector. The fact remains that it will certainly be particularly complex to design and build the link between intergovernmental defence and security on the one hand, and defence as an integrating economic sector on the other.

b. – CSDP Derogations from the Common Law of the CFSP Decision-Making Process[102]

From a legal point of view, the Treaty provides the CSDP with a number of derogations 'from the ordinary law of the CFSP', one of the most important of which is based on the specific criterion *of decisions having military or defence implications. This* concerns the decision-making process under Article 31 TEU, in which paragraph 4 explicitly excludes this type of decision from the derogations to the principle of unanimity provided for in Article 31(2) TEU and from the passerelle clause mechanism provided for in Article 32(3) TEU, which enables the European Council and the Council to extend these derogations. Consequently, the recurring debates on extending the use of majority voting in the field of CFSP through the passerelle clause can only concern civilian CSDP crisis management missions, to the exclusion of military missions and operations.

c. – CSDP Derogations from Ordinary CFSP Law Regarding Financing[103]

While CFSP operational expenditure is charged to the EU budget according to arrangements that have evolved over the history of primary law and that have been marked by strong inter-institutional issues between the two protagonists in the adoption of the budget, this is not the case for expenditure on *operations with military or defence implications.*[104] Thus, in the case of CSDP crisis management missions, only civilian missions are covered by the CFSP budget, while military operations benefit from extra-budgetary funding, which is very limited in nature as it only covers their 'common costs'.[105] This type of mission

---

102 Art. 31(4) TEU.

103 Art. 41 TEU. See the commentary on this provision by A. Potteau in this publication.

104 Art. 41(2) TEU, commented by A. Potteau in this publication.

105 These common costs are generally estimated at around 10% of the total costs of military operations and missions.

remains very largely the responsibility of the States that contribute to it,[106] and clearly raises the question of the implementation of the principle of solidarity for the funding of military operations and missions, which has been covered by the European Peace Facility since the new multiannual financial framework 2021-2027, that succeeded the Athena mechanism in this respect.[107]

d. – Derogations from CFSP Common Law Resulting from Denmark's Opt-Out[108]

Another important specificity of CSDP law resulted from the existence of the 'opt-out' clause established for Denmark, at the time of the 'Edinburgh Compromise' of December 1992 which appears in Article 5 of Protocol No. 22 annexed to the Treaties. Thus, until Denmark renounced its opt-out on 1 July 2022, the law applicable to the CFSP and its CSDP component was significantly affected by the 'Danish exception' and its considerable activation (235 times). This Member State did not participate in the preparation and implementation of EU decisions and actions with military implications adopted by the European Council and the Council. Thus, the unanimity principle governing their decision-making process was implemented without Denmark. Beyond this exclusion from standard-setting activities, Denmark did not participate in the Union's military operations and missions, nor did it make any capabilities available to the Union for these purposes. It did not contribute to the extra-budgetary funding provided by the *ad hoc* Athena mechanism or by the European Peace Facility. It could not participate in permanent structured cooperation under Articles 42(6) and 46 TEU, except as a third country. Denmark was not a member of the European Defence Agency and its status concerning the Torrejon Satellite Centre was not that of a Member State.

On 1 June 2022, Denmark held a referendum on renouncing its 'opt-out' in the field of defence and security, which naturally owes a great deal to Russia's aggression against Ukraine, even though Denmark had been referring to it fairly regularly for some years. The large majority of 66.87% in favour of this renunciation led the Danish State to notify the other Member States, in accordance with Article 7 of the Protocol, of its renunciation of its opt-out with effect from 1 July 2022. As a result, the Union has adopted various decisions necessary to implement some of the effects of this renunciation. One example is the Council Decision of 22 May 2023, which specifies the consequences of renouncing an opt-out for the European Peace Facility and the Torrejon

106 See the commentary on Article 43 TEU by A. Hamonic in this publication.
107 See the commentary by C. Schneider below.
108 Protocol No. 22, Art. 5.

Satellite Centre.[109] Similarly, in another decision dated 23 May 2023,[110] the Council noted Denmark's participation in permanent structured cooperation in accordance with the conditions laid down by the Treaty and by the founding act of this instrument, which implies that Denmark must notify the Council and the High Representative of its application,[111] and present its national implementation plan and its ability to meet the most binding commitments.[112]

II. CFSP/CSDP AREA, COMPETENCES AND ACTS

The CFSP/CSDP and the specific law that governs it are the subject of controversy in the literature and in case law, whether because of the vagueness of its scope and field of application, questions about the non-systemic dimension of its competences (A) or the singularity of its acts (B).

A. AREA AND COMPETENCES OF THE CFSP/CSDP

Questions relating to the field of the CFSP, like those relating to the competences of the Union, have not failed to challenge the doctrine, which has frequently regretted the singular inaccuracies of its domain (1). As for the competences held by the Union under the CFSP, their very existence was sometimes debated, before the Treaty of Lisbon reopened another debate on their exact nature (2).

1. *Imprecise Definition of CFSP/CSDP Areas*

According to the current wording of Article 24(1) TEU, 'the Union's competence in matters of common foreign and security policy shall cover *all areas of foreign policy and all questions relating to the Union's security, including the progressive framing of a common defence policy that might lead to a common defence*'.

---

109 See Decision 2023/991/CFSP of 22 May 2023 on the consequences of Denmark informing the other Member States that it no longer wished to avail itself of Article 5 of Protocol No 22 on the position of Denmark, and amending Decision (CFSP) 2021/509 establishing a European Peace Facility and Decision 2014/401/CFSP on the European Union Satellite Centre.

110 See Decision 2023/1015/CFSP of 23 May 2023 confirming the participation of Denmark in PESCO and amending Decision (CFSP) 2017/2315 establishing permanent structured cooperation (PESCO) and determining the list of participating Member States.

111 Art. 46(3) TEU.

112 Annex Decision (CFSP) 2017/2315/CFSP. See the commentary on Article 46 TEU by Q. Loïez in this publication.

Questions have arisen first of all with regard to the assertion that the CFSP *covers all areas of* foreign policy, whereas these areas have never been the subject of any real theorising, even at the national level, except to sketch out interesting typologies, based on the concept of diplomacy. These, however, have more often than not been devoid of the legal operationality required by EU law and the obsession with the division of competences that characterises it.[113]

While the issue of crisis-management operations and missions has been defined *ratione materiae*, as can be seen from Article 43 TEU,[114] other references to defence and security issues raise questions: one example is the 'CSDP exception' used by the Treaty in Article 31 TEU (mentioned above), which relates to '*decisions having military or defence implications*'. What exactly is the difference between the two concepts, apart from the fact that it is conceivable that the 'area of defence' may cover other non-military aspects? There is also the difficulty of defining what is covered by concepts such as defence, defence policy or European defence.[115] Concerning the latter concept of 'European defence', we also know that it can exist without or with the Union.[116] As far as the latter is concerned, what exact scope should be given to the term 'common' when applied to both *defence policy* and *defence*, given that its integrative dimension cannot be applied in the same way to all aspects of defence, in particular the defence of territorial integrity, which is a reserved competence of the Member States (and/or NATO), without the mutual assistance clause in Article 42(7) TEU changing anything?[117]

On the other hand, on the strength of its experience of economic integration, the Union has been able to open up defence to the economic aspects of the internal market, of research and development and of industrial competitiveness,

---

113 See, for example, the typology proposed by F. Dehousse, which nevertheless leaves open the question of security and defence, which raises other issues: F. Dehousse, 'La politique étrangère et de sécurité commune, l'identité européenne de sécurité et de défense', in J.-V. Louis and M. Dony (eds.), *Commentaire Megret*, vol. 12, *Relations extérieures*, 2nd ed., Brussels, Éditions de l'Université de Bruxelles, 2005, pp. 439 et seq. including pp. 550 et seq.

114 See the commentary on Article 43 TEU, by A. Hamonic in this publication.

115 Under the first subparagraph of Article 42(2) TEU, the 'common security and defence policy' includes the progressive framing of a 'common defence policy of the Union', which will lead to a 'common defence', once the European Council, acting unanimously, has so decided. See the commentary on this provision by E. Bernard in this publication.

116 This is the case, for example, with *European coalitions bringing together European states*, such as the Takuba force (2020–2022) in Mali and the Strait of Hormuz Monitoring Mission (EMASOH), which has been in operation since 2020. See C. Schneider, 'Les ambivalences de la gestion de crise', in A. Hamonic (ed.), *Quelle spécificité de la défense en droit de l'Union*, Rennes, Presses Universitaires de Rennes, pp. 149–175

117 See the commentary on Article 40(7) TEU by J.-C. Martin in this publication.

as shown by the instruments based on the various provisions of the Treaty on the Functioning of the EU (TFEU) discussed in this publication.[118]

Thus, the law of the Union and its CFSP have not really made up for their shortcomings in the absence of a real definition of its foreign policy and defence and security areas, despite certain attempts to clarify them. This was the case with the conclusions of the European Council, issued even before the Maastricht Treaty came into force in June 1992.[119] In particular, the European Council asked which areas could be the subject of 'joint action'. After setting the existence of important common interests as the main and most decisive criterion, the report went on to list several specific CFSP objectives in support of its search for areas for joint action. These included: (i) strengthening the principles of democracy and respect for human and minority rights; promoting regional stability (ii) preventing and resolving conflicts (iii) contributing to more effective international coordination in response to emergencies (iv) and combating arms proliferation and terrorism. It is important to emphasise the particular context of this report, namely the exact delimitation between joint actions and common positions. Nevertheless, it is true that the indeterminacy of the area of the CFSP and its defence component –the CSDP– plays a dynamic and often favourable role for the CFSP/CSDP in its interconnection with the other external policies of the EU, and further fuels conflicts of competence, including that of the choice of legal basis.

2. *The CFSP/CSDP's Remit Has Not Been Properly Clarified*

Since the Maastricht Treaty, part of the doctrine prohibited any idea of the autonomy of the Union's CFSP, which was defined solely as the sum of the foreign policies of the Member States, exercised jointly. Such an analysis has also fuelled the debate on the exact nature of the Union's capacity to conclude treaties, which, after being introduced by the Treaty of Amsterdam, had to be clarified by the Treaty of Nice.[120]

The Treaty of Lisbon has made its own contribution to the autonomous nature of the Union's competences in the field of the CFSP, in particular by

[118] This is the case of the European Defence Fund (see the commentary by S. Rodrigues in this volume), ASAP and EDIRPA (see too the commentary by E. Bernard in this volume), and the EDIP regulation (see the commentary by E. Simon in this publication).

[119] See the conclusions of the European Council of 26 and 27 June 1992, Annex 1, Report to the European Council on the likely development of the Common Foreign and Security Policy (CFSP), aimed at identifying areas for joint action *vis-à-vis* particular countries or groups of countries.

[120] See the addition of paragraph 6 to Article 24 TEU, according to which 'agreements concluded under the conditions laid down in this Article shall be binding on the institutions of the Union'. On this question see J.-V. Louis, 'La politique étrangère et de sécurité commune, l'identité européenne de sécurité et de défense', in J.-V Louis and M. Dony (eds.), *Commentaire Megret*, vol. 12, *Relations extérieures,* 2nd ed., Brussels, Éditions de l'Université

including them expressly in the list of competences it proposes in Article 2 TFEU, without however giving them a place in the categorisation, based on the distinction between exclusive, shared and supporting competences, which it establishes in Articles 3 to 6 TFEU.

It may also be thought that the reciprocity introduced by Article 40 TEU relating to the prohibition of encroachments on the exercise of competences between those of the CFSP and those referred to in Articles 3 to 6 TFEU is part of the affirmation of the existence and autonomy of CFSP competences, as well as of their dimension 'outside the system'.[121] Indeed, the CFSP competences cannot be attached either to the exclusive competences of the Union or to its shared competences.

First of all, concerning the category of exclusive competences, apart from the formal argument of their absence from the list of policies concerned in Article 3 TFEU, declarations No 13 and No 14 relating to foreign and security policy are safeguards laid down by the Member States. Declaration No 13 aims to protect their *responsibilities* in the field of foreign policy (the formulation and conduct of policy and international representation *vis-à-vis* international organisations and third States, as well as the specific nature of their security and defence policy). Declaration 14 stresses that, in addition to the specific rules and procedures referred to in Article 24(1) TEU, the provisions relating to the CFSP, including those concerning the High Representative and the EEAS, do not affect the existing legal basis, responsibilities or competences of each Member State. Lastly, the provisions of Article 352(4) TFEU, which exclude the CFSP/CSDP from the flexibility clause (the latter cannot be used as a basis for achieving a CFSP objective), and which make an explicit reference to the limits of Article 40 TEU and to compliance with them by any act adopted on the basis of the flexibility clause, can be linked to the safeguards used by the Member States to protect their competences.

Secondly, with regard to the category of shared competences, to include the CFSP/CSDP in this category (as some legal analyses have done) is more a misuse of language than a relevant legal analysis. Arguments to this effect have focused on Article 4(1) TFEU, which defines them 'by subtraction'. These would in fact be competences held by the Union when the Treaties confer on it a competence which does not fall within the areas referred to in Articles 3 (exclusive competence) and 6 (supporting competence) TFEU. However, apart

de Bruxelles, 2005, pp. 326 et seq.; J. Raux, 'Capacité internationale de la Communauté européenne et de l'Union, la personnalité internationale', *Jurisclasseur Europe*, fasc. 2200, 11/2002.

[121] See also V. Edjaharian, 'Les compétences dans le traité de Lisbonne: la constitutionnalisation interrogée', in E. Brossset, C. Chevallier-Govers, V. Edjaharian and C. Schneider (eds.), *Le traité de Lisbonne, reconfiguration ou déconstitutionnalisation de l'UE*, Brussels, Bruylant, 2009, pp. 227 et seq.

from the fact that Article 4 TFEU does not include the common foreign and security policy in the list of areas concerned, the very definition of shared competences (*i.e.* that the States exercise theirs to the extent that the Union has not exercised its own)[122] prevents it from being applied to the area of foreign policy. The successive nature of the exercise of competence and not the simultaneous nature of the CFSP precludes it, and it matters little that the principle of pre-emption, which is its expression, is set aside in certain areas of internal policy (research and development) and external policy (development cooperation, economic, technical and financial cooperation and humanitarian action). What is important is the way in which the communicating vessels[123] between the competences of the Union and those of the Member States are regulated. It is indeed the foreign policy of the Member States 'which lies at the heart of the CFSP',[124] the main foundations of which, as evidenced by Article 24(2) TEU, are the development of mutual political solidarity between Member States and the achievement of an ever-increasing degree of convergence between Member States' actions. Ultimately, only the second basis of Article 24(2) TEU, namely the identification of issues of common general interest, escapes this inverted aspiration that characterises the Union's CFSP competence. It is indeed the competences of the Member States and their national foreign policies that essentially underpin the CFSP.

Finally, with regard to the category of supporting competences, the very definition of these competences proposed by Article 6 TFEU highlights their inadequacy with those exercised by the Union in the field of the CFSP. Even though in this case the Union supports, coordinates or supplements the action of the Member States, it has to be said that it is actually the Member States which support the Union's common foreign and security policy[125] in a way that reverses of the logic of Article 6 TFEU.

The facility of resorting to the '*sui generis*' qualification, which could be applied to the Union's competences in the field of the CFSP, is sometimes rightly criticised. However, it is not impossible to propose adding to the official typology of Articles 2 to 6 TFEU another type of competence which could be that of a *parallel competence* to that of the Member States. This would be characterised not by the successive exercise of their respective competences by the Union and the Member States but, on the contrary, by their simultaneous

---

122 The idea here is that States exercise their competences to the extent that the Union has not exercised its own.

123 See the expression borrowed from C. Blumann and L. Dubouis, *Droit institutionnel de l'Union*, 3rd ed., Paris, LexisNexis, 2007, p. 322.

124 See also V. Edjaharian, 'Les compétences dans le traité de Lisbonne: la constitutionnalisation interrogée', in E. Brossset, C. Chevallier-Govers, V. Edjaharian and C. Schneider (eds.), *Le traité de Lisbonne, reconfiguration ou déconstitutionnalisation de l'UE*, Brussels, Bruylant, 2009, p. 243.

125 Art. 24(3) TEU.

exercise. Similarly, another feature of such a parallel competence held by the Union would be the strengthening of the guarantees offered to the Member States as regards the exercise of their own competences, whether in terms of their international representation in third countries and international organisations, the development and implementation of their own foreign policy, or the specific nature of their security and defence policy.

B. CFSP/CSDP LEGAL ACTS

Under the terms of Article 25 TEU, the Union shall conduct the common foreign and security policy, defining the general guidelines[126] and adopting decisions[127] (Section 1). Furthermore, in accordance with Article 37 TEU, the European Union may conclude agreements with one or more States or international organisations in CFSP areas (Section 2).

1. Unilateral Acts

a. – Exclusion of Legislative Acts and Questions about the Legal Value of CFSP/CSDP Acts

In the field of CFSP/CSDP, the exclusion of legislative acts is formally stated twice in Articles 24(1) and 31 TEU, as Claude Blumann points out. This results from the fact that 'the Treaty of Lisbon pays, in a way, for the failure of the Constitutional Treaty'.[128] This Treaty made a very clear distinction between legislative and non-legislative acts, and unquestionably referred decisions to the category of non-legislative acts,[129] based on a *modus operandi* according to which it was the choice of the nature of the act – legislative or non-legislative – that dictated its appropriate procedure. The Treaty of Lisbon reverses this *modus operandi*. It is thus the adoption of the act in accordance with the legislative procedure that determines its nature, which in no way precludes the legislative nature of a decision.[130] The formal exclusion of this nature, in the field of the CFSP, including its CSDP strand, therefore became necessary as soon as it was intended to exclude the association of the Parliament from the adoption of the legal acts of these policies. While the exclusion of legislative

126 Art. 25(a) TEU.
127 Art. 25(b) TEU.
128 See C Blumann, 'La singularité de la décision dans le domaine de la Politique étrangère et de sécurité commune', in I. Govaere, E. Lannon and P. Van Elsuwege (eds.), *The European Union in the world: essay in honour of M. Maresceau*, Leiden, Nijhoff, 2014, pp. 277 et seq.
129 First paragraph of Art. I-33.
130 See Art. 289(3) TFEU.

acts for the CFSP, and therefore the CSDP, is politically understandable, this does not mean that the acts adopted under these policies are devoid of legal value, despite their jurisdictional immunity.

As for questions about the legal value of CFSP acts, they in fact suffer from a lack of clarity, largely fuelled by the exclusion of legislative acts, imprecise terminology, the important place given to *soft law* actions such as general orientations and guidelines, the binding effect of decisions on Member States and, of course, the assertion of the jurisdictional immunity of the CFSP. It is well known that the non-justiciability of an act should not be confused with its lack of legal value.

More specifically, the binding effect of CFSP *decisions* cannot be equated with *binding effect stricto sensu,* but it is not without legal effects. Thus, decisions taken by the Council based on Article 28 TEU *are binding on the Member States,* and their binding dimension is reinforced by the invocability of the *rebus sic stantibus* principle: only the Council can decide to revise the principles and objectives of such decisions. Moreover, the binding nature of these decisions under Article 28 TEU can be assessed in the light of the specific obligations placed on the Member States as regards their national action or position envisaged in application of the Union decision,[131] and their rights in the event of an overriding need linked to developments in a situation or a major difficulty in applying a decision.[132] Decisions under Article 29 TEU are not without constraints for the Member States either, even if they are more flexible or less stringent: the Member States need only *ensure that their national policies are consistent with the Union's position.*

b. – The Importance of 'Soft Law' in the CFSP: General Guidelines,[133] Strategic Lines or Interests[134]

First of all, as regards the 'general guidelines', the Union defines these, under the terms of Article 25(a) TEU, in order to 'conduct the CFSP'. Article 26(1) TEU then states that they shall be defined by the European Council 'including for matters with defence implications'. This guiding power, which is normally distinct from decision-making power, is traditionally exercised by the European Council through its declarations and conclusions, but it is not clear from the provisions of the TEU whether they cover specific measures or *take the form* of decisions.

131 Art. 28(3) TEU.
132 Art. 28(4) TEU.
133 Art. 25 and 26 TEU.
134 Art. 26, 31 and 34 TEU.

The general guidelines refer both to the European Council, which is responsible for formulating them,[135] and to the Council, which, when 'elaborating the CFSP', is responsible for translating the guidelines into decisions which it defines on their basis.[136] It is true, however, that the power conferred on the European Council by Article 26(1) TEU since the Lisbon revision seems to have blurred somewhat the boundaries established by the previous Treaties, which reduced the Council's legal capacity to instruments of soft law. Henceforth, nothing, it seems, prevents the European Council from adopting *decisions that it deems necessary* for these general guidelines. The same applies to the 'strategic guidelines' referred to in paragraphs 1 and 2 of Article 26 TEU.

This is a major difference between the general guidelines and strategic lines referred to in Articles 26(1) TEU and 31(2) TEU of the Lisbon Treaty and the former common strategies introduced by the Treaty of Amsterdam. These latter strategies had in fact been presented as acts distinct from the general guidelines or principles of the CFSP/CSDP, particularly with regard to their more precise objectives, the means they identified and their fixed duration.

c. – The Deceptive Formal Standardisation of Decisions

With regard to unilateral acts, the Treaty of Lisbon standardises terminology. Unlike before the revision, all unilateral acts adopted within the framework of the CFSP, including the CSDP, were described as *decisions*, a type of act also referred to in Article 288 TFEU. However, this unification of the nomenclature of CFSP decisions is in reality a sham, given their diversity.

This diversity can be seen first of all in developments in primary law. It was the Maastricht Treaty that gave the CFSP/CSDP normativity, not in the Kelsenian sense of the existence of a hierarchical legal order, but simply as the capacity recognised for the Union to take, within the framework of the Common Foreign and Security Policy, legal acts producing real effects both in the legal order of the Union and in that of the Member States.[137]

This typology of legal acts inherited from the Maastricht Treaty was based on the distinction between acts involving a common position[138] and those

---

135 Art. 25(1) TEU.

136 Art. 26(2) TEU.

137 This capacity to adopt such acts did not exist in the framework of European political cooperation (EPC) 'codified' by Title III of the Single Act. See P. de Schoutheete, *La coopération politique européenne*, Charleroi, Labor, 1980; J. De Ruyt, *L'acte unique européen*, Brussels, Éditions de l'Université de Bruxelles, 1987, pp. 219 et seq. Although the EPC referred to joint actions and common positions, these were merely objectives assigned to the commitment made by the Member States to consult each other.

138 Art. J.2.

involving joint action.[139] With regard to the latter, they were binding on the States[140] and entailed for them either obligations,[141] or specific rights based, for example, on the existence of an overriding need or difficulty of application, and this 'within the Council'.[142] This is how the Maastricht Treaty began to replace the former complete freedom of Member States with regard to European political cooperation (EPC) with a 'form of loyal cooperation or loyalty specific to the CFSP'. Concerning common positions, the density of the obligations placed on the Member States appeared to be less, since the Member States were only responsible for ensuring that their national positions were *in line with the common positions.*

The boundaries established by the Maastricht Treaty between common positions and joint action have ultimately proved to be rather ambiguous, as has been demonstrated by certain confusions in practice. Above all, the Maastricht Treaty made no provision for acts implementing CFSP/CSDP. They were introduced by the Treaty of Amsterdam but only indirectly:[143] they were mentioned, not in the typology of acts, but under Article 23(2) TEU, as derogations from the unanimity rule required for Council decisions. The Treaty of Amsterdam also gave rise to a new type of CFSP act, namely 'common strategies'.[144] Decided by the European Council, these had the advantage of authorising the Council to derogate from the unanimity rule, in accordance with Article 23 TEU, when adopting common actions or positions or taking 'decisions on the basis thereof'.

After the Lisbon revision, the typology of CFSP acts found in Article 25 TEU, beyond the apparent uniformity inherent in the single denomination of *decision,* still makes distinctions between decisions which define *actions to be taken,* those which define *positions to be taken* and those which lay down *the arrangements for implementing* the first two.

In addition, these decisions may be taken by several bodies: the European Council since the Lisbon revision, the Council, which is of course the decision-making body under ordinary law for the CFSP/CSDP, but also the Political and Security Committee (PSC).

First of all, in accordance with Article 26(1) TEU, the European Council, in addition to the soft law acts which it may take in particular to define the general guidelines of the CFSP and therefore of the CSDP, is empowered to adopt the decisions necessary for that purpose. The European Council's

139 Art. J.3.
140 Art. J.3.4.
141 Obligation to inform and consult on national actions and positions relating to their application.
142 Art. J.3.5.
143 Art. 23(2) TEU.
144 Art. 12 TEU.

decision-making powers are very general in nature compared with the very specific powers[145] conferred on it by the Treaty, which reflect the constant desire of the Member States to curb the 'shift of normative powers' from the Council to the European Council as far as possible. The Council's decision-making power under Article 26 TEU covers *ratione materiae* the Union's strategic interests and the objectives and general guidelines of the CFSP, expressly including issues with defence implications. This power makes the European Council a quasi-common law decision-making body in the field of CFSP/CSDP. The European Council exercises this power unanimously, as it does for all CFSP/CSDP decisions, and not on the basis of consensus, which is the principle by which it operates under common law.[146]

The Council's CFSP decisions, taken on the basis of the general guidelines and strategic guidelines of the European Council, are provided for in Articles 28 and 29 of the TEU.

Those provided for in Article 28 TEU concern *the* Union's *operational action*. They correspond to the former 'joint actions' introduced by the Maastricht Treaty. Referring to a very flexibly defined field, namely *when an international situation so requires*, Article 28 TEU constitutes the legal basis for a number of decisions that may concern CSDP and more broadly defence, in addition to foreign policy: these relate first and foremost to crisis management missions and operations, which also benefit from special legal foundations, namely Articles 42(4) TEU and 43(4) TEU.[147] But it is also true that Article 28 TEU, whether or not it is the only one, is the legal basis used for other decisions, in the same way as the former joint actions. This is the case when it comes to enriching the institutional architecture of the CFSP/CSDP with *ad hoc* security and defence bodies[148] or adopting decisions on the extra-budgetary financing of certain crisis management operations and missions.[149]

The Council decisions provided for in Article 29 TEU *defining 'the approach of the Union to a particular matter of a geographical or thematic nature'* replace the former 'common positions'. They impose on the Member States a degree

---

145 See, for example, Article 7 TEU for the determination of the existence of a serious and persistent breach by a Member State of the values of the Union; Article 18 TEU on the appointment of the High Representative; Article 48(7) TEU on the simplified revision of the Treaties; Article 236 TFEU for the determination of the number of Council formations; Article 283 TFEU and the designation of the ESCB's management bodies.

146 Art. 15(4) TEU.

147 See A. Hamonic's commentary in this publication.

148 See below, *ad hoc* CFSP players such as the Torrejon Centre, the European Institute for Security Studies, the EU Military Staff and the European Security & Defence College.

149 This was the case with the ATHENA mechanism, revised by Council Decision (CFSP) 2015/528 of 22 March 2015, and today with the European Peace Facility (EPF), established by Council Decision (CFSP) 2021/509 of 22 March 2021. See the commentary on these decisions below, and the commentary on Article 41(2) TEU by A. Potteau in this publication.

of constraint that is apparently weaker than that imposed by the decisions in Article 28 TEU, since it is reduced to the simple obligation for them to 'ensure that their national policies conform to the Union positions'. However, decisions of this type often contain very specific measures that it is up to the Member States to implement at the national level. This is best illustrated by the restrictive measures adopted by the Union as part of the CFSP,[150] for which Article 29 TEU is the prior legal basis.

According to the European Court of Justice, the concept of 'Union positions' within the meaning of Article 29 TEU 'lends itself to a broad interpretation' which cannot be confined to acts of a programmatic nature or mere declarations of intent: decisions taken based on this provision may thus provide for measures of such a nature that directly alter the situation of individuals, a fact confirmed by the wording of Article 275(2) TFEU,[151] decisions for which the Council has considerable latitude in defining their purpose.[152]

Finally, the decisions of the Political and Security Committee (PSC), provided for in Article 38(3) of the TEU,[153] are doubly limited. Under this article, they fall within the framework of a delegation of powers by the Council, which authorises the PSC to take *appropriate decisions,* but which does not cover the whole of the CFSP, since these decisions are, *ratione materiae,* limited to defence and security policy alone, and more specifically to the political control and strategic direction of its crisis management operations

150 As a reminder, restrictive measures adopted under the AFSJ have been autonomous from the CFSP since the Lisbon Treaty, in that they no longer require the prior adoption of a CFSP common position.

151 The Court thus defended this broad conception by admitting that Article 29 TEU could serve as a legal basis: to target restrictive measures adopted against persons convicted of misappropriation of public funds, in view of the situation in Egypt (Case T-256/11, *Ezz and Others v Council*, ECLI:EU:T:2014:93); to targeted measures adopted in response to Russia's actions destabilising Ukraine and consisting of restrictions on the export of certain products and technologies and on access to capital markets (Case C-72/15, *Rosneft v Council*, ECLI:EU:C:2017:236); and temporary bans on the broadcasting of certain media content, financed by the Russian government, adopted in reaction to Russia's military aggression against Ukraine on the grounds of their support for that aggression (Case T-125/22, *RT France v Council*, ECLI:EU:T:2022:483).

152 This includes the temporary ban on the broadcasting of certain media, which is a new subject for a restrictive measure based on the CFSP (Case T-125/22, *RT France v Council*, ECLI:EU:T:2022:483). Indeed, if such measures aimed at suspending or sanctioning the broadcasting of content by the media have already been adopted by the Union, it was on another legal basis, namely that of the fight against terrorism in the context of the AFSJ: see Directive (EU) 2017/541 of the European Parliament and of the Council of 15 March 2017 on combating terrorism and replacing Council Framework Decision 2002/475/JHA and amending Council Decision 2005/671/JHA, [2017] *OJ* L88/6.

153 'The Council may authorise the Committee, for the purposes and duration of a crisis management operation, as determined by the Council, to take appropriate decisions concerning the political control and strategic direction of the operation'.

and missions. Moreover, this delegation of competence by the Council has not been the subject of a general legal framework applicable to all operations and missions, since the Council defines it on a case-by-case basis, when each of them is created and for their duration. For example, the PSC may be authorised by a mission's framework decision to take certain 'appropriate decisions'. The most common of these relate to amending the operation's planning documents and appointing heads of mission on a proposal from the High Representative. However, as far as this power of appointment is concerned, there are significant differences between executive military operations and other military or civilian crisis-management missions. In the case of the former, it is the Council which designates the operation commands in the framework decision; the PSC is then only empowered to take subsequent decisions concerning them. By contrast, the latter are very often appointed by the PSC as part of its delegation of powers.[154] Another case of delegation concerns the participation of third States in the mission which the Council alone is empowered to decide:[155] if this is the case, it authorises the PSC to take the relevant decisions to this effect, whether this involves accepting the proposed contributions and/or setting up the Committee of Contributors.

2. *CFSP/CSDP Agreements with Third Parties, International Organisations or States*[156]

Article 37 TEU states that 'the Union may conclude agreements with one or more States or international organisations' in areas covered by the CFSP, including the CSDP. This contrasts in its very watered-down nature with the previous provisions of ex-Article 24 TEU, which had given rise to controversy over the attribution of agreements concluded on this basis to the Union.[157] This new singularity[158] must be seen in the context of the formal unification of the European Union's treaty-based action achieved by Article 218 TFEU.

154 See A. Hamonic, 'Biographie des opérations de gestion de crise de l'Union européenne', in C. Flaesch Mougin (ed.), *Union européenne et sécurité: aspects internes et externes*, Brussels, Bruylant, 2009, pp. 293 et seq. and see by the same author, the commentary on Article 43 TEU in this publication.

155 See C. Schneider, 'La participation des États tiers aux opérations de gestion de grise de l'UE', in I. Bosse-Platière and C. Rapoport (eds.), *L'État tiers en droit de l'Union européenne*, Brussels, Bruylant, 2014, pp. 255 et seq.

156 Art. 37 TEU.

157 They were settled by the Treaty of Nice and the new paragraph 6 of Article 24 TEU, which states that agreements concluded under the conditions laid down in this Article are binding on the institutions of the Union.

158 C. Flaesch-Mougin, 'La négociation et la conclusion des accords internationaux', in N. Aloupi, C. Flaesch-Mougin, C. Kaddous and C. Rapoport (eds.), *Les accords internationaux de l'Union européenne, Commentaire Mégret*, Brussels, Éditions de l'Université libre de Bruxelles, 2019, pp. 183 et seq.; C. Rapoport, 'La procédure de conclusion des

This unification should not, however, be confused with standardisation. It leaves an undeniable specificity of CFSP agreements (a). As for the practice of conventional action by the European Union within the framework of this policy, it essentially covers the field of crisis management (b).

a. – The Specific Nature of CFSP/CSDP Agreements

This specificity of CFSP/CSDP agreements is procedural and is part of the 'institutional imbalance' that characterises the CFSP/CSDP. Admittedly, as in the case of all agreements,[159] the Council is omnipresent in the procedure for concluding CFSP agreements, but with the distinctive feature that it acts unanimously in this area, in accordance with Article 218(8) TFEU, which provides for unanimity voting when necessary in the adoption of actions by the Union. This provision nevertheless seems to leave open the possibility of a CFSP/CSDP agreement being adopted by majority vote in an area where, in accordance with Article 31(2) TEU, a unilateral CFSP/CSDP act can be adopted by a qualified majority. The fact remains that the unanimity requirement of Article 31 TEU, applicable to the decisions which the Council adopts for the conclusion of a CFSP/CSDP agreement, may prove tricky to apply to the conclusion of certain agreements that are particularly dense, with multidimensional content.[160]

The specific procedural features of the conclusion of CFSP/CSDP agreements also affect their negotiation and the role conferred on the Parliament. Thus, in accordance with Article 218(3) TFEU, it is the High Representative who negotiates agreements relating exclusively or principally to the CFSP, including the CSDP, and not the Commission, as is the case for TFEU agreements. The approval of the European Parliament, which is required in cases that have been considerably extended by the provisions of Article 218(6) TFEU,[161] is

accords externes de l'Union européenne: quelle unité après Lisbonne', in I. Govaere, E. Lannon and P. Van Elsuwege (eds.), *The European Union in the world: esay in honour of M. Maresceau*, Leiden, Nijhoff, 2014, pp. 149 et seq.

159 In accordance with Article 218(2), the Council authorises the opening of negotiations, adopts the negotiating directives, authorises the signature and concludes the agreements.

160 See e.g. Case C-244/17, *Commission v Council* (Agreement with Kazakhstan), ECLI:EU:C:2018:662. In this case, the Court rejected the Commission's interpretation that, under Article 218(9) TFEU, any position to be adopted on behalf of the Union in a body set up by an agreement should be subject to majority voting. The Court thus recalled that when an agreement relates exclusively to the CFSP, unanimity is indeed required to adopt such a common position. However, in this case, because the CFSP was only an ancillary component of the partnership agreement in relation to its other dimensions (trade policy, development cooperation), the Court concluded that the Council had wrongly adopted the decision unanimously, and added the legal basis of Article 31(1) TEU.

161 'The Council, on a proposal by the negotiator, shall adopt a decision concluding the agreement. *Except where agreements relate exclusively to the common foreign and security policy* [author's italics], the Council shall adopt the decision concluding the agreement:

excluded for CFSP/CSDP agreements. As we have seen, these have been largely excluded from the objective of democratic legitimisation pursued by the Treaty of Lisbon. The provision of Article 218(6) TFEU nevertheless raises a question in the light of the alternative provided by Article 218(3) TFEU, which refers to agreements relating 'exclusively or principally' to the CSDP.[162] By referring only to agreements relating *exclusively* to the CFSP, Article 218(6) TFEU seems to leave some scope for agreements relating *mainly* to the CFSP, on the understanding that several ambiguities remain as to the distinction between these two types of agreement.

In addition to the approval of the European Parliament, this institution has a right to full and immediate information at all stages of the procedure for the conclusion of an agreement, in accordance with Article 218(10) TFEU.[163] This includes the field of CFSP/CSDP, as the Court of Justice has upheld in several cases.[164]

b. – Conventional CFSP Practice Focused on Defence and Security Policy

An analysis of the European Union's conventional practice reveals a strong predominance of the CSDP, which is deployed in several areas, notably crisis management.

The first of these areas is that of agreements concluded with 'host states' in whose territory the Union deploys a crisis management mission, and which correspond to a well-established practice of states or even international

a) after obtaining consent of the European Parliament in the following cases: i) association agreements; ii) agreement on Union accession to the European Convention for the Protection of Human Rights and Fundamental Freedoms; iii) agreements establishing a specific institutional framework by organising cooperation procedures; iv) agreements with important budgetary implications for the Union; v) agreements covering fields to which either ordinary legislative procedure applies or the special legislative procedure where consent by the European Parliament is required. The European Parliament and the Council may, in an urgent situation, agree upon a time-limit for consent;
(b) after consulting the European Parliament, in other cases. The European Parliament shall deliver its opinion within a time limit which the Council may set depending on the urgency of the matter. In the absence of an opinion within that time-limit, the Council may act'.

162 'The Commission, or the High Representative of the Union for Foreign Affairs and Security Policy where the agreement envisaged relates exclusively or principally to the common foreign and security policy, shall submit recommendations to the Council, which shall adopt a decision authorising the opening of negotiations and, depending on the subject of the agreement envisaged, nominating the Union negotiator or the head of the Union's negotiating team'.

163 'The European Parliament shall be immediately and fully informed at all stages of the procedure'.

164 See in particular. Case C-658/11, *Parliament v Council*, ECLI:EU:C:2014:2025. For the Court, 'the Parliament's involvement in the decision-making process is the reflection, at EU level, of the fundamental democratic principle that the people should participate in the exercise of power through the intermediary of a representative assembly'.

organisations in the area of peace operations. This is reflected in CSDP law, which is committed to a form of standardisation in this area which is all the more interesting, given that the Member States have never undertaken it among themselves.[165] These agreements are referred to as SOFA (*Status of Forces Agreement*) when they concern the status of an armed force for a military operation and as SOMA (Status of Mission Agreement) when they concern the status of a civilian management mission. Their purpose is to specify a set of rules designed to guarantee respect for the sovereignty of the host State, which in return recognises a certain number of rights and privileges for the mission and its agents (including, for the EU, those of its third-party contributors). Three main categories of principles and rules are typically included in such SOFA or SOMA agreements. The first concerns respect for the laws and regulations of the host state, the neutrality and good conduct of the members of the operation and the EU's commitment to refrain from any action incompatible with the objectives of the operation. The second category concerns the rights relating to the free movement of the mission's personnel (often except for locally recruited staff) and its equipment. Finally, the third group of rules relates to liability and therefore to claims for compensation in the event of damage to third parties. These rules are governed by a general principle of amicable settlement organised by the host State and the European force.[166] In a very specific case, that of operation EUFOR Tchad RCA (January 2008 to 15 March 2009), in addition to the two SOFA agreements with the two beneficiary states of this operation, the EU concluded a third agreement with Cameroon, as a 'transit state'. Its purpose was to organise and set the terms for the passage of European force personnel and equipment through Cameroonian territory.

The second area is that of association with crisis management missions and operations conducted by the Union of third States making available to the Union resources in the form of men or equipment for carrying out the missions/operations in question.[167] This type of agreement, which is common in the context of peace operations, is certainly not unique to the Union, but it must nevertheless take account of its specific nature as an international player concerned with preserving its decision-making autonomy. This is a feature of the EU's very specific model, requiring subtle institutional balances, and EU treaty practice in this area has evolved considerably. To learn from bad

165 For a detailed analysis, see A. Cammilleri-Subrenat, *Le droit de la politique européenne de sécurité et de défense*, Paris/Cachan, Lavoisier/Éditions TEC & DOC, 2010.

166 For a detailed presentation of the steps involved in this settlement, including recourse to joint compensation committees and, in the event of failure, recourse to arbitration, *ibid.*, pp. 247 et seq.

167 See C. Schneider, 'La participation des États tiers aux opérations de gestion de grise de l'UE', in I. Bosse-Platière and C. Rapoport (eds.), *L'État tiers en droit de l'Union européenne*, Brussels, Bruylant, 2014.

experiences,[168] framework agreements with third countries have replaced the initial approach of concluding such agreements on a case-by-case basis for each operation.

The challenges inherent in this type of agreement are both technical and political. The aim is to achieve greater efficiency in rapidly setting up operations and improving their quality by ensuring that the capacities made available are optimally matched to their objectives. It is also about strengthening the EU's legitimacy as a crisis management player by offering more and more potential partners the opportunity to come under its flag. Initiated in 2005 for the benefit of limited partners (Norway, Iceland, Ukraine and Canada), the practice of these framework agreements has expanded considerably since the Treaty of Lisbon, particularly as a result of the mandate given by the Council on 23 April 2010 to the HR/VP to negotiate and sign such agreements with some twenty States.[169] A particularly large wave of agreements of this type were signed between 2011 and 2015. The latest agreements concluded in 2019 and 2022 concern Jordan and Vietnam respectively.

In terms of European Union law and its implementation, the existence of such agreements makes it possible to save a number of acts and procedures necessary for the implementation of a contribution from a third country on a case-by-case basis (adoption of the negotiating mandate for an *ad hoc* agreement, negotiation by the High Representative, adoption by the Council of the acts relating to signature and conclusion). In the case of a framework agreement, once the principle of opening up the operation to third countries has been decided by the Council, the implementation by the PSC of the contribution of the third country concerned is considerably simplified: it will be limited to examining requests from the head of mission or operation and the declarations made by third countries with reference to one or other of the provisions of the framework agreement linking them to the EU. The contents of these agreements, beyond a relative formal standardisation, involve some significant material differences: the most important is certainly the limitation of participation to civilian missions.[170]

---

168 This was particularly true of the EUFOR Tchad RCA military operation (January 2008-15 March 2009), which encountered major difficulties in negotiations with Russia: Russia contributed to the operation for an air transport mission on behalf of the European force, involving both the transport of equipment and rescue operations but excluding combat missions. The EUFOR Tchad RCA operation also encountered other difficulties, but of a financial nature.

169 These included the United States, China, Japan, India and Brazil, excluding Russia.

170 This is the case with the EU's agreement with the United States, signed in 2011 as a continuation of their crisis management partnership. The United States has never contributed to an EU military operation, something it cannot imagine politically, although it has participated in several EU civilian management missions (EULEX KOSOVO, EUSEC DRC and EUTM SOMALIA).

The third area is that of agreements on the transfer of persons suspected of acts of piracy.[171] The first of these agreements were concluded under the auspices of the Treaty of Nice,[172] while others were concluded under the Treaty of Lisbon.[173] This explains the formal, procedural and substantive differences. These agreements constitute the judicial component of operation EUNAVFOR Atalanta, which, in accordance with its founding Joint Action, is empowered to make such transfers, in particular to any third State wishing to exercise its jurisdiction in substitution for that of the State (EU Member State or third party) whose vessel was captured as part of its participation in Atalanta. These agreements aim to govern the terms and conditions of the transfer, and are subject to conditionality favouring human political rights.[174] This is certainly demanding but somewhat misleading. It should be remembered that these agreements have particularly enriched the litigation surrounding CFSP agreements, both because of the 'power strategies' of the Parliament and because of the responses given to them by the Court.

Finally, a fourth area is made up of security agreements relating to the exchange of classified information, whether these are permanent agreements with candidate states or partners (states or international organisations) identified as likely to take part in CSDP operations or missions. This type of agreement has given rise to a certain amount of hesitation as to the choice of legal basis, in view of the interference between the CFSP/CSDP and the area of freedom, security and justice (AFSJ). The first agreement concluded with the United States in 2007 was based exclusively on CFSP legislation. A second wave of such agreements, consisting of those concluded in 2009 with Israel and Australia, were concluded on the dual legal basis of CFSP[175] and AFSJ.[176] Since a third wave began in 2010 with the agreements with Lichtenstein and Montenegro, this type of agreement is now founded solely on the legal basis of Article 37 TEU.

---

171 C. Rapoport, 'Le rattachement à la PESC des accords de transfert de l'UE en matière de piraterie maritime', in C. Chevallier Govers and C. Schneider (eds.), *L'Europe et la lutte contre la piraterie maritime*, Paris, Pedone, 2015; I. Bosse-Platière, 'Le volet judiciaire de la lutte contre la piraterie maritime en Somalie', *Mélanges en l'honneur du Professeur Pierre-André Lecoq*, Imprimerie nationale du Nord, 2011, pp. 91 et seq.

172 Art. 24 TEU. It was on the basis of simple exchanges of letters that the EU established links with Kenya ([2008] *OJ* L79/49), on the understanding that these links would be terminated on 20 September 2010, and with the Republic of Seychelles ([2009] *OJ* L315/37).

173 Art. 37 TEU and 218 TFEU. See the EU's agreements with the Republic of Mauritius ([2011] *OJ* L254/3) and with the Republic of Tanzania ([2014] *OJ* L108/1).

174 J. Auvret-Finck, 'La conditionnalité des droits de l''homme dans les accords de l''Union européenne relatifs à la lutte contre la piraterie maritime', in C. Chevallier-Govers and C. Schneider (eds.), *L'Europe et la lutte contre la piraterie maritime*, Paris, Pedone, 2015.

175 Ex-Art. 24 TEU.

176 Ex-Art. 38 TEU.

In addition to the agreements signed with states, there are also agreements with international organisations. These include the European Union's relations with the Western European Union (WEU), the United Nations (UN),[177] the African Union (AU) and, of course, NATO.[178] These partnerships concern institutional cooperation as well as operational cooperation for military or civilian crisis management. They are based on more or less formal instruments, joint declarations or express agreements, and the best known of which are certainly the so-called 'Berlin Plus' agreements with NATO dated 17 March 2003. They have already been put into practice in a wide variety of ways: for example, the EU has developed military operations with NATO assets and capabilities based on the Berlin agreements,[179] civil-military operations in the Darfur region of Sudan and in Somalia in support of AU efforts,[180] military operations in support of UN missions[181] or to prepare for their deployment,[182] as well as civilian missions taking over from the UN[183] or supporting it.[184] As has rightly been emphasised, with the exception of the very specific hypotheses of operations conducted on the basis of the so-called 'Berlin Plus' agreements concluded with NATO, the European Union's cooperation with the UN, the AU and NATO outside Berlin plus is subject to one requirement, namely the operational coordination of the European Union with the other players in the management of the same crisis, coordination which is subject to specific arrangements (points of contact, conditions for exchanges of information, etc.).[185]

III. *AD HOC* CSDP BODIES

Certain *ad hoc* bodies have gradually been created in addition to the institutions which are the constitutional actors of the CFSP/CSDP and whose status and powers are part of the institutional imbalance that governs this policy (see

177 See A. Hamonic, *Les relations entre l'Union européenne et l'ONU en matière de gestion de crise*, Brussels, Bruylant, 2018.

178 See L. Balmond, 'La refondation de la coopération UE/OTAN', in J. Auvret-Finck (ed.), *Vers la relance de la politique de sécurité et de défense commune?*, Brussels, Larcier, 2014, pp. 271 et seq.

179 See operations CONCORDIA (March-December 2003) in Macedonia and EUFOR ALTEA in Bosnia-Herzegovina (still ongoing since December 2004).

180 See the AMIS/EU and AMISOM/EU missions (July 2005–December 2007).

181 See also EUFOR RD CONGO (April–November 2006) in support of MONUC.

182 See also EUFOR TCHAD RCA (January 2008–March 2009) to prepare for the deployment of MINURCAT.

183 See also EUPM BIH since March 2003, following the UNMIBH IPTF in Bosnia; EULEX KOSOVO since December 2008, succeeding UNMIK.

184 See also EUPOL Afghanistan since June 2007 in support of UNAMA.

185 See the contribution by A. Hamonic in this publication.

above, section I). These are for external action in general or more specifically dedicated to the CFSP and its defence component (CSDP). Some of these bodies have found their place in primary EU law, at different stages of its development (A), while others are based on secondary legislation (B).

A. *AD HOC* BODIES BASED ON PRIMARY LAW

1. *The High Representative*[186] *for Foreign Affairs and Security Policy*[187]

From the initial version of this body proposed by the Treaty of Amsterdam, we must first remember that its scope of action was limited to the CFSP/CSDP alone, to the exclusion of the Union's other external policies. This explains the change of name made by the Treaty of Lisbon, which we know was a compromise to do away with the title of *Minister for Foreign Affairs* used in the Treaty establishing the Constitution, which had given rise to all sorts of fantasies. In addition, the initial status of the 'High Representative of the European Union for the CFSP' was marked by its lack of autonomy vis-à-vis the Council and its rotating Presidency, and by the modest nature of the powers conferred on the Representative.[188] These all constituted significant demarcations compared to the High Representative's subsequent rise in power following the Treaty of Lisbon.

Indeed, in addition to the dual role inherited from the Treaty of Amsterdam, combining responsibility for foreign policy on the one hand and defence and security on the other, the status of the High Representative has been enhanced in two additional respects. The first concerns the Commission, of which he/she is not only a member but also a Vice-President (Article 18(3) TEU).

The second element in the strengthening of the High Representative's status is the presidency of the Foreign Affairs Council (FAC), a significant departure from the principle of the rotating presidency of the Council, and undoubtedly one of the most emblematic innovations of the Treaty of Lisbon. It should also be emphasised that this Presidency of the AFAT Council has

186 Art. 15, 17, 18, 21, 24, 26, 27, 32, 36, 38, 43, 44, TEU.

187 E. Poidevin, *Le haut représentant pour la PESC: moteur réel ou leadership par procuration?*, Paris, L'Harmattan, 2010; J. Auvret-Finck, 'Mes perspectives de l'Union européenne en matière d'action extérieure: le haut représentant et le SEAE', in C. Flaesch-Mougin (dir.), *La relance de l'UE et la présidence française*, Brussels, Bruylant, 2011; C. Schneider, 'Le haut représentant', in *Abécédaire de l'Union européenne, Mélanges en l'honneur du Professeur C. Flaesch-Mougin*, Presses de l'Université de Rennes, 2011, pp. 69 et seq.

188 The limited status and powers conferred on this new body did not, however, prevent it from flourishing, it must be said, during the two terms of office of its first incumbent, Javier Solana. With his wealth of experience, he developed a dynamic approach to his role that undoubtedly contributed to its subsequent strengthening.

brought with it the Presidency of the Political and Security Committee (PSC): see below. This new prerogative further underlines the hybrid nature of the High Representative's status, whose powers are no longer limited to foreign and security policy alone but cover all the Union's external policies, including those of the TFEU.

Not surprisingly, the extension of the High Representative's status to cover all external policies is accompanied by new specific powers, both in terms of the right of initiative[189] and in terms of the implementation and management of external relations,[190] as well as the management of its new departments.

This contribution will focus on the functions of the High Representative in strengthening the CFSP and its CSDP component.

In these areas, the new powers of initiative and proposal conferred on the High Representative stand in stark contrast to the previous arrangements under primary law, which reduced the High Representative to the simple role of *assisting* the Council. Some of these powers of initiative of a political nature do not concern standard-setting activities: for example, the HR/VP has the power to convene an extraordinary meeting of the Foreign Affairs Council, either on his/her own initiative or at the request of a Member State.[191] Similarly, the High Representative may ask the PSC to provide an opinion to the Council.[192] As we know, he/she is the key interlocutor for the European Parliament in the exercise of its rights to information and consultation in the field of the CFSP (see above). In addition, the High Representative has inherited a special role as facilitator of consensus in the implementation of the Council's decision-making process and of the provisions of the second subparagraph of Article 31(2) relating to the right of a State to object to the exception of qualified majority voting. Lastly, the contribution of the High Representative to the appointment of special representatives should be emphasised, as this calls for a proposal from him/her to the Council (Art. 33 TEU).

Other powers of initiative and proposal of the High Representative are of particular relevance to the standard-setting activity of the CFSP. To contribute to the development of this policy, the High Representative has, first and foremost, the power to make proposals to the Council,[193] although this power is not exclusive, since it is shared with the Member States.[194]

---

189 For example, a power of proposal for the organisation and operation of the EEAS provided for in Article 27(3) TEU.

190 Under the second subparagraph of Article 21(3) TEU, the High Representative assists the Council and the Commission in their task of ensuring consistency between the various areas of the Union's external action and other policies. See also Article 34(1) TEU.

191 Art. 30(2) TEU.

192 Art. 38(1) TEU.

193 Art. 27(1) TEU.

194 Art. 30 TEU.

To exercise their power of initiative, the High Representative may also have *the support of* the Commission under Article 30 TEU, a situation which is distinct from that of Article 22(2) TEU, which provides for joint proposals justified by the cross-cutting nature of certain Council decisions which may affect both the CFSP/CDP and certain TFEU policies. But the CFSP is also at the origin of the existence of a specific power of joint proposal of the High Representative and the Commission, recalled in Article 215 TFEU, and which concerns restrictive measures which now represent a very dense legal corpus. Finally, and still in the field of CFSP, it is up to the High Representative to submit recommendations with a view to the adoption by the Council of the opening of negotiations on an agreement relating mainly or exclusively to the CFSP and the appointment, depending on the subject of the agreement envisaged, of the negotiator or head of the negotiating team.[195]

Concerning the CSDP in particular, the High Representative has the power of proposal which he/she shares with the Member States. Based on Articles 42(4), 43 and 44 TEU, this power concerns the launch of crisis management missions[196] and the arrangements for setting up and managing the start-up fund intended to finance preparatory activities for EU operational missions from Member States' contributions.

In addition to the powers of initiative, the High Representative also has executive and management powers. They participate with the Member States in the implementation of the CFSP (Article 26(3) TEU) and ensures the implementation of decisions adopted by the European Council and the Council (Article 27(1) TEU). The High Representative is also entitled to use the start-up fund for CSDP missions and operations funded by contributions from the Member States (fourth subparagraph of Article 41(3)), with the authorisation of the Council. Furthermore, in the case of crisis management missions and operations whose implementation the Council has entrusted to a group of volunteer States,[197] the States concerned agree among themselves, '*in association with the High Representative*' on the management of the mission.

As for the contribution of the High Representative to the consistency and coordination activities for the benefit of the CFSP,[198] and more particularly the CSDP, it follows from Article 43(2) TEU which provides that the High Representative shall ensure the coordination of the military and civilian aspects of crisis management missions 'under the authority of the Council and in close and constant contact with the Political and Security Committee' (PSC).

A final category of responsibilities assigned to the High Representative concerns those relating to the authority he/she has over specific CFSP

---

195 Art. 218(3) TFEU.
196 See the commentary by A. Hamonic in this publication.
197 Art. 44 TEU. See the commentary on this provision by N. Clinchamps in this publication.
198 See for the CFSP, the second subparagraph of Art. 26(2) and Art. 32(2) TEU.

and defence bodies. He/she is the Head the European Defence Agency,[199] is responsible for the operational management of the Torrejon Satellite Centre, and President of the Institute for Security and Defence, while the European Security and Defence College (ESDC) operates under their general responsibility.

Over and above the creativity of EU law in attempting to compensate for the labyrinthine singularities of its external action system, it is impossible to ignore the questions it raises, which inevitably affect the status and functions of the High Representative.

The 'too much of a good thing is a bad thing' and the 'in-between' syndromes,[200] which were already problematic when the High Representative's remit covered only the CFSP/CSDP, are now raising new questions. Without doubt, the main one today concerns his/her dual role for foreign policy as well as security and defence policy, while also being involved in the economic aspects of defence within the framework of the TFEU. The latter is tending to become increasingly autonomous from CSDP, though obviously linked to it. How will the High Representative, with highly political responsibilities for external diplomatic and security action via the exploration of the paths of European power, be able to defend his/her prerogatives given the massive expansion of Europe's defence economy, which is doing much to further blur the lines *between Europe, the European Union and defence,* and the exact meaning that the Union's institutional and material law is set to attribute to defence?[201]

2. *The Political and Security Committee (PSC)*[202]

The creation of the PSC owes much to the progress of the European Security and Defence Policy initiated by the European summits in Cologne (June 1999) and Helsinki (December 1999), following the lifting of the British veto at the Franco-British summit in Saint Malo in December 1998. Heir to the former Political Committee (PoCo) for European Political Cooperation (EPC), the PSC is different in a number of respects. Unlike the PoCo, which was made up of the political directors of the foreign ministries of the Member States, the PSC, as it results from the Treaty of Nice, has become a permanent body made up of the deputy permanent representatives of the Member States to the

199 Art. 45 TEU. See the commentary on this provision by A. Hamonic in this publication.

200 See C. Schneider, 'Le haut représentant', in *Abécédaire de l'Union européenne, Mélanges en l'honneur du Professeur C. Flaesch-Mougin*, Presses de l'Université de Rennes, 2011.

201 The conceptual ambiguities inherent in the European dimension of defence should be borne in mind.

202 Art. 38 TEU, 43 TEU and 222 TFEU.

Union, who meet at least twice a week or more frequently when circumstances require (in particular for the scheduling of Foreign Affairs Council meeting).[203]

The founding act of the PSC in application of Article 25 TEU (according to the post-Nice Treaty numbering) is Decision 2001/78/CFSP of 22 January 2001, which describes the PSC as the linchpin of the CFSP and ESDP. This decision is still in force, despite the formal obsolescence of some of its provisions, and it specifies the role, operating arrangements and functions of the PSC.[204] Its role of assisting the Council in monitoring the international situation, which is clearly limited to the field of the CFSP and ESDP, now the CSDP, had nevertheless, in the early days, raised questions about its exact relationship, especially with COREPER,[205] and to a lesser degree with the Commission.[206] Since its creation and the updating of the CFSP institutional architecture brought about by the Treaty of Lisbon and, as far as it is concerned, by Article 38 TEU, the PSC has carried out a range of very diverse tasks and functions. Listed in particular in its founding decision, they are fundamental to the proper functioning of the CFSP,[207] including its defence component.

In the field of CSDP crisis management, for example, the PSC issues directives to the Military Committee and the Committee for Civilian Crisis Management, which may provide it with opinions and recommendations. What is most important are the powers it has under Article 38(2) TEU in terms of political control and strategic direction of CSDP missions and operations under Article 43 TEU,[208] which it exercises under the responsibility of the Council and the High Representative. This function of control and direction

---

203 Prior to the entry into force of the Treaty, the Helsinki European Council had already ratified the new politico-military structures responsible for managing the ESDP, including the PSC, which raised legal questions, particularly with regard to the delegation of powers from the Council to the PSC for the political control and strategic direction of CSDP missions: Such a delegation, endorsed by the Helsinki European Council, could be seen as going beyond the procedures for constitutional revision, which was not the case for military structures, which were not introduced in the Treaty of Nice.

204 See in particular the references to the *Secretary General v High Representative* and his prerogative to 'preside over' the PSC in the event of a crisis 'without prejudice to the prerogatives of the rotating presidency'. The exact composition of the PSC, which remains unclear, nevertheless refers to the fact that it may meet in a formation of political directors.

205 See Article 2 (A) of the appendix to the founding decision, which specifies that, if necessary, the chairman of the PSC may take part in COREPER meetings.

206 In its founding decision of 2001, particular attention was paid to the exercise of its functions *without prejudice to* the powers of COREPER.

207 See in particular the PSC's monitoring of the international situation and contributing, with due regard for COREPER's prerogatives, to the definition of agreed policies by means of opinions and monitoring their implementation, as well as coordinating and monitoring the work of the Council's working parties, whose reports the PSC examines. During times of crises, the PSC may issue directives dealing with the situation and examining all possible options for the Union's response, without prejudice to the decision-making and implementation procedures (COREPER and Commission).

208 See the commentary on this provision by A. Hamonic in this publication.

is accompanied by a possible delegation of power by the Council, as provided for in Article 38(3) TEU, to take appropriate decisions, and has enriched the range of CFSP/CSDP decisions.

The Treaty of Lisbon has 'added' new prerogatives to the PSC based on the new provisions of Article 222 TFEU relating to the solidarity clause.[209] Under Article 222(3) TFEU, it therefore assists the Council in implementing this clause, without prejudice to the powers of COREPER, with the support of the structures developed under the CSDP. This potential contribution from the PSC appears justified because the Union 'shall mobilise all the instruments at its disposal, including the military resources made available by the Member States', following the provisions of Article 222(1) TFEU. Lastly, under Article 222(3) TFEU, the PSC may submit joint opinions to the Council with the Standing Committee of the AFSJ under Article 71 TFEU. This bears witness to the necessary interconnection within the Union between the CSDP and its means and the AFSJ in the overall approach to security, which is all the more justified by the complexity of its system of distributing competences.

3. *The European External Action Service (EEAS)*[210]

The creation of the EEAS is one of the contributions of the Treaty of Lisbon to the CFSP, and is undoubtedly the most commented upon, along with the paradigm shift of the High Representative. It is part of the recurrent debate on the need to strengthen the global approach to the Union's schizophrenic external action and to seek the best ways to give greater effect to its demand for consistency. In the final analysis, the appearance of the EEAS in the institutional landscape of the European Union undoubtedly constitutes a more fundamental innovation than that which governed the strengthening of an already existing body such as the High Representative. It is also true that the creation of the EEAS serves and accompanies the strengthening of the High Representative, who can now 'be assisted' by it in 'fulfilling his [or her] mandate'.[211] This has sometimes led to the EEAS being described as somewhat approximate in terms of its actual status and missions.

The creation of the EEAS is provided for in Article 27(3) of the TEU, and explicitly implied the adoption of a Council Decision to set out the arrangements for its organisation, based on a convoluted decision-making process that favoured inter-institutional strategies, and which lasted some ten months. Under this provision, the initiative for the founding decision of the EEAS lay with the High Representative, the Commission had to approve it

209 See the commentary on this provision by F. Terpan in this publication.

210 Article 27(3) TEU, Declaration No 15 annexed to the Treaty and founding Council Decision (2010/427/EU) of 26 July 2010.

211 Art. 27 TEU.

and the Parliament was simply consulted. However, the Parliament has played a major role and obtained guarantees from the High Representative at the time (Baroness Catherine Ashton), on certain aspects of the functioning of the EEAS.[212]

The EEAS is characterised by institutional and functional hybridity, the result of reconciling the intergovernmental and integrated approaches, as well as the cross-cutting nature of the EU's external action.

This hybridisation can be seen first and foremost in the origins of its agents. The decision of 26 July[213] stipulates that the EEAS is made up of 60% *permanent staff* from the EU institutions and staff from the diplomatic services of the Member States *who enjoy EU staff status*. The EEAS also has 30% *temporary staff* from the Member States, with the remainder made up of *national experts seconded* from *specialised departments* and placed under the authority of the High Representative. Above all, the composition of the EEAS makes room for one of the Parliament's major demands concerning the possibility for its officials to join the EEAS, which was achieved by opening up recruitment to all EU officials and staff from 1 July 2013.[214] Such an opening has contributed to reducing the intergovernmental logic and strengthening the integration logic in the composition of the EEAS, but with a more balanced representation of its institutions and in particular of the Parliament. Finally, special attention (Art. 6) of the founding decision is paid equilibriums to be respected in the recruitment procedures established by the HR/VP in terms of transparency, as well as geographical and gender balance, with particular reference to the fact that the staff of the EEAS should *include a significant number of nationals from all the Member States*.

Hybridity is also apparent in the EEAS's status as an EU body, distinct from the Commission and the Council.[215] The EEAS has the legal capacity to perform its tasks and achieve its objectives, a legal capacity that is not without consequences, especially in terms of litigation.[216] It is treated as an institution as defined by Regulations No 31 (EEC) and No 11 (EAEC), laying

---

212 These guarantees took the form of two statements by the High Representative accompanying the founding decision of the EEAS on 10 July. The first of these statements concerns political accountability. It relates to the sensitive issue of the democratic control of the European Parliament by rationalising and clarifying the Parliament's powers of consultation and information and the High Representative's 'obligations of representation' before the European Parliament, both in plenary and in committee sessions (Council of the EU, 28 July 2010, 12401/1/10 add. 1). The second concerns the procedure for appointing EEAS staff and more specifically heads of delegation and special representatives, for whom a hearing by the EP is possible (Council of the EU, 28 July 2010, 12401/1/10 add. 2).

213 Art. 6.

214 Recital 11 of the founding decision.

215 Art. 1(2) of the founding decision.

216 This means, in particular, that it can be a defendant in an action for annulment under Article 263 TFEU, provided, of course, that the contested act is attributable to it.

down the Staff Regulations of Officials and the Conditions of Employment of Other Servants of the European Communities. The EEAS also enjoys the budgetary autonomy conferred on it by its status as a 'budgetary institution', in accordance with the Financial Regulation applicable to the general budget of the EU. The EEAS therefore has its own section of the EU budget for which the High Representative is the authorising officer and which, separate from the CFSP budget, covers its administrative expenditure alone.

Nevertheless, its organisation, which was the result of a desire to avoid creating it *ab nihilo* while rationalising the Union's external action system, is based on the stripping away of whole sections of the Council and Commission Secretariats. Some of these departments and their respective staff have been transferred to the EEAS, which has made a significant contribution to the hybridisation of the two logics – intergovernmental and integration – giving the EEAS a very special place in the institutional architecture of the Union.[217] Regarding the Council, it should be noted that the EEAS has absorbed the specific structures of the CSDP. These structures, which are expressly attached to it in accordance with the annex to its founding decision, help to give it the image of an 'ersatz' Ministry of Defence. These include the former EU Joint Situation Centre (SitCen) set up within the framework of the WEU and which became INTCEN in 2012; the EU Military Staff (EUMS) set up in 2001; the Civilian Planning and Conduct Capability (CPCC) set up in 2007, and the Military Planning and Conduct Capability (MPCC) set up in 2017. The founding decision of the EEAS requires that it has to provide certain entities with the support that was previously provided by the Council.[218] These include the European Defence Agency, the Security Institute, the European Security and Defence College and the Torrejon Satellite Centre.

As far as the Commission is concerned, it has been 'stripped', not without bitter discussion, of its RELEX Directorate and part of its Development Cooperation Directorate, while retaining all of its development aid departments. It also lost its authority over the EU delegations, which were transferred to the High Representative,[219] the latter now constituting the 'devolved administration' of the EEAS.

The hybridisation of the EEAS is finally functional, to the benefit of the consistency of external action and all its players.

The very complex organisational chart of the EEAS is a significant illustration of this functional hybridisation, which covers all of the Union's *external action* and, in the case of the CFSP, its duality with its CSDP component. The Secretary-General of the EEAS is thus assisted by three Deputy

217 Details of the service transfers are given in the annex to the 26 July decision. See also C. Schneider, *Mélanges en l'honneur de Claude Blumann*, Brussels, Bruylant, 2015.

218 Recital 7 of the EEAS founding decision.

219 Art. 221 TFEU and Art. 5 of the EEAS founding decision.

Secretaries-General, for economic affairs and global issues, for political affairs, and finally for CSDP and crisis management, a department which houses the key civil-military apparatus of this policy and which the founding decision clearly specified was placed 'under the direct *authority and responsibility of the High Representative*'.[220]

The EEAS is commonly – but quite incorrectly – presented as the EU's foreign ministry. These additional responsibilities have contributed to a form of 'militarisation of the EEAS' and have also turned it into a 'mini' defence ministry.

4. *The European Union Delegations*[221]

The EU delegations, which are the expression of the EU's permanent diplomatic representation in third countries and international organisations, constitute the decentralised machinery of the EEAS. They have been attached to the EEAS since the Treaty of Lisbon.[222] In carrying out their functions of representing the Union internationally, they are placed under the authority of the High Representative.[223] Their change of name – they are no longer Commission delegations – testifies to their change of status, as do several clarifications introduced by the founding decision. These include: (i) the opening and closing of delegations (now decided by the High Representative, in agreement with the Council and the Commission);[224] (ii) the assessment of their operation by the Secretary-General of the EEAS;[225] (iii) the special status of the Head of Delegation vis-à-vis the High Representative;[226] (iv) and the composition of their staff.[227]

The organisational and functional complexities of the delegations are essentially inherent in the fragmentation of the Union's external action, which continues to weigh on them beyond the rationalisation effort represented by their attachment to the EEAS. They were quickly highlighted both by Baroness

---

220 Art. 4(3) of the founding decision of the EEAS.

221 Art. 32 and 35 TEU, Art. 5 founding decision of the EEAS (2010/427/EU) of 26 July 2010, Art. 221 TFEU.

222 Art. 5 of the EEAS founding decision.

223 Art. 221 TFEU.

224 Art. 5(1) of the EEAS founding decision. These decisions to open or close do not require a formal act by the Council.

225 Art. 5(5) of the founding decision of the EEAS.

226 In accordance with Article 5(3) of the founding decision, the Head of Delegation receives instructions from the High Representative and the EEAS, but is also responsible for carrying out the instructions given by the Commission in the areas in which it exercises its powers.

227 According to the second subparagraph of Article 5(2) of the founding Decision, the staff of the delegations shall comprise EEAS staff recruited in accordance with the rules of Article 6 of the Decision and Commission staff, 'where appropriate for the implementation of the Union budget and Union policies other than those under the remit of the EEAS'.

Ashton as HR/VP in the reports she submitted in 2011 and 2013,[228] by the work of the Parliament,[229] and above all by the special report of the Court of Auditors.[230] The duality of the financial circuits, which places the delegations under the dual organic and functional dependence of the EEAS and the Commission, has been the main source of difficulty.

In accordance with Article 221(1) TFEU, the delegations are responsible for the Union's international representation vis-à-vis third countries and international organisations. They are now a cog in the particularly labyrinthine international representation of the Union,[231] even if their contribution to this representation is not very precisely defined. Inspired by the classic model of international diplomatic representation, this EU representation nevertheless differs in one respect, namely that delegations do not assume consular functions or diplomatic protection, which are the exclusive preserve of the Member States. Article 5(10) of the founding decision of the EEAS only states 'that upon request by Member States, [delegations shall] support the Member States in their diplomatic relations'.

The contribution of the delegations of the European Union to the CFSP, which is an innovation of the Treaty of Lisbon, is attested by two specific provisions of the TEU. The first is Article 32(3) TEU, which makes the delegations' contributors to the formulation and implementation of common approaches. The second is Article 35(1) TEU, which makes them stakeholders in compliance with and implementation of the decisions of the CFSP, common positions and joint actions. Article 221 TFEU states that the EU delegations shall act in close cooperation with the diplomatic and consular missions of the Member States.

Lastly, the Treaties and the founding decision (Art. 5(9)) attach great importance to *coordination* and *cooperation* between the EU delegations and the diplomatic missions of the Member States, both in terms of common approaches and CFSP common positions and joint actions. Coordination and cooperation, for which the delegations especially are responsible, are part of the requirement for vertical and horizontal consistency in external action laid down in the Treaty to ensure the convergence of European diplomatic action. This diplomatic action is not limited to the central administrations of the external action of the Union and its Member States: it also concerns their representations on the ground. Previously, coordination was the responsibility

---

228 See 'Mid-term review report by the High Representative', in accordance with Article 13(3) of the Council Decision of 26 July 2010 establishing the EEAS, July 2013.

229 See the Report by E. Brok and R. Gualtieri on the mid-term review of the EEAS, 2012/2253 (INI) of 25 March 2013.

230 See also Court of Auditors, Special Report 2014/11 on *The Establishment of the European External Action Service*, 30 June 2014.

231 See D. Bouvier, *La représentation internationale de l'Union européenne*, Brussels, Bruylant, 2020.

of the embassy of the country holding the rotating presidency, and it is now handled by the head of the EU delegation. Regular meetings are held at the level of the decentralised services of the EEAS, reflecting the same shift in responsibilities that has occurred at the central level in favour of the High Representative and the EEAS

5. *EU Special Representatives*[232]

EU Special Representatives (EUSR) are the expression of a practice known as *ad hoc* diplomacy, whereby they are entrusted with a limited mission, *ratione materiae* and *temporis*, in relation to a particular political issue, usually defined geographically, but exceptionally thematically, as shown by the creation of the special representative for human rights. This *ad hoc* diplomacy complements the permanent representation provided by diplomatic missions and constitutes 'the spearhead of crisis prevention and resolution'. The EUSR are one of the many innovations of the Treaty of Amsterdam for the benefit of the CFSP,[233] which did not prevent the Union from using such *ad hoc diplomacy* even before this treaty.[234] The Treaty of Lisbon expressly placed such Special Representatives under the authority of the High Representative,[235] without however settling the question of their attachment to the EEAS.

Special Representatives are appointed by the Council by a majority vote,[236] and, since the Treaty of Lisbon, on a proposal from the High Representative.[237] However, the creation of a new post and the renewal or replacement of its incumbent are naturally based on a consensus between all the parties involved, including the Member States, which are always keen to defend their positions in the balance and distribution of important posts, including the Special Representatives. This is undoubtedly why the High Representative, anxious to retain his/her room for manoeuvre, has sometimes resorted to the palliative of appointing a *special envoy*.

---

232 Art. 31 and 33 TEU. See D. Bouvier, *La représentation internationale de l'Union européenne*, *ibid*., pp. 131 et seq. C. Schneider, 'Les droits fondamentaux frein ou moteur de la PESC: atouts et faiblesses de la diplomatie européenne en matière de droits de l'homme', in J. Andriantsimbozavina (ed.), Paris, Mare & Martin, 2021, pp. 117 et seq.

233 Art. 18 TEU.

234 The first appointments of EU Special Representatives were made in 1996 for the Great Lakes region in Africa and the Middle East peace process, and then in 1998 to monitor the assistance programmes for the Palestinian Authority and the Federal Republic of Yugoslavia. They were seen as a necessity, given both the lack of a 'Mr [or Ms] CFSP' and the lack of foreign policy powers of the delegations.

235 Art. 33 TEU.

236 Art. 31(2) TEU.

237 Art. 33 TEU. This represents a significant reduction in the power of the Council, which until now has had discretionary powers both in creating the post and defining its mandate and in appointing its incumbent.

Described as a 'post-Lisbon anomaly' by Baroness Ashton,[238] the EUSR were strongly opposed because they would compete with the heads of delegation on whose territory they were deployed (a classic criticism of 'duplication' between *ad hoc* diplomacy and permanent diplomacy). Other criticisms included the fact that how they are appointed and the length of their mandate are incompatible with the urgency and flexibility required for crisis management, their exorbitant budgetary burden and their non-integration into the EEAS, which the Council had fought hard to obtain during the negotiations on the creation of the EEAS.

Whatever these misgivings may have been, they all come back to questions about the implementation of consistency within the EU's external action system. Firstly, although they are placed under the authority of the High Representative, and above all because they have not been integrated into the EEAS, Special Representatives continue to maintain privileged links with the PSC, as can be seen from the recurrence in their appointment and terms of office of certain mechanisms.[239] Secondly, there is the question of consistency on the ground, which is somewhat paradoxical given that the Special Representatives were most often conceived of as key players supporting such consistency: many of them have in fact been responsible for coordination missions with CSDP civilian and military operations or for development aid or technical and financial cooperation programmes.

Although complex, some of these consistency issues have been addressed, such as the 'risk of duplication' between the two people in charge in the field, namely the EUSR and the heads of delegation. These issues were addressed using the 'dual role' method used in some non-EU countries. This is how several Special Representatives have combined their duties with the responsibility of head of delegation, as is the case in the African Union (AU),[240] in Afghanistan,[241] in Kosovo[242] and in Bosnia Herzegovina.[243]

It is nonetheless true that the Special Representatives have a special status in the institutional architecture of the external action system. In accordance with the wishes of the Council, they have not been integrated into the EEAS,

238 EEAS, EEAS Review, Brussels, July 2013.

239 See for example: 'The PSC shall maintain a privileged link with the EUSR, and shall be the EUSR's primary point of contact with the Council [...] PSC shall provide the EUSR with strategic guidance and political direction within the framework of the mandate, without prejudice to the powers of the HR'.

240 This is the oldest experiment in combining functions, dating back to Joint Action 2007/805 of 6 December 2007.

241 For Afghanistan, the post of Special Representative, which also includes the responsibility of Head of Delegation, was created in 2010 for a two-year period and extended several times.

242 The Special Representative for Kosovo was created in 2011 for a period of six months and his mandate was changed in 2012 to having the 'dual role' as Head of Delegation.

243 The post of Special Representative for Bosnia is one of the oldest, having been created in 2009, and it was in 2010 that the dual role of Head of Delegation was introduced.

but continue to maintain direct relations with it via the PSC. From a budgetary point of view, they come under the general CFSP budget, which is fairly modest, and together with civilian management missions they account for most of the appropriations.

B. *AD HOC* BODIES BASED ON SECONDARY LEGISLATION

1. *The European Defence Agency*

The European Defence Agency (EDA), a CSDP body dedicated to strengthening the military capabilities of the Member States, is the fruit of the deliberations and proposals of the Convention for a European Constitution, Article III-212 of which provided for the creation of the Agency.[244] The work of the Convention bears witness to the significant contribution of this CSDP body to the institutional law of the EU, in terms of the methods of differentiation, the recurrent debate on the respective merits of intergovernmentalism and integration, and the status of the agencies. Created in advance by Joint Action 2004/251/CFSP of 12 July 2004, the EDA 'made its entry' into primary law thanks to the Treaty of Lisbon and Article 45 TEU.[245]

2. *The Bodies Inherited from WEU*

The competence of the European Union to develop crisis management operations and missions was established by the Treaty of Amsterdam,[246] being directly inspired by the model of the 'Petersberg missions' established by the WEU in 1992.[247] Nevertheless, deprived of any operational capability, the Union could only implement this type of mission thanks to the resources and capabilities of the WEU, with the Treaty providing for the establishment of closer institutional relations between the EU and the WEU, with a view to its eventual integration.

Even before WEU's dissolution on 7 April 2010,[248] the organisation's Council of Ministers decided on 13 November 2000 to end its operational functions and transfer its capabilities in this area to the EU. Some of the

---

244 See C. Schneider, 'Chronique relations extérieures de l'Union européenne, politique européenne de sécurité et de défense', *ADE*, 2003, pp. 434 et seq.

245 See the commentary on this provision by A.-H. Bertana in this publication.

246 Second subparagraph of Art. 17(1) TEU.

247 Petersberg Declaration of the WEU Council, 19 June 1992.

248 The dissolution of WEU is one of the effects of the Lisbon Treaty and of the mutual assistance clause in Article 47(2) TEU: WEU's mutual defence clause (Article V of the 1948 Brussels Treaty), which is more binding than that of the EU, helped to 'keep it alive'. See also C. Schneider, 'Défense', *Répertoire de droit européen*, Paris, Dalloz, 2019.

Union's current agencies are thus 'a legacy of WEU', such as the Institute for Security Studies, the Torrejon Satellite Observation Centre and the Institute for Security Studies. The same applies to SitCen, which became INTCEN in 2012 and has no specific legal basis, apart from the reference to its attachment to the EEAS in the latter's founding decision.

a. – The European Union Satellite Centre (EUSC or SatCen)[249]

Considered by the HR/VP Josep Borrell to be 'the European Union's eye in the sky' and 'a very important element of EU security',[250] this 'EU centre of excellence for geospatial intelligence analysis'[251] was initially set up as a permanent body of the WEU.[252] Its absorption by the EU as the EU Satellite Centre (EUSC) was implemented by Joint Action 2001/5555/CFSP of 20 July 2001, but was repealed in 2014 for reasons of legal clarity.[253] The Centre's headquarters are in Torrejon, Spain, but it also has a liaison office in Brussels.

The EUSC has legal personality enabling it to take legal actions.[254] It is placed under the political supervision of the PSC, which issues political guidelines on its priorities.[255] In operational terms, the Centre comes under the authority of the High Representative who issues instructions to it, in particular based on the guidelines issued by the PSC, but without prejudice to the responsibilities of the Centre's Board and the Director. The Board, which is chaired by the High Representative, is made up of one representative appointed by each Member State and one representative appointed by the Commission. If necessary, it may invite certain CSDP military bodies[256] or other relevant EU bodies, and since

249 Joint Action 2001/555/CFSP of 20 July 2001, repealed by Decision 2014/401/CFSP of 26 June 2014, amended by Decision 2016/2112/CFSP of 1 December 2016.

250 According to the High Representative on 29 August 2023, at an EUSC Board meeting.

251 Ibid.

252 The origins of the Satellite Centre lie in a recommendation by the WEU Parliamentary Assembly in 1988, and its creation was decided by the WEU Council on 27 June 1991.

253 Council Decision 2014/401/CFSP of 26 June 2014 on the European Union Satellite Centre and repealing Joint Action 2001/555/CFSP on the establishment of a European Union Satellite Centre, [2014] *OJ* L188/73. The last amendment to the 2014 Framework Decision was made on 22 May 2023 to take account of Denmark's renunciation of its opt-out on defence matters and its military involvement, and thus to take note of Denmark's accession to the EUSC (Decision 2023/994/CFSP of 22 May 2023, [2023] *OJ* L135/20).

254 Article 5 of the founding joint action. In certain a way, the Torrejon Satellite Centre is making its own particular contribution to the decline in the jurisdictional immunity of the CFSP. Thus, in 2018, in the case *of K.F. v Centre satellitaire de Torrejon,* the Court of First Instance ruled that the EU Satellite Centre (EUSC) in Torrejon was indeed a Union body within the meaning of Article 263 TFEU, whose acts are subject to review as to legality, notwithstanding the existence of a special court; Case T-286/15, ECLI:EU:T:2018:718. See C. Schneider, 'Politique Étrangère et de Sécurité Commune (PESC) et Son Volet Défense (PSDC)', *ADUE*, 2018, pp. 616–619.

255 Art. 3(1) of the founding decision.

256 Chairman of the Military Committee (EUMC) or Director of the Military Staff (EUMS).

2016 external experts to its meetings.[257] Lastly, the EUSC has a Director (Art. 7) who is selected and appointed by the Board based on his/her solid expertise and experience in the fields of geospatial information and imagery, foreign relations and security. The Director generally attends Board meetings.

The EUSC's budget is funded by national contributions from the Member States based on their GNP and by payments for its products and services.[258] Exceptionally, it may receive earmarked contributions and revenue from the general EU budget or from Member States or third countries.

The mission of the EUSC is to support the decision-making process and actions in the field of CFSP and CSDP by providing, at the request of the Council and the High Representative, satellite observation services and products.[259] If a request falls within the CFSP and CSDP field, the Centre may, with the authorisation of the High Representative to which a particular request has been referred, provide services and products to a Member State, the EEAS, the Commission, as well as to EU bodies and agencies, certain associated third countries and international organisations such as the UN, the OSCE, the Organisation for the Prohibition of Chemical Weapons and NATO.

The activity of the EUSC in the performance of its tasks has evolved considerably. Initially somewhat neglected, it is now increasingly called upon to address both the strategic and tactical dimensions of the CFSP and CSDP, in particular by the PSC, the EEAS and the EUMS. As its Director, the Romanian Sorin Ducaru (appointed in 2019), points out, the Centre's '[a]nalysis options cover a wide range: from humanitarian aid, contingency planning and evacuation preparations, to issues of non-proliferation of weapons of mass destruction and their vector technology, general security surveillance and specialised analysis of military capabilities, critical infrastructure or industrial facilities [...]. The Centre also supports EU missions and operations around the world (such as operations Aspide, Irini and Atalanta, or the observation mission in Georgia)'.[260] In particular, the EUSC plays an important role in the Copernicus Security Service supporting EU External and Security Action (SESA).[261] Many Member States, non-EU countries and international organisations have also called on its services, which have proved relevant on several occasions relating to: the presence of chemical weapons and weapons

[257] Decision 2016/2112/CFSP of 1 December 2016, which also provides that the EUSC shall be responsible, after approval by the Administrative Council, for implementing international agreements concluded by the Union in the field of the common foreign and security policy insofar as they relate to the activities of the EUSC (amendment of Article 20 of Decision 2014/401/CFSP).

[258] Art. 10(3) of the founding decision.

[259] Art. 2 of the founding decision.

[260] Le SatCen, carrefour européen du renseignement géospatial, IHEDN, https://ihedn.fr/en/notre-selection/le-satcen-carrefour-europeen-du-renseignement-geospatial/.

[261] See the commentary by A. de Neve in this publication.

of mass destruction in Syria and Iraq, the influx of migrants massing in Libya, the Russian-Georgian conflict,[262] and of course Ukraine.

It is in this context that the Strategic Compass, adopted in March 2022, provides for the strengthening of the EUSC 'to boost our autonomous geospatial intelligence capability',[263] as detailed in the EU Space Strategy for Security and Defence,[264] and in the new European Union Maritime Security Strategy.[265]

b. – The EU Intelligence and Situation Centre

The EU Intelligence and Situation Centre (EU INTCEN) is the intelligence agency of the EU's European External Action Service, reporting to the High Representative.

Its origins lie in the 'transfer' of WEU's *intelligence cell* to the Union as a result of a simple administrative decision by Javier Solana in 1999, when he took up his post as High Representative for the CFSP, and at a time when he was also Secretary General of WEU and of the Council of the European Union.

This is how, in 1999, the modest WEU unit, made up of five people and responsible for analysing information from open sources, joined the brand-new Policy Unit of the EU Council Secretariat as SitCen, as a simple office. After the attacks of 11 September 2001 and following a report by J. Solana in November, SitCen became an independent administrative body, but its staff resources remained as weak as ever. The attacks in Madrid (2004) and London (2005) led to a step change in the SitCen, both from an administrative point of view (it was transformed into a directorate) and in terms of its staff (staff numbers doubled), as well as in terms of the scope of its remit: following a request from the European Council in March 2004, analysis of the terrorist threats became one of its key areas of activity.

The Centre is devoid of any operational capacity on the ground and dedicated to providing and analysing information and assessing geopolitical situations. It cannot therefore be compared with the comprehensive operational intelligence structures that exist in the Member States and which some are calling for the Union. A mere embryo of an intelligence service, its role is reduced to collecting and analysing various sources from the media, the Member States

---

262 See A. Dumoulin and N. Gros-Verheyde, *La politique européenne de sécurité et de défense commune*, Le Dévoluy, Éd. du Villard, 2017, p. 176.

263 'A strategic compass for security and defence', p. 27, https://data.consilium.europa.eu/doc/document/ST-7371-2022-COR-1/fr/pdf.

264 See the commentary by A. de Neve in this publication.

265 See the Council conclusions on the revised EU Maritime Security Strategy (EUMS) and its action plan, 24 October 2023, https://www.consilium.europa.eu/media/67499/st14280-en23.pdf.

and delegations. This analysis involves producing a large number of periodic or specific reports and studies for the High Representative or the Presidency.

SitCen's attachment to the Council Secretariat services transferred to the EEAS is evidenced by its founding decision 2010/427 of 26 July 2010,[266] except for staff assisting the Security Accreditation Authority. In 2012, this attachment led not only to a change of name to INTCEN but also to a restructuring which today is based around four divisions which reflect all of its functions.[267]

From 2020 onwards, in order to draw up the Strategic Compass, INTCEN has worked in particular with the intelligence branch of the EU Military Staff (EUMS) and the national intelligence agencies to produce 'the first-ever comprehensive EU-wide threat analysis',[268] aimed at assessing the strategic risks that the Union faces and will face in the coming decade. This analysis was finalised in November 2020 by the SIAC,[269] and is a classified document drawn up by the EEAS and coordinated within the EEAS by the EU Military Staff. It is important to stress that the analysis has not been approved by the Member States, who have not been given any opportunity to challenge or amend the conclusions of the intelligence specialists.[270] While such an approach, involving forty-two civilian and military intelligence services – including British ones – is standard practice at the national and NATO levels, it was unprecedented at the EU level.[271] It demonstrated the strong links between all the levels of threat, links that havc obviously been strengthened from February 2022 onwards, in the light of the war in Ukraine. The commitments made in the Compass thus aim to improve the anticipation and detection of threats, in particular by strengthening the EU's intelligence capabilities.

c. – European Union Institute for Security Studies[272]

The European Union Institute for Security Studies (EUISS) is the EU agency which analyses foreign, security and defence policy issues. It was set up by the

---

266 Decision establishing the organisation and functioning of the European External Action Service, [2010] *OJ* L201/30.

267 See A. Dumoulin and N. Gros-Verheyde, *La politique européenne de sécurité et de défense commune*, Le Dévoluy, Éd. du Villard, 2017, pp. 165 et seq: these are the functions of open source intelligence, intelligence analysis in charge of providing strategic analyses, crisis monitoring (situation room) and consular crisis management.

268 'A strategic compass for security and defence', p. 7.

269 The Single Intelligence Analysis Capacity (SIAC) is the Union's single intelligence analysis capacity, bringing together civilian and military intelligence.

270 See also D. Fiott and G. Lindstrom, 'Strategic Compass – New Bearings for EU Security and Defence?', *EUISS*, Chaillot Paper No. 171, December 2021, pp. 5–6.

271 E. Bernard, 'La "boussole stratégique", nouveau plan d'action pour la sécurité et la défense de l'UE', *AFDI*, 2023.

272 Council Joint Action 2001/554/CFSP of 20 July 2001, amended by Joint Action 2006/1002/CFSP of 21 December 2006, repealed by Decision 2014/75/CFSP of 10 February 2014.

WEU Council in 1989,[273] on the recommendation of the European Parliament. It is based in Paris. Joint Action 2001/554/CFSP of 20 July 2001 transferred its functions to the Union on the basis of the WEU providing its initial structures.

The Institute has legal personality[274] and an autonomous budget, financed by contributions from the Member States according to their gross national income.[275] It is placed under the political supervision of the PSC,[276] without prejudice to its intellectual independence, which is guaranteed to its Director and researchers.[277] It has a Management Board[278] on which each Member State is represented, as is the Commission, and the Board is chaired by the High Representative who convenes it at least twice a year: it is up to this Board to approve the Institute's annual programme and the long-term work prepared by the Director,[279] as well as its budget.

The Institute's mission has been defined *ratione materiae* and was updated by the 2014 decision[280] with some easily understandable deletions (the reference to the European Security Strategy), and others that may attract attention (supporting the transatlantic dialogue).

In addition, the Institute's contribution to the development of the CFSP, and in particular its defence dimension, has been clarified by a reference to 'conflict prevention and peace policies'. Finally, the scope of the Institute's work has been extended to include 'other external actions of the Union'. In addition to broadening the scope of its research work, the Institute's contribution to the development of strategic thinking is aimed specifically at strengthening the Union's capacity to analyse, forecast and network its external action. The instruments used by the Institute to achieve its mission continue to be the production of political analyses, the organisation of political debates, events and workshops, and information campaigns involving other networks within and outside the Union.

It should be noted that with the revision of the founding joint action in 2006, the Commission was closely involved in the work of the Institute, establishing working relations with it, if necessary, in areas of common interest.[281] This could legitimately be seen as the beginning of the Commission's influence on CFSP/CSDP issues, despite its marginalisation. It is interesting to note that

---

273 Ministerial decision of 13 November 1989.

274 Art. 4 of Decision 2014/75/CFSP.

275 Art. 10 of the aforementioned decision.

276 Art. 3 of the aforementioned decision.

277 Art. 8 of the aforementioned decision.

278 Art. 5 of the aforementioned decision.

279 The Director is appointed by the Board of Directors from among the nationals of the Member States. He/she may be assisted by a deputy director (Art. 6 of the above-mentioned decision).

280 Art. 2 of the aforementioned decision.

281 Art. 18a of the founding decision, added by Joint Action 2006/1002/CFSP of 21 December 2006.

this specific reference to the Commission's association disappeared completely with the 2014 revision/repeal, as if it were now clear that the Commission was a stakeholder in the development of the Union's strategic thinking on security and defence.

The very broad definition of the Institute's field of research leaves room for approaches that may vary according to its research teams and management.

3. *The Legacy of the Nice Summit: Military Crisis Management Bodies*

The CSDP's two main military structures, the Military Committee (EUMC) (a) and the EU Military Staff (EUMS) (b), are the result of the Cologne, Helsinki and Nice summits. In addition to creating the PSC, the latter also established military structures dedicated to crisis management.[282]

a. – The European Union Military Committee (EUMC)[283]

It was at the Nice Summit in December 2000 that the Member States reached an agreement on the creation of an EU Military Committee (EUMC) and its establishment within the Council so that it would be ready to start work as soon as possible. Initially set up for this purpose on an interim basis.[284] The EUMC's definitive founding act on 22 January 2001 was annexed to the Council Decision 2001/79/CFSP.

The EUMC is the highest military body within the Council. It is composed of the Chiefs of Defence Staff of the Member States and meets at this level (known as CHODs, for Chiefs of Defence Staff) when necessary, or at the level of their military delegates (known as MilReps).[285] It has a *permanent* Chairman who is appointed for three years by the Council on the recommendation of the Committee in ECS formation.[286] This permanence was highlighted as a notable exception to the rotating Presidency of the Council. This was the rule up until 2000 with the establishment of the Presidency of the Foreign Affairs Council and Security, entrusted to the High Representative by the Treaty of Lisbon. It appeared justified given the military missions conferred on the EUMC and the specific responsibilities of its President, which call for genuine continuity and are incompatible with the 'ephemeral nature' of the rotating Council Presidency. The founding decision and its annex[287] provide several clarifications regarding the appointment and responsibilities of the

[282] See the commentary by A. Hamonic in this publication.
[283] Decision 2001/79/CFSP of 22 January 2001.
[284] Decision 2000/144/CFSP of 14 February 2000 setting up the Interim Military Body.
[285] Art. 2 of the founding decision.
[286] Art. 3 of the founding decision.
[287] Fourth paragraph of the appendix.

EUMC President. The President is a four-star officer, preferably the Chief of Staff of one of the Member States, 'chosen' by his/her peers in accordance with approved procedures, who recommend him/her for appointment by the Council. The President has specific responsibilities. He/she is accountable to the EUMC, and chairs its meetings in formal formation (ECS), as does his/her representative, who chairs meetings of the Permanent Military Delegates (PMDR).

As spokesman for the EUMC, the Chair participates in the PSC as appropriate, with the right to contribute to discussions. He/she may attend Council meetings when the Council has to take decisions with military implications and acts as military advisor to the High Representative on all military and defence matters. The Chair acts on behalf of the EUMC to give general guidance and direction to the Director General of the Military Staff, and acts as the main point of contact for the Commander of current military operations. He/she is supported administratively by a personal staff, a working group (EUMC Group) and the EU Military Staff.

The tasks and functions of the EUMC are defined in Articles 2 and 3 of the Annex to its founding decision. Within the general framework of its function of directing all EU military activities, the EUMC is responsible for providing the PSC with recommendations and opinions on all military matters within the EU. As a forum for consultation and cooperation between all Member States, and operating on the basis of consensus, the EUMC primarily performs general functions in the field of conflict prevention and crisis management by providing advice and making recommendations to the PSC, at its request or on the EUMC's own initiative in certain areas (military aspects of the development of crisis management concepts, military aspects of the political control and strategic direction of CSDP missions, financial estimates for operations and exercises, military relations with NATO and its non-EU Member States, with EU candidate countries).

Secondly, in crisis management situations and for the launch of an operation, the EUMC issues, at the request of the PSC, an initial directive to the Director General of the Military Staff to define and present strategic military options, assesses these options and forwards them to the PSC with an opinion. Once the option has been selected by the Council, the EUMC authorises the Operation Commander to draw up the planning directive and, on the basis of the assessment carried out by the EUMS, it sends the PSC recommendations and opinions on the Concept of Operations (CONOPS) and the Draft Operation Plan (OPLAN).

Thirdly, in the context of an ongoing military operation, the EUMC monitors proper execution by its commander. It also advises the PSC on the option of ending the operation.

b. – The European Union Military Staff (EUMS)[288]

The European Union Military Staff (EUMS) was set up within the General Secretariat of the Council by Decision 2001/80/CFSP of 22 January 2001, which has been amended several times. The EUMS is described in the Decision as the 'EU's' source of military advice based on consensus'.

Made up of military and non-military personnel seconded from Member States, who must be nationals of the latter,[289] the EUMS works under the direction of the Military Committee (EUMC), to which it is accountable. It has been integrated into the EEAS but reports directly to the High Representative. Seconded military personnel from Member States operate under the same international status as seconded national experts and military personnel. The Director of the EUMS is a 3-star general appointed by the High Representative, who must take into account the interest of the Member States in this function and the delicate balance governing the appointment of other leaders of the CSDP political and military apparatus. The internal organisation of the EUMS was defined relatively precisely by the 2008 decision in six main directorates which faithfully reflect the range of its functions (concept and capabilities, intelligence, operations, a civil-military cell, logistics, communication and information systems).

The EU Military Staff is not a permanent operational headquarters capable of leading and directing EU military operations. Such a structure is one of the elusive aspirations in the history of the CSDP, which the Union has not yet succeeded in achieving and which would testify best to its military integration. Yet the EU still lacks this type of military structure. The withdrawal of the United Kingdom, which has always been blamed for the impossibility of creating it, has altered the situation somewhat, although some Member States that found it convenient to hide behind the British veto have taken up the slack. Nevertheless, beyond the major leap forward for the European Union and its defence that the creation of such a headquarters would represent, the idea of endowing the CSDP with such a capability has progressed in small steps on the basis of compromises setting up modest intermediate structures. This was the case, prior to the creation in 2017 of the Military Planning and Conduct Capability (MPCC, see below), and previously of the establishment within the EUMS of the OpsCentre in 2008, relating to the EU's capacity to carry out early strategic planning at the strategic level for EU-led operations.[290]

---

288 Decision 2001/79/CFSP of 22 January 2001, amended by Decision 2008/298/CFSP of 7 April 2008.

289 Art. 1 to 3 of the founding decision.

290 See Decision 2008/298/CFSP of 7 April 2008, amending the founding Decision of the EUMS of 22 January 2001, in which the Council, after welcoming a report by the High Representative on the EUMS's ability to carry out early strategic planning, took up his

This structure, which was extended until 2016, has not really played a planning and leadership role, but rather a simple support and coordination role, as is clearly demonstrated by its mandate when it was first activated in 2012 for the EU missions in the Horn of Africa (EUCAP Nestor and EUTM Somalia) and the Union's military operation EUNAVFOR Atalanta.[291] The OpsCentre's results have been mixed, with some who have praised its usefulness for its overall approach in the regions concerned, and others who have seen it as a new bureaucratic layer weighing down.[292]

The role of the EUMS is to provide a link between the Military Committee and the military resources made available to the EU. Under the directives issued by the Military Committee, it makes its military expertise available to EU bodies. Concerning its operational functions in support of CSDP missions and operations, it primarily performs three of these functions: early warning, situation assessment and strategic planning. However, the EUMS also ensures that it is in a position to reinforce the national headquarters designated to lead an autonomous operation. It also contributes to the process of developing, evaluating and reviewing capability goals, and taking into account the need for the Member States concerned to ensure consistency with NATO. It is also responsible for monitoring, evaluating and making recommendations on the forces and capabilities made available by the Member States in terms of training, exercises and interoperability. Finally, the EUMS works in close coordination with the European Defence Agency.[293]

4. *The Latest CSDP Creations*

The intensification of its crisis management operations and missions under Article 43 TEU[294] has led the Union to strengthen its capabilities in this area by creating specific bodies, embryos of an 'integrated command' dedicated to the planning and conduct of missions that are both civilian (Section a) and military (Section b). The creation in 2005 of the European Defence College for the coordinated training of personnel specialised in crisis management completes the enrichment of the CSDP apparatus (c).

---

recommendations, including four measures and actions identified in the military opinion.

[291] Decision 2012/173/CFSP of 23 March 2012. The OpsCentre will then be activated for the coordination and support of the military and civilian missions created in the Sahel (EUTM Somalia, EUCAP Sahel Niger and EUCAP Sahel Mali) by Decision 2014/860 CFSP of 1 December 2014.

[292] See A. Dumoulin and N. Gros-Verheyde, *La politique européenne de sécurité et de défense commune*, Le Dévoluy, Éd. du Villard, 2017, pp. 152 et seq.

[293] See the commentary by A.-H. Bertana in this publication.

[294] Ibid.

a. – Civilian Planning and Conduct Capability (CPCC)

Long presented as the hallmark of the Union, the civilian crisis management missions developed on the basis of Article 43 TEU[295] numbered 23 in 2024, 12 of which are still in progress. They provide a wide range of assistance, from police (EUPOL) to border (EUBAM), security service reform (SSR) and capacity building (EUCAP). The creation of a permanent integrated command within the Union for this type of mission did not pose the problem of duplication with NATO, since the latter does not have the instrument of a civilian crisis missions. This is undoubtedly one of the reasons why it was created relatively early in the CSDP's institutional architecture, on the basis of guidelines approved by the Council on 18 June 2007.[296] The CPCC does not therefore have the formal legal basis of a Council decision, which can be explained by the fact that it is simply an administrative organisation of the services of the Council secretariat. It was attached to the EEAS when it was created in 2010, in the same way as the Crisis Management and Planning Directorate (CMPD)[297] and the Military Staff of the European Union.

The CPCC has a staff of just under 100 and is organised around three divisions (mission management, mission support and horizontal coordination). It is headed by a director whose role is to exercise the responsibilities inherent in the operational command of civil management missions, under the authority of the PSC and the High Representative. He/she is systematically entrusted with this function each time a mission of this type is set up. This integrated command covers a whole series of tasks involved in setting up and launching these missions: crisis management concepts and the development of strategic objectives; strategic operational planning; force generation and determination of equipment, financial resources and legal frameworks; assistance to the head of mission in defining the mission plan. Once they have been launched, civilian missions and their Heads of Mission are placed under the authority of the Director of the CPCC, who issues them with instructions and ensures that the decisions taken by the Council and the PSC are implemented effectively. The

295 See the commentary by A. Hamonic in this publication. C. Schneider, 'Les dynamiques ambivalentes de la gestion de crise', in A. Hamonic (ed.), *Quelle spécificité de la défense en droit de l'Union européenne*, Droits européens, Rennes, Presses universitaires de Rennes, 2025, pp. 149–175.

296 Council, 18 June 2007, Presidency report on ESDP, 10910/07.

297 The CMPD is a civil-military crisis management and planning structure bringing together, as its name suggests, two categories of personnel. It was created in 2009 (Foreign Affairs Council; 17 November 2009, doc. 16500/09). It is responsible for the strategic planning of CSDP operations and missions in order to present to the Council, as soon as possible, all possible options for dealing with a crisis. It also plays an important role in involving third parties in CSDP operations and missions, particularly in the negotiation of *ad hoc* or framework agreements. Initially incorporated into the General Secretariat of the Council, it has now been attached to the EEAS.

Director of the CPCC may also make proposals to the PSC for the refocussing and development of the missions' mandates, and for their completion.

Managing civilian crisis management missions is not an easy task. The diversity of the personnel involved (police officers and other internal security specialists, magistrates and other staff from the judicial or customs administrations) makes recruitment more complex. Evaluations of these missions show that some are unable to reach or maintain the staffing levels set by the decision to create them. The financial and accounting management of these missions, which must comply with the strict and highly technical rules of the Commission – which is responsible for implementing the CFSP budget – is another source of difficulties. With a view to improving the deployment and enhancing the effectiveness of civilian missions, the Mission Support Instrument (MSI)[298] was set up in 2016 between the Commission and the EEAS.

b. – Military Planning and Command Capability (MPCC)[299]

The Military Planning and Conduct Capability (MPCC) is one of the first results – relatively modest but perhaps promising – of the CSDP's chaotic history, inherent to it, given the reluctance of the Member States to accept a permanent integrated command for its military operations, such as NATO has. Without this type of structure, the Union has had to fall back on palliatives consisting of *ad hoc* commands, specific to each operation and for its duration only.[300]

The Military Planning and Conduct Capability (MPCC) is a sort of interface with the civilian capability created much earlier in 2007. It is intended to assume responsibility for the planning and conduct of CSDP *military* crisis management *missions*. Although limited in scope, this new CSDP body was the subject of intense negotiations,[301] as evidenced by the terminological precautions taken in its founding decision to avoid disturbing names: the terms 'Headquarters' or 'Commander' were dropped in favour of 'Capability' and 'Director'.

---

298 See conclusions of the Foreign Affairs Council, 18 June 2016, doc. 8022/16.

299 Decision 2017/971/CFSP of 8 June 2017 determining the modalities for the planning and conduct of non-executive mandate military missions conducted by the European Union in the framework of the CSDP, [2017] *OJ* L146/133, 9 June 2017. The legal bases for this decision are Articles 42(4) and 43(2) TEU.

300 This involves, on the one hand, the use of NATO capabilities and assets in accordance with the Berlin plus agreements and, on the other hand, the framework nation system, whereby Member States make some of their assets and capabilities available to the Multinational Operational Command.

301 See N. Gros-Verheyde, 'Couvrez ce QG que je ne saurais voir… le texte sur la MPCC finalisé', B2 PRO, 1 June 2017.

The MPCC does not constitute a truly permanent integrated military command. Its remit, as set out in its founding decision, is limited to operational command of non-executive military missions, recognisable by the acronym EUTM,[302] and therefore excludes executive military operations.[303] When EUTM was set up, it was given operational command of current military missions whose founding decisions were amended to transform their operational command into a simple force command. The missions concerned were EUTM Somalia created in 2010, EUTM Mali created in 2013, and EUTM RCA created in 2016. Subsequently, each of the new military missions was placed under the authority of the MPCC, namely: EUTM Mozambique (July 2021), EUTM Niger (February 2023), EUPM Moldova (April 2023) and the military pillar of the civil-military security and defence initiative with West African countries in the Gulf of Guinea (August 2023).

On the basis of a concept note approved by the Council in March 2017, it is the Director of the EU Military Staff who is designated by the founding decision as the Director of the CMPC. He/she acts under the political control and strategic direction of the PSC in accordance with Article 38 TEU.[304] The task of the MPCC is to assist the PSC in its responsibilities for the strategic direction of military missions by exercising its activities as the commander of these missions (planning and conduct, in particular to set them up, launch and sustain them, and to seek contributors to the mission's forces from among the Member States).

Extending the competences of the MPCC to the command of *executive military operations* would naturally constitute a major step forward in the Union's progress towards a genuine, permanent operational command and a significant qualitative leap in integration into the CSDP. This is not out of the question, as it has already been announced in the Strategic Compass, but once again in a cautious and gradual manner. The latter envisages that the MPCC will be able to assume operational command of at least two small or even medium-scale executive military operations by 2025, in addition to non-executive military missions.[305]

---

302 Art. 1 of the founding decision.

303 See the commentary by A. Hamonic in this publication.

304 Third paragraph of Art. (1) of the founding decision.

305 See also Council of the European Union, 'A strategic security and defence compass for a European Union protecting its citizens, values and interests and contributing to international peace and security', 21 March 2022, doc. 7373/22, p. 19.

c. – The European Security and Defence College (ESDC)[306]

The history of the European Security and Defence College[307] can be traced back to discussions begun in 2003 at the Thessaloniki European Council, which were taken up in an initiative supported in 2004 by four Member States,[308] and given concrete form in the Joint Action of 18 July 2005. The College's mission is to provide staff from the Member States and the European institutions with strategic-level training, so that they can work more effectively within the CSDP framework and develop a common strategic culture.

Statutorily, the ESDC is a 'surprising reality'[309] in view of its differences with comparable bodies in NATO or the Member States, with different statuses as interministerial bodies (see the Institut des hautes études de défense nationale (IHEDN) in France) or attached to the Ministry of Defence (Germany). Unlike these traditional colleges, the ESDC has neither a building, nor a large permanent civilian-military staff, nor a budget to cover this type of major expense. For the most part, its activities are hosted on the premises of the EU Military Staff and it operates under the responsibility of the High Representative.

The structure of the ESDC[310] has a legal capacity,[311] and is based on four bodies: a steering committee, an academic council, a director who is the sole legal representative and is responsible for the administrative and financial management of the College, and a particularly modest secretariat.[312] Clearly, the Academic Council best illustrates the specific nature of the College as a training body.

The originality of the ESDC lies in its organisation in the form of a network,[313] which has sometimes led to it being described as a virtual body: simply put, the totally new idea behind its creation is to bring together in a single network all the experts from the Member States who can offer training. This solution appeared to be not only the least costly, but also attractive because of its flexibility and adaptability to needs, even if it implies special coordination efforts. The ESDC brings together a wide range of partners, including the

---

306 Joint Action 2005/575/CFSP of 18 July 2005, repealed by Joint Action 2008/550/CFSP of 23 June 2008, and Decision 2016/2382/CFSP of 21 December 2016 repealing Decision 2013/189/CFSP.

307 See C. Ciocca, 'Le Collège européen de défense et ses initiatives en matière de lutte contre la piraterie maritime', in C. Chevallier-Govers and C. Schneider (eds.), *L'Europe et la lutte contre la piraterie maritime*, Paris, Pedone, 2015, pp. 91 et seq.

308 Germany, Belgium, France and Luxembourg.

309 C. Ciocca, 'Le Collège européen de défense et ses initiatives en matière de lutte contre la piraterie maritime', in C. Chevallier-Govers and C. Schneider (eds.), *L'Europe et la lutte contre la piraterie maritime*, Paris, Pedone, 2015.

310 Art. 8 of the founding decision.

311 Art. 7 of the founding decision.

312 Originally consisting of two people, its workforce was increased to eight in 2016.

313 Art. 5 of the founding decision.

defence colleges and military academies of the Member States, but this does not mean that it is all there is to it: universities and other institutions in the civilian and military sectors are also part of this network. It is moreover required to establish close links with certain other EU bodies (CEPOL, Frontex, Europol and the Torrejon Satellite Centre). Finally, the European Union Institute for Security Studies cooperates with the College, in particular by making its expertise and capacities available for its training activities.[314]

The training provided by the ESDC is offered to civilian and military personnel from the Member States, but is also open to nationals of candidate countries and, where appropriate, third countries taking part in EU operations and missions.[315] In practice, training needs are identified by the PSC and its Politico-Military Group based on EU policies and their priorities. The courses cover not only the CFSP and its CSDP dimension, but also partnerships and the EU's neighbourhood policy, with a view to highlighting the global approach and in particular the civil-military dimension of crises.

In the first instance, the College organises regular general training, such as high-level training for the CSDP, or training for information officers and public relations officers on CSDP missions. But it also organises ad hoc, targeted training (security sector reform, civilian crisis management, civil-military coordination, maritime security, legal advice for missions and operations, etc.). It should be noted that one of the most recent amendments to the founding decision, which took place in 2018,[316] was to add a new objective to the College, namely to provide the administrations of the Member States with personnel competent in the fields of cyber defence and cybersecurity.

In terms of funding, it should be emphasised that the Member States bear the full cost of their participation in the ESDC.[317] The same applies to participants in its activities and training.[318] As for the EEAS, it bears the costs of accommodating the Director and his/her secretariat on its premises.[319] The College also receives a contribution from the EU budget[320] as well as voluntary contributions[321] to finance specific activities which are earmarked in the budget. Finally, it may apply for research projects in the field of the CFSP and act as coordinator or member of such projects,[322] and the ESDC must indicate the contributions from these projects in its budget.

314 Art. 6 of the founding decision.
315 Art. 4(2) and 10 of the founding decision.
316 See Decision 2018/712/CFSP of 14 May 2018 amending Decision 2016/382, Art. 3(k).
317 Art. 14 of the founding decision.
318 Art. 15 of the founding decision.
319 Ibid.
320 In 2020, the financial reference amount intended to cover ESDC expenditure was €1.88 million.
321 Art. 17 of the founding decision.
322 Art. 18 of the founding decision.

THE COMMON POSITION ON ARMS EXPORT CONTROLS

Council Common Position 2008/944/CFSP of 8 December 2008 defining common rules governing control of exports of military technology and equipment.[1]

Anne MILLET-DEVALLE
Professor at the Université Côte d'Azur, International and European Law Laboratory (LADIE – UPR 7414)

The annual value of arms exports outside the European Union by the 27 Member States[2] was around €20 billion in 2023,[3] making the EU the world's second-largest exporter, with 500,000 people employed in defence companies.[4] Controlling this trade therefore presents particularly sensitive economic and strategic issues for the Member States, which are concerned to preserve their competence in this area (under Article 346 TFEU)[5] and are reluctant to have their exports regulated by the Union. Thus, this control has developed only gradually[6] when the Member States found it was in their interests both in terms

---

1 Council Common Position 2008/944/CFSP of 8 December 2008 defining common rules governing control of exports of military technology and equipment, [2008] *OJ* L335/99. As last amended by Council Decision (CFSP) 2025/779 of 14 April 2025, [2025] *OJ* L239.

2 Data on arms exports by EU Member States can be consulted online on the EEAS COARM website: https://webgate.ec.europa.eu/eeasqap/sense/app/75fd8e6e-68ac-42dd-a078-f616633118bb/sheet/64c1cfa7-bf1a-4300-8600-a0ec26bcf753/state/analysis.

3 Twenty-Sixth Annual Report according to Article 8(2) of Council Common Position 2008/944/CFSP defining common rules governing the control of exports of military technology and equipment, *OJ* C 2025/472, 21.2.2025.

4 Joint Communication from the European Commission and the High Representative of the Union for Foreign Affairs and Security Policy, A new European Defence Industrial Strategy: Achieving EU readiness through a responsive and resilient European Defence Industry, JOIN (2024) 10 final, 5 March 2024.

5 See the commentary on Article 346 TFEU by S. RODRIGQUES in this publication.

6 On the basis of a Franco-German proposal in 1990, the issue of export controls was discussed during the drafting of the Maastricht Treaty. It was then decided that the subject would be considered as an intergovernmental issue within the framework of a common foreign and security policy and not as a trade policy issue. Between 1992 and 1997, the

of security and competition. Reconciling these interests has led them to seek flexible instruments that resolve economic and strategic concerns.

Common Position 2008/944/CFSP is an adaptation of the European Code of Conduct on Arms Exports, adopted in the form of a simple Common Foreign and Security Policy (CFSP) declaration on 8 June 1998, on the initiative of France and the United Kingdom, Europe's leading arms exporters.[7] It defined in detail eight common ethical and security criteria applicable to the national arms export policies of the Member States of the European Union. These criteria had been defined within the framework of European Political Cooperation at the Luxembourg (June 1991) and Lisbon (June 1992) summits, and the Code was then negotiated by an ad hoc group on armaments cooperation. Under the authority of the Political and Security Committee, this group was made up of representatives of the Member States and the Commission

Goods designated as 'armaments' are equipment, components or supplies specifically designed or modified for military use,[8] which differentiates them from dual-use goods.[9] On 13 June 2000, the Council adopted the European Union's first common list of military equipment.[10] It has since been subject to periodic annual review, taking into account similar national or international lists, where appropriate.[11]

The aim of the Code of Conduct was to introduce restraint on conventional arms exports that could contribute, among other things, to human rights violations, internal repression or undermine sustainable development (by exceeding the technical and economic capabilities of the recipient country), while also addressing exports of equipment that could be used for aggression, contribute to regional instability or threaten the security of Member States

---

French and British governments took the view that arms export policy did not require harmonisation at EU level. See S. Bauer, 'L'européanisation des politiques d'exportation d'armement', *AFRI*, 2001, vol. II, pp. 507–523.

7 Council of the European Union, European Union Code of Conduct on Arms Exports, 8 June 2008, 8675/2/98 REV2, PESC 137; see A. Millet-Devalle, 'Codes de conduite et contrôle des exportations d'armement', *Arès*, April 2001, no. 47.

8 This definition of 'specially designed for military use' is the subject of joint harmonisation and interpretation work at European Union level between the various Member States as part of the establishment of the EU Common Military List (see below).

9 See Regulation (EU) 2021/821 of the European Parliament and of the Council of 20 May 2021 setting up a Union regime for the control of exports, brokering, technical assistance, transit and transfers of dual-use items (recast), [2021] *OJ* L206/1. See the commentary on this Regulation in this publication by A. Millet-Devalle under Article 207 TFEU.

10 Council Declaration of 13 June 2000, issued on the occasion of the adoption of the common list of military equipment covered by the European Union code of conduct on arms exports, [2000] *OJ* C191/1,

11 The latest Common Military List of the European Union adopted by the Council on 19 February 2024 (equipment covered by Council Common Position 2008/944/CFSP defining common rules governing the control of exports of military technology and equipment), [2024] *OJ* C/2024/1945.

(the risk of a 'boomerang effect' or diversion to an undesired end-user) and compliance with Member States' international commitments. To facilitate convergence in the application of the criteria, the Code of Conduct created a bilateral consultation mechanism, triggered by a Member State's refusal to export on the basis of these criteria.

This was undoubtedly a significant contribution to the transparency of exports and the promotion of convergence in the national arms export policies of certain Member States,[12] a common approach conceived as constituent element of the Common Foreign and Security Policy (CFSP). However, the exclusively voluntary nature of the system was contested and certain shortcomings criticised, particularly with regard to the export of jointly produced armaments.[13]

Thereafter, in-depth work began on revising the Code to transform it into a binding control instrument, and on 30 June 2005, the Permanent Representatives Committee approved the text of a common position.[14] Yet, the draft was only adopted by the Council in December 2008, reflecting the highly sensitive nature of the issue for the main exporting Member States.

In its resolutions of 13 March and 4 December 2008,[15] the European Parliament noted that 'this issue [had] acquired a new sense of urgency owing to a number of new developments', as the deployment of EU military and civilian missions that could be endangered by weapons exported by Member States. The European Parliament also pointed out that the EU had committed itself in the Lisbon Treaty to acting as a responsible international actor, and denounced – as did a number of non-governmental organisations[16] – France's position, which it accused of using its opposition as a bargaining chip in its

12 Germany adopted 'Political Principles' for arms exports on 30 January 2000, available at: www.auswaertiges-amt.de.

13 As regards exports of jointly produced armaments, France, Germany, Spain, Italy, the United Kingdom and Sweden took the initiative of drawing up a *Letter of Intent between 6 Defence Ministers on Measures to Facilitate the Restructuring of the European Defence Industry* (LoI, 6 July 1998) with the aim of establishing a common regulatory framework for the joint production and export of armaments. This work was the starting point for the negotiation of a final agreement signed on 27 July 2000 in Farnborough (*JORF*, n°268, 18 November 2001), the aim of which was to provide a common and binding political and legal framework to establish an environment favourable to the building of a more competitive European defence industry, by taking concrete measures for cooperation in six areas, including export procedures. For the latter, a mechanism was established for negotiating by consensus on 'white lists' of destinations authorised for the export of each type of equipment produced jointly, before the start of production by all the countries concerned. In drawing up these lists, express reference was made to the criteria of the Code of Conduct (Article 13(2)(a)).

14 [2003] *OJ* L156/79.

15 Available at: https://www.europarl.europa.eu/doceo/document/TA-6-2008-0580_EN.html?redirect

16 *Good conduct? Ten years of the EU Code of Conduct on Arms Exports, June 2008*. Report available at: www.obsarm.org/news/2008/bonneconduite.pdf

efforts to lift the EU arms embargo on China. Paradoxically, it was under a French presidency that the Common Position was finally adopted, without debate and with great secrecy, France having finally sided with the majority position.

Following the adoption of Common Position 2008/944/CFSP, a number of developments resulted in new commitments and obligations for Member States. These included: the entry into force of the Arms Trade Treaty (ATT),[17] to which all Member States are party; the adoption on 19 November 2018 of a revised EU strategy concerning small arms and light weapons and their ammunition;[18] but also the adoption by the United Nations General Assembly of the 2030 Agenda for Sustainable Development, which includes a goal of promoting peaceful societies;[19] and the presentation on 28 May 2018 by the UN Secretary-General of his disarmament programme 'Securing our Common Future'. Among the transparency measures concerning military activities, the latter promotes the communication of information on arms imports and exports.

In order to take account of this new context, the text was revised by Council Decision (CFSP) 2019/1560, adopted on 16 September 2019.[20] This introduced amendments aimed primarily at increasing the transparency and convergence of Member States' export policies.

Under the terms of its revised version (Art. 15), the Common Position is subject to periodic review by the Conventional Arms Exports Subgroup (COARM) of the EU Working Party on Conventional Arms Export. A review therefore began in 2022,[21] in the context of the creation of the European Defence Fund (EDF)[22] and the European Peace Facility (EPF).[23] It focused in particular on the thorny issue of export controls on armaments produced jointly or financed by the EU, on further harmonisation of controls, and also includes an update of the Common Position users' guide.[24]

---

17 The ATT was adopted on 2 April 2013 and entered into force on 24 December 2014.

18 Council of the European Union, 13581/18, CFSP/PESC 985.

19 UNGA, Resolution of 25 September 2015, A/R/70/1.

20 [2019] *OJ* L239/16.

21 Council Conclusions on the review of Council Common Position 2008/944/CFSP of 8 December 2008 on the control of arms exports, adopted in Brussels on 16 September 2019 by the General Affairs Council, Council of the European Union, 12195/19, COARM 154.

22 Regulation (EU) 2021/697 of the European Parliament and of the Council of 29 April 2021 establishing the European Defence Fund and repealing Regulation (EU) 2018/1092, PE/11/2021/INIT, [2021] *OJ* L170/149.

23 Council Decision (CFSP) 2021/509 of 22 March 2021 establishing a European Peace Facility and repealing Decision (CFSP) 2015/528, ST/5212/2021/INI, [2021] *OJ* L102/14.

24 Council of the European Union, User's Guide to Council Common Position 2008/944/CFSP defining common rules governing the control of exports of military technology and equipment, 12189/19, COARM 153, 16 September 2019.

The review process ended in April 2025 with the adoption of Decision (CFSP) 2025/779, which sets out the objective of strengthening cooperation between Member States on rules governing export authorisations, promoting convergence in the field of exports of military technology and equipment, and revising the criteria by which transfer controls are assessed, with a view to achieving 'high common standards' (Recital 8 of the Decision).

Thanks to these successive adaptations, the 2008 Common Position, which is the only binding legal provision on conventional arms exports at regional level, has made it possible to gradually improve the consistency of the EU's export control system (see Section I), but it is still making only a limited contribution to its Europeanisation (Section II).[25]

I. THE CONTRIBUTION OF THE COMMON POSITION TO THE CONSISTENCY OF EU ARMS EXPORT CONTROL POLICY

In 1998, the EU Code of Conduct initiated a process of cooperation on arms exports, both within the Member States and in relations with third countries and international organisations. The adoption of the Common Position and its various revisions subsequently contributed to the organisation of the European arms regimes, thereby promoting the internal (Section A below) and external (Section B) normative consistency of the Union's action on arms exports.

A. THE CONTRIBUTION TO THE INTERNAL NORMATIVE CONSISTENCY OF ARMS EXPORT CONTROLS

The dynamics of the reform of the Common Position expresses the search for both the formal and substantive consistency of arms export controls within the EU.

1. *Formal Consistency*

The adoption of the Common Position in December 2008 made it possible to clarify the division of competences between the Member States and the EU in the area of arms export controls, as well as their legal basis, which determines the decision-making procedures in this area. The text was adopted in the

[25] On the notion of Europeanisation, see in particular C. Radaelli, 'The Europeanization of Public Policy', in K. Featherstone and C. Radaelli, (eds.), *The Politics of Europeanization*, Oxford, Oxford University Press, 2003, pp. 27–56.

context of negotiations between the European Parliament and the EU Council of Ministers on Directive 2009/43/EC on transfers of defence-related products within the EU, which aims to create a uniform European licensing system applicable throughout the EU.[26] The Parliament wanted to include export controls outside the EU in the directive, but a majority of Member States considered that this was a matter for the second pillar and not the Community pillar.[27] The adoption of a binding text under the CFSP pillar therefore made it possible to establish the interpretation of Article 346 TFEU and to achieve a balance between the internal and external aspects, transfers and exports, with two texts which, although different in nature, are equally binding. In addition, the annual report on the application of the Common Position contains information on intra-EU transfers of defence-related products governed by Directive 2009/43/EC.

The adoption of a common position has also made it possible to 'raise' the Code of Conduct to the same normative level as other common positions in the field of arms, within the framework of related texts, in particular joint actions and strategies. The legal framework is multifaceted, including texts relating to both conventional weapons and weapons of mass destruction (WMD). The first category includes the 2002 Council Joint Action on the European Union's contribution to combating the destabilising accumulation and spread of small arms and light weapons,[28] as well as the EU Strategy to combat the illicit accumulation and trafficking of small arms and light weapons (SALW) and their ammunition, adopted by the European Council on 15 and 16 December 2005.[29] With regard to WMD, the 2008 Common Position is also part of the EU Strategy against the Proliferation of Weapons of Mass Destruction of December 2003[30] which identifies the proliferation of these weapons as a major threat and is in line with the Common Position adopted by the Council in the same year, on the non-proliferation of WMD and their means of delivery.[31]

The EU Common Position on common rules governing control of exports of military technology and equipment also has equal status with the Common Position 2003/468/CFSP adopted by the Council on 23 June 2003 on the

---

26 See the contribution by E. Daniel and M. Kieffer in this publication.

27 N. Gros-Verheyde, 'Parliament adopts directive on arms transfers', *Europolitics*, 18 December 2008, no. 3661.

28 Council Joint Action 2002/589/CFSP of 12 July 2002 on the European Union's contribution to combating the destabilising accumulation and spread of small arms and light weapons and repealing Joint Action 1999/34/CFSP, [2002] *OJ* L191/1.

29 Council of the EU, EU Strategy to combat the illicit accumulation and trafficking of SALW and their ammunition, 5319/06, PESC 31, CODUN 4, COARM 5, 13 January 2006.

30 Council of the EU, EU Strategy against the Proliferation of Weapons of Mass Destruction, 15708/03, PESC 768, CODUN 50, CONOP 64, COARM 21, 10 December 2003.

31 Council Common Position 2003/805/CFSP of 17 November 2003 on the universalisation and reinforcement of multilateral agreements in the field of non-proliferation of weapons of mass destruction and means of delivery, [2003] *OJ* L302/34.

control of arms brokering.[32] This Common Position, which aims to regulate arms brokering in order to prevent the circumvention of embargoes on arms exports decreed by the United Nations, the EU or the OSCE, sets out a series of provisions 'commit[ing] States to develop adequate national legislation' thus requiring Member States to take all necessary measures to control brokering activities taking place on their territory or carried out by their nationals. As the Member States have undertaken to transpose the elements of this common position into their national law and, consequently, to regulate the brokering of arms and military equipment, the absence of a common position on arms exports had become problematic, given the points of convergence between the two areas.

The control of brokering organised by a common position and that of arms exports, covered by texts of the same nature, is only one aspect of the strengthening of the formal consistency of the system for moderating the arms trade.

The Common Position (Articles 12 and 13) incorporated into the control system a number of instruments which had been created to improve its operation but which had previously had no binding force: in addition to the EU Common Military List (defining the equipment covered by the control), the Conventional Arms Exports Subgroup (COARM) of the Council Working Party on Non-proliferation and Arms Exports (set up in 1991 and enabling exchanges on all issues relating to conventional arms[33] to help Member States apply the Code) has drawn up a 'user's guide' for officials responsible for issuing export authorisations. It provides a tool for harmonisation, both in terms of notifications of denial of authorisations and consultations and in terms of best practice concerning the interpretation of criteria, end-use controls and arms brokering.[34]

2. *Consistency of Substance*

The Common Position provides a highly inclusive reference framework for the control of all arms-related exports.

The scope of the Code of Conduct had already been extended by Article 1(2) of the Common Position, which sets out the types of exports concerned. National export licences include 'physical' exports (equipment, licences, etc.),

32 [2003] *OJ* L156/79; as early as 2001, the EU had adopted guidelines on the brokering of arms and military equipment.

33 COARM meetings allow Member States to exchange information on their perception of political developments in certain countries.

34 The guide can be consulted on the Council's website under export controls for security purposes: www.consilium.europa.eu/export-controls

but also brokering, transit or transhipment, and intangible transfers of software and technology (by means such as the internet, telephone, etc.).

As regards the control of exports of dual-use items defined by Regulation 2021/821[35] and without prejudice to this Regulation, Council Decisions (CFSP) 2019/1560 and 2025/779 extend the scope of the Common Position's control over such items. Article 6 of the Common Position henceforth provides that the criteria set out in Article 2 and the consultation procedure set out in Article 4 shall also apply to Member States in respect of the dual-use items and technology listed in Annex I to the Regulation, 'where there are serious grounds for believing that the end-user of such goods and technology will be the armed forces or internal security forces or similar entities in the recipient country'. References in the Common Position to military technology or equipment are deemed to cover dual-use goods as well. The Common Position thus sets out the limits of 'communitarisation' in the area of export controls on dual-use items, with the issue still being dealt with in an intergovernmental framework, in which the Regulation is only partially involved, with the criteria defined under the CFSP remaining the relevant elements for deciding whether or not to grant an export authorisation.

With regard to brokering, Common Position 2003/468/CFSP requires Member States, in addition to setting up a system for the exchange of information on brokering activities and establishing appropriate penalties to ensure that controls are effectively enforced, to examine licence applications for specific brokering operations in the light of arms export control provisions. As a further illustration of the overlap between the two areas, COARM agreed in 2007 that the information exchange commitments in Common Position 2003/468/CFSP should be implemented through a mechanism set out in the Code of Conduct on Arms Exports.[36] The latest report on the Code of Conduct presented on 22 November 2008 therefore contained (for the first time) a table taking stock of the implementation of the Common Position on brokering in national legislation. Since the adoption of Common Position 2008/944/CFSP, the annual reports drawn up under Article 8(2) systematically contain details of national implementation of the Common Position on brokering.

The Common Position also provides a general framework for the control of technical assistance related to certain military end-uses, organised by a Council Joint Action.[37] This subjects technical assistance related to WMD to

---

35 See the commentary on this regulation in this publication by A. Millet-Devalle under Article 207 TFEU.

36 Council of the European Union. 2007. *Ninth Annual Report according to operative provision 8 of the European Union Code of Conduct on Arms Exports*. EU Council Document 12919/1/07, Rev. 1. Brussels: Council of the EU, 25 September, Table C, p. 327-8. Available at https://eur-lex.europa.eu/legal-content/EN/TXT/?uri=oj:JOC_2007_253_R_0001_01.

37 Council Joint Action 2000/401/CFSP of 22 June 2000 on the control of technical assistance related to certain military end-uses, [2000] *OJ* L159/216.

controls and allows (Article 3) for the control of technical assistance related to conventional military end-uses and provided in countries under an arms embargo decided by the European Union, the OSCE or the United Nations Security Council.

The European Peace Facility specifies that all assistance, export or transfer measures undertaken in this framework must respect 'the principles laid down in Common Position 2008/944/CFSP and shall be without prejudice to the procedure to be followed by Member States regarding such export or transfer in accordance with that Common Position, including in terms of assessment. Furthermore, such assistance measures shall not affect the discretion of Member States regarding policy on the transfer within the Union, and the export of, military equipment' (Recital 13 and Article 56.3).

Similarly, the regulation establishing the EDF recalls that 'the export of military equipment and technology by the Member States is regulated by Council Common Position 2008/944/CFSP' (Recital 63).

The many provisions relating to the export of arms and dual-use materials thus show a certain consistency within the EU, giving the Union the legitimacy to participate in the development of arms export controls.

B. THE EUROPEAN UNION'S CONTRIBUTION TO THE CONSISTENCY OF ARMS EXPORT CONTROL REGIMES

The exercise of the EU's normative power in the area of arms export controls is clearly demonstrated by the influence of the Common Position on arms export control regimes. This is particularly evident in the promotion of the Common Position among third countries (Section 1), in the support of the Common Position for non-proliferation regimes (Section 2) and in the projection by the EU of its criteria at the universal level, through the Arms Trade Treaty (Section 3).

1. *Promoting the Common Position among Third Countries*

The adoption of Common Position 2008/944/CFSP reinforced Joint Action 2008/230/CFSP adopted on 17 March 2008 by the Council[38] concerning 'support for EU activities in order to promote the control of arms exports and the principles and criteria of the EU Code of Conduct on Arms Exports among

[38] [2008] *OJ* L75/81. This joint action earmarked €500,500 from the general budget of the EU to finance seminars in the field of arms export controls, to promote EU criteria and principles for arms exports and to help third countries to draw up and implement appropriate legislation.

third countries'. Article 11 of Common Position 2008/944/CFSP provides for such promotion, stating that 'Member States shall use their best endeavours to encourage other States which export military technology or equipment to apply the criteria of this Common Position'.

Before the adoption of the Common Position, the momentum created by the 1998 Code to project the criteria defined by the EU beyond its borders was already significant: no fewer than six third countries had decided to join the Code of Conduct process: Bosnia and Herzegovina, Canada, Croatia, the Former Yugoslav Republic of Macedonia, Iceland and Norway.[39] The strengthening of the legal basis for control has obviously contributed to the EU's efforts to promote a responsible approach to exports, and since 2008 four new third countries have officially endorsed the criteria and principles set out in Common Position.[40]

Another way in which the EU can project the mechanisms established by the Common Position is through its support for building the capacity of third States to control arms exports. The EU's activities to promote effective and transparent arms export controls have been the subject of numerous texts and have evolved since 2008.[41] The activities that have been carried out have, in particular, contributed to greater regional cooperation, greater transparency and accountability in accordance with the principles set out in the Common Position and the risk assessment criteria set out therein. The activities in question have generally targeted third countries in the EU's eastern and southern neighbourhood, third countries in Central Asia and Mongolia. Council Decision (CFSP) 2020/1464 of 12 October 2020 on the promotion

39 Tenth Annual Report according to Operative Provision 8 of the European Union Code of Conduct on Arms Exports, (2008/C 300/01).

40 Albania, Bosnia-Herzegovina, Canada, Northern Macedonia, Georgia, Iceland, Montenegro and Norway. Twenty-sixth annual report pursuant to Article 8(2) of Council Common Position 2008/944/CFSP defining common rules governing control of exports of military technology and equipment, ST/16016/2024/INIT, [2025] *OJ* C/2025/472.

41 Council Decision 2013/768/CFSP of 16 December 2013 on EU activities in support of the implementation of the Arms Trade Treaty, in the framework of the European Security Strategy, [2013] *OJ* L341/56; Council Decision (CFSP) 2017/915 of 29 May 2017 on Union outreach activities in support of the of the Arms Trade Treaty, [2017] *OJ* L139/38; Council Joint Action 2008/230/CFSP of 17 March 2008 on support for EU activities in order to promote the control of arms exports and the principles and criteria of the EU Code of Conduct on Arms Exports among third countries, [2008] *OJ* L75/81; Council Decision 2009/1012/CFSP of 22 December 2009 on support for EU activities in order to promote the control of arms exports and the principles and criteria of Common Position 2008/944/CFSP among third countries, [2009] *OJ* L348/16; Council Decision 2012/711/CFSP of 19 November 2012 on support for Union activities in order to promote, among third countries, the control of arms exports and the principles and criteria of Common Position 2008/944/CFSP, [2012] *OJ* L321/62; Council Decision (CFSP) 2015/2309 of 10 December 2015 on the promotion of effective arms export controls, [2015] *OJ* L326/56; Council Decision (CFSP) 2018/101 of 22 January 2018 on the promotion of effective arms export controls, [2018] *OJ* L17/40.

of effective arms export controls[42] thus promotes, through a project for material aid aimed at 'further promoting, among third countries, the criteria and principles set out in Common Position 2008/944/CFSP' (Article 1(2)(a)), an action whose implementation falls within the remit of the EU High Representative for Foreign Affairs and Security Policy/Vice President (HR/VP). Its implementation is entrusted to the German Federal Office of Economics and Export Control, which carries out its tasks under the responsibility of the High Representative

2. *The Common Position's Support for Non-Proliferation Regimes*

The Common Position supports binding arms export control regimes:

> (a) the international obligations of Member States and their commitments to enforce United Nations, European Union and Organisation for Security and Cooperation in Europe arms embargoes; (b) the international obligations of Member States under the Nuclear Non-Proliferation Treaty, the Biological and Toxin Weapons Convention and the Chemical Weapons Convention; (c) the commitment of Member States not to export any form of anti-personnel landmine.[43]

It also supports non-binding arms export control regimes. The first criterion of the Common Position states that:

> An export licence shall be denied if approval would be inconsistent with, inter alia [...] the commitments of Member States in the framework of the Australia Group, the Missile Technology Control Regime, the Zangger Committee, the Nuclear Suppliers Group, the Wassenaar Arrangement and The Hague Code of Conduct against Ballistic Missile Proliferation.

Several of the Member States have made commitments under these agreements, often referred to as 'supplier regimes', which play a very important role in non-proliferation law, but not all of them participate in them and the EU is a member of only one regime (the Australia Group). The Common Position therefore makes it possible to broaden the scope of application of the non-proliferation regimes by imposing on all EU Member States the control lists and criteria established in these non-binding frameworks, thereby making a major contribution to the harmonisation of controls. Under the Wassenaar Arrangement, in particular, which brings together 42 States, the updates of the

---

42 [2020] *OJ* L335/3, amended by Council Decision (CFSP) 2022/848 of 30 May 2022, [2022] *OJ* L148/50, and by Council Decision (CFSP) 2025/208 of 30 January 2025, [2025] *OJ* L2025/208.

43 Common Position 2008/944/CFSP, Art. 2(1).

list of goods subject to export controls (the 'Military List') are systematically transposed into the EU's common list of military equipment.[44]

In addition to this transposition, the common position forms the framework for regular dialogues between COARM and external bodies, including United Nations offices (UNODC), non-governmental organisations (such as the ICRC and *Saferworld*) and companies (*Conflict Armament Research*).

3. *The EU's Projection of the Common Position Criteria in the Arms Trade Treaty*

The Common Position has strengthened the position of the EU and its members in the negotiations on the multilateral Arms Trade Treaty (ATT), enabling it to achieve the adoption of a treaty that harmonises export criteria by aligning them with those of the EU.

In March 2005, COARM set up a contact group. In its conclusions of 3 October 2005, the Council subsequently approved the principle of an Arms Trade Treaty and reiterated this position in its conclusions of 11 December 2006, 18 June 2007 and 10 December 2007. According to United Nations General Assembly resolution 61/89,[45] the Secretary-General sought the views of Member States on the viability, scope and draft parameters of an ATT before establishing the Group of Governmental Experts to examine these issues (seven Member State experts participated in the Group). All EU Member States expressed their views in this process and a joint EU response was submitted,[46] which was taken into account in the report of the Group of Governmental Experts (GGE).[47] In the ATT negotiations, the EU proposed that:

> Member States of the United Nations undertake, in particular, to examine requests for authorisation of exports of conventional arms on which they have to take a decision in a national capacity, in the full exercise of their sovereignty, in the light of a certain number of criteria. These criteria, defined jointly, should be aimed in particular at ensuring that such transfers do not contribute to actions constituting a violation of the fundamental rights recognised by the United Nations Charter,

44 Common Position 2008/944/CFSP, Art. 12.

45 On 6 December 2006, the UN General Assembly adopted resolution 61/89 entitled 'Towards an arms trade treaty: establishing common international standards for the import, export and transfer of conventional arms'.

46 At its meeting on 18 June 2007, the General Affairs and External Council re-emphasised the importance of an Arms Trade Treaty. In a separate EU opinion submitted to the UN Secretary-General, the Council Presidency cited the EU Code of Conduct as a good example of international cooperation in the control of arms exports and argued in favour of an Arms Trade Treaty.

47 Report of the Group of Governmental Experts, A/63/33. Taking stock of the work on establishing common standards towards an Arms Trade Treaty, AG/DSI/3380, 31 October 2008.

that they do not undermine the regional stability of the area concerned or that they undeniably hinder the development of the countries concerned.[48]

This proposal simply transposed the criteria of the European Code of Conduct to the universal level.

However, the support of the Member States and the European Union for a legally binding international treaty was losing political force due to the regional organisation's inability to adopt a legally binding text internally. This was subsequently overcome by the adoption of the Common Position in December 2008

The EU's position was then confirmed by the adoption by the Council on 19 January 2009 of the Decision on support for EU activities in order to promote the process of drawing up an Arms Trade Treaty among third countries, as part of the European security strategy.[49] The text provided for the organisation of several regional events and seminars (in Africa, Asia, Latin America and the Middle East) involving political representatives and members of civil society, researchers and non-governmental organisations, the implementation of which was entrusted by the EU to the United Nations Institute for Disarmament Research.[50] This was done to 'avoid giving the impression that it is trying to impose the criteria defined in the Code of Conduct on other members of the United Nations'.[51]

In fact, the EU played a decisive role in the negotiation of the ATT, illustrating its ability to project internal normative solutions to the universal level.[52]

What the ATT has in common with Common Position 2008/944/CFSP is that it prohibits the authorisation of exports of military equipment if there is an overriding or clear risk that it will be used to commit, or facilitate, serious violations of international humanitarian law and human rights. Despite the reluctance of some States, the EU succeeded – after lengthy discussions – in

---

48 Statement on behalf of the European Union by H.E. Ambassador Eric Danon, Permanent Representative of France to the Conference on Disarmament in Geneva, 63rd session of the United Nations General Assembly, 20 October 2008, in 'La position commune de l'UE du 8 décembre 2008 relative aux règles communes régissant le contrôle des exportations de technologie et d'équipements militaires', *Revue générale de droit international public (RGDIP)*, 2009-1, pp. 95–112.

49 Council Decision 2009/42/CFSP of 19 January 2009, [2009] *OJ* L17/39.

50 'EU support to arms trade treaties', *Europolitics*, no. 3664, p. 15; S. Parker, 'Implications of states' views on an Arms Trade Treaty', UNIDIR, January 2008.

51 See in particular G. Gloser, President-in-Office of the Council, Towards an Arms Trade Treaty, 20 June 2007, available at: www2.hu-berlin.de/francopolis/germanopolis/db/sisdb.cgi?userid=guest&pw=guest&login=Gast&db=fr&view_records=1&ww=on&ID=2519&lang=fr.

52 While for some States (such as the United States), the objective of the ATT was to help regulate legal trade, and for others (such as Russia), it was to combat illegal trade, the EU has ensured that the Treaty targets these two interdependent objectives, which are enshrined in Article 1(a) of the ATT.

imposing the ethical approach of its 2008 Common Position, which is added to the criterion of risk to peace and security. However, while the Treaty requires exports to be assessed based on criteria that are almost identical to those in the EU's Common Position, it actually imposes less restrictive standards, as the Common Position is often more precise. It should be noted in particular that the criterion of the compatibility of the purchase with the level of economic and social development of the purchasing State (known as the sustainable development criterion) appears in the Common Position, but it has not be retained in the ATT.

Since the Treaty was signed, its monitoring and implementation have been included in the annual report drawn up pursuant to Article 8(2) of Council Common Position 2008/944/CFSP, defining common rules governing the control of exports of military technology and equipment.

The EU is convinced that its legal model for non-proliferation can be exported, but this model cannot claim to embody a global paradigm. This strategy often comes up against a logic of legal influence and normative competition, in which the regional organisation is far from always being in a strong position, as the development of its arms export control laws is still limited, being constrained by the CFSP framework.

II. THE LIMITED CONTRIBUTION OF THE COMMON POSITION TO THE EUROPEANISATION OF EXPORT CONTROLS

While export authorisation criteria are defined in the Common Position, decisions to issue licences for the export of military technology and equipment remain a national competence. The principle therefore remains that each Member State should assess applications to export equipment on a case-by-case basis (Article 1(1)). As a result, the binding nature of the Common Position is still very weak because it is largely procedural. The text mobilises the entire spectrum of CFSP action, from elements of supranationalism to the traditional framework of sovereignty, via institutionalised intergovernmentalism.[53] Within this complex framework, and despite the express wishes of Decisions (CFSP) 2019 and 2025, the coordination of export controls between Member States remains partial (Section A) and the monitoring of compliance with the common position is still inadequate (Section B).

---

[53] See in particular S. Bauer, 'L'européanisation des politiques d'exportation d'armements', *Annuaire français de relations internationales*, 2001, vol. 2, pp. 507–523.

A. A PARTIAL COORDINATION OF EXPORT CONTROLS BETWEEN MEMBER STATES

Article 7 of the Common Position sets out obligations to cooperate and promote convergence in the field of exports. These obligations were clarified when the text was amended in 2019. It now calls on Member States to 'exchang[e] relevant information, including information on denial notifications and arms export policies, as well as by identifying possible measures to further increase convergence'. Europeanisation, however, must be put into perspective because of the heterogeneous interpretation of control authorisation criteria (Section 1) and the possibility for one State to circumvent an export ban adopted by another Member State (Section 2). Despite these obstacles, the creation of a European Defence Technological and Industrial Base (EDTIB) is gradually opening up prospects for improved coordination of control (Section 3).

1. National Prerogatives Preserved by a Heterogeneous Interpretation of the Criteria

The transformation of the Code of Conduct into a Common Position included aspects that are binding on the Member States, but this still leaves decision-making to the Member States, while there are no sanctions in the Common Position. Although the Member States are obliged to incorporate the European criteria into their national legislation (which only Belgium did for the Code of Conduct in 2003), constraints remain limited in various ways.

While States must comply with the export criteria set out in the Common Position, it should be emphasised that the obligations defined by the criteria are not identical. For the first four criteria i) respect for international obligations and commitments, ii) respect for human rights and international humanitarian law (IHL), iii) the internal situation of destination countries, and iv) the preservation of peace), the absence of conformity in the situation of the acquiring State implies that 'an export licence shall be denied'. On the other hand, for the last four criteria v) international security, vi) the international behaviour of the buyer country, vii) the risk of misappropriation of technology, and viii) the compatibility of technology exports with the economic level of the buyer), it is simply a matter of the exporting Member State 'taking into account' various assessment factors.

Even in the case of the first four criteria, the obligation to deny an export licence is in fact highly variable, due to the margins of discretion and interpretation left to the Member States by the Common Position.

The first criterion of the Common Position does not raise any difficulties, as the Member States are required to comply with specific international commitments, in particular with regard to the application of arms embargoes decreed by the United Nations Security Council, the Union and the OSCE.[54] Article 2.1 also leaves no room for doubt, stating that an export licence 'shall be denied' if it is incompatible with Member States' international obligations under the Treaty on the Non-Proliferation of Nuclear Weapons, the Biological and Toxin Weapons Convention and the Chemical Weapons Convention, and their commitment not to export any type of anti-personnel landmine. Similarly, a licence shall also be denied if it is incompatible with all the lists produced by non-binding agreements relating to the export of arms or dual-use products (Australia Group, Zangger Committee, Nuclear Suppliers Group, Wassenaar Arrangement and the Hague Code on the Proliferation of Missile Technology).

In the context of the global approach to human rights defined by the second criterion, which includes an examination of respect for human rights and international humanitarian law by the buyer country or the country of final destination, the interpretation leaves so much room for interpretation to the Member States that, in practice, the criterion does not appear to constitute a constraint on national export decisions in these countries.

The reforms to the second criterion introduced by Decision (CFSP) 2025/779 add to the burden on Member States. They must examine the commitment of purchasing States to international human rights instruments – that of the 'human rights situation' – in an approach that is intended to be more realistic and concrete. Thus, Article 2(2) of the 2025 text specifies that exports must be refused if there is a risk that they will be used to 'commit or facilitate internal repression, serious acts of gender-based violence or serious acts of violence against women, children', or other serious violations of human rights 'including against protected groups under international humanitarian law, such as women and children'. However, interpretation of the text remains in the hands of exporting countries.

Numerous examples can be cited in this regard, particularly for exports to Israel and Saudi Arabia. Concerning the latter, since its resolution of 4 October 2018 on the situation in Yemen, it should be recalled that the European Parliament has regularly called on all Member States – but without any results – to refrain from selling arms or any other military equipment to Saudi Arabia, the United Arab Emirates and any other member of the international coalition, as well as to the Yemeni government and other parties to the conflict.[55] Similarly, after the murder of journalist Jamal Khashoggi, only

[54] Full list of arms embargoes available at: https://embargo.grip.org. See also, for the EU, https://www.consilium.europa.eu/fr/topics/sanctions/ and the full list of embargoes decided by the United Nations Security Council: https://main.un.org/securitycouncil/en/content/un-sc-consolidated-list.

[55] Only the governments of Belgium, Denmark, Finland, Germany, Greece, Italy and the Netherlands have adopted measures to restrict their arms exports to countries that are part of the Saudi-led coalition engaged in the war in Yemen.

Germany, Finland and Denmark adopted restrictions on their arms exports to Saudi Arabia.

Even when a decision is taken jointly by the Member States[56] (such as suspending export licences to Egypt for all equipment that could be used for internal repression,[57] and reassessing export licences for equipment covered by Common Position 2008/944/CFSP), companies based in several EU Member States continue to export arms, surveillance technology and other security equipment to Egypt.

The same latitude is left to the Member States for the interpretation of the other criteria: the fragmentation of national positions on exports to Turkey is one illustration of the fluctuations in the assessment of the third criterion (the internal situation in the country of final destination, and existence of tensions or armed conflicts), the fourth criterion (the national security of the Member States), and the sixth criterion (the behaviour of the buyer country towards the international community, and in particular its attitude towards terrorism, the nature of its alliances and respect for international law).

The weakness of the seventh criterion relating to the assessment of the risk that exported equipment may be diverted within the purchasing country or of its re-export under undesirable conditions had given rise to much criticism following the adoption of the Code of Conduct.[58] Article 5 of the 2008 Common Position strengthened the Code, specifying the requirements for applications for authorisation to manufacture under licence in third countries and for end-user certificates, although vigilance in this area was not equal in all Member States. As part of the review of the Common Position (initiated by Decision (CFSP) 2019), the Council adopted[59] a decision establishing a set of common characteristics to be met by end-user certificates for the export of small arms and light weapons (SALW) and their ammunition. This represents real progress towards harmonisation. It should be noted, however, that it concerns only one set of weapons, representing only a tiny proportion of Member States' exports by value.

The major contribution of Council Decision (CFSP) 2025/779 is to provide for stricter end-user verification requirements (Article 5): export authorisation is based on reliable information, accompanied by an end-user certificate or equivalent documentation, with possibilities for subsequent verification.

---

56 This is provided for in Article 9 of the Common Position.

57 See Conclusions of the Foreign Affairs Council of the European Union of 21 August 2013 and of the and of 10 February 2014 on Egypt.

58 See the European Parliament resolution on the Council's Sixth Annual Report according to Operative Provision 8 of the EU Code of Conduct on Arms Exports (2005/2013(INI), [2006] *OJ* C280E/443.

59 Council Decision (CFSP) 2021/38 of 15 January 2021 establishing a common approach on the elements of end-user certificates in the context of the export of small arms and light weapons and their ammunition, [2021] *OJ* L14/4.

Member States 'may require end users to agree to specific verification mechanisms', which nevertheless brings the balance of power between the exporter and the customer into play... Member States must take into account the risk of diversion of the product when granting export authorisation, and this latest amendment is reminiscent of the provisions of Regulation (EU) No 833/2014 concerning sanctions against Russia. These provisions also tend to restrict the granting of authorisations and exemptions in cases of risk of circumvention, in particular through exports via foreign subsidiaries and/or third countries.[60]

A State may also adopt a more restrictive policy (Article 3), but this is extremely rare. Belgium, for example, added to its law transposing the Code of Conduct an additional criterion relating to the presence of child soldiers in the regular army of the importing country.[61]

Compliance with the eight criteria leaves a great deal of room for discretion, and the Common Position is a 'relative standard-setter'.[62] Although COARM, within the Council, promotes ongoing dialogue between Member States on the consistent application of common rules, the inconsistency of national arms export control policies is still self-evident. For the European Parliament, this divergent behaviour by the Member States weakens the European Union's ability to achieve its foreign policy objectives and undermines its credibility as an actor speaking with one voice on the international stage.[63] Article 7(1) of the 2025 decision provides that Member States shall 'exchang[e] relevant information, including information on specific destinations and on denial notifications, arms export policies [...] consulting regarding their risk assessment, as well as by identifying possible measures to further increase convergence and to promote unity and consistency in Union external action'. Thus, if the Decision constitutes an attempt to improve this consistency, it will have to be assessed in the light of its concrete results.

This inconsistency remains particularly evident when one Member State accepts an export refused by another based on common criteria.

---

60 O. Attias, S. Peter and N. Nhari, 'Renforcement du cadre juridique européen sur les exportations de technologies et équipements militaires: les nouvelles orientations de la Décision (PESC) 2025/779', available at: https://www.august-debouzy.com/fr/blog/2196-renforcement-du-cadre-juridique-europeen-sur-les-exportations-de-technologies-et-equipements-militaires-les-nouvelles-orientations-de-la-decision-pesc-2025779.

61 Belgian Law of 5 August 1991 on the import, export, and transit of and against the illegal trade of arms, ammunition, and materials specifically intended for military use or law enforcement purposes and associated technology.

62 P. Weil, 'Vers une normativité relative en droit international', *RGDIP*, 1982, pp. 6–47.

63 European Parliament resolution of 17 September 2020 on Arms exports: implementation of Common Position 2008/944/CFSP (2020/2003(INI), Recital K, [2021] *OJ* C 385/47.

2. *Authorised Circumvention of Export Bans Adopted by a Member State*

Under the terms of Article 4.1 of the Common Position, a State may grant authorisation for 'an essentially identical transaction' to one refused by other Member States within the preceding three years, subject to compliance with a specific prior consultation procedure: before granting authorisation, the State 'shall first consult the Member State or States which issued the denial(s)'. If it nevertheless decides to grant authorisation, it 'shall notify' them, 'giving a detailed explanation of its reasoning'. This information is not provided to all States but within a bilateral framework (except in the case of exports of dual-use goods, which is not specified in the Common Position but can be deduced from a reading of the regulation on the control of exports of dual-use goods and technologies). This specific consultation procedure[64] is carried out via the COARM's online system.

The Common Position continues to reject the 'no undercut' rule (i.e. the rule by which a Member must refuse an export if it has previously been refused by another State on the basis of one of the criteria). This rule nevertheless exists in the Missile Technology Control Regime (MTCR),[65] and, in a non-binding way, within the regime of the Australia Group.[66] This considerably weakens the ambition of the Common Position and raises questions about the consequences of the differences in assessment in the application of the eight criteria.

By contrast, for the EEAS:

> The system already demonstrated that it supports transparency between Member States in relation to specific countries of final destination and end users [...]. Defence companies in Member States are generally aware of the restrictions on arms export policies, and will usually refrain from applying for a licence if they know it is likely to be denied.[67]

---

64 S. Besch and B. Oppenheim, 'Up in arms Warring over Europe's arms export regime', Centre for European Reform, September 2019.

65 In October 1994, the participating states in the Missile Technology Control Regime (MTCR) adopted a 'no undercut' policy to reinforce their guidelines: see https://www.mtcr.info/en/mtcr-guidelines. Such a 'no undercut' policy does not exist in the Wassenaar Arrangement.

66 The 'Australia Group' is an informal body whose aim is to help exporting or trans-shipment countries minimise the risks of contributing to the proliferation of chemical and biological weapons. Its participants have also committed themselves to consultations prior to the export of equipment that another participant has already refused, for possible proliferation reasons. This commitment to consultation is known as the 'no undercut' policy. It does not constitute a binding prohibition.
https://www.dfat.gov.au/publications/minisite/theaustraliagroupnet/site/en/index.html.

67 Twenty-Sixth Annual Report according to Article 8(2) of Council Common Position 2008/944/CFSP defining common rules governing the control of exports of military technology and equipment, [2025] *OJ* C 2025/472, I(5).

The low number of refusals does not therefore indicate the extent to which the export policy is restrictive with regard to certain destinations, but stem rather from the prudence of exporters.

On this major point of circumvention, the common position lies between unilateralism and multilateralism, while preserving the national sovereignty of each State. In this respect, it has the advantage of overcoming the contradictions between the plurality of security systems, but the risk of divergent interpretations of responsibilities in terms of international security is particularly obvious when it comes to exports of goods from the European defence technological and industrial base.

3. *Prospects for Improving Coordination of Control in the Context of Building a European Defence Technological and Industrial Base (EDTIB)*

Several EU initiatives are building cooperation in armaments production and developing capabilities at the EU level, including: the European Defence Industrial Programme (EDIP)[68] and the European Defence Fund, the Permanent Structured Cooperation (PESCO), the Coordinated Annual Review on Defence (CARD), the European Peace Facility, legislative acts such as the 2009 Directives on intra-Community transfers and defence procurement, and the establishment of administrative capabilities, such as the Commission's Directorate-General for Defence Industry and Space (DG DEFIS). These are supplemented by the development of bi- or plurilateral industrial cooperation programmes.

The interactions between the EDTIB and exports are multiple, with exports being necessary for the viability of European industry, which also exposes it to the risk of excessive dependence on orders from third countries, so that it might be less of a priority to fulfil orders from Member States than to fulfil contracts with third countries in the event of a crisis and related shortages.

In terms of export control enforcement, the cooperative programmes between Member States set up on an ad hoc basis have already faced major challenges. It should be remembered that the Common Position had been designed to build an EDTIB, by allowing manufacturers to choose their partners on the basis of their skills, rather than their export situations, which were presumed to be harmonised by the text. However, the Member States concerned are finding it difficult to agree on the conditions for exporting jointly developed products. As part of the review of Common Position 2008/944/

68 Joint Communication to the European Parliament, the Council, the European Economic and Social Committee and the Committee of the Regions – A new European Defence Industrial Strategy: Achieving EU readiness through a responsive and resilient European defence industry, JOIN (2024) 10 final, 5 March 2024.

CFSP, decided by Decision (CFSP) 2019, the Commission, in collaboration with the HR/VP, invited the Member States to:

> explore ways towards the streamlining and gradual further convergence of their arms export control practices, especially for those defence capabilities that are jointly developed. For the same purpose, Member States should also exchange best practice on export control rules for jointly developed capabilities.[69]

At the same time, the Commission went ahead with an assessment of Directive 2009/43/EC on intra-Community transfers, which in its current form does not aim to achieve the highest common standards for controlling arms exports to third countries while facilitating transfers within the European arms market.[70] Through industrial cooperation, it is clear that the Commission's long-standing strategy to intervene in the field of arms, despite Article 346, is asserting itself with regard to export controls.[71] The Commission, like the European Parliament, is also proposing that the export control agreement concluded on 23 October 2019 between France and Germany (joined by Spain in 2021) to resolve their differences over exports to third countries[72] could serve as a template for the Union as a whole.

The recent strengthening of the EDTIB, while not transforming the EU into an exporting entity, has at the very least renewed thinking on cooperation and convergence in the control of exports of military technology and equipment.

The Strategic Compass[73] did not offer any solid prospect of improvement to the lack of Europeanisation in this area. Taking account of the EU's scope for progress in arms control, it simply states the need for coordination: 'We will also bring forward ongoing work towards the streamlining and gradual further convergence of our arms export control practices for defence capabilities jointly developed, in particular in an EU framework, thus ensuring European Defence Fund-funded products will profit from adequate and competitive access to international markets, in line with the 2008 Council Common Position […], and without prejudice to Member States' sovereign decisions'.

---

69 Joint communication, p. 23.

70 Ibid.

71 Some ambiguities have arisen concerning transfers of intellectual property of products developed by the EDF, over which the Commission has a right of scrutiny (it must be informed in advance and if the Commission considers that the transfer is contrary to the interests of the Union, then the financing granted under the Fund will have to be repaid). However, this does not imply that the Commission has any powers over arms exports.

72 Decree no. 2022-1103 of 1 August 2022 publishing the agreement on defence export controls (together with three annexes), signed in Paris on 17 September 2021, *JORF*, No. 0178 of 3 August 2022, text No. 20.

73 Council of the European Union, *A Strategic Compass for Security and Defence – For a European Union that protects its citizens, values and interests and contributes to international peace and security*, 4 May 2022, 7371/22, COR 1.

The EDF and EFF 'change the equation for military exports'.[74] The shortcomings of the Europeanisation of controls become particularly problematic when the States retain responsibility for granting arms export licences, the financing of which is provided by the EU, but when the EU inevitably becomes politically responsible for the proper use of the arms exported, particularly lethal arms.

To bridge this gap, the EU adopted an 'Integrated Methodological Framework' in March 2021, for assessing and identifying the measures and controls required for assistance measures under the EFF. This non-binding framework has not been made public by the EU, but its main elements are presented by the EEAS on its website.[75]

The first principle of the methodological framework is respect for:

> Compliance with all relevant legal instruments and best practices based on national, international, and EU rules, standards and policies in the area of the supply of military equipment, and respect for international law, including international human rights law (IHRL) and International Humanitarian Law (IHL) by the beneficiary. This includes compliance with all Union, national and applicable international arms export control laws and with the international standards established by the Arms Trade Treaty (ATT), including by the beneficiary.

The HR/VP and their administration are responsible for verifying that the exported goods are used in accordance with the commitments made by the beneficiary in the 'arrangements' concluded with the beneficiaries of the EFF and following international law, as well as carrying out evaluations and checks (Article 62 of Decision (CFSP) 2021/509 establishing a European Peace Facility). These controls are defined in the CFSP decision establishing the measure, covering delivery and end-user certificates, diversion and traceability, human rights and utilisation objectives. EU controls are therefore additional to those imposed by the exporting country, in accordance with its national legislation, which must comply with the Common Position and international law.

The HR/VP may suggest to the PSC and the Council that aid be suspended or withdrawn if it considers that the conditions of use are not being complied with. In cases where the beneficiaries do not respect the conditions under which military assistance is provided, particularly with regard to the criteria of the Common Position or the diversion of weapons, the Political and

---

[74] M. Camelo, L. Géhin and F. Santopinto, 'Comment renforcer le rôle de l'UE dans le contrôle des exportations d'armes', *Rapports du GRIP*, 2021-1, Brussels.

[75] https://www.eeas.europa.eu/eeas/questions-and-answers-european-peace-facility%E2%80%99s-integrated-methodological-framework-0_en.

Security Committee (PSC), which is responsible for the political and strategic supervision of the EFF and is hierarchically superior to the actors involved in its implementation, may suspend this assistance and propose to the Council that it be definitively withdrawn (Article 64).

Lastly, Decision (CFSP) 2025/779 provides for 'facilitating mechanisms' that allow joint exports (Article 7.2 of the amended Common Position), though these are not described.

In this 'Integrated Methodology Framework', the EU firmly asserts and details – in the EFF framework alone – the conditionality of its military aid and its monitoring process. At the same time, it seems to want to maintain a degree of discretion in this respect by not publishing the text, thereby relativising the confidence that can be placed in checks on compliance with the common position.

B. AN INADEQUATE CHECK ON COMPLIANCE WITH THE COMMON POSITION

Without going back over the origins of the judicial review of the CFSP, it should be remembered that under the last sentence of the second subparagraph of Article 24(1) TEU and the first subparagraph of Article 275 TFEU, the Court does not in principle have jurisdiction over provisions relating to the CFSP and the acts adopted on their basis. As an act adopted within this intergovernmental framework, the Common Position cannot in principle be subject to judicial review. However, certain developments in the case law of the CJEU could pave the way for an evolution, albeit very limited, in this area (Section 2 below). Public scrutiny of compliance with the text by national parliaments and civil society is all the more necessary given that it is largely beyond the control of the EU courts and often beyond that of national courts.[76] But, reforms in this area have not yet led to real transparency (Section 1).

[76] In France, this control is impossible because export authorisations are considered by the administrative judge to be acts of government (CE, 27 January 2023, req. no. 436098). By contrast, in the United Kingdom, the Court of Appeal obliged the government to review its arms exports to Saudi Arabia in 2019, without however halting them (*R (on the application of Campaign Against the Arms Trade) (Appellant) v Secretary of State for International Trade* [2019] EWCA Civ 1020). Belgium's Council of State annulled several arms export licences to Saudi Arabia on 14 June 2019: Coordination nationale d'action pour la paix et la démocratie and Ligue des droits humains v Région Wallonne, Nos. 244.800, 244.801, 244.802, 244.803, 244.804.

1. *The Inadequate Transparency of Export Controls*

Transparency is a major issue in the control of arms exports, as the publication of export decisions provides EU parliaments and citizens with precise information on the strategic choices made by their respective governments in an area that directly affects their security and their adherence to certain standards and values. For the European Parliament, 'military transparency measures such as reporting on arms exports contribute to cross-border trust-building'.[77]

The information procedure, mentioned as early as 1998 in the Code of Conduct,[78] has been gradually improved under the Common Position, without however becoming entirely satisfactory. It was already made binding with the 2008 Common Position, with each Member State required to provide details of denied export authorisations and the 'reasons for denial'. This information was significantly improved by the revisions of the Position in 2019 and 2025. Indeed, until 2019, each Member State was called on to 'circulate to other Member States in confidence an annual report on its exports of military technology and equipment and on its implementation of this Common Position'. From now on, every year, '[b]y 30 June of each year, each Member State shall submit to the European External Action Service information for the preceding calendar year on its exports of military technology and equipment and on its implementation of this Common Position' (Article 8(1)). However, not all States comply with this obligation, submitting either no reports or incomplete reports.

This information feeds into the European Union's annual report, which is submitted to the Council and published in the 'C' series of the *Official Journal*

---

77 European Parliament resolution of 17 September 2020 on Arms export: implementation of Common Position 2008/944/CFSP (2020/2003(INI), Recital M.

78 Information relating to the criteria has been particularly sensitive for a long time: see the CJEC judgment of 6 December 2001 (C-353/99 P): a Council decision of 4 November 1997 had refused H. Hautala, MEP, access to the report of the COARM working group aimed at obtaining clarification of the eight arms export criteria defined by the Luxembourg and Lisbon European Councils. The General Court, in its judgment of 19 July 1999 in Case T-14/98 *Hautala v Council*, ECLI:EU:T:1999:157, annulled the Council's decision of 4 November 1997, and the Court of Justice upheld the Council's contested judgment. The report had been drawn up under the special European correspondence system COREU (a system adopted in the context of the CFSP pursuant to the provisions of Title V of the Treaty on European Union by the Member States and the Commission in 1995), and so it had not circulated through the usual channels for the distribution of Council documents. The distribution of documents transmitted via the COREU network is limited to a restricted number of authorised recipients in the Member States, the Commission and the General Secretariat of the Council. In addition to confirming the case-law of 17 June 1998 in Case T-174/95 *Svenska Journalistförbundet v Council*, ECLI:EU:T:1998:127, according to which the absence of competence to assess the legality of acts covered by Title V of the Treaty does not preclude the Court's competence to rule on public access to these acts, the contentious nature of the publication of the report led the Council to adopt and publish the Code of Conduct on Arms Exports in June 1998.

of the European Union (pursuant to Article 8.2 of the Common Position). Since October 2020, this report has been available online on the website of the European External Action Service.[79] Its content is virtually identical from year to year, with only the figures provided by the Member States changing. The EEAS database, which contains annually updated information on the value, destination and type of arms export licences, as well as on Member States' actual exports over the period 2013-2019, further enhances transparency by providing more readable representations of the value, military equipment and destination of European arms exports than the annual report

However, this improvement in the transparency of national decisions adopted based on the Common Position criteria is not entirely complete.

The annual reports made public by the Member States provide information on the number of denials, the areas concerned and the criteria on which denials are based. Yet, the lack of standardisation of the reports – called for by the European Parliament and many NGOs for several years – nevertheless persists and contributes to leaving the Member States a great deal of latitude in interpreting the criteria.

Since spring 2022, the EEAS has been managing an internal database containing country pages with relevant information on current and potential destinations for European exports of military equipment. The database, which is intended to contribute to greater convergence in the application of the Common Position by the Member States, is only accessible to EU Member State officials responsible for issuing authorisations and to the EEAS.

As part of the review of the Common Position, the Council decided to establish clear deadlines for the communication of information by Member States, precise standards for the format of the report and new guidelines on the content and process of communicating information. In the autumn of 2022, the Member States agreed on an internal best practice document containing elements for developing a national system for declaring actual exports, although this has not been made public either.

This imperfect transparency does not encourage public control of exports, which is particularly necessary in a context of virtually non-existent judicial control.

---

79 EEAS database: https://webgate.ec.europa.eu/eeasqap/sense/app/75fd8e6e-68ac-42dd-a078-f616633118bb/sheet/ccf79d7b-1f25-4976-bad8-da886dba3654/state/analysis.

2. *The Court's Attempts to Monitor Compliance with the Common Position*

As this is a CFSP text, judicial review of compliance with the Common Position remains excluded in principle,[80] which has led the European Parliament to call for the establishment of a mechanism for EU-level monitoring and control based on full compliance with the eight criteria of the Common Position,[81] without, however, defining the contours of such a mechanism.

It is questionable whether the Court could address the issue indirectly, in particular in the context of a reference for a preliminary ruling. For example, in a case concerning a transfer within the EU, followed by a re-export to a State which is dubious in the light of the criteria of the Common Position, the Court, which has jurisdiction to interpret the Directive on arms transfers within the EU, might be tempted to interpret the criteria set out in the Common Position.

The Court's supervisory ambitions are beginning to be expressed, particularly concerning restrictive measures.

In 2021, in the case of the Bolivarian Republic of Venezuela against the Council of the European Union, the Court (Grand Chamber) judgement on the prohibition on the performance of arms export contracts, held that it was not applicable to contracts concluded prior to the entry into force of a regulation adopting restrictive measures 'provided that they comply with Council Common Position 2008/944/CFSP [...], in particular with the criteria set out in Article 2 thereof' (para. 6). This reference to the criteria of the Common Position may be regarded as a manifestation of the Court's willingness to examine compliance with these criteria.[82]

Above all, in the judgment of 10 September 2024, *Neves 77 Solutions*,[83] the Court (Grand Chamber) recognised its jurisdiction to interpret, in the context of a preliminary ruling, restrictive measures of general application adopted in the context of the CFSP,[84] and also asserted that arms exports fall within the competence of the Union under the TFEU.

---

80 There are two exceptions to the absence of control, one relating to compliance with Article 40 TEU and the other to the legality of Council CFSP decisions providing for restrictive measures against natural or legal persons. See Case C-72/15, *Rosneft*, ECLI:EU:C:2017:236.

81 European Parliament resolution of 17 September 2020 on Arms export: implementation of Common Position 2008/944/CFSP (2020/2003(INI), paras. 19 and 52.

82 Case C-872/19 P, *Bolivarian Republc of Venezuela v Council of the European Union*, ECLI:EU:C:2021:507.

83 Case C-351/22, *Neves 77 Solutions SRL v Agenția Națională de Administrare Fiscală – Direcția Generală Antifraudă Fiscală*, ECLI:EU:C:2024:723.

84 The Court states that it has jurisdiction to interpret, in the context of a reference for a preliminary ruling, a restrictive measure of general application, in so far as it is for the Council to implement that measure, which serves as a basis for national penalty measures imposed on a natural or legal person, in a regulation under Article 215 TFEU. See M. Miłek, 'Interpretation of restrictive measures of general application adopted in the context of the CFSP', News No. 26/2024, Centre for European Legal Studies, 1 October 2024, available at www.ceje.ch.

The Court was responding to a preliminary request concerning the interpretation of provisions of Council Decision 2014/512/CFSP of 31 July 2014 about restrictive measures against Russia, as amended by Council Decision 2014/659/CFSP of 8 September 2014.

In recalling the legal framework applicable to the dispute, the Court began by referring to Common Position 2008/944/CFSP (paragraphs 13-15), essentially from the point of view of its common list of military equipment. It then stated (para. 57) that the arms and military equipment covered by Decision (2014/512) prohibiting their export to Russia fell within the scope of the TFEU, since trade in them

> falls within the remit of the European Union under Articles 114 and 207 TFEU. Those weapons and equipment, set out in the EU Common Military List referred to in Article 12 of Common Position 2008/944 and which acts as a r6eference point for Member States' national military technology and equipment lists, are accordingly subject to the common customs tariff. (Case C-351/22, para. 57)

The Court therefore considered (para. 97) that it had a duty to ensure that the goods whose export to Russia was prohibited did indeed fall within the scope of the EU Common Military List, referred to in Article 12 of Common Position 2008/944, which 'acts as a reference point for the national equipment list' established by Romanian government decrees. The Court also examined the content of this latter list, which was an integral part of the Common Position.

For the time being, this control remains limited to factual questions relating to the Common List, the application of which involves technical rather than political issues.

In the future, however, it cannot be ruled out that the Court will also seek to review certain points of the Common Position in cases concerning exports of dual-use goods,[85] where Member States must take account of the criteria of the Common Position on arms exports. Agreements with third countries that incorporate certain elements of the Common Position, through non-proliferation clauses, could also pave the way for an extension of the Court's jurisdiction, although the Court remains extremely cautious in this area.

The persistent absence of any real overall judicial control of compliance with Common Position 2008/944/CFSP, combined with the varying interpretations of its criteria, gives States a very wide margin for manoeuvre, with their arms exports benefiting from a 'complementarity' mechanism that in reality borders on subsidiarity. EU action in this area is envisaged only for the adoption of regulations imposing restrictive measures in the context of major security crises. In situations considered – often wrongly – to pose less of a threat to

[85] See the commentary on this regulation in this publication by A. Millet-Devalle under Article 207 TFEU.

security, or where unanimity cannot be achieved in the Council, the Member States remain competent to decide whether or not to authorise exports, interpreting the criteria of the Common Position with varying degrees of laxity.

Despite the significant progress made recently by the review process, the Common Position is still an imperfect attempt to reconcile opposing interests, by organising very relative moderation and minimal transparency in arms sales, concepts that remain very different for the exporting states, the EU, companies in the sector and civil society which observes them.[86] Moreover, Member States continue to differ greatly in terms of the organisation of the competent national authorities, interministerial coordination, the existence and performance of compliance departments within companies, and their risk analysis as well as due diligence capabilities. The progress expected from the EU in this area will not be truly assessed until 15 April 2030, when the Common Position will be reviewed once again.

86 See in particular: *Plaidoyer: une occasion unique de mettre fin à l'exception française, appel pour la mise en place d'un contrôle parlementaire des ventes d'armes françaises*, signed by 14 NGOs, 16 November 2020, https://www.actioncontrelafaim.org/presse/une-occasion-unique-de-mettre-fin-a-lexception-francaise-appel-pour-la-mise-en-place-dun-controle-parlementaire-des-ventes-darmes-francaises/.

THE EUROPEAN PEACE FACILITY

Council Decision (CFSP) 2021/509 of 22 March 2021 establishing a European Peace Facility and repealing Decision (CFSP) 2015/528

Catherine SCHNEIDER
Emeritus Professor at the University of Grenoble Alps

The Common Foreign and Security Policy (CFSP) of the European Union (EU) has a budget that is modest in the overall context of funding for external action, particularly given the importance of other items (development cooperation, neighbourhood policy, etc.). This budget mainly covers expenditure on civilian crisis management missions, which account for around 80-90% of it. The remainder of the budget covers funding for special representatives, disarmament actions and a number of services, including the European Defence College. The CFSP budget is governed by the rules set out in Article 41 TEU.[1] Essentially, this provision states that the Union budget shall bear the administrative expenditure of the CFSP and operational expenditure, 'except for such expenditure arising from operations having military or defence implications and cases where the Council unanimously decides otherwise'.

Although the Treaty on European Union (TEU) does not provide any definition of 'operations having military or defence implications', the decision that founded the Athena mechanism (see below) established the principle that the Council would decide on a case-by-case basis whether an operation falls into this category. This is how the extra-budgetary funding of the Common Security and Defence Policy (CSDP) military operations and missions came about.

The exception of military operations and missions means that they are financed by the Member States on the basis of gross national income. This means applying the principle of solidarity to their funding. However, in reality this principle has real limitations: it only concerns a certain category of expenditure – the common costs – incurred by these missions and operations, currently estimated at around 15% of their total cost. The rest of the funding

---

[1] See the commentary on Article 41 TEU by A. POTTEAU in this publication.

is borne by the contributing Member States, and possibly by third-party contributors, although the Union usually decides to exempt them.

Aware of the shortcomings in the effectiveness of solidarity in the implementation of military operations and missions, the Union has tried on several occasions and not without difficulty to remedy the situation. The only way forward, apart from revising the Treaty and Article 41 TEU,[2] which would be acceptable to all the Member States in view of the unanimity requirement, is to extend the list of common costs in an ad hoc, gradual but sufficiently significant manner.

With this in mind, in 2004, a mechanism, called Athena, for financing the common costs of EU operations with military or defence implications was created by Decision 2004/197/CFSP.[3]

This decision was amended several times, notably in 2008, under the French Presidency, and most recently in 2015, before being repealed in 2021 due to the 'absorption' of this mechanism by the European Peace Facility (EPF): see below. It bears witness to the difficulty of reforming the mechanism and the differences of opinion between Member States about this. In addition to seeking to make the EPF more flexible, this always comes back to the question of defining common costs for a fairer distribution of the cost of operations. Despite its efforts, the French Presidency in 2008 was only able to achieve very modest results: '[T]he idea of giving more autonomy to the Operation Commander and the Special Management Committee was limited and the idea of Member States making an advance contribution was abandoned'.[4] As for the progress that has been made, it has been limited to an extension of the common costs, which in reality corresponded to the consolidation of previous practices.

The mechanism had a special committee (Art. 6) in which all the Member States were represented and in which a representative of the European External Action Service (EEAS) and of the Commission took part but did not have the right to vote. Representatives of contributing third countries (like the Member States of the European Economic Area)[5] could participate in the work of the Special Committee, without taking part or voting, as could the Operation Commander.

The mechanism was managed by a 'triumvirate': i) the administrator of Athena, appointed for three years by the Secretary General of the Council (Art. 7), who could be assisted by a deputy if necessary; ii) the operation commander (Art. 8), who exercised his powers on behalf of Athena with regard to the financing of

---

2 It should be remembered that the simplified revision provided for in Article 31(3) TEU authorising the Council to decide unanimously to extend the cases of qualified majority voting in the context of the CFSP is excluded for decisions with military or defence implications (Article 31(4) TEU).

3 Council Decision 2004/197/CFSP of 23 February 2004 establishing a mechanism to administer the financing of the common costs of European Union operations having military or defence implications, [2004] *OJ* L 63/68.

4 See A. Dumoulin and N. Gros-Verheyde, *La politique européenne de sécurité et de défense commune*, Le Dévoluy, Éd. du Villard, 2017, p. 288.

5 For example, Norway has contributed to the EPF up to €101 million, in support of Ukraine.

the common costs of the operation, for which he/she had to submit proposals to the administrator and implement them as authorising officer; and finally, iii) the accounting officer (Art. 9) was responsible for the proper execution of payments, the collection of revenue and the recovery of debts. The draft budget was drawn up by the administrator, with the support of each operational commander, who submitted it to the Special Committee for adoption.

Following Decision 2015/528/CFSP,[6] the common costs assumed have benefited from a new nomenclature organised around four distinct categories of common costs, the last of which, more succinctly, concerns those linked to the winding up of an operation. Each of these categories of common costs was subject to different legal regimes and was listed in very precise and technical terms. Annex I listed 'the common costs borne by Athena whenever they are incurred'.[7] It also stipulated that when no direct link could be established between these costs and a specific operation, the Special Committee could decide to include them in the general budget of the mechanism. Annex II set out the 'operational common costs relating to the preparatory phase of an operation'. These are those costs necessary for exploratory missions[8] carried out by military and civilian personnel with a view to a specific military operation, as well as the medical costs of any emergency medical evacuation. Annex III was the most dense in terms of the common costs covered, which were organised around three specific categories. The first ('Part A') covered 'operational costs relating to the active phase of operations always borne by Athena': these were primarily the additional costs of headquarters in charge of operations, both of which were subject to a particularly precise definition.[9] They also included additional costs due to the support provided to the force in general and incurred as a result of its movement to the place of operation. The second part ('Part B') concerned 'common costs relating to the active phase of a specific operation, borne by Athena when the Council so decides'.[10] Finally, Part C of Annex III referred to operational common costs which could be borne at the request of the Operation Commander and if approved by the Special Committee.[11]

---

6 Council Decision (CFSP) 2015/528 of 27 March 2015 establishing a mechanism to administer the financing of the common costs of European Union operations having military or defence implications (Athena), and repealing Decision 2011/871/CFSP, [2015] *OJ* L84/39.

7 Examples include, but are not limited to, mission expenses incurred by the operation command or its personnel to submit accounts to the Special Committee and compensation paid in respect of compensation claims or legal action.

8 These include, but are not limited to, transport and accommodation, and the recruitment of local staff, particularly for translation.

9 See the extremely precise definitions of the additional costs associated with transport, travel and accommodation.

10 By way of example, and not exhaustively, transport costs to and from the theatre of operations to deploy, support and evacuate the forces required for the operation.

11 Examples include, but are not limited to, essential additional equipment or other essential capabilities, mine removal, as well as the storage and destruction of weapons and munitions collected in the area of operation.

Having failed to consolidate the envisaged broadening of the funding spectrum, the Athena mechanism was abolished and replaced in 2021 by the European Peace Facility (EPF), which also replaces the African Peace Facility (APF), decided in December 2003.[12]

In this context, the objective of the EPF is to consolidate the broadening of the funding spectrum, as recalled in the Strategic Compass adopted in March 2022.[13] This was one of the major innovations achieved during the negotiation of the European Union's 2021-2027 multiannual financial framework, which resulted in the merging of the Athena mechanism and the former APF[14] into a single financial instrument, the new EPF.

The EPF is the result of long and difficult negotiations, which led to a significant retreat from the Commission's proposals.[15] Formally, the founding act of the EPF is Decision (CFSP) 2021/509 of 22 March 2021,[16] a particularly dense document of some sixty pages,[17] which first of all defines the general arrangements for the functioning and organisational structure of the EPF (see Section I below). The decision is also structured around its two main areas of activity, namely military assistance to third parties and the financing of EU military operations and missions by taking over from Athena (Section II).

---

12 Decision No 3/2003 of the ACP-EC Council of Ministers on the use of EDF resources to create a Peace Facility for Africa, [2003] *OJ* L345/108.

13 Council of the EU, 'A strategic compass for security and defence – For a European Union that protects its citizens, values and interests and contributes to international peace and security', doc. 7371/22 of 4 May 2022. On p. 29: 'We undertake to incentivise force generation for military missions and operations, for example […] by expanding the scope of common costs under the European Peace Facility'. On this document, see C. Schneider, 'La politique étrangère et de sécurité commune', *ADUE*, 2021, pp. 346 et seq., and 'Politique étrangère et de sécurité commune', *ADUE*, 2022, pp. 597 et seq.

14 F. Santopinto and J. Marechal, 'L'assistance militaire de l'Union à l'aulne de la facilité européenne pour la Paix', *GRIP*, 2021; C. Schneider, 'Politique étrangère et de sécurité commune (PESC)', *ADUE*, 2020, pp. 583 et seq.; C. Schneider, 'La politique étrangère et de sécurité commune', *ADUE*, 2021, pp. 337 et seq.; C. Schneider, 'Politique étrangère et de sécurité commune', *ADUE*, 2022, pp. 592 et seq. and 617 et seq. C. Schneider; 'La facilité européenne pour la paix (FEP) ou les nouveaux avatars de l'Union et de sa PSDC en tant que contributeur de paix et de sécurité', in L. Potvin-Solis (ed.), *L'Union européenne et la paix*, Brussels, Bruylant, 2023, pp. 439 et seq. and C. Schneider, 'Les dynamiques ambivalentes de la gestion de crise', in A. Hamonic (ed.), *Quelle spécificité de la défense en droit de l'Union européenne*, Droits européens, Rennes, Presses universitaires de Rennes, 2025, pp. 149–175.

15 See C. Schneider, 'Politique étrangère et de sécurité commune (PESC)', *ADUE*, 2020, pp. 583 et seq.; C. Schneider, 'La politique étrangère et de sécurité commune', *ADUE*, 2021, pp. 337 et seq.

16 Council Decision (CFSP) 2021/509 of 22 March 2021 establishing a European Peace Facility and repealing Decision (CFSP) 2015/528, [2021] *OJ* L102/14, as last amended by Council Decision (CFSP) 2024/3185 of 16 December 2024, [2024] *OJ* L2024/3185.

17 The founding decision is built around five titles: the first on the general structure of the new instrument, the second on its budgetary rules, the third on the financing of CSDP operations and missions (which succeeds the Athena mechanism), the fourth on assistance to third parties and finally the last on the final provisions, the most important of which is that they provide for the Council to review the framework decision every three years (Art. 75).

Given its particularly intensive mobilisation, notably for Ukraine, the EPF has seen its resources depleted, leading the Union to react (Section III).

I. A SINGLE MANAGEMENT FRAMEWORK LARGELY INSPIRED BY ATHENA

As Article 1 of its founding decision emphasises, the EPF is a CFSP instrument financed by the Member States and dedicated to preserving peace, preventing conflicts and strengthening international security in accordance with the objective set out in Article 21(2)(c) of the TEU. It is intended to finance the operational expenditure of EU CFSP actions which, following Article 41(2) of the TEU, are not charged to the Union budget. The founding decision sets the financial ceiling for the EPF at €5.69 billion for the period of the multiannual financial framework (2021-2027), the breakdown of which for each year concerned is set out in Annex 1. This ceiling represents a 'significant reduction' compared to the Commission's proposals, but has very quickly raised a problem (see below).

Title 1 (Chapter 2) is also responsible for the organisational structure and general operating procedures of the EPF, which are broadly based on those of Athena,[18] involving in particular the establishment of a Facility Committee (Article 11), albeit with some innovations. From an organisational point of view, the most significant of these is certainly, the creation of two separate administrators appointed for three years by the Secretary-General of the Council: one for CSDP operations, assisted by at least one deputy, and the other for assistance measures. In addition, the founding decision sets out to provide significant clarification on the implementation within of constructive abstention from Articles 31 and 41 TEU[19] (Art. 5 of the Decision),[20] the right of initiative (Art. 6), the legal basis for funding (Art. 7)[21] and consistency (Art. 8).

---

18 In terms of the Athena governance system, the composition of the Committee includes one representative from each Member State. Representatives of the EEAS and the Commission may be invited to meetings, but without voting rights, as well as the EDA when certain points under discussion fall within its sphere of activity. Again as with the Athena mechanism, only those Member States that contribute to missions and operations take part in decisions relating to them.

19 See the commentary on Articles 23 to 40 TEU by C. Schneider, and the commentary on Article 41 TEU by A. Potteau in this publication.

20 See actions brought by Hungary against the Council and the European Peace Facility Committee, alleging infringement of Article 31(1) TEU and of Article 5 of the Council Decision (CFSP) 2021/509: Case T-457/24, [2024] *OJ* C/2024/626 (following an action before the Court which has been dismissed by Order of 11 July 2025, in Case C-319/25, ECLI:EU:C:2025:576) and Case T-605/25, [2025], *OJ* C/2025/5477.

21 The need for a prior basic act of the Council is affirmed on the basis of Article 42 TEU (for operations and missions) and Article 28 TEU (for assistance measures). By way of exception, no basic act is required for the financing of common costs of operations and missions during their preparatory phase.

II. AN INSTRUMENT STRUCTURED AROUND TWO TYPES OF FINANCING

The purpose of the EPF is to finance two main categories of operational expenditure. The first[22] covers the common costs of CSDP military operations and missions under Articles 42(4) and 43 of the TEU and it is in this capacity that the EPF succeeds the Athena mechanism, with the EPF repealing Decision 2015/528 (subsection A). The second category[23] corresponds to assistance measures military and in the field of defence, taken based on Article 28 TEU (B).

A. THE LEGACY OF THE ATHENA MECHANISM: FINANCING THE COMMON COSTS OF EU MILITARY MISSIONS AND OPERATIONS

An important clarification worth highlighting results from Article 4 of the founding decision, according to which the terms EU CSDP operations and missions within the meaning of Article 42 TEU also cover cases where the implementation of a mission is entrusted to a group of Member States in accordance with Article 44 TEU.[24] This mechanism has never yet been used due to the lack of a framework decision defining the complex arrangements for sharing competences between the Union on the one hand and the Member States on the other. The strategic compass of March 2022[25] has made this a priority objective, but the inclusion of this type of mission in the founding decision of the EPF means the Decision does not need to be revised.

Title III of the Decision 2021/509 contains the specific rules governing the funding of operations and missions, which are still based on the concept of common costs. These are the only costs to be covered by the EPF and are particularly modest (see above). They are set out in Annexes III and IV to the Decision, which proposes only slight revisions to the list drawn up by the last Athena decision in 2015, and which do not really help to improve solidarity between Member States to ensure a fairer distribution of the costs of military crisis management. The most significant of these is the definitive inclusion in the list of common costs of certain expenses incurred by battlegroups as a result

22 Art. 1(2)(a).
23 Art. 1(2)(b).
24 See the commentary on Article 44 TEU by N. Clinchamps in this publication.
25 Council of the EU, 'A strategic compass for security and defence – For a European Union that protects its citizens, values and interests and contributes to international peace and security', 21 March 2022, 7371/22, https://data.consilium.europa.eu/doc/document/ST-7371-2022-INIT/fr/pdf.

of their deployment to and redeployment from the theatres of operations. The costs covered are specified in Annex IV, Part A 3 and include, for example, certain transport costs relating to deployment and redeployment,[26] as well as certain operating costs[27] and deployment preparation kits.[28]

B. ASSISTANCE MEASURES PROVIDED BY THE UNION TO THIRD PARTIES IN THE MILITARY AND SECURITY FIELD

Article (1)(2)(b) of Decision 2021/509 defines these measures and covers two types of assistance: assistance to strengthen the military and defence capabilities of third States and international organisations,[29] and assistance to military peace support operations (MPSOs) led by international organisations or third States.[30] This represents a significant expansion, *ratione loci*, *ratione personae* and *ratione materiae*, of the assistance provided by the EU under the former African Peace Facility, but which now covers all regions of the world and no longer just Africa. Nor are its beneficiaries any longer just international organisations, but now also include third countries. Last but not least, the Decision authorises the 'supply of military equipment, or platforms, designed to deliver lethal force'.[31] This is a kind of Copernican revolution in the Union's military and defence assistance, which until now had never been able to take the plunge because of the major differences of opinion between the Member States on this subject; this has been an issue that caused major stumbling blocks during the negotiations, and which delayed the adoption of the Framework Decision.

The differences between the Member States have nevertheless been overcome thanks to a compromise, set out in Articles 59 and 27. The former specifies that the assistance measures relating to the supply of such equipment do not include other items or other forms of support: as the mobilisation of

---

26 The transport costs associated with redeployment include the additional costs associated with transporting battlegroup personnel by land, sea or air to redeploying them from the theatre of operations.

27 More specifically, these are the additional costs associated with the services that are absolutely necessary to provide the necessary support for a battlegroup at air entry points or in tactical areas, logistics areas and maritime assembly areas (for example, the costs of secure storage of equipment and materials, health and catering facilities and general engineering support).

28 For a detailed comparative analysis, see N. Gros-Verheyde, 'Les coûts communs pris en charge pour les missions et opérations militaires (facilité européenne pour la paix)', *B2 PRO*, 28 March 2021.

29 Art. 1(2)(b)(i).

30 Art. 1(2)(b)(ii).

31 Art. 5(3).

the EPF for Ukraine in each of its successive waves has perfectly demonstrated. This has led to the adoption of separate decisions for the supply of lethal weapons on the one hand and for other assistance measures on the other. But it is above all the provisions of Article 27 that have made it possible to overcome the opposition of certain Member States to assistance measures involving the supply of lethal weapons: a State that refrains from adopting an assistance measure is therefore entitled not to contribute to its financing, and it is up to that State to determine other assistance measures to which it will make an additional contribution, which may relate to measures that already exist or those that are planned. The State then presents these to the Council, which approves them. The State concerned shall have a period of six months in which to do this, and if it fails to fulfil this obligation, either the High Representative or other Member States shall take its place in determining the allocation of this additional contribution to other assistance measures. Assistance measures involving the supply of lethal weapons were first and very quickly implemented for Ukraine. They were subsequently extended, on a much more modest scale, to the African continent for the benefit of Niger (June 2022),[32] Rwanda (December 2022),[33] Ghana (July 2023),[34] Benin (September 2023),[35] Somalia (November 2023),[36] Côte d'Ivoire (April 2024),[37]

32 Council Decision (CFSP) 2023/1136 of 8 June 2023 on an assistance measure under the European Peace Facility to support the Nigerien Armed Forces with military equipment designed to deliver lethal force, *OJ* L 149, 9.6.2023, p. 81–84 and Council Decision (CFSP) 2022/1236 of 18 July 2022 on an assistance measure under the European Peace Facility to support the Nigerien Armed Forces, [2022] *OJ* L190121, as respectively repealed by Council Decision (CFSP) 2024/1977 of 15 July 2024, [2024] *OJ* L2024/1977, and by Council Decision (CFSP) 2024/1978 of 15 July 2024, [2024] *OJ* L2024/1978.

33 Council Decision (CFSP) 2022/2354 of 1 December 2022 on an assistance measure under the European Peace Facility to support the deployment of the Rwanda Defence Force in Mozambique, [2022] *OJ* L311/153, as amended by Council Decision (CFSP) 2024/2880 of 18 November 2024, [2024] *OJ* L2024/2880.

34 Council Decision (CFSP) 2023/1440 of 10 July 2023 on an assistance measure under the European Peace Facility to support the Ghana Armed Forces, [2023] *OJ* L176/28. See also since then: Council Decision (CFSP) 2024/1063 of 4 April 2024 on an assistance measure under the European Peace Facility to support the Ghana Armed Forces, [2024] *OJ* L2024/1063.

35 Council Decision (CFSP) 2023/2062 of 25 September 2023 on an assistance measure under the European Peace Facility to support the Beninese Armed Forces, [2023] *OJ* L238/117. See also since then: Council Decision (CFSP) 2024/1455 of 21 May 2024 on an assistance measure under the European Peace Facility to support the Beninese Armed Forces, [2024] *OJ* L2024/1455; Council Decision (CFSP) 2024/1715 of 13 June 2024 on an assistance measure under the European Peace Facility to strengthen the capacities of the Beninese Navy, [2024] *OJ* L2024/1715, and Council Decision (CFSP) 2024/1980 of 15 July 2024 on an assistance measure under the European Peace Facility to support the Beninese Armed Forces with military equipment designed to deliver lethal force, [2024] *OJ* L2024/1980.

36 Council Decision (CFSP) 2023/2680 of 27 November 2023 on an assistance measure under the European Peace Facility to support the Somali National Army with military equipment designed to deliver lethal force, [2023] *OJ* L2023/2680.

37 Council Decision (CFSP) 2024/1248 of 29 April 2024 on an assistance measure under the European Peace Facility to support the Armed Forces of Côte d'Ivoire, [2024] *OJ* L2024/1248.

Kenya (June 2024),[38] Mauritania (July 2024),[39] Congo (November 2024),[40] as well as Egypt (November 2024).[41] The geographical scope has also been extended to Eastern Europe[42] and to the Middle East.[43]

---

38 Council Decision (CFSP) 2024/1794 of 24 June 2024 on an assistance measure under the European Peace Facility to support the Kenya Defence Forces, [2024] *OJ* L2024/1794.

39 Council Decision (CFSP) 2024/2015 of 22 July 2024 on an assistance measure under the European Peace Facility to support the Armed Forces of the Islamic Republic of Mauritania, [2024] *OJ* L2024/2015, and Council Decision (CFSP) 2025/609 of 24 March 2025 on an assistance measure under the European Peace Facility to support the Armed Forces of Mauritania, [2025] *OJ* L2025/609.

40 Council Decision (CFSP) 2024/2840 of 5 November 2024 on an assistance measure under the European Peace Facility to strengthen the capacities of the Navy of the Republic of the Congo in the framework of the Yaoundé Architecture, [2024] *OJ* L2024/2840.

41 Council Decision (CFSP) 2024/2843 of 5 November 2024 on an assistance measure under the European Peace Facility to support the Egyptian Armed Forces, [2024] *OJ* L2024/2843. See also in Africa: Council Decision (CFSP) 2025/1333 of 8 July 2025 on an assistance measure under the European Peace Facility to support the Armed Forces of Senegal, [2025] *OJ* L2025/1333; Council Decision (CFSP) 2025/1340 of 8 July 2025 on an assistance measure under the European Peace Facility to support the Armed Forces of Cabo Verde, [2025] *OJ* L2025/1340; Council Decision (CFSP) 2025/1499 of 18 July 2025 on an assistance measure under the European Peace Facility to support the Togolese Armed Forces, [2025] *OJ* L2025/1499; Council Decision (CFSP) 2025/1554 of 25 July 2025 on an assistance measure under the European Peace Facility to support the Djibouti Armed Forces, [2025] *OJ* L2025/1554; Council Decision (CFSP) 2025/2377 of 24 November 2025 on an assistance measure under the European Peace Facility to support the Armed Forces of the Democratic Republic of the Congo, [2025] *OJ* L2025/2377, Council Decision (CFSP) 2025/2379 of 24 November 2025 on an assistance measure under the European Peace Facility to support the Armed Forces of Chad, [2025] *OJ* L2025/2379 and Council Decision (CFSP) 2025/2506 of 8 December 2025 on an assistance measure under the European Peace Facility to support the Armed Forces of Côte d'Ivoire, [2025] *OJ* L2025/2506.

42 See Council Decision (CFSP) 2022/1093 of 30 June 2022 on an assistance measure under the European Peace Facility to support the Armed Forces of the Republic of Moldova, [2022] *OJ* L176/22, as amended by Council Decision (CFSP) 2024/1049 of 4 April 2024 on an assistance measure under the European Peace Facility to support the Armed Forces of the Republic of Moldova, [2024] *OJ* L2024/1049 and by Council Decision (CFSP) 2025/2353 of 20 November 2025, [2025] *OJ* L2025/2353; Council Decision (CFSP) 2024/1979 of 15 July 2024 on an assistance measure under the European Peace Facility to support the Albanian Armed Forces, [2024] *OJ* L2024/1979, replaced by Council Decision (CFSP) 2025/1562 of 25 July 2025, [2025] *OJ* L2025/1562; Council Decision (CFSP) 2024/2521 of 23 September 2024 on an assistance measure under the European Peace Facility to support the Army of the Republic of North Macedonia, [2024] *OJ* L2024/2521, Council Decision (CFSP) 2025/697 of 7 April 2025 on an assistance measure under the European Peace Facility to support the Armed Forces of the Republic of Moldova, [2025] *OJ* L2025/697, Council Decision (CFSP) 2025/809 of 23 April 2025 on an assistance measure under the European Peace Facility to support the Armed Forces of the Republic of Moldova with military equipment designed to deliver lethal force, [2025] *OJ* L2025/809; Council Decision (CFSP) 2025/823 of 25 April 2025 on an assistance measure under the European Peace Facility to support the Army of the Republic of North Macedonia, [2025] *OJ* L2025/823 and Council Decision (CFSP) 2026/232 of 29 January 2026 on an assistance measure under the European Peace Facility to support the Armed Forces of the Republic of Armenia, [2026] *OJ* L2026/232.

43 See Council Decision (CFSP) 2024/2496 of 23 September 2024 on an assistance measure under the European Peace Facility to support the Lebanese Armed Forces, [2024] *OJ* L2024/2496; Council Decision (CFSP) 2024/2935 of 25 November 2024 on an assistance

The specific rules applicable to these assistance measures are set out in Title IV of the Decision. Article 56 defines their objectives, including: capacity-building, rapid and effective contribution to military responses in crisis situations, contributions to conflict prevention, stabilisation and peace-building, support for security and defence cooperation. It should be noted that particular mention is made of the need for these objectives to be consistent with those of the EU's external action in general.[44]

Assistance measures can take two forms: a specific measure or a general support programme focused on a given geographical area or theme, which in this particular case excludes the supply of equipment and platforms releasing lethal force.[45]

The rules on the suspension of all or part of the financial assistance, which are set out in Article 64 of the Decision, place great emphasis on political conditionality which must be incorporated by the Council into each assistance measure[46] in accordance with a very specific mechanism empowering the Political and Security Committee (PSC)[47] as the EU's High Representative.[48] The PSC is authorised to suspend assistance in several cases: if the beneficiary fails to fulfil its international obligations, in particular with regard to human rights and humanitarian law, or if the situation in the country or regime concerned no longer allows the assistance to be implemented with sufficient guarantees.[49] In emergency cases, the High Representative may suspend assistance pending a subsequent decision by the PSC.[50] It is also worth pointing out that suspension may be implemented if the measure is no longer in the Union's interest.

Lastly, the repeal of the assistance measure is a matter the Council to decide, on the recommendation of the PSC.[51]

measure under the European Peace Facility to support the Jordanian Armed Forces, [2024] *OJ* L2024/2935; Council Decision (CFSP) 2025/129 of 21 January 2025 on an assistance measure under the European Peace Facility to support the Lebanese Armed Forces, [2025] *OJ* L2025/129 and Council Decision (EU) 2025/2387 of 24 November 2025 on an assistance measure under the European Peace Facility to support the Jordanian Armed Forces, [2025] *OJ* L2025/2387.

44 Art. 56(2).

45 Art. 59(6). See, for instance, Council Decision (CFSP) 2024/2034 of 22 July 2024 amending Decision (CFSP) 2022/667 on an assistance measure taking the form of a general programme for support to the African Union under the European Peace Facility for the period 2022-2024, [2024] *OJ* L2024/2034.

46 Art. 64(1).

47 Art. 64(1)(a).

48 Art. 64(1)(b).

49 On 29 July 2023, the EU decided to postpone *indefinitely* its military cooperation with Niger, which in May 2023 had been the first African country to benefit from a €5 million assistance measure involving the supply of munitions for its helicopters, following a military coup.

50 Art. 64(1)(b).

51 Art. 64(2).

III. INTENSIVE MOBILISATION AND DEPLETION OF RESOURCES CALLING FOR REFORM

The allocation of €5.9 billion under the multiannual financial framework (2021–2027) for the EPF, which throughout the negotiations[52] had been considerably reduced compared to the Commission's initial proposals of €10.5 billion, very quickly proved to be insufficient. One of the main reasons for this was that the EPF was very heavily mobilised against Russia's attack on Ukraine, even though it had not been designed to support a high-intensity war effort. By 13 March 2023, the European Union was able to establish that 92% of the initial financial ceiling of the EPF had already been committed, which explains its first re-evaluation that March, followed by two other evaluations on 26 June 2023 and 18 March 2024. These not-inconsiderable increases in the resources allocated to the EPF do not, however, exhaust its reforms: in addition to the necessary increase in its financial ceiling (subsection A), it is also the improvement of its flexibility and the preservation of its global geographical scope that have been sought (B).

A. THE EXHAUSTION OF EPF RESOURCES AND THE INCREASE IN ITS FINANCIAL CEILING

It should be pointed out that on 28 February 2022, just four days after Russia invaded Ukraine, two decisions were taken on a measure of assistance under the European Peace Facility, one to supply lethal weapons to Ukraine[53] and the other to supply non-lethal equipment.[54] For 2022 alone, this first activation was followed by five others[55] for a total amount of €2.8 billion: i.e. more than half the financial ceiling granted to the EPF for the period 2021-2027. The massive mobilisation of the EPF for Ukraine continued in 2023 and 2024, in particular as part of a three-part plan to accelerate the joint procurement and

---

52 For details of these 'cutbacks', see C. Schneider, 'La politique étrangère et de sécurité commune', *ADUE*, 2021, pp. 337–343, and 'Politique étrangère et de sécurité commune', *ADUE*, 2022. pp. 617–622.

53 Council Decision (CFSP) 2022/338 of 28 February 2022 on an assistance measure under the European Peace Facility for the supply to the Ukrainian Armed Forces of military equipment and platforms designed to deliver lethal force, [2022] *OJ* L60/1, as last amended by Council Decision (CFSP) 2023/810 of 13 April 2023, [2023] *OJ* L101/64.

54 Council Decision (CFSP) 2022/339 of 28 February 2022 on an assistance measure under the European Peace Facility to support the Ukrainian armed forces, [2022] *OJ* L61/1, as last amended by Council Decision (CFSP) 2023/229 of 2 February 2023, [2023] *OJ* L32/60.

55 Successively in March, April, May, July and October: see Decision (CFSP) 2022/338 of 28 February 2022, amended on 23 March, 13 April, 23 May, 21 July and 17 October (Decision (CFSP) 2022/1971).

delivery to Ukraine of munitions and missiles. Two of these components[56] each benefited from €1 billion in EPF funding, while the third was financed by the EU budget to the tune of €500 million. In total, and thanks to successive increases in the EPF's financial ceiling, the EPF has allocated €11.1 billion to Ukraine out of its revised overall allocation of €17 billion. There is no doubt that the Ukrainian conflict is directly responsible for the depletion of the FEP's initial resources, necessitating several increases in the financial ceiling set by its founding decision.

The first of these increases follows the decision of 13 March 2023,[57] which was not adopted without difficulty given the differences between the Member States over its terms and conditions, whether relating to its agenda (specific to the EPF or integrated and delayed in the timetable for the mid-term discussions on the multiannual financial framework) or its amount. On 12 December 2022, the Council reached an agreement on the main principles governing this increase, i.e. the need for a Council decision adopted unanimously for amending the founding decision, and the determination of an overall envelope of €5 billion to be implemented gradually.[58]

The decision of 13 March 2023, adopting an increase in the financial ceiling of some €2 billion, raised the financial ceiling for the period 2021-2027 to €7.9 billion. This was followed by the decision of 26 June 2023,[59] adopted much more quickly than expected, which decided on a further increase of €4 billion, bringing the EPF budget to a total of €12 billion. This decision was taken in the particular context of 'the acceleration of the pace of the war in Ukraine and Europe's desire to have an ammunition plan financed largely by the Union'.[60] This new increase brings the EPF budget up to that proposed by the High Representative in 2018, which had been halved by the Member States.

As for the decision of 18 March 2024,[61] introducing a further increase of €5 billion, it brought the EPF to a new level of €17 billion. It is the result of a compromise quite different from the initial proposal by the High Representative,

56 The first part, adopted in March 2023, is intended to reimburse Member States for equipment donated to Ukraine), and the second for the joint procurement of ammunition and missiles from economic operators established in the EU or Norway (May 2023).

57 Council Decision (CFSP) 2023/577 of 13 March 2023 amending Decision (CFSP) 2021/509 establishing a European Peace Facility, [2023] *OJ* L75/23.

58 *Cf.* C. Schneider, 'Politique étrangère et de sécurité commune', *ADUE*, 2022, pp. 591–592. C. Schneider, 'La facilité européenne pour la paix (FEP) ou les nouveaux avatars de l'Union et de sa PSDC en tant que contributeur de paix et de sécurité', in L. Potvin-Solis (ed.), *L'Union européenne et la paix*, Brussels, Bruylant, 2023.

59 Council Decision (EU) 2023/1304 of 26 June 2023 amending Decision (CFSP) 2021/509 establishing a European Peace Facility, [2023] *OJ* L161/66.

60 See N. Gros-Verheyde, 'Facilité européenne pour la paix: le plafond augmenté pour la seconde fois', *B2 PRO*, 27 June 2023.

61 Council Decision (CFSP) 2024/890 of 18 March 2024 amending Decision (CFSP) 2021/509 establishing a European Peace Facility, [2024] *OJ* L2024/890.

who had proposed incorporating into the founding decision a new mechanism in favour of a specific assistance fund for Ukraine. The concept of a specific fund has thus been abandoned in favour of the addition to Article 73 of the founding decision on transitional measures, of a provision which stipulates that €5 billion will be devoted to providing additional support for Ukraine: this is therefore an increase dedicated and earmarked for this support based on a mechanism which, originally, had been introduced mainly to ensure the transition with the Athena mechanism. This earmarking for Ukraine is special in that, in accordance with the invitation from the December 2023 European Council, it covers the two categories of EPF funding, support for the EUMAM Ukraine mission and assistance measures consisting of the reimbursement to Member States of their direct supplies to Ukraine of lethal and non-lethal military equipment, which are reimbursed to them under the EPF assistance measures. It therefore constitutes a derogation from the principle that the two types of EPF financing must be the subject of separate decisions. The decision of 18 March 2024 also recalls that prior to its adoption, strategic guidance was provided in accordance with Article 9 of the founding decision and invites the EPF Committee to decide on the use of this specific amount within one month. Above all, the decision of 18 March 2024 reinforces the *ad hoc* constructive abstention mechanism of the founding decision and Article 27 thereof, which was the condition demanded by Hungary in order to 'lift its veto': constructive abstention does not just cover the supply of equipment delivering lethal force, but all the funding granted under this increase in the EPF earmarked for Ukraine (see Article 1(2)(3)).

Lastly, as part of its resources from miscellaneous revenue (Art. 18.7, b), of the founding decision), since May 2024, another allocation of resources resulting from the revision of CFSP Decision 2014/512 on restrictive measures against Russia: it institutes a mechanism for allocating exceptional and unexpected profits from the immobilisation of Russian assets on the territory of the Union to the benefit of the Union's actions of support for Ukraine, 90% of which is reserved for the EPF.[62]

B. ADAPTING THE EPF IN THE LIGHT OF EXPERIENCE

The latest decisions of 2023 and 2024 also make some revisions to the founding Decision to take into account certain needs and improve the functioning of the EPF. Thus, based on Article 73 of the founding Decision, the Decision of 13 March 2023 extends the common costs of missions and operations to

[62] See Council Decision (CFSP) 2024/1471 of 21 May 2024 on the allocation of the amounts of the financial contribution paid to the European Peace Facility in accordance with Decision (CFSP) 2024/1470, [2024] *OJ* L 2024/1471.

CSDP exercises, for which it proposes a definition in Article 4.[63] At the same time, for the benefit of the 2023 military exercise (MILEX 2023), the Decision of 13 March 2023 provides for exceptional coverage, without prejudice to future decisions on the financing of common costs, certain additional costs of the headquarters and forces participating in the exercise,[64] in addition to the common costs already provided for in Article 45.[65]

However, the two main reforms resulting from the Decision of 13 March 2023 are undoubtedly the extension of pre-financing to assistance measures[66] and the advanced voluntary contributions from Member States.[67] As the decision points out, the aim here is to learn from experience and 'introduce more flexibility in the collection and use of financial contributions from the Member States and in their use by the Facility'.[68] The last reform resulting from the Decision of 16 December 2024 confirms that in addition to the contributions payable by Member States contributing to an operation or assistance measure in accordance with Article 26(5), the Facility may receive three types of alternative contributions:[69] first, 'additional contributions', meaning the additional amounts that are payable by a Member State that abstained from the adoption of an assistance measure and does not contribute to that measure, and that are redirected to other assistance measures, in accordance with Article 26(7), Article 27 and Article 73(10); second, 'advance contributions', meaning contributions paid in advance by Member States on a voluntary basis, in addition to the payments made following a call for contributions, in accordance with Article 29(15); and, third, 'voluntary financial contributions', meaning amounts that may be received in accordance with Article 30. However, an assistance measure may be financed from such additional contributions for up to 50% of its reference amount, unless the

63 See the new Article 4(g), which refers to 'a Union military CSDP exercise or the military component of a civilian CSDP exercise, conducted in accordance with the Exercise Policy of the European Union under the CFSP'.

64 These include transport costs for the battlegroups, the work required for deployment/infrastructure, identification badges in the colours of the Union and the force, and certain operating costs.

65 In its last version resulting from Council Decision (CFSP) 2024/2846 of 5 November 2024, OJ L, 2024/2846, 6 November 2024. The new Article 45(1) states that the common costs of the EU's exercises 'shall be financed through the Facility following the rules and procedures similar to those for operations to which all Member States contribute, and up to an amount to be decided by the Committee for each type of exercise, in particular for the EU Rapid Deployment Capacity (EU RDC), taking into account the agreed EU Programme of Exercises and Exercise-Related Activities under the CFSP. This amount may be exceeded on a case-by-case basis, if allowed by the Committee when approving the budget of an exercise'.

66 Art. 28.

67 New Art. 29(15).

68 Recital 4 of Decision 2023/577/CFSP.

69 New Art. 24a.

Council decides otherwise; and the contributions due by Member States for the measures receiving such additional contributions shall be reduced by the amount of those contributions.[70]

Finally, the need was also felt to take account of an equitable geographical breakdown of EPF financial support, which led to the amendment, by the Decision of 26 June 2023, of Article 2 of the founding decision.[71] This establishes for the first time the principle that the 'financial ceiling shall be used in a manner that preserves the global geographical scope of the Facility and the Union's ability to prevent and swiftly respond to crises and conflicts, primarily but not exclusively in areas that display the most urgent and critical security threats for the Union. This amendment to Article 2 is based on the need to follow the strategic guidelines of the European Council and the Council.'[72] This is the response to repeated requests to secure funding for beneficiaries other than Ukraine. Hungary, for example, had long made its agreement to an increase in the financial ceiling of the EPF (essential for support for Ukraine) conditional on this guarantee.

***

There is no doubt that the EPF is helping to strengthen the CSDP toolbox. It has demonstrated a certain capacity to adapt, firstly by an undeniable refocussing of its initial objectives, which did not include intervention in high-intensity warfare, and then by the fairly rapid increases in its initial financial ceiling. Nevertheless, it will be important to monitor changes in the breakdown of its interventions, both thematically (support for EU operations and missions/ assistance measures) and geographically (Europe with and without Ukraine/ Africa and others).

---

70 New Art. 26(7).

71 In spring 2024, the geographical distribution of assistance measures, raises questions about the 'global vocation' of the EPF: €119 million for Europe (Georgia, Moldova, Macedonia) to which should be added the €11.1 billion for Ukraine; €273 million for Africa (Benin, Côte d'Ivoire, Ghana, Niger, DR Congo, Somalia, the Yaoundé architecture for maritime security in the Gulf of Guinea, and the African Union transition mission in Somalia) and €9 million for Jordan.

72 New Art. 2(3).

ARTICLE 41 TEU: THE FINANCING OF THE COMMON SECURITY AND DEFENCE POLICY

Aymeric POTTEAU
Professor of Law at the University of Lille
Dean of the Faculty of Legal, Political and Social Sciences

Article 41 TEU

1. Administrative expenditure to which the implementation of this Chapter gives rise for the institutions shall be charged to the Union budget.

2. Operating expenditure to which the implementation of this Chapter gives rise shall also be charged to the Union budget, except for such expenditure arising from operations having military or defence implications and cases where the Council acting unanimously decides otherwise.

In cases where expenditure is not charged to the Union budget, it shall be charged to the Member States in accordance with the gross national product scale, unless the Council acting unanimously decides otherwise. As for expenditure arising from operations having military or defence implications, Member States whose representatives in the Council have made a formal declaration under Article 31(1), second subparagraph, shall not be obliged to contribute to the financing thereof.

3. The Council shall adopt a decision establishing the specific procedures for guaranteeing rapid access to appropriations in the Union budget for urgent financing of initiatives in the framework of the common foreign and security policy, and in particular for preparatory activities for the tasks referred to in Article 42(1) and Article 43. It shall act after consulting the European Parliament.

Preparatory activities for the tasks referred to in Article 42(1) and Article 43 which are not charged to the Union budget shall be financed by a start-up fund made up of Member States' contributions.

> The Council shall adopt by a qualified majority, on a proposal from the High Representative of the Union for Foreign Affairs and Security Policy, decisions establishing:
>
> Preparatory activities for the missions referred to in Article 42(1) and Article 43, which are not charged to the Union budget, shall be financed by a start-up fund made up of contributions from the Member States.
>
> The Council shall adopt by qualified majority, on a proposal from the High Representative of the Union for Foreign Affairs and Security Policy, decisions establishing:
>
> **a)** the procedures for setting up and financing the start-up fund, in particular the amounts allocated to the fund;
>
> **b)** the procedures for administering the start-up fund;
>
> **c)** the financial control procedures.
>
> When the task planned in accordance with Article 42(1) and Article 43 cannot be charged to the Union budget, the Council shall authorise the High Representative to use the fund. The High Representative shall report to the Council on the implementation of this remit.

Article 41 of the Treaty on European Union (TEU) is devoted to the financial provisions applicable to the Common Foreign and Security Policy (CFSP), including its defence dimension.[1] It is included in the subdivision dealing with provisions common to the CFSP, in a way reflecting the specific nature of this policy in budgetary and financial terms, and in particular its essentially intergovernmental nature. Indeed, Article 41 removes certain categories of CFSP/CSDP expenditure from the EU budget and requires the Member States to assume them. The fact remains that the terms and financing of this policy, which also has to contend with the dynamics of European integration, did not emerge totally unscathed from the revisions of the Treaties following its establishment by the Maastricht Treaty of 7 February 1992. Whereas the latter laid down the principle of budgeting only for administrative expenditure arising from this policy (current Art. 41(1)), the Treaty of Amsterdam of 2 October 1997 extends the principle to all operational expenditure, subject to two notable exceptions which are still relevant today (current first subparagraph of Art. 41(2)). Having reshaped this provision in particular, the Treaty of Amsterdam also includes an optional exemption from contributions for the benefit of Member States making use of the unique mechanism of constructive abstention which it introduces in the field of CFSP/CSDP (current second subparagraph of Art 41(2)). Since then, the provision has changed relatively little. In perfect continuity with the Treaty establishing a Constitution for

1 The acronym CFSP/CSDP has been chosen to reflect this reality.

Europe, the Treaty of Lisbon merely inserted the current third paragraph, which unusually empowers the Council to establish mechanisms guaranteeing the rapid financing of preparatory activities for Common Security and Defence Policy (CSDP) missions.

The financial provisions relating to the CFSP/CSDP were revised at an early stage to consolidate the budgeting of its expenditure. However, the drafters of the Treaties did not, for all that, keep the same trajectory for it as they did for the expenditure of the other former intergovernmental pillar relating to cooperation on justice and home affairs, which was initially governed by twin prescriptions.[2] While these two areas are still characterised today by contributory exemptions in admittedly different forms, it is only in the case of the CFSP that contributions are coupled with partial non-budgeting. A comparison with the opt-out clauses relating to the area of freedom, security and justice[3] and, for that matter, with enhanced cooperation[4] shows that, although there are adjustment mechanisms,[5] differentiation does not necessarily mean that the policies affected by it have to be debudgetised. If not the basis, then at least the justification must be sought elsewhere, namely in the withdrawal from the EU's integrated budgetary procedures (Section II), which appears to be one of the issues at stake in the financing of CFSP/CSDP expenditure (Section I).

I. FINANCING CFSP/CSDP EXPENDITURE

The provision under review addresses two distinct but interrelated issues: whether or not the EU budget should bear the cost of CFSP/CSDP expenditure (Section A) and the Member States' contribution to that expenditure (Section B). As primary law stands, while debudgeting is undeniably an institutional issue, it also has a financial dimension, as it offers the possibility of modulating Member States' contributions.

---

2 Compare Articles J(11) and K(8) of the original Treaty on European Union.

3 See for example Article 5 of protocol (No 21) on the position of the United Kingdom and Ireland in respect of the area of freedom, security and justice: 'A Member State which is not bound by a measure adopted pursuant to Title V of Part Three of the Treaty on the Functioning of the European Union shall bear no financial consequences of that measure other than administrative costs entailed for the institutions, unless all members of the Council, acting unanimously after consulting the European Parliament, decide otherwise'.

4 Art. 332 TFEU: 'Expenditure resulting from implementation of enhanced cooperation, other than administrative costs entailed for the institutions, shall be borne by the participating Member States, unless all members of the Council, acting unanimously after consulting the European Parliament, decide otherwise'.

5 Art. 11 of Council Regulation (EU, Euratom) No 609/2014 of 26 May 2014 on the methods and procedure for making available the traditional, VAT-based own resource and GNI-based own resources and on the measures to meet cash requirements (recast), [2014] *OJ* L168/39.

A. BUDGETING CFSP/CSDP EXPENDITURE

The budgeting of CFSP/CSDP expenditure is approached by the Treaty on the EU through an initial distinction between 'administrative expenditure' (Section 1) and 'operational expenditure' (*operativer Ausgaben*) (Section 2).

1. The Need to Budget for 'Administrative Expenditure Incurred by the Institutions'

Despite the principle of budgeting CFSP expenditure, the administrative nature of some of this expenditure has an impact on the way it is financed by the EU since, unlike operational expenditure, it theoretically deprives the Council, even when acting unanimously, of the possibility of charging it to the Member States by way of derogation, and therefore of debudgeting such expenditure.

While this *summa divisio* (administrative *vs.* operational) therefore retains a certain importance, it is not so easy to interpret. To define the contours of one of the two components, that of 'administrative expenditure', it might be very tempting to spontaneously refer to the Financial Regulation, in the context of which the Council and the European Parliament define precisely the related concept of 'administrative appropriations'.[6] We could then deduce that administrative expenses include those relating to staff, buildings, their equipment and fluids. This approach is not without its pitfalls, however, since it involves interpreting a distinction of a 'constitutional' nature on the basis of designed legislative provisions, moreover from an at least partially different perspective. Whereas the nature of the expenditure is intended, in Article 41 TEU, to determine whether or not it can be excluded from the EU budget, which is therefore a financial as well as an institutional issue, it is essentially understood in the context of the Financial Regulation from the angle of the budget nomenclature, which does not necessarily have such a resonance.[7]

Furthermore, in interpreting the distinction made in Article 41 TEU, account should no doubt be taken of the terminological asymmetry adopted by the drafters of the Treaties. On the subject of administrative expenditure incurred in implementing the CFSP/CSDP chapter, the Treaty provides a clarification without equivalent for operational expenditure: the administrative expenditure referred to in this primary law stipulation is that incurred 'for the institutions', which might lead one to think that operating expenditure includes operational expenditure if it is incurred in implementing the CFSP/

---

6 Art. 47 of Regulation (EU, Euratom) 2018/1046 of the European Parliament and of the Council of 18 July 2018 on the financial rules applicable to the general budget of the Union, [2018] *OJ* L193/1.

7 See below for the institutional implications of the distinction for the European External Action Service.

CSDP without being incurred 'for the institutions' as such. This is arcane at first sight, but interpretation nevertheless has a certain resonance in the context of the CSDP, which calls on the capabilities provided by the Member States for its operations.[8] Beyond this, the administrative or non-administrative nature of 'expenditure incurred for the institutions' should logically also be interpreted in the light of its circumstantial antonym, which could lead to the inclusion, among operational expenditure, of expenditure which, although materially administrative (expenditure on staff, buildings, fluids, etc.), is nevertheless functionally operational, insofar as it results from joint actions decided – or even to be decided in their actively preparatory dimension – by the EU within the framework of the CFSP/CSDP. From this point of view, operating expenditure resulting from the implementation of the CFSP/CSDP for the institutional structure of the EU would be regarded as administrative, and conversely all expenditure resulting from actions decided on within the framework of the CFSP/CSDP, including operating expenditure, would be regarded as operational. Practice seems to corroborate this hypothesis.

The EU budget thus covers the operating costs of the permanent institutional structures specific to CSDP which have an undeniably military dimension. This is the case for the EU Military Staff integrated into the European External Action Service (EEAS), whose section of the EU budget does indeed authorise, to the tune of €17 million for 2024, appropriations to 'finance the emoluments of the national military experts posted to serve as the European Union Military Staff under CSDP/CFSP'.[9] In the same spirit, it should be noted by way of example that the EU budget authorises appropriations to finance the cost of interpreting for meetings of the Political and Security Committee and the Military Committee,[10] under the heading of operating expenditure of the EEAS, and, in a completely different area, 'this appropriation is intended to cover the cost of acquiring satellite imagery for the EEAS for the purposes of, in particular, crisis prevention and crisis management'.[11] In the budget section of the European Parliament, there are also appropriations dedicated to financing 'cooperation between the European Parliament and the national parliaments in the parliamentary scrutiny of the CFSP/CSDP' as envisaged by primary law.[12] Beyond these few illustrations, which are clearly identifiable from the nomenclature and the accompanying budgetary comments, it is not easy to

---

8 Art. 42(1) TEU.

9 Definitive adoption (EU, Euratom) 2024/207 of the European Union's annual budget for the financial year 2024, [2024] *OJ* L2024/207/2045. Having said that, beyond budgeting, the pooling of expenditure in this case is only partial insofar as seconded experts remain mainly remunerated by their State of nationality.

10 European Union's annual budget for the financial year 2024, p. 2070.

11 Ibid., p. 2068.

12 Ibid., p. 240. See also Articles 9 and 10 of Protocol No. 1 on the role of national parliaments in the European Union.

measure the volume of administrative expenditure incurred by the institutions in implementing the CFSP/CSDP, given that to a large extent this expenditure overlaps with that incurred in implementing other EU actions and policies. This is undoubtedly one of the practical reasons for their budgeting, which can be found *mutatis mutandis* in the separate framework of differentiation mentioned in the introductory remarks.

On the other hand, the expenditure resulting from the appointment of an EU Special Representative decided by the Council in accordance with Article 33 TEU is clearly treated, within the EU budget, as an operational expenditure, including the salary of the person concerned, including his or her team and their travel expenses (see below).[13] It should also be noted that this is required, at least to some extent, by the interinstitutional agreement on the financing of the CFSP/CSDP, which is now incorporated into the agreement on budgetary discipline and concluded periodically on the fringes of the multiannual financial framework.[14] Similarly, in the context of EU operations of a military nature, certain expenditures with an administrative slant, such as travel, accommodation and building maintenance costs, are indeed considered operational if they result from an EU operation and not from the ordinary functioning of the institutions in the context of the CFSP. In this case, this necessarily leads to the non-budgeting of this expenditure, given its military dimension (see below).

A telling illustration of this is the fact that the acquisition of satellite images is included both as operational expenditure for a non-budgeted military mission and, as we have seen, as expenditure covered by the EEAS section of the EU budget. This seems to confirm that the distinction between administrative and operational expenditure is more functional than material. The acquisition of satellite images is covered by the EEAS section of the EU budget, which in principle only includes administrative expenditure,[15] is conceivable given that this service is undoubtedly essential to enable the EU institutions to carry out their CFSP/CSDP functions. By contrast, the expenditure directly involved in the implementation of an EU military mission, as provided for in the operations plan (OPLAN) or requested by the operations commander, is of a different nature.[16]

---

13 European Union's annual budget for the financial year 2024, p. 987.

14 Paragraph 23 of the Interinstitutional Agreement of 16 December 2020 between the European Parliament, the Council of the European Union and the Commission on budgetary discipline, cooperation in budgetary matters and sound financial management as well as on new own resources, including a roadmap for the establishment of new own resources, [2020] *OJ* L433I/33.

15 Article 8(1) of Council Decision 2010/427/EU of 26 July 2010 establishing the organisation and functioning of the European External Action Service, [2010] *OJ* L201/36.

16 Annex IV to Council Decision (CFSP) 2021/509 of 22 March 2021 establishing a European Peace Facility and repealing Decision (CFSP) 2015/528, [2021] *OJ* L102/14.

Beyond this, but doubtless in the same spirit, it has to be said that, although formally applicable 'to the institutions', the principle of budgeting administrative expenditure clearly does not extend to the bodies set up under the CFSP/CSDP, at least in practice.[17] For example, the European Defence Agency,[18] the EU Institute for Security Studies[19] and the EU Satellite Centre,[20][21] which have legal personality and budgetary autonomy, are financed by the Member States, including for their operations, in principle according to the gross national income (GNI) scale. From time to time, however, the EU may have to top up their budgets, for example in return for a service provided, as is explicitly envisaged for the EU Satellite Centre.[22]

2. *Variable Geometry Budgeting for Operational Expenditure*

Unlike the administrative expenditure of the institutions, which must be borne by the EU budget, the Treaty gives the Council of the Union a certain amount of latitude as regards the operational expenditure incurred in implementing the CFSP/CSDP. The present Article 41 TEU limits itself to imposing non-budgeting for operational expenditure 'arising from operations having military or defence implications' (Section a) so that, for other operational expenditure, it leaves to the Council the choice between the two modalities. For these other operational expenses (Section b), however, it is true that, by laying down a principle of budgeting whose political symbolism can undoubtedly not be ignored, it makes non-budgeting – conceived as exceptional – subject to an express unanimous decision by the Council. However, given the importance of this voting method in the field of the CFSP, this significant procedural requirement cannot be seen as completely decisive, in practice.

---

17 The European Defence Agency is in a unique position in that its existence is, in a way, enshrined in Article 45 of the EU Treaty, which does not, however, define its status or operating procedures, which are left to secondary legislation. See below, the criticisms of the European Parliament regarding the choice of state funding. See also the commentary by A.-H. Bertana in this publication.

18 Art. 13 of Council Decision (CFSP) 2015/1835 of 12 October 2015 defining the statute, seat and operational rules of the European Defence Agency (recast), [2015] *OJ* L266/55.

19 Art. 10 of Council Decision 2014/75/CFSP of 10 February 2014 on the European Union Institute for Security Studies, [2014] *OJ* L41/13.

20 Art. 10 of Council Decision 2014/401/CFSP of 26 June 2014 on the European Union Satellite Centre and repealing Joint Action 2001/555/CFSP on the establishment of a European Union Satellite Centre, [2014] *OJ* L188/73.

21 Concerning these bodies, see the commentary on Articles 23 TEU to 40 TEU by C. Schneider in this publication.

22 Ibid.

a. – Imposed Non-Budgeting of Expenditure Relating to 'Operations Having Military or Defence Implications'

The first subparagraph of Article 41(2) TEU thus prohibits the Council of the EU from charging operational expenditure on 'operations having military or defence' to the EU budget.

Introduced by the Treaty of Amsterdam, which at the same time incorporated the 'Petersberg tasks', this prohibition means that, following the second subparagraph of Article 41(2), the Member States are required to bear the operational costs of military crisis management operations. Since 2021, these have been governed by the CFSP/CSDP Decision establishing the European Peace Facility (EPF),[23] but the extra-budgetary funding provided by the Member States is nonetheless only partial, amounting to between 5% and 15%.[24] As was previously the case for Athena,[25] the Member States, are only responsible for the 'common costs' of operations through the PEF,[26] and these costs are therefore the only ones to be shared in a spirit of solidarity based on the principle that each Member State contributes according to its ability to pay, measured in terms of its share of EU GNI (see below). It is true that the other costs are also borne by the Member States, but the logic is far less one of solidarity and far more individual. As the Union depends for its operations on the capacities provided by its Member States, it will be up to those Member States that agree to make these capacities available to assume the non-mutualised financial consequences – i.e. the majority – up to the level of their own commitment. In this respect, the EPF decision nevertheless offers a degree of flexibility by distinguishing between costs that are necessarily shared and must therefore be borne collectively – such as emergency medical evacuations[27] – and costs that are potentially shared, which will only be designated as such on a case-by-case basis, for each operation, either by the Council[28] or by the EPF committee.[29] While the scope of common costs

---

23 Council Decision (CFSP) 2021/509 of 22 March 2021 establishing a European Peace Facility, [2021] *OJ* L102/14, as amended by Council Decisions (CFSP) 2023/577 of 13 March 2023, [2023] *OJ* L75/23; Council Decision 2023/994 of 22 May 2023, [2023] *OJ* L135/120; Council Decision 2023/1304 of 26 June 2023, [2023] *OJ* L161/66; Council Decision 2024/890 of 18 March 2024, [2024] *OJ* L2024/890. See the commentary on this decision by C. Schneider in this publication.

24 European Court of Auditors, 'La défense européenne', Document d'analyse n° 09/2019, p. 24, para. 50.

25 Council Decision (CFSP) 2015/528 of 27 March 2015 establishing a mechanism to administer the financing of common costs of European Union operations having military or defence implications (Athena), [2015] *OJ* L84/39.

26 Art. (1)(2)(a) of Decision 2021/509 cited above.

27 See in this respect Annex IV, Part A, of Decision (CFSP) 2021/509 mentioned above.

28 For example, transport to and from the theatre of operations to deploy, sustain and recover the forces needed for the operation. See in particular Annex IV, Part B, of Decision (CFSP) 2021/509 mentioned above.

29 For example, expenditure incurred in acquiring, renting or refurbishing premises in the theatre of operations (buildings, shelters, tents), to the extent necessary for the forces deployed for the operation. See in particular Annex IV, Part C, of Decision (CFSP) 2021/509 mentioned above.

may therefore be broadened by these two bodies, including where appropriate even beyond what is expressly envisaged in the EPF decision,[30] the fact remains that solidarity can in any event only be expressed with regard to additional costs defined as 'costs other than those which would in any case have been borne [...] independently of the organisation of a Union operation'.[31]

The fact remains that the Treaty does not prohibit the financing by the EU budget of all operational expenditure with military or defence implications: it only imposes non-budgeting on 'expenditure arising from operations' (*Ausgaben für Maßnahmen*) with military or defence implications. In other words, the military nature of an item of operational expenditure is not in itself such as to exclude it from being covered in principle by the EU budget. Furthermore, the operational expenditure must relate to an 'operation' with military or defence implications. Regulating the state financing of CFSP/CSDP expenditure which is not therefore borne by the EU budget, the EPF decision is based precisely on this distinction, since it establishes an extra-budgetary facility to finance not only the common costs of military operations under the CSDP which, under no circumstances could be financed from the EU budget, but also the operational expenditure of other actions in the military and defence field which the Council unanimously decided, by way of derogation, to remove from the EU budget by making them chargeable to the Member States.[32]

This new architecture is accompanied by increased programming in terms of the overall amounts allocated for a period corresponding to that of the Multiannual Financial Framework (MFF), applicable to the EU budget (see below), which makes it possible to take the measure of the financial effort made in a logic of European solidarity. For 2021-2027, the initial EPF decision set a financial ceiling of €5,692 billion (at current prices), which was increased four times during the cycle to reach €17,040 billion in February 2024, i.e. a threefold increase. Despite this very significant increase, which has been encouraged by the deterioration in the geopolitical context, this amount remains quite residual – around 15% – if we compare it with the seven-year ceiling of the 'external actions' heading of the MFF applicable to the EU budget (€101 billion, at 2018 prices), which itself represents less than 10% of the MFF as a whole.[33] Moreover, a reading of the financial reference amounts contained in the acts establishing the eleven current military missions shows that, in terms of volume, expenditure taken on collectively continues to have a clear minority share within the overall EPF envelope. Based on a seven-year projection using the amounts most often allocated on an annual or biennial basis (see table below), they are likely to remain

30 Art. 44(6) and (7) of Decision 2021/509 cited above.

31 Ibid., Art. 44(5).

32 Ibid., in particular Recital 11.

33 Council Regulation (EU, Euratom) 2020/2093 of 17 December 2020 laying down the multiannual financial framework for the years 2021 to 2027, [2020] *OJ* L433I/11, amended by Council Regulation (EU, Euratom) 2024/765 of 29 February 2024, [2024] *OJ* L2024/765.

well below €1 billion out of the €17 billion now available, the vast majority of which will therefore go towards assistance measures of a military nature which, by way of derogation, are not covered by the EU budget (see above).[34]

CSDP missions of a military nature	Financial reference (€ million) and period
Training mission in Somalia (EUTM SOMALIA)	€29.8 million (1 January 2023 to 31 December 2024)
Training mission in Mali (EUTM MALI)	€133.7 million (May 2020 to May 2024)
Training mission in the Central African Republic (EUTM RCA)	€7.8 million (September 2022 to September 2023) €5.2 million (September 2023 to September 2024)
Training mission to Mozambique (EUTM MOZAMBIQUE)	€15.1 million (2021 to 2024)
Naval operation in the north-west Indian Ocean (EUNAVFOR ATALANTA)	€10.4 million (1 January 2023 to 31 December 2024)
Naval operation in the Red Sea, Indian Ocean and Gulf (EUNAVFOR ASPIDES)	€8 million (February 2024 to February 2025)
Naval operation in the central Mediterranean (EUNAVFOR MED IRINI)	€16.9 million (1 April 2021 to 31 March 2023)
Military assistance mission to support for Ukraine (EUMAM UKRAINE)	€106.7 million (October 2022 to October 2024)
Military partnership mission in Niger (EUMPM NIGER)	€27.3 million (December 2022 to December 2025)
Gulf of Guinea security and defence initiative	€0.787 (August 2023 to December 2025)
Military operation in Bosnia-Herzegovina (EUFOR ALTHEA)	Amount not updated in the basic act

Source: author's calculations from basic information.

b. – The Potential Debudgeting of Other Operating Expenses

Regarding operational expenditure other than that relating to operations with military or defence implications, Article 41 TEU lays down the principle of financing by the EU budget, with the exception that it gives the Council the

[34] In 2019, the European Court of Auditors noted that the six active military operations represented, at the time, an annual budget of €78 million for Athena. See European Court of Auditors, 'La défense européenne', Document d'analyse n° 09/2019, pp. 24–25, para. 50.

power to derogate from this principle by deciding unanimously to make such 'other operational expenditure' chargeable to the Member States. Until the establishment of the EPF, the derogation was rarely applied, with the result that a preponderant share of this other CFSP/CSDP expenditure was in fact borne by the EU budget (Section i). Combined in particular with the evolution of the European geopolitical context, the introduction of the EPF, one of the pillars of which is precisely based on the derogation, has significantly changed the situation, since the exception is now used intensively for amounts which are, moreover, extremely significant, to the point of becoming – by far – the largest item of CFSP/CSDP expenditure (Section ii).

i. *Budgeting the Main 'Other Operating Expenses'*

First of all, it should be noted that, even before it became a principle enshrined in the TEU, the budgeting of other operational expenditures was very much favoured by the Council, even if this meant that it had to be decided unanimously, at the time.[35] In a way, the Treaty of Amsterdam formalised the budgetary tropism of the national delegations in this area.

The enshrinement of the principle of budgeting of other operational expenditures was accompanied by an interinstitutional finalisation designed to transcend the dispute between the European Parliament and the Council over the arrangements for bringing these expenditures into the budget (see below). Signed in 1997,[36] the interinstitutional agreement prescribes not only that all such expenditure should be entered in an exclusively dedicated chapter of the Commission's section of the EU budget, but also the broad outlines of its nomenclature, which has the dual advantage of easily identifying the volume of all such expenditure as well as its breakdown, is itself subject to a form of interinstitutional standardisation, albeit one that is periodically updated on the occasion of the renewal of the MFF.[37]

This makes the trajectory of CFSP/CSDP operational expenditure borne by the EU budget all the clearer (see table below). It is now close to €400 million per year, which is considerably more than the operational expenditure on 'operations with military or defence implications' borne collectively by the Member States under Athena and then the EPF (see above). Since the entry into force of the Treaty of Amsterdam, the increase has been continuous, particularly marked between 1998 and 2010 with a tenfold rise (from €25 million

[35] Opinion 1/97 of the Court of Auditors, unpublished but available (only in French) on the Court's website: https://www.eca.europa.eu/Lists/ECADocuments/OP97_01/OP97_01_FR.PDF.

[36] Interinstitutional Agreement of 16 July 1997 between the European Parliament, the Council and the Commission on provisions concerning the financing of the common foreign and security policy, [1997] *OJ* C286/80.

[37] Interinstitutional Agreement of 16 December 2020, cited above.

to €256 million) and, for the last twelve years or so, a relative stabilisation but on the rise (+49% since 2010). Over the entire period, budgeted expenditure on the CFSP/CSDP has thus risen significantly faster than the EU budget itself, attesting during the first phase to the deployment of budgeted joint actions (from 0.03% of the budget in 1998 to 0.198% in 2010) and, during the second phase, to their continued budgetary development up to the present day (0.224% of the EU budget in 2022).

TRAJECTORY OF THE PESC/PSDC CHAPTER WITHIN THE EU BUDGET (In millions of euros)						
	1998	2005	2010	2015	2020	2022
CFSP chapter (payments made)	25	64	256	283	333	383
EU budget (authorised payments)	83,529	89,386	129,088	141,214	153,566	170,603
% of the CFSP/CSDP chapter in the EU budget	0.03	0.07	0.198	0.2	0.216	0.224

Source: author's calculations based on EU budgets.

In line with the nomenclature generally used by the budgetary authority, a distinction should be made between three main categories of CFSP/CSDP operational expenditure borne by the budget: firstly, those relating to the civilian side of security and defence policy, which are by far the costliest (over 85% of the total), and secondly those relating to special representatives, non-proliferation and disarmament, which are relatively residual in volume terms and less dynamic overall.

PESC/PSDC OPERATING EXPENDITURE COVERED BY THE EU BUDGET (Payments made in millions of euros)						
	1998	2005	2010	2015	2020	2022
Civilian CSDP	18	48	222	243	297	357
Special representatives	3	7	23	28	14	12
Non-proliferation and disarmament	4	9	10	11	22	14

Source: author's calculations based on EU budgets.

Under the principle laid down in Article 41 TEU, the civilian missions deployed by the EU under the CSDP are therefore covered by the EU budget. In 2024, the number of such missions was broadly equivalent to the number of military missions (around a dozen), but at a cost (around €350 million) well in excess of that borne collectively by the EPF for the latter, even though military operations as a whole seem to mobilise more human resources than civilian operations.[38] However, the two categories of operation share a common feature in that they both rely on capabilities provided by the Member States which bear the main cost, each according to its individual contribution. To this end, in the context of civilian missions, secondment of national staff is mainly used, on the understanding that, as in the case of military operations, staff deployed in this way remain paid by the State to which they belong. The basic CFSP/CSDP actions for civilian missions inevitably include a clearly standardised clause whereby each member bears the costs of the personnel it seconds, including travel expenses to and from the place of deployment, salaries, medical cover and allowances.[39]

The fact remains that, independently of the possibility of seconding staff from the EU institutions paid by the EU,[40] the pooling of staff costs is nevertheless more important in the context of civilian missions for at least two reasons: the budgeting not only of the daily allowances of seconded staff[41] but also of the remuneration of international or local contract staff recruited with a view, in particular, to making up for the recurrent shortage of seconded staff.[42]

In fact, the EU repeatedly has difficulty filling all the posts available through the secondment of national staff. The work of the European Court

38 The EEAS provides little and/or relatively erratic information on these figures. The European Court of Auditors nevertheless noted that in 2017, 1,800 people were involved in ten civilian operations, while at the same time 3,200 military staff members were involved in six military operations. See European Court of Auditors, 'La défense européenne', Document d'analyse n° 09/2019,, p. 14, point 28.

39 See for example Article 7 of Joint Action 2005/889/CFSP of 12 December 2005 on establishing a European Union Border Assistance Mission for the Rafah Crossing Point (EU BAM Rafah), [2005] *OJ* L327/28, as amended several times; Article 9 of Council Joint Action 2008/124/CFSP of 4 February 2008 on the European Union Rule of Law Mission in Kosovo, EULEX KOSOVO, [2008] *OJ* L42/92, as amended numerous times; Article 7 of Council Decision 2010/452/CFSP of 12 August 2010 on the European Union Monitoring Mission in Georgia (EUMM Georgia), [2010] *OJ* L213/43, as amended numerous times; Art. 7 of Council Decision 2012/389/CFSP of 16 July 2012 on the European Union mission for strengthening regional maritime capacities in the Horn of Africa (EUCAP NESTOR), [2012] *OJ* L187/40, as amended several times; Article 7 of Council Decision 2012/392/CFSP of 16 July 2012 on the European Union CSDP mission in Niger (EUCAP Sahel Niger), [2012] *OJ* L187/48, as amended several times; Article 8 of Council Decision 2014/486/CFSP of 22 July 2014 on the European Union Advisory Mission on Civil Security Sector Reform in Ukraine (EUAM Ukraine), [2014] *OJ* L217/42, as amended several times; Article 6 of Council Decision (CFSP) 2023/162 of 23 January 2023 on a European Union mission in Armenia (EUMA), [2023] *OJ* L22/29; Article 6 of Council Decision (CFSP) 2023/855 of 24 April 2023 on a European Union Partnership Mission in Moldova (EUPM Moldova), [2023] *OJ* L110/30.

40 Ibid.

41 Ibid.

42 Ibid.

of Auditors periodically attests to this.[43] In 2018, for example, the external auditor noted that 30% to 50% of the posts published had not been filled for capacity-building missions in Niger and Mali,[44] stating that 'staffing civilian CSDP Missions is not always a high priority for EU member states'.[45] Being aware of this challenge, the Council and the Member States undertook in 2018, as part of a civilian CSDP pact, to 'increase jointly the number of seconded experts in the missions, aiming to raise the total share of seconded experts to at least 70% of the international mission staff'.[46] But there is still a long way to go. In its latest report on CSDP operations and missions, the EEAS highlighted an 8% increase in the number of seconded personnel since the adoption of the pact, but conceded a parallel 31% increase in the number of contract staff, concluding that the commitment to increase the proportion of seconded experts had not been met.[47] Nonetheless, in the new Pact adopted in May 2023, the Council and the Member States are persevering with their 70% objective, while adding the requirement of 'aiming for 100% seconded personnel in all management, operational and key functional positions'.[48]

Although pathological in terms of the stipulations of the EU Treaty, which state that CSDP missions, including those of a civilian nature, must be based on the capabilities provided by the Member States,[49] the massive use of contract staff to remedy national deficiencies is not without virtue in that, since this is paid for out of the EU budget, it significantly reinforces solidarity in terms of sharing the burden between Member States. The civilian CSDP is not only plagued by a shortage of seconded national staff, it also seems to be faced with major disparities between Member States in terms of the effort made in this area. The European Parliament has expressed concern about this, noting that 'ten Member States currently provide 78% of seconded personnel [while] seventeen Member States only 22%'.[50] In the absence of reliable available data,

43 European Court of Auditors, Special Report No 18/2012 concerning the European Union's assistance to Kosovo related the rule of law, p. 31, para. 87 and Special Report No 7/2015 concerning the EU Police Mission in Afghanistan: mixed results, p. 16, paras 17–18.

44 European Court of Auditors, Special Report No. 15/2018 on strengthening the capacity of the internal security forces in Niger and Mali: only limited and slow progress, pp. 24–25, para. 31.

45 Ibid., p. 26, para. 32.

46 Conclusions of the Council and of the Representatives of the Governments of the Member States, meeting within the Council, on the establishment of a Civilian CSDP Compact, 14305/18 of 19 November 2018, p. 5, para 3.

47 European Union, Common Security and Defence Policy, Missions and operations, Annual Report 2021, p. 22.

48 Conclusions of the Council and of the Representatives of the Governments of the Member States, meeting within the Council, on the establishment of a Civilian CSDP Pact, 9588/23 of 22 May 2023, p. 10, para. 13.

49 Art. 42(1-3) TEU.

50 European Parliament resolution of 18 April 2023 on the implementation of civil CSDP and other forms of Union assistance in the field of civil security, 2022/2196(INI), para. 28.

it is not easy to measure precisely the extent of the disparities in contributions, which should be assessed at the level of all civilian missions in the light of each Member State's share of EU GNI.

The EU budget also covers the cost of equipment for civilian missions, whereas for military operations, the EPF can clearly only do so in a relatively residual way, within the limits, in any case, of additional costs (see above), given the limited concept of 'common costs'. To speed up the deployment of forces and relieve them of some of the administrative burden, this specific civilian nature led the EU to set up a centralised equipment warehouse in 2010,[51] as part of an experiment that was continued from 2012 onwards. The warehouse is mainly intended[52] for non-military missions,[53] and is managed by the Swedish Civil Protection Agency, following a call for tenders. The first task of this warehouse is to maintain a strategic stock of essential equipment and resources (vehicles, IT and communications equipment, personal protective equipment, medical equipment, visibility equipment) needed for deployment in civilian CSDP missions of up to 200 people to any area of operation within 30 days. More generally, it is responsible for acquiring, storing, maintaining and making available all of this equipment to civilian missions.[54] It is naturally paid for from the EU budget, under the CFSP/CSDP chapter, and the warehouse should, according to the financial reference provided for in its basic act, receive around €46 million for four and a half years, i.e. around €10 million a year.

ii. *Debudgeting of Costly Military or Defence-Related Assistance Measures*

So it was not until the establishment of the European Peace Facility that we saw massive recourse – in terms of volume – to the debudgeting of operational expenditure other than that necessarily excluded from the EU budget because it related to 'operations' with military implications.

The EPF is not limited to replacing Athena, and therefore to ensuring the financing by the Member States of the common costs of these EU operations with military implications. It is also designed to ensure the financing by Member States – outside the EU budget, therefore – of assistance measures consisting of strengthening the military capabilities of third States and

---

51 See Council document 13742/12 of 20 September 2012.

52 Accessory to special representatives or other operations decided by the EU in accordance with Article 28 TEU. See Article 1(2) Council Decision (CFSP) 2018/653 of 26 April 2018 on the establishment of a warehouse capability for civilian crisis-management missions, [2018] *OJ* L108/22.

53 Council Decision 2012/698/CFSP of 13 November 2012 on the establishment of a warehouse for civilian crisis management missions, [2012] *OJ* L314/25 (no longer in force).

54 Decision (CFSP) 2018/653 as amended by Council Decision (CFSP) 2021/487 of 22 March 2021 amending and extending Decision (CFSP) 2018/653 on the establishment of a civil crisis management warehouse, [2021] *OJ* L100/13.

international organisations or supporting the military aspects of peace support operations led by international organisations or third States. It is for this reason that the EPF is presented, including in the decision establishing it,[55] as intended to replace the African Peace Facility. The latter was established in 2003, and already provided financial support for peacekeeping operations and capacity-building in Africa through an extra-budgetary instrument, the European Development Fund, which was matched by the Member States but on a different legal basis.[56]

The fact remains that although these assistance measures can be analysed as operational expenditure with military implications, they do not take the form of CSDP 'operations' with their ensuing implications, so their debudgeting is conditional under Article 41 TEU on a unanimous decision by the Council. The EPF Decision formally prescribes this, specifying that the Facility finances the aforementioned assistance measures 'where the Council decides unanimously, pursuant to Article 41(2) TEU, that the operating expenditure arising therefrom shall be charged to the Member States'.[57]

B. CONTRIBUTION TO CFSP/CSDP EXPENDITURE

Although distinct, the question of the States' contributions to the financing of CFSP/CSDP expenditures is not totally disconnected from that of their budgeting (1). The fact remains that CFSP/CSDP expenditures, whether borne by the EU budget or by the Member States, may also be financed by contributions from third States, under certain conditions (2).

1. The Member States' Contribution

In the same spirit, it should no doubt be emphasised that, as the EU is currently financed, the Member States are expected to contribute both to budgeted expenditure (a) and to non-budgeted expenditure (b), it being understood that debudgeting facilitates the modulation of the contribution effort.

a. – Member States' Contributions to EU Budget Expenditure

Where such expenditure is charged to the budget, all members contribute indirectly to it through the own resources system, which in fact includes, as its

---

55 Recital 19 of Decision 2021/509, cited above.

56 See in particular Decision No 3/2003 of the ACP-EC Council of Ministers of 11 December 2003 on the use of resources from the long-term development envelope of the 9th European Development Fund for the creation a Peace Facility for Africa, [2003] *OJ* L345/108.

57 Art. 1(2)(b) of Decision 2021/509, cited above.

main revenue, a form of national contribution based on gross national income.[58] In principle, this applies not only to administrative expenditure but also to 'operating expenditure' (*'dépenses opérationnelles'*; *'operativen Ausgaben'*) if it is charged to the budget (first subparagraph of Article 41(2) TEU).

However, for historical purposes, it should be noted that the situation could have been different in the context of the contributory exemption granted under Protocol No 22 to Denmark, which Denmark eventually renounced. It will be rightly objected that this exemption only applied to operational expenditure arising from decisions and actions with defence implications, so that it mainly concerned expenditure that was not necessarily covered by the EU budget (see above). The fact remains that the expression 'operational expenditure' (*'dépenses opérationnelles'*; *'operativer Ausgaben'*) used in Article 5 of Protocol No 22 is broader than that used in the second subparagraph of Article 41(2) TEU in relation to expenditure which must be borne by the Member States: *expenditure arising from operations* with military implications (*'opérations ayant des implications militaires'*; *'Ausgaben für Maßnahmen'*). Based on such a distinction, it could not be ruled out that certain operational expenditures covered by the budget could be the subject of a contributory exemption, at least in principle – that which did not relate to an 'operation'.

b. – Member States' Contributions to Pooled Expenditure outside the EU Budget

Concerning operational expenditure not covered by the EU budget, the second subparagraph of Article 41(2) TEU establishes the principle of sharing the financial burden between all the Member States based on gross national income. As the EU's own resources system stands, this establishes a form of congruence. Whether the expenditure is borne by the EU budget or directly by the Member States, the contribution (direct or indirect) of each is essentially determined by its relative prosperity.

The option offered to the Council of opting for debudgeting – over and above expenditure on operations with military implications – should therefore *a priori* be exercised by the members more for institutional reasons following budgeting than for reasons of a strictly financial nature.

However, there are two notable exceptions to the principle of applying the GNI mechanism to the financing of expenditure borne by the Member States.

First of all, it should undoubtedly be emphasised that the possibility of opting for the 'debudgeting' of operational expenditure goes hand in hand with the option of modulating the contribution of each of the Member States, called upon to assume directly the financial burden of the expenditure in question.

---

58 Council Decision (EU, Euratom) 2020/2053 of 14 December 2020 on the system of the European Union's own resources, [2020] *OJ* L424/1.

Indeed, while the second subparagraph of Article 41(2) TEU does establish the principle of all Member States contributing according to the GNI-based scale, it nonetheless confers on the Council, always acting unanimously, the power to decide otherwise, and thus to opt for another method of sharing the financial burden between Member States. It cannot therefore be ruled out that the debudgeting is motivated by the desire to use an ad hoc distribution mechanism.

Secondly, it is important to mention the possibility conferred by the TEU on each member to opt out of the obligation to contribute to the financing of CFSP/CSDP expenditure borne directly by the Member States, which necessarily entails having to adjust the GNI mechanism by subtracting the GNI value of those who opt out. This is the financial translation of the constructive abstention provided for in the second subparagraph of Article 31(1) TEU, which allows each delegation to accompany its abstention on CFSP/CSDP matters with a formal declaration exempting it from the obligation to apply the decision adopted.[59] The fact remains that this financial extension of constructive abstention is strictly limited by the second subparagraph of Article 41(2) TEU to expenditure on operations with military implications, which are necessarily excluded from the EU budget. However, this system has not been very popular to date. In 2018, the Commission noted that constructive abstention had only been used once,[60] in 2008, on the initiative of Cyprus in connection with the Joint Action on the rule of law mission in Kosovo (EULEX).[61] This crisis management mission, which was civilian in nature and funded from the EU budget, clearly did not fall within the scope of the contributory exemption expressly provided for in the Constitutional Treaty.

Nevertheless, the recent European Peace Facility demonstrates the possibility of using the first exception mentioned above to extend, not in law but in fact, the scope of the second exception mentioned above. It has to be said that, in accordance with the option available to it under the last sentence of the first subparagraph of Article 41(2) TEU, the Council has decided to make the Member States directly responsible, through the EPF, for a category of operational expenditure – assistance measures – which clearly cannot be regarded as 'operations with military implications', at least in its eyes. By exceptionally excluding from the EU budget expenditure that could – and indeed should – have been borne by the EU, the intergovernmental body is at the same time giving itself the option of derogating from the principle that expenditure incurred by all Member States should be borne according to the

---

59 See the commentary on Articles 23 TEU to 40 TEU by C. Schneider in this publication.

60 Communication from the Commission, 'A stronger global actor: more efficient decision-making for EU Common Foreign and Security Policy', COM(2018) 647 final, 12 September 2018, p. 9.

61 Council Joint Action 2008/124/CFSP/CSDP of 4 February 2008, [2008] *OJ* L42/ 92.

GNI mechanism. Based on this option, which is set out in the first sentence of the second subparagraph of Article 41(2) TEU, the Council is then in a position to extend indirectly, beyond expenditure relating solely to 'operations with military implications', the financial implications of the constructive abstention mechanism of Article 31(1) TEU, which has a broad scope. Here, then, is a 'constitutional' mechanism whose effects and use have been largely revived by secondary legislation, albeit under highly unusual conditions.

Thus, in very practical terms, the EPF Decision provides that, with regard to a very specific category of assistance measures (authorising 'the supply of military equipment or platforms designed to deliver lethal force') the Member State which, having abstained when the measure was adopted, has attached a formal declaration in accordance with Article 31(1) TEU, and so shall not contribute to the financing of the cost of that measure.[62] On the basis of the second subparagraph of Article 41(2) TEU, which in the author views allows for an ad hoc sharing of the financial burden between Member States, the EPF decision could undoubtedly have stopped there. But this would have led to a significant breach in the financial solidarity between Member States, given the high cost of the assistance measures concerned. This is undoubtedly why this specific exemption mechanism is accompanied by a 'voluntary elective commitment',[63] 'exceptional and *sui generis*',[64] by each of the Member States to pay an additional amount towards assistance measures other than those relating to military equipment and platforms releasing lethal force, should it mobilise the mechanism. In short, this leads to a form of earmarking of these additional contributions to a category of expenditure, which is precisely what EU budgetary law prohibits, at least in principle, by prescribing in particular the non-allocation of own resources.[65] In any case, it is clear from the table below that the introduction of this mechanism has helped to increase the use of constructive abstentions, although it is important to find them in the meanders of the Council minutes relating to non-legislative acts that benefit from more limited publicity.

62 Art. 5(3) of Decision 2021/509 cited above.

63 Ibid., Recital 21.

64 Ibid., Recital 24.

65 Art. 7 of Council Decision (EU, Euratom) 2020/2053 of 14 December 2020 on the system of the EU's own resources, [2020] *OJ* L424/1: 'The revenue referred to in Article 2 shall be used without distinction to finance all expenditure entered in the Union's annual budget'.

Basic act authorising assistance measures	**Financial reference (in € millions)**	**Constructive abstention resulting in exemption from contributions**
Council Decision (CFSP) 2022/338 of 28 February 2022 on an assistance measure under the European Peace Facility for the supply to the Ukrainian armed forces of military equipment, and platforms, designed to deliver lethal force, [2022] *OJ* L60/1 (amended seven times).	4,120	Austria, Ireland, Malta (see CM 1944/22) + Hungary (see CM 2408/23).
Council Decision (CFSP) 2022/2245 of 14 November 2022 on an assistance measure under the European Peace Facility to support the Ukrainian armed forces trained by the European Union Military Assistance Mission in support to Ukraine of military equipment, and platforms, designed to deliver lethal force, [2022] *OJ* L294/25 (amended once).	200	Austria, Ireland, Malta, Hungary (see 14945/22 ADD 1)
Council Decision (CFSP) 2023/1136 of 8 June 2023 on an assistance measure under the European Peace Facility to support the Nigerian Armed Forces with military equipment designed to deliver lethal force, [2023] *OJ* L149/81.	4.7	
Council Decision (EU) 2023/2680 of 27 November 2023 on an assistance measure under the European Peace Facility to support the Somali National Army with military equipment designed to deliver lethal force, [2023] *OJ* L2023/2680.	1	
Council Decision (CFSP) 2024/1713 of 13 June 2024 on an assistance measure under the European Peace Facility to support the armed forces of the Republic of Moldova with military equipment designed to deliver lethal force, [2024] *OJ* L2024/1713.	9	Austria, Ireland, Malta (see 8900/24)

This exceptional system is the focus of much attention, albeit somewhat contradictory, from the national delegations.

In its declaration formulated on the occasion of the adoption of the EPF decision, France rightly pointed out that: 'The abstention of a Member State under the second subparagraph of Article 31(1) of the TEU does not affect the financial contribution, which remains payable by the abstaining State, with the exception, provided in the second subparagraph of Article 41(2) of the TEU, of 'expenditure relating to operations having military or defence implications' for which 'Member States whose representatives in the Council have made a formal declaration under the second subparagraph of Article 31(1) shall not be obliged to contribute to [their] financing'. The French delegation added that: 'The ad hoc mechanism established in Article 5(3) of the Decision has no bearing on the interpretation of those provisions of the Treaty'.[66]

Conversely, in the same context of the adoption of the EPF decision, Ireland argued that 'as a matter of law, a Member State availing of the constructive abstention mechanism in the second subparagraph of Article 31(1) of the TEU is not obliged to apply the decision in question, including in respect of financing'.[67]

This raises the question of whether, in general, a constructive abstainer is obliged to contribute to the financing of a decision which, by its position in the decision-making process, it has accepted, in accordance with Article 31 TEU is binding on the Union, without the abstaining country being obliged to apply it. Ireland's response to this question is based solely on Article 31 of the Treaty, whereas France's interpretation is based on a combination of Articles 31 and 41 TEU. Indeed, it is not unreasonable to consider that, by providing for a tax exemption resulting from constructive abstention only for expenditure relating to operations with military implications, Article 41, which is dedicated to the financing of expenditure arising from the implementation of the CFSP/CSDP, has implicitly established the principle that the option not to apply does not entail the option not to finance, outside this precisely defined specific case. This interpretation is, moreover, perfectly consistent with the principle of budgeting operational expenditure, since the constructive abstentionist accepts that the decision commits the Union, which is in principle called upon to assume the financial consequences, without the latter being able, given its singular position, to obtain a contribution adjustment under the own resources system, since Article 41 TEU offers no grounds for supporting such a claim. Exemption from contributions could therefore only be obtained by deciding to make use of the two derogations mentioned above and provided for in that

66 Council Decision establishing a European Peace Facility – Statements, Document 6618/21 of 18 March 2021, p. 5, available on https://data.consilium.europa.eu/doc/document/ST-6618-2021-ADD-1/en/pdf.

67 Ibid., p. 7.

Article, over and above what is explicitly provided for in Article 41 TEU. These include debudgeting and the modulation in the sharing of the financial burden between Member States.

2. *Contributions from Third Countries*

Under certain conditions, the EU authorises third countries to take part in the crisis management operations it deploys or even in assistance measures.[68] To this end, it has been able to conclude a framework agreement on the subject with several countries, in particular Norway,[69] Iceland,[70] Türkiye,[71] Ukraine,[72] Canada,[73] Montenegro,[74] the United States,[75] Serbia,[76] Albania,[77] the Yugoslav Republic of Macedonia,[78] and Colombia.[79]

These agreements include provisions relating to the financial conditions for participation in both civilian missions and military missions. They generally establish the principle that the third country bears all the costs associated

68 See Art. 30 of Decision 2021/509, cited above.

69 Agreement between the European Union and the Kingdom of Norway establishing a framework for the participation of the Kingdom of Norway in the European Union crisis management operations, [2005] *OJ* L67/8.

70 Agreement between the European Union and the Republic of Iceland establishing a framework for the participation of the Republic of Iceland in the European Union crisis management operations, [2005] *OJ* L67/2.

71 Agreement between the European Union and the Republic of Turkey establishing a framework for the participation of the Republic of Turkey in the European Union crisis management operations, [2006] OJ L189/17.

72 Agreement between the European Union and Ukraine establishing a framework for the participation of Ukraine in the European Union crisis management operations, [2005] *OJ* L182/29.

73 Agreement between the European Union and Canada establishing a framework for the participation of Canada in the European Union crisis management operations, [2005] *OJ* L315/21.

74 Agreement between the European Union and Montenegro establishing a framework for the participation of Montenegro in the European Union crisis management operations, [2011] *OJ* L57/2.

75 Framework Agreement between the United States of America and the European Union on the participation of the United States of America in the European Union crisis management operations, [2011] *OJ* L143/72.

76 Agreement between the European Union and the Republic of Serbia establishing a framework for the participation of the Republic of Serbia in the European Union crisis management operations, [2011] *OJ* L163/2.

77 Agreement between the European Union and the Republic of Albania establishing a framework for the participation of the Republic of Albania in the European Union crisis management operations, [2012] *OJ* L169/2.

78 Agreement between the European Union and the former Yugoslav Republic of Macedonia, establishing a framework for the participation of the former Yugoslav Republic of Macedonia in the European Union crisis management operations, [2012] *OJ* L338/3.

79 Agreement between the European Union and the Republic of Colombia establishing a framework for the participation of the Republic of Colombia in the European Union crisis management operations, [2014] *OJ* L251/8.

with its participation, except for those that are jointly financed. However, in principle, the participating third country is asked to contribute to the latter, apart from any daily allowances paid to Member State personnel. Yet, exemption from contributing to the mission's operational budget is generally envisaged in two alternative cases: if the EU considers that the third country is making a substantial contribution to the operation which is essential, or if the participant's gross national income per capita does not exceed that of any of the other Member States. The framework agreements also generally set out the methods for calculating the share of the common costs to be borne by the participating third party, in the form of two formulae, whichever results in the lowest amount: i) a share proportional to the ratio between the GNI of the third party State and the total GNI of all the States contributing to the common costs of the operation, or ii) a share proportional to the ratio between the number of staff of the third party State and the total number of staff employed by all the Member States participating in the operation.

II. THE LEGAL FRAMEWORK FOR CFSP/CSDP EXPENDITURE

The budgeting of CFSP/CSDP expenditure has an impact on its legal regime, both from the point of view of authorisations (Section A) and implementation and control (Section B), even if certain 'Community' standards have taken hold.

A. AUTHORISATIONS

Thus, whether the expenditure is borne by the EU budget or by the Member States, it will be subject to the principle of dual budgetary (Section 1) and regulatory (Section 2) authorisation/basis.

1. Budgetary Basis

a. – Budgetary Authorisation of Expenditure from the EU Budget

The budgeting of CFSP/CSDP expenditure has, from the outset, created a form of hiatus since it has meant that, as far as budgetary authorisation is concerned, certain expenditures arising from a policy defined and implemented in an eminently intergovernmental manner has been subject to fully integrated procedures.

Historically belonging to the category of non-compulsory expenditure in the context of the budgetary procedure inherited from the Treaty of Luxembourg of 22 April 1970, CFSP/CSDP expenditure was in principle, until the entry into force of the Treaty of Lisbon, subject to the final say of the European Parliament. The latter thus obtained, by means of both the budgeting of CFSP/CSDP expenditure and its budgetary prerogatives, a say in a policy in respect of which the EU Treaty confers only a consultative power on it, and a very vague one at that, since the European Parliament must be 'regularly' consulted on the 'main' aspects of the CFSP/CSDP (see Art. 36 TEU).[80]

This hiatus has helped towards the straining of relations between the two parliamentary and intergovernmental arms of the budgetary authority. The European Parliament has been able to criticise the Council of the EU for including certain CFSP/CSDP appropriations in its own section of the budget in such a way as to remove them from the final decision-making power of the Parliament, based on a 'gentlemen's agreement' under which the Council and the European Parliament have mutually undertaken not to interfere in their respective sections.[81] For its part, the European Parliament has not hesitated to place part of the CFSP/CSDP appropriations in the reserve title of the budget, thus making the release of funds conditional on transfers of appropriations during the financial year subject to the consent of the Members of Parliament, and consequently to their consultation.[82]

Following these skirmishes, a tripartite interinstitutional agreement was concluded in 1997.[83] It has since been renewed with a few adjustments and is now incorporated into the interinstitutional agreement on budgetary discipline concluded at the same time as the adoption of the multiannual financial framework.[84] Within this framework, each of the protagonists has had to make concessions.

The Parliament has obtained specific commitments regarding the frequency and consistency of the consultations and information that it must receive in the field of the CFSP. In addition to the five minimum consultative meetings for political dialogue on the CFSP, the High Representative must consult the European Parliament annually on a forward-looking document submitted before 15 June setting out the main aspects and basic choices of the CFSP, including the financial implications for the EU budget and an assessment of the measures launched during the preceding financial year. In addition, following any CFSP/CSDP decision involving expenditure, the High Representative must

80 See the commentary on Articles 23 TEU to 40 TEU by C. Schneider in this publication.
81 Y. Petit, 'Le traité d'Amsterdam et le financement de la PESC/PSDC', *Europe*, January 1998, pp. 5–8.
82 Ibid.
83 Interinstitutional Agreement of 16 July 1997, cited above.
84 Interinstitutional Agreement of 16 December 2020, cited above.

provide the European Parliament within five days with a range of information relating to the costs envisaged, the staff employed, the premises, infrastructure and equipment mobilised.

In return for this strengthening of its information powers, Parliament has made several concessions. Firstly, it had to abandon the practice of placing funds in reserve. Secondly, it accepted a certain restriction on its power to amend the Commission's draft budget. Like the Council, the European Parliament has undertaken, in the absence of an agreement with the representatives of the Member States, to maintain the amount of operating expenditure entered in the previous budget or that proposed by the Commission in the draft budget, whichever is lower. In addition, the signatories have also defined the relevant budget nomenclature by agreement. All CFSP/CSDP operational expenditure must be included in a single chapter of the Commission's section dedicated to this policy, which gives the Commission the freedom to transfer appropriations within this chapter without having to seek authorisation from the two arms of the budgetary authority. However, the agreement proposes – rather than regulates – the structuring of the chapter into several articles, distinguishing between the most important missions and others – emergency measures, preparatory measures and special representatives. This individualisation of CFSP/CSDP operational expenditure within a single chapter is, moreover, enshrined in the Financial Regulation which, in terms of its structure, imposes specific lines only for the most important missions.[85] Thus, in terms of operations, the CFSP/CSDP chapter of the initial 2024 budget comprises three items: EULEX Kosovo (€80 million), the Observer Mission in Georgia (€22 million) and other civilian CSDP missions (€215 million).

The CFSP/CSDP chapter of the EU budget no longer appears to be a significant bone of contention between the two arms of the budgetary authority, which generally do not amend the requests made by the European Commission in the context of the draft budget. However, it should be noted that budgeted CFSP/CSDP expenditure is not a heading (or even a sub-heading) in its own right within the multiannual financial framework, which is in line with the spirit of the multiannual financial framework and the letter of Article 312 TFEU, which prescribes a 'limited number [of categories]' of expenditure corresponding to 'the Union's major sectors of activity'. CFSP/CSDP expenditure thus includes the recurring heading for the EU's external action, so that it is not locked into strict annual ceilings but, conversely, such expenditure does not have a protected envelope.[86] Nevertheless, in its traditional substantial arbitration conclusions on the multiannual financial framework, the European Council does not hesitate to mention an amount which it claims

[85] Art. 52(1)(g) of Regulation 2018/1046, cited above.

[86] However, given the flexibility of the framework, the effects of the ceilings need to be qualified.

to allocate specifically to the CFSP/CSDP, within the host heading, as it did in 2020 for the MFF 2021-2027: in this case €2.375 billion over the period (compared with more than €70 billion for external action). This confirms the contained volume of the budgetary implications of the CFSP/CSDP.[87]

b. – Budgetary Authorisation of Expenditure Borne by the Member States through the EPF

Paradoxical as it may seem at first sight, CFSP/CSDP expenditure paid for by the Member States appears to be subject to a stricter multiannual framework, even though, as it is not part of the EU budget, it is not subject to the multiannual financial framework set out in Article 312 TFEU.

It has to be said that the latter imposes its current seven-year rhythm as if by capillary action, and MFF's disciplinary logic on the European Peace Facility as the entity responsible for the financing by the Member States of operational expenditures relating to the CFSP. The conclusions of the June 2020 European Council are extremely revealing in this respect. Supposedly devoted to the MFF 2021-2027, they nonetheless include an arbitration on the appropriations available under the EPF for this same period (2021-2027).[88] Even more convincing is, of course, the EPF Decision itself, which contains not a 'financial reference' as is de rigueur for the so-called basic acts (see below), but a 'financial ceiling' and an annual breakdown combined with a flexibility mechanism – of the contingency margin type – of the order of 15% in the event of exceptional circumstances, and subject to adjustment of the annual ceilings.[89]

In this respect, it is worth noting that even before the outbreak of war in Ukraine, the multiannual ceiling applicable to the EPF was more than twice as high (€5.6 billion) as the envelope, albeit not formalised, envisaged by the European Council for CFSP/CSDP expenditure (€2.3 billion) and covered by the EU budget. Given the increase in assistance measures for Ukraine, successive revisions of the EPF have widened the gap by an extremely significant proportion (now from 1 to 8).[90]

Like the EU, the EPF not only has a legal personality but also an annual budget, although the way in which it is adopted reflects its singularity as a profoundly intergovernmental entity. In fact, while this tropism is also broadly true of the multiannual framework for the MFF, which is adopted by the Council of the EU acting unanimously after, admittedly, the approval of the European Parliament,[91] the situation is different when it comes to the

[87] Conclusions of the European Council of 17 to 21 July 2020, para. 124, p. 56.
[88] Ibid., para. 126.
[89] Arts. 2 and 17 of Decision 2021/509, as amended.
[90] The multiannual ceiling was raised to €17 billion by Decision (CFSP) 2024/890.
[91] Art. 312 TFEU.

budget. While the arrangements for adopting the EU budget, through the application of qualified majority voting and the co-decision dynamics of the procedure, express the logic of integration to which the budget belongs,[92] those applicable to the EPF budget express deference to state consensualism. The EPF's intergovernmental committee is responsible for unanimously adopting the EPF's annual budget.[93] The EPF Decision adds a strict framework to the budget nomenclature to allow close control by the budgetary authority, in this case by each of the national delegations. To take just one enlightening example, given the rules applicable to transfers during the financial year, each operation or assistance measure must be the subject of a specific title, in such a way that it is necessary to obtain the approval of the Intergovernmental Committee for any change in the destination of the authorised appropriations.[94]

2. *The Normative Basis*

a. – The Legal Basis for Expenditure from the EU Budget

Budgetary authorisation of expenditure is not a sufficient condition for its implementation; it must also have a legislative basis. Based on case law,[95] this principle was enshrined in the Treaty of Lisbon and is now set out in Article 310(3) TFEU: 'The implementation of expenditure shown in the budget shall require the prior adoption of a legally binding Union act providing a legal basis for its action and for the implementation of the corresponding expenditure'. There is no doubt that this principle applies to CFSP/CSDP expenditure charged to the EU budget. This is borne out by the Financial Regulation, to which the aforementioned provision ultimately refers, in particular as regards the definition of exceptions to the said principle.

It must therefore be noted that the Parliament has taken care to extend to the CFSP/CSDP the changes it has made under ordinary law to the principle now expressly set out in the Treaty on the Functioning of the European Union.[96] It is thus open to the budgetary executive to implement, in the field of CFSP/CSDP and in the absence of a basic act, appropriations authorised by the EU budget as long as they relate to preparatory measures 'limited to a short period of time' and aiming 'to establish the conditions for Union action in fulfilment of the objectives of the CFSP, and for the adoption of the necessary legal instruments'.[97] This may involve financing the assessment of operational

92 Art. 314 TFEU.
93 Article 11 of Decision 2021/509 cited above.
94 Ibid., Arts. 18 and 20.
95 Case C-106/96, *United Kingdom v Commission*, ECLI:EU:C:1998:218, ECR p. I-2729.
96 Art. 58 of Regulation 2018/1046, cited above.
97 Ibid., para. 5.

needs, ensuring the rapid initial deployment of resources or creating the conditions on the ground for the launch of the operation, including covering the marginal costs of deploying a team on the ground (insurance, travel and accommodation expenses and daily allowances). While welcome, this flexibility must nevertheless be qualified by the fact that it can only be activated after approval by the Council on a proposal from the High Representative.[98]

Like their equivalents adopted in other areas, the basic acts adopted in the field of CFSP/CSDP include a 'financial reference' defining the envelope available for the action to be taken, within a given period. In so doing, the Council of the EU has adopted the concept (financial reference) used in the Interinstitutional Agreement on budgetary discipline.[99] However, the provisions of the latter do not extend to the CFSP/CSDP since, as its title suggests, they only govern financial entries in 'legislative acts'. Yet, the use of this term should probably be interpreted as meaning that the Council accepts that this is not an amount binding on the budgetary authority but merely a 'reference' illustrating the authors' intentions.[100]

b. – The Legal Basis for Expenditure Borne by Member States

The EPF Decision also formalises the principle of the prior adoption of a basic act in this case for the financing of both an operation and an assistance measure, in the first case based on Articles 42 and 43 of the Treaty on European Union and, in the second case, under Article 28 of that Treaty.[101]

Unsurprisingly, this requirement logically yields to the same imperative of financing preparatory or emergency measures, although it is understood that this does not obviate the need for authorisation from the Council.[102]

Lastly, under the EPF, the basic act formally requires the inclusion of a 'reference amount for the financial resources to be funded under the Facility'.[103]

B. IMPLEMENTATION AND CONTROL

Finally, budgeting CFSP/CSDP expenditure has an impact on how it is implemented and monitored.

---

98 Ibid.
99 Interinstitutional Agreement of 16 December 2020, paras. 17–18.
100 Ibid., para. 19 *mutatis mutandis*.
101 Art. 7(1) of Decision 2021/509, cited above.
102 Ibid.
103 Art. 7(2) of Decision 2021/509, cited above.

1. *Expenditure from the EU Budget*

The implementation of CFSP/CSDP expenditure from the EU budget requires the linkage of at least two provisions of primary law, one relating to the implementation of the CFSP and the other to the implementation of the EU budget. The first lays down the principle that the implementation and even the execution of decisions adopted in the field of CFSP/CSDP is ensured by the High Representative of the EU for Foreign Affairs and Security Policy.[104] The second gives the Commission the power to implement the EU budget.[105] Facilitated by the High Representative's membership of the Commission as Vice-President,[106] the reconciliation/combination of these two stipulations is essentially, if not guaranteed, at least formalised by the decision establishing the organisation and functioning of the European External Action Service (EEAS). Pursuant to the TEU, the EEAS has the function of supporting the High Representative in the fulfilment of his/her mandate.[107] The decision states that while 'actions undertaken under the CFSP/CSDP budget [...] shall be under the responsibility of the High Representative' and of the EEAS under the High Representative's authority. It is the Commission that is responsible for 'their financial implementation' but 'under the authority of the High Representative in his/her capacity as Vice-President of the Commission'.[108] The decision expressly confirms that budget implementation remains the prerogative of the Commission, and the department responsible for implementing the CFSP/ CSDP chapter of the EU budget is 'co-located with the EEAS'.[109] Moreover, although the EEAS is 'a functionally autonomous body of the European Union'[110] and has budgetary autonomy in the form of its own section within the EU budget,[111] its section does not include 'operational expenditure shall remain within the Commission section of the budget'.[112] This organisation is in many ways byzantine but has the merit of synthesising, through the Janus figure of the High Representative, on the one hand, the strong intergovernmental character of CFSP/CSDP expenditure, and on the other hand the integration implied by the assumption of responsibility for this expenditure by an EU budget, in line with 'Community' orthodoxy.

---

104 Art. 26(3) and 27(1) TEU.
105 Art. 317 TFEU.
106 Art. 18(4) TEU.
107 Art. 27(3) TEU.
108 Art. 9(6) of Council Decision (2010/427/EU) of 26 July 2010 establishing the organisation and functioning of the European External Action Service, [2010] *OJ* L201/30.
109 Ibid.
110 Ibid., Art. 1(2).
111 Ibid., Art. 8(1).
112 Ibid.

The latter also prevails when it comes to monitoring the implementation of the budget, including at judicial level.

Based on a strict interpretation of its lack of jurisdiction concerning the CFSP,[113] the Court of Justice of the European Union (CJEU) confirmed, in the context of a dispute about the award of public contracts for the benefit of a civilian crisis management operation, that the CJEU had jurisdiction to rule on the legality of measures relating to the implementation of expenditure which was borne by the EU budget, even if arising from the CFSP/CSDP.[114] It should be noted that these measures were part of the implementation of the provisions relating to public contracts in the Financial Regulation, in respect of which the jurisdiction of the EU's high court could only be impaired by a broad interpretation of the scope of the 'CFSP/CSDP' restriction to the principle of the general jurisdiction of the CJEU to interpret and apply the Treaties.[115]

The fact that CFSP/CSDP expenditure is covered by the EU budget also means that the European Court of Auditors (ECA), which is empowered by Article 287 TFEU to 'examine the accounts of all revenue and expenditure of the Union', has jurisdiction over it. Concerning the CFSP/CSDP, as with other areas of EU competence, the organisation's external auditor uses all the powers available to him/her under the Constitution. Notwithstanding the relatively modest cost to the EU budget, he/she periodically carries out an in-depth examination of certain CSDP operations for which the European Court of Auditors has already issued special reports.[116] More generally, the ECA has been no stranger to the difficulties and debates surrounding the financing of the CFSP/CSDP following its establishment by the Maastricht Treaty. At the request of the European Parliament, in accordance with the current second subparagraph of Article 287(4) of the TFEU, it issued an opinion as early as 1997 on the conditions governing the implementation of expenditure under the CFSP,[117] at the end of which it adopted unambiguous conclusions, in particular regarding the lack of transparency and the questionable nature of the practice of including within the Council section supposedly administrative expenditure for appropriations which were in reality operational and intended to prepare for the deployment of a mission. Again at the request of the European Parliament, the Court of Auditors followed up its conclusions by adopting a special report

---

113 See the commentary on Article 275 TFEU by N. Gros-Verheyde and C. Schneider in this publication.

114 Case C-439/13 P, *Elitaliana SpA v Eulex Kosovo*, ECLI:EU:C:2015:753, para. 50.

115 Ibid., para. 49.

116 See Special Report No 2/96 of the (European) Court of Auditors concerning the accounts of the Administrator and the administration of Mostar by the European Union, [1996] *OJ* C287/1. See, more recently, Special Reports No 15/2018 on strengthening the internal security forces in Niger and Mali, and No 7/2015 on the EU police mission in Afghanistan.

117 Opinion 1/97 of the Court of Auditors, cited above.

on the CFSP/CSDP in 2001, in which it drew up a new assessment.[118] More recently, the Court devoted an 'analysis document' to European defence in which, among other things, it quite clearly suggests that the development of cooperation in this area is taking place at the price of increased complexity to the detriment of effective and comprehensive scrutiny of the CSDP, so much so that it would like to see its auditing powers extended, including, for example, to the European Defence Agency. More generally, the ECA supports, albeit *mezza voce*, the European Parliament's calls for parliamentary scrutiny of the CSDP to be strengthened.[119]

The budgetary control prerogatives of the European Parliament concerning CFSP/CSDP expenditure depend on how this expenditure is financed. As part of the EU's budgetary authority, the institution representing Europe's citizens is invested in accordance with Article 319 TEFU, with the power to 'give a discharge to the Commission in respect of the implementation of the budget' of the EU. This gives MEPs the opportunity, on the one hand, prior to the discharge, to hear the Commission on the implementation of CSDP expenditure charged to the budget and to request any necessary information. On the other hand, it allows MEPs to obtain a report from the budgetary executive on the measures taken following the observations accompanying the discharge. The Parliament does indeed use its powers of budgetary control concerning the CSDP, and in certain cases, to reinforce budgeting as well as its prerogatives. In its resolution accompanying the granting of discharge for the 2019 financial year, for example, it asked the Commission to assess the legality of the Member States' funding of the European Defence Agency, allowing it to state that 'withdrawing the budgetary function from Parliament [...] under Article 42 TEU is possible for the *operating* expenditure only and requires a unanimous decision by the Council'[120] However, in this case, this was not the case insofar as the decision defining the status of the agency – and its method of State financing – was adopted by the Council acting by a qualified majority, under Article 45(2) TEU.

---

118 Special Report No 13/2001 of the (European) Court of Auditors on the Common Foreign and Security Policy, [2001] *OJ* C338/1.

119 European Court of Auditors, 'La défense européenne', Document d'analyse n° 09/2019, paras. 140–141.

120 European Parliament Resolution (EU) 2021/1543 of 29 April 2021 with observations forming an integral part of the decisions on the discharge in respect of the implementation of the general of the European Union budget for the financial year 2019, Section III – Commission and executive agencies, [2021] *OJ* L340/p. 17, para. 487. Emphasis added.

2. *Expenditure Borne by the Member States through the EPF*

Surprising as it may seem, the implementation of expenditures borne by the Member States through the EPF do not escape the 'Community' technostructure completely.

Although it is 'managed under the authority and direction'[121] of an intergovernmental body of its own – i.e. the Facility Committee – the EPF is based on the organisation's political and administrative system, clearly for the sake of consistency and efficiency. The EPF Decision expressly states this and even imposes it: 'The Facility shall make use of the institutions, bodies and agencies of the Union to the greatest possible extent. It shall resort primarily to existing administrative structures and staff of the Union institutions, bodies and agencies, and to staff seconded by Member States [...]'.[122] One might be tempted to see in this provision an illustration of the option given to Member States, outside the exclusive competence of the Union, 'to entrust tasks to the institutions outside the framework of the Union, such as the coordination of collective action undertaken by the Member States or the management of financial assistance'[123] The fact remains that, since its function is to ensure the financing by the Member States of 'EU actions',[124] the EPF was not set up by the Member States but by the EU itself. The EU has indeed provided the EPF with its own legal capacity,[125] which it has accompanied by a special liability regime in contractual matters (i.e. for contracts concluded on behalf of the EPF) and in non-contractual matters (i.e. for damage caused by the implementation of assistance measures or by headquarters and the staff assigned to them in the case of operations).[126] In the author's view, these provisions, which specify that these liabilities 'shall be covered through the Facility, by the contributing Member States and by the contributing third parties where applicable',[127] are less a question of the Council ruling out the very principle of the facility than of the CJEU's jurisdiction[128] to exclude the very principle of the EU's liability[129] towards third parties as a result of action taken by one of its bodies.[130] This is instead of specifying, in the event of a commitment, the financial implications

[121] Art. 10(1) of Decision 2021/509, cited above.

[122] Ibid., Art. 10(2).

[123] Case C-370/12, *Pringle*, ECLI:EU:C:2012:756, para. 158.

[124] Art. 1(1) of Decision 2021/509, cited above.

[125] Ibid., Art. 3(1).

[126] Ibid., Art. 16(3 and 4).

[127] Ibid.

[128] See in this respect the Opinion of Advocate General Ćapeta delivered on 23 November 2023 in Joined Cases C-29/22 P and C-44/22 P, ECLI:EU:C:2023:901.

[129] Except regarding contributors. See Art. 16(2 and 5) of Decision 2021/509, cited above.

[130] See in this respect Case C-370/89, *SGEEM and Etroy v EIB*, ECLI:EU:C:1992:482, Rec. p. I-6211, paras. 13 to 16, as well as, more recently, Case C-597/18 P, *Chrysostomides*, ECLI:EU:C:2020:1028, para. 80: 'The term of 'institution' within the meaning of [Article 340

where appropriate, which logically are borne not by the EU budget but by the Facility as an extra-budgetary instrument directly financed by the Member States.

However, in mobilising the EU's institutional structure in support of the EPF's tasks, the Decision establishing the EPF again distinguishes between operations and assistance measures. Whereas for the former, it is up to the Secretary-General of the Council to appoint the administrator,[131] the accounting officer[132] and the internal auditor[133] for operations, this same prerogative is, in the case of assistance measures, conferred on the High Representative[134] formally entrusted, in accordance with Article 27(1) TEU. This ensures the implementation of the decisions establishing the assistance measures[135] so that the Facility's bipartite budgetary structure corresponds to a double chain of responsibilities as regards implementation. Thus, while the 'Secretary-General of the Council shall provide the administrator for operations and the accounting officer for operations together with the staff and administrative resources needed for them to carry out their functions',[136] for the purpose of 'the financial implementation of the assistance measures' the High Representative benefits from the 'support of the Commission department'[137] located within the EEAS premises (see above). Moreover, it is the head of the Commission's Service for Foreign Policy Instruments department who, naturally on behalf of the Facility, acts as administrator of the assistance measures.[138] This dichotomy results in a sort of integration gradient, no doubt based on the different nature of the two categories of joint actions to be financed, one of which necessarily involves Member States making military capabilities available.

This distinction extends to the method of implementation. For example, with regard to the implementation of the financing of the common costs of an operation, the EPF Decision confers on the operation commander the status of authorising officer,[139] whereas with regard to assistance measures, the method of direct or indirect management is left to the discretion of the Council of the EU. If the latter opts for indirect management, it may entrust implementation

TFEU] encompasses not only the institutions of the Union listed in Article 13(1) TEU, but also all the bodies, offices and agencies of the Union established by, or under, the Treaties and are intended to contribute to the achievement of the European Union's objectives'.

131 Art. 12(1) of Decision 2021/509 cited above.
132 Ibid., Art. 13(1).
133 Ibid., Art. 41(1).
134 Ibid., Art. 12(2); Art. 13(2) and Art. 41(1).
135 Ibid., Art. 10(4).
136 Ibid., Art. 10(3).
137 Ibid., Art. 10(5).
138 https://fpi.ec.europa.eu/what-we-do/european-peace-facility_en (consulted on 20 July 2024).
139 Art. 15 of Decision 2021/509 cited above.

to the services/ bodies of the Member States,[140] to an international organisation, or to a third State or other EU bodies. However, the Council generally opts for indirect management by one or more of the Member States' Ministries of Defence (or their operators). This was the case for the emblematic decision of 28 February 2022 to finance the supply to the Ukrainian armed forces of military equipment and platforms designed to release lethal force.[141]

When it comes to controlling budget implementation, unity prevails. There is no question of relying on the EU's institutional system. The European Court of Auditors has been replaced by a 'college of auditors' responsible for auditing both revenue and expenditure arising from the implementation of the EPF decision, and the accounts of operations and assistance measures. It is up to the Facility Committee to appoint the auditors for a period of three years, renewable once. It is up to the Member States to propose candidates who must be members of a Member State's supreme national audit institution, or be recommended by it.

Based on the report and the audit opinion, it is finally up to the Facility Committee, not the European Parliament, to grant discharge to each director and each operation commander.

140 Including agencies governed by public law or bodies governed by private law with a public service remit, provided that they offer sufficient financial guarantees. See Art. 33(2) of Decision 2021/509 cited above.

141 Art. 4(4) of Council Decision (CFSP) 2022/338 of 28 February 2022 on an assistance measure under the European Peace Facility for the supply to the Ukrainian armed forces of military equipment, and platforms, designed to deliver lethal force, [2022] *OJ* L60/1.

ARTICLE 42 TEU: A GENERAL INTRODUCTION TO THE COMMON SECURITY AND DEFENCE POLICY (CSDP)

Elsa Bernard
Professor of Public Law at the University of Lille
Jean Monnet Chair
Member of the Rights and Perspectives of Law Research Centre (CRDP, ULR 4487)

Article 42 (ex-Article 17 TEU)

1. *The Common Security and Defence Policy shall be an integral part of the Common Foreign and Security Policy. It shall provide the Union with an operational capacity drawing on civilian and military assets. The Union may use them on missions outside the Union for peace-keeping, conflict prevention and strengthening international security in accordance with the principles of the United Nations Charter. The performance of these tasks shall be undertaken using capabilities provided by the Member States.*

2. *The common security and defence policy shall include the progressive framing of a common Union defence policy. This will lead to a common defence, when the European Council, acting unanimously, so decides. It shall in that case recommend to the Member States the adoption of such a decision in accordance with their respective constitutional requirements.*

The policy of the Union in accordance with this Section shall not prejudice the specific character of the security and defence policy of certain Member States and shall respect the obligations of certain Member States, which see their common defence realised in the North Atlantic Treaty Organisation (NATO), under the North Atlantic Treaty and be compatible with the Common Security and Defence Policy established within that framework.

3. *Member States shall make civilian and military capabilities available to the Union for the implementation of the Common Security and Defence Policy, to contribute to the objectives defined by the Council. Those Member States which together establish multinational forces may also make them available to the common security and defence policy.*

Member States shall undertake progressively to improve their military capabilities. The Agency in the field of defence capabilities development, research, acquisition and armaments (hereinafter referred to as 'the European Defence Agency') shall identify operational requirements, shall promote measures to satisfy those requirements, shall contribute to identifying and, where appropriate, implementing any measure needed to strengthen the industrial and technological base of the defence sector, shall participate in defining a European capabilities and armaments policy, and shall assist the Council in evaluating the improvement of military capabilities.

4. *Decisions relating to the common security and defence policy, including those initiating a mission referred to in this Article, shall be adopted by the Council, acting unanimously, on a proposal from the High Representative of the Union for Foreign Affairs and Security Policy or on the initiative from a Member State. The High Representative may propose the use of both national resources and Union instruments, together with the Commission where appropriate.*

5. *The Council may entrust the realisation of a task, within the Union framework, to a group of Member States in order to protect the Union's values and serve its interests. The execution of such a task shall be governed by Article 44.*

6. *Those Member States whose military capability fulfil higher criteria and which have made more binding commitments to one another in this area with a view to the most demanding missions shall establish permanent structured cooperation within the Union framework. Such cooperation shall be governed by Article 46. It shall not affect the provisions of Article 43.*

7. *If a Member State is a victim of armed aggression on its territory, the other Member States shall have towards it an obligation of aid and assistance by all the means in their power, in accordance with Article 51 of the United Nations Charter. This shall not prejudice the specific character of the security and defence policy of certain Member States.*

Commitments and cooperation in this area shall be consistent with commitments under the North Atlantic Treaty Organisation, which, for those States which are members of it, remains the foundation of their collective defence and the forum for its implementation.

Article 42 TEU is the first of the five articles that make up the section of the TEU specifically dedicated to the Common Security and Defence Policy (CSDP).[1] Conceived as a general introduction to this policy, or as a 'guideline',[2] it is made up of seven paragraphs and ten subparagraphs, most of which extend into other provisions of the Treaty. The summary presentation of Article 42 given here is explained not only by the richness of this provision, which implies analysing it by paragraph, by subparagraph, or even in some cases by sentence,[3] but also by the fact that several elements presented in this provision are then taken up and detailed by the four other articles which, with Article 42, make up the section dedicated to the CSDP.

The commentary on Article 42, in its overview, therefore requires numerous references to the commentaries on other provisions: to the commentaries on Articles 43 to 46 TEU[4] but also to that of the preamble to the TEU, which expressly mentions the possible shift from a common defence policy to a common defence 'in accordance with the provisions of Article 42'.[5] Moreover, the first sentence of Article 42, which states that 'the common security and defence policy shall form an integral part of the common foreign and security policy', refers both to the resolution taken by the Member States in the preamble[6] and to the 'common provisions' of the first section of the chapter of the TEU devoted to the common foreign and security policy (CFSP).[7] It is under this section that this statement and the fact that all the provisions applicable to the CFSP are also applicable to security and defence matters, unless the Treaty provides otherwise, have been commented on.[8]

1 The second chapter of Title V of the TEU is entitled 'Specific provisions on the common foreign and security policy'. It contains a first section devoted to 'Common provisions' and a second section devoted to 'Provisions on the common security and defence policy'.

2 H.-J. Blanke and S. Mangiameli (ed.), The Treaty on European Union – A Commentary, Berlin, Springer, 2013, p. 1203.

3 See the commentary on paragraph 2, subparagraph 2 and paragraph 7, subparagraph 2 of this provision, which concerns NATO, by P.-Y. Buchet de Neuilly or the commentary on paragraph 7, subparagraph 1 by J.-C. Martin.

4 See the respective commentaries by A. Hamonic (Article 42(4) and Article 43 TEU), A.-H. Bertana (Article 42(3)(2) and Article 45 TEU), N. Clinchamp (Article 42(5) and Article 44), Q. Loïez (Article 42(6) and Article 46 as well as Protocol 10).

5 See the commentary by E. Bernard. Because of the structure of the book, it has been decided to concentrate most of the commentary on these two provisions (Preamble and Article 42) on the Preamble.

6 The authors of the Treaties state that they are 'resolved to implement a common foreign and security policy, including the progressive framing of a common defence policy [...]'.

7 The reminder that the CFSP includes either 'the progressive framing of a common defence policy, which may lead to a common defence' (Article 24(1)), or 'matters with defence implications' (Article 26(1), or 'the common security and defence policy' (Article 36(2) is regularly mentioned in the Treaty and has been commented on in this publication by C. Schneider under the heading of common provisions.

8 See the commentary by C. Schneider in this publication.

We will therefore confine ourselves in this general presentation to a brief review of the history of this provision (and not that of European defence policy).[9]

Article 42 TEU originated in the Treaty of Maastricht, which was signed in 1992 and entered into force on 1 November 1993. The Treaty on European Union included a CFSP pillar, which in turn included the European Security and Defence Policy (ESDP), which became the Common Security and Defence Policy (CSDP) under the Treaty of Lisbon.

Article J. 4 of the Maastricht version of the TEU stated that the CFSP 'shall include all questions relating to the security of the European Union',[10] while positioning the Western European Union (WEU) as the armed wing and operational component of the European Union.[11] Article J.4(2) states that 'the Union requests the Western European Union (WEU), which is an integral part of the development of the Union, to elaborate and implement decisions and actions of the Union which have defence implications. The Council shall, in agreement with the institutions of the WEU, adopt the necessary practical arrangements'. It is on this point that the provision, which became Article 17 TEU with the Treaty of Amsterdam, then Article 42 TEU with the Treaty of Lisbon, has developed the most.

In 1997, the Treaty of Amsterdam confirmed that the WEU was an integral part of the development of the Union by giving it 'access to an operational capability'. The Treaty also encouraged 'closer institutional relations with the WEU with a view to the possibility of the integration of the WEU into the Union, should the European Council so decide'.[12] This paragraph was deleted by the Treaty of Nice after the decision on integration was taken by the Cologne European Council in June 1999 and, following this decision, integration was decided by the WEU Council in Marseilles in November 2000, shortly before the signing of the Treaty of Nice.

Although the WEU was maintained to ensure both mutual assistance in the event of aggression[13] (which was not provided for in the EU Treaty

---

9 See the commentary on the Preamble in this publication.

10 Article J.4(1). The concept of 'security' encompasses and goes beyond the concept of 'defence', since it covers political, economic, financial, social, environmental and military means. Defence covers the preparation, implementation and use of military force by one or more States. It can therefore be seen as 'the secular arm of a wider security policy', A. Dumoulin, R. Mathieu and G. Sarlet, *La politique européenne de sécurité et de défense (PESD) – De l'opératoire à l'identitaire*, Brussels, Bruylant, 2003, pp. 31–34.

11 On the WEU, see the commentary on the Preamble in this publication.

12 Art. 17(2).

13 In accordance with Article 5 of the modified Brussels Treaty, signed in Paris on 23 October 1954.

prior to the Lisbon revision)[14] and parliamentary scrutiny,[15] the role of this organisation was taken on by the EU bodies. The Treaty of Nice thus drew on the consequences of the Saint Malo Declaration and the desire of the Member States to give the Union a degree of autonomy in defence matters.[16]

Subsequently, as relations between the WEU and the EU diminished, Article 42 TEU resulting from the Lisbon revision no longer referred to the WEU, and Protocol 11 on this provision merely states that 'the European Union shall draw up, together with the Western European Union, arrangements for enhanced cooperation between them'.[17]

On the other hand, a constant feature of Article J.4, then 17, now 42 of the TEU, is the limits that these provisions place on the CSDP. From Maastricht to Lisbon, it is stated in slightly different terms that 'the policy of the Union in accordance with this Article shall not prejudice the specific character of the security and defence policy of certain Member States and shall respect the obligations of certain Member States under the North Atlantic Treaty and be compatible with the common security and defence policy established within that framework'.[18]

The first of these limits relates to the 'specific character of the security and defence policy of certain Member States'. This is not further specified, but obviously covers the neutrality of certain Member States,[19] as well as other specificities, such as Denmark's opt-out from the Common Security and Defence Policy until June 2022[20] or, conceivably, France's nuclear deterrence policy. More generally, it should be remembered that defence issues are primarily a matter for the Member States, and that the CSDP is only secondary to national policies.

The second limitation concerns the obligations arising, for certain Member States, from their membership of NATO and the fact, as recalled again in paragraph 7, sub-paragraph 2 of Article 42, that the commitments made by

---

14 See the commentary on Article 42(7) TEU by J.-C. Martin, in this publication.

15 Article 9 of the aforementioned Brussels Treaty stipulates that 'the Council of the WEU shall submit to an Assembly composed of the Representatives of the Brussels Treaty Powers in the Consultative Assembly of the Council of Europe an annual report on its activities, in particular in the field of arms control'.

16 See the commentary on the preamble in this publication.

17 Deemed redundant in relation to the CSDP, the WEU was dissolved in June 2011.

18 Art. J.4 TEU (Maastricht version, which varies in the wording 'it shall respect the obligations of certain Member States under the North Atlantic Treaty', without adding the reference to 'Member States which consider that their common defence is achieved within the framework of NATO'); Art. 17(1)(3) then (2) TEU (Amsterdam version, then Nice); Art. 4 (2)(2) (Lisbon version).

19 Historically, Austria, Finland, Sweden, Malta and Cyprus have claimed neutrality. With the integration of Finland and Sweden into NATO, the neutrality policy of these states seems to have disappeared. See V. Schwaller, 'Les pays neutres dans la construction européenne, entre rejet européen et redéfinition du concept', *Classe Internationale*, 9 February 2023.

20 See the commentary by C. Schneider in this publication.

Member States under the CSDP must remain consistent with the commitments entered into within NATO 'which, for those States, which are members of it, remains the foundation of their collective defence and the forum for its implementation'.[21]

The implementation of the various guidelines referred to in Article 42 TEU gives rise to mixed results which are analysed in detail in the following comments, from the point of view of the relationship between the CSDP and NATO,[22] CSDP missions and operations,[23] the European Defence Agency,[24] the flexibility mechanism for the CSDP,[25] Permanent Structured Cooperation[26] and finally the mutual defence clause.[27]

21 Article 42 (7)(2) TEU. See the commentary by Y. Buchet de Neuilly, in this publication.
22 See the commentary by Y. Buchet de Neuilly, in this publication.
23 See the commentary by A. Hamonic, in this publication.
24 See the commentary by A.-H. Bertana in this publication.
25 See the commentary by N. Clinchamp in this publication.
26 See the commentary by Q. Loïez, in this publication.
27 See the commentary by J.-C. Martin in this publication.

ARTICLE 42(2)(2) AND 42(7)(2) TEU: EU-NATO RELATIONS

Yves Buchet de Neuilly
Professor at the Université Paris 1 Panthéon Sorbonne

Article 42(2)(2) TEU

The policy of the Union in accordance with this Section shall not prejudice the specific character of the security and defence policy of certain Member States and shall respect the obligations of certain Member States, which see their common defence realised in the North Atlantic Treaty Organisation (NATO), under the North Atlantic Treaty and be compatible with the common security and defence policy established within that framework.

Article 42(7)(2) TEU

Commitments and cooperation in this area shall be consistent with commitments under the North Atlantic Treaty Organisation, which, for those States which are members of it, remains the foundation of their collective defence and the forum for its implementation.

Article 42(2)(2) TEU establishes an explicit link between the European Union and the North Atlantic Treaty Organisation (NATO), reaffirming the primacy of the Atlantic Alliance in matters of collective defence, while nonetheless allowing the EU a genuine margin for manoeuvre and autonomy. The European Union must accommodate the expectations of 'certain' Member States that belong to both organisations (expectations not necessarily shared by all the dual member states)[1] for whom NATO remains the primary defence

[1] On 1 March 2024, NATO and the EU had 23 common members: Belgium, Bulgaria, Croatia, the Czech Republic, Denmark, Estonia, Finland, France, Germany, Greece, Hungary, Italy, Latvia, Lithuania, Luxembourg, the Netherlands, Poland, Portugal, Romania, Slovakia, Slovenia, Spain and Sweden.

framework. It is therefore necessary to avoid any form of incompatibility between EU arrangements and the commitments of these States within NATO.

The EU's subordination to NATO in terms of collective defence is further entrenched in Article 42(7)(2) TEU. This subparagraph no longer refers to the commitments of 'certain' States but extend to all the Member States of the Alliance. The principle of compatibility is replaced by the more binding principle of full compliance. It further clarifies that NATO is not only the body in which the collective defence policy of the dual member states is conceived – which together represented 85% of the EU's Member States and 96.5% of its population in 2024 – but also the organisation tasked with implementing this policy. There is very limited room left for the European Union.

Nevertheless, as the other contributions in this publication make clear, the European Union has not been inactive in the field of security and defence. It should be remembered, however, that this European activity has focused mainly on external security, not on the collective defence of the Member States.[2] For NATO too, territorial defence issues were less prominent in the thirty-year period between the collapse of the Soviet bloc in the early 1990s and the intensification of the war in Ukraine in the early 2020s.[3] During this period, NATO's very relevance was called into question and the organisation owed its survival in part to a reconfiguration and extension of its activities in the field of collective security.[4] In this vast field, the European Union's activities have extended from civilian to military actions, while NATO's have extended from the military to a much broader conception of security, including civilian dimensions.[5] In the grey area of collective security, the two organisations have coexisted, competed and cooperated. The links between the EU and NATO have therefore been built and developed at the margins, on issues that are less politically sensitive and less firmly framed by the treaties.

---

2 Military external security actions are understood here as expeditionary deployments, interventions in third countries or close to their coasts, while defence operations involve putting in place the means for the immediate protection of the territory of European states against direct aggression.

3 In 2024, NATO organised its biggest military exercise since 1988 ('L'OTAN va mener un exercice impliquant 90 000 militaires pendant plusieurs mois', *France info* with *AFP*, 18 January 2024, https://www.francetvinfo.fr/monde/otan/l-otan-annonce-un-exercice-sur-plusieurs-mois-impliquant-90-000-militaires_6311898.html).

4 See for example. J. Eichler, *NATO's Expansion After the Cold War: Geopolitics and Impacts for International Security*, Lausanne, Springer, 2021; E. Hallams, L. Ratti and B. Zyla (eds.), *NATO Beyond 9/11: The Transformation of the Atlantic Alliance*, New York, Palgrave Macmillan, 2013; S. Mayer (ed.), *NATO's Post-Cold War Politics: The Changing Provision of Security*, New York, Palgrave Macmillan, 2014; S. Rynning, *NATO Renewed: The Power and Purpose of Transatlantic Cooperation*, New York, Palgrave Macmillan, 2005.

5 R. McCalla, 'NATO's Persistence after the Cold War' (1996) 50(3), *International Organization*, pp. 445–475; J. Sperling, M. Smith and M. Webber, *NATO's Post-Cold War Trajectory: Decline or Regeneration*, London, Palgrave Macmillan, 2012.

To understand how the EU and NATO are linked, it is necessary to remember that these organisations and their activities are the product of agreements between states, and that states are the constituent units of the international political system,[6] units which claim, with varying degrees of success, control over the legitimate means of violence in a given territory.[7] State and war are interdependent processes. The accumulation of coercive means of warfare, a matter of survival in the face of ever more powerful rivals, has been one of the main factors in the institutionalisation and consolidation of states.[8] Although states almost never have the means to defend themselves against a major military threat on their own, they nonetheless remain the focal point of their populations' security expectations and the main holders of the means of military violence. It is up to the State to protect the integrity of its territory and its population, including through cooperation with other States. As far as European states are concerned, circumstances marked by a resurgence of close-by, high-intensity inter-state conflicts, as in the case of the Yugoslav wars in the 1990s and the Russo-Ukrainian war of the 2020s, have heightened these security expectations and have increased the likelihood of a strengthening of state military capabilities and inter-state military cooperation institutions.[9] These processes feed off each other.

Increasing the means of warfare is not a zero-sum game, contrary to what is suggested by the debates on the links between European integration and security pressures,[10] or the literature on the overlap between collective security organisations.[11] The strengthening of NATO is not necessarily to the detriment of state capabilities and their control of military means, or even to the detriment of other international organisations, in particular the European Union, and vice versa. The European treaties and numerous declarations mention respect for the specific defence policies of some states (neutral states, for example)[12] and the commitments made within the NATO framework by a large number of EU Member States, as well as systematically mentioning NATO's primacy as a collective defence organisation. NATO 'remains the foundation of collective defence for its members', reads the Versailles Declaration of the Heads of State and Government of the European Union, adopted in March 2022, two weeks

6 K. Waltz, *Theory of International Politics*, New York, McGraw Hill, 1979.

7 M. Weber, *Economy and Society*, Paris, Pocket, 2003 (1st ed. 1921 in German).

8 C. Tilly, *Contrainte et capital dans la formation de l'Europe: 990-1990*, Paris, Aubier, 1992.

9 G. Snyder, *Alliance Politics*, 2nd ed., Ithaca, Cornell University Press, 2007; S. Walt, *The Origins of Alliances*, Ithaca, Cornell University Press, 1987.

10 P. Genschel, 'Bellicist integration? The war in Ukraine, the European Union and core state powers' (2022) 29(12) *Journal of European Public Policy*, pp. 1885–1900; R.-D. Kelemen, and K.-R. McNamara, 'State-building and the European Union: Markets, war, and Europe's uneven political development' (2022) 55(6) *Comparative Political Studies*, pp. 963–991.

11 S.-C. Hofmann, 'Overlapping Institutions in the Realm of International Security: The Case of NATO and ESDP' (2009) 7(1) *Perspective on Politics*, pp. 45–52.

12 Three EU Member States are neutral: Austria, Ireland and Malta.

after the full-scale escalation of the Russian-Ukrainian conflict.[13] Similarly, point 8 of the third joint declaration on cooperation between the EU and NATO of 10 January 2023 states: 'NATO remains the foundation of collective defence of its Allies and essential for Euro-Atlantic security'.[14] The elements of language have been stabilised for decades and are set out in the treaties. In terms of collective defence the hierarchy is clear and has never really been questioned.

Yet this primacy of the Atlantic Alliance is far from being an insurmountable obstacle to strengthening European defence. Admittedly, as observers, experts and scholars frequently point out, NATO and the EU are two international organisations that partly overlap: they share some of the same member states, some of their activities, and the same potential geographical scope of intervention (worldwide). However, international organisations often overlap in the same field of activity. It would be useful, but too lengthy to go into here, to add the UN and its Security Council to the equation,[15] and also to mention the countless ad hoc arrangements, such as coalitions of the willing, contact groups and all the more or less integrated coordination mechanisms set up during the management processes of specific conflicts. The relationship between the European Union and NATO needs to be seen in the context of the international field of collective security, characterised both by an increase in the activity of international organisations after the Cold War, and the central and overwhelmingly dominant role of states in decision-making processes.[16]

The availability of several bodies for coordinating military and diplomatic action and a number of instruments for collective action has the advantage for States of widening the range of possibilities, providing them with leverage or an alternative avenue (in the event of a deadlock in an organisation), or allowing them to rely on the synergies and potential for strengthening the cross-cutting actions of several organisations. The main difficulty facing governments is the cost of these mechanisms. However, it must be remembered that no state is capable of dealing with a high-intensity or protracted conflict on its own. States need each other to procure the means of warfare and to conduct large-scale military operations, which may be far from their territory.

All these elements are part of the dynamics at work in the European Union's security and defence policy. All these factors help to explain why the

---

13 Informal Meeting of Heads of State or Government, *Versailles Declaration*, 10 and 11 March 2022, https://www.consilium.europa.eu/fr/press/press-releases/2022/03/11/the-versailles-declaration-10-11-03-2022.

14 Joint Declaration on Cooperation between the EU and NATO, 10 January 2023, https://www.consilium.europa.eu/fr/press/press-releases/2023/01/10/eu-nato-joint-declaration-10-january-2023.

15 See C. Beaucillon's commentary in this publication.

16 Y. Buchet de Neuilly, 'La politique étrangère de l'UE dans le champ de la sécurité internationale', in F. Mérand and R. Schwok, *L'Union européenne et la sécurité internationale. Théories et pratiques*, Geneva, Academia-Bruylant, 2009, pp. 71–86.

strengthening of this policy is not necessarily to the detriment of NATO or the sovereignty of EU Member States. In practice, what is at stake is not so much the transfer of sovereignty to one international organisation or another, but rather the strengthening of coercive state resources, the capacity to mobilise them collectively, the strengthening of the institutions and instruments of international security and defence organisations, and the equally central issue of how these collective resources are controlled and used.

Admittedly, the emergence of European crisis management capabilities and their operational deployment are sometimes perceived as threats to the Atlantic Alliance. Moreover, as we shall see, cooperation between the EU and NATO is rather modest. For the past twenty years or so, competition between the two organisations has been a reality, but this dynamic has not been to the detriment of the other, rival organisation nor to individual states. NATO and the EU have benefited from a wider expansion of expectations in terms of military security, stimulated by the rise of the fight against terrorism,[17] and more recently, by the return of high-intensity warfare in Europe. These dynamics are combined with budgetary constraints that are not necessarily to the detriment of increasing the security capabilities of these organisations. European and North American governments are constantly torn by the tension between budgetary consolidation (particularly in the early 1990s and in the years following the 2008 economic crisis) and the preservation of defence resources. NATO and the EU are part of the state management of this tension.

The EU/NATO relationship is a key parameter in the emergence of a European Security and Defence Policy. This area of European action was initially conceived within the framework of NATO and another collective security organisation, the Western European Union (WEU) (Section I). Its development has subsequently been based in part on competitive cooperation between the EU and NATO (Section II).

I. THE BEGINNINGS AND INSTITUTIONAL FRAMEWORK OF EUROPEAN SECURITY AND DEFENCE AUTONOMY

Recurrent pressure from the American authorities for a better sharing of the financial burden of the military resources invested in the Alliance,[18] and,

---

[17] J. Pomarède, *La fabrique de l'OTAN. Contre-terrorisme et organisation transnationale de la violence*, Brussels, Éditions de l'Université de Bruxelles, 2020.

[18] B. Blankenship, 'The Price of Protection: Explaining Success and Failure of US Alliance Burden-Sharing Pressure' (2022) 30(5) *Security Studies*, pp. 691–724; J. Jakobsen, 'Is European NATO really free-riding? Patterns of material and non-material burden sharing after the Cold War' (2018) 27(4) *European Security*, pp. 490–514.

even more so, the scepticism and disruptive statements made by US President Donald Trump at the end of the 2010s, have raised fears and questions about the solidity of the American commitment to NATO. They have also given renewed vigour to the traditional advocates of greater autonomy for the EU in security matters. From an institutional point of view, such European autonomy was initially conceived within the framework of NATO and in relation to NATO (Section A), while at the same time relying on an organisation that was already available – the Western European Union (Section B).

A. BUILDING EUROPE'S EXTERNAL SECURITY AT THE RIGHT DISTANCE FROM NATO

Can European autonomy be built within NATO or does it necessarily involve building new capabilities within the EU? In the post-Cold War context of the late 1980s, marked by a degree of American disengagement, the option of European autonomy within the Atlantic Alliance was explicitly envisaged. The official aim of the European Security and Defence Identity (ESDI)[19] was to create an autonomous European force within NATO, with a European chain of command and access to NATO assets (which remained essentially American). At the same time, the ESDI was clearly conceived by the American authorities as a means of preserving their leadership.[20] Indeed, many American leaders have never concealed their preference for this ESDI developed within NATO, rather than a more autonomous CSDP created within the framework of the EU.[21] However, the prospect of an ESDI was less compelling for the American military, which was anxious to preserve its control over NATO assets. The Europeans did not obtain the command of joint forces at their headquarters in

[19] The project for a European defence identity emerged with the Hague Platform, adopted on 27 October 1987 by the WEU Member States, Article 4 of which states: 'We need therefore to develop a more cohesive European defence identity…'. After a few years of hesitation, in a context marked by the negotiations on the Treaty on European Union, the ESDI was clearly anchored to NATO. In the final communiqué of the North Atlantic Council meeting of 7 June 1991, the Alliance's foreign ministers reaffirmed the link between the ESDI, European defence and the 'consolidation of the European pillar within the Alliance'. See in particular M. Robles Carrillo, 'The European Security and Defence Identity and WEU-NATO relations' (1998) 51(1/2) *Studia Diplomatica*, pp. 107–124.

[20] J. Howorth, 'The Myth of European Security "Autonomy"' (2014) 1(1) *European Review of International Studies*, pp. 38–45.

[21] At a conference on the future of NATO at the *Royal Institute of International Affairs* in London on 7 October 1999, Assistant Secretary of State Strobe Talbott said: 'We would not want to see an ESDI that comes into being first within NATO but then grows out of NATO and finally grows away from NATO, since that would lead to an ESDI that initially duplicates NATO but that could eventually compete with NATO', (M. Rutten, *From St-Malo to Nice. European defence: core documents*, Chaillot Papers 47, 2001, p. 56).

Naples,[22] as had been envisaged in the initial discussions on ESDI. This further reduced the attractiveness of the ESDI option from the European point of view.

British leaders have always been the most reluctant to develop specifically European military capabilities that would risk duplicating those of NATO. Yet even they agreed, at the end of the Franco-British summit in Saint-Malo in December 1998, that the European Union should have 'the capacity for autonomous decision-making and action'.[23] As Europeans' security priorities were, and are, not always and not necessarily aligned with American security priorities, the European Union had to be able to act where the Americans did not want to. What could be the institutional translation of this expectation of autonomy, in the legal context of Article J.7(1)(3) of the 1997 Treaty of Amsterdam (retained word for word in Article 42 of the TEU), which makes explicit NATO's pre-eminence in matters of collective defence?

In this area, expectations of European autonomy are relatively modest, even among their most ardent supporters. No European government would want to do without the American ally in a major conflict scenario. And even in crisis management, whatever the level of commitment and the format of the operation, the Member States are faced with the crucial and complex issue of the interoperability of forces, the standards of which have long been, and continue to be, developed within the framework of NATO. The development of organisational capacities for military cooperation is costly, in terms of personnel, infrastructure, equipment, budget, know-how, etc. NATO's military resources are much older and more developed than those of the EU. Some European armies are being structured within the NATO framework.

The end of the Cold War saw a reconfiguration of the international field of collective security, increasing the scope for international organisations. In the early 1990s, the rapprochement between Russia and the United States, which lifted the recurrent blockages in the United Nations Security Council, and expectations of military disengagement from external theatres and a reduction in military spending (the 'peace dividend') opened up new prospects for international organisations, first and foremost the UN, in the prevention and resolution of conflicts. Collective security was also a survival solution for NATO, which, with the end of the Soviet era and the disappearance of the rival military organisation of the Warsaw Pact, temporarily lost its appeal

---

22 NATO has two permanent joint force commands in Europe, one in Brunssum in the Netherlands and the other in Naples in Italy. These commands must be ready to plan, conduct and support NATO operations.

23 Joint Declaration at the end of the Franco-British Summit in Saint-Malo, 3–4 December, 1998. It should be noted that at the time, the British Prime Minister, Tony Blair, was taking a constructive stance in European negotiations, particularly those that led to the 1997 Treaty of Amsterdam. See, E. du Réau, 'Saint-Malo, 4 December 1998. Un tournant dans l'histoire des relations franco-britanniques?', *Bulletin de l'Institut Pierre Renouvin*, 2009, no. 30, pp. 147–163.

and its *raison d'être* as a collective defence organisation (except in the eyes of the Eastern European states, which made NATO membership a priority). In the thirty years since then, NATO has developed and implemented collective security capabilities, expanding its repertoire of instruments and conducting out-of-area operations – most substantially in Afghanistan. In Europe, more specifically, the fall of the Berlin Wall, the collapse of the Soviet bloc, and the prospect of German reunification also led to a deepening of institutional links: within a few months, a new treaty, signed in Maastricht on 7 February 1992, replaced the European Communities (ECSC, EEC, EAEC) with a new European Union, one of the pillars of which incorporated the former European Political Cooperation (EPC) into a new Common Foreign and Security Policy (CFSP).

B. WESTERN EUROPEAN UNION, A TRANSITIONAL ORGANISATIONAL SOLUTION

When the Maastricht Treaty was signed on 7 February 1992, the European Union had no military capabilities or instruments of its own. Under the terms of Article J.4 of the Treaty,'[t]he Union requests the Western European Union (WEU), which is an integral part of the development of the Union, to elaborate and implement decisions and actions of the Union which have defence implications'. Coordinated European investment in the international field of collective security began with the WEU, which was given new missions in 1992 at Petersberg, in a context marked by wars in Yugoslavia, including humanitarian, evacuation, peacekeeping and peace-making support.[24] It was also with the WEU that NATO leaders negotiated the first lasting cooperation agreements between NATO and a European organisation. American expectations of reducing their military spending and presence in Europe were reflected in NATO's support for the development of an ESDI and an agreement in principle to make NATO assets available to the WEU. A 'Combined Joint Task Force' (CJTF) concept was adopted by NATO foreign and defence ministers in 1996.[25]

The Petersberg tasks were incorporated into the Treaty of Amsterdam, signed on 2 October 1997. The prospect of WEU integration is mentioned and Article J.7 reaffirms that '[t]he Union will avail itself of the WEU to elaborate and implement decisions and actions of the Union which have defence implications'. A declaration on the WEU is attached to the Treaty, with a series of paragraphs concerning 'relations between WEU and NATO in

---

24 Council of Ministers of Western European Union, *Petersberg Declaration*, Bonn, 19 June 1992.

25 Decisions taken at the Brussels North Atlantic Council, 1994, https://www.nato.int/docu/manuel/1998/201.htm.

the framework of the development of an ESDI within the Atlantic Alliance'. These include consultation mechanisms between WEU and NATO, WEU's participation in NATO defence planning, and operations using NATO assets and capabilities 'under the political control and strategic direction of WEU'.[26]

In practice, the WEU carried out few operations, did not use NATO assets and its activities were gradually transferred to the European Union, as part of a European Security and Defence Policy which emerged in the early 2000s. The few WEU operations in coordination with NATO were deployed in the early 1990s, in the context of the Yugoslav wars, with the main objective of enforcing the arms embargo on Croatia, Bosnia-Herzegovina and the Federal Republic of Yugoslavia, imposed by the United Nations Security Council:[27] in 1992, the NATO Maritime Monitor and WEU operations Sharp Vigilance followed by Sharp Fence; and then from June 1993 to June 1996, the joint WEU and NATO operation, Sharp Guard, with a joint command.

One of the main legacies passed on by the WEU to the EU are the institutional arrangements for the use of NATO assets, first proposed at the 1996 NATO Summit in Berlin and then negotiated at length and formalised as the 'Berlin Plus' arrangements adopted on 17 March 2003. At the Washington Summit on 24 April 1999, the members of the Alliance agreed on arrangements to 'allow the European Union access to the collective assets and capabilities of the Alliance for operations in which the Alliance as a whole is not engaged militarily as an Alliance'.[28]

II. INCREASING SECURITY RESOURCES IN COMPETITIVE COOPERATION BETWEEN THE EU AND NATO

The financial, human, organisational, etc. means of security and warfare are particularly costly. It may seem logical and tempting to build the new European CSDP partly on NATO assets (Section A) and even reciprocally to allow NATO and its Member States access to EU assets (Section B). However, such cooperation is difficult operationalise and the leaders of each of these organisations remain particularly concerned about their decision-making autonomy. This is why the increase in the EU's external security resources

[26] Treaty of Amsterdam amending the Treaty on European Union, the Treaties establishing the European Communities and certain related acts – Declarations adopted by the Conference – Declaration on Western European Union, [1997] *OJ* C340/125.

[27] United Nations Security Council Resolutions 713 (1991), 757 (1992) and 787 (1992).

[28] Washington Summit Communiqué, issued by the Heads of State and Government participating in the meeting of the North Atlantic Council in Washington on 24 April 1999, https://www.nato.int/docu/pr/1999/p99-064f.htm.

has also been based on a dynamic of emulation linked to its competitive relationship with NATO (Section C).

A. ACCESS TO NATO ASSETS: THE 'BERLIN PLUS' ARRANGEMENTS, A DIFFICULT AGREEMENT FOR A FLEETING USE

It took several years to clarify the Berlin Plus arrangements. The American representatives, supported in particular by the British, were keen to ensure continued primacy of NATO and were concerned about the creation of autonomous European planning capabilities. On 8 December 1998, at a meeting of the North Atlantic Council, the US Secretary of State, Madeleine K. Albright, made clear the American position, the '3D rule': no decoupling, duplication or discrimination. Future initiatives should 'avoid pre-empting the Alliance's decision-making process by decoupling ESDI from NATO, avoid duplicating existing capabilities, and avoid any discrimination against non-EU countries'.[29]

There was also reluctance from European states that were members of NATO but not members of the EU, in particular Turkey, whose leaders feared that they would be excluded from future decisions on operations. EU leaders tried to allay these fears by proposing to create inclusive institutional arrangements for consultation and the presence of third-party personnel in 'Berlin Plus' operations, as set out notably in Annex VI of the Presidency report on the European Security and Defence Policy, adopted in Nice in December 2000.[30] However, at the subsequent meeting of the North Atlantic Council, Turkish leaders, concerned about parallel discussions between EU members and candidate countries, mainly Cyprus, blocked the transposition of these European proposals.[31]

After months of difficult negotiations,[32] a compromise was reached and adopted at the European leaders' summit in Copenhagen in December 2002: '[T]he "Berlin Plus" arrangements and the implementation thereof will apply only to those EU Member States which are also either NATO members or

29 https://1997-2001.state.gov/statements/1998/981208.html; M. Albright, 'The Right Balance Will Secure NATO's Future', *Financial Times*, 7 December 1998 (available in M. Rutten, *From St Malo to Nice. European defence: core documents*, Chaillot Papers 47, 2001, p. 10).

30 'Arrangements for non-EU European NATO members and other candidate countries for accession to the EU', *Annex VI to the Presidency Report on the European Security and Defence Policy*, annexed to the *Presidency Conclusions*, Nice European Council, 7, 8 and 9 December 2000.

31 A. Missiroli, 'EU-NATO Cooperation in Crisis Management: No Turkish Delight for ESDP' (2002) 33(1) *Security Dialogue*, pp. 9–26.

32 M. Reichard, 'Some Legal Issues Concerning the EU-NATO Berlin Plus Agreement' (2004) 73 *Nordic Journal of International Law*, pp. 37–67.

parties to the 'Partnership for Peace', and which have consequently concluded bilateral security agreements with NATO'.[33] This solution amounted to excluding two future EU members, Cyprus and Malta, from the arrangement, which was explicitly confirmed by the clarifications made in paragraph 3 of the same declaration: 'The fact that, as things stand at present, Cyprus and Malta will not take part in EU military operations conducted using NATO assets once they have become members of the EU will not, within the limits of the EU Security Regulations, affect the right of their representatives to participate and vote in EU institutions and bodies, including COPS, with regard to decisions which do not concern the implementation of such operations'.[34]

The 'Berlin Plus' arrangements give Europeans access to NATO military resources, including operational command and control structures. As soon as they were adopted, they were used in the Balkans, for the first military operation in the history of the EU: Operation Concordia. On 31 March 2003, the European Union took over Operation Allied Harmony from NATO, whose mission was to maintain peace in the Former Yugoslav Republic of Macedonia. Following the 'Berlin Plus' arrangements, the Command of this European operation was entrusted to the Deputy Supreme Allied Commander Europe (DSACEUR), German Admiral Rainer Fest, and his headquarters were set up in the NATO offices. A second 'Berlin Plus' operation was launched the following year, on 2 December 2004, this time taking over from the NATO Stabilisation Force in Bosnia-Herzegovina. This operation, EUFOR Althea, is the oldest EU military operation still active and the last to be conducted under the 'Berlin Plus' arrangements.

But to achieve the 'Berlin Plus' arrangement, guarantees were given to non-EU members of the Alliance, reducing the EU's autonomy in the decision-making process. Europeans must go through the North Atlantic Council and SHAPE (Supreme Headquarters Allied Powers Europe). They do not have direct access to NATO's operational headquarters,[35] which reduces the value of an 'autonomous' operation using NATO assets. For more than fifteen years, certain Member States, led by France, have pushed for the creation of a European operational military planning capability within the EU. Otherwise, to conduct autonomous military operations, Europeans had to systematically resort to national headquarters, five of which were specifically qualified for European operations. In the name of the principle of non-duplication of NATO capabilities in the EU, the British and their allies on this issue within the EU firmly opposed any creation of an operational military planning centre in

[33] Council Declaration in Annex II to the Presidency Conclusions, *Copenhagen European Council*, 12 and 13 December 2002.

[34] Ibid.

[35] S. Biscop, 'The Future of the Transatlantic Alliance. Not without the European Union' (2020) 14(3) *Strategic Studies Quarterly*, pp. 81–94.

Brussels. Conversely, it was in the name of the EU's autonomy vis-à-vis NATO that other Member States, first and foremost France, generally supported by Belgium, Luxembourg and Spain, regularly called for an institutional strengthening of European security and defence instruments. The deadlock was broken following the 2016 referendum on Brexit, and the EU Member States decided to create a Military Planning and Conduct Capability (MPCC) within the European Union Military Staff, although its prerogatives would initially be limited to the EU's non-executive military missions (mainly training missions).[36] As we can see, European defence is being built in relation to NATO, with and against NATO. By enshrining the primacy of NATO in the European treaties, the Member States are demonstrating this fundamental reality of CSDP: its consubstantial relationship with NATO.

The 2000s saw a vast process of enlargement of both NATO and the EU, to the east and south of Europe. But as the scope of their membership remained – and can only be – different, the evolution and intensity of their cooperation is always dependent on the issues linked to the control of each of the organisations' instruments. Operations of the 'Berlin Plus' type give EU Member States access to NATO assets and NATO members access to classified EU information, which became difficult for the Turkish and Cypriot authorities to accept after the EU's enlargement to include Cyprus in 2004. Relations between the EU and NATO were in a sense 'taken hostage'[37] by the Turkish and Cypriot governments, determined to defend what they considered to be their vital national security interests. Turkish representatives have regularly vetoed the sharing of information with the EU and the participation of Cyprus in EU-NATO meetings. Having been excluded by the Turks from the 'Berlin Plus' arrangements, the Cypriots insisted at length that these arrangements should not be mentioned in the joint EU/NATO declaration of 8 July 2016,[38] and blocked Turkish access to the European Defence Agency. The Cypriot authorities refused any formal EU engagement with NATO beyond the limited 'Berlin Plus' arrangement, which in practice had almost

---

[36] Council Decision (EU) 2017/971 of 8 June 2017 determining the modalities for the planning and conduct of non-executive mandate military missions conducted by the European Union in the framework of the CSDP and amending Decision 2010/96/CFSP on an EU military mission to contribute to the training of Somali security forces; Decision 2013/34/CFSP on an EU military mission to contribute to the training of the Malian armed forces (EUTM Mali); and Decision (CFSP) 2016/610 on an EU CSDP military training mission in the Central African Republic (EUTM CAR) (https://eur-lex.europa.eu/legal-content/EN/TXT/?uri=celex%3A32017D0971). On CSDP missions: see the contribution by A. Hamonic in this publication, on Article 43 TEU.

[37] S.-C. Hofmann, 'The politics of overlapping organizations: Hostage-taking, forum-shopping and brokering' (2019) 26(6) *Journal of European Public Policy*, pp. 883–905.

[38] L.-A. Schuette, 'Shaping institutional overlap: NATO's responses to EU security and defence initiatives since 2014' (2023) 23(3) *British Journal of Politics and International Relations*, pp. 423–443.

fallen into disuse.[39] Similar blockages have also been linked to the complex relationship between Turkey and Greece. In 2020, Turkey vetoed information sharing between NATO's Operation Sea Guardian in the Mediterranean and the EU's maritime operation EUNAVFOR Med Irini.[40]

B. ACCESS TO EUROPEAN UNION RESOURCES: PRESERVING NATO'S DECISION-MAKING AUTONOMY AND PRE-EMINENCE IN DEFENCE MATTERS

In a spirit of reciprocity, some senior members of the Atlantic Alliance have proposed that NATO should be able to use the civilian means of collective security with which the EU is much better equipped. This idea of a reverse 'Berlin Plus' (Berlin Plus reverse) was suggested in 2009 by NATO's Director of Policy Planning, Jamie Shea.[41]

Without going quite so far, certain non-EU members of the Atlantic Alliance, first and foremost the United States, have insisted, on behalf of the security community formed by NATO, on access to European investment and research programmes in the military field.[42] The launch of Permanent Structured Cooperation and the creation of a European Defence Fund (EDF)[43] have been welcomed by NATO as a way of sharing the defence budget burden more effectively among the Allies, provided that these instruments are not reserved for EU Member States and that non-EU members of the Atlantic Alliance can also participate. Initially, these new EU financial instruments were perceived as potentially protectionist measures, aimed at strengthening European industry to the detriment of its international partners, in particular its NATO partners,

---

[39] S. Akgul Acikmese and D. Triantaphyllou, 'The NATO-EU-Turkey trilogy: the impact of the Cyprus conundrum' (2012) 12(4) *Southeast European and Black Sea Studies*, pp. 555–573.

[40] N. Gros-Verheyde, 'La Turquie provoque. L'alliance atlantique s'enrhume. La relation OTAN-UE bloquée', *Bruxelles2*, 3 September 2020, https://club.bruxelles2.eu/2020/09/la-turquie-fonce-lalliance-atlantique-senrhume-la-relation-otan-ue-bloquee.

[41] N. Gros-Verheyde, 'Pour Jamie Shea (OTAN), il faut aller vers un accord "Berlin+ Civil" avec l'UE', *Bruxelles2*, 4 October 2009, https://www.bruxelles2.eu/2009/10/pourjamiesheaotanitisnecessarytowardsaberlincivilagreementwiththeEU.

[42] On PSCs: see the contribution by Q. Loïez's contribution to this work on Articles 42(6) and 46 TEU..

[43] Regulation (EU) 2021/697 of the European Parliament and of the Council of 29 April 2021 establishing the European Defence Fund and repealing Regulation (EU) 2018/1092, [2021] *OJ* L170/149. On this regulation: see the contribution by S. Rodrigues in this publication, under cover of Article 173 TFEU.

first and foremost the United States.[44] A solution allowing third countries access to the PESCO was thus found.[45] Moreover, from the point of view of certain NATO officials, 38 of the first 47 PESCO projects were aligned with the priorities of the Atlantic Alliance.[46] For example, in December 2021, Canada, the United States and Norway were associated with the European military mobility project, the aim of which is to facilitate the movement of troops, personnel, equipment and military assets across EU territory.[47] The capabilities developed thanks to this European financial support are nonetheless national resources that states are never obliged to mobilise for the benefit of a particular operation by an international organisation.[48]

Relations between the EU and NATO depend on two political and institutional dynamics (which are in no way specific to the history of relations between the EU and NATO): on the one hand, the multiplication of international organisations, formal and informal, in the same field of action (in this case the field of collective security)[49] and, on the other hand, the temptation for governments to make links between issues, whether they come under bilateral or multilateral negotiations. In the post-Cold War world, states, while being careful not to pool their military resources, have often stimulated the development of collective crisis management instruments and arenas. These organisations, whose constituent units are states but never exactly the same, have overlapping prerogatives and spheres of action. In each of these arenas, state representatives may have an interest in building links between the items on a specific agenda and other more or less related issues. This temptation is particularly strong for states that are members of one organisation but not of the second, and which also benefit, whatever the organisation, from an intergovernmental decision-making system based on unanimity. For example,

---

44 In May 2019, Ellen Lord, US Under Secretary of Defense for Acquisition, and Andrea L. Thompson, Under Secretary of State for International Security, sent a letter to EU High Representative Frederica Mogherini expressing their concerns about EDF and PESCOs: risks of duplication, non-interoperable military systems, dispersion of defence resources and 'unnecessary competition between the EU and NATO' (N. Gros-Verheyde, 'Les États-Unis tancent les Européens sur leurs initiatives de défense. La lettre américaine décryptée', *Bruxelles2*, 14 May 2019, https://club.bruxelles2.eu/2019/05/les-americains-tancent-les-europeens-sur-leurs-initiatives-de-defense-la-lettre-de-ellen-lord-decryptee).

45 Council Decision (CFSP) 2020/1639 of 5 November 2020 establishing the general conditions under which third States may exceptionally be invited to participate in given PESCO projects, [2020] *OJ* L371/3. See the contribution by Q. Loïez in this publication.

46 L.-A. Schuette, 'Shaping institutional overlap: NATO's responses to EU security and defence initiatives since 2014', (2023) 23(3) *British Journal of Politics and International Relations*, p. 433.

47 Council Decisions (CFSP) 2021 748, 749 and 750 of 6 May 2021, [2021] *OJ* L160/106.

48 T. Tardy, 'European defence: What impact for NATO?', *NATO Defense College Policy Brief*, 5, 2018.

49 N.M. Ewers-Peters, 'Positioning member states in EU-NATO security cooperation: towards a typology' (2023) 32(1) *European Security*, pp. 22–41.

in 2021, Turkey was unable to take part in European permanent structured cooperation on military mobility due to a Greek and Cypriot blockade. The following year, the Turkish authorities made their agreement to the enlargement of NATO to include Finland and Sweden conditional, among other things, on support from these states for Turkish participation in European cooperation on military mobility.[50]

Autonomy is an issue of instrument building and access to the resources of collective external security that lies at the heart of relations between the EU, NATO and their Member States. In terms of security and defence, European strategic autonomy is at once a capability issue, a budgetary issue and a market issue. The primacy of the Atlantic Alliance and the security guarantees provided by the United States are strong incentives for the acquisition of American equipment. The industrial dimension of strategic autonomy is also clear from the first institutional uses of this concept.[51]

The more Europeans seek to develop their collective security and defence instruments in an area where NATO's pre-eminence has never been fundamentally called into question, the more acutely the issues of EU/NATO cooperation arise. Dialogue between the two organisations has gradually developed and become more structured. The main leaders of NATO and the EU signed joint declarations in 2016, 2018 and 2023 to announce their intention to strengthen their cooperation. To give substance to what was constitute this new momentum, 74 concrete actions were identified,[52] and their follow-up was entrusted to teams from NATO and the European External Action Service (EEAS). In the years that followed, few of these actions were completed, including cooperation on military mobility, presented as a

50 'Finland and Sweden commit to support the fullest possible involvement of Türkiye and other non-EU Allies in the existing and prospective initiatives of the European Union's Common Security and Defence Policy, including Türkiye's participation in the PESCO Project on Military Mobility' (para. 8(7) of the *Trilateral Memorandum*, concluded between Turkey, Finland and Sweden under the auspices of the NATO Secretary General, 28 June 2022; https://www.nato.int/nato_static_fl2014/assets/pdf/2022/6/pdf/220628-trilat-memo.pdf).

51 'Europe needs a more integrated, sustainable, innovative and competitive defence technological and industrial base (EDTIB) to develop and sustain defence capabilities. This can also enhance its strategic autonomy and its ability to act with partners' (para. 16 of the *Conclusions of the European Council*, Brussels, 19 and 20 December 2013).

52 In the 2016 declaration, seven areas of cooperation were identified: the fight against hybrid threats, operational cooperation, particularly on maritime issues, cybersecurity and cyberdefence, defence capabilities, the defence industry and defence research, exercises and the strengthening of defence and security capabilities (https://www.nato.int/cps/fr/natohq/official_texts_133163.htm). These areas were broken down into 42 proposals in the Council conclusions on the implementation of the EU/NATO Joint Declaration of 6 December 2016, to which were added 32 proposals one year later in the Council conclusions of 5 December 2017.

'flagship area of EU-NATO cooperation'.[53] This issue has long been of concern to NATO officials, who have faced heavy legal constraints on the crossing of borders between European states of military equipment, as well as problems of compatibility between infrastructures.[54] On these issues, the European Union has broader competences, which it mobilises within the framework of a PESCO. However, we can note that a step has been taken in the institutional operationalisation of this partnership, with the joint establishment of a centre of excellence for the fight against hybrid threats (Hybrid CoE), in Helsinki in 2017. The centre is staffed by EU and NATO personnel.[55]

The development of industrial resources and equipment procurement are partly linked to capability programming. The EU and NATO are both forums for coordinating and formulating capability requirements, where objectives and planning are defined: the Capability Development Plan and the NATO Defence Planning Process. This duality of capability commitment processes is once again a challenge for coordination and competitive cooperation between the EU and NATO. EU Member States that are also members of NATO must at least ensure the compatibility of their commitments in these two forums. In practice, the EU Capability Development Mechanism draws on data on capability requirements identified within NATO.[56] Similarly, some of the EDF's priorities are linked to capability requirements identified through the framework of the Coordinated Annual Review on Defence (CARD) and the Capability Development Plan (CDP), which are themselves informed by NATO priorities, thereby helps this European financial instrument to take account of the expectations expressed within the Atlantic Alliance. In 2017, the High Representative for the CFSP, Federica Mogherini, and the Commissioner for the Internal Market and Industry, Elżbieta Bieńkowska, spoke in NATO arenas to communicate about EDF programming.[57]

---

53 *Eighth progress report on the implementation of the common set of proposals endorsed by EU and NATO Councils on 6 December 2016 and 5 December*, presented to the Council on 16 June 2023.

54 D. Fiott, 'Defence industry, industrial cooperation and military mobility', in G. Lindstrom and T. Tardy (eds.), *The EU and NATO. The essential partners*, Paris, European Union Institute for Security Studies, 2019, pp. 44–51.

55 H. Smith, 'Countering hybrid threats', in G. Lindstrom and T. Tardy (eds.), *The EU and NATO. The essential partners,* Paris, European Union Institute for Security Studies, 2019, pp. 15–24.

56 D. Fiott, 'Defence industry, industrial cooperation and military mobility', in G. Lindstrom and T. Tardy (eds.), *The EU and NATO. The essential partners*, Paris, European Union Institute for Security Studies, 2019, p. 45.

57 Ibid., p. 46.

C. THE EUROPEAN UNION STIMULATED BY ITS COMPETITIVE COOPERATIVE RELATIONSHIP WITH NATO

NATO and the EU are often presented as complementary organisations, each with comparative advantages: on the NATO side, large-scale military capabilities adapted to high-intensity conflicts; on the EU side, more modest military capabilities but a wide range of civilian crisis management resources. These two organisations could then benefit from virtuous cooperation, in the form of a division of labour and sharing of tasks: for NATO the 'robust' operations (in the Balkans, Afghanistan and Libya), and for the EU the more modest security operations associated with a wider range of instruments, from the training of police forces and border control to all aspects of development aid. In practice, the distinctions are not so clear-cut. The division of labour is far from being considered necessarily desirable, and the few cases where it does appear to be at work are the result of the vagaries of separate and autonomous decision-making processes, rather than a concerted policy.[58] This vision of complementarity is very often an ex-post rationalisation or a negotiated argument. In the field of collective security, European actors are seeking to develop their military capabilities, while NATO's range of instruments has been extended to civil protection (intervention in the event of natural disasters) and the strengthening of state capabilities (support for security sector reform).

The EU and NATO have gradually established themselves as collective security organisations, with similar mandates in this area, without geographical restrictions or specialisations. Both organisations are also dependent on the military resources of their Member States, even though they have their own headquarters and planning capabilities, which are much greater for NATO. Those involved point to the risk of duplication, while experts emphasise the lack of efficiency and consistency. But this redundancy and competition are also drivers for the development of capabilities and their use. When an organisation intervenes in Europe (Balkans, Ukraine), Africa (Sudan, Somalia, Libya) or Asia (Afghanistan), managers from the other organisation are encouraged to take initiatives to position themselves, capture resources and seize employment opportunities. Even if, in the majority of cases, state military capabilities are not exclusively reserved for one or other of these organisations, NATO and the EU find themselves in de facto competition for these resources. It is not easy for EU Member States to contribute simultaneously to NATO's rapid reaction force and to the European Union's prepositioned battle group. In the 2000s, Europeans took part in the largest military operation ever deployed by NATO – ISAF in Afghanistan – leaving little room for the EU.

---

[58] G. Lindstrom and T. Tardy (eds), *The EU and NATO. The essential partners*, Paris, European Union Institute for Security Studies, 2019.

At the Prague Summit in November 2002, NATO leaders officially announced the creation of a NATO Response Force (NRF), capable of deploying at sea, in the air and on land in a matter of days, and comprising up to 25,000 troops for crisis evacuation operations, counter-terrorism, deterrence and as a first-entry force in a violent theatre. The NRF was declared operational in November 2006 and has been reformed several times since. At the same time, the Europeans decided to create battlegroups, which are much smaller in size than the NRF (1,500 men, rising to 5,000 under the Strategic Compass approved by the Council in May 2022),[59] but with very similar missions. The European Battlegroups reached full operational capability on 1 January 2007. The coexistence of these two forces may raise questions about the choices made by European states in allocating their resources. But these forces have never been used on the ground because these tools are expensive, given that in the NATO framework and in the EU, the bulk of the costs of operations are borne by the contributing state (the 'costs lie where they fall' principle).[60]

Hesitation and reluctance to mobilise the instruments that had just been created did not prevent NATO and the EU from increasing their activities in the international field of collective security, mounting numerous *ad hoc* operations, often in the same theatres. When these military operations were launched, cooperation between the EU and NATO remained relatively modest, and coordination on the ground has been more or less complicated. For these operations, it was more a form of competition that stimulated initiatives. Through each operation, the EU and NATO have asserted and displayed their capacity to intervene militarily, more or less far from the territory of their Member States. Between 2007 and 2014, the EU and NATO conducted police training operations in Afghanistan: EUPOL Afghanistan[61] and *NATO* Training Mission in Afghanistan (NTM-A).[62] Coordination was difficult, classified information did not circulate, and the Turkish authorities refused the Europeans (who depended on NATO for protection on the ground in Afghanistan) access to the area for which they were responsible. There was no real division of labour, and the two organisations were competing for the resources provided by their joint member states.[63] The EU and NATO

---

59 Council document 7371/22 of 4 May 2022,'A strategic compass on security and defence: For a European Union that protects its citizens, values and interests and contributes to international peace and security'.

60 Y. Buchet de Neuilly, 'The European Union and collective security. Usages, activation et canalisation des ressources militaires expéditionnaires', in A. Bazin and C. Tenenbaum (eds.), *L'Union européenne et la paix*, Paris, Presses de Sciences Po, 2017, pp. 63–86.

61 Council Joint Action 2007/369/CFSP of 30 May 2007 on establishment of the European Union Police Mission in Afghanistan (EUPOL AFGHANISTAN), [2007] *OJ* L139/33.

62 https://www.nato.int/cps/en/natolive/news_52802.htm.

63 T. Aghniashvili, 'Towards More Effective Cooperation? The Role of States in Shaping NATO-EU Interaction and Cooperation' (2016) 15(4) *Connections*, pp. 67–90.

also engaged in lengthy maritime security and counter-piracy operations in the same area, the Gulf of Aden, off the coast of Somalia, under the names EU NAVFOR Atalanta[64] and NATO Operation Ocean Shield. For the EU, this was the first naval military operation with an executive mandate. It was an opportunity to broaden the range of CSDP missions and demonstrate a new European military capability. There was no joint planning or formal division of labour between the EU and NATO, although cooperation and coordination on the ground were considered to be largely satisfactory.[65] Similarly, in the Mediterranean, cooperation between Operation EUNAVFOR MED Irini[66] and NATO's Operation Sea Guardian remained complicated.[67] The competitive relationship between the EU and NATO is reflected in a form of emulation that encourages the leaders of these organisations to take relatively similar initiatives in the same theatres of external operations.

The institutional isomorphy, partly fed by this competitive dynamic, is also expressed in the creation of other European instruments. On 31 May 2022, the European Defence Agency launched its new Hub for EU Defence Innovation (HEDI), which echoes the Defence Innovation Accelerator for the North Atlantic (DIANA), the creation of which was decided at the Brussels summit in 2021. NATO's pre-eminence and Europe's alignment with Atlantic standards can also be seen in the definition, in November 2003, of the legal framework for the status of civilian and military personnel deployed by a Member State on the soil of another Member State (EU Status of Forces Agreement – EU SOFA),[68] which is inspired by the Agreement between the States Parties to the North Atlantic Treaty on the Status of their Forces (NATO Status of Forces Agreement) adopted in 1951,[69] and in the regulation establishing the European

---

64 Council Joint Action 2008/851/CFSP of 10 November 2008 on a European Union military operation to contribute to the deterrence, prevention and repression of acts of piracy and armed robbery off the Somali coast, [2008] *OJ* L301/33.

65 C. Gebhard and S.-J. Smith, 'The two faces of EU-NATO cooperation: Counter-piracy operations off the Somali coast' (2015) 50(1) *Cooperation and Conflict*, pp. 107–127. The authors also point to the practical know-how of sailors who have long been used to cooperating with the navies of other states in multinational operations.

66 Council Decision (CFSP) 2020/472 of 31 March 2020 on a European Union military operation in the Mediterranean (EUNAVFOR MED IRINI), [2020] *OJ* L101/4.

67 N. Gros-Verheyde, 'La coopération UE-OTAN progresse. C'est officiel', *Bruxelles2*, https://club.bruxelles2.eu/2021/06/la-cooperation-ue-otan-progresse-cest-officiel.

68 Agreement between the Member States of the European Union concerning the status of military and civilian staff seconded to the institutions of the European Union, of the headquarters and forces which may be made available to the European Union in the context of the preparation and execution of the tasks referred to in Article 17(2) of the Treaty on European Union, including exercises, and of the military and civilian staff of the Member States put at the disposal of the European Union to act in this context (EU SOFA), [2003] *OJ* C321/6.

69 A. Sari, 'The European Union Status of Force Agreement (EU SOFA)' (2009) 13(3) *Journal of Conflict & Security Law*, pp. 353–391.

Defence Industry Programme (EDIP), which explicitly mentions the need for production capabilities to comply with NATO standards.[70]

CONCLUSION

In the military areas of collective security and defence, states have been careful not to transfer any of their sovereignty to international organisations. NATO, like the EU, remains dependent on negotiations and decisions by governments, on a case-by-case basis, to commit military resources and cooperate on intelligence matters. In this context, marked by the domination of national political authorities, international collective security organisations are necessarily in competition to capture coercive State resources, and their cooperation remains limited. This is all the more the case as states do not hesitate to bypass them or dilute them in ad hoc operations, coalitions of the willing with variable geometry and rules that are renegotiated each time.

In the literature and commentary, it is often said that both the European Union and NATO lack a common strategic vision. The EU has indeed adopted several global strategies (in 2003 and 2016), as well as a strategic compass in 2022. But is it necessary for States to share the same vision and common objectives in order to equip themselves with a genuine common capability? Given the historical processes of political integration of territories (today essentially in the form of the State), it may be seriously doubted. The limits of the European Union are the same as those of NATO: the primacy of states. A common vision is a product of integration, not a prerequisite.

[70] Regulation (EU) 2025/2643 of the European Parliament and of the Council of 16 December 2025 establishing the European Defence Industry Programme and a framework of measures to ensure the timely availability and supply of defence products ('EDIP Regulation') [2025] *OJ* L2025/2643, especially Articles 22(2) and 33.

ARTICLE 42(7)(1) TEU: THE MUTUAL DEFENCE CLAUSE

Jean-Christophe Martin
Professor of public law, Université Côte d'Azur, Laboratoire de droit international et européen (LADIE, UPR 7414), UNESCO Chair in Peace and Development through Law

Article 42(7)(1) TEU

7. If a Member State is the victim of armed aggression on its territory, the other Member States shall have towards it an obligation of aid and assistance by all the means in their power, in accordance with Article 51 of the United Nations Charter. This shall not prejudice the specific character of the security and defence policy of certain Member States.

Since the revision carried out by the Treaty of Lisbon,[1] the Treaty on European Union (TEU) has contained a clause known as the 'mutual defence' or 'mutual assistance' clause,[2] inserted in the last paragraph (7) of Article 42 of the TEU, of which only paragraph 1 is commented on here (the second paragraph, which concerns the relationship with the North Atlantic Treaty Organisation (NATO), is commented on elsewhere).[3]

The inclusion of this clause by the Treaty of Lisbon completes the arrangements for implementing the Common Security and Defence Policy

[1] Article 42(7) of the Treaty of Lisbon reproduces word for word Article I-41 ('Specific provisions on the common security and defence policy')(7) of the Treaty establishing a Constitution for Europe (2005).

[2] Neither of these terms is used in the EU Treaty. The EUR-Lex glossary uses the term 'European defence clause', which is used, for example, in the 'Results of the Council meeting' (3426th Council meeting – Foreign Affairs, 16 and 17 November 2015, 14120/15: https://data.consilium.europa.eu/doc/document/ST-14120-2015-INIT/fr/pdf), and by the European Parliament (e.g. 'European Parliament resolution of 21 January 2016 on the mutual defence clause (Article 42(7) of the Treaty on European Union'), 2015/3034(RSP), [2018] *OJ* C11/89). We will therefore use this formula in this commentary.

[3] See the commentary by Y. Buchet de Neuilly in this publication.

(CSDP) and constitutes a significant step forward for 'European defence' within the Union framework. Although it is often pointed out that the Treaty of Lisbon has introduced an innovation,[4] as no such clause existed in the 'Community' structure prior to this Reform Treaty, it should be remembered that some Member States were already bound by a collective self-defence clause. This is the case, on the one hand, under the Washington Treaty creating the North Atlantic Treaty Organisation, Article 5 of which – only activated once, in response to the attacks in the United States on 11 September 2001 – reads as follows:

> The Parties agree that an armed attack against one or more of them in Europe or North America shall be considered an attack against them all and consequently they agree that, if such an armed attack occurs, each of them, in exercise of the right of individual or collective self-defence recognized by Article 51 of the Charter of the United Nations, will assist the Party or Parties so attacked by taking forthwith, individually and in concert with the other Parties, such action as it deems necessary, including the use of armed force, to restore and maintain the security of the North Atlantic area.

This is the case, on the other hand, in the context of the Treaty of Economic, Social and Cultural Collaboration and Collective Self-Defence (known as the 'Brussels Treaty'), signed in Brussels on 17 March 1948 by five States: Belgium, France, Luxembourg, the Netherlands and the United Kingdom. Although this treaty was not limited to collective defence issues, its main feature was a commitment by the parties to defend each other if one of them fell victim to armed attack in Europe. This treaty, which was not part of the Community construction process, has over time been incorporated into EU law.[5] The 1948 Brussels Treaty was amended by the Treaty of Paris of 23 October 1954, concluded by the five States as well as Italy and the Federal Republic of Germany (as a result of the failure of the European Defence Community), and establishing the Western European Union (WEU) as a new international organisation bringing together ten European States: Belgium, France, Luxembourg, Netherlands, Germany, Portugal, Greece, Spain, Italy and the

4 See, for example, S.B.H. Faure, 'La relance de la défense européenne: par les États, pour les États', *Le Rubicon*, 29 April 2022, https://lerubicon.org/la-relance-de-la-defense-europeenne-par-les-etats-pour-les-etats.

5 The 1992 Treaty on European Union (of Maastricht) specifies that the WEU 'shall be an integral part of the development of the European Union': Art. J.4(2): 'The Union requests the Western European Union (WEU), which is an integral part of the development of the Union, to elaborate and implement decisions and actions of the Union which have defence implications. The Council shall, in agreement with the institutions of the WEU, adopt the necessary practical arrangements'.

United Kingdom. The text of the mutual defence clause (now Article V of the modified Brussels Treaty) was retained:[6]

> If any of the High Contracting Parties should be the object of an armed attack in Europe, the other High Contracting Parties will, in accordance with the provisions of Article 51 of the Charter of the United Nations, afford the Party so attacked all the military and other aid and assistance in their power.

It should be remembered that the WEU was dissolved when the EU Member States decided that all the functions performed by the WEU would henceforth be transferred to the EU.[7] With the entry into force of the Treaty of Lisbon in December 2009, the role of this organisation was fully taken over by the European Union, with the inclusion of the mutual defence clause into the TEU. Thus, by inserting Article 42(7) into the TEU, the Treaty of Lisbon imported into EU law the commitment that some EU Member States had already made by concluding a treaty linked to EU law. As Fabien Terpan puts it, we have witnessed 'a normative transfer from WEU law to EU law'.[8] This is a significant step forward, as it is the first mutual defence clause binding all EU Member States to each other,[9] autonomously from the North Atlantic Treaty.[10] Symbolically important, the clause enables progress to be made towards the objective set out in Article 42(2) of the TEU of common defence and solidarity between Member States in this area.[11]

---

6 This was also the case for Article V, now Article VI, which supplemented the defence clause with details of the legal framework established by the United Nations Charter and the prerogatives of the Security Council.

7 At the end of 2000, the EU took over WEU's crisis prevention and management functions. In November 2010, its Military Staff was disbanded and its operational dimension came to an end. On 31 March 2011, the WEU Member States decided to terminate the organisation, which was dissolved at the end of June 2011.

8 F. Terpan,'Le traité de Lisbonne a-t-il rendu la solidarité possible dans le domaine de la sécurité et de la défense', in E Brosset, R. Mehdi and N. Rubio (eds.), *Solidarité et droit de l'Union européenne. Un principe à l'épreuve*, Confluence des droits, Aix-en-Provence, DICE éditions, 2021, p. 158. Author's translation.

9 F.-X. Priollaud and D. Siritzky, *Le traité de Lisbonne. Texte et commentaire article par article des nouveaux traités européens*, Paris, La Documentation française, 2008, p. 128.

10 According to L. Balmond, '[t]he inclusion of a collective defence mechanism in the text was essential both to complete the Common Security and Defence Policy and to ensure that it did not appear to be purely subsidiary to the Atlantic Alliance, particularly with regard to the Central European countries that joined NATO before joining the Union': 'La défense dans la Constitution européenne', *Perspectives internationales et européennes*, 2006/2. Author's translation.

11 The new security and defence strategy adopted in 2022 ('A strategic compass for security and defence – For a European Union that protects its citizens, values and interests and contributes to international peace and security', doc. 7371/22, 22 March 2022) states: 'Solidarity between Member States is expressed in Article 42(7) of the Treaty on European Union'.

However, this normative transfer is not 'under constant law', as variations have been introduced into the wording. In the French version, for example, whereas the former clause referred to an 'armed attack in Europe' ('*agression armée en Europe*') against one of the States Parties, Article 42(7), refers to an 'armed aggression on its territory' ('*agression armée sur son territoire*'). Similarly, while the wording 'aid and assistance by all the means in their power' is included, the reference to 'military and other' is deleted. There is also a change in the choice of verb and conjugation tense. We also notice a notable change in the English version, where the phrase 'armed attack' is replaced by 'armed aggression'. These terminological choices and the issues they raise call for a detailed analysis of the mutual defence clause, the commentary of which is illuminated by its invocation – the sole occasion to date – by France in the aftermath of the attacks in Paris (Bataclan and Stade de France) on 13 November 2015 and, consequently, how aid and assistance were requested and provided. While the choice made by France to invoke the mutual defence clause rather than the solidarity clause (Article 222 of the Treaty on the Functioning of the European Union (TFEU))[12] may have come as a surprise, it is in itself instructive in terms of the meaning given to the clause and enabled France to set a precedent and thus shape the framework for its implementation.

This chapter looks at the activation of the clause (Section I) and then the aid and assistance commitment and its implementation (Section II).

I. ACTIVATION OF THE MUTUAL DEFENCE CLAUSE

Based on the 'inherent right of self-defence', which is well established in international law (Article 51 of the Charter of the United Nations), Article 42(7) makes the commitment of aid and assistance conditional on the occurrence of armed aggression against a Member State. Although included in a treaty (the TEU) which also sets out very detailed and comprehensive procedures within the European Union, this provision is brief and contains no details as to how the clause is to be invoked.

A. ARMED ATTACK AGAINST A MEMBER STATE

Article 42(7) may be activated '[i]f a Member State is the victim of armed aggression on its territory'. This wording appears rather narrow in that it limits the invocation of the clause to a military operation on the territory of a Member State. Of course, this wording covers the land, sea and air components of the

12 See the commentary by F. Terpan in this publication.

State's territory, including outside Europe,[13] but it excludes attacks against State targets outside its territory, carried out in international spaces, such as the high seas (e.g. attacks against warships cruising on the high seas) or in outer space (attack against a military space object in orbit). States could undoubtedly interpret the provision flexibly if an attack carried out in such international space against one or more craft has the characteristics (particularly in terms of the gravity threshold) of an armed attack.[14] It should also be noted that while the French version consistently uses the concept of '*aggression armée*',[15] which is also the concept used in the French version of Article 51 of the Charter of the United Nations, this is not the case in the English version. The English version of Article 42(7) uses the term 'armed aggression', but this differs from Article 51 of the Charter, which uses the term 'armed attack' (used also in both Article 5 of the Brussels Treaty on the WEU and Article 5 of the North Atlantic Treaty). What legal consequences should be drawn from this variation in terminology in the English version of the clause? The question arises insofar as, in English, the notion of 'armed aggression' is considered by some to be broader than that of 'armed attack'; its use would then have the consequence of lowering the threshold for triggering the mutual defence clause.[16]

On the one hand, this interpretation is based on a semantic variation which is specific to the English language, and the scope of which is moreover not certain. In particular, it appears that the text of the mutual defence clause was prepared in French, so the English version of the clause is the result of a literal translation from the French version. It is therefore difficult to see 'a deliberate attempt to depart from the authentic English wording of the Modified Brussels

---

13 The wording is thus broader than that of Article 5 of the Brussels Treaty on WEU (which refers to'armed aggression in Europe') and Article 5 of the North Atlantic Treaty (which refers to an attack'occurring in Europe or North America'). See J. Auvret-Finck, commentary to Article I-41, in L. Burgorgue-Larsen, A. Levade and F. Picod (eds.), *Traité établissant une Constitution pour l'Europe. Commentaire article par article*, t. 1, Brussels, Bruylant, 2007, pp. 541–542.

14 Under international law, armed aggression is a term reserved for'the most serious forms of the use of force': International Court of Justice (ICJ), 27 June 1986, *Military and Paramilitary Activities in and against Nicaragua (Nicaragua v. United States), ICJ Reports* 1986, p. 101, para. 191.

15 On the contrary, the French version of Article 5 of the North Atlantic Treaty uses the concept of an armed attack, in a translation of the English version that does not correspond to the French text of Article 51 of the United Nations Charter.

16 H. Boddens Hosang and P. Ducheine, 'Implementing Article 42.7 of the Treaty on European Union: Legal Foundations for Mutual Defence in the Face of Modern Threats', *Amsterdam Law School Research Paper*, no. 71, 2020, https://ssrn.com/abstract=3748392. See also S. Clapp and A. Verhelst, 'A comparative analysis of Article 5 Washington Treaty (NATO) and Article 42(7) TEU (EU)', *At a glance*, December 2022, European Parliament Research Service, PE 739.250, p. 1, https://www.europarl.europa.eu/RegData/etudes/ATAG/2022/739250/EPRS_ATA(2022)739250_EN.pdf.

Treaty',[17] which used the concept of 'armed attack'. The importance of this variation in terminology is therefore slight, given the process of drafting the clause, although it cannot be ruled out entirely that it was the result of a deliberate choice by the States during the subsequent stages of negotiation and adoption. Furthermore, the reference in Article 42(7) TEU to Article 51 of the Charter of the United Nations ('in accordance with Article 51 of the Charter of the United Nations') is a reminder that the commitment entered into must be implemented in full compliance with applicable international law (see below). In any event, military action under Article 42(7) TEU must comply with Article 51 of the Charter. It is therefore unconvincing to argue that, in the EU context, Member States have chosen to lower the threshold for triggering self-defence and, consequently, the use of armed force. On the other hand, it is possible to consider that the mutual defence clause in Article 42(7) could indiscriminately encompass self-defence (with reference to Article 51): i.e. the commitment to defend each other by military means and the use of armed force in the face of armed aggression, as part of a broader obligation of assistance in the face of other attacks which do not reach the threshold of armed attack but which would still require assistance by means other than military ones.

This interpretation can be advanced by taking into account another characteristic element of Article 42(7): the desire to extend the commitment by lowering the threshold, through the use of the concept of 'armed aggression' in the English version, would be corroborated by the choice to delete the express reference to military means (which appeared in Article 5 of the Brussels Treaty on the WEU – see below). In short, the aim would be to broaden the scope of the obligation to provide aid and assistance, by lowering the threshold for its invocability and extending it to less serious forms of use of force,[18] to which the other Member States would be called upon to respond by non-military means,[19] outside the narrow scope of Article 51 of the Charter. The contemporary threats of cyber attacks[20] or of hybrid attacks by non-State actors

---

17 A. Sari, 'The Mutual Assistance Clauses of the North Atlantic and EU Treaties: The Challenge of Hybrid Threats' (2019) 10 *Harvard National Security Journal*, p. 418.

18 In the resolution of 22 November 2012 on the European Union's mutual defence and solidarity clauses: Political and Operational Dimensions, the European Parliament takes the view that 'even non-armed attacks, for instance cyberattacks against critical infrastructure, that are launched with the aim of causing severe damage and disruption to a Member State and are identified as coming from an external entity could qualify for being covered by the clause, if the Member State's security is significantly threatened by its consequences, while fully respecting the principle of proportionality' (para. 13, [2015] *OJ* C419/138).

19 A. Sari, 'The Mutual Assistance Clauses of the North Atlantic and EU Treaties: The Challenge of Hybrid Threats', (2019) 10 *Harvard National Security Journal*, p. 417.

20 See also H. Boddens Hosang and P. Ducheine, 'Implementing Article 42(7) of the Treaty on European Union – Legal Foundations for Mutual Defence in the Face of Modern Threats', in *The European Union's Contribution to International Peace and Security, Liber Amicorum in*

illustrate the issues surrounding the interpretation of the clause in this sense. Two interpretations are therefore *a priori* possible, without it being established that the variation between the French and English versions of the text reflects the desire of the EU Member States to move away from the legal regime of self-defence set out in Article 51 of the Charter of the United Nations.

Another important aspect also concerns the controversial definition of the concept of armed aggression. The scope attributed to this notion depends on the choice made between the definition classically limited to an inter-State dimension, and a definition extended to attacks committed by non-State actors, in particular terrorist attacks organised from the territory of a Non-member State. Without reopening the extensive debate on the state of international law in this area (informed by the case law of the International Court of Justice,[21] as well as recent State practices and the reactions they have provoked), it should be emphasised that France's activation of the clause in 2015 made it possible to settle the question with regard to Article 42(7).[22] The interpretation then given unanimously by the EU Member States was clear: the 13 November 2015 terrorist attacks in Paris and Saint-Denis (which claimed 544 victims, 131 dead and 413 injured), committed by non-State actors (the attack had been claimed by the ISIL/Daesh and certainly not meeting the criteria for attribution to a State),[23] could be considered an armed aggression[24] within the meaning of Article 42(7), allowing the mutual defence clause to be invoked. The European External Action Service (EEAS) states quite clearly in its explanatory note on

honour of Gert-Jan van Hegelsom, Leiden, Brill-Nijhoff, 2023, p. 215. It should be noted that, in the 'Strategic Compass' ('A Strategic Compass for Security and Defence – For a European Union that protects its citizens, values and interests and contributes to international peace and security', doc. 7371/22, 22 March 2022), the Member States announced that they would continue 'to conduct regular exercises to further strengthen our mutual assistance in case of an armed aggression, in accordance with Article 42(7) of the Treaty on European Union. This will comprise regular cyber exercises starting from 2022'. These cyber attacks therefore clearly fall within the scope of the mutual defence clause of EU Member States.

21 ICJ, 27 June 1986, *Military and Paramilitary Activities in and against Nicaragua (Nicaragua v. United States of America), ICJ Reports*, 1986, p. 103, para. 195; *Legal Consequences of the Construction of a Wall in the Occupied Palestinian Territory*, Advisory Opinion of 9 July 2004, *ICJ Reports*, 2004, p. 194, para. 139; *ICJ, 19 December 2005, Armed Activities on the Territory of the Congo (DRC v. Uganda), ICJ Reports*, 2005, pp. 222–223, paras. 146–147.

22 H. Boddens Hosang and P. Ducheine, 'Implementing Article 42(7) of the Treaty on European Union – Legal Foundations for Mutual Defence in the Face of Modern Threats', in *The European Union's Contribution to International Peace and Security, Liber Amicorum in honour of Gert-Jan van Hegelsom*, Leiden, Brill-Nijhoff, 2023, p. 215.

23 Draft articles of the International Law Commission on the responsibility of States for internationally wrongful acts, adopted on second reading in 2001, annexed to United Nations General Assembly resolution 56/83, Art. 8 ('Conduct directed or controlled by a State').

24 The classification as armed attack, also submitted by France to the Security Council (doc. S/PV.7565, 20 November 2015), did not give rise to any objections. For a critical analysis of this qualification, see F. Latty, 'Le brouillage des repères du *jus contra bellum*. À propos de l'usage de la force par la France contre Daech', *RGDIP*, 2016/1, pp. 23 and 26.

Article 42(7): 'The attack must originate from abroad and its scope covers attacks by state and non-state actors'.[25]

This leads us to add that, in order to fall within the scope of Article 42(7) and constitute armed aggression, an attack must certainly come from outside the European Union. With regard to the attack of 13 November 2015, President Hollande was careful to point out that '[t]he acts of war on Friday were decided and planned in Syria', after emphasising that they 'were carried out by a jihadist army, the Daesh group', in order to justify the activation of the mutual defence clause, announced in his speech to the French Parliament meeting in Congress on 16 November 2015.[26]

B. THE ACTIVATION PROCEDURE

Article 42(7) contains no procedural indication as to the invocation of the mutual defence clause, unlike the solidarity clause, defined by Article 222 TFEU to react to a terrorist attack or a natural or man-made disaster.[27] The two clauses are very different in scope, with the mutual defence clause being essentially based on an inter-State logic deployed bilaterally, as illustrated by France's invocation of it in November 2015. In his statement to the French Parliament in Congress on 16 November 2015, President Holland said: 'I have asked the Minister of Defence to refer the matter to his European counterparts tomorrow under Article 42(7) of the EU Treaty, which states that when a State is attacked, all Member States must show solidarity'.[28] The following day, the mutual defence clause was formally activated at the Foreign Affairs Council of the European Union (the 'Council'), meeting at the level of defence ministers. All EU Member States agreed to this activation. The minutes of the Council meeting state that 'Ministers expressed their unanimous and full support for France and their readiness to provide all the necessary aid and assistance' and that, according to the High Representative of the Union for Foreign Affairs

---

25 EEAS, 'Article 42(7) TEU – The EU's mutual assistance clause', October 2022, https://www.eeas.europa.eu/sites/default/files/documents/Article%2042%287%29%20TEU%20-The%20EU%27s%20mutual%20assistance%20clause.pdf.

26 Statement by the President of the Republic to Parliament in Congress, 16 November 2015, full transcript: https://www.assemblee-nationale.fr/14/cri/congres/20154001.asp. Author's translation.

27 In addition to the procedural indications it contains, Article 222 TFEU provides that the arrangements for its implementation by the Union shall be defined by a decision adopted by the Council. See the Council Decision of 24 June 2014 on the arrangements for implementation by the Union of the solidarity clause (2014/415/EU, [2014] *OJ* L192/53). See the commentary by F. Terpan in this publication.

28 Statement by the President of the Republic before Parliament in Congress, 16 November 2015, cited above.

and Security Policy, '[n]o formal decision or conclusion by the Council will be required to implement Article 42(7)'.[29]

The situation is thus rather confused and it is difficult to draw clear conclusions as to the procedure for invoking Article 42(7). Basically, 'the invocation by France of the mutual assistance clause in the formal setting of the Council has been considered purely incidental'.[30] The meeting of the Defence Ministers in the Foreign Affairs Council had in fact already been scheduled, and the item entitled 'mutual defence clause (Article 42(7) TEU)' was added to the list of issues to be discussed. This meeting – in a singular configuration of the Council of defence ministers – was an opportunity for the French minister to invoke the clause before all his counterparts gathered together, and no decision was actually adopted by the Council. This confirms that a Council decision is not required for the clause to be activated (which Article 42(7) does not provide for). However, it cannot be argued that France's choice to invoke the clause in the Council does not have a certain, at least symbolic, significance: 'Nevertheless, choosing the Council as the venue can be interpreted as having political, institutional and practical implications, in particular expressing solidarity and readiness to provide assistance according to the EU Treaties'.[31] In the joint press conference held by French Defence Minister Jean-Yves Le Drian and High Representative Federica Mogherini on 17 November 2015, the invocation of Article 42(7) was presented as a 'political act'.[32] But a certain vagueness was maintained insofar as it was also reported that, pragmatically, 'France presented its operational requests to the ambassadors in the Political and Security Committee (PSC) on 24 November 2015'.[33] However, bilateral negotiations were indeed initiated by France on the concrete implementation of the aid and assistance commitment by the other Member States.

It should be added that, in activating the mutual defence clause, EU Member States are also required to comply with the rules of international law governing the use of force in self-defence. Article 42(7) specifies that the commitment to

---

29 Results of the Council meeting: 3426th Council meeting – Foreign Affairs, 16 and 17 November 2015, 14120/15, https://data.consilium.europa.eu/doc/document/ST-14120-2015-INIT/en/pdf.

30 C.-C. Cîrlig, 'The EU's mutual assistance clause first ever activation of Article 42(7) TEU', *Briefing*, November 2015, European Parliament Research Service, PE 572.799, https://www.europarl.europa.eu/RegData/etudes/BRIE/2015/572799/EPRS_BRI(2015)572799_EN.pdf.

31 Ibid.

32 Quoted by P. Chatelet, 'La mise à l'épreuve de l'Union européenne par le terrorisme – Approche française', *Revue de l'Union européenne*, 2016, no. 599, p. 360.

33 The information is attributed to *Europe Defence and Diplomacy*, No. 845, quoted in S.E. Anghel and C.-C. Cîrlig, 'Activation of Article 42(7) TEU: France's request for assistance and Member States' responses', *Briefing*, December 2015, European Parliament Research Service, PE 573.883, https://www.europarl.europa.eu/RegData/etudes/BRIE/2015/573883/EPRS_BRI%282015%29573883_EN.pdf.

aid and assistance must be implemented 'in accordance with Article 51 of the Charter of the United Nations', which deals with the 'inherent right of self-defence' and the conditions under which it may be exercised. While the absence of such a reference would in no way reduce the obligation of EU Member States to comply with this provision, the aim is to clearly include the mutual defence clause in the global legal framework, and to reaffirm its primacy. The reaction in self-defence following the invocation of Article 42(7) must therefore comply with the conditions and limits set out in this provision. In particular, States must 'immediately' bring measures taken in the exercise of the right of self-defence to the attention of the United Nations Security Council (the 'Security Council'). On 20 November 2015, France's representative told the Security Council: 'As I said, the events of 13 November were an armed aggression against France. Our military action, of which we informed the Security Council from the outset and which was justified as legitimate collective self-defence, can now also be characterized as individual self-defence, in accordance with Article 51 of the Charter of the United Nations. [...] In that context, we appeal to Europe. My country has sought and obtained this week from the European Union the first activation in its history of the mutual solidarity clause. [...] We expect Europe to actively engage with us on behalf of our shared security and that of the neighboring countries of Syria'.[34] Moreover, under the terms of Article 51 of the Charter, the mutual defence clause can only be invoked to conduct armed operations 'until the Security Council has taken the measures necessary to maintain international peace and security', at which point the right of self-defence comes to an end. Despite this, the question of the time limit for activating the clause and the procedure for deactivating it is an important matter,[35] particularly for reactionary measures which, by their very nature (measures which would not be contrary to any rule of international law), do not need to be based on self-defence and Article 51 of the Charter.

Of course, even though Article 42(7) refers only to Article 51, Member States are obliged to comply with all the international rules applicable to self-defence. This includes the customary rules that are well established in international case

[34] UN, doc. S/PV.7565, 20 November 2015, pp. 2-3. At this session, the Security Council unanimously adopted resolution 2249 (2015), on a proposal from France, in which it '[c]alls upon Member States that have the capacity to do so to take all necessary measures, in compliance with international law, in particular with the United Nations Charter, [...] on the territory under the control of ISIL also known as Da'esh, in Syria and Iraq, to redouble and coordinate their efforts to prevent and suppress terrorist acts committed specifically by ISIL also known as Da'esh as well as ANF, and all other individuals, groups, undertakings, and entities associated with Al Qaeda' (5).

[35] S.E. Anghel and I.C. Bacian, 'Implemention of the Lisbon Treaty provisions on the Common Security and Defence Policy (CSDP)', *Briefing*, February 2016, European Parliament Research Service, PE 573.285, p. 2, https://www.europarl.europa.eu/RegData/etudes/BRIE/2016/573285/EPRS_BRI(2016)573285_EN.pdf.

law, under which the principles of necessity and proportionality[36] govern the implementation of aid and assistance to the attacked State.

II. THE COMMITMENT TO AID AND ASSISTANCE

To analyse the mutual defence clause we need to look at both the nature and the scope of the commitment made by each EU Member State to the others. This entails asking the questions of whether it is a legal obligation and what it entails; and how it is implemented.

A. THE NATURE OF THE COMMITMENT: 'THE OTHER MEMBER STATES SHALL HAVE [...] AN OBLIGATION'

In ratifying the Treaty of Lisbon, each EU Member State undertook to provide aid and assistance to any other Member State that was the victim of armed aggression. Article 47(2) specifically notes that Member States 'shall have' an 'obligation of aid and assistance by all the means in their power'. The wording used is binding and emphasises the immediacy and force of the obligation.[37] The obligation to provide assistance in the event of armed aggression thus, at first sight, concerns all Member States equally. In the resolution of 22 November 2012 on 'EU mutual defence and solidarity clauses: political and operational dimensions', the European Parliament '[r]eminds the Member States of their unequivocal obligation of aid and assistance by all the means in their power if a Member State is the victim of armed aggression on its territory.[38] The EEAS also states in its introductory note to Article 42(7): 'Once activated it creates a legally binding obligation on all Member States to provide assistance to the attacked Member State'.[39] Admittedly, this interpretation by the EU institutions

---

36 See in particular. ICJ, 27 June 1986, *Military and Paramilitary Activities in and against Nicaragua (Nicaragua v. United States of America)*, *ICJ Reports*, 1986, p. 94, para. 176; *Legality of the Threat or Use of Nuclear Weapons*, Advisory Opinion of 8 July 1996, *ICJ Reports*, 1996, p. 245, para. 41. Generally, see. O. Corten, *Le droit contre la guerre*, 3rd ed., Paris, Pedone, 2020, pp. 747–776.

37 F. Gouttefarde, 'L'invocation de l'article 42 § 7 TUE: la solidarité militaire européenne contre le terrorisme', *Revue Défense Nationale*, 2016/3, no. 788, p. 74. According to J. Auvret-Finck, 'the obligation incumbent on States is strict [...] and diversified from the point of view of the modalities of its implementation (support, punctual or prolonged, direct or indirect, by diplomatic means, economic or financial countermeasures, the use of force...)', commentary to Article I-41, in L. Burgorgue-Larsen, A. Levade and F. Picod (eds.), *Traité établissant une Constitution pour l'Europe. Commentaire article par article*, t. 1, Brussels, Bruylant, 2007, p. 542. Author's translation.

38 Para. 11, [2015] *OJ* C419/138.

39 EEAS, 'Article 42(7) TEU – The EU's mutual assistance clause', October 2022.

and bodies is not in itself binding on the Member States and is not necessarily a faithful expression of the interpretation of the Member States themselves. Some authors therefore consider that the mutual assistance clause does not constitute an obligation. For Fabien Terpan, for example, 'its activation does not create precise and automatic obligations for the Member States. They remain free to choose the means of their assistance, if they choose to provide it'.[40] The very wording of the first subparagraph of Article 42(7) does not indicate that each State may decide to provide assistance or refuse to do so. Instead, the wording chosen ('shall') indicates that the initiative lies with the State that is the victim of the armed attack. Thus, the obligation to provide aid and assistance would be limited to those Member States to which the victim State so requests, on a bilateral basis. This reading is also consistent with the phrase 'by all means within their power', which establishes a measure for the obligation to provide assistance, with regard to the means available to each Member State (see below). This would appear to be quite different, for example, from the provisions of Article 5 of the North Atlantic Treaty, which states that each State 'will assist the Party or Parties so attacked by taking forthwith, individually and in concert with the other Parties, such action as it deems necessary'. Here, it is clear that each State is free to determine the measures it deems necessary to take, which it will implement individually.

Like other collective self-defence clauses, the mutual defence clause between EU Member States probably does not call for an overly rigorous legal approach. It is unlikely that the clause will be the subject of a crystallised dispute between a Member State that has been the object of armed aggression on its territory and one or more other Member States that have not (or not sufficiently) provided the assistance required, with the former then invoking the liability of the latter(s) for failure to fulfil the obligation to provide aid and assistance under Article 42(7) TEU.

Two comments may be made in this regard. Firstly, Article 42(7) states that '[t]his shall not prejudice the specific character of the security and defence policy of certain Member States'. This is intended, in particular, to take account of the historical military neutrality of several Member States.[41] Thus, military means cannot be considered, for these States, as 'means within their power'. The addition of this sentence is intended to safeguard the recognised historical position of certain States and, in so doing, tends to confirm the binding nature of the commitment made in the mutual defence clause.

---

40 Ibid., p. 161.

41 Austria, Ireland, as well as Finland and Sweden, whose position has however evolved following Russia's armed aggression against Ukraine since February 2022. Finland and Sweden renounced their neutrality by becoming members of NATO on 4 April 2023 and 7 March 2024 respectively.

On the other hand, the compulsory nature of a Member State's request for aid raises questions about the legal force of that State's characterisation of its situation as a State under attack. The logic at work is, of course, based on solidarity between Member States and mutual trust, including when it comes to invoking the clause. However, the possibility of disagreement between certain Member States on this qualification and, therefore, on the invocability of the mutual defence clause cannot be ruled out. Yet, the Treaty leaves this question open, as Article 42(7) does not specify anything in this regard. In these circumstances, does the invocation of the clause by a State which considers itself to be the object of armed aggression automatically trigger the obligation of aid and assistance for the other States? Or can another State, because it disputes the existence of armed aggression and therefore the invocability of the clause, refuse to provide aid and assistance? It should be remembered that under the terms of Article 32 TEU, Member States 'shall consult one another within the European Council and the Council on any matter of foreign and security policy of general interest in order to determine a common approach'. Consultation is certainly relevant in this area and, as the mutual defence clause is a strong expression of solidarity between Member States, armed aggression by one of them is certainly of general interest, as is the very question of what constitutes aggression for the purposes of the mutual defence clause. Following the attacks on the Bataclan and the Stade de France in November 2015 and France's invocation of Article 42(7), the Member States consulted each other within the Council, at the level of the Defence Ministers: 'Defence Ministers discussed the reaction to the Paris attacks of 13 November 2015. [...] Ministers expressed their unanimous and full support for France and their readiness to provide all the necessary aid and assistance'.[42] This can be seen as an application of Article 32 TEU and, in any event, such consultation would certainly be an appropriate solution to (or to prevent) a disagreement such as the one envisaged here.

B. THE SCOPE OF THE COMMITMENT: 'AID AND ASSISTANCE BY ALL MEANS IN THEIR POWER'

The wording of the mutual defence clause may appear watered down compared with comparable clauses in the North Atlantic Treaty ('including the use of armed force'), or in the revised Brussels Treaty (WEU), which was referring to 'military or other means'. This is all the more remarkable given that the solidarity clause (Art. 222 TFEU) specifies that the Union must mobilise 'all the instruments at its disposal, including the military resources made available

[42] Results of the Council meeting: 3426th Council meeting – Foreign Affairs, 16 and 17 November 2015, 14120/15, https://data.consilium.europa.eu/doc/document/ST-14120-2015-INIT/en/pdf.

by the Member States' to deal with a terrorist attack and in the event of a natural or man-made disaster. There is no doubt that the phrase 'by all the means in their power' covers means of all kinds, including military means. While the wording may therefore appear weaker, its effect is not to give explicit priority to the military dimension, and indeed international law does not limit the exercise of legitimate self-defence to the use of military force.[43]

From this perspective, the deletion of the reference to military means is the result of a compromise designed to take account of the position of neutrality chosen by certain Member States.[44] The Protocol on the concerns of the Irish people regarding the Treaty of Lisbon, which recognises Ireland's neutrality, is very interesting in this respect: 'It will be for Member States – including Ireland, acting in a spirit of solidarity and without prejudice to its traditional policy of military neutrality – to determine the nature of aid or assistance to be provided to a Member State which is the object of a terrorist attack or the victim of armed aggression on its territory'.[45] The 'means within their power' of neutral States do not include those of a military nature, but they are nonetheless bound by the obligation to provide assistance. On the other hand, for Member States that are not neutral, military means do fall within those 'within their power'.

This criterion of 'means within their power' refers, in short, to the means that each Member State is able to use to assist another Member State which is the victim of armed aggression. On the one hand, this is quite different from what is provided for in Article 5 of the North Atlantic Treaty, which leaves it to each party to the treaty to determine the measures to be taken ('such action as it deems necessary'). In this respect, the mutual defence clause of the TEU appears more ambitious and sets a higher level of commitment

---

43 The legal regime of self-defence established in international law is not limited to an exception to the general prohibition of the threat or use of armed force. Self-defence is also a circumstance precluding wrongfulness under international law of responsibility for internationally wrongful acts. See the ILC Draft Articles on Responsibility of States for Internationally Wrongful Acts, supra, Art. 21 'Self-defence': 'The wrongfulness of an act of a State is precluded if the act constitutes a lawful measure of self-defence taken in conformity with the Charter of the United Nations'. According to the ILC,'[s]elf-defence may justify non-performance of certain obligations other than that under Article 2, paragraph 4, of the Charter of the United Nations, provided that such non-performance is related to the breach of that provision': Commentary on Article 21 of the Draft on the International Responsibility of States for Internationally Wrongful Acts adopted on second reading in 2001, *Report of the International Law Commission on the work of its 53rd session*, Official Records of the General Assembly of the United Nations, A/56/10, 2001, p. 189, para. 2.

44 C.-C. Cîrlig, 'The EU's mutual assistance clause First ever activation of Article 42(7) TEU', *Briefing*, November 2015, European Parliament Research Service, PE 572.799, p. 2. The omission is also clarified by paragraph 2 of Article 42(7), according to which NATO 'remains', for the States which are members of it, 'the foundation of their collective defence and the forum for its implementation'.

45 Protocol on the concerns of the Irish people on the Treaty of Lisbon, [2013] *OJ* L60/132. Article 3(4) states: 'The Treaty of Lisbon does not affect or prejudice Ireland's traditional policy of military neutrality'.

and solidarity for EU Member States. On the other hand, a question of interpretation of the clause arises with regard to the rules of domestic law, generally of constitutional rank, of certain Member States whose use of armed force is subject to parliamentary approval.[46] Are the military assets of a State whose Parliament does not approve their use in response to a request from an attacking Member State 'within its power'? There is every reason to believe that such a legal obstacle would in practice exclude the participation of that State in military operations without it being considered to be in breach of the obligation to provide aid and assistance under Article 42(7) of the TEU.

Unlike the solidarity clause (Art. 222 TFEU), the mutual defence clause was designed to provide aid and assistance between Member States, without any intervention by the EU institutions. Indeed, it is clear from the wording of the clause that the commitment concerns the Member States *ut singuli*, on a bilateral basis, without the EU institutions being assigned a role in its implementation, or EU resources being mentioned. Thus, when it was invoked by France in 2015, Article 42(7) was implemented on a strictly bilateral basis, without any intervention by the institutions. At the 17 November 2015 meeting of the Council in its Foreign Affairs configuration, the High Representative stressed that 'this is not a CSDP operation, but an activation of bilateral aid and assistance'.[47] It is therefore up to the State invoking the clause to ask the other Member States directly for their aid and assistance, specifying the nature of the measures required.[48] In this case, France's requests to the other Member States mainly concerned military operations: participation in air strikes in Syria against Daesh (whereas only France and the United Kingdom had been conducting such strikes until then), support for operations in the Levant (Syria and Iraq) and in the Sahel, but also an increase in the contribution of EU Member States to operations conducted by the EU (civilian and military CSDP missions) and by the United Nations (UN) (peacekeeping missions) in Africa, in order to relieve the commitment of French forces and enable them to be deployed elsewhere. But requests have also been made for non-military means, particularly in the area of intelligence sharing and foreign policy cooperation.[49]

---

46 This was the case, for example, of the United Kingdom (still an EU member at the time) and Germany, whose contribution to military operations at France's request was subject to a vote in Parliament.

47 Results of the Council meeting, doc. 14120/15, *op. cit.* It seems that the High Representative and the EEAS were not involved in the activities related to the activation of Article 42(7), and that the EU Military Committee and Military Staff were not consulted.

48 F. Gouttefarde, 'L'invocation de l'article 42(7), TUE: la solidarité militaire européenne contre le terrorisme', *Revue Défense Nationale*, 2016/3, no. 788, p. 75.

49 See S.E. Anghel and C.-C. Cîrlig, 'Activation de l'article 42, paragraphe 7, du traité sur l'Union européenne: demande d'assistance de la part de la France et réponses des États membres', *Briefing*, November 2015, European Parliament Research Service, PE 572.799. This note contains factual information on the discussions conducted by France with the other Member States, on a bilateral basis, and the resources committed.

That being said, the question may be raised as to the link between the mutual defence clause and the CSDP. As we have pointed out, the clause was inserted into Article 42 TEU, which deals with the CSDP and opens Section 2 of the TEU entitled 'Provisions on the common security and defence policy'. A link is thus established, the contours of which are not clear in the Treaty. Given that States must provide aid and assistance 'by all the means in their power', it is not *a priori* excluded that this could take the form of action under the CSDP, on the basis of Article 42(1). Concerning CSDP missions and operations, the objectives listed in Article 42(1) TEU ('maintaining peace, preventing conflicts and strengthening international security'), however, seem to fall under a different heading, that of crisis management, as indicated by the list (admittedly indicative) given in Article 43 TEU,[50] and in any case pending the building of a common defence by the European Council acting unanimously (Art. 42(2) TEU). However, since the choice of resorting to the CSDP is left to the discretion of the Member States, they could decide by a unanimous decision to act through the CSDP,[51] at least in part.

More broadly, the EEAS interprets the clause as allowing the attacked State to request assistance from the EU institutions: 'The Article itself does not define how it should be implemented. This provides a lot of flexibility for the attacked Member State(s) to implement it in a way that best responds to the respective armed aggression. This is a key strength of this article. While the Treaty does not explicitly foresee a role for EU Institutions in the implementation, the attacked Member State can request such support, for example with regard to coordinating the overall assistance'. In the same vein, the European Parliament, in its resolution of 21 January 2016 'on the mutual defence clause (Article 42(7) of the Treaty on European Union)', '[e]xpresses concerns that managing aid and assistance under the mutual defence clause on a bilateral basis — as in this case — will not be possible for all Member States; calls therefore on the European Council to give impetus to the further development of the mutual defence clause and build on the role of the relevant EU institutions as facilitators'.[52] In the 2012 resolution on this subject, the Parliament already stressed that the institutions could have a role to play and '[t]akes the view that, where collective action is taken to defend a Member State under attack, it should be possible to make use of existing EU crisis management structures where appropriate, and in particular that the

---

[50] CSDP missions 'include joint disarmament actions, humanitarian and rescue missions, military advice and assistance missions, conflict prevention and peacekeeping missions, combat forces missions for crisis management, including peace-making missions and post-conflict stabilisation operations'.

[51] The CSDP decision-making procedure is defined in Article 42(4) of the TEU.

[52] European Parliament resolution of 21 January 2016 on the mutual defence clause (Art. 42(7) TEU), 2015/3034(RSP), [2018] *OJ* C11/ 90, (5). This resolution was adopted by 448 votes in favour, 181 against and 36 abstentions.

possibility of activating an EU Operational Headquarters should be envisaged [...]'.[53] In addition, the European Parliament '[i]nvites the Vice-President/High Representative to propose practical arrangements and guidelines for ensuring an effective response in the event that a Member State invokes the mutual defence clause, as well as an analysis of the role of the EU institutions should that clause be invoked; takes the view that the obligation to provide aid and assistance, expressing political solidarity among Member States, should ensure a rapid decision in Council in support of the Member State under attack; considers that consultations in line with the requirement of Article 32 TEU would serve this purpose, without prejudice to the right of each Member State to provide for its self-defence in the meantime'.[54]

Although no procedural framework has been defined since France invoked the mutual defence clause and the European Parliament renewed its request, it should be noted that, in the 'Prepare together' section of the 'Strategic Compass', the new security and defence strategy which the EU adopted in 2022, the Member States announced that: 'We will continue to invest in our mutual assistance under Article 42(7) of the Treaty on European Union [...]' and '[w]e will continue to conduct regular exercises to further strengthen our mutual assistance in the case of an armed aggression, in accordance with Article 42(7) of the Treaty on European Union'.[55] The investment in question clearly comes under the heading of operational preparation, of strengthening the means of action through which aid and assistance can be provided, rather than that of framing the reaction by legal norms defining the applicable modalities and procedures. This basically confirms that the absence of a precisely established legal framework for organising joint responses to armed aggression, under Article 42(7), is the result of a collective choice – consensual at the very least – by the Member States, which intend to retain a high degree of flexibility in the implementation of the mutual defence clause.

53 Resolution of 22 November 2012 on the European Union's mutual defence and solidarity clauses: political and operational dimensions, [2015] *OJ* C419/ 138, (18).

54 Ibid., para. 17.

55 'A strategic compass for security and defence – For a European Union that protects its citizens, values and interests and contributes to international peace and security', doc. 7371/22, 22 March 2022.

ARTICLE 43 TEU: EU CRISIS MANAGEMENT OPERATIONS

Anne Hamonic
Senior Lecturer, University of Rennes, CNRS, IODE (Institut de l'Ouest: Droit et Europe) – UMR 6262

Article 43 TEU

1. The tasks referred to in Article 42(1), in the course of which the Union may use civilian and military means, shall include joint disarmament operations, humanitarian and rescue tasks, military advice and assistance tasks, conflict prevention and peace-keeping tasks, tasks of combat forces in crisis management, including peace-making, and post-conflict stabilisation. All these tasks may contribute to the fight against terrorism, including by supporting third countries in combating terrorism in their territories.

2. The Council shall adopt decisions relating to the tasks referred to in paragraph 1, defining their objectives and scope and the general conditions for their implementation. The High Representative of the Union for Foreign Affairs and Security Policy, acting under the authority of the Council and in close and constant contact with the Political and Security Committee, shall ensure coordination of the civilian and military aspects of such tasks.

Article 43 of the Treaty on European Union (TEU) was inserted into the Treaty on European Union (EU) by the Treaty of Lisbon, and was presented as a new provision.[1] Paragraph 1, however, takes over, updates and expands the former Article 17(2) TEU from the Treaty of Amsterdam.[2] The latter, for its part, was already largely inspired by the Petersberg Declaration of 19 June

[1] Consolidated version of the Treaty on European Union – Tables of equivalences, [2016] *OJ* C202/363.

[2] 'Questions referred to in this Article shall include humanitarian and rescue tasks, peacekeeping tasks and tasks of combat forces in crisis management, including peacemaking'.

1992, which gave the Western European Union (WEU) a new competence in crisis management by stating that the 'military units of WEU Member States, acting under the authority of WEU, could be employed for: humanitarian and rescue tasks; peacekeeping tasks; tasks of combat forces in crisis management, including peacemaking'.[3]

By incorporating this list of 'Petersberg tasks' into the TEU, the Treaty of Amsterdam gave substance to the European Union's competence in the field of crisis management and to the European Security and Defence Policy (ESDP), of which crisis management was the main competence until the Treaty of Lisbon. Without amending Article 17(2) TEU, but by deleting the provisions of the TEU organising 'recourse [by the EU] to the WEU',[4] the Treaty of Nice then took note of the European Council's choice to develop the Union's 'capacity for autonomous action'.[5] In addition to the setting up of specific bodies[6] and the adoption of the European Security Strategy,[7] this empowerment took shape concretely with the deployment of the EU's first crisis management operations (CMOs) in 2003.[8] Article 43 TEU resulting from the revision carried out by the Treaty of Lisbon, by taking over and significantly expanding the former Article 17(2) TEU, shows that the process of deepening is continuing and that crisis management operations remain an essential part of the ESDP, which has become the Common Security and Defence Policy (CSDP) and which now also includes a mutual assistance dimension[9] and a capacity-building component.[10]

3 WEU Council, 'Petersberg Declaration', Bonn, 19 June 1992, available on the website of the Centre virtuel de la connaissance sur l'Europe (CVCE), https://www.cvce.eu/en/obj/petersberg_declaration_made_by_the_weu_council_of_ministers_bonn_19_june_1992-en-16938094-bb79-41ff-951c-f6c7aae8a97a.html.

4 Art. 17(3) TEU, in the version resulting from the Treaty of Amsterdam, supplemented by the Declaration on Western European Union accompanying the Treaty of Amsterdam, para. 1.

5 European Council Declaration on strengthening the common European policy on security and defence, Annex III to the Presidency Conclusions of the Cologne European Council of 3 and 4 June 1999, accessible via the Council of the Union website, https://www.consilium.europa.eu/media/21070/57886.pdf.

6 The Political and Security Committee (PSC), the EU Military Staff (EUMS) and the EU Military Committee (EUMC) were set up in 2001. See the commentary by C. Schneider in this publication.

7 Council of the European Union, 'The European Security Strategy – A secure Europe in a better world', 12 December 2003, reprinted in *The European Security Strategy – A secure Europe in a better world*, Publications Office, 2009, https://data.europa.eu/doi/10.2860/1402, p. 27.

8 The military operations Concordia in the Former Yugoslav Republic of Macedonia (FYROM) and Artemis in the Democratic Republic of Congo (DRC), and the civilian missions EUPM in Bosnia-Herzegovina and EUPOL Proxima in FYROM. See the appendix at the end of the commentary.

9 Art. 42(7) TEU. See the commentary by J.-C. Martin in this publication.

10 Art. 45 and 46 TEU in particular. See the respective commentaries by A.-H. Bertana and Q. Loïez in this publication.

More specifically, Article 43 TEU, which is closely linked to several paragraphs of Article 42 TEU, fulfils a dual function (Section I); outlines the main characteristics of the Union's crisis management operations (Section II); and introduces the question of the institutions and structures involved in their creation and functioning (Section III).

I. THE DUAL FUNCTION OF ARTICLE 43 TEU

From now on, crisis management competence is the subject of a specifically dedicated provision. Consisting of two paragraphs, Article 43 TEU has a dual function: it provides an (elliptical) presentation of the operational dimension of the CSDP (Section A) and constitutes the legal basis for CFSP decisions on crisis management operations and related structures (Section B).

A. THE (ELLIPTICAL) PRESENTATION OF THE OPERATIONAL DIMENSION OF THE CSDP

Following on from the Petersberg Declaration and the former Article 17(2) TEU, Article 43 TEU is dedicated to the operational dimension of CSDP, and more specifically to the European Union's crisis management operations. However, its presentation is elliptical, not to say incomplete, making it necessary to read Article 43(1) TEU in conjunction with other provisions, as well as to clarify certain terminology, to truly understand its purpose.

First of all, the particular construction of the section dedicated to 'Provisions on the Common Security and Defence Policy', structured around the introductory Article 42 TEU, followed by provisions extending its various paragraphs and subparagraphs, is detrimental to the clarity of the purpose of Article 43 TEU and, consequently, of crisis management operations. Paragraph 1 of Article 43 TEU develops and supplements Article 42 TEU, to which it expressly refers. This explains why Article 43 TEU can be considered as offering 'a more detailed version'[11] of the content of the latter. However, the technique of cross-referencing does not fully compensate for the dispersal of the main characteristics of the Union's crisis management operations and leads to some laconism in Article 43(1) TEU.

In particular, although some of the elements mentioned in Article 42(1) TEU can be found in Article 43 TEU, they are not always included in a clear

11 F. Terpan, 'Article 43 [Tasks and Instruments for Implementing the CSDP]', in H.-J. Blanke and S. Mangiameli (eds.), *The Treaty on European Union (TEU)*, Berlin/Heidelberg, Springer/Verlag, 2013, pp. 1237–1252, spec. p. 1238.

manner, and others are not included at all. For example, the reference to both 'civilian and military' means is found in both provisions. On the other hand, the stipulation that the missions listed take place 'outside the Union' is not included in Article 43 TEU. Admittedly, this characteristic can be deduced from the inclusion of Article 43 TEU among the provisions relating to CSDP, and therefore to the Union's external action. But on reading the text of Article 43 TEU itself, this is apparent only in the wording of one of the types of task that the Union may undertake, namely 'supporting *third countries* in combating terrorism *in their territories*'.[12] Finally, even though it is dedicated to the operational dimension of the CSDP, Article 43 TEU makes no express reference to the Union's 'operational capacity', which refers to all the means – institutional, human, material, financial – enabling the Union to deploy a crisis management operation on its behalf. Nor is reference made to the fact that 'capabilities [are] provided by the Member States', an expression used by Article 42(1) TEU and specified in Article 42(3)(1) TEU.

Understanding the Union's crisis management operations thus requires a cross-reading of Articles 42 and 43(1) TEU, which reduces the completeness and clarity of the latter.

Article 43 TEU also suffers from imprecise terminology. In particular, the Treaty of Lisbon was not used as an opportunity to include the expression 'crisis management operations' in the provision that concern them. Article 43 TEU does not therefore contain any reference to this expression, although it does appear twice in Article 38 TEU on the role of the Political and Security Committee (PSC), which even refers in its second paragraph to 'the crisis management operations referred to in Article 43'. Worse still, although the concept of 'crisis management' is in fact mentioned in Article 43(1) TEU, it is used in a restrictive sense, designating only one type of task that can be carried out by the Union's crisis management operations ('tasks of combat forces in crisis management'), and is therefore a source of confusion rather than clarification.

B. THE LEGAL BASIS FOR ACTS RELATING TO CRISIS MANAGEMENT OPERATIONS AND LINKED STRUCTURES

In just over twenty years, more than forty EU crisis management operations have been set up[13] and, since the entry into force of the Treaty of Lisbon,[14] Article 43 TEU – and more specifically paragraph 2 thereof – forms the legal basis for acts relating to CMOs and linked structures.

[12] Art. 43(1) TEU, in fine. Emphasis added.
[13] See the appendix at the end of this commentary.
[14] Before the Treaty of Lisbon, crisis management operations were usually based on Articles 14 and 25(3) TEU, but there were variations.

Article 43(2) TEU is thus one of the legal bases for Council decisions setting up EU crisis management operations[15] – irrespective of the category[16] to which they belong – but also for the main Council decisions that subsequently mark the life of these deployments:[17] to launch them,[18] to modify their mandates[19] and/or their area of intervention[20] and/or their duration,[21] or to organise their termination.[22] Article 43(2) TEU is then systematically accompanied by Article 42(4) TEU.

The same applies to the decisions relating to various structures linked to the Union's crisis management operations. For example, Article 43(2) TEU, in conjunction with Article 42(4) TEU, was also the legal basis of decisions on the development of the European Security and Defence College (ESDC),[23] the activation of the EU Operations Centre for the Common Security and Defence Policy missions and operations in the Horn of Africa,[24] the establishment of a warehouse for civilian crisis management missions,[25] the planning and conduct arrangements for EU non-executive military CSDP missions which led to the creation of the Military Planning and Conduct Capability (MPCC),[26] or the consideration given to the consequences of the reorganisation of the civilian crisis management structures in the European External Action Service (EEAS)

---

15 For a presentation of their content, see for example Council Decision (CFSP) 2023/855 of 24 April 2023 on a European Union Partnership Mission in Moldova (EUPM Moldova), [2023] *OJ* L110/30.

16 On the different categories of OGC, see Section II.C below.

17 A. Hamonic, 'Biographie des opérations de gestion de crise de l'Union européenne – Éclairages sur les instruments juridiques jalonnant la vie d'une opération', in C. Flaesch-Mougin (ed.), *Union européenne et sécurité: aspects internes et externes*, Brussels, Bruylant, 2009, pp. 293–320.

18 See for example Council Decision (CFSP) 2022/2243 of 14 November 2022 launching the European Union Military Assistance Mission in support of Ukraine (EUMAM Ukraine), [2022] *OJ* L294/21.

19 See for example Council Decision (CFSP) 2022/2441 of 12 December 2022 amending Joint Action 2008/851/CFSP on a European Union military operation to contribute to the deterrence, prevention and repression of acts of piracy and armed robbery off the Somali coast [EUNAVFOR Atalanta], [2022] *OJ* L319/80.

20 See for example Council Decision (CFSP) 2023/2066 of 25 September 2023 amending Decision (CFSP) 2023/1599 on the European Union Security and Defence Initiative in support of West African countries of the Gulf of Guinea [EUSDI], [2023] *OJ* L238/141.

21 See for example Council Decision (CFSP) 2022/2318 of 25 November 2022 amending Decision 2010/452/CFSP on the European Union Monitoring Mission in Georgia (EUMM Georgia), [2022] *OJ* L307/133.

22 Council Decision (CFSP) 2020/471 of 31 March 2020 repealing Decision (CFSP) 2015/778 on a European Union military operation in the Southern Central Mediterranean (EUNAVFOR MED operation SOPHIA), [2020] *OJ* L101/3.

23 Council Decision (CFSP) 2022/1964 of 17 October 2022 amending Decision (CFSP) 2020/1515 establishing a European Security and Defence College, [2022] *OJ* L270/66.

24 Council Decision 2012/173/CFSP of 23 March 2012, [2012] *OJ* L89/66.

25 Council Decision 2012/698/CFSP of 13 November 2012, [2012] *OJ* L314/25.

26 Council Decision (EU) 2017/971 of 8 June 2017, [2017] *OJ* L146/133.

with regard to the function of Civilian Operations Commander for civilian crisis management missions.[27]

To this list of decisions adopted on the basis of Article 43(2) TEU should be added Council Decision (CFSP) 2023/994 of 22 May 2023 'on the consequences of Denmark informing the other Member States that it no longer wishes to avail itself of Article 5 of Protocol 22 on the position of Denmark'.[28] Article 1 states that from 1 July 2022 references to Denmark's opt-out in Council CFSP decisions (including those relating to EU military operations and missions) and 'in decisions adopted by the [PSC] [...] concerning the political control and strategic direction of crisis management operations, as referred to in Articles 42 and 43 TEU, which have defence implications' shall no longer apply.

The use of Article 43(2) TEU as the legal basis for Council decisions makes it possible to distinguish crisis management operations from other deployments with some similar characteristics, but created and conducted under other provisions and instruments of EU law. This is the case of the EU Border Assistance Mission to Moldova and Ukraine (EUBAM Moldova/Ukraine). It has been presented as having '[o]bjectives [...] very similar to other [CSDP] missions'[29] and is even sometimes described as such.[30] However, its constitutive act and the arrangements for its implementation are distinct,[31] in particular in that it was created via a memorandum of understanding signed on 7 October 2005 by the European Commission and the governments of the two States[32] and it is not managed by the CSDP structures.[33] The 'European Union Stabilisation Action in Mopti and Segou' (Mali) (EUSTAMS)[34] is not based on Article 43(2) TEU either, even though the tasks provided for,[35] the conditions

---

27 Council Decision (CFSP) 2022/1625 of 20 September 2022, [2022] *OJ* L244/15.

28 Council Decision (CFSP) 2023/994 of 22 May 2023, [2023] *OJ* L135/120.

29 This clarification has long appeared on the map of current EU missions and operations, to justify the presence of EUBAM Moldova/Ukraine on it. See European Union EEAS, December 2023, https://www.eeas.europa.eu/sites/default/files/styles/full_content_width/public/media/2023/blog%20ghana.jpg?itok=H9d7vQLw.

30 Paragraph 6 of the preamble and point 10 of the Annex to Council Decision (CFSP) 2019/2009 of 2 December 2019 in support of Ukraine's efforts to combat illicit trafficking in weapons, ammunition and explosives, in cooperation with the OSCE, [2019] *OJ* L312/42.

31 See the web page dedicated to the mission: https://eubam.org/who-we-are/#mandate.

32 The 2005 Memorandum and its 2015 Addendum can be accessed at https://eubam.org/publications.

33 This was shown on the map of EU missions and operations in its March 2024 version. See EEAS, Factsheet 'EU Common Security and Defence Policy (CSDP) Missions and Operations', March 2024, https://www.eeas.europa.eu/sites/default/files/documents/2024/EU-mission-and-operation_2024.pdf.

34 Council Decision (CFSP) 2017/1425 of 4 August 2017, [2017] *OJ* L204/90.

35 To advise the Malian authorities and facilitate inter-ministerial coordination, with a view to supporting Malian national policies and plans for the restoration and development of civil administration in the central region of Mali, in line with international standards.

for setting up[36] and the resources required[37] could have justified setting up a CSDP civilian crisis management mission. In financial and practical terms, the EUSTAMS stabilisation action has been likened to such a mission.[38] However, its constituent CFSP decision was based solely on Article 28 TEU and it was 'implemented [...] under the aegis of the EU Delegation to Mali'.[39] These hypotheses of operational deployments outside the CSDP, with objectives and tasks similar to those of the CMOs, have so far remained the exception.[40] Il could be different for the 'coordinated maritime presences' (CMPs).[41] Inaugurated in 2021 in the Gulf of Guinea,[42] and also trialled in the north-west Indian Ocean since 2022,[43] CMPs target areas described by the Council as 'maritime areas of European interest'[44] and they correspond to actions of a 'hybrid nature'.[45] As with EU crisis management operations, the Council ensures political control

36 As with a civilian CSDP mission, EUSTAMS follows a request for intervention from the Host State authorities (in this case the Malian authorities) and was created by the Council of the European Union through a unanimous decision.

37 EUSTAMS had a staff of ten experts 'mainly made up of staff seconded from Member States, EU institutions or the EEAS', and was allocated €3.25 million from the EU budget for 15 months.

38 It was listed under the heading 'CSDP missions' in the Union's budget, among 'other crisis management measures and operations' (Council of the EU, 'CFSP Budget Report – Monthly update as of 30 November 2017, Note from the Commission to delegations', doc. 15736/17, 13 December 2017) and was able to benefit from the support provided by the warehouse for civilian crisis management missions (Decision [CFSP] 2018/653, cited above).

39 Art. 1(1) of Council Decision (CFSP) 2017/1425 of 4 August 2017, cited above.

40 Recourse to this form of CFSP operational deployment was envisaged for other theatres, in particular Iraq, before the civilian mission EUAM Iraq was finally set up. The hypothesis of a 'team placed within the delegation (in the form of a military mission)', instead of a CSDP mission was apparently again considered for the Sahel in 2022. See N. Gros-Verheyde, 'Quel avenir pour les missions EUTM au Sahel? Vers un nouveau format de missions militaires pour la PSDC?', May 2022, *B2 Pro Le quotidien de l'Europe géopolitique*, 21 March 2022, https://club.bruxelles2.eu/2022/03/quel-avenir-pour-les-missions-eutm-au-sahel-vers-un-nouveau-format-de-missions-militaires-pour-la-psdc. In the same year, an 'operational action' based solely on Article 28(1) TEU was set up to support the evacuation of persons in danger in Afghanistan (Council Decision [CFSP] 2022/151 of 3 February 2022 on a European Union action to support the evacuation of certain particularly vulnerable persons from Afghanistan, [2022] *OJ* L25/11), a type of task found in Article 43 TEU.

41 In the Strategic Compass, it is planned to 'expand our Coordinated Maritime Presences to other areas of maritime interest that impact the security of the EU'. Council of the EU, 'A Strategic Compass for Security and Defence – For a European Union that protects its citizens, values and interests and contributes to international peace and security', doc. 7371/22, 21 March 2022, p. 15.

42 Council conclusions launching the pilot case of the Coordinated Maritime Presences concept in the Gulf of Guinea, doc. 5387/21, 25 January 2021.

43 Council conclusions on the implementation of the Coordinated Maritime Presences concept in the north-western Indian Ocean, doc. 6255/22, 21 February 2022, para. 4.

44 Council of the EU, Conclusions on security and defence, doc. 8910/20, 17 June 2020, para. 12.

45 C. Schneider, 'Les dynamiques ambivalentes de la gestion de crise', in A. Hamonic (ed.), *La spécificité de la défense en droit de l'Union européenne*, Rennes, Presses universitaires de Rennes, 2025, spec. p. 171.

and provides strategic guidelines for implementation within the framework of the PSC.[46] In addition, a maritime area of interest coordination cell has been set up within the EU Military Staff,[47] and information sharing is based in particular on the MARSUR network of the European Defence Agency (EDA). However, this is not a deployment based on a CFSP decision and carried out in the name of the Union, but more modestly an action of 'enhanced coordination of naval and air assets'[48] of the Member States already deployed in the maritime area identified. The EU does not assume command of the operation; the resources remain under national command. This new type of initiative, which helps to strengthen the EU's maritime security strategy[49] and contributes to the 'integrated approach to external conflicts and crises',[50] nevertheless also featured on the 2024 map illustrating the Union's 'commitment to security and defence in the world',[51] alongside CSDP crisis management operations and EUBAM Moldova/Ukraine.

II. THE MAIN CHARACTERISTICS OF EU CRISIS MANAGEMENT OPERATIONS

Article 43(1) TEU, read in conjunction with Article 42(1), (3) and (4), sets out the main characteristics of the Union's crisis management operations, which consist of the implementation of various tasks (Section A), outside the Union (Section B), using civilian and military means (Section C), made available to the Union by the States (Section D). Each of these characteristics presents some original features, and the combination of them gives rise to the specificity and variety of EU crisis management operations.

---

46 Council conclusions on the implementation of the Coordinated Maritime Presences concept in the north-western Indian Ocean, para. 11.

47 Council conclusions extending and enhancing the implementation of the Coordinated Maritime Presences concept in the Gulf of Guinea, doc. 6256/22, 21 February 2022, para. 5.

48 EEAS, 'Coordinated maritime presences', *Factsheet*, March 2022, https://www.eeas.europa.eu/sites/default/files/documents/2022-03-coordinated-maritime-presences-newlayout.pdf.

49 Joint Communication to the European Parliament and the Council on the update of the EU Maritime Security Strategy and its Action Plan 'An enhanced EU Maritime Security Strategy for evolving maritime threats', JOIN(2023)8 final, 10 March 2023.

50 Council conclusions of 22 January 2018 on the integrated approach to external conflicts and crises, doc. 5413/18, 22 January 2018.

51 In its March 2024 version. See EEAS, Factsheet 'EU Common Security and Defence Policy (CSDP) Missions and Operations', March 2024, https://www.eeas.europa.eu/sites/default/files/documents/2024/EU-mission-and-operation_2024.pdf.

A. PERFORMING A VARIETY OF TASKS

The presentation of the Union's crisis management competence in Article 43(1) TEU is inherited from the WEU, and consists mainly of a list of tasks that it can carry out through its crisis management operations. While these tasks are still usually referred to as 'Petersberg tasks',[52] the list has been expanded since 1992. In the end, the EU's crisis management operations can perform a wide range of tasks, as Article 43 TEU and related provisions show, as well as the practice developed on the basis of these and earlier provisions.

Firstly, the overall objective of the Union's operational action is set out in Article 42(1) TEU, to which Article 43(1) refers, and states that the Union may have recourse to crisis management operations 'for peace-keeping, conflict prevention and strengthening international security in accordance with the principles of the United Nations Charter [UNC]'. This general objective allows for a broad understanding of the scope of EU crisis management operations, since it covers the whole spectrum of the maintenance of international peace and security, allowing recourse to these operations both upstream and during the height of a conflict, as well as downstream.

Secondly, the list of tasks in Article 43(1) TEU itself confirms this broad approach. Indeed, before being extended by the Treaty of Lisbon, the list of Petersberg tasks inherited from WEU was limited to 'humanitarian and rescue tasks; peacekeeping tasks; tasks of combat forces in crisis management, including peacemaking' – i.e. tasks essentially involving military means. The Union's autonomy in crisis management has been accompanied by a new concept of crisis management, based on a dual civilian-military dimension,[53] which continues to be one of the EU's hallmarks in this area, and which constitutes a definite added value. The Treaty of Lisbon's addition of references to 'conflict prevention' and 'post-conflict stabilisation' tasks, in which civilian means can play an essential role, reflects the importance of civilian crisis management within the CSDP framework. The list of tasks in Article 43(1) TEU now covers the entire security continuum and thus the various components of the maintenance of international peace and security, identified by the UN Secretary-General in the 1992 Agenda for Peace,[54] even if the vocabulary chosen is not strictly identical.[55]

---

52 Emphasis added.

53 See Section II.C below.

54 UNSG, 'An Agenda for Peace: Preventive Diplomacy, Peacemaking and Peacekeeping', Report submitted by the Secretary-General, doc. A/47/277-S/24111, 17 June 1992. B. Boutros-Ghali distinguished between preventive diplomacy, *peacemaking*, *peacekeeping* and post-conflict *peacebuilding*.

55 A. Hamonic, *Les relations entre l'Union européenne et l'ONU dans le domaine de la gestion des crises*, Brussels, Bruylant, 2018, spec. pp. 77–78, notes 223 and 224.

Moreover, the original version of the Petersberg task list already combined a time-related approach (through tasks identified in relation to the moment of intervention: peacekeeping or peacemaking), and a material identification (designating the type of action as humanitarian, evacuation or combat related). This dual approach was reinforced by the Treaty of Lisbon, which not only extended the spectrum upstream and downstream, with conflict prevention and stabilisation at the end of conflicts, but also added 'joint disarmament actions' and 'military advice and assistance missions', as well as 'the fight against terrorism', presented as a cross-cutting concern to which all the other tasks may respond.

Thirdly, the diversity of tasks that can be carried out by the Union through its crisis management operations is further reinforced by the fact that the list in Article 43(1) TEU is non-exhaustive. The variety of practice shows that it has always been non-exhaustive, and the Treaty of Lisbon has maintained the term 'include' at the beginning of the list of possible tasks. As early as the first EU crisis management operations in the early 2000s, it became clear that, while some of them clearly fell within one of the types of task on the Petersberg list,[56] others did not. This was notably the case for various civilian missions whose mandates could not be covered by a list inherited from a military organisation.[57] The updating of the list by the Treaty of Lisbon was therefore partly a matter of codification,[58] and partly a matter of anticipation[59] and openness. Since the Treaty of Lisbon entered into force, several new tasks have been added to the list, but innovations have also continued, such as the diversification of the tasks

---

[56] For example, Operation Artemis in the Democratic Republic of Congo, which was authorised by the UN on the basis of Chapter VII of the UN Charter, had a robust mandate to provide military security for camps for displaced persons, to get Bunia airport back into operation and to protect civilians and humanitarian and UN personnel, or EUFOR Tchad/RCA operation, which had a humanitarian mandate that included helping to protect civilians in danger and facilitating the delivery of humanitarian aid and the free movement of humanitarian personnel.

[57] These include rule of law missions such as EUJUST Themis, deployed in Georgia in 2004–2005, and EULEX Kosovo, created in 2008.

[58] In this way, we can consider that 'peacekeeping' covers the border assistance tasks already carried out by the EUBAM Rafah mission since 2005 and the ceasefire monitoring tasks carried out by the EUMM Georgia mission from 2008.

[59] The first military mission, EUTM Somalia, was decided on in February 2010, just a few weeks after the entry into force of the Treaty of Lisbon, which added 'military advice and assistance tasks' to Article 43 TEU.

performed by the Union's naval operations,[60] or the inclusion of tasks relating to cybersecurity.[61]

Fourthly and lastly, the variety of the tasks carried out by crisis management operations is matched by a variety in the intensity of the Union's involvement through them. EU CMOs may be given executive or non-executive mandates. In the case of military deployments, this distinction forms the basis for the difference between 'military operations', in which force may be used, and 'military missions', which essentially provide military advice and training.[62] The Union's ability to take on both types of mandate is reflected in Article 43 TEU, in the references to 'missions of combat forces for crisis management', on the one hand, and to 'missions of military advice and assistance', on the other. The Union's civilian missions are usually non-executive missions. They play an impartial monitoring role (of borders and/or ceasefires), or advise, support or train the authorities of third countries on whose territory they are deployed. But they do not replace the authorities of the third country. The only exception to date is the civilian rule of law mission EULEX Kosovo, which was initially given 'executive responsibilities',[63] enabling it in particular to 'revers[e] or annu[l] operational decisions taken by the competent Kosovo authorities',[64] or to 'us[e] executive powers to investigate, prosecute and adjudicate on criminal and civil matters'.[65]

B. OUTSIDE THE EU

Although Article 43 TEU remains ambiguous on this point,[66] EU crisis management operations would take place 'outside the Union', as specified in Article 42(1) TEU to which it expressly refers. This geographical scope requires some clarification.

---

60 The naval operation EUNAVFOR MED IRINI set up in 2020 aims to contribute to the prevention of arms trafficking, to the implementation of UN measures to prevent the illicit export of petroleum fom Libya, to assist in the development of the capacities and in the training of the Libyan Coast Guard and Navy in law enforcement tasks at sea, and to contribute to the disruption of the business model of human smuggling and trafficking networks. (Art. 1 of Council Decision [CFSP] 2020/472 of 31 March 2020 on a European Union military operation in the Mediterranean [EUNAVFOR MED IRINI], [2020] *OJ* L101/4).

61 The mandate of the European Union Partnership Mission in Moldova (EUPM Moldova) ([2023] *OJ* L110/30), for example.

62 See Section II.C below.

63 Art. 2(2) of Council Joint Action 2008/124/CFSP of 4 February 2008 on the European Union Rule of Law Mission in Kosovo, EULEX Kosovo, [2008] *OJ* L42/92, in its initial version.

64 Ibid., Art. 3(b).

65 EEAS, *CSDP – Missions and operations annual report 2017*, p. 12, https://www.eeas.europa.eu/sites/default/files/csdp_annual_report_2017_web_en_2.pdf.

66 See above, Section I.B.1.

First of all, it should be emphasised that the ability to intervene, including militarily, outside the territory of its Member States is unusual for a regional security organisation. Indeed, Chapter VIII of the United Nations Charter[67] and the key acts of several regional entities[68] conceive of regional agreements and organisations as intended to ensure regional security, which itself contributes to the maintenance of international peace and security. As early as 1999, however, the UN Department of Peacekeeping Operations (DPKO) recognised the specificity of the European Union in this respect, stating, after identifying 'Europe' as its region of intervention, that the Union 'may also carry out activities in other regions'.[69] In recognition of its success in ensuring peace and security between its own Member States, the Union's ability to intervene 'outside the area' does of course imply compliance with the conditions governing the legality of such deployments under international law, which vary according to the type of CMO envisaged.[70] In practice, the EU has deployed operations and missions to contribute to crisis management in different regions of the world,[71] in particular[72] in the Western Balkans,[73] in

67 Article 52 CNU of the Charter thus admits the 'regional action' of regional agreements or bodies and the 'peaceful settlement of local disputes' through them.

68 Thus, according to Article 3 of the Constitutive Act of the African Union, one of its objectives is to 'promote peace, security and stability *on the continent*' [emphasis added] (Art. 3 of the Constitutive Act of the African Union, signed in Lomé on 11 July 2000, UNTS, vol. 2158, p. I-37733); in the Helsinki Summit Declaration of July 1992, the Heads of State and Government of the Member States of the CSCE (now the OSCE) considered that '[t]he Council and the Committee of Senior Officials have already established for the CSCE an important role in dealing with crises which have developed *within our area* [emphasis added] (Para. 13 of the Helsinki Summit Declaration, 'The Challenges of Change', accessible via OSCE website, https://resources.osce.org/sites/default/files/f/documents/7/c/39530.pdf).

69 UNSG, Department of Peacekeeping Operations (DPKO), 'Cooperation between the United Nations and regional organizations/arrangements in a peacekeeping environment – Suggested Principles And Mechanisms', March 1999, spec. p. 21. Only WEU had the same clarification (p. 22).

70 See Section II.C below.

71 See the EEAS map illustrating 'the Union's commitment to security and defence in the world': EEAS, Factsheet 'EU Common Security and Defence Policy (CSDP) Missions and Operations', April 2025, https://www.eeas.europa.eu/sites/default/files/documents/2025/EU-mission-and-operation_2025.pdf.

72 It has not intervened on the American continent or in Oceania; it has only intervened twice in Asia, via the EU monitoring mission in Aceh (Indonesia) (Aceh Monitoring Mission – AMM) and the police mission in Afghanistan (EUPOL Afghanistan).

73 In the Western Balkans, the EU has set up six crisis management operations (2 military operations and 4 civilian missions). On 1 January 2025, two were still underway (the EUFOR Althea military operation and the EULEX Kosovo civilian mission).

Africa[74] and in the Middle East,[75] and then in Eastern Europe and the Southern Caucasus,[76] thus identifying preferred areas of intervention and a form of regionalisation of crisis management.

Secondly, the deployment of crisis management operations 'outside the EU' covers several types of areas. Many of the European Union's crisis management operations have taken place or are taking place on the territory of a third country, in response to an internal crisis, and may therefore involve its land, sea and/or air territory, or even cyberspace. Deployments may also involve several third countries, for example when the mission is tasked with monitoring a border or a ceasefire. The EU also regularly adopts a regional approach, extending the readiness zone,[77] or occasionally the action zone, of a CMO to another third country,[78] deploying an operation on the land territory[79] or off the coasts[80] of several third countries, or even setting up a regional coordination cell within its CMOs.[81] In addition, some of the Union's naval

---

74 In Africa or off its coasts, the EU has decided on twenty-six crisis management operations (9 military operations [including EUFOR Libya, which was not launched in the end]), 6 military missions, 10 civilian missions and 2 civilian-military missions). On 1 January 2025, eleven operations were underway: 3 naval operations (EUNAVFOR Atalanta, EUNAVFOR MED IRINI and EUNAVFOR ASPIDES); 3 military missions (EUTM Somalia, EUTM RCA and EUMAM Mozambique); 4 civilian missions (EUCAP Somalia, EUCAP Sahel Mali, EUAM RCA and EUBAM Libya), and 1 civilian-military mission (EUSDI in the Gulf of Guinea).

75 In the Middle East, the EU has set up four crisis management operations, all civilian. On 1 January 2025, three were still in progress (EUBAM Rafah, EUPOL COPPS, EUAM Iraq). In addition, the area of operation of the EU maritime security operation to preserve freedom of navigation in the context of the Red Sea crisis (EUNAVFOR ASPIDES) 'shall comprise the Baab al-Mandab Strait and the Strait of Hormuz, as well as international waters in the Red Sea, the Gulf of Aden, the Arabian Sea, the Gulf of Oman and the Persian Gulf' (Art. 1(3) of Council Decision [CFSP] 2024/583 of 8 February 2024 on a European Union maritime security operation to safeguard freedom of navigation in relation to the Red Sea crisis [EUNAVFOR ASPIDES], [2024] *OJ* L2024/583).

76 In Eastern Europe and the Southern Caucasus, the EU has set up six crisis management operations (1 military mission and 5 civilian missions). On 1 January 2025, five were underway (the EUMAM Ukraine military mission and four civilian missions: EUMM Georgia, EUAM Ukraine, EUPM Moldova and EUMA Armenia).

77 Part of the EUFOR RDCongo operation was stationed in Gabon.

78 Between October 2022 and February 2023, the EUMM Georgia mission monitored the international border between Armenia and Azerbaijan, and then deployed a team to Armenia.

79 Operation EUFOR Tchad/RCA was deployed in both States, while the area of deployment of the European Union Security and Defence Initiative for the countries of West Africa in the Gulf of Guinea (EUSDI) initially covered Ghana and Benin, before being extended to Côte d'Ivoire and Togo.

80 When EUNAVFOR Atalanta was set up in 2008, it was deployed 'up to 500 nautical miles off the Somali coast and neighbouring countries' (Article 1(2) of Council Joint Action 2008/851/CFSP of 10 November 2008, [2008] *OJ* L301/3).

81 A Regional Advisory and Coordination Cell for the Sahel (RACC) has been set up as part of the EUCAP Sahel Mali mission, in order to 'support the G5 Sahel structures and countries' (Council Decision [CFSP] 2019/762 of 13 May 2019, *OJ* L125/18). Then, the EU concluded

operations may take place on the high seas, and therefore outside the territory of any third State.

Finally, it should be noted that the characteristic that EU crisis management operations take place 'outside the EU' does not prevent some of them from taking place, in whole or in part, on the territory of EU Member States. Thus, in April 2022, when the mandate of the civilian mission EUAM Ukraine was extended to support the Ukrainian authorities in facilitating the investigation and prosecution of any international crimes committed in the context of military aggression, it was decided that 'elements of EUAM Ukraine may temporarily *conduct their activities from the territories* of the Republic of Moldova and *of Member States*'.[82] Moreover, the European Union Military Assistance Mission in support of Ukraine (EUMAM Ukraine), created in October 2022, 'operates on the territory of the Member States'.[83] Admittedly, this choice is linked to 'exceptional circumstances'[84] and is intended to be 'temporary';[85] it has enabled the training objectives initially set[86] to be exceeded; above all, it reduces the risk of the Union being considered as cobelligerent.[87] However, it reflects a flexible interpretation, to say the least, of the characteristic of EU crisis management operations expressly mentioned in Article 42(1) TEU, according to which they take place 'outside the Union'.

C. WITH CIVILIAN AND MILITARY MEANS

While the extension of WEU's competences to crisis management was confined to an essentially military approach, that of the European Union was fairly quickly envisaged as twofold, being able to rely on both military and civilian

an agreement with Mauritania on the establishment and functioning of the European Union Regional Advisory and Coordination Cell deployed in Nouakchott to support the G5 Sahel structures (see Council Decision (CFSP) 2024/226 of 9 June 2023, [2024] *OJ* L2024/226).

82 New wording of Article 2*a*(2)(c) of Decision 2014/486/CFSP on the European Union Advisory Mission for Civilian Security Sector Reform Ukraine (EUAM Ukraine), following the amendment made by Council Decision (CFSP) 2022/638 of 13 April 2022, [2022] *OJ* L117/ 38. Emphasis added.

83 Art. 1(5), of Council Decision (CFSP) 2022/1968 of 17 October 2022 on a European Union military assistance mission in support of Ukraine (EUMAM Ukraine), [2022] *OJ* L270/85.

84 Ibid. Para. 10 of the preamble.

85 Ibid. Article 1(5) states that the mission shall operate in the territory of the Member States '[u]ntil the Council decides otherwise and amends this Decision accordingly'.

86 While the mission was supposed to train 30,000 soldiers by the end of 2023, 34,000 had already been trained by November 2023. See also Council of the EU, Press release, 'European Peace Facility: Council gives green light to additional funding for training of Ukrainian armed forces under EUMAM Ukraine', 28 November 2023.

87 N. Gros-Verheyde, 'Difficulté politique pour la mission d'assistance aux forces ukrainiennes (EUMAM Ukraine)', *B2 Pro Le quotidien de l'Europe géopolitique*, 29 September 2022, https://club.bruxelles2.eu/2022/09/exclusif-retard-a-lallumage-pour-la-future-mission-militaire-europeenne-eumam-ukraine.

means. As the Treaty of Amsterdam simply repeats the Petersberg list of tasks, this dual approach was not expressly mentioned. Nor does it appear in the Final Declaration of the Franco-British Summit in Saint-Malo of 4 December 1998,[88] or in the Declaration adopted at the end of the Cologne European Council of 4 June 1999, although these were essential stages in the Union's autonomy in crisis management. On the other hand, this duality was established when the Headline Goals 2003 were set in December 1999,[89] and then in the European Security Strategy (ESS) of 12 December 2003, in which the possibility of 'developing operations involving both military and civilian capabilities'[90] is described as a way to 'add particular value'.[91] By inserting a reference to 'civilian and military means' in Article 43(1) TEU and to 'civilian and military assests' in Article 42(1) TEU, the Treaty of Lisbon codified this specificity of the European Union, which is thus able to use a variety of resources to support different crisis management operations under the CSDP.

The means – or capabilities – in question are diverse, in response to the varied tasks that the EU can take on through its crisis management operations.

Military means consist mainly of armed forces personnel and their equipment, which must be adapted to the characteristics of the deployment (task involving possible use of force or simply a military training/advisory activity; land or naval intervention, etc.). The many tools put in place within the EU framework since 2016 to strengthen the military capabilities of both Member States and third countries highlight the importance of the existence and availability of equipment capable of releasing lethal force,[92] but also of additional equipment and supplies, for medical purposes or to facilitate the transport of forces and materials, for example.[93]

Civilian means are both less obvious and (yet) even more varied. At the Santa Maria da Feira European Council in June 2000, the civilian dimension of EU crisis management was described as covering four main areas (police, strengthening the rule of law, civil protection and civil administration)[94] to

---

88 Joint Declaration on Defence issued at the British-French Summit, Saint-Malo, 4 December 1998, https://www.cvce.eu/obj/declaration_franco_britannique_de_saint_malo_4_decembre_1998-fr-f3cd16fb-fc37-4d52-936f-c8e9bc80f24f.html.

89 See Section II.D below.

90 Council of the European Union, 'European Security Strategy – A secure Europe in a better world', 12 December 2003, Publications Office, 2009, https://data.europa.eu/doi/10.2860/1402.

91 Ibid.

92 See C. Schneider's commentary on the European Peace Facility in this publication.

93 See, for example, the various projects under the Permanent Structured Cooperation (see the commentary by Q. Loiez in this publication) or the equipment financed via the European Peace Facility (see the commentary by C. Schneider in this publication).

94 Santa Maria da Feira European Council, 19-20 June, 2000, Presidency Conclusions, Annex 1, Appendix 3: 'the study to define concrete targets in the area of civilian aspects of crisis management', available at https://www.cvce.eu/content/publication/2007/6/12/042a8da3-def7-44ac-9011-130fed885052/publishable_en.pdf.

which were added monitoring and security sector reform. These tasks require a wide range of resources: police officers, magistrates, customs officers, humanitarian workers, experts in various fields such as conflict analysis or transitional justice, the fight against terrorism,[95] and now also in cybersecurity and the fight against hybrid threats.[96]

This duality of capabilities gives rise to a diversity of categories of EU crisis management operations.

In the course of EU practice, several categories of CMO have emerged. The duality of 'civilian and military assets' that can be mobilised first gave rise to two categories of EU crisis management operations, inaugurated in 2003: 'civilian missions' and 'military operations'. The former fulfil their mandates using civilian means, while the latter require military means. As several provisions of the TEU lay down specific rules for decisions 'with military implications or in the field of defence', two distinct regimes apply.

These two categories of crisis management operation differ firstly in terms of their legality under international law: prior authorisation from the Security Council is required for military operations where the tasks undertaken may involve the use of force; for civilian missions, an invitation from the third country to intervene on its territory is sufficient.

The funding arrangements are also different: while all expenditure on civilian missions is funded from the EU budget, only the administrative expenditure of military operations are, under Article 41 TEU.[97] The operational expenditure of military operations is borne solely by the States contributing to the operation, each for the costs resulting from its contribution ('costs lie where they fall' principle), with the exception of the 'common costs' which are collectively funded by all the Member States via the European Peace Facility (EPF)[98] which, in this respect, has replaced the Athena mechanism created in 2004.[99]

---

95 For example, for the EU military mission to contribute to the training of the Malian armed forces (EUTM Mali) (Council Decision 2013/34/CFSP of 17 January 2013, [2013] *OJ* L14/19) or for the European Union security and defence initiative for West African countries in the Gulf of Guinea (Council Decision [CFSP] 2023/1599 of 3 August 2023, cited above).

96 For example, for the EUPM Moldova mission to strengthen the resilience of the security sector in the areas of crisis management and hybrid threats (Council Decision [CFSP] 2023/855, cited above).

97 See the commentary by A. Potteau in this publication.

98 Council Decision (CFSP) 2021/509 of 22 March 2021 establishing a European Peace Facility and repealing Decision (CFSP) 2015/528, [2021] *OJ* L102/14. See the commentaries on the European Peace Facility by C. Schneider and on Article 41 TEU by A. Potteau in this publication.

99 Council Decision (CFSP) 2015/528 of 27 March 2015 establishing a mechanism to administer the financing of the common costs of European Union operations having military or defence implications (Athena), and repealing Decision 2011/871/CFSP, [2015] *OJ* L84/39.

Finally, in terms of command, a Civilian Planning and Conduct Capability (CPCC) was established in 2007, before becoming the Civilian Operations Headquarters (CivOpsHQ) in March 2025; its Managing Director acts as Civilian Operations Commander for all the Union's civilian missions. Based on the CPCC model, the Military Planning and Conduct Capability (MPCC) was created in 2017. However, while the MPCC was immediately given responsibility for the Union's military missions,[100] the situation was different for military operations. Due to the reluctance of certain Member States and its limited resources, it was only possible to envisage a gradual extension of the MPCC's role to military operations. These were initially excluded from the competence of the MPCC. Then, in 2018, it was accepted that the MPCC could also plan and conduct 'one executive military CSDP operation limited to EU Battlegroup size' from the end of 2020.[101] In the Strategic Compass of May 2022, a further step seems to have been taken. The extension remains gradual, since it is planned that '[b]y 2025, [the MPCC] will be able to plan and conduct all non-executive mandate military missions *and two small-scale executive mandate operations or one medium-scale executive mandate operation, as well as live exercises*',[102] before '[i]n a second phase',[103] it will be able to do so for 'additional executive mandate operations'.[104] It also states that the MPCC 'should be considered as the preferred command and control structure'.[105] In practice, the MPCC had been involved in some exercises,[106] but it had not yet been given responsibility for the Operational Headquarters (OHQ) at the strategic level for an EU military operation. The EU therefore continues to use one of the five pre-identified national operation headquarters,[107] or NATO's SHAPE for its military operations.[108]

---

[100] Council Decision (CFSP) 2017/971 of 8 June 2017 determining the planning and conduct arrangements for EU non-executive military CSDP missions, [2017] *OJ* L146/133. See below.

[101] Council conclusions of 19 November 2018 on Security and Defence in the context of the EU Global Strategy, doc. 13978/18, 19 November 2018.

[102] Council of the European Union, 'A Strategic Compass for security and defence – For a European Union that protects its citizens, values and interests and contributes to international peace and security', doc. 7371/22, 21 March 2022, p. 19. Emphasis added.

[103] Ibid.

[104] Ibid.

[105] Ibid., p. 16.

[106] EEAS, 'Military Exercise 2022 (MILEX 22)', https://www.eeas.europa.eu/eeas/military-exercise-2022-milex-22_en; EEAS, 'Annual Progress Report on the Implementation of the Strategic Compass for Security and Defence', doc. 6891/23, 27 February 2023, p. 4.

[107] Five Member State headquarters can be used for EU military operations: Germany (Potsdam), Spain (Rota), France (Mont Valérien), Greece (Larissa) and Italy (Rome). On 1 January 2025, the Operation Headquarters for EUNAVFOR MED IRINI is based in Rome. After being based in the United Kingdom (Northwood) and following Brexit, since 2019 EUNAVFOR Atalanta's Operation Headquarters has been based in Rota, with the exception of the Maritime Security Centre – Horn of Africa (MSCHOA), which is based in Brest, France. The OHQ of EUNAVFOR ASPIDES is located in Greece.

[108] In the context of the 'Berlin Plus' arrangements, see Section II.D below.

Since 2003, the European Union has deployed twenty-five civilian missions, whose acronyms[109] demonstrate the variety of tasks performed and resources mobilised: the Union has carried out police missions (EUPOL, EUPAT, EUP[olice]M,), rule of law missions (EUJUST, EULEX), advisory missions (EUAM), monitoring missions (EUMM) including border assistance missions (EUBAM), missions to strengthen civilian capabilities in the security sector (EUAVSEC, EUCAP, EUP[artnership]M) or to support reform of this sector (EUSEC, EUSSR, EUAM).[110] On 1 January 2025, twelve EU civilian missions were underway.[111] In order to 'enhance the civilian CSDP missions' effectiveness, impact, flexibility and robustness',[112] a Civilian CSDP Compact was adopted in 2018,[113] followed by a second one in 2023,[114] which lists various 'commitments by the Council and the Member States'.[115] For example, the 2023 Civilian CSDP Pact includes commitments to include human rights impact and human rights risk analysis in all planning documents for civilian CSDP missions,[116] the strengthening of the human resources capacity of the Civilian Staff,[117] the establishment of a regular and structured civilian capability development process,[118] and the EU's ability to deploy 200 civilian experts within 30 days by 2027.[119]

---

109 The meaning of the various acronyms can be found in the EU Military Committee Glossary: Council of the European Union, 'EUMC Glossary of acronyms and definitions – Revision 2024', doc. 17117/24, 20 December 2024.

110 See the appendix at the end of this commentary.

111 EUAM Iraq, EUAM RCA, EUAM Ukraine, EUBAM Libya, EUBAM Rafah, EUCAP Sahel Mali, EUCAP Somalia, EULEX Kosovo, EUMA Armenia, EUMM Georgia, EUPM Moldova, EUPOL COPPS. EUCAP Sahel Niger was withdrawn before the end of its mandate, which was due to last until September 2024. See the mission's website, https://www.eucap-sahel.eu and N. Gros-Verheyde, 'Après une fausse perquisition de la junte nigérienne, le retrait de la mission EUCAP Sahel Niger accéléré', *B2 Pro Le quotidien de l'Europe géopolitique*, 29 February 2024, https://club.bruxelles2.eu/2024/02/actualite-apres-une-fausse-perquisition-de-la-junte-nigerienne-le-retrait-de-la-mission-eucap-sahel-niger-accelere.

112 Conclusions of the Council and of the Representatives of the Governments of the Member States, meeting within the Council, on the establishment of a Civilian CSDP Compact, doc. 9588/23, 22 May 2023, p. 2.

113 Conclusions of the Council and of the Representatives of the Governments of the Member States, meeting within the Council, on the establishment of a Civilian CSDP Compact, doc. 14305/18 of 19 November 2018. T. Smit, *Strengthening EU civilian crisis management: the civilian CSDP compact and beyond*, SIPRI Insights on Peace and Security, no. 2021/5, November 2021.

114 Conclusions of the Council and of the Representatives of the Governments of the Member States, meeting within the Council, on the establishment of a Civilian CSDP Compact, doc. 9588/23, 22 May 2023, p. 16.

115 Ibid., p. 7.

116 Ibid., p. 19(10).

117 Ibid., p. 22(16)(a).

118 Ibid., p. 21(15).

119 Ibid., p. 16(4).

Military operations, which also began in 2003, initially consisted of deploying forces on the territory of third countries to carry out various types of tasks (EUFOR), before naval operations were also deployed (EUNAVFOR). In just over twenty years, the EU has decided on eleven military operations and deployed ten,[120] four of which were still underway on 1 January 2025.[121] Developments relating to EU military deployments[122] include the disappearance of robust land operations[123] in favour of naval operations[124] and the development, from the early 2010s onwards, of a third category of CMOs: the military missions.

These 'military missions' constitute a sort of hybrid category, in that their legal regime borrows from both that of civilian missions and that of military operations, as their name itself reflects. They involve the deployment of military means, but under a non-executive mandate: i.e. without the use of force or the performance of tasks on behalf of the authorities of the third country. Their tasks are usually to provide military training (EUTM), military advice (EUMAM) and/or support for the development of military structures (EUMPM) for the armed forces of a third country. As such, they are sometimes supplemented by assistance measures under the European Peace Facility, which finances the supply of military equipment, where appropriate as capable of delivering lethal force, to armed forces trained by the EU military mission.[125] Because they involve the use of military resources, the rules governing the funding of military operations apply, and the chain of command for military

---

[120] The launch of Operation EUFOR Libya was conditional on a request to that effect from the United Nations Office for the Coordination of Humanitarian Affairs (OCHA) (Council Decision 2011/210/CFSP of 1 April 2011 on a European Union military operation in support of humanitarian assistance operations in response to the crisis situation in Libya [Operation EUFOR Libya], [2011] *OJ* L89/17). However, this request was not made and the operation was therefore not deployed.

[121] EUFOR Althea, EUNAVFOR MED IRINI, EUNAVFOR Atalanta and EUNAVFOR ASPIDES.

[122] D. Fiott, 'Military CSDP Operations: Strategy, Financing, Effectiveness', in S. Blockmans and P. Koutrakos (eds.), *Research Handbook on the EU's Common Foreign and Security Policy*, Cheltenham, Edward Elgar, 2018, pp. 111–131.

[123] EUFOR Althea, in Bosnia and Herzegovina, has a mandate primarily to act as a deterrent and to contribute to a safe and secure environment, within the framework of the Stabilisation and Association Process (Article 1(1) of Council Joint Action 2004/570/CFSP of 12 July 2004 on the European Union military operation in Bosnia and Herzegovina, [2004] *OJ* L252/10).

[124] Three of the four current operations are naval operations. They can include policing activities at sea, such as boarding, inspection, arrest and seizure.

[125] See e.g. Council Decision (CFSP) 2021/2032 of 19 November 2021 on an assistance measure under the European Peace Facility to support military units trained by the EU Training Mission in Mozambique, [2021] *OJ* L415/25 and Council Decision (CFSP) 2022/2245 of 14 November 2022 on an assistance measure under the European Peace Facility to support the Ukrainian Armed Forces trained by the European Union Military Assistance Mission in support of Ukraine with military equipment, and platforms, designed to deliver lethal force, [2022] *OJ* L294/25. Through these assistance measures, the EPF succeeds the African Peace Facility (APF), with a scope of action that is no longer limited geographically. See the commentary by C. Schneider on the European Peace Facility in this publication.

missions, like that for military operations, includes two commanders.[126] However, because they carry out non-executive tasks, they are 'missions' whose legality is conditional only on the agreement of the host third country to intervene on its territory. In addition, the Member States have agreed that command and control at the strategic level of all military missions should be provided by a single structure, the Military Planning and Conduct Capability (MPCC), modelled on the CPCC for civilian missions. The Director of the EU Military Staff (EUMS) is the Director of the MPCC and, as such, acts as Mission Commander for EU military missions.[127] Military missions were inaugurated in Africa in 2010 with the EUTM Somalia mission, and they have gradually multiplied on this continent, before being implemented in Europe in 2022 with EUMAM Ukraine. On 1 January 2025, four EU military missions were ongoing,[128] and three had ended.[129] Today, they are one of the vectors of the dynamism of the Union's crisis management, and are emerging as sources of significant innovation.[130]

While this trilogy of categories of crisis management operations (military operations/civilian missions/military missions) seemed to have stabilised, a new type of EU crisis management operation came into being in 2023.[131] The European Union Security and Defence Initiative in support of West African countries in the Gulf of Guinea (EUSDI) aims to 'assist West African countries [in the region] in developing the adequate capabilities within their security and defence forces to contain and respond to the pressure exercised by terrorist

---

126 See Section III.A below.

127 Council Decision (CFSP) 2017/971 of 8 June 2017 determining the planning and conduct arrangements of EU non-executive military CSDP missions [...], [2017] *OJ* L146/133, Art. 2(1).

128 EUMAM Ukraine, EUTM Mozambique, EUTM RCA, EUTM Somalia.

129 EUMAM RCA, EUTM Mali and EUMPM Niger. The first has been replaced by EUTM RCA. The other two came to an end because of the political and security situation in the country: EUTM Mali was not extended in May 2024 (EEAS, Press release 'Mali: Communiqué de presse sur le non-renouvellement du mandat d'EUTM Mali', 8 May 2024, https://www.eeas.europa.eu/eeas/mali-communiqu%C3%A9-de-presse-sur-le-non-renouvellement-du-mandat-d%E2%80%99eutm-mali_und_en); the decision setting up EUMPM Niger was repealed before the planned end of the mission's mandate, 'the Union personnel of this mission [having been] redeployed to Europe on 17 December 2023' (Council Decision (CFSP) 2024/1498 of 27 May 2024 repealing Decision (CFSP) 2022/2444 on a European Union military partnership mission in Niger (EUMPM Niger), [2024] *OJ* L2024/1498).

130 See above, Section II.B for EUMAM Ukraine. See also A. Hamonic, 'Les missions militaires de l'Union européenne, une catégorie remarquable d'opérations de gestion de crise', in M. Ailincai, C. Chevallier-Govers and V. Adjaharian-Kanaa (eds.), *Les Europes: de l'intérieur, vers d'extérieur. Mélanges en l'honneur de Catherine Schneider*, Paris, Mare & Marin, 2021, pp. 585–608.

131 See the EEAS map illustrating 'the Union's commitment to security and defence in the world': EEAS, Factsheet 'EU Common Security and Defence Policy (CSDP) Missions and Operations', April 2025, https://www.eeas.europa.eu/sites/default/files/documents/2025/EU-mission-and-operation_2025.pdf.

armed groups'.[132] It is intended to contribute to the training, support and strengthening of both the civilian security forces and the military forces of the target States in the Gulf of Guinea region. The Initiative therefore has both a civilian and a military pillar. In a way, it is both a civilian and a military mission, and therefore it shares and combines their respective characteristics. Described as a 'mission',[133] it is deployed on the territory of African States in the target zone, provided it has been invited to do so.[134] But the mission's two pillars are distinct in terms of funding,[135] and command and control.[136] The Joint Support Coordination Cell (JSCC), 'co-chaired for the Initiative by the Civilian Operations Commander and the Military Commander, shall ensure the unity of the chain of command'.[137] Such a combination of two elements – civilian and military – within the same CMO had already been tried out with the European Union's civil-military support action to the African Union mission in the Darfur region of Sudan, and then in Somalia from mid-2005 to the end of 2007.[138] In addition to its mixed nature, which confirms the added value of the Union's capacity to deploy civilian and military means, EUSDI offers a new illustration of a crisis management operation with a regional scope: initially involving Benin and Ghana, it was rapidly extended to Côte d'Ivoire and Togo, and may be extended to various other 'West African countries of the Gulf of Guinea'.[139] Finally, the EUSDI is also a concrete expression of the integrated approach that the EU is promoting in terms of external conflict and crisis management,[140] since it is designed to be 'complemented by the

---

132 Art. 1(1) of Council Decision (CFSP) 2023/1599 of 3 August 2023 on EUSDI, cited above.

133 Ibid., para. 2 of the preamble.

134 Ibid., Art. 1(4).

135 Ibid., Arts. 10 and 15.

136 The civilian pillar is under the strategic command and control of the Civilian Operations Commander, who is now the Managing Director of the CivOpsHQ, which is made available for the planning and conduct of this pillar. The military pillar is under the strategic command and control of the Military Commander, who is the Director of the MPCC, which is responsible for the operational planning and conduct of this pillar. However, 'for the purposes of the initiative', the CPCC and the MPCC are 'reinforced' respectively by a civilian command and support cell and a military command and support cell, whose heads exercise command and control, at operational level, of the corresponding pillar. Thus, the Head of the civilian command and support cell exercises, for the civilian pillar of the mission, the same functions as the Head of Mission for a civilian CSDP mission (Article 6 of Decision (CFSP) 2023/1599, cited above); the Head of the military command and support cell exercises, for the military pillar of the mission, the same functions as the Force Commander of the mission for a military CSDP mission (Article 13 of Decision (CFSP) 2023/1599, cited above).

137 Art. 4(4) of Decision 2023/1599, cited above.

138 Council Joint Action 2005/557/CFSP of 18 July 2005 on the European Union civilian-military supporting action to the African Union mission in the Darfur region of Sudan, [2005] *OJ* L188/46.

139 Art. (1)(4) of Council Decision (CFSP) 2023/1599 of 3 August 2023), cited above.

140 Council conclusions of 22 January 2018 on the Integrated Approach to External Conflicts and Crises, doc. 5413/18 of 22 January 2018.

deployment of Military Advisers in Union delegations, in conjunction with assistance measures under the European Peace Facility for the provision of military equipment and in synergy with security-related projects'.[141] The armed forces of the four countries benefiting from the EUSDI are recipients of assistance measures under the EPF, and the EUSDI should facilitate their implementation.[142]

D. MADE AVAILABLE TO THE UNION BY THE STATES

Although Article 43 TEU is silent on this point, Article 42(1) TEU, to which it refers, and the first subparagraph of Article 42(3) TEU respectively specify that the implementation of CSDP, and in particular the performance of the tasks carried out by the Union's crisis management operations, 'shall be undertaken using capabilities provided by the Member States', which they 'shall make [...] available to the Union'. This feature of the Union's 'operational capacity'[143] is a manifestation of the intergovernmental character that continues to mark CSDP and is customary in security organisations capable of deploying peacekeeping or crisis management operations or missions. It does, however, require some clarification as regards the method used, the States concerned and the status of the personnel made available for EU crisis management operations.

First of all, the method of 'making available' capabilities to the Union must be seen in the context of the objective of autonomy sought under the ESDP from the end of the 1990s onwards, and revived in 2022. A turning point in the history of the ESDP came when the Member States accepted that the Union should have a 'capacity for autonomous action' in conflict prevention and crisis management. This was first set out in the Final Declaration of the Franco-British Summit in Saint-Malo on 4 December 1998,[144] which symbolised the end of the 'British lock'. The ambition was then taken up by all EU Member States in the Declaration adopted on 4 June 1999 at the end of the Cologne European Council.[145] The Helsinki European Council in December 1999 subsequently emphasised that the process of developing an autonomous EU capability in the context of the ESDP 'does

---

141 Para. 2 of the preamble to Council Decision (CFSP) 2023/1599 of 3 August 2023), cited above.

142 Art. 2(4) of Council Decision (CFSP) 2023/1599 of 3 August 2023), cited above.

143 Art. 42(1) TEU.

144 Joint Declaration on Defence issued at the British-French Summit, Saint-Malo, 4 December 1998, https://www.cvce.eu/obj/declaration_franco_britannique_de_saint_malo_4_decembre_1998-fr-f3cd16fb-fc37-4d52-936f-c8e9bc80f24f.html.

145 European Council Declaration on strengthening the common European policy on security and defence, Annex III to the Presidency Conclusions of the Cologne European Council of 3 and 4 June 1999, accessible via the Council of the Union website, https://www.consilium.europa.eu/media/21070/57886.pdf.

not imply the creation of a European army',[146] and therefore does not imply the transfer of national forces to the Union, nor their merging, as was reiterated when the Treaty of Lisbon was adopted.[147] It does, however, require the Union to have the human and material capabilities necessary to deploy and conduct, in its own name, crisis management missions and operations outside the Union. To this end, it is therefore the Member States that make capabilities available to the Union and, in order to ensure the sufficiency, predictability and interoperability of the capabilities that the Union may have recourse to within the framework of the ESDP/CSDP. The method chosen therefore has been to establish capability objectives. In the military sphere, the Helsinki European Council in 1999 set the 'Headline Goal 2003', aimed at enabling the deployment of up to 60,000 forces by 2003;[148] then the 'Headline Goal 2010'[149] set in 2004 focused on rapid reaction capabilities, in particular giving impetus to the creation of the battlegroups concept.[150] With regard to civilian crisis management capabilities, engagement objectives were set as early as 2000 in each of the four areas identified at the Santa Maria da Feira European Council,[151] supplemented in 2004 by the 'Civilian Headline Goal 2008'.[152] This led in particular to the concept of Civilian Response Teams (CRTs),[153] and then in 2007 the 'New Civilian Headline Goal 2010'.[154] With these objectives,

---

146 Presidency Conclusions of the Helsinki European Council of 10-11 December 1999, para. 27, accessible via the European Parliament website, https://www.europarl.europa.eu/summits/hel1_en.htm.

147 See the 'Protocol on the concerns of the Irish people on the Treaty of Lisbon', [2013] *OJ* L60/131, in which it is specified that the latter 'does not provide for the creation of a European army [...]'.

148 More specifically, the Member States undertook 'to be able, by 2003, to deploy within less than sixty days, and to sustain for at least one year, forces up to corps level (60,000 persons). These forces should be militarily self-sustaining, with the necessary command, control and intelligence capabilities, logistics and other combat units and, if necessary, air and naval elements' (Helsinki European Council of 10 and 11 December 1999, Presidency Conclusions, para. 28).

149 Council, 'Headline Goal 2010', 6309/6/04 REV 6, 4 May 2004.

150 EUMC, 'EU Battlegroups Concept', 10501/04, 14 June 2004.

151 In the area of police, the Member States undertook to provide up to 5,000 police officers, 1,400 of whom could be deployed within 30 days; to strengthen the rule of law, the aim was to replace, train and assist failing local institutions, with the support of 300 experts; in the area of civil protection, disaster assessment teams, a European resource coordination centre and intervention teams of up to 2,000 experts were deemed necessary to provide assistance for humanitarian actions; for civil administration, the objective (not quantified) was to create a pool of experts that could be rapidly mobilised to act where local administrations would be unable to do so in times of crisis. See the Presidency Conclusions of the Santa Maria da Feira European Council, June 2000.

152 Approved by the European Council on 17 December 2004, 15863/04, 7 December 2004.

153 General Secretariat of the Council, 'Civilian Headline Goal 2008 – Multifunctional Civilian Crisis Management Resources in an Integrated Format – Civilian Response Teams', 10462/05, 23 June 2005.

154 Approved by the Council on 19 November 2007, 14823/07, 9 November 2007.

however, the EU Member States have made only 'a political commitment'[155] to make 'voluntary contributions'[156] to the catalogues of forces and capabilities that can be made available to the EU. And while several dozen EU CMOs have indeed been deployed, the figures set out in the objectives have not been achieved and/or the objectives achieved have not been translated into reality.[157]

In the Declaration on strengthening capabilities adopted by the Council on 11 December 2008, the objective is still expressed in terms of mobilisable personnel over a given period, to which is added a list of the types of operations and missions that the Union should be able to plan and conduct simultaneously,[158] which reflects the Union's level of ambition in this area. The entry into force of the Treaty of Lisbon and the implementation of various defence innovations since 2016 have not fundamentally altered the approach. Following on from the EU's Global Strategy (EUGS), the implementation plan on security and defence has set a 'new level of ambition',[159] implying various 'concrete actions' including that of 'clarifying and completing capability priorities',[160] in order to identify capability shortfalls. There is also a 'non-exhaustive' list of the different types of CSDP civilian missions and military operations that the EU should be able to carry out simultaneously.[161] The 2018 Civilian CSDP Compact and its 2019 Action Plan identified 22 commitments, including the ability to 'launch a new mission of up to 200 personnel in any area of operation within 30 days after a Council decision'.[162] The new Civilian CSDP Compact of 2023 states that '[i]n 2027, the EU will be able to deploy 200 experts within 30 days'.[163] The Strategic Compass, adopted in March 2022 against a backdrop of geopolitical upheaval, is intended to 'enhance the EU's strategic autonomy' and to this end sets out various security and defence objectives and the means of achieving them. These include, for example,

---

155 Meeting of EU Defence Ministers, Sintra, 28 February 2000, 'Food for thought Paper': 'The Headline Goal expressed at Helsinki represents a *political* commitment by the Member States'. Emphasis added.

156 Capabilities Commitment Conference, Brussels, 20-21 November, 2000, Declaration, para. 4.

157 Battlegroup rotations have been organised but these have never been deployed as part of EU crisis management operations.

158 Council, 'Draft Declaration on Strengthening Capabilities', 16840/08, 5 December 2008, p. 2.

159 High Representative, 'Implementation Plan on Security and Defence', doc. 14392/16, 14 November 2016.

160 Ibid., p. 21.

161 Ibid., pp. 16–17.

162 Conclusions of the Council and of the Representatives of the Governments of the Member States, meeting within the Council, on the establishment of a Civilian CSDP Compact, doc. 14305/18 of 19 November 2018, para 11. See also European Commission and High Representative, 'Joint action plan implementing the civilian CSDP Compact', doc. SWD(2019) 173 final, 30 April 2019.

163 Conclusions of the Council and of the Representatives of the Governments of the Member States, meeting within the Council, on the establishment of a Civil CSDP Compact, doc. 9588/23, 22 May 2023, p. 16.

the ambition to have, 'an EU Rapid Deployment Capacity allowing the swift deployment of a modular force of up to 5,000 troops in a non-permissive environment',[164] which was declared operational in May 2025.[165]

Despite the proliferation of 'commitments', the principle remains that of the 'provision' of capabilities by the Member States for EU crisis management operations, and there is no legal obligation to achieve these capability objectives, or even to systematically provide capabilities for each of the EU's crisis management operations. In practice, each Member State remains free to decide whether or not to contribute to each new crisis management operation and its development. This freedom, which safeguards the sovereignty of the Member States, also reflects a form of realism, linked to the variety of Member States' defence positions and resources. For example, some EU Member States favour a position of neutrality and/or have few capabilities – particularly military capabilities. Others wish to preserve their autonomy of decision and action to be able to contribute to operations in other frameworks – in particular the UN, but above all NATO – or to carry them out in their own name, and must therefore deal with the 'principle of a single set of forces'[166] from which they must draw. The principle of crisis management resources being 'made available' by States sometimes complicates the design of a CMO, reduces its ambition and/or delays its launch.[167] However, this has not prevented the EU from deploying more than forty CMOs since 2003.[168]

Secondly, the identification of the 'States' that can make resources available to the Union for its crisis management operations needs to be clarified.

As is expressly stated in Article 32(1) TEU, to which Article 43(1) TEU refers, and the first subparagraph of Article 42(3) TEU, the States concerned are first and foremost, and obviously, the 'Member States' of the Union. And,

---

164 Council of the European Union, 'A Strategic Compass for security and defence – For a European Union that protects its citizens, values and interests and contributes to international peace and security', doc. 7371/22, 21 March 2022, p. 19.

165 EEAS, Press Release, 'Common Security and Defence Policy: EU Rapid Deployment Capacity becomes operational', 20 May 2025, https://www.eeas.europa.eu/eeas/common-security-and-defence-policy-eu-rapid-deployment-capacity-becomes-operational_en.

166 Protocol (No. 10) on Permanent Structured Cooperation established by Article 42 of the Treaty on European Union. See also Council of the European Union, 'A strategic compass for security and defence – For a European Union that protects its citizens, values and interests and contributes to international peace and security', doc. 7371/22, 21 March 2022, p. 30: 'In line with the single set of forces principle, these forces remain in the hands of the Member States and can also be deployed in other frameworks'. Thus, 'European nations do not have two armies and two defence budgets, one for each organisation [EU and NATO]' (A. Papaioannou, 'Strengthening EU-NATO relations', *NATO Review – Opinion, Analysis and Debate on Security Issues*, 16 July 2019, https://archives.nato.int/nato-review-strengthening-eu-nato-relations).

167 For the EUFOR Tchad/RCA, for example, after five force generation conferences, ambitions were scaled back, and Russia's contribution (with a team of up to 120 troops and, above all, four helicopters) proved decisive.

168 See the appendix at the end of this commentary.

since Denmark abandoned its defence opt-out in 2022, all Member States can indeed do so, in favour of both civilian and military deployments. However, this explicit reference is not exclusive; the provision of assets may concern different types of States and involve other players.

For example, in the context of cooperation between the European Union and NATO, the 'Berlin plus' arrangements,[169] concluded on 17 March 2003, provide for NATO capabilities to be made available for the planning and command of EU military operations. For instance, the EU's Concordia military operation in the Former Yugoslav Republic of Macedonia was 'carried out with recourse to NATO assets and capabilities, on the basis agreed with NATO',[170] as was operation EUFOR Althea in Bosnia-Herzegovina, which continues to benefit from them.[171] Since 2019, the Vice-Chief of Staff of Supreme Headquarters Allied Powers Europe (SHAPE) has been the Operation Commander for EUFOR Althea.[172]

In addition, the first subparagraph of Article 42(3) TEU states that '[t]hose Member States which together establish multinational forces may also make them available to the common security and defence policy', a hypothesis which has also been put into practice on several occasions. This is the case, for example, of Eurocorps which brings together eleven European States[173] and describes itself as 'a multinational, fully deployable and highly autonomous headquarters, [...] prepared to plan and conduct military operations across full operational and intensity spectrum [...] *to the benefit of international organisations, especially the European Union and NATO*'.[174] It states it has been deployed on two EU military missions (EUTM Mali and EUTM CAR),[175] and was ready to take on the role of force headquarters for an EU Battlegroup in 2016 and 2017, an experience repeated in 2025.[176] Eurogendfor, for its part, states it is a 'flexible tool can act under military command or civil authority to guarantee public security, and maintenance of public order in crisis management operations. *[It] is first and foremost, at the disposal of the EU*, but it could also respond to requests by the UN, OSCE, NATO, and other

169 NATO, 'The NATO-EU Strategic Partnership', in *The Istanbul Summit Reader's Guide*, June 2004, https://archives.nato.int/istanbul-summit-readers-guide.

170 Council Joint Action 2003/92/CFSP of 27 January 2003 on the EU military operation in the Former Yugoslav Republic of Macedonia ([2003] *OJ* L34/26), Art. 1(3).

171 Council Joint Action 2004/570/CFSP of 12 July 2004, cited above, Art. 1(3).

172 Political and Security Committee Decision (CFSP) 2019/264 of 7 February 2019 on the appointment of the EU Operation Commander for the European Union military operation in Bosnia and Herzegovina [...], [2019] *OJ* L44/12.

173 Six framework nations (Belgium, France, Germany, Luxembourg, Poland and Spain) and five associate nations (Austria, Greece, Italy, Romania and Turkey).

174 See https://www.eurocorps.org/ on the Eurocorps website. Emphasis added.

175 Ibid., https://www.eurocorps.org/operations/european-union/.

176 Ibid., https://www.eurocorps.org/readiness/european-battle-group/.

international organisations or ad-hoc coalitions'.[177] It brings together nine European States[178] and has contributed to no fewer than fifteen EU operations and missions, both military and civilian.[179] These pre-constituted multinational forces make the capabilities of Member States available to the EU, as well as to third countries. But the latter can also contribute individually to EU CMOs.

Third countries are also invited to participate in most EU crisis management operations,[180] which thus become a vehicle for a form of internationalisation of EU crisis management.[181] Based on an agreement establishing a framework for its participation in EU crisis management operations in general, or an ad hoc agreement providing for its participation in a given CMO, a third country may thus make capabilities available to the EU to contribute to one or several of its military operations, military missions and civilian missions.[182] In this case, the contributing third State 'shall associate itself' with the constituent act of the CMO, as well as with its amendments. It then benefits from a form of alignment with the status of Member States in the context of the mission or operation. It is free to decide whether or not to make a contribution and to choose the nature and extent of that contribution; it may also decide to modify or withdraw it during an operation or mission. When contributing to a crisis management operation, in principle,[183] third States 'shall have the same rights and obligations as [contributing] EU Member States with regard to the day-to-day management'[184] of the mission or operation. As such, they are members of the Committee of Contributors. However, they are not among the members of the Council or the PSC, which adopt the main decisions relating to crisis management operations.

---

177 See https://eurogendfor.org/eurogendfor-operational-concept/ on the Eurogendfor website. Emphasis added.

178 Seven Member States (Spain, France, Italy, the Netherlands, Poland, Portugal and Romania), one Partner State (Lithuania) and one Observer State (Türkiye).

179 See the list of past and current missions in question: https://eurogendfor.org/current-and-past-missions/.

180 In the constituent acts of the EU CMOs, there is usually an article entitled 'Participation of third countries'.

181 A. Hamonic, *Les relations entre l'Union européenne et l'ONU dans le domaine de la gestion des crises*, Brussels, Bruylant, 2018, spec. pp. 704-737.

182 On these agreements, see the commentary by C. Schneider in this publication.

183 In some cases, alignment with the rights and obligations of participating Member States is limited to third States making 'significant military contributions'. See, for example, Article 8(4) of Council Decision (CFSP) 2022/1968 of 17 October 2022 on EUMAM Ukraine, cited above.

184 See, for example, Article 9(2) of Decision (CFSP) 2023/855 concerning the EUPM Moldova mission.

Thirdly and lastly, it is important to return to certain aspects[185] of the status of the staff thus made available as part of the Union's crisis management operations, which is the result of a combination of several legal instruments.

Some elements are to be found in the constituent act of the EU crisis management operation itself. Some of them state[186] that '[a]ll seconded staff shall remain under the full command of the national authorities of the seconding State in accordance with national rules, the Union institution concerned, or the European External Action Service (EEAS). Those authorities shall transfer Operational Control of their staff to the [Civilian or Military] Operation Commander'.[187] Operational control is thus distinguished from full control, and the State retains in particular the power to recruit and withdraw seconded personnel, as well as administrative and disciplinary authority over them, and exclusive jurisdiction in criminal matters.[188] It is also specified that '[t]he Member State, the Union institution, or the EEAS respectively shall be responsible for answering any claims linked to the secondment from or concerning the members of staff whom they have seconded, and for bringing any action against such persons'.[189]

The status of military and civilian personnel made available by the States is then the subject of several agreements, some concluded between the Member States, others between the European Union and third countries involved in its crisis management operations. The first agreement between EU Member States, SOFA UE,[190] sets out the status of military and civilian staff who are on the territory of (another) Member State in the context of the preparation or execution of EU crisis management operations. This is the case, for example,

185 On the financial aspects, see the commentary on Article 41 TEU by A. Potteau in this publication.

186 In this respect, the constituent acts for civilian missions are much more developed than those for military missions and operations. However, the parallelism can be seen in Council Decision (CFSP) 2023/1599 of 3 August 2023 on an EU security and defence initiative for the countries of West Africa in the Gulf of Guinea (EUSDI) ([2023] *OJ* L196/25), which has both a civilian pillar and a military pillar.

187 See for example Articles 5(6) (for the civilian pillar) and 12(6) (for the military pillar) of Council Decision (CFSP) 2023/1599 of 3 August 2023) on the EUSDI, cited above, p. 25.

188 A. Claeys-Bouuaert, 'Responsabilité pour violations du DIH dans le cadre des opérations de l'Union européenne – Question de l'attribution du fait internationalement illicite', in A.-S. Millet-Devalle, *L'Union européenne et le droit international humanitaire*, Paris, Pedone, 2010, pp. 119-136, spec. p. 123.

189 See, for example, Article 6(2) of Council Decision (CFSP) 2023/162 of 23 January 2023 on a European Union mission to Armenia (EUMA), [2023] *OJ* L22/29.

190 Agreement between the Member States of the European Union concerning the status of military and civilian staff seconded to the institutions of the European Union, of the headquarters and forces which may be made available to the European Union in the context of the preparation and execution of the tasks referred to in Article 17(2) of the Treaty on European Union, including exercises, and of the military and civilian staff of the Member States put at the disposal of the European Union to act in this context (EU SOFA), [2003] *OJ* C321/6.

of personnel made available to national headquarters used for EU military operations.[191] More unusually, this is also the case for the units and personnel of the EUMAM Ukraine military mission, to which the EU SOFA[192] applies, since exceptionally this CMO takes place on the territory of the Member States. For example, the agreement contains provisions on the entry, stay and departure of personnel, identification details, the carrying of weapons and certain privileges and immunities. But it also contains rules for determining the competent jurisdiction between the State of origin and the State of stay, depending on the personnel and the offence committed, as well as those relating to the waiver by Member States of claims for compensation against another Member State for damage caused to property or persons in connection with the preparation and execution of EU crisis management operations. On this last point, another agreement between Member States concerns the waiver of claims for compensation relating to damage to property and personnel on the territory of third countries where crisis management operations are conducted or on the high seas.[193]

Over and above this specific issue, the status of civilian and military personnel in the theatre of operations results from a status of force agreement (SOFA) or status of mission agreement (SOMA) concluded by the EU with the third State (or States) on whose territory the CMO is deployed[194] or transits.[195] Based on its model agreements (one for SOFAs[196] and one for SOMAs[197]), the provisions of which will generally be taken over, the Union will negotiate a CFSP agreement in which the operation or mission and its personnel will undertake to respect the laws and regulations of the host State, but also rules on the identification of EU operation personnel, border crossings and travel on the territory of the host State, or on the carrying of weapons and the use of force for military deployments. The agreements also contain privileges, immunities and other guarantees relating to the proper conduct of the mission

---

191 See Section II.C above.

192 Art. 9 of Council Decision (CFSP) 2022/1968 of 17 October 2022, cited above.

193 Agreement between the Member States of the European Union on claims for compensation brought by a Member State against another Member State for damage to property owned, used or exploited by it or injury or death of its military or civilian personnel in the context of an EU crisis management operation – Declaration by the Member States, [2004] *OJ* C116/1.

194 See for example the Agreement between the European Union and the Republic of Moldova on the status of the European Union Partnership Mission in Moldova (EUPM Moldova), [2023] *OJ* L2023/2204.

195 For example, an agreement has been concluded with Cameroon on the status of European Union-led forces in transit within the territory, as part of EUFOR RCA ([2008] *OJ* L57/31).

196 Council of the EU, 'Draft model agreement on the status of the European Union-led forces between the European Union and a Host State', 11894/07, 20 July 2007.

197 Council of the EU, 'Agreement between the European Union and the Host State on the status of the civilian crisis management mission conducted in the European Union by the Host State', 16323/08, 15 December 2008.

or operation, offering a particularly protective status.[198] In addition to the inviolability of facilities, archives and correspondence, the model agreements[199] stipulate that the personnel of the EU CMOs are 'exempt from social security provisions' and 'from any form of taxation in the Host State on the salary and emoluments'. They also enjoy 'immunity from the criminal jurisdiction of the Host State under all circumstances' and 'immunity from civil and administrative jurisdiction in the Host State in respect of words spoken or written and all acts performed by them in the exercise of their official functions', as well as immunity from execution. It is nevertheless specified that '[t]he immunity [...] from the jurisdiction of the Host State does not exempt them from the jurisdictions of the Sending States', and that '[t]he competent authorities of a Sending State shall have the right to exercise on the territory of the Host State all the criminal jurisdiction and disciplinary powers conferred on them by the law of the Sending State with regard to all [...] personnel subject to the relevant law of the Sending State'.

Lastly, since the contributing third State associates itself with the constituent act of the crisis management operation, its status is aligned with that of an EU Member State, as is that of the capabilities made available. Thus, the status of personnel deployed by a contributing third State on the territory of the host third State is governed by the agreement on the status of the mission or forces that the latter has concluded with the EU. This is specified in the agreement between the EU and the contributing third State on its participation in crisis management operations which, for its part, governs in particular the status of the personnel and forces of the third State seconded to the headquarters or command elements located outside the State(s) in which the CMO is taking place, but also addresses certain questions of jurisdiction and the waiver of claims against any State participating in an EU operation or mission, and vice versa.[200]

III. THE INSTITUTIONS AND STRUCTURES INVOLVED

The second paragraph of Article 43 TEU is an innovation of the Treaty of Lisbon, constituting a sort of detailing of the institutional provisions relating to the CFSP in general, and the CSDP in particular, especially of Article 42(4),

---

198 S. Aurel, 'Status of forces and status of mission agreements Under the ESDP: the EU's evolving practice' (2008) 19(1) *EJIL*, pp. 67–100, spec. pp. 67 and 98–100.

199 The following extracts are taken from the 'Draft model agreement on the status of the European Union-led forces [...]', cited above, Art. 6 and 8.

200 See, for example, the Agreement between the European Union and the Republic of Peru establishing a framework for the participation of the Republic of Peru in the European Union crisis management operations, [2022] *OJ* L292/14.

for acts relating to crisis management operations. Article 43(2) thus recalls the principal role of the Council of the Union and that of the Political and Security Committee (PSC) which supports it (Section A) and refers to the plural involvement of the High Representative of the Union for Foreign Affairs and Security Policy (HR/VP or High Representative) in the preparation and conduct of the CMOs (Section B).[201] Without going back on the impetus provided by the European Council,[202] Article 43(2) thus reaffirms the fundamentally intergovernmental nature of the process. In so doing, it makes no mention of the involvement of the Union's supranational institutions, which are nonetheless no longer totally unrelated to the EU crisis management operations (Section C).

A. THE MAIN ROLE OF THE COUNCIL, SUPPORTED BY THE PSC

By virtue of Article 42(4) TEU, under the CSDP, decision-making power lies with the Council, which adopts decisions unanimously. While this provision states that this applies in particular to decisions 'initiating a mission', Article 43(2) TEU confirms the procedure, but above all specifies the scope of the decisions concerned in the context of crisis management operations. In so doing, it also outlines the scope of decisions whose adoption may, for its part, be delegated to the PSC.

Thus, according to Article 43(2) TEU, the Council 'shall adopt decisions [relating to crisis management operations] defining their objectives and scope and the general conditions for their implementation'. The Council, and through it the Member States, thus intend to retain control over the creation and development of crisis management operations. Although Article 43(2) TEU is silent on the matter, adoption requires unanimity within the Council, in accordance with Article 42(4) TEU, which itself takes over the rule in the first subparagraph of Article 31(1) TEU.[203] Unanimity then means the agreement of all the EU Member States, not just the Member States contributing to the operation or mission. Constructive abstention is applicable to decisions relating to any crisis management operation, and was used by Cyprus when adopting the constituent act of the EULEX Kosovo civilian mission in 2008 and

---

[201] For a detailed presentation of the procedures for CSDP crisis management operations, see Council 'Suggestions for crisis management procedures for CSDP crisis management operations', doc. 7660/13 REV2, 18 June 2013. See also F. Moreno, 'How to plan and launch a CSDP mission or operation', in J. Rehrl, *Handbook on CSDP*, 4th ed., Publication of the Federal Ministry of Defence of the Republic of Austria, 2021, pp. 80–85.

[202] Art. 26(1) TEU. See the commentary by C. Schneider in this publication.

[203] See the commentary by C. Schneider in this publication.

by Hungary in 2022 when creating the EUMAM Ukraine military mission.[204] On the other hand, the derogations for recourse to qualified majority voting, provided for in Article 31(2) and (3) TEU, are excluded for 'decisions having military or defence implications'.[205] For other crisis management operations (i.e. civilian missions), suggestions in favour of moving to qualified majority voting have not yet been taken up.[206]

The Council, which has political control and strategic direction of the CMOs, approves the Crisis Management Concept,[207] and then adopts the decision to set up the EU crisis management operation. In addition to the reasons for deployment in the preamble, this decision usually includes a first article describing the CMO's 'mission', generally followed by one or two articles detailing the CMO's 'mandate', 'objectives' and/or 'missions'. This is followed by a series of articles describing the procedures for implementing the operation or mission, in particular as regards the 'chain of command and structure', the 'Civilian Operations Commander' and the 'Head of Mission' and 'staff', or the 'designation of the headquarters' and the 'appointment of the EU [Military Mission or Operation] Commander', the status of personnel, 'political control and strategic direction', 'participation of third States', 'financial arrangements', 'status of the mission [or of Union-led personnel]', 'consistency of the Union's response and coordination', 'release of information', as well as 'entry into force and duration'.

As specified in Article 42(4) TEU, the Council also adopts the decision to launch the operation or mission. As the CMO is implemented, it is again the Council that adopts decisions amending the constituent decision as regards the objectives of the operation or mission, its mandate or its duration. Like

204 Council of the European Union (Foreign Affairs), draft minutes, 17 October 2022, doc. 13777/22 ADD 1, 27 October 2022, p. 6 and p. 7. R.A. Wessel and V. Szép, *The implementation of Article 31 of the Treaty on European Union and the use of Qualified Majority Voting: Towards a more effective Common Foreign and Security Policy*, Study Requested by the AFCO committee of the European Parliament, 2022, spec. pp. 61–63.

205 Art. 31(4) TEU.

206 See the Communication from the Commission, 'A stronger global actor: a more efficient decision-making for EU Common Foreign and Security Policy', COM(2018) 647 final, 12 September 2018; R.A. Wessel and V. Szép, *The implementation of Article 31 of the Treaty on European Union and the use of Qualified Majority Voting: Towards a more effective Common Foreign and Security Policy?*, Study Requested by the AFCO committee of the European Parliament, 2022; European Parliament resolution of 22 November 2023 on the European Parliament's plans for revising the Treaties, doc. P9 TA(2023)0427; European Parliament, Resolution of 2 April 2025 on the implementation of the common security and defence policy – annual report 2024, doc. P10_TA(2025)0058.

207 The Crisis Management Concept (CMC) is the conceptual framework describing the CSDP activity to be undertaken in response to a given crisis, defining the strategic political objectives of the CSDP engagement and proposing one or more options for achieving them. See also EEAS, 'EU Concept for Military Command and Control – Rev 8', doc. 8798/19, 23 April 2019, para. 7.

the initial decision, these decisions are based on Articles 43(2) TEU and 42(4) TEU. However, the same does not apply to Council decisions on the signing and conclusion of agreements which also form part of the arrangements for implementing the crisis management operation (essentially agreements on the status of forces or the mission, agreements on the participation of third States and, where appropriate, agreements on the transfer of persons apprehended by an EU CMO). These fall under the unified procedure for the conclusion of international agreements of the Union under Article 218 TFEU,[208] and have as their substantive legal basis Article 37 TEU. Finally, the termination of the CMO may also give rise to a Council decision based on Articles 43(2) and 42(4) TEU.[209] On the other hand, it is rare for the Council to adopt decisions on the appointment of heads and commanders of operations and missions;[210] these are among the categories of decisions whose adoption is usually delegated to the PSC.

Article 38 TEU sets out the PSC, that is the 'linchpin'[211] of the CSDP. It 'shall exercise, under the responsibility of the Council and of the High Representative, the political control and strategic direction of the crisis management operations referred to in Article 43 [TEU]'. In this capacity, the PSC may be authorised by the Council 'for the purpose and for the duration of a crisis management operation, [...] to take the relevant decisions concerning the political control and strategic direction of the operation', which are then based on Article 38 TEU. This authorisation appears systematically in the constituent decisions of EU crisis management operations and usually covers decisions on amending planning documents, the chain of command and the rules of engagement, and on appointing the Operation or Mission Commander, Force Commander or Head of Mission. The PSC is also responsible for adopting decisions on accepting contributions from third States and setting up a Committee of Contributors. The PSC reports to the Council; the EU Military Committee (EUMC) or the Civilian Operations Commander and Head of Mission report(s) to the PSC on the conduct of the operation or mission.

---

208 More specifically, they are agreements that 'relate exclusively [...] to the [CFSP]', for which paragraphs 3 and 6 of Article 218 TFEU lay down specific rules.

209 Council Decision (CFSP) 2020/471 of 31 March 2020, cited above.

210 However, this sometimes happens. See, for example, Council Decision (CFSP) 2020/718 of 28 May 2020 appointing the EU Force Commander of the European Union military operation in the Mediterranean (EUNAVFOR MED IRINI), [2020] *OJ* L168/64.

211 European Council Nice, 7–10 December, 2000, 'Conclusions of the Presidency, Annex III – Political and Security Committee to Annex VI – Report on ESDP', https://www.consilium.europa.eu/ueDocs/cms_Data/docs/pressData/en/ec/00400-r1.%20ann.en0.htm.

It is thus under the authority of the Council and the PSC that the chain of command and the operational and tactical command and control (C2) of the Union's crisis management operations are exercised.[212]

Outside the area of operation, the Operation Commander for military operations, the Mission Commander for military missions or the Civilian Operations Commander for civilian missions is responsible for developing the Concept of Operations (CONOPS), the Operation Plan (OPLAN), the Rules of Engagement (RoE) and the force generation process; he/she coordinates the deployment, sustainment, redeployment and termination of the operation or mission. He/she heads the operation headquarters, the strategic-level command and control structure responsible for the operational planning and conduct of the operation or mission. For civilian missions, this is now the CivOpsHQ, located within the EEAS; its Managing Director is thus the Civilian Operations Commander for all civilian CSDP missions. For military missions, this function is performed by the CMPC, which is located within the EU Military Staff (EUMS); its Director is thus the Mission Commander for all EU military missions, and should gradually become the Mission Commander for military operations. However, as the competence of the CMPC in this respect is only progressive, for military operations this role is still, for the time being, the responsibility of one of the national headquarters made available to the Union or, exceptionally, of NATO's SHAPE.[213]

In-theatre command and control is exercised by the Force Commander for military operations, the Mission Force Commander for military missions, or the Head of Mission for civilian missions. He/she acts under the command of the Operation Commander or Civilian Operations Commander, and exercises command and control over the personnel, teams and units provided by the contributing States, along with being responsible for the day-to-day management of the mission, including its budgetary aspects, as well as administrative and logistical responsibility.

Under the authority of the Council and in close contact with the PSC, the High Representative of the Union for Foreign Affairs and Security Policy (HR/VP) is also involved. Article 43(2) of the TEU reflects the multifaceted involvement of the High Representative of the Union in EU crisis management operations.

---

212 For a detailed presentation of the command and control concepts and architecture for EU CMOs, see EEAS, 'Guidelines for Command and Control Structure for Civilian CSDP Missions', doc. 5095/23, 6 January 2023, and EEAS, 'EU Concept for Military Command and Control – Rev 8', doc. 8798/19, 23 April 2019.

213 See Section II.C above.

B. THE PLURAL INVOLVEMENT OF THE HIGH REPRESENTATIVE OF THE UNION

Both Articles 43(2) TEU and 42(4) TEU refer to an aspect of the multifaceted involvement of the High Representative of the Union in the creation and implementation of the Union's crisis management operations, as a result of the fact that he/she 'shall conduct the Union's common foreign and security policy. He[/she] shall contribute by his proposals to the development of that policy, which he[/she] shall carry out as mandated by the Council. The same shall apply to the common security and defence policy'.[214] The HR/VP is thus the 'orchestra conductor'[215] of the CSDP.

First of all, Article 42(4) TEU provides that the High Representative has the power of initiative for CSDP decisions, which he/she shares with each of the Member States. Since the entry into force of the Treaty of Lisbon, the decisions establishing the Union's crisis management operations, but also usually the other Council decisions marking the life of these operations and missions[216] and certain decisions of the PSC,[217] thus refer to 'the proposal of the [HR/VP]'. The High Representative's power of initiative also applies to agreements. In the case of international agreements concluded by the Union for the implementation of its operations and missions, which are agreements 'relat[ing] exclusively to the [CFSP]' according to the terminology of Article 218 TFEU, the High Representative 'shall submit recommendations to the Council' prior to the opening of negotiations[218] and is in principle designated as negotiator. This means that he/she is the author of the proposal for a decision on the signature and conclusion of the agreement,[219] and where appropriate, of the proposal for a decision on the suspension of the agreement.[220] Again according to Article 42(4) TEU, '[t]he High Representative may propose the use of both national resources and Union instruments, together with the Commission where appropriate'. The decision establishing a European Peace Facility (EPF),[221] which governs the financing of EU military operations and missions, but also allows for the adoption of military assistance measures for

---

214 Art. 18(2) TEU.

215 A. Dumoulin and N. Gros-Verheyde, *La politique européenne de sécurité et de Common defence – Parce que l'Europe vaut bien une défense*, Le Dévoluy, Éd. du Villard, 2017, spec. p. 109. Translated from French.

216 Decisions initiating a mission are expressly covered by Article 42(4) TEU. This also applies to decisions amending or terminating the mandate of the mission or operation. See Section I.B.2 above.

217 This is the case for decisions appointing the Head of Mission of civilian missions.

218 Art. 218(3) TFEU.

219 Art. 218(5) and (6) TFEU.

220 Art. 218(9) TFEU.

221 Council Decision (CFSP) 2021/509 of 22 March 2021, cited above.

third countries,[222] was adopted 'having regard to the proposal from the High Representative of the Union for Foreign Affairs and Security Policy, supported by the European Commission'. As a welcome extension of his/her power of initiative, the High Representative's role as Chair of the Council's Foreign Affairs (including Defence) configuration enables him/her to set the agenda for its meetings.

Secondly, the High Representative is also involved in the 'political control and strategic direction' of EU crisis management operations. Alongside the Council, the PSC, the EUMC and the EUMS, the High Representative is one of the 'permanent actors at the strategic level with responsibilities relating to C2 (control and command)'.[223] More specifically, according to the dedicated article of the constituent decisions, it is '[u]nder the responsibility of the Council and the HR'[224] that the PSC exercises the political control and strategic direction of the mission or operation. The Managing Director of the Civilian Operations Headquarters (CivOpsHQ) as Civilian Operations Commander for civilian missions, on the one hand, and the Military Commander as Head of the CMPC, on the other hand, exercise command and control at the strategic level for the planning and conduct of civilian and military missions respectively, 'under the political control and strategic direction of the PSC and overall authority of the High Representative'.[225] They report to the Council through the HR/VP.[226] In addition, the High Representative proposes the names of the Heads of Mission.[227] The PSC is chaired by a representative of the HR/VP, and the HR/VP or his/her representative chairs the Committees of Contributors of the CMOs.

To carry out his various responsibilities and tasks, the High Representative 'shall be assisted by a European External Action Service',[228] whose general administration includes 'the Crisis Management and Planning Directorate, the Civilian Planning and Conduct Capability, the European Union Military Staff and the European Union Situation Centre, placed under the direct

222 See the commentary on Article 41 TEU by A. Potteau and the commentary on the European Peace Facility by C. Schneider in this publication.

223 EEAS, 'EU Concept for Military Command and Control – Rev 8', doc. 8798/19, 23 April 2019, pt 17. See also Committee for Civilian Aspects of Crisis Management (CIVCOM), 'Draft Guidelines for Command and Control Structure for EU Civilian Operations in Crisis Management', 9919/07 DCL 1, 23 May 2007, para. 13.

224 See, for example, Article 10(1) of Council Decision 2010/452/CFSP of 12 August 2010 on the European Union Monitoring Mission in Georgia (EUMM Georgia), cited above.

225 Articles 5(3) and 12 of Council Decision (CFSP) 2023/1599 of 3 August 2023 on EUSDI), cited above.

226 Ibid., Art. 5(5), for the Civilian Operations Commander and Art. 12(5), for the Military Commander.

227 See, for example, the visa for PSC Decision 2023/2784 of 8 December 2023 appointing the Head of Mission of the European Union Border Assistance Mission in Libya (EUBAM Libya/2/2023), [2023] *OJ* L2023/2784.

228 Art. 27(3) TEU.

authority and responsibility of the High Representative'.[229] In addition, the High Representative 'may ask the PSC for an opinion on the international situation';[230] the CivOpsHQ assists and advises him/her for civilian missions, and military expertise is provided by the EUMS for military operations and missions.

The High Representative is also involved in the communication and exchange of information in the context of the conduct of EU crisis management operations. He/she is authorised to communicate or exchange with third States associated or designated by the PSC, other organisations and bodies,[231] or even other operations deployed in an area,[232] unclassified documents and/or classified information or documents, up to the level of classification and under the conditions specified in the constituent act of each crisis management operation.[233] To this end, it may enter into the necessary arrangements.[234] The HR may also delegate these tasks relating to the communication and exchange of information 'to staff of the EEAS, to the Civilian Operations Commander or to the Military Commander'.[235]

Lastly, under Article 43(2) of the TEU, the High Representative is responsible for 'ensur[ing] coordination of the civilian and military aspects' of the Union's crisis-management operations, an extension of his responsibility for 'ensur[ing] the unity, consistency and effectiveness of action by the Union'[236] in CFSP matters, and more generally 'the consistency of the Union's external action'.[237] Decisions creating EU crisis management operations usually include an article on 'Consistency of the Union's response and coordination',[238] which states that '[t]he High Representative shall ensure the implementation of this Decision and its consistency with the Union's external action as a whole, including

229 Art. 4(3)(a) of Council Decision 2010/427/EU of 26 July 2010 establishing the organisation and functioning of the European External Action Service, [2010] *OJ* L201/30.

230 Art. 38 TEU.

231 Such as the United Nations or Interpol. See for example Article 15(5) and (6) of the consolidated version of Council Decision 2013/233/CFSP of 22 May 2013 on the European Union Border Assistance Mission in Libya (EUBAM Libya), [2013] *OJ* L138/15.

232 Such as 'Operation Prosperity Guardian and [...] the Combined Maritime Forces' in the case of EUNAVFOR ASPIDES (see Article 10(3) of Council Decision (CFSP) 2024/583 of 8 February 2024 on Operation EUNAVFOR ASPIDES, cited above) or 'NATO Security Assistance and Training for Ukraine (NSATU)' in the case of EUMAM Ukraine (see Council Decision (CFSP) 2024/2876 of 8 November 2024 on EUMAM Ukraine ([2024] *OJ* L2024/2876).

233 For example, Art. 20(2) of Council Decision (CFSP) 2023/1599 of 3 August 2023 on EUSDI), cited above.

234 Ibid.

235 Ibid., Art. 20(4).

236 Art. 26(2)(2) TEU.

237 Art. 18(4) TEU.

238 See, for example, Art. 17 of Council Decision (CFSP) 2023/1599 of 3 August 2023 on EUSDI, cited above.

the Union's development programmes and its humanitarian assistance programmes'[239] or 'the Union's assistance programmes'.[240] Reference may also be made to the role of the Head of the EU Delegation and to coordination with other EU CSDP operations and missions in the area of intervention,[241] as well as with the representatives and activities of the international partners[242] and, where appropriate, with some Member States.[243]

C. THE PARTICIPATION OF SUPRANATIONAL INSTITUTIONS

For EU crisis management operations, Article 43(2) TEU sets out the characteristics of the intergovernmental method, which is particularly prevalent in CSDP, especially for decisions with military or defence implications. It is therefore not surprising that the institutions representing the supranational approach – the European Parliament, the European Commission and the EU Court of Justice – do not appear in Article 43(2) TEU on crisis management operations. However, this does not mean that these institutions have no role to play in crisis management operations.

This is the case, first of all, of the European Parliament and the European Commission. According to the second subparagraph of Article 24(1) TEU, they have '[s]pecific roles [...] defined by the Treaties'[244] for CFSP, a cryptic formula which reflects their marginal involvement, which is not, however, non-existent as regards the Union's crisis management operations.

On the one hand, the European Parliament is not involved in the decision-making process since 'the adoption of legislative acts shall be excluded' in CFSP matters. However, it does have certain means of information and expression

239 Ibid.

240 See for example Article 15(1) of Council Decision (CFSP) 2023/855 of 24 April 2023 on a European Union Partnership Mission in Moldova (EUPM Moldova), cited above.

241 See, for example, Article 14(3) of Council Decision (CFSP) 2019/2110 of 9 December 2019 on the European Union CSDP Advisory Mission in the Central African Republic (EUAM CAR) ([2019] *OJ* L318/141), which refers to EUTM CAR.

242 In the decision establishing operation EUNAVFOR ASPIDES, reference is made to 'the United Nations, the authorities of the countries in the region, and other multinational and bilateral actors, including the Gulf Cooperation Council, the League of Arab States, the United States of America and the United Kingdom' (Art. 6(2) of Council Decision (CFSP) 2024/583 of 8 February 2024).

243 See, for example, Article 7(4) of Council Decision 2013/34/CFSP of 17 January 2013 on the EUTM Mali mission, referring to 'Member States' bilateral activities in Mali, as well as with other international actors in the region, in particular the UN, the African Union (AU), ECOWAS and bilateral actors including the United States and Canada, and with key regional actors'.

244 Article 24(1)(2) TEU. M. Riddervold and G. Rosén, 'Beyond Intergovernmental Cooperation: The Influence of the European Parliament and the Commission on EU Foreign and Security Policies' (2015) 20(3) *European Foreign Affairs Review*, pp. 399–418.

concerning the CFSP and CSDP,[245] and therefore crisis management operations. The Treaties provide that the European Parliament 'shall regularly consult [...] on the main aspects and the basic choices of the common foreign and security policy and the common security and defence policy and inform it of how those policies evolve'.[246] The Treaty of Lisbon also added CSDP to the agenda for the debate on the progress made in implementing the CFSP (held twice a year), pursuant to Article 36(2) TEU, which also states that '[t]he European Parliament may address questions or make recommendations to the Council or the High Representative'. Through its numerous questions, resolutions and regular reports, the institution responsible for 'democratic scrutiny of the European Union's external action'[247] can express its positions, concerns and criticisms regarding crisis management operations in particular,[248] even if these are limited vectors of influence.[249] The European Parliament 'shall [also] be immediately and fully informed at all stages of the procedure'[250] for the negotiation and conclusion of external agreements, a procedural rule which the Court of Justice has described as an 'essentiel procedural requirement',[251] in the context of disputes concerning CFSP agreements concluded for the implementation of a crisis management operation,[252] in respect of which the European Parliament is not otherwise involved.[253] Then, in its capacity as

245 See for example N. Clinchamps, 'CSDP and the European Parliament in the light of the Lisbon Treaty', in N. Clinchamps and P.-Y. Monjal (eds.), *L'autonomie stratégique de l'Union européenne. Perspectives, responsabilité, ambitions et limites de la défense européenne*, Brussels, Larcier, 2015, pp. 55–72; C. Moser and S. Blockmans, 'The Extent of the European Parliament's Competence in Common Security and Defence Policy', Policy Department for External Relations, European Parliament, 2022; H. Flavier, 'L'implication du Parlement européen en matière de défense. Derrière le Parlement, les citoyens?', in A. Hamonic, *La spécificité de la défense en droit de l'Union européenne*, Rennes, Presses universitaires de Rennes, 2025.

246 Art. 36(1) TEU. See the commentary by C. Schneider in this publication.

247 Case C-658/11, *Parliament v Council*, ECLI:EU:C:2014:2025, para. 79; Case C-263/14, *Parliament v Council*, ECLI:EU:C:2016:435, para. 80.

248 See the Annual report on the implementation of the CSDP (doc. A9-0403/2023 of 6 December 2023 for the 2023 annual report). See also, for example, the European Parliament Resolution of 18 April 2023 on the implementation of civilian CSDP and other EU civilian security assistance, doc. P9_TA(2023)0106, 18 April 2023.

249 A. Hamonic, 'Politique étrangère et de sécurité commune et parlementarisation de l'Union européenne', in I. Bosse-Platière (ed.), *La parlementarisation des processus d'intégration régionale – Approche comparée Europe, Afrique, Amériques*, Droits européens, Rennes, Presses universitaires de Rennes, 2020, pp. 295–332.

250 Art. 218(10) TFEU.

251 Case C-658/11, *Parliament v Council*, ECLI:EU:C:2014:2025, para. 80; Case C-263/14, *Parliament v Council*, ECLI:EU:C:2016:435, para. 84.

252 Both cases concerned CFSP agreements, concluded with the Republic of Mauritius and the United Republic of Tanzania respectively, on the conditions of transfer of suspected pirates and associated seized property from the European Union-led naval force to the third country and on the conditions of suspected pirates after transfer.

253 Case C-658/11, *Parliament v Council*, ECLI:EU:C:2014:2025, paras. 84–85.

budgetary co-authority, the European Parliament takes part in the vote on administrative expenditure arising from all the crisis management operations and on operational expenditure arising from the Union's civilian missions,[254] on which it is consulted and informed.[255] The European Parliament regularly criticises the structure of the CFSP budget and deplores the insufficient evolution of its size.[256] It can even postpone or refuse to grant discharge to the Commission for the implementation of the budget.[257] In a resolution of November 2023, the Parliament proposed various ambitious changes to the CSDP, including its funding by the Union 'through a dedicated budget under parliamentary co-decision and scrutiny'.[258] Finally, and more indirectly, the communitisation of the Union's defence policy,[259] which gives rise to the adoption of regulations via the ordinary legislative procedure, offers the European Parliament a role in the development of initiatives to strengthen the defence capabilities of the Member States. And these could then be made available to the Union for its crisis management operations.

The trend towards the communitisation of defence also favours the involvement of the European Commission, in particular through its power of initiative, which enables it to draw up proposals for regulations aimed at strengthening the European Defence Technological and Industrial Base (EDTIB),[260] but also to withdraw them, if necessary, if the amendments envisaged by the co-legislators risk distorting its proposals. Furthermore, when, in the context of the CSDP, the High Representative proposes recourse to national resources and EU instruments, he/she may do so 'together with the Commission where appropriate'.[261] Above all, the Commission's

---

254 In accordance with Article 41 TEU. See the commentary by A. Potteau in this publication.

255 Interinstitutional Agreement between the European Parliament, the Council of the European Union and the European Commission on budgetary discipline, cooperation in budgetary matters and sound financial management as well as on new own resources, including a roadmap for the establishment of new own resources, [2020] *OJ* L433I/28, para. 24.

256 Report on the implementation of the Common foreign and security policy – annual report 2023, doc. A9-0389/2023, 4 December 2023, paras. 34 and 35.

257 It has already made use of this prerogative, in particular to express its disagreement with the categorisation of CMO expenditure as administrative or operational (Resolution of the European Parliament of 23 April 2009 with observations forming an integral part of the Decision on discharge in respect of the implementation of the European Union general budget for the financial year 2007, Section II; Council, para. 2, [2009] *OJ* L255/18).

258 European Parliament resolution of 22 November 2023 on the European Parliament's plans for revision of the Treaties, doc. P9_TA(2023)0427, pt 22 of the resolution and annex (amendment 51 concerning Article 42(1) TEU).

259 E. Bernard, 'La communautarisation de la défense européenne dans le contexte de la guerre en Ukraine', *RTD eur.*, 2023/3, pp. 325–350. See in particular the commentaries by S. Rodrigues on the Regulation establishing the European Defence Fund, by E. Bernard on the ASAP and EDIRPA Regulations, and by E. Simon on the EDIP Regulation, in this publication.

260 Ibid.

261 Art. 42(4) TEU. See Section III.B *above*.

power to implement the budget finds expression in various ways in the implementation of EU crisis management operations, and more specifically civilian missions.[262] For the latter, the financial provisions in the constituent act state that 'all expenditure shall be managed in accordance with the rules and procedures applicable to the general budget of the Union'. In so doing, the mission may award contracts and conclude technical agreements with Member States, the host State or participating third States, in particular for the supply of equipment, services and premises. However, this is '[s]ubject to the Commission's approval'.[263] In addition, each CSDP mission 'shall be responsible for the implementation of its budget',[264] but '[t]o this end, [it] shall sign an agreement with the Commission';[265] and the mission 'shall report fully to, and be supervised by, the Commission on the financial activities undertaken in the framework of the agreement'.[266]

As for the Court of Justice of the European Union (CJEU), Article 24(1)(2) TEU, supplemented by Article 275 TFEU, lays down the principle that it has no jurisdiction over provisions and acts relating to the CFSP,[267] and therefore the CSDP. However, the Court of Justice (Court) stressed that these provisions 'introduce a derogation from the rule of the general jurisdiction which Article 19 TEU confers on the Court of justice to ensure that in the interpretation and application of the Treaties the law is observed and they must, therefore, be interpreted narrowly'.[268]

In recent years, the CSDP has gradually come under the jurisdiction of the CJEU,[269] through various disputes relating to crisis management operations, and the CJEU has then extended its jurisdiction.[270]

---

262 See the above-mentioned commentary by A. Potteau in this publication.

263 See for example Article 13(2) of Council Decision (CFSP) 2023/855 of 24 April 2023 on a European Union Partnership Mission in Moldova (EUPM Moldova), cited above.

264 Ibid., Art. 13(3).

265 Ibid.

266 Ibid., Art. 13(4).

267 Subject to two exceptions mentioned in Article 24 TEU and specified in Article 275 TFEU, which do not directly concern the Union's CMOs, but concern 'monitoring compliance with Article 40 [TEU]' and 'reviewing the legality of decisions providing for restrictives measures against natural or legal persons.

268 Case C-439/13 P, *Elitaliana SpA v EULEX Kosovo*, ECLI:EU:C:2015:753, para. 42; Case C-455/14 P, *H. v Council, Commission and the EUPM Bosnia-Herzegovina*, ECLI:EU:C:2016:569, para. 40. See in particular. I. Bosse-Platière, 'Les exceptions à l'incompétence de la Cour de justice en matière de politique étrangère et de sécurité commune (PESC)', in E. Carpano and G. Marti (eds.), *L'exception en droit de l'Union européenne*, Rennes, Presses universitaires de Rennes, 2019, pp. 95–114.

269 See the commentary on Article 275 TFEU by N. Gros-Verheyde and C. Schneider in this publication.

270 F. Favière, 'L'atténuation de la spécificité de la défense par la Cour de justice de l'Union européenne', in A. Hamonic, *La spécificité de la défense en droit de l'Union européenne*, Rennes, Presses universitaires de Rennes, 2025.

On the question of the litigation status of these CMOs, in 2015 the Court confirmed the interpretation of the General Court (GC), which considered that a crisis management operation did not have legal personality and was a 'mission, of limited duration, which could not be a "body, office or agency" within the meaning of the first paragraph of Article 263 TFEU',[271] and therefore not a party in an action for annulment before the CJEU. Since then, however, the General Court, noting in particular the development of the legal capacity of the Union's civilian missions (as reflected in their constituent decisions),[272] has recognised its jurisdiction to hear several actions brought against such missions,[273] without, however, clearly deciding whether or not they are 'bodies, offices or agencies' of the Union.[274]

In addition, through various cases involving several civilian crisis management missions, the CJEU has declared its jurisdiction in increasingly varied disputes. This applies first and foremost to disputes relating to the management of mission personnel. The General Court has agreed to hear cases in which the relationship arose from an employment contract containing an arbitration clause conferring jurisdiction on the CJEU to settle disputes arising therefrom, thus enabling it to recognise the contractual liability of a mission within the meaning of Article 340(1) TFEU.[275] In addition, relying in particular on the values of equality and the rule of law to which effective judicial protection contributes, the Court held that it also had jurisdiction to hear actions for annulment and damages concerning personnel management measures taken by a crisis management mission, even in respect of staff seconded by the Member States, since 'staff members seconded by the Member States and those seconded by the EU institutions are subject to the same rules

271 Case C-439/13 P, *Elitaliana SpA v EULEX Kosovo*, ECLI:EU:C:2015:753, para. 59.

272 In the decisions establishing EU civilian missions, an article now states that '[a]s required in order to implement this Decision, [the mission] shall have the capacity to procure services and supplies, enter into contracts and administrative arrangements, employ staff, hold bank accounts, acquire and dispose of assets, discharge its liabilities and be a party to legal proceedings' (see, for example, Art. 12a of the consolidated version of Council Decision 2012/392/CFSP of 16 July 2012 on the European Union CSDP mission in Niger (EUCAP Sahel Niger), [2012] *OJ* L187/48).

273 Case T-763/16, *PY v EUCAP Sahel Niger*, ECLI:EU:T:2018:181, paras. 50–54. See also, for example, Case T-165/20, *JC v EUCAP Somalia*, ECLI:EU:T:2022:453; Case T-194/20, *JF v EUCAP Somalia*, ECLI:EU:T:2022:454.

274 At issue in the cases in question was the contractual relationship between the mission and a member of staff, with an employment contract containing an arbitration clause providing for the jurisdiction of the CJEU; the actions were therefore upheld as being based on Article 272 TFEU.

275 Case T-763/16, *PY v EUCAP Sahel Niger*, ECLI:EU:T:2018:181; Case T-165/20, *JC v EUCAP Somalia*, ECLI:EU:T:2022:453; Case T-194/20, *JF v EUCAP Somalia*, ECLI: EU:T:2022:454; Case T-602/15 RENV, *Liam Jenkinson v Council, Commission, EEAS and EULEX Kosovo*, ECLI:EU:T:2021:764. See the commentary on Article 270 TFEU by N. Gros-Verheyde in this publication.

so far as concerns the performance of their duties "at theatre level"',[276] and disputes concerning the latter fall within the jurisdiction of the CJEU under Article 270 TFEU.[277] The Court has also excluded from the scope of the jurisdictional immunity of Articles 24 TEU and 275 TFEU acts relating to the award of public contracts adopted in the context of a civilian mission of the Union, insofar as such a contract falls within the scope of the provisions of the Financial Regulation on the award of public contracts, for the interpretation and application of which the Court has jurisdiction.[278] Finally, the Court also agreed to answer questions on the interpretation of several provisions of the instrument creating a civilian mission of the European Union, leading it to consider the mission 'as responsible and therefore as defendant in any action relating to the consequences of the implementation of the mission entrusted to it'.[279]

In two other joined cases, the General Court and the Court were confronted with the thorny issue of the non-contractual liability of a mission for damage allegedly suffered as a result of acts and omissions committed in the implementation of its mandate. More specifically, it is, in the present case, the inadequacy of the investigations carried out by the EULEX Kosovo civilian mission into the disappearance and murder of members of the applicants' family, which, according to the applicants, constituted a breach of various fundamental rights protected by the European Convention for the Protection of Human Rights and Fundamental Freedoms (ECHR) and the Charter of Fundamental Rights of the European Union.[280] Taking up a distinction already outlined,[281] the General Court concluded that it 'manifestly lack[ed] jurisdiction' to hear such a claim for compensation, on the grounds that, on this occasion, the action 'ar[ose] from acts or conduct which fall within the scope of political or strategic issues connected with defining the activities, priorities and resources' of the mission,[282] and not from 'acts or conduct which are purely personnel management matters',[283] nor in an act 'adopted albeit for

276 Case C-455/14 P, *H. v Council, Commission and the EUPM Bosnia and Herzegovina*, ECLI:EU:C:2016:569, para. 50. Case T-371/22, *Montanari v EUCAP Sahel Niger*, ECLI:EU:T:2024:494, para. 46.

277 Ibid., para. 44. See the commentary by N. Gros-Verheyde in this publication.

278 Case C-439/13 P, *Elitaliana SpA v EULEX Kosovo*, ECLI:EU:C:2015:753, paras. 48–49.

279 Case C-283/20, *CO and Others v MJ, Commission, EEAS, Council, EULEX Kosovo*, ECLI:EU:C:2022:126, para. 47.

280 Case T-771/20, *KS and KD v Council of the European Union and Others*, ECLI:EU:T:2021:798.

281 Case T-271/10 R, *H v Council and Commission*, ECLI:EU:T:2010:315, para. 25. The General Court distinguished 'purely administrative decisions which are taken in relation to staff management within the [mission], which would be clearly separable from the 'political' measures taken as part of the CFSP'.

282 Case T-771/20, *KS and KD v Council of the European Union and Others*, ECLI:EU:T:2021:798, para. 28.

283 Ibid., para. 35. The General Court refers to Case C-455/14 P, *H. v Council, Commission and the EUPM Bosnia and Herzegovina*, cited above.

operational reasons by a CFSP body, but based on provisions covered by the [TFEU]'.[284] Thus, according to the General Court, in this case, the CFSP did not merely represent 'the context'[285] of the contested acts, the legality of which could be assessed in the light of the provisions of the TFEU or secondary legislation; it constituted the very basis of the contested acts and conducts which, as such, had to be covered by the jurisdictional immunity organised by the TEU and the TFEU. And it added that the consequent lack of jurisdiction of the CJEU could not be set aside 'solely on the basis that such recognition would [...] be the only way of guaranteeing [the appellants] effective judicial protection'.[286] In the context of the appeals brought by the appellants and the Commission, Advocate General T. Capeta argued on the contrary that the General Court should have accepted jurisdiction. Following a line of reasoning strongly influenced by the 'broader context of the ongoing negotiations on the accession of the European Union's to the [ECHR]',[287] she took the view that the 'constitutional principles of the EU legal order, principally the rule of law, which includes the right to effective judicial protection, and the principle requiring respect for fundamental rights in all EU policies'[288] allow the jurisdiction of the CJEU to be limited 'only exceptionally',[289] and that this cannot be the case for actions for damages brought in respect of CFSP acts alleged to violate the fundamental rights of individuals.[290] The Court's ruling was eagerly awaited, not least because it could 'break the deadlock' blocking the Union's accession to the ECHR. However, with regard more specifically to the jurisdictional status of crisis management operations, the judgment also offers significant advances. In the Grand Chamber judgment of 10 September

---

284 Ibid., para. 36. The General Court refers Case C-439/13 P, *Elitaliana SpA v EULEX Kosovo*, cited above.

285 Ibid., para. 34.

286 Ibid., para. 40.

287 Opinion of Advocate General T. Capeta, 23 November 2023, Joined Cases *KS and KD v Council and Others* (C-29/22 P) and *Commission v KS, KD and Others* (C-44/22 P), ECLI:EU:C:2023:901, para. 4, 24–26 and 145–153. It recalls Opinion 2/13 of 18 December 2014, ECLI:EU:C:2014:2454), in which the Court 'had left open the question of the compatibility of [the] draft Accession Treaty with the relevant Treaty provisions on the CFSP [...]' considering that 'it had not yet had the opportunity to define the extent to which its jurisdiction is limited by Article 24(1) TEU and 275 TFEU' (pt 25 of the Opinion). It went on to stress that the CFSP was 'the only [remaining] topic' following the unanimous provisional agreement in March within the '46+1' group (para. 26). On Opinion 2/13, see I. Bosse-Platière and A. Hervé, 'La CJUE juge le projet d'adhésion de l'Union à la Convention européenne des droits de l'homme incompatible avec les traités: quelques réflexions concernant l'action extérieure de l'UE', chronicle 'L'action extérieure de l'Union européenne', *RTD eur.*, January-March 2015, p. 220.

288 Opinion of Advocate General T. Capeta, 23 November 2023, Joined Cases *KS and KD v Council and Others* (C-29/22 P) and *Commission v KS, KD and Others* (C-44/22 P), cited above, para. 155.

289 Ibid.

290 Ibid., para. 89.

2024,[291] the Court in a way mapped out a 'third way' between the diametrically opposed visions of the General Court and of the Advocate General.

Firstly, it firmly reaffirmed the specific nature of the CFSP deriving from the Treaties and held that 'the claim that the acts or omissions which are the subject of an action brought by an individual infringe that individual's fundamental rights is not in itself sufficient for the Court of Justice of the European Union to declare that it has jurisdiction to hear and determine that action [...]; otherwise, the last sentence of the second subparagraph of Article 24(1) TEU and the first paragraph of Article 275 TFEU would be deprived of their effectiveness in part and the principles of conferral and of institutional balance infringed'.[292] It also added that these two articles may 'be regarded as *leges speciales* in relation to Articles 268 and 340 TFEU',[293] implying that actions for non-contractual liability are also subject to the limitation on the Court's jurisdiction over the CFSP. By refusing to allow the invocation of an allegation of fundamental rights to automatically confer jurisdiction on the CJEU in relation to actions concerning CFSP acts, the Court has a priori supported the limitation of the jurisdiction of the Union's courts in CFSP matters, including in relation to crisis management operations.

However, at a second stage, the Court accepted in part the objections criticising the General Court's restrictive and selective reading of the case-law relating to CFSP and CSDP acts, and thus recognised the jurisdiction of the CJEU in respect of certain acts or omissions occurring in the context of the implementation of a crisis management operation. More specifically, the Court appropriately described the steps in the reasoning to be followed in the event of an action concerning acts or omissions falling within the scope of the CFSP. Unsurprisingly, it explained that it is first necessary to 'ascertain, [...], whether the situation at issue falls within one of the situations provided for in [Articles 24 TEU and 275 TFEU]',[294] namely for the review of compliance with Article 40 TEU and for actions concerning the review of the legality of decisions providing for restrictive measures against natural or legal persons. It went on to state that, if not, 'it is necessary [then] to assess whether [...] the jurisdiction of the Court of Justice of the European Union may be based on the fact that the acts and omissions at issue are not directly related to the political or strategic choices made by the institutions, bodies, offices and agencies of the Union in the context of the CFSP, and in particular the CSDP'.[295] In fact, according

[291] Joined Cases C-29/22 P and C-44/22 P, *KS and KD v Council and Others* and *Commission v KS and Others*, ECLI:EU:C:2024:725.

[292] Ibid., para. 73. For a more detailed analysis of this part of the judgment, see the commentary by N. Gros-Verheyde and C. Schneider on Article 275 TFEU, in this publication.

[293] Ibid., para. 91.

[294] Ibid., para. 115.

[295] Ibid., para. 116.

to the Court, the CJEU 'does not have jurisdiction'[296] 'to assess the legality of, or interpret, acts or omissions directly related to the conduct, definition or implementation of the CFSP, and especially the CSDP, that is to say, in particular the identification of the European Union's strategic interests and the definition of both the actions to be taken and the positions to be adopted by the European Union as well as of the general guidelines of the CFSP, within the meaning [of various articles relating to the CFSP, including Articles 42 and 43 TEU]'.[297] It concluded by stressing that this solution is consistent with the CFSP provisions of the Treaty, in terms of both their wording and the context in which they are set, and the purpose they pursue.[298] The Court also took the opportunity to emphasise that this solution 'enables the effectiveness of the provisions to be preserved, without, however, unduly prejudicing the right to an effective remedy'.[299] The Court's reasoning is not confined to actions relating to EU crisis management operations, but undoubtedly applies to them. By adopting a direct link to political or strategic choices as a criterion for recognising the jurisdiction of the CJEU, the Court is moving closer to the approach of the General Court.[300] By indicating what falls within the scope of these political or strategic choices,[301] it provides valuable guidance, even if, by offering only a non-exhaustive list[302] and by not specifying what is meant by the 'direct' nature of the connection, the Court leaves room for a certain degree of discretion (and imprecision).

Above all, however, it should be noted that the Court rejected any overall assessment of the acts and omissions at issue in order to conclude that the CJEU lacks jurisdiction, contrary to what the General Court of First Instance did. Instead, it required a 'specific analysis of each of the acts and omissions falling within the scope of the CFSP, and in particular the CSDP'[303] referred to in the action, while emphasising that 'taking account of the fact that the aim of legal certainty does not require that the Courts of the European Union have to consider the substance of the case in order to establish whether they have jurisdiction'.[304] It then applied this immediately to the case in point. It thus

296 Ibid., para. 117.
297 Ibid., para. 118.
298 Ibid., para. 119.
299 Ibid., para. 119.
300 See above.
301 '[T]he conduct, [...] definition or [...] implementation of the CFSP, and especially the CSDP, that is to say, in particular, the identification of the Union's strategic interests and the definition of the actions to be taken and the positions to be adopted by the European Union as well as of the general guidelines of the CFSP' (para. 118).
302 This is reflected in the use of 'in particular' (pt 118).
303 Joined Cases C-29/22 P and C-44/22 P, *KS and KD v Council and Others* and *Commission v KS and Others*, cited above, para. 121.
304 Ibid., para. 121.

ruled that the identification of the resources made available to a mission[305] and the decision to revoke its executive mandate[306] were directly linked to political or strategic choices, which the CJEU cannot therefore examine. On the other hand, the mission's capacity to employ staff (and the decisions it entails) 'constitutes an act of day-to-day management'[307] which is not directly linked to political and strategic choices. The same is true of the absence of provisions for legal aid, which is a matter of 'purely procedural rules',[308] the lack of enforcement powers conferred on the review panel or of remedies for breaches found by it to have been committed, which relate to 'an aspect of [the mission's] administrative management',[309] or failure to take remedial action to remedy the breaches of fundamental rights found by the review panel and the misuse or abuse of power in the absence of a serious legal examination of the case, which, according to the Court, 'concern the failure to adopt individual measures relating to the particular situations [of the applicants]'.[310] These are therefore not directly related to the political or strategic choices made in the context of the EULEX Kosovo mission. The acts and omissions may therefore be subject to review by the CJEU, and the General Court's order is therefore partially annulled.

While ensuring immunity from jurisdiction for certain types of decisions, the Court's concrete analysis shows the variety of reasons why acts and omissions may, for their part, be considered as not directly related to the political and strategic choices relating to an CMO. In doing so, the Court reinforces the accountability and therefore the legitimacy of CMOs. By continuing to widen the breach in the jurisdictional immunity of CMOs, it is also contributing to the 'communitisation' of the CSDP.

---

305 Ibid., para. 126.
306 Ibid., para. 136.
307 Ibid., paras. 127 and 128.
308 Ibid., para. 130.
309 Ibid., para. 131.
310 Ibid., para. 133.

Appendix

List of the EU Crisis Management Operations (CMOs) of the European Union

(On 1 January 2025 – by category and alphabetical order of acronym)
(*in brackets: year of adoption of the act creating the operation or mission – year of end of the operation or mission if completed*)

- <u>**Military operations**</u>

- **Artemis** (*June 2003-September 2003*): European Union military operation in the Democratic Republic of Congo
- **Concordia** (*March 2003-December 2003*): European Union military operation in the Former Yugoslav Republic of Macedonia
- **EUFOR Althea** (*2004-…*): European Union military operation in Bosnia and Herzegovina
- **EUFOR Libya** (*2011-not launched*): European Union military operation in support of humanitarian assistance operations in response to the crisis situation in Libya
- **EUFOR RCA** (*2014-2015*): European Union military operation in the Central African Republic
- **EUFOR RD Congo** (*April 2006-November 2006*): European Union military operation in support of the United Nations Organisation Mission in the Democratic Republic of Congo (MONUC) during the electoral process
- **EUFOR Tchad/RCA** (*2007-2009*): European Union military operation in the Republic of Chad and in the Central African Republic
- **EUNAVFOR ASPIDES** (*2024-…*): European Union maritime security operation to safeguard freedom of navigation in relation to the Red Sea crisis
- **EUNAVFOR Atalanta** (*2008-…*): European Union military operation to contribute to maritime security in the West Indian Ocean and in the Red Sea; previously (until 2022) European Union military operation to contribute to the deterrence, prevention and repression of acts of piracy and armed robbery off the Somali coast.
- **EUNAVFOR MED IRINI** (*2020-…*): European Union military operation in the Mediterranean
- **EUNAVFOR MED Operation Sophia** (*2015-2020*): European Union military operation in the Southern Central Mediterranean

- <u>**Military missions**</u>

- **EUMAM Mozambique** (*2024-…*): European Union military assistance mission in Mozambique; previously **EUTM Mozambique** (*2021-2024*): European Union military training mission in Mozambique.

- **EUMAM RCA** (*2015-2016*): European Union CSDP military advisory mission in the Central African Republic
- **EUMAM Ukraine** (*2022-...*): European Union military assistance mission in support of Ukraine
- **EUMPM Niger** (*2022-2023*): European Union military partnership mission in Niger
- **EUTM Mali** (*2013-2024*): European Union military mission to contribute to the training of the Malian armed forces
- **EUTM RCA** (*2016-...*): European Union CSDP military training mission in the Central African Republic
- **EUTM Somalia** (*2010-...*): European Union military mission to contribute to the training of the Somali security forces

• **Civilian missions**

- **AMM Aceh** (*2005-2006*): European Union monitoring mission in Aceh (Indonesia)
- **EU SSR GUINEA-BISSAU** (*2008-2010*): European Union mission in support of security sector reform in the Republic of Guinea-Bissau
- **EUAM Iraq** (*2017-...*): European Union advisory mission in support of security sector reform in Iraq
- **EUAM RCA** (*2019-...*): European Union CSDP advisory mission in the Central African Republic
- **EUAM Ukraine** (*2014-...*): European Union advisory mission for civilian security sector reform in Ukraine
- **EUAVSEC South Sudan** (*2012-2014*): European Union aviation security CSDP mission in South Sudan
- **EUBAM Libya** (*2013-...*): European Union integrated border management assistance mission in Libya
- **EUBAM Rafah** (*2005-...*): European Union border assistance mission at the Rafah crossing point
- **EUCAP Sahel Mali** (*2014-...*): European Union CSDP mission in Mali
- **EUCAP Sahel Niger** (*2012-2024*): European Union CSDP mission in Niger
- **EUCAP Somalia** (*2012-...*): European Union capacity-building mission in Somalia; *previously* **EUCAP NESTOR** (*2012-2016*): European Union mission on regional maritime capacity building in the Horn of Africa.
- **EUJUST LEX Iraq** (*2005-2013*): European Union Integrated Rule of Law Mission for Iraq
- **EUJUST Themis** (*2004-2005*): European Union Rule of Law Mission in Georgia
- **EULEX Kosovo** (*2008-...*): European Union rule of law mission in Kosovo
- **EUMA Armenia** (*2023-...*): European Union mission in Armenia
- **EUMM Georgia** (*2008-...*): European Union Monitoring Mission in Georgia

- **EUPAT** (*2005-2006*): European Union police advisory mission in the former Yugoslav Republic of Macedonia (fYROM)
- **EUPM BiH** (*2002-2012*): European Union Police Mission in Bosnia and Herzegovina
- **EUPM Moldova** (*2023-...*): European Union partnership mission in Moldova
- **EUPOL Afghanistan** (*2010-2017*): European Union police mission in Afghanistan
- **EUPOL COPPS** (*2005-...*): European Union police mission for the Palestinian territories
- **EUPOL Kinshasa** (*2004-2006*): European Union police mission in Kinshasa (DRC)
- **EUPOL Proxima** (*2003-2005*): European Union police mission in the former Yugoslav Republic of Macedonia
- **EUPOL RD Congo** (*2007-2014*): European Union police mission undertaken in the framework of reform of the security sector (SSR) and its interface with the system of justice in the Democratic Republic of Congo.
- **EUSEC RD Congo** (*2005-2016*): European Union mission to provide advice and assistance for security sector reform in the Democratic Republic of Congo

• **<u>Civil-military missions</u>**

- **AMIS EU supporting action** (*2005-2007*): European Union civilian-military supporting action to the African Union mission in the Darfur region of Sudan, which became (*in April 2007*) the **AMIS/AMISOM EU supporting action** (*April 2007-December 2007*): European Union civilian-military supporting action to the African Union mission in the Darfur region of Sudan and in Somalia (AMIS/AMISOM)
- **EUSDI** (*2023-...*): European Union security and defence initiative in support of West African countries in the Gulf of Guinea

ARTICLE 44 TEU: THE FLEXIBILITY MECHANISM FOR THE CSDP

Nicolas Clinchamps
Professor of Public Law
IDPS, Sorbonne Paris Nord University

Article 44 TEU

1. Within the framework of decisions adopted in accordance with Article 43, the Council may entrust the implementation of a task to a group of Member States which are willing and have the necessary capabilities for such a task. Those Member States, in association with the High Representative of the Union for Foreign Affairs and Security Policy, shall agree among themselves on the management of the task.

2. The Member States participating in the task shall keep the Council regularly informed of its progress or at the request of another Member State. Those States shall inform the Council immediately should the completion of the task entails major consequences or require amendment of the objective, scope or conditions determined for the task in the decisions referred to in paragraph 1. In such cases, the Council shall adopt the necessary decisions.

Flexibility defeated by sovereignty! In the name of a certain flexibility sought by the Treaty of Lisbon, a group of volunteer Member States, mandated by the Council of the European Union (EU), can be entrusted with the execution of a mission 'in order to protect the Union's values and serve its interests' (Art. 42(5) TEU). The aim is to launch missions under the Common Security and Defence Policy (CSDP) in a tighter format. The reference to the EU's values and interests refers to the principles on which it is based: 'In its relations with the wider world, the Union shall uphold and promote its values and interests [...]. It shall contribute to peace, security [...], solidarity and mutual respect among peoples, [...] the protection of human rights, [...] as well as [...] the strict observance and development of international law, including respect for the principles of the United Nations Charter' (Art. 3(5) TEU).[1] The operational dimension of CSDP is part of this contribution. In its external relations, it acts in order 'to safeguard its values, fundamental interests, security, independence and integrity' (Art. 21(2)(a) TEU). Under the Common Foreign and Security Policy (CFSP), the Member States 'shall ensure, through the convergence of their actions, that the Union is able to assert its interests and values on the international scene' (Article 32(1) TEU). This reference to the EU's values and interests therefore goes beyond the simple flexibility mechanism. From this point of view, the reference would be better placed in Article 42(1), which defines the CSDP as a whole, while implementation of the flexibility mechanism is covered by Article 44. The Council of the EU-Foreign Affairs emphasises that this article 'provides a potential additional modality for the EU and its Member States as a security provider, making use of the flexibility of the Union framework'.[2] However, this flexibility does not seem to appeal to the Member States, which have never used this tool. What is the reason for this reluctance? The answer lies in the choice of a formula based on the logic of enhanced cooperation (Section I below). As with enhanced cooperation in the field of defence,[3] the implementation of this approach has so far failed (II).

I. A MECHANISM BASED ON THE LOGIC OF ENHANCED COOPERATION

The flexibility mechanism illustrates the variable-geometry CSDP envisaged by the Lisbon Treaty, following the logic of enhanced cooperation. This inspiration permeates the principles (Section A), which find their limits in the procedure (Section B).

A. INSPIRATION IN PRINCIPLE

The Lisbon Treaty fills a gap. The flexibility mechanism enables volunteer states to move forward by speeding up the implementation of operations.[4] This possibility of urgent action presupposes that the volunteer States have

---

1 See the commentary by C. Beaucillon in this publication.

2 Council of the EU – Foreign Affairs of 18 May 2015, conclusions, doc. n° 8971/15, Brussels, 18 May 2015, para. 17, j, p. 11.

3 Apart from defence, some enhanced cooperation has been implemented, in particular that relating to the European Financial Public Prosecutor's Office. Council Regulation (EU) 2017/1939 of 12 October 2017 implementing enhanced cooperation with regard to the establishment of the European Public Prosecutor's Office, [2017] *OJ* L283/. 1.

4 T. Tardy, 'In groups we trust: Implementing Article 44 of the Lisbon Treaty', *Institute for Security Studies EU*, Brief no. 27, 2014, p. 2.

the capabilities to be deployed, particularly in the military field. These are Member States 'which are willing and have the necessary capability for such a task' (Art. 44(1) TEU). They can mobilise the forces and establish the command structures. These missions are carried out within the framework of 'decisions adopted in accordance with Article 43 TEU' (ibid.).[5] This means that these specific missions can be launched within the general framework of CSDP missions covering the expanded[6] tasks: 'joint disarmament operations, humanitarian and rescue tasks, military advice and assistance tasks, conflict prevention and peace-keeping tasks, tasks of combat forces in crisis management, including peace-making and post-conflict stabilisation' (Art. 43(1) TEU). The Lisbon Treaty also states: 'All these tasks may contribute to the fight against terrorism, including by supporting third countries in combating terrorism on their territory' (ibid.). The flexibility mechanism therefore does not create new categories of CSDP missions. It also aligns with their funding rules: the EU budget for civilian missions (unless the EU Council unanimously decides otherwise) and State contributions (Art. 41(2) TEU) under the Athena mechanism,[7] which was succeeded by the European Peace Facility[8] for military missions. Preparatory activities for the latter are financed by 'a start-up fund made up of Member States' contributions' (Art. 41(3) TEU). Moreover, beyond the reference to Member States, these missions are not closed, a priori, to the participation of third States. However, there is nothing to prevent recourse to capability or financial support from other Member States, or the extension of the mission to them a posteriori. Lastly, the flexibility of the mechanism allows for changes during the course of the mission: the participating Member States 'shall inform the Council immediately should the completion of the task entail major consequences or require amendment of the objective, scope and conditions determined for the task [...]' (Art. 44(2) TEU). But, this flexibility is subject to a decision by the Council (ibid.) and therefore to unanimity among its members (see below).

---

5 See the commentary by A. Hamonic in this publication.

6 These missions were defined by the Foreign and Defence Ministers of the Western European Union (WEU) meeting in Bonn on 19 June 1992: 'military units of the WEU Member States, acting under the authority of the WEU, could be employed for humanitarian or rescue tasks; peacekeeping tasks; tasks of combat forces for crisis management, including peacemaking', Petersberg Declaration, Bonn, 19 June 1992, pt. II, 4. They were transferred to the EU by the Treaty of Amsterdam (Declaration on WEU), then extended by the Treaty of Lisbon (Art. 43).

7 Council Decision (CFSP) 2015/528 of 27 March 2015 establishing a mechanism to administer the financing of the common costs of European Union operations having military or defence implications (Athena), and repealing Decision 2011/871/CFSP, [2015] *OJ L*84/ 39.

8 Article 74 of Council Decision (CFSP) 2021/509 of 22 March 2021 establishing a European Peace Facility and repealing Decision (CFSP) 2015/528, [2021] *OJ* L102/ 14. See the commentary by C. Schneider in this publication.

The flexibility mechanism is part of the broad vision of a multi-speed CSDP, alongside other tools inspired by the logic of enhanced cooperation. In 2002, during the work of the Convention on the Future of Europe, in the context of enlargement to 15 (1995) and soon to 25 (2004), the Franco-German proposal presented by the foreign ministers, Dominique de Villepin and Joschka Fischer, was aimed in particular at introducing greater flexibility through recourse to the mechanism of enhanced cooperation in the field of the European Security and Defence Policy (ESDP): 'This would allow a group of Member States to develop enhanced cooperation which would be open to the rest of the Member States or even to the Union as a whole, and would at the same time establish a link with the EU's existing institutions and policies. [...] In addition, the use of other flexibility instruments within the framework of the Treaty should also be examined for the ESDP. Specific rules should be laid down for the use of flexibility instruments within the Treaty in launching and conducting military operations'.[9] Working Group VIII on Defence then proposed 'a form of closer cooperation between Member States [...] wishing to carry out the most demanding tasks and fulfilling the requirements for such a commitment to be credible'.[10] This gave rise to the flexibility mechanism.

More broadly, the idea of a differentiated approach at the origin of enhanced cooperation dates back to the mid-1970s. In 1975, the Tindemans report on economic and monetary policy noted that 'it is impossible at the present time to submit a credible programme of action if it is deemed absolutely necessary that in every case all the stages should be reached by all the States at the same time'. Those States 'which are able to progress have a duty to forge ahead'.[11] The principle of enhanced cooperation was 'constitutionalised'[12] by the Treaty of Amsterdam (Title VII TEU). This partially removed the 'taboos [...] on the traditional postulates of the unity and uniformity of Community law'[13] without, however, going so far as to include the second and third pillars. 'While the differences between Member States are greater in the CFSP than in any other area, the Treaty of Amsterdam therefore gave up on managing the heterogeneity of ambitions and interests that enlargement will only exacerbate'.[14] The Treaty of Nice then extended enhanced cooperation to the CFSP within the limits of 'the implementation of a joint action or a common

9 D. de Villepin and J. Fischer, *Joint Franco-German proposals for the European Convention in the field of the European Security and Defence Policy*, CONV 422/02, Brussels, 22 November 2002, pp. 3–4.

10 *Final report of Working Group VIII 'Defence'*, European Convention, CONV 461/02, Brussels, 16 December 2002, (54), p. 19.

11 L. Tindemans, *The European Union*, Report to the European Council, 29 December 1975, *ECB*, Brussels, European Commission, Supplement 1/76, p. 21.

12 F. Chaltiel, 'Le traité d'Amsterdam et la coopération renforcée', *RMCUE*, 1998, p. 289.

13 V. Constantinesco, 'Les clauses de coopération renforcée', *RTDE*, 1997, p. 751.

14 F. de la Serre, 'Une Europe ou plusieurs?', *Politique étrangère*, 1999, no. 1, p. 27.

position' (Art. 27, B, TEU) while excluding it, at the express request of the United Kingdom, from the field of defence.[15] This gap was finally filled by the Treaty of Lisbon, which opens them up to the CSDP (Art. 329(2)(1) TFEU). From this point of view, the flexibility mechanism is an operational lever resulting from the extension of their scope to the CSDP. It is also part of a set of provisions introduced by the Treaty of Lisbon and aligned with the logic of enhanced cooperation, particularly in the area of capabilities, through the permanent structured cooperation procedure (or PESCO)[16] and the recognition of the European Defence Agency (EDA).

Permanent structured cooperation is open to Member States whose 'military capabilities fulfil higher criteria and which have made more binding commitments to one another in this area with a view to the most demanding missions' (Art. 42(6) TEU). Member States involved in permanent structured cooperation undertake jointly to increase their investment, bring their defence instruments closer together, to strengthen the interoperability of equipment, cooperate to make good capability shortfalls and participate in equipment programmes within the framework of the European Defence Agency (EDA; Article 2 of Protocol No. 10 on [permanent structured cooperation] established by Article 42 TEU). Like the flexibility mechanism, permanent structured cooperation makes it possible to bring together Member States wishing to move forward and to welcome, where appropriate, those wishing to participate at a later stage (Article 46(3) TEU). Basically, however, it is more restrictive in terms of the conditions it imposes on Member States. On the other hand, the procedure is more flexible because permanent structured cooperation is adopted by a decision of the Council of the EU acting by qualified majority after consultation of the High Representative of the Union for Foreign Affairs and Security Policy/Vice-President of the Commission (HR/VP) (2).

The differentiated organic approach to capabilities has been institutionalised in two stages. Created outside the EU on 12 November 1996, the Joint Armaments Cooperation Organisation (OCCAR)[17] brings together several EU Member States (France, Germany, the United Kingdom, Italy, Belgium and Spain) to conduct cooperative programmes. Following this model, on 12 July 2004 the Council set up the EDA to give the EU global capability ambitions before it was recognised by the Treaty of Lisbon.[18] Under primary law, the EDA is tasked with bringing Member States together to work on joint projects (Art. 45(2) TEU). Envisaged 'as an important element towards the development

[15] X. Latour, 'Coopération renforcée et politique européenne de sécurité et de défense', *Droit et défense*, 2000, p. 27.
[16] See the commentary by Q. Loïez in this publication.
[17] OCCAR subsequently took the form of an international organisation. Convention of 9 September 1998 establishing [OCCAR], entered into force on 28 January 2001.
[18] See the commentary by F. Liberti in this publication.

of more flexible and effective European military resources',[19] it is competent to carry out ad hoc Category A projects or programmes, 'which shall presume general participation by the participating Member States';[20] or Category B projects or programmes where one or more Member States 'intend to establish an ad hoc project or programme within the Agency's remit'.[21] An opt-in/opt-out procedure provides essential flexibility to take account of Member States' strategic divergences. In principle, the differentiated capability approach followed by permanent structured cooperation or the EDA is reflected, at an organic level, by recourse to the flexibility mechanism. This is in line with the logic of enhanced cooperation. However, this inspiration comes up against procedural limits.

B. THE PROCEDURAL LIMITS OF THIS INSPIRATION

Inspired by the logic of enhanced cooperation, the flexibility mechanism suffers from the same limitations. These are inherent in the rules of intergovernmental cooperation that govern the implementation of all CSDP missions. Thus, the legal basis for the delegated tasks of the flexibility mechanism is a unanimous decision of the EU Council. The Treaty of Lisbon takes care to specify that this procedure, which encompasses the whole of the CFSP,[22] concerns decisions relating to the CSDP, 'including those initiating a mission' (Art. 42(4) TEU). As an integral part of the CFSP, the CSDP is subject to the principle of intergovernmental cooperation. Diplomacy, security and defence are sovereign functions of the State and cannot escape its sovereignty. Consequently, each Member State has a right of veto. However, since the Treaty of Amsterdam (Art. 23(1) TEU), this right can be relaxed by the possibility of 'constructive abstention' in order to limit blockages. Under the Treaty of Lisbon, a Member State which abstains 'shall not be obliged to apply the decision, but shall accept that the decision commits the Union' (Art. 31(2) TEU). The Strategic Compass adopted in May 2022 refers precisely to this concerning the implementation of the flexibility mechanism: 'More broadly, we must also strive for greater flexibility in our decision-making process, without compromising on political and financial solidarity. We will therefore use the potential afforded by the EU Treaties, including constructive abstention. We will in particular decide on practical modalities for implementing Article 44 of the Treaty on European

---

19 Council Joint Action 2004/551/CFSP of 12 July 2004 on the establishment of the European Defense Agency, (2), [2004] *OJ* L245/17.

20 Ibid., Art. 20(1).

21 Ibid., Art. 21(1).

22 Art. 31(1) TEU: 'Decisions under this Chapter [on specific provisions concerning the CFSP] shall be taken by the European Council and by the Council acting unanimously, except where this Chapter provides otherwise [...]'.

Union, in accordance with CSDP decision making, to allow a group of willing and able Member States to plan and conduct a mission or operation within the EU framework and under the political oversight of the Council'.[23] The combination of constructive abstention with the flexibility mechanism is supposed to increase the operational effectiveness of CSDP. However, this 'institutional dynamic',[24] derived from UN practice, has proved to be only relatively effective, insofar as it does not make it possible to circumvent the veto of a Member State.[25] Nevertheless, if a State resorts to this particular form of abstention, a decision can be taken. The States concerned may accompany their abstention with a formal declaration. In this way, they accept that the decision is binding on the EU, but are not obliged to apply it (Art. 31(2) TEU).[26] Despite this precaution, its use remains limited.[27]

Basically, the elements of the mandate given to the volunteer Member States participating in the flexibility mechanism do not depart from those established in the context of the classic CSDP missions. The Council defines 'their objectives and scope and the general conditions for their implementation' (Art. 43(2)), leaving the Member States to agree among themselves on the management of the mission (Art. 44(1)). The Council's mandate sets out the objectives of the mission and identifies the partners (States, international organisations such as the UN, NATO, the African Union, etc.). It designates the commander and the location of the headquarters. It assesses the cost of the task, and sets the date on which it will come into effect and its deadline. It defines the political control and strategic direction entrusted to the Political and Security Committee (PSC), under the responsibility of the Council and the HR/VP (Art. 38(2) TEU), as well as the military direction entrusted to the EU Military Committee (EUMC).[28] The consistency of the EU's external action is the joint responsibility of the Foreign Affairs Council (Art. 16(6)(3) TEU) and the HR/VP (Art. 18(4) TEU). The latter consults and informs the European

---

[23] General Secretariat of the Council, 'A strategic compass on security and defence – For a European Union that protects its citizens, values and interests and contributes to international peace and security', doc. no. 7371/22 COR 1, Brussels, 4 May 2022, p. 14.

[24] S. Sur, 'Le Conseil de sécurité: blocage, renouveau et avenir', *Pouvoirs*, 2004, no. 109, p. 70.

[25] There is also a limit: 'If the members of the Council qualifying their abstention in this way represent at least one third of the Member States comprising at least one third of the population of the Union, the decision shall not be adopted'. Art. 31(1) TEU.

[26] The text adds: 'In a spirit of mutual solidarity, the Member State concerned shall refrain from any action likely to conflict with or impede Union action based on that Decision and the other Member States shall respect its position'. Ibid.

[27] At the European Council meeting on 14 December 2023, Hungary abstained for the first time on Ukraine's application to join the EU, allowing accession negotiations to begin. At the suggestion of German Chancellor Olaf Scholz, Hungarian Prime Minister Victor Orbán left the room at the time of the vote. However, he vetoed the adoption of €50 billion in financial support for Kyiv.

[28] Annex to the Council Decision of 22 January 2001 setting up the Military Committee of the European Union (2001/79/CFSP), [2001] *OJ* L27/ 4.

Parliament, which may ask questions and make recommendations (Art. 36 TEU). Although the HR/VP is involved in missions falling under the flexibility mechanism (Article 44(1) TEU), his/her role remains that of ensuring, 'under the authority of the Council and in close and permanent contact with the Political and Security Committee, shall ensure coordination of the civilian and military aspects of such tasks' (Article 43(2) TEU). Although Article 44 TEU does not expressly refer to this, there is nothing to prevent the HR/VP from exercising his/her power of initiative (Article 42(4) TEU). The procedures of the flexibility mechanism are therefore aligned with the rules governing the classic missions of the CSDP.

In the final analysis, this alignment is simply an extension of that achieved through enhanced cooperation on the same rules, resulting from the constraints of intergovernmental cooperation. Similarly, the decision to use enhanced cooperation is taken by the Council acting unanimously on the opinion of the HR/VP, which gives its opinion 'on the consistency of the enhanced cooperation envisaged with the [CFSP] of the Union', and by the Commission, which gives its opinion 'on the consistency of the enhanced cooperation envisaged with the other policies of the Union'. As the European Parliament has no legislative competence in the area of the CFSP (Article 24(1)(2) TEU), it is kept informed of the request (Article 329(2)(2) TFEU). On the other hand, like all enhanced cooperation, CSDP cooperation is subject to a threshold of at least nine Member States participating (Article 20(2) TEU). Like permanent structured cooperation, the delegated tasks of the flexibility mechanism do not require any threshold. They can therefore, a priori, be entrusted to two Member States. This is where the essential difference lies.

The effectiveness sought through the use of the flexibility mechanism would require going further. The differentiation dynamic of this mechanism is hampered by the sovereignty of the Member States, preserved by unanimous voting within the Council. The objective of efficiency can only be achieved at the cost of an in-depth reform of the functioning of the CSDP by admitting that this mechanism can be activated by a majority vote. This loss of sovereignty could be compensated for by giving greater functional freedom to the volunteer states by entrusting them with the task of defining certain rules that are usually included in the clauses of the mandate defined by the Council. This could concern the modalities of operations, in particular command structures and the organisation of the forces involved. It would then be necessary to obtain a prior agreement negotiated in advance within the Political and Security Committee (PSC).[29] In the absence of significant progress in this direction, the flexibility of the mechanism risks remaining more apparent than real. This

29 See the commentary by C. Schneider in this publication.

admittedly legitimate attachment to sovereignty no doubt explains the failure of its implementation.

II. THE FAILURE OF ITS IMPLEMENTATION

In practice, Article 42(5) TEU has never been implemented in any way, either in the context of land tasks/missions or maritime tasks/missions, whether or not they have an executive mandate (combat missions). This shortcoming is not isolated. Only one permanent structured cooperation has been launched to date. It has brought together all the Member States except Malta.[30] No 'classic' enhanced cooperation (Article 329(2) TFEU) has been implemented in the field of CSDP. The European start-up fund, which could facilitate the financing of operations covered by the flexibility mechanism, has not been created despite requests from the European Parliament.[31] The failure to use these procedures is therefore indicative of the Member States' difficulty in conceiving, in a 'pioneering' spirit, a differentiated way of operating the CSDP. The added value in terms of the capacity of the flexibility mechanism remains to be proven (Section A below). The result is an operational failure (Section B).

A. QUESTIONABLE ADDED VALUE IN TERMS OF CAPACITY

In terms of capabilities, the flexibility mechanism struggles to distinguish itself from the already tight format of traditional CSDP operations. 'In fact, most missions and operations bring together only some of the Member States, without there even being any need to formally invoke Article 42(5). And if we look at the personnel deployed, we see that a small number of States provide the bulk of CSDP resources'.[32] In this sense, Article 44 merely codifies

---

[30] The joint notification of 11 November 2017 triggering permanent structured cooperation was initially signed by 23 Member States before being supplemented by notification letters of 7 December 2017 sent to the Council and HR/VP Federica Mogherini by Ireland and Portugal. In May 2023, Denmark joined the permanent structured cooperation. Council Decision (CFSP) 2023/1015 of 23 May 2023 confirming the participation of Denmark in the PESCO, and amending Decision (CFSP) 2017/2315 establishing permanent structured cooperation (PESCO) and determining the list of participating Member States, [2023] *OJ* L136/73.

[31] See, for example, the European Parliament resolution of 21 November 2013 on the implementation of [CSDP] (according to the annual report from the Council to the European Parliament on [CFSP]) (14605/1/2012 – 2013/2105(INI)), (7).

[32] F. Terpan, 'Le traité de Lisbonne a-t-il rendu la solidarité possible dans le domaine de la sécurité et de la défense', in E. Brosset, R. Mehdi and N. Rubio (eds.), *Solidarité et droit de l'Union européenne: un principe à l'épreuve*, Confluence des droits, Aix-en-Provence, DICE Éditions, 2021, p. 162.

practice. 'In fact, the possibility for a group of MS to carry out a mission in a third country is not new at all. In the 1990s, the treaty of Maastricht gave de WEU the responsibility to develop the Security and Defence policy, and to carry out operations in the framework of the Petersberg Tasks'.[33] This aspect, linked to the size of the missions, calls into question the relevance of using the flexibility mechanism which, from this point of view, gives the impression of a 'duplication' effect.

The objective of the flexibility mechanism is not limited to the dimensional approach alone. Above all, it aims to promote the EU's responsiveness by mandating a coalition of willing Member States. 'Generally speaking, this mechanism could be useful for taking flexible and rapid action when a rapid response from the Union is required'.[34] With the emphasis on speed and efficiency, operations under the flexibility mechanism are naturally designed to mobilise reduced capabilities in the format of the EU Battlegroups (EUBGs). These have their origins in the rapid reaction capability decided at the Helsinki European Council on 10 and 11 December 1999. The aim was to be able 'to provide smaller rapid reaction elements with a very high degree of availability'.[35] Following Operation Artemis in the Democratic Republic of Congo in 2003,[36] the rapid reaction concept was further developed at the Brussels European Council on 17 and 18 June 2004,[37] which approved the *Headline Goal 2010* for the establishment of EUWGs by 2007. These were envisaged as 'a specific form of rapid reaction, consisting of a battalion-sized joint force grouping'.[38] The decision had to be taken within five days of the European Council's approval of the crisis management concept, and the EUWGs deployed within ten days of this decision.[39] At the instigation of France, the UK and Germany, the EUWG concept was defined by the EU Military Staff and approved by the EUMC. A single document on the EUWG concept was adopted in October 2006. In 2009, the European Council called for 'increasing the effectiveness, visibility and

---

33 F. Terpan: 'In fact, the possibility for a group of MS to carry out a mission in a third country is not new at all. In the 1990s, the treaty of Maastricht gave the WEU the responsibility to develop the Security and Defence policy, and to carry out operations in the framework of the Petersberg Tasks', 'Art. 44 TEU-L – Implementation of CSDP by a Group of Member States', in H.-J. Blanke and S. Magianelli (eds.), *The Treaty on European Union – A Commentary*, Berlin, Springer, 2013, p. 1255.

34 Towards a European Defence Union – A White Paper as a first step, Directorate-General for External Policies, Thematic Department, doc. EP No 535.011, April 2016, p. 37.

35 Presidency progress report to the Helsinki European Council on strengthening the common European security and defence policy, Helsinki European Council, Presidency conclusions, 10 and 11 December 1999, Annex IV.

36 This was the first autonomous CSDP military operation to be conducted outside Europe.

37 Brussels European Council of 17 and 18 June 2004, Presidency conclusions, doc. no. 10679/04, Brussels, 18 June 2004, para. 60, p. 13.

38 Headline Goal 2010, Council of the EU, Secretariat, doc. no. 6309/6/04, Brussels, 4 May 2004, p. 3.

39 Ibid.

impact of CSDP [...] by strengthening the EU's ability to deploy appropriate civilian and military capabilities and personnel rapidly and effectively across the full spectrum of crisis management actions'.[40] The EUWGs have been fully operational since 1 January 2007. The plan is to have two EUBGs on standby every six months, to be able to project 1,500 troops up to 5,000 kilometres away and conduct an autonomous mission for one to three months. 'This is a fundamental advance on the Helsinki headline goal, in that the European Rapid Reaction Force, as it is improperly called, is primarily a theoretical pool of troops, while the battlegroups will be directly mobilisable'.[41]

However, due to a lack of political will and sufficient funding, no EUBGs have been deployed and standby duty is not always provided.[42] By way of comparison, to deal with the crisis in Ukraine, NATO deployed four battalion-level multinational battlegroups in Estonia, Latvia, Lithuania and Poland in 2017, followed by four additional battlegroups in Bulgaria, Hungary, Romania and Slovakia in February 2022, following the Russian invasion. The Strategic Compass also calls for adjustments to the format of the EU's Rapid Deployment Capacity (RDC), see above: 'A substantial modification of the EU Battlegroups should lead to a more robust and flexible instrument, for instance through tailored force packages including land, maritime and air components, different levels of operational readiness and longer stand-by periods. A comprehensive and complete overview of all available elements will give us the flexibility to tailor our force to the nature of the crisis and the requirements and objectives of the operation decided by the Council, using substantially modified EU Battlegroups, Member States' military forces and capabilities or a combination of the two'.[43]

The war in Ukraine, rising tensions in the Balkans and Donald Trump's re-election to the White House are making Europeans face up to their responsibilities. However, this does not yet seem to be enough to motivate them to make use of the capability tools that can be put at the service of the flexibility mechanism.

More broadly, this mechanism is an extension of the ambitious programme set out in the *Headline Goal 2010* of 2004[44] and confirmed by the declaration

40 Brussels European Council of 13 and 14 December 2012, Presidency conclusions, doc. EUCO 205/12, Brussels, 14 December 2012, para. 24, p. 10.

41 J. Michel and J. Rivière, Rapport d'information sur les nouveaux défis de la construction de l'Europe de la défense, AN, RI n° 2531, 27 September 2005, p. 31.

42 This was the case in the first half of 2021 and the first half of 2022. R. Le Gleut and H. Conway-Mouret, Rapport d'information sur 'Quelle boussole stratégique pour l'Union européenne?', RI, S, No. 753, 7 July 2021, p. 60.

43 'A strategic compass on security and defence – For a European Union that protects its citizens, values and interests and contributes to international peace and security', cited above.

44 Brussels European Council of 17 and 18 June 2004, ibid.

of 8 December 2008[45] consisting of the deployment of 60,000 troops in 60 days for a major operation.[46] The aim was to be able to plan and conduct operations simultaneously:

'two major stabilisation and reconstruction operations, with a suitable civilian component, supported by a maximum of 10,000 troops for at least two years;

- two rapid response operations of limited duration using inter alia the EU's battle groups;

- an emergency operation for the evacuation of European nationals (in less than ten days), bearing in mind the primary role of each Member State as regards its nationals and making use of the consular lead State concept;

- a maritime or air surveillance/interdiction mission;

- a civil-military humanitarian assistance operation lasting up to 90 days;

- around a dozen ESDP civilian missions (inter alia police, rule of law, civil administration, civil protection, security sector reform and observation missions) of varying formats, inter alia in a rapid reaction situation, including a major mission (possibly up to 3,000 experts), which could last several years'.[47]

However, this ambition has not been followed up in practice. The logic of cooperation requiring unanimity forces the Council to vote for the lowest common denominator. Enhanced cooperation could have made up for the shortfall in capabilities. To date, the EU has failed to realise its ambitions at both ends of the spectrum. On the one hand, the *Headline Goal 2010* has never been achieved. On the other hand, the deployment of the battlegroups has been limited to carrying out exercises. All this has contributed to the operational failure of the flexibility mechanism.

B. AN OPERATIONAL FAILURE

The logic of cooperation stifles isolated initiatives, a priori, when an operation is launched and, a posteriori, if a change in its scope appears necessary. While the flexibility mechanism claims to be effective and flexible, it remains subject to the doxa of unanimity. Article 44 TEU does not specify when it intends to 'entrust' the implementation of the flexibility mechanism to a group of States. Consequently, the room for manoeuvre of the latter depends on the mandate defined by the Council of the EU. Furthermore, the volunteer Member States

---

[45] Council Declaration of 8 December 2008 on strengthening [ESDP] capabilities (16840/08) annexed to the Presidency Conclusions of the European Council of 11 and 12 December 2008, 17271/08, Brussels, 12 December 2008.

[46] This objective was first set by the Heads of State and Government at the Helsinki European Council, which set an initial deadline of 2003. Helsinki European Council, para. 28.

[47] Council statement (16840/08), cited above.

must report regularly to the HR/VP on the results of a mission, which remains under the political control and strategic direction of the PSC (Art. 44(2) TEU), the central operational body reporting to the Council, and therefore to the Member States. Once again, this is a reminder of how traditional CSDP tasks/missions operate (see above). In principle, information is provided every six months. However, the logic of the flexibility mechanism would require the role of the PSC to be redefined to give volunteer states real operational room for manoeuvre. Yet, the Lisbon Treaty is silent on this point. Although sovereign, the Member States are subject to a variable geometry of autonomy. This contradiction may explain their reticence about this mechanism and, more broadly, their reluctance to venture into enhanced cooperation.

Operation EUTM Mali is a perfect illustration of this. In October 2012, the European Council decided that the crisis in Mali posed 'an immediate threat to the Sahel region as well as to West and North Africa and to Europe'.[48] The urgency would have justified recourse to the flexibility mechanism. 'In Mali, the ideal conditions were in place for the deployment of an [EU] battlegroup: a solid legal framework; European consensus; and a request from the legitimate authorities of the state concerned. For many observers, Mali was a test case for European defence. And Europe did not pass it'.[49] France alone decided to become involved by launching Operation Serval in January 2013. 'The truth is that it is indisputable that for the first time in the history of the [EU], one of its Member States, France, decided on its own initiative to launch a military operation in Africa, in Mali, and that the other Member States of the Union supported it. The EU was unable to intervene militarily in Mali'.[50] The European Parliament deplores this: 'The situation in Mali is a missed opportunity to use for the first time EU battlegroups'.[51]

The operational reality of the CSDP is too often limited to missions which, in most cases, are relatively modest in scale.[52] However, the preparation of traditional CSDP operations is hardly compatible with the urgency of the crises they are supposed to combat. In 2008, the EUFOR Tchad/RCA operation would require six months of negotiations by the Member States between the decision by the EU Council and its implementation on the ground. In 2014, it took two months to mobilise 750 soldiers for operation EUFOR RCA.[53] On 1 April 2011, the

48 Conclusions of the European Council of 18 and 19 October 2012, para. 21, EUCO 156/12.

49 D. Reiner, J. Gautier, A. Vallini and X. Pintat, Rapport d'information fait par le groupe de travail: 'Quelle Europe, pour quelle défense?', S, RI no. 713, 3 July 2013, p. 18.

50 Y. Petit, 'Le rôle de l'Union européenne dans la crise malienne', *Civitas Europa*, 2013, no. 31, p. 182.

51 European Parliament resolution of 12 September 2013 on EU's military structures: state of play and future prospects (2012/2319(INI)), para. 18.

52 See the commentary by A. Hamonic in this publication.

53 On the launch of these operations: B. Emptaz, 'Opérations militaires européennes: bilan contrasté ou ambitions perdues?', *RDN*, 2015, No. 781, p. 96.

EU Council decided to launch Operation EUFOR Libya. It was never implemented because the Member States could not agree on whether it should be humanitarian or military in nature.[54] They therefore made it conditional on authorisation from the UN Office for the Coordination of Humanitarian Affairs, knowing that the latter was unlikely to give the green light. These stumbling blocks fully justify recourse to the flexibility mechanism, which in principle enables faster and more effective action to be taken.

To facilitate operations under the flexibility mechanism, a new operational tool is now being considered. The Strategic Compass provides for the creation of an EU Rapid Deployment Capacity (RDC) under the command of the Military Planning and Conduct Capability (MPCC). Currently limited to operations with a non-executive mandate,[55] the competence of the MPCC should be extended to operations with an executive mandate to become a genuine European Headquarters.[56] The aim will be to 'rapidly deploy up to 5,000 troops in hostile environments in response to different types of crisis'.[57] This would include 'land, air and maritime components, as well as the strategic assets required'.[58] This would make it easier to implement the flexibility mechanism, especially as, according to the European Parliament, the 'decision-making on the deployment of the EU RDC based on Article 44 TEU also allows for the involvement of third countries in EU RDC missions where necessary and desired'.[59] The operational scenarios envisaged will initially concern rescue and evacuation operations, as well as the initial phase of stabilisation operations. The RDC could also take part in humanitarian missions to meet needs arising from natural disasters or armed conflict. It is to be based on the modified EUWGs (see above) and the 'pre-identified Member States' military forces and capabilities, in line with the single set of forces principle',[60] which consists of placing forces under a single command. The aim is to ensure that recourse to the RDC does not lead to the mobilisation of state forces already deployed as part of a NATO operation. Both types of operation could be combined. Given the failure of the battlegroups, the European Parliament considers that the RDC 'should not be viewed as a revised EU Battlegroups concept'.[61] In

---

54 Article 1 of Council Decision 2011/210/CFSP of 1 April 2011 on an European Union military operation in support of humanitarian assistance in response to the crisis situation in Libya (Operation EUFOR Libya), [2011] *OJ* L89/ 17.

55 Art. 1 of Council Decision (EU) 2017/971 of 8 June 2017 determining the planning and conduct arrangements for EU non-executive military CSDP missions e [...], [2017] *OJ* L146/ 3.

56 'A strategic compass on security and defence', cited above, p. 16.

57 Ibid., p. 3.

58 Ibid., p. 14.

59 European Parliament resolution of 19 April 2023 on the EU Rapid Deployment Capacity, EU Battlegroups and Article 44 of the TEU: the way forward (2022/2145(INI)), para. 17.

60 'A strategic security and defence compass', cited above, p. 14.

61 European Parliament resolution of 19 April 2023, para. 5.

October 2023, a first crisis management exercise (MILEX) involving 2,800 soldiers, 25 aircraft and six ships from nineteen Member States was conducted from the Rota naval base in Cadiz, southern Spain. On paper, the RDC has been operational since January 2025, but its deployment remains dependent on the willingness of Member States. The European Parliament sees it as an essential tool for the credibility of CSDP, and 'stresses the importance of the EU having the necessary flexible, robust and credible instruments, capabilities, and command and control structure to act effectively and respond rapidly and decisively to prevent and manage crises in order to assert itself as a more credible security and defence actor and serve and protect the Union's citizens, interests, principles and the values enshrined in Article 21 TEU across the world'.[62]

Finally, the urgency to which it is supposed to respond raises the question of whether the flexibility mechanism could be activated with the mutual defence clause (Art. 42(7) TEU).[63] This hypothesis has been put forward: 'Article 42(7) TEU could be also viewed in connection with Article 44 TEU (and also Article 42(5) TEU), whereby the Council may entrust the implementation of a task, i.e. a CSDP mission/operation, to a group of willing states or with Article 43(1) TEU, whereby the EU's CSDP operations "may contribute to the fight against terrorism, including by supporting third countries in combatting terrorism in their territories"'.[64] However, a priori this prospect seems unlikely. The activation of this clause by the President of the French Republic, François Hollande, following the attacks of 13 November 2015, was a first, but of essentially media significance. Beyond the announcement effect, the HR/VP, Federica Mogherini, considered that this decision did not imply recourse to a CSDP mission but was a matter of 'activating bilateral aid and assistance'.[65] The intergovernmental response to such a request does not involve decisions taken by the EU institutions. The EEAS can simply provide assistance in coordinating the actions taken by the Member States.

***

Both in its principles and in its implementation, the flexibility mechanism is locked in by the unanimity rule. State sovereignty is preserved at the cost of immobility. However, the idea of reform in favour of a more integrated CFSP

[62] Para. 1.
[63] See the commentary by J.-C. Martin in this publication.
[64] See C.-C. Cîrlig, 'The EU's mutual assistance clause. First ever activation of Article 42(7) TEU', European Parliament Research Service, Briefing, November 2015, p. 4.
[65] Outcome of the Council meeting – Foreign Affairs, Brussels, 16 and 17 November 2015, doc. no. 14120/15, p. 6.

is being put forward, notably in Germany[66] and, to a certain extent, in France.[67] This would raise the question of its extension to the CSDP. The logic would lead to the flexibility mechanism coming under the qualified majority or any other alternative formula to unanimity within the Council. 'It would thus be conceivable for a Member State to submit directly to the PSC an operation conceived with a few other partner states, which would save a considerable amount of time by doing away with prior studies and discussions between Member States with a view to establishing a concept of operation'.[68] The flexibility mechanism could also be activated by 'cooperation building blocks' contributed by CSDP to national, NATO or UN operations. 'As long as an EUTM mission works in the same direction as a national operation or an ad hoc operation, it would not be abnormal for it to be able to contribute'.[69] It will take a great deal of boldness to convince Member States to agree to limits on their sovereignty in an area as sensitive as defence. In the meantime, we must rely on what already exists and follow the incantations of the European Parliament which '[c]alls on the VP/HR and the Member States to unleash the full potential of the provisions of the Treaty relating to CSDP and to give serious consideration to implementation arrangements for Article 44 TEU on entrusting the implementation of a CSDP task to a group of Member States to make the CSDP more flexible and efficient in the field, while maintaining a strong collective European dimension'.[70] The introduction of the flexibility mechanism has undoubtedly been hastily described as a 'decisive step'[71] in the differentiated implementation of CSDP. State sovereignty therefore prevails today. Time will tell whether the flexibility mechanism will eventually be able to override it.

---

66 Adopted in Germany in 2021, the 'tricolour' coalition contract between the Liberals (FDP), the *Greens* and the Social Democrats (SPD) proposes extending qualified majority voting within the Council to the CFSP. Mehr Fortschritt wagen – Bündnis für Freiheit, Gerechtigkeit und Nachhaltigkeit, Koalitionsvertrag 2021 – 2025 Zwischen der Sozialdemokratischen Partei Deutschlands (SPD), Bündnis 90 / Die Grünen und Den Freien Demokraten (FDP), p. 108.

67 Since 2017, Emmanuel Macron has been defending his vision of European sovereignty, which he describes as 'real' without specifying what this would mean beyond 'the ability to exist in today's world to defend our values and interests' (Speech for a sovereign, united and democratic Europe, Paris, La Sorbonne, 26 September 2017, https://www.elysee.fr). In his 'Strasbourg oath' delivered before the European Parliament, he called for the emergence of a sovereign Europe that would be a 'power open to the world', advocating the generalisation of qualified majority voting 'for our main public policies' (Declaration on European integration and the conflict in Ukraine, Strasbourg, 9 May 2022, https://www.elysee.fr).

68 R. Le Gleut and H. Conway-Mouret, 'Quelle boussole stratégique pour l'Union européenne', RI, S, No. 753, 7 July 2021, p. 56.

69 Ibid., p. 57.

70 European Parliament resolution of 18 January 2023 on the implementation of common security and defence policy- annual report 2022 (2022/2050(INI)), para. 29.

71 J. Pueyo and Y. Fromion, Rapport d'information sur l'Europe de la défense à la veille du Livre blanc, AN, RI no. 536, 12 December 2021, p. 14.

ARTICLE 45 TEU: THE EUROPEAN DEFENCE AGENCY

Anne-Hélène Bertana
Postdoctoral researcher student at the University of Bordeaux

Article 45 TEU

1. The European Defence Agency referred to in Article 42(3), subject to the authority of the Council, shall have as its task to:

a) contribute to identifying the Member States' military capability objectives and evaluating observance of the capability commitments given by the Member States;

b) promote harmonisation of operational needs and adoption of effective, compatible procurement methods;

c) propose multilateral projects to fulfil the objectives in terms of military capabilities, ensure coordination of the programmes implemented by the Member States and management of specific cooperation programmes;

d) support defence technology research, and coordinate and plan joint research activities and the study of technical solutions meeting future operational needs;

e) contribute to identifying and, if necessary, implementing any useful measure for strengthening the industrial and technological base of the defence sector and for improving the effectiveness of military expenditure.

Decision (CFSP) 2015/1835

Council Decision (CFSP) 2015/1835 of 12 October 2015 defining the statute, seat and operating rules of the European Defence Agency (recast of Council Decision 2011/411/CFSP of 12 July 2011 defining the statute, seat and operating rules of the European Defence Agency and repealing Joint Action 2004/551/CFSP).

The existence of an Agency in the field of defence capabilities development, research, acquisition and armaments, commonly referred to as the European Defence Agency (EDA), seems unavoidable given the strategic importance of the defence industry for the development of cooperation between States and the strengthening of their capabilities. This is borne out by the fact that the Maastricht Treaty referred to it as early as 1992 and entrusted its creation to the Western European Union (WEU).[1]

Before the EDA was set up, subsidiary bodies of the WEU were created, namely the Western European Armaments Group in 1993 and the Western European Armaments Organisation in 1996. At the same time, a Franco-German initiative led to the gradual creation, between 1993 and 2001, of the Organisation for Joint Armament Cooperation (known by its French acronym OCCAR, or Organisation Conjointe de Coopération en matière d'Armement) for the management of collaborative programmes.[2] Within the European Union, it was with the Joint Declaration of the 'Pralines Summit' of 29 April 2003 that Germany, France, Belgium and Luxembourg urged the Convention on the Future of the EU and the Intergovernmental Conference (responsible for drafting the Treaty establishing a Constitution for Europe (TECE), to provide for the creation of a European Agency for the Development and Acquisition of Military Capabilities. At the time, this initiative was seen as a way of relaunching defence cooperation during the crisis following the war in Iraq.[3] They wanted it to support EU Member States in increasing their military capabilities, strengthening interoperability and cooperation between their armed forces, and more generally in the 'creation of an environment favourable to a competitive European defence industry'.[4] This was subsequently taken up in the Conclusions of the Thessaloniki European Council of 19 and 20 June 2003.[5] Although the TECE therefore provided for the creation of a European

---

1 Para. 5, 'Declaration on Western European Union' (1st), attached to the Treaty on European Union, signed in Maastricht on 7 February 1992, [1992] *OJ* C191/ 107.

2 The Convention establishing the OCCAR was signed in September 1998, and entered into force in January 2001, between Germany, France, Italy and the United Kingdom. Belgium and Spain subsequently became member states.

3 A. Dumoulin and N. Gros-Verheyde, *La politique européenne de sécurité et de défense commune*, Le Dévoluy, Éd. du Villard, 2017, p. 169.

4 Brussels Declaration following the Meeting of the Heads of State and Government of Germany, France, Luxembourg and Belgium on European Defence, known as the 'Pralines' summit, 29 April 2003.

5 European Council, *Presidency Conclusions of the Thessaloniki European Council of 19 and 20 June 2003*, *BO*, 23 June 2003, PE 333.583, para. 65, p. 27.

Defence Agency,[6] it was created in advance at the request of the Council[7] and by a Joint Action of July 2004.[8]

The value of the EDA now seems to be confirmed by three observations: its enshrinement in the Treaty on European Union (TEU), the scope of its tasks and the participation of many States. It is incorporated in primary law in Articles 42(3) and 45 of the TEU,[9] while a Council Decision supplements these articles.[10] Of the four agencies[11] established under the Common Foreign and Security Policy (CFSP), including the Common Security and Defence Policy (CSDP), it is the only one mentioned by the Treaty of Lisbon in 2007. This seems to reflect not only the importance it represents for the Member States, but also the political role it should play.[12] It has also undeniably strengthened the EDA's position within CSDP and with the Member States.[13]

The same is true of the 'attractive and innovative' missions[14] assigned to the EDA. Not only has it replaced the Armaments Group and the Western European Armaments Organisation[15] in their role of control and cooperation, but it has also been tasked with identifying operational requirements, strengthening the European Defence Technological and Industrial Base (EDTIB) and assisting the Council in evaluating the improvement of military capabilities. It has also

---

6 Art. III-212 TECE, [2003] *OJ* C169/. It should be noted that although this Treaty never entered into force, the provisions of Article 45 TEU concerning the EDA are identical.

7 Council of the EU, *Council Conclusions on ESDP, including the Agency in the field of defence capabilities development, research, acquisition and armaments*, 2541st Council meeting – External Relations – 14500/03, 17 November 2003, p. 7.

8 Council Joint Action (CFSP) 2004/551 of 12 July 20004 on the establishment of the European Defence Agency, [2004] *OJ* L245/17.

9 It is also referred to in Article 42(3)(2) TEU. Its full name is 'Agency in the field of defence capabilities development, research, acquisition and armaments', but the TEU provides for it to be called the 'European Defence Agency', which is also used in secondary EU legislation.

10 Council Decision (CFSP) 2015/1835 of 12 October 2015 defining the status, seat and operating rules of the European Defence Agency, [2015] *OJ* L266/55. It replaces a previous decision from 2011, Council Decision (CFSP) 2011/411 of 12 July 2011 defining the statute, seat and modalities of operation of the European Defence Agency and repealing Joint Action 2004/551/CFSP, [2011] *OJ* L183/16.

11 The other three are the EU Satellite Centre, the EU Institute for Security Studies and the European Security and Defence College. See the commentary by Catherine Schneider in this publication.

12 E. Aalto, 'Towards a common defence? Legal foundations after the Lisbon Treaty', in L. Rubini and M. Trybus (eds.), *The Treaty of Lisbon and the future of European law and policy*, Cheltenham, Edward Elgar, 2012, p. 314; A. Dumoulin and N. Gros-Verheyde, *La politique européenne de sécurité et de défense commune*, Le Dévoluy, Éd. du Villard, 2017, p. 169.

13 Remarks reported from an interview with an ACN representative in May 2013. K. Vlachos-Dengler, 'EDA and armaments collaboration', in N. Karampekios and I. Oikonomou (eds.), *The European defence agency*, London, Routledge, 2015, p. 99.

14 A. Cammilleri-Subrenat, *Le droit de la politique européenne de sécurité et de défense dans le cadre du traité de Lisbonne*, Paris/Cachan, Lavoisier/Éditions TEC & DOC, 2010, p. 60.

15 They ceased operating in 2005 and 2006 respectively. A. De Nève, *L'Agence européenne de défense et la coopération dans le domaine capacitaire*, Paris, L'Harmattan, 2010, p. 35.

been involved in defining a European capabilities and armaments policy.[16] This agency is therefore not limited to armaments cooperation, but can deal with all military capabilities, and its political role has been affirmed.

Finally, the interest shown by the Member States in the EDA can be deduced from their membership of the agency: although it is optional, all the EU Member States are members.[17] Even Denmark, which only lifted its CFSP opt-out in 2022,[18] joined the EDA in 2023.[19] It is similarly noteworthy that the EDA has also signed administrative arrangements authorising the participation of third countries[20] and maintains relations with international organisations,[21] which confirms its apparent attractiveness.

If the EDA is supposed to have a predominant place within the CSDP, it is because of evolutions in defence budgets in the Union and in the security context. For several years now, none of the EU Member States has been able to finance on its own a national defence industry, which would enable it to be strategically autonomous.[22] Cooperation must therefore enable them to reduce the fragmentation of their research and technological innovation programmes, as well as limiting the diversity of military capabilities, which prevents economies of scale and leads to cases of harmful competition.[23] The EDA's role is therefore to help Member States make European defence more efficient by strengthening the EDTIB.[24]

Nevertheless, despite the need for such cooperation and the apparent enthusiasm of the States for the EDA, the latter suffers from national dissensions. These were evident from the outset, with 'final discussions' taking

---

16 These tasks are listed in Article 42(3)(2) of the TEU and Article 2 of Decision (CFSP) 2015/1835, cited above.

17 Art. 45(2) TEU.

18 Following Russia's armed aggression in Ukraine, the decision to lift the opt-out was taken in a national referendum, with 66.90% of the vote in favour. N. Gros-Verheyde, 'Le retour plein et entier du Danemark dans le giron de la PSDC. Velkommen', *Bruxelles2*, 1 June 2022.

19 EDA, *Annual report 2022*, p. 22.

20 These are Norway (2006), Switzerland (2012), Serbia (2013), Ukraine (2015) and the United States (2023). EDA, 'Who we are – Third Parties', https://eda.europa.eu/who-we-are/third-parties (consulted on 22 April 2024).

21 In particular, it signed an administrative arrangement with OCCAR in 2012, a memorandum of understanding with NATO's Improvised Explosive Devices Centre of Excellence (2017) and has exchanged letters with NATO in various fields. European Defence Agency, 'Who we are – Third Parties', https://eda.europa.eu/who-we-are/third-parties (accessed on 22 April 2024).

22 J.-P. Maulny and N. Gros-Verheyde, 'L'échec de l'Agence européenne de défense est-il irrémédiable?', *Bruxelles2*, 9 May 2016.

23 A. De Nève, *L'Agence européenne de défense et la coopération dans le domaine capacitaire*, Paris, L'Harmattan, 2010, p. 55.

24 D. Fiott, 'The European Commission and the European Defence Agency' (2015) 53(3) *Journal of Common Market Studies*, p. 542; A. Barrinha, 'The EDA and the discursive construction of European defence and security', in N. Karampekios and I. Oikonomou (eds.), *The European defence agency*, London, Routledge, 2015, p. 27.

place up to two hours before the adoption of the Joint Action 2004. They concerned the internal organisation of the Agency, the staff it should have, but above all the role it should play. Some Member States wanted the Agency to be limited to the role of 'adviser', others wanted it to act more as a 'coordinator', and still others wanted it to be an 'executor'.[25] In particular, a compromise had to be found between the position of France, which wanted 'to have a solid top-down steering instrument for the development of capabilities', and that of the United Kingdom, which wanted 'to reduce investment in the European institutions to a minimum'.[26]

These divergences have resulted in an Agency with limited resources, despite the strategic importance of the competencies entrusted to it. What is more, it has relatively low visibility. While this is understandable in the eyes of the general public and the non-specialist media,[27] since the Agency is involved in technical fields, the scarcity of scientific works devoted to it is more revealing.[28]

So, after two decades of existence and with a mixed record, questions about the place and role of the EDA still remain. These questions come up against the value that the Member States seem to have placed on the EDA, particularly after it was enshrined in Article 45 of the TEU.

Ultimately, the Agency seems to be subject to two paradoxes. Firstly, the Member States of the European Union have entrusted it with essential missions, which are gradually being increased, but these ambitions are at odds with the control they exercise and the lack of resources they grant it (Section I). This first inconsistency has a direct impact on the second, which is that despite the number and variety of activities it carries out, the EDA's scope remains limited (Section II).

I. AMBITIONS SUBJECT TO INTERGOVERNMENTALITY

Initially tasked in 2004 with defining a European armaments policy and helping to ensure sufficient military capabilities to meet the European

---

25 A. De Nève, *L'Agence européenne de défense et la coopération dans le domaine capacitaire*, Paris, L'Harmattan, 2010, p. 35.

26 Advisory Council on International Questions, *European Defence Cooperation – Sovereignty and the ability to act*, Government of the Netherlands, 2012, p. 17.

27 Alain de Nève's observation in 2010 that the EDA was not well known is still valid in 2024. See A. De Nève, *L'Agence européenne de défense et la coopération dans le domaine capacitaire*, Paris, L'Harmattan, 2010, p. 25.

28 With the notable exception of two works, one by Alain de Nève and the other by Nikolaos Karampekios and Iraklis Oikonomou. Both note the lack of attention paid to the EDA. See A. De Nève, *L'Agence européenne de défense et la coopération dans le domaine capacitaire*, Paris, L'Harmattan, 2010, p. 25; N. Karampekios and I. Oikonomou (eds.), *The European defence agency*, London, Routledge, 2015, p. 1.

Union's political ambitions,[29] the EDA's missions have subsequently expanded (Section A). However, the States that entrusted it with this important role limit its achievements by not giving it the necessary latitude (Section B).

A. GRADUAL EXPANSION OF ESSENTIAL MISSIONS

Since its creation, the EDA's role has been affirmed and enhanced, not only by the TEU and the 2015 decision[30] governing it, but also by Council and European Council conclusions, the establishment of the Permanent Structured Cooperation (PESCO),[31] and the *Long-Term Review* drawn up by the EDA in 2017,[32] and approved by the Council of the European Union.[33] In addition, its recent *2024 Long-Term Review* provides for the consolidation of its involvement within the Union.[34] For the time being, the Council has called for its implementation, stressing the political impetus contained in this text and the importance of the EDA's role.[35] This gradual increase is made possible by the formulation of its missions and tasks in the second subparagraph of Article 42(3) and in Article 45(1), since each may in fact cover a number of activities.

The EDA's remit now covers all defence capabilities, research, acquisition and armaments.[36] As a result, it acts in a number of ways. For the member states, the EDA defines and prioritises operational requirements; it produces expert reports leading to concrete proposals; it oversees projects to develop joint capabilities and technological research; it ensures coordination and consistency between national viewpoints and between defence initiatives; and it monitors compliance with their commitments. The EDA is also responsible

---

29 A. De Nève, *L'Agence européenne de défense et la coopération dans le domaine capacitaire*, Paris, L'Harmattan, 2010, p. 39.

30 Decision (CFSP) 2015/1835, cited above.

31 Council Decision (CFSP) 2017/2315 of 11 December 2017 establishing permanent structured cooperation (PESCO) and determining the list of participating Member States, [2017] *OJ* L331/57, p. 63.

32 EDA, *Long-Term Review of the Agency – Conclusions and Recommendations*, 18 May 2017, https://eda.europa.eu/docs/default-source/documents/ltr-conclusions-and-recommendations.pdf (accessed 20 February 2025).

33 Council of the EU, *Council conclusions on security and defence in the context of the EU's overall strategy*, 9178/17, 18 May 2017, paras. 16–23; Results of the Council meeting, 3538th Foreign Affairs Council meeting, Defence issues, 9396/17, 18 May 2017, p. 4.

34 EDA, *2024 Long-Term Review – EDA as the Intergovernmental Defence Nexus at EU level*, 2024, https://eda.europa.eu/docs/default-source/documents/2024-long-term-review-of-the-european-defence-agency.pdf (accessed 20 February 2025).

35 Council of the European Union, *Council Conclusions on EU Security and Defence*, 9225/24, 27 May 2024, para. 7.

36 A. Dumoulin and N. Gros-Verheyde, *La politique européenne de sécurité et de défense commune*, Le Dévoluy, Éd. du Villard, 2017, p. 169.

for more political missions, as part of the strengthening of the EDTIB. Finally, it provides support for CSDP operations.

The definition of operational requirements is one of the first tasks assigned by the TEU[37] and taken over by the 2015 decision. In this context, the EDA provides a Capability Development Plan (CDP),[38] making it possible to identify future security threats and the capabilities available and those to be developed accordingly.[39] As provided for in *2017 Long-term Review*, the EDA now includes capability priorities in this plan.

Secondly, the Member States regularly call on the EDA to provide expertise and make proposals. For example, in 2013, the European Council asked the EDA to study ways of promoting more effective cooperation in joint procurement projects.[40] In 2016, it asked the EDA to put forward proposals to improve the CDP, the decision-making mechanisms promoting state cooperation in various areas,[41] security of supply at European level and, more specifically, collaborative programmes.[42]

These can be developed within the EDA, which oversees all stages of the project: research and development, definition of common standards and requirements, planning and industrial development.[43] Member States can also entrust the EDA with the development of specific projects for which they have taken the initiative.[44] Ultimately, therefore, it operates on the basis of 'intergovernmental networking',[45] whether in terms of military capabilities or defence technology research.[46] In both these areas, the EDA's role was

---

37 Art. 42(3)(2) and Art. 45(1)(a) TEU.

38 Art. 5(3)(a)(ii), Decision (CFSP) 2015/1835, cited above. It should be noted that Article 5.3, a, i, of the same decision referred to the Capacity Development Mechanism. However, the Union has gradually abandoned this mechanism in favour of the CDP. European Parliament, *Defence of the European Union: the process of implementing the White Paper*, study PE 603.871, December 2018, p. 10.

39 EDA, 'What we do – EU defence initiatives', https://eda.europa.eu/what-we-do/EU-defence-initiatives (accessed on 22 April 2024).

40 L. Chappell and P. Petrov, 'The EDA and military capability development: Making pooling and sharing work', in N. Karampekios and I. Oikonomou (eds.), *The European defence agency*, London, Routledge, 2015, p. 196.

41 More specifically, the areas targeted were standardisation, certification, testing and evaluation, training and military education.

42 European Council, *Conclusions of 15 December 2016*, EUCO 34/16, 15 December 2016. The Council had made the same requests: see Council of the EU, *Conclusions on the implementation of the EU's comprehensive strategy in the field of security and defence*, 14149/16, 14 November 2016.

43 For a presentation of the programmes, see European Defence Agency, 'What we do – Capability development', https://eda.europa.eu/what-we-do/capability-development (consulted on 22 April 2024).

44 Art. 9.1(f) of Decision (CFSP) 2015/1835, cited above.

45 Original quote: 'intergovernmental networking'. D. Fiott, 'The European Commission and the European Defence Agency', (2015) 53(3) *Journal of Common Market Studies*, p. 545.

46 As provided for in Article 5.3(c) and Article 5.3(d) respectively of Decision (CFSP) 2015/1835, cited above.

strengthened in 2017: firstly by the creation of PESCO, in which the member states undertook to use the EDA as a 'European forum for the development of joint capabilities';[47] and secondly by the *Long-term Review*, which reflects the desire for the EDA to be the preferred structure for technology and capability development activities.[48]

In addition, the Agency has powers for the purposes of coordination and consistency, particularly in its role as co-secretary of PESCO, which was not directly provided for in the TEU.[49] This concerns national viewpoints, for example for the development of European airspace,[50] but also for its initiatives and those of other institutional frameworks.[51] The 2015 decision also tasked it with ensuring overall consistency between its activities and other EU policies that may have an impact on defence capabilities.[52] In this respect, it is trying to establish itself as an interface between the participating Member States and the Commission or other EU agencies.[53] The *2024 Long-Term Review* places particular emphasis on this mission, which should make the EDA the preferred body for harmonising state positions and providing European expertise in the field of defence.[54]

The EDA also has powers to monitor compliance with national commitments. Indeed, Article 42(3) TEU stipulates not only that States must progressively improve their military capabilities, but also that the EDA assists the Council in evaluating these improvements.[55] The EDA also fulfils this function with regard to the contributions of participating Member States to PESCO, in particular through the Coordinated Annual Defence Review (CARD).[56]

The EDA also has a more political role in strengthening the EDTIB, since it is responsible for contributing to the creation of a European defence equipment

---

47 Para. 18, 'Annex – List of ambitious and more binding common commitments undertaken by the participating Member States in the five areas defined in Article 2 of Protocol No 10', Decision (CFSP) 2017/2315, cited above. See the commentary on Article 46 TEU by Q. Loïez in this publication.

48 Para. 10, EDA, *Long-term Review of the Agency – Conclusions and Recommendations*, 18 May 2017.

49 The EDA provides the secretariat for the PSC together with the European External Action Service, including the EU Military Staff. Para. 2.2.1 of Annex III 'Governance', and Article 7.1, Decision (CFSP) 2017/2315, cited above.

50 Council of the EU, *Council Conclusions (Defence) on CSDP*, 8971/15, 18 May 2015, para. 19.

51 Art. 7(3)(b) Decision (CFSP) 2017/2315, cited above.

52 Art. 5(3)(g) Decision (CFSP) 2015/1835, cited above.

53 EDA, *Long-term review of the Agency – Conclusions and recommendations*, 18 May 2017, para. 11.

54 EDA, *Long term review – EDA as the intergovernmental Defence Nexus at EU level*, 2024, p. 6.

55 This mission is set out in Article 45(1)(a) of the TEU and Article 2(2) of Decision (CFSP) 2015/1835, cited above.

56 Art. 3, Protocol No. 10 on permanent structured cooperation established by Article 42 TEU.

market, drawing up policies and strategies, and developing and harmonising the relevant state procedures.[57]

Finally, it can provide more technical support for CSDP operations.[58] This support is provided in two different ways: i) by giving access to projects and activities developed within the EDA; or ii) by providing contractual support for the award of contracts.[59]

From this perspective, it is undeniable that the EDA's missions are numerous, diversified and vital. Given this, coupled with its enshrinement in the TEU and the importance of the EDTIB in strengthening European defence, it would be legitimate to expect the EDA to have significant resources and to play a leading role. However, the Member States of the Union, which have defined these missions, seem to be putting the brakes on its activities.

B. RESTRICTIONS IMPOSED BY PARTICIPATING MEMBER STATES

The EDA's efficiency is limited for three reasons which demonstrate its dependence on the will of national states: its intergovernmental nature, the absence of any power of coercion over the States and its moderate own resources.

Firstly, the Agency is intergovernmental rather than supranational, as evidenced by the fact that, like the rest of the CSDP, it is enshrined in the TEU rather than the TFEU. The way it operates proves this, since it is the ministers, meeting in the Council of the Union, who control it politically by giving it guidelines.[60] It can also receive instructions from the Heads of State and Government when the European Council so decides in its conclusions.[61] In both cases, decisions are adopted unanimously, meaning that each State has a *de facto* veto. While the High Representative holds the Presidency, the implementation of the Council's decisions and the day-to-day management of the EDA are the responsibility of a Steering Committee made up of representatives of the participating Member States and a representative of the Commission, who is excluded from voting.[62] At this level, decisions are normally taken by qualified majority, with the notable exception of those

---

57 Art. 5(3)(e) Decision (CFSP) 2015/1835, cited above.

58 Art. 5(3)(i) Decision (CFSP) 2015/1835, cited above.

59 EDA, 'What we do – Support to operations', https://eda.europa.eu/what-we-do/support-to-operations (accessed on 22 April 2024).

60 Art. 4(3) Decision (CFSP) 2015/1835, cited above.

61 A. Dumoulin and N. Gros-Verheyde, *La politique européenne de sécurité et de défense commune*, Le Dévoluy, Éd. du Villard, 2017, p. 171.

62 Art. 8(1) and 9, Decision (CFSP) 2015/1835, cited above.

concerning the Agency's general budget[63] or when a State objects 'for important and substantiated national policy reasons',[64] in which case the decision is taken by the Council unanimously. This last exception is all the easier to implement because the *important* nature of the decision is a matter for each State to decide and seems not very restrictive compared with the requirement of 'vital and stated reasons of national policy'[65] mentioned in the TEU to circumvent qualified majority voting in CFSP matters. The reference to this provision in the *2024 Long-Term Review*, which even devotes its final paragraph to it, confirms the desire of States to be able to use it.[66]

While it may initially have been considered necessary for the Member States to exercise this control in order to ensure their accession to the EDA,[67] the unanimity requirement is now widely considered to be an impediment to its effectiveness.[68] Indeed, the complexity of reaching agreement among twenty-seven Member States and the predominance of national interests regularly lead to delays[69] or national retreats in times of crisis.[70] Ultimately, the latter are a 'sword of Damocles' that has hung over the establishment of a common EDTIB since the creation of the EDA.[71] As the EDA is required to reflect these state wishes, it is obliged to adopt an attitude of 'constructive reserve'.[72]

Secondly, the Agency is subject to the will of States to respect their own commitments, which are already weakened by imprecision, since it has no power of constraint. For example, although Article 42(3) of the TEU stipulates that states must progressively improve their military capabilities, there is no specific reference to this improvement. Within the framework of PESCO, 26 States[73] have entered into more binding commitments regarding their defence budgets, cooperation, operational capabilities and the development of capabilities and

---

63 Art. 9(2) and 9(1)(b), Decision (CFSP) 2015/1835, cited above.

64 Art. 9(3) Decision (CFSP) 2015/1835, cited above.

65 Art. 31(2) TEU. Emphasis by the author.

66 EDA, *Long term review – EDA as the intergovernmental Defence Nexus at EU level*, 2024.

67 A. Georgopoulos, 'EDA and EU defence procurement integration', in N. Karampekios and I. Oikonomou (eds.), *The European defence agency*, London, Routledge, 2015, p. 132.

68 See for example: A. Dumoulin and N. Gros-Verheyde, *La politique européenne de sécurité et de défense commune*, Le Dévoluy, Éd. du Villard, 2017, p. 171; F. Lureau, 'Une industrie de défense compétitive, condition et enjeu d'une politique européenne de défense', *Annales des Mines – Réalités industrielles*, Institut Mines-Télécom, 2018, p. 40; Cour des Comptes, *La coopération européenne en matière d'armement. Un renforcement nécessaire, soumis à des conditions exigeantes*, Paris, La Documentation française, 2018, p. 75.

69 J. Domecq, 'Les défis de l'AED: mutations technologiques, nouvelles menaces et évolutions géostratégiques', *Revue Défense Nationale*, 2016, no. 789, p. 108.

70 Ibid., p. 106.

71 P. Platzgummer, 'The EDA and defence offsets: Trailing after the Commission', in N. Karampekios and I. Oikonomou (eds.), *The European defence agency*, London, Routledge, 2015, p. 207.

72 A. De Nève, *L'Agence européenne de défense et la coopération dans le domaine capacitaire*, Paris, L'Harmattan, 2010, p. 69.

73 All EU Member States except Malta.

the defence industry.[74] While these commitments are numerous, they rarely include precise provisions and deadlines for implementation, leaving States considerable room for interpretation. Moreover, some are collective, which means that no State is bound by a specific objective.[75]

The evaluation carried out by the AED[76] also has its shortcomings. First of all, the CARD is only voluntary. States are simply required to support it 'as far as possible', and individual constraints must be taken into account.[77] Secondly, there are no sanctions in the event of a breach of the commitments. The jurisdiction of the Court of Justice of the European Union (CJEU) is expressly excluded,[78] and even the phenomenon of 'naming and shaming' is not observable here.[79]

As a result, states can violate their commitments with legal impunity. For example, when they failed to meet the increase in defence investment spending agreed under the EDA in 2007, this requirement simply became a target again when the PESCO was launched in 2017.[80] EDA documents also frequently admit that they do not have access to all the necessary state data that would enable them to compile their reports.[81]

Finally, the Agency lacks resources. It is mainly funded by contributions from the participating states, based on the gross national income scale,[82] and its budget is voted unanimously. The fear that it will take on too much importance and manage its own research programmes itself has led to numerous blockages and forced it to keep its budget low.[83] For example, in some cases the Member States have been unable to reach agreement and the budget renewal has been based on decisions taken in previous years, pending a consensus on the three-year financial framework.[84] As for the budget itself, while it has

---

74 Decision (CFSP) 2017/2315, cited above.

75 A. Dumoulin and Q. Loïez, *La coopération structurée permanente (CSP): enjeux politiques, juridiques et capacitaires*, Paris, Pedone, 2022, p. 56.

76 Art. 45(1)(a) TEU.

77 Para. 7, 'Annex – List of ambitious and more binding common commitments undertaken by the participating Member States in the five areas defined in Article 2 of Protocol No 10', Decision (CFSP) 2017/2315, cited above.

78 Art. 24(1) TEU. See the commentary on this article by C. Schneider in this publication.

79 A. Dumoulin and Q. Loïez, *La coopération structurée permanente (CSP): enjeux politiques, juridiques et capacitaires*, Paris, Pedone, 2022, p. 62.

80 Ibid., p. 56.

81 For a recent example, see EDA, *Defence data 2022 -, Key findings and analysis*, 2023.

82 Art. 13(9)(a) Decision (CFSP) 2015/1835, cited above.

83 A. De Nève, *L'Agence européenne de défense et la coopération dans le domaine capacitaire*, Paris, L'Harmattan, 2010, p. 71.

84 See for 2019: EDA, 'Latest News – Outcome of EDA Ministerial Steering Board,' November 20, 2018, https://www.eda.europa.eu/info-hub/press-centre/latest-news/2018/11/20/outcome-of-eda-ministerial-steering-board (accessed 18 April 2024).

increased slightly since the UK left the European Union,[85] it will only reach €44.788 million in 2023.[86] By comparison, the defence budget of the Member States that same year was €270 billion;[87] while the administrative budget of the OCCAR was €74.359 million.[88]

In addition to the fact that this budget is very limited, it is mainly spent on running the Agency. This represented between 93% and 95% of the budget from 2009 to 2020 and has only fallen to between 81% and 85% since 2021.[89] It should be noted, however, that the EDA can also manage funds provided for ad hoc projects or programmes, which can be much larger and in fact reached an unprecedented €296,498 million in 2023.[90] However, these additions do not give the EDA any latitude, and former director Jorge Domecq[91] deplored the EDA's inability to finance cooperative programmes itself.[92]

The number of employees is also rather modest.[93] By 2023, it had 188,[94] but by comparison, the OCCAR has more than 300 staff members.[95]

As a result, the resources allocated to the EDA do not always allow it to carry out the full range of its tasks.[96] The *2017 Long-Term Review* rightly emphasised that it should have adequate resources, even mentioning the possibility of its administrative costs being covered by the EU budget rather than by contributions from participating states.[97] Despite these limitations, the Commission remains very active and has been able to translate the many tasks entrusted to it into action. While it must therefore be acknowledged that it has had some successes, its record over the last two decades remains mixed, not least because its lack of resources means that it has to compete with other institutions.

---

85 A. Dumoulin and N. Gros-Verheyde, *La politique européenne de sécurité et de défense commune,* Le Dévoluy, Éd. du Villard, 2017, p. 172.

86 EDA, *Annual report 2023*, 24 April 2024, p. 27.

87 European Council, 'A European defence for our geopolitical union: address by President Charles Michel to the EDA annual conference', 30 November 2023.

88 OCCAR, *Business Plan 2023*, p. 55.

89 Calculations based on data provided by the EDA. EDA, 'Who we are – Budget', https://eda.europa.eu/who-we-are/Budget (accessed on 24 April 2024).

90 Only contributions directly managed by the EDA are taken into account. EDA, *Annual report 2023*, 24 April 2024, p. 27.

91 Jorge Domecq was director of the EDA from 2015 to 2020.

92 J. Domecq, 'Les défis de l'AED: mutations technologiques, nouvelles menaces et évolutions géostratégiques', *Revue Défense Nationale*, 2016, no. 789, p. 105.

93 A. Dumoulin and N. Gros-Verheyde, *La politique européenne de sécurité et de défense commune,* Le Dévoluy, Éd. du Villard, 2017, p. 172.

94 EDA, *Annual report 2023*, 24 April 2024, p. 28.

95 Direction générale de l'armement du ministère des Armées (France), *Dossier d'informations,* Paris, February 2022, p. 5.

96 K. Vlachos-Dengler, 'EDA and armaments collaboration', in N. Karampekios and I. Oikonomou (eds.), *The European defence agency*, London, Routledge, 2015, p. 99.

97 EDA, *Long-term Review of the Agency – Conclusions and recommendations*, 18 May 2017, paras. 12, 22 and 23.

II. MULTIPLE ACTIVITIES IN COMPETITION WITH OTHER INSTITUTIONS

To fulfil the missions entrusted to it, the Agency has carried out various actions and continues to act in a wide range of areas. However, the proliferation of its initiatives seems to reflect a lack of clarity in the definition of its role (subsection A). While this may give the impression that the Agency has finally succeeded in establishing itself, this lack of clarity also makes it more vulnerable to other institutions that tend to overshadow it, particularly the European Commission (B).

A. A VARIETY OF ACHIEVEMENTS REVEALING AN UNCLEAR ROLE

Despite the EDA's functional and budgetary constraints, it has accomplished many tasks since its creation, following the provisions of the TEU, and several observers have praised its achievements.

As early as 2010, Alain de Nève argued that the EDA had 'succeeded in defining its own agenda and had demonstrated its ability to guide programmatic convergence', as well as 'bringing together the points of view of the Member States'.[98] It is also recognised that it has established itself as a 'trusted partner'[99] of the latter, thanks to its expertise, which enables the EDA to provide relevant information and advice, but also thanks to its 'concrete initiatives and tangible results'.[100] Ultimately, it has contributed to harmonising the European defence market and national requirements, as well as streamlining Member States' approaches to their capability shortfalls.[101] More specifically, it has influenced defence industry standards in three ways: by providing important information to Member States or the Commission; by directly influencing the content and direction of standards adopted by the Commission; and by assisting Member States in applying EU standards.[102]

---

98 A. De Nève, *L'Agence européenne de défense et la coopération dans le domaine capacitaire*, Paris, L'Harmattan, 2010, p. 142.

99 Original quote: 'trusted partner'. L. Chappell and P. Petrov, 'The EDA and military capability development: Making pooling and sharing work', in N. Karampekios and I. Oikonomou (eds.), *The European defence agency*, London, Routledge, 2015, p. 200.

100 Original quote: 'concrete initiatives and tangible results'. Reported from an interview with an ACN representative. K. Vlachos-Dengler, 'EDA and armaments collaboration', in N. Karampekios and I. Oikonomou (eds.), *The European defence agency*, London, Routledge, 2015, p. 99.

101 Ibid., p. 98.

102 A. Georgopoulos, 'EDA and EU defence procurement integration', in N. Karampekios and I. Oikonomou (eds.), *The European defence agency*, London, Routledge, 2015, p. 131.

Nevertheless, while the EDA carries out a wide range of activities, a study of its diversity suggests that its role is still not clearly defined, two decades after its creation. Indeed, to give a more concrete idea of its actions, by way of example and without claiming to be exhaustive, it is possible to cite several of the Agency's achievements.

It has drafted many useful texts for states, such as codes of conduct. The first of these concerned defence procurement and good practice in the supply chain in 2006; another concerned offsets in 2009; the next concerned the pooling and sharing of capabilities in 2012;[103] and yet another text focused on prioritisation in 2014. The EDA also drafted two strategies in 2007 and 2008, the first on the Union's technological and industrial base, and the second on armaments cooperation. It has also developed a Framework Agreement on security of supply between Member States,[104] and a Hub for EU Defence Innovation (HEDI).[105]

The EDA has also established itself as a bank of resources, which it collects in particular during the Coordinated Annual Review of Defence (CARD). Its data is considered the most reliable[106] and is used by authors for economic analysis.[107]

Concerning the concrete development of joint projects and programmes, the EDA is the initiator of the VAT exemption for projects developed within it and bringing added value to the EDTIB.[108] In practice, it has managed 93 collaborative projects, capabilities or research, in 2023.[109] The EDA also facilitates joint procurement by setting up agreements for a fast-track procedure for the joint procurement of artillery ammunition; joint procurement of chemical, biological, radiological and nuclear products; or military equipment.[110]

As part of its role in defining defence priorities, in 2023 it worked on the revision of the Capacity Development Plan (CDP), resulting in the definition

---

103 A. Barrinha, 'The EDA and the discursive construction of European defence and security', in N. Karampekios and I. Oikonomou (eds.), *The European defence agency*, London, Routledge, 2015, p. 35.

104 The first version from 2006 was updated in 2013. EDA, 'What we do – Security of Supply', https://eda.europa.eu/what-we-do/all-activities/activities-search/security-of-supply (accessed on 25 April 2024).

105 EDA, *Annual report 2022*, 2023, p. 3.

106 J. Droff and J. Malizard, 'Qui porte le fardeau?', *Revue française d'économie*, XXXIV, 2019, p. 119.

107 See for example: ibid.; F. Lureau, 'Une industrie de défense compétitive, condition et enjeu d'une politique européenne de défense', *Annales des Mines – Réalités industrielles*, Institut Mines-Télécom, 2018.

108 This mechanism previously existed within NATO, but not within the EU. J. Domecq, 'Les défis de l'AED: mutations technologiques, nouvelles menaces et évolutions géostratégiques', *Revue Défense Nationale*, 2016, no. 789, p. 105.

109 EDA, *Annual report 2023*, 2024, p. 10.

110 Ibid., p. 7.

of twenty-two priorities for the development of defence capabilities. It also carried out its annual *Key Strategic Activities* (KSA) cycle, targeting capability and research areas for analysis.[111] Finally, its *Capability Technology Groups* (CapTechs) have continued to implement technology roadmaps and are currently negotiating forty-eight new technology research projects.[112]

The EDA also provides support to governments in several ways. It manages tactical and training courses in various fields, such as air transport and cyber defence.[113] It can also help them overcome administrative obstacles to military mobility, in line with NATO.[114]

Ultimately, therefore, the EDA oscillates 'between impetus and incentive, coordination and expertise, and even control and evaluation of military capabilities',[115] because the participating Member States have different visions and expectations.[116] The initial lack of precision in Articles 43(2)(2) and 45(1) TEU has not therefore been overcome by the transposition of the tasks entrusted to it into concrete actions. It would appear that all these tasks have been entrusted to it without establishing clear priorities or drawing lessons from previous successes and failures.[117] The EDA is trying to do this for itself, and set out five main tasks in its *2024 Long-Term Review*.[118] However, they do not cover all of its activities, and the document does not specifically address the resources needed to carry out these tasks efficiently. Without a clear and assertive role, the EDA is subject to potential rivalry with other institutions that share some of its competences.

---

111 Ibid., p. 4.

112 Ibid., p. 14.

113 For more on this subject, see ibid, p. 18; and EDA, 'What we do – Training & Exercises', https://eda.europa.eu/what-we-do/training-exercises (accessed 25 April 2024).

114 EDA, *Annual Report 2023*, 2024, p. 20.

115 A. Dumoulin and Q. Loïez, *La coopération structurée permanente (CSP): enjeux politiques, juridiques et capacitaires*, Paris, Pedone, 2022, p. 172.

116 J. Domecq, 'Les défis de l'AED: mutations technologiques, nouvelles menaces et évolutions géostratégiques', *Revue Défense Nationale*, 2016, no. 789, p. 103.

117 A. Dumoulin and Q. Loïez, *La coopération structurée permanente (CSP): enjeux politiques, juridiques et capacitaires*, Paris, Pedone, 2022, p. 172.

118 These five core tasks are: 1) identifying shared needs and priorities at EU level, to ensure that EU Member States' armed forces have the capabilities they actually require; 2) enabling collaborative defence research, technology, and innovation, to prepare the future of EU defence; 3) harmonising requirements and engaging in joint capability development, while ensuring interoperability; 4) aggregating demand towards joint procurement to fill capabilities shortfalls; finally 5) interfacing with EU civilian and defence policies and voicing Ministries of Defence's joint positions. EDA, *2024 Long-Term Review – EDA as the intergovernmental Defence Nexus at EU level*, 2024.

B. HARMFUL INSTITUTIONAL COMPETITION

Although the creation of the EDA was necessary and it remains a unique agency, this does not mean that it is alone in its field of competence. Yet the TEU makes no specific provision for cohabitation or collaboration with other agencies. The only indication in Article 45(2) is brief, since it simply states that the EDA 'shall carry out its tasks in liaison with the Commission where necessary'. As for the 2015 decision, which sets out how the EDA is to operate, it refers to it but, again, remains terse. The EDA has therefore had to establish itself, without a clear definition of its role,[119] with few resources and alongside other bodies that are sometimes better established.[120] These include international organisations such as the OCCAR and NATO, and EU institutions such as the Commission.

Collaboration with the OCCAR, whose remit is to facilitate 'the management of cooperation arrangements for armaments programmes and technology demonstrations',[121] seems fairly natural. Its remit and the number of its member states are smaller, and their cooperation 'ensures the continuity of capability development projects to strengthen the [EDTIB]'.[122] Although it is not mentioned in the TEU, the 2015 decision refers to it on several occasions as a privileged partner of the EDA.[123] It is also cited as an example of potential guests at meetings of the Steering Committee.[124] In addition, there has been an administrative arrangement between the two bodies since 2012.

With NATO, by contrast, there is more competition, since it has several bodies with missions similar to those of the EDA: the NATO Support and Procurement Agency (NSPA), the NATO Standardisation Office (NSO), the Defence Innovation Accelerator for the North Atlantic (DIANA) and the Information and Communications Agency (NCIA).[125] As a result, and given the EDA's more limited resources, these entities have sometimes been favoured by states that are members of both organisations at the same time. For example, the EDA has suspended its publications concerning the establishment of common

---

[119] A. De Nève, *L'Agence européenne de défense et la coopération dans le domaine capacitaire*, Paris, L'Harmattan, 2010, p. 42.

[120] A. Georgopoulos, 'EDA and EU defence procurement integration', in N. Karampekios and I. Oikonomou (eds.), *The European defence agency*, London, Routledge, 2015, p. 185.

[121] A. De Nève, *L'Agence européenne de défense et la coopération dans le domaine capacitaire*, Paris, L'Harmattan, 2010, p. 89.

[122] A. Cammilleri-Subrenat, *Le droit de la politique européenne de sécurité et de défense dans le cadre du traité de Lisbonne*, Paris/Cachan, Lavoisier/Éditions TEC & DOC, 2010, p. 63.

[123] (7) of the Preamble and Article 26(2), Decision (CFSP) 2015/1835, cited above.

[124] Art. 8(7)(b) Decision (CFSP) 2015/1835, cited above.

[125] NATO, 'What we do – NATO's agencies', https://www.nato.int/cps/en/natohq/topics_66470.htm?selectedLocale=fr (consulted on 25 April 2024).

armaments standards and has taken over NATO's STANAG standards.[126] On the other hand, the EDA has established itself more as a forum for collective armaments projects.[127] Consequently, although NATO is not mentioned in Articles 42(3) and 45 TEU, it is planned that it too will be invited to meetings of the Steering Board on matters of common interest,[128] and that administrative arrangements will be signed.[129] The *2024 Long-Term Review* again insists on the signing of such arrangements, which are necessary to ensure the consistency of the actions undertaken by the various agencies. It also states that the EDA is a key contributor to cooperation between the EU and NATO.[130]

Within the EU, the EDA works with other bodies. These include the European External Action Service, of which the EU Military Staff is a member, the EU Military Committee,[131] and more recently the European Investment Bank, with which it signed a programme agreement in 2019 establishing a cooperative financial mechanism.[132]

Relations with the Commission, on the other hand, are more complex, even though it is the only one expressly referred to in Article 45(2) TEU, while the 2015 decision refers to their consultation on several occasions[133] and includes an Article 24 dedicated to their relations. Under the terms of the agreement, the Commission is a non-voting member of the EDA's Steering Committee and may participate in some of the projects or programmes. Moreover, both the EDA and Commission should work together to share their expertise. In 2016, EDA Director Jorge Domecq stated that he had 'established a relationship of trust with the European Commission'.[134]

However, there seems to be some tension between these two bodies, whose areas of competence may overlap. In fact, the Commission's actions concerning the internal market intervene in the field of defence, while the EDA's missions concern defence procurement.[135] Both therefore play a role for

[126] A. Georgopoulos, 'EDA and EU defence procurement integration', in N. Karampekios and I. Oikonomou (eds.), *The European defence agency*, London, Routledge, 2015, p. 177.

[127] Ibid., p. 178.

[128] Art. 8(7)(a) Decision (CFSP) 2015/1835, cited above.

[129] Art. 26(3) Decision (CFSP) 2015/1835, cited above.

[130] EDA, *2024 Long-Term Review – EDA as the intergovernmental Defence Nexus at EU level*, 2024, p. 7.

[131] EDA, *Long-Term Review of the Agency – Conclusions and recommendations*, 18 May 2017, p. 1.

[132] EDA, 'EIB signs Cooperative Financial Mechanism (CFM) arrangement', December 2019, https://eda.europa.eu/news-and-events/news/2019/12/09/eib-signs-cooperative-financial-mechanism-(cfm)-arrangement (accessed 25 April 2024).

[133] Art. 5(d)(v) and Art. 5(e), Decision (CFSP) 2015/1835, cited above.

[134] J. Domecq, 'Les défis de l'AED: mutations technologiques, nouvelles menaces et évolutions géostratégiques', *Revue Défense Nationale*, 2016, no. 789, p. 105.

[135] A. Cammilleri-Subrenat, *Le droit de la politique européenne de sécurité et de défense dans le cadre du traité de Lisbonne*, Paris/Cachan, Lavoisier/Éditions TEC & DOC, p. 63.

the EDTIB, with actions that may overlap.[136] Three cumulative factors place them in a competitive position: the EDA operates according to a different intergovernmental logic, while the Commission operates according to a supranational logic;[137] the Member States may exacerbate tensions by preferring one or other of the institutions, depending on the initiatives developed or the circumstances;[138] finally, the resources of the Commission are far greater than those of the EDA, whether in terms of its capacity to issue standards or its budget,[139] which reinforces the feeling of 'rivalry between unequal partners' to the detriment of the EDA.[140]

As a result, the role of the EDA sometimes seems to be called into question by the Commission's growing involvement in the defence industry. This is not a recent development, since the Commission drafted a communication in 1996 proposing to contribute to the establishment of such a European armaments agency and the implementation of its activities.[141] Since then, it has become involved in the defence industry through directives, commissioned policy studies, formal and informal working relationships with other players, communications and financial investments.[142] The first Van der Leyen Commission has included, for the first time, a Directorate-General for Defence Industry and Space (DG DEFIS) and has drafted a New European Defence Industrial Strategy (EDIS), along with the High Representative.[143] Since 2024, there is now a Commissioner for Defence and Space in charge of overseeing the implementation of the EDIS. Some commentators believe that the Commission

---

136 A. De Nève, *L'Agence européenne de défense et la coopération dans le domaine capacitaire*, Paris, L'Harmattan, 2010, p. 142.

137 The tensions between institutions falling under these two logics are classic. D. Fiott, 'The European Commission and the European Defence Agency', (2015) 53(3) *Journal of Common Market Studies*, p. 542.

138 Ibid., p. 555.

139 J. Domecq, 'Les défis de l'AED: mutations technologiques, nouvelles menaces et évolutions géostratégiques', *Revue Défense Nationale*, 2016, no. 789, p. 103.

140 Original quote: '*rivalry of unequal partners*'. Remarks reported from an interview with an EDA representative in 2013. D. Fiott, 'The European Commission and the European Defence Agency', (2015) 53(3) *Journal of Common Market Studies*, p. 544. See also. J.-P. Maulny and N. Gros-Verheyde, 'L'échec de l'Agence européenne de défense est-il irrémédiable', *Bruxelles2, 9 May 2016*.

141 Commission of the European Communities, *The Challenges Facing the European Defence-Related Industry, a Contribution for Action at European Level*, COM(96) 10 final, Brussels, 24 January 1996.

142 For a more detailed presentation of these Commission actions, see D. Fiott, 'The European Commission and the European Defence Agency', (2015) 53(3) *Journal of Common Market Studies*, p. 545. See also. E. Bernard, 'La communautarisation de la défense européenne dans le contexte de la guerre en Ukraine', *RTDE*, 2023/4, pp. 325–350.

143 European Commission and High Representative, *Joint communication to the European Parliament, the Council, the European Economic and Social Committee and the Committee of the Regions – A new European Defence Industrial Strategy: Achieving EU readiness through a responsive and resilient European Defence Industry*, JOIN(2024) 10 final, 5 March 2024.

is deliberately encroaching on the EDA's competences by extending its own.[144] There have even been cases where the work of the former has rendered that of the latter obsolete, as in the case of the regulation of offsets, when a directive[145] was adopted that sometimes contravenes the EDA's Code of Conduct on Offsets.[146]

In addition, the Commission only moderately involves the EDA in its initiatives. While this was understandable at the time of its first 'Defence Package' in 2007, when the Agency was a newcomer,[147] the situation hardly seems to have improved. However, in 2017, the EDA's *Long-term Review* urged the Commission 'to make full use of the existing structures and networks of expertise of the Agency'[148] in its areas of activity.

At present, the EDA is only marginally involved in the Commission's latest initiatives which are the European Defence Fund (EDF),[149] the EDIRPA[150] and ASAP[151] regulations, and the latest, European Defence Industry Programme (EDIP) regulation.[152] It is mentioned in its role as an expert, and sometimes as an executor, but without acquiring a privileged position.

---

144 A. Georgopoulos, 'EDA and EU defence procurement integration', EDA and EU defence procurement integration'p. 183; D. Fiott, 'The European Commission and the European Defence Agency', (2015) 53(3) *Journal of Common Market Studies*, p. 544.

145 Directive (EC) 2009/81 of the European Parliament and of the Council of 13 July 2009 on the coordination procedures for the award of certain works contracts, supply contracts and service contracts by contracting authorities or entities in the fields of defence and security, and amending Directives 2004/17/EC and 2004/18/EC, [2009] *OJ* L216/76.

146 P. Platzgummer, 'The EDA and defence offsets: Trailing after the Commission', in N. Karampekios and I. Oikonomou (eds.), *The European defence agency*, London, Routledge, 2015, p. 237.

147 A. De Nève, *L'Agence européenne de défense et la coopération dans le domaine capacitaire*, Paris, L'Harmattan, 2010, p. 143.

148 Full quote: 'to make full use of the existing structures and networks of expertise of the Agency and to acknowledge its enhanced relevance for the identification, prioritisation and development into technical specifications of overarching capability and R&T priorities as well as their implementation regarding EU funded activities'. EDA, *Long-term review of the Agency – Conclusions and recommendations*, 18 May 2017.

149 Regulation (EU) 2021/697 of the European Parliament and of the Council of 29 April 2021 establishing the European Defence Fund and repealing Regulation (EU) 2018/1092, [2021] *OJ* L170/149. See the commentary by S. Rodridues in this publication.

150 Regulation (EU) 2023/2418 of the European Parliament and of the Council of 18 October 2023 on the establishment of an instrument to strengthen the European defence industry through joint procurement (EDIRPA), [2023] *OJ L2023/2418*. See the commentary by E. Bernard in this publication.

151 Regulation (EU) 2023/1525 of the European Parliament and of the Council of 20 July 2023 on supporting ammunition production (ASAP), [2023] *OJ* L185/ 7. See E. Bernard's commentary in this publication.

152 Regulation (EU) 2025/2643 of the European Parliament and of the Council of 16 December 2025 establishing the European Defence Industry Programme and a framework of measures to ensure the timely availability and supply of defence products ('EDIP Regulation'), [2025] *OJ* L2025/2643.

As regards the EDF, it acts as an observer on the Committee, assists the Commission in drafting calls for proposals and indirectly manages some of the projects funded.[153] In the EDIRPA regulations and ASAP, the EDA is associated with the task force for joint procurement in the field of armaments, but is simply invited to share its views and expertise with the Committee.[154] Finally, in the EDIP regulation,[155] it is stated that the Commission will often rely on the KSAs developed within the EDA,[156] which will be represented in the Defence Security of Supply Board[157], and is also one of the entities eligible for funding.[158] On the other hand, the EDA will still only be invited to provide its view and expertise to the Committee, as an observer.[159]

Ultimately, the EDA may be condemned to 'working more and more as a subcontractor to the European Commission', which needs its scientific skills.[160] This situation is potentially problematic, because the Commission's approach is based on the logic of markets and industrial priorities, whereas the intrinsic specificities of the defence industry lead to different logics. The defence market should not therefore be regulated by analogy like the civilian industrial market.[161] Daniel Fiott has therefore called for the establishment of a 'structured dialogue' between the two bodies, which is not provided for in the TEU.[162] For its part, the EDA has demonstrated its desire to be more involved in the Commission's initiatives. Indeed, its *2024 Long-Term Review* strongly emphasises the expertise it can contribute to the defence industry, expressing the wish to be more involved in the EDF, and stating that the EDA will take forward the activities developed thanks to the ASAP and EDIRPA regulations.[163]

Be that as it may, the role and place of the EDA still do not seem to be firmly established, despite two decades spent multiplying its activities in response to the missions entrusted to it. There are a variety of opinions as to its potential evolution: it could become a political forum for the lasting harmonisation of

---

153 EDA, *Annual report 2023*, 2024, p. 8.

154 Art. 16 of Regulation (EU) 2023/2418, above; Art. 16 of Regulation (EU) 2023/1525, above.

155 See the commentary by E. Simon in this publication.

156 Paras. 47, 50, 58 and 59 of the Regulation, above.

157 Ibid., Art. 76.

158 Ibid., Art. 12.

159 Ibid., Art. 77.

160 J.-P. Maulny and N. Gros-Verheyde, 'L'échec de l'Agence européenne de défense est-il irrémédiable', *Bruxelles2, 9 May 2016.*

161 Remarks reported after an interview with an EDA representative in 2014. D. Fiott, 'The European Commission and the European Defence Agency', (2015) 53(3) *Journal of Common Market Studies*, p. 550.

162 Original quote: 'structured dialogue'. Ibid., p. 550.

163 EDA, *Long term review – EDA as the intergovernmental Defence Nexus at EU level*, 2024, pp. 2 and 6.

the wishes and interests of the Member States,[164] in particular by associating the EDA more closely with the national headquarters;[165] or it could become a 'future organisational melting pot for all ESDP competences, beyond the capability aspect alone',[166] by integrating it with the Union's other politico-military institutions; or it could become a 'genuine European procurement agency',[167] which for some should be a delegated agency of the Commission.[168] While there are several ideas for this intergovernmental agency, which has a mixed record, it would be risky to make any predictions. Like the rest of defence cooperation within the EU, it is subject to the wills of the Member States. And these can change radically depending on the context, since 'the Union is consolidated through crises',[169] whether they result from the strategic position of the United States, the rise of Euroscepticism, the outbreak of conflicts or a financial shock that makes cooperation more urgent. Currently, in the light of the Council conclusions of 27 May 2024, the defence ministers of the Member States appear to be in favour of consolidating the EDA, since they have announced that they wish to make greater use of it, supporting the *2024 Long-Term Review* and reaffirming the importance of the EDA's role within the Union.[170]

---

164 Cour des Comptes, 'La coopération européenne en matière d'armement. Un renforcement nécessaire, soumis à des conditions exigeantes', Paris, La Documentation française, April 2018.

165 F. Lureau, 'Une industrie de défense compétitive, condition et enjeu d'une politique européenne de défense', *Annales des Mines – Réalités industrielles*, Institut Mines-Télécom, 2018, p. 38.

166 A. De Nève, *L'Agence européenne de défense et la coopération dans le domaine capacitaire*, Paris, L'Harmattan, 2010, p. 112.

167 N. Gros-Verheyde, 'Face à la menace Trump: aux armes Européens! Neuf pistes pour réagir', *Bruxelles2*, 11 February 2024.

168 J.-P. Maulny and N. Gros-Verheyde, 'L'échec de l'Agence européenne de défense est-il irrémédiable', *Bruxelles2, 9 May 2016*.

169 E. Bernard, 'L'autonomie stratégique de l'Union européenne à l'épreuve d'une double crise: entre confiance et méfiance', in E. Bernard and F. Grabrias, *La confiance en temps de crise*, Brussels, Bruylant, 2021, p. 307.

170 Council of the European Union, *Council Conclusions on EU Security and Defence*, 9225/24, 27 May 2024, p. 6.

ARTICLE 46 TEU: PERMANENT STRUCTURED COOPERATION

Quentin Loïez[1]
Legal and Policy Officer at the European Commission (DG DEFIS)

Article 46 TEU

1. Those Member States which wish to participate in the permanent structured cooperation referred to in Article 42(6), which fulfil the criteria and have made the commitments on military capabilities set out in the Protocol on permanent structured cooperation, shall notify their intention to the Council and to the High Representative of the Union for Foreign Affairs and Security Policy.

2. Within three months following the notification referred to in paragraph 1 the Council shall adopt a decision establishing permanent structured cooperation and determining the list of participating Member States. The Council shall act by a qualified majority after consulting the High Representative.

3. Any Member State which, at a later stage, wishes to participate in the permanent structured cooperation shall notify its intention to the Council and to the High Representative.

The Council shall adopt a decision confirming the participation of the Member State concerned which fulfils the criteria and makes the commitments referred to in Articles 1 and 2 of the Protocol on permanent structured cooperation. The Council shall act by a qualified majority after consulting the High Representative. Only members of the Council representing the participating Member States shall take part in the vote.

A qualified majority shall be defined in accordance with Article 238(3)(a) of the Treaty on the Functioning of the European Union.

1 This analysis is provided in a personal capacity and reflects the views of the author only. In no way can it be regarded as the official position of the European Commission.

> **4.** If a participating Member State no longer fulfils the criteria or is no longer able to meet the commitments referred to in Articles 1 and 2 of the Protocol on permanent structured cooperation, the Council may adopt a decision suspending the participation of the Member State concerned.
> The Council shall act by a qualified majority. Only members of the Council representing the participating Member States, with the exception of the Member State in question, shall take part in the vote.
> A qualified majority shall be defined in accordance with Article 238(3)(a) of the Treaty on the Functioning of the European Union.
> **5.** Any participating Member State which wishes to withdraw from permanent structured cooperation shall notify its intention to the Council, which shall take note that the Member State in question has ceased to participate.
> **6.** The decisions and recommendations of the Council within the framework of permanent structured cooperation, other than those provided for in paragraphs 2 to 5, shall be adopted by unanimity. For the purposes of this paragraph, unanimity shall be constituted by the votes of the representatives of the participating Member States only.

Although the genesis of its provisions can be traced back to the Treaty establishing a Constitution for Europe (TECE)[2] of 2004, which never entered into force, permanent structured cooperation (PESCO) made its real entry into the primary law of the European Union (EU) with the Treaty of Lisbon.[3] Between 2009, when the latter came into force, and 2017, PESCO remained a simple option, freely available to the Member States. However, the geopolitical context facing the EU in the second decade of the 21st century[4] finally led the Council to take up this option.

The creation of PESCO took place in a climate of political will on the part of all those involved strengthening the European Union's action in defence. The EU Global Strategy[5] presented by the High Representative of the Union for Foreign Affairs and Security Policy (hereinafter 'the High Representative' or HR/VP), Ms Federica Mogherini, set out a new strategic

2 Treaty establishing a Constitution for Europe, [2004] *OJ* C310/1.

3 Treaty of Lisbon amending the Treaty on European Union and the Treaty establishing the European Community, signed at Lisbon, 13 December 2007, pp. 1-271.

4 Examples include the military intervention in Libya (2011) and its consequences, the Syrian civil war (which began in 2011), Russia's annexation of Crimea (2014), the wave of terrorist attacks in Paris and Brussels (2015), the election of Donald Trump in the United States of America (2016), and the referendum on the United Kingdom's exit from the European Union (BREXIT) (2016).

5 Shared vision, common action: a stronger Europe – A global strategy for the European Union's foreign and security policy, 2016.

framework at the European level from June 2016, to create new momentum in defence cooperation within the European Union. Following on from this, the European Commission also launched its European Defence Action Plan in November 2016,[6] announcing the creation of a European Defence Fund (EDF).[7] It was under these favourable political circumstances that the Council decided to create PESCO in December 2017, by activating the relevant provisions in the Treaty on European Union (TEU) as well as its annexed Protocol Number 10. With this Council decision,[8] PESCO enters the secondary law of the European Union.

The Council has made no secret of its expectations of PESCO, which it describes as 'a major step forward in strengthening the common defence policy'. It also considers that PESCO 'could be an element in a possible move towards a common defence'. According to the Council, PESCO also provides 'an ambitious, binding and inclusive European legal framework for investment in the security and defence of the territory of the European Union and its citizens. It also provides all Member States with an essential political framework contributing to the improvement of their respective military resources and defence capabilities through well-coordinated initiatives and concrete projects based on more binding commitments. The development of the defence capabilities of the Member States of the Union will also benefit NATO'.[9] In these few lines we find the three main characteristics of PESCO, as shaped by secondary law: modularity, inclusiveness and ambition. However, far from being irreconcilable objectives, it seems difficult for PESCO to reconcile these three characteristics effectively in practice.

The existence of more binding commitments made by the Member States participating in PESCO, the adoption of numerous projects within this framework and the establishment of a system for evaluating and supervising the implementation of commitments and projects are all elements that currently characterise the operation of PESCO, but whose effectiveness can sometimes seem relative. The purpose of this contribution is therefore to try to answer the following question: to what extent does PESCO, which is inclusive and modular, manage to remain ambitious and effective at the same time?

In an attempt to provide some answers, we need to examine both the body of EU law relating to PESCO and the practical developments to which its implementation by the Member States and the Council has led. Thus, after

---

6 European Defence Action Plan, Brussels, 30 November 2016, COM(2016) 950 final.

7 Regulation (EU) 2021/697 of the European Parliament and of the Council of 29 April 2021 establishing the European Defence Fund and repealing Regulation (EU) 2018/1092, [2021] *OJ* L170/149 (EDF Regulation); see the commentary by S. Rodrigues in this volume.

8 Council Decision (CFSP) 2017/2315 of 11 December 2017 establishing permanent structured cooperation (PESCO) and determining the list of participating Member States, [2017] *OJ* L331/57 (Decision (CFSP) 2017/2315).

9 Ibid.

examining the two characteristics that have been particularly asserted since 2017, namely the inclusiveness and modularity of PESCO (Section I), we will seek to understand whether and how PESCO can also be considered an ambitious and effective framework for cooperation (Section II).

I. AN INCLUSIVE AND MODULAR PESCO

A. A PESCO THAT HAS BECOME PARTICULARLY INCLUSIVE SINCE 2017

In the preparatory work for the Treaty establishing a Constitution for Europe (TECE) there was a clear desire to make possible a form of 'closer cooperation between Member States, open to all Member States wishing to carry out the most demanding tasks and fulfilling the requirements for such a commitment to be credible'.[10] This avant-garde spirit was reflected in the text of the TECE by giving Member States the option of creating a permanent structured cooperation (PESCO).

This possibility was included in the Treaty of Lisbon, which replicated the provisions relating to PESCO. Primary law thus remained faithful to the avant-garde spirit which had motivated the existence of PESCO from the outset. The persistence in primary law of two characteristic elements of this logic still bears witness to this original spirit.

The first characteristic can be described as a 'flexibility clause' for creating PESCO. The purpose of this flexibility clause is to facilitate the emergence of a group of capable and willing Member States. There is no minimum number of participating Member States required to set up PESCO. This makes it considerably easier for a small number of Member States, a core group of motivated Member States, to consider setting up PESCO. In addition, the vote to create PESCO is by qualified majority.[11]

However, the governance of PESCO, at least for its day-to-day operation as provided for in Article 46(6) TEU, appears to be the counterpart of the flexibility that governs the process of setting it up. Once established, PESCO operates on the basis of unanimity. Once again, the rigidity of this intergovernmental system reflects the intention of the drafters of the Treaty not to encourage the

---

10 Working Group VIII 'Defence', Final Report by the Chairman of Working Group VIII 'Defence' to the Members of the Convention, CONV 461/02 – WG VIII 22, Brussels, 16 December 2002, para. 54 (Working Group VIII 'Defence').

11 Art. 46(2) TEU.

emergence of a PESCO comprising too many participating Member States. A PESCO that is too inclusive has two major disadvantages:[12]

- The uselessness of the flexibility clause for the creation of PESCO (the only advantage of qualified majority voting is that it allows the creation of PESCO in the absence of unanimity among the Member States).
- Governance that is more complex to implement (the greater the number of participating Member States, the more difficult it will be to achieve unanimity for the day-to-day running of PESCO).

A comparison with enhanced cooperation, illustrated in Table 1, highlights the advantages of the flexibility clause in PESCO, since enhanced cooperation appears to be its mirror image. Enhanced cooperation seems far less likely to encourage the emergence of a vanguard group.

Table 1 – Comparison between PESCO and enhanced cooperation

	PESCO	Enhanced cooperation
Creation conditions	There is no minimum number of participating Member States required to create PESCO	At least nine participating Member States are required to create enhanced cooperation (see Art. 20(2) TEU)
	Decision to create PESCO by qualified majority	For enhanced cooperation within the framework of the Common Foreign and Security Policy (CFSP), the decision to create enhanced cooperation is taken unanimously (see Article 329(2) of the Treaty on the Functioning of the EU).

The second characteristic is the existence of criteria for participation in PESCO, the aim of which is to filter out the most capable Member States and ensure that PESCO has a certain degree of homogeneity among its members (rather like the convergence criteria for the euro zone).[13] The need to meet the conditions for participation again supports the view that PESCO is conceived as a vanguard in which only the most capable Member States (i.e. those meeting the conditions for participation) can take part in cooperation.[14]

---

12 A PESCO that might be considered too inclusive would have a greater number of participating Member States than is strictly necessary to obtain a qualified majority for the creation of cooperation.

13 In fact, some members of the working group referred to a 'defence Euro-zone' when they envisaged the group as the vanguard in defence matters. See. Working Group VIII 'Defence', para. 54, cited above.

14 Protocol (No. 10) on Permanent Structured Cooperation established by Article 42 TEU, Art. 1 and Art. 2.

However, in 2017, despite the flexibility clause and adopting a flexible interpretation of the participation criteria, the Council ultimately did not wish to adhere to the original spirit of the primary law on PESCO. The Council opted for the creation of a particularly inclusive PESCO, bringing together 25 participating Member States. In 2023, Denmark, in line with its decision to participate fully in the EU's Common Security and Defence Policy (CSDP), was accepted by the Council as the 26th Member State to participate in PESCO.[15] Today, 26 of the 27 current EU Member States are members of PESCO.[16]

By creating a particularly inclusive PESCO in 2017, the Council finally responded with a framework almost identical to that of the CSDP, exposed to the same difficulties of unanimous governance. The complexity of intergovernmental governance by 25, and then 26, Member States was already apparent in the early years of PESCO. A famous example of this was the adoption of the decision on the conditions governing the participation of third countries in PESCO projects,[17] which was more than two years behind schedule.[18]

Back in December 2017, the Council planned to adopt a decision on the exceptional participation of third countries in PESCO projects.[19] While a core set of conditions had been imposed, in particular by Article 4(2)(g) of Decision (CFSP) 2017/2315,[20] the Council still had to adopt a decision enabling it to determine precisely the degree of inclusiveness of PESCO with regard to third States.

The Council had apparently not anticipated the difficulty it would have in bringing this set of rules to fruition, since in March 2018 it had planned to reach a decision on the matter by the end of 2018.[21] The Council in fact took two years to achieve this result. This was due to political differences

15 Council Decision (CFSP) 2023/1015 of 23 May 2023 confirming the participation of Denmark in PESCO and amending Decision (CFSP) 2017/2315 establishing permanent structured cooperation (PESCO) and determining the list of participating Member States, [2023] *OJ* L136/73.

16 Malta remains the last Member State not to be part of PESCO.

17 Council Decision (CFSP) 2020/1639 of 5 November 2020 establishing the general conditions under which third States could exceptionally be invited to participate in individual PESCO projects, [2020] *OJ* L371/3 (Decision (CFSP) 2020/1639).

18 Council Recommendation of 6 March 2018 concerning a roadmap for the implementation of PESCO, [2018] *OJ* C88/1, para. 13.

19 Decision (CFSP) 2017/2315, Art. 4(2)(g) and Art. 9(1), cited above.

20 These include providing 'substantial added value to the project', 'helping to strengthen PESCO and CSDP' and 'fulfilling more binding commitments'.

21 As evidenced by the Recommendation of 6 March 2018: 'The work to develop these general conditions [for the exceptional participation of third States in given projects] should start as soon as the common set of governance rules for the projects and the sequencing of the fulfilment of commitments are in place by June 2018 and, subject to a further assessment by the Council, a Decision should in principle be adopted before the end of 2018'.

between the participating Member States (which were unable to agree on a compromise)[22] and external geopolitical pressures on the EU.[23]

By overcoming these governance difficulties, the Council nonetheless succeeded in adopting a decision on the subject. Article 3 of Decision (CFSP) 2020/1639 sets out no less than eight cumulative conditions that third countries must meet if they wish to participate in a PESCO project. As Table 2 shows, these conditions are designed to ensure that only third States making a significant contribution and respecting the EU's commitments can participate in PESCO. The most likely potential third States are European states geopolitically close to the EU and non-EU members of NATO, with the likely exception of Turkey as reflected in the fourth condition as set out in Table 2. Each of the conditions is strictly verified and assessed by the Council, which retains control, under the unanimity rule, of the decision on whether or not to open up PESCO projects to the participation of third countries.

Table 2 – The eight conditions for third State participation in a PESCO project

Condition	Logic of the condition
Substantial added value	The third State's participation must make a significant contribution to the project.
Strengthening the CSDP	The third State must contribute to the Common Security and Defence Policy (CSDP).
Compliance with more stringent commitments	The third State must respect the commitments made by the Member States. Decision (CFSP) 2020/1639 specifies that the third State's participation must 'in particular' be consistent with the commitments that PESCO project helps to fulfil.
Shared EU values and objectives	The third State must share the EU's values and have a political dialogue on security and defence issues. This condition appears to be a means of excluding from cooperation any third State that would jeopardise the security interests of the Union or its Member States (this condition can be seen in the light of the tensions in the Eastern Mediterranean in 2020 between Greece and Turkey, both of which are members of NATO).[24]

[22] V. Mahieu, 'La participation des pays tiers au sein de la PESCO', *Éclairage du GRIP*, 30 March 2020.

[23] D. Fiott, 'The Poison Pill – EU defence on US terms?', EUISS Brief, June 2019.

[24] E. Pommiers, 'Pourquoi la Grèce et la Turquie s'affrontent en Méditerranée orientale', *Le Monde*, 14 September 2020.

Condition	Logic of the condition
No dependencies	The participation must not create dependencies for the Union. This condition prevents the creation of a form of dependence on the third State, but also aims to prevent the third State from imposing restrictions 'on a Member State of the Union as regards the purchase of armaments, research and development of capabilities, or the use and export of armaments or capabilities and technologies, which would impede progress or prevent the employability, jointly or otherwise, export or operational deployment of capabilities developed in the context of PESCO project'.
Agreement on information security	An information security agreement must be in place.
Administrative arrangement with the European Defence Agency (EDA)	If the project is supported by the EDA, an administrative arrangement must be made.
Legal consistency with PESCO as a whole	The third State must undertake to comply with certain provisions of Decision (CFSP) 2017/2315 and Decision (CFSP) 2018/909.[25] This should ensure a certain degree of overall legal consistency within PESCO project in which a third State might participate.

At their request, the participation of four NATO countries – the United States, Canada, Norway and the United Kingdom – as well as the participation of Switzerland, was accepted by seven different Council decisions.[26] These third countries are participating in the military mobility project, coordinated by the Netherlands, which involves the largest number of participating Member States (24) and covers an important area in EU-NATO cooperation, as well as in

---

[25] 'It has undertaken, in its request for participation referred to in Article 2(1) of this Decision, to ensure compliance with certain provisions of Decision (CFSP) 2017/2315 and Decision (CFSP) 2018/909'. Decision (CFSP) 2020/1639, Art. 3(h), cited above.

[26] Council Decision (CFSP) 2021/749 of 6 May 2021 on the participation of the Kingdom of Norway in the PESCO project Military Mobility', [2021] *OJ* L160/109; Council Decision (CFSP) 2021/748 of 6 May 2021 on the participation of Canada in the PESCO project Military Mobility, [2021] *OJ* L160/106; Council Decision (CFSP) 2021/750 of 6 May 2021 on the participation of the United States of America in the PESCO project Military Mobility, [2021] *OJ* L160/112; Council Decision (CFSP) 2022/2244 of 14 November 2022 on the participation of the United Kingdom of Great Britain and Northern Ireland in the PESCO project Military Mobility, [2022] *OJ* L294/22; Council Decision (CFSP) 2023/385 of 20 February 2023 on the participation of Canada in the PESCO project Network of Logistic Hubs in Europe and Support to Operations, [2023] *OJ* L53/14; Council Decision (CFSP) 2025/75 of 13 January 2025 on the participation of Switzerland in the PESCO project Military Mobility, [2025] *OJ* L2025/75; Council Decision (CFSP) 2025/967 of 20 May 2025 on the participation of Switzerland in the PESCO project Cyber Ranges Federations, [2025] *OJ* L2025/967.

the European Logistics Platforms and Operations Support Network project (Canada) and in the Cyber Ranges Federations project (Switzerland).

While the inclusiveness of PESCO is evident in terms of the number of participating Member States, this inclusiveness does not necessarily appear to be transposable to the opening up of PESCO to third States. In fact, the broad inclusiveness of the PESCO vis-à-vis EU Member States, coupled with rigid governance marked by unanimity, ultimately limits the openness of the PESCO to non-EU countries.

The sensitive issue of opening up PESCO's projects to third countries reflects the importance of modularity within PESCO.

B. MODULARITY: A FEATURE THAT HAS BECOME CENTRAL TO PESCO

Although primary law did not specifically provide for this possibility, the concept appears to be at the heart of PESCO as developed by secondary law. A glance at the decisions and recommendations relating to PESCO projects shows the extent to which this modular approach has become central to the operation of PESCO.

Table 3 – The centrality of modularity in PESCO secondary law

Secondary law relating to the PESCO	Main contribution	Link with modularity
Council Decision (CFSP) 2017/2315 of 11 December 2017 establishing permanent structured cooperation (PESCO) and determining the list of participating Member States	Establishes PESCO and sets out its operating procedures; lists the more binding commitments of the participating Member States; presents the principles and governance of PESCO	Introducing the modular dimension of the PESCO
Council Recommendation of 6 March 2018 concerning a roadmap for the implementation of PESCO	Defines the next steps to start implementing PESCO	Addresses the next stages in the modularity of PESCO (e.g. common set of governance rules for projects, general conditions for the exceptional participation of third countries in given projects).

Secondary law relating to the PESCO	Main contribution	Link with modularity
Council Decision (CFSP) 2018/340 of 6 March 2018 establishing the list of projects to be developed under PESCO	Draws up the initial list of 17 PESCO projects	Materialises the modularity of the PESCO by establishing the list of PESCO projects
Council Decision (CFSP) 2018/909 of 25 June 2018 establishing a common set of governance rules for PESCO projects	Enables common rules to be established for the governance of PESCO projects	Establishes a harmonised governance framework to limit differences between PESCO projects in this area
Council Recommendation of 15 October 2018 concerning the sequencing of the fulfilment of the more binding commitments undertaken in the framework of permanent structured cooperation (PESCO) and specifying more precise objectives	Specifies the terms and timetable for implementing the more binding commitments for the first phase of PESCO	Addresses the modularity of PESCO from the point of view of the implementation of more binding commitments
Council Decision (CFSP) 2018/1797 of 19 November 2018 amending and updating Decision (CFSP) 2018/340 establishing the list of projects to be developed under PESCO	Updates the list of PESCO projects with 17 new projects	Materialises the modularity of the PESCO by establishing/updating the list of PESCO projects
Council Recommendation of 14 May 2019 assessing the progress made by the participating Member States to fulfil commitments undertaken in the framework of permanent structured cooperation (PESCO)	Assesses and makes recommendations on the implementation of PESCO by participating Member States	Contains recommendations on the implementation of projects and on improving the practice of participating Member States in this area
Council Decision (CFSP) 2019/1909 of 12 November 2019 amending and updating Decision (CFSP) 2018/340 establishing the list of projects to be developed under PESCO	Updates the list of PESCO projects with 13 new projects	Materialises the modularity of the PESCO by establishing/updating the list of PESCO projects

Secondary law relating to the PESCO	Main contribution	Link with modularity
Council Recommendation of 15 June 2020 assessing the progress made by the participating Member States to fulfil commitments undertaken in the framework of permanent structured cooperation (PESCO) 2020/C	Evaluates and makes recommendations the implementation of PESCO by participating Member States	Contains recommendations on the implementation of projects and on improving the practice of participating Member States in this area.
Council Decision (CFSP) 2020/1639 of 5 November 2020 establishing the general conditions under which third States could exceptionally be invited to participate in individual PESCO projects	Sets out the conditions for exceptional participation by a third State in a given PESCO project	Defines the degree of inclusivity of the modularity of PESCO with regard to third countries
Council Decision (CFSP) 2020/1746 of 20 November 2020 amending and updating Decision (CFSP) 2018/340 establishing the list of projects to be set up under the PESCO	Updates the list of PESCO projects by closing 1 project	Establishes the modularity of the PESCO by establishing/updating the list of PESCO projects
Council Decision (CFSP) 2021/749 of 6 May 2021 on the participation of the Kingdom of Norway in the PESCO project Military Mobility	Opens the PESCO Military Mobility project to participation by the Kingdom of Norway	Acknowledges the exceptional participation of a third State in a given PESCO project
Council Decision (CFSP) 2021/748 of 6 May 2021 on the participation of Canada in the PESCO project Military Mobility	Opens the PESCO Military Mobility project to Canadian participation	Acknowledges the exceptional participation of a third State in a given PESCO project
Council Decision (CFSP) 2021/750 of 6 May 2021 on the participation of the United States of America in the PESCO project Military Mobility	Opens up the PESCO Military Mobility project to participation by the United States of America	Acknowledges the exceptional participation of a third State in a given PESCO project
Council Recommendation of 16 November 2021 assessing the progress made by the participating Member States to fulfil commitments undertaken in the framework of permanent structured cooperation (PESCO) 2021/C 464/02	Assesses and makes recommendations on the implementation of PESCO by participating Member States	Contains recommendations on the implementation of projects and on improving the practice of participating Member States in this area

Secondary law relating to the PESCO	**Main contribution**	**Link with modularity**
Council Recommendation of 16 November 2021 concerning the sequencing of the fulfilment of the more binding commitments undertaken in the framework of permanent structured cooperation (PESCO) and specifying more precise objectives, and repealing the Recommendation of 15 October 2018 2021/C 464/01	Specifies the arrangements and timetable for implementing the more binding commitments for the second phase of PESCO	Addresses the modularity of PESCO from the point of view of the implementation of more binding commitments
Council Decision (CFSP) 2021/2008 of 16 November 2021 amending and updating Decision (CFSP) 2018/340 establishing the list of projects to be set up under the PESCO	Updates the list of PESCO projects with 14 new projects	Establishes the modularity of the PESCO by establishing/updating the list of PESCO projects
Council Recommendation of 14 November 2022 assessing the progress made by the participating Member States to fulfil commitments undertaken in the framework of permanent structured cooperation (PESCO) 2022/C 433/02	Assesses and makes recommendations on the implementation of PESCO by participating Member States	Contains recommendations on the implementation of projects and on improving the practice of participating Member States in this area
Council Decision (CFSP) 2022/2244 of 14 November 2022 on the participation of the United Kingdom of Great Britain and Northern Ireland in PESCO project Military Mobility	Opens up the PESCO project Military Mobility to UK participation	Acknowledges the exceptional participation of a third State in a given PESCO project
Council Decision (CFSP) 2023/385 of 20 February 2023 on the participation of Canada in the PESCO project Network of Logistic Hubs in Europe and Support to Operations	Opens the PESCO project Network of Logistics Hubs in Europe and Support to Operations to Canadian participation	Acknowledges the exceptional participation of a third State in a given PESCO project
Council Decision (CFSP) 2023/995 of 22 May 2023 amending and updating Decision (CFSP) 2018/340 establishing the list of projects to be developed under PESCO	Updates the list of PESCO projects with 11 new projects and by closing 3 projects	Establishes the modularity of the PESCO by establishing/updating the list of PESCO projects

Secondary law relating to the PESCO	Main contribution	Link with modularity
Council Decision (CFSP) 2023/1015 of 23 May 2023 confirming the participation of Denmark in PESCO, and amending Decision (CFSP) 2017/2315 establishing permanent structured cooperation (PESCO) and determining the list of participating Member States	Acknowledges Denmark's participation in PESCO	n.a.
Council Recommendation of 13 November 2023 assessing the progress made by the participating Member States to fulfil commitments undertaken in the framework of the permanent structured cooperation (PESCO)	Assesses and makes recommendations on the implementation of PESCO by participating Member States	Contains recommendations on the implementation of projects and on improving the practice of participating Member States in this area
Council Decision (CFSP) 2024/1972 of 15 July 2024 amending and updating Decision (CFSP) 2018/340 establishing the list of projects to be developed under the PESCO	Updates the list of PESCO projects by closing 2 projects	Establishes the modularity of the PESCO by establishing/updating the list of PESCO projects
Council Recommendation of 18 November 2024 assessing the progress made by the participating Member States to fulfil commitments undertaken in the framework of the permanent structured cooperation (PESCO)	Assesses and makes recommendations on the implementation of PESCO by participating Member States	Contains recommendations on the implementation of projects and on improving the practice of participating Member States in this area
Council Decision (CFSP) 2025/75 of 13 January 2025 on the participation of Switzerland in the PESCO project Military Mobility	Opens the PESCO project Military Mobility to the participation of Switzerland	Acknowledges the exceptional participation of a third State in a given PESCO project
Council Decision (CFSP) 2025/967 of 20 May 2025 on the participation of Switzerland in the PESCO project Cyber Ranges Federations	Opens the PESCO project Cyber Ranges Federations to the participation of Switzerland	Acknowledges the exceptional participation of a third State in a given PESCO project

Secondary law relating to the PESCO	Main contribution	Link with modularity
Council Decision (CFSP) 2025/1107 of 27 May 2025 amending and updating Decision (CFSP) 2018/340 establishing the list of projects to be developed under PESCO	Updates the list of PESCO projects with 11 new projects and by closing 2 projects	Establishes the modularity of the PESCO by establishing/updating the list of PESCO projects

Modularity is addressed in more than 96% of the secondary acts relating to PESCO,[27] and marks a turning point in relation to the implementation of PESCO as envisaged by the drafters of primary law. It also reflects the fact that the modularity of PESCO is mobilising considerably both the Council and the participating Member States, which are in the driving seat when it comes to proposing and then implementing PESCO projects.

These projects are intended to give practical expression to compliance with the PESCO participation criteria laid down in primary law. PESCO projects demonstrate 'both support for capability development and the provision of substantial support within means and capabilities to Common Security and Defence Policy operations and missions'.[28] These 'concrete common projects', which are 'potentially capitalising on existing regional clusters',[29] should lead to the establishment, in the literal sense of the term, of sectoral, structured and permanent cooperation.[30] The effects of PESCO projects are therefore intended to be long-lasting, even once they have been completed.

As shown in Table 4, PESCO led to the adoption of a total of 83 projects, 75 of which are still being implemented (the eight remaining projects having been closed). These projects have been adopted gradually, in waves, since the launch of PESCO in 2017. It has taken no fewer than six waves of project adoption to reach this impressive number.

---

27 64% of the secondary laws relating to PESCO deal directly with PESCO projects or the modularity of PESCO, and 32% of the secondary laws relating to PESCO deal with other aspects concerning PESCO projects.

28 Decision (CFSP) 2017/2315, cited above.

29 Decision (CFSP) 2017/2315, cited above.

30 'For those projects approaching their completion, having ensured successful deliverables, the PESCO secretariat could facilitate discussions on the use of delivered capabilities and related structures, including possible follow-on projects. The Council also suggests that having reached their objectives, thus establishing permanent and structured cooperation, projects could be closed'. Council Recommendation of 13 November 2023 assessing the progress made by the participating Member States in fulfilling their commitments under permanent structured cooperation (PESCO), ST/13647/2023/INIT, [2023] *OJ* C2023/994, para. 10 (Recommendation of 13 November 2023).

Table 4 – Broad categories of PESCO projects

Project categories	Number of projects in progress	Number of projects closed	Total
Training and facilities	9	3	12
Land, training and systems	13	2	15
Maritime sector	11	0	11
Air sector, systems	13	1	14
Cyber, command, control, communications, IT, intelligence, surveillance and reconnaissance	12	0	12
Strategic enablers & force multipliers	13	2	15
Space sector	4	0	4
Total	75	8	83

While the adoption of 83 projects may, at first sight, be seen as a success for PESCO, it can also be seen as a sign of the difficulty in prioritising the most structuring projects and those most likely to contribute to the objectives of PESCO.

It is true that, on the basis of proposals from the Member States, the High Representative of the Union for Foreign Affairs and Security Policy (HR) is supposed to identify 'the most ambitious project proposals, which contribute to the EU's level of ambition and which are most likely to strengthen Europe's strategic autonomy' by recommending them to the Council for adoption.[31] However, this recommendation by the HR is not binding on the Council. Moreover, this recommendation is incidental in that the HR is not legally bound to issue one.[32] It is therefore the participating Member States that control the adoption process. They control it both upstream (the draft proposal comes from the participating Member States),[33] and downstream (the decision establishing the draft PESCOs is taken by the Council). However, in a context where the decision to adopt projects remains subject to intergovernmental

[31] By virtue of their institutional position as both Vice-President of the European Commission and President of the Foreign Affairs Council.

[32] 'The High Representative may make a Recommendation concerning the identification and evaluation of PESCO projects', Decision (CFSP) 2017/2315, Art. 5(1), cited above.

[33] 'Participating Member States may propose any project *they consider useful to the objectives of PESCO*', Decision (CFSP) 2017/2315, cited above.

governance,[34] it is understandable that the Council may find it difficult to select only a limited number of projects with real European added value. This project selection process can even lead to some surprising results. Indeed, by the Council's own admission, in 2020 only 36 of the 47 existing PESCO projects were 'considered to contribute to the implementation of the EU Capability Development Priorities, with 24 of them directly addressing the HICGs [high-impact capability objectives] and 12 indirectly'.[35] As some observers have pointed out, this left 11 projects (i.e. almost a quarter of the 47 projects at the time) with no link whatsoever with the EU's capability development priorities.[36] This is despite the fact that consistency with the EU's Capability Development Plan (CDP) is an important element of the PESCO.[37]

In addition, the inflation in the number of projects can also have the effect of dispersing and diluting the cooperation efforts of the participating Member States. Indeed, the multiplication of participation in PESCO projects may prove to be a difficulty for certain participating Member States, whose resources (for example human and financial) they can dedicate to the implementation of projects are not unlimited. This dispersal of effort by participating Member States could ultimately affect project implementation. In addition, participating Member States with insufficient resources to participate could find themselves particularly affected by this inflation in the number of projects, which in turn could lead to an increased influence of the Member States with the greatest capacity to participate in numerous projects. This tendency, which has been noted by some observers,[38] may seem paradoxical for a PESCO which claims to be so inclusive.

The inflation in the number of PESCO projects is also exacerbated by the difficulty participating Member States have in revitalising or withdrawing PESCO projects that do not produce any concrete results. Although secondary law introduced the modular approach to PESCO, it does not provide for a specific procedure to deal with this type of situation.

[34] Decisions to adopt projects are taken 'by unanimity, as constituted by the votes of the representatives of the participating Member States', Decision (CFSP) 2017/2315, cited above.

[35] Council Recommendation of 15 June 2020 assessing the progress made by the participating Member States in fulfilling their commitments under permanent structured cooperation (PESCO), 2020/C 204/01, [2020] *OJ* C204/1, para. 11 (Recommendation of 15 June 2020).

[36] S. Blockmans and C. Dylan Macchiarini, 'PESCO: A Force for Positive Integration in EU Defence' (2021) 26 *European Foreign Affairs Review*, special issue, pp. 87–110.

[37] Decision (CFSP) 2017/2315, Commitments No 2 and No 15, cited above.

[38] Over the first three waves of projects, the data collected by these authors tends to show that France, Italy, Spain and Germany stand out as the most active participating Member States, shifting the centre of gravity of PESCO towards Western Europe. See S. Blockmans and C. Dylan Macchiarini, 'PESCO: A Force for Positive Integration in EU Defence', (2021) 26 *European Foreign Affairs Review*, special issue.

This is all the more disturbing given that the Council Recommendation of 15 June 2020 (2020 Recommendation)[39] already noted the lack of significant progress on many projects,[40] a situation which still persisted in 2022 for some projects.[41] Such a lack of progress in the implementation of projects constitutes a risk to the 'relevance, effectiveness and credibility of all PESCO projects', as the 2022 Recommendation admits between the lines. Nevertheless, it seems that improvements have been noted on this point, as shown by the November 2023 Recommendation in which the Council, '[n]oting the PESCO Projects Progress Report of 11 July 2023, [...] underlines the adaptability and effectiveness of PESCO as a cooperation framework, with visible progress in PESCO projects across all domains'. A positive trend moderately confirmed in the Recommendation of 18 November 2024 (2024 Recommendation).[42]

Nevertheless, several avenues have had to be explored in an attempt to rationalise the modularity of PESCO. The first of these is to encourage Member States to develop more structuring and strategic projects. In its 2022 Recommendation, the Council encouraged 'participating Member States to use the fifth wave of PESCO projects [...] to launch strategically relevant projects aimed at delivering critical capabilities and improving the interoperability of forces, also in line with the EU's Capability Development Priorities derived from the CDP, and the guidance agreed in the Strategic Compass'. If the strategic importance of the projects is measured by the limited number of projects adopted per wave, Table 5 shows that the fifth and sixth waves did slightly better than previous waves in this respect.

39 Recommendation of 15 June 2020, cited above.

40 'Three projects have already reached Initial Operational Capability (IOC) and 23 are planned to reach IOC in the timeframe 2020-2023. However, more than two-thirds (30) of the projects remain at their ideation phase, including some which were already established in March and November 2018', Recommendation of 15 June 2020, para. 11, cited above.

41 '[T]he Council notes that a number of other projects continue to face difficulties in their implementation, including delays in reaching project objectives. The Council highlights that pMS [participating Member States] should undertake enhanced efforts to deliver tangible results as planned, especially for those projects officially established in 2018 that have not yet rendered any concrete deliverables'. Council Recommendation of 14 November 2022 assessing the progress made by the participating Member States in fulfilling their commitments under permanent structured cooperation (PESCO) 2022/C 433/02, [2022] *OJ* C433/ 6 (Recommendation of 14 November 2022).

42 '[T]he Council welcomes the projects' overall progress across all domains, with a significant number of projects having advanced to the execution phase. The Council also notes that over the past year, PESCO projects have continued to yield deliverables while some report delays'. Council Recommendation of 18 November 2024 assessing the progress made by the participating Member States to fulfil commitments undertaken in the framework of the permanent structured cooperation (PESCO), [2024] OJ, C2024/6982. (Recommendation of November 2024).

Table 5 – Waves of PESCO projects

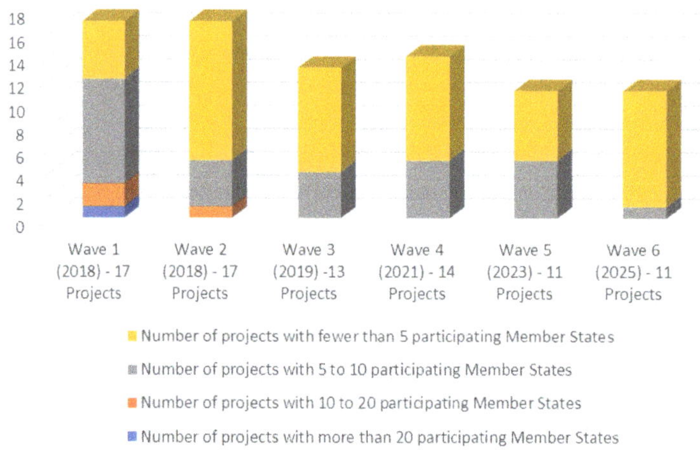

On the other hand, if strategic importance is measured by the ability of projects to bring together a large number of participating Member States, it can be seen that the number of projects with fewer than five participating Member States remains high or is even worsening (see the sixth wave in Table 5). The difficulty of selecting strategic projects could explain why, in its Recommendation of 13 November 2023 (2023 Recommendation), following the adoption of the fifth wave of projects and with a view to future waves of PESCO projects, the Council felt it necessary to reiterate 'the necessity for the upcoming projects to be strategically relevant, in line with the Strategic Compass and reflecting the current geopolitical context, as well as connected to the EU Capability Development Priorities'. In its 2024 Recommendation, the Council insisted again on a similar message, encouraging participating Member States to 'consider new ambitious projects of strategic relevance'.[43]

The second option is to group projects together, or even merge them. The aim is to pool the resources of certain projects, exploiting possible synergies and avoiding duplication. This is an interesting prospect given that participation in several projects is likely to mobilise a large number of resources at national level. This option has been repeated on several occasions (in 2020,[44] 2021[45] and

43 Recommendation of 18 November 2024, cited above.
44 Recommendation of 15 June 2020, see above.
45 Council Recommendation of 16 November 2021 assessing progress made by the participating Member States to fulfil commitments undertaken in the framework of permanent structured cooperation (PESCO), 2021/C 464/02, ST/12724/2021/INIT, [2021] *OJ* C464/10, para. 14 (Recommendation of 16 November 2021).

in 2022[46]). However, it has to be said that the participating Member States have never yet grouped or merged several projects. In fact, the participating Member States appear to be reluctant to merge with other projects, even at the cost of a gain in resources and efficiency.

A third option is to close PESCO projects that have achieved their objectives or show no significant progress in implementation. It is interesting to note that the Council has regularly referred to this possibility since its 2020 Recommendation. If the initiative to close a PESCO project seems to come only from the will of its participants, this only takes effect after the adoption by the Council of a decision to update the list establishing the PESCO projects. To date, only eight projects have been closed, so this rationalisation option seems to have been little used at this stage.

A fourth option for streamlining the modularity of PESCO is to have more regular and longer pauses between waves of project adoption. In 2019, a pause in the adoption of new PESCO projects was decided and implemented.[47] The opportunity to move from annual to biennial adoption was also an option considered as part of the 2020 Strategic Review of the PESCO. This approach was followed up. Persisting in adopting new projects, wave after wave, does not seem consistent with the fact that certain projects are sometimes persistently behind schedule and that, as the Council pointed out in 2022, the majority of current projects are not expected to produce any concrete effects by 2025.[48] This initial rationalisation of PESCO's modularity is therefore welcome.

The final option for streamlining the modularity of PESCO is outlined in the 2024 Recommendation, and consists in adopting more mature projects with a clear timeline.[49] The Council notes that the efficiency of this approach 'was demonstrated by several projects adopted in May 2023 that are already making progress, and one project that started implementation in the PESCO framework from the execution phase'.

---

46 Recommendation of 14 November 2022, see above.

47 This pause was mentioned in point 12 of the Council Recommendation of 14 May 2019: 'After 2019 [...], the next call for PESCO projects should be launched in 2021 [...]. In the light of further experience, the participating Member States will then consider the possibility of moving to a biennial process'.

48 'The Council notes that [...] overall progress was made with regard to projects, with 18 of them, across all domains, already reaching execution phase, and two having already reached their full operational capability. The Council also welcomes that nearly half of the projects are expected to deliver concrete results by 2025. This includes 77 % of the projects (20 out of 26) identified in the Council Conclusions of 20 November 2020 on the PESCO Strategic Review 2020 as expected to deliver in this timeframe'. Recommendation of 14 November 2022, para. 10, cited above.

49 'The Council highlights that a key element for the success of PESCO projects is a well-established proposal with an appropriate level of maturity, and a clear timeline'. Recommendation of November 2024, cited above.

So, while from a legal point of view the modular PESCO is intended to be an ambitious framework, its practical implementation sometimes comes up against the reality of the limits of a highly consensual form of governance, based as it is on the principle of unanimity.

II. AN AMBITIOUS PESCO

A. A LESS THAN OBVIOUS AMBITION GIVEN THE WAY PESCO OPERATES

Under primary law, the Member States participating in PESCO commit themselves to five areas of cooperation as set out in Table 6. Some authors consider that Article 2 of Protocol No. 10 'imposes five areas of 'cooperation' [...] which together constitute and structure the integration process'.[50] Secondary law has considerably supplemented primary law. Indeed, as of 2017, the Council Decision sets out a list of twenty more binding commitments entered into by the participating Member States and divided between the different areas of cooperation, as shown in Table 6.

Table 6 – The more binding commitments of PESCO

Fields of cooperation	Number of more binding commitments	Summary of more binding commitments
Budget	5	Increase defence budgets, devote 20% of defence spending to equipment, increase joint projects to develop strategic capabilities, approach 2% of defence spending on research and technology (R&T), and regularly review the relevance of these financial commitments.
Equipment	6	Play a leading role in the development of capabilities within the EU via the Coordinated Annual Defence Review (CARD), support the CARD, promote the commitment of the European Defence Fund (EDF), establish harmonised specifications for joint projects, study the joint use of existing capabilities, and step up cooperation on cyber defence.

[50] F. Mauro and F. Santopinto, 'Permanent Structured Cooperation National perspectives and state of play', Brussels, European Parliament, study, July 2017, p. 18.

Fields of cooperation	Number of more binding commitments	Summary of more binding commitments
Operational	3	Making units available to achieve the EU's level of ambition, creating a tool for identifying available capabilities, speeding up national political commitment, supporting CSDP operations/missions in various ways, contributing to EU Battlegroups (EUBGs), standardising military transport, defining common assessment criteria for EUBGs, establishing common technical and operational standards, strengthening participation in multinational structures, and adopting an ambitious approach to the joint funding of missions/operations.
Capacity gaps	3	Filling the gaps identified by the Capacity Development Plan (CDP) and the CARD, strengthening European strategic autonomy and the European Defence Technological and Industrial Base (EDTIB), examining as a priority a collaborative approach to filling national gaps, and participating in at least one strategic capabilities PESCO project.
Industrial	3	Use the European Defence Agency (EDA) to develop joint capabilities, consider OCCAR for the management of armaments programmes, ensure that capability projects strengthen the EDTIB by avoiding duplication, and ensure that programmes benefit entities that bring added value to Europe.

As stipulated in Article 3 of Decision (CFSP) 2017/2315, these twenty commitments are legally binding on the Member States participating in the PESCO. However, this binding force of the commitments only has real effect if it is accompanied by a means of monitoring and forcing the participating Member States to respect these commitments in practice.

In terms of control, secondary law is quite specific. First of all, it introduces a 'phased approach' with 'realistic and binding objectives for each phase'.[51] The secondary law even echoes the original spirit of PESCO by stating that this 'realistic phased approach is key to preserve the participation of a vanguard of Member States in PESCO'. This is because some of the commitments 'can be achieved more quickly than others'. In concrete terms, this means 'two respective phases (periods 2018-2021 and 2021-2025)' that 'will allow for the sequencing of commitments'. At the end of the second phase (i.e. after 2025) a commitment review procedure is planned. This could be an opportunity for

[51] Decision (CFSP) 2017/2315, Annex III, cited above.

the participating Member States to decide on 'new commitments, with a view to embark on a new stage towards European security and defence integration'.

As part of this phased approach, the law also provides that 'binding nature of PESCO commitments will be ensured by an annual regular assessment conducted by the High Representative of the Union for Foreign Affairs and Security Policy and supported, in particular, by the European Defence Agency (EDA), for the capability development aspects (notably described in Article 3 of Protocol 10), and EEAS, including European Union Military Staff (EUMS) and other CSDP structures, for the operational aspects of PESCO'. Articles 3 and 6 of Decision (CFSP) 2017/2315 organise this monitoring and evaluation process in very concrete terms.

The assessment mechanism is based on two levels:

- The first level is the national implementation plan. This is a document specific to each participating Member State, produced annually to organise the implementation of commitments at national level. This document is subject to major transparency requirements, as it must be accessible to all participating Member States. It is one of the tangible elements on which the Annual Report presented by the High Representative to the Council in its PESCO configuration is based.
- The Annual Report and the Strategic Review constitute the second level. As stated in Decision (CFSP) 2017/2315: 'The High Representative shall present an annual report on PESCO to the Council', which 'shall describe the status of PESCO implementation, including the fulfilment, by each participating Member State, of its commitments, in accordance with its National Implementation Plan'. This report 'will serve as a basis for Council Recommendations and decisions adopted in accordance with Article 46 of the TEU'. In addition, 'at the end of each phase (2021; 2025), a Strategic Review exercise will be conducted assessing the respect of the commitments foreseen to have been fulfilled during that phase'.

In order to facilitate the evaluation procedure, the commitments have also been detailed 'through more precise objectives set among participating Member States'[52] at the start of the first phase in 2018 and of the second phase in 2021 in the context of two Council recommendations. Each year, on the basis of the High Representative's annual report, the Council is therefore in a position to adopt its recommendations assessing the progress made by the participating Member States in meeting the commitments to which they have subscribed. In 2021, this Recommendation also took account of the Strategic Review that was carried out at the end of the first phase.

Despite the very diplomatic language used to comment on the collective performance of the participating Member States, it has to be said that these

[52] Decision (CFSP) 2017/2315, cited above.

recommendations have sometimes referred to certain difficulties encountered by the participating Member States. For example, the Council sometimes referred to the difficulty of implementing PESCO projects (*see* part I B of this commentary). Furthermore, although the Council often seems to be satisfied overall with the progress made by the participating Member States in its annual recommendations,[53] it may nevertheless be possible to detect, sometimes between the lines, certain prospects for improvement in the collective performance of the participating Member States, as shown by the few examples mentioned in Table 7.

Table 7 – Areas for improvement in the 2023 and 2024 Recommendations

Fields of cooperation	Selected examples of areas for improvement (taken from the Recommendations)	
	2023 Recommendation	2024 Recommendation
Budget	– The 'Council reiterates the need to spend more and better in defence'. – The 'Council calls for a combined effort by all the participating Member States to reverse the decline in defence Research and Technology spending from 1,7% to 1,1%, remaining well below the 2% collective benchmark'. – 'Boosting research, technology, development and innovation, as well as acquisition [...] should remain a priority for' participating Member States.	– The Council observes that '[d]espite an overall increase of 28% in EU defence research and technology investment in 2024, most pMS contributions towards reaching the collective benchmark remain below 2%, with an overall 1,6% of total defence expenditure. The pMS have been spending more, but not more together: the increased defence expenditure and investment have not been translated into more collaborative projects. – The Council 'recalls that boosting research, technology, development and innovation, as well as acquisition, particularly in cooperation among pMS, should remain a priority for the pMS, while striking the right balance between long-term innovation for future capabilities and adequate quantities of military equipment and stockpiles, also with a view to strengthening the European Defence Technological and Industrial Base (EDTIB)'.

53 For instance: 'The Council underlines that the participating Member States have stepped up their efforts towards the fulfilment of the more binding commitments, including through the PESCO projects which demonstrate progress in all relevant domains'. Recommendation of 13 November 2023, cited above.

Fields of cooperation	Selected examples of areas for improvement (taken from the Recommendations)	
	2023 Recommendation	2024 Recommendation
Equipment	– Participating Member States 'are encouraged to make full use of the EU prioritisation tools and initiatives, notably the EU Capability Development Plan (CDP) […], as well as recommendations of the Coordinated Annual Review on Defence (CARD)'.	– The Council 'recalls that pMS are encouraged to make full use of the EU prioritisation tools and initiatives, notably the EU Capability Development Plan (CDP) which serves as a central reference for EU capability development, taking into account the Headline Goal Process, as well as recommendations of the Coordinated Annual Review on Defence (CARD) to inform national planners'.
Operational	n.a.	– The Council 'encourages pMS to consider taking on the responsibility as framework nation for the EU Battlegroups'.
Capacity gaps	– Participating Member States 'are encouraged to address more specifically strategic capability shortfalls, namely the High Impact Capability Goals'. – Participating Member States 'have not yet sufficiently prioritised a European collaborative approach in addressing capability gaps'.	– 'while many pMS are reassessing their policies and strategies to make better use of a European collaborative approach in addressing national capability gaps, for the majority of pMS a European collaborative approach is still not sufficiently prioritised. The Council thus calls on the pMS to use their growing defence budgets to increase investments in European collaborative solutions, thus contributing to a more coherent EU defence landscape and to reducing technological and industrial dependencies'.
Industrial	– Participating Member States 'are also invited to continue their involvement in cooperation programmes that have a positive impact on the EDTIB, including by considering those programmes in their acquisition strategies and procedures'.	– The Council 'strongly encourages pMS to increase efforts to ensure that their cooperation programmes and acquisition strategies have a positive impact on EDTIB, and to make best use of existing and future EU financial tools in this regard, including the European Defence Fund and those envisaged in the Regulation proposed by the Commission 'establishing the European Defence Industry Programme and a framework of measures to ensure the timely availability and supply of defence products'.

Wherever the Council 'calls', 'recalls', 'invites', 'encourages' or 'reaffirms', it is likely that the participating Member States have not collectively acted fully satisfactorily and have not necessarily applied the guidance provided in the past annual recommendations. Such an impression can be supported by statements made the Council itself, like for instance in the Recommendation of November 2024, where it 'acknowledges that further progress is needed for the fulfilment of all commitments by the end of the second PESCO initial phase, in 2025', or in its 2023 Recommendation where it 'further call[s] on each pMS [participating Member State] to take into account the findings and recommendations presented in the Annual Report, and to review and update its contribution to the fulfilment of the more binding commitments'. The latter reminder alone highlights a problem from which the whole system of evaluation put in place by secondary law suffers, namely the absence of a genuine constraint to force participating Member States to comply with their commitments.

The Council's recommendations have no binding legal force, and the only real sanction, provided for by primary law[54] and specified by secondary law,[55] that of suspending the participation of a participating Member State, seems never to have been officially envisaged. However, this 'last resort' solution would allow the Council to 'suspend the participation of a Member State [which] no longer fulfils the criteria, given beforehand a clearly defined timeframe for individual consultation and reaction measures, or is no longer able or willing to meet PESCO commitments and obligations'. This sanction is all the more interesting in that the Council can take the decision by a qualified majority of the participating Member States (excluding the participating Member State concerned).

Nevertheless, in practice, the very consensual operation of PESCO does not, at this stage, create an atmosphere that is genuinely likely to exploit the deterrent and coercive potential of this sanction. Once again, the flexibility envisaged by primary law is not really exploited in practice by the participating Member States, which may in turn have a negative effect on the effective implementation of PESCO commitments and, through this, the real ambition of PESCO.

If the annual recommendations seem to have a moderate impact, what about the Strategic Review exercises? The outcomes of the initial PESCO Strategic Review, approved by the Council in its Conclusions of 20 November 2020, showed that 'progress towards meeting [the more binding commitments] [...] was insufficient for [participating Member States] to step up the efforts to fulfil all the more binding commitments'. Given this, the discussions surrounding

[54] Article 46(4) TEU.

[55] Decision (CFSP) 2017/2315, Art. 6(4), cited above.

the Strategic Review also highlighted the importance of maintaining a certain political momentum around PESCO to preserve its ambition as much as possible. To this end, the possibility was even raised that every two years, the national implementation plans could be accompanied by a high-level political declaration in which the participating Member States 'could outline main achievements and state specific national priorities and contributions', an approach that was eventually implemented, as noted in the November 2024 Recommendation.[56]

With the latest Strategic Review, it seems that the Council considers that a new approach is needed. In its November 2024 Conclusions on the latest PESCO Strategic Review,[57] the Council indicated that it was necessary to adjust PESCO in view of its new phase, starting in 2026, with a specific focus on its 'commitments, projects, and working methods'.

- On the commitments, the Council recommends a 'revised set of commitments', that will need to indicate clear and measurable goals to enhance implementation and transparency, thus ultimately contributing to increased visibility and enhanced political ownership.
- On PESCO projects, the Conclusions also emphasized 'the need for improved project quality'. The Council provided or repeated some key messages to better streamline the PESCO modularity, like for instance, the importance to 'promote the development of strategic and impactful projects', the fact that 'project proposals should include clear and measurable objectives and timelines, set by the project members to stimulate timely progress'. It also encouraged participating Member States 'to launch a new project with preferably at least three participants' and 'to close projects that are underperforming or that are no longer considered relevant'.
- On the working methods, the Conclusions insisted notably on the need for an 'updated and simplified [national implementation plan] template, in order to make the [national implementation plans] more politically focused, concise, and future-oriented'. The Council also called for a 'stronger and more effective role of the PESCO secretariat'.

It remains uncertain how this guidance would help the High Representative to propose, by May 2025, relevant amendments to the PESCO legal framework, in particular the Decision (CFSP) 2017/2315 establishing PESCO and the

[56] 'The Council notes that, in line with the biennial cycle, all pMS have accompanied their NIPs with a high-level political statement, outlining main achievements and stating specific national priorities and contributions to the fulfilment of the more binding commitments'. Council Recommendation of 18 November 2024, cited above.

[57] Council Conclusions on the PESCO Strategic Review, 14375/24, Brussels, 18 November 2024.

Decision (CFSP) 2018/909 establishing a common set of governance rules for PESCO projects.[58]

Despite the phased approach that structures the implementation of PESCO, the ambition of this cooperation framework should also be measured by its ability to respond to current defence challenges. In this respect, PESCO's record may appear rather slim.

Given that the Member States consider an inclusive PESCO as 'the most important instrument to foster common security and defence',[59] it seems legitimate to expect that PESCO will provide an important response to the challenges posed in particular by the war of aggression that Russia is currently waging against Ukraine.

Nevertheless, rather than being a framework for cooperation mobilised to respond to the consequences of this conflict, PESCO appears to be more a framework for cooperation in which the Member States are only just beginning to draw some lessons from this conflict. Indeed, the November 2023 Recommendation only notes timid developments and implications of the conflict for PESCO. For example, 'the Council notes that [the 2023] Annual Report reflects on the *first implications* of Russia's ongoing war of aggression against Ukraine for pMS' security and defence policies and projects' (author's emphasis). The Council goes on to state that 'this is illustrated by the *initial* changes in pMS' existing plans to secure capabilities required for high-intensity warfare, including strategic enablers, their *intention* to adjust national defence industrial policies and strategies'. This recommendation, which comes almost 21 months after the start of the Russian invasion, does not suggest a clear willingness on the part of the participating Member States to make rapid use of the PESCO framework to adapt to the consequences of the conflict.

The Council also noted that some PESCO projects were making a modest contribution to the response to the challenges posed by this conflict,[60] and welcomed 'the fact that addressing the capability areas highlighted by the lessons observed from Russia's ongoing war of aggression against Ukraine is already within the remit of some of the ongoing PESCO projects'. On this last point, the opposite would have been surprising given the very broad scope of capabilities covered by all 66 PESCO projects (as illustrated by Table 4).

---

[58] Council Decision (CFSP) 2018/909 of 25 June 2018 establishing a common set of governance rules for PESCO projects, [2018] *OJ* L161/3741

[59] Notification on permanent structured cooperation (PESCO) to the Council and to the High Representative of the Union for foreign affairs and security policy, Decision (CFSP) 2017/2315, cited above.

[60] It is noted, for example, that some of the capabilities 'such as those set up under the PESCO projects concerning the European Medical Command and Computer Incident Rapid Response Teams, have already been used or activated in support of EU CSDP missions and operations, namely EUMAM Ukraine'. Decision (CFSP) 2017/2315, para. 9, cited above.

Although the Council notes, again in its 2023 Recommendation, that '[i]n the current geopolitical context, PESCO is a key framework for defence cooperation and for enhancing the pMS' defence capabilities that is flexible and adaptable', PESCO does not appear to be the preferred framework for Member States' response to the challenges of the war in Ukraine and the return of high-intensity conflict. It is this relative passivity on the part of PESCO that the Council seems to acknowledge, albeit half-heartedly, when it states that given 'the geopolitical context and new efforts in EU defence, *ensuring political momentum* and *enhanced pMS' ownership* is essential for PESCO to remain a truly strategic initiative' (author's emphasis). A message that the Council confirmed in its Recommendation of 2024.[61]

It is worth noting that the Council, in its November 2024 Conclusions on the latest PESCO Strategic Review, showed awareness of the need to improve the way PESCO should contribute to the EU's response to the new geopolitical context. It clearly stressed, in these Conclusions, that 'PESCO should, where applicable, also contribute to the wider EU efforts aimed at addressing Ukraine's military needs' and encouraged 'participating Member States [...] to facilitate Ukraine's participation in PESCO projects, within the current legal framework related to third States' participation'. Such an evolution of PESCO would notably lead to 'the progressive integration of the Ukrainian defence technological and industrial base into the EDTIB'. To achieve the latter objective, as well as to enhance and improve the overall impact of PESCO, participating Member States should be able to better rely on other EU defence initiatives.

B. OPTIMISING THE OPERATION OF PESCO THROUGH OTHER EU DEFENCE INITIATIVES

The Coordinated Annual Review on Defence (CARD) was created in 2017 as part of the implementation of the 2016 Global Strategy. It is a process enabling Member States, on a voluntary basis, to share information about their expenditure, investment and cooperation efforts in the defence sector. Thanks to the analytical work carried out by the EDA in close coordination with the EUMS and the EEAS, the CARD should make it possible to increase the transparency and visibility of Member States' defence spending, capability

[61] 'The Council reaffirms the guidance outlined in its Recommendation of 13 November 2023, in particular as set out in paragraphs 20 to 23 thereof [...]. The Council urges the pMS to address that guidance' Council Recommendation of 18 November 2024 assessing the progress made by the participating Member States to fulfil commitments undertaken in the framework of the permanent structured cooperation (PESCO), cited above.

development planning and capability cooperation, and to identify prospects for cooperation opportunities.

No fewer than four PESCO commitments provide for participating Member States not only to contribute to the CARD but also to exploit its results. For example, as set out in Decision (CFSP) 2017/2315, the participating Member States all pledged to 'play a substantial role in capability development within the EU, including within the framework of CARD' and to 'support the CARD to the maximum extent'.

In terms of their contribution to the CARD, the performance of the participating Member States still seems to leave room for improvement. Indeed, the 2022 report shows that the CARD still often presents a fragmented vision, particularly when it comes to data that is essential for PESCO, i.e. the rate of investment in collaborative defence programmes.[62]

However, it is in the exploitation of the results of the CARD that the Member States really seem to have to improve. Although the Council notes in its 2022 Recommendation that 'participating Member States have shown some improvement in the use of EU capacity development tools and initiatives', it nevertheless regularly invites participating Member States to make use of the results of the CARD, for example in its 2022 Recommendation, in which it noted pMS 'have made modest progress in their uptake of the Union's capability planning and development tools and processes as orientation for national planning and decision-making', but at the same time recalled that participating Member States (pMS) 'are encouraged to step up their efforts towards a more systematic and active use of these instruments, including the CARD recommendations'. As another example, the Council also recalled in its November 2023 Recommendation that PESCO projects 'should take advantage of the opportunities for collaboration identified by the CARD for the joint development of defence capabilities'. The 2022 CARD Report also noted that 'only modest progress was made to turn collaborative opportunities presented in the 2020 CARD cycle into concrete cooperation' and that 'no improved coherence of the EU defence landscape has yet been observed'. The 2022CARD Report also stated that 'Member States implement their plans largely at national level' and that they 'generally consider cooperation only when it coincides with national plans, benefits national industry, or consolidates a strategic partnership'.

The latest developments do not tend to show a significant improvement in the participating Member States' practice. In its 2024 Recommendation, the Council felt the need, once again, to underline 'that the collaborative opportunities identified through CARD should guide the Member States for

[62] 30% of investment in defence programmes was not communicated in the CARD, which makes it difficult to have an overall view of cooperation on defence programmes. See the CARD 2022 report (2022-card-report.pdf (europa.eu)).

new PESCO projects, and the possible continuation and expansion in scope of the existing ones'. All these observations and repeated messages seem to suggest, to say the least, that the participating Member States are finding it difficult to exploit the opportunities offered by CARD. The 2024 CARD Report also emphasised the fact that 'greater harmonisation of national defence planning remains necessary' and that 'Member States must work together to align their operational requirements and timelines, including in the context of collaborative frameworks such as PESCO'.[63] Already the 2020 CARD Report made a rather harsh observation when it stated that 'cooperation remains the exception rather than the norm'. This trend has unfortunately been observed once again by the Council itself in its 2024 Recommendation, where it bluntly stated that '[participating Member States] have been spending more, but not more together'. The ambition of PESCO to exploit the potential offered by the CARD therefore seems somewhat perfectible.

In addition, from 2017, secondary law prepared the possibility for PESCO to interact with the EDF and its precursor programme the European Defence Industrial Development Programme (EDIDP).[64] Some of the commitments stressed the need to exploit the opportunities offered by the EDF. This is the case for commitment No. 3, which states that 'joint and "collaborative" strategic defence capabilities projects [...] should be supported through the European Defence Fund if required and as appropriate'. Commitment 8 calls for 'the intensive involvement of a future European Defence Fund in multinational procurement with identified EU added value'. The PESCO projects Progress Report of July 2024 clearly presents how the two defence initiatives are expected to divide up their work: 'While the EDF aims at incentivising industrial cooperation, PESCO projects [...] focus more on aspects such as policy, concepts, harmonising requirements, or training'.[65] However, given the proliferation of PESCO capability projects,[66] whose European added value or structuring dimension is not always obvious, it can be difficult to be convinced that the participating Member States have really succeeded in creating conditions favourable to this interaction with the EDF. In fact, Recital 5 of Decision (CFSP) 2017/2315 sums up the participating Member States' expectations of the EDF. It states that '[i]ncreasing joint and collaborative defence capability development projects is among the binding commitments under PESCO. Such projects may be supported by contributions

63 See the 2024 CARD Report (card-report-2024.pdf (europa.eu)).

64 Regulation (EU) 2018/1092 of the European Parliament and of the Council of 18 July 2018 establishing the European Defence Industrial Development Programme aiming at supporting the competitiveness and innovation capacity of the Union's defence industry, [2018] *OJ* L200/30 (EDIDP Regulation).

65 See the PESCO Projects Progress Report – PESCO Secretariat documentation for public release July 2024 (PESCO-Projects-Progress-Report_Public_Release_.pdf (europa.eu))

66 More than half of the 75 PESCO projects have a capability development dimension.

from the Union budget in compliance with the Treaties and the relevant Union instruments and programmes'. It is therefore clear that for participating Member States, financial support from the EDF will always be welcome to assist PESCO projects related to capacity development. This financial support was made all the more attractive by the fact that the EDF and the EDIDP provided for a funding bonus for projects with the PESCO banner.[67]

With the second wave of projects, the possibility of financial support from the EDF generated a certain amount of enthusiasm among the participating Member States. They sought to propose projects that would enable them to pre-empt the PESCO 'label' for their project, in order to potentially benefit from the EDF financial bonus.[68] As Sven Biscop reveals, by proposing projects within PESCO, 'Member States hope to get their hands on the EDF'.[69] The prospect of financial support probably encouraged some participating Member States to quickly promote projects that would involve their national industry as soon as possible. Some authors have been able to demonstrate that in 2019, most of the participating Member States coordinating projects expected their project to benefit from the EDF.[70] It should be noted that at that time the proposed financial envelope for the EDF was particularly attractive. The amount envisaged for the EDF was close to €13 billion. This was around €4 billion more than the amount that was finally retained under the 2021-2027 multiannual financial framework. The high expectations of the participating Member States, coupled with the lower-than-anticipated amount from the EDF, raises a number of questions. *What will happen to* the sustainability of projects that do not receive financial support from the EDF, and competition between small and large PESCO projects? Here again, we can see the risks associated with inflation in the number of PESCO projects.

In view of this, it seemed necessary to concentrate the action of the EDF on a limited number of relevant PESCO projects.[71] In practice, as Table 10 illustrates, the Commission tends to adopt a balanced approach, with an average of 57% of projects funded by the EDF/EDIDP having a link with

[67] Art. 13 of the EDF Regulation and Art. 11 of the EDIDP Regulation, cited above.

[68] Interview conducted by the author in January 2019.

[69] S. Biscop, 'European Defence and PESCO: Don't Waste the Chance', *EU Integration and Differentiation for Effectiveness and Accountability*, Egmont – Royal Institute for International Relations, May 2020.

[70] L. Béraud-Sudreau, Y.-S. Efstathiou and C. Hannigan, 'Keeping the momentum in European defence collaboration: an early assessment of PESCO implementation', *The International Institute for Strategic Studies*, May 2019.

[71] '[T]he EDF is a substantial enough amount to steer Member States' investment decisions in the right direction only if it is concentrated on a small set of key projects. If the money is spread out over dozens of projects every year, it will not make much of a difference'. S. Biscop, 'European Defence and PESCO: Don't Waste the Chance', *EU Integration and Differentiation for Effectiveness and Accountability*, Egmont – Royal Institute for International Relations, May 2020.

PESCO projects. It should be noted that different EDF projects can sometimes be linked to the same PESCO projects or to several different PESCO projects. For example, in 2023 the EDF financed 14 projects linked to 20 different PESCO projects.

Table 10 – EDF projects or EDIDP linked to PESCO projects

	Total EDF or EDIDP budget allocated (in millions of euros)	EDF budget or EDIDP allocated to projects linked to PESCO projects (in millions of euros)	% of EDF budget or EDIDP linked to PESCO projects	Number of projects funded by EDF or EDIDP	Number of projects funded by EDF or EDIDP linked to PESCO projects	% of EDF projects or EDIDP linked to PESCO projects
EDF 2024	910	n.a	n.a	62	13	20%
EDF 2023	1,031	594.8	58%	54	14	26%
EDF 2022	832	487.5	59%	41	11	27%
EDF 2021	1,200	623	52%	61	15	25%
EDIDP 2020	158	99.9	63%	26	15	58%
EDIDP 2019	200	159	80%	16	9	56%
EDF AND EDIDP 2019-2023	3,421	1,964.2	57%	198	64	32%

The EDF Interim Evaluation confirmed the extent to which EDF has become an essential source of funding for PESCO projects, stating that 'EDF has emerged as the primary implementation tool for PESCO'.[72] A trend also confirmed on the side of PESCO, where the PESCO projects Progress Report of July 2024 indicates that the 'majority of projects report either having a link to projects that have been awarded or likely to apply for EU funding under the [EDIDP] and the [EDF]'. Nevertheless, beyond this financial contribution to projects linked to the modularity of PESCO, the European executive seems

[72] Commission Staff Working Document Evaluation – Interim Evaluation of the European Defence Fund, SWD(2025) 151 final, Brussels, 17 June 2025.

to have taken the measure of the side effects of the PESCO funding bonus in the EDF regulation. Indeed, in its communication of 15 February 2022,[73] the Commission states that it will consider 'reinforcing the current system of EDF bonuses, in order to provide a financial incentive on condition that Member States commit to jointly acquire and/or own defence capabilities under development', specifying that this commitment should go beyond the simple intention to acquire the end product or to use the technology in a coordinated manner (as EDF already provides). Rather than simply reinforcing the current EDF bonus system, the aim is to strengthen its conditionality. The European Commission's objective is also quite clear: 'This would provide stronger incentives to ensure that the collaboration continues beyond the R&D phases, to acquisitions, as well as operations and maintenance'. In other words, only the most promising PESCO projects in terms of the commitment of its participating Member States to cooperate beyond capability development would be rewarded. This reinforced conditionality appears to be consistent with the PESCO commitments.[74] However, because such an approach would have likely required an amendment to the EDF regulation (through the ordinary legislative procedure) in the context of the EDF Interim Evaluation, it appears that the Commission has favoured a non-legislative adjustments to the EDF and rather decided to focus on 'the way the PESCO bonus is evaluated' in the implementation of the EDF,[75] with the aim of improving and strengthening the assessment of the link between the EDF proposal and the PESCO project. An approach that echoes the Council Conclusions of November 2024 which 'stresses the importance of defining clear links between relevant PESCO projects and EDF proposals'.

Emergency measures that were adopted in response to the most immediate consequences of the conflict in Ukraine include: i) the regulation on support for the production of ammunition (ASAP),[76] aimed at increasing European production capacities in the field of ammunition and missiles; and ii) the regulation on the establishment of an instrument to strengthen the European defence industry through joint procurement (EDIRPA),[77] aimed at encouraging Member States to jointly purchase the most urgent and critical defence

---

73 The Commission's contribution to European defence, COM(2022) 60 final, Strasbourg, 15 February 2022.

74 Decision (CFSP) 2017/2315, Commitments Nos 15, 16, 19 and 20.

75 Commission Staff Working Document Evaluation – Interim Evaluation of the European Defence Fund, cited above.

76 Regulation (EU) 2023/1525 of the European Parliament and of the Council of 20 July 2023 on supporting ammunition production ASAP) ([2023] *OJ* L185/7). See the commentary on this regulation by E. Bernard in this publication.

77 Regulation (EU) 2023/2418 of the European Parliament and of the Council of 18 October 2023 on establishing an instrument for the reinforcement of the European defence industry through joint procurement (EDIRPA), [2023] *OJ* L2023/2418. See the commentary on this regulation by E. Bernard in this publication.

products resulting from the conflict. As such, these regulations do not create any funding bonuses (like the EDF/EDIDP) or other special links with PESCO. On the other hand, in its Recommendation of November 2023, the Council reminded the Member States participating in PESCO to take advantage of these new instruments,[78] and even 'to take forward, within the framework of PESCO where possible, potential new opportunities in relation to joint procurement, in full consistency with EDA programmes and with Regulation (EU) No 2023/2418 [...], and the ramping-up of EDTIB production capacity, in full consistency with Regulation (EU) 2023/1525' [i.e. ASAP].

While the interactions between PESCO and the EDIRPA and ASAP programmes are not particularly well developed, PESCO could interact more intensively with the European Commission's future defence industry programmes. For example, in its proposal for a regulation on the establishment of the European Defence Industry Programme (EDIP),[79] the Commission has envisaged several elements that could have a greater or lesser impact on PESCO.

The EDIP regulation, as adopted, provides indeed for the extension of the financial support logic of ASAP and EDIRPA beyond 2025 (until 2027), as well as an extension of the type of products that can be supported. This means that financial support under the EDIRPA logic will no longer be limited solely to the most urgent and critical products, and financial support under the ASAP logic will no longer be limited solely to munitions and missiles. This wider coverage means that certain PESCO projects will be eligible to benefit from these new funding opportunities. This prospect is made all the more realistic by the fact that the proposal for a regulation provides for a funding bonus,[80] when the action financed is carried out as part of a project stemming from the PESCO.[81] It is worth noting that in its November 2024 Conclusions on the latest Strategic Review, the Council encourages participating Member States 'to explore ways of applying other EU financial tools and instruments, such as

78 'The Council highlights that the reactiveness and resilience of the EDTIB should be bolstered to face high-intensity warfare scenarios and encourages the pMS to take advantage of new initiatives to ramp up EU defence industrial production capacity. The pMS are also invited to continue their involvement in cooperation programmes that have a positive impact on the EDTIB, including by considering those programmes in their acquisition strategies and procedures'. Recommendation of 13 November 2023.

79 Regulation (EU) 2025/2643 of the European Parliament and of the Council of 16 December 2025 establishing the European Defence Industry Programme and a framework of measures to ensure the timely availability and supply of defence products ('EDIP Regulation'), [2025] *OJ* L2025/2643.

80 Proposed EDIP regulation, Art. 17.

81 It should be noted that the proposed EDIP regulation stipulates that this funding bonus only applies to projects that did 'not benefit from a comparable increased funding rate in another EU funding programme'. It would therefore appear to be forbidden for the same PESCO project to combine a funding bonus under the EDF with a funding bonus under the EDIP. Finally, Article 20 of the EDIP Regulation does not refer explicitly to a bonus for PESCO projects.

the EDIP proposed by the Commission, to increase collaborative projects, to cooperate to mitigate capability shortfalls, to support aggregating demand, and to step up joint procurement'.

The EDIP Regulation also contains a new legal framework to facilitate cooperation between Member States on armaments programmes throughout the life cycle of the equipment concerned. This mechanism, known as the 'Structure for European Armaments Programmes' (SEAP), could complement and reinforce the action of participating Member States in the context of PESCO, and in particular its modular dimension. Thus, as explained in the joint communication from the European Commission and the HR presenting a new strategy for the European defence industry[82] (EDIS), 'the Commission will make available a new legal framework – the [...] SEAP – as a vehicle to underpin and strengthen defence cooperation, including in the context of PESCO, if so agreed by Member States'. Indeed, by 'pooling [European] demand for defence products throughout their life cycle', the SEAP could become a relevant legal framework, available to participating Member States to carry out their PESCO project. A PESCO project with the SEAP label could thus benefit from a number of significant advantages, as shown in Table 11.

Table 11 – Benefits of SEAP

Benefits	Corresponding article in the EDIP regulation
Several types of SEAP-specific funding and SEAP-related funding bonuses as part of EDIP financial support	Article 11(2) and (3) Article 13(1)
Definition of specific public purchasing rules	Article 47
Exemption from VAT and/or excise duty for the joint acquisition of jointly-owned equipment	Article 45(1)(c)

It should be noted that the possibility of defining its own public procurement rules by derogating from Directive 2009/81/EC on defence procurement[83] appears to be a relevant advantage given that, as pointed out

[82] Joint Communication to the European Parliament, the Council, the European Economic and Social Committee and the Committee of the Regions, 'A new European Defence Industrial Strategy: Achieving EU readiness through a responsive and resilient European Defence Industry', JOIN/2024/10 final, see the commentary on this strategy by F. Liberti in this publication.

[83] Directive 2009/81/EC of the European Parliament and of the Council of 13 July 2009 on the coordination of procedures for the award of certain works contracts, supply contracts and service contracts by contracting authorities or entities in the fields of defence and

in the CARD's 2022 report and confirmed in CARD's 2024 report,[84] 'many [participating Member States] regard European collaborative approaches as *more time consuming* and *more complex*'[85] (author's italics), which more often than not leads them to opt 'for national solutions or non-EU suppliers', in contradiction with the spirit of their more binding commitments. The SEAP therefore complements the modular framework of the PESCO with its own advantages.

Furthermore, Member States cooperating in the context of a SEAP must also maintain this cooperation throughout 'the lifecycle of the defence product or technology, until its decommissioning'.[86] This may provide an opportunity to strengthen the modularity of PESCO. In effect, by using the SEAP framework to conduct a PESCO capability project, the participating Member States would be committing themselves to cooperating throughout the life cycle of the equipment concerned. This assurance of a lasting commitment from the Member States participating in a PESCO project thanks to the SEAP, in addition to a wide range of possible financial support from the EDIP, could therefore encourage the emergence of PESCO projects which would thus establish 'permanent and structured' cooperation.

With the CARD, the EDF and the arrival of the new EDIP and EDIS initiatives, there is considerable potential for PESCO to continue to optimise its operation and effectiveness. With this in mind, it is interesting to note that EDIS has already announced that '[i]n the context of the ongoing PESCO Strategic Review, the High Representative could recommend the participating Member States to strengthen the more binding commitments related to the EDTIB and to consider possible new commitments, notably on joint procurement from the EDTIB, in line with the ambition of the present strategy'. It will be interesting to examine whether the High Representative, in line with the EDIS and the guidance outlined by the Council in its November 2024 Conclusions on the Strategic Review, will strengthen the PESCO commitments accordingly. This could potentially help to create new conditions for a revitalized and more streamlined approach to the second phase of PESCO, set to commence in 2026.

---

security, and amending Directives 2004/17/EC and 2004/18/EC, [2009] *OJ* L216/76. See the commentary on this directive by S. Rodrigues in this publication.

84 '[C]ollaborative procurement, which tends to be perceived as more complex and time-consuming'. See 2024 CARD Report, cited above.

85 See 2022 CARD report, cited above.

86 EDIP regulation, Art. 41(1)(a).

PART II

Treaty on the Functioning of the European Union (TFEU)

ARTICLE 16 TFEU: HOW TO MAKE THE DEFENCE 'GDPR COMPATIBLE'?

Stéphane Rodrigues
Senior lecturer (HDR) at the Université Paris 1 Panthéon-Sorbonne
Member of the Sorbonne Institute for Research in International and European Law (IREDIES-EA 4536)
Member of the Brussels Bar

Article 16

1. Everyone has the right to the protection of personal data concerning them.

2. The European Parliament and the Council, acting in accordance with the ordinary legislative procedure, shall lay down the rules relating to the protection of individuals with regard to the processing of personal data by Union institutions, bodies, offices and agencies, and by the Member States when carrying out activities which fall within the scope of Union law, and the rules relating to the free movement of such data. Compliance with these rules is subject to the control by independent authorities.

The rules adopted on the basis of this Article shall be without prejudice to the specific rules laid down in Article 39 of the Treaty on European Union.

Article 16 TFEU is one of the provisions of general application in Part One 'Principles' of the TFEU. In its current wording, it stems from the Treaty of Lisbon, and in part from the 1997 Treaty of Amsterdam (see former Article 286 of the EC Treaty). Its first paragraph recognises the right of every individual to the protection of his or her personal data. In so doing, it echoes Article 8 of the Charter of Fundamental Rights of the EU (hereinafter 'the Charter' or 'CFREU'), which makes this a fundamental right, closely linked to the right to respect for private and family life enshrined in Article 7 of the Charter and

Article 8 of the 1950 European Convention on Human Rights (hereinafter 'ECHR').

The first subparagraph of the second paragraph of Article 16 TFEU then empowers the EU co-legislators, using the ordinary legislative procedure, to establish a common legal framework for the protection of personal data. An initial common legal framework, albeit imperfect and incomplete, had already been established by Directive 95/46/EC.[1] This was repealed and replaced by Regulation (EU) 2016/679 of 27 April 2016 known as the General Data Protection Regulation ('GDPR'),[2] which came into force on 25 May 2018.[3] As the Court's case-law has consistently emphasised, the objective of GDPR is 'ensuring a high level of protection of the fundamental rights and freedoms of natural persons, in particular their right to privacy with respect to the processing of personal data'.[4]

The question of its application to the field of the CFSP is addressed by Recital 16 of GDPR, which states that it 'does not apply to the processing of personal data by the Member States when carrying out their activities in relation to the common foreign and security policy of the Union', including therefore in application of the common security and defence policy. This exclusion is in line with the second paragraph of Article 16 TFEU, which refers to Article 39 TEU.

This last provision was introduced with the Lisbon Treaty of 2007, and is one of its innovations. The negotiating mandate of the Intergovernmental Conference of 26 June 2007 stated that 'a specific legal basis for the protection of personal data in the field of the CFSP will be provided', with particular reference to 'the processing of such data by the Member States when carrying

1 Directive 95/46/EC of the European Parliament and of the Council of 24 October 1995 on the protection of individuals with regard to the processing of personal data and on the free movement of such data, [1995] *OJ* L281/31. Legal basis: Art. 100 A TEC.

2 See Regulation (EU) 2016/679 of the European Parliament and of the Council of 27 April 2016 on the protection of individuals with regard to the processing of personal data and on the free movement of such data, and repealing Directive 95/46/EC, [2016] *OJ* L119/1; corrigendum [2018] *OJ* L127/2.

3 See also Proposal for a regulation from the European Parliament and from the Council laying down additional procedural rules relating to the enforcement of Regulation (EU) 2016/679 – COM(2023) 348 final of 4 July 2023, Proposal amending Regulations (EU) 2016/679, (EU) 2016/1036, (EU) 2016/1037, (EU) 2017/1129, (EU) 2023/1542 and (EU) 2024/573 as regards the extension of certain mitigating measures available for small and medium sized enterprises to small mid-cap enterprises and further simplification measures – COM(2025)501 final of 21 May 2025 and Proposal Proposal amending Regulations (EU) 2016/679, (EU) 2018/1724, (EU) 2018/1725, (EU) 2023/2854 and Directives 2002/58/EC, (EU) 2022/2555 and (EU) 2022/2557 as regards the simplification of the digital legislative framework, and repealing Regulations (EU) 2018/1807, (EU) 2019/1150, (EU) 2022/868, and Directive (EU) 2019/1024 (Digital Omnibus – COM(2025) 837 final of 19 November 2025.

4 See in this sense, for example: Case C-604/22, *IAB Europe*, ECLI:EU:C:2024:214, para. 53; Joined Cases C-17/22 and C-18/22, *HTB Neunte Immobilien Portfolio*, ECLI:EU:C:2024:738, para. 31 and Case C-247/23, *Deldits*, ECLI:EU:C:2025:172, para. 27.

out activities which fall under the CFSP and ESDP and the movement of such data'.[5]

The aim is not to exempt the CFSP from any obligation to protect personal data. Article 39 TEU provides a special legal basis for the Council alone, by way of derogation from Article 16(2) TFEU, to adopt a decision laying down specific rules whose scope is limited to the processing of personal data solely by the Member States. It should therefore be understood that the general rules continue to apply to the institutions, bodies, offices and agencies of the Union, including in the context of the CFSP.[6] This is the case in particular with Regulation (EU) 2018/1725 of the European Parliament and of the Council of 23 October 2018 on the protection of individuals with regard to the processing of personal data by the Union institutions, bodies, offices and agencies and on the free movement of such data.[7]

Without going into detail about the obligations of the EU institutions, bodies, offices and agencies with regard to the protection of personal data, attention should be drawn to Article 25 of Regulation (EU) 2018/1725, which provides that the internal rules of these bodies may limit the application of some of the rights recognised to individuals whose data are processed, provided that such a limitation 'respects the essence of the fundamental rights and freedoms and is a necessary and proportionate measure in a democratic society to safeguard [in particular] the national security, public security or defence of the Member States'.[8] For example, the Steering Board of the European Defence Agency adopted a decision along these lines as part of its internal workings.[9]

However, to date, the Council has still not adopted the decision referred to in Article 39 TEU, 'despite the mandatory nature of this provision' because of the wording used: 'the Council shall adopt'.[10] The Council is therefore in a

---

5 Council document no. 11218/07 of 26 June 2007, fn. 7. p. 6.

6 See in this regard: M. de Serpa Soares, 'Artigo 39 TUE', in M. Lopes Porto and G. Anastácio (eds.), *Tratado de Lisboa anotado e comentado*, Coimbra, Almedina, 2012, pp. 151–152, spec. p. 151.

7 [2018] *OJ* L295/39. This Regulation repeals Regulation (EC) No 45/2001 and Decision No 1247/2002/EC.

8 This derogation for defence activities can be found in other secondary legislation on the protection of personal data, such as Directive 2002/58/EC of the European Parliament and of the Council of 12 July 2002 concerning the processing of personal data and the protection of privacy in the electronic communications sector (Directive on privacy and electronic communications), [2002] *OJ* L201/37 – see Art. 15(1)).

9 Decision of the Steering Board of the European Defence Agency of 24February 2020 on the adoption of internal rules concerning restrictions of certain rights of data subjects in relation to processing of personal data in the framework of the functioning of the EDA, [2020] *OJ* L109/28. On the EDA: see the commentary on Article 45 TEU by A.-H.Bertana.

10 See in this regard: G. Marhic, 'L'article 39 TUE n'est pas au ciel!', in S. Marquardt and S. Blockmans (eds.), *The European Union's Contribution to International Peace and Security. Liber Amicorum in honour of Gert-Jan van Hegelsom*, Leiden, Brill & Nijhoff, 2023, pp. 164–186, spec. p. 164.

situation of circumscribed powers,[11] and to date could be considered to be in a situation of failure to act, within the meaning of Article 265 TFEU.[12] Does this mean that Member States are currently exempt from any requirement to protect personal data in the exercise of their CFSP-related activities? *A priori*, 'no', as it should be remembered that the Charter, including the aforementioned Article 8, has the same binding legal value as the Treaties (see Article 6(1) TEU) and is binding on the Member States 'when they are implementing Union law' (see Article 51(1) CFREU). Accordingly, for some authors, the obligations arising from Article 8 CFREU are sufficiently clear to apply and 'the Council's abstention to date cannot therefore have any harmful consequences in this respect'.[13] In other words, in the absence of specific rules, the general rules would apply.[14]

In this respect, attention needs to be paid to two provisions of the GDPR in relation to defence issues. First, Article 23(1) of GDPR states that Union or Member State law to which the data controller or processor is subject may restrict (by way of a legislative measure) the scope of some obligations and rights provided for in GDPR (e.g. information to be provided, right of access, right to be forgotten, etc.), 'when such a restriction respects the essence of the fundamental rights and freedoms and is a necessary and proportionate measure in a democratic society to safeguard'. This is notably the case for national security, defence or public security. Second, Article 45 GDPR is related to the possible transfer of personal data to a third country or an international organisation 'where the Commission has decided that the third country, a territory or one or more specified sectors within that third country, or the international organisation in question ensures an adequate level of protection'.

11 See by analogy: ruling of the Case C-351/22, *Neves 77 Solutions*, ECLI:EU:C:2024:723, para. 46, concerning Article 215(1) TFEU in relation to restrictive measures in the context of economic and financial relations with one or more third countries: 'In that regard, it is apparent from the clear wording of Article 215(1) TFEU, particularly the use of 'shall adopt', distinct from the terms 'may adopt' used in paragraph 2 of that article, that it falls to the Council to adopt the necessary measures referred to in paragraph 1 of that article to give effect to a CFSP decision setting out the European Union's position regarding the interruption or reduction of economic and financial relations with a third country. That institution therefore has, in the situation covered by that paragraph, circumscribed powers'.

12 For an initial application of the former Article 175 TEC (now Article 265 TFEU) to a failure by the Council to legislate, see Case 13/83, *European Parliament v Council of the European Communities*, ECLI:EU:C:1985:220. One may ask why the Commission, guardian of the Treaties, and/or the European Parliament did not consider initiating such a procedure.

13 G. Marhic, 'L'article 39 TUE n'est pas au ciel !', in S. Marquardt and S. Blockmans (eds.), *The European Union's Contribution to International Peace and Security. Liber Amicorum in honour of Gert-Jan van Hegelsom*, Leiden, Brill & Nijhoff, 2023, p. 165.

14 See by analogy: Case 167-73, *Commission v France*, ECLI:EU:C:1974:35, para. 32: '[...] whilst under Article 84(2) [of the EEC Treaty], therefore, sea and air transport are, so long as the Council has not decided otherwise, is excluded from the rules of Title IV of Part Two of the Treaty relating to the common transport policy, it remains, on the same basis as the other modes of transport, subject to the general rules of the Treaty [...]'.

When assessing the adequacy of the level of protection, the Commission shall, in particular, take account of relevant legislation, both general and sectoral, including concerning public security, defence or national security (see Article 45(2)(a) of GDPR).

It must also be possible to ensure the effective application of the rules protecting personal data: Article 39 TEU specifies in this respect that '[c]ompliance with these rules shall be subject to the control of independent authorities', according to the same formula used in the second sentence of the first paragraph of Article 16(2) TFEU. As regards the Union's institutions, bodies, offices and agencies, Regulation (EU) 2018/1725 established a European Data Protection Supervisor (EDPS: see Articles 52 to 60). In the case of Member States acting within the framework of the CFSP, the question of supervision by an independent authority seems to arise. In the absence of a decision yet adopted by the Council on the basis of Article 39 TEU, should we consider that the national authorities under ordinary law responsible for the protection of personal data (following the example of the Commission Nationale Informatique et Libertés – CNIL, in France) are competent? The combination of Articles 8 and 51(1) of the Charter, mentioned above, argue in favour of this. In any event, this seems to us to be an interpretation in harmony with the objective of 'effective and comprehensive protection of data subjects' which serves as a guide for the Court of Justice in applying the GDPR.[15] If the Member States are not willing to accept this, they could always strive to set up an ad hoc regime in the context of the decision that the Council must adopt in order to comply with the requirement of Article 39 TEU.[16]

---

15 See e.g.: Case C-231/22, *État belge (données traitées par un journal officiel)*, ECLI:EU:C:2024:7, para. 28.

16 It should be noted that the forthcoming decision should cover not only the issue 'data protection', but also the question of the 'free movement of data'. At present, defence activities are excluded from the scope of most secondary legislation that ensures the free movement of data. One example is Directive (EU) 2019/1024 of the European Parliament and of the Council of 20 June 2019 on open data and the re-use of public sector information (recast), [2019] OJ L172/56 (see Art. 1(2), pt d (i)); Regulation (EU) 2022/868 of the European Parliament and of the Council of 30 May 2022 on European data governance and amending Regulation (EU) 2018/1724 (Data Governance Act), [2022] *OJ* L152/1 (see Art. 3(2)(d)), or Regulation (EU) 2023/2854 of the European Parliament and of the Council of 13 December 2023 on harmonised rules on fair access to and fair use of data and amending Regulation (EU) 2017/2394 and Directive (EU) 2020/1828 (Data Act), [2023] *OJ* L2023/2854, (see Art. (1)(6)).

ARTICLES 49 TO 62 TFEU AND DIRECTIVE 2009/81/EC: EUROPEAN REGULATIONS APPLICABLE TO PUBLIC DEFENCE AND SECURITY CONTRACTS[1]

Stéphane Rodrigues
Senior Lecturer at the Université Paris 1 Panthéon-Sorbonne
Member of the Institut de recherche en droit international and European Law (IREDIES-EA 4536)
Member of the Brussels Bar

Article 49

Within the framework of the provisions set out below, restrictions on the freedom of establishment of nationals of a Member State in the territory of another Member State shall be prohibited. Such prohibition shall also apply to restrictions on the setting-up of agencies, branches or subsidiaries by nationals of any Member State established in the territory of any Member State.

Freedom of establishment shall include the right to take up and pursue activities as self-employed persons and to set up and manage undertakings, in particular companies or firms within the meaning of the second paragraph of Article 54, under the conditions laid down for its own nationals by the law of the country where such establishment is effected, subject to the provisions of the Chapter relating to capital

1 Directive 2009/81/EC of the European Parliament and of the Council of 13 July 2009 on the coordination of procedures for the award of certain works contracts, supply contracts and service contracts by contracting authorities or entities in the fields of defence and security, and amending Directives 2004/17/EC and 2004/18/EC, [2009] *OJ* L216/ 76. This directive refers to former Articles 47(2), 55 and 95 of the EEC Treaty, now Articles 53, 62 and 114 TFEU respectively.

Article 50

1. In order to attain freedom of establishment as regards a particular activity, the European Parliament and the Council, acting in accordance with the ordinary legislative procedure and after consulting the Economic and Social Committee, shall act by means of directives.

2. The European Parliament, the Council and the Commission shall carry out the duties devolving upon them under the preceding provisions, in particular:

a) by according, as a general rule, priority treatment to activities where freedom of establishment makes a particularly valuable contribution to the development of production and trade;

b) by ensuring close cooperation between the competent authorities in the Member States in order to ascertain the particular situation within the Union of the various activities concerned;

c) by abolishing those administrative procedures and practices, whether resulting from national legislation or from agreements previously concluded between Member States, the maintenance of which would form an obstacle to freedom of establishment;

d) by ensuring that workers of one Member State employed in the territory of another Member State may remain in that territory for the purpose of taking up activities therein as self-employed persons, where they satisfy the conditions which they would be required to satisfy if they were entering that State at the time when they intended to take up such activities;

e) by enabling a national of one Member State to acquire and use land and buildings situated in the territory of another Member State, in so far as this does not conflict with the principles laid down in Article 39(2);

f) by effecting the progressive abolition of restrictions on freedom of establishment in every branch of activity under consideration, both as regards the conditions for setting up agencies, branches or subsidiaries in the territory of a Member State and as regards the subsidiaries in the territory of a Member State and as regards the conditions governing the entry of personnel belonging to the main establishment into managerial or supervisory posts in such agencies, branches or subsidiaries;

g) by coordinating to the necessary extent the safeguards which, for the protection of the interests of members and others, are required by Member States of companies or firms within the meaning of the second paragraph of Article 54 with a view to making such safeguards equivalent throughout the Union;

h) by satisfying themselves that the conditions of establishment are not distorted by aids granted by Member States

Article 51

The provisions of this Chapter shall not apply, so far as any given Member State is concerned, to activities which in that State are connected, even occasionally, with the exercise of official authority.

The European Parliament and the Council, acting in accordance with the ordinary legislative procedure, may rule that the provisions of this Chapter shall not apply to certain activities.

Article 52

1. The provisions of this chapter and measures taken in pursuance thereof shall not prejudice to the applicability of provisions laid down by law, regulations or administrative action providing for special treatment for foreign nationals on grounds of public policy, public security or public health.

2. The European Parliament and the Council shall, acting in accordance with the ordinary legislative procedure, issue directives for the coordination of the abovementioned provisions.

Article 53

1. In order to make it easier for persons to take up and pursue activities as self-employed persons, the European Parliament and the Council shall, acting in accordance with the ordinary legislative procedure, issue directives for the mutual recognition of diplomas, certificates and other evidence of formal qualifications and for the coordination of the provisions laid down by law, regulation or administrative action in Member States concerning the taking-up and pursuit of activities as self-employed persons.

2. In the case of the medical and allied and pharmaceutical professions, the progressive abolition of restrictions shall be dependent upon coordination of the conditions for their exercise in the various Member States.

Article 54

Companies or firms formed in accordance with the law of a Member State and having their registered office, central administration or principal place of business within the Union shall, for the purposes of this Chapter, be treated in the same way as natural persons who are nationals of Member States.

'Companies or firms' means companies or firms constituted under civil or commercial law, including cooperative societies, and other legal persons governed by public or private law, save for those which are non-profit-making.

Article 55

Member States shall accord nationals of the other Member States the same treatment as their own nationals as regards participation in the capital of companies or firms within the meaning of Article 54, without prejudice to the application of the other provisions of the Treaties.

Article 56

Within the framework of the provisions set out below, restrictions on freedom to provide services within the Union shall be prohibited in respect of nationals of Member States who are established in a Member State other than that of the person for whom the services are intended.

The European Parliament and the Council, acting in accordance with the ordinary legislative procedure, may extend the provisions of the Chapter to nationals of a third country who provide services and who are established within the Union.

Article 57

Services shall be considered to be 'services' within the meaning of the Treaties where they are normally provided for remuneration, in so far as they are not governed by the provisions relating to freedom of movement for goods, capital and persons.

'Services' shall in particular include:

a) activities of an industrial character;

b) activities of a commercial character,

c) activities of craftsmen,

d) activities of the professions.

Without prejudice to the provisions of the Chapter relating to the right of establishment, the person providing a service may, in order to do so, temporarily pursue his activity in the Member State where the service is provided, under the same conditions as are imposed by that State on its own nationals.

Article 58

1. Freedom to provide services in the field of transport shall be governed by the provisions of the Title relating to transport.

2. The liberalisation of banking and insurance services connected with movements of capital shall be effected in step with the liberalisation of movement of capital.

Article 59

1. In order to achieve the liberalisation of a specific service, the European Parliament and the Council, acting in accordance with the ordinary legislative procedure and after consulting the Economic and Social Committee, shall issue directives.

2. As regards the directives referred to in paragraph 1, priority shall as a general rule be given to those services which directly affect production costs or the liberalisation of which helps to promote trade in goods.

Article 60

The Member States shall endeavour to undertake the liberalisation of services beyond the extent required by the directives issued pursuant to Article 59(1), if their general economic situation and the situation of the economic sector concerned so permit.

To this end, the Commission shall make recommendations to the Member States concerned.

Article 61

As long as restrictions on freedom to provide services have not been abolished, each Member State shall apply such restrictions without distinction on grounds of nationality or residence to all persons providing services within the meaning of the first paragraph of Article 56.

Article 62

The provisions of Articles 51 to 54 shall apply to the matters covered by this Chapter.

Establishing an internal market is one of the objectives assigned to the Union by Article 3(3) TEU. For the Court of Justice, this is an 'essential objective of the Treaty'.[2] This internal market is defined by Article 26(2) TFEU as 'an area without internal frontiers in which the free movement of goods, persons, services and capital is ensured in accordance with the provisions of the Treaties'. It also includes 'a system ensuring that competition is not distorted' (in accordance with Protocol 27 on the internal market and competition).

To implement this objective of an internal market through the exercise of shared competence (see Article 4(2)(a) TFEU), the Union uses two integration approaches: on the one hand, the enactment, through primary law, of

2 See Joined Cases C-403/08 and C-429/08, *Football Association Premier League Ltd and Others*, ECLI:EU:C:2011:631, para. 115.

prohibitions and obligations concerning what not to do (negative integration) and, on the other, the adoption, through secondary law, of measures for the approximation of national laws (positive integration through harmonisation).[3]

Articles 49 to 62 TFEU are part of this dual approach to implementing the right of establishment and the freedom to provide services. Firstly, they prohibit in principle all 'restrictions on the freedom of establishment of nationals of a Member State in the territory of another Member State' (see Article 49(1) TFEU) and on the freedom to provide services within the Union 'in respect of nationals of Member States who are established in a Member State other than that of the person for whom the services are intended' (see Article 56(1) TFEU). Secondly, in order to facilitate access to and pursuit of activities as self-employed persons, the European Parliament and the Council, acting in accordance with the ordinary legislative procedure, shall 'issue directives for the mutual recognition of diplomas, certificates and other evidence of formal qualifications, and for the coordination of the provisions laid down by law, regulation or administrative action in Member States concerning the taking-up and pursuit of activities as self-employed persons' (see Article 53(1) TFEU on the right of establishment, to which Article 62 TFEU refers for the freedom to provide services). It was in this context that the directives were adopted, firstly to coordinate and then to harmonise the rules applicable to procedures for the award of contracts by contracting authorities, in respect of public contracts whose estimated value exceeds certain thresholds.

The intervention of EU law in the sphere of public procurement, when primary law ignores this sector, is understandable first and foremost for economic reasons. According to Commission estimates, public procurement accounts for around 20% of EU GDP (around €2.4 trillion per year).[4] The impact on the internal market is therefore significant. Furthermore, the intervention of the European lawmaker is explained by the need to ensure that the principles inherent in the internal market (equal treatment and free movement) are respected in practice[5] and that the award of public contracts is open to competition.[6]

Without going into detail about the origins of secondary legislation in this sector, it should be remembered that the first texts were adopted at the very

---

3 See the commentary on Article 114 TFEU by S. Rodrigues.

4 2010 estimates quoted by the Commission in its 1st annual report on the implementation of the public procurement directives: SWD(2012) 342 final of 9 October 2012.

5 Thus, the Court has 'held that that the purpose of coordinating at Community level the procedures for the award of public contracts is to eliminate barriers to the freedom to provide services and goods and therefore to protect the interests of traders established in a Member State who wish to offer goods or services to contracting authorities established in another Member State' (Case C-380/98, *University of Cambridge*, ECLI:EU:C:2000:529(16)).

6 See Case C-324/98, *Telaustria Verlags GmbH*, ECLI:EU:C:2000:669(62): the aim is to 'ensure, for the benefit of any potential tenderer, a degree of advertising sufficient to enable the services market to be opened up to competition and the impartiality of procurement procedures to be reviewed'. On the links between competition law and public procurement

beginning of the 1970s, with a first directive devoted to public supply contracts (Directive 70/32/EEC)[7] followed by a second for public works contracts (Directive 71/305/EEC).[8] Their scope was then gradually extended, firstly to cover litigation by approximating review procedures (Directive 89/665/EC),[9] then to include new so-called special sectors (initially water, energy, telecommunications and transport: see Directive 90/531/EC),[10] and above all the services sector (Directive 92/50/EC).[11]

Since then, a continuous process of codification has been undertaken, with three series of reforms in 1993,[12] 2004[13] and 2014. Positive law is thus made up of three new directives from February 2014, responding to a concern for modernisation:[14] Directive 2014/23/EU on the award of concession contracts,[15] Directive 2014/24/EU on the award of public contracts and repealing Directive

law: V. Bridoux, *Droit de la commande publique et droit de la concurrence de l'Union européenne. Étude sur une dynamique commune*, foreword by A.-S. Choné-Grimaldi and C. Bovet, preface by C. Prieto and S. Rodrigues, *Concurrences*, 2021.

7 Commission Directive 70/32/EEC of 17 December 1969 on the provision of goods to the State, to local authorities and other official bodies, [1970] *OJ* L13/1.

8 Council Directive 71/305/EEC of 26 July 1971 concerning the co-ordination of procedures for the award of public works contracts, [1971] *OJ* L185/5.

9 Council Directive 89/665/EEC of 21 December 1989 on the coordination of the laws, regulations and administrative provisions relating to the application of review procedures to the award of public supply and public works contracts, [1989] *OJ* L395/33, as last amended by Directive 2007/66/EC of the European Parliament and of the Council of 11 December 2007 [...] with regard to improving the effectiveness of review procedures concerning the award of public contracts, [2007] *OJ* L335/31. See also Council Directive 92/13/EEC of 25 February 1992 coordinating the laws, regulations and administrative provisions relating to the application of Community rules on the procurement procedures of entities operating in the water, energy, transport and telecommunications sectors, [1992] *OJ* L76/14.

10 Council Directive 90/531/EEC of 17 September 1990 on the procurement procedures of entities operating in the water, energy, transport and telecommunications sectors, [1990] *OJ* L297/1.

11 Council Directive 92/50/EEC of 18 June 1992 relating to the coordination of procedures for the award of public service contracts, [1992] *OJ* L209/1.

12 Council Directive 93/36/EEC of 14 June 1993 coordinating procedures for the award of public supply contracts, [1993] *OJ* L199/1; Council Directive 93/37/EEC of 14 June 1993 concerning the coordination of procedures for the award of public works contracts, [1993] *OJ* L199/54 and Council Directive 93/38/EEC of 14 June 1993 coordinating the procurement procedures of entities operating in the water, energy, transport and telecommunications sectors, [1993] *OJ* L199/84, all based on the former Article 100a TEC.

13 Directive 2004/17/EC of the European Parliament and of the Council of 31 March 2004 coordinating the procurement procedures of entities operating in the water, energy, transport and postal services sectors, [2004] *OJ* L134/1 and Directive 2004/18/EC of the European Parliament and of the Council of 31 March 2004 on the coordination of procedures for the award of public works contracts, public supply contracts and public service contracts, [2004] *OJ* L134/114, both based on the former Articles 47-2, 55 and 95 TEC.

14 Following the Commission's Green Paper of 27 January 2011 on modernising EU public procurement policy: 'Towards a more efficient European Procurement Market' COM(2011)15 final.

15 Directive 2014/23/EU of the European Parliament and of the Council of 26 February 2014 on the award of concession contracts, [2014] *OJ* L94/1.

2004/18/EC[16] and Directive 2014/25/EU on the procurement of entities operating in the water, energy, transport and postal services sectors and repealing Directive 2004/17/EC.[17]

Between the last two reforms came the adoption of a directive on defence and security procurement: Directive 2009/81/EC of 13 July 2009.[18] The origins of this instrument can be traced back to a study carried out by the European Commission in 2004,[19] based on a threefold observation: public defence contracts (around a fifth of all public purchases) are characterised by compartmentalisation at the national level, by specific features that differentiate them from other public contracts,[20] and by a legal framework that is complex to apply.[21] To remedy this, two options were proposed: either simply clarify the existing legal framework, or establish specific rules adapted to the characteristics of defence. The second option was chosen with Directive 2009/81/EC, the scope of which will be extended to the security sector by amendment of the European Parliament.

---

16 Directive 2014/24/EU of the European Parliament and of the Council of 26 February 2014 on the award of public contracts and repealing Directive 2004/18/EC, *[2014] OJ* L94/65.

17 Directive 2014/25/EU of the European Parliament and of the Council of 26 February 2014 on the procurement of entities operating in the water, energy, transport and postal services sectors and repealing Directive 2004/17/EC, [2014] *OJ* L94/243. See also Commission Implementing Decision (EU) 2016/1804 of 10 October 2016 on the detailed rules for the application of Articles 34 and 35 of Directive 2014/25/EU of the European Parliament and of the Council on the procurement by entities operating in the water, energy, transport and postal services sectors ([2016] *OJ* L275/39), which provides for an exclusion procedure for activities directly subject to competition.

18 Directive 2009/81/EC of the European Parliament and of the Council of 13 July 2009 on the coordination of procedures for the award of certain works contracts, supply contracts and service contracts by contracting authorities or entities in the fields of defence and security, and amending Directives 2004/17/EC and 2004/18/EC, [2009] *OJ* L216/76.

19 See the Commission's Green Paper on defence procurement: COM(2004) 608, 23 September 2004.

20 As underlined by economic doctrine: 'Armament markets are not very competitive at the national level. The market logic is most often that of a thwarted monopsony (a very limited number of companies facing a single customer), or that of a bilateral monopoly (a single customer and a single supplier)'. Furthermore, 'the balance of power between the State and a single supplier is affected by two major difficulties likely to fuel mistrust on both sides: the specificity of assets and asymmetries of information' (A. Quinet, *Économie de la guerre*, preface by General T. Burkhard, Paris, Economica, 2023, pp. 151–153).

21 Added to this is the so-called 'agent-principal' dilemma, from which it follows that 'agents (i.e. defence companies) seek to extract excessive profits and/or use public funds to acquire resources that will enable them to win future contracts' from the State (the 'principal'), which is often 'imperfectly informed' and generally exercises limited control over these companies (O. Schmitt, *Préparer la guerre. Stratégie, innovation et puissance militaire à l'époque contemporaine*, Paris, PUF, 2024, spec. pp. 230 and 428).

The adoption of Directive 2009/81/EC illustrates what some authors have described as the repressive approach to integration in EU law,[22] although it does differentiate from that applied to so-called special sectors, 'in that it does not concern markets excluded from the scope of the general directive, but reduces the material scope of the latter'.[23]

It is therefore appropriate to set out, firstly, the special regime of Directive 2009/81/EC (Section I) and, secondly, the other instruments of secondary legislation likely to apply to defence contracts (Section II).

I. THE SPECIAL REGIME UNDER DIRECTIVE 2009/81/EC[24]

Directive 2009/81/EC was adopted as part of the '2009 Defence Package',[25] which also includes a review of other instruments relating to export controls[26] and intra-Community transfers.[27] In so doing, it contributes to the gradual

---

22 See in this regard: E. Simon, *Rôles et fonctions du droit de l'Union européenne dans l'intégration des politiques d'acquisition d'armement*, PhD thesis, Paris, Université Paris 1 Panthéon-Sorbonne, defended on 13 July 2017, under the supervision of V. de Beaufort and S. Rodrigues, spec. p. 194. The author draws in particular on the work of M. Blauberger and M. Weiss, 'If you can't beat me, join me! - How the Commission pushed and pulled member states into legislating defence procurement' (2013) 20(8) *Journal of European Public Policy*, p. 8.

23 E. Simon, *Rôles et fonctions du droit de l'Union européenne dans l'intégration des politiques d'acquisition d'armement*, PhD thesis, Paris, Université Paris 1 Panthéon-Sorbonne, defended on 13 July 2017, p. 197.

24 On this directive, see in particular: E. Bodard, *La nouvelle réglementation des marchés publics de la défense*, dissertation of the Institut d'études politiques de Strasbourg, 2009; B. Heuninckx, 'Évolutions récentes du droit européen des marchés publics de Défense', *Pyramides, Revue du Centre d'études et de recherches en administration publique*, 2011, no. 21, pp. 139–172; S. Rodrigues, 'La directive sur les marchés publics dans les domaines de la défense et de la sécurité. Ou de l'art difficile de rentrer dans le rang (du marché intérieur)', *Europe*, 2009, study no. 10, pp. 4–8 and M. Trybus, *Buying defence and security in Europe: the EU defence and security procurement directive in context*, Cambridge, Cambridge University Press, 2014.

25 J. Cats, 'Le "paquet défense": le marché intérieur au service de la défense européenne?', *Revue du marché commun et de l'Union européenne*, October-November 2009, no. 352, pp. 564–573.

26 See Council Regulation (EC) No 428/2009 of 5 May 2009 setting up a Community regime for the control of exports, transfer, brokering and transit of dual-use items (recast), [2009] *OJ* L134/1, repealed and replaced by Regulation (EU) 2021/821 of the European Parliament and of the Council of 20 May 2021 setting up a Union regime for the control of exports, brokering, technical assistance, transit and transfers of dual-use items (recast), [2021] *OJ* L206/1. See the commentary on this regulation in this publication by A. Millet-Devalle under Article 207 TFEU.

27 See Directive 2009/43/EC of the European Parliament and of the Council of 6 May 2009 simplifying terms and conditions of transfers of defence-related products within the Community, [2009] *OJ* L1461. See the commentary on this directive in this publication, by E. Daniel and M. Kieffer under Article 114 TFEU.

establishment of a 'European defence equipment market', which is considered 'essential for strengthening the European Defence Technological and Industrial Base and developing the military capabilities needed to implement the European Security and Defence Policy' (Recital 2 of the Directive).[28]

Subject to Articles 30, 45, 46, 55 and 296 of the EC Treaty (now, respectively, Articles 36, 51, 52, 62 and 346 of the TFEU), the scope of the Directive (see Article 2) covers the supply of military equipment[29] and sensitive equipment,[30] including their spare parts, components and/or sub-assemblies, works, supplies and services directly connected with any such equipment for all or part of its life cycle, as well as works and services intended for specifically military purposes or sensitive works and services. This Directive shall apply to contracts which have a value excluding value-added tax (VAT) estimated to be no less than the following thresholds: EUR 443 000 for supply and service contracts, and EUR 5 538 000 for works contracts.[31]

The main challenge faced by the authors of the directive was to satisfy both the security requirements of the Member States and the obligations arising from the Treaty (equal treatment, free movement, free competition), a balance that the application of the existing directives seemed difficult to strike.[32] As a result, the directive now provides for specific rules to take account of security requirements in terms of information and supply, aiming to lighten or simplify procedures for some of the activities in question, and providing appropriate arrangements for subcontracting situations.

A. INFORMATION SECURITY AND SECURITY OF SUPPLY

In terms of security requirements, the Directive provides a framework for the handling of classified information, while applying the principle of mutual recognition to security clearances issued by the competent authorities of the Member States.[33] However, the contracting authority may still impose its

28 The EDTIB is estimated to generate annual sales of €70 billion, export volumes of over €28 billion and employ around 500,000 people (SIPRI figures for 2021).

29 'Military equipment' is defined as equipment 'specifically designed or adapted for military purposes, intended for use as weapons, munitions or war material' (see Article 1(6) of Directive 2009/81/EC).

30 Sensitive' means equipment, works and services 'intended for security purposes which involve, require and/or contain classified information' (see Art. 1(7) of Directive 2009/81/EC).

31 Commission Delegated Regulation (EU) 2023/2510 of 15 November 2023 amending Directive 2009/81/EC of the European Parliament and of the Council in respect of the thresholds for supply, service and works contracts3, [202] *OJ* L2023/2510.

32 In this sense: S. de La Rosa, *Droit européen de la commande publique*, Brussels, Bruylant, 3rd ed., 2025, spec. para. 448, p. 376.

33 Directive 2009/81/EC, Art. 22.

requirements for the protection of classified information as a condition for selecting candidates.[34]

The same applies to conditions relating to the security of supply,[35] where the contracting authority/entity may require, for example, certification or documents demonstrating that the tenderer will be able to fulfil the obligations relating to the export, transfer and transit of goods associated with the contract. These documents may include any additional documents from the Member State(s) concerned; an undertaking by the tenderer to put in place and/or maintain the necessary capacity to cope with any increase in the needs of the contracting authority/entity as a result of a crisis situation, on terms and conditions to be agreed; or an undertaking by the tenderer to maintain, modernise or adapt the supplies covered by the contract.

B. STREAMLINING PROCEDURES

As far as streamlining procedures is concerned, research and development (R&D) activities, which are essential in the defence sector, are the main beneficiaries, in the form of a dual system of exclusion and exception. Firstly, contracts awarded as part of a cooperation programme based on R&D activities carried out jointly by at least two Member States to develop a new product and, where appropriate, to work on subsequent stages of all or part of the product's life cycle, are excluded from the scope of the Directive.[36] Bi- or multilateral cooperation programmes, such as those developed within OCCAR or through permanent structured cooperation PESCO, are thus exempt from competitive tendering requirements (PESCO).[37] For the Commission itself, these programmes 'are an effective means to foster market consolidation and competitiveness'.[38] It therefore also encourages them, to a certain extent, in

34 Ibid., Art. 42.

35 Ibid., Art. 23.

36 Ibid., Art. 13(c), which also requires the Member States concerned to notify the Commission of the share of R&D expenditure in the overall cost of the programme, the cost-sharing agreement and each Member State's proposed share of the purchase, if any. Outside the R&D sector, contracts awarded under the PSC could also be excluded from the scope of the Directive as government-to-government contracts, as referred to in Article 13(f) of Directive 2009/81/EC (see on this subject the Commission's guidance on government-to-government procurement in the fields of defence and security, published in the [2016] *OJ* C450/1).

37 See commentary on Articles 42(6) and 46 TEU and Protocol No 10.

38 Cf. COM(2013) 542 final, cited above, p. 6. See also: Commission guidelines for cooperation-based procurement in the fields of defence and security, published in the [2019] *OJ* C157/1, with an amended version published in the [2022] *OJ* C374/1. These guidelines provide details on central purchasing bodies (*see* Art. 10 of Directive 2009/81/EC), on the exclusion of R&D programmes for the development of new products and on contracts awarded through international organisations.

the same way as the use of central purchasing bodies under the conditions set out in the Directive for joint procurement, including via the European Defence Agency (EDA).[39] Such a derogation may also be considered to extend to the new areas of cooperation opened up by Regulation (EU) 2023/1525 of the European Parliament and of the Council of 20 July 2023 on support for ammunition production (ASPA), and known as the 'ASAP Regulation',[40] and by Regulation (EU) 2023/2418 of the European Parliament and of the Council of 18 October 2023 on the establishment of an instrument to strengthen the European defence industry through joint procurement (EDIRPA).[41]

In addition to this exclusion scheme, there is an exception scheme which allows contracting authorities/entities to use the negotiated procedure without publication of a contract notice in the case of supply and service contracts for R&D services, other than those referred to in Article 13,[42] and for products manufactured solely for research and development purposes (with the exception of quantity production to establish the commercial viability of the product or to recover research and development costs).[43]

In the minds of EU legislators, the aim of these exceptional provisions is clearly to encourage R&D as a 'key way of strengthening the European Defence Technological and Industrial Base', thus justifying 'maximum flexibility in the award of contracts for research supplies and services'.[44]

In addition, for all other defence contracts, recourse may be had to the competitive dialogue procedure,[45] which is similar to that provided for in the other directives, but which may be applied more often insofar as it concerns 'particularly complex' contracts. For these, recourse to the restricted procedure or the negotiated procedure with publication of a contract notice will not enable the contract to be awarded, when the contracting authority/entity is objectively unable to define in advance the technical means capable of meeting its needs and objectives, and/or to establish the legal and/or financial package for a project. In such cases, a dialogue is established with the candidates admitted

---

39 Directive 2009/81/EC, Art. 10. On the EDA: see the commentary in this publication on Article 45 TEU by H. Bertana.

40 [2023] OJ L185/7. On ASAP, see E. Bernard in this publication.

41 [2023] *OJ* L2023/2418. On EDIRPA, see E. Bernard in this publication

42 This includes services undertaken as part of a cooperation programme, as mentioned above, but also R&D services 'other than those where the benefits accrue exclusively to the contracting authority/entity for its use in the conduct of its own affairs, on condition that the service provided is wholly remunerated by the contracting authority/entity' (Article 13(j) of Directive 2009/81/EC).

43 Directive 2009/81/EC, Art. 28(2). It should be noted that, by analogy with the non-defence public procurement directives, this procedure may also be used, in particular, in the event of a prior unsuccessful procedure, in urgent cases resulting from crisis situations or 'when, for technical reasons or reasons connected with the protection of exclusive rights, the contract may be awarded only to a particular economic operator'.

44 Ibid., Recital 55.

45 Ibid., Art. 27.

to this procedure, with a view to developing one or more solutions capable of meeting the said needs and on the basis of which the selected candidates are invited to submit a tender.

However, the Commission maintains a watchful eye, favouring a restrictive interpretation and excluding any abusive practice aimed at circumventing the Directive.[46] In this respect, we believe that the general principles of EU law applicable to public procurement (in particular the principles of non-discrimination and minimum transparency)[47] must continue to prevail.[48] This is why the Commission has, for example, opened infringement proceedings against the Czech Republic concerning a deemed abusive application of the derogation relating to government-to-government contracts in Directive 2009/81/EC, in the context of the purchase of military helicopters by direct award. The Commission considered that this was also an infringement of the principles of non-discrimination, equal treatment and transparency, in that EU companies were prevented from submitting tenders and competing effectively for the award of this contract, by being obliged to cooperate only with national companies.[49]

Finally, it should be added that the Russian war against Ukraine led to the introduction of a temporary exception mechanism (until 30 June 2025) to facilitate joint procurement during the ammunition supply crisis. Article 14 of the ASAP Regulation provides for two derogation clauses for Directive 2009/81/EC '[w]here at least two Member States enter into an agreement to commonly procure relevant defence products and where the extreme urgency deriving from the crisis resulting from Russia's war of aggression against Ukraine prevents the use of any of the procedures provided for by Directive 2009/81/EC for the conclusion of a framework agreement'. The first derogation concerns the second subparagraph of Article 29(2) of Directive 2009/81/EC: it allows a contracting authority/entity 'may modify an existing framework agreement which has been concluded following one of the procedures

---

46 Cf. COM(2013) 542 final, p. 7.

47 With reference, by analogy, to the case *Telaustria*, cited above, and to the Commission's 2006 interpretative communication on the Community law applicable to contract awards not subject or not fully subject to the public procurement directives, [2006] *OJ* C179/2. See in the same vein: commentary on Article 346 TFEU and F. Terpan, 'La CJUE et les marchés publics de défense: l'encadrement des intérêts nationaux de sécurité', *RTDE*, 2016, vol. 52, no. 3, pp. 495–512.

48 Along similar lines, with regard to contracts awarded under the aegis of the EDA, see B. Heuninckx, 'Évolutions récentes du droit européen des marchés publics de Défense', *Pyramides, Revue du Centre d'études et de recherches en administration publique*, 2011, no. 21, spec. pp. 182–183, which is based on Council Decision 2007/643/CFSP of 18 September 2007 of the financial rules of the European Defence Agency and on the procurement rules and on rules on financial contributions from the operational budget of the European Defence Agency, [2007] *OJ* L269/ 1.

49 See Commission press release of 7 February 2024 on the INFR(2023)4017 procedure against the Czech Republic.

provided for by Article 25 of that Directive so that its provisions may apply to contracting authorities/entities which are not originally party to the framework agreement'. The second derogation concerns the third subparagraph of the same Article 29(2) and authorises a contracting authority/entity to 'make substantial amendments to the quantities laid down in an existing framework agreement insofar as that is strictly necessary for the application of paragraph 2 of this Article. Where quantities laid down in an existing framework agreement are substantially modified pursuant to this paragraph, any economic operator that meets the contracting authority's/entity's conditions initially laid down in the public procurement procedure for the framework agreement'.[50] To avoid abuses in the application of these derogations, the principle of non-discrimination concerning additional quantities must be respected, particularly in relations between the contracting authorities/entities of the Member States concerned, and competition must not be prevented, restricted or distorted. Despite these precautions, the question arises as to whether Pandora's box has not been opened to perpetuate these crisis clauses.[51] Proof of this is the inclusion of these clauses in Council Regulation (EU) 2025/1106 of 27 May 2025 establishing the Security Action for Europe (SAFE) through the Reinforcement of the European Defence Industry Instrument[52] and in the new regulation establishing a European Defence Industry Programme (EDIP).[53]

---

50 To do this, the contracting authority/entity must open up this possibility by means of an *ad hoc* notice published in the *Official Journal of the European Union*.

51 In this regard: P. De Baecke and S. Rodrigues, 'French Procurement Rules and war in Ukraine: a subtle evolution' (2023) 32(6) *Public Procurement Law Review*, Special Issue on Ukraine, pp. 418–428.

52 [2025] *OJ* L2025/1106; in particular Articles 18 and 19.

53 See Regulation (EU) 2025/2643 of the European Parliament and of the Council of 16 December 2025 establishing the European Defence Industry Programme and a framework of measures to ensure the timely availability and supply of defence products ('EDIP Regulation') [2025] *OJ* L2025/2643, in particular Article 52. See the commentary on this proposal by E. Simon in this publication. This Regulation is backed up by the new strategy adopted on the same day and entitled 'A new European Defence Industrial Strategy: Achieving EU readiness through a responsive and resilient European Defence Industry' (EDIS): see the Joint Communication JOIN(2024)10 final from the European Commission and the High Representative of the Union for Foreign Affairs and Security Policy, which refers to an 'extension' of the derogation mechanism provided for in the regulation ASAP for Directive 2009/81/EC, as an 'Industrial Solidarity Clause' (see p. 14). In addition to those exemptions, the EDIP Regulation contains the establishment of a 'Structure for European Armament Programme' (SEAP), with a view to fostering the competitiveness of the EDTIB and of the Ukrainian DTIB by aggregating the demand for defence products throughout their lifecycle. Accordingly, the procurement made by a SEAP will be considered as a government-to-government contract as referred to in Article 13, point (f) of Directive 2009/81/EC.

C. TAKING ACCOUNT OF THE REALITIES OF THE SECTOR: SMES AND SUBCONTRACTING

We feel it is worth highlighting another special provision relating to subcontracting arrangements, which are particularly common in the European defence sector, whose fabric includes many small and medium-sized enterprises (SMEs).[54]

In the legislator's view, it may be 'appropriate for the contracting authorities/entities to oblige the successful tenderer to organise transparent and non-discriminatory competitive tendering when awarding subcontracts to third parties' and 'appropriate for the option of subcontracting, which the tenderer may avail himself of, should be accompanied by the possibility for the Member State to allow or require its contracting authorities/entities to request that subcontracts representing at least a certain proportion of the value of the contract be awarded to third parties, it being understood that affiliated undertakings are not considered to be third parties'.[55]

In practical terms, this means that the contracting authority/entity can require subcontracting to represent up to 30% of the value of the contract concerned.[56]

This special regime must be seen in the context of the Directive's encouragement of the development and dissemination of 'best practice between Member States and European industry with a view to encouraging free movement and competitiveness on subcontracting markets within the EU, as well as efficient management of suppliers and SMEs with a view to obtaining the best value for money'.[57]

D. HOW IS IT IMPLEMENTED? WHAT ARE THE RESULTS?

Directive 2009/81/EC had to be transposed into national law by 21 August 2011. However, as the Commission noted, 'the vast majority of Member States have experienced difficulties in transposing within the deadline set'.[58] In fact,

[54] In France, nearly 4,000 SMEs are involved in the defence sector.

[55] Ibid., Recital 40.

[56] Ibid., Art. 21.4.

[57] Ibid., Recital 40. See also in this sense: Commission Recommendation (EU) 2018/624 of 20 April 2018 on cross-border market access for sub-suppliers SMEs in the defence sector ([2018] *OJ* L102/87), which recommends in particular encouraging subcontracting through pre-information and division into lots and which encourages Member States to also use the European Structural and Investment Funds to support SMEs, for example by developing regional clusters of excellence.

[58] See Report from the Commission on the transposition of Directive 2009/81/EC: COM(2012) 565 final, 2 October 2012, spec. p. 10.

the joint report by the Commission and the High Representative of the Union for Foreign Affairs and Security Policy of 5 May 2015 on the implementation of the 2013 Defence Communication noted that large defence procurement contracts were still being managed in the Member States without applying the 2009 Directive.[59] This led the Commission to open several infringement proceedings in January 2018.[60]

However, in its first report on the application of the Directive,[61] the Commission welcomed the fact that, between 2011 and 2015, the value of public contracts awarded in accordance with the Directive had increased more than tenfold, reaching a value of around €30.85 billion over this period (compared with an average annual total of around €80 billion over the same period). There were however large disparities across countries, with the United Kingdom ensuring that more than 50% of the value of contracts were awarded in accordance with the Directive, whereas Germany's record was the weakest. That said, a closer analysis of the data shows that 'the objectives of the Directive have only been partially achieved': on the one hand, the proportion of public contracts awarded after genuine competitive tendering was only around 3.3% of the total expenditure concerned and, on the other, only around 10% of the value of contracts awarded under the Directive had been won directly by foreign companies.[62]

On this last point, it is notable that certain Member States, including France first and foremost, do not hesitate to call for a form of European preference, on the basis of what might be described as an enterprising reading of Recital 18 of the Directive. With reference to Article 296 of the EC Treaty (now Article 346 of the TFEU) and Article XXIII(1) of the Agreement on Government Procurement (GPA), Recital 18 concludes within the framework of the World Trade Organisation (WTO) that 'Member States retain the power to decide whether or not their contracting authority/entity may allow economic operators from third countries to participate in contract award procedures'.

59 Commission and High Representative, Report on the implementation of the European Commission Communication on Defence, 5 May 2015, spec. p. 2.

60 See Commission press release No IP/18/357 of 25 January 2018. The countries concerned included Denmark, Italy, the Netherlands, Poland and Portugal.

61 European Commission, Report 'on the implementation of Directive 2009/81/EC on public procurement in the fields of defence and security, in comply with Article 73(2) of that Directive', COM(2016) 762 final of 30 November 2016.

62 It should be noted that this observation also seems to apply in application of the framework directive 2014/24/EU, on reading the European Court of Auditors' special report 28/2023 of 25 October 2023, entitled Public procurement in the EU. Decline in competition for works, goods and services contracts awarded between 2011 and 2021. The ECA estimates that the level of competition in these public contracts has decreased over the last decade due in particular to a significant overall increase in single-bidder contracts (42%), a high level of direct award of contracts (16%) and a low number of direct cross-border public contracts between Member States (5%).

In any case, the Commission did not consider it appropriate to envisage a legislative amendment, preferring to redouble its educational efforts by adopting guidelines or recommendations. The European Parliament has been more prescriptive. In a report on the implementation of Directive 2009/81/EC, it considered that 'the Commission should assume its responsibility for monitoring the necessity and proportionality of exclusions invoked by the Member States in their awarding of contracts outside the scope of the Defence Procurement Directive', and that 'some aspects of the implementation of the Defence Procurement Directive could be improved, such as the Member States' use of the open procedure, innovation partnerships or other new procedures as provided for in Directive 2014/24/EC, and encourages Member States to consistently apply that directive whenever possible'. However, it also concluded that no revision of the Directive was necessary at this stage, 'as the existing regulatory framework should be sufficient if correctly implemented and used'.[63]

However, it seems to the author that the recommendations made by the European Court of Auditors in its aforementioned Special Report No. 28/2023, although aimed solely at Framework Directive 2014/24/EU, could also be relevant to Directive 2009/81/EC. This applies in particular to the recommendations made to the Commission to 'close the gaps in the public procurement data collected', to 'improve its monitoring tools to allow better analysis' and finally to 'deepen the root cause analysis and put forward measures to overcome key obstacles to competition in public procurement'.[64]

To conclude this brief overview of Directive 2009/81/EC, it should be added that litigation over its interpretation before the Court of Justice is still confidential. To author's knowledge, only one preliminary ruling case has led to a judgment,[65] on 15 September 2022,[66] concerning in particular the system for checking the suitability of participants in a public procurement procedure (Article 38 of the Directive) and the possibility of rejecting abnormally low tenders (Article 49 of the Directive), without the application of these provisions presenting any originality or specificity in relation to the other public procurement directives.

---

[63] Parliament report 2019/2204(INI) of 24 March 2021 on the implementation of Directives 2009/81/EC and 2009/43/EC.

[64] European Court of Auditors, 'Public procurement in the EU: Less competition for contracts awarded for works, goods and services in the 10 years up to 2021', *Special Report*, 28, EN, 2023.

[65] A second case was brought in 2022 but resulted in an order of inadmissibility: see Case C-521/22, *KONŠTRUKTA – Defence, a.s.*, ECLI:EU:C:2023:94.

[66] Case C-669/20, *Veridos*, ECLI:EU:C:2022:684.

II. APPLICATION OF OTHER PUBLIC PROCUREMENT DIRECTIVES TO THE DEFENCE SECTOR

Outside the scope of Directive 2009/81/EC, the other defence contracts remain subject to the other three directives on procurement procedures (Section A). In addition, the litigation aspect is directly inspired by the pre-existing directives on review procedures (Section B).

A. APPLICATION OF OTHER PUBLIC PROCUREMENT DIRECTIVES

The common feature of the general directives is that they specify that they apply in principle to public defence contracts not covered by Directive 2009/81/EC, but with exceptions linked to the protection of essential security interests within the meaning of Article 346 of the TFEU,[67] and by regulating the specific case of mixed contracts involving aspects relating to defence or security.

1. *Protection of Essential Security Interests*

If we look at Framework Directive 2014/24/EU(Art. 15),[68] it does not apply on the one hand to 'the protection of the essential security interests of a Member State cannot be guaranteed by less intrusive measures, for instance by imposing requirements aimed at protecting the confidential nature of information which the contracting authority makes available in a contract award procedure as provided for in this Directive'. On the other hand, it does not apply when the Directive 'would oblige a Member State to supply information the disclosure of which it considers contrary to the essential interests of its security'.

To the author's knowledge,[69] the Court of Justice had the opportunity for the first time to rule on this provision, in the context of a case for failure to fulfil obligations brought by the Commission. This concerned the Polish authorities invoking their rules to allow contracts for the production of official

---

67 See the commentary on this article in this publication by S. Rodrigues.

68 To be read in conjunction with Articles 10 and 21 of Directive 2014/23/EU (concessions) and Articles 20 and 24 to 27 of Directive 2014/25/EU (special sectors).

69 See, however, Case C-187/16, *Commission v Austria* (State Printing Office), ECLI:EU:C:2018:194, which ruled in particular on Article 14 of Directive 2004/18/EC, relating to contracts declared to be secret or the performance of which must be accompanied by special security measures or where the protection of the essential interests of a Member State so requires.

documents, printed matter and other stamps and markings to be awarded without competition.[70]

The Court's reasoning led it to distinguish between two categories of documents. First, as regards excise stamps, legal notices, control stickers, ballot papers, holographic signs on voting right certificates and microprocessor systems with software for managing public documents, computer systems and databases necessary for the use of public documents, the Court considered that applying the derogation in Article 15(3) of Directive 2014/24/EU is disproportionate in the light of the objectives put forward, in particular the continuity of the supply of official documents, confidentiality and the security and safety of its citizens. In the Court's view, in fact, other provisions of Directive 2014/24/EU already make it possible to address the aforementioned concerns, for example by authorising the contracting authority to impose an obligation of secrecy and compliance with appropriate technical specifications and selection criteria.

The Court ruled differently for a second category of documents, including: the personal documents of military personnel and their identity cards, the service cards of police officers, border guards, State security agents, internal security agency agents, intelligence agency agents, military counter-intelligence service agents and career military personnel appointed to a post in this service, military intelligence service agents and career military personnel appointed to a post in this service, and members of the military police. In this category, the Court found that 'those documents present a direct and close link to the objective of protecting national security, with the result that these may justify additional confidentiality requirements' and 'can render indispensable a limitation on the disclosure of the characteristics of such documents and the information that they contain – including, in particular, the identity of those agents and officers – with the result that such documents must be regarded as having a particularly high level of sensitivity which requires greater protection against, inter alia, leaks and falsification' (para. 108 of the judgment). For these documents, the proportionality test is thus met. Poland could therefore apply Article 15(3) of Directive 2014/24/EU.

2. *Mixed Markets*

As regards mixed contracts, apart from those awarded or organised under international rules for which Directive 2014/24/EU does not apply (Art. 17), the applicable regime will depend on whether the different parts of a given public contract are objectively separable. Where this is the case, contracting

70 Case C-601/21, *Commission v Poland*, ECLI:EU:C:2023:629, which also provided the Court an opportunity to clarify the concept of protection of the essential security interests of the Member States within the meaning of Article 346 TFEU.

authorities have the choice between awarding separate contracts for the different parts of the contract or awarding a single contract. The latter case must then fall under either Article 346 TFEU or Directive 2009/81/EC and be 'justified for objective reasons' (see Art. 16 of Directive 2014/24/EU).[71]

Similarly, where the various parts of a given contract are objectively inseparable, the contract may be awarded without applying Directive 2014/24/EU where it includes elements falling within the application of Article 346 TFEU of the Union, or, if not, in accordance with Directive 2009/81/EC.

B. THE LITIGATION ASPECT INSPIRED BY THE 'REMEDIES' DIRECTIVES[72]

As explained in Recital 72 of Directive 2009/81/EC, '[c]ompliance with transparency and competitive obligations [of tendering] should be ensured by an effective review system, based on the system provided for in Directives 89/665/EEC and 92/13/EEC', referred to above as the 'Remedies Directives'.

Title IV on the rules applicable to appeals (Articles 55 to 64) pursues the same objective: accessibility of the appeals procedures 'at least to any person having or having had an interest in obtaining a particular contract who has been or risks being harmed by an alleged infringement' of the public procurement rules (Art. 55).

As emphasised by the Court of Justice in its case law on Directive 89/665/EC, applicable by analogy, there is 'a review of the lawfulness of decisions adopted by contracting authorities, the purpose of which is to ensure that the relevant rules of EU law or national provisions transposing those rules are complied with. It is not possible for such review to be confined to a simple examination of whether the decisions adopted by contracting authorities are arbitrary'. This does not exclude the possibility for the national legislature 'grant the competent national courts and tribunals more extensive powers for the purpose of reviewing whether a measure was expedient'.[73]

---

[71] See judgment of 18 December 2025, Case C-769/23, *Mara*, ECLI:EU:C:2025:984, in particular para. 50 which states that 'The rules on conflict between Directive 2009/81 and Directive 2014/24 laid down in Article 16 of the latter directive are more recent and, moreover, more detailed than those contained in Article 3 of Directive 2009/81. Article 16 of Directive 2014/24 therefore expresses the intention of the EU legislature at the time of adoption of that directive and must be applied to the detriment of Article 3(1) of Directive 2009/81, which [...] has a different scope, but must be regarded as having been superseded by the legislative developments brought about by Directive 2014/24'.

[72] On these so-called 'Remedies' directives: S. de La Rosa, *Droit européen de la commande publique*, Brussels, Bruylant, 2017, spec. pp. 405–427.

[73] See Case C-440/13, *Croce Amica One Italia Srl v Azienda Regionale Emergenza Urgenza (AREU)*, ECLI:EU:C:2014:2435, para. 46.

To this end, minimum rules are laid down concerning, in particular: the powers to be conferred on the competent authorities (corrective or preventive interim measures, annulment of unlawful decisions and/or award of damages); as well as the standstill period between the awarding of a contract decision and the conclusion of the contract and the time limit for lodging an appeal. In addition, certain serious infringements (failure to publish a contract notice, prevention of pre-contractual review, etc.)[74] must be penalised, at the very least, by the contract in question having no effect. It is specified that, in accordance with the procedural autonomy of the Member States,[75] the penalties must, in any event, be 'effective, proportionate and dissuasive' and consist either in imposing financial penalties on the contracting authority[76] or in shortening the duration of the contract.

C. FOR THE RECORD: INTERNATIONAL PUBLIC CONTRACTS AND FOREIGN SUBSIDIES

Finally, reference should be made to two other instruments that may also affect defence procurement: Regulation (EU) 2022/1031 establishing an instrument for international public procurement (IMPI);[77] and Regulation (EU) 2022/2560 on foreign subsidies distorting the internal market.[78] Readers should refer to the respective comments on these two regulations in this publication.

---

74 These may also justify intervention by the Commission (the so-called corrective mechanism under Article 3 of Directive 89/665/EC).

75 Although subject to the principles of equivalence and effectiveness in the light of the right to an effective remedy (Article 47 of the Charter of Fundamental Rights of the European Union). See, for example, Joined Cases C-145 and 149/08, *Club Hotel Loutraki AE and Others*, ECLI:EU:C:2010:247, para. 74.

76 On the system of fines: see in particular Case C-263/19, *T-Systems Magyarország and Others*, ECLI:EU:C:2020:373.

77 Regulation (EU) 2022/1031 of the European Parliament and of the Council of 23 June 2022 on access to public contracts and concessions in the European Union for economic operators, goods and services from third countries and establishing procedures to facilitate negotiations in relation to access to public contracts and concessions in third countries for economic operators, goods and services from the European Union (International Public Procurement Instrument – IMPI), [2022] *OJ* L173/1. See M. Morales, 'Publication of the instrument on international public procurement: an offensive tool in the service of reciprocity', *Europe*, 2023, no. 2, study 1, pp. 5–9. On the opening of the first investigation under the IMPI against several Chinese public contracts in the field of medical devices: Commission press release IP/24/2044 of 24 April 2024.

78 Regulation (EU) 2022/2560 of the European Parliament and of the Council of 14 December 2022 on foreign subsidies distorting the internal market, [2022] *OJ* L330/1. See the commentary on this regulation in this publication, by S. Rodrigues, under Article 114 TFEU.

III. CONCLUSION

Public procurement in the defence sector was becoming a key issue in the context of the Ukraine war, justifying the adoption of the abovementioned instruments like ASAP and EDIRPA or of the EDIP Regulation with a view to encouraging joint procurement. The European Commission and the High Representative have confirmed that trend in their Joint White Paper for 'European Defence Readiness 2030', adopted on 19 March 2025,[79] providing a framework for the 'ReArm Europe' plan announced by the President of the Commission on 4 March 2025[80] and endorsed by the Extraordinary European Council of 6 March 2025. Explaining that "[r]egulatory simplification and harmonisation must focus both on rules and procedures that are specific to the defence sector, and on the impact on the defence industry of EU policies and regulations that are not defence-specific, but which impede the European defence technological and industrial base (EDTIB) from responding with maximum agility to the current heightened needs",[81] the Commission, first, has adopted, on 17 June 2025, a Defence Omnibus Simplification proposal, including the simplification of Directive 2009/81/EC (see the box below); and, secondly, will present another revision of that directive for 2026,[82] still in order to support the defence industry, to overcome the weaknesses identified (fragmentation, under-investment…), by taking into account the Competitiveness Compass[83] recommendation to introduce a European preference.[84]

---

79 Document JOIN(2025) 120 final.

80 See Press statement 25/673 by President von der Leyen on the defence package, on 4 March 2025.

81 See JOIN(2025) 120 final, p. 9.

82 It should be noted that the Commission work programme 2025 has already announced an overall evaluation of the Public Procurement Directives for the third quarter of 2025. See Annex II to the Commission work programme 2025, *Moving forward together: A Bolder, Simpler, Faster Union*, document COM(2025) 45 final, 11 February 2025.

83 See Commission Communication, *A Competitiveness Compass for the EU*, document COM(2025) 30 final, 30 January 2025.

84 See JOIN(2025) 120 final, p. 13. The report by Mario Draghi to the European Commission on *The future of European competitiveness*, issued on 9 September 2024, recommends to 'introduc[ing] a reinforced European preference principle and substantive incentive mechanisms to valorise European defence solutions and excellence over non-EU solutions' (see Part B| In-depth analysis and recommendations, p. 169).

Postscript, October 2025

In its communication *Defence Readiness Omnibus* adopted on 17 June 2025,[85] the European Commission put forward simplification proposals in defence-specific legislation and programmes, as well as in non-defence-specific laws to remove regulatory barriers and facilitate EU defence readiness and industrial buildup. One of these proposals is about amending Directive 2009/81/EC.[86] As explained in the proposal, the main amendments would be the following:

- The thresholds of Directive 2009/81/EC will be raised to enable Member States to focus on critical contracts and reduce the administrative burden on the industry for smaller procurement procedures. The current threshold for supply and service contracts (€443,000) will be replaced by €900,000, and the one for works contracts (€5,538,000) by €7 million.
- The open procedure and dynamic purchasing system, based on Directive 2014/24 will be introduced to enhance the range of tools at the disposal of the Member States.
- A modified and more flexible innovation partnership procedure will be introduced, based on Directive 2014/24, to support the procurement of innovative solutions.
- A simplified procedure will be introduced for the direct procurement of innovative products or services that result from competitive parallel research and development projects.
- A temporary derogation will be introduced to allow Member States to use the negotiated procedure without prior publication for common procurements, including off-the-shelf procurement. This will be available for the procurement of identical defence products or products subject only to minor modifications conducted by at least three Member States.
- The provisions related to Member States joining cooperative programmes based on R&D, after the end of the R&D phase, will be codified in Directive 2009/81/EC.
- The rules governing framework procurement agreements will be clarified, and the maximum duration of a framework agreement will be extended from 7 to 10 years.
- The statistical reporting obligations related to defence procurement will be reduced to ease the administrative burden for Member States.

---

85 European Commission, Communication, *Defence Readiness Omnibus*, COM(2025)820 final, 17 June 2025.

86 European Commission, Proposal for a Directive of the European Parliament and of the Council amending Directives 2009/43/EC and 2009/81/EC, as regards the simplification of intra-EU transfers of defence-related products and the simplification of security and defence procurement, COM(2025)823 final, 17 June 2025.

Besides, in their joint communication of 16 October 2025 named 'Preserving Peace – Defence Readiness Roadmap 2030',[87] the European Commission and the High Representative announced an evaluation of the Directive 2009/81/EC by end 2026, paving the way to a review of the text. See also: Commission work programme 2026, 'Europe's Independence Moment', of 21 October 2025.[88]

[87] JOIN(2025) 27 final.
[88] COM(2025)870 final.

ARTICLES 101 TO 109 TFEU: WHEN COMPETITION LAW ENTERS THE DEFENCE SECTOR

Renaud Bellais

PhD in economics and associate researcher at ENSTA Bretagne and CESICE, Grenoble Alpes University

and

Stéphane Rodrigues

Senior Lecturer at the Université Paris 1 Panthéon-Sorbonne
Member of the Sorbonne Institute for Research in International and European Law (IREDIES-EA 4536)
Member of the Brussels Bar

Article 101

1. The following shall be prohibited as incompatible with the internal market: all agreements between undertakings, decisions by associations of undertakings and concerted practices which may affect trade between Member States and which have as their object or effect the prevention, restriction or distortion of competition within the internal market, and in particular those which:

a) directly or indirectly fix purchase or selling prices or any other trading conditions;

b) limit or control production, markets, technical development, or investment;

c) share markets or sources of supply;

d) apply dissimilar conditions to equivalent transactions with other trading parties, thereby placing them at a competitive disadvantage;

e) make the conclusion of contracts subject to acceptance by the other parties of supplementary obligations which, by their nature or according to commercial usage, have no connection with the subject of such contracts.

2. Any agreements or decisions prohibited pursuant to this Article shall be automatically void.

3. The provisions of paragraph 1 may, however, be declared inapplicable in the case of:

– any agreement or category of agreements between undertakings,

– any decision or category of decisions by associations of undertakings,

– any concerted practice or category of concerted practices,

which contributes to improving the production or distribution of goods or to promoting technical or economic progress, while allowing consumers a fair share of the resulting benefit, and which does not:

a) impose on the undertakings concerned restrictions which are not indispensable to the attainment of these objectives;

b) afford such undertakings the possibility of eliminating competition in respect of a substantial part of the products in question.

Article 102

Any abuse by one or more undertakings of a dominant position within the internal market or in a substantial part of it shall be prohibited as incompatible with the internal market in so far as it may affect trade between Member States.

Such abuse may, in particular, consist in:

a) directly or indirectly imposing unfair purchase or selling prices or other unfair trading conditions;

b) limiting production, markets or technical development to the prejudice of consumers;

c) applying dissimilar conditions to equivalent transactions with other trading parties, thereby placing them at a competitive disadvantage;

d) making the conclusion of contracts subject to acceptance by the other parties of supplementary obligations which, by their nature or according to commercial usage, have no connection with the subject of such contracts.

Article 103

The appropriate regulations or directives to give effect to the principles set out in Articles 101 and 102 shall be laid down by the Council, on a proposal from the Commission and after consulting the European Parliament.

1. The regulations or directives referred to in paragraph 1 shall be designed in particular:

a) to ensure compliance with the prohibitions laid down in Article 101(1) and in Article 102 by making provision for fines and periodic penalty payments;

b) to lay down detailed rules for the application of Article 101(3), taking into account the need to ensure effective supervision on the one hand, and to simplify administration to the greatest possible extent on the other;

c) to define, if need be, in the various branches of the economy, the scope of the provisions of Articles 101 and 102;

d) to define the respective functions of the Commission and of the Court of Justice of the European Union in applying the provisions laid down in this paragraph;

e) to determine the relationship between national laws and the provisions contained in this Section or adopted pursuant to this Article.

Article 104

Until the entry into force of the provisions adopted in pursuance of Article 103, the authorities in Member States shall rule on the admissibility of agreements, decisions and concerted practices and on abuse of a dominant position in the internal market in accordance with the law of their country and with the provisions of Article 101, in particular paragraph 3, and of Article 102.

Article 105

1. Without prejudice to Article 104, the Commission shall ensure the application of the principles laid down in Articles 101 and 102. On application by a Member State or on its own initiative, and in cooperation with the competent authorities in the Member States, which shall give it their assistance, the Commission shall investigate cases of suspected infringement of these principles. If it finds that there has been an infringement, it shall propose appropriate measures to bring it to an end.

2. If the infringement is not brought to an end, the Commission shall record such infringement of the principles in a reasoned decision. The Commission may publish its decision and authorise Member States to take the measures, the conditions and details of which it shall determine, needed to remedy the situation.

3. The Commission may adopt regulations relating to the categories of agreement in respect of which the Council has adopted a regulation or a directive pursuant to Article 103(2)(b).

Article 106

1. In the case of public undertakings and undertakings to which Member States grant special or exclusive rights, Member States shall neither enact nor maintain in force any measure contrary to the rules contained in the Treaties, in particular to those rules provided for in Article 18 and Articles 101 to 109.

2. Undertakings entrusted with the operation of services of general economic interest or having the character of a revenue-producing monopoly shall be subject to the rules contained in the Treaties, in particular to the rules on competition, in so far as the application of such rules does not obstruct the performance, in law or in fact, of the particular tasks assigned to them. The development of trade must not be affected to such an extent as would be contrary to the interests of the Union.

3. The Commission shall ensure the application of the provisions of this Article and shall, where necessary, address appropriate directives or decisions to Member States.

Article 107

1. Save as otherwise provided in the Treaties, any aid granted by a Member State or through State resources in any form whatsoever which distorts or threatens to distort competition by favouring certain undertakings or the production of certain goods shall, in so far as it affects trade between Member States, be incompatible with the internal market.

a) aid granted to the economy of certain areas of the Federal Republic of Germany affected by the division of Germany, in so far as such aid is required in order to compensate for the economic disadvantages caused by that division. Five years after the entry into force of the Treaty of Lisbon, the Council, acting on a proposal from the Commission, may adopt a decision repealing this point.

2. The following may be considered to be compatible with the internal market:

a) aid to promote the economic development of areas where the standard of living is abnormally low or where there is serious underemployment, and of the regions referred to in Article 349, in view of their structural, economic and social situation;

b) aid to promote the execution of an important project of common European interest or to remedy a serious disturbance in the economy of a Member State;

c) aid to facilitate the development of certain economic activities or of certain economic areas, where such aid does not adversely affect trading conditions to an extent contrary to the common interest;

d) aid to promote culture and heritage conservation where such aid does not affect trading conditions and competition in the Union to an extent that is contrary to the common interest;

e) such other categories of aid as may be specified by decision of the Council on a proposal from the Commission.

Article 108

1. The Commission shall, in cooperation with Member States, keep under constant review all systems of aid existing in those States. It shall propose to the latter any appropriate measures required by the progressive development or by the functioning of the internal market.

2. If, after giving notice to the parties concerned to submit their comments, the Commission finds that aid granted by a State or through State resources is not compatible with the internal market having regard to Article 107, or that such aid is being misused, it shall decide that the State concerned shall abolish or alter such aid within a period of time to be determined by the Commission.

If the State concerned does not comply with this decision within the prescribed time, the Commission or any other interested State may, in derogation from the provisions of Articles 258 and 259, refer the matter to the Court of Justice of the European Union direct.

On application by a Member State, the Council may, acting unanimously, decide that aid which that State is granting or intends to grant shall be considered to be compatible with the internal market, in derogation from the provisions of Article 107 or from the regulations provided for in Article 109, if such a decision is justified by exceptional circumstances. If, as regards the aid in question, the Commission has already initiated the procedure provided for in the first subparagraph of this paragraph, the fact that the State concerned has made its application to the Council shall have the effect of suspending that procedure until the Council has made its attitude known.

If, however, the Council has not made its attitude known within three months of the said application being made, the Commission shall give its decision on the case.

3. The Commission shall be informed, in sufficient time to enable it to submit its comments, of any plans to grant or alter aid. If it considers that any such plan is not compatible with the internal market having regard to Article 107, it shall without delay initiate the procedure provided for in paragraph 2. The Member State concerned shall not put its proposed measures into effect until this procedure has resulted in a final decision.

4. The Commission may adopt regulations relating to the categories of State aid that the Council has, pursuant to Article 109, determined may be exempted from the procedure provided for by paragraph 3 of this Article.

Article 109

The Council, on a proposal from the Commission and after consulting the European Parliament, may make any appropriate regulations for the application of Articles 107 and 108 and may in particular determine the conditions in which Article 108(3) shall apply and the categories of aid exempted from this procedure.

The establishment of an internal market is one of the objectives assigned to the European Union (see Article 3(3) of the Treaty on European Union, hereinafter 'TEU').[1] It includes 'a system ensuring that competition is not distorted' (see the preamble to Protocol No 27 on the internal market and competition, annexed to the TEU and to the Treaty on the Functioning of the European Union, hereinafter 'TFEU'). According to the case law, undistorted competition 'implies the existence on the market of *workable* competition, that is to say the degree of competition necessary to ensure the observance of the basic requirements and attainment of the objectives of the Treaty, in particular the creation of a single market achieving conditions similar to those of a domestic market'.[2]

To this end, common rules on competition are laid down by Articles 101 to 109 TFEU (within Chapter 1 of Title VII of Part Two of the TFEU), as part of the exercise of an exclusive competence conferred on the Union (see Article 3(1)(b) of the TFEU, which refers to 'the establishing of the competition rules necessary for the functioning of the internal market').

Apart from the case where the provisions of Article 346 TFEU apply,[3] the defence sector is not, *a priori,* exempt from the application of the competition rules laid down by the TFEU. Indeed, for the Commission, strengthening the internal market in defence clearly involves 'combating distortions of competition'.[4] Moreover, pursuant to case-law, the mere existence of sectoral rules (like regulations or directives adopted in the defence sector on Articles 114 or 173 TFEU, for example), in no way means that an anti-competitive conduct in this sector is re-exempted from the competition rules laid down by the Treaties, irrespective of whether or not those sectoral rules are applicable to those conducts.[5]

The competition's common rules are of two kinds: on the one hand, those applicable to undertakings (Articles 101 to 106 TFEU) discussed in Section I below, and, on the other, those relating to aid granted by Member States (Articles 107 to 109 TFEU), examined in Section II. In addition, there is a specific regime for undertakings entrusted with the operation of services of general economic interest (hereinafter 'SGEIs'), Section III.

---

1 See the commentary on Article 114 TFEU by S.Rodrigues in this publication.

2 To this effect: Case 26-76, *Metro v Commission*, ECLI:EU:C:1977:167, para. 20.

3 See commentary on Article 346 TFEU.

4 Commission Communication of 24 July 2013, entitled 'Towards a more competitive and efficient defence and security sector': COM(2013) 542 final, spec. p. 7.

5 See, by analogy: Case C-220/24, *Aeroportul Internaţional 'Avram Iancu' Cluj*, ECLI:EU:C:2025:124, para. 27, referring to sectoral rules related to air transport.

I. COMPETITION RULES APPLICABLE TO COMPANIES IN THE DEFENCE SECTOR[6]

Insofar as a player in the defence sector is likely to qualify as an undertaking within the meaning of Articles 101 and 102 TFEU (Section A), it must comply with the prohibitions laid down by these provisions (Section B), on pain of prosecution and sanctions by the European Commission (Section C), and must also submit to the merger control regime (Section D).

A. QUALIFICATION AS A COMPANY UNDER THE COMPETITION RULES

The concept of an undertaking is central to the application of the competition rules. However, the drafters of the Treaties did not provide any definition. It therefore fell to the Court to do so. According to a now well-established formula, an 'undertaking' within the meaning of Articles 101 and 102 TFEU (as indeed within the meaning of Article 107 TFEU, see below) is as 'every entity engaged in an economic activity, regardless of the legal status of the entity and the way in which it is financed',[7] it being specified that this involves 'carrying on economic activities of an industrial or commercial nature by offering goods or services on the market'.[8]

Exclusion from the scope of economic activities therefore allows for exclusion from classification as an undertaking, and hence from the competition rules. In this respect, it is clear from the Court's case law that two broad categories of activities can be considered non-economic: on the one hand, those involving the exercise of an 'exclusively social function'[9] and, on the other, those involving 'the exercise of powers relating to [...] control and supervision [...] which are typically those of a public authority'.[10]

In the light of this legal framework, the question of the applicability of the competition rules to players in the defence sector does not arise so much for private companies operating in this sector as for certain public bodies,

---

6 On these rules, see D. Bosco and C. Prieto, *Traité de droit européen de la concurrence. Ententes, abus de position dominante. Concentrations*, Brussels, Bruylant, 2024.

7 To this end, see Case C-41/90, *Klaus Höfner*, ECLI:EU:C:1991:161, para. 21.

8 See Case 118/85, *Commission of the European Communities v Italian Republic*, ECLI:EU:C:1987:283, para. 7.

9 See Joined Cases C-159/91 and 160/91, *Poucet and Pistre*, ECLI:EU:C:1993:63, para. 18. It should be noted that the absence of a profit motive is not sufficient to deprive an entity of its status as an undertaking within the meaning of the competition rules of the Treaty: see Case C-67/96, *Albany*, ECLI:EU:C:1999:430, para. 85, concerning a sectoral pension fund benefiting military personnel in particular.

10 See Case C-364/92, *SAT Fluggesellschaft v Eurocontrol*, ECLI:EU:C:1994:7, para. 30.

such as France's Directorate General for Armaments (Direction Générale de l'Armement, DGA). By way of analogy, reference may be made to Case C-118/85 *Commission v Italy,*[11] in which the *Amministrazione autonoma dei monopoli di Stato* was classified as a (public) undertaking because it was involved in an economic activity consisting of offering goods and services on the market in the manufactured tobacco sector, irrespective of the fact that it did not have a legal personality separate from that of the State.

The question may also arise for internal government industrial activities that are contracted out: e.g. part of the maintenance of military aircraft and helicopters in France, carried out by the Ateliers industriels de l'aéronautique, which is part of the Service Industriel de l'Aéronautique (SIAé) of the French Ministry of Defence. The exclusive relationship with the State could be considered as unfair competition and constitute an undue monopoly in relation to private French and European companies capable of offering similar services, at least for some of the activities concerned, although it is difficult to separate these from the operational dimensions that may therefore be covered by Article 346 of the TFEU.

B. PROHIBITION OF ANTI-COMPETITIVE AGREEMENTS AND OF DOMINANT POSITION ABUSE

Two types of conduct by undertakings are prohibited by the TFEU: anti-competitive agreements (Section 1) and dominant position abuse (Section 2).

1. Prohibition of Anti-Competitive Agreements (Article 101 TFEU)

The first paragraph of Article 101 TFEU describes the conditions constituting an infringement of the prohibition of anti-competitive conduct (a). The third paragraph of the article provides for derogations allowing undertakings to enter certain agreements (b).

a. – Conditions of the Offence

Three conditions must be met cumulatively for an infringement of Article 101 TFEU to occur.

Firstly, it is necessary to identify an agreement (written or verbal) between undertakings, a decision by associations of undertakings,[12] or a so-called

[11] See Case 118/85, *Commission of the European Communities v Italian Republic,* ECLI:EU:C:1987:283.

[12] Such as a sports federation: Case C-214/21 P, *International Skating Union v Commission,* ECLI:EU:C:2023:1012, para. 93.

concerted practice between undertakings each enjoying genuine commercial autonomy.[13]

Secondly, this conduct must actually or potentially affect trade between Member States,[14] even if it only concerns the territory of a single State (restriction of access to that territory), or even if the undertakings involved are established outside the territory of the European Union, in the application of the so-called internal effect rule, and in compliance with the principle of territoriality of international public law.[15]

Thirdly, the conduct in question must have the aim or effect of restricting competition. Certain cases are described in Article 101(1) TFEU by way of illustration: price fixing, restrictions on production, market sharing, inequality of trading conditions, bundling of services, etc. The Court's interpretation of this criterion is particularly wide-ranging: 'In order to decide whether an agreement is to be considered as prohibited by reason of the distortion of competition which is its object or effect, it is necessary to examine the competition within the actual context in which it would occur in the absence of the agreement in dispute'.[16] It is therefore essential to look at the evidence of a loss of autonomy on the part of the players and the real impact of their agreement on the market. It should be added that the Commission has identified reference thresholds (in terms of market share) below which an agreement may be considered to be of 'minor importance' which does not appreciably restrict competition:[17] for example, when the combined market share held by the parties to the agreement does not exceed 10% on any of the relevant markets affected by the agreement between competitors, or 15% in the case of an agreement between non-competitors.

b. – Derogations (outside the SGEI regime)

Article 101(3) TFEU provides that a cartel may be deemed to comply with Union law if it contributes to improving the production or distribution of goods or to promoting economic progress, 'while allowing consumers a fair share of the resulting benefit'.

However, two conditions must be met cumulatively: firstly, the cartel must not 'impose on the undertakings concerned restrictions which are not

---

13 See Case T-325/01, *Daimler Chrysler*, ECLI:EU:T:2005:322, para. 88.

14 On this criterion: Commission Communication, Guidelines on the effect on trade concept contained in Articles 81 and 82 of the Treaty, [2004] *OJ* C101/81.

15 See Joined Cases C-89/85, C-104/85, C-114/85, C-116/85, C-117/85 and C-125/85 to C-129/85, *Ahlström Osakeyhtiö and Others v Commission*, ECLI:EU:C:1988:447, paras. 16–18.

16 See Case 99/79 *SA Lancôme v Etos*, ECLI:EU:C:1980:193, para. 24.

17 Commission – Notice on agreements of minor importance which do not appreciably restrict competition within the meaning of Article 101(1) of the Treaty on the Functioning of the European Union (de Minimis Notice), [2014] *OJ* C291/1.

indispensable to the attainment of these objectives'; secondly, it must not 'afford such undertakings the possibility of eliminating competition in respect of a substantial part of the products in question'.

In practice, these conditions establish a 'cost-benefit' balance of the cartel, in the sense that the 'improvement must in particular show appreciable objective advantages of such a character as to compensate for the disadvantages which they cause in the field of competition'.[18]

In the area of defence, the evolution of the European Union's position on the concept of strategic autonomy since 2016 could lead to the justification of certain industrial concentration decisions to guarantee the security of supply. Indeed, armaments-related production depends on niche markets that do not necessarily guarantee the sustainability of these activities based on national markets alone, even though they may be essential to strategic autonomy. In addition, a multiplication of production units in Europe can lead to a volume of activity below the viability threshold for each of them.

Given changes in the quantities produced and the costs associated with innovation and dedicated industrial facilities, grouping together companies from different countries may be the necessary condition to ensure the sustainability of the corresponding supplies (sometimes with specialisation in centres of excellence between different countries to achieve the minimum critical size), at the risk of eventually depending on a supplier from outside the EU.

The creation of the company MBDA illustrates this approach through a Franco-British concentration of missile activities, made necessary by a collapse in orders in the 1990s and by the growing cost of missile development. This was particularly so for the Scalp EG/Storm Shadow cruise missiles, whose development was becoming incompatible with the budgetary resources of France or the United Kingdom alone.[19] At the time, the companies involved in the creation of MBDA held the largest market share in Europe.

Similarly, the question may arise with the creation of KNDS by the merger of Nexter (France) and KMW (Germany) in battle tanks or that of Naviris between Naval Group (France) and Fincantieri (Italy) in surface ships, even if the market power of the entities thus created is less than that of MBDA on a European scale.

However, the legitimacy of the strategic autonomy argument and the scope of activities that may be eligible have yet to be clarified. For example, in September 2023, the European Commission imposed a fine of €1.2 million on Diehl (Germany) and RUAG (Switzerland) under Article 101 of the TFEU.[20] For fourteen years, the two companies had colluded to share the European hand grenade market.

---

18 See Joined Cases 56/64 and 58/64, *Consten and Grundig*, p. 502 of the 1966 ECR.

19 R. Bellais, 'MBDA's Industrial Model and European Defence' (2022) 33(7) *Defence and Peace Economics*, pp. 876–893.

20 https://ec.europa.eu/commission/presscorner/detail/fr/ip_23_4531.

To obtain an exemption on this basis, the first Regulation of 1962 laying down detailed rules for the application of former Articles 85 and 86 of the EC Treaty (now Articles 101 and 102 of the TFEU)[21] provided for a procedure of prior notification of draft agreements to the Commission. This was replaced on 1 May 2004 by a system of legal exceptions.[22] The Commission no longer has exclusive competence to apply Article 101(3) TFEU, the direct effect of which is recognised, leading to a 'decentralisation' of its provisions in favour of the competent courts of the Member States and the national competition authorities, which are now called upon to cooperate within a European Competition Network (ECN).[23]

This reform has been accompanied by a strengthening of the Commission's powers of investigation and sanction (see below) and by a development of block exemptions adopted by the Commission based on an authorisation from the Council, pursuant to Article 103 TFEU. These exemptions are laid down in regulations and describe the conditions to be met before Article 101(1) TFEU can be declared inapplicable to certain types of agreements or cartels.

For example, reference may be made to Commission Regulation (EU) No 316/2014 on certain categories of technology transfer agreements,[24] Commission Regulation (EU) 2022/720 on certain categories of vertical agreements and concerted practices,[25] or Commission Regulations (EU) 2023/1066 and 2023/1067 on certain categories of research and development agreements respectively,[26] and on specialisation agreements.[27]

---

21 Council Regulation (EEC) No 17/62 implementing Articles 85 and 86 of the Treaty, [1962] *OJ* 13//204.

22 Council Regulation (EC) No 1/2003 of 16 December 2002 on the implementation of the rules on competition laid down in Articles 81 and 82 of the Treaty, [2003] *OJ* L1/1. See also: Commission Notice, Guidelines on the application of Article 81(3) of the Treaty, [2004] *OJ* C101/97.

23 See also: Commission Notice on cooperation within the Network of Competition Authorities, [2004] *OJ* C101/43, and Commission Notice on cooperation between the Commission and the national courts in applying Articles 81 and 82 of the EC Treaty, [2004] *OJ* C101/54. See also: Directive (EU) 2019/1 of the European Parliament and of the Council of 11 December 2018 to empower Member States' competition authorities to enforce competition rules more effectively and to ensure the proper functioning of the internal market, [2019] *OJ* L11/3.

24 Commission Regulation (EU) No 316/2014 of 21 March 2014 on the application of Article 101(3) of the Treaty on the Functioning of the European Union to categories of technology transfer agreements, [2014] *OJ* L93/17.

25 Commission Regulation (EU) 2022/720 of 10 May 2022 on the application of Article 101(3) of the Treaty on the Functioning of the European Union to categories of vertical agreements and concerted practices, [2022] *OJ* L134/4.

26 Commission Regulation (EU) 2023/1066 of 1 June 2023 on the application of Article 101(3) of the Treaty on the Functioning of the European Union to certain categories of research and development agreements, [2023] *OJ* L143/9.

27 Commission Regulation (EU) 2023/1067 of 1 June 2023 on the application of Article 101(3) of the Treaty on the Functioning of the European Union to certain categories of specialisation agreements, [2023] *OJ* L143/20.

2. *Prohibition of Abuse of a Dominant Position (Article 102 TFEU)*

The first paragraph of Article 102 TFEU prohibits 'abuse by one or more undertakings of a dominant position within the internal market or in a substantial part of it'. The same indicative list of examples of anti-competitive agreements (see above) is used to illustrate cases of abuse of a dominant position.[28]

The case law test highlights the dual criterion of dominance and dependence: 'An abuse may be committed if an undertaking in a dominant position strengthens that position to such an extent that the degree of dominance thus achieved substantially hampers competition, i.e. leaves only undertakings whose conduct is dependent on the dominant undertaking'.[29]

Several undertakings may be considered to be responsible for an abuse of a dominant position. This is referred to as collective dominance.[30]

The Commission and the European Court of Justice use a range of indicators to identify abusive situations of domination. The most common is market share. However, other factors may also be taken into account, such as the fact that the undertaking is a 'benchmark' undertaking or exercises economic power, enabling it to 'behave to an appreciable extent independently of its competitors, customers and, ultimately, consumers'.[31]

But infringement of Article 102 TFEU also presupposes that the identified abuse affects trade between Member States. The identification of the relevant reference market is therefore crucial, in order to take account of the degree of substitutability in the eyes of consumers, both from the point of view of the product and the geography of the market.[32]

In this respect, the relevant market in the defence industry sector is not always easy to identify. This is due in particular to the fact that this sector has atypical economic characteristics both on the demand side (with the frequent existence of monopsony and significant countervailing buying power) and on the supply side (with the existence of restricted oligopolies and high barriers to entry).[33]

---

28 See also: Communication from the Commission, 'Guidance on the Commission's enforcement priorities in applying Article 82 of the EC Treaty to abusive exclusionary conduct by dominant undertakings', [2009] *OJ* C45/7.

29 See Case 6/72, *Europemballage Corporation and Continental Can Company v Commission*, ECLI:EU:C:1973:22, p. 247 of the 1973 ECR.

30 See Case 30/87, *Corine Bodson v Pompes funèbres des régions libérées*, ECLI:EU:C:1988:225, paras. 26–29.

31 See Case 27/76, *United Brands v Commission* (so-called 'Chiquita bananas' case), ECLI:EU:C:1978:22, para. 65.

32 On this concept see the Commission Notice on the definition of the relevant market for the purposes of Union competition law, C/2023/6789, [2024] *OJ* C2024/1645.

33 In this sense: G. Arnoux, *Le droit européen de la concurrence et l'industrie de la défense*, PhD thesis, Université Paris 1 Panthéon-Sorbonne, 2011, spec. pp. 394–418.

If the scope of the arms markets is defined *de facto* on a national and not a European basis, we can speak of thwarted monopolies for companies in the sector, since States can decide to open up to competition from European and above all non-European companies. Their apparent dominant position, resulting from industrial consolidation since the 1990s, depends in fact on the goodwill of the monopsony through the use it can make of Directive 2009/81/EC or, more often, of Article 346 of the TFEU.[34] This is particularly the case when a country opts for over-the-counter negotiations with a third country, notably in the context of an FMS contract (*Foreign Military Sales*) with the United States.

While MBDA had a monopoly on the anti-tank missile segment in France, in 2009 the DGA decided to put its Milan ER offer in competition with the Spike from Rafael (Israel) and the Javelin from Raytheon (USA). This led to the decision to acquire Javelins, which were produced in the United States.[35] The concept of a dominant position must therefore be approached with caution in the arms sector, given the legal levers available to governments to redefine the economic contours of the market when awarding a public contract.

C. PROSECUTION AND PENALTIES FOR BREACHES OF COMPETITION RULES

For cartels prohibited by Article 101 TFEU, the second paragraph of this provision provides for a strict sanction: the automatic nullity of the agreement.

Secondary legislation, in particular Regulation (EC) No 1/2003,[36] also gives the Commission the power to impose financial penalties on undertakings that infringe Articles 101 and 102 of the TFEU.

This power to impose sanctions is generally exercised during or at the end of an investigation procedure initiated by the Commission, either on its own initiative or following a complaint from a third party (very often a competitor of the targeted company or companies).[37] The powers of investigation are wide-ranging: requests for information, hearings, on-site visits (business premises

---

34 Even if some authors mention 'the absence of impact of the defence exception on the applicability of Articles 101 and 102 TFEU on the defence industry' (see G. Arnoux, *Le droit européen de la concurrence et l'industrie de la défense*, *ibid.*, spec. p. 136).

35 https://www.opex360.com/2009/10/23/larmee-de-terre-fait-le-choix-du-missile-javelin.

36 See also: Commission Regulation (EC) No 773/2004 of 7 April 2004 relating to the conduct of proceedings by the Commission pursuant to Articles 81 and 82 of the EC Treaty, [2004] *OJ* L123/18 and Commission notice on best practices for the conduct of proceedings concerning Articles 101 and 102 of the TFEU, OJ C308/6.

37 See the Commission notice on the handling of complaints lodged under Articles 81 and 82 of the EC Treaty, OJ C101/65.

and the homes of management staff),[38] filing under seals, seizure of any data medium, etc. In the event of obstruction of the investigation or a procedural incident, fines may be imposed up to a maximum of 1% of the turnover of the company in question, as well as periodic penalty payments up to a maximum of 5% of turnover.[39] These sanctions may be accompanied by interim measures.

In the interests of legal certainty, the Commission has adopted guidelines on settlement measures[40] and the calculation of fines.[41] While recognising that the Commission is free to increase the level of fines 'in order to reinforce their deterrent effect',[42] the European Court of Justice may be called upon to exercise full jurisdiction under Article 31 of Regulation 1/2003, which empowers it, in addition to simply reviewing the legality of the penalty, to substitute its assessment for that of the Commission and, consequently, 'to cancel, reduce or increase the fine imposed where the question of the amount of the fine is before it'.[43]

It should be noted that in September 2023, the Commission sanctioned for the first time a cartel in the defence sector, and imposed a fine on Diehl of EUR 1.2 million for participating in a cartel concerning the sale of military hand grenades together with its competitor RUAG. RUAG was not fined as it revealed the cartel to the Commission under the leniency programme. The Commission found that the companies split national markets across the EEA between themselves during almost 14 years. Both companies admitted their involvement in the cartel and agreed to settle the case.[44]

---

38 On 23 November 2021, the Commission announced that it had carried out unannounced inspections at the premises of a company in the defence sector, on suspicion of a cartel, but without any further details: see press release IP/21/6241 of 23 November 2021.

39 See, for example, Commission press release IP/23/4531 of 21 September 2023, 'Antitrust: Commission fines defence company €1.2 million cartel settlement' (Case AT.40760).

40 Commission Notice on the conduct of settlement procedures in view of the adoption of decisions pursuant to Article 7 and Article 23 of Council Regulation (EC) No 1/2003 in cartel cases, [2008] *OJ* C167/1.

41 Guidelines on the method of setting fines imposed pursuant to Article 23(2)(a) of Regulation (EC) No 1/2003, [2006] *OJ* C210/2. See also: Commission Notice on immunity from fines and reduction of fines in cartel cases, *[2006] OJ* C298/17.

42 See Case T-203/01, *Michelin v Commission*, ECLI:EU:T:2003:250, para. 254.

43 See Joined Cases T-117/07 and T-121/07, *Areva and Others* and *Alstom v European Commission*, ECLI:EU:T:2011:69, para. 318 and the case law cited.

44 See Annex to the Commission's report on Competition Policy 2023, SWD(2024) 53 final of 6 March 2024, p. 14.

D. PREVENTIVE MERGER CONTROL[45]

Based on the principle that prevention is better than cure, in 1989 the Commission obtained a mandate from the Council to monitor certain mergers, which could lead to abuse of a dominant position.[46] Since then, the system has been based on Regulation 139/2004Council which came into force on 1 May 2004.[47]

The basic rule is that prior notification to the Commission is compulsory for mergers with a 'Community dimension', irrespective of the nationality of the undertakings involved and the location of the activities forming the subject of the merger.[48]

Three types of concentration are concerned: i) a merger between undertakings, ii) the acquisition of a holding by one undertaking in order to acquire control of another undertaking, and iii) the creation of a joint venture (which to perform 'on a lasting basis all the functions of an autonomous economic entity', as specified in Article 3(4) of the 2004 merger Regulation).

To define the Community dimension of the operation, reference must be made to thresholds (see Article 1 of the 2004 Regulation): i.e. primarily a worldwide turnover of more than €5 billion for all the undertakings concerned, it being understood that at least two of these undertakings have an individual turnover in the European Union of more than €250 million, unless each of the undertakings concerned achieves more than two-thirds of its total turnover in the European Union within one and the same Member State.[49]

Once notified, the proposed concentration is suspended until the Commission, subject to certain deadlines (which vary according to the

45 See the 'Mergers' section of Regulation (EU) 2022/2560 of the European Parliament and of the Council of 14 December 2022 on foreign subsidies distorting the internal market, in [2022] *OJ* L330/1. See A. Reindl and I. Van Damme, 'The EU Foreign Subsidies Regulation', *Concurrences*, 2024, spec. pp. 73–110 and V. Carvalho and E. Tricot, 'Contrôle des concentrations d'entreprises: comment anticiper le contrôle des subventions étrangères?', *Dictionnaire permanent – Droit européen des affaires*, bulletin n° 416, November 2023, pp. 1–3.

46 Council Regulation (EEC) No 4064/89 of 21 December 1989 on the control of concentrations between undertakings, [1989] *OJ* L395/1.

47 Council Regulation (EC) No 139/2004 of 20 January 2004 on the control of concentrations between undertakings, [2004] *OJ* L24/1. See also: Commission Implementing Regulation (EU) 2023/914 of 20 April 2023 implementing Council Regulation (EC) No 139/2004 on the control of concentrations between undertakings and repealing Commission Regulation (EC) No 802/2004, [2023] *OJ* L119/22, and Codified Jurisdictional Notice of the Commission on Council Regulation (EC) No 139/2004 on the control of concentrations between undertakings, [2008] *OJ* C95/1.

48 See Case T-102/96, *Gencor v Commission*, ECLI:EU:T:1999:65, para. 74.

49 Note: these thresholds are reduced to €2.5 billion and €100 million respectively if, in at least three Member States, the individual turnover of at least two companies exceeds €25 million and the individual EU turnover of at least two companies exceeds €100 million.

simplified or non-simplified nature of the procedure chosen),[50] and, in general, after consulting interested third parties (notified by means of a notice published in the OJ),[51] adopts a decision on whether or not to authorise the operation: it is understood that in practice the most common case is of authorisation subject to conditions. The undertakings concerned give commitments which the Commission considers necessary to ensure that there will be no significant impediment to 'impede effective competition in the common market or in a substantial part of it, in particular as a result of the creation or strengthening of a dominant position' (Art. 2 of the 2004 regulation). Thus, for example, a commitment may consist of the sale of assets to competitors or a withdrawal from certain segments of the market(s) concerned.[52]

To guide the Commission's analysis, the proper definition of the relevant market or the market in question is a necessary prerequisite for assessing the effects on competition of a merger.[53] It follows in particular from the case law that 'the market in the products affected by the merger must take account of the overall economic context so as to make it possible to assess the actual economic power of the undertaking or undertakings in question and, for that purpose, it is necessary first to define the products which, although incapable of being substituted for other products, are sufficiently interchangeable with the undertaking's own products, both as regards their objective characteristics and the competitive conditions and the structure of supply and demand on the market'.[54] The degree of competition existing in the relevant market at the time a merger is notified is therefore a decisive factor in determining whether a situation of collective dominance has arisen, particularly if there is stable demand with low volatility.

By way of example, reference is made to two recent Commission decisions applying the 2004 Regulation in the defence sector. The first decision, adopted on 22 December 2022, unconditionally authorised the acquisition of joint control of Aubert & Duval (specialising in high-end metallurgical products, including forged bars and powders) by the consortium formed by Airbus,

---

50 See Commission Notice on simplified treatment of certain concentrations under Council Regulation (EC) No 139/2004 on the control of concentrations between undertakings, [2023] *OJ* C160/1.

51 See for example, prior notification of a concentration, Case M.12130 – JOHN COCKERILL DEFENSE / FN HERSTAL / THALES / LS2, as published in *OJ* C/2025/6767 of 22 December 2025.

52 See Communication from the Commission on remedies acceptable under Council Regulation (EC) No 139/2004 and under Commission Regulation (EC) No 802/2004, [2008] *OJ* C267/1.

53 See Commission notice on the definition of relevant market for the purposes of Community competition law, [1997] *OJ* C372/5.

54 See Case T-342/99, *Airtours v Commission*, ECLI:EU:T:2002:146, para. 20.

Safran and Tikehau Ace Capital (TAC) France.[55] The Commission concluded that there was no risk of 'foreclosure' of customers for forged fuselage and wing parts, or for certain parts or infrastructures in the space sector.

The other decision, dated 22 December 2023, authorised the acquisition of joint control of Jeumont Electric's military activities by Framatome SAS and Naval Group SA (all three being based in France), and the acquisition of sole control of Jeumont Electric's other activities by Framatome SAS. The Commission considered that the transaction would have a limited impact on competition on the markets where the companies are active, namely the design of electrical equipment used for power generation or in the defence sector, for the propulsion and power supply of submarines and surface ships. As it pointed out: 'Although the transaction gives rise to several vertical links [...] (i) Jeumont's market share remains limited; (ii) many alternative suppliers will remain active; and (iii) Framatome and Naval Group account for only a small share of demand for this type of equipment'.[56]

The difficulty in the armaments sector stems from the fact that a large number of companies are not exclusively dependent on this sector, but are dual-use companies in the sense that they operate simultaneously in the military and civil markets. This intersection of markets and product portfolios is reinforced by the technical proximity of products on these two markets, and even the existence of common platforms that can be militarised.

In the helicopter sector, for example, the Guépard Light Utility Helicopter (HIL) programme, launched in 2017 by the French Defence Ministry, is a military adaptation of the Airbus Helicopters H160, a purely civilian programme. Eurocopter had already won the tender for the United States Army Light Utility Helicopter in 2006 with its UH-72 Lakota project, which is a militarised derivative of the EC145. Its main competitor, Leonardo Helicopters (formerly Agusta Westland), also offers such military derivatives.

While these mergers between civil and military activities allow for economies of scale and scope, they also blur market boundaries and create overlapping powers for the authorities. On the one hand, the European Commission considers itself legitimate to control mergers that have an impact on civilian markets. On the other hand, Member States may consider that defence interests take precedence over competition law, in particular by invoking Article 346

55 Commission press release MEX/23/22 of 3 January 2023. The notification was published in the [2022] *OJ* C452/40, under reference M.10760. The authorisation decision is announced in the [2023] *OJ* C2023/1211.

56 Commission press release MEX/24/3 of 3 January 2024. The notification was published in the [2023] *OJ* C2023/1208, under reference M.11262.

TFEU.[57] Everything therefore depends on how the authorities approach this grey area when assessing proposed mergers.

II. RULES APPLICABLE TO STATE AID[58] IN THE DEFENCE SECTOR

Article 107 TFEU lays down the principle that State aid is incompatible with the internal market under certain conditions (Section A). There are, however, exceptions to this principle, from which the beneficiaries of such aid in the defence sector may seek to benefit (Section B). All of these rules are subject to guidance from the Commission (Section C).

A. PRINCIPLE OF INCOMPATIBILITY OF STATE AID WITH THE INTERNAL MARKET

Article 107 TFEU states that 'save as otherwise provided in the Treaties, any aid granted by a Member State or through State resources in any form whatsoever which distorts or threatens to distort competition shall, insofar as it affects trade between Member States, be incompatible with the internal market', by favouring certain undertakings or the production of certain goods.

In the light of established case law, it emerges that the classification of a measure as 'State aid' requires four conditions to be met cumulatively: 'there must, first, be an intervention by the State or through State resources; second, the intervention must be liable to affect trade between Member States; third, it must confer an advantage on the recipient; and fourth, it must distort or threaten to distort competition'.[59]

With regard to the first condition, only advantages granted directly or indirectly through State resources or constituting an additional burden for the State are to be considered as aid. It is therefore necessary to check whether there is a sufficiently direct link between the advantage granted to the beneficiary, on the one hand, and a reduction in the State budget, or even a sufficiently concrete economic risk of burdens being placed on it, on the other hand.

---

57 Even if, according to some authors, merger control is 'de facto freed from the defence exception' (G. Arnoux, *Le droit européen de la concurrence et l'industrie de la défense*, PhD thesis, Université Paris 1 Panthéon-Sorbonne, 2011, spec. p. 92).

58 On these rules, see: A. Cartier-Bresson, *Droit des aides publiques aux entreprises*, Thémis-Droit, Paris, PUF, 2020 and M. Karpenschif, *Manuel de droit européen des aides d'État*, 4th ed., Brussels, Bruylant, 2021.

59 See to this effect, for example, Case C-522/13, *Ministerio de Defensa and Navantia*, ECLI:EU:C:2014:2262, para. 20.

Thus, for example, a property tax exemption for a warship maintenance company introduced by a Member State at the request of its Ministry of Defence constitutes a public intervention which leads to the alleviation of a burden which should normally be borne by the costs of the undertaking, and, consequently, to a reduction in the budget of the public authority concerned.[60]

The second condition relating to the impact on trade between Member States is often analysed in conjunction with the fourth condition relating to the impact on competition. The European Court of Justice emphasises that it is not necessary to establish that the aid in question has an actual impact on trade between Member States and that competition is actually distorted, but only to examine whether the aid is likely to affect trade between Member States and distort competition; this is the case, in particular, where the aid in question strengthens the position of an undertaking compared with that of other undertakings competing in intra-Community trade, which must then be regarded as affected by the aid. Thus, in the *Navantia case*, cited above, the Court found that the shipbuilding sector was a market open to competition and trade between Member States, on which the undertaking benefiting from the tax exemption at issue was therefore in competition with other undertakings, as regards both its civil and military activities. In these circumstances, the exemption was considered 'liable to affect such trade and to distort competition' between Member States.[61]

As for the third condition, it implies the granting of an advantage to the beneficiary of the aid, which includes any intervention which, in whatever form, is likely to favour companies directly or indirectly, or which must be considered as an economic advantage that the beneficiary company would not have obtained under normal market conditions. Thus, for example, the property tax exemption enjoyed by a warship maintenance company has the effect of directly alleviating, without any other intervention being necessary, the charges which normally burden the costs of a company in an identical situation to its own. The exemption thus confers an economic advantage on the company in question.[62] However, this advantage must be selective and not the result of a general measure justified by the nature or general scheme of the system of charges to which it applies. In the aforementioned example of the property tax exemption, the Court held that such an exemption for State-owned property used for national defence purposes did not appear to be directly related to the objectives of the property tax itself.[63]

---

60 Ibid., para. 50.
61 Ibid., paras. 51–54.
62 Ibid., para. 26.
63 Ibid., para. 44.

In contrast, France's research tax credit (CIR) benefits defence companies, but is a general measure open to any company with eligible expenditure, regardless of nationality or the nature of its activities, operating in France.

B. DEROGATIONS FROM THE PRINCIPLE OF INCOMPATIBILITY (OUTSIDE THE SGEI REGIME)

Article 107 TFEU provides for two possible sources of derogation: i) certain categories of aid are considered to be compatible with the law as a whole; and ii) other aid may be considered to be compatible with the internal market on a case-by-case basis.

Article 107(2) TFEU therefore considers the following to be compatible: 'aid having a social character, granted to individual consumers, provided that it is granted without discrimination related to the origin of the products concerned'; 'aid to make good the damage caused by natural disasters or exceptional occurrences'; and 'aid granted to the economy of certain areas of the Federal Republic of Germany affected by the division of Germany, in so far as such aid is required in order to compensate for the economic disadvantages caused by that division'.

On the other hand, 'the following may be considered compatible with the internal market' under Article 107(3) TFEU: 'aid to promote the economic development of areas where the standard of living is abnormally low or where there is serious underemployment', and the outermost regions, 'in view of their structural, economic and social situation'; 'aid to promote the execution of an important project of common European interest or to remedy a serious disturbance in the economy of a Member State'; 'aid to facilitate the development of certain economic activities or of certain economic areas, where such aid does not adversely affect trading conditions to an extent contrary to the common interest'; 'aid to promote culture and heritage conservation where such aid does not affect trading conditions and competition in the Union to an extent contrary to the common interest'; while 'other categories of aid as may be specified by decision of the Council on a proposal from the Commission'. As far as the author is aware, no Council decision has yet been adopted in the field of defence.

In order to benefit from a derogation under Article 107(3) TFEU, State aid projects must be notified in advance to the European Commission, which will examine their compatibility with the internal market in order to authorise them, with or without conditions (see below). To simplify this procedure and in the interests of legal certainty, the Commission may be authorised by the Council to draw up exemption (notification) regulations for certain categories of State aid, specifying the conditions for compatibility. This is the purpose of Commission Regulation (EU) No 651/2014, known as the General Block

Exemption Regulation (or GBER).[64] The sixteen categories covered include, for example, aid for SMEs, environmental protection; research,[65] development and innovation,[66] training[67] and aid for local infrastructure or European territorial cooperation projects. All these categories can, *a priori,* be applied to the defence industry.

Reference should also be made to Commission Regulation (EU) 2023/2831 on the application of Articles 107 and 108 of the TFEU to *de minimis aid* ('*De Minimis* Regulation').[68] Pursuant to that regulation, aid granted by a Member State to a single undertaking of less than EUR 300,000 over a period of three fiscal years are considered as not meeting not all the criteria of Article 107(1) of the TFEU and therefore are not subject to the notification requirement laid down in Article 108(3) of the TFEU.[69] A similar regulation also applies to *de minimis* aid granted to an undertaking providing an SGEI: in this case, the reference threshold is raised to €750,000.[70]

C. THE COMMISSION'S POWERS UNDER STATE AID RULES

Pursuant to Article 108 TFEU, the Commission, together with the Member States, carries out an ongoing review of aid schemes existing in those States. As part of this review, it may find that aid is incompatible or is being misused. It will then invite the Member State concerned to abolish or amend the aid in question. It may also propose any appropriate measure required by the progressive development or functioning of the internal market.

---

[64] Commission Regulation (EU) No 651/2014 of 17 June 2014 declaring certain categories of aid compatible with the internal market in application of Articles 107 and 108 of the Treaty, [2014] *OJ* L187/1, as last amended by Commission Regulation (EU) 2023/1315 of 23 June 2023, [2023] *OJ* L167/1.

[65] See, on the basis of the regime prior to the 2014 GBER: Commission Decision 2008/806/EC of 12 March 2008 on a State aid scheme implemented by Italy for the aeronautical industry, including the defence contractor *Agusta Westland*, [2008] *OJ* L284/1.

[66] This category covers aid intended to co-finance of a research and development project financed by the European Defence Fund (FEDEF) or the European Defence Industrial Development Programme (EDIDP) (see Art. *25(6)* of Regulation (EU) 651/2014). See the commentary on Article 173 TFEU for a presentation of the FEDEF and the PEDID.

[67] For an application case under the regime prior to the 2014 GBER: notification XT 55/04 on the granting of training aid to *BAE Systems Marine Submarines*, [2005] *OJ* C270/39.

[68] Commission Regulation (EU) No 1407/2013 of 18 December 2013 on the application of Articles 107 and 108 of the Treaty on the Functioning of the European Union to aid *de minimis*, [2013] *OJ* L352/1.

[69] Commission Regulation (EU) 2023/2831 of 13 December 2023, [2023] *OJ* L2023/2831.

[70] Commission Regulation (EU) 2023/2832 of 13 December 2023 on the application of Articles 107 and 108 of the Treaty on the Functioning of the European Union to *de minimis aid* granted to undertakings providing services of general economic interest, [2023] *OJ* L2023/2832.

In addition, as mentioned above, Article 108 TFEU requires the Commission to be notified of any plans to grant or alter aid. The Commission may also receive a complaint against aid that has not been notified.[71] If it considers that a proposal is not compatible with the internal market, it initiates a formal investigation procedure. The Member State concerned may not put its proposed measures into effect until this procedure has resulted in a final decision.

This entire procedure is set out in Regulation (EU) 2015/1589 Council laying down detailed rules for the application of Article 108 of the TFEU,[72] while distinguishing between notified aid and non-notified aid, which is considered to be unlawful. In the latter case, the Commission may, after giving the Member State concerned the opportunity to submit its comments, adopt a decision requiring the Member State to suspend payment of any unlawful aid or to recover the amount provisionally, until it has decided on the compatibility of the aid with the internal market. In the event of a negative decision on unlawful aid, the Commission will decide that the Member State concerned must take all necessary measures to recover the aid (with interest) from the beneficiary, subject to a ten-year limitation period.

Under Article 108(2) TFEU, if a Member State does not comply within the prescribed period with a decision of non-compatibility or misuse of an aid measure adopted by the Commission, the Commission or any other Member State concerned may bring the matter directly before the Court of Justice of the European Union, by way of derogation from Articles 258 and 259 TFEU: i.e. without having to initiate any prior administrative procedure.[73] As with the application of Articles 101 and 102 TFEU, the Commission has powers of investigation and sanction, with the possibility of imposing fines on the companies concerned or periodic penalty payments (up to a maximum of 1% and 5% respectively of their total turnover in their last financial year), subject to a limitation period of three years.

Finally, at the request of a Member State, the Council, acting unanimously, may still decide that an aid measure which that State has implemented or

---

[71] See, for example, in the context of Case T-26/01, the complaint by *Fiocchi munizioni SpA*, an Italian company active in the manufacture and marketing of arms and munitions, concerning subsidies granted by the Kingdom of Spain to *Empresa Nacional Santa Barbara*, a Spanish military production company (Case T-26/01, *Fiocchi munizioni v Commission*, ECLI:EU:T:2003:248).

[72] Council Regulation (EU) 2015/1589 of 13 July 2015 laying down detailed rules for the application of Article 108 of the Treaty on the Functioning of the European Union (codified text), [2015] *OJ* L248/9.

[73] For a case in the defence sector: Case C-485/10, *Commission v Greece*, ECLI:EU:C:2012:395, for failure to comply with Decision 2009/610/EC, Commission Decision of 2 July 2008 on the measures C 16/04 (ex NN 29/04, CP 71/02 and CP 133/05) granted by Greece to Hellenic Shipyards SA[2009] *OJ* L225/104). Greece was subsequently fined €10 million and ordered to pay a penalty payment of €7,294,000 every six months for failing to comply with the Court's first judgment (see Case C-93/17, *Commission v Greece*, ECLI:EU:C:2018:903).

intends to implement must be considered compatible with the internal market, in derogation from the provisions of Article 107 TFEU or the regulations provided for in Article 109 TFEU, but only 'if exceptional circumstances justify such a decision'. To the author's knowledge, this option has not yet been used in the defence sector.

III. THE SGEI REGIME[74]

Article 106(2) TFEU[75] provides for special arrangements for undertakings operating a service of general economic interest (SGEI).[76] As the Court has stated, the objective of such a scheme is 'to reconcile the Member States' interest in using certain undertakings, in particular in the public sector, as an instrument of economic or fiscal policy with the Community' s interest in ensuring compliance with the rules on competition and the preservation of the unity of the Common Market'.[77] It is intended to allow derogations from any rule of the Treaty, not just the competition rules, including the rules applicable to State aid.[78]

As the authors of the Treaties did not define the concept of an undertaking entrusted with the management of an SGEI, case law has gradually defined it. In particular, this has led to a functional rather than purely organic approach: the management of an SGEI implies the assumption of specific obligations or constraints in the public interest. For example, Régie belge des Postes was considered to be an undertaking entrusted with the management of an SGEI

---

74 For a summary of EU law on SGEIs: S. Rodrigues, 'Les services d'intérêt (économique) général de Rome à Lisbonne: de l'indifférence à la reconnaissance?', dossier '60 ans du traité de Rome', *Revue de l'Union européenne*, May 2018, no. 618, pp. 283–292.

75 Article 106 TFEU contains two further paragraphs. The first paragraph requires Member States to treat public undertakings and undertakings to which Member States grant special or exclusive rights in the same way as private undertakings, in particular as regards compliance with the competition rules. For a recent case of interpretation: Case C-510/22, *Romaqua Group*, ECLI:EU:C:2023:694, concerning exclusive concessions to exploit mineral water. As for the third paragraph of Article 106 TFEU, it confers on the Commission a specific supervisory power in the application of this provision, with the possibility of adopting, 'where necessary', appropriate directives or decisions addressed to the Member States. Case law has recognised that the Commission has a wide discretion in exercising this power (see Case C-202/88, *France v Commission*, ECLI:EU:C:1991:120; Case C-107/95 P, *Bundesverband der Bilanzbuchhalter v Commission*, ECLI:EU:C:1997:71).

76 As well as for companies managing a tax monopoly, i.e. those which benefit from an exclusive right whose purpose is to feed a public budget providing resources to the State, following the example of the tax monopoly on tobacco and alcohol in certain Member States.

77 See Case C-202/88, *France v Commission*, ECLI:EU:C:1991:120, para. 12.

78 See to this effect Case 78/76, *Steinicke and Weinlig*, ECLI:EU:C:1977:52, para. 18 and Case T-106/95, *Fédération française des sociétés d'assurances (FFSA) e.a.*, ECLI:EU:T:1997:23, para. 170.

insofar as it had 'the obligation to collect, carry and distribute mail on behalf of all users throughout the territory of the Member State concerned, at uniform tariffs and on similar quality conditions, irrespective of the specific situations or the degree of economic profitability of each individual operation'.[79]

Such obligations may derive from a legislative or regulatory text, from a public law concession,[80] or even from an international convention incorporated into national law by statute.[81]

Two cumulative conditions are required for undertakings managing an SGEI to be able to derogate from the rules of the TFEU: firstly, it must be demonstrated that the application of these rules 'obstruct the performance, in law or in fact, of the particular tasks assigned to them'; secondly, 'the development of trade must not be affected to such an extent as would be contrary to the interests of the Union'.

As regards the first condition, the Court has provided some clarification. It is necessary to examine 'the extent to which a restriction on competition or even the exclusion of all competition from other economic operators is necessary in order to allow the holder of the exclusive right to perform its task of general interest and in particular to have the benefit of economically acceptable conditions'.[82] In addition, 'it is necessary to take into consideration the economic conditions in which the undertaking operates, in particular the costs it has to bear and the legislation, particularly concerning the environment, to which it is subject'.[83] Finally, 'it is sufficient that the application of those rules obstruct the performance, in law or in fact, of the special obligations incumbent upon that undertaking. It is not necessary that the survival of the undertaking itself be threatened'.[84]

The increasing number of cases in which the derogation for SGEIs in the field of State aid has been used has led the Court to define a special category of public service compensation which, under certain conditions, may escape classification as State aid under Article 107 TFEU. According to the Altmark case law, public subsidies intended to enable the management of an SGEI do not fall within the scope of this provision 'where a State measure must be regarded as compensation for the services provided by the recipient undertakings in order to discharge public service obligations'.

---

79 See Case C-320/91, *Corbeau*, ECLI:EU:C:1993:198, para. 15.

80 See Case C-393/92, *Commune d'Almelo*, ECLI:EU:C:1994:171, para. 47 (in this case an electricity distribution concession).

81 See in this respect Joined Cases C-147/97 and 148/97, *Deutsche Post*, ECLI:EU:C:2000:74, para. 44 (here the Universal Postal Convention).

82 See Case C-320/91, *Corbeau*, ECLI:EU:C:1993:198, para. 16.

83 See Case C-393/92, *Commune d'Almelo*, ECLI:EU:C:1994:171, para. 49.

84 See Case C-159/94, *Commission v France*, ECLI:EU:C:1997:501, para. 59 (concerning the exclusive rights to import and export gas and electricity granted to EDF-GDF).

For the purposes of applying this criterion, the cumulative meeting of four conditions is required, as follows: 'First, the recipient undertaking must actually have public service obligations to discharge, and the obligations must be clearly defined [...]; Second, the parameters on the basis of which the compensation is calculated must be established in advance in an objective and transparent manner [...]; Third, the compensation cannot exceed what is necessary to cover all or part of the costs incurred in the discharge of public service obligations, taking into account the relevant receipts and a reasonable profit for discharging those obligations [...]; Fourth, where the undertaking which is to discharge public service obligations, in a specific case, is not chosen pursuant to a public procurement procedure which would allow for the selection of the tenderer capable of providing those services at the least cost to the community, the level of compensation needed must be determined on the basis of an analysis of the costs which a typical undertaking, well run and adequately provided with [...] would have incurred in discharging those obligations, taking into account the relevant receipts and a reasonable profit for discharging the obligations'.[85]

As a result, in 2005, the Commission adopted a 'package' of rules to make the system of public service compensation and other aid granted to an undertaking managing an SGEI more secure, pointing out in particular that public service compensation which does not meet the 'Altmark criteria' is subject to the application of the rules on State aid, but may be declared compatible with the internal market, in particular by virtue of Article 106(2) TFEU.[86] This 'SGEI package' was revised in 2011: see in particular Commission Decision 2012/21/EU,[87] two interpretative communications[88] and the *de minimis* Regulation, revised in 2023, cited above.[89]

These latest developments should be seen in the broader context of the contributions made by the Treaty of Lisbon (2007) to the consolidation of a European status for SGEIs. Article 14 TFEU, the previous version of which (Article 16 of the EC Treaty) already recognised SGEIs as part of the EU's shared values, conferred on the EU a new power to establish common conditions and principles enabling undertakings managing an SGEI to fulfil their missions,

---

85 See in this respect the leading judgment of the Court of 24 July 2003, Case C-280/00, *Altmark Trans and Regierungspräsidium Magdeburg*, ECLI:EU:C:2003:415.

86 See also Joined Cases T-568/08 and T-573/08, *M6 and TF1 v Commission*, ECLI:EU:T:2010:272, para. 62.

87 Commission Decision 2012/21/EU of 20 December 2011 on the application of Article 106(2) of the Treaty on the Functioning of the European Union to State aid in the form of public service compensation granted to certain undertakings entrusted with the operation of services of general economic interest, [2012] *OJ* L7/3.

88 Communication from the Commission on the application of European Union State aid rules to compensation granted for the provision of services of general economic interest ([2012] *OJ* C8/4) and EU Framework for State aid in the form of public service compensation (2011) ([2012] *OJ* C8/15).

89 Commission Regulation (EU) 2023/2832, cited above.

'without prejudice to the competence of Member States, in compliance with the Treaties, to provide, to commission and to fund such services'. A protocol (No. 27) has been added to reiterate this competence of the Member States and exclude the application of the Treaty rules to non-economic services of general interest. Finally, Article 36 of the Charter of Fundamental Rights of the European Union, which now has the same legal value as the Treaties (see Article 6(1) TEU), requires the Union to recognise and respect access to SGEIs 'as provided for in national laws and practices, in accordance with the Treaties, in order to promote the social and territorial cohesion of the Union'.

To the best of the author's knowledge, the Commission's decision-making practice and the cases brought before the Court of Justice have not given rise to a case for the application of the derogation for SGEIs in the defence industry sector.[90]

[90] In his above-mentioned thesis, M. Arnoux speaks of the imposition by States on defence industrialists of 'quasi-public service obligations', but considers that Article 106(2) TFEU is not 'a relevant legal basis for establishing the compatibility of military State aid' (G. Arnoux, *Le droit européen de la concurrence et l'industrie de la défense*, PhD thesis, Université Paris 1 Panthéon-Sorbonne, 2011, pp. 369–370).

ARTICLE 114 TFEU: A LEGAL BASIS AS A REFERENCE FOR REGULATING THE EUROPEAN DEFENCE INDUSTRY

Stéphane RODRIGUES
Senior Lecturer at the Université Paris 1 Panthéon-Sorbonne
Member of the Sorbonne Institute for Research in International and European Law (IREDIES-EA 4536)
Member of the Brussels Bar

Article 114

1. Save where otherwise provided in the Treaties, the following provisions shall apply for the achievement of the objectives set out in Article 26. The European Parliament and the Council shall, acting in accordance with the ordinary legislative procedure and after consulting the Economic and Social Committee, adopt the measures for the approximation of the provisions laid down by law, regulation or administrative action in Member States which have as their object the establishment and functioning of the internal market.

2. Paragraph 1 shall not apply to fiscal provisions, to those relating to the free movement of persons nor to those relating to the rights and interests of employed persons.

3. The Commission, in its proposals envisaged in paragraph 1 concerning health, safety, environmental protection and consumer protection, will take as a base a high level of protection, taking account in particular of any new development based on scientific facts. Within their respective powers, the European Parliament and the Council will also seek to achieve this objective.

4. If, after the adoption of a harmonisation measure by the European Parliament and the Council, by the Council or by the Commission, a Member State deems it necessary to maintain national provisions on grounds of major needs referred to in Article 36, or relating to the protection of the environment or the working environment, it shall notify the Commission of these provisions as well as the grounds for maintaining them.

> **5.** Moreover, without prejudice to paragraph 4, if, after the adoption of a harmonisation measure by the European Parliament and the Council, by the Council or by the Commission, a Member State deems it necessary to introduce national provisions based on new scientific evidence relating to the protection of the environment or the working environment on grounds of a problem specific to that Member State arising after the adoption of the harmonisation measure, it shall notify the Commission of the envisaged provisions as well as the grounds for introducing them.
>
> **6.** The Commission shall, within six months of the notifications as referred to in paragraphs 4 and 5, approve or reject the national provisions involved after having verified whether or not they are a means of arbitrary discrimination or a disguised restriction on trade between Member States and whether or not they shall constitute an obstacle to the functioning of the internal market.
>
> In the absence of a decision by the Commission within this period the national provisions referred to in paragraphs 4 and 5 shall be deemed to have been approved.
>
> When justified by the complexity of the matter and in the absence of danger for human health, the Commission may notify the Member State concerned that the period referred to in this paragraph may be extended for a further period of up to six months.
>
> **7.** When, pursuant to paragraph 6, a Member State is authorised to maintain or introduce national provisions derogating from a harmonisation measure, the Commission shall immediately examine whether to propose an adaptation to that measure.
>
> **8.** When a Member State raises a specific problem on public health in a field which has been the subject of prior harmonisation measures, it shall bring it to the attention of the Commission which shall immediately examine whether to propose appropriate measures to the Council.
>
> **9.** By way of derogation from the procedure laid down in Articles 258 and 259, the Commission and any Member State may bring the matter directly before the Court of Justice of the European Union if it considers that another Member State is making improper use of the powers provided for in this Article.
>
> **10.** The harmonisation measures referred to above shall, in appropriate cases, include a safeguard clause authorising the Member States to take, for one or more of the non-economic reasons referred to in Article 36, provisional measures subject to a Union control procedure.

The former Article 3(1)(h) of the Treaty establishing the European Community (TEC) stated that the activities of the Community shall include 'the approximation of the laws of Member States to the extent required for the functioning of the common market'. This wording was dropped by the Treaty of Lisbon from the list of objectives assigned to the Union by Article 3 of the Treaty on European Union (TEU). However, Chapter 3 in Title VII of Part Three of the Treaty on the Functioning of the European Union (TFEU) is devoted to the approximation of laws. Article 114 TFEU is one of the five articles that make up this chapter.

This approximation of legislation corresponds to what is commonly referred to as harmonisation as a mode of positive integration of the internal market through secondary legislation, in contrast to the mode of negative integration which results from primary legislation and which consists of enacting prohibitions and prescriptions on what not to do (prohibitions of obstacles to free movement, restrictions on free competition, etc.).[1]

The approximation of national regulations has always been envisaged as an integration tool from the inception of the Treaties and is linked to the implementation of certain EU actions or policies. Examples include, but are not limited to: Articles 43 TFEU (agricultural policy), 48 TFEU (social security), 50-2 TFEU (company law), 81 and 83 TFEU (judicial cooperation in civil and criminal matters), 91 TFEU (transport), 113 TFEU (indirect taxation), 118 TFEU (creation of European intellectual property rights), 133 TFEU ('measures necessary for the use of the euro as a single currency'), and 207 TFEU (trade policy),[2] etc.

In addition to these legal bases for sectoral harmonisation, there are two more general legal bases. First, from what can be described as 'historical' basis, former Article 100 TCEE, then Article 94 TEC, now Article 115 TFEU provides the legal grounds for directives on the approximation of national provisions which 'directly effect the establishment or functioning of the internal market' may be adopted by the Council alone (with the simple consultation of the European Parliament). Second, a more recent legal basis, introduced by the Single European Act as Article 100a of the TECE, then Article 95 TEC, and now Article 114 TFEU, covers measures relating to the approximation of national provisions 'which have as their object the establishment and functioning of the internal market', which may be adopted under the ordinary legislative procedure. Article 114 TFEU has thus become the common-law legal basis for harmonisation, which is preferred in order to achieve the internal market

1 For a variation of this dual integrative approach in the field of defence see E. Simon, *Rôles et fonctions du droit de l'Union européenne dans l'intégration des politiques d'acquisition d'armement*, PhD thesis, Paris, Université Paris 1 Panthéon-Sorbonne, defended on 13 July 2017, under the supervision of Viviane de Beaufort and Stéphane Rodrigues. The author mainly draws on the doctrine of the Italian legal theorist N. Bobbio, on the dual repressive and promotional function of law.

2 See the commentary on this article by S. Robert in this publication.

objectives of Article 26 TFEU, although three areas are excluded: taxation, the free movement of persons and the rights and interests of employed persons.[3] Thus, in its proposal for a Directive on defence procurement (now Directive 2009/81/EC), the Commission justified recourse to Article 95 TEC (in addition to Articles 47(2) and 55 TEC) because these were provisions 'designed to ensure that the procedures used for the public procurement of goods and services comply with the principles of the free movement of goods, freedom of establishment and freedom to provide services'.[4]

In order to present the general regime of Article 114 TFEU, it is necessary to define the scope of harmonisation (Section I), to describe the harmonisation procedures (Section II) and to specify the derogating provisions (Section III), in the light especially of the instruments of secondary legislation having a direct or indirect impact on the defence sector.

I. THE SCOPE OF HARMONISATION

With Article 114 TFEU, the case law of the Court explains that 'the authors of the Treaty intended to confer on the Community legislature a discretion, depending on the general context and the specific circumstances of the matter to be harmonised, as regards the harmonisation technique most appropriate for achieving the desired result, in particular in fields which are characterised by complex technical features. That discretion may be used in particular to choose the most appropriate harmonisation technique where the proposed approximation requires physical, chemical or biological analyses to be made and scientific developments in the field concerned to be taken into account. Such evaluations relating to the safety of products correspond to the objective imposed on the Community legislature by Article 95(3) EC of ensuring a high level of protection of health [...] where the Community legislature provides for a harmonisation which comprises several stages, for instance the fixing of a number of essential criteria set out in a basic regulation followed by scientific evaluation of the substances concerned and the adoption of a positive list of substances authorised throughout the Community, two conditions must be satisfied. First, the Community legislature must determine in the basic act the essential elements of the harmonising measure in question. Second, the

3 Areas which may, however, be covered by harmonisation directives but on the basis of other provisions, in particular Article 115 TFEU, cited above.

4 Directive 2009/81/EC of the European Parliament and of the Council of 13 July 2009 on the coordination of procedures for the award of certain works contracts, supply contracts and service contracts by contracting authorities or entities in the fields of defence and security, and amending Directives 2004/17/EC and 2004/18/EC, [2009] *OJ* L216/76. See the commentary on this directive in the commentary on Articles 49 to 62 of the TFEU by S. Rodrigues in this publication.

mechanism for implementing those elements must be designed in such a way that it leads to a harmonisation within the meaning of Article 95 EC. That is the case where the Community legislature establishes the detailed rules for making decisions at each stage of such an authorisation procedure, and determines and circumscribes precisely the powers of the Commission as the body which has to take the final decision. That applies in particular where the harmonisation in question consists in drawing up a list of products authorised throughout the Community to the exclusion of all other products'.[5]

To illustrate this last point in the field of defence, reference can be made to Directive 2009/43/EC simplifying the conditions for transfers of defence-related products within the Community,[6] with a regularly updated list of the products concerned.[7]

However, the Court does not recognise that the Union's legislature has a general power to harmonise: harmonisation measures must be 'intended to improve the conditions for the establishment and functioning of the internal market. To construe that article as meaning that it vests in the Community legislature a general power to regulate the internal market would not only be contrary to the express wording of the provisions cited above but would also be incompatible with the principle embodied in Article 3b of the EC Treaty (now Article 5 EC)[8] that the powers of the Community are limited to those specifically conferred on it'.[9]

Furthermore, the case law states that 'the mere fact that an act may affect the establishment or functioning of the internal market is not sufficient to justify using that provision as the basis for the act' (i.e. Article 100a; now Article 114 TFEU).[10] Article 114 TFEU may be 'used as a legal basis only where it is actually and objectively apparent from the legal act that its purpose is to

5 See Case C-66/04, *United Kingdom v Parliament and Council*, ECLI:EU:C:2005:743, paras. 45–49, concerning Regulation 2065/2003 on smoke flavourings used or intended for use in or on foods. See also in the same sense: Case C-482/17, *Czech Republic v European Parliament and Council of the EU*, ECLI:EU:C:2019:1035, paras. 60–62, concerning Directive (EU) 2017/853 of the European Parliament and of the Council of 17 May 2017 amending Council Directive 91/477/EEC on control of the acquisition and possession of weapons.

6 Directive 2009/43/EC of the European Parliament and of the Council of 6 May 2009 simplifying terms and conditions of transfers of defence-related products within the Community, [2009] *OJ* L146/1. See the commentary on this directive in this publication by E. Daniel and M. Kieffer.

7 See most recently: Commission Delegated Directive (EU) 2023/277 of 5 October 2022 amending Directive 2009/43/EC of the European Parliament and of the Council as regards the updating of the list of defence-related products in line with the updated Common Military List of the European Union of 21 February 2022, [2023] *OJ* L42/1.

8 Today: Art. 5.1 TFEU.

9 See Case C-376/98, *Germany v Parliament and Council*, ECLI:EU:C:2000:544, para. 83.

10 See Case C-426/93, *Germany v Commission*, ECLI:EU:C:1995:367, para. 33.

improve the conditions for the establishment and functioning of the internal market'.[11]

This is the case in particular 'where there are obstacles to trade or it is likely that such obstacles will emerge in future because the Member States have taken or are about to take divergent measures with respect to a product or a class of products such as to ensure different levels of protection and thereby prevent the product or products concerned from moving freely within the Community, Article 95 EC authorises the Community legislature to intervene by adopting appropriate measures, in compliance with Article 95(3) EC and with the legal principles mentioned in the Treaty or identified in the case-law'.[12]

In so doing, recourse to Article 114 TFEU may be motivated by both corrective and preventive considerations: EU legislators may have recourse to it in particular in the event of divergences between national rules where these are such as to hinder fundamental freedoms, but also 'if the aim is to prevent the emergence of such obstacles to trade resulting from the divergent development of national laws. However, the emergence of such obstacles must be likely and the measure in question must be designed to prevent them'.[13] This is how the Commission justified recourse to Article 114 TFEU in its proposal for a regulation on the establishment of the action to support the production of ammunition[14] (now the ASAP regulation),[15] by arguing that 'divergent national legislation, in particular regarding the certification of defence products, intra-EU transfer of products and related components as well as divergent implementation of Union law have proven to become bottlenecks for European relevant defence products supply chains and obstacles to interoperability. As a result, it is necessary to adopt Union-harmonising legislation based on Article 114 of the TFEU to ensuring the functioning of the internal market, by avoiding shortages of relevant defence products in the Union'.[16]

Furthermore, according to the case law, 'the Union legislature may deem it necessary to provide for the establishment of a Community body responsible for contributing to the implementation of a process of harmonisation'.[17]

The coexistence of Article 114 TFEU with other possible legal bases for the approximation of national rules is fuelling a dispute as to which legal basis is relevant. Three rules of interpretation are favoured by the Court of

---

11 See Case C-217/04, *United Kingdom v Parliament and Council*, ECLI:EU:C:2006:279, para. 42.

12 See Case C-434/02, *Arnold André*, ECLI:EU:C:2004:800, para. 34.

13 See Case C-58/08, *Vodafone and Others*, ECLI:EU:C:2010:321, paras. 32–33.

14 COM(2023) 237 final, 3 May 2023.

15 Regulation (EU) 2023/1525 of the European Parliament and of the Council of 20 July 2023 on supporting ammunition production (ASAP), [2023] *OJ* L185/7. See the commentary on this regulation by E. Bernard in this publication.

16 See Section 2, pp. 4–5 of COM(2023) 237 final, 3 May 2023.

17 See Case C-217/04, *United Kingdom v Parliament and Council*, ECLI:EU:C:2006:279, para. 44.

Justice: firstly, the rule of *lex specialis*, in that the specific legal basis must take precedence over the general legal basis;[18] secondly, the rule that the principal objective must take precedence over the ancillary objective;[19] and thirdly, the rule of democracy, which requires preference to be given to the legal basis that allows the most active participation by the European Parliament.[20]

Finally, it should be added that in certain cases, where there are equivalent objectives, a dual legal basis may be accepted.[21] Thus, for example, the ASAP Regulation mentioned above is based on both Article 114 TFEU and Article 173(3) TFEU, on industrial policy,[22] corresponding to each of the two pillars of this instrument of secondary legislation (harmonisation to avoid shortages of certain defence products and strengthening the responsiveness and capacity of the EDTIB to guarantee the availability and timely supply of these products).[23] The same applies to the regulation establishing a European Defence Industry Programme (EDIP) and a framework of measures to ensure the availability and timely supply of defence products.[24] This is based on three pillars, each with its own legal basis: Article 114 TFEU for the pillar relating

---

18 See the judgment in Case C-376/98, cited above, which annulled the 1998 'Tobacco Advertising' Directive on the grounds that it had been adopted on the basis of Article 100a TEC, in that it imposed prohibition measures that were too general and went beyond the scope of eliminating obstacles to the free movement of advertising media or distortions of competition in the tobacco products market.

19 See Case C-137/12, *Commission v Council*, ECLI:EU:C:2013:675, which annuls Council Decision 2011/853/EU on the signing, on behalf of the Union, of the European Convention on the legal protection of services based on, or consisting of, conditional access, for having been adopted on the basis of Article 114 TFEU instead of Article 207 TFEU (common trade policy). This is insofar as 'the primary objective of the Convention is not to improve the functioning of the internal market, but to extend legal protection of the relevant services beyond the territory of the European Union and thereby to promote international trade in those services' (para. 67).

20 See Case C-300/89, *Commission v Council*, ECLI:EU:C:1991:244, concerning Directive 89/428 on the disposal of titanium dioxide waste. For the Court, the aim was to ensure '[t]he involvement of the European Parliament in the legislative process of the Community, would thus [not] be jeopardized'(see point 20 of the judgment). This rule of interpretation seems to have fallen into disuse given the generalisation of the ordinary legislative procedure (co-decision by the Council and the European Parliament) with the Treaty of Lisbon.

21 See Case C-242/87, *Commission v Council*, ECLI:EU:C:1989:217, concerning the adoption of the Erasmus programme, based on the former Articles 128 and 235 EEC.

22 See the commentary by D. Fiott in this publication.

23 See the commentary by E. Bernard in this publication.

24 See Regulation (EU) 2025/2643 of the European Parliament and of the Council of 16 December 2025 establishing the European Defence Industry Programme and a framework of measures to ensure the timely availability and supply of defence products ('EDIP Regulation') [2025] *OJ* L2025/2643. See the commentary by E. Simon in this publication. This new regulation was backed up by the new strategy adopted on the same day and entitled 'A new European Defence Industrial Strategy: Achieving EU readiness through a responsive and resilient European Defence Industry' (EDIS): see joint communication JOIN(2024)10 final from the European Commission and the High Representative of the Union for Foreign Affairs and Security Policy. See the commentary on Article 173 TFEU by D. Fiott in this publication.

to the internal market in defence equipment,[25] Article 173 TFEU for the pillar relating to the competitiveness of the European Defence Technological and Industrial Base (EDTIB) and Article 212 TFEU[26] for the section concerning assistance to third countries, in this case Ukraine.[27]

A final hypothesis is that of evolving legal bases, where an act of secondary legislation undergoes an extension of its scope which necessitates recourse to one or more new legal foundations. Reference may be made here to the proposal to recast Regulation (EU) 2019/452 on the screening of foreign investments.[28] This regulation is currently based on Article 207(2) of the TFEU, under the EU's common trade policy,[29] which includes foreign direct investment. However, as the Commission now wishes to include other investments in the scope of the Regulation (in particular investments made through EU subsidiaries controlled by third-country investors) and to harmonise certain standards and procedural deadlines, recourse to Article 114 TFEU is being sought.[30]

II. HARMONISATION METHODS

Harmonisation methods underwent a major change at the end of the 1970s, culminating in the Single European Act.

---

25 From a number of angles, the main ones being: security of supply (with the introduction of an EU-wide strategic stocks regime, the identification and monitoring of critical industrial capacities in the supply chains of certain defence products, and a crisis management mechanism), the certification of defence products and the simplification of the reopening of existing and future framework contracts with the EDTIB to other Member States. It should be noted that the 'crisis management' aspect is reminiscent of the proposal for a regulation establishing a single market instrument for emergency situations presented by the Commission in 2022 (see COM(2022) 459 final, 19 September 2022), based in particular on Article 114 TFEU, Article 2(8) of which states that the new text will be 'without prejudice to the Member States' responsibility for safeguarding national security and their power to safeguard other essential State functions, including ensuring the territorial integrity of the State and maintaining law and order'.

26 See the commentary on this article S. Robert in this publication.

27 For the sake of completeness, Article 322(1) TFEU is also referred to as a legal basis in view of the budgetary aspects involved in financing the programme and assistance to Ukraine. See the commentary on Article 41 TEU by A. Potteau in this publication.

28 Regulation (EU) 2019/452 of the European Parliament and of the Council of 19 March 2019 establishing a framework for the screening of foreign direct investments in the Union, [2019] *OJ* L79I/1. See the commentary on this regulation by S. Robert, in this publication.

29 See the commentary on this article S. Robert in this publication.

30 See the explanatory memorandum to the Proposal for a Regulation of the European Parliament and of the Council on screening of foreign investment in the Union and repealing Regulation (EU) 2019/452 of the European Parliament and of the Council, COM(2024) 23 final, 24 January 2024, spec. pp. 11–12. On this proposal see A. Coskun, 'La proposition de nouveau règlement sur le filtrage des investissements étrangers dans l'Union: vers une européanisation de la sécurité économique?', *Europe*, 2024, No. 4, Study No. 3.

The initial practice (1958-1983) was to apply the former Article 100 EEC (now Article 115 TFEU), which required unanimity within the Council (with simple consultation of the European Parliament and the European Economic and Social Committee), and recourse to the use of directives as a single instrument. The harmonisation sought was intended to be total and detailed, which meant that implementation was complex and the procedure lengthy. It should be noted that Article 115 TFEU can still be applied today where Article 114 TFEU or a specific legal basis cannot be applied.[31]

The famous judgment in *Cassis de Dijon by* the Court of Justice in 1979,[32] by highlighting the principle of mutual recognition,[33] led to de facto harmonisation (sometimes referred to as 'imperfect harmonisation'), which the Commission enshrined through a system of standard equivalence in a communication of 3 October 1980.[34] The latter's implementation was facilitated by the introduction of a system of prior notification of technical rules and standards inspired by the former Article 97 TEC (now Article 117 TFEU). This was the purpose of Council Directive 83/189 of 28 March 1983 which was repealed and replaced by Directive 98/34/EC of the European Parliament and of the Council of 22 June 1998 laying down a procedure for the provision of information in the field of technical standards and regulations; itself amended by Directive 98/48 of 20 July 1998 to extend it to rules on information society services and finally repealed and replaced by Directive (EU) 2015/1535 of the European Parliament and of the Council of 9 September 2015 (codified text).[35]

Without going into the details of this notification system, it may simply be pointed out that it means that a technical rule or standard falling within the scope of the directive and which has not been notified cannot be applied to an individual, and that the national court is obliged to refuse to apply it.[36]

Above all, however, the Single European Act (1986) introduced Article 100a of the EC Treaty, now Article 114 TFEU, to provide for another means of harmonisation on the basis of measures adopted by qualified majority in

---

31 For example, in the area of harmonisation tax see Council Directive 2011/96/EU of 30 November 2011 on the common system of taxation applicable in the case of parent companies and subsidiaries of different Member States (recast), [2011] *OJ* L345/8; amended by Council Directive (EU) 2015/121 of 27 January 2015, [2015] *OJ* L21/1.

32 Case 120/78, *Rewe-Zentral AG*, ECLI:EU:1979:42.

33 Ibid., para. 14 of the judgment: 'There is therefore no valid reason why, provided that they have been lawfully produced and marketed in one of the Member States, alcoholic beverages should not be introduced into any other Member State; the sale of such products may not be subject to a legal prohibition [...]'.

34 Confirmed and updated by the Commission interpretative communication on facilitating the access of products to the markets of other Member States: the practical application of mutual recognition, ([2003] OJ C265/2) and by the communication of 14 February 2007 on the new 'LCM package': COM(2007) 35.

35 [2015] *OJ* L241/1.

36 See Case C-194/94, *C.I.A. Security*, ECLI:EU:1996:172 and Case C-303/04, *Lidl Italia Srl*, ECLI:EU:2005:528.

the Council, in co-decision with the European Parliament (since the Treaty of Lisbon, under the ordinary legislative procedure). However, three areas are excluded: taxation, the free movement of persons and measures relating to the rights and interests of employees.

Article 114(3) TFEU also sets a general objective of a high level of protection for health, safety, the environment and consumers. The resulting new approach now focuses on certain requirements considered to be essential and of collective interest (health, safety, environmental and consumer protection), with referral to the Commission for the adoption of more detailed technical requirements.[37] In this respect, the Commission relies on a technical standardisation process,[38] involving European standardisation bodies[39] which, on the basis of a mandate from the Commission, adopt technical standards[40] that are then be published in the *Official Journal of the European Union* (*OJEU*) at the Commission's initiative. As a result, products complying with these standards enjoy a presumption of conformity with the essential requirements of the corresponding directive.[41]

All of these procedures have been codified in Regulation (EU) No 1025/2012 of the European Parliament and of the Council of 25 October 2012 on European standardisation,[42] which has extended the scope of European standards to services (including ICT) and lays down rules for cooperation between the European and national standardisation bodies and the Commission.

The issue of technical standardisation in the defence field is still not given much prominence, even though the cooperation between the Commission and the European Defence Agency (EDA) includes projects in this area,[43] and one of the objectives of the European Defence Fund (EDF) is to contribute

---

37 This new approach would be confirmed in a Council resolution of 10 November 2003.

38 As explained in several communications: COM(2004) 674 of 18 October 2004 and COM(2008) 133 of 11 March 2008 ('Towards an increased contribution from standardisation to innovation in Europe').

39 There are three: the European Committee for Standardisation (CEN), the European Committee for Electromagnetic Standardisation (CENELEC) and the European Telecommunications Standards Institute (ETSI).

40 To date, around 22,000 standards have been adopted by CEN-CENELEC, of which some 4,000 have been made mandatory by the Commission. In addition, 30% of these standards are transcriptions of international ISO standards for the European territory.

41 For an explanatory summary of the process see Case C-185/08, *Latchways plc and Others*, ECLI:EU:2010:619, para. 31.

42 Directive amending Council Directives 89/686/EEC and 93/15/EEC and Directives 94/9/EC, 94/25/EC, 95/16/EC, 97/23/EC, 98/34/EC, 2004/22/EC, 2007/23/EC, 2009/23/EC and 2009/105/EC of the European Parliament and of the Council and repealing Council Decision 87/95/EEC and Decision No 1673/2006/EC of the European Parliament and of the Council, [2012] *OJ* L316/12.

43 See, for example, the pilot project for the standardisation of a remotely piloted aircraft system (RPAS) and a detection and avoidance system (DAA), with a budget of 434,000 euros in 2016-2018 (project PP-15-STAN-CERT-01). The EDA also has a system for identifying

to an 'increase in the standardisation of defence systems and a greater interoperability between Member States' capabilities'.[44] A case in point is the *European Initiative for Collaborative Air Combat Standardisation* (EICACS), led by Dassault Aviation, to which the European Union is contributing nearly €75 million.

It should be added that the relaunch of NATO-EU cooperation[45] could help to enhance the value of joint standardisation work.[46] It is interesting to note in this respect that the new European Defence Industry Strategy of March 2024 (EDIS, mentioned above) devotes a section to the issue of technical standardisation, emphasising the complementarity of the EDA's work on standards with that of NATO.[47]

III. DEROGATIONS FROM HARMONISATION

Unlike Article 115 TFEU, Article 114 TFEU provides for certain derogations, of which there are two variants: either a Member State will be authorised not to apply the harmonisation measure under certain conditions, or it will be able to benefit from a safeguard clause provided for in the measure itself.

As regards the possibility of a Member State refusing to apply a harmonisation measure (see Art. 114(4) to (9) TFEU), there are two possible scenarios, which are not mutually exclusive. First, it may rely on 'major needs' referred to in Article 36 TFEU,[48] for the protection of the environment or the working environment justifying the maintenance of national provisions (the *status quo* prior to the harmonisation measure). Second, a Member State it may be faced with a 'specific problem' in the field of environmental protection or in work settings following the adoption of the harmonisation measure, leading the Member State to introduce national provisions 'based on new scientific

best practice in standardisation, under the acronym 'EDSTAR' (for 'EDA-managed European Defence Standards Reference system'). On the EDA: see the contribution by F. Liberti in this publication.

44 See Art. 3(2)(b) of Regulation (EU) 2021/697 of the European Parliament and of the Council of 29 April 2021 establishing the European Defence Fund and repealing Regulation (EU) 2018/1092, [2021] *OJ* L170/149. See S. Rodrigues's commentary on the EDF in this publication.

45 See the commentary on the second subparagraph of Article 42(2) and the second subparagraph of Article 42(7) TEU on EU-NATO relations by Y. Buchet de Neuilly, in this publication.

46 See the work of the Nato Standardisation Office (NSO), which records the standardisation agreements (STANAGs) negotiated between NATO member states.

47 See Section 2.2.2 of document JOIN (2024)10 final of 5 March 2024, cited above.

48 Article 36 TFEU provides an exhaustive list of grounds: public morality, public policy, public security, the protection of health and life of humans, animals or plants, the protection of national treasures possessing artistic, historic or archaeological value, or the protection of industrial and commercial property.

evidence' (post-harmonisation hypothesis). The national provisions in question must then be notified to the Commission, which must ensure that there is no arbitrary discrimination or disguised restriction on trade and that there are no obstacles to the functioning of the internal market; the derogation measure is deemed to have been approved if the Commission fails to react within six months of notification (unless the delay is extended on public health grounds). The Commission may also propose adapting a harmonisation measure that poses a problem for a Member State, particularly where public health is at stake. Finally, it should be noted that the Commission has the power to bring an action for failure to fulfil obligations directly before the Court of Justice if it finds that a Member State is 'misusing' the derogations.

As regards safeguard clauses, Article 114(10) TFEU provides that they may be provided for 'in appropriate cases' in the harmonisation measure to authorise Member States to take provisional measures, 'for one or more of the non-economic reasons referred to in Article 36 [TFEU]'. This would seem to exclude justification for the protection of industrial and commercial property. However, it does include the justification of public security, which can thus be incorporated in a harmonisation text when, for example, it refers to Article 346 TFEU on the protection of the essential security interests of the Member States.[49] In any event, a Member State wishing to rely on the safeguard clause must also notify its legislation to the Commission, which will check that it complies with the conditions set out in the said clause.

***

Given that the defence sector has an economic dimension, particularly where defence equipment is concerned, the Commission advocated the idea (as early as 1996) that '[b]y facilitating intra-Community trade, the completion of a "European defence market" should facilitate both cooperation and integration in the European defence-related industry'.[50] With this in mind, in 1997 the Commission advocated an 'EU defence industry strategy',[51] followed in 2003 by an 'EU defence equipment policy'.[52]

---

49 For example, in this sense: Directive 2014/24/EU of the European Parliament and of the Council of 26 February 2014 on public procurement and repealing Directive 2004/18/EC, [2014] *OJ* L94/65. Article 1(3) of this Directive states that its implementation '[t]he application of this Directive is subject to Article 346 [TFEU]'. See the commentary on Article 346 TFEU in this publication, by S. Rodrigues.

50 European Commission, 'The challenges facing European defence-related industry, a contribution for action at European level', Communication of 24 January 1996, COM(96) 10 final, spec. para. 4.1.2, p. 22.

51 European Commission, 'Implementing the Union's Defence Industrial Strategy', Communication of 4 December 1997, COM(97) 583 final.

52 European Commission, 'European Defence – Industrial and Market Issues – Towards an EU Defence Equipment Policy', Communication of 11 March 2003, COM(2003) 113 final.

While the creation of this internal defence market has subsequently focused on strengthening the competitiveness of this sector,[53] the issue of harmonisation remains central to the Commission's initiatives and will be developed along two main dimensions set out in its December 2007 'Defence Package' (see the above-mentioned Communication): first, the coordination of public procurement procedures in the fields of defence and security, with the adoption of Directive 2009/81/EC (cited above), and, second, the simplification of conditions for transfers of defence-related products within the EU, with the adoption of Directive 2009/43/EC (cited above). Since then, other instruments of secondary legislation with a direct or indirect impact on the defence sector have been adopted on the basis, in whole or in part, of Article 114 TFEU. In chronological order of adoption, and without claiming to be exhaustive,[54] they are presented and commented on below:

- Regulation (EU) 2022/2560 on foreign subsidies distorting the internal market;[55]
- Regulation (EU) on support for the production of ammunition (known as the ASAP Regulation);[56]

---

53 See in this regard: European Commission, 'Strategy for a stronger and more competitive European defence industry, Communication of 5 December 2007', COM(2007) 764 final and 'Towards a more competitive and efficient defence and security sector', Communication of 24 July 2013, COM(2013) 542 final. Since then, the competitiveness objective has remained a leitmotiv for the European Commission, particularly in its 2016 'European Defence Action Plan' (see Communication of 30 November 2016, COM(2016) 950 final), in its 2022 'Contribution to Defence Europe' (see Communication COM(2022) 60 final, 15 February 2022) in the European defence industry strategy (EDIS) adopted on 5 March 2024 (abovementioned) and in the Joint White Paper for European Defence Readiness 2030, adopted by the European Commission and the High Representative of the Union for foreign affairs and security policy, on 19 March 2025 (see document JOINT(2025) 120 final).

54 We could also refer to Regulation (EU) 2024/1252 of the European Parliament and of the Council of 11 April 2024 establishing a framework for ensuring a secure and sustainable supply of critical raw materials and amending Regulations (EU) No 168/2013, (EU) 2018/858, (EU) 2018/1724 and (EU) 2019/1020 ([2024] *OJ* L2024/1252), which includes among 'strategic technologies' key technologies essential 'for applications in the aerospace and defence sectors' (Art. 2, para. 30 of the Regulation) and which defines a methodology for selecting strategic raw materials on the basis of their importance for defence and aerospace applications (see Section 2 of Annex I to the Regulation). See also Regulation (EU) 2019/881 of the European Parliament and of the Council of 17 April 2019 on ENISA (the European Union Agency for Cybersecurity) and on information and communications technology cybersecurity certification and repealing Regulation (EU) No 526/2013 (Cybersecurity Act),[2019] *OJ* L151/15.

55 Regulation (EU) 2022/2560 of the European Parliament and of the Council of 14 December 2022 on foreign subsidies distorting the internal market, [2022] *OJ* L330/1. Note: Article 207 TFEU is also another legal basis (see the commentary on Article 207 TFEU by S. Robert-Cuendet in this publication).

56 Regulation (EU) 2023/1525 of the European Parliament and of the Council of 20 July 2023 on supporting ammunition production (ASAP), [2023] *OJ* L185/7. Note: it also has Article 173 TFEU as another legal basis (see the commentary on Article 173 TFEU by D. Fiott in this publication).

- the Regulation establishing a European Defence Industry Programme (EDIP).[57]

Further use of Article 114 TFEU is expected with a dedicated Defence Omnibus Simplification proposal by June 2025, as announced by the abovementioned Joint White Paper for European Defence Readiness 2030, which considers that "Regulatory simplification and harmonisation must focus both on rules and procedures that are specific to the defence sector, and on the impact on the defence industry of EU policies and regulations that are not defence-specific, but which impede the European defence technological and industrial base (EDTIB) from responding with maximum agility to the current heightened needs". Several options would be considered, such as increasing the cross certification of defence products and facilitating mutual recognition of certification where appropriate; enabling the rapid grant of construction and environmental permits for defence industrial projects as a matter of public-interest priority; ensuring the timely and lawful availability and usability of all necessary materials and other inputs in the supply chain of the EDTIB, in particular for essential uses for which adequate substitutes are not available; or removing obstacles to the availability at relevant times and locations of military personnel.

Last, in this context, the EU directives on defence and sensitive security procurement (see Directive 2009/81/EC) and on intra-EU transfers of defence-related products (see Directive 2009/43/EC) will also be subject to regulatory simplification and harmonisation.

Postscript, June 2025

In its communication *Defence Readiness Omnibus* adopted on 17 June 2025,[58] the European Commission put forward simplification proposals in defence-specific legislation and programmes, as well as in non-defence-specific laws to remove regulatory barriers and facilitate EU defence readiness and industrial buildup. Apart from a proposal amending Directives 2009/43/EC and 2009/81/EC,[59] the proposal for a regulation on the acceleration of permit-granting for defence readiness projects, based on Article 114 TFEU, stands out.[60]

---

57 See Regulation (EU) 2025/2643 of the European Parliament and of the Council of 16 December 2025 establishing the European Defence Industry Programme and a framework of measures to ensure the timely availability and supply of defence products ('EDIP Regulation') [2025] *OJ* L2025/2643, and the commentary by E. Simon in this publication.

58 European Commission, Communication, *Defence Readiness Omnibus*, COM(2025) 820 final, 17 June 2025.

59 European Commission, *Proposal for amending Directives 2009/43/EC and 2009/81/EC, as regards the simplification of intra-EU transfers of defence-related products and the simplification of security and defence procurement*, COM(2025) 823 final, 17 June 2025. See the commentaries on these directives in this publication.

60 European Commission, *Proposal for a regulation of the European Parliament and of the Council on the acceleration of permit-granting for defence readiness projects*, COM(2025) 821 final, 17 June 2025.

In a nutshell, this proposal sets up streamlined permitting processes for defence readiness projects. All defence readiness projects will benefit from Member States designating a national competent authority acting as a single point of contact, in charge of the coordination and facilitation of permitting, guiding economic operators, ensuring that information is publicly accessible, and that all documents can be digitally submitted. Detailed timelines for permitting procedures are also established (with a standard timeline of 60 days).

DIRECTIVE 2009/43/EC SIMPLIFYING TERMS AND CONDITIONS OF TRANSFERS OF DEFENCE-RELATED PRODUCTS WITHIN THE COMMUNITY: A BLUEPRINT FOR EUROPEANISING CONTROLS ON THE MOVEMENT OF MILITARY EQUIPMENT

Directive 2009/43/EC of the European Parliament and of the Council of 6 May 2009 simplifying terms and conditions of transfers of defence-related products within the Community[1]

Elise Daniel

PhD in public law and a civil servant in France's Ministry of the Economy and Finance

and

Maeve Kieffer

PhD in public law and a civil servant in France's Ministry of Ecological Transition and Territorial Cohesion

Adopted under the French Presidency of the Council of the European Union, Directive 2009/43/EC of the European Parliament and of the Council of 6 May 2009 simplifying terms and conditions of transfers of defence-related products within the Community came into force in June 2009, also known as

[1] Disclaimer: Any opinions, findings, and conclusion or recommendations expressed in this material are those of the authors and do not necessarily reflect the view of their current or former employers or those of the French Government.

the 'Transfers Directive'. It was due to be transposed by 30 June 2011 and its provisions were to be applied from 30 June 2012. However, by that date, only 20 of the EU's 27 Member States at the time had notified the Commission of national transposition measures. It was not until 2016 that all national legislation was brought into line, and for some Member States only after the European Commission had launched infringement proceedings for failure to notify under Article 258 TFEU.[2]

The directive is divided into six chapters (1/ Subject matter, scope and definitions; 2/ Transfer licences; 3/ Information, certification and export after transfer; 4/ Customs procedures and administrative cooperation; 5/ Updating the list of defence-related products; 6/ Final provisions), twenty articles and an annex containing the list of defence-related products, the circulation of which is regulated within the internal market.

Together with Directive 2009/81/EC of the European Parliament and of the Council of 13 July 2009 on the coordination of procedures for the award of certain works contracts, supply contracts and service contracts by contracting authorities or entities in the fields of defence and security, and amending Directives 2004/17/EC and 2004/18/EC (known as the 'Defence Procurement Directive'),[3] Directive 2009/43/EC constitutes what is commonly known as the 'defence package'. The two Directives are based on the 'Strategy for a stronger and more competitive European defence industry'[4] and they share a common goal: to develop a European security and defence policy based on a European defence market. The two directives are complementary: 'opening up a State's public procurement markets only makes sense if products can cross the borders of that State'.[5] The aim of the transfers Directive is indeed to make it easier for defence-related goods to cross the internal borders of the

2 The seven Member States late in transposing the transfers Directive were Belgium, Denmark, Finland, Italy, Luxembourg, Poland and Romania; European Commission, 'Report from the Commission to the European Parliament and the Council on the transposition of Directive 2009/43/EC simplifying terms and conditions of transfers of defence-related products within the European Union', Brussels, 29 June 2012, COM(2012) 359 final, pp. 16–20.

3 Directive 2009/81/EC of the European Parliament and of the Council of 13 July 2009 on the coordination of procedures for the award of certain works contracts, supply contracts and service contracts by contracting authorities or entities in the fields of defence and security, and amending Directives 2004/17/EC and 2004/18/EC, p. 76. For more on this Directive, see S. Rodrigues in this publication.

4 Communication from the Commission to the European Parliament, the Council, the European Economic and Social Committee and the Committee of the Regions, 'Strategy for a stronger and more competitive European defence industry', 5 December 2007, COM(2007) 764 final. Back in 1997, the Commission published a communication entitled 'Implementing the European Union's strategy on defence-related industries' in which it advocated, for the first time, the creation of a European defence equipment market. This communication remained a dead letter due to the formal opposition of the European Council.

5 J. Cats, 'Le 'paquet défense': le marché intérieur au service de la défense européenne?', *RMCUE*, 2009, p. 564.

European Union (EU) by inviting national authorities of the Member States to 'harmonise the conditions for intra-Community transfers, with a view to achieving a 'stronger and more competitive' European defence industry'.[6]

The legal basis for the transfers Directive is Article 114 TFEU (formerly Art. 95 TEC), which allows Member States' legislation to be harmonised to ensure the proper functioning of the internal market. The approach is therefore initially economic, aiming to enhance the functioning of the European defence equipment market, to promote the integration of the European defence supply chain and to strengthen security of supply, by simplifying the rules and procedures relating to the intra-EU transfer of defence-related products.

With its twenty articles, the transfers Directive is much shorter than the complementary defence procurement Directive, which has seventy-five articles. Nevertheless, it represents a major step forward in European defence integration, bringing the movement of defence-related products within the 'Community' sphere, whereas they were previously covered by the exceptions provided for in Articles 30, 45, 46, 55 and above all 296 of the Treaty establishing the European Community (TEC) (now Article 346 of the Treaty on the Functioning of the European Union – TFEU), which provides that 'any Member State may take such measures as it considers necessary for the protection of the essential interests of its security which are connected with the production of or trade in arms, munitions and war material'.[7] The extensive interpretation of this article by some Member States had enabled them to protect their defence industries from opening up to European competition.

Implementation of the transfers Directive has also to be coordinated with Council Common Position 2008/944/CFSP of 8 December 2008 defining common rules governing control of exports of technology and military equipment.[8] The directive, which deals with transfers, harmonises the conditions for crossing EU's internal borders, while the common position, on exports, addresses the conditions for crossing EU's external borders. Several provisions of the Directive refer to the Common Position, as the transfer of a defence-related product is generally a prerequisite for exporting it. 'Defence-related products', 'technologies and military equipment' or, more simply, 'war material' are intended for use in armed conflict zones which, for several decades now, have been located outside European borders.

By regulating the internal market and taking exports into account, the transfers Directive lays the foundations for integrated control of the movement of war material at the European level (Section I). However, European

[6] H.-L. Goffinet, 'La directive simplifiant les transferts intracommunautaires de produits liés à la défense', *Note d'Analyse du GRIP*, 2010, p. 3.

[7] Art. 346(1)(b) TFEU. See the contribution by S. Rodrigues in this publication.

[8] Council Common Position 2008/944/CFSP of 8 December 2008 defining common rules governing control of exports of military technology and equipment, [2008] *OJ* L335/99.

harmonisation remains limited, due to legal impediments, both internal to the text of the directive and linked to the existence of international forums informing European law. This is despite the current political context, which seems increasingly favourable to the development of a genuine European policy in this area (Section II).

I. THE INPUTS OF THE TRANSFERS DIRECTIVE: SETTING THE FOUNDATION FOR A EUROPEANISATION OF CONTROLS ON THE MOVEMENT OF WAR MATERIAL

Directive 2009/43/EC gives concrete form to the internal defence market by explicitly introducing procedural harmonisation of national controls on the movement of war material based on the principle of mutual trust (Section A). It goes even further by implicitly promoting consistency between internal controls on transfers carried out by national authorities and external controls on exports (Section B).

A. IMPLEMENTING PROCEDURAL HARMONISATION OF CONTROLS TO ENABLE THE CREATION OF AN INTERNAL DEFENCE MARKET

Directive 2009/43/EC aims to create a genuine internal market for defence-related products by establishing a common licensing system (1) and a certification system (2).

1. *Establishing a Common Licensing System*

The transfers Directive's main contribution is the establishment of a common system of transfer licences within the EU, enabling the de-compartmentalisation of national legislations, a source of complexity and even of comparative disadvantage between European manufacturers and manufacturers from third countries which may have access to a vast unified domestic market. The system only applies to transfers, i.e. 'any transmission or movement of a defence-related product from a supplier to a recipient in another Member State'.[9] The circulation of defence-related products between Member States (as well as

9 Art. 3(2) of the Transfers Directive.

Norway and Iceland)[10] and third States is qualified as exports, and in this case it is appropriate to apply Common Position 2008/944/CFSP, cited above. A difference is thus made between the situation within or outside the European Union, whereas before the Directive came into force, Member States' licensing policies largely made no distinction between the export of these products outside the European Union and their circulation within the Union. The transfers Directive therefore enables European companies to benefit from the advantages of the European Union's internal market.

All transfers of defence-related products are subject to a licence, defined as 'an authorisation by a national authority of a Member State for suppliers to transfer defence-related products to a recipient in another Member State'.[11] However, certain transfers may benefit from licence exemptions. These specific situations are listed in Article 4(2) of the transfers Directive.[12]

The exit licence granted by the Member State is valid throughout the territory of the EU and 'no further authorisation for passage through other Member States or entrance onto the territory of other Member States should be required'.[13] Mutual trust is at the heart of this system, and controls by the importing State are prohibited.

Three types of licences can be used: general licences, global licences and individual licences.

General transfer licences (Art. 5 of the transfers Directive) authorise suppliers established in one Member State to transfer defence-related products, specified in the licence, to categories of recipients located in another Member State. The directive lists several categories of recipients or destinations that should benefit from general licences: armed forces, certified companies, and trade fairs (transfers for demonstrations, evaluation or exhibition purposes).[14]

---

10 The directive also applies to these two States of the European Economic Area, but not to Liechtenstein.

11 Art. 3(5) of the Transfers Directive.

12 The specific situations exist: when the supplier or recipient is a public institution or part of the armed forces; when deliveries are made by the European Union, the North Atlantic Treaty Organisation (NATO), the International Atomic Energy Agency (IAEA) or other intergovernmental organisations for the purpose of carrying out their missions; the transfer is necessary for the implementation of an armaments cooperation programme between Member States; the transfer is linked to humanitarian aid in the event of a disaster or made as a donation in the context of an emergency situation; the transfer is necessary for the purposes of repair, maintenance, exhibition or demonstration, or after these operations. The Directive also allows the Commission, at the request of a Member State or on its own initiative, to include additional exemptions where the transfer takes place under conditions that do not affect public policy or public security, where the requirement for prior authorisation has become incompatible with Member States' international commitments following the adoption of the Transfers Directive, or where this amendment is necessary in the interests of intergovernmental cooperation.

13 Recital 17 of the Transfers Directive.

14 Art. 5(2) Directive 2009/43/EC.

General licences are formalised by an act of national law listing the products and recipients or uses concerned.[15] Manufacturers transferring one of the listed products to one of the categories of recipients envisaged do not therefore have to make a specific request to the national authorities, at the time of the transfer. However, they may be subject to certain specific formalities, such as notification prior to the first transfer. This type of licence radically simplifies procedures for suppliers and enables national authorities to focus controls on transfers considered to be more sensitive. As stated in Recital 29 of the Directive, the aim is 'the progressive replacement of individual ex-ante control by general ex-post control in the Member State of origin of the defence-related products [...]'.

Global transfer licences (Art. 6 of the transfers Directive), on the other hand, are prior authorisations issued by the national authority of a Member State to an individual supplier, at the latter's request, for the transfer of specified products, without quantitative limits, to specified recipients for a renewable period of three years. The potential for simplification of global transfer licences lies in the fact that they do not relate to a single consignment, but can be used to cover several transfers over a longer period. They can be particularly useful for routine deliveries to regular customers or for small- and medium-sized enterprises (SMEs) with a limited catalogue of products. These licences are also published in an act of domestic law which takes the form of an individual decision addressed to the supplier requesting it, specifying the defence-related products or categories of products to which the global transfer licence applies, as well as the authorised recipients or categories of recipients.

Lastly, individual transfer licences (Article 7 of the transfers Directive) take the classic form of export licences. They are an authorisation issued by a national authority to an individual supplier for a single transfer of a specified quantity of products. They are to be used only in the cases specified in Article 7: when limited to a single transfer, when for the protection of the essential security interests of the Member State or for reasons of public policy required, or when necessary to comply with the international obligations and commitments of the Member States. Individual transfer licences may also be used where a Member State has serious grounds for believing that the supplier will not be able to fulfil all the conditions necessary for obtaining a global or general transfer licence.

The Commission's latest report on the evaluation of the transfers Directive (in 2016), indicates that during the period 2012-2014, between 500 and

[15] In French law, these are interministerial decrees: for example, the decree of 6 January 2012 on the general licence for the transfer of defence-related products to the European Union for exhibition and demonstration purposes at international trade fairs, or the decree of 6 January 2012 on the general licence for the transfer of defence-related products to the armed forces of a Member State or to a contracting authority in the field of defence.

600 general transfer licences were issued each year in 21 Member States.[16] Moreover, 1,475 notifications of the first use of general transfer licences were recorded in the 24 Member States for which complete data was available.

This system of control through the issue of customs authorisations is supplemented by a certification mechanism available to certain manufacturers, enabling them to benefit from a less restrictive authorisation regime.

2. *Setting Up a Common Certification System*

The second contribution of the transfers Directive is the certification of certain companies established on the territory of the European Union. Article 9 states that certification makes it possible to establish 'the reliability of the recipient undertaking, in particular as regards its capacity to observe export limitations of defence-related products received under a transfer licence from another Member State'.[17] The criteria for assessing the reliability of an undertaking are set out in Article 9(2) of the Transfers Directive.

While certification is issued by national authorities, these apply common European criteria. Like licences, certification is based on the principle of mutual recognition of certifications between the 27 Member States, with certification issued by one State allowing certified companies to receive transfers of equipment (under a general licence) from the 26 other Member States. Certification enables companies to benefit from the general transfer licence system. It allows control to be moved from *de ante* to *ex ante*, by validating recipients *a priori,* without any licence application.

Member States must designate the competent authorities responsible for certifying recipients of defence-related products established on their territory under general transfer licences issued by other Member States. The authorities responsible for certification vary depending on the Member State: they may be not only the Ministry of Defence (as in Greece, France, Slovenia and Portugal), but also the Ministry of Industry (the Czech Republic and Spain), or the Ministry of Economic Affairs (Austria, the Netherlands, Slovakia and Lithuania).

The Member States are also required to set up a process for controlling that the company complies with the certification criteria. This control mechanism must be carried out at least every three years and preferably during the first

---

16 European Commission, 'Report from the Commission to the European Parliament and the Council, Evaluation of Directive 2009/43/EC of the European Parliament and of the Council of 6 May 2009 simplifying terms and conditions of transfers of defence-related products within the Community', COM(2016) 760 final, 30 November 2016.

17 Art. 9(2), of the Transfers Directive.

year following the granting of the certificate (Art. 9(5)).[18] These are *a posteriori* verifications, in the name of mutual trust. Certification is thus based on a dual control *ex ante* and *ex post*.

Member States are obliged to publish and regularly update the list of certified recipients and to notify the Commission, the European Parliament and the other Member States. The Directive also requires the Commission to make a central register of recipients certified by the Member States available to the public on its website (Art. 9(8)). This database is called CERTIDER, and is maintained by Member States, with the European Commission providing technical support only.

Some have feared that transnational manufacturers established in several Member States might be tempted to choose the countries with the most flexible certification procedures for integrating their equipment. There would then have been a risk of relocating production capacity to these countries. However, this risk has proved to be relatively limited. Previous reports from European institutions do not mention such practices.

Moreover, certification does not appear to be relevant for all companies. The process is restrictive, not least because of the regular controls carried out by the national authorities. Article 9(2)(b) of the Directive stipulates that certified companies must demonstrate that they are engaged in 'a relevant industrial activity', which the Commission and all the Member States interpret as implying that their main activity is manufacturing and excluding any company that is purely a trader or only carries out intermediation activities.[19] Certification is therefore mainly aimed at product integrators: i.e. companies that centralise materials from different manufacturers to integrate them into a final product. The aim of certified companies is to facilitate trade with their European suppliers.[20]

In the end, the use of certification has been lower and slower than expected.

---

[18] J. Seniora, 'Intra-Community transfers of defence-related products: one year of implementation of the Directive', *Note d'Analyse du GRIP*, 25 June 2013, Brussels, p. 6.

[19] Senate Report No. 306 on behalf of the Committee on Foreign Affairs, Defence and Armed Forces on the draft law on the control of imports and exports of war material and assimilated material, the simplification of transfers of defence-related products in the European Union and defence and security markets, by J. de Rohan, 2011, p. 83.

[20] For example, '[f]or France, here are the questions companies should ask themselves before embarking on a certification process: "Am I an integrator of defence-related products? Will my European suppliers be able to send me defence-related products using the general licence for certified companies in force in their countries?"'; J. Seniora, 'Transferts intra-communautaires des produits liés à la défense: un an de mise en œuvre de la Directive', *Note d'Analyse du GRIP*, 25 June 2013, Brussels, p. 5.

In 2016, almost half of the Member States had no experience of the certification process, i.e. no certified companies.[21] Only 55 companies had been certified in Europe, half of them in just two Member States – Germany (14) and France (12) – and half of the Member States had no certified companies. In February 2024, there were 74 certified companies, including 16 in Germany and 15 in France.[22]

The industry considers the certification process to be costly and time-consuming.[23] Some have justified this disappointing record by pointing out that Member States have carried out few awareness-raising campaigns among their companies to explain how the certification process works and what its objectives are; that a certain reluctance to certify may be due to the fact that a director is personally liable, a practice that is not widespread in Europe unlike in the United States; that some companies whose main activity does not involve defence-related products do not want to be certified to protect their image, so as not to be perceived as defence companies.[24]

Finally, the system put in place by the transfers Directive is binding. Article 16 requires penalties to be imposed on companies that fail to comply with the procedures for controlling the movement of war material. Although the definition of penalties is left to the Member States, the same article stipulates that the penalties must be effective, proportionate and dissuasive. In practice, depending on the Member State, penalties consist of administrative fines (in Hungary and the Czech Republic) or administrative fines combined with prison sentences (in Ireland, Malta and Sweden).[25]

The procedural harmonisation of controls, based on the principle of mutual trust, is helping to remove internal borders in the internal market for defence-related products. But the contributions of the transfers Directive go beyond the internal market, as it establishes a link with war material exports via the common list of military equipment and by encouraging exchanges between

21 European Commission, 'Report from the Commission to the European Parliament and the Council: Evaluation of Directive 2009/43/EC of the European Parliament and of the Council of 6 May 2009 simplifying terms and conditions of transfers of defence-related products within the Community', COM(2016) 760 final, 30 November 2016, p. 5.

22 The list is available at https://webgate.ec.europa.eu/certider/public/recipientList.

23 European Commission, 'Report from the Commission to the European Parliament and the Council, Evaluation of Directive 2009/43/EC of the European Parliament and of the Council of 6 May 2009 simplifying terms and conditions of transfers of defence-related products within the Community', COM(2016) 760 final, 30 November 2016, p. 7.

24 J. Seniora, 'Intra-Community transfers of defence-related products: one year of implementation of the Directive', *Note d'Analyse du GRIP*, 25 June 2013, Brussels, p. 7.

25 In France, Article L 2339-1 of the Defence Code provides for criminal penalties. The penalties are high: a maximum of five years' imprisonment and a fine of seventy-five thousand euros for the heaviest penalties. A company that fails to keep its export registers up to date, or that violates a non-re-export commitment, is liable to heavy criminal penalties.

national authorities. The Directive thus puts in place the beginnings of a European approach to controlling the circulation of war material.[26]

B. ENCOURAGING CONSISTENCY BETWEEN CONTROLS ON TRANSFERS AND EXPORTS OF WAR MATERIAL

The transfers Directive contains numerous references to the aforementioned Council Common Position 2008/944/CFSP. It even takes over the export control regime indirectly. The Directive is in fact working towards greater consistency in controlling the movement of war material at European level through the common list of defence-related products (Section 1), the ricochet regulation of exports outside EU territory (Section 2) and the institutionalisation of a forum for exchanges between national authorities (Section 3).

1. *The Europeanisation of Controls through the Introduction of a European List of Controlled Equipment Common to Transfers and Exports*

The third major contribution of the Directive is the European definition of defence-related products through the list in Annex 1, which determines the material scope of controls. Articles 2, on the scope of the transfers Directive, and Article 3, defining the concepts used in the text, both simply refer to the Annex to define what defence-related products are.

From a substantive standpoint, the list is a highly technical compilation of products and equipment classified as war material. The list is precise and exhaustive.[27] Only equipment specifically identified in the list is considered war material. Within each category, specifications are made to further refine the classification and whether or not the equipment belongs on the list of defence-related equipment. The list also combines the express inclusion and exclusion of certain equipment. It also contains interpretative notes to help national authorities and manufacturers classify equipment. Some of the weapons listed can sometimes be included in other categories of equipment.

---

26 See also H.-L. Goffinet, 'La directive simplifiant les transferts intracommunautaires de produits liés à la défense', *Note d'Analyse du GRIP*, 2010.

27 For example, the first category of equipment, 'ML1', for the first item in the 'military list', refers to 'smooth-bore weapons with a calibre of less than 20 mm, other arms and automatic weapons with a calibre of 12.7 mm (calibre 0.50 inches) or less and accessories, as follows, and specially designed components therefor'. The phrase 'specially designed', which appears repeatedly in the list, should be understood as meaning 'specially designed for military use'. The second category, 'ML2', refers to 'smooth-bore weapons with a calibre of 20mm or more, other weapons or armament with a calibre greater than 12.7 mm (calibre 0.50 inches), projectors and accessories, as follows, specially designed therefor'.

Some weapons are classified as war material and also as firearms.[28] The listed products include, evidently, military equipment of all kinds (tanks, machine guns, protective equipment, computer software, etc.), but also parts of said equipment (bolts, tape, etc.), the material needed to maintain and keep the equipment operational, and substances such as fuels.

Listing products is an insider's exercise. The European Commission also asks national experts to check the work of interpreters to ensure that no mistakes have been made. This verification is not superfluous, as errors are common, and European Commission staff lack expertise in this area, despite the creation of a Directorate-General dedicated to defence issues in 2021, the Directorate-General *for Defence Industry and Space* (DG DEFIS). The uniform interpretation of the list is essential, as it determines the application of the directive's provisions to the equipment in question. The list is therefore intended for both customs authorities and manufacturers, who are responsible for submitting licence applications to the national authorities.

The 'common list of defence-related products' is updated annually by the European Commission in accordance with the provisions of Article 13((1) and (2)) of the transfers Directive, which reproduces the procedure set out in the Interinstitutional Agreement on Better Lawmaking,[29] by means of a delegated directive.[30]

Article 13 of the transfers Directive specifies that the list of defence-related products must 'strictly correspond to the Common Military List of the European Union'. This reference, which was made by the French authorities when the directive was transferred to the system of delegated acts in 2019,[31] is due to the existence, in the past, of disparities between the list annexed to the directive (relating to the war material that may circulate under licence within the internal market), and the list of war material annexed to Common Position 2008/944/CFSP (concerning the material that may enter or leave European territory under licence). The European list annexed to the transfers Directive has its origins in the list adopted by the Council of the European Union on exports.

---

28 In particular within the meaning of Directive (EU) 2021/555 of the European Parliament and of the Council of 24 March 2021 on control of the acquisition and possession of weapons ([2021] *OJ* L115/1), Article 2(2) of which states that it does not apply to the acquisition or possession, in accordance with national law, of weapons and ammunition by the armed forces, the police or public authorities, or to transfers governed by Directive 2009/43/EC.

29 Interinstitutional Agreement between the European Parliament, the Council of the European Union and the European Commission on Better Law-Making, 13 April 2016, [2016] *OJ* L123/1.

30 The latest is Commission Delegated Directive (EU) 2023/277 of 5 October 2022 amending Directive 2009/43/EC of the European Parliament and of the Council as regards updating the list of defence-related products in accordance with the updated Common Military List of the European Union of 21 February 2022, [2023] *OJ* L42/1.

31 On this subject, see below.

Without the strict control of national experts, the differences that may have existed between these two lists, due in particular to problems of translation or of copying the names of the equipment listed, could have led to aberrant situations in which equipment entering EU territory could not circulate there, or worse still, equipment was subject to a licence to circulate between Member States whereas it was not subject to a licence to leave EU territory. In other words, a licence was required for the transfer of equipment, but not for its export.

Similarly, excessive delays in transposing the list annexed to the directive by the Commission from the list annexed to the common position may have rendered the transfer list obsolete even before it came into force. The list of equipment subject to export controls is generally adopted by the Council in February.[32] However, the list annexed to the transfer Directive was adopted in June of the following year. As a result, for a year and a half, the equipment subject to control within the internal market was not the same as that controlled at the EU's external borders. Moreover, from one year to the next, equipment considered to be a military product that saw its use become more widespread and more common, joined the list of dual-use items (DUIs), and was therefore no longer subject to a movement regime as strict as that for war material.[33] A long transposition period eventually means that certain goods are subject to stricter rules within the EU than when exported to third countries.

The existence of an identical list for transfers and exports is one of the conditions for the development of a genuine European policy for controlling the movement of war material.

The links between transfers and exports are essential. War material is, by its very nature, intended for use outside the territory of the European Union. The transfers Directive does not ignore this destination. In fact, it seeks to ensure that national authorities' controls on transfers and exports of war material are consistent.

2. *The First Steps towards the Europeanisation of Controls through the Inclusion of Export Controls in the Transfers Directive*

The defence market is international by nature. The equipment is not intended for domestic use, but is destined to be used in conflict zones. Since the European Union has not experienced war on its territory since the creation of the European Coal and Steel Community (ECSC) in 1951, the production of

---

32 The latest common list was adopted by the Council in February 2024, [2024] *OJ* C2024/1945.

33 List annexed to Regulation (EU) 2021/821 of the European Parliament and of the Council of 20 May 2021 setting up a Union regime for the control of exports, brokering, technical assistance, transit and transfers of dual-use items (recast), [2021] *OJ* L206/1. On this regulation, see the contribution by A. Millet-Devalle in this publication.

war material by European manufacturers, even when purchased by European armies, is destined for use outside European territory. Equipment transferred between EU Member States is therefore destined to be exported.

Such international shipment is taken into account in the transfers Directive. Thus, although it applies to intra-EU transfers of defence-related products, it makes the link with exports of such equipment outside EU territory: the control of intra-EU transfers of defence-related products requires consideration of the control of exports of war material.

Chapter III of the Directive expressly concerns post-transfer exports. This is despite Article 1(2), which defines the purpose of the Directive, stating that 'this Directive shall not affect the discretion of Member States as regards policy on the export of defence-related products' and Recital 30 of the Directive, which recalls that the principles governing the export of equipment from EU territory are set out in Common Position 2008/944/CFSP. Firstly, Article 8 of the Directive allows the State issuing the transfer licence to restrict the export of equipment to third States. A State may therefore attach an obligation to provide information to a transfer licence if the equipment leaves EU territory after being transferred to another Member State; it may even prohibit such re-exportation. This article establishes the right of national authorities to know the final destination and use of the material.[34] Article 10 guarantees the operationality of Article 8 by stipulating that a Member State issuing an export licence must control whether any such export restrictions exist in a transfer licence previously issued for the exported equipment or one of its components. If such an export restriction exists, the exporting State must secure the agreement of the transferring Member State before authorising the export. These procedures ensure consistency between circulation within the internal market and the export authorisations issued by the Member States. Finally, Article 11, which provides the legal basis for customs control of exports of defence-related products, makes the exporting State responsible for controlling the legality of transfer licences issued by any other Member State for the movement of the good within the EU.

Through these three articles, the transfers Directive therefore indirectly regulates the export of defence-related products. These regulations encourage the introduction of export licences similar to those imposed for transfers[35] and promote exchanges between national authorities. Council Common Position 2008/944/CFSP also encourages communication between Member States, particularly on refusals to grant licences and the reasons for such refusals.

---

34 On this issue, see D. Callamand, 'La problématique destination et utilisation finales dans les exportations d'armement', *Rapport du GRIP*, 2008/4; as well as I. Berkol and V. Moreau, 'Contrôles post-exportation lors des transferts d'armement: épreuves d'arrivée et monitoring de l'utilisation finale', *Rapport du GRIP*, 2009/4.

35 Art. 1 of the Directive even defines the concept of 'export licences'.

However, the transfers Directive institutionalises a forum for discussion and exchange for the Member States, by creating a committee, which will become an expert group in 2021.

3. *The Institutionalisation of a Forum to Promote Consistency between National Transfer and Export Policies*

Article 13a of the transfers Directive establishes a group of experts who must be consulted by the European Commission before the adoption of any delegated act implementing the provisions of the Directive. In 2019, this group of experts replaced the transfers committee provided for in Article 14 of the directive, which has now been abolished. However, the understanding of its role by DG DEFIS, which heads the expert group, goes beyond recording the work carried out by the Commission. Following the example of DG GROW, when it headed the transfers Committee, DG DEFIS is using the expert group to further harmonise national practices, in particular by encouraging Member States to share their best practices and disseminate national data, such as licence refusals.

The agenda for the sessions is proposed by the European Commission, but Member States can make an active contribution. Without betraying the content of the discussions held between the Member States in the transfers Committee, it should be noted that the Committee's meetings provide an opportunity to point out the difficulties encountered by national manufacturers as a result of licence refusals by the customs authorities of other Member States, which limit or delay the manufacture of equipment. Pieces of military equipment are in fact complex items, which very often combine components manufactured in several Member States or third countries. These exchanges also enable the adoption of European Commission recommendations, which are not binding,[36] but constitute guidelines providing details on the different types of licences or certification criteria, to improve the harmonisation of national regulations and practices.[37]

---

[36] In accordance with Article 288 TFEU.

[37] The recommendations adopted to date are as follows: Commission Recommendation (EU) 2016/2123 of 30 November 2016 on the harmonisation of the scope of and conditions for general transfer licences for armed forces and contracting authorities as referred to in point (a) of Article 5(2) of Directive 2009/43/EC of the European Parliament and of the Council (notified under document number C(2016) 7711), [2016] *OJ* L329/101; Commission Recommendation (EU) 2016/2124 of 30 November 2016 on the harmonisation of the scope and conditions concerning for general transfer licences for certified recipients referred to in Article 9 of Directive 2009/43/EC of the European Parliament and of the Council [notified under document number C(2016) 7728], [2016] *OJ* L329/105; Commission Recommendation (EU) 2018/2050 of 19 December 2018 on aligning the scope and conditions concerning for general transfer licences for the purposes of demonstration and evaluation as referred to in point (c) of Article 5(2) of Directive 2009/43/EC of the European Parliament and of the

Discussions in expert groups also provide an opportunity for Member States and the Council to share developments in export controls. For example, the progress of work on revising Council Common Position 2008/944/CFSP, when it is carried out by the Council Working Group on Conventional Arms Exports (COARM), is regularly presented to the transfers Expert Group.

Thus, the Transfers expert group encourages the gradual development of an EU-wide policy on the transfer and export of war material.

More broadly, the links between transfers and exports established by the transfers Directive help to ensure that controls on the movement of war material are consistent across Europe and lay the foundations for a European policy in this area. However, at this stage, war material transfer and export policies are still largely in the hands of the Member States.

II. THE LIMITS OF THE TRANSFERS DIRECTIVE: THE INEVITABLE MAINTENANCE OF STATE CONTROL OVER THE CIRCULATION OF WAR MATERIAL?

Both the provisions of the Directive and its sources allow national authorities to exert considerable influence over its implementation (Section A). In addition to these legal limits, which hamper integration, there are political limits which are tending to diminish, opening up the prospect of a real Europeanisation of controls on the movement of military equipment (Section B).

A. LEGAL LIMITS TO THE EUROPEANISATION OF THE MOVEMENT OF WAR MATERIAL

The provisions of the directive were drafted to guarantee a wide margin of interpretation for national authorities. However, as well as taking advantage of this freedom, the Member States contribute, upstream, through their participation in international organisations, to informing European regulations

Council [notified under document number C(2018) 8598], [2018] *OJ* L327/89; Commission Recommendation (EU) 2018/2051 of 19 December 2018 on aligning the scope of and conditions for general transfer licences for the purposes of repair and maintenance as referred to in point (d) of Article 5(2) of Directive 2009/43/EC of the European Parliament and of the Council [notified under document number C(2018) 8610], [208] *OJ* L327/94; Commission Recommendation (EU) 2018/2052 of 19 December 2018 on aligning the scope of and conditions for general transfer licences for the purpose of exhibition as referred to in point (c) of Article 5(2) of Directive 2009/43/EC of the European Parliament and of the Council [notified under document number C(2018) 8611], [2018] *OJ* L327/98.

independently of the institutions. The limits to the Europeanisation of the circulation of war material are therefore both internal to the Directive (Section 1) and external to it (Section 2).

1. *Internal Limits to the Directive: Respect for the 'Sovereign or Political' Discretion of National Authorities*

The provisions of the transfers Directive are drafted in such a way as to leave the national authorities considerable room for manoeuvre. It is important, as Recitals 17 and 18 emphasise, that the freedom of Member States to grant or refuse a licence is respected, as is their choice of the type of licence granted, as well as the conditions of the transfer. Recital 28 reiterates this: '[T]he margin of manoeuvre of Member States regarding the definition of the conditions of general, global and individual transfer licences should be sufficiently flexible to allow for further cooperation efforts within the existing international export control framework. Since the decision to authorise or refuse an export is and should remain the prerogative of each Member State, such cooperation should result only from the voluntary coordination of export policies'.

This objective of extensive compliance with national transfer and export policies is given concrete form by several provisions that allow Member States to derogate, or even opt out from provisions of the Directive.

For example, the transfers Directive places particular emphasis on the grounds of public policy or public security, which traditionally justify a Member State being able to derogate from the application of EU law.[38] These grounds even form the basis for a 'right of unilateral suspension' of a decision taken by another Member State.[39] Article 15 of the transfers Directive, entitled 'Safeguard measures', provides that where a Member State considers that there is a serious risk that a certified recipient in another Member State will not comply with a condition attached to a general transfer licence, or where it considers that public policy, public security or its essential security interests could be threatened, it shall inform the other Member State and ask it to assess the situation.[40] If doubts persist, despite the response from the national authorities, the Member State initiating the control may provisionally suspend the effects of its general transfer licence with regard to the recipient(s) in question.

---

38 Art. 4(7)(b) and Art. 15.

39 Senate Report No. 306 on behalf of the Committee on Foreign Affairs, Defence and Armed Forces on the draft law on the control of imports and exports of war material and assimilated material, the simplification of transfers of defence-related products in the European Union and defence and security markets, by J. de Rohan, 2011, p. 42.

40 Within the meaning of Art. 346 TFEU.

Secondly and most importantly, apart from this exceptional suspension on grounds of public order and security, the Directive places the burden of all the mechanisms it introduces very largely on national authorities. For example, Article 5 governing general transfer licences sets out four cases in which Member States are required to adopt licences. However, this list is not exhaustive, and Member States may create other general transfer licences for any reason they wish. The directive does not seek to create a European transfer licence, or even a European transfer licence label. The principle of the general transfer licence is European, but its implementation is specific to each Member State.[41]

Member States may also specify the transfer conditions required to benefit from a general licence. Not only do the categories of general licence vary from one Member State to another, but so do the conditions for benefiting from them and how they are used. These conditions include for example, criteria prohibiting the use of a general transfer licence[42] or the requirement of prior notification to the national authorities when an company uses a general transfer licence for the first time.[43] Similarly, the granting of a global licence is generally subject to the prior transmission of a certain amount of information to the national authorities for examination of the file, which is not specified in any way in the Directive. The control *ex ante* of transfers established by the Directive is therefore based, at least in terms of the substance of the criteria to be applied, on the assessment of each Member State. The same applies to individual licences. The transfers Directive does not specify the material criteria for control. It only lays down procedural rules, which may also be adapted by each Member State. Unlike Council Common Position 2008/944/CFSP, which does not harmonise the procedural conditions for exports, but formalises eight criteria for the substantive assessment of licence applications, the directive merely proposes procedures for issuing licences, but leaves almost total discretion regarding the substantive criteria for issuing licences.

Finally, the transfers Directive is not binding on the Member States as to the end to be achieved, other than to introduce controls on the movement of equipment, but it does specify the means to be implemented, despite what Article 288(3) TFEU says about this type of secondary legislation.

---

41 This led the first commentators on the directive to fear the development of *forum shopping* among defence manufacturers: H.-L. Goffinet, 'La directive simplifiant les transferts intracommunautaires de produits liés à la défense', *Note d'Analyse du GRIP*, 2010.

42 For example, the general licence issued by the French authorities for the transfer of defence-related products to certified companies (LGTFR 102) stipulates that the licence may not be used to contravene France's international commitments or to transfer the source codes of war material. The LGTFR 102 also includes non-re-export clauses or specific technical clauses for certain armaments, for example.

43 This principle of first notification is set out in Article 5(4) of Directive 2009/43/EC.

Its provisions are designed to guarantee the freedom of States to develop a national policy for controlling the movement of war material. Recital 6 and Article 1(2) make it clear that the transfer and export policy for defence-related products remains national. The directive is concerned only with rules and procedures.

This results from the will of the Member States, which is unsurprising in the defence sector.[44] The transfers Directive shows a strong national influence, reflected in its 46 recitals, which express the sensitivity of the debates that led to the negotiation of the text. Recital 7 states that 'harmonisation of the relevant laws and regulations of the Member States should not prejudice the international obligations and commitments of the Member States nor their discretion as regards their export policy for defence-related products'. Recital 8 adds that 'Member States should remain entitled to pursue and further develop intergovernmental cooperation, whilst complying with the provisions of this Directive'. Recital 11 states that the Directive respects the international commitments of the Member States. Recital 14 guarantees that '[t]his Directive should not prejudice the application of provisions necessary on grounds of public policy or public security. In the light of the nature and features of defence-related products, grounds of public policy, such as the safety of transport, the safety of storage, the risk of diversion and the prevention of crime, are of particular relevance for the purposes of this Directive'. Recital 39 further provides that '[i]f a Member State of origin has a reasonable doubt as to whether a certified recipient will comply with a condition attached to its general transfer licence, or where a licensing Member State considers that public policy, public security or its essential security interests could be affected, it should not only inform the other Member States and the Commission, but should also be able to provisionally suspend the effect of any transfer licence benefiting that recipient, having regard to its responsibility for the preservation of human rights, peace, security and stability'.

The text of the transfers Directive, because of the will of those who drafted it, therefore contains the limits to the integration of control over the circulation of war material. What is more, the influence of national policies is not limited to the implementation of the directive. Member States also exert influence on the Directive from the international legal order, through their participation in international agreements that influence European provisions.

---

44 This desire to guarantee the development of a national policy can be found in numerous texts specific to defence. See, for example, on Member States' export policy: Articles 20(9) and 23(3) of Regulation (EU) 2021/697 of the European Parliament and of the Council of 29 April 2021 establishing the European Defence Fund and repealing Regulation (EU) 2018/1092 ([2021] *OJ* L170/149) or Article 56(3) of Council Decision (CFSP) 2021/509 of 22 March 2021 establishing a European Peace Facility and repealing Decision (CFSP) 2015/528 ([2021] *OJ* L102/14).

2. *The External Limits of the Directive: The Influence of the Member States on the International Regulations which are the Source of the Directive*

The movement of war material is controlled at the international level by various instruments, with the Wassenaar Arrangement having a particular influence on European legislation.

This Arrangement is a multilateral agreement on the export control of conventional arms and sensitive dual-use goods and technologies (i.e. for both civilian and military use), and the control of conventional arms and war material. Set up in 1996 by 33 States, it now has 42 members. The European Union is not represented, as competence in this area remains mainly national, and the many Member States that participate sit alone. 'The Wassenaar Arrangement has been established in order to contribute to regional and international security and stability, by promoting transparency and greater responsibility in transfers of conventional arms and dual-use goods and technologies, thus preventing destabilising accumulations'.[45]

Like the European instruments, the Wassenaar Arrangement calls for controls to be carried out in the country of the final destination of the goods to take account of the risks of regional and international destabilisation associated with exports. The Arrangement uses two main procedural techniques: i) the call for harmonised controls on the movement of goods, based on the sharing of information between national authorities, and ii) the definition of a list of goods to be controlled. These two techniques are reminiscent of the procedures put in place at the European level by the transfers Directive.

The Declaration establishing the Wassenaar Arrangement states that participating States shall meet regularly to ensure that transfers of conventional arms and dual-use goods and technology are conducted responsibly and with respect for regional and international peace and security. To this end, States party to the Arrangement must exchange information voluntarily and regularly on licences, refusals they oppose, as well as the reasons for such refusals. The explicit aim is to better coordinate national policies. Such mechanisms are also provided for in Article 12 of the transfers Directive, which requires Member States to set up, in conjunction with the Commission, direct cooperation and the exchange of information between national authorities.

The second main contribution of the Arrangement is the annual adoption of a list of dual-use items and a list of conventional arms whose circulation the States Parties agree to control.[46] The list of conventional weapons determines

---

45 First paragraph of the objectives of the Arrangement as described in its 'Initial Elements' adopted by the plenary meeting on 11 and 12 July 1996 and amended exceptionally by the plenary meeting on 6 and 7 December 2001.

46 In principle, goods no longer included in the military equipment list are included in the dual-use goods list.

the adoption of the European control lists. The latter transpose the list adopted at Wassenaar. The transposition timetable is, in principle, as follows: the lists are negotiated each year in December at Wassenaar; the Council transposes the list of war material for exports at the beginning of the year (generally in February), by updating the annex to Council Common Position 2008/944/CFSP; then, in the spring, the European Commission updates the common list of defence-related products annexed to the transfers Directive, taking over the content of the list of military equipment annexed to the Common Position.

The content of the list annexed to Council Common Position 2008/944/CFSP is not necessarily identical to that of the list adopted at Wassenaar, as the EU Council may decide to extend the list of equipment controlled at the European level. By contrast, the content of the list of defence-related equipment annexed to the transfers directive, must be 'strictly' identical to that adopted by the Council.[47]

The European texts were negotiated after the Wassenaar Arrangement was put in place, and set out at the EU level the commitments made by the Member States at Wassenaar.

The influence of another international body, and through it that of the Member States, should also be mentioned, namely the LoI (*Letter of Intent).* The organisation was set up by France, Germany, Italy, Spain, Sweden and the United Kingdom, which signed a letter of intent and related agreement on 6 July 1998 to support industrial restructuring in the defence sector. The LoI framework enables the States Parties to adopt joint recommendations to facilitate the development of the European Defence Technological and Industrial Base (EDTIB). To this end, the signatory states are discussing export and transfer procedures, with the aim of harmonising them. This agreement has not been called into question by the adoption of Common Position 2008/944/CFSP in 2008 nor that of the transfers Directive in 2009. On the contrary, meetings of the LoI States were generally held in conjunction with those of the transfers Committee. As long as the United Kingdom was an EU Member State at least, the LoI group even acted as a sort of antechamber to the committee, being able to discuss within a restricted committee the proposed recommendations put forward by the European Commission and working on the needs for changes to European regulations or practices identified in the transfers committee.

The implementation of European regulations thus remains largely in the hands of the Member States, and transfer and export policies are still exclusively national. However, the European and international political context is becoming more favourable to the development of an integrated European policy in this area.

---

47 See above.

B. POLITICAL LIMITS TO THE EUROPEANISATION OF THE CIRCULATION OF WAR MATERIAL

The Commission's 2016 report on the implementation of the transfers Directive concluded that the text had met with only moderate success among national authorities. This reflected the political reluctance of the Member States to Europeanise the control of the circulation of war material. Such a preservation of national control is also tolerated by the European Commission (Section 1). However, the European context has evolved rapidly in recent years, becoming increasingly favourable and even asking for the development of a genuine European policy on the transfer and export of war material. In other words, the Europeanisation of the movement of war material seems increasingly possible (Section 2).

1. National Political Obstacles to Harmonisation: The Reluctance of Member States to Fully Apply the Directive

The transfers Directive has a special evaluation measure enabling the European Commission to review its implementation five years after its entry into force (i.e. in 2016), and to report to the European Parliament and the Council. The Commission's report could have been accompanied by a legislative proposal to influence the Directive's impact on the development of a European defence equipment market and a European defence technological and industrial base (EDTIB). However, in its report, the European Commission considered that while it was not necessary to amend the directive, it was essential to focus efforts on improving its implementation. The report not only concluded that the directive's influence on the development of an EDTIB in Europe was not yet visible, but also highlighted a number of obstacles to the effective application of the directive on transfers. The main difficulties stem from the lack of harmonisation in the implementation of general transfer licences in the Member States, the slowness in taking account of the new licensing and certification options, and the variable use of any prior authorisation exemptions depending on the Member State. In addition, transfers between Member States remain a complex issue that continues to create a significant administrative burden. The directive leaves a wide margin of discretion to the national authorities for its implementation, leading to disparities in national control regimes that the institutionalisation of a forum for exchanges between Member States has not been able to avoid. For example, the European Commission's report notes that, while the number of global transfer licences issued during the period 2012-2014 is high, five States issued no global licences during the evaluation period and four issued nearly 200 or more each. Similarly, there were significant differences in the number of general transfer licences: eleven

Member States recorded no notifications at all, while three Member States recorded more than 100. In addition, the vast majority of transfers (around 90%) were still carried out using individual transfer licences, while only a small proportion were carried out using global transfer licences (<5%) and general transfer licences (<10%). Individual transfer licences were due to be replaced by new tools, but they remain the main form of transfer authorisation in Europe.[48]

As the 2016 report shows, Member States are tending to maintain previous practices and are favouring a national approach to controlling the movement of defence-related products, to the detriment of harmonising this control at European level. Against this backdrop, the European Parliament called on the Commission to make it a priority to follow up the recommendations on the scope and conditions of general transfer licences, including by considering the possibility of transforming the recommendations into binding provisions.[49] This has still not been done.

Political reluctance on the part of the Member States, or their difficulties in overcoming the hurdle of genuine mutual trust, can be explained in particular by the strategic interest represented by the trade in war material. From an economic point of view, arms exports account for a very large proportion of Member States' trade balances. In 2021, for example, they represented €10.2 billion for France, with European purchases accounting for only around 20% of the total. In terms of trade, France exports more than it transfers. Germany exported €4.4 billion, but only in the first half of 2022, which on an annual basis is broadly equivalent to French exports. Transfers, on the other hand, accounted for almost 60% of this amount. Russia's neighbouring Member States have been investing massively in rearmament since the invasion of Ukraine.[50] These investments illustrate this, as do a number of the objectives of Common Position 2008/944/CFSP: the circulation of war material also presents a security risk, in terms of regional destabilisation or the diversion of weapons by terrorist organisations. Each State therefore has a strong security interest in maintaining control over this trade.

48 European Commission, 'Report from the Commission to the European Parliament and the Council, Evaluation of Directive 2009/43/EC of the European Parliament and of the Council of 6 May 2009 simplifying terms and conditions of transfers of defence-related products within the Community', COM(2016) 760 final, 30 November 2016, p. 5.

49 European Parliament, Committee on the Internal Market and Consumer Protection, 'Report on the implementation of Directive 2009/81/EC, concerning procurement in the fields of defence and security, and Directive 2009/43/EC, concerning the transfer of defence-related products (2019/2204(INI))', 8 March 2021, para. 21.

50 https://www.gifas.fr/press-summary/la-pologne-passe-des-commandes-massives-d-armement; https://www.lemonde.fr/international/article/2023/11/26/comment-la-guerre-en-ukraine-redessine-les-flux-du-rearmement-mondial_6202422_3210.html.

Finally, there are also issues linked to the historical link between the State and the defence industry, at least for those countries with a developed defence industry, including France.[51]

The European Commission is sensitive to these national considerations and is listening to the Member States. In the transfers group, and before that in the Committee, the Commission has been keen to encourage constructive exchanges and a proactive attitude on the part of the Member States. The Commission seems to consider that the transfers Directive is still work in progress. By contrast, the Commission does not feel this way about the defence procurement Directive. The meetings of the group or, at the time, the committee, were much more formal. It is more a question of Member States being accountable to the European Commission. Within the framework of the transfers, the Commission adopts a less firm stance, encouraging Member States to exchange information.[52] For example, the Commission allowed the Member States to contribute extensively to the evaluation of the Article 17 Directive, which resulted in the report published in 2016.[53]

This consultative position is also illustrated by the differences in the application of the text tolerated by the Commission. For example, Germany has transposed the common list of military equipment into two lists. The first, in accordance with the annexe to the directive, is intended to make equipment subject to the rules set out in the directive. However, it does not contain all the equipment in Annex 1 of the directive. Some equipment has been taken out and included in a second list, which simply lists the equipment banned from circulation on German territory. The Commission has been informed of this second list, the existence of which the German representatives make no secret of during discussions in the expert group, and which they justify by Germany's particular sensitivity in this area, due to its history. France also has two lists. It has added space equipment to the list annexed to the transfers directive.

---

51 The links between the French State and the major French defence industrialists are still very close, not to say organic. The Minister of Defence, the Minister of Foreign Affairs or the President of the Republic can act as the French defence industry's sales representatives by concluding arms sales with other states, including European states. Not forgetting examples such as the failed sale of French submarines to Australia, or the about-turn by the Belgian army which, after choosing French machine guns, finally opted for the German offer, or the French government's attempt to sell Rafale planes to Belgium: https://www.challenges.fr/entreprise/defense/f-35-en-belgique-pourquoi-le-rafale-ne-pouvait-pas-gagner_622026.

52 These impressions are based on the authors' participation in the Transfers Directive and the Defence Procurement Directive committees and verified with former colleagues. It would not appear that the change from a committee to an expert group has altered the Commission's position vis-à-vis the Member States when it comes to implementing the Transfers Directive.

53 See below; European Commission, 'Report from the Commission to the European Parliament and the Council, Evaluation of Directive 2009/43/EC of the European Parliament and of the Council of 6 May 2009 simplifying terms and conditions of transfers of defence-related products within the Community', COM(2016) 760 final, 30 November 2016.

This second list, which extends the range of equipment subject to the transfers Directive, is set out in a second part of the national decree transposing the common list of military equipment.[54] The European Commission even tolerates the existence of transfer licences that disregard the spirit of the Directive by calling into question the fundamental rule that import controls must cease,[55] in the application of the principle of mutual trust. Germany requires a general licence for the entry and transit of weapons of war. Hungary requires transit licences for certain categories of products and has maintained entry licences.[56]

The political stances of the Member States, which tend to preserve national approaches to controlling the movement of war material, and which are tolerated by the European Commission, could however change as the European context evolves and becomes more conducive to the integration of controls on a continental scale.

2. *A More Favourable European Context for a Truly European Control of the Circulation of Defence-Related Products?*

In addition to the inherent ratchet effect of European integration, which nevertheless clashes with political will, recent regulatory developments and political attempts do show that the European context is evolving in favour of a genuine Europeanisation of control, or even making such Europeanisation progressively necessary. European defence has been strengthened in particular since 2017.[57]

A letter from Ursula van der Leyen, the Defence Minister of the Federal Republic of Germany at the time, to the European Commission called for a

54 Order of 27 June 2012 on the list of war material and assimilated material subject to prior export authorisation and defence-related products subject to prior transfer authorisation, Part Two: other used material.

55 This rule is set out in Article 4(1) of the Directive. The objective is set out in Recital 17: 'Member States should be free to deny or grant prior authorisation. In line with the principles establishing the internal market, such authorisation should be valid throughout the Community and no further authorisation for passage through other Member States or entrance onto the territory of other Member States should be required'.

56 European Commission, 'Report from the Commission to the European Parliament and the Council on the transposition of Directive 2009/43/EC simplifying terms and conditions for transfer of defence-related products within the EU', Brussels, 29 June 2012, COM(2012) 359 final, p. 7.

57 On the construction of a European defence / a European defence law / the Europeanisation of defence, see in particular: E. Bernard, 'La communautarisation de la défense européenne dans le contexte de la guerre en Ukraine', *RTDE*, 2023/3, p. 325; A. Cammilleri-Subrenat, *Le droit de la politique européenne de sécurité et de défense dans le cadre du traité de Lisbonne*, Paris/Cachan, Lavoisier/Éditions TEC & DOC, 2010; É. Daniel, *La mise en œuvre de la compétence opérationnelle de l'Union européenne en matière de PESC: singularités et cohérences*, thesis, 2016; B. Irondelle, 'L'Europe de la défense', in J. Ziller (ed.), *L'Union européenne*, Paris, Édition Traité de Lisbonne, La Documentation française, 2008, pp. 202–207; A. Hamonic, 'Union européenne et défense: un État membre de (presque) perdu; dix

strengthening of the European Union's transport infrastructure to facilitate the movement of armed forces within Europe. This letter gave rise to several parallel programmes under the European Defence Agency (EDA), to remove administrative obstacles to the movement of military personnel (two technical arrangements on mobility military were signed in 2021),[58] and by the European Commission, to finance a resizing of Member States' road infrastructures through the MIE-T regulation.[59] Improving the movement of European military personnel inevitably raises the issue of improving the movement of war material.[60] Under the transfers Directive, armed forces can benefit from a licence exemption or a general transfer licence, depending on the circumstances.[61] However, not all countries have introduced these exemptions or derogations from the individual licence principle. Some States even prohibit the movement of uniformed members of foreign armed forces on their territory.[62]

With the Russian invasion of Ukraine, defence issues have been given greater prominence at EU level and the adoption of legislative acts has accelerated.[63] In February 2022, the Commission published a roadmap on

---

innovations de (re)trouvées', *RTDE*, 2019, p. 783; M. Saoudi, 'La politique européenne de défense à la lumière du CFP 2021-2027: vers un droit européen de la défense?', *Les champs de mars*, 2021/1, No. 36, pp. 147–169.

58 The first technical arrangement concerns military mobility. It was led by the Netherlands. The second technical arrangement was led by Germany. Its aim is to develop military hubs throughout the EU, enabling mobilised armies that have to cross European territory to be accommodated in suitable conditions. The EDA is continuing its work in this area. On 30 January 2024, it organised a symposium in Brussels on military mobility.

59 Regulation (EU) 2021/1153 of the European Parliament and of the Council of 7 July 2021 establishing the Connecting Europe Facility and repealing Regulations (EU) No 1316/2013 and (EU) No 283/2014 ([2021] *OJ* L249/38): the European Interconnection Facility (EIF), also known as the *Connecting Europe Facility* (CEF), supports European infrastructure projects of common interest in the transport, energy and telecommunications sectors. It has a budget of €33.7 billion for the period 2021-2027. As part of the Multiannual Financial Framework (MFF) 2021-2027, a specific budget of €1.74 billion has been allocated to boost military mobility in the EU. See https://www.touteleurope.eu/economie-et-social/le-mecanisme-pour-l-interconnexion-en-europe-mie-un-programme-pour-les-infrastructures-europeenne. See the contribution by S. de La Rosa in this publication on this regulation, based in particular on Article 172 TFEU.

60 É. Daniel and M. Kieffer, 'La libre circulation du militaire dans l'Union européenne', *Les champs de Mars*, 2021/1, no. 36, pp. 197–201.

61 See Art. 4(2), and Art. 5 of the Transfers Directive.

62 During the preparatory work for these various agreements, Ireland and Germany raised the issue of such national bans on all or part of their territory.

63 On this subject, see in particular. A. Hamonic, 'L'agression armée de l'Ukraine, un révélateur de l'Union européenne en tant qu'acteur de défense?', *Le club des juristes*, 18 March 2022 (article available at https://www.leclubdesjuristes.com/politique/lagression-armee-de-lukraine-un-revelateur-de-lunion-europeenne-en-tant-quacteur-de-defense-787) and A.-H. Bertana, 'L'impact de la guerre en Ukraine sur la coopération européenne en matière de défense: simple sursaut ou véritable éveil?', *Revue de l'Union européenne*, 2023, pp. 44–51.

critical technologies for security and defence.[64] The aim is to enable the whole of Europe and its immediate neighbourhood to rearm. Here again, the issue of the circulation of war material is unavoidable. In July 2023, the ammunition production support regulation (ASAP) came into force.[65] This regulation aims to strengthen the EDTIB as a matter of urgency by mobilising €500 million from the EU budget for European defence industries for the production of ground-to-ground ammunition, artillery ammunition and missiles.[66] In October 2023, the regulation on the establishment of an instrument to strengthen the European Defence Industry Reinforcement Through Common Procurement Act (EDIRPA) entered into force.[67] Its purpose is to strengthen the European defence industry through joint procurement. This regulation is a financial instrument that encourages Member States to engage in joint defence procurement. The question of a European licence and a European authority competent to issue it inevitably arises in connection with the implementation of this regulation.

The European institutions are therefore rapidly taking up the issue of trade in war material and, consequently, its circulation. If these issues are settled at the European level, then it would seem consistent for the regulation of the movement of war material to be fully Europeanised.

The European Parliament has on several occasions called for greater Europeanisation of arms transfers and exports, under the impetus in particular of its Security and Defence Subcommittee (SEDE), which is very active in this area.[68] In its resolution of 25 March 2021 on public procurement in the fields of defence and security and transfers of defence-related products, the Parliament called on the Member States to step up intra-EU defence procurement and research and development cooperation, as well as to increase the level of interoperability of their armies.[69] Furthermore, in 2020, in a report on the

---

64 Communication from the Commission to the European Parliament, the Council, the European Economic and Social Committee and the Committee of the Regions, *Roadmap on critical technologies for security and defence*, COM(2022) 61 final, 15 December 2022.

65 Regulation (EU) 2023/1525 of the European Parliament and of the Council of 20 July 2023 on supporting ammunition production (ASAP), [2023] OJ, L185/7. See the contribution by E. Bernard in this publication.

66 Combined reading of Articles 1 and 5 of Regulation (EU) 2023/1525, cited above.

67 Regulation (EU) 2023/2418 of the European Parliament and of the Council of 18 October 2023 on establishing an instrument for the reinforcement of the European defence industry through common procurement (EDIRPA), [2023] OJ L2023/2418. See also the contribution by E. Bernard in this publication.

68 On the SEDE subcommittee, see: K. Von Wagau, 'Le Parlement européen et la PESD – Le rôle de la sous-commission de la sécurité et défense (SEDE)', in S. Dagand, K. von Wagau, I. Bosse-Platière and C. Caballero-Bourdot, 'Le Parlement européen dans la PSDC', *Cahiers de l'IRSEM*, November 2010, No. 4, pp. 17–29.

69 European Parliament resolution of 25 March 2021 on the implementation of Directive 2009/81/EC, concerning public procurement in the fields of defence and security and Directive 2009/43/EC, concerning the transfer of defence-related products (2019/2204(INI)), [2021] *OJ* C494/54.

implementation of the BDU Regulation, the transfers Directive and Common Position 2008/944/CFSP, Hannah Neumann MEP for the Europe Ecology Group proposed the adoption of a regulation governing transfers and exports of military equipment.[70]

In addition to the creation of DG DEFIS, the European Commission is also strengthening its position in this area. It has set up a number of working groups on military equipment, including the Critical Technologies Observatory and the Task Force for Joint Defence Procurement.[71] With regard to the transfers Directive in particular, although the Commission has no plans to change the text of the Directive,[72] it recently stood up to the Member States at the institutional level by imposing the creation of a group of experts instead of maintaining the committee requested by the Member States. Admittedly, this was simply a matter of bringing the directive into line with the comitology rules adopted after the entry into force of the Lisbon Treaty,[73] but it could be seen as a sign that the Commission is strengthening its control over the circulation of war material. The Commission has firmly opposed compliance with the 'Better Law-making' agreement[74] and demanded that it be given a delegated power, enabling it 'to adopt non-legislative acts of general application to supplement or amend certain non-essential elements of the legislative act'[75] and not an implementing power, which it may use 'where uniform conditions for implementing legally binding Union acts are needed'.[76] The representatives of the Member States have attempted to argue that Annex 1 to the Directive, which lists the equipment subject to the certification and licensing regimes established by the Directive, is

70 See: https://www.europarl.europa.eu/doceo/document/A-9-2020-0137_FR.html#_section1, https://old.robert-schuman.eu//fr/doc/divers/La-gouvernance-du-Fonds-europeen-de-defense.pdf, https://www.euractiv.com/section/defence-and-security/interview/sede-rapporteur-eu-badly-needs-common-rules-transparency-in-arms-export.

71 European Parliament, Committee on Foreign Affairs, Report on Arms Exports: Implementation of Common Position 2008/944/CFSP (2020/2003(INI)), 17 July 2020; https://www.europarl.europa.eu/news/fr/press-room/20200910IPR86831/exportations-d-armes-de-l-ue-plus-de-controle-et-de-transparence: 'We simply say: Where EU money is involved in arms development, we also need an enforceable mechanism for EU control of any future exports. This would be based on the restrictive application of the eight existing criteria of the EU Common Position on arms exports and allow for sanctions for cases where member states do not comply with these rules'.

72 The Commission regularly confirms to national authorities at meetings of the Transfers Expert Group that negotiations on the Transfers Directive are not currently being reopened.

73 In particular Regulation (EU) No 182/2011 of the European Parliament and of the Council of 16 February 2011 laying down the rules and general principles concerning mechanisms for control by Member States of the Commission's exercise of implementing powers, [2011] *OJ* L55/13.

74 The conditions for the use of implementing acts and delegated acts were set out in an inter-institutional agreement entitled 'Better Lawmaking', which is in turn set out in guidelines and a toolbox.

75 Art. 290 TFEU.

76 Art. 291 TFEU.

an essential element of the Directive and that its adoption at the EU level, and not in each Member State, is justified by the need to ensure uniform conditions for implementing the Directive. However, the Commission has adhered to a strict application of the Interinstitutional Agreement on the criteria for the application of Articles 290 and 291 TFEU,[77] point II.B.1 of which states that '[i]f the legislator confers the power to amend a legislative act on the Commission, that power can only be exercised by delegated acts, including where that power to amend relates to the annexes, as they are an integral part of legislative acts'. The Member States' main fear was that abolishing the committee, which could justify a more political level of representation than the group of experts, would reduce the role of the Member States and increase that of the Commission, a fear exacerbated by the concomitant creation of DG DEFIS.

The creation of DG DEFIS has not, for the moment, altered the Commission's approach within the transfers expert group. The Commission remains attentive to and respectful of national positions. However, the fact that there is now a Directorate-General dedicated to defence issues will necessarily help increase the skills of Commission staff in these areas. By gaining expertise in the highly technical subjects of defence, including the circulation of war material and the issues involved, the Commission and, beyond that, the Union, will necessarily have greater legitimacy to drive forward a genuine European policy on the transfer and export of war material. Recently published by the Commission, the Defence Readiness Omnibus Act (17 June 2025) proposes to improve Europe's ability to act quickly, coordinate more effectively and ensure its defence industry can deliver at speed and scale, and could indeed be a manifestation of the Commission's increasing technical expertise.[78]

Recent institutional developments, which have been both the product of and the driving force behind the adoption of several European acts in the field of defence in recent years, coupled with changes in the international geopolitical context, particularly the political situation at the borders of the European Union, make the question of developing a genuine integrated European policy on the movement of war material all the more pressing.

---

77 Interinstitutional Agreement between the European Parliament, the Council of the Union and the European Commission of 18 June 2019 on non-binding criteria for the application of Articles 290 and 291 of the Treaty on the Functioning of the European Union, [2019] *OJ* C223/1.

78 https://ec.europa.eu/commission/presscorner/detail/en/ip_25_1518.

REGULATION (EU) 2022/2560 ON FOREIGN SUBSIDIES DISTORTING THE INTERNAL MARKET: AN INSTRUMENT OF ECONOMIC WARFARE

Regulation (EU) 2022/2560 of the European Parliament and of the Council of 14 December 2022 on foreign subsidies distorting the internal market

Stéphane RODRIGUES
Senior Lecturer at the Université Paris 1 Panthéon-Sorbonne
Member of the Sorbonne Institute for Research in International and European Law (IREDIES-EA 4536)
Member of the Brussels Bar

As the Commission points out, the European Union 'is pursuing a model of open strategic autonomy by shaping the system of global economic governance and by developing mutually beneficial bilateral relations, while protecting its internal market from unfair and abusive practices [...].' In recent years, foreign subsidies appear in some instances to have had a distortive impact on EU's internal market, creating an uneven playing field for competition.[1] To examine this issue, the Commission launched a public debate in 2020 on the basis of a White Paper[2] which identified a 'legislative gap' in EU rules on competition, trade and public procurement, which would effectively prevent the EU from taking action when foreign subsidies distort the internal market, in particular by financing mergers or public procurement bids.

Following this consultation, on 5 May 2021,[3] the Commission presented a proposal for a Regulation on foreign subsidies distorting the internal market

1 Extract from the explanatory memorandum to the proposal for a regulation on foreign subsidies distorting the internal market: Commission Communication COM(2021) 223 final, 5 May 2021.

2 White Paper on establishing a level playing field for foreign subsidies: Commission Communication COM(2020) 253 final of 17 June 2020.

3 COM(2021) 223 final, cited above.

basing it on Articles 114 TFEU (internal market) and 207 TFEU (trade policy).[4] This proposal led to the adoption by the European Parliament and the Council of Regulation (EU) 2022/2560 (hereinafter 'the Regulation'), on 14 December 2022.[5] It has been applicable since 12 July 2023 and has been supplemented by an implementing regulation from the Commission.[6]

After defining the purpose and scope of the regulation (Section I), this chapter analyses its operational provisions (Section II).

I. PURPOSE AND SCOPE OF REGULATION (EU) 2022/2560

The purpose of the Regulation (see Article 1) is to contribute to the proper functioning of the internal market 'by establishing a harmonised framework to address distortions caused, directly or indirectly, by foreign subsidies,[7] with a view to ensuring a level playing field'. To this end, it lays down the rules and procedures for investigating and remedying foreign subsidies that distort the internal market, which may affect all economic activities, particularly in two cases covered by specific provisions: mergers and procedures for the award of public contracts or concessions.

This commentary focuses on the provisions relating to public contracts and concessions (hereinafter 'public procurement contracts' or 'the contracts').[8] In this respect, the Regulation (see Recital 41) specifies that, despite the particular regime for defence and security contracts covered by Directive 2009/81/EC (see above), 'it should be possible to examine the foreign subsidies in the context of such contracts in an ex officio review', as only contracts exempted by the said Directive or for which the conditions for the application of Article 346 TFEU[9] are met are not covered by the Regulation.

---

[4] See the commentary on Article 207 TFEU by S. Robert, in this publication.

[5] Regulation (EU) 2022/2560 of the European Parliament and of the Council of 14 December 2022 on foreign subsidies distorting the internal market, [2022] *OJ* L330/1. See also three statements by the institutions, [2022] *OJ* C491/6. For a detailed commentary: A. Reindl and I. Van Damme, 'The EU Foreign Subsidies Regulation', *Concurrences*, 2024, spec. pp. 111–142 on the 'public procurement' section.

[6] See Commission Implementing Regulation (EU) 2023/1441 of 10 July 2023 on the detailed arrangements for the conduct of proceeding by the Commission pursuant to Regulation (EU) 2022/2560, [2023] *OJ* L177/1, as corrected by Commission Implementing Regulation (EU) 2023/2414 of 25 October 2023, [2023] *OJ* L2023/2414.

[7] This covers foreign subsidies granted to undertakings, including public undertakings directly or indirectly controlled by the State, which carry out an economic activity in the internal market. In particular, an undertaking which merges with or acquires control of an undertaking established in the Union, or an undertaking which participates in a procedure for the award of public contracts is deemed to be carrying out an economic activity in the internal market or concessions within the Union, (see Article 1(2) of the Regulation).

[8] For the 'concentrations' section, see the commentary on Articles 101 to 109 TFEU (R. Bellais and S. Rodrigues).

[9] See the commentary on Article 346 TFEU (S. Rodrigues) in this publication.

II. A SYSTEM ESTABLISHED BY REGULATION (EU) 2022/2560

The system is twofold: first, there is a general procedure for the Commission's ex officio review of all public contracts, including those in the defence and security sectors; and second, there is a specific procedure from which contracts covered by Directive 2009/81/EC are excluded.

A. EX OFFICIO EXAMINATION PROCEDURE (RULES 9 TO 18 OF THE REGULATION)

The Commission may, on its own initiative, examine information from any source, including the Member States, a natural or legal person or an association, concerning alleged foreign subsidies distorting the internal market. Unlike the specific procedure set out below, an ex officio examination can only take place in respect of a contract that has already been awarded and cannot lead to the annulment of the decision awarding it.

The procedure may involve two stages. The first stage consists of a preliminary examination, during which the Commission will gather all relevant information (see Article 13 of the Regulation, on requests for information) and carry out inspections inside (see Article 14 of the Regulation) and outside the Union (see Article 15 of the Regulation). If this provides the Commission with sufficient evidence that a company has benefited from a foreign subsidy distorting the internal market,[10] it will move on to the second stage, that of an in-depth investigation, possibly accompanied by provisional measures to avoid 'irreparable damage' (see Article 12 of the Regulation). A notice will then be published in the *OJEU*, with a set period for collecting views. After this, if its initial analysis is confirmed, the Commission may adopt either a decision imposing remedial measures,[11] or a decision accepting commitments from the company under investigation, provided that they 'fully and effectively remedy the distortion in the internal market', including repayment of the subsidy in

---

[10] It should be noted that the Commission may also decide not to go further, 'based on a balancing of 'the negative effects of a foreign subsidy in terms of distortion in the internal market' [...] and 'against the positive effects of the subsidy on the development of the relevant subsidised economic activity concerned in the internal market, while considering other positive effects of the foreign subsidy such as the broader positive on relevant policy objectives, in particular those of the Union' (see Art. 6 of the Regulation).

[11] See the non-exhaustive list of remedies in Article 7 of the Regulation: granting access to infrastructure, or a licence, which has been acquired as a result of, foreign subsidies, or has benefited from distorting the internal market; reducing capacity or market presence, including by temporarily restricting commercial activity; prohibiting certain investments; disposing of certain assets, etc.

question (Art. 11(3) of the Regulation).[12] In all other cases, the Commission will close the investigation with a decision not to raise any objections.

Finally, it should be added that the Commission's investigative powers are accompanied by the power to impose financial penalties (see Article 17 of the Regulation), inspired by the competition enforcement regime.[13] The Commission can impose fines on companies that refuse to cooperate, that wilfully or through negligence provide incomplete, inaccurate or misleading information, that refuse to respond to a request for information or to submit to an inspection, or that fail to comply with an undertaking given or a provisional or remedial measure. These penalties may vary in amount, with a ceiling not exceeding, for fines, 1% or 10% (depending on the seriousness of the infringement of the regulation) of the total turnover achieved by the company concerned during the previous financial year, and 5% of the same turnover for fines.

B. SPECIFIC NOTIFICATION/DECLARATION PROCEDURE (ARTICLES 27 TO 33 OF THE REGULATION)

Chapter 4 of the Regulation sets out a specific regime for certain contracts with foreign subsidies distorting the internal market in the context of public procurement procedures or concessions, outside the scope of Directive 2009/81/EC.

Foreign subsidies 'that cause or risk causing a distortion in a public procurement procedure shall be understood as foreign subsidies that enable an economic operator to submit a tender that is unduly advantageous in relation to the works, supplies or services concerned' (Art. 27 of the Regulation), are assessed on the basis of the non-exhaustive list of indicators set out in Article 4 of the Regulation, with reference to the last three years. In this respect, if over this period the total amount considered does not exceed €4 million, it will be considered as 'unlikely to distort the internal market' (Article 4(2) of the Regulation), and not at all if this same amount does not exceed €200,000 (Article 4(3) of the Regulation).[14]

---

12 Reference to the same indicative list in Article 7 of the Regulation, see above.

13 Council Regulation (EC) No 1/2003 of 16 December 2002 on the implementation of the rules on competition laid down in Articles 81 and 82 of the Treaty, [2003] *OJ* L1/1. On borrowings from competition law see L. Idot, 'Le règlement relatif aux subventions étrangères faussant le marché intérieur: un nouvel outil en droit de la concurrence?', *Europe*, Étude 4, no. 6, June 2023, pp. 5–10.

14 By reference to the so-called *de minimis* threshold in Article 3(2) of Commission Regulation (EU) No 1407/2013 of 18 December 2013 on the application of Articles 107 and 108 of the Treaty on the Functioning of the European Union to *de minimis* aid, [2013] *OJ* L352/1. This regulation expired on 31 December 2023. It was replaced on 1 January 2024, for a period

Another limitation of the scope of the Regulation is that it sets a main threshold for notification. The estimated value of the contract concerned must be equal to or greater than €250 million (Art. 28(1) of the Regulation). If this threshold is reached, the contracting authority/entity must indicate in the contract or concession notice or, in the case of a procedure without prior publication, in the contract or concession documents, that economic operators are subject to an obligation to notify subsidies that meet the conditions of the Regulation or to declare subsidies that do not (see the procedure in Article 29 of the Regulation, applicable from 12 October 2023). The contracting authority must immediately send this notification to the European Commission[15] and also inform it of any suspicions it may have regarding a declaration.

It will be up to the Commission to carry out a preliminary examination to decide whether to open an in-depth investigation.[16] If it opens such an investigation, it will have a period of 90 working days to take a decision, during which time the disputed contract may not be awarded (the 'stand still' clause of Article 32(2) of the Regulation, which stipulates that the contract may be awarded after this period). The Commission has three options: it may find that the subsidy does not distort the market; it may find, on the contrary, that this is the case, but that the economic operator concerned has offered sufficient commitments to remedy fully and effectively the distortion of the internal market; and finally it may adopt a decision prohibiting the award of the contract or concession to the economic operator concerned. In this case, the contracting authority/entity will have to reject the tender and may, if it had previously judged it to be economically the most advantageous, award the contract or concession to the economic operator, not covered by a procedure under the Regulation, who submitted the second best tender.

---

of seven years, by Commission Regulation (EU) 2023/2831 of 13 December 2023 on the application of Articles 107 and 108 of the Treaty on the Functioning of the European Union to *de minimis* aid, [2023] *OJ* L2023/2831, which raises the reference threshold to €300,000.

15 However, it can also launch an ex officio procedure on the basis of its own information.

16 On 16 February 2024, the Commission announced that it had opened its first in-depth investigation under Regulation (EU) 2022/2560, following a notification by CRRC Qingdao Sifang Locomotive Co, Ltd, a subsidiary of CRRC Corporation, a Chinese state-owned train manufacturer. It concerns a public procurement procedure launched by the Bulgarian Ministry of Transport and Communications for the supply of twenty reversible electric trains as well as related maintenance and personnel training services over a period of fifteen years, at a value of approximately 1.2 billion leva (€610 million). See European Commission press release IP/24/887 of 16 February 2024. Following this, CRRC decided to withdraw from the tender in question: see statement by European Commissioner Thierry Breton dated 26 March 2024, STATEMENT/24/1729. See two other investigations opened on 3 April 2024 following notifications by the Chinese groups ENEVO and Shanghai Electric, in connection with a public contract in Romania for the design, construction and operation of a photovoltaic park, financed by the European Modernisation Fund: *see* European Commission press release IP/24/1803 of 3 April 2024.

The general system of financial penalties set out in Article 17 of the Regulation also applies. Thus, an economic operator who, wilfully or through negligence, has provided inaccurate or misleading information in a notification or declaration made based on the Regulation, may be fined an amount not exceeding 1% of its total turnover during the previous financial year. The fine may be higher, but may not exceed 10% of the same turnover, if an operator, again either wilfully or through negligence, has failed to comply with, or has circumvented or attempted to circumvent, its notification obligation under the Regulation.

***

Between now and January 2026, following consultation with stakeholders and Member States, the Commission will publish guidelines concerning in particular the application of criteria for determining the existence of a distortion, the application of the balancing test and the assessment of a distortion in a procedure for the award of public contracts or concessions (see Article 46 of the Regulation). They will be welcome in the name of legal certainty for businesses, which must now incorporate this new procedure into their obligations for any financial contribution received from a third country.[17]

In so doing, Regulation (EU) 2022/2560 is, in the author's view, part of a general movement to equip the European Union with instruments of economic warfare and thus falls within what might be called the European law of 'atypical warfare'.[18]

Postscript August 2025

The European Commission has launched on 12 August 2025, its first review of the Foreign Subsidies Regulation, with public consultation until 18 November 2025.[19]

The review report would focus on: (i) the assessment of foreign subsidies that distort the internal market, (ii) the application of the balancing test (i.e. whether positive effects of the foreign subsidy counterbalance its distortive effects), (iii) the review of foreign subsidies with a possible distortive effect in the internal market on the Commission's own initiative, (iv) the notification thresholds and, (v) more generally, the level of complexity of the rules and the costs incurred by businesses.

---

[17] See also V. Carvalho and E. Tricot, 'Contrôle des concentrations d'entreprises: comment anticiper le contrôle des subventions étrangères?', *Dictionnaire permanent – Droit européen des affaires*, bulletin no. 416, November 2023, pp. 1–3.

[18] To use the formula of D. Mainguy, *Droit de la 'guerre atypique'*, Paris, LGDJ-Lextenso, 2023, spec. pp. 155–185 (economic sanctions).

[19] See Commission Press Release IP/25/1954 of 12 August 2025.

ARTICLE 122 TFEU: EXCEPTIONAL FINANCIAL ASSISTANCE TO MEMBER STATES

Frédéric ALLEMAND
Researcher at the Faculty of Law, Economics and Finance of the University of Luxembourg
Co-director of the Robert Schuman Initiative – Jean Monnet Centre of Excellence

Article 122 (ex Article 100 TEC)

1. Without prejudice to any other procedures provided for in the Treaties, the Council, on a proposal from the Commission, may decide, in a spirit of solidarity between Member States, upon the measures appropriate to the economic situation, in particular if severe difficulties arise in the supply of certain products, notably in the area of energy.

2. Where a Member State is in difficulties or is seriously threatened with severe difficulties caused by natural disasters or exceptional occurrences beyond its control, the Council, on a proposal from the Commission, may grant, under certain conditions, Union financial assistance to the Member State concerned. The President of the Council shall inform the European Parliament of the decision taken.

In the fourth century CE, Vegetius, a high-ranking official of the Late Roman Empire, published *Epitoma rei militaris*, a summary of Roman military tradition and the conduct of war during the reign of Theodosius.[1] The work was intended to contribute to the recovery and preservation of an empire weakened by military inadequacy, statism and the gradual erosion of classical

1 S. JANNIARD, 'Végèce et les transformations de l'art de la guerre aux IVe et Ve siècles après J.-C.', *Antiquité tardive. Revue internationale d'Histoire et d'Archéologie (IVe-VIIe siècle)*, 2008, vol. 16,

culture.[2] It quickly established itself as an important treatise on military art and retained a certain authority until the 16th century, and even to this day, through its maxim 'Si vis pacem, para bellum ('If you want peace, prepare for war'). This paraphrase of one of the recommendations made in Book III points out the moral, physical and material disinvestment in the military, in favour of civil functions:

> But the calm of a long peace led some to the charms of leisure, others to civil employment. Thus, the practice of military exercises, first neglected and then abandoned, eventually fell into oblivion. This situation, which dates back to the last century, is not surprising when one considers that after the First Punic War, a peace lasting more than twenty years, by removing the habit of arms, plunged the Romans, who had been victorious everywhere, into such weakness that they were unable, in the Second Punic War, to stand up to Hannibal.[3]

Fifteen hundred years later, the same observation of reduced deterrence capabilities and the need for collective rearmament is striking the European Union and its Member States. The rise of global risks, Russia's illegal aggression against Ukraine, the limited effects of economic and financial sanctions against Russia, Belarus and their leaders and, since early 2025, political uncertainty over the United States's commitment to NATO have all made it necessary for Europeans to strengthen their defence capabilities.[4] 'We are in an era of rearmament', said Ursula von der Leyen in March 2025, when she presented the main lines of the future White Paper on European defence. 'And Europe is ready to massively boost its defence spending. Both, to respond to the short-term urgency to act and to support Ukraine but also to address the long-term need to take on much more responsibility for our own European security'.[5]

More than in any other field, the availability of budgetary resources is key in defence. 'A war fought without a good reserve of money has only a faint breath of life. The sinews of war are money,' suggests Brother Jean to Grandgousier

---

2 See, for example: R. Paribeni, *L'Italia Imperiale da Ottaviano a Teodosio*, Milan, A. Mondadori, 1938, pp. 682 et seq.; E. Stein, *Histoire du Bas-Empire*, vol. I, *De l'Etat Romain à l'Etat Byzantin (284-476)*, Bruges, Desclée de Brouwer, 1959.

3 Vegetius, *Traité de l'art militaire*, Livre Ier, 'Chapitre 28: Avantages de la pratique des armes'. Available on the website *L'Antiquité grecque et latine du Moyen-Âge*, edited by P. Remacle, P. Renault, F.-D. Fournier et al.: https://remacle.org/bloodwolf/erudits/vegece/livre1.htm. (Author's translation.)

4 Meeting of Heads of State or Government, 'Versailles Declaration', 10 and 11 March 2022; Conclusions of the Extraordinary European Council of 6 March 2025, EUCO 6/25, paras. 4–10; also: Council of the European Union, 'A Strategic Compass for Security and Defence. For a European Union that protects its citizens, values and interests and contributes to international peace and security', Brussels, 21 March 2022; European Commission, White Paper on European Defence/Readiness 2030, Brussels, 19 March 2025.

5 U. von der Leyen, Statement by the President of the European Commission on the defence package, Brussels, 4 March 2025.

in *Gargantua*.[6] Nowadays, this is precisely one of Europe's main weaknesses lies. Since 1994, European treaties have required Member States to act in accordance with the principle of sound public finances[7] and to avoid excessive public deficits.[8] Public spending on defence is not subject to any specific legal treatment and is included in the calculation of the public accounts balance. This has resulted in strong pressure on military budgets,[9] which is reinforced each time an economic recession forces a consolidation of public finances in order to meet national and/or European budgetary targets. As noted by the European Commission and the High Representative of the Union for Foreign Affairs in 2022, the budget cuts implemented in the wake of the 2008-2009 economic and financial crisis resulted in a total underinvestment in defence of around €160 billion over the period 2009-2018.[10] The national measures taken to support economic activity in response to Covid-19 have also left public finances in very diverse situations. Among the Member States with the largest military budgets in the EU, four have public debt levels of over 100% (France, Italy, Spain and Greece), which limits their room for manoeuvre.[11] As for Germany, the growth of its public spending has been limited since 2009 by its 'constitutional debt brake', which prohibits annual net borrowing of more than 0.35% of GDP.[12]

---

6 F. Rabelais, *La vie très horrifique du grand Gargantua père de Pantagruel*, Chapitre XLVI: Comment Grandgousier traita humainement Toucquedillon prisonnier, 1534. In this chapter, Grandgousier, the embodiment of the ideal Renaissance ruler, denounces the warlike ambitions of his neighbour and advocates international relations based on mutual respect and cooperation. Toucquedillon, an envoy from the neighbouring kingdom taken prisoner by Brother Jean, is freed by Grandgousier, who pays the monk the ransom he was entitled to demand. (Author's translation.)

7 Art. 119(3) TFEU; also: European Council Resolution on the Stability and Growth Pact, Amsterdam, 17 June 1997, Section I.

8 Art. 126(1) TFEU.

9 For example: France, Ministry of Defence, White Paper on Defence, 1994, p. 141.

10 European Commission and High Representative for Foreign Affairs, Joint Communication on the Defence Investment Gaps Analysis and Way Forward, JOIN(2022) 24 final, 18 May 2022.

11 According to Eurostat, the debt ratios for these countries in 2024 were 113.0%, 135.3%, 101.8% and 153.6% respectively. In the cases of Greece and Spain, the deterioration in their financial situation is mainly linked to the public debt crisis that both countries experienced between 2010 and 2015.

12 In March 2025, Germany relaxed the conditions for borrowing to finance a major investment programme, particularly in the defence sector. For an overview of the main features of this reform, see European Commission, *Spring 2025 Economic Forecast*, Brussels, 19 May 2025, spec. Chapter 'The potential economic impact of the reform of Germany's fiscal framework'. Available at: https://economy-finance.ec.europa.eu/economic-forecast-and-surveys/economic-forecasts/spring-2025-economic-forecast-moderate-growth-amid-global-economic-uncertainty/potential-economic-impact-reform-germanys-fiscal-framework_en.

The defence of freedom and peace on the European continent cannot be hampered by a lack of resources.[13] Financial stability is an objective to be pursued by economic and budgetary policies,[14] which are designed to achieve the general objectives of the Union, i.e. the promotion of peace, its values and the well-being of its peoples.[15] Given national financial constraints, the Commission proposes five action points in its White Paper on Defence to support massive, sustainable public and private investment in the Union and, in doing so, ensure the credibility of the Union's military deterrence and meet Ukraine's defence equipment needs:[16] the creation of an extra-budgetary financial instrument with a financial capacity of €150 billion (the SAFE instrument);[17] the relaxation of European budgetary discipline rules to facilitate an increase in public investment spending on defence at national level;[18] the reallocation of part of the Cohesion Funds available for the period 2021-2027 to productive investments related to security and defence;[19] a greater contribution from the European Investment Bank and a simplification of procedures;[20] and also the improvement of financing conditions for private companies through the completion of the Savings and Investment Union.[21] To date, only the SAFE financial instrument, the activation of the flexibility clause of the Stability and Growth Pact (SGP) and the strengthening of the European Investment Bank's financial policy in favour of the European Defence Industrial Base (EDTIB) have been implemented.[22]

---

13 Statement by F. Merz at the conclusion of the agreement on debt brake reform, quoted in 'Germany: Parties agree on historic debt deal', *Deutsche Welle*, 14 March 2025.

14 Case C-370/12, *Pringle*, ECLI:EU:C:2012:756, para. 135.

15 Art. 119(1) and 120 TFEU.

16 European Commission, White Paper on European Defence/Readiness 2030, Brussels, 19 March 2025p. 16.

17 Proposal for a Council Regulation establishing the Security Action for Europe (SAFE) through the reinforcement of European defence industry Instrument, COM(2025) 122 final, 19 March 2025.

18 Communication from the Commission on 'Accommodating increased defence expenditure within the Stability and Growth Pact', Brussels, C(2025) 2000 final, 19 March 2025.

19 Communication from the Commission on 'A Modernised Cohesion policy: The mid-term review', COM(2025) 163 final, 1 April 2025.

20 The Commission presented a legislative simplification package relating to the defence industry (the Defence Readiness Omnibus) on 17 and 23 June 2025. It includes a communication, three proposals for legislative acts, four proposals for delegated acts of the Commission and an interpretative notice on the application of non-financial reporting obligations by the defence industries. See the European Commission's dedicated web page: Defence Readiness Omnibus, available at: https://defence-industry-space.ec.europa.eu/eu-defence-industry/defence-readiness-omnibus_en.

21 Communication from the Commission on the 'Savings and Investments Union', COM(2025) 124 final, 19 March 2025.

22 See Council Regulation (EU) 2025/1106 of 27 May 2025 establishing the Security Action for Europe (SAFE) through the Reinforcement of the European Defence Industry Instrument, [2025] *OJ* L2025/1106; Council of the EU, 'Council activates flexibility in EU fiscal rules for 15 member states to increase defence spending', Press Release, 8 July 2025. Available

The SAFE financial instrument is undoubtedly as disruptive as the SURE Regulation (Support to mitigate Unemployment Risks in an Emergency) and the NextGenerationEU (NGEU) instruments were when they were adopted. Since the Versailles Summit in March 2022, European support measures have consisted of financial assistance granted under the European Peace Facility to the Ukrainian armed forces,[23] or to EU instruments financially supporting the European defence industry (ASAP[24] and EDIRPA[25] instruments). In spring 2024, the Commission proposed to extend the logic of these two instruments in a more structured and long-term perspective, in the form of the European Defence Industry Programme (EDIP).[26] These measures are in addition to the European Defence Fund.[27] The maximum budgetary envelopes for these instruments range from €300 million to €4.2 billion. All these measures are taken either under the CFSP[28] or under industrial policy (Article 173(3) TFEU), in this case, possibly in conjunction with other legal bases.[29] As for the SAFE instrument, it provides financial assistance to Member States in the form of loans with a maximum maturity of 45 years. Its granting is conditional on the submission of a national investment plan for the European defence industry. The assistance is financed by loans raised by the Union on the financial markets or from financial institutions. The financial arrangement follows the back-to-back model: repayment by the Member States receiving Union

at: https://www.consilium.europa.eu/en/press/press-releases/2025/07/08/council-activates-flexibility-in-eu-fiscal-rules-for-15-member-states-to-increase-defence-spending; and also: European Investment Bank, 'EIB steps up financing for European security and defence and critical raw materials', Press Release, 21 March 2025. Available at: https://www.eib.org/en/press/all/2025-156-eib-steps-up-financing-for-european-security-and-defence-and-critical-raw-materials.

23 Council Decision (CFSP) 2022/338 of 28 February 2022 on an assistance measure under the European Peace Facility for the supply to the Ukrainian Armed Forces of military equipment, and platforms, designed to deliver lethal force, [2022] *OJ* L60/1; last amended by Council Decision (CFSP) 2023/810 of 13 April 2023, [2023] *OJ* L101/64.

24 Regulation (EU) 2023/1525 of the European Parliament and of the Council of 20 July 2023 on supporting ammunition production (ASAP), [2023] *OJ* L185/7.

25 Regulation (EU) 2023/2418 of the European Parliament and of the Council of 18 October 2023 on establishing an instrument for the reinforcement of the European defence industry through common procurement (EDIRPA), [2023] *OJ* L2023/2418.

26 Proposal for a Regulation of the European Parliament and of the Council establishing the European Defence Industry Programme and a framework of measures to ensure the timely availability and supply of defence products ('EDIP'), COM(2024) 150 final, 5 March 2024. Since then, that proposal was adopted. See: Regulation (EU) 2025/2643 of the European Parliament and of the Council of 16 December 2025 establishing the European Defence Industry Programme and a framework of measures to ensure the timely availability and supply of defence products ('EDIP Regulation'), [2025] *OJ* L2025/2643.

27 Regulation (EU) 2021/697 of the European Parliament and of the Council of 29 April 2021 establishing the European Defence Fund and repealing Regulation (EU) 2018/1092, [2021] *OJ* L170/149; lastly modified by Regulation (EU) 2024/795 of the European Parliament and of the Council of 29 February 2024, [2024] *OJ* L795/1.

28 Art. 28(1) and Art. 41(2) TEU.

29 For example, Articles 114 TFEU, 212(2) and 322(1) TFEU for the EPID instrument; Articles 182(4), 183 and 188 TFEU for the European Defence Fund.

financial assistance enables the Union to repay its own loans. The maximum amount of assistance is limited to €150 billion. However, unlike the ASAP and EDIRPA instruments, SAFE is based on Article 122 TFEU. This provision confers autonomous executive powers on the Council, from which the European Parliament is excluded.[30] Conversely, Article 173(3) TFEU requires the ordinary legislative procedure to be followed, with the Parliament and the Council on an equal footing.

During the negotiation of the proposal for the SAFE Regulation, the European Parliament expressed its serious concerns about the use of Article 122 TFEU for the adoption of this act, arguing that the conditions for the application of each of its two paragraphs were neither met nor justified. The Union also had other legal bases for adopting this legislative proposal, it was pointed out.[31] Following the adoption of the latter by the Council on 27 May 2025, the following month the European Parliament's Committee on Legal Affairs recommended that the Parliament refer the matter to the Court of Justice for annulment.[32] Finally, at the end of August 2025, Parliament lodged a request with the Court of Justice for the annulment of the SAFE Regulation.[33]

In order to shed light on this debate, it is necessary to first recall the origins of Article 122 TFEU (Section 1), and then discuss its use since 2009, distinguishing between the exercise of crisis management powers (Section 2) and the power to grant Union financial assistance to Member States (Section 3). The possibilities for the European Parliament to be involved in the exercise of these powers are discussed in the conclusion (Section 5).

I. ORIGINS AND DEVELOPMENT OF ARTICLE 122 TFEU

Article 122 is one of seven provisions in Chapter 1, entitled 'Economic policy', of Title VIII on economic and monetary policy, in Part Three of the Treaty on the Functioning of the European Union. This article, along with almost all of the articles in Title VIII, was inserted by the Maastricht Treaty into the Treaty establishing the European Community, replacing the former Title II on economic policy and its various chapters, which dated from 1957. The wording of paragraph 1 of Article 122 TFEU is based on Article 103(2) to (4) of the Treaty establishing the European Economic Community (Section A), while paragraph 2 reflects the specific requirements of the economic and monetary union established by the Maastricht Treaty (Section B).

---

30 M. Chamon, *The use of Article 122 TFEU. Institutional implications and impact on democratic accountability*, Study requested by the AFCO committee, PE 753.307, September 2023.

31 Letter from Roberta Metsola, President of the European Parliament, to Ursula von der Leyen, President of the European Commission, ref. D 200557, 5 May 2025.

32 European Parliament, Committee on Legal Affairs, Minutes of the meeting of 24 June 2025, JURI_PV(2025)0164_1, para. 11.

33 See Case C-560/25, *European Parliament v Council of the EU.*

A. ARTICLE 103 OF THE TREATY ESTABLISHING THE EUROPEAN ECONOMIC COMMUNITY (TEC), THE INSPIRATION FOR ARTICLE 122(1) TFEU

1. *The Negotiation of Article 103 TEC*

The negotiators of the Treaty establishing the European Economic Community were aware that the full realisation of the common market would not be without obstacles. Meeting this objective within the timeframe agreed by all Member States would require some adaptation procedures 'to enable such adjustments in the application of the Treaty as circumstances may render necessary', in addition to the possibility of maintaining or introducing certain temporary derogations beyond the transitional period.[34] These procedures adressed the concerns expressed by France about the internal imbalances that could be caused by the opening of national markets.[35] To this end, Paris proposed that Member States retain the autonomous power to maintain a system of export subsidies and import taxes and to terminate it when the economic difficulties ceased.[36] Faced with opposition from other national delegations, the French negotiators defended the establishment of equalisation schemes between several companies or, alternatively, Community financial mechanisms where these proved necessary for the implementation of measures to manage crisis situations and product shortages, such mechanisms being decided by the Council on a proposal from the Commission. Similar mechanisms could be established or maintained by Member States, subject to notification to the Commission and compatibility with the rules of the Treaty.

In the draft treaty submitted in January 1957, the management of crises and shortage situations was covered by three provisions. These recognised the primary responsibility of Member States to take action. However, their autonomy was limited by the obligation to consult each other before taking any action and by the recommendation to take measures (ideally indirect measures) to regularise the situation (Article X of the draft treaty). Community action was subsidiary and required two conditions to be met before it could be initiated: the Council had unanimously to decide that national measures were insufficient to manage the situation and that the crisis or shortage was serious (Article X+1 of the draft treaty). The Council, acting by a qualified majority on

[34] Intergovernmental Committee set up by the Messina Conference, *Report of the Heads of Delegation to the Ministers for Foreign Affairs*, Brussels, 21 April 1956, available at: https://www.cvce.eu/s/14g.

[35] L. Warlouzet, 'La France et les négociations du traité de Rome (1955-1957)', in CVCE, *Les traités de l'Union européenne: textes, travaux préparatoires, témoignages*, Luxembourg, 2016.

[36] Draft minutes of the Paris Conference (20-21 October 1956). Historical archives of the Council of the European Union. File: Negotiations on the Treaties establishing the EEC and the EAEC (1955-1957), CM3. Conference of Foreign Ministers, Paris, 20-21 October 1956, CM3/NEGO/095.

a proposal from the Commission, could then decide on appropriate measures such as the application of production quotas, the allocation of resources, minimum or maximum prices, or import or export programmes both within the Community and in relation to third countries.[37] These measures, it was specified, had to be examined in conjunction with the other provisions of the Treaty, in particular those relating to the common commercial policy. The final provision (Article X+2 of the draft treaty) reiterated the obligation of Member States to implement Council decisions. A very concise formulation of Articles X and X+1 was presented by the German delegation. It linked crisis management powers to economic policy. The subsidiary nature of Community intervention in relation to that of the Member States was retained. This proposal had been revised on the basis of a French proposal which reintroduced concerns relating to supply difficulties in paragraph 4. The aim was to draw lessons from the 1956 Suez crisis and the problems of oil transport.[38] Although the final wording of Article 103 TEC was silent on the types of measures that the Council could take under paragraph 2, an interpretative statement specified that the delegations unanimously recognise that these measures included, 'inter alia, the establishment of financial mechanisms'.[39]

Article 103 in the version adopted in the EEC Treaty reads as follows:

1. Member States shall regard their conjunctural policies as a matter of common concern. They shall consult each other and the Commission on the measures to be taken in the light of prevailing circumstances.

2. Without prejudice to any other procedures provided for in this Treaty, the Council may, acting unanimously on a proposal from the Commission, decide on measures appropriate to the situation.

3. Acting by a qualified majority on a proposal from the Commission, the Council shall, where required, issue any directives needed to give effect to the measures decided upon under paragraph 2.

4. The procedures provided for in this Article shall also apply if any difficulty should arise in the supply of certain products.

---

37 Intergovernmental Conference on the Common Market and Euratom, Common Market Group, *French proposal on cases of crisis or shortage within the Common Market*, Brussels, 17 January 1957. Historical archives of the Council of the European Union. File: Negotiations on the Treaties establishing the EEC and the EAEC (1955-1957), CM3/NEGO-241.

38 Highlighted by F. Martucci, 'Article 100 EC', in I. Pingel (ed.), *Commentaire article par article des traités UE et CE*, 2nd ed., Basel/Paris/Brussels, Helbing Lichtenhahn/Dalloz/Bruylant, 2010, p. 852.

39 Intergovernmental Conference on the Common Market and Euratom, Committee of Heads of Delegation, *Draft articles on short-term economic policy and supply difficulties drawn up by the Common Market Group*, Brussels, 5 February 1957. Historical archives of the Council of the European Union. File: Negotiations on the treaties establishing the EEC and the EAEC (1955-1957), CM3/NEGO-241.

2. *The Application of Article 103 TEC until the Maastricht Treaty*

Until it was replaced by the Maastricht Treaty, this provision was applied more than 140 times, starting in 1960. Measures relating to mutual consultation between Member States or to guidelines for economic policy remained rare (twelve over the entire period).[40] Most of the Council's measures were in response to supply crises affecting a particular sector (fishing), an entire national economy (difficulties in supplying potatoes) or all Member States of the Community (the energy crises of 1974 and 1979). On several occasions, Article 103 was used instead of Article 235 of the ECSC Treaty to adopt interim measures to preserve the rights of economic operators pending the entry into force of the definitive legal regime. This was particularly the case when the common fisheries policy was established in the late 1970s, in the context of the negotiation of fishing agreements between the Community and third countries.[41] The situation or risk of shortage was in itself sufficient grounds for Council intervention, particularly when products essential to economic life (petroleum products) were concerned.[42] However, this reason was generally linked to potential or actual economic effects, such as an increase in production costs and the cost of living or the balance of payments. The intensity of these effects was left to the discretion of the Council and did not appear to be a determining factor for action.[43] As regards 'circumstances' other than supply difficulties, their definition was again subject to the Council's power of interpretation. In practice, the circumstances taken into account consisted of 'capital movements of an exceptional magnitude'[44] or fluctuations in the currencies of Member States.[45] Whether in relation to supply difficulties or

---

[40] See, for example, Council Decision (1960/301) of 9 March 1960 on co-ordination of the conjunctural policies of the Member States, [1960] *OJ* 31/764; Council Directive 74/121/EEC of 18 February 1974 on stability, growth and full employment in the Community, [1974] *OJ* L63/19.

[41] Council Regulation (EEC) 1779/77/EEC of 2 August 1977 laying down interim conservation and management measures for herring fishing in the Irish Sea, [1977] *OJ* L196/4.

[42] See, for example: recital (1) of Council Directive (75/339/EEC) of 20 May 1975 obliging the Member States to maintain minimum stocks of fossil fuel at thermal power stations, [1975] *OJ* L153/35.

[43] Thus, the decline in green bean production due to the drought of summer 1976 justified Community intervention, given the risks of rising living costs and the 'threat to the Community's supply of these preserves'! More than protecting consumers, the measure aimed to preserve the agri-food sector. See Council Regulation (2226/76/EEC) of 9 December 1976 temporarily and partially suspending the autonomous Common Customs Tariff duties on preserved beans in pods, [1976] *OJ* L251/5.

[44] Recital (1) of Council Directive (72/156/EEC) of 21 March 1972 on regulating international capital flows and neutralizing their undesirable effects on domestic liquidity, [1972] *OJ* L91/13.

[45] Council Regulation (3450/73/EEC) of 17 December 1973 amending Regulation (EEC) No 974/71 as regards the level of prices for agricultural products in Italy following developments in the monetary situation, [1973] *OJ* L353/25.

the state of the economic situation, the urgency of intervention was generally emphasised to justify the application of Article 103 instead of the appropriate legal basis under the sectoral policy affected by the crisis.[46]

That being said, it should be noted that the Council was under no obligation to act but had the power to take appropriate measures 'in the common interest and not in the interest of a specific group of economic operators'.[47] Consequently, it was under no obligation to compensate for all the effects of a crisis suffered by businesses or consumers in the Member States concerned.[48] As the Court of Justice emphasised in the *Rewe Zentral* judgment, Article 103(2) conferred on the Council a power of economic management to prevent or mitigate short-term fluctuations in the economy and thus contribute to the attainment of the objectives of the Treaty and the achievements of economic integration.[49] This Community management power was made necessary by the reduction in the scope of Member States' economic policies as areas of economic activity become common (common market, agricultural policy),[50] and by the impossibility for Member States to intervene autonomously.[51]

The power of management was not to be confused with the power to coordinate the economic policies of Member States. It did not allow for any transfer of powers from the States to the Union: it could only be exercised within the limits of the Union's powers. Its scope was nonetheless considerable, given the economic dimension of most of the Union's areas of intervention. 'Economic policy may cover all sectors of the economy', concluded Advocate General (AG) Roemer in the *Balkan-Import* case.[52] Practice showed that this management power had been used to establish agri-monetary measures, set up financial support mechanisms, introduce derogations from the common customs tariff, define measures to conserve fish stocks, require the constitution of stocks of petroleum products, set targets for reducing primary energy consumption and establish performance targets for heat generators. All of these measures could have been adopted on other legal bases in the provisions of the EEC Treaty governing the relevant Community sectoral policies. In view of the risk of misuse of powers, the Court of Justice clarified the conditions for

46 See, for example: Recital (6) of Council Regulation (EEC) No 3152/78 of 21 December 1978 laying down certain interim measures for the conservation and management of fishery resources applicable to vessels flying the flag of Spain for the period 1 to 31 January 1979, [1978] *OJ* L374/24.
47 Joined Cases 9 and 11/71, *Grands Moulins de Paris*, ECLI:EU:C:1972:52, para. 33.
48 Ibid., para. 32; see also: Case 43/72, *Merkur Aussenhandel*, ECLI:EU:C:1973:108.
49 Case 10/73, *Rewe Zentral*, ECLI:EU:C:1973:111, para. 14; also: Case 5/73, *Balkan-Import*, ECLI:EU:C:1973:109, para. 17; and Case 9/73, *Schlüter*, ECLI:EU:C:1973:110, para. 12.
50 Ibid.
51 For example: Case 31/74, *Galli*, ECLI:EU:C:1975:8, para. 23; Joined Cases 88 to 90/75, *SADAM*, ECLI:EU:C:1976:32; Case 154/77, *Public Prosecutor v P. Dechman*, ECLI:EU:C:1978:145, para. 22.
52 Opinion of AG Roemer in Case 5/73, *Balkan-Import*, ECLI:EU:C:1973:71.

the use of Article 103(2): the suddenness of the events facing the Council, the urgency of the measures to be taken, the seriousness of the situation, the close link between the area concerned and the economic policy, and the absence of any adequate provision in the sectoral policy concerned.[53] Finally, the pursuit of a short-term stabilisation objective required that the appropriate measures be exclusively temporary, since they responded to a deterioration in the short-term economic balance. They should remain in force for as long as the risks or the crisis situation persisted.[54] On the other hand, making them permanent (i.e. turning management measures into regulatory measures), required that they be incorporated into the relevant sectoral policy framework.

B. THE EXPLICIT FORMALISATION OF EU FINANCIAL ASSISTANCE, REFLECTING THE REQUIREMENTS OF ECONOMIC AND MONETARY UNION

Article 103 remained unchanged until the Maastricht Treaty. Although it recognised the European Community's monetary capacity, the Single European Act left the provisions on economic policy unchanged and referred any changes necessary for the development of economic and monetary policy to a future constitutional revision.[55] This was achieved with the Maastricht Treaty. Inserted by Article G, point 25, into the EC Treaty, the new Article 103a defines the legal regime applicable to the Council's economic management powers (paragraph 1). It also makes explicit the Community's power to provide financial assistance (paragraph 2). The obligation of coordination between Member States and the power granted to the Council for this purpose are dealt with in separate provisions (Articles 102a and 103 TEC).

1. *The Negotiation of Article 103a TEC*

In general, the wording of Article 103a reflects a desire to strengthen the conditions for its implementation. Economic management powers were intended to respond to the state of the *economy*, whereas Article 103 TEC referred only to 'the situation'. Supply difficulties had to be 'serious'. The wording of paragraph 2 addresses the same concerns. The principle of financial assistance was set out in the Delors Report on Economic and Monetary Union. Sharing a single currency requires sufficient convergence in economic

[53] Case 5/73, *Balkan-Import*, ECLI:EU:C:1973:109, para. 14; Case 10/73, *Rewe Zentral*, ECLI:EU:C:1973:111, para. 15.

[54] See, for example, the medium-term financial assistance mechanism established in 1971 and extended until 1988.

[55] Art. 20 of the Single European Act.

conditions.[56] Cohesion funds are intended to support structural changes in national economies to a certain extent: regional policy is not aimed at subsidising incomes or compensating for inequalities in purchasing power, but at equalising production conditions.[57] As for cyclical adjustments (employment, production), these were to be brought about by market forces, under the effect of the full realisation of the free movement of persons and capital. However, the report considers that these various dynamics may be insufficient in certain circumstances. 'In order to reduce adjustment burdens temporarily, it might be necessary in certain circumstances to provide financing flow through official channels. Such financial support would be additional to what might come from spontaneous capital flows or external borrowing and should be granted on terms and conditions that would prompt the recipient to intensify its adjustment efforts'.[58] It was therefore recommended that, in cooperation with the European Parliament, the Council may take measures to implement Community structural policies as well as decisions on Community loans, which would replace the 1971 medium-term assistance mechanism.[59]

The draft treaty presented by the Luxembourg Presidency of the Council endorsed this idea and proposed amending Article 103 TEC by adding two paragraphs on financial assistance after the provisions on economic policy coordination. Such assistance would be granted to Member States experiencing difficulties or a serious threat of difficulties due to events beyond their control.[60] It would take the form of a support programme accompanied by budgetary intervention or special loans. The financial assistance mechanism was detailed by the Commission in its contribution to the work of future intergovernmental conferences on economic and monetary union and political union. It proposed replacing Article 108 TEC on mutual assistance with a financial support mechanism. This new financial mechanism 'would be activated in the event of serious problems in one or more Member States or if economic convergence required a particular effort by the Community to back up national adjustment strategies, so as to provide positive conditionality [...] The mechanism will provide support for national efforts'.[61] The draft provision consisted of three paragraphs: the first gave the Council the power to grant, under certain

---

56 Committee for the Study of Economic and Monetary Union [Delors Committee], *Report on Economic and Monetary Union in the European Community*, Brussels, 17 April 1989, para. 29.

57 Ibid.

58 Ibid.

59 Ibid., para. 59.

60 Conference of the Representatives of the Governments of the Member States – Political Union – Economic and Monetary Union. *Draft Treaty on European Union (reference document of the Luxembourg Presidency)*, CONF-UP-UEM 2008/91, 18 June 1991, specifically draft Article 103.

61 European Commission, 'Intergovernmental conferences: contributions by the Commission', *Bull. EC*, 2/91, 1991, p. 53.

conditions, financial assistance to a Member State facing difficulties or serious risks of difficulties. The Council decides by qualified majority, after assessment by the Commission. The general conditions governing the granting of financial assistance shall be decided by the Council, in cooperation with the European Parliament. In accordance with the same procedure, the Council could establish a (permanent) borrowing facility to finance specific loans granted to Member States as financial assistance.

The Commission's proposal served as a basis for the negotiations of the intergovernmental conference on Economic and Monetary Unio (EMU). Several developments are worth noting. On the one hand, Community financial assistance was dealt with in a separate provision from those on economic policy coordination and mutual assistance. The aim was to take account of the closer coordination of economic policies and to avoid any confusion between financial assistance and mutual assistance, the latter being reserved for Member States which did not participate fully in EMU. Secondly, the conditions for activating financial assistance were strengthened, since 'serious difficulties' were now required. This strengthening was the counterpart to the change from unanimity to qualified majority voting in the Council. Finally, the Council's power to establish a borrowing system was abolished, as it was considered to be covered by the power to grant financial assistance. The European Parliament's cooperation in the granting of financial assistance was reduced to mere *ex post* information.

The fundamental political decisions were taken at the ministerial meeting in Scheveningen in early December 1991. The point of contention was that the financial assistance procedure did not distinguish between the different causes of a Member State's financial difficulties, namely natural disasters and events of similar magnitude on the one hand, and 'exceptional events' on the other. Germany objected that accepting these 'events' without further conditions would open the door to financial claims and represent a leap into the unknown that could undermine the Community budgetary discipline regime.[62] Unanimity within the Council must be required to activate financial assistance.[63] This guarantee seemed unfair to Luxembourg and contrary to the principle of solidarity when applied to natural disasters. On a proposal from the Luxembourg representative, Jean-Claude Juncker, the text of Article 103a was reworded so that the granting of financial assistance in the event of exceptional

62 See also: J. Pipkorn, 'Legal arrangements in the Treaty of Maastricht for the effectiveness of the EMU', [1994] 31 *CML Rev.*, pp. 263 et seq.

63 Ministerial meeting in Scheveningen, Netherlands, 30 November and 1 December, and Brussels, 2 and 3 December 1991 -Verbatim, Historical Archives of the Council of the Union, CM3 NEGO, NEGO 7, 13.2, spec. Reel 608 of 3 December 1991, p. [136].

occurrences would require unanimity, and in the event of natural disasters, a qualified majority.[64]

2. *The Break with the Nice Treaty Approach*

The Treaty of Amsterdam left the wording of Article 103a TEC unchanged. Only its numbering has been changed (Article 100 TEC). However, the Treaty of Nice marked a significant departure from the trade-off negotiated at Maastricht: unanimity in the Council was replaced by qualified majority voting, both for the adoption of measures appropriate to the economic situation (paragraph 1) and for the granting of financial assistance (paragraph 2). The removal of different treatment depending on the facts giving rise to the assistance simplified the wording of this provision. However, the Parliament remained only 'informed' of decisions taken in this area.[65] Germany's change of position may come as a surprise. Two circumstances explained it: the fact that Article 103 TEC had not been actively invoked since 1991;[66] in the context of an enlarged Union, maintaining unanimity in the Council made it more difficult to activate financial assistance measures.[67] The most recent amendment to Article 100 EC, now Article 122 TFEU, was introduced by the Treaty of Lisbon. It specifies that measures appropriate to the economic situation shall be taken 'in a spirit of solidarity between Member States' and that the difficulties giving rise to them may be linked to the supply of certain products, 'notably in the area of energy'. These clarifications respond to the concerns of the Member States of Central and Eastern Europe, which are faced with the uncertainty of Russian gas supplies.[68] They do not alter the scope of this provision. Since the 1970s, it has been used to 'establish real solidarity between Member States in the event of difficulties in the supply [of energy products]'.[69]

---

[64] Ibid., p. [137].

[65] Art. 2(5) of the Treaty of Nice.

[66] Paragraph 1 on measures appropriate to the economic situation has been used four times to repeal measures to manage the energy crisis of the 1970s, and once to amend Directive 68/414/EEC on the storage of crude oil and petroleum products.

[67] See 'Adapting the Institutions to make a success of enlargement' – Commission opinion in accordance with Article 48 of the Treaty on European Union on the calling of a Conference of Representatives of the Governments of the Member States to amend the Treaties, COM(2000) 34 final, 21 January 2000, para. 10.

[68] 'Gas: Europe feels the first effects of the cut-off of supplies between Russia and Ukraine', *Le Monde*, 1 January 2006.

[69] Recital 2 of Council Decision (77/186/EEC) of 14 February 1977 on the exporting of crude oil and petroleum products from one Member State to another in the event of supply difficulties, [1977] *OJ* L61/23; also, in the early 2000s, following the publication of the Green Paper 'Towards a European strategy for the security of energy supply': Council Directive 2004/67/EC of 26 April 2004 concerning measures to safeguard security of natural gas

II. ARTICLE 122 TFEU AND ECONOMIC POLICY COORDINATION

Article 122 TFEU is inserted in Chapter 1, entitled Economic Policy, after the provisions on the coordination of economic policies (Articles 120 and 121) and before those establishing discipline of fiscal policies through market mechanism (Articles 123 to 125) and through fiscal rules and procedures (Article 126). This central position reflects the specific function of Article 122 within the economic policy coordination framework: to fill the gaps in economic policy coordination without reducing Member States' responsibility for their budgetary policies.

In order to achieve the objectives set out in Article 3 TEU, in particular the establishment of an economic and monetary union whose currency is the euro, the Member States and the Union must act to establish 'an economic policy'.[70] This policy takes a hybrid form, combining three elements: close coordination of Member States' economic policies, the internal market and the definition of common objectives.

The first and third elements refer to two distinct categories of competence: the Member States' exclusive competence to conduct their economic policies[71] and the Union's competence to coordinate national economic policies.[72] It is important to note the drafters' emphasis on the central responsibility of Member States in exercising coordination competence: according to Article 5(1) TFEU, 'The *Member States* shall coordinate their economic policies within the Union' (author's emphasis). The wording of this coordination competence contrasts with that used in the field of employment policy, where '*the Union* shall take measures to ensure coordination',[73] and in the field of social policy, where '*the Union* may take initiatives to ensure coordination'.[74] From this perspective, the management of the economic situation and the adoption of appropriate economic measures are primarily the responsibility of the Member States. The Union shall ensure that national policies are aimed at stability by establishing an appropriate economic environment (i.e. the internal market) and by exercising its coordinating powers. However, the coordination of economic policies cannot constitute a single economic policy such as the single monetary policy does, as this would render the national policies on which it is based

supply, [2004] *OJ* L127/92. Based on Article 100 TEC, this directive is part of the effort to 'genuine solidarity between Member States in major emergency supply situations' (Recital 13).

70 Art. 119(1) TFEU.

71 Arts. 120 and 121(1) TFEU.

72 Art. 5(1) TFEU.

73 Art. 5(2) TFEU.

74 Art. 5(3) TFEU.

meaningless.[75] In other words, it does confer legal competence on the Union to decide on national economic policy measures. By positioning coordination competence between shared competences (Article 4 TFEU) and supporting competences (Article 6 TFEU), the Treaty symbolically marks the two legal limits of Union action in the field of economic policy: it cannot decide on the content of Member States' economic policies, nor can it ignore them. In this in-between, the Union institutions are empowered to adopt procedural measures in respect of Member States, including binding measures.[76]

The deepening of the internal market is making national economies more interdependent. At the same time, it is reducing the areas where Member States can take action. The Court of Justice has said that national measures to deal with economic downturns cannot cover areas that have become common.[77] This makes it even more important to have 'closer coordination'.[78]

The Union's sectoral policies may provide for cyclical interventions for their implementation, in addition to structural measures.[79] However, these interventions pursue the specific objectives of the sectoral policies concerned; they do not necessarily correspond to the objectives of economic policy at large. The guarantee of security of supply under the common agricultural policy aims 'to ensure the food independence of the peoples of the Member States from third countries'.[80] In the context of economic policy, security of supply is crucial for price stability, control of production costs and the maintenance of consumer purchasing power.[81]

The competence to coordinate economic policies does not authorise any substantive measures in the areas reserved for the Member States. The ordinary powers of guidance, surveillance, discipline and sanction conferred on the Council and the Commission ensure the coordination of economic policies and sustained convergence of the economic performances of the Member States. Procedures for preventing, reacting to and correcting economic situations are

---

75 F. Martucci, *L'ordre économique et monétaire de l'Union européenne*, Brussels, Bruylant 2015, p. 192, pp. 297 and seq.

76 See, to that effect: Joined Cases 281, 283, 284, 285 and 287/85, *Germany and Others v Commission*, ECLI:EU:C:1987:351, paras. 28 and 29, which concerned a Commission decision establishing a procedure for prior notification and consultation on the migration policies of Member States, based on Article 118 of the ECSC Treaty. That provision required the Commission to promote close cooperation between Member States in the social field.

77 See, for example: Case 31/74, *Galli*, ECLI:EU:C:1975:8, paras. 23 and 24.

78 Arts. 121(3) and 136(1) TFEU.

79 Case 5/73, *Balkan-Import*, ECLI:EU:C:1973:109, para. 12; Case 9/73, *Schlüter*, ECLI:EU:C:1973:110, para. 9; Case 10/73, *Rewe Zentral*, ECLI:EU:C:1973:111, para. 12, concerning the common agricultural policy.

80 Y. Petit, 'Agriculture', *Répertoire de droit européen*, Dalloz, December 2002 (updated in February 2023), para. 90.

81 See, for example: Council Decision (66/272/EEC) of 21 April 1966 authorising the Kingdom of the Netherlands to levy a tax on exports of potatoes to other Member States, [1966] *OJ* 79/1207.

established for this purpose. The Council shall recommend broad economic policy guidelines (BEPGs) for the Member States and the Union.[82] It shall monitor economic developments in each Member State and in the Union on the basis of the Commission's analyses. Opinions or recommendations may be addressed to any Member State whose economic policy is not consistent with the BEPGs or if it threatens the proper functioning of EMU.[83] The Council, acting on a proposal from the Commission, may temporarily authorise a Member State to deviate from its economic and budgetary objectives if exceptional circumstances beyond its control have a budgetary impact.[84] A significant deterioration in the economic situation and a serious deterioration in the public finances of a Member State shall continue to be addressed through the usual instruments of Articles 121 and 126 TFEU.[85] Member States experiencing or threatened with serious financial stability difficulties are subject to enhanced surveillance under the coordination powers of Article 121 TFEU.[86] The same applies to Member States receiving financial assistance.[87] As regards the economic policies of the Union (i.e. sectoral policies that may have economic effects), Article 121 logically only allows for recommendations to be made. The BEPGs call on the European institutions to act in accordance with the appropriate legal bases.[88] The multilateral surveillance procedure referred to in Article 121(3) TFEU concerns only the economic policies of the Member States. It leaves open the question of the adjustment of an EU sectoral policy whose economic effects adversely affect an economic situation in the Union or, conversely, may contribute to redressing an economic situation that has deteriorated or is threatened with deterioration.

Article 122 addresses two shortcomings in the powers of coordination and discipline. Paragraph 1 provides a cross-cutting legal basis enabling the

---

82 Art. 121(2) TFEU.

83 Art. 121(4) TFEU.

84 Art. 26 of Regulation (EU) 2024/1263 of the European Parliament and of the Council, on the effective coordination of economic policies and on multilateral budgetary surveillance and repealing Council Regulation (EC) No 1466/97, [2024] *OJ* L2024/1263.

85 Regarding Greece between 2010 and 2025, see: European Commission, Excessive deficit procedure and Greece – Closed procedure, updated: 2025. Available at: https://economy-finance.ec.europa.eu/economic-and-fiscal-governance/stability-and-growth-pact/corrective-arm-excessive-deficit-procedure/excessive-deficit-procedures-overview/greece_en.

86 Art. 3 of Regulation (EU) No 472/2013 of the European Parliament and of the Council of 21 May 2013 on the strengthening of economic and budgetary surveillance of Member States in the euro area experiencing or threatened with serious difficulties with respect to their financial stability, [2013] *OJ* L140/1.

87 Arts. 6 and 7 of Regulation (EU) No 472/2013 of the European Parliament and of the Council, ibid.

88 For application, see Council Recommendation (EU) 2015/1184 of 14 July 2015 on broad guidelines for the economic policies of the Member States and of the European Union, [2015] *OJ* L192/27, spec. Guideline No 3: Removing key barriers to sustainable growth and jobs at Union level.

Council to take appropriate management measures in response to the economic situation in all sectors of the economy covered by Union law. Paragraph 2 enables the Union to respond to a situation where a Member State, which is experiencing or is seriously threatened with serious difficulties, does not have the financial means to keep its economic policy consistent with the requirements of economic policy coordination and fiscal discipline. In both cases, Article 122, as belonging to the chapter on economic policy and, more broadly, to the title on economic and monetary policy, aims to achieve the objectives and principles thereof: the proper functioning of EMU through the achievement of close coordination of economic policies, the maintenance of fiscal discipline and, ultimately, the financial stability of the monetary union.[89]

III. ARTICLE 122(1) TFEU: EXCEPTIONAL MANAGEMENT POWERS IN THE EVENT OF ECONOMIC DIFFICULTIES

The activation of crisis management powers is based on the assumption that there are difficulties affecting the economic situation (Section A). The diversity of possible difficulties requires the recognition of broad powers of intervention to prevent or deal with them (Section B). These exceptional powers must be reconciled with the Union's other powers of economic intervention (Section C).

A. CONDITIONS OF APPLICATION

The wording of Article 122(1) TFEU is notable for its vagueness. This was hardly surprising, given the very subject matter of this provision: 'the economic situation'. The concept is not defined by the Treaties but is defined in secondary legislation for the purposes of monitoring the economic performance and policies of Member States.[90] It refers to the state of all economic activities[91] (production, employment, trade balance, price levels, purchasing power, etc.) as measured by economic indicators.[92] The factors behind economic developments are many and varied, both internal and external to Member States, specific to one State or common to several or even to the Union as a whole. This means that the economic situation is constantly changing. It is dynamic and, as such,

[89] Case C-370/12, *Pringle*, ECLI:EU:C:2012:756, para. 135.

[90] Article 4 of Regulation (EU) 2024/1263, cited aboe.

[91] See the opinion of AG Roemer, Case 5/73, *Balkan-Import*, ECLI:EU:C:1973:71.

[92] Banque de France, 'La conjoncture économique' (The economic situation), updated: December 2024. Available at: https://www.banque-france.fr/fr/statistiques/themes-statistiques-et-series-webstat-associees/la-conjoncture-economique.

subject to continuous monitoring by the Council, under Article 121(3) TFEU. In the absence of further clarification, the 'economic situation' referred to in Article 122 TFEU may be that of a Member State, several Member States or the Union as a whole. There is also nothing to prevent the specific situation of a territory of a Member State from being taken into account too, provided that there is a common interest in doing so, as was the case with the measures adopted at the end of 1970 for the French department of French Guiana in the fisheries sector.[93]

Not every change in the economic situation triggers the activation of Article 122(1) TFEU. Some changes are desirable, such as an increase in the growth rate, a reduction in the unemployment rate, price stability, etc. They reflect the achievement of the socio-economic objectives of the Treaties as set out in Article 3 TEU and specified in operational terms in the BEPGs. Only a negative development in the economic situation justifies recourse to this provision, as is implicit in the reference to the existence of 'serious difficulties in the supply of certain products'. A threshold of seriousness must be reached before intervention becomes necessary.[94] It should be noted that it is not necessary for a deterioration to have been observed in order for Community intervention to be justified. The identification of a threat or contemporary 'challenges' allows preventive measures to be adopted, as practice shows.[95]

The nature of the difficulties affecting the economic situation is provided for illustrative purposes. The choice of an example of difficulties rather than a categorical definition of the difficulties to be taken into account is explained, firstly, by the impossibility of foreseeing every single circumstance giving rise to the deterioration in 'the economic situation' – or else the definition would be so broad and general that it would lose all usefulness. Secondly, a list of difficulties would have reduced the scope and usefulness of the economic management powers. In practice, the Council does not always specify in detail the difficulties affecting the economic situation or the causal link between the situation and the difficulties encountered. Some points seem self-evident.[96]

---

93 Council Regulation (EEC) 3153/78 of 21 December 1978 laying down certain interim measures for the conservation and management of fishery resources applicable to vessels flying the flag of certain non-member countries in the 200 nautical-mile zone off the coast of the French department of Guiana, [1978] *OJ* L374/31.

94 Legal Service of the Council of the European Union, Opinion on the proposals relating to Next Generation EU, doc. 9062/20, 24 June 2020, para. 121, spec. fn. 69.

95 Recital 5 of Council Regulation (EEC) 974/71 of 12 May 1971 on certain measures of conjunctural policy to be taken in agriculture following the temporary widening of the margins of fluctuation for the currencies of certain Member States, [1971] OJ L106/1; European Parliament resolution of 22 November 2012 on EU mutual defence and solidarity clauses: political and operational dimensions, P7_TA(2012)0456, para. 31.

96 Recital 2 of Council Directive 98/93/EC of 14 December 1998 amending Directive 68/414/EEC imposing an obligation on Member States of the EEC to maintain minimum stocks of crude oil and/or petroleum products, [1998] OJ L358/100.

For example, with regard to the security of energy supplies, Directive 98/93/EC refers to the risk of a significant increase in the price of crude oil and petroleum products on the international markets which would be 'likely to cause serious disruption of the economic activity of the Community' (Article 1(2)). Six years later, Directive 2004/67 refers in very general terms to the need to take action in the event of 'any difficulty which reduces gas supplies [that] could seriously disrupt the economic activity of the Community'.[97] Regulation (EU) 2016/369 on the provision of emergency assistance within the Union refers to natural disasters such as climate change or large-scale migration flows at the Union's borders as factors that 'may cause serious economic difficulties.[98] The Commission justifies the use of Article 122 TFEU as the legal basis for the SAFE Regulation by citing 'the sudden deterioration of the security environment of the Union since the beginning of 2025' and the 'massive and potentially destabilising consequences for the supply of defence products essential for the interests of the Union and its Member States [...] which could have serious repercussions on public finances'.[99] Recital 8 of the Regulation establishes the link between fiscal constraints and the economic situation, in a wording inspired by Article 122(1): 'As a consequence, there is a growing need to accelerate, in a spirit of solidarity, the provision of Union support to those Member States that are likely to be threatened by serious difficulties due to the massive public investments needed, which may have an impact on their economic situation'.[100] It could be argued that increased public spending is likely to support the economic situation in the short and medium term, thereby counterbalancing the recessionary effects of geopolitical uncertainties. However, the regulation avoids this criticism by pointing to the fragile fiscal situation of several Member States and the economic effects that a deterioration in their public debt sustainability could cause.[101]

B. THE BROAD SCOPE OF CRISIS MANAGEMENT POWERS

Pursuant to Article 122 TFEU, the Council may take 'appropriate measures' in response to the economic situation. The multifactorial nature of the difficulties causing the economic disturbances requires that the Council be given the broadest possible management powers. In the dispute over the 1973 system of compensatory amounts, the Court ruled that the powers reserved to the

97 Recital 2 of Council Directive 2004/67/EC, cited above.

98 Recital 4 of Council Regulation (EU) 2016/369 of 15 March 2016 on the provision of emergency support within the Union, [2016] *OJ* L70/1.

99 Explanatory memorandum to the proposal for a Council Regulation (EU) 2025/122 final, 19 March 2025.

100 SAFE Regulation, cited above.

101 Recital 9 of the SAFE Regulation.

Member States in the monetary field did not preclude the Council from having 'the powers necessary to take, in principle, the measures of a conjunctural nature which may prove necessary for the maintenance of the objectives of the Treaty'.[102] It went on to state that 'without such a possibility, which is inherent in any economic management, the institutions would be unable to fulfil the tasks assigned to them in these areas'.[103] With regard to areas that have become common, such as the common agricultural policy, the Court accepted the Council's intervention on the basis of Article 103 TEC, on an interim basis, due to the urgency of the situation and the absence of immediately available economic measures in the sector concerned.[104] Insofar as Article 122(1) TFEU is a continuation of Article 103 TCEE, the solution adopted by the Court applies by analogy. Thus, in order to address supply difficulties, the Council is using Article 122(1) TFEU in 2022 for a series of measures that would normally fall within the scope of energy policy,[105] health policy,[106] cohesion policy or civil protection.[107]

Article 122(1) TFEU does not impose any form for measures to manage the economic situation. The Council is free to adopt any type of legal act, whether binding or non-binding. In practice, crisis management requires the adoption of binding acts. As one author has observed, directives are preferred for the adoption of preventive measures and regulations and decisions for reactive measures.[108]

In terms of content, measures may consist of new substantive obligations or amendments to existing provisions in the form of temporary derogations.

The 'appropriateness' of measures constitutes a limit on economic management powers. Negatively speaking, measures must address the difficulties causing the economic downturn or aim to reduce its economic effects. Taken within the framework of Chapter 1 on economic policy, they must be economic in nature:[109] i.e. they must relate to economic activities. In the past, this limitation has been applied flexibly. In order to reduce the rate of

---

102 Case 5/73, *Balkan-Import*, ECLI:EU:C:1973:109, Case 9/73, *Schlüter*, ECLI:EU:C:1973:110 and Case 10/73, *Rewe Zentral*, ECLI:EU:C:1973:111.

103 Ibid.

104 Ibid.

105 See, for example: Council Directive 2004/67/EC, above n. 68; Council Regulation (EU) 2022/1369 of 5 August 2022 on coordinated demand-reduction measures for gas, [2022] *OJ* L206/1; Council Regulation (EU) 2022/2577 of 22 December 2022 laying down a framework to accelerate the deployment of renewable energy, [2022] OJ L335/36.

106 Council Regulation (EU) 2022/2372 of 24 October 2022 on a framework of measures for ensuring the supply of crisis-relevant medical countermeasures in the event of a public health emergency at Union level, [2022] *OJ* L314/64.

107 See Recital 5 of Council Regulation (EU) 2016/369, cited above.

108 F. Martucci, 'Article 100 EEC', in I. Pingel (ed.), *Commentaire article par article des traités UE et CE*, 2nd ed., Basel/Paris/Brussels, Helbing Lichtenhahn/Dalloz/Bruylant, 2010, para. 4.

109 Legal Service of the Council of the European Union, Opinion on the proposals relating to Next Generation EU, doc. 9062/20, 24 June 2020, para. 121.

domestic energy consumption and the energy dependence of the Communities, Directive 78/170/EEC lays down minimum efficiency requirements for energy generators (in particular hot-water boilers).[110] In its opinion on the use of Article 122 TFEU, the Council's Legal Service concluded that the NextGenerationEU instrument is economic in nature insofar as it finances economic recovery measures.[111] Some could argue that, in detail, some of the measures financed primarily pursue climate objectives.

The final aspect to be addressed is that the measures under Article 122(1) TFEU must be proportionate to the severity of the situation. Their duration is limited to the time necessary to restore the economic situation or prevent any future crisis in the event of persistent difficulties.[112] Article 122(1) allows only the adoption of temporary measures: any permanent economic management measures must be based on the substantive legal bases of relevant sectoral policies.[113] However, a distinction seems possible depending on whether the measures are intended to prevent the economic situation from deteriorating as a result of difficulties or to provide an immediate response to risks that have materialised. In practice, the permanence of economic management measures seems to be accepted in areas where the Union has no competence to act. Council Directive 73/238/EEC of 24 July 1973 on measures to mitigate the effects of difficulties in the supply of crude oil and petroleum products does not include an expiry date. The same applies to Council Directive 2009/119/EC, which replaces it and was also adopted on the basis of Article 100 TEC in the absence of Union competence in the area of energy.[114]

---

110 Council Directive (78/170/EEC) of 13 February 1978 on the performance of heat generators for space heating and the production of hot water in new or existing non-industrial buildings and on the insulation of heat and domestic hot-water distribution in new non-industrial buildings, [1978] OJ L52/32.

111 Legal Service of the Council of the European Union, Opinion on the proposals relating to Next Generation EU, doc. 9062/20, 24 June 2020, para. 139.

112 Thus, the period of application of certain provisions of the package of management measures taken in response to the 2022 energy crisis has been extended by one year until 30 June 2025. This extension is justified by the continuing risks to energy supply.

113 See Council Regulation (EEC) No 3450/73 (cited above), which makes the intervention or purchase prices for Italian agricultural products permanent. To this end, it repeals a Council regulation based Article 103 EEC Treaty, that determined the monetary compensation amounts applicable to these products. Regulation 3450/73 is based on Articles 28, 43, 103 and 235 of the EEC Treaty.

114 In 2018, Directive 2009/119/EC was amended by Regulation (EU) 2018/1999 of the European Parliament and of the Council based on substantive legal bases relating to energy policy (Arts. 192(1) and 194(2) TFEU).

C. RECONCILING MANAGEMENT POWERS WITH OTHER POWERS OF INTERVENTION IN RESPONSE TO ECONOMIC DIFFICULTIES

The relationship between Article 122(1) TFEU and other substantive legal bases remains a complex issue.[115] According to the treaties, the use of Article 122(1) TFEU is 'without prejudice to other procedures'. Advocate General Roemer euphemistically observed that 'wording of the expression "without prejudice to" is not entirely clear'. Two interpretations are possible: Article 122(1) has a supplementary scope concerning other provisions of the Treaty providing for powers of economic intervention.[116] The exercise of this economic management power presupposes that the Council first verifies that the measure envisaged cannot be adopted based on another provision. According to a second interpretation, the application of Article 122(1) TFEU is parallel to that of other provisions allowing for the adoption of temporary measures.[117] As the Advocate General justified in his conclusions in the *Balkan-Import* case:

> Measures relating to economic policy have a very broad scope. However, that being so, it seems inconceivable to interpret Article 103 as meaning that the measures in question could be based solely on that provision and that it would often be necessary to comply with other procedural rules (such as those in the agricultural sector requiring consultation of Parliament). In reality, such fragmentation, which would considerably slow down the procedure, is unacceptable if the measures relating to economic policy are to have a rapid effect. It therefore appears that, in principle, we must consider correct the view that, provided that the objectives are geared towards economic policy, Article 103 may be validly applied independently of other provisions of the Treaty and in parallel with them.[118] (our translation)

In this case, the Court of Justice did not confirm the principle of parallel application of Article 103 TEC with other relevant provisions, namely Articles 40 and 43 TEC. When faced with difficulties in a specific sector, the appropriate measures must 'normally' be taken within the powers conferred on the European institutions in that area. This order of priority between the provisions of sectoral economic policies and Article 122(1) TFEU is set

115 For a discussion of the controversies: A. Weber, *Schutznormen und Wirtschaftsintegration*, Baden-Baden, Nomos, 1982, pp. 132 et seq. Cited in A. Weber and S. Pilz, 'Article 122 [Solidarity]', in R. Böttner and H.-J. Blanke (eds.), *Treaty on the Functioning of the European Union – A Commentary*, Cham, Springer, 2025, p. 599.

116 In this sense, F. Martucci, 'Article 100 EEC', in I. Pingel (ed.), *Commentaire article par article des traités UE et CE*, 2nd ed., Basel/Paris/Brussels, Helbing Lichtenhahn/Dalloz/Bruylant, 2010, para. 7.

117 See the interpretations of the Council and the Commission in the opinion of AG Roemer in Case 5/73, *Balkan-Import*, ECLI:EU:C:1973:71.

118 Opinion of AG Roemer, ibid.

aside when the urgency of the situation so requires. In disputes concerning compensation amounts, the Court of Justice noted in this regard the absence of any preventive mechanism established under the common agricultural policy, the time needed to adopt appropriate measures in this area and the urgency of action. In light of this context, 'it may be considered that the Council was entitled to make use, on an interim basis, of the powers conferred on it by Article 103 of the Treaty'.

In practice, the argument of urgency is a decisive factor in basing measures appropriate to the economic situation on Article 122, rather than on another provision. Urgency may be due to the suddenness of events, the slowness of other applicable procedures, the end of the parliamentary session, the time needed for the permanent legal regime to enter into force, etc.[119] The challenge is to take swift action to limit the worsening of economic disturbances, their spread and/or the undermining of elements of the acquis Communautaire.[120] The assessment of urgency remains relative, particularly when the measures taken are preventive. For example, the funding made available by the NextGenerationEU instrument to support economic recovery must be committed by the end of 2023 at the latest, and implemented by the end of 2026 at the latest.[121] Similarly, the SAFE instrument emphasises the urgency of committing massive public expenditure to strengthen the BITDE... and at the same time recalls the regular findings made over several years on 'financial, industrial and capability shortcomings in the defence sector'.[122]

IV. ARTICLE 122(2) TFEU: THE UNION'S POWER TO PROVIDE FINANCIAL ASSISTANCE

The power to provide financial assistance under Article 122(2) TFEU is one of the most obvious expressions of the principle of solidarity. This provision remained inactive until the public debt crisis of 2010. Since then, it has been used on several occasions to establish financing instruments enabling the Union to channel the appropriate financial resources to the financial assistance

119 See Recital 2 of Council Regulation (EEC) No 341/78 of 20 February 1978 laying down certain interim measures for the conservation and management of fishery resources applicable to vessels flying the flag of Spain, for the period 21 February to 31 May 1978, [1978] OJ L49/1.

120 Case 5/73, *Balkan-Import*, ECLI:EU:C:1973:109.

121 Art. 3 of Council Regulation (EU) 2020/2094 of 14 December 2020 establishing a European Union Recovery Instrument to support the recovery in the aftermath of the COVID-19 crisis ('NGEU Regulation'), [2020] *OJ* L433I/23.

122 Recital 3 of the SAFE Regulation, cited above.

needs of Member States.[123] Financial assistance is subject to tension between two conflicting requirements: the liberal logic of Member States' own direct responsibility for their budgets and the social imperative of solidarity in European integration. The wording of Article 122(2) TFEU reconciles these two dimensions through the strict conditions for its triggering (Section A) and the arrangements for granting financial assistance (Section B).

A. CONDITIONS FOR TRIGGERING ARTICLE 122(2) TFEU

The activation of Article 122(2) TFEU requires that a Member State be experiencing 'difficulties or [being] threatened with severe difficulties' (Section 1). Two categories of causes are identified: natural disasters and 'exceptional occurrences beyond [the] control' of the Member State concerned (Section 2).

1. *The Existence of Current or Potential Difficulties*

Once again, the Treaties leave the concept of 'difficulties' undefined. As in the case of Article 122(1), this vagueness suggests that a variety of 'difficulties' are accepted and that no specific type is excluded. Consequently, the difficulties referred to and identified under Article 122(1) TFEU may also be considered for Article 122(2). However, the very purpose of this provision presupposes that the 'difficulties' place a constraint on the public finances of the Member State concerned. They may thus consist of 'a severe deterioration in the borrowing conditions of the Member State concerned',[124] 'a sudden and sharp increase in public expenditure of the Member State concerned',[125] a marked decline in GDP, a decline in the employment rate, disruptions in supply chains[126] or insufficient availability of strategic products.[127]

Article 122(2) sets out separate requirements depending on whether the difficulties are current or potential. In the latter case, the threats must be 'serious' (i.e. highly probable) and the difficulties 'severe'. The aim is to avoid activating the procedure for hypothetical events with limited effects on

[123] Council Regulation (EU) No 407/2010 of 11 May 2010 establishing a European financial stabilisation mechanism (the 'EFSM Regulation'), [2010] *OJ* L118/1; Council Regulation (EU) 2020/672 of 19 May 2020 on the establishment of a European instrument for temporary support to mitigate unemployment risks in an emergency (SURE) following the COVID-19 outbreak, [2020] *OJ* L159/1; Council Regulation (EU) 2020/2094 of 14 December 2020; and, lastly, Council Regulation (EU) 2025/1106.

[124] Recital 4 of the EFSM Regulation, cited above.

[125] Recital 7 of the SURE Regulation, cited above.

[126] Recital 2 of the NGEU Regulation, cited above.

[127] Recital 8 of the SAFE Regulation, cited above.

a Member State's financial situation. It should be noted that the rewriting of Article 100 TEC by the Treaty of Nice removed the condition of 'serious difficulties' when the triggering occurrence is a natural disaster.

2. *Causes of Difficulties: Natural Disasters and Exceptional Occurrences beyond the Control of the Member State*

The granting of financial assistance by the Union to a Member State affected by a natural disaster is self-evident in a Community with a shared destiny. As indicated in Section 2, this circumstance was the first one invoked to justify granting the Union the power to provide financial assistance. In the absence of a definition, the term 'natural disaster' must be understood in its common meaning to refer to a disaster resulting from an event of natural origin: flood, drought, fire, storm, earthquake, volcanic eruption, tsunami, etc. The concept of disaster refers to an event of abnormal intensity that causes significant damage and whose consequences exceed the usual response and repair capabilities. From this perspective, the concept differs from human disasters (migration flows, terrorist attacks) or technological disasters (nuclear accidents, power failures, internet failures). These events would be included in the catch-all category of 'exceptional occurrences beyond the control of the Member State'.

This being said, Council Regulation (EU) 2016/369, adopted on the basis of Article 122(1) TFEU, establishes a framework for emergency assistance in the event of man-made or natural disasters. Some may be surprised that a financial assistance instrument could be based on Article 122(1) rather than Article 122(2). In this regard, it should be noted that the negotiators of the Maastricht Treaty were concerned about the disincentive effect of financial assistance on budgetary discipline. Consequently, Article 122(2) stipulates that financial assistance must be granted subject to certain conditions, regardless of the causes of the beneficiary Member State's financial difficulties. The treaty does not specify the nature or content of the conditions. However, imposing economic policy conditions on a state facing financial difficulties due to events beyond its control implicitly suggests that the government is, in one way or another, responsible for its situation. Conversely, Article 122(1) does not lay down any conditions for the granting of emergency measures.

The benefit of financial assistance for 'exceptional occurrences' responds to requests from Member States with the greatest economic convergence needs (Portugal, Spain, Greece) for the creation of a mechanism to stabilise the economy. The aim was to enable the Member States concerned to cope with idiosyncratic shocks as they arose or materialised.[128] Although the idea was

[128] See Conference of Representatives of the Governments of the Member States – Economic and Monetary Union, Proposal by the Portuguese delegation on Article 3, Brussels, EMU/2/91, 15 January 1991.

retained in Article 122(2), it came at the price of three reservations, only two of which are retained in the current wording of that provision. Exceptional occurences must be beyond the control of the States, which excludes financial assistance to States whose financial difficulties are the result of their own fiscal indiscipline. In this respect, the triggering event is similar to the case of force majeure recognised elsewhere in EU law. Financial assistance is accompanied by conditions agreed between the European institutions and the beneficiary State. The last condition – deleted by the Treaty of Nice – provided that the granting of financial assistance was subject to a unanimous vote by the Council.

Examples of 'exceptional occurrences beyond the control of the State' recognised to date by the Council include the global financial and economic crisis, pandemics and military conflicts initiated by a third country. As regards the causal link between the difficulties and the exceptional occurences, it is sufficient that these events are the main, but not the sole cause of the difficulties. Thus, the ESFM Regulation states that '[t]he deepening of the financial crisis has led to a severe deterioration of the borrowing conditions of several Member States beyond what can be explained by economic fundamentals'.[129]

It should be noted that the procedure under Article 126 TFEU on excessive deficits provides that the Council shall take into account the presence of exceptional circumstances when assessing compliance by Member States with their budgetary obligations. The regular application of this provision, together with the details provided by the legislation supplementing the implementation of Article 126, is likely to inform the Council's practice when acting on the basis of Article 122(2) TFEU.

Article 126(2)(a) TFEU allows the public deficit criterion to be considered to have been met if the excess over the reference value of 3% of GDP is only exceptional and temporary, and provided that it remains close to the reference value. Neither the Treaty nor the Protocol (No 12) on the excessive deficit procedure specify the concepts of 'exceptional', 'temporary' and 'close to the reference value'. Regulation (EC) No 1467/97 of 1997, as amended in 2024, specifies that the exceptional nature of the excess lies in the circumstances in which it occurs. Two categories of circumstances are envisaged: 'an unusual circumstance independent of the Member State concerned and with a significant impact on the financial position of the general government' and 'a severe economic downturn in the euro area or in the Union as a whole'.[130] The first circumstance refers to natural disasters and 'any other event of a catastrophic nature'.[131] In practice, this circumstance has allowed for a wide

[129] Recital 4 of the ESFM Regulation, cited above.

[130] Art. 2 of Council Regulation (EC) No 1467/97 of 7 July 1997 on speeding up and clarifying the implementation of the excessive deficit procedure, [1997] *OJ* L209/6; last amended by Council Regulation (EU) 2024/1264 of 29 April 2024, [2024] *OJ* L2024/1264.

[131] Ibid., p. 18.

range of events to be considered: the 2015 migration crisis, terrorist attacks, methodological changes during the transition to the European system of accounts 2010[132] and, more anecdotally, a legal-technical error in the recovery of tax arrears equal to 0.3% of GDP.[133] It is not enough for a fact to be unusual and outside the control of the government to be classified as exceptional in terms of fiscal discipline. Its occurrence must have a 'major impact' on public finances. The aim is to ensure that there is a proportionate relationship between the event invoked and the activation of the excessive deficit procedure and to limit the risk of moral hazard: a circumstance with a low budgetary impact is normally manageable if the Member State has sufficient budgetary leeway under the preventive arm of the SGP. Thus, the floods in Germany in the summer of 2002 were not classified as exceptional circumstances because they did not have a significant budgetary impact.[134] The same was true of the surprise annual inflation rate of -0.5% measured in Spain in 2016.[135]

The second circumstance referred to in Article 126 TFEU relates to an economic fact. In 1996, the Commission specifically considered the cases of the deterioration of the economic situation in Germany following reunification and in Finland following the collapse of its export markets in the former USSR. This circumstance was also invoked concerning the subprime mortgage crisis in autumn 2008. Regulation (EC) No 1467/97 originally defined a 'severe economic downturn' as an annual decline in real GDP of at least 2%. In 2005, this definition was relaxed to refer to a negative annual GDP growth rate or a negative 'output gap' over a prolonged period. In 2011, the extension of the power granted by the legislator to the Commission and the Council to take into account the existence of exceptional circumstances in the prevention of excessive deficits resulted in a tightening of the definition. A severe economic downturn must now occur 'in the euro area or in the Union as a whole'. This definition excludes asymmetric economic crises: i.e. those whose effects are limited to a single Member State.

In conclusion, the existence of difficulties or a serious threat of severe difficulties does not entitle a Member State to financial assistance from the

---

[132] The impact of the transition to ESA 2010 was significant in Belgium and Finland. See Belgium Report prepared in accordance with Article 126(3) of the Treaty, COM(2015) 112 final, 27 February 2015; and on Finland, COM(2015) 803 final, 16 November 2015.

[133] Commission Report on Denmark in accordance with Article 126(3) of the Treaty, COM(2015) 801 final, 16 November 2015.

[134] Report from the Commission, Excessive deficit in Germany. Report prepared in accordance with Article 104(3) of the Treaty, SEC(2002) 1245 final, 19 November 2002 (Declassified on 15 November 2006), p. 2, note 1. The economic cost of the floods in Bavaria was estimated at over €9 billion (0.45% of GDP) and the budgetary cost for Germany alone at 0.1% of GDP. More fundamentally, an early warning procedure had been initiated against Germany as early as 2001 due to the risk of exceeding the reference value.

[135] Council Implementing Decision (EU) 2017/2351 of 9 August 2016 on imposing a fine on Spain for failure to take effective action to address an excessive deficit, [2017] *OJ* L336/27.

Union. The decision to grant or refuse financial assistance, as well as the terms and conditions of such assistance, is the sole prerogative of the Council.

B. THE TERMS AND CONDITIONS FOR GRANTING UNION FINANCIAL ASSISTANCE

Article 122(1) TFEU authorises the Council to take 'appropriate measures' in response to the economic situation. Similarly, Article 122(2) gives the Council broad discretion in choosing the form or content of financial assistance (Section 1). At most, the Treaties indicate that assistance must be granted 'subject to certain conditions' (Section 2).

1. The Form and Content of Financial Assistance

In the absence of any provisions in the Treaties on financial assistance, reference should be made to the Financial Regulation of the Union.[136] Under Article 223, 'Financial assistance by the Union to Member States or third countries shall be in accordance with pre-defined conditions and take the form of a loan or a credit line or any other instrument deemed appropriate to ensure the effectiveness of the support'. Financial instruments are any financial support measures taken by the Union and financed from the Union budget.[137] They may take the form of equity or quasi-equity investments, loans or guarantees, or other risk-sharing instruments. They may, where appropriate, be combined with other forms of financial support or with funds under shared management or with funds from the European Development Fund. The urgency of the situation requires that priority be given to financing instruments that can be implemented quickly and easily: loans, credit lines and guarantees. Grants are not included among the possible forms of assistance. The fact that they are, by definition, 'financial contribution[s] *by way of donation*' (author's emphasis) contradicts the principles relating to the conditionality of assistance.[138]

Under the Financial Regulation, financial assistance may take several forms. According to one approach, assistance is granted on a case-by-case basis. Each assistance measure reflects the discussions between the requesting State and the EU institutions on the amount granted, the disbursement arrangements, the conditions to be met by the beneficiary, the monitoring of the proper implementation of the conditionality, etc. Another approach is based on the

136 Regulation (EU, Euratom) 2024/2509 of the European Parliament and of the Council of 23 September 2024 on the financial rules applicable to the general budget of the Union, [2024] *OJ* L2024/2509.

137 Ibid., Art. 2(30).

138 See below.

establishment of a general framework for granting financial assistance. The terms and conditions for granting assistance are the same for all beneficiary Member States. This approach is particularly suitable for preventing or remedying difficulties caused to several Member States by the same triggering event. It was applied to provide financial assistance to Member States in the context of COVID or in the context of strengthening the EDTIB. The financial instrument is adopted in the form of a regulation.

Financial assistance is an instrument of solidarity at the discretion of the Council. Requests for assistance submitted by Member States do not necessarily have to be granted in full. As the Court of Justice has rules in its case law, the appropriate measures referred to in Article 122(1) do not have to compensate for all the adverse effects of the deterioration in the economic situation.[139] On the other hand, assistance measures must aim to reduce difficulties or mitigate their effects. Does this mean that the Union is authorised to grant financial support to a Member State in any area? Crises are unpredictable and multifaceted. The objective of Article 122 TFEU to support a Member State in difficulty would be called into question if the Council were unable to take regulatory or budgetary measures in any area of Union competence. The sector of the production of arms, ammunition or military equipment, as well as related services, does not exclude Union intervention, whether in relation to the internal market, transport policy or industrial policy.[140] Article 41(2) TEU prohibits operational expenditure with military or defence implications from being charged to the Union budget. The granting of financial assistance in accordance with Article 122 TFEU does not have the effect of charging military expenditure to the Union budget: such expenditure remains the sole responsibility of the Member States, and the financial support they have received from the Union must be reimbursed. In practice, the Commission considered basing the ASAP Regulation on Article 122 TFEU, drawing inspiration from the solution adopted for the joint purchase of vaccines during COVID-19. This option was ultimately abandoned in favour of the more traditional legal basis of Article 173 TFEU. Several reasons were given for this change: the desire not to exclude the European Parliament from the adoption of a central initiative for European defence; the commitment of the European Parliament to examine the text under the urgent procedure.[141]

---

139 Case 43/72, *Merkur Aussenhandel*, ECLI:EU:C:1973:108.

140 See in particular: S. Rodrigues, 'European Defence Fund, public procurement, military mobility, etc.', in A. Hamonic (ed.), *La spécificité de la défense en droit de l'Union européenne*, Rennes, Presses Universitaires de Rennes, 2025, pp. 223–244.

141 On the negotiation of the ASAP Regulation, see E. Bernard, 'La communautarisation de la défense européenne dans le contexte de la guerre en Ukraine', *RTDE*, July-September 2023, pp. 325–350.

Finally, financial assistance measures taken in response to specific difficulties are, by their very nature, temporary.[142] In its *Pringle* judgment, the Court of Justice emphasises in this regard that

> 'Article 122(2) TFEU does not constitute an appropriate legal basis for the establishment of a stability mechanism of the kind envisaged by that decision. The fact that the mechanism envisaged is to be permanent and that its objectives are to safeguard the financial stability of the euro area as a whole means that such action cannot be taken by the Union on the basis of that provision of the FEU Treaty.'[143]

The temporary nature of the measures adopted under Article 122 TFEU appeared to be called into question with the adoption of Council Regulation (EU) 2022/2372 of 24 October 2022 on a framework of measures for ensuring the supply of crisis-relevant medical countermeasures.[144] In 2021, the Commission established the Health Emergency Preparedness and Response Authority (HERA) as a new internal service.[145] In view of the criticism regarding the decision-making and budgetary autonomy of this structure in relation to the Commission, Regulation (EU) 2022/2372, in its review clause, provides for an assessment of the need to establish HERA as a separate entity and invites the Commission to submit, if appropriate, proposals to amend this Regulation or to make further proposals.[146] In its resolution on the *COVID-19 pandemic: lessons learned and recommendations for the future*, the European Parliament expressed concern that Article 122 TFEU could be used as a basis for institutionalising HERA, given the central role of this authority for the European Health Union.[147] The Commission's 2025 evaluation concluded that there was no need to change the status of HERA.[148]

2. *Conditions Attached to the Granting of Financial Assistance*

Under Article 122(2) TFEU, the granting of financial assistance must be accompanied by 'certain conditions' defined by the Council. The vagueness

---

142 See, for example: Article 1 of Regulation (EU) 2022/2578 of the European Parliament and of the Council of 22 December 2022 establishing a market correction mechanism to protect Union citizens and the economy against excessively high prices, [2022] *OJ* L 335/45.

143 Case C-370/12, *Pringle*, ECLI:EU:C:2012:756, para. 65.

144 [2022] OJ L314/64.

145 Commission Decision of 16 September 2021 establishing the Health Emergency Preparedness and Response Authority, [2021] *OJ* CI 393/3.

146 Article 16 of Regulation (EU) 2022/2372, cited above.

147 European Parliament resolution of 12 July 2023 on the COVID-19 pandemic: lessons learned and recommendations for the future (2022/2076(INI)), [2024] *OJ* C/2024/4003, para. 74.

148 Report from the Commission, Review of the implementation of the operations of the Health Emergency Preparedness and Response Authority, COM(2025) 147 final, 26.3.2025, point 5.3.

of this wording gives the Council a wide discretion to adapt the conditions to the nature of the difficulties encountered and the budgetary situation of the beneficiary State. Thus, the conditions laid down in the SURE Regulation are limited to verifying that the deterioration in public finances is due to measures taken to contain Covid-19.[149] Conversely, the SAFE Regulation is based on the partnership approach applied in the preventive arm of the SGP or in the implementation of the NGEU Regulation: the granting of financial assistance is conditional on the development of an investment plan for the European defence industry. Under this plan, Member States detail their measures implementing the objectives of the financial assistance at the national level. Approval by the Council and proper implementation are conditions for the disbursement of the assistance in instalments.[150] The implementation of conditionality implies a power of supervision and recommendation on the part of the institutions responsible for implementing the assistance.

The Financial Regulation lays down a uniform framework for the implementation of assistance by the Commission.[151] It provides, in particular, that, except in exceptional circumstances, loans shall be disbursed in instalments, provided that the conditions governing the financial assistance are met. Where the conditions are not met, the disbursement of assistance may be suspended or cancelled.

V. DEMOCRATIC SCRUTINY OF THE APPLICATION OF ARTICLE 122 TFEU

Economic and monetary union is not a policy area like any other. Despite the fact that economic policy and monetary policy are included in the Community section of the Treaty, the institutional mechanisms of EMU differ in several respects from the traditional Community method. The highly political dimension of monetary unification, the retention by Member States of their competence in economic policy,[152] the desire of some negotiators of the Maastricht Treaty to ensure that the ECB's interlocutor was an intergovernmental body, and the debates surrounding the integration of the EMU into the Community pillar[153] have led to an original result in terms of the division of economic and monetary responsibilities: a 'combination of

---

149 Art. 6 of the SURE Regulation, cited above.

150 Art. 12 of the SAFE Regulation, cited above.

151 Art. 233 of the Financial Regulation, cited above.

152 See Arts. 2(3), 5(1), 119(1), 120 and 121(1) TFEU.

153 See J.-V. Louis, 'Union économique et monétaire', in J. Megret, M. Waelbroeck and J.-V. Louis et al. (eds.), *Droit de la CEE* ('Commentaire Mégret'), 2nd ed., Brussels, Editions de l'Université libre de Bruxelles, 1995, 6, pp. 20 and seq.

supranationalism and intergovernmentalism'.[154] The most sensitive institutional expression of the influence of intergovernmentalism in EMU lies in the unusual place that the Treaties and practice reserve for non-legislative procedures and the marginalisation of the European Parliament.[155]

The choice of procedure for the application of Article 122 TFEU follows this logic: the exercise of economic management powers and the granting of financial assistance are the sole discretion of the Council, acting by qualified majority on a proposal from the Commission. At most, the adoption of a financial assistance measure is subject to notification of the European Parliament by the President of the Council. This notification is justified by the parliamentary responsibilities for budgetary control.

The NGEU and SAFE financial instruments pursue longer-term objectives, such as the Union's technological catch-up, the acceleration of the ecological transition and the establishment of a genuine European defence. It is argued that these objectives will strengthen the Union's resilience in the event of future difficulties. These two instruments are undoubtedly part of a crisis context marked by urgency. At the same time, many of the measures they recommend as conditionalities have long been identified as necessary. However, both economic policy measures and measures in the defence sector are primarily the responsibility of national governments and only marginally fall within the remit of the EU. The NGEU and SAFE instruments seek to overcome national resistance to change by providing financial incentives for action. Nevertheless, the scale of the transformation required in many strategic areas[156] calls for long-term action that cannot be achieved through the use of Article 122 TFEU. This provision allows for a response to specific difficulties encountered by one or more Member States, but not to short-sighted or ill-advised public policy choices. Article 122 TFEU cannot be used in place of the legal bases provided for establishing sectoral public policies (industrial, agricultural, etc.) When presenting the main lines of the next multiannual financial framework (MFF), the President of the Commission emphasised the unsatisfactory nature of solutions based on Article 122 TFEU.

> We have witnessed crisis since the beginning of my mandate – it started with Covid-19, then we had a heavy energy crisis, then the Russian war in Ukraine. And

---

154 F. Snyder, 'EMU – Metaphor for European Union? Institutions, Rules and Types of Regulations', in R. Dehousse (ed.). *Europe after Maastricht. An Ever Closer Union?* Munich, Beck, 1994, spec. p. 68.

155 See F. Allemand and F. Martucci, 'La mutation de la fonction parlementaire: le rôle des parlements dans la gouvernance économique' (The changing role of parliament: the role of parliaments in economic governance), in J.-B. Auby and P. Idoux, *Le gouvernement économique européen*, Brussels, Bruylant 2017.

156 See in particular: M. Draghi, *The Future of European Competitiveness*, 2 parts, Brussels, 9 September 2024.

> each time, it was extremely difficult to react quickly and with the financial firepower that was necessary. Because, as you know, our budget today is designed in such a way that 90% of resources are fixed. This budget was designed in 2018-2019, but we are now living with this 90% fixed. What we did then was to try to use Article 122, which is suboptimal; it is not the best instrument to have for such severe crisis. This is why we are creating a dedicated crisis mechanism with a firepower of up to almost EUR 400 billion. Because crises are no longer the exception, they are the norm, and we have learnt the lesson.[157]

Pending the adoption of the new MFF 2028-2034, the European Parliament's involvement in the development of measures based on Article 122 TFEU has undergone some changes. In parallel with the negotiation of the NGEU instrument, the European Parliament secured the establishment of an ad hoc budgetary procedure for exchanging views with the Council and the Commission on the budgetary implications of measures taken on the basis of Article 122 TFEU.[158] The procedure consists of two stages. The first stage concerns the assessment of the implications of the measures for the Union budget. The Commission undertakes to attach a financial statement to any legislative proposal adopted pursuant to Article 122. If the Council or, more likely, the European Parliament considers that the impact is 'significant', either may convene a meeting of a joint committee to which the European Commission is invited. The discretionary power granted to the Council in implementing the two paragraphs of Article 122 TFEU limits the potential of this type of mechanism. The meetings should allow for 'a constructive dialogue with a view to reaching a common understanding of the budgetary implications of the envisaged legal act'. It can be inferred from the purpose of these exchanges that they will focus on the amounts and form of the assistance measures, as well as the financing arrangements. However, the appropriateness of the measure is not a matter for discussion. The discussions should not be prolonged unnecessarily, given the urgency of the situation. In any event, the procedure may not exceed two months.

In addition, the European Parliament and the Commission have committed to improving their cooperation. In a joint statement by their respective presidents, it has been agreed that the Commission will 'provide comprehensive justification and information on the exceptional cases where the proposals

---

157 Statement by President von der Leyen on the next long-term EU budget, Brussels, 16 July 2025.

158 Joint declaration of the European Parliament, the Council and the Commission on budgetary scrutiny of new proposals based on Article 122 TFEU with potential appreciable implications for the Union budget, [2020] *OJ* C444I/5.

by the Commission are based on Article 122 TFEU.[159] The strengthening of the exchange of information for the benefit of the European Parliament is accompanied by a subsequent amendment to its internal assessment procedures. In accordance with Rule 138 of its Rules of Procedure, the President of the Parliament may invite the Commission to make a statement to the assembly when it intends to adopt a proposal for a legal act based on Article 122 TFEU. The statement provides an opportunity to justify the reasons for the choice of legal basis. The statement must be made before the proposal is adopted by the College of Commissioners, which allows for the content of the measures to be amended if Parliament has concerns about the choice of legal basis. Furthermore, given the possible budgetary implications of measures taken under Article 122 TFEU, the Commissioner responsible is invited to report on the implementation of these measures no later than three months after their adoption and at regular intervals thereafter.

Finally, the Council retains the option of consulting the European Parliament before adopting a measure based on Article 122 TFEU. The opinion delivered by the Parliament is not binding on the Council. This option has rarely been used to date.[160]

---

159 Joint statement by European Commission President von der Leyen and European Parliament President Metsola on the revision of the Interinstitutional Framework Agreement, Brussels, ref. STATEMENT/24/5404, 21 October 2024.

160 It was applied in particular when adopting Council Directive 98/93/EC.

THE SECURITY ACTION FOR EUROPE (SAFE) THROUGH THE REINFORCEMENT OF THE EUROPEAN DEFENCE INDUSTRY INSTRUMENT

Council Regulation (EU) 2025/1106 of 27 May 2025 establishing the Security Action for Europe (SAFE) through the Reinforcement of the European Defence Industry Instrument

Daniel FIOTT
Professor, Centre for Security, Diplomacy and Strategy (CSDS), Vrije Universiteit Brussel
Non-resident Senior Fellow, Real Instituto Elcano

I. THE RATIONALE FOR THE SAFE REGULATION

In the context of Europe's deteriorating security and geopolitical situation, the European Commission proposed a Security Action for Europe (SAFE) Regulation on 19 March 2025.[1] The SAFE Regulation sets out a new financial tool for the European Union (EU), which will see the EU issue loans for defence investment for the first time. Indeed, the SAFE instrument will be endowed with up to €150 billion in loans to be utilised by EU Member States and third states to scale up defence production in critical defence capability areas, to reduce the fragmentation of the European defence market and to enhance the Union's strategic autonomy in defence. As a first for the EU, the SAFE loan

[1] Commission of the European Communities, 'Proposal for a Council Regulation establishing the Security Action for Europe (SAFE) through the reinforcement of the European Defence Industry Instrument', COM(2025) 122 final of 19 March 2025. See also the subsequent SAFE Council Regulation – Council of the EU 'Council Regulation establishing the Security Action for Europe (SAFE) through the Reinforcement of the European Defence Industry Instrument', Council Regulation (EU) 2025/1106, 27 May 2025.

instrument will include repayment schedules of up to 45 years, and come with a 10-year grace period with no repayments on interest being made. As with all EU-level defence investment tools, access to the SAFE loan instrument comes with a series of conditions including, as a principle,[2] the need for at least two participating countries to address the priority capability areas first set out by President Von der Leyen,[3] subsequently endorsed by the European Council,[4] and then reaffirmed in the EU's White Paper on European Defence.[5] These conditions respect a minimum level of autonomy and security controls. This chapter discusses the emergence of the SAFE Regulation, and considers some of the opportunities and challenges emerging from the new instrument.

II. THE EMERGENCE OF THE SAFE REGULATION

Given the ongoing Russian invasion of Ukraine and some fundamental shifts in the transatlantic relationship, the EU has been considering new ways of financing defence in Europe. Indeed, as a consequence of Russia's war on Ukraine, the EU has introduced, modified or accelerated a range of new and/or existing tools to assist EU Member States in stimulating defence production and innovation in key capability and technology areas. The European Commission, in particular, has been investing in key defence innovation domains – both before and after the Russian invasion – via the European Defence Fund (EDF), which started in 2021. Through the Fund, the EU has invested in key weapons domains including ground, air and naval combat capabilities. Moreover, the Union has also dedicated EDF funding to key technology areas such as cyberdefence and space. In addition to the EDF, the Union has adapted other financial tools such as the European Peace Facility (EPF) to assist with the acquisition of ammunition, missiles and other military equipment that is necessary for the defence of Ukraine. Permanent Structured Cooperation (PESCO) projects also address some of the Union's key capability objectives, although there remain questions about PESCO's overall effectiveness.

---

2 It should be noted that in the SAFE Regulation (27 May 2025) there is a derogation under Article 4 (3) that allows for 'procurements [to be] carried out by one Member State' under the SAFE instrument should a procurement contract be signed no later than 30 May 2026.

3 Commission of the European Communities, 'Letter to the European Council', 4 March 2025. See: https://ec.europa.eu/commission/presscorner/api/files/attachment/880628/Letter%20by%20President%20von%20der%20Leyen%20on%20defence.pdf.

4 European Council, 'Conclusions of the Special meeting of the European Council', EUCO 6/25, 6 March 2025.

5 Commission of the European Communities and High Representative of the Union for Foreign Affairs and Security Policy, 'Joint White Paper for European Defence Readiness 2030', JOIN(2025) 120 final of 19 March 2025.

Indeed, the Union has not remained static in the area of defence investment, and it has sought to build on and complement tools such as the EDF, EPF and PESCO. For example, the European Commission established financial tools to assist EU Member States in stimulating ammunition and missile production, as well as to provide assistance with capability development and support for defence SMEs. Such tools included the introduction of the €500 million Act in Support of Ammunition Production (ASAP), the €310 million European Defence Industry Reinforcement through Common Procurement Act (EDIRPA) and schemes such as the EU Defence Innovation Scheme (EUDIS). In many respects, tools such as ASAP and EDIRPA have been designed to test the ground for the Union in supporting defence capability development and production efforts. Indeed, both ASAP and EDIRPA were seen as precursor programmes for the European Defence Industry Programme (EDIP) Regulation, which was introduced in 2025.[6] EDIP is widely seen as the follow-on instrument from the EDF, so that the Union can provide financial assistance along the full spectrum of defence production – from R&D and prototyping (under the EDF) to development, commercialisation and maintenance (under the EDIP).

Although each of these financial instruments is set to substantially assist EU Member States with collaborative defence innovation efforts and joint capability development, the re-election of Donald Trump in the United States (US) in 2024 and the ongoing war in Ukraine have placed considerable pressure on EU leaders to move more swiftly and boldly on defence investment. Within a NATO context, President Trump campaigned on a pledge to force European allies to increase their defence investment levels from 2 per cent of gross domestic product (GDP) (agreed at the NATO Wales Summit in 2014) to 5 per cent of GDP (agreed at the 2025 Hague NATO Summit). EU Member States found themselves in the difficult position of having to drastically increase their defence spending, but to do so in such a way as to ensure that investments would benefit the European defence market. Indeed, although several EU-NATO nations continue to procure US-made defence equipment, a growing sense of the need to ensure European autonomy in defence production has taken root, especially since the 2022 Versailles Declaration, which stressed the importance of building up the European Defence Technological and Industrial Base (EDTIB).

Politically, then, the EU is faced with a need to prove its worth in defence investments, but it needs to do so with more ambition and urgency – hence the SAFE loan instrument. Indeed, when the European Commission presented its 'ReArm Europe' plan on 6 March 2025, it did so within a dynamic transatlantic

---

[6] See Regulation (EU) 2025/2643 of the European Parliament and of the Council of 16 December 2025 establishing the European Defence Industry Programme and a framework of measures to ensure the timely availability and supply of defence products ('EDIP Regulation'), [2025] *OJ* L2025/2643, and the contribution by E. Simon in this publication.

relationship with the US. March 2025 saw the creation of a 'coalition of the willing' during the 2 March London Summit, which was called in the wake of US political signals that it would no longer substantially support Ukraine with military equipment or offer Kyiv any security guarantees. Here, it is worth recalling the rather unceremonious meeting in the Oval Office between Ukrainian President Zelensky and President Trump on 28 February 2025, which resulted in worsened US-Ukraine relations. The decision by the US to downscale its support for Ukraine and to push for a peace agreement above the heads of European countries led leaders in several EU countries to call for more Union support for Ukraine. In addition, March 2025 was a month of further trade tensions between the US and the EU, with President Trump calling for the imposition of trade tariffs on EU steel and aluminium, in addition to other products.

With such political pressures in mind, and before a Special European Council was called in Brussels on 6 March 2025, the President of the European Commission, Ursula von der Leyen, presented the 'ReArm Europe Plan' through a formal letter to the European Council, sent on 4 March 2025. Although this initiative would go on to be renamed the 'Readiness 2030' plan when it was formally unveiled on 28 March 2025, the raft of initiatives took many in Europe by surprise. Indeed, President von der Leyen presented a €800 billion package of defence investment initiatives ahead of the Special European Council to assert the EU's autonomy in defence amid growing US hesitancy about supporting European security. It is certainly true that the €800 billion pledge for more EU defence investment came as an unprecedented announcement, especially given that the EDF was only endowed with €8 billion, while sums received by ASAP and EDIRPA combined amounted to less than €1 billion. In short, the '€800 billion' figure promised to place the EU in the 'big league' of defence spenders, especially given that the Union as a whole invested €279 billion in defence in 2023.[7]

It is as part of the 'ReArm Europe' plan that President von der Leyen first presented the SAFE loan instrument idea, with a budget of €150 billion, which would represent a large part of the overall €800 billion spending pledge. The remaining €650 billion would, it was argued by the President, be generated from a relaxation of the Union's Stability and Growth Pact (SGP) rules that limited EU Member States' ability to accrue more national debt for defence. In fact, the 'ReArm Europe' plan stipulated that the European Commission would provide some fiscal headroom for EU Member States to spend more on defence without triggering the SGP's 'excessive deficit procedure'. To be more precise, this part of the 'ReArm Europe' plan would provide EU Member States with flexibility in the SGP for up to four years, with a possible extension if necessary. Indeed, the flexibility under the National Escape Clause will be

[7] European Defence Agency, 'EDA Defence Data', 2024. See: https://eda.europa.eu/publications-and-data/defence-data.

capped at 1.5% of GDP, so that each year activation of the clause would allow EU Member States to mobilise an additional defence expenditure by up to 1.5% of GDP.[8]

Finally, the symbolism of the EU investing €800 billion in defence resonates with existing political developments in the EU and in the transatlantic relationship. First, the former and present European Commissioners for defence spoke about the need for the Union to invest in the region of €100-500 billion, especially if the EU wants to be perceived as a serious actor in defence. In this respect, a total of €800 billion seemingly puts the EU in a different league of defence investments, and it has not been lost on observers that the figure of €800 billion is close to what the US spends on defence every year. Secondly, the idea that the EU should borrow/lend money for defence investments was relatively new, but was arguably only made possible because of shifts in Germany's approach to defence. For years, Berlin had seen itself as the leader of the 'frugal states' that argued against borrowing or incurring debt, lest the EU's overall credit rating become damaged in the process. However, this changed in March 2025 when the German parliament voted in favour of changing the country's 'debt brake' rules to allow for an injection of €500 billion in defence and infrastructure.[9] This shift in Germany's debt ceiling rules appeared to coincide with the European Commission's decision to move ahead with the SAFE Regulation. And here, we should acknowledge that the €650 billion in additional investment foreseen by the Commission under the activation of the National Escape Clause covers a great deal of the additional €500 billion announced by Germany.[10] Yet in contrast to these national developments, the Commission has steadfastly maintained that EU-level investments – such as the SAFE instrument – should be used for collaborative EU defence efforts.

III. THE SAFE REGULATION

The SAFE Regulation, as established by the Council of the EU on 27 May 2025, represents a landmark legislative measure aimed at reinforcing the EDTIB. Introduced under the Polish Presidency of the Council of the EU, the

---

8 European Commission, 'Communication accommodating increased defence expenditure within the Stability and Growth Pact', C(2025) 2000 final, 19 March 2025, p. 5.

9 S. Kinkartz, 'Defense, infrastructure: Germany plans record investment', DW News, 8 July 2025. See https://www.dw.com/en/defense-infrastructure-germany-plans-record-investment/a-73196730.

10 D. Fiott, 'Spending Our Way Out of a Crisis? The Challenges and Benefits of ReArming Europe', CSDS Policy Brief, No. 4, 2025. See https://csds.vub.be/publication/spending-our-way-out-of-a-crisis-the-challenges-and-benefits-of-rearming-europe/; see also Council of the EU, 'Council Recommendations allowing Member States to deviate from the maximum growth rates of net expenditure as set by the Council under Regulation (EU) 2024/1263 (activation of the national escape clause)', 10342/3/25, 4 July 2025.

SAFE Regulation establishes a comprehensive financial mechanism designed to enhance defence preparedness, autonomy and industrial resilience among EU Member States. In this respect, SAFE builds on and supports existing EU defence investment mechanisms, including the EDF, EDIRPA and ASAP. In particular, one can observe the same market intervention logics introduced by EDIRPA and ASAP in Article 4(1) of the SAFE Regulation, which stresses the need to 'speed up the adjustment of the defence industry to structural changes' and to 'improve the timely availability of defence products'.[11] Central to the SAFE Regulation is the provision of financial assistance amounting to up to €150 billion in the form of long-term loans. These loans are repayable over 45 years, with an additional ten-year initial grace period, thereby ensuring affordability and sustained investment in the defence sector.

Given the security challenges facing the EU, the SAFE instrument is to be used for the common procurement of the Union's most urgent capability needs including air and missile defence, artillery systems, ammunition and missiles, drones and counter-drone systems, military mobility, artificial intelligence, quantum computing, cyber and electronic warfare, strategic enablers, space-based assets and critical infrastructure protection.[12] These defence capability areas were outlined in the EU's Defence White Paper and endorsed by the European Council, as it underlined the need to rapidly enhance the Union's defence readiness.[13] These capability areas also correspond to NATO capability targets, and so SAFE can be considered as an important means of meeting NATO defence planning objectives among European allies. More precisely, these capability areas can be broadly divided into two categories: 1) for short-term capabilities such as ammunition, missiles and drones, which are in short supply in Europe but necessary for defending Europe and supporting Ukraine; and 2) strategic platforms that will enhance European defence over the longer-term, such as in the domains of naval and air platforms and emerging and disruptive technology fields like artificial intelligence and electronic warfare capabilities.

To access SAFE loans, EU Member States are required to submit detailed European defence industry investment plans to the European Commission, demonstrating their defence capability needs and the alignment of their proposed expenditures with the SAFE Regulation's objectives. Under Article 7(2) and (3), the European defence industry investment plan submitted to the European

---

11 Council Regulation (EU) 2025/1106, cited above.

12 D. Fiott, 'Going it Alone, Doing So Divided? The Era of Uncertainties and Europe's Defence Industrial Politics', CSDS Policy Brief, No. 8, 2025. See: https://csds.vub.be/publication/going-it-alone-doing-so-divided-the-era-of-uncertainties-and-europes-defence-industrial-politics/.

13 European Council, 'Conclusions', 20 March 2025. See https://www.consilium.europa.eu/media/viyhc2m4/20250320-european-council-conclusions-en.pdf.

Commission should give a reasoned and substantiated case for the type of defence product(s) to be developed, the associated costs and a description of how the planned investment activities will contribute to strengthening security of supply and resilience, especially by facilitating access to the defence market for SMEs, mid-caps and new defence players.[14] Here, the SAFE Regulation imposes certain financial safeguards on Member States applying for a SAFE loan, such as a ceiling that restricts the top three Member State recipients from receiving more than 60% of the total funds, thus promoting equitable distribution across the Union. The eligibility criteria for participation in SAFE-backed procurement activities are indeed strictly delineated, indicating that the Commission will have to assess each investment plan, as per Articles (2) and (4) in the SAFE Regulation.

Additionally, the SAFE Regulation allows for a limited inclusion of third-country components, capped at 35% of the overall procurement value, to preserve the Union's strategic autonomy. Here, one should also recall that contractors and subcontractors must be legally established and operational within the EU, the European Economic Area (EEA), the European Free Trade Association (EFTA) or Ukraine. Moreover, their executive management structures must also be based within these jurisdictions. Nevertheless, openness to third countries was a particularly sensitive matter for negotiators, as there is general disagreement among co-legislators on how open/closed EU defence industrial initiatives should be, although Article 16 (11) does stress that 'contractors have the ability to decide, without restrictions imposed by third countries or by third-country entities, on the definition, adaptation and evolution of the design of the defence product procured'.[15] This is in line with the expectations of European industry, which has been supportive of SAFE, when it asked that 'Europe should retain the ability to decide, without restrictions, on design definition, adaptation and evolution'.[16] In this case, SAFE introduces a preliminary obligation for the EU and any third country to enter into a Security and Defence Partnership, which sets out a general political framework for cooperation and aligns the EU and third countries on values and political principles (the EU, for example, has such partnerships with Canada, Moldova, Japan, South Korea, the United Kingdom and others). While the SAFE Regulation appears more open than the EDF in terms of third-country participation, it remains unclear today what role such non-EU countries can play. Interestingly, however, it is obvious under SAFE that any third countries that do want to participate in SAFE, subject to a bilateral or multilateral

---

14 Council Regulation (EU) 2025/1106, cited above.

15 Council Regulation (EU) 2025/1106, cited above.

16 ASD Europe 'Industry views on the proposed SAFE instrument', IRIS Commentary, 22 April 2025. See https://www.asd-europe.org/news-media/publications/asd-position-papers/industry-views-on-the-proposed-safe-instrument/.

agreement (see Article 17 (1) and (2), would be required to make a financial contribution. This contribution, as per Article 17 (4), would be classed as 'external assigned revenues',[17] which implies that such revenues would be used to support and reinforce the EDTIB and Ukraine's defence industry (as stated by Article 21 (5) of the Financial Regulation).[18]

In light of the urgent geopolitical context, the SAFE Regulation authorises the use of expedited procurement procedures, notably through negotiated contracts without prior publication, thereby accelerating the acquisition process. Here, it should be noted that the SAFE Regulation is part of wider European Commission efforts to simplify the procedures for defence procurement, cooperation and transfers in the EU, as set out in the Defence Readiness Omnibus. The European Commission's 'Defence Readiness Omnibus,' published in June 2025, proposes a comprehensive set of measures to streamline EU defence regulation and unlock up to €800 billion in investments by 2030. Drawing on the EU White Paper on European Defence, the package includes fast-track permitting, simplified access to EU defence funding, incentives for joint procurement and streamlined intra-EU transfers. This will also permit a revision of the Defence Procurement Directive (2009/81/EC) in 2026. The Omnibus also clarifies how environmental and financial regulations apply to defence and aims to improve private investment through refined eligibility under InvestEU. These reforms collectively aim to accelerate capability development and cross-border defence cooperation.[19]

A significant fiscal provision within the SAFE Regulation is the exemption of defence-related acquisitions from Value Added Tax (VAT). This exemption applies to both intra-Community transactions and imports, with suppliers retaining the right to deduct VAT on upstream inputs. The legal basis of the SAFE Regulation rests on Article 122 of the Treaty on the Functioning of the European Union (TFEU). This article (see the chapter by Frédéric Allemand in this publication) is designed to allow EU Member States to act in a 'spirit of solidarity' by adopting measures that respond to 'severe difficulties [...] in the supply of certain products'. Again, 'severe difficulties' in this respect have been premised on the idea that the European defence sector has difficulties producing enough military equipment to meet the threat from Russia. It is on this legal basis that the European Commission and Council of the EU have agreed to develop SAFE, especially given the additional time pressures imposed

---

[17] Council Regulation (EU) 2025/1106, cited above. See also F. Santoponto, 'The EU's SAFE Rearmament Programme and Its Potential Consequences', IRIS Commentary, 28 May 2025. See https://www.iris-france.org/en/le-programme-de-rearmement-safe-de-lue-et-ses-consequences-potentielles/.

[18] European Union, 'Regulation of 18 July 2018 on the financial rules applicable to the general budget of the Union', Regulation (EU, Euratom) 2018/1046, 18 July 2018.

[19] Commission of the European Communities, 'Communication on the Defence Readiness Omnibus', COM(2025) 820 final, 17 June 2025.

on Europe by the election of President Trump and the shifts in US security policy towards Europe and NATO.

IV. CHALLENGES AND OPPORTUNITIES

Naturally, it will take time to assess fully the benefits of the SAFE loan instrument, as there is a need to see the instrument used in practice by EU Member States. Still, there remain concerns about how effective the tool will be in practice. The first challenge is the financial amount contained in the SAFE instrument, which, according to some (albeit US-based) analysts, is still insufficient.[20] Despite €150 billion being the most substantial EU-level defence financing tool in existence, it is claimed that this amount does not fully meet the military investment needs of Europe, especially if the additional €650 billion purported to result from the relaxed SGP rules do not materialise. Still, the amount of €150 billion is significant, and it is more likely that more substantial challenges to SAFE lie elsewhere. For example, SAFE is seen as a short-term measure to support the European defence industry, but it remains to be seen whether it will have a major impact on addressing long-standing market challenges such as duplication and fragmentation. It is clear that EU Member States, while now having access to additional capital, still need to collaborate more intensely and to align their military procurement needs.

The biggest challenge facing SAFE is indeed whether EU Member States will show interest in applying for loans. Countries with low borrowing costs may not necessarily be attracted by the loans offered under SAFE, and EU Member States with stronger credit may simply seek to finance their defence modernisation domestically. Indeed, one analysis has shown that the Eurozone ten-year bond yield in March 2025 was 3.22%, while Germany was only borrowing at 2.68% in the same month.[21] Many other EU Member States can also borrow more cheaply than the rate being offered under SAFE. The positive news is that the EU has a strong credit rating. Borrowing through the Union allows members to access loans at preferential rates, much lower than might be possible on the open market, and the experience of the Covid-19-era Support to mitigate Unemployment Risks in an Emergency (SURE) mechanism

---

20 T. Burman, 'Expert Sounds Alarm on $170 Billion European Defense Plan', Newsweek, 20 May 2025. See: https://www.newsweek.com/expert-defense-spending-europe-military-2074517#:~:text=%22While%20politically%20important%2C%20the%20€150%20billion%20fund,to%20meet%20Europe's%20defense%20ambitions%2C%22%20Muharremi%20said.

21 D. Fiott, 'Going it Alone, Doing So Divided? The Era of Uncertainties and Europe's Defence Industrial Politics', CSDS Policy Brief, No. 8, 2025. See https://csds.vub.be/publication/going-it-alone-doing-so-divided-the-era-of-uncertainties-and-europes-defence-industrial-politics/. See also J. Arnal, 'Beyond Nostalgia: Making the Most of the EU's Defence Spending Boom' (2025) 60(3) *Intereconomics*, pp. 138–139.

shows that a majority of Member States do indeed apply for EU-backed loans in times of crisis. This will certainly benefit those EU Member States with weaker credit ratings, and this could be a lifeline for financially constrained EU Member States that are faced with the pressure to modernise their defences while also maintaining fiscal discipline. Finally, we should also not exclude the fact that Member States may still participate in SAFE-financed collaborative efforts, even if they do not apply for a SAFE loan directly. Indeed, nothing is stopping a Member State that can borrow more cheaply than the EU's rates from collaborating with Member States that have applied for a SAFE loan.

However, the introduction of SAFE loans could also have a positive impact on the Union's overall indebtedness, as the ability to spread the costs over a long period would ensure that the Union does not incur any further debt (i.e. instead of having to increase the size of the EU budget to accommodate additional defence spending). We should also consider that loans operate under a different logic to grants, as loans mean repayments and repayments can best be made by investing in capabilities or technologies that can provide some form of return on investment. In this sense, there is an added pressure under SAFE to ensure that loans are used in the most productive ways possible. Still, it is also true that loans only defer expenditures over a longer period and/or to some distant point in the future – yet, they still need to be repaid, regardless of the short-term fiscal flexibility they may create.[22] Here, it will be critical that SAFE loans are deployed rapidly to ensure that the investment can reach critical areas of investment quickly. The positive news here is that SAFE comes with a pre-financing possibility (see Article 11), which will allow Member States to request up to 15% of pre-financing from the loan support to kick-start defence projects in a timely fashion. The risk is that any long, drawn-out process will not allow EU Member States and Europe's defence industry to rapidly enhance defence production in a short time frame.

There is also the challenge of how SAFE loans will be reflected in EU Member States' defence budgets, as SAFE is a loan-making rather than grant-making instrument. Indeed, under the EDF, grants are made to industry consortia, and there is no need for repayment. Accordingly, grants show up in EU Member State defence budget accounting as income, whereas a loan would need to be repaid, and thus it will be classified as an expense. There is also a risk that EU Member States will seek a loan from the SAFE instrument to pay for existing projects rather than generating new defence capabilities. Taking loans under the SAFE instrument could allow EU Member States to boost their defence spending in the short term, especially as loans will appear in national accounts as expenditure. This may, in the short term, contribute

---

22 J. Arnal, 'Beyond Nostalgia: Making the Most of the EU's Defence Spending Boom' (2025) 60(3) *Intereconomics*, pp. 138–139.

to the pressure on NATO to increase defence spending. Indeed, the Hague NATO Summit in June 2025 resulted in a new investment target of 5% of GDP (replacing the 2% of GDP target agreed at the NATO Wales Summit in 2014). Applying for SAFE loans could add a short-term boost to defence expenditure, but this possibility should not cloud the real importance of ensuring that SAFE-backed investments do indeed go to developing European defence capabilities and stimulating European defence production.

Another challenge with SAFE is ensuring consistency with the raft of other EU defence investment schemes including the EDF, PESCO and the EDIP. It will be necessary to ensure that SAFE and other EU instruments focus on delivering the capability priorities contained in the EU White Paper on European Defence and endorsed by the European Council.[23] It may not presently be clear how SAFE will relate to the EDIP and whether loans under SAFE could be utilised to (part) fund common projects in the EDIP. Indeed, for SAFE to make a lasting contribution to the EDTIB, it should work in close coordination with other EU defence investment initiatives to ensure a minimum level of security of supply in the European defence market.[24] Here, there will also be a need to assess how SAFE loans will relate to other EU loan-making facilities, such as those instruments offered by the European Investment Bank (EIB) under the Strategic European Security Initiative (SESI). Here, some €8 billion in loans are also being made available by the EIB, albeit for defence investments that fall below the threshold of military equipment (e.g. logistics, manufacturing sites, etc.).

Despite the challenges outlined here, there are a number of opportunities associated with the SAFE instrument. First, it is not at all clear that EU Member States will decide to apply for SAFE loans based solely on the borrowing costs involved. Indeed, there are political reasons to believe that a 45-year repayable loan, even at a slightly higher borrowing rate, would still be politically lucrative for EU Member States. This is because the instrument can be used to support European defence producers and for them to engage in joint development – thus, the loan instrument can be seen as a means to the end of more EU defence collaboration. The SAFE Regulation is set up in such a way as to support the European defence sector by providing a minimum level of security of supply and providing opportunities for cross-border cooperation. Interestingly, SAFE introduces an 'anti-concentration' mechanism 'under which the three largest beneficiaries of the mechanism may not borrow more than 60% of the total

---

[23] 'Conclusions of the Special meeting of the European Council', cited above.

[24] D. Fiott, 'Sovereignty by Design? Security of Supply in Defence in the European Union', ARES Group Paper, No. 113, 2025. See: https://www.iris-france.org/wp-content/uploads/2025/05/ARES_2025_05_113_Security_Supply_PolicyPaper.pdf.

€150 billion available'.[25] This ensures that medium and small EU Member States will have an opportunity to benefit from SAFE too. Indeed, analysis already shows that EU Member States seeking to develop their national defence industrial bases would be well-placed to benefit from SAFE loans.[26]

V. THE SAFE REGULATION AND CONTROVERSY

Although the SAFE loan instrument marks a new avenue for EU defence industrial cooperation, it is not without controversy. In particular, the fact that the SAFE Regulation is based on Article 122 TFEU has led to contention in the European Parliament, which, at the time of writing, has voted on taking legal action against the Council of the EU and European Commission (see the contribution on Article 122 by F. Allemand in this publication).[27] The Parliament's Committee on Legal Affairs has argued that recourse to Article 122 TFEU unnecessarily excludes the European Parliament 'from the decision-making process' on the SAFE Regulation. In essence, Article 122 TFEU provides the Regulation with two legal bases namely: 1) enabling the Council to adopt measures based on a Commission proposal, without the involvement of the European Parliament; and 2) providing for policy and financial means to address economic difficulties.[28] When designing the SAFE instrument, the Commission decided Article 122 TFEU was required as a legal basis to speed up the regulatory adoption process, and to address the 'economic difficulties' facing the European defence market.

One cannot doubt that the European defence market is facing substantial economic difficulties, especially after decades of neglect and under-investment, although quite what 'economic difficulties' specifically mean in the European defence market context is open to interpretation. Nevertheless, the discussion about the validity of Article 122 in the case of the SAFE instrument does give rise to some broader reflections on the agility of the ordinary legislative procedure to respond speedily in times of crisis. On the one hand, the experience of adopting the ASAP Regulation under Article 173 TFEU demonstrates that

---

25 L. Maslanka, 'Imperfect Balance: The EU's Defence Loan Mechanism (SAFE)', OSW, 28 May 2025. See https://www.osw.waw.pl/en/publikacje/analyses/2025-05-28/imperfect-balance-eus-defence-loan-mechanism-safe.

26 A. Koziol, 'SAFE Gives New Impetus to EU Security and Defence', PISM, 29 May 2025. See https://www.pism.pl/publications/safe-gives-new-impetus-to-eu-security-and-defence.

27 Socialists & Democrats, 'European Parliament votes to take legal action after being excluded from decision-making process of EU defence funding', 24 June 2025. See https://www.socialistsanddemocrats.eu/newsroom/european-parliament-votes-take-legal-action-after-being-excluded-decision-making-process.

28 R. Mańko, 'Legal Bases in Article 122 TFEU: Tackling Emergencies Through Executive Acts', European Parliamentary Research Service, 11 April 2025. See https://www.europarl.europa.eu/thinktank/en/document/EPRS_BRI(2025)769579.

the co-legislators were able to adopt a vital EU-financing tool in a relatively rapid fashion. On the other hand, the experience of adopting EDIRPA and EDIP raises questions about the speed of efficient adoption. No one doubts the essential need to involve the European Parliament in legislative processes in defence, but whether the ordinary legislative procedure is currently geared to adopting legislation most efficiently is a legitimate question. Indeed, during the financial crisis and the Covid-19 pandemic, Article 122 TFEU was used to rapidly launch Union financial support. Whether such speed of action can become the norm in EU defence industrial policy remains to be seen.

ARTICLES 170 TO 172 TFEU: TRANS-EUROPEAN NETWORKS AND DEVELOPMENT OF MILITARY MOBILITY

Stéphane de La Rosa
Professor at the Université Paris-Est Créteil, Jean Monnet Chair
Director of the MIL

and

Quentin Loïez[1]
Legal and Policy Officer at the European Commission (DG DEFIS)

> **Article 170**
>
> **1.** To help achieve the objectives referred to in Articles 26 and 174 and to enable citizens of the Union, economic operators and regional and local communities to derive full benefit from the setting-up of an area without internal frontiers, the Union shall contribute to the establishment and development of trans-European networks in the areas of transport, telecommunications and energy infrastructures.
>
> **2.** Within the framework of a system of open and competitive markets, action by the Union shall aim at promoting the interconnection and interoperability of national networks as well as access to such networks. It shall take account in particular of the need to link island, landlocked and peripheral regions with the central regions of the Union.

1 This analysis, which is provided in a personal capacity, reflects the views only of the author, and can in no way be regarded as the official position of the European Commission.

Article 171

1. In order to achieve the objectives referred to in Article 170, the Union:

– establishes a set of guidelines covering the objectives, priorities and broad lines of actions envisaged in the field of trans-European networks; these guidelines identify projects of common interest;

– implements any action that may prove necessary to ensure the interoperability of networks, particularly in the field of harmonising technical standards;

– may support projects of common interest supported by the Member States and defined within the framework of the guidelines referred to in the first indent, in particular in the form of feasibility studies, loan guarantees or interest-rate subsidies; the Union may also contribute to the financing of specific transport infrastructure projects in the Member States through the Cohesion Fund set up in accordance with Article 177.

EU action takes into account the potential economic viability of projects.

2. In order to achieve the objectives referred to in Article 170, the Union:

– shall establish a series of guidelines covering the objectives, priorities and broad lines of measures envisaged in the sphere of trans-European networks; these guidelines shall identify projects of common interest,

– shall implement any measures that may prove necessary to ensure the interoperability of the networks, in particular in the field of technical standardisation,

– may support projects of common interest supported by Member States, which are identified in the framework of the guidelines referred to in the first indent, particularly through feasibility studies, loan guarantees or interest-rate subsidies; the Union may also contribute, through the Cohesion Fund set up pursuant to Article 177, to the financing of specific projects in Member States in the area of transport infrastructure.

The Union's activities shall take into account the potential economic viability of the projects.

3. Member States shall coordinate among themselves, in liaison with the Commission, policies pursued at national level which may have a significant impact on the achievement of the objectives referred to in Article 170. The Commission may, in close cooperation with the Member States, take any useful initiative to promote such coordination.

4. The Union may decide to cooperate with third countries to promote projects of common interest and ensure the interoperability of networks.

5. Member States shall, in liaison with the Commission, coordinate among themselves the policies pursued at national level which may have a significant impact on the achievement of the objectives referred to in Article 170. The Commission may, in close cooperation with the Member State, take any useful initiative to promote such coordination.

6. The Union may decide to cooperate with third countries to promote projects of mutual interest and to ensure the interoperability of networks.

Article 172

The guidelines and other measures referred to in Article 171(1) shall be adopted by the European Parliament and the Council, acting in accordance with the ordinary legislative procedure and after consulting the Economic and Social Committee and the Committee of the Regions.

Guidelines and projects of common interest which relate to the territory of a Member State shall require the approval of the Member State concerned.

I. SCOPE AND MEANING OF THE COMPETENCE OF 'TRANS-EUROPEAN NETWORKS' IN EUROPEAN UNION LAW

Since its introduction by the Single European Act in 1986, the Union's economic and social cohesion policy has been relatively stable, centred on the implementation of the various Structural Funds: the ERDF (European Regional Development Fund), the ESF (European Social Fund), the EAGGF (European Agricultural Guidance and Guarantee Fund); and, since the Maastricht Treaty, the Cohesion Fund for the new Member States. Issues relating to the development and funding of infrastructure within and between Member States have historically been covered by the ERDF, based on the principle of additionality between national and European funding.[2]

With the Maastricht Treaty (1992), cohesion policy was supplemented by the introduction of a more specific policy: the development of trans-European networks. In order to 'derive full benefit from the setting up of an area without internal frontiers, Article 129b of the EC Treaty gave the Community the power to develop trans-European networks in the transport, telecommunications and energy infrastructure sectors'.[3] At the end of the Cold War, there was the conviction that it was appropriate to take advantage of the 'peace dividend', and network policy was barely associated with defence issues. The latter were only covered, in a fragmentary way, by the provisions relating to the CFSP.

2 On the principles applicable to the Funds and the history of cohesion policy, see N. Rubio, *Le contrôle des fonds européen de cohésion: évolutions, enjeux et perspectives*, Travaux du CERIC, Brussels, Bruylant, 2013; S. de La Rosa, 'Politique de cohésion économique, sociale et territoriale', *JurisClasseur Europe*, January 2023, Fasc. 2110. See also the commentary on Article 175 TFEU by S. Rodrigues, in this publication.

3 On the introduction of the trans-European network policy by the Maastricht Treaty, see C. Mestre and Y. Petit, 'Commentary on Title XII', in V. Constantinesco, R. Kovar and D. Simon, *Treaty on European Union. Commentaire article par article*, Paris, Economica, 1995.

The Treaty of Lisbon (2007) added a 'territorial' strand to cohesion policy, which is set out in Article 174(3) of the TFEU: in the implementation and allocation of the Structural Funds, particular attention must be paid to rural areas, areas affected by industrial transition and regions which suffer from severe and permanent natural or demographic handicaps, such as the EU's northernmost regions with low population densities, as well as islands, cross-border and mountain regions. Apart from primary legislation, the EU enlargement to Eastern Europe has also been supported by an ever-increasing link between cohesion policy and the Union's investment policy. These funds are now fully integrated into the national recovery and facility plans, and their allocation must be integrated in accordance with the content of the recommendations adopted for each State, as part of the European Semester coordinating economic and social policies.

In addition, the policy on trans-European networks has been significantly extended and clarified. In order to achieve the objectives of the internal market (Article 26 TFEU) and cohesion policy (Article 174 TFEU), the aim of this shared competence is for the Union to 'contribute to the establishment and development of trans-European networks in the areas of transport, telecommunications and energy infrastructures'. The aim of this policy is centred on the linkage and interconnection of networks: according to the wording of Article 170(2) TFEU, recalled at the beginning of this contribution, the action of the Union takes into account the geographical constraints and isolation of the various territories.

Designed in this way, the network's remit is intended to support the development and interoperability of major infrastructures. Often associated with fairly technical issues, the scope of this policy will not be truly defined until it is the subject of a horizontal regulation on the identification and funding of common infrastructure: e.g. as in the case of transport: Regulation 1315/2013 on the development of trans-European transport networks.[4]

This general text, which is essential for assessing European network policy, concerns 'the development of a trans-European transport network comprising a dual-layer structure consisting of the comprehensive network and of the core network, the latter being established on the basis of the comprehensive network' (Art. 1). The deployment of the comprehensive network, which takes the form of 'European corridors', is based on the identification by the Member States of 'projects of common interest', which are financed by the Union in return for compliance with requirements in terms of infrastructure content, management and interoperability.

4 Regulation (EU) No 1315/2013 of the European Parliament and of the Council of 11 December 2013 on Union guidelines for the development of the trans-European transport network, [2013] *OJ* L348/1.

The few judgments relating to Regulation 1315/2013 show that this text is interpreted in the light of a general purpose – common in internal market law – relating to the removal of barriers between Member States of the Union. In the first case concerning this text, *United Kingdom v Parliament and Council*, Advocate General Y. Bot emphasised that '[t]he establishment and development of the trans-European networks, and the TEN-T [policy] in particular, is designed to facilitate the interconnection of national networks so as to overcome any obstacles to the free movement of goods and persons. Such obstacles are frequently geographical, as in the case of the Alps between France and Italy, or technical, such as the existence of a variety of national on-board signalling and speed-control systems for railway transport, which enable trains to react to signals transmitted from the ground. Such barriers are necessarily an impediment to the establishment of the internal market'.[5]

This general objective has two consequences. Firstly, the definition of projects of common interest, which are the subject of EU funding and form part of the definition of eligible infrastructure by the Member States, must demonstrate 'European added value': i.e. characterise a project which, in addition to the potential value for the Member State in question alone, 'leads to a significant improvement of either transport connections or transport flows between the Member States which can be demonstrated by reference to improvements in 'efficiency, sustainability, competitiveness or cohesion'. The State is therefore obliged to plan its network development projects from a European perspective and cannot, in isolation, describe a network as being of common interest.[6] Secondly, where infrastructure networks fall within the scope of Regulation 1315/2013 and are linked to the comprehensive network, States are required to maintain their accessibility to all modes of transport and may not reduce either capacity or access links: for example, an inland port that is part of the comprehensive network and served by a rail link may not lose its rail service, at the risk of undermining the objective of enhancing the value

---

5 Opinion presented by AG Bot, Case C-121/14, *United Kingdom v Council and Parliament*, ECLI:EU:C:2015:526.

6 Case C-121/14, *United Kingdom v Council and Parliament*, ECLI:EU:C:2015:749, para. 51: '[I]n accordance with the objective of contributing to the establishment and development of trans-European networks in the area of transport infrastructure, referred to in Article 170(1) TFEU, it is apparent from recital 8 in the preamble to that regulation that the trans-European transport network must be developed through the creation of new transport infrastructure, through the rehabilitation and upgrading of existing infrastructure and through measures promoting its resource-efficient use'. It should be added that although the State cannot consider a project to be of common interest in isolation, the fact remains that, under Article 172 TFEU, 'Guidelines and projects of common interest which relate to the territory of a Member State shall require the approval of the Member State concerned'.

of the networks and the need to make them interoperable, between States and between the various existing modes of transport.[7]

II. LINKING NETWORK POLICY WITH MILITARY MOBILITY: QUALIFYING DUAL-USE NETWORKS

The European Union's initiative on military mobility was sketched out in June 2016 in the overall strategy for the European Union's foreign and security policy,[8] and then formalised in the Joint Communication 'Improving Military Mobility in the European Union'[9] adopted in 2017 and the first Action Plan on Military Mobility presented in 2018.[10] It would lead to the mobilisation of network policy, and more specifically the use of trans-European transport networks, to develop the coordination and mobility of armed forces between States. This initiative coincides with a 'strategic' awakening on the part of the Commission and the Member States, which were finally taking the measure of the risks of destabilisation arising from Russia's invasion of Crimea and the multiplication of systemic threats.

In the Joint Communication presented in 2017 by the Commission and the High Representative for Foreign Affairs and Security Policy, it was stated that 'in order to be prepared for crises including through military exercises and to react to them, it is necessary to ensure that those decisions can be taken fast and that, when taken, troops and equipment can move swiftly and smoothly'.[11] This imperative of interoperability and rapid accessibility of transport infrastructures for military purposes immediately establishes a functional and inseparable link between the military mobility programme and the development of network policy within the meaning of the Treaties.

---

7 Case C-229/21, *Port of Brussels*, ECLI:EU:C:2022:471, para. 68: 'Member States must, where feasible, aim to ensure interconnection between, inter alia, rail, road and, as appropriate, inland waterway infrastructure, both for passenger transport and for freight transport'.

8 In the 2016 definition of the 'Comprehensive Strategy for the European Union's Foreign and Security Policy', the Council, while not using the expression 'military mobility', already affirmed the need for a 'responsive Union' in terms of defence. To this end, the declaration calls on states to develop 'the capacity for rapid response also by tackling the procedural, financial and political obstacles which prevent the deployment of the Battlegroups, hamper force generation and reduce the effectiveness of CSDP military operations', see Council of the EU, 28 June 2016, *A comprehensive strategy for the European Union's foreign and security policy*, 10715/16, p. 42.

9 Joint Communication to the European Parliament and the Council Improving Military Mobility in the European Union, JOIN(2017) 41 final.

10 Joint Communication to the European Parliament and the Council on the Action Plan on Military Mobility, JOIN(2018) 05 final.

11 Joint Communication to the European Parliament and the Council entitled 'Improving Military Mobility in the European Union', JOIN(2017) 41 final, cited above.

The integration of military issues into network policy was presented in the first action plan on military mobility, where it was clearly stated that 'Transport infrastructure policy offers a clear opportunity to increase synergies between defence needs and existing Union policies, and in particular the trans-European transport network (TEN-T). In this context, there is scope for demonstrating the EU's added value, and ensuring a more efficient use of public money'. It led to a broadening of the objectives assigned to the latter, as described in Article 171 TFEU. According to this provision, to achieve the general objectives of Article 170 TFEU, the Union's main task is to support projects of common interest supported by the Member States, through funding and the definition of a common normative framework for interoperability.

The general objectives set out in Title XVI of the TFEU concern interoperability, financial support through dedicated loans and funding, common accessibility and security rules. In addition, taking into account the means of military mobility, certain networks must be considered as dual-use under the first action plan. As one of the key actions of the first Action plan, it was decided that the Commission, in conjunction with the Member States, the European External Action Service (EEAS) and the EU Military Staff (EUMS), would identify the 'gaps between the current technical requirements applicable to the trans-European transport network on the one hand, and what would be adequate for military transport on the other'. The Commission was also in charge of identifying 'the parts of the trans-European transport network suitable for military transport, including necessary upgrades of existing infrastructure'. This use of civilian infrastructures required the latter to meet the technical and material requirements of military use.[12] This has led to the adoption of criteria for use for military purposes, corresponding to requirements approved by the Council, covering the use of dual-use infrastructure such as ports, airports, terminals, rail links and waterways.[13]

In August 2021, the Commission adopted an implementing regulation defining the applicable requirements for the dual use of certain infrastructures. Regulation 2021/1328 establishes several criteria that must be met by certain infrastructures before they can be considered as dual-use.[14] These include

---

12 Joint Report to the European Parliament and the Council on the implementation of the Action Plan on Military Mobility from October 2020 to September 2021, JOIN (2021) 26 final, 24 September 2021, para. 6: '[T]he addition of the military layer of the EU military transport network data onto the interactive TENtec map viewer enables the EU Member States to more easily identify the bottlenecks and vulnerable areas on the trans-European transport network'.

13 Military requirements for military mobility inside and outside the Union, 4 July 2019, approved by the Council on 15 July 2019.

14 Commission Implementing Regulation 2021/1328 of 10 August 2021 specifying the infrastructure requirements applicable to certain categories of dual-use infrastructure actions under Regulation 2021/1153, [2021] *OJ* L288/37.

permanent operating capacity and the configuration of runways (length, width, surface) for aerial infrastructures, vessel draught, depth of quays and unloading capacity for ports, as well as the availability of electrical power, track gauge, axle loads and the number of platforms per station for rail infrastructure.

As a result, a form of dissociation in European network policy has emerged. Certain heavy infrastructures, insofar as they meet precise and enhanced capacity and availability requirements, are considered to be of dual-use and may be the subject of specific funding. At the same time, others are lighter but central to interoperability issues and fall outside the scope of defence issues. The definition of technical criteria for accepting an infrastructure as dual-use is gradually becoming a central issue: the fact that certain networks are not suitable for the passage of troops or military equipment, or that certain States oppose movements because their infrastructures are unavailable, can constitute major bottlenecks when there is an urgent need to transfer military resources to certain flanks of the Union. Following Russia's unlawful invasion of Ukraine, the Commission and the High Representative tabled the action plan on military mobility 2.0.[15] Building on the progress made since 2017, this Action Plan 2.0 was intended to open the next chapter of work on military mobility for the period 2022-2026.

Therefore, the efforts initiated in 2017 on military mobility were pursued and led to notable developments, including the full confirmation of the integration of military mobility into European network policy with the adoption of Regulation (EU) 2024/1679,[16] which repealed Regulation 1315/2013. Discussed under the ordinary legislative procedure following Article 172 TFEU,[17] these new guidelines for the development of the TEN-T stipulate that '[t]he trans-European transport network shall be planned, developed and operated in a resource-efficient way, and in accordance with the applicable Union and national environmental requirements, through: [...] the taking into account of possible synergies with the dual-use of infrastructure identified in the Military Requirements for Military Mobility within and beyond the EU'.[18] Thereby, as outlined in the 2025 Joint Report on the implementation of the Action Plan on Military Mobility 2.0, Regulation 2024/1679 proves to

15 Joint Communication to the European Parliament and the Council, Action plan on military mobility 2.0, JOIN(2022) 48 final.

16 Regulation (EU) 2024/1679 of the European Parliament and of the Council of 13 June 2024 on Union guidelines for the development of the trans-European transport network, amending Regulations (EU) 2021/1153 and (EU) No 913/2010 and repealing Regulation (EU) No 1315/2013, [2024] *OJ* L2024/1679. (Union guidelines for the development of the trans-European transport network).

17 Art. 172(1) TFEU: 'The guidelines and other measures referred to in Article 171(1) shall be adopted by the European Parliament and the Council, acting in accordance with the ordinary legislative procedure and after consulting the Economic and Social Committee and the Committee of the Regions'.

18 Union guidelines for the development of the trans-European transport network, Art. 5(1)(f).

be innovative by providing four key elements to support military mobility within and beyond the EU: 'Firstly, it anchors within EU law the notion of a military mobility transport network; secondly, through its new Article 48 on military mobility, it mandates the Commission to identify priority military mobility corridors; thirdly, it sets the TEN-T on the path of becoming a largely dual-use transport infrastructure network, notably by requiring the Member States to consider military mobility needs when constructing or upgrading infrastructure on the TEN-T; and fourthly, it strengthens and aligns several transport infrastructure requirements with Military Requirements, especially for rail; and in some instances the updated maps also reflect the military needs, most notably with extensions into neighbouring countries Ukraine and Moldova'.[19] However, this formal and explicit inclusion of military mobility issues in the scope of Regulation 2024/1679 required the establishment of specific procedures.

Given the sensitivity of the information and data required for the support of dual-use infrastructures, it was necessary that the full technical details, specific to military mobility, be adopted through alternative processes than the one usually provided for under the TEN-T procedures. By way of example, the latest joint report on the implementation of the Action Plan on Military Mobility 2.0, presented in March 2025, explains the process that has been followed to identify the four priority military mobility corridors,[20] for which the Commission services and the EEAS set out a three-step approach: '(i) the first step was to identify the main corridors for short-notice and large-scale movements of military personnel and materiel in the event of a crisis or conflict or for military exercises; (ii) the second step to identify gaps in the infrastructure on the main corridors identified as priority for military movements and: (iii) the third step to identify the actions to close the gaps and ensure that military personnel and materiel can move smoothly for military purposes'. The Commission, together with the EU Military Staff representing the EEAS, 'held two meetings with Member States, in October 2023 and July 2024, each time followed by consultations with NATO, in particular with the Joint Support and Enabling Command […]. On this basis, the Commission services and the EEAS finalised the identification of priority military mobility corridors'. This corresponded to the accomplishment of the first step. Then, 'the four priority military mobility corridors identified were presented to and subsequently endorsed by the EU Military Committee in October 2024. These new priority corridors were included in the revised Annex II of the Military Requirements, which were adopted by the Council on 17 March'. The identification of these four corridors was essential, as they help to 'guide and prioritise future

19 Joint Report to the European Parliament and the Council on the implementation of the Action Plan on Military Mobility 2.0, JOIN(2025) 11 final.

20 Namely the Northern, Central Northern, Central Southern and Eastern Corridors.

investments in the military mobility network at both EU and national levels' which are related to the second and third steps.

Given the sensitive, confidential and strategic nature of military mobility, the institutions had to demonstrate a degree of normative engineering in order, on the one hand, to keep dual-use infrastructures within the scope of the 'common' law on trans-European networks, as defined in Articles 170 et seq. TFEU, and, on the other hand, to identify the elements of confidentiality and specificity of the rules specific to these infrastructures, if necessary by relying on the military expertise of relevant EU bodies, Member States, and regular consultations with NATO.[21] In this respect, the structured dialogue between the EU and NATO has become a reference framework, as emphasised by the tenth Progress Report on EU/NATO cooperation in June 2025.[22]

III. THE USE AND DEVELOPMENT OF DUAL-USE NETWORKS: THE REGULATORY AND FUNDING SUPPORT CHALLENGES

The recognition of dual-use infrastructures in the context of network policy raises two important questions at the implementation stage.

Firstly, the interoperability of networks requires cross-border movements of troops or equipment to be carried out rapidly. So far, Member States have remained competent on such matters, the passage of troops, equipment and military support through a national territory requiring the agreement of the transit State. Therefore, it is in this context that the European Defence Agency (EDA)[23] has played an important role in optimising permission procedures for cross-border movements. As explained in the latest Joint Report on the implementation of the Action Plan on Military Mobility 2.0, the EDA Category A-Programme on 'Optimising Cross-Border Movement Permission Procedures in Europe' has continued making progress to simplify

---

21 On NATO-EU relations: see the commentary by Y. Buchet de Neuilly in this publication.

22 Tenth progress report on the implementation of the common set of proposals endorsed by EU and NATO Councils on 6 December 2016 and 5 December 2017, 10 June 2025, spec. p. 8: 'Military mobility continued to be a flagship project. Russia's war of aggression against Ukraine has demonstrated the importance of rapid and unhindered movement of military forces, along with their equipment and supplies. Both organisations acknowledge the importance of strengthening infrastructure and addressing procedural and regulatory impediments to military movement. The Structured Dialogue on Military Mobility continued to serve as an effective tool for focused discussions on shared priorities and respective work strands, such as military requirements, transport infrastructure, transport of dangerous goods, simplification of customs procedures and cross-border movement permissions, engagement in exercises, and host-nation support' (available at https://www.nato.int/nato_static_fl2014/assets/pdf/2025/6/pdf/250605-progress-report-nr10-EU-NATO.pdf).

23 On the EDA, see the commentary by A.-H. Bertana in this publication.

and harmonise military mobility procedures across Europe. The Joint Report indicates that '27 contributing Member States, including Norway, have signed the Programme Arrangement for cross-border movement permissions' and that this has resulted in the adoption of 'Technical Arrangements' (TAs), one for Surface and one for Air, which have been signed by 26 and 25 Member States respectively (including Norway). The Joint Report finally highlights that another TA for the maritime domain is in an 'advanced state of negotiation'. Each TA describes a desired objective to be reached when it comes to military cross-border movement-related processes, while allowing participants to take the appropriate national measures to attain this goal, in line with their national position. The deployment of these TAs will undoubtedly lead to revisions of internal texts, such as the regulatory provisions of the Defence Code in French law, relating to authorisations for passage or overflight.[24]

This work complements the strategic-level efforts of Member States through PESCO's military mobility project. Notably, this project is the largest PESCO initiative, with 25 participating Member States, as well as NATO allies like the US, Canada, Norway, the UK and Switzerland.[25] Geographically, it brings together many countries interested in military mobility. According to the latest Joint Report on Military Mobility 2.0, this project has established a National Point of Contact Network which will utilise the EDA's Cross Border Movement Permission TAs.

Several Member States have also taken a bottom-up approach outside the EU framework, responding to the new NATO Regional Plans[26] agreed at the 2023 Vilnius Summit. The Netherlands, Germany and Poland were the first to act, signing a letter of intent on 30 January 2024, to establish the Dutch-German-Polish corridor and address cross-border movement-related issues.[27]

---

[24] See, for example, the recent Order of 13 April 2023 on activities subject to the authorisation provided for in Article R. 1333-4 of the French Defence Code, concerning Category I and II nuclear materials in import and export facilities, or present in a vitally important point designated under the national energy sector security directive.

[25] PESCO also provides a framework for related projects, such as the Network of Logistic Hubs in Europe and Support to Operations, as well as initiatives to enhance European strategic lift capabilities, including the Future Mid-size Tactical Cargo, Strategic Air Transport Outsized Cargo, and Next Generation Medium Helicopter projects

[26] See NATO-Topic: Deterrence and defence: 'These plans direct how NATO will deter and defend against any aggressor from any direction, explaining how, in the event of a crisis, Allied forces would defend forward and defeat complex threats across NATO territory. They also set out specifically what will be expected of Allies in a crisis. Driven by the increasingly complex threat environment, this is a larger, more demanding, ask of Allies than NATO has made since the end of the Cold War. The plans ensure that Allies can provide the right forces at the right time and in the right places'.

[27] A Sollfrank and S. Boeke, 'Enablement and Logistics as Critical Success Factors for Military Operations: Comparing Russian and NATO Approaches' (2024) 169(7) *The RUSI Journal*, pp. 10–22. 'The letter outlines four key areas, in which the participating states aim to align regulations and synchronise procedures: (i) cross-border movement permissions; (ii) coordination of movement assets; (iii) infrastructure; and (iv) information sharing'.

Similar cooperative actions have also emerged among other Member States, as well as with non-EU NATO allies.[28]

Secondly, and in line with the overall aim of cohesion and network policy, the development of dual-use networks requires the deployment of specific funding instruments to enable Member States to bring certain infrastructures up to the standards and requirements required for military mobility.

This is the background to the Connecting Europe Facility (hereinafter CEF), set up by Regulation 2021/1153.[29] Based notably on the Union's Trans-European Networks competence (Art. 172 TFEU), the objectives of the CEF are to build, develop, modernise and complete trans-European networks in the transport, energy and digital sectors, and to facilitate cross-border cooperation in the field of renewable energies.[30] One of its specific objectives in the transport sector includes 'adapt[ing] parts of the TEN-T for the dual use of transport infrastructure with a view to improving both civil and military mobility'.[31] During the negotiations on the Multiannual Financial Framework for the period 2021-2027, a significant cut was decided for military mobility, moving from €6.5 billion to €1.69 billion in current prices (€1.5 billion in 2018 prices).[32] This decision was considered by analysts to go against the EU's crucial need for military mobility.[33] Therefore, while having an overall budget of over €33 billion for the period 2021-2027, the CEF Regulation would only allocate a significantly smaller share of this amount to the financial support for dual-use infrastructures.

The CEF Regulation defines specific eligibility rules for its financial support to dual-use infrastructure. One or more Member States, or legal entities established in Member States could apply for funding for actions which 'relate to the sections or nodes identified by Member States in the Annexes to the Military Requirements for Military Mobility within and beyond the EU as adopted by the Council on 20 November 2018, or any subsequent list adopted thereafter, and to any further indicative list of priority projects that are

28 'Enablement and Logistics as Critical Success Factors for Military Operations: Comparing Russian and NATO Approaches', cited above: 'Other corridors have followed since, with two letters of intent signed on the fringes of the Washington Summit: one by Italy, Albania, North Macedonia and Bulgaria; and another by Greece, Bulgaria and Romania. More corridors are being developed in parallel, and all use the first letter of intent between the Netherlands, Germany and Poland as a template'.

29 Regulation No 2021/1153 of the European Parliament and of the Council of 7 July 2021 establishing a Connecting Europe Facility and repealing Regulations No 1316/2013 and No 283/2014, [2021] OJ L249/38.

30 Regulation (EU) 2021/1153, Art. 3(1).

31 Ibid., Art. 3(2).

32 Special meeting of the European Council (17, 18, 19, 20 and 21 July 2020), Conclusions.

33 ECA Special report 04/2025: EU military mobility – Full speed not reached due to design weaknesses and obstacles en route, 5 February 2025.

identified by Member States in accordance with the Military Mobility Action Plan'.[34] Hence, the CEF intervenes in this framework to provide financial support to enable the construction of new infrastructure or to upgrade existing infrastructures in line with the usage requirements identified in Implementing Regulation 2021/1328, which was adopted in accordance with Article 12(2) of the CEF Regulation.

In total, the CEF has funded 95 different projects located in 21 different Member States, through three different waves of calls for projects, as reflected in Table 1. Examples of projects, that have received funding (and only in France or Belgium) include the renovation of the Mussuguet tunnel between Cassis and Aubagne by SNCF Réseau in 2022 and the renovation of rail infrastructure in the port of Antwerp,[35] then in 2023, the adaptation of infrastructure in the Port of La Rochelle to dual-use purposes,[36] and in 2024, the modernisation of marshalling yards by SNCF Réseau in France and the improvement of rail links between the ports of Antwerp and Zeebruge.[37]

[34] Ibid., Art. 12.

[35] Commission Implementing Decision on the selection of Military Mobility projects following the 2021 call for proposals for grands under the Connecting Europe Facility – Transport sector pursuant to Implementing Decision C(2021)5763, C(2022) 3261 final, 25 May 2022.

[36] Commission Implementing Decision of 11April 2023 on the selection of Military Mobility projects following the 2023 call for proposals for grants under the Connecting Europe Facility – Transport sector pursuant to Implementing Decision C(2021)5763, C(2023) 2298 final.

[37] Commission Implementing Decision of 7March 2024 on the selection of Military Mobility projects following the 2023 call for proposals for grants under the Connecting Europe Facility – Transport sector pursuant to Implementing Decision C(2023)4886, C(2024) 1421 final.

Table 1 – Overview of EU-funded military mobility projects under CEF (Source ECA)

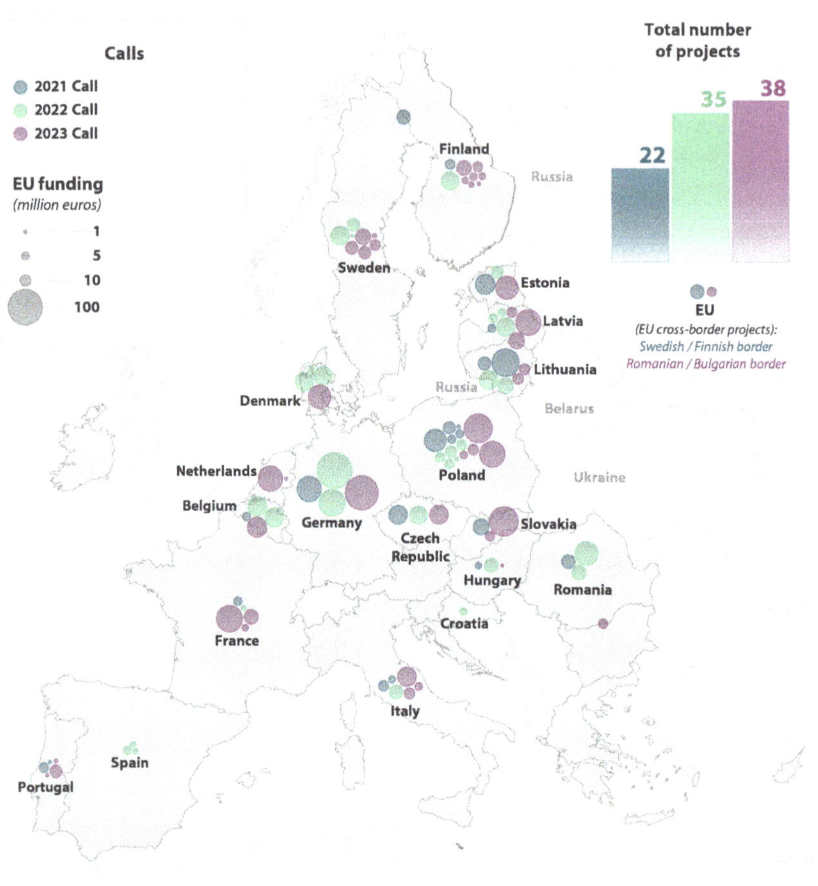

However, a recent Report from the European Court of Auditors, presented in February 2025, highlighted a series of issues connected to CEF financial support to military mobility. For instance, it stressed that the military assessment and geostrategic dimension were not sufficiently taken into account in the selection of dual-use infrastructure projects under CEF. This is an issue which reflects the complexity of using the TEN-T's financial instrument (for the first time) to support dual-use infrastructure projects. The official reply of the European Commission to the latter observation was to 'consider the extent to which it is possible to give additional weight to the military relevance of projects, as part of the preparation of the next proposals and calls'. Despite these difficulties, the ECA report recognised that '[the ECF] funding of dual-use military mobility infrastructure projects was welcomed by all member state representatives [...], who regarded it as complementary to NATO and inter-governmental military mobility activities'. This shows that while ECF financial support to military mobility was modest, it was nevertheless an important first step in the right direction, to start addressing the EU's needs on military mobility.

IV. THE FUTURE OF MILITARY MOBILITY: MOVING BEYOND THE TEN-T FRAMEWORK

While significant progress has been made in implementing the two action plans on military mobility, the new Commission (installed in 2024) expressed renewed and heightened ambitions for this topic. The primary objective is to collaborate with Member States to strengthen military mobility by eliminating all remaining obstacles, as well as to promote a comprehensive, whole-of-government approach to facilitate the swift movement of military personnel and equipment.

The Joint White Paper for European Defence Readiness 2030[38] provides even more explicit guidance on addressing the ongoing challenges affecting military movement within the EU. It offers fresh perspectives on each of the traditional approaches to overcoming military mobility hurdles, presenting new ways to tackle these issues:

- Regarding infrastructures, the White Paper recalls that the EU has designated four priority multi-modal corridors for military mobility, which are crucial for short-notice and large-scale movements of troops and equipment. However, it emphasises that these corridors require 'substantial and urgent' investments to facilitate the efficient movement of troops and military equipment. Specifically, the White Paper identifies 500 hot-spot projects within these priority corridors, including the widening of railway tunnels, reinforcement of road and railway bridges, and expansion of port and airport terminals, which need to be upgraded urgently. Furthermore, the White Paper stresses the importance of ensuring the security, maintenance, and repair of these infrastructures to guarantee their operational readiness. Additionally, it underscores the dual-use dimension and potential of these infrastructures, which can serve both military and civilian purposes, highlighting the benefits of investing in infrastructure that can support multiple uses.[39]

[38] Joint White Paper for European Defence Readiness 2030, JOIN(2025) 120 final.

[39] Ibid: 'Strengthening the logistics of the armed forces also matches the need to make our economy more connected and competitive – a perfect fit in terms of dual *use*'.

- On regulatory aspects, the white paper indicates that 'the EU and Member States need to immediately simplify and streamline regulations and procedures and ensure priority access for the armed forces to transport facilities, networks and assets'. The use of the word 'immediately' is interesting and hints at a different approach to that adopted so far, namely the TAs, which are non-binding initiatives and which tend to take time to be implemented. It is worth noting that the White Paper announces a review of the existing EU legislation in order to better reflect and accommodate the needs of military mobility in the EU law.
- Regarding regulatory aspects, the White Paper emphasises that the EU and Member States must 'immediately' simplify and streamline regulations and procedures to ensure priority access for armed forces to transport facilities, networks, and assets. The use of the word 'immediately' is again noteworthy, as it suggests a shift towards a more urgent and decisive approach. The White Paper announces a comprehensive review of existing EU legislation to better align it with the needs of military mobility, ensuring that EU law effectively supports and facilitates the movement of military personnel and equipment.
- Regarding the reinforcement of capabilities related to military mobility, the White Paper unequivocally states that it is essential to enhance the availability of specialised and dual-use transport assets across all modes of transportation. To achieve this, the White Paper proposes that the EU can play a facilitating role in promoting joint procurement initiatives, pre-contracting assets, and encouraging the use of uniform design standards for dual-use capabilities.

However, the true innovation of the White Paper on military mobility lies in its statement which outlines the implementation plan for the newly announced developments. Specifically, the White Paper indicates that the EU would adopt a Joint Communication on military mobility, accompanied by necessary legislative initiatives, by the end of 2025. This intention was already taking shape by mid-2025, as evidenced by the European Commission's launch of a targeted consultation on 12 June 2025, in collaboration with the High Representative and the European Defence Agency (EDA).[40] The consultation aims to prepare a comprehensive military mobility package, which will comprise the Joint Communication that presents the overall package, and outlines concrete actions for the years to come. Furthermore, a regulation proposal has been announced to entail targeted amendments to EU legislation, including transport legislation, to better support military mobility. These legislative amendments are intended to contribute to a 'whole-of-government' approach

[40] European Commission, Press release, EU addressing military mobility challenges Brussels, 12 June 2025.

at the EU level, ensuring a coordinated and effective response to the challenges of military mobility. The regulation proposal should also establish a new regulatory framework for military mobility. The proposed regulation aims to harmonise national procedures and rules, and introduce emergency measures to ensure uninterrupted military movements in Europe. This is notably not the first time the EU has expressed its intention to develop an emergency framework for military mobility. Recently, in its EU stockpile strategy,[41] the EU emphasised the need to create adaptable policies and regulatory frameworks for cross-border movement in times of crisis and recognised that this approach is crucial for facilitating seamless EU-wide cross-border transport of military equipment and personnel. The proposed regulation also takes into account the dual-use dimension of military mobility, as it will consider the impact of military movements on the civilian side. The European Commission's intention to propose a Regulation, rather than a Directive, suggests a desire to address regulatory issues affecting military mobility in a more direct and immediate manner, echoing the White Paper's call to 'immediately' address these challenges.

At the time of writing this contribution (July 2025, for the English version of the publication), the legal basis for the proposed regulation remains unknown. Although it has not been announced, it is possible that the TEN-T provisions of the TFEU could again serve as a potential legal basis for adopting the envisioned measures. As previously demonstrated, the TEN-T has proven to be a valuable instrument in supporting the development of dual-use infrastructures and identifying priority corridors for military mobility. Its provisions could potentially be leveraged again to provide a legal foundation for the proposed regulation, building on the existing framework and expertise. However, other legal bases could also be suitable for supporting the adoption of measures focused on the transportation of military equipment and personnel, particularly those related to the EU's common transport policy. Recent precedents, such as the use of Article 91(1)(d) TFEU to establish the Social Climate Fund as one of its legal bases,[42] demonstrate that the common transport policy can be extended to other areas related to transportation. Moreover, the common transport policy has already been used to adopt proposals for transport rules addressing defence issues, such as the Regulation proposal on

41 Communication from the Commission to the European Parliament, the Council, the European Economic And Social Committee and the Committee of the Regions, EU stockpiling strategy: Boosting the EU's material preparedness for crises, COM(2025) 528 final.

42 Regulation (EU) 2023/955 of the European Parliament and of the Council of 10 May 2023 establishing a Social Climate Fund and amending Regulation (EU) 2021/1060, [2023] *OJ* L130/1.

> the use of railway infrastructure capacity in the single European railway area,[43] which includes a provision on reprioritising access to rail infrastructures in the event of a defence crisis. While using the common transport policy as a legal basis would require an extensive interpretation of Articles 91 TFEU (for road, rail, and inland water transports) and Article 100 TFEU (for air and sea transport), it could be argued that this would not contradict Article 90 TFEU, which states that the objectives of the Treaties should be pursued within the framework of a common transport policy. The Treaty objectives, notably the promotion of peace and the well-being of the Union's peoples,[44] are closely linked to the EU's ability to ensure its defence readiness, which can be achieved through enhanced military mobility. Therefore, integrating the objective of harmonising the rules on the transport of military equipment and personnel into the common transport policy would not appear entirely inappropriate. Nevertheless, while these arguments suggest that the EU's common transport policy could also become a suitable framework candidate for improving military mobility, a delicate balance would need to be struck. The proposed Regulation would need to carefully avoid encroaching on the Common Security and Defence Policy (CSDP) framework, focusing instead on the transport aspects of military movements and likely emphasising the cross-border and dual use dimensions of these transportation activities. Furthermore, it would require Member States to increasingly address various aspects of military mobility within a 'community' framework, rather than relying solely on the CSDP framework, while still maintaining Article 346 TFEU[45] as a safeguard to protect their essential security interests.

The European Commission and the High Representative's renewed ambition to enhance military mobility extends beyond the preparation of the Military Mobility package, announced for the end of 2025. Firstly, it should be noted that the Security Action For Europe (SAFE) regulation,[46] adopted in May 2025, provides a €150 billion loan instrument to support Member States in enhancing their defence readiness, with military mobility being one of the eligible areas for investment. This regulation clearly acknowledges the importance of military mobility, allowing Member States to access funding to improve their military mobility capabilities or infrastructures. Secondly, on 15 July 2025, the European Parliament and the Council of the EU reached an agreement[47] on the Commission's proposal to update the priorities and modify the current cycle of

43 Proposal for a Regulation of the European Parliament and of the Council on the use of railway infrastructure capacity in the single European railway area, amending Directive 2012/34/EU and repealing Regulation (EU) No 913/2010, COM(2023) 443 final.

44 Art. 3 TEU.

45 See the commentary on Article 346 TFEU by S. Rodrigues in this publication.

46 Council Regulation (EU) 2025/1106 of 27 May 2025 establishing the Security Action for Europe (SAFE) through the Reinforcement of the European Defence Industry Instrument, [2025] *OJ* L2025/1106.

47 See: https://www.europarl.europa.eu/news/en/press-room/20250714IPR29627/cohesion-funding-deal-on-mid-term-update-responding-to-new-challenges.

EU cohesion funding.[48] This agreement will provide Member States and regions with greater flexibility to allocate funds to new priorities, including defence industrial capabilities and military mobility, following its official adoption. Thirdly, military mobility also became a key priority for the upcoming negotiations on the next Multi-Annual Framework (MFF) for the period 2028-2034. While military mobility suffered significant cuts during the previous MFF negotiations, this time the Commission has proposed an ambitious allocation under the next MFF-CEF. As highlighted by the Commissioner for Sustainable Transport and Tourism during his speech to the European Parliament's Transport and Tourism Committee on 16 July 2025,[49] the next MFF-CEF will dedicate a substantial share of its proposed budget to supporting military mobility. Specifically, €17.65 billion is earmarked for the development and upgrading of dual-use infrastructures, representing a tenfold increase compared to the current MFF. This should help to facilitate the urgent investments called for by the White Paper. In addition to infrastructure support, the Commission also proposes to enhance military mobility on the capability side, as requested in the White Paper. The proposed European Competitiveness Fund[50] includes a specific activity for 'Military Logistics Enablement and Support' under its chapter on Support for Resilience and Security, Defence Industry, and Space. This activity will cover initiatives such as incentivising the procurement of military mobility-related capabilities.[51] This proposal directly echoes the White Paper's call to improve access to military mobility-related assets, demonstrating the Commission's commitment to a comprehensive approach to enhancing military mobility.

While the Commission and the High Representative have demonstrated a renewed commitment to enhancing military mobility, the extent to which the Council and the European Parliament will support the proposed expansion of EU action in this area remains to be seen in the coming years. It is certain, however, that the EU's ability to 'demonstrate [its] readiness and deterrence'[52] will be directly tied to its capacity to strengthen military mobility in the years ahead.

---

48 Proposal for a Regulation of the European Parliament and of the Council amending Regulations (EU) 2021/1058 and (EU) 2021/1056 as regards specific measures to address strategic challenges in the context of the mid-term review, COM(2025) 123 final.

49 European Commission – Speech, Commissioner Tzitzikostas' speech in the EP TRAN Committee on the next MFF and its impact on transport and tourism, Brussels, 16 July 2025.

50 Proposal for a Regulation of the European Parliament and of the Council on establishing the European Competitiveness Fund (ECF), including the specific programme for defence research and innovation activities, repealing Regulations (EU) 2021/522, (EU) 2021/694, (EU) 2021/697, (EU) 2021/783, repealing provisions of Regulations (EU) 2021/696, (EU) 2023/588, and amending Regulation (EU) [EDIP], COM(2025) 555 final.

51 Ibid., Art. 49(1)(a).

52 Joint White Paper for European Defence Readiness 2030, JOIN(2025) 120 final, cited above.

Addendum – Update as of November 2025

Following the call of the Joint White Paper on European Defence-Readiness 2030, the Defence-Readiness Roadmap[53] of 16 October 2025 indicated clear objectives and milestones, including the announcement of a Military Mobility package for November 2025. This also followed the 26 June 2025 European Council's invitation to the Commission and the High Representative to present further proposals to strengthen military mobility, enabling defence equipment and personnel to be moved efficiently across the Union.[54]

Therefore, on 19 November 2025, the Commission and the High Representative presented the Military Mobility package, composed of a Joint Communication[55] and a Regulation proposal.[56] The Joint Communication is consistent with the Defence-Readiness Roadmap, indicating that the package aims to establish, by the end of 2027, an EU-wide Military Mobility Area. This is presented as a step towards the longer-term objective of a Military Schengen. The overall goal of this Military Schengen is to ensure that improving military mobility will reinforce the Union's overall deterrence capabilities.

The Regulation proposal puts forward a comprehensive set of measures to facilitate the transport of equipment, goods and personnel for military purposes, while minimising and mitigating the impact of such transport on civilian traffic. It addresses the different regulatory, infrastructure and capability related issues, already outlined by the White Paper. Here are some of the envisaged measures:

– Streamlining cross-border military transport is one of the main strands of the Regulation proposal. The objective is to secure a clear process for cross-border military transport operations within a maximum of three working days, compared to the usual several tens of days, including the 45 days identified by the European Court of Auditors in its report. The permission procedures will be set out in a single rulebook applicable to all 27 Member States, significantly simplifying the work of armed forces moving across borders within the EU. The Regulation also foresees streamlined customs formalities and ensures that the same rules apply to military transport whether carried out directly by the armed forces or by civilian contractors, again simplifying procedures for the latter.

53 Join(2025) 27 final – Joint communication to the European Parliament, the European Council and the Council – Preserving Peace – Defence Readiness Roadmap 2030.

54 EUCO 12/25 – European Council meeting (26 June 2025) – Conclusions.

55 Joint Communication to the European Parliament and the Council on Military Mobility, JOIN 2025 – 846 final.

56 Proposal for a Regulation of the European Parliament and of the Council on establishing a framework of measures to facilitate the transport of military equipment, goods and personnel across the Union, COM 2025 – 847 final.

- The Regulation is also proposed to establish an emergency framework, the European Military Mobility Enhanced Response System (EMERS), to provide an efficient, coordinated and effective mechanism to facilitate military transport in temporary, extraordinary and urgent situations. EMERS may be activated by the Council of the European Union, following an assessment and proposal by the Commission, when a significant increase in military movements is expected or occurring. The measures under EMERS are ambitious: for example, Member States would shift from permission requests for cross-border military movements to simple notifications six hours before the movement takes place. EMERS will also ensure priority access for the armed forces to all relevant infrastructure to enable the fastest possible execution of military transport operations.
- In addition, the Regulation clearly takes into account the transatlantic dimension, with several types of extensions envisaged for NATO allies that are not EU Member States.
- As already envisaged in the White Paper, the Regulation proposal includes measures to foster solidarity and capability sharing between Member States. It establishes a solidarity pool of shared transport and logistics capabilities to address capability gaps faced by Member States in performing military transport operations, taking direct inspiration from the experience of the European Civil Protection Pool and rescEU under the Union Civil Protection Mechanism.[57] The Pool will be composed of Member State capabilities on a voluntary basis, as well as possible Union-owned or contracted capabilities, following the rescEU model. The Pool will require financial incentives, envisaged under the future European Competitiveness Fund. The provisions of the latter on military mobility will therefore be crucial to ensure that the Solidarity Pool becomes an attractive framework for all Member States.
- The Regulation proposal also foresees measures to improve infrastructure readiness and protection. It sets out rules to enhance the preparedness of dual-use transport infrastructure. Here also the interaction with the future Connecting Europe Facility appears crucial. Moreover, the Regulation proposal entails provisions to identify and better protect strategic dual-use infrastructure against all hazards and threats.

[57] Regulation (EU) 2021/836 of the European Parliament and of the Council of 20 May 2021 amending Decision No 1313/2013/EU on a Union Civil Protection Mechanism.

The Regulation proposal relies on Articles 91 and 100(2) TFEU and therefore constitutes a common transport policy proposal. The Commission justifies this approach by the Regulation's focus on the transport of military equipment, goods and personnel across the Union. It observes that Member States' armed forces rely heavily on dual-use transport infrastructure and equipment to perform military transport operations. By recognising this dual-use dimension, the Commission considers that the common transport policy can be mobilised and developed to support the specific needs of military transport. In addition, rules on cross-border military transport need to be integrated and developed within the common transport policy at Union level, in particular to take account of the specificities of transport carried out on behalf of the armed forces by civil companies, and to ensure that the impact on civilian transport is minimised and mitigated as far as possible. In light of the above, the Regulation is proposed under the common transport policy to establish measures and lay down appropriate provisions aimed at facilitating military transport in the Union and across its external borders while minimising and mitigating its impact on civilian transport.

It remains to be seen how the co-legislators will conduct negotiations on this proposal. A key challenge will be ensuring coherence with the wider set of initiatives designed to reinforce military mobility, including those to be supported under the next MFF through the Connecting Europe Facility and the European Competitiveness Fund. As highlighted these initiatives are mutually dependent, and alignment across them will be essential. All actors – including the Commission – will therefore need to actively ensure consistency across the different negotiation strands and funding frameworks. What is already clear is that, once adopted, the Regulation will represent another step in broadening the scope and concrete operational dimension of the European Defence Union.

ARTICLE 173 TFEU: THE EUROPEAN DEFENCE INDUSTRY

PART ONE: A LEGAL BASIS TO STRENGTHEN THE COMPETITIVENESS OF THE EUROPEAN DEFENCE INDUSTRY

Daniel Fiott
Professor, Centre for Security, Diplomacy and Strategy (CSDS), Vrije Universiteit Brussel
Non-resident Senior Fellow, Real Instituto Elcano

PART TWO: A NEW STRATEGY FOR THE EUROPEAN DEFENCE INDUSTRIAL (EDIS) TO PREPARE THE UNION FOR ANY EVENTUALITY

Fabio Liberti[1]
Policy Officer, Directorate-General for Defence Industry and Space (DG DEFIS), European Commission

Article 173 TFEU

1. The Union and the Member States shall ensure that the conditions necessary for the competitiveness of the Union's industry exist.

For that purpose, in accordance with a system of open and competitive markets, their action shall be aimed at:

– speeding up the adjustment of industry to structural changes,

– encouraging an environment favourable to initiative and to the development of undertakings throughout the Union, particularly small and medium-sized undertakings,

[1] This analysis, which is provided in a personal capacity, reflects the views only of the author, and can under no circumstances be regarded as the official position of the European Commission.

– encouraging an environment favourable to cooperation between undertakings,

– fostering better exploitation of the industrial potential of policies of innovation, research and technological development.

2. The Member States shall consult each other in liaison with the Commission and, where necessary, shall coordinate their action. The Commission may take any useful initiative to promote such coordination, in particular initiatives aiming at the establishment of guidelines and indicators, the organisation of exchange of best practice, and the preparation of the necessary elements for periodic monitoring and evaluation. The European Parliament shall be kept fully informed.

3. The Union shall contribute to the achievement of the objectives set out in paragraph 1 through the policies and activities it pursues under other provisions of the Treaties. The European Parliament and the Council, acting in accordance with the ordinary legislative procedure and after consulting the Economic and Social Committee, may decide on specific measures in support of action taken in the Member States to achieve the objectives set out in paragraph 1, excluding any harmonisation of the laws and regulations of the Member States.

This Title shall not provide a basis for the introduction by the Union of any measure which could lead to a distortion of competition or contains tax provisions or provisions relating to the rights and interests of employed persons.

I. A LEGAL BASIS FOR STRENGTHENING THE COMPETITIVENESS OF THE EUROPEAN DEFENCE INDUSTRY

Article 173 TFEU is the only provision in Title XVII devoted to industry in Part Three of the TFEU. It has its origins in the Treaty of Maastricht (1992), under Article 130 of the EC Treaty, which became Article 157 of the EC Treaty following the Treaty of Amsterdam (1997). It echoes the first reflections developed by the Commission in 1990[2] and in 1994[3] in favour of a European

[2] Commission of the European Communities, 'Industrial policy in an open and competitive environment – Guidelines for a common approach', COM(1990) 556 final, 16 November 1990.

[3] Commission of the European Communities, 'An Industrial Competitiveness Policy for the European Union', COM(1994) 319 final, 14 September 1994.

industrial policy.[4] The Treaty of Lisbon (2007) made this policy a supporting competence of the European Union (see Art. 6(b) TFEU). Consequently, it does not replace that of the Member States in this area (see Art. 2(5) TFEU) and cannot lead to the adoption of measures to harmonise national regulations (see Art. 173(3) TFEU).

Consequently, most of the acts adopted on the basis of Article 173 TFEU (or its predecessors) consist of support measures, particularly financial support, especially for small and medium-sized enterprises (SMEs).[5] It has also been used as a legal basis to encourage strategic investment by the private sector, particularly in response to financial crises.[6]

In a spirit of financial and strategic support, the Commission has gradually mobilised Article 173 TFEU in the field of defence, proposing in 2017 to the European Parliament and the Council the adoption of a European Defence Industrial Development Programme aimed at supporting the competitiveness and innovation capacity of the EU defence industry (EDIDP).[7] This became Regulation (EU) 2018/1092 of the European Parliament and of the Council of 18 July 2018.[8] The programme, scheduled for 2019-2020, was to be the forerunner of the European Defence Fund (EDF).[9]

The creation and development of the EDIDP and subsequently the EDF represented a major step forward in European defence cooperation and EU defence industrial policy. For the first time in its history, the European Union (EU) was directly funding defence research and development (R&D)

---

4 See also: European Commission, 'For a European industrial renaissance', COM(2014) 14 final of 22 September 2014 and 'A new industrial strategy for Europe', COM(2020) 102 final of 10 March 2020, which focuses on the defence and space industry as part of strengthening the EU's industrial and strategic autonomy.

5 See in this sense: Regulation (EU) No 1287/2013 of the European Parliament and of the Council of 11 December 2013 establishing a Programme for the Competitiveness of Enterprises and small and medium-sized enterprises (COSME) (2014–2020), [2013] *OJ* L347/33, repealed and replaced by Regulation (EU) 2021/690 of the European Parliament and of the Council of 28 April 2021 establishing a programme for the internal market, competitiveness of enterprises, including small and medium-sized enterprises, the area of plants, animals, food and feed, and European statistics (Single Market Programme) and repealing Regulations (EU) No 99/2013, (EU) No 1287/2013, (EU) No 254/2014 and (EU) No 652/2014.

6 See in this sense, in the context of the Juncker Plan, Regulation (EU) 2015/1017 of the European Parliament and of the Council of 25 June 2015 on the European Fund for Strategic Investments, the European Investment Advice Hub and the European Investment Project Portal and amending Regulations (EU) No 1291/2013 and (EU) No 1316/2013, [2015] *OJ* L169/1.

7 See COM(2017) 294 final of 7 June 2017.

8 [2018] *OJ* L200/30.

9 Regulation (EU) 2021/697 of the European Parliament and of the Council of 29 April 2021 establishing the European Defence Fund and repealing Regulation (EU) 2018/1092 ([2021] *OJ* L170/149). On this regulation see the commentary by S. Rodrigues in this publication.

from its own budget. The fact that the EU has developed, since 2015,[10] a financial tool to stimulate defence industrial cooperation between European industry and EU Member States 'marks a radical change in the way the EU thinks about and supports defence'.[11] To date, the EDF has enabled investments worth €2 billion for the joint development of R&D in areas such as air combat, air and missile defence, cyberspace, information superiority, digital transformation, disruptive technologies, naval and land capabilities and space defence capabilities.[12] The EDF has been so successful to date that the institutions and Member States agreed on a financial top-up to the fund during the mid-term review of the Multiannual Financial Framework (MFF). Originally, the fund had been allocated €8 billion for the period 2021-2027, but thanks to the 'Strategic Technologies for Europe Platform' (STEP)[13] and the mid-term review of the MFF, this amount was increased by €1.5 billion for a total fund of €9.5 billion up to 2027;[14] although the additional investment will be allocated to the European Defence Industry Programme (EDIP),[15] up to 2027.

However, the EDF not only represents a new financial tool for the EU in the field of defence, it also symbolises profound changes in the way Member States and EU institutions perceive the European defence market. In fact,

10 In June 2015, a Preparatory Action in Defence Research (PADR) was launched by the Commission was launched with a budget line of around €90 million for 2017–2019. It was not based on Article 173, but on the EU's Financial Regulation (see Arts. 58(2)(b), and 110, 125 and 181 of Regulation (EU, Euratom) 2018/1046 of the European Parliament and of the Council of 18 July 2018 on the financial rules applicable to the general budget of the Union, amending Regulations (EU) No 1296/2013, (EU) No 1301/2013, (EU) No 1303/2013, (EU) No 1304/2013, (EU) No 1309/2013, (EU) No 1316/2013, (EU) No 223/2014, (EU) No 283/2014 and Decision No 541/2014/EU, and repealing Regulation (EU, Euratom) No 966/20121, [2018] *OJ* L193/1) On this action: R. Bellais and D. Fiott, 'A "Game Changer"? The EU's preparatory action on defence research', *Policy Paper*, April 2016, Armament Industry European Research group (ARES).

11 D. Fiott, 'Promoting European Defence Cooperation and the Promise of Financial Incentives', *ARES Group Commentary*, No. 16, 2017, p. 2. See: https://www.iris-france.org/wp-content/uploads/2017/05/ARES-16-Comment-DFiott-may-2017.pdf.

12 D. Fiott, 'Invest and innovate? Spain and the European Defence Fund', Real Instituto Elcano Analysis, No. 81, 2023. See https://media.realinstitutoelcano.org/wp-content/uploads/2023/08/investing-and-innovating-spain-and-the-european-defence-fund-elcano-royal-institute.pdf.

13 Regulation (EU) 2024/795 of the European Parliament and of the Council of 29 February 2024 establishing the 'Strategic Technologies for Europe' platform (STEP). See: https://eur-lex.europa.eu/eli/reg/2024/795/oj.

14 A. Pugnet, 'European Defence to Benefit from Slight EU Budget Increase', *Euractiv*, 21 June 2023. See https://www.euractiv.com/section/defence-and-security/news/european-defence-to-benefit-from-slight-eu-budget-increase.

15 Regulation (EU) 2025/2643 of the European Parliament and of the Council of 16 December 2025 establishing the European Defence Industry Programme and a framework of measures to ensure the timely availability and supply of defence products ('EDIP Regulation'), [2025] *OJ* L2025/2643.

the alignment of the political and industrial interests of the Member States and the political entrepreneurship of the European Commission and the European Parliament highlights a confluence of political interests. This level of entrepreneurship and political will is by no means novel for the EU, as the European Commission had throughout the 1990s called for synergies[16] between Europe's civil and defence sectors and insisted on the development of the European defence sector as an essential element of the Union's overall industrial and technological competitiveness.[17] In this respect, the agreement on the need for the European Defence Fund was also partly stimulated by geopolitical factors such as Russia's first invasion of Ukraine in 2014, as well as the election of Donald Trump in the United States and the Brexit referendum in 2016.

In order to legally justify the role of the supranational EU institutions in defence-related matters, the EU institutions and Member States have made constructive use of Article 173 TFEU. In essence, Article 173(1) TFEU states that '[t]he Union and the Member States shall ensure that the conditions necessary for the competitiveness of the Union's industry exist' and that this objective is to be achieved through open and competitive markets: 1) speeding up the adjustment of industry to structural changes; 2) encouraging an environment favourable to small and medium-sized enterprises (SMEs); 3) encouraging industrial cooperation across borders; and 4) making better use of industrial potential through innovation, research and technological development. All of these factors are relevant to how the EU has developed its role in defence and industrial policy since at least 2016. However, while the EDF was primarily intended to support industry, the current focus on the EDIP, as well as preparatory initiatives such as the Ammunition Production Support Act (ASAP),[18] and the European Defence Industry Reinforcement Common Procurement Act (EDIRPA)[19] have responded to the effects of Russia's war on Ukraine since February 2022.

---

16 European Commission, 'Communication on the action plan on synergies between the civil, space and defence industries', Brussels, COM(2021) 70 final, 22 February 2022, p. 5. See https://commission.europa.eu/document/download/2353ded9-0e39-4d35-a46c-67c62779afe1_en?filename=action_plan_on_synergies_en.pdf.

17 D. Fiott and M. Ketselidis, 'EU civil-defence Synergies: Understanding the Challenges and Drivers of Change', *ARES Group Policy Paper*, No. 74, 2022, p. 21. See https:// www.iris-france.org/wp-content/uploads/2022/04/74-Policy-Paper-Synergies-March-2022.pdf.

18 Regulation (EU) 2023/1525 of the European Parliament and of the Council of 20 July 2023 on supporting for ammunition production (ASAP), [202] *OJ* L185/7. See the contribution by E. Bernard in this publication.

19 Regulation (EU) 2023/2418 of the European Parliament and of the Council of 18 October 2023 on the establishment of an instrument to strengthen the European defence industry through joint procurement (EDIRPA), [2023] *OJ* L2023/2418. See: S. Clapp, 'Reinforcing the European Defence Industry', European Parliament Research Service, June 2023, https://www.europarl.europa.eu/thinktank/en/document/EPRS_BRI (2023) 749805 and contribution by E. Bernard, in this publication.

To understand why Article 173 TFEU has been used to justify this role and why this is an important development in the Union's defence and industrial policy, it is necessary to examine other articles of the Union Treaties which have been interpreted as imposing a general prohibition on the use of the Union budget to finance military or defence policy. Specifically, Article 41(2) of the Treaty on European Union (TEU) provides that 'expenditure arising from operations having military or defence implications' may not be charged to the Union budget.[20] This has been interpreted as imposing a general prohibition on the use of the Union budget for defence purposes, but the wording is very specific in referring to 'operations', which does not automatically equate to industrial defence policy. In fact, Article 173 TFEU and Article 182 TFEU authorise investment from the EU budget for research, innovation and development.[21] The current reality, with investments continuing to be made from the EU budget via the EDF, is that the Union is effectively funding defence and industrial cooperation via a legal basis provided by the EU Treaties, and in particular by the Treaty on the Functioning of the European Union (TFEU).

This chapter shows how the European Commission, the EU Member States and the European Parliament have agreed to use Article 173 of the TFEU as the main legal basis for founding the EDF. This is done by examining the genesis of the European Defence Fund, with an overview of how the fund fits into the Union's overall approach to defence and industrial policy. There follows a discussion of the future of EU defence and industrial policy to examine how new instruments, such as EDIP,[22] can play a role in supporting the European Defence Technological and Industrial Base (EDTIB).

A. UNDERSTANDING THE RELEVANCE OF ARTICLE 173 TFEU AND EU ACTION IN THE FIELD OF DEFENCE AND INDUSTRY

The creation of the EDF after 2016 marked a pivotal moment in the development of EU defence and industrial policy. For some academics, the advent of the fund represented a specific historical moment in which institutions such as the European Commission sought to address the economic concerns that had been growing in the European defence sector.[23] Indeed, concerns such as market fragmentation and increasing competition in the international defence market

---

20 See the commentary by A. Potteau in this publication.

21 See the commentary by F. Andreone and A. Ferrazzoli in this publication.

22 Regulation (EU) 2025/2643 of the European Parliament and of the Council of 16 December 2025 establishing the European Defence Industry Programme and a framework of measures to ensure the timely availability and supply of defence products ('EDIP Regulation'), [2025] *OJ* L2025/2643.

23 P. Haroche, 'Supranationalism Strikes Back: A neo Functionalist Account of the European Defence Fund' (2020) 27(6) *Journal of European Public Policy*, pp. 853–872.

enabled the Commission to offer supranational solutions to Member States. In this respect, the idea of mobilising Article 173 of the TFEU for the European Defence Fund comes as little surprise, as there is a close relationship between wider concerns about Europe's industrial competitiveness and its specific concerns in the defence sector.[24] Other authors have built on these ideas by pointing out that the European Commission's involvement in defence sector policy has led to a blurring of the boundaries between inter-governmentalism and supra-nationalism, with interesting implications for how governments frame their national sovereignty in the defence sector at EU level.[25]

Yet, as other academics have observed, the European Commission has been able to justify industrial defence policy through an 'efficiency framework', not least because governments still regard defence and budgetary policies as central to state policy and sovereignty.[26] Thus, while EU Member States recognised that the EDF would contribute to the efficiency of the Union's defence market, they did not endorse ideas that fell outside the scope of Article 173 TFEU, especially those previously put forward by the Commission, such as joint ownership of the Union's defence assets.[27] In this sense, the EU Member States wished to affirm the industrial and competitive dimensions of the European Defence Fund, rather than any politico-military justification, which could theoretically be used to delimit their sovereignty in defence matters.[28]

Other analysts have been less surprised by the nature of the legal basis for the European Defence Fund. Indeed, some have pointed to how the European Union – and the Commission in particular – has always tended to emphasise the industrial competitiveness dimensions of European defence and industrial initiatives.[29] In 2009, for example, two directives were adopted to further stimulate public procurement in the defence field,[30] and defence transfers in

---

24 Ibid.

25 C. Håkansson, 'The European Commission's New Role in EU Security and Defence Cooperation: the Case of the European Defence Fund' (2021) 30(4) *European Security*, pp. 589–608.

26 C. Hoeffler, 'Beyond the Regulatory State? The European Defence Fund and National Military Capacities' (2023) 30(7) *Journal of European Public Policy*, pp. 1281–1304.

27 Ibid.

28 E. Sabatino, 'The European Defence Fund: A Step Towards a Single Market for Defence?' (2022) 44(1) *Journal of European Integration*, pp. 133–148.

29 D. Fiott, 'Financing Rhetoric? The European Defence Fund and Dual-Use Technologies', in A. Calcara, R. Csernatoni and C. Lavallée (eds.), *Emerging Security Technologies and EU Governance: Actors, Practices and Processes*, London, Routledge, 2020, pp. 42–57.

30 Directive 2009/81/EC of the European Parliament and of the Council of 13 July 2009 on the coordination of procedures for the award of certain works contracts, supply contracts and service contracts by contracting authorities or entities in the fields of defence and security and amending Directives 2004/17/EC and 2004/18/EC, [2009] *OJ* L216/76. See the commentary by S. Rodrigues in this publication.

the EU.[31] In doing so, the EU has essentially grafted part of its wider Single Market policies onto the defence sector. For example, Directive 2009/81/EC on in the field of defence was essentially based on the Union's already well-established public procurement directives, which stressed the importance of developing the competitiveness of the single market by liberalising cross-border trade in military equipment and technology and calling for non-discrimination of European suppliers of defence equipment. This development also reflects the long-standing importance of dual-use technologies, which blur the boundaries between the commercial and defence sectors.

This has enabled the European Commission and, to a lesser extent, the European Parliament, to extend their action and the relevance thereof in the defence sector, by insisting on the 'dual-use paradigm' as a means of circumventing the strictly intergovernmental aspects of the Union Treaties, such as Article 346 TFEU[32] and Article 42 TEU. Article 42 TEU contains the legal provisions relating to the Common Security and Defence Policy (CSDP), which does not provide for a role for the European Commission in defence matters.[33] Instead, Article 42(3) TEU emphasises the essential role of intergovernmental agencies such as the European Defence Agency, which are directly responsible for the 'defence capabilities development, research, acquisition and armaments'.[34] Indeed, Article 42(3) also calls on the Agency – rather than the Commission – to 'identify operational requirements' and implement 'any measure needed to strengthen the industrial and technological base of the defence sector'. However, by stressing the need to strengthen the industrial competitiveness of the European defence sector, the Commission and the European Parliament have also been able to use Article 173 TFEU to strengthen their role in defence and industrial policy: in the case of the EDF, this has happened with the agreement of the European Council and the EU Member States.

B. FINDING A POLITICAL AND LEGAL BASIS FOR EUROPEAN UNION INVESTMENT IN THE FIELD OF DEFENCE

Article 173 of the TFEU has therefore become the fundamental legal basis for the Union's industrial and defence policy. This policy takes the form of multiple initiatives, but the main interest here is the European Defence Fund (EDF). As mentioned above, Article 173(1) of the TFEU defines the general objectives

31 Directive 2009/43/EC of the European Parliament and of the Council of 6 May 2009 on simplifying terms and conditions of transfers of defence-related products within the Community, [2009] *OJ* L146/1. See the commentary by E. Daniel and M. Kieffer, in this publication.

32 See the contribution by S. Rodrigues in this publication.

33 D. Fiott, 'The European Commission and the European Defence Agency A Case of Rivalry?' (2015) 53(3) *Journal of Common Market Studies*, pp. 542–557.

34 See the commentary on the AED by A-H. Bertana in this publication.

of the Union's industrial and competitiveness policy. In doing so, it stresses the importance of open and competitive markets and emphasises cross-border cooperation in the field of technology and research, in particular SMEs.[35] At first sight, paragraph Article 173(1) seems to run counter to the specific characteristics of the defence market, which tends to have a high degree of direct State intervention. In this respect, the defence market does not operate like other economic sectors, since in most cases there is only one public purchaser. This means that the defence sector does not operate in the 'open and competitive' way of markets, as provided for in the EU Treaties.

However, when Article 173 TFEU is read in conjunction with Article 182 TFEU, which requires the use of Union investment through the multi-annual financial framework for technological and scientific purposes, the Union's institutions have argued in favour of funding the defence sector. In this respect, we should consider that 'competitive markets' is an expression that can be applied on a more global basis, meaning that the European defence sector faces strong competition from allies, partners and competitors in international defence markets. For example, in a joint communication published on 18 May 2022 to analyse the defence investment gaps facing the EU, the High Representative of the Union for Foreign Affairs and Security Policy and Vice-President of the European Commission observed that '[d]espite the overall competitiveness of the sector, difficulties and gaps exist. Defence companies are still structured mainly along national borders, benefiting from a close relationship with national governments [...], the EDTIB remains highly fragmented, especially outside the aeronautics and missile sectors. This greatly reduces its ability to improve its competitiveness through pooling of R&D and economies of scale in production'.[36]

Another aspect of Article 173 TFEU that should be taken into account when considering its applicability to the defence sector is the emphasis on cooperation between EU Member States. Articles 173(2) and 173(3) TFEU provide for the participation of Union bodies such as the European Commission as contributors to technological and scientific cooperation between Member States. As stated in Article 173(2) TFEU, 'the Commission may take any useful initiative to promote' cooperation between Member States in the field of technology, research and development. This raises the question of the extent

---

35 It is instructive to note that Article 173 TFEU has been used more widely to adopt EU acts in favour of SMEs. See, for example, Regulation (EU) 2021/690 of the European Parliament and of the Council of 28 April 2021 establishing a programme for the internal market, competitiveness of enterprises, including small and medium-sized enterprises, the area of plants, animal, food and feed sectors and European statistics (Single Market Programme). See https://eur-lex.europa.eu/legal-content/EN/TXT/?uri=CELEX%3A32021R0690.

36 European Commission/HR/VP, 'Joint Communication on Defence Investment Gaps Analysis and Way Forward', Brussels, JOIN(2022) 24 final, 18 May 2022, p. 5. See https://commission.europa.eu/document/download/4bcf9a69-ed82-4a74-836f-b85bb16725f6_en?filename=join join.

to which the European Commission is required to stimulate and financially support cooperation between EU Member States in the field of defence and industry. In this respect, we should not only consider the Commission as the important institution of the Union to drive forward the Union's defence and industrial efforts, but also the European Parliament, with its crucial role in managing the Union's budget and MFF. It is another key supranational actor that has used Article 173 TFEU as a legal basis to release funds at EU level for the defence sector.[37]

The importance of cooperation in the field of defence and industry has been well expressed by the Heads of State and Government through the European Council. In fact, in its conclusions of 15 December 2016, the European Council invited the Commission to present proposals for the creation of the European Defence Fund.[38] In June 2017, the European Council went further by recognising that the 'joint development of capability projects commonly agreed by Member States to fill the existing major shortfalls and develop the technologies of the future is crucial to fulfil the level of ambition of the EU' in security and defence.[39] This is a particularly important statement by the European Council, as it reinforces the idea that institutional bodies such as the European Commission should be involved in the defence sector. In this sense, while Article 173 of the TFEU can be seen as an essential legal basis for building the EDF, the EU Member States and the European Parliament have demonstrated strong political will to free up investment at the EU level, from the EU budget for the defence sector.

While Article 173 of the TFEU offers a narrow interpretation of cooperation in the field of defence and industry based on research and

---

37 As confirmed by the setting up of the 'Strategic Technologies for Europe Platform (STEP)', by Regulation (EU) 2024/795, mentioned above, which commits the European Union. See also the European Parliament resolution of 28 February 2024 'Implementation of the common security and defence policy – annual report 2023' (2023/2119 (INI)). In point 45 of this report, the European Parliament '[p]oints out that the EDIRPA and ASAP can only be a first step towards improving the EDTIB's capacities to supply Member States with the products and quantities needed and should be complemented with further initiatives, including a European Defence Industrial Strategy (EDIS) coupled with the long-term and comprehensive EDIP for which adequate funding needs to be ensured, as well as an effective regulatory framework aimed at encouraging innovation, boosting production and ensuring smarter and more efficient public investments; calls, in that regard, on the EU Member States to provide the necessary funds to all European defence instruments in the upcoming MFF revision; regrets that the EDIP has still not been proposed by the Commission; calls for the fast and efficient implementation of the EDIRPA and ASAP; fully supports the proposed creation of a EUR 100 billion common defence fund aimed at immediately ramping up domestic arms and ammunition production'.

38 European Council, 'Conclusions', Brussels, EUCO 34/16, 15 December 2016. See https://www.consilium.europa.eu/media/21929/15-euco-conclusions-final.pdf.

39 European Council, 'Conclusions', Brussels, EUCO 8/17, 23 June 2017. See https://www.consilium.europa.eu/media/23985/22-23-euco-final-conclusions.pdf.

technology, the EDF responds to some of the (geo)political objectives developed by the EU in recent years. As the EDF Regulation states, the 'aim of the Fund is to enhance the competitiveness, innovation, efficiency and technological autonomy of the Union's defence industry, thereby contributing to the Union's strategic autonomy'. The EU seeks to achieve this objective 'supporting the cross-border cooperation between Member States as well as cooperation between enterprises, research centres, national administrations, international organisations and universities throughout the Union'.[40] Thus, the interpretation of Article 173 TFEU and Article 182 TFEU may include other policy objectives, which are not entirely economic or industrial. Indeed, in a report drawn up by a group of experts advising the EU on the steps to be taken prior to the creation of the EDF, it was observed that the multitude of security risks and dependencies facing the Union means that: 'Since no European country can afford to maintain a full-spectrum defence industrial base on its own, the logical solution is to work with like-minded partners and improve defence cooperation by making the most effective use of the tools available to the Union'.[41] In this respect, it is becoming virtually impossible to separate the geopolitical and industrial motivations of EU-funded schemes for the European defence sector.

C. THE FUTURE OF EUROPEAN UNION DEFENCE AND INDUSTRIAL POLICY

Today, the European Defence Fund has become an essential part of the EU's growing role and interest in defence and industrial cooperation. Until now, the Fund's legal and political basis has been based primarily on the objective of promoting cooperation in research, technology and development. As shown here, this is understandable in the context of the EDF, given that it invests in upstream R&D through to prototyping. In this sense, the fund does not finance the development of capabilities up to the commercialisation phase, which means that it remains within the limits of Article 173 TFEU. However, this logic may not extend to some of the defence and industrial initiatives currently being developed by the European Commission. For example, the EDIP Regulation is designed to continue to stimulate cooperation between EU Member States when the

---

40 European Union, 'Regulation establishing the European Defence Fund', Brussels, Regulation (EU) 2021/697, 29 April 2021, p. 2. See https://eur-lex.europa.eu/legal-content/EN/TXT/PDF/?uri=CELEX:32021R0697.

41 EU Institute for Security Studies/European Commission, 'Group of Personalities: European Defence Research – The Case for an EU Defence R&T Programme', February 2016, p. 36. See https://op.europa.eu/en/publication-detail/-/publication/acbeac0e-faf0-11e5-b713-01aa75ed71a1.

EDF ends.[42] In other words, the EDIP is designed to continue the process of cooperation and investment, from prototyping through to development and commercialisation. This additional step, although necessary to the logic of a cradle-to-grave approach to EU defence and industrial cooperation, is not necessarily covered by the legal logic of Article 173 TFEU.

What is proposed with the EDIP is a programme that will lead to joint defence procurement.[43] Drawing on lessons learned from the joint procurement of medical equipment during the Covid-19 pandemic and munitions, following Russia's invasion of Ukraine, the EU is seeking to put in place incentives for EU Member States to collaborate on the production of military capabilities. The EDIP will initially be endowed with €1.5 billion to 2027, but its longer-term financing is unclear. Although political statements have called for €100 billion for EDIP,[44] there is no guarantee that this financial envelope will be approved by the Member States, or that the funding will come directly from the EU budget.[45] Indeed, there have also been political statements suggesting that the EU should experiment with 'defence bonds' to raise capital on the markets.

So far, the preparatory programmes in place to support the EDIP provide important information on the legal basis that will be mobilised. The EU has developed the ASAP[46] and the EDIRPA.[47] The ASAP is endowed with €500 million (until 2025) to support the increase in the ammunition and missile production capacities of the EDTIB, mainly to support the Ukrainian army; while the EDIRPA devoted €300 million (until the end of 2024) to encourage Member States to acquire the most urgent and critical defence products jointly from the EDTIB. The ASAP was adopted in July 2023 and, like the EDF, has its legal basis in Article 173(3) of the TFEU,[48] Recital 8 of which in the regulation establishing the ASAP aims to support the Union 'to increase its volume of production, reduce its lead production time and address potential bottlenecks'

---

42 See the commentary by E. Simon in this publication.

43 See in particular Articles 11 and 35 of the EDIP Regulation.

44 A. Pugnet, 'Breton pitches EUR 100 billion fund for defence industry cooperation', www.euractiv.com, published on 10 January 2024 and updated on 5 March 2024.

45 Finally, the EDIP Regulation contains a financial envelope of €1,500 million for actions to strengthen the EDTIB until 31 December 2027 (see Art. 3 of the EDIP Regulation).

46 Regulation (EU) 2023/1525 of the European Parliament and of the Council of 20 July 2023 on support for the production of ammunition (ASAP), [2023] *OJ* L185/7. See the contribution by E. Bernard in this publication.

47 Regulation (EU) 2023/2418 of the European Parliament and of the Council of 18 October 2023 establishing an instrument for the reinforcement of the European defence industry through common procurement (EDIRPA), [2023] *OJ* L2023/2418. See S. Clapp, 'Reinforcing the European Defence Industry', European Parliament Research Service, June 2023, https://www.europarl.europa.eu/thinktank/en/document/EPRS_BRI (2023) 749805 and contribution by E. Bernard in this publication.

48 With Article 114 of the TFEU, relating to the establishment of the internal market: on this article, see the commentary by S. Rodrigues in this publication.

in the production of ammunition.[49] In this respect, a key element of the EDIP has been legally justified based on improving the EU's competitiveness and industrial readiness in the defence sector.

Similarly, EDIRPA was adopted in October 2023 and is also based on Article 173 TFEU, which emphasises the need to support the competitiveness of European industry.[50] In fact, the regulation relating to EDIRPA makes it possible to justify Article 173 TFEU as the legal basis for the act. Indeed, the regulation recalls that data from the European Defence Agency (EDA) showed that in 2020, EU Member States invested 13% less (or €4.1 billion) in collaborative defence procurement compared to 2019 data. The regulation points out that this level of joint procurement 'is well below the 35% benchmark to which Member States have committed themselves' and states that, without action, 'fragmentation of the demand side of the defence market results into a series of problems and inefficiencies, including on the supply side, while increasing maintenance costs of a plethora of different systems'.[51] On this basis, the EDIRPA regulation makes it clear that '[I]f this current trend is not addressed, it will continue to significantly undermine the competitiveness of the EDTIB and risks affecting its market prospects in the next decade'.[52] Once again, an essential element of the Union's defence and industrial policy and initiatives is justified based on Article 173 TFEU.

Regarding the legal basis for EDIP, it is a combination of Article 173 TFEU (on EDTIB), Article 114 TFEU (on the European Defence Equipment Market, EDEM) and Article 212 TFEU (on the Ukrainian DTIB) and Article 322 TFEU (on financial provisions). In addition to Article 173 TFEU, Article 114 TFEU deals with the 'functioning of the internal market' and, in particular, of the EDEM and, since Russia's war against Ukraine, there has been a strong need to adapt the EDEM to the geopolitical context of the war, including a 'general increase for defence equipment and a potential future peak of demand for specific defence products in the Union and possibly at global scale'.[53] Article 212 TFEU responds

[49] European Commission, 'Regulation on establishing the Act in Support of Ammunition Production', Brussels, COM(2023) final, 3 May 2023. See https://eur-lex.europa.eu/legal-content/EN/TXT/PDF/?uri=CELEX:52023PC0237.

[50] European Commission, 'Regulation establishing the Act to strengthen the European defence industry through joint procurement', Brussels, COM(2022) 349 final, 18 July 2022. See https://eur-lex.europa.eu/legal-content/EN/TXT/PDF/?uri=CELEX:52022PC0349.

[51] European Commission, 'Regulation on establishing the European defence industry through common Procurement Act', Brussels, COM(2022) 349 final, 18 July 2022, p. 3. See https://eur-lex.europa.eu/legal-content/EN/TXT/PDF/?uri=CELEX:52022PC0349.

[52] Ibid., p. 3.

[53] European Commission, 'Proposal for a Regulation establishing the European Defence Industrial Development Programme (EDIDP), COM(2024) 150 final, Brussels, 5 March 2024. See https://defence-industry-space.ec.europa.eu/document/download/6cd3b158-d11a-4ac4-8298-91491e5fa424_en?filename=EDIP%20Proposal%20for%20a%20Regulation.pdf.

to the logic of the need to respond to the war in Ukraine by focusing on financial assistance to third countries.

These legal bases remain the main method of supporting the EU defence industry, but, following the war against Ukraine, there has been increasing pressure to remedy the current legal restrictions on the purchase of defence equipment from the EU budget. In particular, as noted above, Article 41(2) TEU prohibits investment from the budget to finance 'operations having military or defence implications'.[54] It is difficult to know what the term 'operations' means in practice. From one point of view, it can be interpreted literally as the funding of military operations, but it has also been seen as having wider implications. For example, should the financing of military capabilities from the EU budget be used in the context of an EU military operation under Article 41(2) TEU or not? Removing this restriction would undoubtedly facilitate the financing of all aspects of European security and defence, and the existing legal bases under the CSDP provisions are not in a position to provide a solution that goes beyond the restriction provided for in Article 41(2).

For example, while Article 42(2) TEU refers to the 'progressive framing of a common Union defence policy', this will lead to 'a common defence, when the European Council, acting unanimously, so decides', this does not imply investment at the EU level, although it may have recourse to extra-budgetary mechanisms similar to the European Peace Facility. The problem is also that, to date, Article 42(2) of the TEU has not been expressly formulated by the European Council and there is no doubt that Member States could agree a single definition of what 'common defence' means in the EU context, particularly because many Member States still have a preference for security guarantees under NATO. The same question arises in relation to Article 42(7) TEU, which provides that '[i]f a Member State is the victim of armed aggression on its territory, the other Member States shall have an obligation of aid and *assistance by all* the means in their power' (emphasis added), including military means.[55] Even then, any military capability financed by the Union to comply with Article 42(7) TEU would qualify as the financing of 'operations'.[56]

For these reasons, the use of Article 173 TFEU and related articles for European defence and industrial cooperation will remain crucial. What is remarkable, however, is that the provisions of the Treaties that make extensive reference to industrial competitiveness remain relevant to the geopolitical challenges facing the EU. At the Versailles summit held in the wake of Russia's

---

54 For example, H. Foy, 'EU look to bypass Treaty ban on purchase arms to support Ukraine', *Financial Times*, 21 March 2024, see www.ft.com/content/b1f5a276-c1c8-44fc-9d07-d0d42b578314.

55 See the contribution by J.C. Martin in this publication.

56 R. Le Gluet and H. Conway-Mouret, 'European defence: the challenge of strategic autonomy', https://www.senat.fr/rap/r18-626/r18-626.html.

invasion of Ukraine in February 2022, the European Council stressed the importance of developing Europe's competitiveness in the field of defence and industry for the specific geopolitical purposes of defending Europe. Indeed, in the Versailles Declaration of March 2022, the European Council called for redoubled efforts to 'resolutely invest more and better in defence capabilities and innovative technologies'.[57] In this respect, the European Council called for an increase in defence spending, more joint investment, synergies between civil, space and defence research and innovation, the development of emerging and innovative technologies and measures to 'strengthen and develop our defence industry'.[58] It should be remembered that while the main messages from the European Council contained in the Versailles Declaration are hardly new, the sense of urgency surrounding them has been heightened by the return of war to Europe's borders. In this sense, the imperatives of industrial competitiveness and the geopolitical drivers of cooperation have been reinforced.[59]

This same logic was developed with the publication on 5 March 2024 of the new European Defence Industry Strategy (EDIS), which stressed that a 'strong European defence industry[60] is an essential pre-requisite for achieving defence readiness'.[61] These objectives were further underlined by the European Council in its conclusions of 21-22 March 2024, in which it called for strengthening the EDTIB by increasing defence spending, improving access to private and public funding, developing public procurement and joint investment, enhancing interoperability, European defence market integration and supply chains, and addressing skills shortages in the defence sector.[62] It is therefore clear that, within the framework of the current legal basis, much can be achieved at the EU level in the field of security and defence.

---

57 European Council, 'Versailles Declaration', Versailles, 10 and 11 March 2022, p. 3. See https://www.consilium.europa.eu/media/54773/20220311-versailles-declaration-en.pdf.

58 Ibid., p. 3.

59 D. Fiott and L. Simón, 'EU Defence After Versailles: an Agenda for the Future', In-Depth Study, European Parliament, 2023, p. 17. See https://cris.vub.be/ws/portalfiles/portal/105712510/_2023_EU_Defence_After_Versailles.pdf.

60 European Commission/HR/VP, Joint Communication on a new European Defence Industrial Strategy: Achieving EU readiness through a responsive and resilient European Defence Industry', JOIN(2024) 10 final, 5 March 2024, p. 2. See https://eur-lex.europa.eu/legal-content/FR/ALL/?uri=JOIN%3A2024%3A10%3AFIN.

61 See the second part of this contribution.

62 European Council, 'Conclusions - 21-22 March 2024', EUCO 7/24, Brussels, 22 March 2024, pp. 4–5. See https://www.consilium.europa.eu/media/70894/euco-conclusions-2122032024-fr.pdf.

CONCLUDING REMARKS

In conclusion, Article 173 TFEU has become a solid legal basis for developing EU defence and industrial policy and initiatives. The blurring of the boundaries between institutional roles and capabilities, commercial and defence technologies and industrial and geopolitical motivations is fully embedded in the framework of Article 173 TFEU. This will have shown how Article 173 TFEU guided and supported the creation of the European Defence Fund, but it is also likely to continue to be used in the future, as has already been the case for the EDIP Regulation. However, as we have also observed, we must recognise that the use of Article 173 TFEU for defence, while clearly specifying the need to invest in the Union's industrial competitiveness in all economic areas, has only been possible because of a high degree of political unity between the Union's institutions and the EU Member States. To promote the industrial competitiveness of the defence sector in Europe, the Member States have seized the opportunity to use the EU budget for both industrial and geopolitical defence purposes.

In many ways, the combination of the Covid-19 pandemic and Russia's war on Ukraine has only increased the growing importance of the defence sector. While learning valuable lessons about security of supply, technological sovereignty and defence, the EU continues to see a blurring between economics and politics. Although politics and economics are rarely separable, the current geopolitical climate means that industrial policy has become an intensely political affair. We have seen this with the massive public subsidies and legislation promoted by both China and the US to support their national strategic industrial sector and their commercial operators. So while Article 173 TFEU can be seen as an interesting case study of how EU institutions, such as the European Commission, have enhanced their role in defence policy, it also reflects the rapidly changing geopolitical contours of the global economy. Whether the original drafters of the EU treaties could have foreseen the need to take account of defence and industrial policy is unclear, but we should at least acknowledge that the insistence on including industrial competitiveness in the treaties has benefited efforts to strengthen European defence.

While the use of Article 173 of the TFEU is the result, among other things, of the EU's desire to use industrial leverage to adapt to its geopolitical environment, the development of EDIS is another recent and particularly revealing example of this trend.

II. THE NEW EUROPEAN DEFENCE INDUSTRIAL STRATEGY (EDIS): PREPARING THE UNION FOR ANY EVENTUALITY

Faced with a geopolitical climate marked by the return of the possibility of a high-intensity conflict on European soil, potentially involving the territorial integrity of Member States, the Commission is developing its intervention in support of the competitiveness of the European Defence Technological and Industrial Base (EDTIB). The new European Defence Industrial Strategy (EDIS), presented by the Commission and the High Representative of the European Union for Foreign Affairs and Security Policy on 5 March 2024, aims to strengthen the readiness of the EDTIB in the face of the constantly deteriorating security environment in Europe. To this end, it aims to give structure to some of the emergency measures adopted by the Commission in response to the Russian aggression in Ukraine (in particular the intervention logic of the ASAP and EDIRPA programmes),[63] while completing the Union's intervention in support of cooperation in the field of defence. With EDIS and the accompanying *European Defence Industry Programme* (EDIP),[64] the Commission has set ambitious objectives in terms of cooperation, and has put in place structural support for the competitiveness of the European defence industry, supporting cooperation from the initial phases of an armaments programme (research and technology) through to the purchase and joint ownership of equipment. With EDIS and the EDIP programme, the Commission is encouraging Member States to spend more, better and together in Europe. It is proposing a framework to help Member States meet these industrial policy objectives.

The European Commission has gradually expanded its intervention in support of the competitiveness of the European defence industry since 2016 and the presentation of the European Defence Action Plan.[65] This intervention can be broadly divided into three phases: action to promote the Union's strategic autonomy; the emergency response to the Russian invasion of Ukraine; and finally, the implementation of a structural response to the need to increase European preparedness in the defence field.

In the first phase, between 2016 and 2022, the Commission used the financial leverage of the EU budget for the first time to support the competitiveness of the European defence industry. The November 2016 Plan announced the creation of the European Defence Fund, which became a reality in April 2021

63 See E. Bernard's commentary in this publication.

64 See the commentary by E. Simon in this publication.

65 Communication from the Commission to the European Parliament, the European Council, the Council, the European Economic and Social Committee and the Committee of the Regions, European Defence Action Plan, COM(2016) 950 Final, 30 November 2016.

with the approval by the co-legislators of Regulation 2021/697.[66] The fund itself was preceded by a Preparatory Action on Defence Research (PADR)[67] and the European Defence Industry Development Programme (EDIDP),[68] endowed respectively with €90 million and €500 million.

The aim of the European Defence Fund and the Commission's actions in this first phase is to defragment the industrial offer within the European defence equipment market. Through financial support for cross-border cooperation, the Commission hopes to improve the quality of European products through additional investment in research and development, and the creation of new partnerships leading to better market prospects for companies often operating essentially on a national scale. This increase in competitiveness should enable the collaborative preparation of future military capabilities, but above all the strengthening of the Union's strategic autonomy.

Along the same lines, the European Commission presented a new 'defence package' in 2022, consisting of two communications on a 'Roadmap on critical technologies for security and defence',[69] and the 'Commission contribution to European defence'.[70] In these communications, and especially in the Roadmap, the emphasis is again on preparing for the future and reducing critical dependencies. In the Roadmap, the Commission proposes in particular to identify and monitor technologies critical to security and defence.

The Russian invasion of Ukraine shows that the preparation for the future, via the European Defence Fund, and the objective of increasing the Union's strategic autonomy must be strengthened further, as well as being accompanied by urgent measures to ensure that the EDTIB can provide States with what they need to ensure their security. In May 2022, three months after the start of Russia's aggression, the Commission and the High Representative presented a

---

66 Regulation (EU) 2021/697 of the European Parliament and of the Council of 29 April 2021 establishing the European Defence Fund and repealing Regulation (EU) 2018/1092 ([2021] *OJ* L170/149). On this regulation, see the commentary by S. Rodrigues in this publication.

67 For an overview of the programme's objectives and results, see https://defence-industry-space.ec.europa.eu/eu-defence-industry/preparatory-action-defence-research-padr_en.

68 For an overview of the programme's objectives and results, see https://defence-industry-space.ec.europa.eu/eu-defence-industry/european-defence-industrial-development-programme-edidp_en.

69 Communication from the Commission to the European Parliament, the European Council, the Council, the European Economic and Social Committee and the Committee of the Regions, 'Roadmap on critical technologies for security and defence', Strasbourg, 15 February 2022, COM(2022) 61 final.

70 Communication from the Commission to the European Parliament, the European Council, the Council, the European Economic and Social Committee and the Committee of the Regions Commission contribution to European defence, Strasbourg, 15 February 2022 COM(2022) 60 final.

joint communication on defence investment shortfalls.[71] The communication describes the situation resulting from Russia's invasion of Ukraine, and analyses the result of several decades of under-investment in defence in Europe, listing the resulting industrial and capability shortfalls. The EDTIB was geared to producing in limited capacities, adapted to peacetime, and risks not being able to meet the new needs of Member States' armed forces. The latter finally increased their national defence budgets, and rushed to obtain ammunition of all calibres, which is generating demand that the industry cannot meet, while crowding out the smallest Member States.

To remedy this situation, the Commission proposed the creation of a *task force* on defence procurement, and in July 2022 presented a proposal for a regulation to support cooperation in defence equipment procurement. This emergency instrument (EDIRPA) was not approved by the co-legislators until 18 months later, mainly because of a delay on the part of the European Parliament due to a conflict between committees over the allocation of the issue.

EDIRPA has been complemented by the ASAP programme, which has provided financial support for the ramp-up of industrial production in the munitions and missile sectors, the result of a dramatic appeal by President Zelensky at the European Council in February 2023.

EDIRPA and ASAP have the merit of testing the EU's new interventionism and responding to urgent needs, but they suffer from limited budgets (€300 million for EDIRPA, €500 million for ASAP) and limited timeframes (end of June 2025 for ASAP, end of 2025 for EDIRPA). Their sector of intervention (the most urgent and critical defence equipment for EDIRPA, munitions and missiles for ASAP) is also limited.

Given the duration of the conflict in Ukraine, it has become increasingly clear that there is a need to increase the readiness of Europe's armed forces, and consequently of European industry. To achieve this, a common response at the European level, both structural and long-term, is required. To this end, in March 2024, the College of Commissioners approved the new Strategy, as well as the EDIP Programme, which is its first direct translation. With these two texts, the Commission has entered a third phase of intervention, long-term preparation (Section I). The current phase is that of implementing this new strategy (Section II).

---

71 Communication from the Commission to the European Parliament, the European Council, the Council, the European Economic and Social Committee and the Committee of the Regions on the Defense Investment Gaps Analysis and Way Forward, 18 May 2022 JOIN(2022) 24 final.

A. FROM EMERGENCY RESPONSE TO PREPAREDNESS: A PARADIGM SHIFT

The watchword of the new European Strategy is defence preparedness, an imperative for the Member States' defence apparatus in the new geopolitical context. With the EDIS Strategy and the EDIP Programme,[72] the Commission is showing that it is ready to assume its responsibilities in strengthening the European defence industry, an essential prerequisite for completing defence preparedness.

To do this, the European Defence Industrial Strategy (EDIS) first analyses the European defence market, and in particular its players: the Member States ('demand') and industry ('supply'). After addressing the question of financing, the Strategy analyses the issue of integrating defence preparations into European society and EU policies. It also addresses the issue of partnerships. The Strategy mixes analysis, presenting a framework of the situation, with concrete measures designed to improve the existing situation and contribute to meeting the objectives set out in the text.

As far as 'demand' for defence products is concerned, the Strategy stresses that the Member States are still a long way from meeting the commitments they have made in the context of NATO, the European Defence Agency and Permanent Structured Cooperation (PESCO), particularly as regards cooperation in the procurement of defence equipment. Several Member States have yet to meet the target of devoting 2% of GDP to defence, but there is a clear trend towards increasing budgets. However, Member States continue to spend in an essentially 'national' way, which is detrimental to the interoperability and visibility of the European defence industry. Worse still, since the Russian invasion of Ukraine, the Member States have used the additional budgets massively to buy non-European systems.

To deal with this situation, the Strategy sets out the need for Member States to invest more, better and together at the European level. In what has become one of the Strategy's slogans, 'better' corresponds to the need to invest in capability priorities identified by States collectively, while 'together' and 'European' are easily translated into cooperation in development and procurement, as well as the need to support the EDTIB.

To achieve these objectives, the strategy presents a series of innovative instruments, from the new joint procurement programming function to European defence projects of common interest. In addition, the logic behind the EDIRPA programme has been extended through the EDIP programme. This extension is not only temporary, but above all concerns the military capabilities that can be the subject of cooperation in the acquisition phase. Whereas

[72] See E. Simon's commentary on the Commission's proposal in this publication.

EDIRPA was limited to the most urgent and critical defence capabilities (notably munitions and missiles), EDIP has broadened the spectrum to include all defence equipment.

The Strategy also advocates the creation of the Structure for European Armament Programme (SEAP) to provide Member States with the possibility of benefiting from a standardised context for the management of armaments programmes, with a series of bonuses on offer ranging from VAT exemption in the event of joint ownership of equipment to funding under the EDIP. Finally, a European mechanism for military sales will enable states to have at their disposal industrial preparation reserves in the defence field, to increase the availability and speed up the delivery of defence products manufactured in the EU. This mechanism also includes the creation of a catalogue of defence products produced by the EDTIB and a standard regime applicable to future defence contracts and framework agreements with EU-based manufacturers.

With this mechanism, the Commission hopes to put the EDTIB back on an equal footing with foreign companies, particularly American, which benefit from the so-called *Foreign Military Sales* mechanism that enables states wishing to acquire a product developed by American industry to benefit from simplified purchasing procedures and rapid deliveries – an important selling point at a time when European states are trying to reinforce their armed forces as a matter of urgency.

On the industrial side (the supply side of the European defence market), the Strategy aims to see European industry increase its production rates and volumes. To achieve this, the Commission is extending the intervention logic of the ASAP programme to all defence products, beyond munitions and ground-to-ground missiles.

In addition, the Strategy states that the EDIP programme will support the development of '*ever-warm facilities*' or ready-to-use production capacity. These facilities are needed to avoid a massive increase in production capacity to meet a peak in demand. As it would be difficult to justify maintaining such production lines in peacetime, the Commission is proposing to support manufacturers in being ready for such production peaks, for example by building up stocks or developing facilities that can be mobilised on a permanent basis.

The need for even greater support for innovative technologies is also part of the Strategy, in two ways. First, the Strategy puts in place specific measures for innovative small and medium-sized enterprises (SMEs), such as the Fund to Accelerate defence Supply chain Transformation (FAST) (fund for the acceleration of the transformation of supply chains in the defence sector) to improve access to credit (loans and capital investment) for SMEs working in the defence sector. Furthermore, the Strategy indicates that the EDIP programme will support the industrialisation of prototypes resulting from cooperation in the research and development phase, supported by the European Defence Fund to ensure the continuity of the collaborative effort beyond the R&D phase.

Finally, to enable companies to produce more and faster, the Strategy has announced the creation of an EU-wide security of supply regime. Indeed, the economic marginalisation of the defence sector in terms of volume, compared with other sectors, often makes it difficult for defence companies to gain priority access to raw materials or critical components (such as electronic chips, for example) that they need in very limited volumes. Furthermore, faced with a drastic reduction in orders from European governments, European defence companies have often maintained their competitiveness thanks to export orders. Striking the right balance between the need to maintain a strong reputation on international markets (and therefore to fulfil export orders, even when there is an urgent need in Europe) and responding to security crises on the European continent is an extremely complex issue. The system proposed by the Commission recognises this complexity by differentiating between requirements for components and/or raw materials (for which a system of prioritisation of orders is provided) and requirements for defence products. For the latter, non-binding measures are mentioned.

This scheme not only responds to a clearly identified need, but also to a request made by the co-legislators during the discussions on the ASAP programme. At the time, the Council called for the 'regulatory pillar' of this programme to be abandoned, as it already provided for the Commission to introduce the possibility of prioritising orders, calling for in-depth preparatory work and consultation with the Member States. The Parliament, which was in favour of mapping the industrial base and establishing a system for prioritising orders, finally accepted the Council's request in return for a commitment to re-examine the issue as soon as possible[73] Following the extensive consultation that preceded EDIS and EDIP, the Commission revised its proposal, proposing a gradual and proportionate regime.

Finally, the Strategy stresses the need to 'normalise' defence particularly, but not only, within EU policies. This part of the strategy puts forward a message whose necessity cannot be underestimated. The Strategy states that '[t]he European defence industry is a crucial contributor to resilience, security, and social sustainability. There will be no economic prosperity without peace on the continent, and the EDTIB role in this respect needs to be fully acknowledged in the Union's regulatory environment and policies'. Specifically, the Strategy calls for a change in the lending policy of the European Investment Bank (EIB), which to this day excludes financing for weapons, munitions, equipment or infrastructure dedicated to military use, an exclusion that seems anachronistic in the current security context and that runs counter to the role given by the Treaties to the EIB of supporting the policies of the Union.

---

[73] See the commentary on the regulation ASAP by E. Bernard in this publication.

B. IMPLEMENTING AND ASSESSING THE STRATEGY

The strategy is now in its implementation phase. This largely depends on the implementation of the EDIP programme, which is currently under discussion with the co-legislators, with adoption scheduled for mid-2025 at the earliest. At the same time, some of the measures announced (hackathons,[74] the creation of an innovation office in Kyiv) are already taking shape, while others are being discussed with the European External Action Service (EEAS), the European Defence Agency and the Member States.

The new strategy presented by the Commission and the High Representative is in line with the intellectual continuity of the communications presented since 2016. The observation that the market is fragmented, that States and industries need to cooperate more, and the imperative of reducing strategic dependencies, have been repeated since 2016 and were reaffirmed again in 2022 in the joint communication on the analysis of investment gaps. EDIS, on the other hand, marks a break with the instruments proposed. While essential but partial actions have been presented by the Commission since the 2016 Action Plan, EDIS comes full circle and presents a coherent set of instruments to support cooperation in armament programmes, from the upstream research phase through to development, industrialisation, acquisition, maintenance in operational condition and finally the withdrawal of systems.

The Commission has set targets against which the success of the Strategy can be measured. For example, based on the observation that Member States do little to cooperate in the area of procurement,[75] EDIS has set a target of 40% of their equipment expenditure to be devoted to collaborative procurement.

To bolster the competitiveness of the EDTIB, and reverse the current trend whereby States spend almost 80% of their budgets[76] on non-European products,[77] EDIS asserts that States should ensure that at least 50% of their defence investment benefits the EDTIB by 2030, and 60% by 2035.

Finally, to ensure that collaborative but strictly national procurement does not enable Member States to meet the first two parameters, the Strategy also asserts that by 2030, the value of defence-related intra-EU trade should

74 During a hackathon, specialists get together to discuss a specific problem: in this case, how to apply innovation to the defence sector.

75 According to the 2021 defence data presented by the European Defence Agency (EDA), the Member States devoted 18% of their equipment spending to collaborative procurement, compared with the 35% target set by the Member States themselves in 2007 within the EDA framework.

76 The Strategy states that '78% of the defence acquisitions by EU Member States between the start of Russia's war of aggression and June 2023 were made from outside the EU, with the US alone representing 63%'.

77 This compares with 60% previously, as indicated in the Communication on the analysis of investment gaps in the defence sector for 2022, cited above.

represent at least 35% of the value of the European defence market (compared with 15% today).

It is important to emphasise that these three numerical targets are political guidelines and not legal obligations. In comparison, federal laws in the United States require the government to select products where the cost of domestic components must exceed a certain percentage of the total cost.

Member States reacted to the presentation of the Strategy at the Enlarged Foreign Affairs Council with Defence Ministers on 27 May 2024. In its conclusions, the Council 'welcomes the presentation of the joint communication from the European Commission and the High Representative on a new strategy for the European defence industry and calls for progress on all work concerning this document in coordination with the Member States'.[78]

At the same time, the Council recalled not only the mandate received by the Commission from the Heads of State and Government in March 2024,[79] but also that 'EDTIB needs significant, sustained investments from the Member States and, without prejudging the next Multiannual Financial Framework, the Union, to underpin the EU's defence readiness'. Finally, the Council stressed 'the importance of adequate and consistent financing for the EU's defence readiness'.

These conclusions confirm that the implementation of a Strategy leading to a state of readiness for the Union cannot be done without strong political will and sufficient budgets.

As far as political will is concerned, the Commission has shown since 2019 that support for the defence industry is becoming a priority. This trend has even accelerated during its term of office. While Ursula von der Leyen's Commission began its term by focusing on the ecological and digital transition, Russian aggression in Ukraine has put defence issues centre stage. On the part of the Member States, there seems to be a tension between acceptance of the objective benefits of European cooperation and the desire to retain as much control as possible over the sector, via intergovernmental mechanisms. The Commission's presentation of a large number of measures aimed at changing the behaviour of Member States may be perceived by some as a desire to interfere. While the consultation that preceded EDIS and EDIP helped to clear up certain misunderstandings, a constant effort to educate and exchange information will undoubtedly be necessary to apply the measures announced as effectively as possible.

As far as the budget is concerned, the seriousness of the international situation has prompted certain heads of European states or governments (notably the Estonian Prime Minister, Kaja Kallas who became High

[78] Council conclusions on EU security and defence, 27 May 2024.

[79] It 'recalls the invitation by the European Council of March 2024 to explore all options for mobilising funding and report back by June'.

Representative of the European Union for Foreign Affairs and Security Policy in December 2024) to propose exceptional instruments for financing European defence, in particular by raising funds on the financial markets through the issue of common bonds. Such an idea, taken up by French President Emmanuel Macron, would undoubtedly be a major step forward in filling the existing investment gaps, but it requires a unanimous decision by the 27 Member States.

More generally, a massive increase in the budget for EU programmes in support of the EDTIB during the next multiannual financial framework (2028-2034) seems to be the keystone of success for the European Strategy. Without an increase in the funds available for the European Defence Fund and, even more so, for EDIP, it will be difficult for these programmes to have the impact needed to bring about the transformations within the EDTIB and bring about lasting changes in the behaviour of governments and industry.

THE EUROPEAN DEFENCE FUND

Regulation (EU) 2021/697 of the European Parliament and of the Council of 29 April 2021 establishing the European Defence Fund and repealing Regulation (EU) 2018/1092, [2021] *OJ* L170/149.

Stéphane Rodrigues
Senior Lecturer at Université Paris 1 Panthéon-Sorbonne
Member of the Sorbonne Institute for Research in International and European Law (IREDIES-EA 4536)
Member of the Brussels Bar

In line with the positions it has expressed since the mid-1990s,[1] the Commission announced a 'new deal for European defence'[2] in 2014. Two years later presented a 'European Defence Action Plan'[3] in which it explained that it wanted to ensure not only the full application of existing instruments relating to free movement[4] and free competition,[5] but it also set out to make use of other competences linked to the internal market, in particular those that

1 See the following communications from the European Commission: 'The challenges facing the European defence-related industries, a contribution for action at European level', COM(96) 10 final, 24 January 1996; 'Implementing the Union's defence industrial strategy', COM(97) 583 final, 4 December 1997; 'European Defence – Industrial and Market Issues – Towards an EU Defence Equipment Policy', COM(2003) 113 final, 11 March 2003; 'A strategy for a stronger and more competitive European defence industry', COM(2007) 764 final, 5 December 2007 and 'Towards a more competitive and efficient defence and security sector', COM(2013) 542 final, 24 July 2013.

2 European Commission, 'A new deal for European Defence Roadmap for Communication COM (2013) 542...', cited above; Communication COM(2014) 387 final, 24 June 2014.

3 European Commission, 'European Defence Action Plan', Communication of 30 November 2016, COM(2016) 950 final.

4 See the commentary in this publication on Articles 49 to 62 TFEU and the commentary on Directives 2009/43/EC (transfers of defence-related products within the EU) and 2009/81/EC (defence and security procurement) by S. Rodrigues.

5 See the commentary on Articles 101 to 109 TFEU by R. Bellais and S. Rodrigues in this publication.

it can implement in the context of research and development policy (R&D) policy,[6] and of the Union's industrial policy.

It was therefore by favouring both an industrial and R&D approach that the Commission lifted the veil on the creation of a European Defence Fund (EDF) in response to the concerns expressed by President Juncker in his State of the Union address on 14 September 2016: 'The European defence market suffers from fragmentation and insufficient industrial collaboration. A more efficient use of public money and a stronger industrial base could be achieved by strengthening the Defence Single Market, reducing duplications and improving the competitiveness of the EU defence industry'. Indeed, the Commission had estimated the cost of the lack of cooperation at between €25 billion and €100 billion: 'Without a sustained investment in defence, the European industry risks lacking the technological ability to build the next generation of critical defence capabilities. Ultimately, this will affect the strategic autonomy of the Union and its ability to act as a security provider'.[7] A link was thus established with the emerging and still vague concept of strategic autonomy: the EDF was therefore to help to consolidate a European defence technological and industrial base (EDTIB).[8]

It should be noted that no reference to a specific legal basis was made at this stage by the Commission, any more than in its communication of June 2017 confirming the launch of the EDF.[9] The combined use of Articles 173 (industrial policy),[10] 182(4) (specific research programme), 183 (multiannual research framework programme) and 188(2) (use of the ordinary legislative procedure to adopt the abovementioned programmes) of the TFEU was revealed only when the Commission adopted its legislative proposal in June 2018.[11]

However, the question of the legal basis is essential to legitimising and justifying the intervention of the Union's co-legislators in a field – that of defence – where intergovernmentalism is the order of the day, under the sole

6 See commentary on Articles 179 to 190 TFEU by F. Andreone and A. Ferrazzoli in this publication.

7 COM (2016) 950 final, p. 3.

8 As confirmed by the European Council in its conclusions of 19-20 December 2018, para. 16.

9 Communication from the Commission to the European Parliament, the Council, the European Economic and Social Committee and the Committee of the Regions, *Launching the European Defence Fund*, COM(2017) 295 final, 7 June 2017, hereinafter 'the EDF Communication'. For an analysis of this project: S. Rodrigues, 'The European Defence Fund: a turning point for the European Union?', 25 January 2018, www.blogdroiteuropeen.com.

10 It is this provision alone that will serve as the legal basis for Regulation (EU) 2023/2418 of the European Parliament and of the Council of 18 October 2023 on the establishment of an instrument to strengthen the European defence industry through joint procurement ('EDIRPA'): see E. Bernard, 'La communautarisation de la défense européenne dans le contexte de la guerre en Ukraine', *RTDE*, 2023/3, pp. 325–350, spec. pp. 330–334 and commentary on this regulation by E. Simon, in this publication.

11 European Commission, Proposal for a Regulation of the European Parliament and of the Council establishing the European Defence Fund: COM(2018) 476 final, 13 June 2018.

leadership of the Council and the High Representative for Foreign Affairs and Security Policy (hereinafter 'the High Representative' or 'HR'). Furthermore, several observers have rightly pointed out that '[t]he idea of Community funding for military research is not self-evident, especially in a European Union whose primary objective is to 'promote peace' and whose action is geared more towards the civilian world than the military world'.[12]

Indeed, the Commission had carefully prepared the ground[13] by taking an increasing interest in so-called dual-use activities to emphasise 'the possible interactions between civil and military research and the dual-use potential of space'[14] and then in security activities more generally, from both internal and external perspectives.[15] This is how it began in mobilising the EU's Framework Programme for Research and Development (FP8), which covers the period 2014-2020 (known as 'Horizon 2020' and with a budget of around €77 billion),[16] to find the necessary funding for a Preparatory Action *on Defence Research* Defence (hereinafter PADR),[17] which is considered essential for CSDP operations to achieve synergies with national research programmes.[18]

The PADR was implemented over the period 2017-2018, and would then pave the way for the period 2019-2020, for the European Defence Industrial Development Programme (EDIDP) aimed at supporting the competitiveness

12 A. Dumoulin and N. Gros-Verheyde, *La politique européenne de sécurité et de défense commune*, Le Dévoluy, Éd. du Villard, 2017, p. 419.

13 On the Commission's progressive approach in this area: F. Santopinto, 'Le financement de la recherche de défense par l'UE', note d'analyse, Groupe de recherche et d'information sur la paix et la sécurité (GRIP), March 2016.

14 See in this connection: Communication from the European Commission, 'European Defence – Industrial and Market Issues – Towards an EU Defence Equipment Policy', document COM(2003) 113 final, 11 March 2003, spec. p. 5.

15 See the European Commission communication of 3 February 2004, 'Towards a programme to advance European security through research and technology', document COM (2004) 72 final. On this programme, see in particular. H. Bauduin, *Retour d'expérience: le programme européen de recherche en matière de sécurité. Étude de la participation et des performances françaises*, 2013, available at http://cache.media.education.gouv.fr/file/Securite/72/8/RAPPORT_-_Retex_PERS_-_mars_2014_307728.pdf (consulted on 24 January 2024).

16 See Regulation (EU) No 1290/2013 of the European Parliament and of the Council of 11 December 2013 laying down the rules for participation and dissemination in 'Horizon 2020' – the Framework Programmme for Research and Innovation (2014-2020) and Regulation (EU) No 1291/2013 of the European Parliament and of the Council of 11 December 2013 Horizon 2020 – the Framework Programme for Research and Innovation, [2013] *OJ* L347/81.

17 European Commission, Decision C(2017) 2262 final of 11 April 2017 on the financing of the Preparatory Action on Defence Research ' and the use of unit costs for the year 2017.

18 For more see R. Bellais and D. Fiott, 'A 'Game Changer'? The EU's preparatory action on defence research', Policy Paper, April 2016, Armament Industry European Research group (ARES). See also commentary on Articles 179 to 190 TFEU.

and innovation capacity of the EU defence industry,[19] with a budget of almost €500 million.[20]

EDF was created to take over from EDIDP after 2020, with a budget of €7.9 billion for 2021-2027, divided between €2.6 billion for research and €5.3 billion for development.[21] On the occasion of the review of the 2021-2027 Multiannual Financial Framework (MFF),[22] the Council decided to increase the EDF budget by €1.5 billion, enabling €3.151 billion to be allocated to research and €6.302 billion to development actions.[23] It should be noted that this budgetary 'boost' was allocated to calls for proposals or to the granting of funding in support of investments that contribute to the objectives of the new 'Strategic Technologies for Europe' platform (known as STEP) established at the same time as the revision of the 2021-2027 MFF.[24]

Essentially in terms of objectives and legal framework, the EDF is a continuation of the EDIDP (Section I).[25] Its implementation allows us to draw some initial lessons that will be useful for the long-term financing by the EU of a genuine European defence industry strategy (Section II).

---

19 Regulation (EU) 2018/1092 of the European Parliament and of the Council of 18 July 2018 establishing the European Defence Industrial Development Programme aimed at supporting the competitiveness and innovation capacity of the Union's defence industry (EDIDP), [2018] *OJ* L200/30. See the commentary on the EDIDP above.

20 Commission Implementing Decision C(2019)2205 of 19 March 2019 on the financing of EDIDP and the adoption of the work programme for the years 2019 and 2020.

21 The Commission had proposed a more ambitious budget of around €13 billion.

22 Council Regulation (EU, Euratom) 2024/765 of 29 February 2024 amending Regulation (EU, Euratom) 2020/2093 laying down the multiannual financial framework for the years 2021 to 2027, [2024] *OJ* L2024/765.

23 This translates into an additional amount of €376 million in the amended EU budget for 2024: see the Commission's proposal to this effect of 29 February 2024, COM(2024) 80 final.

24 Regulation (EU) 2024/795 of the European Parliament and of the Council of 29 February 2024 establishing the Strategic Technologies for Europe Platform (STEP) and amending Directive 2003/87/EC and Regulations (EU) 2021/1058, (EU) 2021/1056, (EU) 2021/1057, (EU) No 1303/2013, (EU) No 223/2014, (EU) 2021/1060, (EU) 2021/523, (EU) 2021/695, (EU) 2021/697 and (EU) 2021/241, [2024] *OJ* L2024/795. This platform aims to 'support critical and emerging strategic technologies and their respective value chains in relevant sectors' (Art. 1 of the STEP regulation), by mobilising resources under eleven existing EU programmes, including the EDF. Its implementation is accompanied by the creation of a so-called 'sovereignty label', which will serve as a quality label to help projects attract public and private investment by certifying their contribution to the STEP objectives and also to help improve access to EU funding, in particular by facilitating the cumulation or combination of funding from several EU instruments (see Recital 11 of the STEP Regulation). See also: Communication from the Commission – Guidance Note concerning certain provisions of Regulation (EU) 2024/795 establishing the Strategic Technologies for Europe Platform (STEP), [2024] *OJ* C2024/3209 and Second Guidance Note on the STEP clarifying elements of Regulation (EU) 2024/795 and Commission Communication C/2024/3209, [2025] *OJ* C/2025/6798.

25 See also. F. Mauro and E. Simon, study for the European Parliament, doc. PE 653.638, May 2021: 'Review of the Preparatory Action on Defence Industrial Development Programme (EDIDP): lessons for the implementation of the European Defence Fund (EDF)'.

I. OBJECTIVES AND LEGAL STATUS OF THE EDF

We will look successively at the objectives assigned to the ERD (Section A), the eligible entities (B) and actions (C), the award criteria (D), the co-financing rates (E) and, lastly, the question of ownership of the results obtained at the end of the project (F).

A. OBJECTIVES

According to Article 3 of the Regulation, the EDF has a general objective: 'to foster the competitiveness, efficiency and innovation capacity of the European defence technological and industrial base (EDTIB) throughout the Union, which contributes to the Union strategic autonomy and its freedom of action, by supporting collaborative actions and cross-border cooperation between legal entities throughout the Union, in particular SMEs and mid-caps, as well as by strengthening and improving the agility of both defence supply and value chains, widening cross-border cooperation between legal entities and fostering the better exploitation of the industrial potential of innovation, research and technological development, at each stage of the industrial life cycle of defence products and technologies'.

There are also two specific objectives: on the one hand, 'to support collaborative research that could significantly boost the performance of future capabilities throughout the Union, aiming to maximise innovation and introduce new defence products and technologies, including disruptive technologies for defence, and aiming to make the most efficient use of defence research spending in the Union' and, on the other hand, 'to support the collaborative development of defence products and technologies, thus contributing to the greater efficiency of defence spending within the Union, achieving greater economies of scale, reducing the risk of unnecessary duplication and thereby fostering the market uptake of European defence products and technologies and reducing the fragmentation of defence products and technologies throughout the Union, ultimately leading to an increase in the standardisation of defence systems and a greater interoperability between Member States' capabilities'.

To achieve these objectives, the EDF is implemented by the European Commission under direct management, with some exceptions, in accordance with the EU Financial Regulation[26] and may therefore allocate funding using

---

26 By reference, at the time of the adoption of the EDF, to Regulation (EU, Euratom) 2018/1046 of the European Parliament and of the Council of 18 July 2018 on the financial rules applicable to the general budget of the Union, amending Regulations (EU) No 1296/2013, (EU) No 1301/2013, (EU) No 1303/2013, (EU) No 1304/2013, (EU) No 1309/2013, (EU)

grants, prizes and contracts and, where appropriate, given the specific nature of the action, financial instruments within the framework of so-called mixed operations.[27]

B. ELIGIBLE ENTITIES

The definition of eligible legal entities (Art. 9 of the Regulation) is based on the idea of European preference: this primarily concerns recipients and subcontractors taking part in actions that are established in the European Union or an associated country (member of the European Free Trade Association – EFTA).[28] Accordingly, the infrastructures, facilities, assets and resources of recipients and subcontractors participating in an action supported by the EDF must be located on the territory of a Member State or an associated country for the entire duration of the action, and their executive management structures must be established in the Union or an associated country. Recipients and subcontractors participating in an action must not be subject to the control of a non-associated third country or a non-associated third country entity.

Echoing the concerns of several of the European Union's partners, including the United States, a derogation has been introduced. It allows a legal entity established in the EU or an associated country but controlled by a non-associated third country or an entity in a non-associated third country to be eligible for EDF, provided that guarantees approved by the Member State or associated country in which it is established in accordance with its national procedures are made available to the Commission. These guarantees must provide assurances that 'the involvement in an action of such a legal entity would not contravene the security and defence interests of the Union and its Member States as established in the framework of the CFSP pursuant to Title V of the TEU, or the objectives set out in Article 3 of this Regulation'.

To this end, it must be ensured that control over the legal entity is not exercised in a way that impedes or limits its ability to carry out the action and deliver results, that imposes restrictions on its infrastructure, facilities, assets,

No 1316/2013, (EU) No 223/2014, (EU) No 283/2014 and Decision No 541/2014/EU, and repealing Regulation (EU, Euratom) No 966/2012, [2018] *OJ* L193/1. That regulation has been repealed and replaced by Regulation (EU, Euratom) 2024/2509 of the European Parliament and of the Council of 23 September 2024 on the financial rules applicable to the general budget of the Union (recast), [2024] *OJ* L2024/2509.

27 See Article 8 of Regulation (EU) 2021/697 . A 'blending' operation, within the meaning of Title X of the EU Financial Regulation, makes it possible to combine forms of non-reimbursable aid or financial instruments from the EU budget with forms of reimbursable aid from development financial institutions or other public financial institutions, as well as commercial financial institutions and commercial investors.

28 Like Norway, for example, which was already a member of the APCD.

resources, intellectual property or know-how needed for the purposes of the action, or that undermines the capabilities and standards it needs to carry out the action. In addition, the non-associated third country or a non-associated third country entity seeking support from the EDF may not have access to sensitive information relating to the action.[29]

In addition, as a standard requirement for responding to a call for projects financed by the EU, the EDF regulation requires the constitution of a consortium made up of at least three eligible legal entities established in at least three different Member States or associated countries. At least three of these eligible legal entities established in at least two different Member States or associated countries are not, for the entire duration of the action, directly or indirectly controlled by the same legal entity and do not control each other.

C. ELIGIBLE ACTIONS

Eligible actions (Art. 10 of the regulation)[30] fall into nine categories, listed as follows:

- activities that aim to create, underpin and improve knowledge, products and technologies, including disruptive technologies for defence, which can achieve significant effects in the area of defence;
- activities that aim to increase interoperability and resilience, including secured production and exchange of data, to master critical defence technologies, to strengthen the security of supply or to enable the effective exploitation of results for defence products and technologies;
- studies, such as feasibility studies to explore the feasibility of new or upgraded products, technologies, processes, services and solutions;
- the design of a defence product, tangible or intangible component or technology as well as the definition of the technical specifications on which such a design has been developed, including any partial tests for risk reduction in an industrial or representative environment;
- the system prototyping of a defence product, tangible or intangible component or technology;
- the testing of a defence product, tangible or intangible component or technology;
- the qualification of a defence product, tangible or intangible component or technology;

[29] Employees or other persons taking part in the action must have national security clearance issued by a Member State or associated country, where applicable.

[30] See also Art. 21 of the EDF regulation providing for additional eligibility criteria for development actions.

- the certification of a defence product, tangible or intangible component or technology;
- the development of technologies or assets increasing efficiency across the life cycle of defence products and technologies.

D. AWARD CRITERIA

Once the consortium made up of eligible entities and the competitive calls for proposals have been drawn up in accordance with the EU Financial Regulation and published (see below), the Commission must take into account a series of award criteria (Art. 11 of the Regulation):[31]

- contributing to excellence or breakthrough potential in the field of defence, in particular, if it is demonstrated that the expected results of the proposed action offer significant advantages over existing defence products or technologies;
- contributing to the innovation and technological development of the European defence industry, in particular, if it is demonstrated that the proposed action involves innovative or novel approaches and concepts, new technological improvements that hold promise for the future, or the use of technologies or concepts that have not previously been used in the defence sector, while avoiding unnecessary duplication;
- contributing to the competitiveness of the European defence industry, if it is demonstrated that the proposed action has a positive balance in terms of cost-effectiveness and efficiency, thus creating new market opportunities in the EU and beyond and accelerating the growth of companies throughout the EU;
- contributing to the autonomy of the EDTIB, including by increasing non-dependence on sources outside the EU and enhancing security of supply, and to safeguarding the EU's security and defence interests, in line with the objectives of the EDF;
- contributing to the establishment of new cross-border cooperation between legal entities established in Member States or associated countries, in particular SMEs and mid-caps whose participation in the action is substantial, as recipients, subcontractors or as other legal entities in the supply chain, and which are established in Member States or associated countries other than those in which the legal entities cooperating in a consortium which are not SMEs or mid-caps are established; and, finally,
- contributing to the quality and effectiveness of the implementation of the action.

[31] See also Art. 22 of the EDF regulation providing for additional award criteria for development actions.

E. CO-FINANCING RATES

As with all regulations governing the granting of EU financial support, the EDF regulation contains provisions relating to the co-financing rate for selected projects. The principle is that funding may cover up to 100% of eligible costs. However, there are two exceptions: the co-financing rate is reduced to a maximum of 20% for prototyping and 80% for testing, qualification and certification.

In addition, there is a bonus mechanism. For example, a selected project that is already part of a permanent structured cooperation project can benefit from a 10% bonus.[32] The same applies when at least 15% of the total eligible costs of the activity are allocated to mid-cap companies established in Member States or associated countries. And where at least 10% of the total eligible costs of the activity are allocated to SMEs established in Member States or associated countries, the percentage of the total eligible costs of the activity allocated to these SMEs may be doubled.

F. OWNERSHIP OF RESULTS

Finally, there is one last particularly sensitive aspect of the EDF system: ownership of the results of EU-funded actions.

In the case of research activities (Art. 20 of the regulation), the principle is that the results are the property of the recipients who produced them, unless the support granted by the EU was in the form of a public contract. Echoing the restrictive eligibility provisions mentioned above, it is specified that these results may not be subject to 'any control or restriction by a non-associated third country or by a non-associated third-country entity, directly, or indirectly through one or more intermediate legal entities, including in terms of technology transfer'.

The same applies to the results of development actions, over which the EU cannot claim any intellectual property rights (Art. 23 of the regulation).

II. IMPLEMENTATION OF THE EDF

As part of the first work programme for 2021, the Commission identified no fewer than 17 themes, and 142 proposals were submitted. The Commission

[32] See the commentary on Articles 42(6) and 46 TEU by Q. Loiez, in this publication.

selected 61 projects,[33] involving around 700 companies (40% of which are SMEs) from 26 Member States.[34] Of these projects, 31 are devoted to research (for €322 million) and 30 to development (for €845 million). Examples include the EDOCC (military projects), EDINAF (naval combat), HYDEF (the hypersonic defence interceptor) and NEUMANN (air power and propulsion).

The second work programme was adopted in May 2022, with a budget of €924 million for 33 themes, structured around eight calls for proposals which were opened in June 2022 and evaluated in spring 2023.[35] The results were presented in June 2023: 134 proposals were received from 550 entities (39% of which were SMEs), while 24 research projects, and 14 capability development projects were finally selected, for a budget of €317 million and €514 million respectively.[36]

Following on from this, on 7 June 2022 the first part of the third work programme for 2023 was adopted, with a budget of €255.5 million (respectively €213mn for capability development and €42.5mn for research).[37] This was supplemented on 29 March 2023 by a second part, with a larger budget, of €789 million (respectively €511.9mn for capability development and €277.1mn for research).[38] This work programme covers 34 themes structured around four thematic calls for proposals and three calls focusing on disruptive technologies and SMEs. Priorities include space surveillance and, in the naval sector, the development of the prototype for the European Patrol Corvette (EPC). An EU Defence Innovation Scheme (EUDIS) has also been set up, with a budget of €2 billion, 74% of which is funded by the EDF, the remainder by the Member States (4.5%), as well as private and public investors (21.5%). A partnership

33 See the list of 61 projects annexed to the Commission's press release IP/22/4595 of 20 July 2022. The first disputes have arisen between the promoters of some of the rejected projects: see for example Case T-614/22, *MBDA France v Commission* (EDF-2021-AIRDEF-D project/endo-atmospheric interceptor) (removal order of 8 September 2023); Case T-617/22, *Safran Aircraft Engines v Commission*, ECLI:EU:T:2024:629 (EDF-2021-ENERENV-D-PES-ALPES project/innovative propulsion system for air combat systems) and Case T-134/23, *Institut Jožef Stefan v European Commission*, ECLI:EU:T:2024:907 (EDF-2021-MCBRN-R). On these disputes: R. Chaker, 'Le Fonds européen de la défense: genèse, ambitions et premier bilan', *Revue de l'Union européenne*, 2023, no. 670, pp. 398–399.

34 Malta was the only country not to submit a project.

35 Examples include the development of space-based missile early warning and Earth observation capabilities, a European naval surveillance capability, a toolbox for cyber defence and information warfare, on-board electronic warfare, collaborative combat for land forces, sustainable components for submarine applications, and so on.

36 See Commission press release IP/23/3481 of 26 June 2023 and O. Jehin, 'FEDEF 2023: 41 projets industriels de défense vont se partager 832 millions', *B2 Pro Le quotidien de l'Europe géopolitique*, 28 June 2023.

37 Commission implementing decision C(2022) 3659 final, 7 June 2022.

38 Commission implementing decision C(2023) 2296 final of 29 March 2023.

has been established between EUDIS and the Hub for EU Defence Innovation (HEDI) within, the European Defence Agency (EDA).[39]

The results of the calls launched in 2023 were made public by the Commission on 16 May 2024: 54 joint European R&D projects were selected for a total of just over €1 billion.[40] The projects with the most funding include: the EMISSARY for the development of a set of sensors and space command and control software (coordinated by Italy's Leonardo for €100 million over 48 months); the HYDIS project, for studies into a new hypersonic missile interceptor (coordinated by France's MBDA for €80 million over 36 months); and the ACTUS project, for the development of technologies for tactical airborne drone systems (coordinated by Greece's Intracom Defense AE for €42 million over 48 months).

The fourth work programme, was presented on 15 March 2024 by the European Commission.[41] It comprises 6 thematic calls for proposals and 2 calls for proposals aimed at SMEs. Of the 16 major thematic categories selected, the ones with the most funding should be highlighted: information superiority (€181 million to develop new-generation multifunctional transceiver software and a MALE drone equipped with ISTAR resources);[42] air combat (€150 million, in particular to design a next generation of helicopters) and land combat (€130 million, in particular for new intelligent weapons and munitions systems and a new generation of armoured infantry fighting vehicles).[43] The budget envelope for 2024 was increased to €1.1 billion,[44] including €225 million to support start-ups under EUDIS.

Finally, the fifth Work Programme for 2025 was adopted on 29 January 2025 with a budgetary allocation of €1.065 billion.[45] It addresses 33 call topics in total, structured along seven thematic calls for proposals, two non-thematic calls for proposals and two actions in support of the Alliance for Defence Medical Countermeasures. The focus is on enabling technologies related

---

39 On the EDA, see the commentary on Article 45 TEU by A.-H. Bertana in this publication.

40 See European Commission press release IP/24/2666 of 15 May 2023.

41 See European Commission press release IP/24/1495 of 15 March 2024 and European Commission implementing decision C(2024) 1702 final of the same date. Note: a first part of the 2024 programme was the subject of an implementing decision C(2023) 4252 final of the European Commission on 21 June 2023.

42 ISTAR: Intelligence, Surveillance, Target Acquisition and Reconnaissance.

43 For details of the 16 themes see O. Jehin, 'Décryptage: appel à propositions 2024 au titre du FEDef. Priority to development', www.club.bruxelles2.eu (consulted on 18 March 2024).

44 Norway is contributing around €33.7 million.

45 See Commission Implementing Decision C(2025) 568 final of 29 January 2025 on the financing of the European Defence Fund and the adoption of the work programme for 2025 – Part 2 and amending Implementing Decisions C(2023) 2296 final and C(2024) 1702 final as regards financial support to third parties. See also Annex 2 to that decision with an indicative multiannual perspective 2025-2027 and Commission Press Release IP/25/376 of 30 January 2025: 'More than €1 billion from the European Defence Fund to develop next generation defence technologies and innovation'.

to autonomous triage and evacuation of injured personnel, multifunctional information distribution system, human-AI dialogue, chiplets for defence applications, soldier systems, and great-depth enabling technologies. In terms of budgetary priorities, around €100 million will finance future challenges in the fields of ground combat, space, air combat and energy resilience and environmental transition; and more than €40 million are allocated to R&D efforts in critical areas in the current and future operational context, such as cyber, naval combat, underwater warfare, simulation and training, advanced passive and active sensors. Moreover, 4% of the EDF 2025 budget will be dedicated to a call addressing disruptive technologies. In addition, around 6% will support two non-thematic calls on innovative and future defence solutions, inviting specifically SMEs to apply for research and development actions. Last, but not least, the EDF 2025 Work Programme will keep on supporting defence innovation through EUDIS, providing grants and services for start-ups, scale-ups, SMEs, research & technology organisations, accelerators and other non-traditional actors to help them overcome defence market entry barriers, bring ideas to the market and make a difference to EU security and defence.[46]

It is difficult make an initial assessment of the EDF, even if only provisionally.[47] From a macroeconomic point of view, before the implementation of the fourth programme, we can count 101 projects in progress for €4.3 billion disbursed. From a more qualitative point of view, according to data processed by the Foundation for Strategic Research (FRS) for the first four years of operation (2021-2024), it can be seen that the top 4 Member States during this period of time in terms of participation are France, Italy, Germany and Spain. As for the total funding to SMEs, it was increasing, from 18% in EDF 2021 to 27% in EDF 2024. This is in line with the increase of the EDF budget, with €840 million earmarked for SME-led projects between 2023 and 2027. In January 2024, a Defence Equity Facility was set up in partnership with the European Investment Bank (EIB) Group,[48] providing €175 million (of which €75 million is matched by the European Investment Fund, a subsidiary of the EIB). The aim is to attract additional private investment of up to €500 million for European SMEs.[49]

---

46 It should be noted also that half of the proposed call topics for 2025 will support the objectives of STEP in the field of digital technologies and deep-tech innovation, clean and resource-efficient technologies and biotechnologies.

47 For an attempt at a general mid-term review: N.-J. Brehon, 'Le soutien européen à l'industrie de défense. Bilan à mi-parcours du fonds européen de défense', Schuman Paper No. 779, 10 February 2025 and 'Les inflexions préoccupantes du fonds européen de défense', Schuman Paper No 801, 8 September 2025.

48 H. Masson, *European Defence Fund: Assessmentafter four Calls For Proposals (2021-2022)*, Foundation for Strategic Research, Défense &Industries, No. 21, July 2025.

49 This mechanism is reminiscent of the CASSINI Fund, co-managed by the Commission and the EIF since 2022 to boost investment in space companies. On the EU's space policy: see the commentary on Article 189 TFEU by A. de Neve in this publication.

Be that as it may, as some observers have pointed out, 'comparisons remain tricky: each project is specific and variations in budgetary envelopes lead to significant disparities'.[50] Nevertheless, two brief comments may be added. Firstly, while defence industry players appear to be on board,[51] the fact remains that the available budget envelopes are not being fully mobilised. For the year 2022, only €832 million will have been shared out of a total available budget of €924 million. Secondly, even if the Commission seems to welcome this in the name of consistency with the objectives of the Strategic Compass,[52] several of the EDF projects selected are linked to PESCO projects (11 in 2022), so the question of overlap for display reasons may arise.

As provided for in Article 29 of Regulation (EU) 2021/697, an interim evaluation of the Fund must be carried out 'once there is sufficient information available about its implementation, but no later than four years after the start of the implementation period of the Fund'. The Commission launched a consultation procedure which began on 24 January 2024 and ended on 21 February 2024.[53] The report should include an assessment of the governance of the fund, the lessons learned from the EDIDP and the PADR, the implementation rates, and the results in terms of project allocation, including the degree of participation of SMEs and mid-caps and their level of cross-border participation. It will also provide an opportunity to take stock of the countries of origin of recipients, the number of countries participating in individual projects and the distribution of intellectual property rights created. In the light of the results of the consultation, expected in the first half of 2025, the Commission will be able to present proposals for appropriate amendments to the Regulation, before having to carry out a final evaluation at the end of the implementation period, and by 31 December 2031 at the latest, and prepare a report on the implementation of the fund.

***

In conclusion, to date, EDF has had the merit of launching 'a European defence innovation dynamic',[54] while at the same time paving the way for a form of

---

50 R. Mielcarek, 'Decoding. European Defence Fund. Outline of funding dynamics', www.bruxelles2.eu (consulted on 12 February 2024).

51 R. Chaker, 'Le Fonds européen de la défense: genèse, ambitions et premier bilan', *Revue de l'Union européenne*, 2023, no. 670, p. 400.

52 See Council document of 21 March 2022, 'Strategic Compass on Security and Defence – For a European Union that protects its citizens, its values and its interests, and contributes to international peace and security'.

53 With some thirty contributions collected and available at the following Internet address: https://ec.europa.eu/info/law/better-regulation/have-your-say/initiatives/13928-Fonds-europeen-de-la-defense-evaluation-intermediaire/feedback_fr?p_id=32501457 (consulted on 24 February 2024).

54 R. Chaker, 'Le Fonds européen de la défense: genèse, ambitions et premier bilan', *Revue de l'Union européenne*, 2023, no. 670, p. 400.

sustainable funding for defence capability research and development, as confirmed by the proposal for a new European Defence Industry Programme (EDIP), presented by the Commission on 5 March 2024 for a new European Defence Industry Strategy (EDIS), presented by the Commission on 5 March 2024,[55] published the same day by the European Commission and the High Representative.[56] The proposal states that the new programme will complement the EDF, in particular by supporting the projects it finances at a later stage in the life cycle of defence equipment.[57] In addition, it will draw on the experience of the equity facility co-financed by the EDF and the EIF (see above), to establish the new Fund to Accelerate defence Supply chain Transformation (FAST), to strengthen the security of supply within the Member States and the EU.[58]

For the time being, the budget announced for financing EDIP may seem modest: €1.5 billion for 2025-2027.[59] This is a far cry from the estimate of needs put forward by Commissioner Thierry Breton at €100 billion for the period after 2027.[60] But perhaps the key issue lies elsewhere. EDF will have marked a 'fundamental change', insofar as the Union's intervention is evolving 'from a supply-side policy, characterised by normative action aimed at establishing a defence market at EU level, to a demand-side policy, marked by the provision of public funding as part of an industrial policy'.[61] And 'for the time being, this mini-revolution is being carried out tactfully so as not to offend the sensitivities of the Member States, which are traditionally the masters of the game in this area':[62] 'it is a skilful approach to go through investment without encroaching on national sovereignty'.[63]

55 Communication from the Commission, Proposal for a Regulation of the European Parliament and of the Council establishing the European Defence Industrial Programme and a framework of measures to ensure the timely availability and supply of defence products, COM(2024) 150 final of 5 March 2024. See E. Simon's commentary of this proposal in this publication.

56 Joint Communication from the Commission and the High Representative of the Union for Foreign Affairs and Security Policy, 'A new European Defence Industrial Strategy: Achieving EU readiness through a responsive and resilient European Defence Industry', JOIN(2024) 10 final of 5 March 2024.

57 Objective highlighted by EDIS (see Section 3.2.2.).

58 See the explanatory memorandum, p. 3 and Recital 29 of the abovementioned proposal for an EDIP regulation.

59 See Art. 5 of the proposed EDIP regulation cited above.

60 P. Jacqué, 'UE: Thierry Breton propose un fonds de 100 milliards d'euros pour développer la défense européenne', *Le Monde*, www.lemonde.fr (accessed on 12 January 2024).

61 F. Mauro, 'Où en est la recherche européenne de défense?', analysis note, Groupe de recherche et d'information sur la paix et la sécurité (GRIP), March 2017, spec. p. 2.

62 S. Rodrigues, 'The European Defence Fund: a turning point for the European Union', 25 January 2018, www.blogdroiteuropeen.com.

63 O. Marty, 'La défense européenne a peut-être trouvé son embryon', *Les Echos*, Le point de vue, 15 December 2016, p. 12.

Postscript, December 2025

On 22 April 2025, the European Commission has adopted a proposal amending Regulations (EU) 2021/694, (EU) 2021/695, (EU) 2021/697, (EU) 2021/1153, (EU) 2023/1525 and 2024/795, as regards incentivising defence-related investments in the EU budget to implement the ReArm Europe Plan.[64] This EDF amendment aims to enable cumulation of funding between the EDF and other Union programmes for the same action and introduces the possibility to transfer resources allocated to Member States under cohesion policy funds to the EDF.

On 17 June 2025, the European Commission has released a communication entitled "*Defence Readiness Omnibus*"[65] to put forward simplification proposals in defence-specific legislation and programmes, as well as in non-defence-specific laws to remove regulatory barriers and facilitate EU defence readiness and industrial buildup. One of these proposals is about amending Regulation (EU)2021/697.[66] As explained by the Commission, the proposed changes aim to:

- clarify and simplify award criteria, introducing the possibility of selecting only the most relevant award criteria, and implementing the EDF through annual or multi-annual work programmes;
- clarify the rules applicable to direct awards;
- facilitate the use of indirect management;
- simplify pre-commercial procurement and access rights of co-financing Member States to the results of development projects;
- make costs for testing activities conducted outside of the Union territory (e.g. in Ukraine) eligible for funding.

On the same day, the Commission adopted an interim evaluation report of the EDF,[67] pointing out notably that, '[w]hile the EDF is still a relatively young programme (none of the EDF projects have been completed yet), its relevance for the Member States' armed forces is already evidenced by its role in developing new defence technologies and products that address critical gaps in all capability domains. The take up of EDF precursors projects' results by the armed forces of the Member States gives a strong

64 COM(2025) 188 final.

65 European Commission, Communication, *Defence Readiness Omnibus*, COM(2025) 820 final; 17 June 2025.

66 European Commission, Proposal for a regulation of the European Parliament and of the Council amending Regulations (EC) No 1907/2006, (EC) No 1272/2008, (EU) No 528/2012, (EU) 2019/1021 and (EU) 2021/697 as regards defence readiness and facilitating defence investments and conditions for defence industry, COM(2025) 822 final, 17 June 2025.

67 European Commission, Report, The European Defence Fund: supporting the development of the defence capabilities of tomorrow. Interim evaluation of the European Defence Fund, COM(2025) 299 final, SEC(2025) 169 fin and SWD(2025) 151 final, of 17 June 2025.

indication for its potential'. In this regard, the Commission recalls, inter alia, that EDF actions are expected to develop more than 50 prototypes, which constitute the technology and capability blocks for next generation defence capabilities. The Commission concluded that the EDF 'has successfully brought together defence R&D under a single, medium to long-term and well-recognised programme, contributing to a coherent and more integrated EU defence R&D landscape' and announces that, in close cooperation with the Member States, it will work on 'developing a stronger link with procurement (where relevant jointly) by the Member States' armed forces of the results and outcomes of EDF projects'.
Then after, on 16 July 2025, the European Commission has adopted a proposal for a regulation of the European Parliament and of the Council on establishing the European Competitiveness Fund ('ECF'), including the specific programme for defence research and innovation activities, repealing Regulations (EU) 2021/522, (EU) 2021/694, (EU) 2021/697, (EU) 2021/783, repealing provisions of Regulations (EU) 2021/696, (EU) 2023/588, and amending Regulation (EU) [EDIP].[68] The ECF will replace the EDF by a specific programme on defence research and innovation referred to in Article 182(3) TFEU,[69] with effect from 1 January 2028.
On 17 December 2025, the European Commission has adopted an implementing decision on the financing of the EDF and the adoption of the work programme for 2026 (see document C(2025) 8719 final). This is the sixth EDF Work Programme which addresses 31 topics in total, organised around ten calls, one action to focus on threats from hypersonic glide vehicles, and two actions in support of the EU Alliance for defence medical countermeasures, for a total budget of 1 billion EUR.
Last, on 29 December 2025, the Regulation (EU) 2025/2643 of 16 December 2025 establishing the European Defence Industry Programme and a framework of measures to ensure the timely availability and supply of defence products ('EDIP Regulation') has been published (OJ L/2025/2643).

68 COM(2025) 555 final.

69 See commentary of Articles 179 to 190 TFUE in this publication, by F. Andreone and A. Ferrazzolli.

THE ASAP REGULATION: EU SUPPORT FOR AMMUNITION PRODUCTION

Regulation (EU) 2023/1525 of the European Parliament and of the Council of 20 July 2023 on supporting ammunition production (ASAP).[1]

Elsa Bernard

Professor of Public Law at the University of Lille
Jean Monnet Chair
Member of the Rights and Perspectives of Law Research Centre (CRDP, ULR 4487)

Echoing President Zelensky's call when he came to Brussels for an extraordinary European Council meeting, one year after the start of Russia's invasion of Ukraine, European leaders took note of the urgent need to supply Kyev with missiles and ammunition, defence products consumed in very large quantities by the Ukrainian army to resist Moscow.[2]

Faced with the prospect of European stocks running out and the inability of Member States to produce sufficient quantities of these defence products to meet Ukraine's needs, the European Union has set up a scheme to support production capacity. Proposed in May 2023,[3] the regulation on support for ammunition production, known as 'ASAP', was adopted on 20 July 2023.[4]

A year earlier, on 19 July 2022, the European Commission had presented its proposal for a regulation 'establishing an instrument for the reinforcement of the European defence industry through common procurement',[5] known as

1 Regulation (EU) 2023/1525 of the European Parliament), [2023] *OJ* L185/7.

2 At that time (February 2023), Ukraine was firing up to 7,000 artillery shells a day, a quarter of what the Russian forces were firing.

3 Document COM(2023) 237 final of 3 May 2023.

4 'Act in Support of Ammunition Production'.

5 Regulation (EU) 2023/2418 of the European Parliament and of the Council of 18 October 2023 on establishing an instrument for the reinforcement of the European defence industry through common procurement (EDIRPA), [2023] *OJ* L2023/2418.

EDIRPA.[6] This proposal, like the later ASAP regulation, was in response to the invitation made by the Heads of State or Government in March 2022 to the Commission, to present an analysis of defence investment gaps and to propose 'any further initiative necessary to strengthen the European defence industrial and technological base' (EDTIB).[7]

Discussions on the EDIRPA instrument had already been underway for several months when the decision was taken to act more specifically on ammunition production in the EU. Thus, the objectives and needs of the European defence industry were already known. The joint communication 'on the Defence Investment Gaps Analysis and Way Forward', presented on 18 May 2022, also provided for the establishment by the Commission and the High Representative of the Union for Foreign Affairs and Security Policy ('the High Representative')[8] of a 'task force' for joint defence procurement.[9] This task force was directed to 'work with Member States to support the coordination of their very short-term procurement needs to face the new security situation'.[10] It did so in two stages, focusing firstly on coordinating European demand, 'to avoid a race to secure orders which would result in spiralling prices', and secondly by establishing 'an aggregate estimate of needs' by mapping and supporting the increase in EU industrial production capacity required to meet these needs. The proposed ASAP regulation was designed, in part, on the basis of the results produced by the task force.[11] In particular, the task force was able to provide some initial responses in terms of production capacity in the sector,[12] which were subsequently clarified during the 'tour' of European ammunition producers conducted by then Commissioner Thierry

---

6 See the commentary on this regulation by E. Bernard in this publication. For a combined analysis of the ASAP and EDIRPA instruments, see E. Bernard, 'La communautarisation de la défense européenne dans le contexte de la guerre en Ukraine', *Revue Trimestrielle de Droit Européen (RTDE)*, 2023/4, pp. 325–350.

7 Informal Meeting of Heads of State or Government, Versailles Declaration, 10-11 March 2022.

8 The High Representative chairs the European Defence Agency, which already has experience in this area since it was created in 2004, specifically to support cooperative European defence projects. See the commentary by A.-H. Bertana in this publication.

9 Joint Communication to the European Parliament, the European Council, the Council, the European Economic and Social Committee and the Committee of the Regions on the Defence Investment Gaps Analysis and the Way Forward, JOIN(2022) 24 final, 18 May 2022.

10 Ibid.

11 'The proposal draws on the lessons learned from the Joint Communication on the Defence investment gaps analysis and way forward of 18 May 2022 and builds on the work undertaken in the framework of the Defence Joint Procurement Task Force, established immediately after the publication of the above-mentioned Joint Communication', Explanatory Memorandum to the proposal for a Regulation, COM(2023) 237 final, 3 May 2023.

12 'The Defence Joint Procurement Task Force has initiated the mapping of the EU industry's manufacturing capacities, including in the area of ground-to-ground and artillery ammunition, as well as missiles', Explanatory Memorandum to the proposal for the regulation in question.

Breton, whose portfolio included the Directorate-General for Defence Industry and Space (DG DEFIS).[13]

In their joint communication of 18 May 2022, the European Commission and the High Representative already proposed new possibilities for Member States 'to engage with industry to step up their production capacity to meet the increased needs, based on consolidated and more predictable demand'. As Member States 'start adapting their planning processes to take into account the new security landscape', the Communication states, 'it is paramount to set up a more structured approach [...] to deliver on this new ambition in a coordinated way'.[14]

However, the planning of ammunition production did not give rise to as rapid an initiative as the joint procurement of defence products. One year after the start of the war, ammunition and missile production capacities had not really been increased in the Member States of the European Union. It was not until the winter of 2023, following suggestions from then Estonian Prime Minister Kaja Kallas,[15] that a three-part 'Munitions Plan' was agreed. The first was to urgently supply Ukraine with ammunition; the second was to acquire this ammunition jointly; the third was to produce more of it.

While the first two components, consisting respectively of the supply of ammunition to Ukraine and joint procurement, are covered by the European Peace Facility[16] – outside the EU budget – and therefore fall within the scope of the CFSP and CSDP, the third component falls within the supranational sphere. It aims to support the ramping up of production of these defence products by European industry to enable Member States to replenish their stocks and rapidly supply Ukraine, and to enable European industry to increase the predictability of government orders and to benefit from partial coverage of their production by the European budget.

To this end, in March 2023 the Council invited the Commission to present 'concrete proposals to urgently support the ramp-up of manufacturing capacities of the European defence industry, secure supply chains, facilitate efficient procurement procedures, address shortfalls in production capacities and promote investments, including, where appropriate, by mobilising the

---

13 'I initiated a tour on the ground to get a good understanding of Europe's industrial capacities. I set out to see each of the 15 identified players to check their capacity, challenge them and understand what they needed to increase and accelerate their output', Act in Support of Ammunition Production (ASAP), Press conference by Commissioner Thierry Breton, 3 May 2023 (europa.eu).

14 Joint Communication on the Defence Investment Gaps Analysis and the Way Forward, JOIN(2022) 24 final, 18 May 2022, cited above, 5.4.

15 See the comments made to journalists in February 2023: V. Malingre and P. Jacqué, 'Guerre en Ukraine: pour accélérer la production de munitions à destination de Kiev, Bruxelles envisage d'effectuer des achats en commun', *Le Monde*, 12 February 2023.

16 See the commentary by C. Schneider in this publication.

Union budget'.[17] Although the figure is not mentioned in the ASAP regulation, then Commissioner Thierry Breton indicated on several occasions that the aim of this third part of the plan was to increase the EU's production capacity for missiles and ammunition to one million shells per year.[18] As the regulation states, 'joint efforts to enable Member States to replenish their depleted stocks and to support Ukraine can only be effective if the EU supply side can deliver on time the required defence products'.[19] The ASAP instrument, designed to meet the objectives of this third part of the plan, therefore complements EDIRPA – which it incorporates in many respects – by supporting the supply of ammunition, rather than demand.

Proposed by the Commission of 3 May 2023 and scheduled to be applied 'as soon as possible' (or 'ASAP'), the 'Regulation of the European Parliament and of the Council on supporting ammunition production' was adopted two and a half months later, on 20 July 2023. Given the urgent need to produce these defence products, and in order to avoid complications similar to those that arose during the vote on the EDIRPA proposal in the European Parliament,[20] the text proposed by the Commission without a prior impact assessment, was the subject of an urgent procedure within the European Parliament,[21] before being adopted by a large majority[22] on 1 June 2023, without amendment. This was despite proposed amendments from certain political groups.[23] The Council, on the other hand, made major cuts to the Commission's proposal, particularly in its regulatory dimension. While the ASAP Regulation, like the EDIRPA Regulation, is based on Article 173(3) of the TFEU,[24] insofar as it involves implementing measures to enable European industry to adapt rapidly

---

17 Note on *Delivery and joint procurement of ammunition for Ukraine*, as approved by the Council on 20 March 2023, 7632/23.

18 See, for example, the press conference of 3 May 2023. In March 2024, the Commission announced that with the support of ASAP, Europe should reach an annual production capacity of 2 million shells by the end of 2025. See the press release, consulted on 10 May 2024.
https://ec.europa.eu/commission/presscorner/detail/fr/IP_24_1495

19 Explanatory Memorandum, Proposal for an ASAP Regulation cited above, p. 1.

20 See the commentary on this regulation by E. Bernard in this publication.

21 In accordance with Article 163 of the European Parliament's Rules of Procedure and at the request of the European People's Party (EPP), then the Liberals of the Renew/Renaissance Group.

22 446 votes in favour, 67 against and 112 abstentions.

23 The Social Democrats, the Greens/EFA and the GUE/NGL. The Parliament simply asked for – and obtained – a few minor changes to the Commission's proposal, in particular a bonus for small and medium-sized enterprises in the context of financing rates and the abandonment of a derogation from labour law that was linked to increases in production rates.

24 This provision authorises the European Parliament and the Council to decide on specific measures to support action taken in the Member States to achieve the objectives referred to in Paragraph 1 of Article 173, in particular to speed up the adjustment of industry to structural change.

to structural change, it also has a regulatory pillar, which justifies its second legal basis: Article 114 of the TFEU.[25]

With a budget of €500 million, of which €240 million comes from the budget initially earmarked for EDIRPA,[26] and €260 million from the European Defence Fund,[27] the ASAP instrument sets up an aid scheme for production capacity and a ramp-up fund for a short period (from 25 July 2023 to 30 June 2025).[28] Its role is to finance increases in production capacity for ground-to-ground ammunition, artillery ammunition and missiles.[29] While the Commission's proposal was ambitious in view of its stated objectives (Section I), the regulation adopted is much less so following the Council's amendments, particularly with regard to the regulatory pillar (Section II). The ASAP instrument has been implemented swiftly to allow it to have an impact on European production capacity for ammunition and missiles (Section III).

I. AN AMBITIOUS PROPOSAL

On several occasions, voices from the highest levels of the European Commission have suggested that, like Covid-19, the war in Ukraine requires urgent action, and that what had been done to speed up the development and availability of vaccines should be done with ammunition.[30] However, the EU's

---

25 See the Commission proposal, p. 5. Article 114 TFEU concerns measures for the approximation of the laws of the Member States which have as their object the establishment and functioning of the internal market. See the commentary on this article by S. Rodrigues in this publication.

26 See the commentary on this regulation by E. Bernard in this publication. The remaining €260 million were taken from the European Defence Fund.

27 Regulation (EU) 2021/697 of the European Parliament and of the Council of 29 April 2021 establishing the European Defence Fund and repealing Regulation (EU) 2018/1092, [2021] *OJ* L170/149. See the commentary on this regulation by S. Rodrigues in this publication.

28 Art. 5(1) of the ASAP Regulation. Under the terms of Article 7(2) of the ASAP Regulation, actions started before the date of submission of the proposal for such actions may be financed by the ASAP, provided that they did not start before 20 March 2023 (the date on which the Council approved the munitions plan), and that they were not completed before the grant agreement was signed.

29 According to the definition of 'relevant defence products' given in Art. 2(12) of the Regulation. This broad definition, given the number and variety of existing missiles, may cover nuclear missiles (although some Member States would undoubtedly oppose this) and should enable ASAP to support the production of NATO-standard ammunition (155 mm calibre shells) and Soviet-standard ammunition (152 mm calibre shells), which are widely used in Ukraine and are still produced in the former Eastern bloc Member States.

30 Ursula von der Leyen used 'the example of Community aid for vaccine production during the Covid-19 pandemic, which she wants to apply to ammunition', S. Kauffman and T. Wieder, 'À Munich, les alliés de l'Ukraine veulent relancer la production de munitions', *Le Monde*, 20 February 2023. See also Commissioner Thierry Breton's remarks to the

'Vaccine Strategy'[31] was based on two pillars, one supporting the production of vaccines in the EU by means of advance purchase contracts concluded with producers via an emergency aid instrument; the other enabling the EU's regulatory framework to be adapted to the emergency, in order to 'accelerate the development, authorisation and availability of vaccines'.[32]

However, munitions are not vaccines and their purchase, unlike that of vaccines, cannot be financed by the EU budget.[33] This explains why the Commission was unable to manage the three components of the ammunition plan itself, and that the first two components were financed by the European Peace Facility, outside the EU budget. Furthermore, Regulation (EU) 2020/521, on which the EU Vaccine Strategy was based, had Article 122(1) TFEU as its legal basis. This provision reserves decision-making to the Council and excludes the European Parliament, 'if severe difficulties arise in the supply of certain products, notably in the area of energy'.[34] While the war in Ukraine is indeed the cause of such 'supply difficulties' for ammunition and missiles, the exclusion of the institution with European democratic legitimacy from a project as sensitive as ASAP would have been problematic. The fact that the ASAP funds were partly taken from EDIRPA, an instrument itself co-adopted by the European Parliament, would have added a further difficulty to this sidelining.

Contrary to what had been announced, the Commission did not proceed with ammunition as it had done with vaccines. It has more traditionally based its proposal for regulation on an 'Industry' pillar, namely Article 173(3) TFEU. However, since this provision expressly excludes any harmonisation of the laws and regulations of the Member States, the Commission's proposal also includes a regulatory pillar or 'Internal Market' pillar, based on Article 114 TFEU and comprising both Union -harmonising legislation 'to ensuring the functioning of the internal market, by avoiding shortages of relevant defence products in the Union' and 'measures aimed at establishing requirements to

European Parliament on 8 May 2023: 'As we have done with vaccines, only collective and resolute action to invest in the industrial base will enable us to achieve our objectives', https://www.europarl.europa.eu/doceo/document/CRE-9-2023-05-08-ITM-012_EN.html.

31 The legal basis for the 'EU Vaccine Strategy' was Council Regulation (EU) 2020/521 of 14 April 2020 activating the emergency support under Regulation (EU) 2016/369 and amending its provisions taking into the COVID-19 outbreak, [2020] *OJ* L117/3.

32 Communication from the Commission EU strategy for vaccines against COVID-19, COM(2020) 245 final, 17 June 2020.

33 Unless an interpretation of Article 41(2) TEU is adopted that is different from the current one, which has not been the case. See the commentary on this article by A. Potteau in this publication.

34 Under the terms of this provision, 'the Council, on a proposal from the Commission, may decide, in a spirit of solidarity between Member States, upon the measures appropriate to the economic situation, in particular if severe difficulties arise in the supply of certain products, notably in the area of energy'.

secure the timely and lasting availability of the relevant defence products'.[35] Indeed, when Member States take measures to preserve their stocks of missiles and ammunition, 'divergent national legislation, in particular regarding the certification of defence products, intra-EU transfer of products and related components as well as divergent implementation of Union law have proven to become bottlenecks for European relevant defence products supply chains and obstacles to interoperability'.[36] The measures proposed by the Commission were therefore aimed at monitoring the availability of missiles, ammunition and their components in the Member States, as has recently been planned for other products (outside the defence sector) in order to facilitate the Union's resilience in a context of crisis.[37]

The proposed ASAP regulation provided, first of all, in Article 13,[38] that the Commission could identify the companies in the entire supply chain of the defence products concerned. This 'mapping' would have enabled it to monitor[39] the production capacities of companies 'continuously' and to identify any problems in the production chain. The Commission could also have requested information from the Member States[40] and from companies established within them,[41] responses to these requests being obligatory.

Another provision of the proposed regulation, Article 14 entitled 'Priority Rated Orders', provided that the Commission could, at the request of Member States[42] wishing to acquire the defence products concerned and encountering 'serious difficulties' in doing so, due to shortages or serious risks of shortages, 'require an undertaking to accept, or prioritise an order for supply-critical defence products', provided that the supply difficulties in question were likely to compromise the security of the Union and its Member States. The Commission

---

35 See the explanatory memorandum to the proposed ASAP regulation cited above.

36 Ibid.

37 See e.g. Regulation (EU) 2023/1781 of the European Parliament and of the Council of 13 September 2023 establishing a framework of measures to strengthen the European semiconductor ecosystem and amending Regulation (EU) 2021/694 (Chips Act), [2023] *OJ* L2229/1, spec. Chapter IV, Crisis monitoring and response. In the field of defence, such measures have existed in the United States since the Defense Production Act of 1950.

38 Article entitled 'Identifying needs, mapping and capacity monitoring'.

39 Under the terms of Art. 13, as proposed.

40 Proposal for a Regulation, Art. 13(5).

41 Proposal for a Regulation, Art. 13(4).

42 Under Article 14(1) of the proposal, 'where at least three Member States which have entered or are considering entering into an agreement to commonly procure relevant defence products, or where a Member State which has procured or is considering to procure for the purpose of transferring required relevant defence products to Ukraine face severe difficulties either in the placing of the order or in the execution of the contract due to shortages or serious risks of shortages of supply-critical defence products and these difficulties may undermine the security of the Union and of its Member States, they may ask the Commission to require an undertaking to accept, or to prioritise an order of supply-critical defence products.

could have adopted an Implementing Act obliging the concerned undertakings 'to accept or perform the priority rated order, at a fair and reasonable price', in the event of a refusal to execute the order.[43] Failure to comply with this act could have led to the imposition of a penalty payment on the company,[44] after it had been given the opportunity to make its point of view known.[45] Overly ambitious and no doubt perceived as too intrusive in national ammunition production, the measures relating to mapping and priority orders did not survive the Council's scrutiny.

The proposal to abolish national authorisation usually required for transfers within the Union of two types of defence-related products[46] for the duration of the ASAP, met with a similar fate.

If the 'Industry' pillar has undergone fewer changes than the regulatory pillar, this is mainly due to the fact that, at the time of the drafting of the ASAP regulation by the Commission, its proposal for the EDIRPA had already been the subject of negotiations between the European Parliament and the Council for several months. The Commission was therefore aware of the reservations of the co-legislators, particularly those relating to the non-financing of defence products controlled by third countries or entities from third countries.[47] Thus, in the proposed ASAP regulation, as in the regulation that would subsequently be adopted, the exclusion from financial support by the ASAP fund for entities established in, or controlled by, a non-associated third country or an entity from a non-associated third country,[48] does not concern subcontractors. Given that the production of ammunition and missiles depends on components from third countries and that the objective is to increase the production of products for which subcontractors are already working, it was accepted at the proposal stage that ASAP could finance the production of ammunition even when, in the supply chain, subcontractors are controlled by third countries or entities from third countries. Imposing new collaborations exclusively with European subcontractors would certainly have benefited the EDTIB, but would not have made it possible to meet the urgent requirement, which was moreover assigned to a short-term instrument.

---

43 Proposal for a Regulation, Art. 14(3)(b).

44 Proposal for a Regulation, Art. 15.

45 Proposal for a Regulation, Art. 16.

46 Proposal for a Regulation, Art. 20. The products concerned are, on the one hand, 'ammunition and fuse setting devices, and specially designed components therefore, as listed in the third category of the Annex of the Directive 2009/43/EC (third category of the EU Military List – ML3) and, on the other hand, 'missiles and related equipment and accessories, and specially designed components therefore, as listed in the fourth category of the Annex of the Directive 2009/43/EC (fourth category of the EU Military List – ML4)'. See the commentary on this directive by E. Daniel and M. Kieffer in this publication.

47 On this point, we refer you to our commentary on the EDIRPA Regulation in this publication.

48 ASAP Regulation, Art. 10 (1 and 2). This criterion is also found in the EDIRPA Regulation.

However, as in its proposal for the EDIRPA regulation,[49] the Commission had proposed that the ASAP Regulation prohibit any restriction by a non-associated third country or an entity of a non-associated third country[50] on defence products and technologies financed by the European budget via this instrument.[51] Such restrictions undermine the autonomy of Member States in the use, maintenance and management of defence products, in this case in relation to ASAP, ammunition and missiles. Nevertheless, the co-legislators of the ASAP Regulation wished to be more permissive than the Commission.[52]

As regards not defence products but entities participating in an action supported under the ASAP, in its proposal for the ASAP Regulation, the Commission wished to exclude undertakings controlled by a non-associated third country or by an entity of a non-associated third country as it had previously done in its proposal for the EDIRPA Regulation. Although it provided for a derogation from this principle,[53] the Commission was thus in line with the objective of using the ASAP instrument to strengthen the European defence industry while limiting dependence on third countries and entities from those countries. Contrary to what was subsequently requested by the Council and is now set out in Article 10(1) of the Regulation, in its proposal the Commission had therefore not provided for European funds to be able to finance, via the ASAP, undertakings subject to the control of a non-associated third country or of an undertaking from such a country, which had simply been subject to screening within the meaning of Regulation (EU) 2019/452

49 Proposal for an EDIRPA Regulation Art. 8(9).

50 ASAP is open to 'associated countries', i.e. members of the European Free Trade Association who are members of the European Economic Area (EEA), in accordance with the conditions laid down in the Agreement on the European Economic Area; Article 3 of the Regulation.

51 Proposal for an ASAP Regulation, Article 10(3). The Commission has thus taken over the rules of the EDF concerning restrictions. The regulation establishing the EDF refers on several occasions to the fact that actions financed by the fund may not be subject to restrictions on defence products and technologies, whatever their nature, by third countries or entities; see Recital 8 of the Regulation, as well as Articles 9(4), 10(2), 20(3), and 23(2).

52 See Section II below.

53 According to Article 10(2) of the ASAP Regulation, an undertaking established in the EU but controlled by third parties (and which has not been screened within the meaning of Regulation 2019/452 on screening of foreign direct investment in the EU) may still participate in an action supported by ASAP 'if guarantees, approved by the Member State or the associated country in which the undertaking is established are made available to the Commission in accordance with national procedures'. The guarantees in question must, in particular, make it possible to ensure that the participation of the undertaking concerned is not contrary either to the interests of the Union and its Member States in the field of security and defence as defined in the framework of the CFSP or to the objectives set out in the ASAP Regulation. In particular, they certify that, for the purposes of an action, measures are in place to ensure that, on the one hand, the recipient is able to carry out the action without restrictions concerning its infrastructure and facilities and, on the other hand, a non-associated third country or an undertaking of such a third country cannot have access to sensitive or classified information relating to the action. Art. 9(6) and (7) of the EDIRPA Regulation includes this condition.

on the screening of foreign direct investment into the Union,[54] and, where necessary, mitigating measures. The automaticity of this possibility offered by the legislator (since it is not a derogation) allows Member States to acquire missiles and ammunition from entities controlled by third parties. While it is easy to understand the value of this openness in enabling Member States to obtain emergency supplies, it is also easy to see the value of the Commission's more restrictive approach for European industry and for the Union's strategic autonomy. At the end of the trialogue, the regulation finally adopted is the result of compromise and reconciliation between the two objectives of urgently producing more missiles and ammunition on the one hand, and strengthening the EDTIB on the other.

II. A CONCILIATORY SETTLEMENT

The regulatory pillar of the proposed ASAP Regulation presented by the European Commission is the main victim of the conciliation that had to take place in the trialogue and more specifically in the negotiations with and within the Council. Opposition to the Regulation of the internal market reflected the desire of Member States - led by France and Germany - to retain control over production methods, supplies, transfers of components essential to the production of ammunition, and the destination of ammunition produced.

The mapping proposed by the Commission fizzled out.[55] Similarly, the Council rejected the Commission's proposal on priority orders, even though it provided that such orders could not be imposed without the agreement of the Member State in which the company concerned was established.[56] Generally speaking, the conciliation aimed to allow Member States to retain more power over the production of ammunition than the Commission's proposal allowed, even at the risk of jeopardising the objectives announced in the ammunition plan.[57]

Stripped of its substance, the regulatory pillar, as it appears in the adopted regulation, is reduced to two articles. The first aims to speed up the procedure for granting authorisations by Member States in order to guarantee the

54 Regulation (EU) 2019/452 of the European Parliament and of the Council of 19 March 2019 establishing a framework for the screening of foreign direct investments into the Union, [2019] *OJ* L791/1. See the commentary on this regulation by S. Robert in this publication.

55 See Section I above.

56 Proposal for a regulation, Art. 14(2).

57 See also O. Jehin, 'Le fonds ASAP pour les munitions dépouillé de sa substance. France, Allemagne, Pologne à l'assaut de la proposition Breton', *Blog B2*, 9 June 2023, and, by the same author, 'ASAP, l'instrument adopté en urgence pour accroître la production de munitions', *Blog B2*, 25 July 2023.

availability and timely supply of missiles and ammunition.[58] The second aims to facilitate joint procurement of ammunition and missiles by at least two Member States where the extreme urgency resulting from the war in Ukraine prevents recourse to one of the procedures provided for in Directive 2009/81/EC on public procurement in the field of defence.[59] Where appropriate, the Directive provides for derogations to allow existing framework agreements to be opened directly – without reopening competition – to states that were not originally party to the agreement,[60] and to permit substantial amendments to the quantities specified in the original contract.[61]

As for the industry pillar to which €500 million are dedicated, it is planned that a maximum amount of €50 million can be used as a 'blending operation' within the framework of a so-called 'Ramp-up Fund' provided for in the Regulation.[62] This fund, which was supposed to be managed indirectly, was designed to overcome the difficulties encountered in obtaining loans in the defence sector by offering loan solutions. Its objective was to unlock public and private investment to 'support the increase of manufacturing capacities in the ammunition and missiles sector by providing opportunities for increased availability of funds to companies across the value chains'.[63] However, as later stated in the Report on the implementation of ASAP Regulation, 'the Commission was not able to identify a fully suitable option to implement such a Fund in line with the ASAP objectives and its urgent timeline. Indeed, it would have implied indirect management by an entrusted implementing partner under InvestEU able to operate in the entire Union, such as the European Investment Fund and European Investment Bank, but their exclusion policies on ammunition unfortunately preclude them as potential candidates. In addition, the Ramp-up Fund appeared unattractive for implementing partners due to the limited budget (very high administrative burden) and narrow scope of the product (limited ecosystem of ammunition producers and suppliers)'.[64]

Although the role of the European Investment Bank (EIB) is to finance European projects, its support for the European defence industry 'beyond its

---

58 Art. 13 of the ASAP Regulation.

59 Directive 2009/81/EC of the European Parliament and of the Council of 13 July 2009 on the coordination of procedures for the award of certain works contracts, supply contracts and service contracts by contracting authorities or entities in the fields of defence and security, and amending Directives 2004/17/EC and 2004/18/EC, [2009] *OJ* L216/76. See the commentary on this directive by S. Rodrigues in this publication.

60 Art. 14(2) of the ASAP Regulation.

61 Art. 14(3) of the ASAP Regulation.

62 Art. 5 (2) of the ASAP Regulation.

63 Recital 37 of the ASAP Regulation.

64 Report from the Commission to the European Parliament and the Council on the implementation of Regulation (EU) 2023/1525 of the European Parliament and of the Council of 20 July 2023 on supporting ammunition production (ASAP), 8 July 2024, COM(2024) 296 final, p. 11.

current dual-use support' remained controversial,[65] as it was not possible to include the EIB in the Regulation due to disagreements between the Member States:[66] it is simply mentioned – conditionally – in the recitals of the Regulation. It is therefore likely that the provisions relating to the Ramp-up Fund and its blending mechanism were included in the Regulation with a view to blending the funds of ASAP funds with those of the national investment banks.

The remaining €450 million in funds (*at minimum*) are managed directly.[67] Drawn from the European budget, these funds can be used to finance, up to 35% of the cost of increasing or modernising ammunition and missile production capacity, via the ASAP instrument. This amount may reach 40% for the production capacities of the components of these defence products and the raw materials used in their manufacture, provided that these components are entirely intended for the production of the defence products concerned.[68] A funding rate increased by a further 10 percentage points may be granted to an action if it meets certain specific criteria, namely if it contributes to the creation of new cross-border cooperation between entities established in Member States or associated countries; if the applicants give priority to orders resulting from the joint acquisition of the defence products concerned by at least three Member States or associated countries, or to those resulting from the acquisition of ammunition and/or missiles by at least one Member State with a view to their transfer to Ukraine; if the funding benefits an SME or, in the case of a consortium, a majority of SMEs.[69] In addition, full cost coverage is provided for activities related to improving access to finance for economic operators producing or making available ammunition and missiles.[70]

Six types of action are eligible for ASAP financial support, ranging from the optimisation of existing production capacity to the training, retraining or professional development of personnel in connection with the activities in question, including the establishment of cross-border industrial partnerships or the creation and provision of manufacturing capacity reserved for ammunition and missiles. Although they are varied in nature, the actions eligible for ASAP funding are exclusively linked to the production capacities for ammunition and missiles, including their components and the corresponding raw materials.[71] All of them must make it possible to remedy 'identified bottlenecks in production

---

65 See the commentary on Articles 308 and 309 TFEU by S. Rodrigues in this publication.

66 In a declaration accompanying the regulation, Austria, Ireland, Luxembourg and Malta indicated that they were not in favour of 'the EIB increasing its support beyond the support it currently provides for dual use'. See the declarations of the Member States, https://data.consilium.europa.eu/doc/document/ST-11787-2023-ADD-2-REV-1/fr/pdf.

67 ASAP Regulation, Art. 7.

68 ASAP Regulation, Art. 9(1).

69 These criteria are listed in Article 9(2) of the ASAP Regulation.

70 ASAP Regulation, Art. 9(2), last paragraph.

71 The six types of eligible actions are listed in Article 8(3) of the Regulation.

capacities and supply chains with a view to securing and accelerating the production of relevant defence products in order to ensure their effective supply and timely availability'.[72]

Actions prohibited by applicable international law, those aimed at the acquisition of autonomous lethal weapons without the possibility of significant human control over selection and engagement decisions during strikes targeting human beings,[73] and those already fully funded by other public or private sources are ineligible for funding under the instrument.

With regard to the restrictions that may be imposed by a non-associated third country or an undertaking from a non-associated third country[74] on ASAP-funded ammunition, the co-legislators have reduced the scope of the prohibitions the Commission had proposed[75] to restrictions on the use of defence products only.[76] They have also introduced a rather ambiguous formula concerning export restrictions. The latter are not prohibited by the Regulation, but Article 10(6) of the Regulation states that the beneficiary of ASAP support 'shall make every effort to ensure that the action funded under the Instrument will allow for the delivery of outputs to Ukraine'. The wording is the result of lively discussions within the Council on whether or not to authorise restrictions on the export of ammunition and missiles produced using components from third countries – which the Commission was not in favour of – even though the objective and raison d'être of ASAP is precisely to export this type of defence product to Ukraine.

Finally, the ASAP Regulation lays down the criteria for allocating the funds, which the Commission, assisted by a committee,[77] applied under the work programme adopted on 18 October 2023.[78]

---

72 ASAP Regulation, Art. 8(2).

73 ASAP Regulation, Article 8(4). These criteria are identical to those in the EDIRPA Regulation.

74 ASAP is open to 'associated countries', i.e. members of the European Free Trade Association who are members of the European Economic Area (EEA), in accordance with the conditions laid down in the Agreement on the European Economic Area; Article 3 of the Regulation.

75 See Section I above.

76 Article 10(6) of the ASAP Regulation states that 'the instrument shall not financially support the ramp-up of production capacities for relevant defence products that are subject to a restriction by a non-associated third country or a non-associated third country entity that limits Member States' *ability to use them*'. Emphasis added.

77 ASAP Regulation, Art. 16.

78 In accordance with Article 11 of the ASAP Regulation, Article 11. See https://ec.europa.eu/commission/presscorner/detail/fr/ip_23_5105.

III. A HASTY IMPLEMENTATION

As with the drafting of the regulation, the implementation of the ASAP instrument was carried out as quickly as circumstances dictated. The Commission set out on the work programme provided for in the Regulation as soon as it was adopted, in July 2023. This programme, which lays out 'the funding priorities taking into account the work of the Defence Joint Procurement Task Force',[79] was adopted by the Commission by means of an implementing act,[80] on 18 October 2023.[81] It is based on five types of call for projects (explosives, powders, shells, missiles, certification and reconditioning tests for artillery ammunition), each with an indicative budget (from €190 million for explosives to €4.35 million for certification and reconditioning tests).

In order to respond to the urgency, tighter deadlines than usual were imposed,[82] not only for the submission of project proposals by industry,[83] but also for the evaluation by the Commission of the proposals submitted. The Commission was therefore able to present the thirty-one projects selected from the five themes on 15 March 2024.[84] As a result of this presentation, the budget of €513 million, allocated by the European Union and Norway, made it possible to mobilise a total of €1.4 billion in investments, thanks to the expected co-financing from industry, which are used to tackle bottlenecks and increase ammunition and missile production capacity in Europe.[85]

The Commission estimated that 'thanks to the measures already taken, European annual production capacity for 155 mm shells had already reached 1 million shells per year by January 2024'.[86] In June 2024, then Commissioner Thierry Breton estimated that production capacity would reach 1.7 million 155 mm shells in Europe by the end of 2024, and 2.5 million by 'the turn of the year 2025', a level of production that he considered 'comparable' to Russia's production of this type of ammunition.[87]

79 ASAP Regulation, Art. 12(2).

80 ASAP Regulation, Art. 12(3).

81 Commission implementing Decision of 18 October 2023, on the financing of the instrument on supporting ammunition production (asap) established by Regulation (eu) 2023/1525 of the european parliament and of the council and the adoption of the work programme for 2023–2025, C(2023) 7320 final, 18 October 2023.

82 For example, the deadlines for calls for projects under the European Defence Fund.

83 The deadline for submission of proposals was set to 13 December 2023 17.00 CET.

84 see the Commission press release: 'Commission allocates €500 million to ramp up ammunition production, out of a total of €2 billion to strengthen the EU defence industry', 15 March 2024, https://ec.europa.eu/commission/presscorner/detail/en/ip_24_1495 a list of these projects is available at https://defence-industry-space.ec.europa.eu/document/download/b694b109-fa2c-493e-bf1e-87768ae6469e_en?filename=asap%20factsheet.pdf.

85 And not just within the EU, since Norway is a major beneficiary of ASAP funds.

86 Press release of 15 March 2024, cited above.

87 Dialogue with Thierry Breton on European geopolitics, Dialogue: European Geopolitics, Paris Air Forum Edition 2024, 17 June 2024.

While it is difficult to know exactly what the figures are, it is important to remember that unlike the results of Strands 1 (supply of ammunition) and 2 (joint acquisition of ammunition) of the ammunition plan, the results of Strand 3 are not immediate and require more time, since the aim is not simply to supply Ukraine from existing stocks or to jointly purchase products already available but to produce them.

The evaluation report on the implementation of ASAP and its results, which was presented by the Commission on 8 July 2024,[88] does not give production figures, but considers that the thirty-one projects selected for funding under ASAP provide a good basis for achieving the objectives and, more importantly, that they substantially increase munitions production capacity, as well as their respective supply chains. In the report, the Commission concludes that the implementation of ASAP has demonstrated the effectiveness of an emergency instrument in the defence industry, as well as the possibility of setting up calls for projects for specific industrial needs in compliance with the comitology process. Despite the constraints – notably those linked to the timetable – and over and above the recommendations made, the report concludes with the observation that the ASAP programme 'is a very good demonstration of the Commission's ability to act urgently and in full compliance with the legal framework'.

Nevertheless, as the report also notes, some proposals which scored above the threshold could not be financed due to the limited size of the available budget. Supporting these proposals would require an increase in the ASAP allocation of €240 million. According to the report, these projects could have added around 40% of powder production, more than 100% of shell and shell body production, and a substantial additional amount of production capacity for various missile systems.

Figures such as these highlight the very real consequences of funding that fall far short of what is needed to achieve the stated objectives.

Furthermore, as already indicated, the report states that the Ramp-up Fund provided for in Article 15 of the ASAP Regulation could not be set up for the reasons mentioned above.

On 22 April 2025, in order to implement the ReArm Europe Plan, the Commission proposed a new Regulation[89] amending several funding

[88] Report from the Commission to the European Parliament and the Council on the implementation of Regulation (EU) 2023/1525 of the European Parliament and of the Council of 20 July 2023 on supporting ammunition production (ASAP), 8 July 2024, COM(2024) 296 final

[89] Proposal for a Regulation of the European Parliament and of the Council amending Regulations (EU) 2021/694, (EU) 2021/695, (EU) 2021/697, (EU) 2021/1153, (EU) 2023/1525 and 2024/795, as regards incentivising defence-related investments in the EU budget to implement the ReArm Europe Plan, COM/2025/188 final.

programmes[90] including ASAP. On 18 December 2025, the Council formally adopted the regulation incentivising defence-related investments in the EU budget to implement the ReArm Europe Plan.[91] The Regulation introduces additional flexibility in using EU Funding under Cohesion Policy to bolster the European defence industry. It includes in particular a clause which allows Member States to transfer resources allocated to them under cohesion policy funds to these two programmes, on a voluntary basis. Furthermore, if adopted, the ASAP's duration would be extended until 31 December 2026.

After this date, another programme has to replace ASAP as well as EDIRPA. This is what the co-legislators committed to in July 2023, when the ASAP Regulation was adopted. In a joint statement, the Council and the European Parliament pointed out that the ASAP Regulation provides an immediate response to the urgent need to ramp up production in the context of the challenges posed by the war in Ukraine, by putting in place a temporary instrument to facilitate industrial investment. They then invited the Commission to present 'as soon as possible any further initiatives necessary to strengthen the EDTIB, including adequate financing, for instance in the context of the European Defence Investment Programme, as well as a legal framework aimed at ensuring security of supply and supporting ammunition production'.[92] This is what has been done with the regulation for a European Defence Industry Programme (EDIP).[93] This regulation, which covers a wider field than just ammunition and missiles, is consistent with ASAP's rationale for intervention to support the European defence industry by providing financial backing for investment in the sector's production capacity.

---

90 The Digital Europe Programme (DEP), Horizon Europe, European Defence Fund (EDF), Connecting Europe Facility, Strategic Technologies for Europe Platform (STEP) and ASAP.

91 https://www.consilium.europa.eu/en/press/press-releases/2025/12/18/council-adopts-measures-to-incentivise-and-simplify-defence-investments-in-the-eu/?utm_source=chatgpt.com.

92 Joint statement of the European Parliament and of the Council, 17 July 2023, (2023/C 260/01), [2023] *OJ* C260/1.

93 Regulation (EU) 2025/2643 of the European Parliament and of the Council of 16 December 2025 establishing the European Defence Industry Programme and a framework of measures to ensure the timely availability and supply of defence products ('EDIP Regulation'), [2025] *OJ* L2025/2643, see the commentary by E. Simon in this publication.

THE EDIRPA REGULATION

Regulation (EU) 2023/2418 of the European Parliament and of the Council of 18 October 2023 on establishing an instrument for the reinforcement of the European defence industry through common procurement (EDIRPA)[1]

Elsa BERNARD
Professor of Public Law at the University of Lille
Jean Monnet Chair
Member of the Rights and Perspectives of Law Research Centre (CRDP, ULR 4487)

Along with the ASAP,[2] the European defence industry reinforcement through common procurement act, known as EDIRPA, is one of the two temporary instruments established by regulations of the European Parliament and of the Council in 2023 to adapt the EU's Defence Technological and Industrial Base (EDTIB) to support a high-intensity conflict and enable it to 'address in particular the most urgent and critical defence product needs'.[3] EDIRPA, with a budget of EUR 300 million, allows for the partial reimbursement from the European Union (EU or Union) budget to Member States when the joint procurement of defence products involves a consortium of at least three Member States. It stems from the awareness, in the aftermath of Russia's invasion of Ukraine,[4] of the defence industrial and capability gaps in the EU

1 Regulation (EU) 2023/2418 of the European Parliament and of the Council of 18 October 2023 on establishing an instrument for the reinforcement of the European defence industry through common procurement (EDIRPA), [2023] OJ L2023/2418.

2 See the commentary on Regulation (EU) 2023/1525 of the European Parliament and of the Council of 20 July 2023 on support to ammunition production (ASAP) by E. BERNARD in this publication.

3 Article 3(2) of the Regulation. For an analysis of the ASAP and EDIRPA instruments, see E. BERNARD, 'La communautarisation de la défense européenne dans le contexte de la guerre en Ukraine', *Revue Trimestrielle de Droit Européen (RTDE)*, 2023/4, pp. 325–350.

4 Defence capabilities refer to military assets, including the necessary material, equipment and technology. They do not include defence operations or other elements necessary to manage defence capabilities such as training, personnel and logistics. See the Communication from the Commission to the European Parliament, the European Council, the Council, the European Economic and Social Committee and the Committee of the Regions. European Defence Action Plan, COM(2016) 950 final, fn. 24.

and the detrimental effects of fragmented defence procurement. Meeting in Versailles on 10 and 11 March 2022, approximately two weeks after the start of the war in Ukraine, the Heads of State or Government of the European Union decided, among other things, to intensify cooperation between them through joint defence projects.[5] To this end, they asked the Commission, in coordination with the European Defence Agency, to analyse defence investment gaps, presented to them on 18 May 2022, in a joint communication from the Commission and the High Representative of the Union for Foreign Affairs and Security Policy ('the High Representative').[6]

While the Communication acknowledges announcements on increases in Member States' defence budgets,[7] it also mentions the concern that the EU may repeat 'past mistakes that led to inefficiencies, duplications and dependencies'.[8] Indeed, 'based on the historical record, there is [...] a risk that Member States opt for national solutions, because of industrial and security of supply considerations, or, when not available privilege "off-the shelf" non-EU solutions given the sense of urgency, at the expense of possible EU solutions that may have equivalent lead times'.[9] Addressing the capability and industrial gaps in the Member States means not only planning and developing capabilities, but also strengthening cooperation between them in order to reduce the fragmentation of the European defence market: i.e. to quote the usual slogan of the European Commission, 'to invest more, better, together and European'.[10]

This call for a common defence industry in the EU, however, does not date from the war in Ukraine. For several years, European leaders have been aware, on the one hand, that European defence spending 'has historically resulted in lower efficiency and output in comparison with that of our allies and of our competitors'[11] and, on the other hand, that the lack of cooperation in this area costs tens of billions of Euros per year.[12]

---

5 Informal meeting of Heads of State or Government, Versailles Declaration, 10–11 March 2022.

6 Joint Communication to the European Parliament, the European Council, the Council, the European Economic and Social Committee and the Committee of the Regions on the Defence Investment Gaps Analysis and the Way Forward, JOIN(2022) 24 final, 18 May 2022.

7 See NATO press release of 7 July 2023, Defence spending of NATO countries (2014–2023).

8 Joint Communication, 2022, cited above.

9 Ibid.

10 These terms are regularly reflected in the Commission's European defence documents. See, most recently, the European Defence Industrial Strategy, JOIN(2024) 10 final, of 5 March 2024.

11 Joint Communication, 2022, cited above.

12 'Between EUR 25 and 100 billion per year, depending on the areas concerned', said then President of the European Commission Jean-Claude Juncker, 'State of the Union Address 2016: Towards a better Europe – a Europe that protects, empowers and defends', 14 September 2016.

To remedy this, in 2007 Member States in the European Defence Agency already set the target of jointly purchasing 35% of their total capital expenditure. Although this target was renewed in 2017 in the framework of Permanent Structured Cooperation[13] and in line with the increase in European defence spending, in 2020 the joint purchase of equipment still represented only 11% of the total purchase of equipment (22% in 2023), while the rest was spent on a national basis.

As the war in Ukraine has dramatically increased the need to strengthen Member States' defence capabilities and consolidate the EDTIB, the European Council[14] called on the Commission to propose a regulation establishing a short-term instrument to incentivise Member States to jointly procure defence products through the EU budget.[15] To this end, a Task Force[16] established by the Commission and the High Representative[17] engaged in a dialogue with Member States and the defence industry to assess short-term needs, coordinate them and support joint procurement.

By publishing its proposal for a regulation on 19 July 2022[18] – without a prior impact assessment due to the urgency[19] – the Commission announced, through then Commissioner Thierry Breton, that the text should be the subject of swift negotiations between the European Parliament and the Council with a view to being implemented by the end of 2022. However, the Regulation was finally adopted only on 18 October 2023, due to tensions in the European Parliament between the ITRE committee (Industry) and SEDE (Defence Security) then subcommittee. The examination of the proposal for a regulation by the assembly was thus extended until the end of April 2023, when negotiations with the Council could finally begin. The regulation was therefore only adopted on 18 October 2023, which is why the budget originally intended to cover the years 2022 to 2024 now applies to the period from the entry into

---

13 See Q. Loïez's commentary on Article 46 TEU in this publication.

14 See the conclusions of the European Council of 30–31 May 2022.

15 According to Article 2 of the Regulation, 'defence products' are products falling within the scope of Article 2 of Directive 2009/81/EC, including combat medical equipment, that is to say, military equipment and sensitive equipment, including spare parts, components, and/or sub-assemblies thereof, contracts awarded in fields which have as their object either works, supplies and services directly related to such equipment, works and services intended for specifically military purposes, or sensitive works and services.

16 Task Force on Defence Joint Procurement.

17 The High Representative chairs the European Defence Agency, which was established in 2004 to support cooperative European defence projects. See A.-H. Bertana's commentary on Article 45 TEU in this publication.

18 Proposal for a Regulation of the European Parliament and of the Council on establishing the European Defence Industry Reinforcement through Common Procurement Act, COM(2022) 349 final, 19 July 2022.

19 This is despite the Swedish government's criticism, accessed on 8 May 2024, www.europarl.europa.eu/RegData/etudes/BRIE/2023/739294/EPRS_BRI (2023) 739294-EN.pdf

force of the text until 31 December 2025,[20] and has been reduced due to the transfer of part of the funds to ASAP, the creation of which was considered during the overly lengthy negotiations on EDIRPA.[21]

In substance, EDIRPA aims, as has been said, to encourage *cooperation* between Member States *in defence procurement*. However, the negotiations on the Regulation have highlighted the tension between two potentially contradictory objectives.

The first objective is to strengthen the European Defence Technological and Industrial Base (EDTIB), encouraging Member States to buy not only 'together' but also 'European'. Indeed, the acquisition of defence products outside the EU creates dependencies on countries whose positions and interests in conflicts may differ from those of European states. In addition, such products purchased from third parties may be subject to restrictions, whether on their use, their maintenance, their modification or their export, which undermines the strategic autonomy of the European Union.

The second objective is to replenish, as a matter of urgency, national stockpiles of equipment and weapons, which may involve sourcing from third countries and companies controlled by those countries, provided that they can supply the defence products sought.

Logically given its role in the legal order of the European Union, the Commission has, in its proposal for a Regulation, prioritised the first objective, namely the strengthening of European industry through the EDIRPA instrument. However, its desire to protect the autonomy of the Union did not withstand the wish of the Member States to be able to equip themselves urgently by obtaining, if necessary, products already available on the market, even if they were not European, as evidenced by the content of the EDIRPA Regulation as adopted. Therefore, while the EDIRPA undeniably supports common defence procurement (Section I), it is not as focused on strengthening the EDTIB as proposed by the European Commission (Section II). A few months after its implementation began, the programme appears capable of encouraging joint purchases, but tangible results have yet to materialise (Section III).

I. A WELCOME SUPPORT FOR COMMON DEFENCE PROCUREMENT

Originally expected to have a budget of EUR 500 million, drawn from the Multiannual Financial Framework 2021-2027, EDIRPA saw its budget reduced to EUR 300 million to support the ASAP, envisaged almost seven months after

20 Art.1of the EDIRPA Regulation.
21 See below.

the publication of the EDIRPA proposal by the Commission.[22] However, this fund allows the European Union to provide financial support to Member States' defence joint procurement until the end of 2025 from the Union's budget[23] – and not from the Member States, as is the case of the European Peace Facility, for example.

The legal basis for the Regulation is Article 173(3) TFEU, which authorises the European Parliament and the Council to decide on specific measures to support action in the Member States to achieve the objectives referred to in Article 173(1), namely, in particular, to "speeding up the adjustment of industry to structural changes". In this case, the structural change in the markets justifying the establishment of EDIRPA stems from Russia's invasion of Ukraine, which requires, as stated in the Regulation, accelerating the strengthening of the EDTIB.[24]

In order to be eligible for financial support from EDIRPA, common procurement of defence products must fulfil certain conditions.

Firstly, they must be made by EU Member States (or their public entities)[25] as well as associated third countries that apply to participate in the Programme.[26] Indeed, EDIRPA beneficiaries cannot be 'legal entities', as is the case under the European Defence Fund.

Secondly, in order to be eligible for funding, joint procurement actions must, be carried out by a consortium of at least three Member States, irrespective of whether the cooperation between them is new or whether it is a continuation of an already existing cooperation.[27] Thus, funding may in particular benefit retroactively an action undertaken before the date of the request for funds for the action in question, provided, however, that it did not start before the beginning of the war in Ukraine on 24 February 2022 and was not completed before the signature of the grant agreement.[28] Acquisitions must also address the most urgent and critical defence product needs.[29] Those needs prohibited by international law or those aiming at the acquisition of lethal autonomous weapons without the possibility of meaningful human control over selection

---

22 Of the initial budget, EUR 240 million were redirected, after negotiation, by the European Commission to ASAP. During the final negotiations, EUR 40 million were finally added to reach a total budget for EDIRPA of EUR 300 million.

23 See the commentaries by C. Schneider and A. Potteau, in this publication.

24 See Recital 10 of the Regulation.

25 Art. 10 of the Regulation.

26 For Iceland, Liechtenstein and Norway, the instrument is 'open to the participation of Member States and members of the European Free Trade Association which are members of the European Economic Area', Article 5 of the Regulation.

27 Art. 8(1)(C) of the Regulation. In the case of existing cooperation, it must be extended to at least one new Member State or associated country (Art. 8 (1)(b)).

28 Art. 6(3).

29 Art. 8(1)(a).

and engagement decisions in strikes against human beings are not eligible for funding from the EDIRPA programme.[30]

Once the common procurement is eligible for funding by EDIRPA, the amount of the financial contribution awarded shall be established, taking into account the collaborative nature of the common procurement and the need to create the necessary incentive effect to induce cooperation.[31] This amount is therefore not automatically proportional to the cost of acquisition. On the contrary, it depends on factors such as the complexity of the common public market,[32] the characteristics of the cooperation and its effects in terms of the interoperability of acquisitions or long-term investment for industry,[33] or the number of participating Member States and associated countries.[34] In addition, the contribution of EDIRPA to each action may not exceed either 15% of the total financial envelope of EDIRPA (i.e. EUR 45 million) or 15% of the estimated value of the common procurement.[35]

An agent appointed by the Member States of the consortium shall be responsible for awarding contracts and concluding, on their behalf, the contract with the contractors.[36] The latter, like subcontractors involved in common procurement, must fulfil certain criteria. In order to ensure that acquisitions primarily benefit the European defence industry, and in accordance with what is implied by the legal basis of the Regulation (Article 173(3) TFEU, cited above), these contractors must be established and have their management structures in the Union or in an associated country and must not be subject to control by a non-associated third country or by a non-associated third country entity.[37]

---

30 Art. 8(2)(a) and (b).

31 Art. 6(2).

32 Art. 7(2)(a).

33 Art. 7(2)(b).

34 Or the inclusion of additional Member States and associated countries in existing cooperation, Art. 7(2)(c).

35 Art. 7(3). By way of derogation, however, that contribution may amount to up to 20 % of the total financial envelope of EDIRPA and up to 20 % of the estimated value of the common procurement in two cases: where Ukraine or Moldova is one of the beneficiaries of additional quantities under the procurement action, and where at least 15% of the estimated value of the common market is awarded to small or medium-sized enterprises, as contractors or subcontractors (Art. 7(4)(a) and (b)).

36 Article 9(1) specifies that the Regulation is without prejudice to the rules on the coordination of procedures for the award of certain works contracts, supply contracts and service contracts by contracting authorities or entities in the fields of defence and security, as laid down in particular in Directive 2009/81/EC, cited above.

37 The definition of 'control' given in Article 2.2 of the Regulation refers to the control of a contractor or subcontractor. It is defined as the ability to exercise decisive influence over a contractor or subcontractor, directly or indirectly through one or more intermediate legal entities.

Furthermore, while defence products (and their components) that are subject to common procurement can be purchased from non-associated third countries (or entities from such countries), they should not be restricted to use by those countries or entities, which would limit the ability of Member States to use them.[38] Moreover, the cost of components originating in the Union or associated countries must not be less than 65% of the estimated value of the final product. This should be a difficult condition to implement and control as it requires a thorough knowledge of the goods concerned and the ability to trace the origin of often complex defence systems.[39] Customs rules on the origin of products will be mobilised here.

Finally, none of its components 'shall come from non-associated third countries which contravene the security and defence interests of the Union and its Member States or which do not respect good neighbourly relations'.[40]

However, derogations from the rules on contractors, subcontractors and components of defence products are provided for in the Regulation, which, as will be seen, reduces EDIRPA's support for the EDTIB.[41]

It is for the Commission, assisted by a committee,[42] to assess the quality of the projects submitted to it for funding by EDIRPA. To this end, Article 11 of the Regulation lays down the criteria for the awarding of grants, including the number of States participating in the common market (Article 11(1)(a)), the estimated value of the contract (Article 11(1)(b)), a demonstration that the acquisition contributes to the recovery of stocks and the strengthening of the EDTIB, so that it can meet in particular the most urgent and critical needs for defence products (Article 11(1) (c)) and a demonstration of the contribution of the action to the recovery of stocks (Article 11(1)(d)).[43]

Undoubtedly, the Regulation is designed to support Member States' common procurement in the defence sector from the EU budget. However, it does not guarantee that such acquisitions benefit exclusively the European defence industry and thus strengthen the EDTIB.

The purpose of the provision which forms the legal basis of the Regulation, namely Article 173(3) TFEU, is 'that the conditions necessary for the competitiveness of the Union's industry exist'.[44] Moreover, the Joint Communication of the Commission and the High Representative that preceded the EDIRPA proposal states that measures enabling joint action on defence investment and acquisition 'are critical to ensure that Europe can field stronger

---

38 Art. 9(10).
39 They are high-tech products, involving a large number of components.
40 Art. 9(12).
41 Arts. 9(5), 9(6) and 9(11) of the Rules of Procedure. See Section II below.
42 Art. 16.
43 Art. 11(1)(C).
44 Art. 173(1) TFEU.

and more interoperable defence capabilities while enhancing the European defence industrial and technological base (EDTIB), which are both essential for Europe's long-term security and strategic autonomy'.[45] The EDIRPA project therefore involved financing acquisitions from the European defence industry and not from the defence industry of third countries. Furthermore, the search for strategic autonomy means not only that contractors and subcontractors involved in programmes financed by the EU budget are not controlled by non-associated third countries or by one of their entities, but also that restrictions are imposed by those same countries or entities on the products and technologies resulting from those programmes. Vigilance is therefore required with regard to the legal entities (contractors and subcontractors) with which Member States conclude agreements, in particular if, although established in the Union, those entities are controlled by a non-associated third country or by an entity from one of those countries. Vigilance is also required with regard to defence products and technologies acquired where they may be subject to restrictions preventing European States that have jointly purchased them from using them freely, if they come wholly or partly from non-associated third countries or entities from such countries.

The proposal for a regulation presented by the European Commission in July 2022 demonstrates this dual vigilance and the desire to pursue the objective of strengthening the European defence industry, above all with the EDIRPA instrument. This is not surprising given the legal basis of the act and since the Commission, which is excluded from the Common Security and Defence Policy (CSDP), has competence in the field of industry. It is clear from reading its proposal that the European defence industry should not be sacrificed to the backdrop of the replenishment of stocks, as a matter of urgency.

Thus, the Commission's proposal first prohibits contractors and subcontractors involved in the common procurement – and necessarily established in the Union – from being subject to control by a non-associated third country or by an entity from such a country.[46] Contrary to what ultimately prevails in the Regulation, the Commission proposal does not open participation in the acquisition financed by the EDIRPA Fund to contractors and subcontractors, subject to control by third parties but subject to a screening within the meaning of Regulation 2019/452 on the screening of foreign direct investments into the Union and, where appropriate, to 'mitigating measures'

45 Communication on Defence Investment Gaps Analysis and the Way Forward, 18 May 2022.

46 Art. 8(5) of the proposal for a Regulation on EDIRPA. This reflects the rules of the European Defence Fund relating to the entities from which Member States can jointly purchase. A derogation is provided for in the proposed EDIRPA Regulation (Article 8(5)) but is conditional on the contractor or subcontractor in question providing guarantees approved by the Member State or associated third country in which the contractor is established.

taking into account the objectives of each of its Regulations.[47] On the contrary, the co-legislators allow Member States to procure defence products from a wide range of entities controlled by third parties, which may be able to meet the needs faster than European entities. The objective of the replenishment of stocks therefore prevails here, for the European Parliament and the Council, over that of strengthening the EDTIB and the independence of the Union.

Secondly, in its proposal for the EDIRPA Regulation – and indeed in its proposal for the ASAP Regulation[48] – the Commission has prohibited any restrictions, by entities or third countries, on products and technologies financed by the fund.[49] Such a ban, which also prevails in the context of the European Defence Fund,[50] avoids financing from the European budget of defence products under the control of third States,[51] which of course contributes to the EU's independence in security and defence. Again, the co-legislators did not wish to exercise the same vigilance as the Commission. They limited themselves to restrictions on the use of defence products, which suggests on the contrary that other restrictions, including export restrictions, are permissible.[52] Moreover, even this prohibition of restrictions on use is subject to a derogation for 'urgent and critical' defence products, 'taking into account the current situation and the urgency to procure with the support of the Instrument'.[53] The co-legislators – and in particular the Member States meeting in the Council – have therefore given priority to the possibility of acquiring weapons that could be quickly exported to a country at war, including non-European armaments on which they do not have full autonomy. Such an approach raises the question of the relevance of the legal basis of the Regulation, which, it should be recalled, refers to 'the competitiveness of *the Union* industry'.

---

47 Art. 9(5) of the EDIRPA Regulation, which refers to Regulation (EU) 2019/452 of the European Parliament and of the Council of 19 March 2019 establishing a framework for the screening of foreign direct investments into the Union, [2019] *OJ* L79/1.

48 See the commentary on this Regulation by E. Bernard in this publication.

49 Art. 8(9) of the proposal for a Regulation on EDIRPA.

50 See Recital 8 of the Regulation establishing the European Defence Fund, as well as Articles 9(4), 10(2), 20(3) and 23(2), cited above.

51 Like the so-called 'ITAR products', the name of the ITAR standard, which allows the United States to monitor the sensitive defence equipment that it exports (including its re-export).

52 Under Article 9(10) of the Regulation, 'common procurement procedures and contracts shall also include a requirement that the defence product is not subject to a restriction imposed by a non-associated third country or a non-associated third country entity [...] which limits a Member State's ability to use that defence product'.

53 Art. 9(10) of the EDIRPA Regulation. Two conditions are laid down for this derogation: first, that the members of the consortium commit to exploring the feasibility of replacing these restricted components by components that are not restricted and originate in the EU and, secondly, that the purchased products have been used before 24 February 2022 within the armed forces of a majority of the Member States participating in the common procurement.

II. AN IMPLEMENTATION EFFECTIVE IN THREE AREAS

In accordance with the EDIRPA Regulation, the Commission is responsible for the adoption of the work programme by means of an implementation act.[54] On 15 March 2024, the Commission adopted an implementation decision on the financing of EDIRPA and the adoption of the work programme for 2024-2025.[55]

The EDIRPA budget, which ultimately amounts to EUR 310 million, is divided into three priority areas of EUR 103.2 million each. The first area concerns the replenishment of ammunition stocks,[56] bearing in mind that in order to be eligible, the acquisition project must have a minimum value of EUR 120 million. Under the second area, projects worth at least EUR 150 million can be financed for the development of anti-aircraft and missile defence systems.[57] The last area aims to support joint purchase contracts for the development of all types of combat platforms, tanks, armoured vehicles, support vehicles and military systems, including in the context of the replacement of Soviet systems. This means funding projects worth at least EUR 150 million.

In response to the EDIRPA call for proposals, Member States and Norway had submitted twelve proposals by the deadline of 25 July 2024. Four months later, on 14 November 2024, the European Commission approved funding for five cross-border projects related to the common procurement of air and missile defence systems, ammunition and platforms.[58] Each selected project will receive EUR 60 million, for a total of EUR 300 million in EU funding. However, these five projects represent a combined procurement value of over EUR 11 billion, which illustrates the significant leverage effect of EU funding. For the Commission, 'EDIRPA's EUR 300 million investment has incentivized a commitment over thirty-six times larger, demonstrating the programme's effectiveness in driving substantial defence investments across

---

54 Art. 12.

55 C(2024) 1700 final, 15 June 2021. See also the annex to the decision,//defence-industry-space.ec.europa.eu/document/download/9af5891e-3880-454d-a062-3a88e2d89392_en?filename=EDIRPA%20WP%20Annex.pdf.

56 Both for light weapons ammunition (up to 12.7 mm) and for tank, anti-tank, mortar, missile and artillery ammunition.

57 Including for MANPAD portable air defence systems, anti-missile batteries, anti-drone systems, anti-aircraft defence ammunition and defence radars.

58 Commission Implementing Decision of 29.11.2024 establishing the list of proposals selected for funding and the proposals placed on the reserve list under the Instrument for the reinforcement of the European defence industry through common Procurement (EDIRPA) established by the Regulation (EU) 2023/2418 following the calls for proposals EDF-EDIRPA-2024-FNLC-AMD, EDF- EDIRPA-2024-FNLC-AMMO and EDF-EDIRPA-2024-FNLC-LSP launched under the work programme adopted by the Decision C(2024)1700, C(2024) 8314 final.

the EU'.[59] Another source of satisfaction for the Commission comes from the involvement of a high number of Member States in the selected EDIRPA projects: twenty of them, including states which had never engaged in common defence procurements projects before, are involved. Furthermore, not only three Member States are participating in each project (which is the minimum legal requirement) but, on average six of them are taking part. According to the Commission, this illustrates 'EDIRPA's role in encouraging collaboration among Member States to address critical capability gaps'.

Indeed, to bolster joint air and missile defence capabilities, two projects were selected: one to support the common procurement of 'Mistral' very short-range air defence systems by nine Member States[60] and one for the common procurement of IRIS-T SLM medium-range air defence systems by six Member States.[61]

Another project selected by four Member States will support the procurement of the Common Armoured Vehicle System (CAVS), a modern armoured carrier for protected troop transport.[62]

Finally, regarding the common procurement of ammunition, EDIRPA supports two distinct projects, one involving six Member States called 'CPoA 155mm',[63] and the so named project 'HE 155mm' involving four Member States.[64]

One can, of course, welcome with the Commission 'the first-ever EU-funded projects supporting common procurement of critical defence products by the Member States'[65] but one may also regret that the EDIRPA fund is limited to only EUR 300 million. Indeed, several other proposals, which the Commission

---

59 'EU Boosts Defence Readiness with First Ever Financial Support for Common Defence Procurement', Press Release, 14 November 2024, https://ec.europa.eu/commission/presscorner/detail/en/ip_24_5827.

60 The 'MISTRAL' project includes France, Belgium, Cyprus, Denmark, Estonia, Spain, Hungary, Slovenia, Romania, https://defence-industry-space.ec.europa.eu/edirpa-mistral_en.

61 Project 'JAMIE' (for 'Joint Air Missile Defence Initiative in Europe), will result in the common procurement of IRIS-T SLM medium-range air defence systems by six Member States (Germany, Austria, Slovenia, Belgium, Estonia, Latvia). These are systems for protection against air threats such as combat aircraft, attack helicopters and unmanned air systems, https://defence-industry-space.ec.europa.eu/edirpa-jamie_en.

62 Germany, Finland, Latvia, Sweden; https://defence-industry-space.ec.europa.eu/edirpa-cavs_en.

63 Denmark, Netherlands, Italy, Poland, Lithuania, Hungary, https://defence-industry-space.ec.europa.eu/edirpa-cpoa155mm_en.

64 Germany, Estonia, Denmark, Netherlands; https://defence-industry-space.ec.europa.eu/edirpa-he-155mm_en.

65 'EU boosts defence readiness with first ever financial support for common defence procurement', Press Release, 14 November 2024, cited above.

itself described as 'promising' by the Commission could not be selected due to a lack of available funding.[66]

At the end of 2026, the Commission will evaluate the implementation of the EDIRPA instrument and submit a report to the European Parliament and the Council analysing the impact and effectiveness of the actions undertaken.[67] It will then be time to judge the effectiveness of this short-term instrument, which will no longer finance actions by that date. It will have been replaced, like ASAP, by the long-term programme, which was requested by the legislators in July 2023,[68] and which is the subject of a Regulation for a European Defence Industry Programme (EDIP).[69]

---

[66] These projects were added to a reserve list which makes them identifiable for potential future funding.

[67] Art. 14(2)(C) of the Regulation.

[68] See the Joint Statement of the European Parliament and the Council, 17 July 2023, 11 787/23 ADD 1, Interinstitutional file 2023/0140 (COD). See also the commentary on the ASAP Regulation by E. Bernard in this publication.

[69] Regulation (EU) 2025/2643 of the European Parliament and of the Council of 16 December 2025 establishing the European Defence Industry Programme and a framework of measures to ensure the timely availability and supply of defence products ('EDIP Regulation'), [2025] *OJ* L2025/2643, see the commentary by E. Simon in this publication.

REGULATION ESTABLISHING A PROGRAMME FOR THE EUROPEAN DEFENCE INDUSTRY AND A FRAMEWORK FOR MEASURES TO ENSURE THE AVAILABILITY AND TIMELY SUPPLY OF DEFENCE PRODUCTS (EDIP): AN INSTRUMENT FOR TRANSITION AND TRANSFORMATION[1]

Edouard SIMON[2]
Team Leader, Defence Industrial Policy, European Commission (DG DEFIS)

The proposal for a regulation establishing a programme for the European defence industry and a framework for measures to ensure the availability and timely delivery of defence products (EDIP),[3] was adopted on 5 March 2024 alongside the European Defence Industrial Strategy (EDIS),[4] and the EDIP

1 Editors' note: Regulation (EU) 2025/2643 establishing the EDIP programme was adopted on 16 December 2025, at a late stage in the preparation of this volume. The commentary on the proposed regulation, originally published in the French edition (November 2024), has therefore been revised in light of the final text, albeit without the benefit of a full in-depth analysis. For an initial critical analysis of the EDIP Regulation, see L. CASTELLANOS-JANKIEWICZ, A. CARROZZINI, L. BOZZI and A. GUZMÁN MUTIS, 'ReArm Europe and the Rule of Law' (2026) 1(1) *EDSeQ - European Defence & Security Law & Policy Quarterly*, pp. 4–19, DOI: https://doi.org/10.21552/edseq/2026/1/4.

2 This analysis is presented in a personal capacity and reflects only the author's views. It cannot be considered as the official position of the European Commission.

3 Proposal for a Regulation of the European Parliament and of the Council on establishing the European Defence Industry Programme and a framework for measures to ensure the availability and timely provision of defence products ('EDIP'), COM/2024/150 final (EDIP Regulation proposal).

4 Joint Communication to the European Parliament, the Council, the European Economic and Social Committee and the Committee of the Regions, 'A new European Defence Industrial Strategy: Achieving EU readiness through responsive and resilient European

aims to be the EDIS's main implementation instrument. While seeking to achieve the long-term objectives of the strategy, EDIP also perpetuates the recent support given to the European defence industry under the current Multiannual Financial Framework (MFF), thus making it possible to 'reconcile the urgent with the long term',[5] (Section I below).

It is in this spirit that the proposed EDIP regulation is intended to be an instrument of transition and transformation. The Commission sees this as an opportunity to roll out a whole range of concrete measures, grouped around four main pillars: a programmatic pillar, in which the Commission draws on its most recent experience to support the competitiveness of the European and Ukrainian defence industries (Section II); a legal framework to support cooperation between Member States throughout the life cycle of defence equipment (Section III); a security of supply regime that takes full advantage of the internal market (Section IV); and a governance pillar to ensure Member State participation at every stage of the Regulation's implementation (Section V).

I. EDIP: AN INSTRUMENT FOR TRANSFORMATION AND TRANSITION

A. AN INSTRUMENT OF TRANSFORMATION

The proposed EDIP Regulation builds on the findings and solutions developed by the strategy (EDIS) and pursues its objectives. Consequently, *defence readiness*, particularly *defence industrial readiness*, is at the heart of the Commission's approach, in line with the Granada Declaration. The other major objective here is support for Ukraine, and this is perhaps the main innovation in the Commission's text: defining an instrument to support the industrial base of a third country and linking it to a programme supporting the European industrial base.

The legal bases of the proposed EDIP Regulation reflect the different aspects of this contribution to industrial preparedness in the field of defence:

- Article 173 TFEU aims to support the competitiveness of the European Defence Industrial and Technological Base (EDTIB), in particular by accelerating its adaptation to the structural changes brought about by the sudden deterioration of Europe's security environment.
- Article 114 TFEU aims to ensure the availability of defence products and services, particularly in times of crisis, by improving the conditions for the functioning of the internal market.

Defence Industry', JOIN/2024/10 final, ('A new European Defence Industrial Strategy'), see F. Liberti's contribution in this publication.

5 Proposal for an EDIP Regulation, explanatory memorandum, see above.

- Article 212 TFEU provides support for the restoration, reconstruction and modernisation of Ukraine's defence industrial base, thereby paving the way for its gradual but rapid integration into the EDTIB.
- Finally, recourse to Article 322 TFEU allows for the use of other financial resources, in particular to finance actions supporting the specific needs of the Ukrainian industrial base.

B. A TRANSITIONAL INSTRUMENT

In many respects, the proposed EDIP Regulation can be seen as a transitional instrument between the short and medium-term urgent needs and responses to the structural problems of the EDTIB.

First and foremost, the proposed EDIP Regulation should be seen as a bridge between the instruments adopted as a matter of urgency to respond to the immediate needs resulting from the Russian invasion of Ukraine (EDIRPA and ASAP) and the next Multiannual Financial Framework, which will run from 2028 onwards. In this sense, the financial support measures are based on a twofold logic. On the one hand, they aim to ensure the continuity of ASAP and EDIRPA emergency support measures until the end of the current MFF (31 December 2027).[6] On the other hand, they aim to prepare for the future of existing instruments by targeting an ambitious ramp-up of the various European defence industrial policy instruments (from the EDF to the future EDIP).

The budget proposed by the Commission for EDIP reflects this hybrid nature. With €1.5 billion, EDIP almost doubles the resources available until 2025 to support the industrial base.[7] However, as the strategy points out, this budget is nowhere near sufficient to meet the funding needs required to support the transformation of Europe's defence industry necessary to ensure defence readiness.[8]

Furthermore, this only concerns the budget available to support the adaptation of the EDTIB to the new security context. Support for the specific needs of the Ukrainian industrial base does not have a dedicated budget in the Commission's proposal (Art. 5(1)(b)). This paradoxical situation, where one of

---

6 See the commentary by E. Bernard in this publication.

7 EDIRPA has a budget of €350 million and ASAP a budget of €500 million.

8 'This [EDIP] budget, given the scale of the effort needed to ensure the defence industrial readiness across the Union, has to be considered as a bridge – limited in scale – towards the next Multi-Annual Financial Framework. Given that the security challenges faced by Europe are likely to remain, it is important that the next MFF includes an ambitious financial envelope on defence with relevant budgets for the successors of both EDF and EDIP for the period from 2028 onwards', cited above. 'In this context, the European Council invites the Council and the Commission to explore all options for mobilising funds and report back by June,' European Council meeting (21 and 22 March 2024) – Conclusions, EUCO 7/24, Brussels, 22 March 2024.

the main objectives of the proposed regulation has no budget, should be resolved by the possibility of allocating external resources (Art. 6(1)), and in particular the interest payments generated by the freezing of Russian assets. These are currently estimated at €3 billion per year, which could be distributed by the Council among the various instruments and programmes supporting Ukraine (European Peace Facility[9] and its Ukraine Assistance Fund,[10] the Facility for Ukraine[11] and EDIP).

Beyond the budgetary aspects, it should be noted that the material and temporal scope of the text also ensures a form of evolution of the emergency instruments towards being a tool for transforming the EDTIB. Indeed, the measures in the proposed EDIP Regulation are not limited to 'ground-to-ground and artillery ammunitions as well as missiles' (ASAP) or to 'the most urgent and critical defence product needs' (EDIRPA). It is, in fact, inclusion on the European Union Military List[12] that determines whether equipment qualifies as a 'defence product' within the meaning of the Regulation. The scope of the EDIP proposal is therefore much broader than that of the emergency instruments. Finally, the proposed regulation not only provides for the text to apply from 2025 (i.e. before the end of the emergency instruments), but also for its support to be retroactive from the date of its adoption by the College (5 March 2024). The retroactive nature of the support measures is particularly important in order not to artificially delay the implementation of actions potentially eligible for EDIP support.

II. FIRST PILLAR: FINANCIAL SUPPORT FOR THE DEFENCE INDUSTRY (ARTICLES 3 TO 21)

The first pillar of the proposed EDIP Regulation provides for a set of measures to support the defence industry using the European budget. This pillar consists of two components: a programme to support the competitiveness of the European defence industry (the programme) and an instrument to meet the specific needs of the Ukrainian defence industry (the instrument for support to Ukraine).

---

9 Council Decision (CFSP) 2021/509 of 22 March 2021 establishing a European Peace Facility, and repealing Decision (CFSP) 2015/528, [2021] *OJ* L102/14, see C. Schneider's contribution in this publication.

10 'Ukraine Assistance Fund: Council allocates €5 billion under the European Peace Facility to support Ukraine militarily', Press release, Council of the European Union, 18 March 2024.

11 Regulation (EU) 2024/792 of the European Parliament and of the Council of 29 February 2024 establishing the Ukraine Facility, [2024] *OJ* L2024/792.

12 Common Military List of the European Union adopted by the Council on 20 February 2023 (equipment covered by Council Common Position 2008/944/CFSP defining common rules governing the control of exports of military technology and equipment) (updating and replacing the Common Military List of the European Union adopted by the Council on 21 February 2022, [2022] *OJ* C100/3) (CFSP) 2023/C 72/02, [2023] *OJ* C72/2; Directive 2009/43/EC of the European Parliament and of the Council of 6 May 2009 simplifying terms and conditions of transfers of defence-related products within the Community, [2009] *OJ* L146/1, Annex – List of defence-related products.

A. ONE PILLAR, TWO VECTORS

The creation of two separate vectors is a direct consequence of the different legal bases used (Articles 173 TFEU and 212 TFEU respectively) and the specific objectives that derive from them: support for the competitiveness of European industry and the acceleration of its adaptation, on the one hand, and support for the recovery, reconstruction and modernisation of Ukrainian industry, on the other. The budgetary sources for these two vectors must also be different: Title V of the EU budget for the programme supporting the competitiveness of European industry and Title VI for the instrument of support for Ukraine. Furthermore, the eligible entities also differ due to distinct legal bases. Under the programme, entities eligible for European support must be based in the EU or in a country associated with the programme. Under the instrument, entities must be based in the EU or in Ukraine to be eligible.

Despite these differences, the programme and the instrument have a great many similarities. Starting with the type of actions supported (eligible actions – Articles 11 to 15 and 19), which are the same, albeit with a few exceptions.[13]

B. ELIGIBLE ACTIONS

Actions eligible under the programme and the instrument are based on two main approaches. On the one hand, the proposed EDIP regulation aims to extend the approach of the EDIRPA and ASAP emergency instruments by broadening their principle of application to all products included on the European Union's military list.

On the other hand, the Commission's proposal introduces new eligible actions that can be seen as trial balloons for the next Multiannual Financial Framework, for which the budget available for the defence industry support is expected to increase significantly. Among these new features, it is worth noting in particular the possibility of supporting the industrialisation and commercialisation of products developed under EU-funded actions (Art. 11(3)(c)). This action ensures continuity of support for projects that have benefited from the European Defence Fund beyond the prototype stage, and ensures that these projects will result in products that will actually be acquired by the armed forces of Member States.

The Commission also proposes the establishment of a European military sales mechanism (Art. 14), which appears to be intended to replicate the advantages of the US Foreign Military Sale (FMS) mechanism for the benefit of the EDITB. Under EDIP, the European budget could support the establishment

13 The Ukraine Support Instrument cannot finance either European defence projects of common interest (Art. 15) or the FAST fund (Art. 19).

of genuine 'European strategic reserves' (or industrial preparedness reserves in the field of defence), which should ensure the greater availability of defence products manufactured by the EDIB.

Finally, without being exhaustive, it is worth noting the possibility of supporting the deployment of European Defence Projects of Common Interest (Art. 15), which makes it possible to support projects aimed at ensuring the provision of defence capabilities, at European level, which are actually European in nature, and which no Member State can provide on its own. An example of such capabilities could be a European air defence shield supported by (the former) Commissioner Thierry Breton.[14]

III. SECOND PILLAR: THE LEGAL FRAMEWORK OF THE STRUCTURES FOR EUROPEAN ARMAMENT PROGRAMME (ARTICLES 22 TO 33)

The second pillar of the proposed EDIP regulation is an innovation. It involves the creation of a new legal framework: the Structure for European Armament Programmes (SEAP).

This framework, largely inspired by that of the European Research Infrastructure Consortia,[15] aims to support Member States in their cooperation efforts throughout the life cycle of a defence product by offering a flexible and voluntary framework with a number of advantages. A SEAP may thus have the following tasks: joint procurement of defence products, technologies or services, joint management of the life cycle of defence products and, possibly, management of industrial preparedness stocks in the field of defence (Art. 22). It is possible to create one at any stage of a product's life cycle (including after the acquisition of a product). However, any stage of the life cycle of a product covered by a SEAP must be carried out jointly once the SEAP has been established.

The proposed EDIP Regulation provides for a limited number of conditions for establishing a SEAP, allowing for a degree of flexibility for Member States, associated States and Ukraine (Art. 23). A SEAP must therefore contribute to achieving the capability priorities defined in the CFSP. It must be composed of at least three States, including at least two Member States. And it must cover all stages of the life cycle of a defence product after its creation.

---

14 See the hearing of Commissioner Thierry Breton by the Defence and Armed Forces Committee of the French National Assembly, 4 June 2024. Mr Breton was Commissioner of Internal Market from 2019 to 2024.

15 Council Regulation (EC) No 723/2009 of 25 June 2009 on a Community legal framework for a European Research Infrastructure Consortium (ERIC), [2009] *OJ* L206/1.

In return, a SEAP enjoys a number of advantages. Some are financial and linked to the first pillar of the proposed EDIP regulation. For example, the Commission's text proposes specific support for these structures, in particular 'for the purpose of managing and maintaining a Defence Industrial Readiness Pool' (Art. 11(5)(f)). This action could also serve as a basis for financial support for the establishment of a SEAP. In addition, the proposed regulation provides for an increased funding rate (bonus) when an action is carried out within the framework of a SEAP and another when the States participating in a SEAP have developed a 'common approach to exports for defence products developed and acquired' within that framework.

However, the Commission's proposal also introduces several non-financial benefits aimed at simplifying cooperation within the framework of a SEAP. Firstly, for actions requiring a consortium of at least three eligible entities (defence cooperation actions, support for the industrialisation and commercialisation of defence products developed under actions financed by the Union, and activities aimed at increasing interoperability and interchangeability): this criterion is waived for SEAPs. These are effectively, by design, a consortium of three States. This derogation greatly simplifies the process of applying for and implementing an action supported by an EU programme. Furthermore, a SEAP benefits from a total exemption from the Directive on defence and security procurement, allowing for greater flexibility in the conduct of cooperation. Finally, a SEAP is recognised as an international organisation within the meaning of the VAT Directive and, as such, when it acquires a defence product on its own account (i.e. it will retain ownership), it can benefit from a VAT exemption (Art. 24(1)(d)).

IV. THIRD PILLAR: LEVERAGING THE INTERNAL MARKET FRAMEWORK TO SUPPORT SECURITY OF SUPPLY (ARTICLES 34 TO 56)

The third pillar of the proposed EDIP Regulation recommends the implementation of a European security of supply regime at the internal market level. The need for this European regime stems primarily from the increasing cross-border organisation of defence production supply chains. The upper levels of these supply chains remain largely organised on a national basis, resulting in a fragmented EDTIB that is unable to take full advantage of the potential of an integrated internal market. However, the situation becomes much more complex as one moves further down these supply chains. Indeed, one of the main insights from the 'Ammunition initiative' is that, for numerous military components, dual-use items and raw materials, defence supply chains are already integrated across borders, functioning at minimum on a European scale and frequently on a global level. This continental organisation of defence supply chains is also likely to increase in the coming years as defence industrial policy instruments (EDF, ASAP, EDIRPA and EDIP) take effect.

Since supply chains are intended to be organised at the level of the internal market, the need to ensure a level of security of supply at this level appears to be a factor in terms of both reliability (and therefore a criterion for choice) for Member States and competitiveness for these supply chains. This reality is recognised at the highest political level in Europe, since, as early as 2013, the European Council called for the implementation of such a regime,[16] a position echoed by the European Parliament on several occasions.[17] Although the Member States were not then prepared to see the European Commission take action in an area widely perceived (even today) as falling within the sphere of national sovereignty,[18] the deterioration in the security situation and the difficulties in ensuring the supply of ammunition (in particular 155 mm shells) by the EDTIB led the Council, together with the European Parliament, to ask the Commission to take action in this area.[19]

It is in this context that the Commission has proposed to build on the experience of the security of supply and crisis management frameworks adopted at European level in either a sectoral (semiconductors,[20] health[21] and

16 European Council, 19 and 20 December 2013 – Conclusions, EUCO 217/13, Brussels, 20 December 2013.

17 For example: 'urge the Commission to present, without delay, a security of supply regime for defence as demanded by the European Council in 2013, and which has become a matter of utmost urgency given the current security situation', Report on a European Parliament recommendation to the Council and the Vice-President of the Commission / High Representative of the Union for Foreign Affairs and Security Policy on the EU's Foreign, Security and Defence Policy after the Russian invasion of Ukraine, Report – A9-0164/2022, 2022/2039(INI), European Parliament, 25 May 2022; or 'Recalls that in 2013 the European Council called on the Commission to develop a roadmap for a comprehensive EU-wide security of supply regime, which, unfortunately, has never been presented; urges the Commission to present this roadmap without further delay', Report on Critical technologies for security and defence: state of play and future challenges, Report – A9-0120/2023, 2022/2079(INI), European Parliament, 4 April 2023.

18 'The Commission takes note of Member States' unwillingness to go beyond such a political commitment at this stage and agree on an EU-wide regime on Security of Supply.' European Defence Action Plan, Brussels, 30 November 2016, COM (2016) 950 final.

19 'The European Parliament and the Council therefore call on the Commission to consider, as appropriate, putting forward as soon as possible any further initiatives necessary to strengthen the EDTIB, including adequate financing, for instance in the context of the European Defence Investment Programme, as well as a legal framework aimed at ensuring security of supply and supporting ammunition production,' Joint statement of the European Parliament and the Council on the adoption of the Regulation on support for ammunition production (ASAP), Annex to the legislative resolution, 13 July 2023 – Strasbourg.

20 Regulation (EU) 2023/1781 of the European Parliament and of the Council of 13 September 2023 establishing a framework of measures for strengthening Europe's semiconductor ecosystem and amending Regulation (EU) 2021/694 (Chips Act), [2023] *OJ* L229/1.

21 Council Regulation (EU) 2022/2372 of 24 October 2022 on a framework of measures for ensuring the supply of crisis-relevant medical countermeasures in the event of a public health emergency at Union level, [2022] *OJ* L314/64.

critical raw materials[22]) or horizontal[23] context. The proposed EDIP Regulation is based on three types of measures:

- *Preparatory measures (Articles 34 to 39)*: these are mainly aimed at facilitating and accelerating the acquisition of EDIP defence products by extending and broadening the possibility introduced by the ASAP Regulation to reopen framework agreements for the benefit of other Member States or Ukraine (Article 34). The EDIP proposal also sets out a framework for the use of the possibility offered to Member States by the new Financial Regulation to request the Commission to acquire defence products on their behalf or with them (Articles 35 to 37).
- *Mapping and supply chain monitoring measures (Articles 40 to 42)*: the process proposed by the Commission is broadly similar to that adopted by the co-legislators in the *Chips Act*, which already has direct implications for particularly sensitive defence supply chains. Responsibility for mapping and monitoring is thus shared between the Commission and the Member States, which remain responsible in particular for identifying and monitoring key market players (Art. 42). It should be noted that the proposed regulation does not provide for an exhaustive mapping of the EDTIB and its supply chains. It focuses on key defence products identified by Member States within the framework of the European Defence Preparedness Council (Art. 58).
- *A framework for crisis management (Articles 43 to 56)*: the Commission's proposed regulation provides for two modes for the crisis management framework aimed at combating the fragmentation of the internal market in times of crisis.

The first mode ('supply crisis – prevention and mitigation', Articles 43 to 47) provides for measures when a disruption in the supply of a product that is not a defence product (e.g. a dual-use component or raw material) materialises or is about to materialise. The aim is to be able to arbitrate between defence and civilian supply chains for access to these products (requests for information, priority orders).

The second mode ('security-related supply crisis', Articles 48 to 54) focuses on supply disruptions and supply risks for defence products when the shortage is linked to the emergence of a security crisis. In addition to the measures contained in the supply crisis, the security-related supply crisis provides for specific measures for defence products. Each of these measures must be explicitly activated by the Council before the Commission can implement them.

---

22 Regulation (EU) 2024/1252 of the European Parliament and of the Council of 11 April 2024 establishing a framework for ensuring a secure and sustainable supply of critical raw materials and amending Regulations (EU) No 168/2013, (EU) 2018/858, (EU) 2018/1724 and (EU) 2019/1020, [2024] *OJ* L2024/1252.

23 SMEI/SURMI: Council and Parliament strike a provisional deal on crisis preparedness, Council of the European Union, Press release, 1 February 2024.

V. FOURTH PILLAR: A EUROPEAN DEFENCE PREPAREDNESS COUNCIL TO ENSURE FULLY PARTNERSHIP-BASED GOVERNANCE (ARTICLE 58)

Finally, the proposed EDIP Regulation provides for a specific governance framework to complement the traditional comitology framework as provided for in Article 291 TFEU.

The proposed regulation provides that several Commission decisions for the implementation of the regulation shall be adopted after a positive opinion from a committee composed of representatives of the Member States. This is the case, for example, for the work programmes of the Programme and the Instrument or for priority orders (Art. 47). The use of comitology is standard practice for the implementation of European programmes, particularly in the field of the defence industry. For the activation of the two modes of the crisis framework, the proposed EDIP Regulation provides for the use of Council implementing acts.

However, beyond the use of the comitology framework, the Commission proposes the establishment of a European Defence Preparedness Council (composed of representatives of the Member States) whose role is to assist and advise the Commission in the implementation of the EDIP, and in particular the security of supply regime. Such a function (purely advisory) goes well beyond the role of the programme committee and is intended to ensure that Member States remain informed and involved at every stage of the implementation of a framework that is particularly sensitive for them.

The proposed EDIP Regulation is now in the hands of the co-legislators. It must be discussed and negotiated before the Regulation is adopted, probably in 2025.

VI. UPDATE: OUTCOME OF THE LEGISLATIVE PROCEDURE

On 29 December 2025, the Regulation (EU) 2025/2643 of 16 December 2025 establishing the European Defence Industry Programme and a framework of measures to ensure the timely availability and supply of defence products ('EDIP Regulation') has been published.[24] The text resulting from the negotiations between the European Parliament and the Council respects the ambition of

[24] Regulation (EU) 2025/2643 of the European Parliament and of the Council of 16 December 2025 establishing the European Defence Industry Programme and a framework of measures to ensure the timely availability and supply of defence products ('EDIP Regulation'), [2025] *OJ* L2025/2643.

the Commission's proposal while incorporating three main modifications to the Commission's proposals.

- **Structure of the Regulation**

The first type of changes brought by co-legislators to the Commission's proposal concerns the structure of the Regulation. Whereas the structure in chapters of the Commission's proposal reflected the different logics of intervention (use of the Union budget, voluntary legal framework (SEAP) and Security of Supply (SoS) framework), the co-legislators decided to break up the chapter on the use of the Union budget into four different chapters:

- A chapter dedicated to the EDIP programme itself, focusing exclusively on the actions supporting the competitiveness of the EDTIB. It is worth noting that certain provisions on the possibility for the Commission to participate in defence procurements have been moved by the co-legislators from the SoS chapter to the EDIP chapter, hence confirming their link to the broader objective of supporting EDTIB competitiveness. However, the content remains quite close to the Commission's proposal.
- A chapter for the Ukraine Support Instrument (USI) mostly replicates the structure and content of the EDIP programme, and only adapts to the specificities of supporting the recovery, reconstruction and modernisation of the Ukrainian DTIB. These changes, even though optically important, bring more clarity to the specific structure and functioning of the Instrument, but remain in line with the policy intent of the Commission's proposal.
- A chapter on the European Defence Projects of Common Interest (EDPCI): the article on EDPCI has been significantly modified by the co-legislators. In particular, the identification of EDPCIs has been completely transformed: whereas they were to be proposed by the Commission in the Work Programme in the initial proposal, the final text foresees that the Council may identify them through implementing powers. The criteria for these projects, as well as the activities potentially supported by the Union's budget, have been further clarified.
- A chapter on the EU military sales mechanism (EU MSM): unlike EDPCIs, the transformation of the article on the EU MSM into a dedicated article does not reflect any significant changes in substance. This new chapter only brings more visibility to a set of measures which, admittedly, goes beyond the sole use of the Union's budget.

- **Eligibility conditions on products:**

As with previous texts adopted since February 2022, eligibility conditions on products have been one of the most debated issues within and between the Council and the European Parliament. Whereas eligibility conditions for entities have been remarkably stable since 2022 (with the notable exception of requirements applying to certain subcontractors), eligibility requirements on products supported with EU funding have significantly evolved since the 'EDF blueprint'. Accordingly, the Union budget cannot support products which are 'subject to control or restriction by a non-associated third country or a non-associated third-country entity'.

With ASAP and EDIRPA, the co-legislators agreed on solutions based on the 'EDF blueprint' adapted to the temporary and short-term character of the instruments, and in order to take into account the nature of existing European supply chains. Both instruments limit the principle of absence of restrictions to restrictions of use (which limit the ability of Member States to use the defence product concerned). In EDIRPA, co-legislators also introduced a derogation to this principle.

With the EDIP, the co-legislators have departed from the EDF blueprint to use other eligibility requirements for products. This takes into account the internationalisation of existing European defence supply chains and pursues the objective of the EDF of ensuring the freedom of use by the armed forces of Member States:

- By requiring that no more than 35% of the content of a defence product originates from outside the Union, the EDIP Regulation (as with EDIRPA) aims at limiting the possibility of third countries interfering in the sourcing of EU defence supply chains.
- By introducing the EU design authority (the contractor or beneficiary has the ability to decide, without restrictions, on the definition, adaptation and evolution of the design of the defence products concerned), the EDIP Regulation ensures that restrictions from non-EU sources can be mitigated.

This 'EDIP blueprint' is likely to set a new standard for future EU programmes focusing on post-R&D phases.

• **Security of Supply**:

On security of supply, it is noticeable that the co-legislators have kept most of the ambition and proposals of the Commission. However, they have made several changes:

- They significantly *reinforced the internal market narrative* of this chapter, notably by introducing a large number of recitals, explicating the link between the substantive measures and the legal basis of this chapter (Article 114 TFEU).
- They reinforced the *guarantees for industry and Member States* in several of the measures introduced (in particular, priority-rated orders and requests).

The co-legislators have also reinforced the role of Member States in the mapping and monitoring of actions. The Member State of an establishment now acts as the intermediary between the Commission and national industries. However, the Commission has the possibility and leeway to challenge production inputs, incentivising Member States and industry to fully cooperate in the process.

Even though these changes have introduced further complexity to the Security of Supply framework, making it probably less efficient, they aim at reinforcing the buy-in from Member States. This buy-in is absolutely key for the success of the SoS framework and the achievement of the internal market for defence, as it aims at building trust between Member States and the Commission, as well as between Member States.

ARTICLES 174 TO 178 TFEU: WHEN COHESION POLICY SUPPORTS THE DEFENCE SECTOR

Stéphane Rodrigues
Senior Lecturer at the Université Paris 1 Panthéon-Sorbonne
Member of the Sorbonne Institute for Research in International and European Law (IREDIES-EA 4536)
Member of the Brussels Bar

Article 174

In order to promote its overall harmonious development, the Union shall develop and pursue its actions leading to the strengthening of its economic, social and territorial cohesion.

In particular, the Union shall aim at reducing disparities between the levels of development of the various regions and the backwardness of the least favoured regions.

Among the regions concerned, particular attention shall be paid to rural areas, areas affected by industrial transition, and regions which suffer from severe and permanent natural or demographic handicaps such as the northernmost regions with very low population density and island, cross-border and mountain regions.

Article 175

Member States shall conduct their economic policies and shall coordinate them in such a way as, in addition, to attain the objectives set out in Article 174. The formulation and implementation of the Union's policies and actions and the implementation of the internal market shall take into account the objectives set out in Article 174 and shall contribute to their achievement. The Union shall also support the achievement of these objectives by the action it takes through the Structural Funds (European Agricultural Guidance and Guarantee Fund, Guidance Section; European Social Fund; European Regional Development Fund), the European Investment Bank and the other existing Financial Instruments.

The Commission shall submit a report to the European Parliament, the Council, the Economic and Social Committee and the Committee of the Regions every three years on the progress made towards achieving economic, social and territorial cohesion and on the manner in which the various means provided for in this Article have contributed to it. This report shall, if necessary, be accompanied by appropriate proposals.

If specific actions prove necessary outside the Funds and without prejudice to the measures decided upon within the framework of the other Union policies, such actions may be adopted by the European Parliament and the Council acting in accordance with the ordinary legislative procedure and after consulting the Economic and Social Committee and the Committee of the Regions.

Article 176

The European Regional Development Fund is intended to help to redress the main regional imbalances in the Union through participation in the development and structural adjustment of regions whose development is lagging behind and in the conversion of declining industrial regions.

Article 177

Without prejudice to Article 178, the European Parliament and the Council, acting by means of regulations in accordance with the ordinary legislative procedure and consulting the Economic and Social Committee and the Committee of the Regions, shall define the tasks, priority objectives and the organisation of the Structural Funds, which may involve grouping the Funds. The general rules applicable to them and the provisions necessary to ensure their effectiveness and the coordination of the Funds with one another and with the other existing Financial Instruments shall also be defined by the same procedure.

A Cohesion Fund set up in accordance with the same procedure shall provide a financial contribution to projects in the fields of environment and trans-European networks in the area of transport infrastructure.

Article 178

Implementing regulations relating to the European Regional Development Fund shall be taken by the European Parliament and the Council, acting in accordance with the ordinary legislative procedure and after consulting the Economic and Social Committee and the Committee of the Regions.

With regard to the European Agricultural Guidance and Guarantee Fund, Guidance Section, and the European Social Fund, Articles 43 and 164 respectively shall continue to apply.

Article 174 TFEU forms part of Title XVIII on economic, social and territorial cohesion in Part Two of the TFEU (Articles 174 to 178 TFEU). It constitutes the main legal basis for the exercise by the European Union of a shared competence within the meaning of Articles 2(2) and 4(2)(c) TFEU, aimed at achieving one of the objectives assigned to the EU by the third subparagraph of Article 3(3) TEU, namely the promotion of 'economic, social and territorial cohesion, and solidarity among Member States'.[1] The aim is to respond to an economic reality, namely the disparities in wealth within the EU,[2] by taking specific action, in particular through financial instruments such as the European Structural and Investment Funds (ESF).

Apart from a reference in the preamble and in Article 2 of the EEC Treaty to the idea of reducing development disparities between regions, the 1957 Treaty of Rome did not contain a legal basis dedicated to cohesion. This was even though one of the first structural funds established in the name of social policy, the European Social Fund (ESF: ex-Article 146 EC, now Article 162 TFEU), was already seeking to meet this objective.

It was not until the Single European Act of 1986 that economic and social cohesion (formerly Articles 130A to 130E of the EC Treaty) was included as a Community competence. The Treaty of Maastricht (1992) added a reference to rural areas and a specific protocol, and the Treaty of Amsterdam (1997) added a reference to islands. Finally, the Treaty of Lisbon (2007) introduced the current wording of Articles 174 to 178 of the TFEU, explicitly emphasising the territorial dimension of cohesion and confirming the protocol dedicated to this competence (Protocol No. 28).[3]

Under the EU's multiannual financial framework for 2021-2027, the EU's so-called 'regional' policy will mobilise €378 billion, making it the second

---

1 See C. Boutayeb, 'Retour sur un tropisme: la solidarité dans le domaine de la cohésion économique, sociale et territoriale', in *Concurrence et Europe – Liber Amicorum Laurence Idot*, vol. II, Paris, Concurrences, 2022, spec. pp. 261–272.

2 According to EUROSTAT figures for 2019: expressed in terms of purchasing power standards, GDP per capita in the 240 NUTS2 regions of the EU27 ranged from 32% of the EU27 average in Mayotte to 260% of this average in Luxembourg (press release STAT/34/2019 of 26 February 2019).

3 On this policy, see in particular W. Delfaa, '60 ans de politique régionale européenne', *Revue du droit de l'UE*, 4/2018, pp. 11–33 and S. de La Rosa, 'Politique de cohésion économique, sociale et territoriale. Cadre juridique et organisation générale', *JurisClasseur Europe*, 2012, fasc. 2210, and M. Jouen, *La politique européenne de cohésion*, Réflexe Europe, Paris, La Documentation française, 2011. See also the European Court of Auditors' Special Report No. 7/2020 of 26 February 2020 on the implementation of cohesion policy.

largest item of expenditure.[4] It is implemented in particular by Regulation (EU) 2021/1060 laying down common provisions for the ESF.[5]

Without going into further detail about the regulatory framework, it should be emphasised, as was done in the new European Defence Industrial Strategy (EDIS) of March 2024,[6] that the European Defence Technological and Industrial Base (EDTIB) may benefit from EU funding under the ESF, in line with the objectives assigned to these funds.[7] This chapter focuses on five of these main funds, in chronological order of creation: the European Social Fund (already mentioned), the European Regional Development Fund (ERDF), the European Cohesion Fund, the European Globalisation Adjustment Fund and the InvestEU programme. It gives some examples of projects in the defence sector, co-financed by the EU (according to the principle of capping its intervention), and managed with the Member States (according to the so-called shared management method).[8]

I. THE EUROPEAN SOCIAL FUND (ESF+)

The European Social Fund (ESF), created in 1962, has been given the name 'ESF+' for the period 2021-2027. It has a budget of €99.3 billion for this period, and its implementing regulation (Regulation (EU) 2021/1957)[9] sets out two general objectives: i) to help Member States and regions achieve high levels of

---

4 Council Regulation (EU, Euratom) 2020/2093 of 17 December 2020 laying down the multiannual financial framework for the years 2021 to 2027, [2020] *OJ* L433I/11.

5 Regulation (EU) 2021/1060 of the European Parliament and of the Council of 24 June 2021 laying down common provisions on the European Regional Development Fund, the European Social Fund Plus, the Cohesion Fund, the Just Transition Fund and the European Maritime, Fisheries and Aquaculture Fund and financial rules for those and for the Asylum, Migration and Integration Fund, the Internal Security Fund and the Instrument for Financial Support for Border Management and Visa Policy, [2021] *OJ* L231/159; corrigendum, [2021] *OJ* L261/58. See also the Commission Implementing Decision (EU) 2021/1130 of 5 July 2021 setting out the list of regions eligible for funding from the European Regional Development Fund and the European Social Fund Plus and of Member States eligible for funding from the Cohesion Fund for the period 2021-2027, which established the annual breakdown of overall resources by Member State. The budget earmarked for France is approximately €18.4 billion for 2021–2027.

6 See Joint Communication [by the European Commission and the High Representative of the Union for Foreign Affairs and Security Policy of 5 March 2024] to the European Parliament, the Council, the European Economic and Social Committee and the Committee of the Regions, 'A new European Defence Industrial Strategy: Achieving EU readiness through a responsive and resilient European Defence Industry' JOIN(2024) 10 final, 5 March 2024, in particular Section 5.1.3.

7 EDIS estimates the EDTIB in 2021 at €70 billion in annual sales and €28 billion in export volumes (see p. 4).

8 See the Internet platform providing access to all public information relating to European cohesion funding: https://kohesio.ec.europa.eu/fr.

9 Regulation (EU) 2021/1057 of the European Parliament and of the Council of 24 June 2021 establishing the European Social Fund plus (ESF+) and repealing Regulation (EU) No 1296/2013, [2021] *OJ* L231/21.

employment, fair social protection, a skilled and resilient workforce prepared for the world of work and inclusive and cohesive societies aiming to eradicate poverty and implement the principles set out in the European Social Charter; and ii) to support and complement Member States' policies aimed at ensuring equal opportunities, equal access to the labour market, fair and quality working conditions and social protection and inclusion, and thus provide added value to these policies, with particular emphasis on inclusive and quality education and training, lifelong learning, investment in children and young people and access to basic services.

Projects in the field of defence co-financed by ESF+ are still underdeveloped. One example is the support provided during the previous programming period (2014-2020) to the public defence integration establishment in France, whose total budget of over €156 million was matched by almost €50 million from the ESF to promote the social and professional integration of young volunteers. The same ESF+ commitment can be seen over the period 2021-2027, with 80% co-funding of the 'Service militaire adapté (SMA)' scheme, which is a military social and professional integration scheme for young people in overseas France who face the greatest hurdles in entering the job market and obtaining qualifications. The 2023 budget for the SMA scheme in Réunion was €20 million, of which €16 million was funded by the ESF+.

ESF+ support may not necessarily be directly visible in the defence field, but could appear through civilian projects that may have a military dimension or prove useful to the defence world. In this respect, reference can be made to the creation in 2021 in France's Eure department of a metallurgy production school, to train specialist technicians that SMEs supplying the armed forces may also need, given the lack of qualified personnel in this sector. Supported by France's Trade Association in Metallurgy Industries and Professions (*Union des industries et métiers de la métallurgie* or UIMM), this project has received ESF+ funding of €411,147 (out of a total budget of €616,721).

Since February 2022, the war in Ukraine has also led some neighbouring regions to call on the ESF+ to manage the flow of migrants from that country. For example, the 'Lubelskie helps Ukraine' project, run by the Lublin Social Action Centre (Poland), received ESF+ funding in 2022-2023 (€840,180 out of a total budget of €988,447) and will have enabled 800 Ukrainian migrants to be received and socially integrated.

II. THE EUROPEAN REGIONAL DEVELOPMENT FUND (ERDF)

The European Regional Development Fund (ERDF), created in 1975, has since been renewed regularly and currently covers the period 2021-2027 on the basis of Regulation (EU) 2021/1058,[10] which provides it with a budget of €200.4 billion.[11]

The ERDF has two main tasks: firstly, to contribute to the overall objective of strengthening the economic, social and territorial cohesion of the Union; and secondly, to help reduce the gap between the levels of development of the various regions of the Union and the backwardness of the least favoured regions by contributing to the structural adjustment of regions whose development is lagging behind and to the conversion of declining industrial regions. This includes promoting sustainable development and meeting environmental challenges. In this way, the ERDF should contribute to the move towards a more competitive, greener and more connected EU.

In practical terms, the ERDF can co-finance: investment in infrastructure; activities to promote applied research and innovation, including industrial research, experimental development and feasibility studies; investment in access to services; productive investment in SMEs; investment aimed at preserving existing jobs and creating new ones; and equipment, software as well as intangible assets, and so on.

However, certain activities are explicitly and restrictively excluded, such as the decommissioning or construction of nuclear power stations, the production, processing and marketing of tobacco and tobacco products, a company in difficulty, investments in the elimination of waste by landfill, or linked to the production, processing, transport, distribution, storage or combustion of fossil fuels, with certain exceptions. Defence activities are not included in these exclusions.

In 2016-2019, for example, the ERDF was able to co-fund the IMATOP project, a collaborative project between the University of Poitiers and the company SAGEM, to support research into the optimisation of optronic devices aimed at improving the anti-glare, demisting and hydrophobicity properties that can be applied to binoculars, rifle scopes and infrared detectors. The ERDF will contribute 40% of the total budget of around €595,000.

Another example is provided by the SEMCHA project, during the 2014-2020 programming period, which enabled the *Conseil régional du Grand-Est* (in France) to revitalise an area of the city of Châlons-en-Champagne, following the sale by the Ministry of Defence of a large proportion of its property in the area. The ERDF covered 40% of the total cost of the operation (which was approximately €740,000).

---

10 Regulation (EU) 2021/1058 of the European Parliament and of the Council of 24 June 2021 on the European Regional Development Fund and the Cohesion Fund, [2021] *OJ* L231/60.

11 Including €8 billion earmarked for European territorial cooperation (INTEREG): see Regulation (EU) of the European Parliament and of the Council of 24 June 2021, [2021] *OJ* L231/94.

Even more directly and operationally, the ERDF co-financed 41% (of the total budget of €828.47 million) of the SYDDRE project (in 2019-2022), which enabled Normandy SMEs DRONEXTR and ARELIS to develop an innovative detection solution for the new generations of drones or unmanned aerial vehicles (in particular WIFI UAVs), in line with the expectations of the French Ministry of Defence's Directorate General for Armaments.

III. THE COHESION FUND

The Cohesion Fund is the heir to the cohesion financial instrument established in 1993, and has been perpetuated ever since, with each renewal of the EU's multiannual financial framework. For the period 2021-2027, Regulation (EU) No 2021/1058, referred to above, provides it with a budget of €42.6 billion and has confirmed its primary purpose: to provide financial support to the least developed Member States (i.e. those whose gross national income per capita is less than 90% of the average gross income per capita in the EU) for projects, half of which are in the field of the environment and the other half in trans-European transport networks (TEN-T). As such, the Cohesion Fund must contribute 37% of the expenditure supported by the EU to achieve its climate protection objectives.[12]

Sharing the same exclusions of eligible activities as those applicable to the ERDF (see above), the Cohesion Fund can therefore potentially be mobilised for projects in defence, in the broadest sense of the term. For example, Ireland's Defence Employment Support (DES) programme, which was aimed at unemployed people aged between 18 and 24 during the 2014-2020 programming period, received 66% of its funding from the ESF (for a total budget of €840,000).

IV. THE EUROPEAN GLOBALISATION ADJUSTMENT FUND

Created in 2006 at France's request in particular, in the wake of the social crisis caused by the restructuring and relocation plan of the Hewlett-Packard group, the European Globalisation Adjustment Fund for redundant workers (EGF) has since been extended.[13] Its remit is to intervene in the event

[12] See also Articles 170 to 172 TFEU and the commentary thereon by S. de La Rosa in this publication.

[13] Regulation (EU) 2021/691 of the European Parliament and of the Council of 28 April 2021, [2021] *OJ* L153/48. See the latest EGF activity report: COM(2023) 482 final of 11 August 2023, for the years 2021–2022 and the proposal for amending the regulation as regards

of large-scale restructuring involving the cessation of activity of at least 200 redundant workers or self-employed workers, over a reference period of four or six months (depending on the level of development of the region concerned and whether or not SMEs are affected).[14] The measures implemented will aim to facilitate the reintegration into the labour market of those made redundant, in particular by financing training, individualised services to help find a job, outplacement, business creation or even the takeover of businesses by employees. Special measures of limited duration may also be covered, in the form of allowances (job search, mobility, childcare, subsistence, etc.). However, measures that are not conditional on the active participation of the target beneficiaries in job-seeking or training activities and measures that are the responsibility of companies under national law or collective agreements are excluded.

It should also be noted that the EGF is mobilised on a case-by-case basis at the request of the Member State concerned, outside the MFF, with an annual ceiling originally set at €500 million, which has been reduced to €186 million for 2021-2027. The maximum co-financing rate is the highest rate for ESF+ in the Member State concerned, or at least 60%.

We will refer to two examples of EGF allocations: the first example is that of the German metallurgy group GMH Guss, a partner in particular of the KNDS group, the European leader in land defence, with an EGF intervention in 2021 to the tune of €1,081,706 for a wave of redundancies within this group.[15] The second example comes from France, where the EGF mobilised €3,745,264 in 2022 for redundancies within the European Airbus group.[16]

V. THE INVESTEU PROGRAMME

In response to the global financial crisis (2007-2009) and its aftershocks, an investment plan for Europe was agreed in 2014,[17] which led to the creation of the European Fund for Strategic Investments (EFSI) the following year. Managed

---

support to workers affected by imminent job displacement in enterprises undergoing restructuring: COM(2025) 140 final of 1 April 2025.

14 It should be noted that the EGF cannot be mobilised when public sector employees are made redundant as a result of budget cuts decided by a Member State, as may be the case for a Ministry of Defence or the Armed Forces.

15 Decision (EU) 2021/1021 of the European Parliament and of the Council of 8 June 2021 on the mobilisation of the European Globalisation Adjustment Fund following the application submitted by Germany – EGF/2020/003 DE/GMH Guss, [2021] *OJ* L224/14.

16 Decision (EU) 2022/359 of the European Parliament and of the Council of 16 February 2022 on the mobilisation of the European Globalisation Adjustment Fund for Displaced Workers following an application from France – EGF/2021/005 FR/Airbus, [2022] *OJ* L68/15.

17 Communication from the Commission, An Investment Plan for Europe, COM(2014) 903 final of 26 November 2014.

by the European Investment Bank[18] under the terms of an agreement with the Commission, it was initially endowed with €21 billion, via an EU guarantee mechanism in particular, with the aim of stimulating investment to the tune of €315 billion, before being extended until 2020 with a new investment target of €500 billion. It was finally made permanent with the 2021-2027 MFF, through the adoption of a dedicated programme known as InvestEU.[19]

Among the areas likely to benefit from InvestEU is explicitly 'the development of the defence industry in order to contribute to the Union's strategic autonomy'.[20] Support can therefore be given to the defence industry supply chain in the EU, in particular through financial support for SMEs and mid-cap companies; for companies involved in disruptive technology projects in the defence sector and closely related dual-use technologies; for the defence sector supply chain when the entities concerned are involved in collaborative research and development projects in this field, including those financed by the European Defence Fund,[21] and for training and research infrastructures in the defence field. It should be noted that as defence qualifies as a public good, InvestEU is entitled to intervene in this sector to remedy market failures or sub-optimal investment situations, in compliance with the EU Financial Regulation.[22] However, it cannot be mobilised for the use, development or

---

18 Regulation (EU) 2015/1017 of the European Parliament and of the Council of 25 June 2015 on the European Fund for Strategic Investments, the European Investment Advice Hub and the European Investment Project Portal and amending Regulations (EU) No 1291/2013 and (EU) No 1316/2013, OJ L169/1. It should be noted that, in addition to Article 175 TFEU, this Regulation is also based on Articles 172 and 173 TFEU: see the commentary on these articles in this publication, respectively, by S. de La Rosa and D. Fiott.

19 Regulation (EU) 2021/523 of the European Parliament and of the Council of 24 March 2021 establishing the InvestEU Programme and amending Regulation (EU) 2015/1017, [2021] *OJ* L107/30. Double legal basis: Arts. 173 and 175 TFEU. See also Commission Delegated Regulation (EU) 2021/1078 of 14 April 2021 supplementing Regulation (EU) 2021/523 of the European Parliament and of the Council by setting out the investment guidelines for the InvestEU Fund, [2021] *OJ* L 234/18, as amended by Commission Delegated Regulation (EU) 2025/1774 of 28 August 2025, as regards strategic investments in the field of defence set out in the investment guidelines for the InvestEU Fund, [2025] *OJ* L 2025/1774.

20 See point 13 of Annex II to Regulation (EU) 2021/523, cited above.

21 Regulation (EU) 2021/697 of the European Parliament and of the Council of 29 April 2021 establishing the European Defence Fund and repealing Regulation (EU) 2018/1092, [2021] *OJ* L170/149. See the commentary on this regulation by S. Rodrigues in this publication.

22 See Annex V of Regulation (EU) 2021/523, cited above, which refers to Article 209(2)(a) of the EU Financial Regulation (see Regulation (EU, Euratom) 2018/1046 of the European Parliament and of the Council of 18 July 2018 on the financial rules applicable to the general budget of the Union, amending Regulations (EU) No 1296/2013, (EU) No 1301/2013, (EU) No 1303/2013, (EU) No 1304/2013, (EU) No 1309/2013, (EU) No 1316/2013, (EU) No 223/2014, (EU) No 283/2014 and Decision No 541/2014/EU, and repealing Regulation (EU, Euratom) No 966/2012, [2018] *OJ* L193/1. That latter text has been repealed and replaced by Regulation (EU, Euratom) 2024/2509 of the European Parliament and of the Council of 23 September 2024 on the financial rules applicable to the general budget of the Union (recast), *OJ* L2024/2509.

production of products and technologies in the field of defence, which are prohibited by the applicable international law.

The InvestEU web portal provides little information on projects in the defence sector.[23] Two projects stand out: the Celtonn project (INPO-20232976), which aims to develop cutting-edge high-frequency and millimetre-wave solutions for the space, radar, defence and telecommunications industries. This project, with a budget of €1.5 million, is being carried out by a start-up hosted by the innovation centre at the University of Limerick (Ireland). Secondly, the PowerUp project, led by three Estonian, French and Polish SMEs, to develop new-generation generators based on fuel cells (EIPP-2020154) for the maritime, automotive and military industries, with a budget of €1 million.

Finally, other projects with a civilian dimension could also lead to military applications, such as the Franco-Iberian Allpriv project (INPO-20232976) which, with an estimated budget of €2.4 million, aims to innovate in the protection of medical equipment in hospitals to enable them to continue operating in the event of a cyber-attack.

***

The coming years should see an increase in the number of projects eligible for ESIF funding in the field of defence. Indeed, the new European Defence Industrial Strategy (EDIS) (2024), mentioned above, states that the Commission will consider including or maintaining defence preparedness, security and resilience as an explicit strategic objective in future relevant EU programmes to ensure that they fully support the EDTIB and that implementing partners and intermediaries (in the case of indirect management) do not face obstacles in pursuing these objectives.

The Joint White Paper for European Defence Readiness 2030, adopted on 19 March 2025 by the European Commission and the High Representative,[24] confirms that cohesion policy should contribute to defence and security capabilities, by funding security and defence-related investments 'that contribute to regional development as defence industries often create research and development and industrial ecosystems which benefit Europe's regions and communities'. With this in mind, the White Paper invites the EU co-legislators to consider some changes to the EU cohesion funds, within the framework of the mid-term review of the EU cohesion policy.[25] To that purpose, on 1 April 2025, the European Commission presented a proposal for amending, inter

---

23 https://ec.europa.eu/investeuportal/desktop/en/index.html (consulted on 17 March 2024).

24 JOIN(2025) 120 final.

25 See Commission Communication, 'A modernised Cohesion policy: The mid-term review', COM(2025) 163 final, 1 April 2025.

alia, Regulation (EU) 2021/1058.[26] Two new specific objectives will be created within the existing scope of the ERDF support. The first new specific objective will allow Member States to reprogramme under their 2021-2027 programmes under the Investments for jobs and growth goal amounts for enhancing productive capacities in enterprises in the defence sector without restriction in terms of geography or size of the enterprise. Productive investments in enterprises other than SMEs and made in all EU regions should also be able to access financial support for defence industry projects of common interest under EDIP and reinforce Europe's overall defence and preparedness capacities. The second new specific objective related to defence will contribute to building resilient defence or dual use infrastructure to foster military mobility in the EU. To encourage Member States to implement those new objectives, they will, when using the proposed framework, benefit from an additional one-off pre-financing of 30% of the amounts programmed under the dedicated priority and the possibility to apply a Union financing of up to 100% regarding both specific objectives – provided that the programme amendment is submitted in 2025.

We think this reform is a step in the right direction[27] even if it is not without its flaws.[28] What remains to be done is to better communicate and inform potential project sponsors of funding opportunities and to convince the companies concerned to play the game of putting together ESIF applications and ensuring the transparency of the funding applied for and obtained.[29]

---

[26] See Proposal for a regulation of the European Parliament and of the Council amending Regulations (EU) 2021/1058 and (EU) 2021/1056 as regards specific measures to address strategic challenges in the context of the mid-term review, COM(2025) 123 final, 1 April 2025.

[27] See also in the right direction, the proposal from the Commission to allow the Recovery and Resilience Facility (RRF) (see Regulation (EU) 2021/241 of the European Parliament and of the Council of 12 February 2021 establishing the Recovery and Resilience Facility,[2021] *OJ* L57/17) to support voluntary national contributions to the future European Defence Industry Programme (EDIP). Therefore, the contribution to EDIP in such a case would be considered an RRF investment. See: Communication from the Commission, *NextGenerationEU – The road to 2026*, COM(2025) 310 final, 4 June 2025, Section 3.2.

[28] See on that proposal, the opinion 02/2025 of the European Court of Auditors of 30 April 2025, which makes a number of criticisms on the absence of an impact assessment, the risk to further widening the scope of the EU cohesion policy and diverting resources from its core mission of reducing regional disparities, as well as the risk of adding further to the fragmentation of cohesion policy programmes. Besides, the ECA insists on several sources of legal uncertainty: the proposal does not clarify how these investments would contribute to the objective of cohesion to strengthen territorial, economic and social cohesion as set out in the TFEU; the proposal does not include, for defence investments, any derogations from the horizontal principles stated in Regulation (EU) 2021/1060 (e.g. the 'do no significant harm' environment principle, the application of the General Block Exemption Regulation (GBER) in case of state aids, transparency obligations, etc.). Last, the proposal does not establish any eligibility criteria on the country of establishment of entities supported for dual-use or defence capability projects and does not make any reference to EDIS.

[29] See Art. 38 of the EU Financial Regulation, cited above.

Postscript December 2025

The European Parliament and the Council have adopted, on 18 September 2025:

- Regulation (EU) 2025/1913 amending Regulation (EU) 2021/1057 establishing the European Social Fund Plus (ESF+) as regards specific measures to address strategic challenges.[30] Member States may now use the ESF+ 'to provide support for the development of skills in civil preparedness, in the defence industry including for dual-use capabilities, and in cybersecurity under dedicated priorities, prioritising skills related to dual-use capabilities and civil preparedness'.
- Regulation (EU) 2025/1914 of the European Parliament and of the Council of 18 September 2025 amending Regulations (EU) 2021/1058 and (EU) 2021/1056 as regards specific measures to address strategic challenges in the context of the mid-term review.[31] New specific objectives are defined for the ERDF and the Cohesion Fund as follows: enhancing industrial capacities to foster defence capabilities, prioritising capabilities of a dual-use nature, developing resilient defence infrastructure, including to foster military mobility in the Union, as well as enhancing civil preparedness.

It may be interesting to note that 'given the urgent need to enable crucial investments, in particular in defence capabilities in the context of pressing geopolitical challenges',[32] those Regulations entered into force on the day following that of its publication in the Official Journal of the European Union.

Last, on 29 December 2025, the Regulation (EU) 2025/2643 of 16 December 2025 establishing the European Defence Industry Programme and a framework of measures to ensure the timely availability and supply of defence products ('EDIP Regulation') has been published (OJ L/2025/2643).

30 [2025] *OJ* L2025/1913.
31 [2025] *OJ* L2025/1914.
32 See Recital 18 of Regulation (EU)2025/1913 and Recital 24 of Regulation (EU)2025/1914.

ARTICLES 179 TO 190 TFEU: EU RESEARCH AND DEVELOPMENT POLICY IN DEFENCE

Fabrice ANDREONE
Doctor of Law, HDR
Adviser/Senior Expert at the European Commission[1]

and

Angelo FERRAZZOLI
Legal Analyst at the European Commission[2]

Article 179

1. The Union shall have the objective of strengthening its scientific and technological bases by achieving a European research area in which researchers, scientific knowledge and technology circulate freely, and encouraging it to become more competitive, including in its industry, while promoting all the research activities deemed necessary by virtue of other Chapters of the Treaties.

2. For this purpose the Union shall, throughout the Union, encourage undertakings, including small and medium-sized undertakings, research centres and universities in their research and technological development activities of high quality; it shall support their efforts to cooperate with one another, aiming, notably, at permitting researchers to cooperate freely across borders and at enabling undertakings to exploit the internal market potential to the full, in particular through the opening-up of national public contracts, the definition of common standards and the removal of legal and fiscal obstacles to that cooperation.

---

1 This article is written in a strictly personal capacity by the author. It does not commit the Commission or the European Union in any way.

2 This article is written in a strictly personal capacity by the author. It does not commit the Commission or the European Union in any way.

All Union activities under the Treaties in the area of research and technological development, including demonstration projects, shall be decided on and implemented in accordance with the provisions of this Title.

Article 180

In pursuing these objectives, the Union shall carry out the following activities, complementing the activities carried out in the Member States:

a) implementation of research, technological development and demonstration programmes, by promoting cooperation with and between undertakings, research centres and universities;

b) promotion of cooperation in the field of Union research, technological development and demonstration with third countries and international organisations;

c) dissemination and optimisation of the results of activities in Union research, technological development and demonstration;

d) stimulation of the training and mobility of researchers in the Union.

Article 181

1. The Union and the Member States shall coordinate their research and technological development activities so as to ensure that national policies and Union policy are mutually consistent.

2. In close cooperation with the Member State, the Commission may take any useful initiative to promote the coordination referred to in paragraph 1, in particular initiatives aiming at the establishment of guidelines and indicators, the organisation of exchange of best practice, and the preparation of the necessary elements for periodic monitoring and evaluation. The European Parliament shall be kept fully informed.

Article 182

1. A multiannual framework programme, setting out all the activities of the Union, shall be adopted by the European Parliament and the Council, acting in accordance with the ordinary legislative procedure after consulting the Economic and Social Committee. The framework programme shall:

– establish the scientific and technological objectives to be achieved by the activities provided for in Article 180 and fix the relevant priorities;

– indicate the broad lines of such activities,

– fix the maximum overall amount and the detailed rules for Union financial participation in the framework programme and the respective shares in each of the activities provided for.

2. The framework programme shall be adapted or supplemented as the situation changes.

3. The framework programme shall be implemented through specific programmes developed within each activity. Each specific programme shall define the detailed rules for implementing it, fix its duration and provide for the means deemed necessary. The sum of the amounts deemed necessary, fixed in the specific programmes, may not exceed the overall maximum amount fixed for the framework programme and each activity.

4. The Council, acting in accordance with a special legislative procedure and after consulting the European Parliament and the Economic and Social Committee, shall adopt the specific programmes.

5. As a complement to the activities planned in the multiannual framework programme, the European Parliament and the Council, acting in accordance with the ordinary legislative procedure and after consulting the Economic and Social Committee, shall establish the measures necessary for the implementation of the European research area.

Article 183

For the implementation of the multiannual framework programme the Union shall:

– determine the rules for the participation of undertakings, research centres and universities,

– lay down the rules governing the dissemination of research results.

Article 184

In implementing the multiannual framework programme, supplementary programmes may be decided on involving the participation of certain Member States only, which shall finance them subject to possible Union participation.

The Union shall adopt the rules applicable to supplementary programmes, particularly as regards the dissemination of knowledge and access by other Member States.

Article 185

In implementing the multiannual framework programme, the Union may make provision, in agreement with the Member States concerned, for participation in research and development programmes undertaken by several Member States, including participation in the structures created for the execution of those programmes.

Article 186

In implementing the multiannual framework programme the Union may make provision for cooperation in Union research, technological development and demonstration with third countries or international organisations.

The detailed arrangements for such cooperation may be the subject of agreements between the Union and the third parties concerned.

Article 187

The Union may set up joint undertakings or any other structure necessary for the efficient execution of Union research, technological development and demonstration programmes.

Article 188

The Council, on a proposal from the Commission and after consulting the European Parliament and the Economic and Social Committee, shall adopt the provisions referred to in Article 187.

The European Parliament and the Council, acting in accordance with the ordinary legislative procedure and after consulting the Economic and Social Committee, shall adopt the provisions referred to in Articles 183, 184 and 185. Adoption of the supplementary programmes shall require the agreement of the Member States concerned.

Article 189

1. To promote scientific and technical progress, industrial competitiveness and the implementation of its policies, the Union shall draw up a European space policy. To this end, it may promote joint initiatives, support research and technological development and coordinate the efforts needed for the exploration and exploitation of space.

2. To contribute to attaining the objectives referred to in paragraph 1, the European Parliament and the Council, acting in accordance with the ordinary legislative procedure, shall establish the necessary measures, which may take the form of a European space programme, excluding any harmonisation of the laws and regulations of the Member States.

3. The Union shall establish any appropriate relations with the European Space Agency.

4. This Article shall be without prejudice to the other provisions of this Title.

Article 190

At the beginning of each year the Commission shall send a report to the European Parliament and to the Council. The report shall include information on research and technological development activities and the dissemination of results during the previous year, and the work programme for the current year.

Defence research has a number of distinctive features compared with civilian research. These stem from its strategic orientation, its importance in terms of internal and external security, and its impact on the development of technologies in general, and their repercussions on civil society in particular.

On the one hand, this type of research aims to develop emerging and disruptive technologies that are likely to transform military capabilities, offering a significant strategic advantage to the state that possesses them. On the other hand, defence research plays a crucial role in innovation, not only by responding to immediate needs, but also by exploring innovative ideas that can lead to significant breakthroughs. It therefore requires an environment conducive to 'ideation', where researchers can envisage new applications.

As a result, defence R&D stimulates innovation in the industrial sector, particularly in cutting-edge technologies. It also benefits from special collaboration between developers (government defence agencies and their industrial partners) and end-users (armed forces).

In addition, it is strongly driven by defence policy objectives and operational needs, which require, at the very least, long-term planning. Defence research is, of course, characterised by a high degree of confidentiality due to the imperative of national security; this distinguishes it, at least in part, from civilian research and links it to the strategic autonomy of key players who thus ensure an important basis of sovereign power.

However, if we distinguish between civil and defence research, we can see that there is a great deal of porosity between them, allowing for mutual enrichment and sometimes even making it difficult to distinguish between them. In this respect, we might recall the quotation attributed to Talleyrand: 'We call military everything that is not civilian'.

With this duality established, it is hardly surprising that the research sectors linked to defence include aeronautics, electronics, nuclear power, cybersecurity and, more recently, artificial intelligence.

Today, the European Union once again finds itself at a crossroads, faced with growing geopolitical challenges and ever more rapidly evolving technologies, as well as the emergence of new threats. In this new context, support for defence-related research is crucial, as it helps to strengthen 'the competitiveness, efficiency and innovation capacity of the European Defence Technological and Industrial Base (EDTIB) throughout the Union, which contributes to the Union's strategic autonomy'.[3] This reinforcement requires in-depth cooperation to meet the costs associated with research and development, as well as the risks associated with the research phase for technologies at a low level of maturity.

3 Regulation (EU) 2021/697 of the European Parliament and of the Council of 29 April 2021 establishing the European Defence Fund and repealing Regulation (EU) 2018/1092, [2021] *OJ* L170/149, Art. 3.

It is therefore important to explore the Union's recent initiatives, such as the European Defence Fund (EDF) in its dimension of support for research[4] and the proposal to integrate dual-use research, whose applications may have both civilian and military uses, in the future Framework Programme for Research and Development (FP10), underlining the EU's efforts to consolidate its defence capabilities, stimulate technological innovation and ensure its economic security.

These steps reflect a desire to adapt the EU's legal and financial framework to contemporary reality, where the distinction between civil and military applications is becoming increasingly blurred. Articles 179 to 190 TFEU, grouped in Title XIX entitled 'Research, Technological Development and Space', have already served as the legal basis for the EDF regulation and the harmonisation of the internal defence market.

These provisions have created a basis for the EU's strategic autonomy in research, development and space[5] which we explore below as follows: after a presentation of the general principles guiding European defence research (Section I), the chapter will focus on the definition and implementation of support actions in this area (Section II).

I. THE GENERAL PRINCIPLES OF EUROPEAN RESEARCH AND DEFENCE UNION

A. THE OBJECTIVES OF THE EUROPEAN UNION'S RESEARCH POLICY

The Single European Act (Art. 130f) already contained provisions relating to the objectives of European Community (EC) research policy. However, the concept of a European Research Area (ERA)[6] was launched in earnest by the European Commission in a communication entitled 'Towards a European Research Area' of 19 July 2000.[7] The aim was to remedy the overlapping and fragmented nature of Member States' national research and innovation systems, in the context of the Lisbon strategy.[8] This text can be seen as the

---

4 See the commentary by S. Rodrigues on the European Defence Fund in this publication.

5 On the specific features of space policy, see the contribution by A. de Neve in this publication.

6 The acronym ERA stands for European Research Area.

7 Communication from the Commission to the Council, the European Parliament, the Economic and Social Committee and the Committee of the Regions, 'Towards a European Research Area', COM(2000) 6 final, 18 January 2000, followed by the Council Resolution (2000/C 205/01) on establishing a European area of research and innovation, 15 June 2000, [2000] *OJ* C205/1.

8 European Council, 'Presidency Conclusions', Lisbon Summit, 23 and 24 March 2000.

lead-in for the changes to EU primary law that were made in the context of the Lisbon Treaty. The wording of Article 179 TFEU makes the creation of the ERA the main objective of the Treaty in the field of research. It is *de facto* the political dimension of this Union action.[9]

The aim of the EU's Framework Programmes for Research and Technological Development (FPRDT), set out in Articles 182 and 183 TFEU,[10] is to support the development and establishment of the European Research Area. It is also one of the largest items in the EU budget: around €95.5 billion between 2021 and 2027[11] under the current multiannual financial framework (MFF).[12]

The creation of a European Research Area[13] provided for in Article 179 TFEU is based on the following three pillars: i) the creation of an 'internal market' for research, a genuine area of free movement of knowledge, researchers and technologies, designed to strengthen cooperation, stimulate competition and optimise the allocation of resources; ii) the restructuring of the European research fabric, essentially through better coordination of national research activities and policies; and iii) the development of a European policy that goes beyond the funding of research activities and covers all aspects of other national and European research policies.[14] The link between research and defence policies can therefore be found in the third strand of the European Research Area, although the legal basis of Article 179 TFEU does not *expressly* concern the Defence Union.

---

9 As highlighted by the proposal for the next Framework Programme: 'It is an objective of the Union to strengthen its scientific and technological bases by strengthening the European research area (ERA) in which researchers, scientific knowledge and technology circulate freely [...]'. European Commission, Proposal for a Regulation of the European Parliament and of the Council establishing Horizon Europe, the Framework Programme for Research and Innovation, for the period 2028–2034 laying down its rules for participation and dissemination, and repealing Regulation (EU) 2021/695, Brussels, 16 July 2025, COM(2025) 543 final, 2025/0543(COD), CELEX: 52025PC0543, accompanying documents: {SEC(2025) 555}, {SWD(2025) 555}, {SWD(2025) 556}, Explanatory Memorandum.

10 See below.

11 European Commission, Directorate-General for Research and Innovation, *Horizon Europe, budget: Horizon Europe – the most ambitious EU research & innovation programme ever*, Publications Office of the European Union, 2021, https://data.europa.eu/doi/10.2777/109078, consulted in February 2024.

12 Council Regulation (EU, Euratom) 2020/2093 of 17 December 2020 laying down the multiannual financial framework for the years 2021 to 2027, [2020] *OJ* L433I/11. See latest amended proposal for a Council Regulation amending Regulation (EU, Euratom) 2020/2093 laying down the multiannual financial framework for the years 2021 to 2027, COM(2026) 21 final.

13 Communication from the European Commission to the European Parliament, the Council, the European Economic and Social Committee and the Committee of the Regions, 'A new ERA for research and innovation', COM(2020) 628 final, Brussels, 30 September 2020.

14 For more details on the latest actions taken, see the DG R&I annual report published on 19 June 2023, available at https://commission.europa.eu/publications/annual-activity-report-2022-research-and-innovation_en?prefLang=fr (consulted in February 2024).

Article 179 TFEU also refers to the competitiveness of European industry, which could be improved by strengthening its research base. It could be argued that defence industries are also concerned; at the very least, they are not excluded from the scope of this provision. Furthermore, industries that produce goods based on dual technologies are certainly concerned.

However, it should be noted that the European co-legislators and the Commission have chosen in particular to retain the legal basis of Article 173(3) TFEU relating to the industrial competitiveness of the Union, in general, which therefore also applies to the EDTIB,[15] to establish the European Defence Fund, the European Defence Industrial Development Programme (EDIDP) and the EDIRPA.[16] This sidelines Article 179 TFEU, whose objective is more limited. It aims in fact at strengthening the Union's scientific and technological bases, in particular to develop its competitiveness, as well as that of its industry. The provisions of Article 179 TFEU therefore appear to be much more limited than those of Article 173 TFEU[17] in providing a legal basis for the creation of the EDF and the EDIDP.

Finally, primary law provides for the possibility of adopting harmonising legislation to create a European Research Area.[18] This is subject to the ordinary legislative procedure, after consultation of the European Economic and Social Committee (EESC), as defined in Article 182(5) TFEU.

An example of this is the recent proposal for a Council Recommendation on improving the safety of research,[19] the legal basis for which is Article 182(5) and the first and second sentences of Article 292 TFEU.

Although this proposal is not specifically aimed at the defence sector, its objectives remain relevant because they concern security and, in particular, the undesirable transfer of knowledge, know-how and critical technologies that could affect the security of the EU and its Member States, for example, if they are sent to third countries for military purposes.

---

15 See above.

16 See below. Regulation (EU) 2023/2418 of the European Parliament and of the Council of 18 October 2023 on establishing an instrument to strengthen the European defence industry through common procurement (EDIRPA), [2023] *OJ L2023/2418*. On this regulation see the commentary by E. Bernard in this publication.

17 See the contribution by D. Fiott and F. Liberti on Article 173 TFEU in this publication.

18 On the question of harmonisation, with regard to the specific features of space policy, see the contribution by A. de Neve in this publication.

19 Council Recommendation of 23 May 2024 on enhancing research security, (C/2024/3510), [2024] *OJ* C/2024/3510.

B. THE LIMITS TO THE UNION'S ACTION AS LAID DOWN BY PRIMARY LAW: THE NECESSARY COMPLEMENTARITY WITH THE RESEARCH ACTIVITIES OF THE MEMBER STATES (ARTICLES 180(1) TFEU AND 181(1) TFEU)

Article 180(1) TFEU places a limit on EU action in the field of research: it must complement the policies of the Member States. Thus, the Union's competence to take action in this area does not have the effect of preventing the Member States from exercising their own competence, in accordance with Article 4(3) TFEU. A peculiarity can be identified here with regard to the framework of the Union's competences in the context of Article 2(2) TFEU with the introduction by Article 4(3) TFEU of a less extensive shared competence.

The logical consequence of the two above-mentioned provisions is the obligation for the Union and its Member States to coordinate in the field of research to ensure the consistency of national and EU policies (Art. 181 TFEU). This is an obligation because the wording of this provision uses the present tense, which makes it imperative not only for the Member States but also for the Union. It should also be noted that the field of research lends itself to the open method of coordination (OMC).[20]

In addition, in the context of the Intergovernmental Conference at the origin of the Treaty of Lisbon, the Declaration on Article 179 TFEU states:

> 'The Conference agrees that the Union's action in the area of research and technological development will pay due respect to the fundamental orientations and choices of the research policies of the Member States.'

In order to implement this coordination provided for in primary law, the Commission, in collaboration with the Member States, may draw up guidelines and indicators, organise the exchange of best practice and prepare the necessary elements for the evaluation of research policies, which is also the subject of an annual report (see Art. 190 TFEU).[21]

Article 181(2) TFEU states that the Commission may take initiatives, in collaboration with the Member States, in support of the coordination obligation set out in Article 181(1). More specifically, it shall establish indicators and issue guidelines in the field of the European Research Area (ERA). The Commission also regularly adopts reports on the functioning of the ERA in

[20] To this end, see the Green Paper of 4 April 2007 on 'The European Research Area: New Perspectives' [COM(2007) 161 final – Not published in the *Official Journal*] and, more recently, see Council Recommendation (EU) 2012/2415 of 2 December 2022 on the guiding principles for knowledge valorisation, [2022] *OJ* L317/141.

[21] See below.

which it monitors the various indicators and produces the relevant statistics.[22] Moreover, it regularly evaluates the framework programme.[23][24]

These provisions do not currently cover defence-related research activities. However, it is certain that if the Union were to decide to develop a research policy for dual-use goods in the context of the next framework programme,[25] it would then be necessary to ensure the consistency of the different levels of research policy, as prescribed by the aforementioned provisions of primary law. The provisions of the second paragraph of Article 181 TFEU could also be applied to dual-use research in the next FP, with restrictions on information due to the sensitivity of the defence sector.

II. DEFINITION AND IMPLEMENTATION OF ACTIONS TO SUPPORT DEFENCE RESEARCH AND THE DEFENCE UNION

A. DEFINITION OF EU ACTIONS IN THE FIELD OF RESEARCH: SUPPORT FOR THE EUROPEAN UNION'S RESEARCH OBJECTIVES AS DEFINED IN ARTICLE 179 TFEU

Article 180 TFEU lists the actions which implement the objectives of the Union's research policy as set out in Article 179 TFEU.[26] They are then specified in Articles 182 to 189 TFEU.

Article 180 TFEU provides for the definition and implementation of a European research, development and demonstration programme that is a driving force for promoting cooperation between/with businesses, universities and research centres. It should be noted that the aim is not only to support fundamental research but also more applied research (demonstration activities), with a view to competitiveness, as mentioned in Articles 173 and 179 TFEU.

Article 180 TFEU also refers to international cooperation with third countries and international organisations as a category of activities that make it

22 Available at https://european-research-area.ec.europa.eu/era-monitoring-reports (consulted in February 2024).

23 As provided for in Article 190 (see above), a monitoring mechanism is provided for in the Treaties and takes the form of communications from the Commission. See the Report from the Commission to the European Parliament and the Council, 'Annual Report on Research and Technological Development Activities of the European Union and the Monitoring of Horizon Europe and Horizon 2020 in 2022', COM(2023) 277 final, Brussels, 31 May 2023.

24 See below.

25 Ibid.

26 See above.

possible to implement the objectives of EU research policy. Article 186 TFEU[27] then sets out the details of this international cooperation.

Finally, the provisions of Article 180 TFEU mention research dissemination and exploitation activities and the mobility of researchers, which are two major pillars of the European Research Area.[28] *De facto*, these aspects are implemented directly by the Framework Programme.

It should be noted that the provisions of the EU Treaties that define research activities and their limits do not explicitly mention defence research, although they do not formally exclude it. Defence policy, *strict speaking*, clearly falls within the scope of Article 41 TEU.[29] Primary law therefore makes a distinction between research and defence, which depend on different and identified legal bases. Consequently, at this stage, while developments in research may obviously have implications for security and defence, and they remain distinct from military and security issues. apart from in dual-use areas.

B. MECHANISMS FOR IMPLEMENTING EUROPEAN RESEARCH POLICY

1. The European Union's Research Framework Programme

a. – The Union's Research Framework Programme as Defined in Articles 180(a) TFEU, 182(1) to (4) and 183 TFEU

The European Union's Framework Programme for Research and Development (FPRD), defined in Articles 182 and 183 TFEU, lays down the scientific guidelines for EU-funded research, the broad outlines of this research, the level of funding and the rules for the participation of the various players involved in this policy (training and mobility of researchers). It also sets out the rules for exploiting and disseminating EU-funded research. The implementation of the research activities defined in points c) and d) of Article 180 TFEU is therefore covered by the Framework Programme and not by a separate legal basis in the context of the Treaty.

The framework programme is multiannual, with no specific duration indicated in the provisions mentioned. Today, its seven-year duration is aligned

---

27 See below.

28 Communication from the European Commission to the European Parliament, the Council, the European Economic and Social Committee and the Committee of the Regions, 'A new ERA for research and innovation', cited above. See also, on the question of researcher mobility, the Council Recommendation of 18 December 2023 on a European framework to attract and retain researchers, innovation and entrepreneurial talents in Europe, (C/2023/1640). For recent developments, see the DG R&I annual report, cited above.

29 See the commentary by A. Potteau in this publication.

with that of the Multiannual Financial Framework (MFF). Article 182(2) TFEU states that these actions shall be implemented through specific programmes. Each programme lays down its own operating procedures and maximum budgetary amounts (expenditure ceilings).

The distinction made by EU primary law between framework programmes and specific programmes has an institutional consequence. The TFEU provides for the ordinary legislative procedure to be used to adopt the framework programme (Article 188(2) TFEU) and a special legislative procedure (consultation of the European Parliament and the EESC) to adopt the specific programmes (Article 182(4) TFEU).

At this stage, it is important to consider the potential links between the Framework Programme and defence research.

The European Union's current research programme has its origins in the ECSC Treaty (Articles 50 and 55 ECSC) and the EAEC Treaty (Articles 2 and 4(1) EAEC), which deal with nuclear research in the civil sector only.[30] There is also a reference to a research policy in the agricultural field in the provisions of the EEC Treaty (Art. 41 EEC).

As a reminder, from 1986 onwards, the Single European Act provided a solid legal basis for European research policy (Title VI, Art. 130 F) to 130 Q of the TEC).[31] Moreover, this basis has not been fundamentally revised by successive constitutional changes until the Treaty of Lisbon.

At the turn of the 2000s, the Union was an organisation whose main objective was to promote peace through trade and development. Issues relating to defence fall within its remit only through the CSDP and the free movement of goods with a dual-use component. From the outset, it does not appear that the European research programme was intended to risk supporting defence research.

From the end of the 1990s onwards, activities with a dual component have been high on the European agenda. As early as 2003, the Commission showed an interest in the links between civil and military research, particularly in the field of space[32] but also in internal and external security issues.[33] However, the idea of European defence research remains at an embryonic stage.

30 See the commentary on the EAEC Treaty in this publication by A. Popov.

31 See above.

32 Communication from the Commission to the Council, the European Parliament, the European Economic and Social Committee and the Committee of the Regions, 'European Defence – Industrial and Market Issues – Towards an EU Defence Equipment Policy', COM(2003) 113 final, Brussels, 11 March 2003. On the space dimension of research, see the contribution by A. de Neve in this publication (commentary on Article 189 TFEU).

33 Communication from the Commission to the Council and the European Parliament, 'Area of Freedom, Security and Justice: Assessment of the Tampere programme and future orientations', COM(2004) 0401 final, 2 June 2004.

For the first time, FP7 (2007–2013) includes a theme devoted to security within the specific 'cooperation' programme[34] and a theme relating to space, the dual aspects of which are indisputable. However, the text does not include the word 'defence'. Instead, it covers activities relating to European home affairs policy (police, justice, etc.). There are plans to support the development of satellite surveillance and early warning systems and techniques, including for the safety of citizens in terms of environmental management and security. There is also support for the development of space telescopes and detectors, and for data analysis in the space sciences, whose dual dimension is obvious to all. The 10th theme of the 'cooperation programme' aims to guarantee the security of citizens in the face of terrorism and crime. It refers to the European security strategy entitled 'A secure Europe in a better world',[35] adopted by the European Council, the aim of which is to respond to the need to put in place a security strategy comprising measures in both the civilian and defence fields. The text also states that the research funded will remain civilian. The time has not yet come to fund military research. However, the funding of dual-use civilian research is not ruled out. In this case, it is even planned to decide on cooperation with the European Defence Agency (EDA).[36]

Thus, with FP7 or Seventh Framework Programme (2007-2013), the Commission ventured into the field of defence for the first time through Articles 182 and 183 TFEU, which confer powers on the EU in the area of European research. However, this foray into defence policy, which was previously the preserve of the Member States, was still very timid. Indeed, Article 45(1) TEU confers on the EDA[37] competences in the field of defence-related research.[38] However, although the Commission was moving into defence issues by the back door, let there be no mistake: this was the start of a process that would give rise fifteen years later to the European Defence Fund.[39]

---

34 The search for new technological solutions in the field of security will focus on four areas: protection against terrorism and crime; security of infrastructures and utilities; border security; and restoring security in the event of a crisis.

35 Council of the European Union, 'European Security Strategy: A Secure Europe in a Better World', Brussels, [Not published in the *Official Journal*].

36 European Council, Presidency Conclusions of 19 and 20 December 2013, EUCO 217/13, CO EUR 15, CONCL 8, forwarded by the General Secretariat of the Council to delegations, Brussels, 20 December 2013.

37 See Art. 45(1) TEU: 'd) support defence technology research, and coordinate and plan joint research activities and the study of technical solutions meeting future operational requirements; e) contribute to identifying and, if necessary, implementing any useful measure for strengthening the industrial and technological base of the defence sector and for improving the effectiveness of military spending'.

38 See the commentary on Article 45 TEU by A.-H. Bertana in this publication.

39 See below.

Since September 2011 and the conclusion of the cooperation agreement with the EDA,[40] the European Commission has been involved in supporting research into dual technologies, for which the Agency is the prime contractor. This involves activities such as protection against the so-called NRBC-E threat (nuclear, radiological, biological, chemical and explosive), drone systems and cyber defence (ESSOR programme).

In its Communication of 24 July 2013 'Towards a more competitive and efficient defence and security sector',[41] the Commission noted the existence of numerous synergies between civil and military research, leading to the necessary coordination in the context of the 'security' strand of FP7 and research activities in the field of European defence. By way of example, this text mentions the work that has been carried out on CBRN-E threats, cyber defence in the context of the Common Security and Defence Policy (CSDP) and its synergies with cybersecurity. Several activities in this area have also been announced as part of the Union's cybersecurity strategy.[42]

In addition, the Communication mentions for the first time the possibility of funding a preparatory action on defence capabilities essential for CSDP operations, to seek synergies with national research programmes. It proposes that the Commission, together with the Member States, the EEAS and the EDA, should define the content and modalities of such an action. This action falls outside the traditional scope of the Framework Programme, which concerns civil research. Since the adoption of the ECSC Treaty, this is the first Commission text to mention the possibility of adopting a research action in the field of defence. The conclusions of the European Council of 19 and 20 December 2013[43] validate this approach.

Since 2016, the European Commission's involvement in defence has been supported at the highest political level. In his State of the Union address in autumn 2016,[44] Jean-Claude Juncker stated his desire to develop a European defence policy. To make this political statement operational, the Commission

40 Coordination agreement (European Framework cooperation) available at: https://eda.europa.eu/news-and-events/news/11-09-16/EDA_and_the_Commission_signed_a_European_Framework_Cooperation_coordination_letter_yesterday. See also N. Karampekios *et al* (eds.), *The Emergence of EU Defense Research Policy*, Innovation, Technology, and Knowledge Management, Switzerland, Springer, 2018, https://doi.org/10.1007/978-3-319-68807-7_14.

41 European Commission, 'Towards a more competitive and efficient defence and security sector', COM(2013) 542 final, Brussels, 24 July 2013 and SWD(2013) 219.

42 Examples include aspects relating to interdependence and sectoral cooperation, as well as information sharing and collaboration. These points in particular highlight the need for close cooperation and improved information sharing to tackle cybersecurity challenges in a context of increasing interdependence. In this respect, it should be emphasised that the strategy aims to establish a solid framework for strengthening Europe's digital security, based on the commitment of all the players concerned, at both national and European level.

43 European Council, Presidency Conclusions of 19 and 20 December 2013, para. 18.

44 The State of the Union Address 2016: 'Towards a better Europe – A Europe that Protects, Empowers and Defends', Strasbourg, 14 September 2016.

adopted an initial communication on the 'European Defence Action Plan' on 30 November 2016.[45] This was quickly followed by a second communication, in June 2017, entitled 'Launch of the European Defence Fund'[46] which already provided for further preparatory action in the field of defence.

Initially, the Commission decided that the research component of the European Defence Fund would consist of a preparatory action worth €90 million between 2017 and 2019,[47] including €25 million in the first year,[48] €40 million in 2018 and €25 million in 2019. The Commission signed a delegation agreement with the European Defence Agency on 31 May 2017. In the context of an indirect management mode, it delegates the management of the preparatory action to this body. The approach adopted for this action is similar to that adopted for the Framework Programme: call for proposals, evaluations and award of grants to one or more consortia.[49] The first calls were published on 7 June 2017 and the first grant agreements were signed at the end of 2017. For the implementation of the Preparatory Action, the Commission was assisted by a group of experts from the Member States which foreshadowed the comitology rules,[50] and by an Advisory Group bringing together experts from industry, research and technology organisations, universities, the EDA and the European External Action Service (EEAS). Regulation (EU) 2021/697 of the European Parliament and of the Council of 29 April 2021 formally established the European Defence Fund.

Secondly, the aforementioned 2017 Commission Communication provided for the adoption of a capability strand with the *European Defence Industrial Development Programme (EDIDP)*, with a budget of €245 million in 2019 and €255 million in 2020, in line with the conclusions of the Group of Personalities on European Defence Research,[51] and the European Parliament's report on

---

45 European Commission, 'European Defence Action Plan', Brussels, 30 November 2016.

46 European Commission, 'Launch of the European Defence Fund', COM(2017) 295 final, Brussels, 7 June 2017.

47 Conclusions of the European Council of 19 and 20 December 2013, EUCO 217/13.

48 Commission Decision on the financing of the 'Preparatory action on Defence Research and the use of unit costs for 2017' (C(2017) 2262 of 11 April 2017). It constitutes a funding decision for the year 2017. An annex to the decision provides a detailed description of the areas of intervention for 2017.

49 See below.

50 Regulation (EU) No 182/2011 of the European Parliament and of the Council of 16 February 2011 laying down the rules and general principles concerning mechanisms for control by Member States of the Commission's exercise of implementing powers, [2011] *OJ* L55/13.

51 See European Union Institute for Security Studies, Report of the group of personalities on the preparatory action for CSDP-related research: the case for an EU-funded defence R&T programme: catalysing cooperation, enabling capabilities, sustaining competitiveness, European Union Institute for Security Studies, 2016, available at https://data.europa.eu/doi/10.2815/65051 (accessed February 2024).

the Defence Union.[52] Regulation (EU) 2018/1092[53] of the European Parliament and of the Council establishes the European Defence Industrial Development Programme.

This unprecedented financial effort in the field of defence is monitored in the context of the new Multiannual Financial Framework 2021-2027, adopted by the Council in December 2020. Heading V of this multiannual programming document sets a budget of €13.185 billion for security and defence. The EDF regulation has a budget of €7.9 billion for research (Art. 4 of the EDF regulation).[54]

As already mentioned, Article 173(3) TFEU is one of the legal bases of the EDF. This provision of the Treaty concerns the competitiveness of European industry, in this case defence (EDTIB),[55] and actions to support Member States in this area. It is envisaged that the funding of the specific defence research programme will be separate from the Framework Programme. Consequently, the EDF constitutes an EU research programme, distinct from the Framework Programme provided for in Articles 182 and 183 TFEU, both in terms of its legal basis and its funding.

It should be noted that the citations of this text also refer to Article 188(2) TFEU for recourse to the ordinary legislative procedure, as is the case for the Framework Programme. They also refer to Article 183 TFEU, which sets out the rules for implementing the FP.

The way in which the two research programmes are implemented (the EDF and FPRTD) is very similar.

In both cases, the European Commission adopts work programmes that define the strategic research priorities. The Commission adopts the EDF work programme as well as the various work programmes relating to each of the specific the FPRTD (Art. 182(3) TFEU). It should be noted that the methods for adopting these documents are similar for both the EDF and the FPRD. Indeed, Article 24 of the Regulation establishing the EDF provides that the annual work programmes shall be adopted by the Commission using an implementing act (*décision d'exécution*, in French), following the provisions of Article 291 TFEU and the framework set out in Regulation (EU) No 182/2011 of the European Parliament and of the Council of 16 February 2011 laying down the rules and

52 See the European Parliament's resolution of 22 November 2016 on 'The European Defence Union' [2016/2052(INI)], which states that 'the European Defence Research Programme will need a total budget of at least €500 million per year over this period in order to be credible and have a substantial impact'.

53 Regulation (EU) 2018/1092 of the European Parliament and of the Council of 18 July 2018 establishing the European Defence Industrial Development Programme aiming at supporting the competitiveness and innovation capacity of the Union's defence industry, [2018] *OJ* L200/30.

54 Regulation (EU) 2021/697, cited above.

55 See above.

general principles concerning mechanisms for control by Member States of the Commission's exercise of implementing powers. The same applies to each of the FPRD work programmes adopted using an implementing decision, the last of which was adopted on 31 March 2023.[56]

The preparation of these strategy documents and the supervision of the two programmes are the responsibility of the Commission's departments for both the EDF and the framework programme, in this case a recently created Directorate-General called DEFIS for the European Defence Fund and DG R&I (formerly RTD) for the FPRTD.

The implementation of the EDF is modelled on the Research Framework Programme: calls for proposals, evaluation of proposals by external experts based on the criterion of excellence, and grants awarded to research consortia.

It should be noted that the legislator did not wish, at least initially, to use an indirect management method, as was the case with the preparatory action, which was implemented by the EDA. The EDF is managed directly by the Commission's departments, whereas the administrative and financial management of the Framework Programme is the responsibility of the European Commission's six executive agencies. The legislator could have entrusted the management of the EDF to one of the existing agencies or created a new executive agency responsible solely for actions under the European Defence Fund. It rejected this option, as well as indirect management by the EDA, no doubt for reasons of political sensitivity.

The management of the EDF is supervised by a Programme Committee, composed of representatives of the Member States, which is subject to the provisions on comitology in accordance with the provisions of Regulation (EU) No 182/2011.[57] The same applies to the specific programmes of the FPRTD, which are overseen by Programme Committees established in the context of the same regulation.

Although the legal bases used by the Union to establish the Framework Programme and the EDF are distinct, they are nonetheless two EU research programmes. Furthermore, EU legislators decided to use the provisions of Articles 182 and 183 TFEU applicable to the Framework Programme to make the EDF operational. The implementation of this fund therefore follows the rules defined for the Framework Programme, with the few adaptations mentioned above.

Following the European Defence Fund's second call for projects, 41 collaborative defence research and development projects were selected for funding, receiving EU support of around €832 million.[58] Examples include the

[56] C(2023) 2178 final.

[57] See above.

[58] See the results of the EDF's calls for projects, available at https://defence-industry-space.ec.europa.eu/funding-and-grants/calls-proposals/result-edf-2022-calls-proposals_en?prefLang=fr.

ODIN'S EYE II project, a European space-based missile warning system, and the LATACC project, which aims to improve collaboration between armed forces, including autonomous systems, at different levels, in the context of high-intensity conflicts. It is also worth mentioning that the EU Defence Innovation Scheme (EUDIS),[59] developed under the EDF, with a budget of €2 billion,[60] defines a set of instruments set up in favour of SMEs and start-ups, in order to offer them more opportunities to access EDF funding.

Following the rise in tensions on the international scene over the last few years, there has been a new impetus in thinking about the synergies to be established between the EDF and the Framework Programme.

While Horizon Europe already mentions possible links within the strict framework of research, between the civil and defence fields, but also with other existing instruments,[61][62] the Commission recently proposed exploring new options.

In line with this approach, it has adopted a White Paper proposing options for strengthening and supporting R&D in the field of dual-use technologies which can be used for both civilian and military purposes.[63]

This document builds on reflections already initiated in 2018.[64] It has developed rapidly through various communications dealing with areas of the Common Foreign and Security Policy (CFSP) at the intersection of related policies of the internal market, research and industry, and particularly the space industry.[65]

---

59 https://eudis.europa.eu/index_en#factsheet.

60 €1.46 billion from the EDF and €500 million from other public and private sources.

61 See, for example, the Communication from the Commission, 'Action Plan on synergies between the civil, defence and space industries', COM(2021) 70 of 22 February 2021.

62 More specifically, the self-standing Research and Innovation Framework Program covering the years 2028-2034, '[…] will be tightly connected to the components of the ECF [European Competitiveness Fund, also focusing on defence] to ensure a seamless investment journey from idea to market'. European Commission, Proposal for a Regulation of the European Parliament and of the Council on establishing the European Competitiveness Fund ('ECF'), including the specific programme for defence research and innovation activities, repealing Regulations (EU) 2021/522, (EU) 2021/694, (EU) 2021/697, (EU) 2021/783, repealing provisions of Regulations (EU) 2021/696, (EU) 2023/588, and amending Regulation (EU) [EDIP], Brussels, 16 July 2025, COM(2025) 555 final.

63 European Commission White Paper 'On options for enhancing support for research and development involving technologies with dual-use potential', COM(2024) 27 final, Brussels, 24 January 2024. The text sets out possible options for stepping up support for research and development in the field of potential dual-use technologies.

64 Proposal for a Regulation of the European Parliament and of the Council establishing the Horizon Europe – the Framework Programme for Research and Innovation, laying down its rules for participation and dissemination, COM(2018) 435 final, 7 June 2018.

65 See the following communications: the Communication from the Commission to the European Parliament, the Council, the European Economic and Social Committee and the Committee of the Regions on the 'Action Plan on synergies between the civil, space and defence industries', COM(2021) 70 final, Brussels, 22 February 2021; the Communication from the Commission to the European Parliament, the Council, the European Economic

In the course of these discussions, the Commission developed the objective to be pursued. The aim is to mutually enrich the civil, space and defence sectors, to increase the effectiveness of investment through results.[66] To achieve this, it is proposing to rely on greater complementarity between programmes, which logically includes dual-use technologies.

In this context, the White Paper launches a public consultation that paves the way for a reassessment of the current R&D support framework to better align European initiatives with contemporary geopolitical challenges and the objectives of the European economic security strategy. Thus, the historic distinction between civil and defence research, as articulated in the Treaties and embodied in the Framework Programme, finds in this White Paper an opportunity for re-examination, from the angle of interoperability and complementarity; while at the same time highlighting the need for more appropriate instruments to encourage cross-fertilisation between the civil and defence sectors.

These changes will have consequences for the next Framework Programme (FP10), which is already being prepared by the European Commission (DG R&I). It is also likely to raise questions about the participation or modes of participation of third countries in this programme (Art. 186 TFEU).[67]

On 5 March 2024, the European Commission and the High Representative of the Union for Foreign Affairs and Security Policy adopted a joint communication on a new European Defence Industrial Strategy (EDIS)[68] with the aim of increasing the EU's preparedness for its new security environment through a responsive, resilient and innovative European defence industry.

---

and Social Committee and the Committee of the Regions on the 'Roadmap on critical technologies for security and defence', COM(2022) 61 final, Strasbourg, 15 February 2022; the Joint Communication to the European Parliament, the European Council, the Council, the European Economic and Social Committee and the Committee of the Regions on the 'Defense Investment Gaps Analysis and the Way Forward', JOIN(2022) 24 final, Brussels, 18 May 2022; the Commission Staff Working Document, 'First progress report on the implementation of the Action Plan on synergies between the civil, defence and space industries', SWD(2022) 362 final, Brussels, 10 November 2022; the Communication from the Commission to the European Parliament, the Council, the European Economic and Social Committee and the Committee of the Regions on 'A new European Innovation Agenda', COM(2022) 332 final, Strasbourg, 5 July 2022; the joint Communication to the European Parliament and the Council on the 'European Union Space Strategy for Security and Defence', JOIN(2023) 9 final, Brussels, 10 March 2023 and the joint Communication to the European Parliament and the Council on the 'European Economic Security Strategy', JOIN(2023) 20 final, Brussels, 20 June 2023.

66 For questions relating to developments between research and the field of space, see the commentary by A. de Neve in this publication.

67 See below.

68 Joint Communication to the European Parliament, the Council, the European Economic and Social Committee and the Committee of the Regions, 'A new European Defence Industrial Strategy: Achieving EU readiness through a responsive and resilient European Defence Industry', JOIN(2024) 10 final, Brussels, 5 March 2024.

EDIS places particular emphasis on the importance of defence research and innovation.

The strategy underlines the need for the EU to remain at the forefront of defence innovation, in particular by supporting a competitive and resilient European defence industry and technology sector. It also highlights the importance of the European Defence Fund and collaborative projects in stimulating innovation, with particular emphasis on support for SMEs and the exploitation of civil innovation cycles for defence applications (an action already undertaken under EUDIS). Finally, EDIS stresses the importance of the next MFF including an ambitious financial envelope for defence, in particular to provide the successor to EDF with a budget commensurate with innovation needs.

In light of these announcements and the approach developed within EDIS, EDF as well as EUDIS will likely continue to be at the very heart of the Union's defence research policy and action.

b. – Programmes Complementary to the EU Research Framework Programme (Articles 184 TFEU and 188(2) TFEU)

To conclude with the implementation of the objectives of the European Research Area defined in Article 179 TFEU, it should be noted that Article 184 TFEU provides that the implementation of the Framework Programme allows the Union to adopt research programmes complementary to the FP, in which only certain Member States participate. It is thus stipulated that the EU may support such programmes, although this is not obligatory. The adoption of these complementary programmes is identical to that of the framework programme. It must include rules applicable to the dissemination of knowledge (see Art. 180(c) TFEU)[69] and to access by other Member States that have not participated in the financing of these complementary programmes.

These are adopted through the ordinary legislative procedure, after consultation of the EESC. The second sentence of Article 188(2) states that such adoption requires the agreement of the Member States concerned, although the text does not specify how this agreement is to be obtained.

Moreover, this provision could provide an interesting framework for the future development of defence research and, more specifically, support programmes for the development of dual-use goods, along the lines of what already exists in cybersecurity.[70]

---

[69] See above.

[70] Ibid.

2. *International Cooperation Activities as Defined in Articles 180(b) TFEU and 186 TFEU*

Article 180(b) TFEU provides that international cooperation activities shall be implemented in the context of the Framework Programme. This objective is made operational by the provisions of Article 186 TFEU, which enable the EU to deploy its research policy beyond its borders.

The EU cooperates closely with third countries and international organisations in the field of R&D, notably through specific agreements. These collaborations enable legal entities located outside EU territory to participate in calls for proposals under the Framework Programme for Research and Technological Development (FPRTD), based on specific geographical or thematic criteria. The European Commission also concludes bilateral scientific cooperation agreements.[71]

Unlike the Framework Programme, which promotes international cooperation in the context of Article 186 TFEU, the Defence Fund does not, strictly speaking, provide for the development of an international cooperation policy as does the Framework Programme. Given the sensitivity of the field of defence-related research, the Defence Fund does not authorise the participation of legal entities established outside the EU, except under the specific conditions set out in Article 9(6) of the Regulation establishing the EDF. However, companies located in the territory of EFTA may participate in the activities of the European Defence Fund under the Agreement on the European Economic Area (EEA). This is, of course, a very special case, as these third countries are very close to the EU in terms of both values and geography.

Moreover, it seems quite clear that if the next Framework Programme were to fund research in the dual or defence field, as mentioned in the White Paper of 24 January 2024, limitations would be imposed on international cooperation and on the exploitation and dissemination of results in this field of research, following the example of the provisions that prevail for actions under the EDF.[72]

---

71 COM(2021) 252 of 18 May 2021.

72 Recital 57 and Articles 2.24, 9.3, 9.4 and 10.2 of the Regulation establishing the EDF: see above.

3. *Actions in Support of Research Taking the Form of Partnerships as Defined in Articles 185 and 187 TFEU*

It is important to mention here the actions in support of research which take the form of partnerships. These are provided for in Articles 185[73] and 187[74] TFEU. While these actions have not yet been used in the field of defence, they could, in the medium term, constitute policy development instruments for defence research.

There are two types of partnership provided for in treaty law. Firstly, Article 185 TFEU gives concrete form to the provisions of Article 181(1) TFEU[75] on the coordination of Member States' research programmes. The *de facto* aim of this provision is to enable the EU to participate in research programmes launched by one or more of its Member States and thus to support partnerships between public research players within the EU.

Secondly, to achieve the objective set out in Article 181(1) TFEU, Article 187 TFEU allows the Union to set up 'joint undertakings or any other structure' necessary for the proper execution of its research programmes. This provision is used as an instrument for associating private funds with research and innovation policies and promoting the use of 'public-private partnerships' (PPPs), unlike the legal basis provided for in Article 185 TFEU. Institutionalised partnerships are established only when other forms of partnership prove unsuitable. They are implemented by dedicated structures, created specifically based on a Council Regulation, in accordance with the provisions of Article 188(1) TFEU.

The joint ventures created to date are not linked to European research in the field of dual technologies or defence.[76] However, it should be noted that some of these entities have dual aspects or even a defence-related dimension.

---

[73] 'In implementing the multiannual framework programme, the Union may make provision, in agreement with the Member States concerned, for participation in research and development programmes undertaken by several Member States, including participation in the structures created for the execution of those programmes'.

[74] 'The Union may set up joint undertakings or any other structure necessary for the efficient execution of the Union's research, technological development and demonstration programmes'.

[75] 'The Union and the Member States shall coordinate their research and technological development activities so as to ensure that national policies and Union policy are mutually consistent'.

[76] See Council Regulation (EU) 2021/2085 of 19 November 2021 establishing the Joint Undertakings under Horizon Europe and repealing Regulations (EC) No 219/2007, (EU) No 557/2014, (EU) No 558/2014, (EU) No 559/2014, (EU) No 560/2014, (EU) No 561/2014 and (EU) No 642/2014 (known as the 'Single Basic Act (SBA)'), [2021] *OJ* L427/17. This legislative instrument provides for the establishment and immediate start of operations of the following nine Joint Undertakings: Circular Bio-based Europe; Clean Aviation; Clean Hydrogen; Europe's Rail; Global Health EDCTP3; Innovative Health Initiative; Key Digital Technologies; Single European Sky ATM Research 3; Smart Networks and Services.

One example is the *Single European Sky* Joint Undertaking, which aims to improve air traffic management (ATM) and air navigation services (ANS). Mainly oriented towards the civil aspects of air traffic management, its application has *de facto* important implications for defence and security. Thus, close cooperation between civil and military uses of airspace is necessary and recognised within the framework of this initiative.[77]

It should also be noted that the 'Structure for European armaments programmes' chapter of the regulation on the establishment of the European Defence Industry Programme and of a framework of measures to ensure the availability and timely delivery of defence-related products (EDIP)[78] is largely inspired by the ERIC (European Research Infrastructure Consortium) concept. This constitutes the EU legal framework applicable to a European research infrastructure,[79][80] in the context of Article 187 TFEU. This civil research initiative has therefore largely served as a model for developments not only in defence research, but also for defence industrial policy as a whole.

In addition to support for research activities, primary legislation provides for an annual report on R&D activities, based legally on Article 190 TFEU.[81] It focuses on assessing the impact and effectiveness of EU research initiatives.[82] It has been noted that it does not include information on the EDF, nor on dual research or research in the field of defence. In fact, following an identical approach, Article 28(3) of the Regulation establishing the EDF[83] provides

---

77 Against this background, please also see the current advance in AI related matters where the scope of Council Regulation 2024/1732 is being widen to enable the Union to '[...] respond to new technological developments and strategic imperatives, namely the significant scale-up of AI-optimised compute capacity in Europe [...]' in European Commission, Proposal for a Council Regulation on amending Council Regulation (EU) 2021/1173 of 13 July 2021 on establishing the European High Performance Computing Joint Undertaking and repealing Regulation (EU) 2018/1488, Brussels, 15 July 2025, COM(2025) 414 final.

78 Regulation (EU) 2025/2643 of the European Parliament and of the Council of 16 December 2025 establishing the European Defence Industry Programme and a framework of measures to ensure the timely availability and supply of defence products ('EDIP Regulation'), [2025] *OJ* L2025/2643.

79 Council Regulation (EU) No 1261/2013 of 2 December 2013 amending Regulation (EC) No 723/2009 concerning the Community legal framework for a European Research Infrastructures Consortium (ERIC), [2013] *OJ* L326.

80 https://research-and-innovation.ec.europa.eu/strategy/strategy-2020-2024/our-digital-future/european-research-infrastructures/eric_en.

81 At the beginning of each year, the Commission presents a report to the European Parliament and the Council. This report should cover in particular the activities carried out in research and technological development, as well as the dissemination of results during the previous year and the work programme for the current year.

82 Report from the Commission to the European Parliament and the Council, Annual Report on Research and Technological Development Activities of the European Union and Monitoring Horizon Europe and Horizon 2020 in 2022, COM(2023) 277, 31 May 2023.

83 See above.

for an annual report on its implementation, separate from the report on the Framework Programme.

CONCLUSION

In the current context in which the European Union is seeking to strengthen its defence research capabilities, notably through the European Defence Fund and the Commission's proposal to include dual-use research in the next Framework Programme (FP10), we are witnessing a significant development in the EU's legal and political framework. Indeed, the European Commission's proposed support for dual-use technologies in the context of FP10, set out in a White Paper of 24 January 2024 is designed to strengthen the EU's strategic autonomy. It marks the beginnings of a crucial new stage in the development of a Defence Union. *Ultimately,* this approach reflects a new reality in which European defence is taking centre stage on the Union's agenda, calling into question the distinction that prevailed until recently between civil and military research. These possible legal and political developments raise questions about the potential synergies between civil and military research and contribute not only to the EU's strategic autonomy but also to its economic security and prosperity, in a tense geopolitical climate. By recognising the importance of this duality and initiating discussions on the framework for funding and regulating research into dual-use technologies, the EU is demonstrating its ability to anticipate and respond to future challenges, while ensuring a balanced and ethical approach to dual-use research.

ARTICLE 189 TFEU: EUROPEAN SPACE POLICY

Alain De Neve
Researcher at the Centre for Security and Defence Studies (CESD) at the Royal Higher Institute for Defence (Brussels)

Article 189 TFEU

1. To promote scientific and technical progress, industrial competitiveness and the implementation of its policies, the Union shall draw up a European space policy. To this end, it may promote joint initiatives, support research and technological development and coordinate the efforts needed for the exploration and exploitation of space.

2. To contribute to attaining the objectives referred to in paragraph 1, the European Parliament and the Council, acting in accordance with the ordinary legislative procedure, shall establish the necessary measures, which may take the form of a European space programme, excluding any harmonisation of the laws and regulations of the Member States.

3. The Union shall establish any appropriate relations with the European Space Agency.

4. This Article shall be without prejudice to the other provisions of this Title.

For a long time, the space sector was considered exclusively from the point of view of its societal, economic and scientific dimensions, but it was slow to gain recognition as a sector of strategic importance for the European Union, which had no formally declared competence in this area until the adoption of the Lisbon Treaty. Indeed, since the beginnings of the Ariane launcher programme and the creation of the European Space Agency (ESA)[1] in 1975, space has remained the prerogative, even the reserved domain, of a few European nations with a solid and dedicated industrial and technological base. Unlike in the

[1] In French: *Agence spatiale européenne.*

United States, where space has a long-term vision, the development process of the European space sector has mainly been the result of an incremental and programmatic approach whose political guidance has never been easy to read, either for European institutional players, national authorities or outside observers.[2] For several decades, therefore, European space policy has mainly been an 'approach', or at best a 'public policy by default', to use the terms employed by Bertand de Montluc and Florent Perache.[3] In other words, it has been an *ad hoc* solution steered by heterogeneous players, be they national agencies, the ESA, the European Commission or industrial operators. In the absence of an integrative approach, European space policy has been built up over time, based on segmented programmatic convergences and mainly steered by the Member States who were investing in the sector.[4]

As far as defence is concerned, an examination of the various milestones that led to the gradual definition of a European space policy reveals an even more edifying fact: Europe's space policy has been built, not without difficulty, through fragmented programmes. Whether in the field of observation or telecommunications, European military space programmes have always been the initiative of the Member States. In a few limited cases, and without the model adopted being transposable from project to project, they have either accepted the arrival of partners from the European Union, or agreed to exchange capabilities for programming rights.[5] In the field of telecommunications, it has to be admitted that cooperation has been even more limited, since no convergence on the model of the observation sector has been achieved.[6] It is a truism that those Member States with a sufficiently developed industrial and technological base have given priority to defining national military space capabilities, without systematically seeking partners within the European Union.

These failures in no way mean that there is no momentum for Europeanisation. Convergences have emerged, and the European Space Agency owes its existence to one of them, since it was created out of the merger between the *European Launcher Development Organisation* (ELDO) and the *European Space Research Organisation* (ESRO). However, for both strategic and budgetary

---

2 M. Brandenburg and S. Lieberman, 'Critical Spaces: European and U.S. Institutions for Outer Space' (2022) 20(1) *Astropolitics – The International Journal of Space Politics and Policy*, pp. 93–111.

3 B. De Montluc and F. Perache, 'L'espace, facteur d'intégration pour la gestion de la sécurité en Europe', *Réalités industrielles*, May 2006, pp. 61–65.

4 Ibid., pp. 61–65.

5 Take, for example, the agreements between Germany (SAR-Lupe) and Italy (Cosmo-Skymed) on the one hand, and France (Hélios 2 and Pléiades-HR) on the other.

6 It would be more accurate to say that France, Germany and Spain came very close to co-operating in the field of military telecommunications. However, when Germany and Spain withdrew during the project, France was forced to develop the Syracuse satellite programme on its own.

reasons, all efforts to define a space policy that was even remotely integrated at European level came up against the – often unacknowledged – reluctance of European states. This reluctance was mainly due to the differences between Member States in terms of their industrial and technological bases, with only some of them having the operational resources required to conduct space activities. This is why the preservation of an intergovernmental institutional structure such as the ESA has proved fundamental, as it enabled those States that so wished to contribute to optional programmes with variable geometry. However, space applications in the field of security and defence have long suffered from a lack of harmonisation and convergence of vision between the EU and ESA Member States. In a way, Article II of the ESA Convention establishing the European Space Agency has acted as a brake on any ambition to gear the Agency's programmes more assertively towards security and defence objectives.[7] This limited, albeit real, drive towards Europeanisation has therefore mainly focused on programmes designed to fulfil utilitarian or scientific civilian missions.

Nevertheless, over the past two decades, the EU's institutions, operational structures and military capabilities have grown in strength. Despite the political divergences – sometimes difficult to overcome – that it has faced, a common foreign and security policy (CFSP) and its defence component (ESDP) have come into being and have achieved a certain degree of emancipation. The various crises that emerged in the immediate post-Cold War period, and later in the post-9/11 era, have demonstrated that space-based resources are now essential for anticipating, dealing with and planning for crises. The dependence of modern military organisations on space is such that it now calls for the development of policies aimed at guaranteeing the autonomous access of these military organisations to the orbits and frequencies required to conduct operations.

The Embryo of a European Space Policy

As far as space policy is concerned, the Lisbon Treaty represents the final fruit of the first embryonic initiatives undertaken before 2009, marked by programmatic impasses and essential lessons learned from the strategic context. It illustrates a gradual path towards a more integrated and coherent vision of European space activity within the institutional framework of the European Union. It is therefore useful to understand the different stages that eventually led the Member States to building space action as a shared EU competence. It should be noted that the integration of security and defence issues into the

[7] Article II of the Convention states that the 'purpose of the Agency shall be to provide for and to promote, for exclusively peaceful purposes, cooperation among European States in space research and technology and their space applications, with a view to their being used for scientific purposes and for operational space application systems'.

European space policy currently being developed has proved to be a gradual process, marked by slow progress that is sometimes out of step with the importance of the issues at stake. Clearly, the dichotomy between civilian aspirations and defence requirements has given rise to substantial debate, reflecting the complexity of harmonising sometimes divergent objectives within a unified space strategy.

To single out one act that could be considered as the embryo of this post-Lisbon space policy, there is no doubt that the resolution on strengthening the synergy between ESA and the European Community of June 1998, adopted by the Council of the European Union and the ESA Council, would be the best example.[8] For the first time, the ESA was officially given responsibility for developing and implementing a long-term space policy, while the European Community was given legal, economic and social responsibility for regulating space-related markets. Strengthening the consistency of the European approach to space (the notion of policy was not yet clearly mentioned) was therefore at the heart of the debates that followed from May 1999 onwards. These debates highlighted the lack of consensus between the main European players, as well as the delays in the design, funding and launch of innovative projects and applications. These were the factors that prompted the European states, in close cooperation with ESA, to establish for the first time a European strategy for space, which came into being in September 2000. Entitled 'Europe and Space: turning to a new chapter',[9] the European Commission's communication on a joint space strategy fully acknowledged the role of satellite information in implementing European policies. It should be noted, however, that among the policies mentioned, security and defence policy was not specifically named. The three objectives around which the Commission's communication was structured were: i) strengthening the basis of space activities, ii) increasing scientific knowledge, and iii) extending the benefits of space to markets and society.

Later, in November 2000, the Council[10] and the ESA Council[11] endorsed these objectives, and the ESA Council supported the establishment of a cooperation structure between ESA and the European Commission. The Council therefore asked the Commission to set up a joint *task force* with ESA.

An expert report for the ESA Director General recommended nothing less than Europe integrating its space activities into a wider economic and political

[8] Council Resolution of 22 June 1998 on the reinforcement of the synergy between the European Space Agency and the European Community, 98/C 224/01, [1998] *OJ* C224/1.

[9] COM(2000) 597 – C5-0146/2001 – 2001/2072(COS).

[10] Council Resolution of 16 November 2000 on the European Strategy for Space, [2000] *OJ* C371/2.

[11] ESA Council Resolution on a European Strategy for Space, ESA/C-M/CXLVIII/Res.1, 16 November 2000.

strategy. To this end, it was suggested that the EU's political role in space policy should be strengthened by giving the European Council responsibility for defining a European space policy, while ESA should become Europe's space agency. The experts also proposed that the Commission should define the regulatory framework for space activities and unite the interests of users around a single strategy. It was also proposed that the European Parliament should be able to discuss and review European space policy on a regular basis.

An essential step towards further integration of the European space sector was taken on 25 November 2003, when the European Community and ESA adopted a Framework Agreement, which entered into force on 28 May 2004.[12] The aim of this agreement was to provide a basis for an overall European space policy and for effective and beneficial cooperation between the two parties. The agreement created a strategic partnership between supply (ESA) and demand for space systems (from the European Community). It formally established the Space Council, a joint secretariat to replace the Joint *Task Force*, and a High Level Space Policy Group to replace the *Joint Space Strategy Advisory Group* (JSSAG). The agreement, which lasted four years, would be renewed automatically.

This slow evolution of the European space sector towards greater and greater integration subsequently took place against a backdrop of institutional and geopolitical upheaval. On the institutional front, the failure to adopt a European constitution de *facto* postponed integration projects in the space sector for several years. Meanwhile, profound changes in the structure of the space market (launchers, satellites, services) and in the paradigms that had previously governed the sector made the adaptation of the European space sector particularly urgent.[13] This paradigm shift was the consequence of an unprecedented combination of several phenomena with which the European Union must contend if it is to place its space policy at the service of a common security and defence policy (CSDP) and genuine strategic autonomy.[14]

A contested space

The first phenomenon, which has certainly been present since the early days of the conquest of space, but which has become more radical over the last two decades, is the growing number of oppositions between the players in the sector. Outer space is confirmed as the place where conflicts between powers

---

12 Council Decision of 29 April 2004 on the conclusion of the Framework Agreement between the European Community and the European Space Agency, [2004] *OJ* L261/63.

13 J.C. Moltz, 'The Changing Dynamics of Twenty-First Century Space Power' (2019) 12(1) *Journal of Strategic Security*, pp. 15–43; X. Pasco, 'L'espace, domaine de confrontation stratégique', *Revue Défense Nationale*, Comité d'études de Défense Nationale, 2020, no. 385, pp. 59–63.

14 Institut Montaigne, 'Space: Europe wakes up', Note, February 2020.

are expressed.[15] The ASAT test carried out by Russia on 15 November 2021 using a *Nudol-type* missile against one of its decommissioned communications satellites (Kosmos 1408) was no more and no less than a warning issued by Moscow at a time when the country's armed forces were gathering on the borders of Ukraine. According to several intelligence sources, the cyber-attack on 24 February 2022, which permanently affected the Ka-SAT network operated by Viasat, was also carried out by Russia.[16]

More generally, the competition between the world's major space powers has resulted in growing rivalry over the allocation of orbits and frequencies. New entrants to the space sector are challenging the dominant position held until recently by the traditional powers: the United States, Russia and Europe – who are no longer the only ones to control the entire spectrum of key space functions. If Europe is to achieve strategic autonomy in the field of security and defence, it will have to build up the autonomy of its space assets in the context of growing rivalry between the powers. Europe will only be able to achieve this autonomy of access to and exploitation of space through the development of high-performance instruments for the surveillance and observation of enemy systems. This is in the knowledge that, in strictly material terms, no satellite can be defended or protected. For example, since 2017, the Russian *Luch-Olymp* satellite has been carrying out regular and repeated co-orbital manoeuvres close to satellites owned by third countries, whose retaliatory options are limited and consist of detecting the type of information or intelligence that the Russian satellite is 'sucking in'.

---

15 A. Kerrest, 'Actualités du droit de l'espace: la responsabilité des États du fait de la destruction de satellites dans l'espace', *Annuaire français de droit international*, 2009, vol. 55, pp. 615–626; M. Krepon and C. Clary, *Space Assurance or Space Dominance? The Case Against Weaponizing Space*, Washington, The Henry L. Stimson Center, 2003; M. Jaluzot, F. Choudat, P.-S. Perono and P. Touraine, *Les nouvelles dynamiques de puissance dans le domaine spatial*, Paris, École de Guerre Économique, Promotion MSIE-31, December 2019.

16 J.A. Guerrero Saade and M. Van Amerongen, 'AcidRain | A Modem Wiper Rains Down on Europe', 31 March 2022, https://www.sentinelone.com/blog/author/jags; 'Russian cyber operations against Ukraine', Declaration by the High Representative on behalf of the European Union, Brussels, Council of the EU, 10 May 2022.

A hyper-competitive space

Europe's space actions that emerged from the Lisbon Treaty are part of a hyper-competitive context. This situation is the result of two phenomena: the democratisation of production techniques and the growing diversity of the players involved.

The uses to which space is put have also changed and multiplied. It is worth mentioning the transformations in the technological ecosystem over the past two decades. First of all, there has been the increasing miniaturisation of the computer system components on board satellites. The latest design and manufacturing techniques have enabled the development of increasingly miniaturised, powerful and energy-efficient hardware. A satellite is nothing more than a computer in orbit. These developments have led to the mass production of micro- and nanosatellites, for which lighter, less expensive launchers have proved more suitable, creating a new market for the deployment of satellites serving a growing number of countries.

Production techniques based on 3D printing and laser sintering have also revolutionised satellite manufacturing and development costs. Whereas in the past, the design of a range of satellites was mainly the result of government orders for a small number of units, now new manufacturing processes allow larger volumes and, consequently, economies of scale that were previously difficult to envisage.

As satellites have become smaller, the cost of putting them into orbit has fallen considerably. Players such as Orbital ATK and SpaceX have taken advantage of this phenomenon and entered this niche market by also working on less expensive, modular and reusable launchers (in the case of SpaceX). Management models based on the vertical integration of manufacturing processes, as well as production lines from sectors outside the space industry, have made such feats possible.

Today, private space flight is raising major questions.[17] Discredited during its first years of activity (notably by European industries and their political representatives), SpaceX now symbolises this rush into space. However, it is important to remember that SpaceX remains essentially an industrial tool at the service of NASA and the US Department of Defense, whose public orders are vital to the company. It is even, in a way, one of the industrial spearheads of US defence policy. This should remind us – and Europe when it considers building and/or preserving its autonomy in this sector – that space is first and foremost a field whose achievements depend on a high level of government orders, particularly for defence purposes.

---

[17] J.-M. Bockel, *The Future of the Space Industry*, NATO Parliamentary Assembly, Economic and Security Committee, 173 ESC 18 E Fin, 17 November 2018.

The space activism of a growing number of governments seeking to benefit from the services provided by the sector and the enthusiasm of private players from the New Space sector are generating major tensions over the allocation of orbits and frequencies. Such tensions already exist in low-Earth and geostationary orbits and are jeopardising the safety of near-Earth space by increasing the risk of cascade collisions.[18] Such phenomena, even if accidental, could generate unprecedented crises between States that suspect each other of deliberately attacking each other's satellites. With more than 2,600 satellites in low earth orbit, the situation could prove explosive. To this end, Europe intends to work on developing a *Space Traffic Management* (STM) system that will enable it to identify and track objects in orbit and determine the exact circumstances in which collisions may occur in the future. While several EU Member States have certain STM technological building blocks and have thus enabled EU satellites to avoid collisions, it is essential to coordinate them to ensure that Europe as a whole has fully autonomous access to and surveillance of space, thereby providing it with a coordinated instrument for preventing crises resulting from outer space incidents.

By institutionalising space policy as a shared competence of the European Union, Article 189 of the TFEU has in fact structured the dynamic cooperation that already existed between certain Member States, notably through the activities of the European Space Agency (ESA). This legal recognition therefore formalises a European space policy that had previously been steered on an *ad hoc* basis by various players.

This chapter focuses on three areas. The first examines how the legal framework of the Lisbon Treaty has strengthened space-related initiatives and activities within the EU and brought to the fore the strategic importance of space as an area of common interest.

A second focuses on the 'Security & Defence' dimension of European space policy post-Lisbon. The changing geopolitical context and the rise of new technologies have given increasing importance to the 'defence' and 'strategic' dimensions of space competence. This section explores how the EU has stepped up its involvement in these areas of the space sector, notably through initiatives such as the Strategic Compass and the Joint Communication to the European Parliament on Security and Defence in Space. Issues relating to the surveillance, resilience and protection of space infrastructures will also be examined, underlining the growing integration of defence considerations into European space policy.

The third and final part of this contribution will look at how Article 189 of the TFEU could prove to be a springboard for more comprehensive EU

---

[18] A. De Neve, *Crowded and Dangerous Orbits: European Space Governance at a Time of Potentially Saturating Programs*, Paris, IFRI, February 2022.

regulation in the field of space. The formulation of an EU space law represents the next step in the evolution of European space policy. However, this ambition has been hampered by divergences between Member States, delaying the timetable for the conception and adoption of this regulation. This section will analyse the challenges inherent in harmonising national legal frameworks, legal uncertainties and political obstacles. It will also discuss why a European space law is essential to ensure strategic autonomy, build resilience and guarantee security in the European space sector.

I. THE EUROPEAN AREA IN THE TREATY OF LISBON

The Treaty of Lisbon, which came into force in 2009, marks a decisive step in the consolidation and expansion of European space policy, providing a stronger legal framework for space-related initiatives and activities within the European Union (EU). By explicitly including space policy among its competences in Article 189, the Treaty on the Functioning of the EU (TFEU) recognises the strategic importance of space as an area of common interest, thereby encouraging collaboration between the Member States and the European space industry. This formal integration underlines the EU's recognition of space not only as a security and defence issue, but also as a key driver for science, technology, the economy and society as a whole. As a result, the Lisbon Treaty facilitates a unified and coordinated approach to contemporary space challenges, such as earth surveillance, satellite navigation and space exploration, while promoting innovation and competitiveness within the European space sector.

It should be added that European space policy has also benefited from a series of institutional innovations introduced by the Treaty of Lisbon. One of the most fundamental is undoubtedly that of conferring legal personality on the European Union, enabling it to negotiate and conclude international treaties. It provides the EU with a set of essential instruments for implementing its space policy. But it is also important to understand how the Treaty of Lisbon defines the Union's competence in the field of space. This is expressed in Article 189 TFEU: '[T]o promote scientific and technical progress, industrial competitiveness and the implementation of its policies, the Union shall draw up a European space policy'. Article 189(2) also gives the European Parliament a greater role in this area, stating that the European Parliament and the Council 'shall establish the necessary measures, which may take the form of a European space programme, excluding any harmonisation of the laws and regulations of the Member States'. It is paragraph 3 of Article 4 TFEU that further clarifies the competence of the European Union in the field of space. This article specifies that this is a shared competence which, unlike the Union's other shared competences, in no way pre-empts the ability of the Member States to exercise their own competence in this area (a reservation which was already included in the terms in which paragraph 2 of Article 189 ended). In fact, as a general rule, in the case of 'normal' shared competences, the Member States refrain from exercising their competences as soon as the Union chooses to exercise its own. This is clearly not the case in the field of space. Moreover, the principles of subsidiarity and proportionality apply to space as they do to any other shared competence. The principle of subsidiarity means that the Union can only act if it can do so more effectively than the Member States. The Member States, and among them the players with a dedicated industrial and technological base, see their sovereign prerogatives in the space field preserved, with the European Union acting only in those segments where collective coordination is required. The principle of proportionality requires that the content and form of EU action should not exceed what is necessary to achieve the objectives pursued.

Nevertheless, since the Lisbon Treaty revision, the Treaties now give the European Union a very explicit mandate in space matters. It is thus in a position to define policies and actions and implement genuine programmes to coordinate the efforts of the Member States, optimise resources and maximise the benefits of space activity for the Union as a whole. This includes the development of major projects such as Galileo (the satellite navigation system that represents a European alternative to the United States' GPS), and Copernicus (the Earth observation programme that plays a crucial role in managing natural disasters, monitoring the environment and supporting European security). In short, the Lisbon Treaty enables the EU to play a leading role on the international space scene, promoting a competitive space industry and contributing to scientific research, security and the well-being of European citizens.

It is important to dwell a little on the institutional specificity of the European Union's shared competence in the field of space. In reality, this is the result of the coordination of two approaches – one intergovernmental, the other supranational – which are often said to be difficult to reconcile. Institutionally, the ESA operates as an intergovernmental organisation. The European Union, on the other hand, uses a supranational mode of governance, notably through the actions undertaken by the European Commission.[19] The balance between these two forms of governance is the result of a particularly complex and fragile alchemy. The European Space Agency's budget is based

[19] M. Brandenburg and S. Lieberman, 'Critical Spaces: European and U.S. Institutions for Outer Space', (2022) 20(1) *Astropolitics – The International Journal of Space Politics and Policy*.

on contributions from its Member States,[20] in line with their gross domestic product. This budget enables the ESA to undertake programmes based on the mandate entrusted to it. However, the ESA also provides for a system of *fair returns* for contributors to optional programmes. A country without a national space agency can therefore choose to allocate its contribution to companies or sectors of activity that are important to its national economy. In this way, the ESA, which uses commercial entities to develop the equipment included in its programmes, pays these companies up to the level of the share dedicated by the Member State on whose territory they are established. Clearly, such an approach is incompatible at first sight with the European Union's desire to encourage the development of a free European market – a central dimension of European integration. However, there is pragmatic cooperation between the European Union and the ESA, enabling them to work together to develop European space capabilities. Some observers even see this as a form of harmonisation, making cooperation effective by guaranteeing both its economic efficiency and its technical virtues, and thereby bringing States with different interests and objectives into line with a common higher objective.[21] However, this does not always enable the realisation of all the ambitions that might be expected of Europe in space.

II. THE 'SECURITY & DEFENCE' DIMENSION OF EUROPEAN SPACE POLICY AFTER LISBON

Granting the European Union a shared competence, albeit specific, in space matters is also part of the strengthening of the EU as a security and defence player. The growing importance of space within the Union should enable the sector to be strengthened as an instrument of the Common Security and Defence Policy (CSDP). The aim here is to provide the European Union with the means to monitor and protect its critical space infrastructures, guarantee its strategic autonomy and increase its capacity to act independently on the international stage. By developing autonomous space capabilities, such as secure communications, surveillance and reconnaissance systems, the EU aims to strengthen its security posture, its resilience in the face of potential threats and its ability to contribute to global stability. This also implies better coordination with Member States' national defence policies and the implementation of

---

20 The ESA member states are: Austria, Belgium, the Czech Republic, Denmark, Estonia, Finland, France, Germany, Greece, Hungary, Ireland, Italy, Latvia, Lithuania, Luxembourg, the Netherlands, Norway, Poland, Portugal, Romania, Spain, Sweden, Switzerland and the United Kingdom.

21 S. Zabusky, *Launching Europe: An Ethnography of European Cooperation in Space Science*, Princeton, Princeton University Press, 1995, p. 54.

joint projects that can serve both civilian and military objectives, underlining the crucial role of space in responding to contemporary and future security challenges.

It should be noted that the Treaty of Lisbon created the post of High Representative of the Union for Foreign Affairs and Security Policy/Vice-President of the European Commission (the 'High Representative' or HR/VP). The High Representative also chairs the European Defence Agency (EDA), as well as the Foreign Affairs Council. The HR/VP is assisted by a European External Action Service, which is responsible for coordinating and ensuring the consistency of the Union's external policies on security issues.[22] Although security and defence issues are not the driving force behind European space policy, all the frameworks have been established to ensure that the space sector will eventually converge with the Union's politico-military needs.

Like the wider field of industry, space policy has for a long time been seen by the European Commission as a back door to dealing with defence and security issues, and space policy has recently seen its status evolve in the context of debates between the Member States and the European institutions. The deterioration of the security environment over the last decade, as well as the profound structural changes that have led to a diversification of space players, both public and private, are the main factors that explain the recent institutional developments in the European space sector.

Since the outbreak of the conflict in Ukraine provoked by Russian aggression,[23] Europe has significantly stepped up its commitment to the security and defence dimensions of its space sector. This tense geopolitical situation has acted as a catalyst, prompting European nations to accelerate the development and implementation of advanced space technologies. The aim of this drive is not only to guarantee strategic autonomy in space, but also to improve surveillance, communications and intelligence capabilities for the continent's security. This development marks a turning point in the way Europe perceives and integrates space into its defence policy, underlining the crucial importance of this environment in modern security strategies. For example, the Versailles Declaration of 11 March 2022 was already an opportunity for the leaders of the Member States of the European Union, reacting to Russia's attack on Ukraine on 24 February 2022, to stress the need to strengthen the security and defence dimensions of space industries and activities.[24] Later, the

---

[22] On these institutional aspects, see the commentary on Articles 23 to 40 TEU by C. Schneider, in this publication.

[23] A conflict that has also demonstrated the fragility of the cooperation with Russia in the space sector. On this subject, see European Space Policy Institute, *The War in Ukraine and the European Space Sector*, Vienna, ESPI Briefs 57, May 2022; *The War in Ukraine from a Space Cybersecurity Perspective*, Vienna, ESPI Report 84, October 2022.

[24] Informal Meeting of Heads of State or Government, Versailles Declaration, 10–11 March 2022.

European Commission's Strategic Compass on the European Union's security and defence, published on 21 March, clearly identified space as an increasingly competitive area with major defence implications.

The European Union's efforts were later reinforced by additional collaborative programmes. For example, at the 2022 Ministerial Council of the European Space Agency, various space-related defensive initiatives were put forward, inviting member countries to participate.

Moreover, the very course of Russia's offensive against Ukraine clearly demonstrated the crucial role of space as a strategic resource. This confrontation also highlighted the significant and crucial impact of commercial resources – such as the Starlink secure communications network – alongside state resources and strategies, underlining the need for ongoing collaboration and interaction between the public and private domains, particularly when it comes to technical and operational skills in the space domain.[25]

Europe's growing awareness of the critical dimension of space for security and defence is reflected in the Joint Communication to the European Parliament and the Council published on 10 March 2023.[26] Soberly entitled 'European Union Strategy for Security and Defence in Space', this communication highlights how the European Union must see itself – and must be seen – as a key player in the field of space in the service of security and defence. The document recognises that space is an increasingly contested sphere, where the security of space infrastructures is becoming paramount for the functionality of economies and the implementation of European public policies, including the defence of Europe.

The Joint Communication stresses the importance of protecting space infrastructures against emerging threats, such as anti-satellite capabilities developed by other nations (the communication explicitly refers to the case of China as an illustration in support of its point). In response to these threats, the European Union must therefore seek to strengthen the resilience of its space systems. This includes protection against cyber-attacks, recognising that space and related terrestrial infrastructures are particularly vulnerable. To strengthen this resilience, the EU plans to put in place an EU-wide security framework for the protection of space systems. This framework will propose information sharing and cooperation on space security incidents. It will also

[25] Opinion of the European Economic and Social Committee, 'EU Space Strategy for Security and Defence', Joint Communication to the European Parliament and the Council on the European Union Space Strategy for Security and Defence, JOIN(2023) 9 final, CCMI/215, rapporteur: Maurizio Mensi; co-rapporteur: Jean Pie, 2023.

[26] Joint Communication to the European Parliament and the Council, 'European Union Space Strategy for Security and Defence', JOIN(2023) 9 final, European Commission, Brussels, 10 March 2023.

be based on the application of existing European directives and regulations on the resilience of critical entities and cybersecurity.[27]

However determined the European Union may be to guarantee the security of its space infrastructures, it must place particular emphasis on increasing its technological autonomy in the space sector by reducing its strategic dependence on third countries. This means strengthening European industrial capabilities and improving coordination between the European Defence Agency,[28] the ESA, and other agencies[29] to develop critical space technologies. One of the priorities in this area is the management of space transit, a sector in which the United States has predominant technological resources. In its conclusions, the EU Security and Defence Council, at its meeting on 27 May 2024 (9225/24), rightly recalled that '[w]hile recalling that Space Domain Awareness is a sovereign prerogative, the Council welcomes the efforts by relevant Member States to share information with the EU in this field. It encourages the collaborative development of additional dedicated capabilities required for Member States' Space Domain Awareness and reiterates its support for reinforcing EU Space Surveillance and Tracking capabilities of objects in orbit.

It seems that Europe has taken the measure of the strategic, commercial and geopolitical dimensions of Space Traffic Management (STM), which is not limited to the sustainability of outer space, but also includes questions concerning Europe's future autonomy in access to and use of space. European national players have already developed several policies and initiatives aimed at directly or indirectly addressing STM-related concerns. However, the EU has been slow to develop provisions aimed at establishing a concerted and coordinated STM strategy. This delay in developing an appropriate regulatory framework is not without consequences.

Firstly, it could jeopardise the sustainability of Europe's autonomous access to and use of space. By depending on the US regulatory framework, European space actors would not be able to meet some of the most stringent requirements

---

27 Regulation (EU) 2022/2554 of the European Parliament and of the Council of 14 December 2022 on the digital operational resilience for the financial sector and amending Regulations (EC) No 1060/2009, (EU) No 648/2012, (EU) No 600/2014, (EU) No 909/2014 and (EU) 2016/1011; Directive (EU) 2022/2555 of the European Parliament and of the Council of 14 December 2022 on measures for a high common level of cybersecurity across the Union, amending Regulation (EU) No 910/2014 and Directive (EU) 2018/1972, and repealing Directive (EU) 2016/1148 (SRI 2 Directive); Directive (EU) 2022/2557 of the European Parliament and of the Council of 14 December 2022 on the resilience of critical entities and repealing Council Directive 2008/114/EC [2022] *OJ* L333/1.

28 See the commentary on Article 45 TEU by A.-H. Bertana in this publication.

29 Examples include the European Union Agency for the Space Programme, the European Union Satellite Centre (SatCen, based in Torrjéon de Ardoz), the European Aviation Safety Agency (EASA) and the European Agency for the Operational Management of Large-scale IT Systems (eu-LISA).

unless they relied exclusively on US data to operate. With no choice but to rely on US directives, Europe's sovereignty, interests and needs could be put at risk.

Furthermore, it is more than likely that insurance companies could push for the adoption of the highest level of services to better manage their financial risks. In this context, they would be inclined to promote the use of the 'enhanced' services defined by the United States. In addition, the future competitiveness of European satellite manufacturing could be threatened if companies were forced to use US STM data or to apply for a US STM licence, with the possibility of this being refused.

Finally, there are also considerable risks for European launch service providers. They could suffer the competitive disadvantage of not having their launch windows and collision avoidances certified by the US authorities. Concerning *Space Situational Awareness* (SSA), many European players are heavily dependent on data-sharing agreements signed with the United States. These agreements include ministries and armed forces (of Belgium, Denmark, France, Germany, Italy, Netherlands, Norway, Spain, and the United Kingdom), European intergovernmental organisations (ESA, EUMETSAT), commercial satellite operators and launch service providers. From the American point of view, these SSA-sharing agreements are powerful instruments of leadership.

In the long term, European companies could fall behind US companies in acquiring critical market share, with US companies likely to dominate the SSA/STM tendering market through contracts with the US Department of Commerce[30] to develop a paid 'enhanced' level of service to complement the basic level of service offered. In such a scenario, US companies would enjoy a decisive competitive advantage that could seriously erode the attractiveness of the European space industry.

It is therefore essential to guarantee the value of Europe's space infrastructure and the future competitiveness of European space programmes.[31] A study by the European Commission revealed that more than 10% of the EU's GDP depends on space infrastructure and services.[32] The Council also pointed out that 'space systems and services are crucial to the functioning of our society, economy, and security and defence'.[33] This wording may seem

---

[30] This is the US federal government department responsible for trade and industry.

[31] C. Mölling, F. Schimmel and T. Schütz, *The Role of Space as a Global Common Good for Critical Infrastructure and Industry – A Workshop Report*, *Strategic Compass*, DGAP Report, No. 21, October 2021.

[32] Directorate-General for Internal Market, Industry, Entrepreneurship and SMEs (European Commission), PriceWaterhouseCoopers (PwC), *Dependence of the European Economy on Space Infrastructures – Potential Impacts of Space Assets Loss*, Brussels, European Commission, 2017, https://op.europa.eu/en/publication-detail/-/publication/e5450aac-0d4d-11e8-966a-01aa75ed71a1/language-en.

[33] General Secretariat of the Council, *Council Conclusions on EU Security and Defence*, Brussels, Council of the European Union, 27 May 2024, 9225/24, p. 23.

trivial, but it is of obvious importance in the current context. Any loss of space capabilities or control over them, whether as a result of deliberate aggression or material failure, would result in substantial economic loss. The need to protect space assets and secure the benefits they generate calls for strong and decisive measures in a wide variety of areas, including technology, the rule of law and standardisation. In addition, the development of European space programmes over the period 2014–2021 (Galileo, EGNOS, Copernicus) and the launch of new initiatives (such as GOVSATCOM, and future IRIS2) require EU Member States to take the necessary action to strengthen space security.

These actions should also strengthen user confidence in European space-based services. To this end, the European Union must adopt provisions to guarantee not only a certified level of performance, but also the long-term availability of space-based services. Furthermore, at a time when the European Union is trying to implement a credible common security and defence policy, to which space assets make an essential, if not vital, contribution, it should meet the most stringent security and safety requirements for government and defence users.

In its communication adopted at its plenary session on 12 July 2023,[34] the European Economic and Social Committee (EESC) once again reiterated the strategic importance of space as a key factor enabling European decision-makers to act independently and in an informed manner, particularly in crisis management and the preservation of security. In the EESC's view, this recognition implies the urgent need to develop a robust European space policy, while calling for greater involvement of civil society to legitimise and strengthen public support for civilian applications of space technologies. Given the need for strategic autonomy, the EESC reiterates that Europe must consolidate its independence in space by integrating civil, military, national and European efforts, both public and private, to improve security. This context justifies the strengthening of public-private partnerships and cooperation with countries sharing common values. The EESC warns of the increased risk of attacks against space infrastructures, which threaten the essential services provided by satellites, underlining the crucial importance of protecting European space capabilities against potential vulnerabilities. The Committee calls on Member States to assume their role in maintaining global peace and security by strengthening their sovereignty in the use of space. This means ensuring the resilience of the European space industry and securing critical supplies and infrastructure, with the priority objective of guaranteeing sovereign and sustainable access to space for Europe.

[34] Opinion of the European Economic and Social Committee on the Joint Communication to the European Parliament and the Council on the European Union space strategy for security and defence, JOIN(2023) 9 final, (2023/C 349/23).

In addition to reiterating the strategic nature of space infrastructures, which had already been the subject of a communication from the European Commission in 2011,[35] the EESC recalls the diversity of threats that are likely to weigh on space infrastructures, thereby justifying, without expressly mentioning it, the European Union's growing competence in this sector. While welcoming the steps taken to carry out an annual analysis of the space threat landscape (which it considers essential for understanding the hostile environment in which space and terrestrial infrastructures and services are and will be evolving), the EESC stresses the need to increase the resilience and protection of space systems and services in the EU. In its view, this should include the development of an EU-wide security framework, information sharing and cooperation on space security incidents, strengthening the technological sovereignty of the EU space sector, better identification of security risks in the EU space sector and, finally, the development of capabilities, including autonomous EU access to space in order to increase resilience.

III. ARTICLE 189 OF THE TFEU AS A SPRINGBOARD FOR MORE COMPLETE REGULATION OF THE EUROPEAN UNION IN THE SPACE SECTOR

Today, the European Union is characterised by a kaleidoscope of regulations governing space activities: eleven of its Member States have specific legal frameworks designed to regulate orbital operations, operators and space objects. It should be emphasised that, with the exception of Latvia, all European nations are committed to the 1967 Space Treaty, a founding pact that prescribes a series of essential duties. With the rise of non-governmental players in the space arena, close collaboration between European states is becoming imperative if they are to honour their international commitments.

It was in response to these challenges that the European Commission, on 25 June 2025, adopted the EU Space Act, establishing for the first time a common European framework for resilience, security, and sustainability in outer space. Initially proposed as a future directive by the President of the European Commission, Ursula von der Leyen, in her letter of intent to the Presidency of the Council of the European Union on 13 September 2023,[36] the EU Commission opted for a "regulation" in order to guarantee a uniform implementation in all member states.

---

[35] P.A. Slann, 'Anticipating Uncertainty: The Security of European Critical Outer Space Infrastructures', *Space Policy*, 2016, no. 35, pp. 6–14.

[36] State of the Union 2023 – *Letter of Intent*, Brussels, European Commission, 13 September 2023, see https://state-of-the-union.ec.europa.eu/state-union-2023_en for access.

According to the Commission's work programme for 2024, published in October 2023, the projected space bill was supposed to be completed in the first quarter of 2024. Although no specific information on the content of the initial proposed legislation was available, a targeted consultation was launched between October and November 2023 to gather the views of stakeholders who could be affected by a European space law, including satellite operators and manufacturers, launch service providers and scientists. Since its announcement, EU Member States and space operators active in the EU were eagerly awaiting such legislation and, with it, the changes it could bring. At the European Space Conference in January 2024, it was mentioned that the European Commission would present a draft law by March 2024.[37] That same month, the French Parliament adopted a resolution in favour of the adoption of a European space law.[38] On 9 April, however, the Commissioner for Industry, Defence and Space,[39] Thierry Breton, addressing the European Parliament's Committee on Industry, Research and Energy (ITRE), stated that the presentation of this EU space regulation would be delayed, probably until the summer and possibly even postponed until after the European elections in June 2024. The justification put forward for this postponement was that more time seemed necessary to bring all the players together around a common vision.

Whatever the timeframe, a European space law – as it was initially presented – should have had to overcome numerous hurdles to become functional and beneficial. Several EU Member States already have national space legislation and are actively engaged in space activities, while a growing number are adopting national frameworks and expanding their presence in the space sector. In a highly regulated environment, where countries have long established and enforced national laws, the practical implementation of a space law at the EU level was anything but straightforward, which is precisely why the Commission chose to proceed through a regulation rather than a directive.. There were indeed many difficulties in establishing regulation at the European level.[40]

---

37 Speech by Commissioner Breton – EU Space: the Top 5 Priorities for 2024 and Beyond, Brussels, European Space Conference 2024, 23 January 2024, https://ec.europa.eu/commission/presscorner/detail/en/speech_24_368.

38 Proposition de résolution européenne (n° 1944); rapport de Mme Cécile Rilhac, au nom de la commission des affaires européennes (n° 1991); texte considéré comme adopté par la commission des affaires économiques le 15 janvier 2024; discussion et adoption le 5 mars 2024 (TA n° 249), https://www.legifrance.gouv.fr/download/file/oT90hilQlNGLdFIZevDKGSa7L0MNomMd5FrZzLuw-aY=/JOETEXTE.

39 Mission letter from President von der Leyen to Thierry Breton, Brussels, 1 December 2019, https://commissioners.ec.europa.eu/document/download/9e3944aa-6986-4498-ace6-1a11e5320b69_en?filename=president-elect_von_der_leyens_mission_letter_to_thierry_breton_en.pdf.

40 D. Stefoudi, 'EU Space Law – Three reasons against, three reasons in favour', EJIL:Talk!, 29 April 2024, https://www.ejiltalk.org/eu-space-law-three-reasons-against-three-reasons-in-favour.

The first is the absence of full EU competence in space matters. The EU's competence in space is, as we know, defined by Article 189 of the TFEU. According to this article, the EU may establish a European space policy, promote research and development, and coordinate efforts in the field of space exploration and exploitation. However, any harmonisation of the laws and regulations of EU Member States is explicitly excluded from EU competence. The proposed European space regulation would instead be based on Articles 114 and 191 of the TFEU. These articles concern the harmonisation of internal market rules and environmental protection respectively. Space activities undoubtedly have implications for the internal market and the environment, and EU Member States often include them in their national frameworks, particularly as part of the licensing process. For example, operators seeking authorisation may be required to provide information on their commercial status or follow debris mitigation guidelines. Despite certain aspects of the space sector affecting EU competence in the internal market and the environment, the exclusion of EU Member States' space laws and regulations from harmonisation persists. Consequently, drawing a clear distinction between space matters regulated at a national level and those regulated at the EU level may prove unrealistic.

A second major difficulty is the high degree of legal uncertainty affecting the development of the space sector in Europe. National and international laws governing space activities aim to provide legal certainty for states, international organisations and private companies operating in the space field. Almost half of the EU Member States have adopted national frameworks covering space activities within their jurisdiction, and several others are in the process of adopting them. These laws serve to implement Article VI of the Outer Space Treaty (1967), which obliges states to authorise and supervise their national activities in space. While there are similarities in the scope and content of the national frameworks – including provisions relating to the licensing of space activities, liability and insurance issues, debris mitigation requirements and space object registration processes – there are also significant variations. Some frameworks focus on specific types of activity, such as the use of space resources or the operation of launch bases. Consequently, attempting even *minimal* harmonisation is complex and potentially counterproductive. Although space regulation at the EU level does not aim to achieve such harmonisation, the simplification of licensing procedures has been mentioned among its priorities. In addition, addressing resilience, safety and sustainability without affecting the existing space debris and safety provisions already incorporated into national frameworks and applied by several operators presents challenges. At present, due to the lack of clarity on its content, the draft European Space Regulation acts as a destabilising factor, and its potentially disruptive impact on existing national frameworks cannot be accurately assessed.

A final difficulty is undoubtedly the lack of political and legal opportunity. EU Member States develop their space laws and policies with a medium to long-term perspective, and the absence of a clear timetable certainly impacts their plans, affecting their space priorities and national industry.

Morevoer, ambitious space legislation at the EU level is also expected to enshrine a natural extension of the EU's mission to position it among the world's space players. There are three main reasons for this.

The first is the need to achieve real strategic autonomy. In the current geopolitical context, autonomous space capabilities are of paramount importance, given the number of civil, commercial and defence applications that depend on space technology. The European Union has long managed the EU Space Programme, providing reliable Earth observation data and applications via Copernicus, enhanced geolocation services via Galileo and EGNOS, secure connectivity via GOVSATCOM (and, tomorrow, the future IRIS2 constellation), and essential space situational awareness for space missions. The EU Space Programme not only promotes the take-up of satellite applications, but also provides autonomous space capabilities for the EU and its Member States. It is governed by the Regulation establishing the EU Space Programme and the European Union Space Programme Agency (EUSPA),[41] which, among other things, lays down the conditions for access to EU space data and services and guarantees a high level of security for its various components. While the space programmes of individual states and their private companies must comply with broader national frameworks, the EU space programme operates outside these regulations. The implementation of a European regulation for space could guarantee an equivalent level of regulatory protection for the EU space programme, an important asset for the EU's autonomy in space, but also for security and defence needs.

A second reason is the search for an acceptable level of resilience, security and sustainability to secure the benefits of space technology and maintain the accessibility of Earth orbits, while preserving the space environment. Several EU Member States have put in place national frameworks with measures that address these three pillars. A legislative framework at the European level would ensure that all EU Member States implement at least minimum measures in this respect. Such coordination is essential, especially given the high level of cooperation in space between EU Member States, which could benefit from simplified regulation.

A third and final reason would be to achieve a uniform approach to space. In addition to establishing a minimum level of regulation, a European

41 Regulation (EU) 2021/696 of the European Parliament and of the Council of 28 April 2021 establishing the Union Space Programme and the European Union Agency for the Space Programme and repealing Regulations (EU) No 912/2010, (EU) No 1285/2013 and (EU) No 377/2014 and Decision No 541/2014/EU, [2021] *OJ* L170/69.

regulation on space would promote a unified position, particularly concerning resilience, security and sustainability. Such a cohesive approach to space would also facilitate the adoption and implementation of other EU policies, such as the EU Space Strategy for Security and Defence, the EU approach to space traffic management, as well as other policy initiatives leveraging space, such as the Green Pact for Europe.

The lack of detail and the ongoing delays in presenting a draft EU space law are in many ways reminiscent of the preparatory work on a European space code of conduct that was undertaken twice, in 2008 and 2014, to no avail. This delay once again exposed the EU's difficulty in speaking with one voice, as well as its tendency to retreat into a wait-and-see posture. Such an option would be difficult to sustain in the long term, given that we are talking about a European space law. Indeed, the difficulties inherent in such a project have been known for a long time. As we all know, it is essential to tackle, in particular, the issue of the competitiveness of the European space sector and that of the financing by EU public funds of the American private sector in charge of launching European satellite capacities. The answer to the question of whether an EU space law is necessary should therefore be obvious. However, by forcing the postponement of the project, the EU Member States, seem to have indicated that this is far from being the case.

With the adoption of the long-awaited EU Space Act on 25 June 2025 – regardless of the form it ultimately took – the European Commission marked a historic milestone in the governance of European space activities.[42] For the first time, the Union maximises its chance to establish a single market for space services and data, inspired by the thirteen national space legislations that already exist across Europe. Presented by Commissioner for Defence and Space Andrius Kubilius, the regulation aims to introduce a coherent and binding framework to ensure resilience, security, and sustainability in outer space, effectively transforming space into a fully integrated component of the EU Single Market. The expected regulation was designed to overcome the initial concerns expressed by countries such as Germany and Italy. It establishes common operational and environmental standards for all space operators active in the EU, including foreign entities such as Starlink, covering areas such as collision avoidance, debris mitigation, end-of-life management, cybersecurity, and environmental impact assessment. The legislation introduces a comprehensive risk management framework throughout the lifecycle of space missions and promotes the development of a 'European Space Resilience Network (EUSRN)' to strengthen coordination between the Commission, the European Space Agency, and national authorities. Although the regulation excludes military

42 'Actualité – La Commission européenne place sur orbite un "code de la route" pour l'espace', *B2 Pro, Le quotidien de l'Europe géopolitique*, June 2025, https://club.bruxelles2.eu/2025/06/actualite-la-commission-europeenne-place-sur-orbite-un-code-de-la-route-pour-lespace/.

activities under the national security clause, it sets a strategic precedent by positioning Europe as a global leader in responsible space governance, while fostering industrial competitiveness, sustainability, and innovation across the European space economy.

It remains to be seen, however, whether this ambitious framework will be sufficient to enable the European Union and its Member States to move toward genuine strategic autonomy in the space sector – one that would also allow them to achieve the 'reconquête à marche forcée' evoked by French President Emmanuel Macron.[43]

CONCLUSION

The history of European space development shows a complex evolution, shaped by divergent national interests and gradual institutional cooperation. Despite fragmented beginnings and slow integration, the Treaty of Lisbon and subsequent initiatives marked a decisive step forward, giving the European Union explicit competence in space, thereby enhancing its stature on the international stage. Article 189 of the TFEU represents a major, albeit imperfect, development of the European Union's competences in this field. However, the sudden changes in the strategic context and the transformation of the players in the global space market should lead to greater integration and greater regulatory consistency at the EU level.

While preserving the autonomy of the Member States, this shared competence paves the way for more coordinated policies and a more strategic use of space as a lever for security, defence and technological progress. Recent developments should mark the culmination of a process of 'securitisation' of the European space domain, which has meant that space is no longer seen simply as a field for civil and scientific activities, but as a key issue in terms of European defence and strategic autonomy.[44]

Space, once seen primarily as an arena for scientific exploration and technical cooperation, is now firmly recognised as a key strategic domain for Europe – as the recent Draghi report has again emphasised. Current and future challenges – whether related to security, defence, or environmental sustainability – demand a unified and robust European response. In this context, the adoption by the European Commission on 25 June 2025 of the long-awaited EU Space Act, in

---

43 'Actualité espace: l'Europe doit mener une "reconquête à marche forcée"', *Bruxelles2*, June 2025, https://club.bruxelles2.eu/en/2025/06/actualite-espace-leurope-doit-mener-une-reconquete-a-marche-forcee-emmanuel-macron/.

44 N. Klimburg-Witjes, 'Shifting articulations of space and security: boundary work in European space policy making' (2021) 30(4) *European Security*, pp. 526–546, DOI:10.1080/09662839.2021.1890039.

the form of a regulation rather than a directive, marks a decisive step towards establishing a coherent framework for the governance of space activities within the Union. By setting out common rules for resilience, safety, and sustainability in orbit, the Act aims to foster Europe's strategic autonomy in the face of global space powers while supporting the competitiveness and collective prosperity of its Member States.

Yet, despite its historic character, the EU Space Act also raises a number of uncertainties. Its effective implementation will depend on Member States' willingness to align their national frameworks, on the industry's capacity to adapt to new compliance requirements, and on the Union's ability to reconcile ambition with pragmatism. Questions also remain as to whether this regulation alone will be sufficient to ensure Europe's leadership in a sector evolving at unprecedented speed. In short, although the EU has now equipped itself with a long-overdue 'code of conduct' for space, its journey toward true strategic autonomy and global influence in this domain remains very much a work in progress.

ARTICLE 207 TFEU: THE COMMON COMMERCIAL POLICY AND THE COMMON SECURITY AND DEFENCE POLICY

Sabrina ROBERT

Professor of law at Nantes University

Member of the Law and Social Change Research Centre

Associate member of IREDIES – Université Paris 1

> **Article 207 TFEU**
>
> **1.** The common commercial policy shall be based on uniform principles, particularly with regard to changes in tariff rates, the conclusion of tariff and trade agreements relating to trade in goods and services, and the commercial aspects of intellectual property, foreign direct investment, the achievement of uniformity in measures of liberalisation, export policy and measures to protect trade such as those to be taken in the event of dumping or subsidies. The common commercial policy shall be conducted in the context of the principles and objectives of the Union's external action.
>
> **2.** The European Parliament and the Council, acting by means of regulations in accordance with the ordinary legislative procedure, shall adopt the measures defining the framework for implementing the common commercial policy.
>
> **3.** Where agreements with one or more third countries or international organisations need to be negotiated and concluded, Article 218 shall apply, subject to the special provisions of this Article.
>
> The Commission shall make recommendations to the Council, which shall authorise it to open the necessary negotiations. The Council and the Commission shall be responsible for ensuring that the agreements negotiated are compatible with internal Union policies and rules.

> The Commission shall conduct these negotiations in consultation with a special committee appointed by the Council to assist the Commission in this task and within the framework of such directives as the Council may issue to it. The Commission shall report regularly to the special committee and to the European Parliament on the progress of negotiations.
>
> **4.** For the negotiation and conclusion of the agreements referred to in paragraph 3, the Council shall act by a qualified majority.
>
> For the negotiation and conclusion of agreements in the fields of trade in services and the commercial aspects of intellectual property, as well as foreign direct investment, the Council shall act unanimously where such agreements include provisions for which unanimity is required for the adoption of internal rules.
>
> The Council shall also act unanimously for the negotiation and conclusion of agreements:
>
> **a)** in the field of trade in cultural and audiovisual services, where these agreements risk prejudicing the Union's cultural and linguistic diversity;
>
> **b)** in the field of trade in social, education and health services, where these agreements risk seriously disturbing the national organisation of such services and prejudicing the responsibility of Member States to deliver them.
>
> **5.** The negotiation and conclusion of international agreements in the field of transport shall be subject to Title VI of Part Three and to Article 218.
>
> **6.** The exercise of the competences conferred by this Article in the field of the common commercial policy shall not affect the delimitation of competences between the Union and the Member States, and shall not lead to harmonisation of legislative or regulatory provisions of the Member States in so far as the Treaties exclude such harmonisation.

Article 207 TFEU relates to the European Union's common commercial (or trade) policy, which falls within the scope of its exclusive competences. This provision does not, therefore, come under those directly concerning the Common Security and Defence Policy (CSDP). However, it is clear that the two policies intersect, sometimes very closely: the economy is increasingly penetrating security issues, and the European Union's openness to external economic relations (whether in the area of trade in goods, services, intellectual property rights or foreign direct investment) is both a powerful lever for strengthening its defence capabilities (both internally and in the EU's external sphere of influence), as well as being a potential source for undermining the Union's strategic autonomy. The many recent developments in the common trade policy are not misleading on this. If the European Union seems to be gradually converting to controlled free trade, it is both out of a concern to strengthen the resilience of the European economy in the face of the successive shocks experienced by Member States in recent years, and in order to adapt better to the new geo-economic dimension of global security. Two regulations of the European Parliament and the Council reflect this intertwining of the common commercial policy and the CSDP: Regulation (EU) 2019/452 of 19 March 2019 establishing a framework for screening foreign direct investment in the Union and Regulation (EU) 2021/821 of 20 May 2021 setting up a Union regime for the control of exports, brokering, technical assistance, transit and transfers of dual-use items.

SCREENING FOREIGN DIRECT INVESTMENT IN EUROPE'S DEFENCE SECTOR

Regulation (EU) 2019/452 of the European Parliament and of the Council of 19 March 2019 establishing a framework for the screening of foreign direct investments into the Union

Sabrina Robert
Professor of law at Nantes University
Member of the Law and Social Change Research Centre
Associate member of IREDIES – Université Paris 1

Regulation (EU) 2019/452 of the European Parliament and of the Council of 19 March 2019 establishing a framework for the screening of foreign direct investments into the Union[1] (hereafter the '2019 Regulation' or 'Regulation 2019/452') was not adopted under the Common Security and Defence Policy (CSDP), but under the Common Commercial Policy of Article 207 TFEU (CCP). Since the entry into force of the Lisbon Treaty, this policy has encompassed foreign direct investment (FDI) and enables the European Union (EU) to define the conditions of access for such FDI to the internal market. Given that the EU is the main place of attraction for foreign investment[2] and that its market is the most open in the world, due to the universal nature of the freedom of

1 Regulation (EU) 2019/452 of the European Parliament and of the Council of 19 March 2019 establishing a framework for the screening of foreign direct investments into the Union, [2019] *OJ* L79I/1.

2 Just under €140 billion of inward FDI in 2022 out of a global total of €1,200 billion. European Commission, Third annual report on the screening of foreign direct investments into the EU, COM(2023) 590 final, 19 October 2023, p. 2. This represents just under 50,000 transactions in 2023, compared with 5,420 in 2015. FDI flows have slowed since 2021 for the European Union, but also for the rest of the world economy. Fourth annual report on the screening of foreign direct investments into the EU, COM(2024) 464 final, 17 October 2024, pp. 2–4.

movement of capital enshrined in Article 63(1) TFEU,[3] the adoption of an FDI screening mechanism could seem un-European in its very nature. This type of mechanism may take the form of any 'instrument of general application, such as a law or regulation, and accompanying administrative requirements, implementing rules or guidelines setting out the terms, conditions and procedures to assess, investigate, authorise, condition, prohibit or unwind foreign direct investment'.[4] Before the adoption of the 2019 Regulation, several Member States were already carrying out such screening at national level, and three of them (France, Germany and Italy)[5] managed to convince the Commission, and then the other Member States, that such a mechanism was necessary at EU level.[6]

The tighter control that can be exercised over inward FDI may be explained first and foremost by a profound change in the concepts of defence and security. These are no longer limited to military risks, but encompass the fight against numerous hybrid threats. They include risks to economic security, while technological and industrial independence are also crucial, and FDI is seen as a potential threat. This obviously applies to foreign investment in defence, but also in many other sectors deemed sensitive (transport, infrastructure, energy, access to raw materials, telecommunications, health, media, etc.). This broad understanding explains why the EU now considers investment screening to be a key element in the defence of its strategic autonomy.[7]

Another reason why the EU has set up an FDI screening mechanism is that several Member States have been exposed to a certain degree of politicisation of investment operations carried out on their territory: an increase in investments

3 'Within the framework of the provisions set out in this Chapter, all restrictions on the movement of capital between Member States and between Member States and third countries shall be prohibited'.

4 Regulation 2019/452, Art. 2(4).

5 See the joint letter sent by France, Germany and Italy to the European Commission in February 2017: https://www.bmwk.de/Redaktion/DE/Downloads/S-T/schreiben-de-fr-it-an-malmstroem.pdf?__blob=publicationFile&v=4.

6 R. Bismuth, 'Reading between the lines of the EU regulation establishing a framework for screening FDI into the Union', in J. Bourgeois (ed.), *EU Framework for Foreign Direct Investment Control*, Alphen aan den Rijn, Wolters Kluwer, 2019, pp. 104–107.

7 Although the EU's strategic documents on European defence and security do not go into much detail on this point, they refer to it almost systematically. See in particular the Communication from the Commission, 'Advancing European economic security: an introduction of five new initiatives', COM(2024) 22 final, 24 January 2024, p. 2; Council of the European Union, 'A strategic compass for security and defence – For a European Union that protects its citizens, its values and its interests, and contributes to international peace and security', 21 March 2022, p. 35; Joint Communication from the European Commission and the High Representative of the Union for Foreign Affairs and Security Policy on the 'European Economic Security Strategy', JOIN(2023) 20 final, 20 June 2023, pp. 8–9. For an analysis of the link between FDI screening and the protection of the EU's strategic autonomy see S. Robert, 'Foreign investment control procedures as a tool for enforcing EU strategic autonomy' (2023) 8 *European Papers*, pp. 513–523.

made by state-owned companies (or more broadly by companies controlled by states) and by sovereign wealth funds;[8] the deployment of offensive strategies by certain foreign companies to extend their influence abroad, etc.

Chinese companies have been mainly at the centre of the concerns raised by these strategies. Jean-Claude Juncker's 2017 State of the Union speech left no doubt that the adoption of Regulation 2019/452 was primarily motivated by the need to deal with Chinese economic expansionism, pointing out that:

> If a foreign, state-owned, company wants to purchase a European port, part of our energy infrastructure or a defence technology firm, this should only happen in transparency, with scrutiny and debate. It is a political responsibility to know what is going on in our own backyard so that we can protect our collective security if needed.[9]

The President of the Commission alluded to a number of remarkable 'takeovers' by Chinese companies, including:[10] the purchase of the port of Piraeus by Cosco,[11] the (short-lived) acquisition of Toulouse airport by Casil Europe[12] and the purchase of the German robotics company Kuka by Midea.[13]

Regulation 2019/452 was therefore adopted to address the risk that the globalisation of trade and the resulting interdependencies could be used for coercive purposes.[14] It applies to all FDI, whatever its origin, that may threaten European security. This may include what the Commission calls 'predatory acquisitions'[15] that undermine the EU's economic autonomy by diverting the exploitation of the sectors concerned from meeting the needs of Europe's populations; investments that can be described as 'interference' or that

---

8 See the *Reflection Paper on Harnessing Globalisation* of 10 May 2017, in which the Commission expresses its concerns about the rise of investments made by state-owned enterprises. COM(2017) 240, p. 15.

9 State of the Union Address 2017, http://europa.eu/rapid/press-release_SPEECH-17-3165_en.htm.

10 Chinese investment in Europe jumped 21% between 2017 and 2018. P.M. Gadocha, 'Assessing the EU framework regulation for the screening of foreign direct investment – What is the effect on Chinese investors?' (2020) 6(1) *The Chinese Journal of Global Governance*, p. 45.

11 China COSCO Shipping Corporation Limited is China's largest shipowner.

12 Casil Europe is owned by two Chinese companies, Shandong Hi-Speed Group and Friedmann Pacific AM. In December 2015, Casil Europe sold the airport to a French group, Eiffage. From the outset, the Chinese takeover was designed to be purely commercial and speculative.

13 Midea is a Chinese company specialising in the production of domestic appliances and air conditioners.

14 H. Farrell and A.L. Newman, 'Weaponized interdependence. How global economic networks shape State coercion', *International Security*, 2019, p. 45.

15 Commission Communication C/2020/1981 of 25 March 2020, Guidance to the Member States concerning foreign direct investment and free movement of capital from third countries, and the protection of Europe's strategic assets, ahead of the application of Regulation (EU) 2019/452 (FDI Screening Regulation), para. 4.

threaten political independence (in the telecommunications or media sectors for example), that aim to influence or manipulate opinions in Europe; or investments that can be described as being for 'circumvention', which interfere with the dissemination of Europe's values and the protection of its interests abroad (in the case, for example, of a foreign company that transfers technology without regard for the interests of the Union). This classification inferred from the 2019 regulation is reminiscent of the four categories of risk identified by the Commission in January 2024 in the *Economic Security Package*: 1) the risks to the resilience of supply chains; 2) the risks to the physical and cyber-security of critical infrastructure; 3) the risk for technology security and of technology leakage (to countries that do not share the EU's values); and 4) the risk of weaponisation of economic dependencies and the risk of economic coercion.[16]

Regulation 2019/452 is in fact part of a European regulatory framework currently being consolidated, which aims to better control free trade and strengthen the EU's ability to act in a globalised and open market, which presents both opportunities and risks for its strategic autonomy. Thus, Regulation 2019/452 together with other measures mark a profound change in the EU's economic policy. The latter include the Regulation against economic coercion,[17] the Regulation on foreign subsidies,[18] the instrument on international public procurement,[19] the Regulation on dual-use goods,[20] the Regulation on critical raw materials,[21] the European Commission's guidance on 'killer acquisitions',[22] and the Commission's recommendations on 5G.[23]

---

16 Communication from the Commission, Advancing European Economic Security..., cited above, p. 1.

17 Regulation (EU) 2023/2675 of 22 November 2023 on the protection of the Union and its Member States from economic coercion by third countries, [2023] *OJ* L2023/2675.

18 Regulation (EU) 2022/2560 of 14 December 2022 on foreign subsidies distorting the internal market, [2022] *OJ* L330/1. See the commentary on this regulation by S. Rodrigues in this publication.

19 Regulation (EU) 2022/1031 of the European Parliament and of the Council of 23 June 2022 on the access of third-country economic operators, goods and services to the Union's public procurement and concession markets and procedures supporting negotiations on access of Union economic operators, goods and services to the public procurement and concession markets of third countries, [2022] *OJ* L173/1.

20 Regulation (EU) 2021/821 of the European Parliament and of the Council of 20 May 2021 setting up a Union regime for the control of exports, brokering, technical assistance, transit and transfer of dual-use items, [2021] *OJ* L206/1. See the commentary on this regulation by A. Millet-Devalle in this publication.

21 Regulation (EU) 2024/1252 of the European Parliament and of the Council of 11 April 2024 establishing a framework for ensuring a secure and sustainable supply of critical raw materials and amending Regulations (EU) No 168/2013, (EU) 2018/858, (EU) 2018/1724 and (EU) 2019/1020.

22 Communication from the Commission Guidance on the application of the referral mechanism set out in Article 22 of the Merger Regulation to certain categories of cases 2021/C 113/01, 31 March 2021.

23 Commission Recommendation (EU) 2019/534 of 26 March 2019, Cybersecurity of 5G networks.

The Commission clearly intends to break with its traditional 'naïveté' towards liberalisation and globalisation, and make European defence and security a priority, even if this affects the liberal foundations of EU law.

Furthermore, the 2019 Regulation is not a static document. As soon as it was adopted, it was bound to evolve. In the first three years of its implementation, the instrument was adapted to the emergence of new security challenges through the Commission's 'doctrine', concerning: the Covid-19 pandemic,[24] the war between Russia and Ukraine,[25] and the deployment of 5G.[26] From the outset, the adoption of a new regulation that would deepen the EU's screening system at the Union level had been envisaged,[27] and in January 2024, the Commission unveiled its proposal for a new regulation.[28] This could lead to substantial changes to the existing system.[29]

For the time being, however, the system put in place is modest.[30] It is far from being comparable to the model in this area, namely the American screening mechanism, placed under the responsibility of the Committee on Foreign Investment in the United States (CFIUS) and the President of the United States, which constitutes a decisive weapon in the defence of the American economy.[31] As the title of Regulation 2019/452 indicates, its purpose is to establish a 'framework' for investment screening, not a European screening mechanism. In other words, the scheme is an umbrella tool that is not intended to replace national mechanisms. Its main purpose is to enable cooperation

24 Communication C/2020/1981 of 25 March 2020, Guidance to the Member States concerning foreign direct investment and free movement of capital from third countries, and the protection of Europe's strategic assets, ahead of the application of Regulation (EU) 2019/452.

25 Communication 2022/C 151 I/01 of 6 April 2022, Guidelines for Member States concerning foreign direct investment from Russia and Belarus in view of the military aggression against Ukraine and the restrictive measures laid down in the recent Council Regulations on sanctions.

26 Cybersecurity of 5G networks.

27 Article 15(1) of the Regulation entrusts the Commission with the task of evaluating the operation and effectiveness of the Regulation and reporting to the European Parliament and the Council.

28 Proposal for a Regulation on screening foreign investment in the Union, repealing Regulation 2019/452, COM(2024) 23 final, 21 January 2024. This proposal was drawn up following a number of evaluations carried out under the aegis of the Commission. These included a targeted consultation of Member States and stakeholders from 14 June to 21 July 2023. An evaluation was carried out by the OECD, *Framework for screening foreign direct investment into the EU. Assessing effectiveness and efficiency*, November 2022. At the time of writing, the legislative process is underway in the European Parliament, whose Committee on International Trade adopted the text in April 2025.

29 These developments are examined in this commentary.

30 A. Hervé, 'Mise en place d'un mécanisme de filtrage des investissements: quand l'Union européenne montre ses dents… de lait', *RTDE,* 2019, p. 749.

31 For a comparative analysis of the US screening mechanism and Regulation 2019/452, see J. Jacobs, 'Tiptoeing the line between national security and protectionism: a comparative approach to foreign direct investment screening in the United States and European Union' (2019) 47(02) *International Journal of Legal Information,* pp. 105–117.

between Member States and the EU and to coordinate procedures. Moreover, responsibility for screening FDI remains in the hands of the Member States.[32] The Commission's role is subsidiary, not decision-making.

There are two main reasons for this unambitious approach. The first is that the screening of foreign investment must not call into question the fundamental rule of the free movement of capital. Limitations to this freedom can only be introduced in exceptional circumstances. Among these, harm to public policy and national security makes it possible to take account of the objective of defence and economic security, but in a necessarily restrictive manner. The 2019 Regulation therefore had to strike the right balance between detecting and mitigating the security risks associated with FDI and keeping the European market open to such transactions. The second reason relates to the delicate link that the Regulation establishes between the EU's exclusive competence to define common commercial policy and the sovereign right of Member States to protect their public policy and national security, as recognised by Articles 4(2) TEU[33] and 346 TFEU.[34] In other words, while it is up to the EU to regulate FDI, it is up to the Member States to be able to control it for security purposes. Thus, with Regulation 2019/452, the EU exercised its exclusive competence in the field of FDI and immediately returned it to the Member States.[35]

To understand more precisely how the screening of FDI in the Union operates, under the control of the European framework and the Commission, this commentary will first present the purpose of the 2019 Regulation: the control of FDI likely to constitute a threat to security in the Union (Section I), and secondly, the methods of screening; The latter are the responsibility of the Member States, within the framework of their national procedures, but under the control of the Commission, which aspires to an increasingly decisive role in this area (Section II).

---

32 Art. 1(3) of Regulation 2019/452

33 See B. Warusfel's commentary on this article in this publication.

34 See the commentary on this article by S. Rodrigues in this publication.

35 On the complex relationship between the competences of the EU and those of the Member States and on the legal basis for the adoption of the screening framework, see T. Destailleur, 'Une occasion manquée pour l'Union de s'affirmer en tant qu'acteur international du droit des investissements étrangers', *R.T.D.E.*, 2020, pp. 89 et seq; R. Bismuth, 'Reading between the lines of the EU regulation establishing a framework for screening FDI into the Union', in J. Bourgeois (ed.), *EU Framework for Foreign Direct Investment Control*, Alphen aan den Rijn, Wolters Kluwer, 2019, pp. 107–108, pp. 111–112.

I. FOREIGN DIRECT INVESTMENT AND ECONOMIC SECURITY RISKS IN EUROPE

Regulation 2019/452 bases the possibility of screening FDI on Article 65(1)(b) TFEU: i.e. the protection of public policy and public security in the Member States. Although this is a derogation from the free movement of capital, the text enshrines a broad concept of security (Section A). On the other hand, while the material scope of the Regulation may also appear broad, there are limits which may affect the effectiveness of FDI screening in Europe (Section B).

A. THE CONCEPT OF ECONOMIC SECURITY IN REGULATION 2019/452

1. Public Order, Public Security and Economic Security

Regulation 2019/452 does not provide any definition of public policy or public security. This is not unique to European regulation. Neither national investment screening mechanisms in Europe and elsewhere,[36] nor investment treaties where the notion of public security is also present to justify certain barriers to foreign investment,[37] offer such a definition. These instruments use a multitude of different expressions which are considered equivalent: 'national interest', 'public policy and public security', 'public order and security', 'essential interests of the State' and 'public safety'.[38]

The absence of a definition stems from the fact that public policy and public security are concepts whose content is a matter for the sovereign power of the State invoking it. The Court of Justice of the European Union (CJEU) systematically reiterates this in its decisions on Article 65(1) TFEU: 'Member States are still, in principle, free to determine the requirements of public policy and public security in the light of their national needs'.[39] And since public policy and public security are closely linked to States' conception of their sovereignty, the content of these concepts is necessarily evolving.

---

36 UNCTAD, 'National security-related screening mechanisms for foreign investment. An analysis of recent policy developments', *Investment Policy Monitor*, December 2019, special issue, p. 9.

37 UNCTAD, 'The Protection of National Security in IIAs', UNCTAD series on international investment policies for development, 2009, p. 73.

38 UNCTAD, 'National security-related screening mechanisms for foreign investment. An analysis of recent policy developments', *Investment Policy Monitor*, December 2019, special issue, p. 9.

39 Case C-54/99, *Association Eglise de scientologie de Paris and Scientology International Reserves Trust v Prime Minister*, ECLI:EU:C:2000:124, para. 17; Case C-106/22, *Xella Magyarország Építőanyagipari Kft. v Innovációs és Technológiai* Miniszter, ECLI:EU:C:2023:568, para. 66.

Originally, national security or public security was primarily concerned with protection against military threats to the territory of the State.[40] But this concept has evolved.[41] In both domestic and international law, public security now covers protection against multiple threats such as those to a State's economy or the well-being of its population.[42] The Covid-19 crisis revealed that the national security of States can also depend on their ability to respond – from a health and economic point of view, both immediately and in the long term – to supply needs that are sometimes prosaic (the supply of surgical masks, for example) and sometimes more fundamental (pharmaceutical research in particular). In the spring of 2020, governments made several changes to their national investment screening mechanisms, but this was not purely in response to the Covid-19 pandemic.[43] Many of these changes have since been maintained or even strengthened,[44] demonstrating that preserving the economic independence of governments is now one of their essential security interests.

However, the shift from the notion of public security to that of economic security raises questions about the risk of a resurgence of economic protectionism. This risk is all the greater given that the dividing line between the two is far from obvious. For the CJEU, there is no doubt that 'purely economic grounds, such as, in particular, promotion of the national economy or its proper functioning, cannot serve as justification for an obstacle to one of the fundamental freedoms enshrined in the Treaties'. However, 'reasons of an economic nature in the pursuit of an objective in the public interest or the guarantee of a service of general interest may constitute an overriding reason in the public interest capable of justifying an obstacle to one of the fundamental freedoms enshrined in the Treaties'.[45] The distinction between 'purely economic grounds' and 'economic grounds pursuing an objective of general interest' seems very fragile, especially when the protection of economic

---

40 D.A. Baldwin, 'The concept of security' (1997) 23(1) *Rev. Int'L Stud.* 1997, p. 5; UNCTAD, 'The Protection of National Security in IIAs', UNCTAD series on international investment policies for development, 2009, p. 26.

41 J. Ma, 'International investment and national security review' (2021) 52 *Vanderbilt Journal of Transnational Law,* pp. 899–948.

42 UNCTAD, 'The Protection of National Security in IIAs', UNCTAD series on international investment policies for development, 2009, p. 7.

43 OECD, 'Investment Screening in Times of COVID - and Beyond', 23 June 2020; UNCTAD, 'Investment Policy Responses to the COVID-19 Pandemic', *Investment Policy Monitor*, May 2020, special issue no. 4.

44 Reference can be made to the work of the *CELIS Institute*, which carries out detailed analyses of national screening mechanisms and reports on their constant evolution: https://www.celis.institute/

45 Case C-563/17, *Associação Peço a Palavra e.a.*, ECLI:EU:C:2019:144, para. 70; Case C-106/22, *Xella Magyarország Építőanyagipari Kft. v Innovációs és Technológiai Miniszter*, ECLI:EU:C:2023:568, para. 65.

security involves promoting the independence and resilience of the national economy.

The European Commission seems to have become accustomed to this mixing of genres. It will be remembered that when the French 'anti-takeover' decree was adopted in 2006,[46] which aimed to amend the French Monetary and Financial Code to extend the list of sectors likely to be subject to control by the Minister for the Economy, the Commission asked France to amend the decree so that it would be less restrictive of the free movement of capital (the aim was to remove casinos from the list of activities subject to ministerial authorisation).[47]But when the 'Montebourg decree' was adopted in 2014,[48] characteristic of a genuine return to 'economic patriotism', the Commission did not complete the examination procedure. More recently, in the face of all-out reactions from Member States to increase their level of investment controls during the Covid-19 pandemic, the Commission has adopted the extensive conceptions of economic security implemented by the Member States. It has even encouraged them,[49] which could be interpreted as a desire to define a new geo-economic strategy.[50]

This broad conception of economic security also raises questions as to its compatibility with Article 65 TFEU. While it is for the Member States to define what constitutes their security, the Court has consistently held that:

> [I]n the EU context and, in particular, as derogations from a fundamental freedom enshrined in the TFEU, be interpreted strictly, so that their scope cannot be determined unilaterally by each Member State without any control by the EU institutions.[51]

Regulation 2019/452 sets out several conditions under which FDI may be considered a threat to economic security.[52] But these conditions lack precision, to the extent that FDI falling within their scope seems to be subject to a presumption of a threat to security. This presumption does not

[46] Decree no. 2005-1739 of 30 December 2005.

[47] A. Lienhard, 'La European Commission demande à la France de modifier son décret anti-OPA', *Dalloz actualité*, 5 November 2006.

[48] Decree no. 2014-479 of 14 May 2014.

[49] Communication C/2020/1981 of 25 March 2020, cited above.

[50] P. Jaïs, 'Investissements directs étrangers: la renaissance du souverainisme', *Le Club des juristes*, Blog du Coronavirus, 4 May 2020, www.leclubdesjuristes.com; P.M. Gadocha, 'Assessing the EU framework regulation for the screening of foreign direct investment – What is the effect on Chinese investors?' (2020) 6(1) *The Chinese Journal of Global Governance*, p. 38.

[51] Case C-54/99, *Association Eglise de scientologie de Paris and Scientology International Reserves Trust v Prime Minister*, ECLI:EU:C:2000:124, para. 17; Case C-106/22, *Xella Magyarország Építőanyagipari Kft. v Innovációs és Technológiai Miniszter*, ECLI:EU:C:2023:568, para. 66. Emphasis added.

[52] See Section B.1) and 2) below.

seem compatible with the restrictive approach that should be adopted when implementing derogations to the free movement of capital.

II. ECONOMIC SECURITY IN THE MEMBER STATES AND ECONOMIC SECURITY IN THE EUROPEAN UNION

The economic security addressed in the 2019 Regulation is that of individual Member States. It follows that the Regulation allows a Member State to send comments to another Member State when the former considers a planned or executed FDI project in the latter likely to affect its security, whether or not the project is subject to screening.[53] The cooperation procedure is fundamental, since the Regulation does not allow a State to screen FDI carried out on the territory of another State. The proposal for a new Regulation goes some way towards remedying this situation, since it provides that in such a case, the State which fears for its security or public order will be able to initiate, on its own initiative, a procedure relating to an FDI project in the other Member State.[54] The proposed regulation does not, however, go so far as to grant this State a genuine right of screening, which would be enforceable against the other Member State in which the investment is located.

Regulation 2019/452 also aims to ensure security in the European Union, when a FDI is likely to affect the security of more than one Member State. In such cases, the Commission may issue an opinion to the Member State concerned by the FDI, whether or not it carries out screening.[55]

Ultimately, the European framework for screening investments makes it possible to reinforce the idea of the security of the European Union, irrespective of the identification of one or more Member States under particular threat. In reality, the procedures set out in Regulation 2019/452 bear little resemblance to this dimension. At most, Article 8 allows the Commission to issue an opinion on FDI likely to affect 'projects or programmes of interest to the Union'. The list of these projects concerns outer space, artificial intelligence, transport, defence, telecommunications and energy, and is annexed to the Regulation.[56] It is more in the Commission's doctrine that this dimension has been strengthened. The guidance adopted for the Covid-19 pandemic was deeply imbued with it. The

---

53 Art. 6(2) and Art. 7(1).

54 Art. 9(1).

55 Art. 6(3) and Art. 7(2).

56 These include the following programmes: Galileo, EGNOS, Copernicus, Horizon 2020, TEN-T, TEN-E, Trans-European Telecommunication Networks, European Defence Industrial Development Programme, Permanent Structured Cooperation. This list is amply extended in the proposal for a new Regulation (Annex I).

Commission referred to what might be called 'European national security', stressing the need to preserve the capacity to meet the needs of populations not only at the national level but also, and above all, at the regional level:

> [T]oday more than ever, the EU's openness to foreign investment needs to be balanced by appropriate screening tools. In the context of the COVID-19 emergency, there could be an increased risk of attempts to acquire healthcare capacities (for example for the productions of medical or protective equipment) or related industries such as research establishments (for instance developing vaccines) via foreign direct investment [bold in original text]. Vigilance is required to ensure that any such FDI does not have a harmful impact on *the EU's capacity to cover the health needs of its citizens.* [emphasis added][57]

Other elements of this doctrine suggest that the Commission could also develop an offensive conception of the Union's security.[58] For example, in its guidance on FDI from Russia and Belarus adopted in April 2022, it calls on the Member States to systematically examine these operations.[59] This process raises questions, irrespective of the legitimacy of the treatment of Russian and Belarusian investments. The Commission is playing on the blurred distinction between the sanction regimes and the screening of investments for economic security purposes.[60] While one of the objectives of the 2019 Regulation is to increase the transparency of national screening procedures, the Commission's position is ambivalent. The way in which it envisages the mobilisation of screening mechanisms in the context of the deployment of 5G on the territory of the Member States gives the same impression of a hardening of its position. The Communication on securing 5G calls for a systematic examination of all investments in this area.[61] This position is reminiscent of the European Parliament's March 2019 resolution on the security threats posed by China's

---

57 Para. 4 of the communication.

58 On the fact that the FDI screening framework could be used as an instrument of 'economic warfare': P.M. Gadocha, 'Assessing the EU framework regulation for the screening of foreign direct investment – What is the effect on Chinese investors?' (2020) 6(1) *The Chinese Journal of Global Governance*, p. 38. Compare this with a similar analysis of the US screening system: J. Jacobs, 'Tiptoeing the line between national security and protectionism: a comparative approach to foreign direct investment screening in the United States and European Union' (2019) 47(02) *International Journal of Legal Information*, p. 105.

59 Which account for a tiny proportion of inward FDI. In 2022, of all screened FDI transactions in Europe, 1.4% came from Russian investors and 0.2% from Belarusian investors. Third annual report on screening foreign direct investment in the EU, COM(2023) 590 final, 19 October 2023, p. 25.

60 S. Robert-Cuendet, 'Unilateral and extraterritorial sanctions and international investment law', in C. Beaucillon (ed.), *Research handbook on unilateral / extraterritorial sanctions and international law*, Cheltenham, Edward Elgar Publishing, 2021, pp. 212–213.

61 *Secure 5G Deployment in the EU,* cited above, para. 9, which in reality is not its responsibility, since the Commission does not itself have the power to carry out screening. See below Section II.A.2).

growing technological presence in the EU, which itself refers to the US position denouncing genuine 'economic aggression' on the part of China, particularly in the field of telecommunications.[62]

A. FDI LIKELY TO THREATEN ECONOMIC SECURITY IN THE EUROPEAN UNION

Regulation 2019/452 sets out an indicative list of factors that may be taken into account to identify FDI 'likely to affect security or public order'.[63] These factors correspond firstly to a list of sectors that may be deemed sensitive from a security point of view. Generally speaking, these are sectors considered essential to the economy, social well-being, national security and the performance of the essential functions of government. Without the list being exhaustive, Article 4 of the Regulation thus mentions critical infrastructures, critical technologies and dual-use items as defined by Regulation 428/2009, the supply of critical inputs, access to sensitive information and the freedom and pluralism of the media. However, practice shows that the sectors in which the majority of screening operations take place only partially correspond to this list. During the first four years of operation of the European framework, it was mainly manufacturing industry, information and communication technologies, specialised activities (such as legal and accounting firms and consultancies), wholesale and retail trade and transport and warehousing that fell within the scope of the screening procedures.[64]

Article 4 of the Regulation adds other factors that may be taken into account to determine whether an investment risks undermining one of these sectors: the fact that the foreign investor is controlled directly or indirectly by a foreign government; the fact that the investor has already participated in activities undermining security or public order in a Member State; and the fact that there is a serious risk that the foreign investor will engage in illegal or criminal activities.

Two points need to be detailed here. Firstly, these criteria are only indicative. States are not obliged to refer to them and nothing prevents a State from authorising a FDI project by an investor who is, for example, subject to

---

62 White House, Office of Trade and Manufacturing Policy Report, *How China's Economic Aggression Threatens the Technologies and Intellectual Property of the United States and the World*, June 2018, https://trumpwhitehouse.archives.gov/briefings-statements/office-trade-manufacturing-policy-report-chinas-economic-aggression-threatens-technologies-intellectual-property-united-states-world/

63 Art. 4(2).

64 Third Annual Report on Screening Foreign Direct Investment in the European Union, cited above, p. 18; Fourth Annual Report on Screening Foreign Direct Investment in the European Union, cited above, p. 6.

European sanctions. In contrast, the proposal for a new regulation requires Member States to refer to these more detailed factors. In particular, the proposal requires that account be taken of the existence, against the foreign investor, of European sanctions taken pursuant to Article 215 TFEU, without prejudice to the decision to be taken by the State carrying out the screening.[65]

Secondly, it is not certain that these criteria are sufficient to meet the requirements of the case law of the CJEU. The CJEU considers that 'public policy and public security may be relied on *only where there is a genuine and sufficiently serious threat to a fundamental interest of society*' [author's emphasis].[66] However, the notion of FDI 'likely to affect security or public order' seems broader than the standard 'genuine and sufficiently serious threat'.[67] The first concept authorises a general analysis, not necessarily detailed, which does not have to lead to the identification of an actual risk; the Court of Justice's standard, on the other hand, requires a detailed examination of the concrete effects that the operation could have on national security.

This possible mismatch between the Regulation and Article 65(1) TFEU, as interpreted by the CJEU, came to the fore in the recent case of *Xella Magyarorszá*. The Hungarian investor had been refused the right to acquire 100% of the shares of another Hungarian company operating in the mining sector. The Minister's refusal was based, on the one hand, on the fact that *Xella Magyarorszá* was in fact controlled by investors from non-EU countries and, on the other hand, on the fact that such a takeover undermined the security of supply of raw materials for the construction sector. As this was an 'intra-EU' investment, the Court pointed out that Regulation 2019/452 did not apply. Consequently, the Hungarian decision had to be analysed solely in the light of the TFEU, which does not allow the objective of securing supplies of basic raw materials (i.e. gravel, sand and clay) to be regarded as a public security objective (unlike the security of energy or oil supplies).[68] A reading of this judgment raises the question of whether the Court's analysis might have been different if it had had to assess the situation based on the 2019 Regulation; and if so, whether the Regulation is compatible with the TFEU.

---

65 Art. 13 of the proposed new regulation.

66 Case C-54/99, *Association Eglise de scientologie de Paris and Scientology International Reserves Trust v Prime Minister*, ECLI:EU:C:2000:124, pt. 17; Case C-106/22, *Xella Magyarország Építőanyagipari Kft. v Innovációs és Technológiai Miniszter*, ECLI:EU:C:2023:568, para. 66. Emphasis added.

67 See the analysis of the European Court of Auditors, Special Report, 'Screening foreign direct investments in the EU', 2023, p. 21. The framework is in place, but important limits prevent the effective management of risks to security and public order.

68 Case C-106/22, *Xella Magyarország Építőanyagipari Kft. v Innovációs és Technológiai Miniszter*, ECLI:EU:C:2023:568, para. 69.

B. DIRECT AND FOREIGN INVESTMENT

Regulation 2019/452 applies only to foreign *direct* investment, since the scope of the Common Commercial Policy is limited to such transactions. FDI is defined as follows in the regulation:

> 'foreign direct investment' means an investment of any kind by a foreign investor aiming to establish or to maintain lasting and direct links between the foreign investor and the entrepreneur to whom or the undertaking to which the capital is made available in order to carry on an economic activity in a Member State, including investments which enable effective participation in the management or control of a company carrying out an economic activity.[69]

The absence of a precise definition is symptomatic of all international investment law, and here it is probably deliberate. This is in order to bring within the scope of the Regulation as many transactions as possible whose common feature is to enable investors to exercise a decisive influence over the management of their investments. FDI covers both greenfield investments, which involve the creation of new economic units, as well as the acquisition of existing companies. But FDI can also take the form of a concession agreement, the exploitation of intellectual property rights or licence agreements. International case law on investment protection is the best illustration of this extreme diversity,[70] which the 2019 Regulation does not intend to limit.

Conversely, portfolio investments, which the CJEU defines as 'the acquisition of shares on the capital market solely with the intention of making a financial investment without any intention to influence the management and control of the undertaking',[71] are excluded from the scope of the Regulation. Member States have retained competence in this area. However, this does not prevent them from screening such transactions in accordance with the conditions laid down in their domestic law. Furthermore, the distinction between FDI and portfolio investment can be difficult to draw. Identifying a threshold below which the investor cannot exercise decisive influence depends on many factors and is assessed on a case-by-case basis. Moreover, recent government practice has shown that States do not hesitate to lower these thresholds in order to bring a greater number of transactions within the scope of their screening system.[72]

---

69 Art. 2(1).

70 A. de Nanteuil, *Droit international de l'investissement*, 3th ed., Paris, Pedone, 2020, pp. 175–203.

71 Joined Cases C-282/04 and C-283/04, *Commission v Kingdom of the Netherlands*, ECLI:EU:C:2006:608, para. 19.

72 In France, Decree no. 2020-892 of 22 July 2020 lowered the foreign investment control threshold from 25% to 10%.

In practice, some of the investment transactions notified to the Commission for screening are portfolio investments.[73]

The assessment of the foreign nationality of the investor is an even more delicate issue. The 2019 Regulation adopts a formal conception of the foreign nationality of an investor,[74] its scope being limited to investments made by undertakings incorporated or otherwise organised in accordance with the law of a third country.[75] In practice, the Commission's assessment shows that the majority of investments subject to screening come from the United States, the United Kingdom, China, Japan, offshore financial centres (such as the Cayman Islands, Liechtenstein or Monaco) and Canada. However, the Commission also notes a trend towards diversification in the remaining share of controlled FDI.[76]

Conversely, the Regulation does not apply to investments made by European subsidiaries of foreign companies. This exclusion was firmly reiterated by the CJEU in the *Xella Magyarország* case. However, the circumstances of the case could have raised doubts as to whether only European interests were at stake: at the end of a chain involving a Hungarian company, a German company and a Luxembourg company was a company from Bermuda. Yet, the CJEU ruled out the relevance of the control criterion in assessing the foreignness of the investor.

This is a major shortcoming of the 2019 Regulation, since foreign investments are currently characterised by legal arrangements that variously complex, and the nationality of investors is a highly manipulable concept, or at least one that can be optimised. In its proposal for a new regulation, the Commission intends to remedy this by extending the scope of the text to investments made in the Union through foreign control, which covers investments made by the European subsidiaries of foreign investors.[77]

This extension would enable the European system to be better adapted to the reality of international investment operations. However, it is not without its difficulties. The relationship with freedom of establishment is likely to be tricky. From the moment that screening applies to intra-EU investments, it

---

73 European Court of Auditors, Special Report, 'Screening foreign direct investments in the EU', 2023, p. 24.

74 In accordance with the case law of the International Court of Justice, which considers that only the formal criteria of the place of incorporation and the place of the registered office should be used to determine the nationality of a legal person (to the exclusion of the criterion of control). *Barcelona Traction, Light and Power Company, Limited*, Judgment of 5 February 1970, *I.C.J. Reports* 1970, p. 3.

75 Case C-106/22, *Xella Magyarország Építőanyagipari Kft. v Innovációs és Technológiai Miniszter*, ECLI:EU:C:2023:568, para. 32.

76 Third annual report on screening foreign direct investment in the European Union, p. 22 and Fourth annual report on screening foreign direct investment in the European Union, pp. 4–5.

77 Art. 2(3).

interacts with the fundamental principles of the internal market.[78] European companies, even those controlled by foreign interests, enjoy freedom of establishment on the territory of all Member States. Screening an operation carried out by such a company could therefore constitute an obstacle to that freedom. This was the situation in the *Xella Magyarország* case, in which the Court stated its position on the provisions of the TFEU relating to freedom of establishment:

> (these provisions) must be interpreted as precluding a foreign investment filtering mechanism provided for by the legislation of a Member State by means of which a resident company which is a member of a group of companies established in several Member States, over which an undertaking of a third country has decisive influence, may be prohibited from acquiring ownership of another resident company regarded as strategic, on the ground that the acquisition harms or risks harming the national interest in ensuring the security of supply to the construction sector, in particular at the local level, with respect to basic raw materials such as gravel, sand and clay.

The Court therefore recognises the primacy of the principle of freedom of establishment over the exceptional restrictions that may be placed on the free movement of capital. And it is not certain that it would have reached a different conclusion if Regulation 2019/452 had been applicable to intra-EU investments.

III. SCREENING FDI AND PROTECTING ECONOMIC SECURITY IN EUROPE

Investment screening is the responsibility of the Member States. However, although the Commission has only limited powers, it seems to aspire to a greater role (Section A). This could enhance the effectiveness of national systems, which are currently very disparate (Section B).

A. SCREENING AUTHORITIES

1. The National Authorities of the Member States

Under Article 3(1) of the 2019 Regulation, States 'may maintain, amend or adopt mechanisms to screen foreign direct investment in their territory'. In other words, Member States are under no obligation to introduce such

[78] The proposal for a new regulation is based on both Article 207 TFEU and Article 114 TFEU. On the latter article, see the commentary by S. Rodrigues in this publication.

mechanisms. However, the Commission's ambition with the implementation of the European framework has been to encourage those Member States that did not yet have such a mechanism to put one in place. In its 2023 third evaluation report, the Commission stressed that the very effectiveness of national systems depends on this.[79] If not all countries had such a mechanism, foreign investors could resort to circumvention strategies by engaging in a certain form of forum shopping. In addition, in the case of FDI this poses security risks *in* the EU,[80] the fact that it is impossible to enter into a process of cooperation with the various States concerned partly undermines the very purpose of the Regulation.

Before the Regulation was adopted, fourteen Member States had a screening mechanism in place,[81] but by the end of 2024 this number had risen to twenty-four. By the same date, the other three Member States – Croatia, Cyprus and Greece – had embarked on (more or less advanced) legislative processes aimed at establishing such a system.[82] From this point of view, the incentive objective of the Regulation has clearly been achieved. Nevertheless, it should be noted that in its proposal for a new regulation, the Commission wants the adoption of a screening mechanism to become mandatory for Member States.[83]

However, even if a screening system exists at national level, the Member States are under no obligation to screen FDI likely to present a risk to European economic security. At the very least, Member States have so much margin of discretion in identifying investments likely to threaten economic security that they are not in fact under any such obligation. Indeed, the only obligation laid down in Regulation 2019/452 is that of notifying the other Member States and the Commission of FDI that is subject to screening.[84]

Finally, it should be emphasised that the identity of the national screening authorities varies from one country to another. In general, screening is placed under the authority of the minister in charge of the economy, who defers to an interministerial committee, the composition of which is not always known.[85]

79 Third annual report on screening foreign direct investment in the European Union, p. 8.

80 See above, Section I.A.2.

81 In 2019, UNCTAD counted around thirty such schemes worldwide. This figure may seem low. But in reality, the countries that are the main recipients of foreign investment all have such schemes in place today. The fact that the vast majority are European countries confirms the EU's great attractiveness. UNCTAD, 'National Security-Related Screening Mechanisms for Foreign Investment. An Analysis of Recent Policy Developments', *Investment Policy Monitor*, Special Issue, December 2019, p. 4.

82 The European Commission maintains an up-to-date list of screening mechanisms and the legislative and regulatory processes underway: https://circabc.europa.eu/rest/download/7e72cdb4-65d4-4eb1-910b-bed119c45d47

83 Art. 3(1).

84 Art. 6(1).

85 In France, this is the Interministerial Committee for Foreign Investment in France, whose membership is not public.

However, screening may also fall under the responsibility of several ministries.[86] In some cases, more than one authority may be responsible for controlling FDI. This is the case, for example, when the transaction falls within the scope of competition regulations. In a few rare cases, the national competition authorities may themselves be responsible for screening.[87] More frequently, however, these authorities must cooperate with the screening authorities, within the framework of procedures that are more or less formalised.[88]

2. *The European Commission*

The role of the Commission is defined in Articles 6 to 8 of the Regulation. The Commission has no decision-making powers or right of veto. The most it can do is issue opinions to the State responsible for screening,[89] which the latter is not obliged to follow.[90] It must simply 'take due account' of them. The wording is significantly different when it comes to the opinions issued by the Commission on FDI likely to affect projects or programmes of interest to the EU. Here, Member States are required to take 'the utmost account' of the Commission's opinion.[91] But the opinion is not binding. The proposal for a new regulation strengthens the scope of these opinions by requiring Member States to give them 'the utmost attention'[92] and, above all, to give reasons for refusing to follow them.[93]

In practice, it is difficult to determine whether these opinions are, on the whole, followed or not by the Member States. They are confidential[94] and the Commission does not provide this information in its evaluation reports. The most that can be said is that the proportion of screening procedures notified

86 The Danish Act on Screening FDI of May 2021, for example, stipulates that the decision whether or not to authorise an FDI project that falls under the screening procedure must be negotiated by the Minister for Industry, the Minister for Finance, the Minister for Foreign Affairs and the Minister for Defence.

87 This is the case in Poland, where the *Office of Competition and Consumer Protection* (UOKiK) carries out the screening.

88 In France, for example, although cooperation has been established, there is no formalised procedure to govern exchanges between Multicom4, the office in charge of screening within the Ministry of the Economy, and the Competition Authority. On the other hand, in Romania, coordination procedures are clearly detailed.

89 Article 6(3) of the Regulation concerning FDI subject to screening and Article 7(2) concerning FDI not subject to screening.

90 The opinion in question falls within the scope of Article 288 TFEU: 'Recommendations and opinions shall have no binding force'.

91 Art. 8(2)(c).

92 Article 7(5) of the Proposal for a new regulation provides that the State 'shall give utmost consideration' to the opinion, whereas Articles 6(9) and 7(7) of Regulation 2019/452 only requires it to 'shall give due consideration' to the opinion.

93 Art. 7(8)(b)(ii).

94 Art. 10 of the Regulations.

to the Commission that result in an opinion is extremely low.[95] However, it can sometimes be assumed that Member States do not hesitate to ignore the Commission's recommendations. For example, the authorisation given by Germany to the Chinese investor Cosco to buy a substantial part of the port of Hamburg was given despite the strong reservations expressed publicly by the Commission.[96]

The very first version of the draft regulation on investment screening provided that the Commission itself could oppose specific FDI projects.[97] At the time, this proposal was premature, as some Member States were opposed to the very idea of European regulations on screening. Above all, giving the Commission such a power of decision could conflict with the division of powers between the Member States and the Union. The proposal for a new regulation in no way alters the division of powers set out in Regulation 2019/452, even if the Commission is given the right to initiate, on its own initiative, a procedure to examine a FDI that has not been notified under the cooperation mechanism. This examination procedure is not equivalent to a screening procedure, since it only authorises the Commission to issue an opinion to the interested State.[98]

The European framework for the screening of FDI therefore gives the Commission only limited powers of support. However, it is quite clear from the Commission's doctrine that it aspires to a consolidated role: firstly, by seeking to strengthen the authority of its opinions. For example, in its guidance on the Covid-19 pandemic, the Commission emphasised that its opinions 'have to be taken into utmost account by the Member States',[99] a phrase that is repeated in the proposal for a new regulation; secondly, by adopting an offensive approach to the mobilisation of national screening mechanisms, as previously emphasised in relation to Russian and Belarusian investment and investment in 5G;[100] and finally, by playing on the grey area between the exclusive competence of the Member States to defend their security and the strengthening of the EU's competence to defend European security. In its communications, the Commission uses formulas that imply that it itself has

---

95 Less than 2% for files examined in 2023. Fourth Assessment Report, p. 25.

96 J. Packroff, 'Hamburg port terminal takeover divides Berlin and Brussels', 21 October 2022. https://www.euractiv.com/section/eu-china/news/hamburg-port-terminal-takeover-divides-berlin-and-brussels/.

97 Art. 3(2) of the first draft regulation stipulated that one of the provisions of the very first draft regulation provided that the Commission may screen foreign direct investment likely to affect projects or programmes of interest to the Union for reasons of security or public policy.

98 Art. 9(3).

99 Guidance of 25 March 2020, Appendix para. 2.

100 See above, Section I.A.1.

screening powers.[101] This is by no means the case, but it does show that it considers its coordination and monitoring role to be essential for screening FDI in Europe.

B. SCREENING DEVICES

1. *Coordination of National Procedures*

The purpose of the 2019 Regulation is not to harmonise national screening mechanisms. Its aim is to rationalise and to set up a basic coordination of these mechanisms, in order to ensure legal certainty for FDI, which continues to benefit from the assumption that is adds value to the national economies of host countries.

It should be emphasised that the screening procedures which existed prior to the Regulation were often not very transparent (or even known), sometimes not formalised, and did not allow the investors concerned to be duly involved or even to be able to appeal against the final decision. To remedy this, the 2019 Regulation establishes the principle that these procedures must be transparent, non-discriminatory, held within a reasonable time, adversarial and that the final decision must be open to appeal.[102] It obliges Member States to notify the Commission of their national systems, as well as any changes made to them.[103]

Despite these basic requirements, which are not monitored by the Commission, the various national screening mechanisms remain very disparate. The duration of screening processes varies enormously. Some national systems are only sector-specific, so that they do not cover all the transactions referred to in Regulation 2019/452. Not all national schemes cover greenfield investments.[104] There are significant differences in the thresholds for triggering supervision and many other discrepancies.[105] All this affects the effectiveness of FDI control at EU level.[106]

This is why the Commission is seeking to enter a phase of genuine harmonisation in procedures with its proposal for a new regulation. The fact

---

101 For example, in its communication on 5G, it states that it will 'monitor foreign investment in 5G' (p. 11). In its Second Annual Evaluation Report of 2022, it considers that '(A)rticle 7 allows the European Commission *the right to screen ex officio* investments of which it is aware in a Member State' (emphasis added). Second annual report on screening foreign direct investment in the EU, COM(2022) 433 final, 1 September 2022, p. 22.

102 Art. 3.

103 Art. 3(7) and (8).

104 This is the case in France, Germany, Portugal and the Czech Republic.

105 OECD, 'Framework for Screening Foreign Direct Investment into the EU: Assessing Effectiveness and Efficiency', 1 January 2022.

106 European Court of Auditors, Special Report, 'Screening foreign direct investments in the EU', 2023, p. 20.

that the new regulation is also based on Article 114 TFEU should facilitate this approach, since it authorises the alignment of national laws for security purposes. As it stands, however, the proposal for a new regulation merely strengthens the 'minimum requirements' that national systems must meet (in particular, the need to give reasons for decisions adopted at the end of the screening process, which is not currently systematic).[107] This is therefore only the first step towards harmonisation.

2. *Cooperation between Member States and between Member States and the Commission*

National screening systems rarely take into account the interests of other Member States and, more generally, the European dimension of security.[108] Yet this is the essential objective of the European framework. The cooperation dimension of the 2019 Regulation is therefore fundamental.

This system is based on the obligation for Member States to notify the Commission and the other Member States of any FDI that is subject to screening,[109] providing detailed information on the operation planned.[110] On this basis, the Commission or the other Member States can assess whether the operation is likely to affect security beyond the screening State alone and issue an opinion in the case of the former or comments in the case of the latter.[111] The exchange of information via national contact points is crucial. This system enables risks to be detected which would otherwise go unnoticed because of the complexity of ownership structures, the influence of public authorities, criminal intentions, cross-border vulnerabilities and critical dependencies.[112] In practice, the number of notifications increases from year to year, which may be interpreted as a good assimilation by the Member States of the operation of the FDI screening framework.[113]

However, the potential for cooperation is still limited, mainly because the notification requirement only applies to screened investments. As a result, access to information on unscreened FDI – a decision which is at the discretion of the relevant State – is not immediate. Admittedly, the Commission or

---

107 Art. 4.

108 Only the Lithuanian, German and Czech systems do so, the first two allowing the national authorities to carry out screening even if the investment in question does not present a risk to the country's security. OECD, 'Framework for Screening Foreign Direct Investment into the EU. Assessing Effectiveness and Efficiency', p. 47.

109 Art. 6(1).

110 Art. 9.

111 On how the Commission carries out this examination, see the explanations given in its third annual report on FDI screening, p. 20.

112 European Court of Auditors, Special Report, 'Screening foreign direct investments in the EU', 2023, p. 19.

113 Fourth annual report on screening foreign direct investment in the European Union, p. 13.

the other Member States may ask the relevant State to provide them with the information they need to assess a transaction.[114] Furthermore, they may themselves be in possession of relevant information (in which case they must share it with the State concerned). However, if the FDI has not been notified, it may also be that the Commission or the other Member States are simply unaware of the transaction. There is also provision for the other Member States and the Commission to issue comments or opinions fifteen months after the FDI has been carried out. This possibility goes some way towards closing the loopholes in the cooperation arrangements. However, once the FDI has been completed, it is much more complex, assuming that the relevant State wishes to do so, to require changes to the investment by the foreign investor.[115] Extending the notification obligation to all FDI likely to present security risks, as envisaged in the proposal for a new regulation, would make the cooperation mechanism more effective from this point of view.

C. THE CONSEQUENCES OF SCREENING

At the end of the screening process, governments have three options: to authorise the FDI, to authorise it with mitigating measures, or to oppose it. In practice, the overwhelming majority of screened FDI is authorised unconditionally,[116] with only 10% of authorisations being granted subject to conditions and a tiny proportion of transactions (1% in 2022 and 2023) being blocked.[117]

This low proportion should come as no surprise. Worldwide, there are few examples of foreign investment projects being rejected outright.[118] Under the US system, the President of the United States has exercised his right of veto on only five occasions.[119] The implementation of a screening procedure is a last resort. Before doing so, informal negotiations may take place between the

---

114 Art. 7(5).

115 This could clash with the standards of investment protection guaranteed by investment treaties. S. Robert-Cuendet, 'La crise de la Covid-19 comme révélateur du renforcement de la souveraineté économique des Etats: l'exemple des mécanismes de filtrage des investissements étrangers', *JDI*, 2021, pp. 58–59.

116 In 2022, 86% of FDI was screened: Third annual report on screening foreign direct investment in the Union, COM(2023) 590 final, 19 October 2023, p. 13; in 2023, the proportion was 85%. (Fourth report, p. 13)

117 Idem.

118 See the list drawn up by UNCTAD for the period 2016-2019: 'National security-related screening mechanisms for foreign investment. An analysis of recent policy developments', Investment Policy Monitor, December 2019, special issue, pp. 13–15.

119 A.P. Larson and D.M. Marchick, 'Foreign investment and national Security. Getting the balance right', Council on Foreign Relations, The Bernard and Irene Schwartz Series on American Competitiveness, 18 July 2006, p. 15, https://www.cfr.org/report/foreign-investment-and-national-security.

foreign investor and the government to define the terms of an FDI project in a way that is compatible with the government's conditions. Conversely, however, some deals may be halted prematurely in the face of fierce political and public opposition. For example, the French economy minister 'vetoed' the takeover of the Carrefour group by Canada's Couche-tard in 2021, without any formal screening procedure. Furthermore, before the formal activation of a screening procedure, requests for sensitive information addressed to the foreign investor may also act as a deterrent. We should therefore not underestimate the number of FDI projects that are abandoned for reasons of confidentiality. In its fourth report on the operation of Regulation 2019/452, the Commission states that 4% of requests for approval are withdrawn before a formal decision is taken.[120]

Lastlyy, it should be emphasised that although *ex-post* screening systems are rare, Regulation 2019/452 does authorise them. At least that is how the Commission understands it, with its guidance on the Covid-19 pandemic stressing that:

> It is important to keep in mind that, in case a foreign investment does not undergo a national screening process, the Regulation stipulates that Member States and the Commission may provide comments and opinions within 15 months after the foreign investment has been completed. *This can lead to the adoption of measures by the Member State where the investment has taken place*, including the necessary mitigating measures.[121] (added emphasis)

To allow this, however, it would seem necessary for the national provisions themselves to provide for their application *a posteriori*, in respect of an investment that has already been made. Moreover, imposing new conditions on an investor during the course of operations raises questions of legal certainty and compatibility with international investment protection law.[122]

120 Fourth report, p. 13.

121 Annex to the guidance, para. 3. Emphasis added.

122 S. Robert-Cuendet, 'La crise de la Covid-19 comme révélateur du renforcement de la souveraineté économique des Etats: l'exemple des mécanismes de filtrage des investissements étrangers', *JDI*, 2021, pp. 58–59.

DUAL-USE GOODS REGULATION: EUROPEAN CONTROL OF DUAL-USE GOODS

Regulation (EU) 2021/821 of the European Parliament and of the Council of 20 May 2021 setting up a Union regime for the control of exports, brokering, technical assistance, transit and transfer of dual-use items (recast)[1]

Anne Millet-Devalle
Professor at the Université Côte d'Azur
International and European Law Laboratory (LADIE – UPR 7414)

The recasting of the 2009 Regulation[2] in 2021 for setting up a Union regime to control exports, brokering, technical assistance, transit and transfer of dual-use items (DUIs) took place against a backdrop of evolving legal, technological, commercial and geostrategic issues relating to the control of these items. These had already led the European Union (EU) to amend substantially its legislation, adopted in 1994,[3] on a number of occasions.

The Regulation (EU) 2021/821 of 2021 (hereafter 'the Regulation')[4] was preceded in 2011 by the publication of a Green Paper[5] initiating a wide-ranging public debate on the export control system in the EU, then in 2014

1 Regulation (EU) 2021/821 of the European Parliament and of the Council of 20 May 2021 setting up a Union regime for the control of exports, brokering, technical assistance, transit and transfers with regard to dual-use items (recast), [2021] *OJ* L206/1. As last amended by Commission Delegated Regulation (EU) 2024/2547 of 5 September 2024, as regards the list of dual-use items, [2024] *OJ* L2024/2547.

2 Council Regulation (EC) No 428/2009 of 5 May 2009 setting up a Community regime for the control of exports, transfers, brokering and transit of dual-use items, [2009] *OJ* L134/1.

3 Regulation (EC) No 3381/94, [1994] *OJ* L367/1, based on Article 133 TEC, amended by Regulation (EC) No 837/95, [1995] *OJ* L90/1, Decision 94/942/CFSP, [1994] OJ L367/8, as last amended by Decision 2000/243/CFSP, [2000] *OJ* L82/1; Council Regulation (EC) No 1334/2000 of 22 June 2000 setting up a Community regime for the control of exports of dual-use items and technology, [2000] *OJ* L159/1.

4 [2021] *OJ* L206/1.

5 Commission, Green Paper, 'The dual-use export control system of the European Union: ensuring security and competitiveness in a changing world', COM(2011) 393 final, 30 June 2011.

by a Commission communication on the review of export control policy,[6] and subsequently by a proposal on the modernisation of the Union's export controls.[7] Over four years it was negotiated between the Commission, the European Parliament and the Council, a period which revealed tensions between institutions representing different interests in several respects.[8] A preliminary political agreement was finally reached on 9 November 2020, and the Parliament adopted at first reading the legislative resolution recasting Regulation 428/2009 on 25 March 2021.[9] This was followed by adoption in the Council on 10 May 2021.[10]

Since then, there has been a flurry of EU activity in this area, including: a recommendation on internal compliance programmes for research controls on dual-use items under the Regulation:[11] a communication on 'the European economic security strategy' of 20 June 2023; a recommendation;[12] a White Paper on export controls in January 2024;[13] and related Council conclusions approved on 30 May 2024.[14]

The goods covered by the Regulation[15] are defined in the 2021 regulation as 'items, including software and technology, which can be used for both civil

---

6 Communication from the Commission to the Council and the European Parliament, 'The Review of export control policy: ensuring security and competitiveness in a changing world', COM(2014) 244 final, 24 April 2014.

7 Commission proposal on modernising EU export controls, COM(2016)616, 28.9.2016. http://eur-lex.europa.eu/legal-content/EN/TXT/?qid=1476175365847&uri=CELEX:52016PC0616.

8 See, for example, Report from the Commission to the European Parliament and the Council on the implementation of Regulation (EC) No 428/2009 setting up a Community regime for the control of exports, transfers, brokering and transit of dual-use items, COM(2018) 852 final, 14 December 2018.

9 Parliament adopts text on export controls, brokering, technical assistance, transit and transfer of dual-use goods, 25 March 2021: https://www.europarl.europa.eu/doceo/document/TA-9-2021-0101_EN.html.

10 Council press release, 10 May 2021, available at: https://www.consilium.europa.eu/fr/press/press-releases/2021/05/10/trade-of-dual-use-items-new-eu-rules-adopted/.

11 Commission Recommendation (EU) 2021/1700 of 15 September 2021 on internal compliance programmes for controls of research involving dual-use items under Regulation (EU) 2021/821 of the European Parliament and of the Council setting up a Union regime for the control of exports, brokering, technical assistance, transit and transfer of dual-use items, [2021] *OJ* L338/1.

12 Joint Communication from the European Commission and the High Representative of the Union for Foreign Affairs and Security Policy to the European Parliament and the Council on 'The European Economic Security Strategy' of 20 June 2023, JOIN(2023) 20 final.

13 European Commission, White Paper on export controls, COM(2024) 25 final, 24 January 2024.

14 Council of the European Union, doc. 9439/24.

15 Regulation (EU) 2019/125 of the European Parliament and of the Council of 16 January 2019 concerning trade in certain goods which could be used for capital punishment, torture or other cruel, inhuman or degrading treatment or punishment (the so-called 'Anti-Torture Regulation') states in Article 11 that Annex III, which defines the list of goods which could be used to inflict torture or other inhuman or degrading treatment or punishment, does not include DUIs. These are governed by Regulation EC No 428/2009 – now 2021/821 – and

and military purposes, and includes items which can be used for the design, development, production or use of nuclear, chemical or biological weapons or their means of delivery, including all items which can be used for both non-explosive uses and assisting in any way in the manufacture of nuclear weapons or other nuclear explosive devices'.[16] This definition is the culmination of a gradual evolution, first incorporating concerns about nuclear proliferation and then about other weapons of mass destruction (WMD). The 1994 regulation simply defined DUIs as 'goods capable of both civilian and military use' (Art. 2). The successive regulations of 2000 and 2009 then included goods that could 'be used in any manner whatsoever in the manufacture of nuclear weapons'.[17] Regulation 2021/821 brought the concept of DUI into line with the overall approach to non-proliferation defined by the EU in its 2003 strategy against the proliferation of WMD'[18] and with the binding legal basis provided by United Nations Security Council Resolution 1540 (2004).[19] The text also reveals particular vigilance about cyber-surveillance assets[20] and control of the provision of technical assistance.

This change in definition is not limited to goods, with the definition of 'exporter' extended, for example, to natural persons and researchers involved in dual-use technology transfers. Significantly moreover, it means that the Regulation is much more than just a necessary update of an ageing text. Instead, it is a clear advance by the EU on the diplomatic chessboard of

goods governed by Common Position 2008/944/CFSP. The same applies to Article 18 on goods which could be used for the purpose of capital punishment. However, it should be noted that in France, since 1July 2020, the authority responsible for receiving and processing applications from operators subject to the provisions of Regulation 2019/125, as well as for classifying the goods concerned and issuing authorisations and refusals to export or import, is the Ministry of the Economy's dual-use goods department (SBDU, Service des Dual-use items). The SBDU has replaced the French Customs Department, which had been responsible for these matters until that date.

16 Art. 2 of Regulation (EU) 2021/821.

17 This inclusion, from 2000 onwards, of a concern for nuclear proliferation in the area of dual use was all the more expected as the first interest shown by the Communities in the control of DUIs concerned intra-Community transfers of recovered plutonium and uranium enriched above 20%, as well as installations, the main components of crucial importance, technology linked to reprocessing, enrichment and the production of heavy water in a Joint Policy Statement adopted on 20 November 1984.

18 http://www.consilium.europa.eu/ueDocs/cms_Data/docs/pressdata/fr/misc/78341.pdf

19 United Nations Security Council, S/RES/1540 (2004), 28 April 2004. The resolution, based on Chapter VII of the Charter, states that the 'proliferation of nuclear, chemical and biological weapons, as well as their means of delivery, constitutes a threat to international peace and security'. It calls on all States to establish, develop, review and maintain appropriate effective national export controls and transhipment controls over nuclear, chemical or biological weapons and their means of delivery, including appropriate laws and regulations to control export, transit, transhipment and re-export.

20 Against this backdrop, on 16 October 2024 the Commission published guidelines for the export of cyber-surveillance goods: https://policy.trade.ec.europa.eu/news/commission-publishes-guidelines-cyber-surveillance-exporters-2024-10-16_en.

non-proliferation, or at the very least a crucial element in a coherent framework that the EU is gradually putting in place. It confirms the Union's place among the major players in the development of international disarmament law, the fight against proliferation and the Union's preventive approach. Very early on, the EU signalled its desire to promote high-level common standards in the field of non-proliferation, with the adoption of the first common criteria relating to arms exports, by the Luxembourg and Lisbon European Councils respectively in in 1991 and 1992.[21] Since then, the EU's involvement in this area has manifested itself at two levels: the development of regional law and support for the universal legal framework for disarmament and non-proliferation. This support was affirmed in particular in the Global Strategy for the European Union's Foreign and Security Policy (or European Union Global Strategy, EUGS) of 2016[22] or Decision (CFSP) 2017/809 supporting the implementation of Resolution 1540 (2004). Furthermore, the support was illustrated for example by the positions defended during the negotiation of the Arms Trade Treaty in 2013, or in cooperation on WMD issues with the North Atlantic Treaty Organisation (NATO), the United Nations (UN) and other regional organisations, as well as in the context of multilateral initiatives on proliferation issues.

Within the EU, this approach is implemented by more specific, operational measures of a different nature depending on whether DUIs or weapons are involved. Article 346(1)(b) TFEU[23] allows any Member State to 'take such measures as it considers necessary for the protection of the essential interests of its security which are connected with the production of or trade in arms, munitions and war material; such measures shall not adversely affect the conditions of competition in the internal market regarding products which are not intended for specifically military purposes'. This obliges the EU to act primarily in this area under its Common Foreign and Security Policy (CFSP). In this context, the EU defined a Code of Conduct in 1998 on arms exports,[24]

---

21 A. Millet-Devalle, 'L'UE et le contrôle des exportations d'armements et de biens et technologies à double usage', in J.-C. Martin (ed.), *La gestion des frontières extérieures de l'Union européenne. Défis et perspectives en matière de sécurité et de sûreté*, Paris, Pedone, 2012, pp. 47–71.

22 'The EU will actively participate in export control regimes, strengthen common rules governing Member States' export policies of military – including dual-use – equipment and technologies, and support export control authorities in third countries and technical bodies that sustain arms control regimes'.

23 See the commentary on Article 346 TFEU by S. Rodrigues in this publication.

24 The European Code of Conduct on arms exports was adopted in the form of a Common Foreign and Security Policy (CFSP) declaration on 8 June 1998, at the initiative of France and the United Kingdom, Europe's leading arms exporters. EU Code of Conduct on Arms Exports (EU Code), 8 June 2008: http://www.consilium.europa.eu/uedocs/cmsUpload/08675r2en8.pdf

which became a Common Position in December 2008,[25] and a Council Common Position (2003/468/CFSP) of 23 June 2003 on the control of arms brokering.[26] The distinction remains a key one, despite: i) the Commission's determination to use Community law – in the sense of the former first pillar – to ensure the construction of a European security and defence market, through specific rules on free movement and competition, enabling supply and demand to be matched to guarantee autonomy; and ii) despite the highly restrictive interpretation by the Court of Justice of the European Union (CJEU) of the provisions excluding arms from the application of internal market rules and the gradual subjection of arms to directives organising the internal market.

The legal basis for the Regulation is therefore Article 207(2) of the TFEU.[27] It places this issue within the framework of the common commercial policy, which is an exclusive Union competence, 'conducted in the context of the principles and objectives of the Union's external action' (Article 207(1) TFEU). These justify an export regime in this area that derogates from the liberal principles applicable to civil goods.[28]

The Regulation provides that Member States shall adopt measures to implement specific provisions and that the relevant information shall be published in the *Official Journal of the European Union*. As part of their implementing powers, Member States may therefore adopt a variety of measures, both in terms of export authorisation procedures, transfers, transit and brokering, and in terms of their content. Nearly 140,000 export authorisations are granted each year, compared with around 800 export refusals (0.04% of the value of all authorised extra-EU27 exports), around forty of which relate to cyber-surveillance goods.[29] Authorisations are centralised in France,[30] but

[25] Council Common Position 2008/944/CFSP of 8 December 2008 defining common rules governing control of exports of military technology and equipment, [2008] *OJ* L335/99.

[26] [2003] *OJ* L156/79.

[27] See the commentary on Article 207 TFEU by S. Robert in this publication.

[28] Case C-83/94, *Criminal proceedings against Peter Leifer, Reinhold Otto Krauskopf and Otto Holzer*, ECLI:EU:C:1995:329, paras. 10 and 11; Case C-70/94, *Fritz Werner Industrie-Ausrüstungen GmbH v Federal Republic of Germany*, ECLI:EU:C:1995:328, para. 10. In these judgments, the Court confirmed that the rules on the control of DUI were part of the common commercial policy, even though they were intended to achieve foreign and security policy objectives. See in particular C. Kaddous, S. Ahmed, M. Miłek, S. Notario and A. Słowik, 'Droit et contentieux de la politique commerciale commune', *Annuaire de droit de l'UE*, 2022, pp. 631–702; P. Musquar, *Politique commerciale de l'Union européenne*, Brussels, Larcier, 2020; M. Mondélice, O. Bichsel and O. Delas, *L'Union européenne, puissance globale dans les relations internationales et transatlantiques*, Brussels, Bruylant, 2023.

[29] Commission, Report on the implementation of Regulation (EU) 2021/821, COM(2025) 19 final, 30 January 2025.

[30] See, for example the Order of 13 December 2001, as amended, on the control of exports to third countries and the transfer to EU Member States of dual-use goods and technologies, which sets out the formalities to be completed by persons exporting to third countries or dispatching to EU Member States; the two decrees of 31 July 2014, relating to exports of

are regional in Belgium for example. These margins for manoeuvre on the part of the Member States are indicative of their reluctance to allow the EU to control goods that are largely part of a defence market, and to which many of them wish to apply the same relative freedom as they have with regard to arms exports under Common Position 2008/944/CFSP.[31] Despite its binding nature, Common Position 2008/944/CFSP gives them considerable discretion,[32] as illustrated in recent years by the proliferation of legal proceedings relating to authorisations for arms exports to Saudi Arabia and Israel. The procedural framework of the 2021 Regulation is similar in certain respects, while retaining a real specificity for DUIs. The very broad nature of the concept of the European armaments and security market and the ambitions to build a European defence technological and industrial base (EDTIB) thus call into question the consistency of the EU since the disappearance of its former 'pillars' and the permeability of the various categories of EU standards.

The ambivalence of DUIs, which are the main potential source of the proliferation of conventional weapons and weapons of mass destruction, means that the control of their exports faces two conflicting constraints: i) non-proliferation, which is necessary for European and international security, and ii) support for trade, which is essential for totally legitimate applications. As the Commission pointed out in its communication preceding the 2021 regulation,[33] the EU is a major producer and exporter of DUIs and as such plays an important role in controlling these exports. In 2022, these goods accounted for 2% of extra-EU exports of goods, worth €147 billion,[34] including €57.3 billion in exports authorised by the Member States under the Regulation. The Strategic Compass, which was prepared at the same time as the 2021 regulation, highlighted the objective of 'strengthen[ing] dual-use

helicopters and their spare parts to third countries and relating to exports of tear gas and riot control agents to third countries; the circular of 16 November 2021 relating to the export and transfer of dual-use goods and technologies.

31 See A. Millet-Devalle's commentary on the common position in this publication.

32 The transformation of the code of conduct into a common position includes aspects that are binding on the Member States, but this is done at the discretion of the Member States and there is no possibility of sanctions. The Member States are now obliged to incorporate the European criteria into their national legislation, but when it comes to export decisions, the elements of constraint are extremely limited. See A. Millet-Devalle, 'À propos de la position commune de l'UE relative aux règles communes régissant le contrôle des exportations de technologies et d'équipements militaires du 8 décembre 2008', *RGDIP*, 2009-1, pp. 95–112.

33 Communication from the Commission to the Council and the European Parliament, Review of export control policy: ensuring security and competitiveness in a changing world, COM(2014) 244 final, 24 April 2014.

34 Commission staff working document, Statistical update on dual use-export control (2021), SWD(2023) 341 final, 19 October 2023.

innovation',[35] particularly in the space sector, and that of 'invest[ment] in dual-use technologies', considered essential 'as our strategic competitors are rapidly investing in critical technologies'.[36] Export controls must therefore be based on a balanced assessment of the heterogeneous issues at stake, determined by a context that is both internal to the EU and influenced by the regulations of its trading and security partners, or by the behaviour of states perceived as threats or as simply as competitors. The Commission's White Paper of 24 January 2024 on export controls highlights in particular the change in circumstances brought about by Russia's war of aggression against Ukraine,[37] its consequences for relations between the EU and China, and the move towards strategic use of controls.

As a result, since 2022, the issue has been part of a broader EU economic security plan based on three pillars: promoting the Union's competitiveness, guarding against risks and forging partnerships with the widest possible range of countries in order to safeguard common economic security interests. DUI export measures are seen by the EU as part of the 'trade toolbox' that the EU is working to strengthen, including through specific strategies.[38]

The DUI export control regime is clearly a mechanism used in response to national commercial and security concerns.[39] Since the World War II, export control regimes have been used by States, in particular the United States and EU Member States, as a mechanism for implementing national or regional security policies to limit the proliferation of weapons and restrict the technological development of States that are hostile or threaten international or regional security. As early as 1979, the United States promulgated the *Export Administration Regulations* (EAR)[40] on the control of exports of DUIs. In 2020, China also adopted a law on the control of exports of sensitive technologies.[41]

---

35 Council of the European Union, *A Strategic Compass for Security and Defence*, 4 May 2022, 7371/22 COR 1, p. 24. See in particular E. Bernard, 'La "boussole stratégique", nouveau plan d'action pour la sécurité et la défense de l'Union européenne', in J.-C. Martin (ed.), 'Union européenne et droit international', *AFDI*, 2022, pp. 570–583.

36 Ibid., p. 34. It should also be pointed out that, at national level, the Minister for the Economy, Finance and Industrial and Digital Sovereignty stated in the 2023 report to Parliament on French DUI exports (July 2023) that 'their control must focus on supporting our export businesses', particularly in the aerospace and civil nuclear sectors, p. 3.

37 COM(2024) 25 final, cited above.

38 See, for example, European Parliament resolution of 16 September 2021 on a new EU-China strategy (2021/2037 (INI)).

39 See D.E. McDaniel, United States Technology Export Control: An Assessment, Westport, Paeger, 1993, pp. 3–8; O. Jankowitsch-Prevor and M. Quentin (eds.), *European Dual-Use Trade Controls. Beyond Materiality and Borders*, Brussels, Peter Lang, 2013.

40 Export Administration Regulations (EAR), 15 CFR. paras. 730–799.

41 Export Control Law of the People's Republic of China, Order of the President of the People's Republic of China No. 58, 17 October 2020, effective 1 December 2020: http://www.npc.gov.cn/englishnpc/c23934/202112/63aff482fece44a591b45810fa2c25c4.shtml.

The rules developed by the EU are marked by tensions between the interests defended in this area by certain Member States and by the organisation.

The export of DUIs is governed by a wide range of legal instruments, both at the international level and under the national law of major exporting states such as the United States, China and France. This raises questions about the relationship between the various non-proliferation regimes and EU law (Section I). These complex normative relationships, guided by the ambiguous combination of national interests in non-proliferation and trade, have constrained the EU in its ambitions to transform its export control regime of DUI, calling for an analysis of the contributions of the new regulation to the non-proliferation regime from the Commission's praxeological perspective (Section II).

I. THE FRAGILE RELATIONSHIP BETWEEN REGULATION 2021/821 AND OTHER NON-PROLIFERATION REGIMES

While the texts and mechanisms adopted at the international level to better control the trade in DUIs and prevent proliferation are still patchy, national standards, at least those of the main players in this trade, are much more developed. Until the war in Ukraine, the relationship between EU law and international non-proliferation regimes and within the Union itself posed few difficulties, being the subject of a relative consensus at both the multilateral and European level, a consensus that is now being called into question (Section A). On the other hand, the extraterritorial dimension of certain third-country regimes has, since the inception of these texts, given rise to conflicts between them and EU law (Section B).

A. CHALLENGES TO THE RELATIONSHIP BETWEEN REGULATION 2021/821 AND INTERNATIONAL REGIMES AND WITHIN MEMBER STATES

The multilateral regimes on which the EU bases its lists of goods subject to export authorisation are founded on the rule of consensus. Russia's participation in these regimes is now blocking virtually all developments (Section 1). In the context of a conflict that makes it even more urgent to develop the control lists, and in which the Member States are acting increasingly unilaterally, the Commission is calling for a transformation of the relationship between the export regimes and that of the EU, to avoid 'the risk of a patchwork of controls'[42] and to achieve genuine coordination as soon as possible (2).

[42] White Paper, 4(1).

1. *The Conflict in Ukraine is Blocking the Link between the Regulation and Multilateral Regimes for the Control of DUIs*

The relationship between the 2021 Regulation and the international control regimes is essentially based on the establishment by this text (as by the previous regulations) of a common list (Annex I of the Regulation) of DUIs subject to an export authorisation. This list results from the compilation of the lists of the international control regimes.[43] It is updated annually by the Commission, using delegated acts, to take account of technological and geopolitical developments within the various regimes.

The European list of dual-use goods and technologies thus incorporates into the European legal order the lists resulting from the work of non-binding non-proliferation regimes in which EU Member States participate. These regimes concern different categories of goods: sensitive, industrial and cryptology goods for the Wassenaar Arrangement,[44] missile technology for the Missile Technology Control Regime (MTCR), goods related to nuclear technologies for the Nuclear Suppliers Group (London Club or NSG), and chemical and biological goods for the Australia Group.

The EU participates in or supports, in different ways, these non-binding multilateral regimes, which operate based on consensus and whose texts are then implemented uniformly in the EU. Within the Nuclear Suppliers Group, for example, the Commission participates in meetings defining the lists simply as an observer. On the other hand, the EU is a member of the Australia Group, along with 42 States that are all parties to the conventions banning biological weapons (1972) and chemical weapons (1993). This Group is an informal body whose aim is to help exporting or trans-shipment countries minimise the risks of contributing to proliferation through 'common lists of regulated products', drawn up during consultations between Group members and regularly revised. With regard to trade within the EU, it is envisaged that each Member State will apply the guidelines in accordance with its commitments as a member of the Union.[45] Concerning the Wassenaar Arrangement, within which lists have been proposed, discussed and then voted on by the representatives of the

---

43 The list is divided into ten categories: nuclear facilities and equipment, special materials and related equipment, materials processing, electronics, computers, telecommunications and information security, sensors and lasers, navigation and aeroelectronics, marine, aerospace and propulsion.

44 Wassenaar Arrangement on Export Controls for Conventional Arms and Dual-Use Goods and Technologies, Public Documents, vol. II, compiled by the Wassenaar Arrangement Secretariat, 2024. The Technical Group of Experts (WA-EG) is responsible for proposing annual updates of the Arrangement's control lists. It meets at least twice a year, for two-week sessions; the Plenary Assembly (WA-PLM) takes the decisions proposed by the various groups when it meets in December. All decisions within the Wassenaar Arrangement are taken by consensus, and it takes an average of 3 years for the States to agree on a revision.

45 https://www.dfat.gov.au/publications/minisite/theaustraliagroupnet/site/fr/directrices.html.

administrations of the forty-two participating States since 1996, Regulation (EC) No 1334/2000 of 22 June 2000 provides that the principles of export control and the list of controlled dual-use items and technologies, as defined by the Arrangement, are binding on all EU Member States. Within the MTCR, which brings together 35 States, 22 of which are EU Member States, a common list of goods and technologies is defined ('the Technical Annex'). In line with its 2003 strategy against the proliferation of weapons of mass destruction, the EU also adopted Decision (CFSP) 2017/2370 in December 2017, in support of the Hague Code of Conduct against Ballistic Missile Proliferation (HCOC). The annual meetings discuss ways to increase the effectiveness of national export licensing measures and aim to prevent would-be proliferators from obtaining the components needed for chemical and biological weapons programmes.

This direct or indirect participation by the EU in the work of non-proliferation regimes has nevertheless become a matter of concern for the Commission in recent years. Thus in 2023, it proposed, in the context of its joint communication on a European strategy for economic security, to 'stimulate discussions and actions in favour of European coordination in the field of export control, while fully respecting existing multilateral regimes and Member States' prerogatives'[46] in order to address as a priority technology security risks and technology leaks.[47]

Indeed, as the 2024 White Paper points out, the global context for export controls has changed radically. Faced with Russia's war of aggression against Ukraine, the EU quickly imposed export restrictions on dual-use and sensitive goods, essential to curbing Russia's medium and long-term war efforts.[48] However, the need for the EU to have a system capable of producing rapid and uniform results has become clear. The Commission considers that the 'ability of the multilateral export control regimes to deliver new decisions on items subject to controls and to keep pace with technological developments has been hampered by certain members, creating gaps in the adoption of new export controls at multilateral level'.[49] The Wassenaar Arrangements, both the

[46] European Commission, 'Commission proposes new initiatives to strengthen economic security', Press Release, 24 January 2024.

[47] European Commission and High Representative, Joint Communication to the Parliament and the Council on the European Economic Security Strategy, JOIN(2023) 20 final, cited above. This provides a framework for assessing and addressing – in a proportionate, accurate and targeted manner – risks to the EU's economic security, while ensuring that the EU remains one of the most open and attractive destinations for business and investment.

[48] Commission Delegated Regulation (EU) 2022/699 of 3 May 2022 amending Regulation (EU) 2021/821 of the European Parliament and of the Council by removing Russia as a destination from the scope of Union general export authorisations C/2022/2885, [2022] *OJ* L130I/1. This text was adopted '[i]n light of Russia's illegal attack on Ukraine's territorial integrity, sovereignty and independence and the respective threats to the Union's essential security interests'.

[49] White Paper, p. 2.

MTCR and the NSG, of which Russia is a member, are systematically blocked by Russia's opposition to changes to the lists.

In its White Paper of January 2024, the Commission therefore proposes that the EU should introduce new controls into the list in Annex I of the 2021 Regulation, which would be amended either under the ordinary legislative procedure or by a delegated act. The introduction of new goods to be subject to export controls in the list in Annex I would standardise controls in the Member States and help to level the playing field between EU exporters. In its conclusions of 30 May 2024, and 'without necessarily agreeing with or precluding further Council discussion on the White Paper's analysis of the international export control system' (point A), the Council considered that this amendment could be envisaged, clearly favouring the route of a delegated act (paragraphs 1-2 of Council Conclusions, 9439/24). However, the latest delegated regulation of 5 September 2024 does not reflect this boldness on the part of the Commission, and only incorporates the minor amendments that may have been adopted recently by the multilateral regimes.[50]

The quasi-blocking of these regimes has encouraged several Member States to take individual measures that are not anchored in these regimes, which increases the risk of fragmentation of the single market and, more generally, reduces the effectiveness of the multilateral export control system.

2. *The Economic and Strategic Risks Posed by Emerging Technologies Are Transforming the Way DUIs Are Monitored within the EU*

One of the objectives of the 2021 regulation was to improve cooperation between the Commission and the Member States. Cooperation had already been established, back in the 2009 Regulation, within the framework of a Dual-Use Coordination Group (DCG) chaired by the Commission and made up of one representative from each Member State. This was aimed to examine questions relating to the legislation by consulting exporters, brokers, technical assistance providers and other relevant persons and bodies, or by setting up technical expert groups, in particular the 'Emerging Technologies Expert Group' (ETEG), to exchange information with Member States on risk assessments of emerging technologies. The Commission has also set up a platform, a secure and encrypted system to support cooperation and the exchange of information between national authorities and the Commission. Guidelines and best practice recommendations to ensure the effectiveness and consistency of the system will also be published by the Commission and the Council.

---

50 Commission Delegated Regulation (EU) 2024/2547 of 5 September 2024 amending Regulation (EU) 2021/821 of the European Parliament and of the Council as regards the list of dual-use items, C/2024/6093, [2024] *OJ* L2024/2547.

In addition to this consultation, the 2021 Regulation organises the relationship between the EU and its Member States, which must inform the European Commission of the national authorities empowered to grant export authorisations and to prohibit the transit of 'non-Community' dual-use items, of the measures they are taking to apply the Regulation. They must also take all measures, in collaboration with the Commission, to establish direct cooperation and exchange of information between national authorities to ensure the effectiveness, consistency and enforcement of export controls and to provide the Commission with the information necessary for the preparation of its annual report. States must also take into account the EU's international obligations and commitments, in particular the relevant non-proliferation regimes and export controls, any sanctions imposed by the EU, but also by the Organisation for Security and Cooperation in Europe (OSCE) or the UN, in their decisions to authorise or refuse to authorise exports.

However, the DUI list, which is common to all Member States, can be supplemented by national lists subjecting goods to the export control regime, such as helicopters and their main parts for France,[51] a possibility referred to as the 'catch-all' clause, which already existed before the 2021 regulation.

Yet, such unilateral measures were very rare in the EU and – unlike in the US – had historically only been used to achieve narrowly defined security or human rights objectives. Sustained country-specific controls outside of sanctions regimes or arms embargoes were not part of the policy of the EU and its Member States. Since the adoption of the EU's economic security strategy, it has become clear that several Member States have made greater use[52] of this possibility, which could undermine the consistency and effectiveness of the European regime.

The Regulation provides for this 'catch-all' clause for cyber-surveillance goods not listed in Annex I, if the competent national authority informs the exporter that 'the items in question are or may be intended, in their entirety or in part, for use in connection with internal repression and/or the commission of serious violations of human rights and international humanitarian law'.[53] With the stated aim of improving the control of cyber-surveillance goods, the text allows, for new autonomous EU controls on these goods, if all Member States adopt coordinated actions. But this provision has not yet been implemented due to a lack of agreement between States.

---

[51] Ministry of the Economy, Finance and Industrial and Digital Sovereignty, portal of the Directorate-General for Enterprise: https://www.entreprises.gouv.fr/fr/echanges-commerciaux-et-reglementation/service-des-biens-double-usage/bien-est-est-il-double-usage#:~:text=La%20liste%20des%20biens%20à,pièces%20principales%20pour%20la%20France.

[52] Information on measures taken by Member States in accordance with Articles 4, 5, 6, 7, 8, 9, 11, 12, 22 and 23 of the Dual-Use Regulation, [2023] *OJ* C208/06.

[53] Art. 5(1) of the 2021 Regulation.

In addition to cyber-surveillance goods, the 2021 Regulation also introduced a mechanism to facilitate the coordination of national export controls at EU level, and this is one of its most innovative elements. The adoption by Member States of a ban on or authorisation requirement for DUIs not listed in Annex I for reasons relating to public security, in particular the prevention of terrorist acts, or the safeguarding of human rights,[54] may lead to coordination of the controls provided for in the national lists (Articles 9 and 10).

On the one hand, the Commission publishes an annual information note containing all the 'national measures' notified to it by the Member States,[55] which has no legal effect in the other Member States. It also publishes a 'compilation of national control lists',[56] which allows Member States to impose authorisation obligations by reference to the national control lists of other Member States included in the compilation, without having to adopt their own national controls. This possibility falls far short of coordinating national controls throughout the EU, with serious implications for competitiveness and possible autonomy in the field of critical technologies. Companies in the quantum technology sector, for example, which are subject to export authorisations and bans in the country where they are based, could be tempted to set up in another country that does not adopt these national lists. The text makes no provision for constraints, deadlines or procedures, which creates uncertainty for States and exporters alike, and a strong likelihood of forum shopping within the EU. In its White Paper, the Commission pays particular attention to this mechanism and its implementation and regrets that the regulation does not require Member States to inform and consult each other or the Commission before adopting these national lists.

These lists are all the more sensitive in that they may also reflect pressure exerted by non-EU countries to align with their own regimes.

B. THE CONFLICTING RELATIONSHIP BETWEEN EU LAW ON DUAL-USE CONTROLS AND THE LAW OF NON-EU COUNTRIES

With third countries, the Commission and the Member States use the exchange of information and best practices, capacity building and awareness raising to promote global convergence on DUIs. Nevertheless, problems of the coexistence of rules of different origins are posed by the regulations of States

54 Art. 9.1 of Regulation (EU) 2021/821.

55 Information on measures taken by Member States in accordance with Articles 4, 5, 6, 7, 8, 9, 11, 12, 22 and 23 of the Dual-Use Regulation', [2023] *OJ* C208/06; and C/2024/5881.

56 Establishment of national control lists under Article 9(4) of the Dual-Use Regulation, [2023] *OJ* C2023/441; and C/2024/5880.

that have adopted texts with extraterritorial effect, which constitute a lever of power used both as a tool of coercive diplomacy and to control technologies and their markets.

The US DUI control system is governed by the Export Control Reform Act (ECRA), passed in 2018.[57] It repealed the Export Administration Act (EAA) of 1979, which until then had been the export control legislation applicable to DUI.[58] Under ECRA, the provisions of which are implemented by the Export Administration Regulations (EAR), the President of the United States has the authority to control the exports of DUIs.[59] The EAR mainly concerns the control of exports of DUIs, defined as goods 'that ha[ve] civil applications as well as terrorism and military or weapons of mass destruction (WMD)-related applications'.[60] The regulations are not limited to the control of these goods, and may also apply to certain purely civilian items, or to military items.[61] The administrative authority responsible for implementing WMD export controls on behalf of the President of the United States is the Secretary of Commerce, and his Industry and Security Office, which defines the Commerce Control List of controlled items and foreign persons and end-uses considered a threat to the national security and foreign policy of the United States. Licences are required to export and re-export items on this list, and unauthorised exports, re-exports and transfers of controlled items are prohibited. As soon as a foreign product includes controlled items, it is subject to a compulsory licence for export and re-export, which gives this regulation extraterritorial scope, as the US administration can block the sale of equipment produced by a non-US manufacturer to a third country, if the equipment includes a component, technical data or software of US origin.

57 Export Control Reform Act (ECRA), Pub. Law 115-232, 132 Stat. 1653, Subtitle B., Part I, 2018, 50 USC Ch. 58 (2018).

58 The DUI's export control system, which expired in 2001, was maintained between 2001 and 2018 by a presidential declaration of a 'national emergency' through the invocation of the International Emergency Economic Powers Act (IEEPA). See, for example, H.E. Moyer and L.A Mabry, 'Export controls as instruments of foreign policy: the history, legal issues, and policy lessons of three recent cases' (1983) 15(1) *Law and Policy in International Business*, p. 60; I.F. Fergusson and P.K. Kerr, 'The U.S. Export Control System and the Export Control Reform Initiative', Congressional Research Service, 28 January 2020: https://crsreports.congress.gov/product/pdf/R/R41916.

59 ECRA, 50 USC, Ch. 58, cited above, para. 4812(a)(1): 'the President shall control: (1) the export, reexport, and in-country transfer of items subject to the jurisdiction of the United States, whether by United States persons or by foreign persons'.

60 EAR, cited above, 15 CFR, para. 730.3.

61 The precise description of what is 'subject to the EAR' is in para. 34.3, which does not limit the EAR to controlling only dual-use items. [...] Thus, items subject to the EAR include purely civilian items, items with both civil and military, terrorism or potential WMD-related applications, and items that are exclusively used for military applications but that do not warrant control under the International Traffic in Arms Regulations (ITAR)'.

Following the US model of extraterritoriality, a 2020 Chinese law on export control of sensitive technologies[62] provided that retaliatory measures can be imposed on any country that misuses its export control measures towards China.[63]

This extraterritorial application has long been problematic and the source of numerous disputes.[64] In its White Paper of January 2024, the Commission raised new concerns about an increase, since the adoption of the 2021 Regulation, in the use by China and the United States of unilateral export controls on new goods not listed by the non-proliferation regimes, 'in some cases because of growing national security considerations and in other cases in order to address new risks posed by emerging technologies'.[65]

This unilateral approach has an undeniable impact on the ability of EU companies to export these cutting-edge technologies and components, as illustrated by the case of the ban on the export of certain technologies to China.

Beginning with a decision by the Dutch government[66] to revoke the licence for the shipment to China of machines not listed in the Wassenaar Arrangement and Annex I of the 2021 Regulation (essential for manufacturing the most advanced chips related to quantum technology), the Netherlands was the first European country to join the United States in imposing export

62 Export Control Law of the People's Republic of China, Order of the President of the People's Republic of China No. 58, 17 October 2020, effective 1 December 2020: http://www.npc.gov.cn/englishnpc/c23934/202112/63aff482fece44a591b45810fa2c25c4.shtml.

63 Article 48 of the Export Control Law of the People's Republic of China: 'Where any country or region endangers the national security or interest of the People's Republic of China by abusing export control measures, the People's Republic of China may take counter measures against such a country or region according to the actual circumstances'. See e.g. U.S. Department of State, 'The Chinese Communist Party's Military-Civil Fusion Policy', accessed 8 March 2023: https://2017-2021.state.gov/military-civil-fusion/index.html.

64 See also E.L. Hirschhorn, B.J. Egan, E.J Krauland, *U.S. Export Controls & Economic Sanctions*, 4th ed., Oxford, Oxford University Press, 2022.

65 White Paper, cited above, 3(2). The US Department of Commerce has officially justified its restrictions on semiconductors by linking advanced semiconductor technologies to WMD development, China's military modernisation and human rights abuses. It should be noted, however, that since the 2018 export control reform, ECRA, beyond its long-established goals of preventing the proliferation of WMD and military and dual-use technologies, has established new authorities to impose export controls for the explicit purpose of preserving US military superiority, strengthening the US industrial base, maintaining US technological leadership, and advancing US foreign policy objectives. ECRA was drafted with China and the challenges it poses to economic security in mind, and the Commerce Department is now charged, on an ongoing basis, with identifying 'emerging and core technologies [that are] critical to the national security of the United States' that should be controlled, particularly with respect to China: https://ecfr.eu/publication/the-power-of-control-how-the-eu-can-shape-the-new-era-of-strategic-export-restrictions/.

66 Letter from the Dutch Minister for Foreign Trade and Development Cooperation of 8 March 2023 to the Dutch Parliament: https://open.overheid.nl/documenten/oep-7b25ba07017fbcc4a9d285cc013849f6516f03bd/pdf.

restrictions on advanced semiconductor equipment.[67] While the stated aim has been to prevent the acquisition of chips likely to be used in weapons, the export restrictions on this type of technology imposed by the United States (since October 2022) mark a strategic change in the use of the post-Cold War export control policy. Already, under the first Trump administration, the US had introduced technology blockades against China, and the Biden administration has continued this use of export controls as a strategic tool[68] to contain China's competitiveness. The United States provides for a licence exception that authorises exports to countries that have export controls equivalent to their own on certain emerging technologies, which constitutes an instrument of pressure that led Spain (from 2023),[69] then France (2023),[70] as well as Finland and Italy (2024),[71] to adopt almost identical regulations to restrict exports of quantum computers, in the application of Article 9 of Regulation 2021/821, and therefore invoking risks to public security.

These decisions highlight a series of new challenges for the EU and its Member States, which are increasingly caught in the crossfire, with the United States putting pressure on its allies to align with its policy towards China. This in return threatens to put certain goods on its control list.[72] Given the highly integrated nature of the EU's single market, there is a risk that Chinese measures against one Member State will contaminate others, as illustrated

[67] The United States then further tightened these measures in October 2023 and September 2024. Bureau of Industry and Security, US Department of Commerce, https://www.bis.doc.gov/index.php/documents/about-bis/newsroom/press-releases/3355-2023-10-17-bis-press-release-acs-and-sme-rules-final-js/file. See also https://www.ecinews.fr/fr/les-usa-controlent-les-exportations-de-technologie-quantique/.

[68] National Security Strategy (NSS), 12 October 2022: https://www.whitehouse.gov/wp-content/uploads/2022/11/8-November-Combined-PDF-for-Upload.pdf. The CHIPS and Science Act of 2022 (117th Congress Public Law 167, U.S. Government Publishing Office) also employs, in a new hybrid approach, with export controls to a specific country, China: https://www.govinfo.gov/content/pkg/PLAW-117publ167/html/PLAW-117publ167.html.

[69] Ministerial Decree ICT/534/2023 of 26 May 2023, available at: https://www.boe.es/boe/dias/2023/05/31/pdfs/BOE-A-2023-12785.pdf.

[70] Order of 2 February 2024 on exports to third countries of goods and technologies associated with quantum computing and its enabling technologies and equipment for the design, development, production, testing and inspection of advanced electronic components, published in the *JORF* of 10 February 2024, entered into force on 1 March 2024, amended by the Order of 27 March 2025 published in the Official Journal of the French Republic (JORF) No. 0077 of 30 March 2025, entered into force on 1 April 2025.

[71] https://www.borenius.com/legal-alerts/2024/07/08/finnish-export-controls-adapt-to-technological-developments-amid-geopolitical-tensions/.

[72] These are DUIs for which China enjoys an asymmetric influence compared to Europe, including rare earth magnets, photovoltaic solar equipment, genetic modification technologies, quantum computers and automatic driving software, on which the EU depends for the production of electric vehicles, industrial robotics, drones and medical devices.

in another area by the dispute with Lithuania.[73] National decisions could be challenged at the WTO by China. Because of the EU's single trade policy, the European Commission would then have to defend national positions at the WTO, and the consequences of a WTO decision could be borne by the EU as a whole.

However, it should be emphasised that the potential conflict arising from the coexistence of export control regimes can sometimes be mitigated: 'the EU has stepped-up cooperation with international partners as part of its efforts to uphold international security, for instance under the EU-US Trade and Technology Council[74] and the development of a global coalition coordinating export restrictions on sensitive goods'.[75]

The 2021 Regulation thus fits into a network of national and international relations and standards, both within and outside the EU, which have been disrupted since the adoption of the text by the geopolitical context and advances in new technologies,[76] leading the Commission to make a measured assessment of the Regulation's contribution to the European export control regime of DUI, in order to propose improvements.

II. THE PERFECTIBLE CONTRIBUTION OF REGULATION 2021/821 TO THE EUROPEAN EXPORT CONTROL REGIME FOR DUIS

The assessment of the implementation of the 2021 Regulation made by the Commission in its White Paper of January 2024 explores the problematic consequences of the persistent attachment of Member States to a sovereign assessment of the appropriateness of exporting DUIs, which permeates the text and now calls for reform (Section B). This contextualised assessment is marked by the consequences of the war in Ukraine, by the military-civilian integration of the EU's systemic rivals, by the fact that a narrow conception of national

73 On 31 January 2022, the EU initiated proceedings against the People's Republic of China before the World Trade Organisation for its discriminatory trade practices against Lithuania, which also affected other exports from the single market. https://www.wto.org/french/news_f/news22_f/ds610rfc_31jan22_f.html.

74 Established at the EU-US Summit in Brussels on 15 June 2021 to deepen transatlantic trade and economic relations based on shared values, the Council is a forum for coordinating approaches to key global trade, economic and technology issues. It met for the first time in Pittsburgh on 29 September 2021 and established an ambitious joint declaration, including cooperation on export controls. One of the ten working groups is dedicated to export controls. The Council's work highlights the existence of a new forum for consultation, involving industry and academics, with an approach to controls motivated less by issues of public security than by economic security.

75 White Paper, p. 2.

76 C.P. Bown, 'The Challenge of Export Controls', *Finance & Development*, IMF, June 2023.

security has been overtaken by export control policy and by developments in relations between the United States and China. It nevertheless leaves unresolved the older question, inherent to the issue, of how to reconcile human security and support for exports of DUIs, which has not been neglected but has only been very partially resolved by the 2021 text (Section A).

A. STRIKING A BALANCE BETWEEN STRENGTHENING HUMAN SECURITY AND SUPPORTING EXPORTS OF DUI

When presenting the new UN disarmament programme 'Securing Our Common Future' in 2018, UN Secretary-General António Guterres suggested adopting a disarmament model based on human security: 'Just as the notion of security has evolved to place humans at its centre, the objectives and language of disarmament need to evolve in order to contribute to human, national and collective security in the 21st century'.[77] This link between disarmament and human security highlights this relatively recent conception of security, complementing its traditional state-centric meaning. The concept was defined for the first time in 1994 by the UNDP's Human Development Report,[78] and renews the notion of security, which should no longer be restricted to the state and military framework and go beyond the dichotomy between internal and external security. It has since been the subject of much debate and interpretation.[79] The EU has asserted an original regional approach to human security, with the right of arms as its conceptual foundation. For example, it used the concept in the negotiations on the Anti-Personnel Landmines Convention, and the 2003 European Security Strategy implicitly incorporated it,[80] as did certain specific arms law instruments, in particular the EU Strategy against Illicit Small Arms and Light Weapons and their Ammunition, adopted on 13 January 2006.[81] While an express reference to human security appears for the first time in the 2019 analysis of the implementation of the 2016 Comprehensive Security Strategy, this notion was not formally asserted in the 2021 Regulation. However, the Commission claims it considering 'evolving towards a "human security" approach recognising that security and human

---

77 International Action Network on Small Arms (IANSA), 'Quick Guide to Small Arms Issues in 'Securing our Common Future': Secretary General António Guterres' Agenda and Disarmament Programme', 2019, p. 4.

78 UNDP, *Human Development Report*, Paris, Economica, 1994.

79 T. Owen, 'The difficulties and benefits of defining and assessing human security', *Human Rights, Human Security and Disarmament*, UNIDIR, 2004, p. 17.

80 'The internal and external aspects of security are inextricably linked [...] security is a necessary condition for development' because in 'many cases, economic failure is linked to political problems and violent conflict'.

81 Council of the European Union, 5319/06.

rights are inextricably interlinked'. It notes that 'the "human security" approach intends to place people at the heart of the EU's export control policy, in particular by recognising the interlinkages between human rights, peace and security'.[82] However, this rapprochement between arms and DUI export controls, which are now also subject to human rights criteria being taken into account in the export authorisation decision, is accompanied by support for DUI exports through the organisation of relations with the producers of these goods, whose competitiveness the EU is particularly concerned not to hinder. It may thus be recalled that the title of the Commission's 2014 communication (COM(2014) 244 final), 'Review of export control policy: ensuring security and competitiveness in a changing world', clearly displayed the desire to combine these two a priori opposing objectives.

1. *Bringing DUI Export Criteria into Line with Those for Weapons in Terms of Human Security*

The EU is a major producer and exporter of arms. Since 1998, it has therefore been concerned to include in its Code of Conduct on the control of arms exports security and human rights criteria determining export authorisation. Ten years later, this code was transformed into a CFSP common position,[83] to make it binding, and including eight common, detailed ethical and security criteria applicable to Member States' national arms export policies. Among these criteria,[84] the 1998 Code mentioned 'compliance with its international commitments [...] including under international humanitarian law applicable to international and non-international armed conflicts'[85] as part of the buyer's behaviour towards international society. The Common Position of December 2008 increased the number of references to human rights, explicitly including in the criterion of respect for human rights the criterion of respect for international humanitarian law (IHL) by buyer countries or countries of final destination. In this way, EU law gradually incorporated IHL concerns, initially used as a security index to assess the stability of an area, before becoming an autonomous objective in 2008 for the control of arms exports.

---

82 Communication from the Commission to the Council and the European Parliament, Review of export control policy: ensuring security and competitiveness in a changing world, COM(2014) 244 final, 24 April 2014.

83 Common Position 2008/944/CFSP of 8 December 2008, cited above.

84 These eight criteria relate to respect for international commitments, human rights, the internal and regional situation, the security of Member States, behaviour towards the international community, attitude towards terrorism, nature of alliances, respect for international law, risk of diversion or re-export, compatibility with technical and economic capacities.

85 Council, European Union Code of Conduct on Arms Export, 8675/2/98, PESC 137, COARM 13, 5 June 1998, Criterion 6.

Until the 2021 regulation, on the other hand, the control of DUI exports was based mainly on national security issues alone, in line with the American approach to control in this area. However, as Julien Ancelin has written, 'whether it is a question of an authoritarian regime restricting freedoms in order to reinforce its domination, or a non-state armed group extending its capacity to cause harm, DUIs are a prime vector for infringements of rights and freedoms'.[86]

It is true that since the 2000 DUI Regulation, a Member State could prohibit or make subject to authorisation the export of DUIs not on the common list for reasons relating to public security or the protection of human rights (Article 5.1 of the Regulation, Article 8.1 of the 2009 Regulation), but human rights and international humanitarian law are now expressly included in the common criteria defined by the 2021 Regulation, which States should take into account (Recital 2). Article 5.1 thus opens up the possibility of making the export of cyber-surveillance goods not listed in Annex I subject to authorisation if they may be intended for use involving the violation of these rights. Article 9 also provides that 'a Member State may prohibit or impose an authorisation requirement on the export of dual-use items not listed in Annex I, for [...] human rights considerations'. This approach to protecting human rights is particularly reinforced by Article 10, which states that authorisation is required for export if a Member State imposes an export authorisation on the basis of a national control list under Article 9, published by the Commission, and if the exporter has been informed by the competent authority that the goods are intended for uses of concern.

In addition to operationalising the concept of human security, this transformation of the regulation has made it possible to reduce the original material division of non-proliferation law into arms law and DUI law, consolidating this sensitive legal regime. Human security thus appears to be a new lever for the development and coherent implementation of this law, an observation that needs to be put into perspective,[87] in the light of the

[86] J. Ancelin, 'L'Union européenne et les Dual-use items: La politique commerciale commune à l'aune de la sécurité humaine', *La Revue des droits de l'homme*, Actualités Droits-Libertés, published online on 18 October 2017 at: http://journals.openedition.org/revdh/3290.

[87] In particular, it should be emphasised that, as far as DUIs are concerned, the EU has not considered adopting the 'no undercut' principle whereby, if a member state of a non-proliferation regime refuses an export authorisation, this prohibition applies to all partner states. The MTCR, on the other hand, provides for this 'no undercut' rule, which implies non-competition between suppliers in the event of a previous refusal, and after prior consultation. The Australia Group is the only system where the decision to refuse is genuinely binding on all countries. The non-circumvention rule is strictly applied: if one country refuses an export, its partners must also refuse it. In contrast, the 2008 EU Common Position on Arms Exports provides that a Member State's refusal to grant an export licence may be overridden by another Member State acting in its place to honour the arms sales contract. A State wishing to grant a licence for an export that is 'essentially identical' to a

consistency between the attention paid to respect for human security and the support provided by the Regulation for the activities of European industries associated with control mechanisms.

2. *Support for DUI Exporters Affected by Export Controls*

In earlier versions of the regulation, the EU had already attempted to strike a balance between security and trade support. Considering that export controls are a decisive factor in competitiveness, the 2021 Regulation attempts to reconcile these conflicting imperatives by making those involved more accountable through several mechanisms.

The text explicitly recognises that 'The contribution of exporters, brokers, providers of technical assistance or other relevant stakeholders to the overall aim of trade controls is crucial',[88] requiring them to adopt an 'internal compliance programme' (ICP)[89] to assess the risks associated with exports themselves and to take 'reasonable care' by putting in place 'transaction screening measures'.[90] The adoption of an ICP is taken into account by the competent authorities in their decision to grant a licence. The Regulation (Article 5.2) also states that '[w]here an exporter is aware, according to its due diligence findings, that cyber-surveillance items which the exporter proposes to export, not listed in Annex I, are intended, in their entirety or in part', for use involving internal repression and/or the commission of serious and systematic violations of human rights and international humanitarian law, then the exporter must inform the competent authority. The latter will then decide whether or not to authorise the export in question. The text thus imposes specific obligations on exporters, but modulates them 'in a proportionate manner' according to the risks and the size of companies, and increases the clarity of the mechanisms and the predictability of authorisations to facilitate operations.

The regulation simplifies and harmonises the procedures for granting authorisations. It provides for five types of authorisation valid throughout the EU customs area (general authorisation for exports to countries that do

transaction that has been previously refused by another Member State over the last three years simply needs to consult the latter first. If, after consultation, that State persists in its intention to export, it must notify its decision and explain its position to the State that issued the first refusal. The final decision to grant or refuse authorisation therefore remains the sovereign decision of each State.

88 Para. 7 of the preamble to the 2021 Regulation.

89 Art. 2.21 of the Regulation; Commission Recommendation 2021/1700 of 15 September 2021 on internal compliance programmes for controls of research involving dual-use items under Regulation (EU) 2021/821, [2021] *OJ* L338/1; Commission Recommendation 2019/1318 of 30 July 2019 on internal compliance programmes for dual-use trade controls, [2019] *OJ* L205/15.

90 Para. 7 of the preamble to the 2021 Regulation.

not pose difficulties;[91] national general export authorisations, which must be compatible with general export authorisations and if they do not cover the export of software and dual-use technologies to certain countries; individual or global authorisation granted to an exporter for two years, for the export of one or more DUIs to an end-user in a third country or of several goods, countries and end-users; large-scale project authorisations, granted to a specific exporter, for a type or category of dual-use goods which may be valid for exports to one or more specific end-users in one or more specified third countries for large-scale projects). Exporters applying for an authorisation must provide the authorities with full information and keep detailed records.

The regulation also structures the relationship with the private sector, by providing that exporters, brokers and assistance providers may be consulted by the 'dual-use' coordination group chaired by the Commission and made up of one representative from each Member State.

However, this association of economic actors is modulated, as it distinguishes between them according to their nature. The Regulation is based on the American model of 'deemed export' provided for in the EAR regulation.[92] But by extending the controls on the provision of technical assistance within the EU beyond the supply or transfer of technology or technical data, it introduces controls on European exporters providing technical assistance not outside the customs territory of the Union but within it, where the importer is not a European resident and is temporarily present on EU territory.

This last remark highlights the strategic autonomy dimension of the Regulation, but it is not exclusive of the preservation of the sovereignty of the Member States, which is still prevalent, and which feeds into a half-hearted assessment of the Regulation's contributions in terms of non-proliferation.

B. THE PERSISTENT ATTACHMENT OF MEMBER STATES TO THEIR SOVEREIGN ASSESSMENT OF THE DESIRABILITY OF EXPORTING

In its overall assessment of the effectiveness of the control regime, the Commission expressed strong concern about the new national controls established by some States outside the multilateral framework, creating a risk of control fragmentation within the EU, and threatening the single market.[93] On 20 June 2023, the Commission and the High Representative (HR/VP)

---

91 Among these general authorisations, the 2021 regulation introduces two new authorisations for the intra-group export of certain software and technology (EU007) and for the export of certain goods incorporating cryptographic functions (EU008).

92 EAR, para. 734.13(b).

93 COM(2024) 25 final, cited above, p. 3.

had already adopted the Communication on a European Economic Security Strategy,[94] proposing faster and coordinated action and full exploitation of the potential of the 2021 Regulation. The Commission then clarified the analysis and presented concrete proposals in its White Paper of April 2024, in an attempt to mitigate the impact of the lack of a common approach to export controls (Section 1). This has been accompanied by strong reluctance to increase the transparency of national decisions taken by EU Member States in granting authorisations (Section 2).

1. *The Continuing Lack of a Common Approach to Control*

In all the documents presented in recent years, the Commission has stressed both the need for and the shortcomings of a common approach to the objectives and procedures of export controls on DUIs. In the White Paper of April 2024, it goes so far as to affirm the need for a 'uniform [...] controls system' (4(1)).

It is interesting to note that the common definition of DUIs to be subject to export controls is negotiated and adopted by the Member States in a framework outside the EU, in their participation in non-binding multilateral non-proliferation regimes. These controls are then mechanically transposed within the EU in Annex I to the Regulation. In its Communication on the European Economic Security Strategy, the Commission deplored the fact that, in addition to the current deadlock in these regimes, the EU's effectiveness is hampered by the fact that it is only a member of one of these regimes and an observer in another, and that the lists drawn up by these regimes do not reflect the positions of all the Member States, some of which are not members.

The boldness shown by the Commission in its White Paper is largely due to the evolution of the context, the measures adopted by the EU against Russia.[95] This marks a new common voluntary approach, and an important political change, considerably widening the traditional scope of export restrictions beyond military and dual-use goods, to include a series of advanced commercial technologies (electronics, computing, telecommunications, information security, sensors, lasers, aeronautical and maritime technologies). The EU's 11th package of economic and individual restrictive measures[96] further extended

94 Commission and High Representative, Joint Communication to the Parliament and the Council on the European Economic Security Strategy, JOIN(2023) 20 final, cited above.

95 Council Regulation (EU) 2022/328 of 25 February 2022 amending Regulation (EU) No 833/2014 concerning restrictive measures in view of Russia's actions destabilising the situation in Ukraine, ST/6561/2022/INIT, [2022] *OJ* L49/1.

96 [2023] *OJ* L159I. Since December 2023, a new clause relating to dual-use goods and advanced technological goods used in Russian military systems has applied to EU exporters and contractually prohibits the re-export to Russia and the re-export for use in Russia of a limited number of goods as part of a sale, supply, transfer or export to a third country, with the exception of partner countries.

the list to include goods likely to contribute to the technological strengthening of Russia's defence and security sector.[97] Since the end of the Cold War, restrictions on the export of DUIs have never been used by the EU with such strategic ambition, on such a scale, with such coordination between allies, or against an economy the size of Russia's. They demonstrate a strong desire for trade and technology policy to support security imperatives.

While the EU has been united in adopting export restrictions as part of a sanctions regime against Russia, it is far from being as consistent with regard to China. Many EU Member States share US concerns about the security threat posed by China, but there is no full alignment between the EU and the US, or between all EU Member States, to make use of the opportunities opened up by the 2021 Regulation to establish strategic export controls of European technology using non-proliferation text. Despite the clarifications provided on DUI export controls by the President of the Commission in her founding speech on EU-China relations,[98] Member States continue to adapt their national lists to their security analyses on a discretionary basis, through the catch-all clause (mentioned above). This leaves the EU vulnerable both to leaks of sensitive technologies and to national uses of the Regulation that do not take account of their consequences for other States or the Union itself.

In its White Paper of April 2024, the Commission was at liberty to point out that neither the multilateral regimes nor the implementation of the coordination mechanism of Articles 9 and 10 create a rule of general application or a public rule. This leaves States too much latitude, which places them in a weak position concerning pressure from powerful partners.

---

97 This list now covers electronic components, semiconductor materials, manufacturing and testing equipment for electronic integrated circuits and printed circuit boards, precursors of energetic materials and precursors of chemical weapons, optical components, navigational instruments, metals used in the defence sector and marine equipment. The June 2023 package also added 87 entities to the list of those directly supporting Russia's military-industrial complex in that country's war of aggression against Ukraine. This list now includes entities in third countries that produce and export drones to Russia, as well as other parties involved in circumventing sanctions and supplying electronic components to Russia.

98 Ursula Von der Leyen, Speech on EU-China relations to the Mercator Institute for China Studies and the European Policy Centre, 30 March 2023: 'we know there are some areas where trade and investment poses risks to our economic and national security, particularly in the context of China's explicit fusion of its military and commercial sectors. This is true for certain sensitive technologies, dual-use goods or even investment which comes with forced technology or knowledge transfers [...] The European Union needs to define its future relationship with China and other countries in sensitive high-tech areas such as microelectronics, quantum computing, robotics, artificial intelligence, biotech, – you name it. Where dual-use purposes cannot be excluded or human rights might be implicated, there will need to be a clear line on whether investments or exports are in our own security interests', at: https://ec.europa.eu/commission/presscorner/detail/%E2%80%8Cen/speech_23_2063.

The proposals put forward by the Commission have already been followed to a very limited extent as regards the establishment of a political coordination forum for export controls:[99] the Council's Working Party on Dual-Use Goods has been designated as the forum for discussions on export controls, and the Council is particularly keen to emphasise its central role in the ongoing discussions.[100] This forum for examining the strategic and foreign policy dimensions of export control policy makes it possible to find an institutional solution to the difficulties posed by the overlap between trade and security policies.

The other responses proposed by the Commission, the most important ones, received a more cautious welcome from the Council. The Commission had raised the question of the appropriateness of adopting an additional legal provision to the 2021 Regulation, allowing the introduction of new common controls. The aim is both to extend Annex I of the Regulation to goods whose controls could not be adopted by the multilateral regimes because of Russia's opposition, and to define a mechanism for better coordination of the new national control lists to facilitate the coordination of controls between Member States under Articles 9 and 10 of the Regulation, to enable the national authorities to take account of the risks or repercussions of their decisions for the other Member States and the Union. '[W]ithout prejudice to any overarching views from the Council on a European Economic Security Strategy and the role of export control therein' (point C), and without rejecting the adoption of a delegated act (see above, I.A.1.), the Council's position expressed on 30 May 2024 defends more the competence of the Member States as regards controls: 'voluntary coordination of national control lists should be without prejudice to the Member State's ability to act in response to national security concerns' (para. 5) and 'make full use of existing instruments' (para 9). The Council thus prioritises 'coordination among Member States in fully implementing of the current Regulation' (point E).

The Commission's proposal in the White Paper to increase transparency in the adoption of new national lists[101] is part of its drive to improve processes in this area.

2. *Persistent Limits to the Transparency of Control Processes*

One of the main objectives of the 2021 Regulation is to strengthen the exchange of relevant information and to introduce greater transparency (Recitals 2, 34, 35, Chapter VII 'Transparency, outreach, monitoring, evaluation').

---

99 White Paper, para. 5(2).

100 Council of the European Union, doc. 9439/24, point B and paras. 3, 4, 8 and 12.

101 White Paper, para. 4(1).

It should be emphasised that this transparency is already considerably greater than that organised by the EU in the area of arms export controls. Unlike the DUI list, the list of arms, munitions and war material, which was unanimously drawn up by the Council in 1958, has never been officially published or updated.[102] It was simply made public for the first time in 2001 following a question from an MEP.[103]

However, the transparency of dual-use goods is still considered unsatisfactory by the Commission, which is responsible for drawing up the annual report on the implementation of the Regulation, in consultation with the Dual-Use Coordination Group.

This report will include the number, value and destination of authorisations and refused applications. For the first time, the 2021 Regulation provides that the publication of an annual Union report on the implementation of controls should contain relevant information on the granting of authorisations and the monitoring of the application of controls under the Regulation (Article 26). Nevertheless, account must be taken of the need to ensure the protection of the confidentiality of certain data, in particular where the transmission or publication of data relating to the granting of authorisations could have an impact on defence, foreign policy and national security concerns or jeopardise the protection of sensitive personal and commercial information. The second subparagraph of Article 26(2) specifies the information that should generally be included in the EU's annual report. Unsatisfied with the information received, in January 2024 the Commission adopted a recommendation on the preparation of the EU annual report on export controls of DUI, asking Member States 'to take into account the non-binding guidance' on the subject,[104] especially as regards data collection. The Commission's guidance takes account of the fact that the competent authorities of the Member States have varying practices with regard to public reporting on a national basis. Moreover, this is without prejudice to the exchange of information between Member States and the Commission which aims to 'enhance the efficiency of the Union export control regime and to ensure the consistent and effective implementation and enforcement of control throughout the customs territory of the Union', in accordance with Article 23 of Regulation 2021/821.

---

102 The list of products intended for specifically military purposes, adopted in 1958 (Council Decision 255/58) and intended for Member States, itemises the products covered by Article 346. The fact that this list is not updated gives Member States greater room for manoeuvre.

103 Written question by Bart Staes MEP (Greens/EFA). [2001] *OJ* C364E/85.

104 Commission Recommendation (EU) 2024/214 of 10 January 2024 on guidelines setting out the methodology for data gathering and processing for the preparation of the annual report on the control of exports, brokering, technical assistance, transit and transfer of dual-use items pursuant to Regulation (EU) 2021/821 of the European Parliament and of the Council, [2024] *OJ* L2024/214.

The Regulation improves transparency concerning cyber-surveillance assets, to which a specific section of the annual report is dedicated, including the number of requests received in each Member State, as well as the list of all destinations targeted by these requests and the Member States concerned.

The Regulation provided for a very gradual timetable enabling the Commission to evaluate its implementation. The first evaluation of cyber-surveillance authorisations was not scheduled until after 10 September 2024 (Article 26.4). In addition, the full evaluation of the Regulation by the Commission was to be carried out between 10 September 2026 and 10 September 2028, with the Commission having to submit these two evaluations to the European Parliament, the Council and the European Economic and Social Committee. This timetable pushed back transparency, which the Commission had already circumvented with the publication, in April 2024, of its White Paper. This document proposed to formally bring forward the evaluation to the first quarter of 2025, in order to examine and, possibly afterwards, make new proposals to remedy the shortcomings of the Regulation. Council simply 'took note' of this,[105] believing that priority should be given to implementing the regulation before carrying out an assessment. Nevertheless, in accordance with its wishes, the Commission published the first report on the application of the Regulation at the end of January 2025.[106]

The publication of this report certainly attests to the improved transmission of information from the Member States to the EU, but the fact remains that it contains more information on the buyer Member States than on the seller Member States, revealing many gaps in Member States' policies, particularly in terms of refusing exports or the volume of exports. For civil society and NGOs observing these transactions, the overall impression remains of having insufficient sources of information.

The intense legislative activity on the part of the EU institutions and the Member States in the area of export controls of DUIs since the adoption of Regulation 2021/821 is indicative of the fact that these controls are more crucial than ever, as the stakes have largely shifted in recent years from non-proliferation to economic security. While a future recast is out of the question, the text has at least been adapted by the Commission's activism. The aim is to take advantage of the current flexibility of the Regulation to take account of the rapid changes in national laws and technologies and the blockages in multilateral regimes, in a context of upheaval – the extent of which the EU is only just beginning to grasp. This requires new policy options to be defined for a common understanding of 'public security', based on the adoption of

[105] Council of the European Union, doc. 9439/24, para. 10.

[106] Commission, Report on the application of Regulation (EU) 2021/821, COM(2025) 19 final, 30 January 2025.

effective rules and agile adaptation mechanisms. Implementing such a risk-reduction approach will involve trade-offs that are already proving difficult, notably between limiting strategic dependencies and preserving peaceful relations.

ARTICLE 212 TFEU: A NEW LEGAL BASIS FOR REGULATING THE EUROPEAN DEFENCE INDUSTRY?

Sabrina Robert
Professor of Law at Nantes University
Member of the Law and Social Change Research Centre
Associate member of IREDIES – Université Paris 1

Article 212 TFEU

1. Without prejudice to the other provisions of the Treaties, and in particular Articles 208 to 211, the Union shall carry out economic, financial and technical cooperation measures, including assistance, in particular financial assistance, with third countries other than developing countries. Such measures shall be consistent with the development policy of the Union and shall be carried out within the framework of the principles and objectives of its external action. The Union's operations and those of the Member States shall complement and reinforce each other.

2. The European Parliament and the Council, acting in accordance with the ordinary legislative procedure, shall adopt the measures necessary for the implementation of paragraph 1.

3. Within their respective spheres of competence, the Union and the Member States shall cooperate with third countries and the competent international organisations. The arrangements for Union cooperation may be the subject of agreements between the Union and the third parties concerned.

The first subparagraph shall be without prejudice to the Member States' competence to negotiate in international bodies and to conclude international agreements.

Along with Article 213 TFEU, Article 212 TFEU constitutes Chapter 2 on Economic, Financial and Technical Cooperation with Third Countries, of Title III of the TFEU. This chapter is dedicated to cooperation with third countries and humanitarian aid, as part of Part Five of the TFEU on the Union's external action. It supplements the provisions on European development aid, the main objectives of which are to reduce and eradicate poverty (Articles 208 to 211 TFEU).[1] But it also differs in that it covers economic, financial and technical cooperation with third countries apart from developing countries. This aspect of external cooperation is designed as a vehicle for disseminating the principles that are consubstantial with the creation of the Union: democracy, the rule of law, and the universality and indivisibility of human rights and fundamental freedoms.[2] Maintaining security in Europe is necessarily a prerequisite for disseminating these values.

Article 212 TFEU therefore allows the European Parliament and the Council to adopt measures falling within the scope of European defence on this basis. This is the case of several acts adopted in favour of macro-financial assistance to Ukraine. Ukraine has been receiving this assistance for several years, under the European Neighbourhood Policy, and initially without the security aspect being predominant. But since 2022, the scope of European assistance to Ukraine has changed radically. On 24 February 2022 – coincidentally since this was also the date of the start of Russian aggression in Ukraine – the European Parliament and the Council adopted Decision 2022/313 granting new macro-financial assistance to Ukraine.[3] This time, the aid was intended to help Ukraine which was shaken by severe economic difficulties following the Covid-19 pandemic, but also destabilised by 'prolonged security threats at its border with Russia'.[4] Subsequently, this security dimension became predominant, as with the adoption of Regulation (EU) 2022/2463 of 14 December 2022 establishing a support instrument for Ukraine for 2023 (macro-financial assistance +).[5] Mention should also be made of the adoption of the Ukraine facility in February 2024 (Regulation (EU) 2024/792 of the European Parliament and of the Council), the purpose of which is to provide financial support to Ukraine to strengthen its economic and social resilience after the Russian aggression, and

1 Article 212 TFEU was introduced by the Nice Treaty (2000), taking over, but supplementing and clarifying, the former Article 181a TEC, which alone formed Title XXI of the EC Treaty on economic, financial and technical cooperation with third countries.

2 Article 21 TEU, to which Article 212 TFEU implicitly refers by emphasising the 'principles and objectives' of the EU's external action (Article 212(1) TFEU).

3 Decision (EU) 2022/313 of the European Parliament and of the Council of 24 February 2022 providing macro-financial assistance to Ukraine, [2022] *OJ* L55/4.

4 See Recital 3 of Decision (EU) 2022/313.

5 Regulation (EU) 2022/2463 of the European Parliament and of the Council of 14 December 2022 establishing an instrument for providing support for Ukraine for 2023 (macro-financial assistance +), [2022] *OJ* L322/1.

to prepare for its accession to the EU. The facility is conditional on Ukraine respecting the fundamental values defended by the Union.[6]

In addition to micro-financial assistance initiatives, Article 212 TFEU also serves as the legal basis for the new industry and defence programme (EDIP).[7] Although it is not the only basis, the fact that this programme is linked to this provision confirms that it can now be classed as one of the relevant provisions for consolidating European defence. The European Commission has decided to mobilise Article 212 TFEU as part of its proposal for a regulation to contribute to the recovery, reconstruction and modernisation of Ukraine's defence technological and industrial base. With this decision, it was proposed to mobilise the EU budget to support the Ukrainian defence industry.

The objective is to translate this support into a dedicated instrument for Ukraine following the same logic of leveraging the European budget within the framework of the regulation on the establishment of an instrument to strengthen the European defence industry through joint procurement (EDIRPA),[8] and the Regulation on supporting ammunition production (ASAP).[9] This openness makes it possible for Ukraine to be involved in joint purchases by Member States in the case of EDIRPA-type support, and for companies from the Ukrainian defence industry to be involved alongside European industry in the case of ASAP-type support.

The approach adopted here makes a de facto contribution to Ukraine's war effort, in particular by strengthening and modernising its production capacity. However, this support is also presented as a way of preparing the integration of the Ukrainian defence technological and industrial base into that of the Union. This is in line with the approach announced in the new strategy for the European defence industry,[10] which aims to further strengthen ties with Ukraine by reinforcing industrial cooperation.

---

6 Art. 5(1) of the Regulation.

7 Regulation (EU) 2025/2643 of the European Parliament and of the Council of 16 December 2025 establishing the European Defence Industry Programme and a framework of measures to ensure the timely availability and supply of defence products ('EDIP Regulation'), [2025] *OJ* L2025/2643. See the commentary by E. Simon in this publication.

8 See the commentary on the EDIRPA regulation by E. Bernard in this publication.

9 See E. Bernard's commentary on the ASAP regulation in this publication.

10 See F. Liberti's commentary on the EDIS strategy in this publication.

ARTICLE 222 TFEU: THE SOLIDARITY CLAUSE

Declaration No 37 annexed to the TFEU
Council Decision 2014/415/EU of 24 June 2014 on the arrangements for the implementation by the Union of the solidarity clause [2014] *OJ*, L192/53.

Fabien TERPAN
Professor of Public Law, Sciences Po Grenoble – UGA, CESICE, Jean Monnet Chair in European Union Law and Politics

Article 222 TFEU

1. The Union and its Member States shall act jointly in a spirit of solidarity if a Member State is the object of a terrorist attack or the victim of a natural or man-made disaster. The Union shall mobilise all the instruments at its disposal, including the military resources made available by the Member States, to:

a) – prevent the terrorist threat in the territory of the Member States;
– protect democratic institutions and the civilian population from any terrorist attack;
– assist a Member State in its territory, at the request of its political authorities, in the event of a terrorist attack;

b) assist a Member State in its territory, at the request of its political authorities, in the event of a natural or man-made disaster.

2. Should a Member State be the object of a terrorist attack or the victim of a natural or man-made disaster, the other Member States shall assist it at the request of its political authorities. To that end, the Member States shall coordinate between themselves in the Council.

3. The arrangements for the implementation by the Union of the solidarity clause shall be defined by a decision adopted by the Council acting on a joint proposal by the Commission and the High Representative of the Union for Foreign Affairs and Security Policy. The Council shall act in accordance with Article 31(1) of the Treaty on European Union where this decision has defence implications. The European Parliament shall be informed.

For the purposes of this paragraph and without prejudice to Article 240, the Council shall be assisted by the Political and Security Committee with the support of the structures developed in the context of the common security and defence policy and by the Committee referred to in Article 71; the two committees shall, if necessary, submit joint opinions.

4. The European Council shall regularly assess the threats facing the Union in order to enable the Union and its Member States to take effective action.

Declaration No 37 annexed to the TFEU

Without prejudice to the measures adopted by the Union to comply with its solidarity obligation towards a Member State which is the object of a terrorist attack or the victim of natural or man-made disaster, none of the provisions of Article 222 is intended to affect the right of another Member State to choose the most appropriate means to comply with its own solidarity obligation towards that Member State.

Council Decision 2014/415/EU of 24 June 2014 on the arrangements for the implementation by the Union of the solidarity clause, *OJ*, L 192, 1 July 2014, pp. 53-58.

Article 222 TFEU provides for a solidarity clause in the event of a terrorist attack or a natural or man-made disaster. The genesis of this article lies in the context of the terrorist attacks in the United States on 11 September 2001, as well as the attacks on European territory in Madrid on 11 March 2004 and in London on 7 July 2005. The idea of a solidarity clause was incorporated into the work of the Convention on the Future of Europe, which was tasked with drawing up a draft treaty establishing a Constitution for Europe between February 2002 and June 2003. The primary aim of these discussions was to provide for a form of solidarity in the event of a terrorist attack, and thus to provide a response commensurate with the stakes involved. However, the scope of solidarity was eventually extended to natural and man-made disasters.[1] At that time, the European Union already had a civil-protection mechanism,[2] as well as a solidarity fund:[3] the idea was therefore to strengthen existing instruments through a mechanism seen as an interface capable of coordinating the various instruments.

1 P. Hilpold, 'Filling a Buzzword with Life: The Implementation of the Solidarity Clause in Article 222 TFEU' (2015) 42(3) *Legal Issues of Economic Integration*, p. 218.

2 Decision 2007/779/EC Euratom of 8 November 2007 establishing a Community civil protection mechanism, [2007] *OJ* L314/9.

3 Council Regulation (EC) 2012/2002 of 11 November 2002 establishing the European Union Solidarity Fund, [2002] *OJ* L311/3.

Given that the Constitutional Treaty was not ratified, it was not until the Treaty of Lisbon (2007) that the solidarity clause was incorporated into the Union's primary law, in a form identical to that provided for in the Constitutional Treaty. Solidarity was nevertheless mentioned in advance, at a political level, in a declaration on solidarity against terrorism, adopted by the European Council on 25 March 2004.[4] Today, the solidarity clause appears in the Treaty on the Functioning of the European Union (TFEU) and is therefore not included in the provisions relating to the Common Security and Defence Policy (CSDP),[5] which are set out in Articles 42 to 46 of the Treaty on European Union (Title V, Chapter 2, Section 2). However, as we shall see, this does indeed concern the field of security and defence, despite the reticence shown by certain Member States during the negotiations on the Constitutional Treaty.[6]

It is insofar as it contributes to the development of the EU's defence dimension that Article 222 TFEU will be analysed here. The proposed reading will take into account Declaration No 37 annexed to the TFEU, as well as Council Decision 2014/415/EU of 24 June 2014.[7] The latter was adopted based on a proposal from the Commission and the High Representative,[8] and with the support of the Political and Security Committee, the structures developed in the framework of the CSDP and the Standing Committee on Operational Cooperation on Internal Security, as provided for in Article 222(3) of the TFEU. This decision defines the rules and procedures for the implementation of the solidarity clause by the Union (and not by the Member States). More broadly, the solidarity clause will be situated in relation to the Treaty system, to clarify as far as possible its relationship with the CSDP and other policies (Section I). The invocation of the clause will then be presented (Section II), followed by its scope and effectiveness (Section III).

---

4 European Council, Declaration on combating terrorism, Brussels, 25 March 2004. See M. Ekengren, 'New Security challenges and the need for new forms of EU cooperation: the solidarity declaration against terrorism and the open method of coordination' (2006) 15(1) *European security*, pp. 89–111.

5 A. Cammilleri-Subrenat, *Le droit de la politique européenne de sécurité et de défense dans le cadre du traité de Lisbonne*, Paris/Cachan, Lavoisier/Éditions TEC & DOC, 2010; P. Koutrakos, *The EU Common Security and Defence Policy*, Oxford, Oxford University Press, 2013; J. Auvret-Finck (dir.), *Vers une relance de la politique de sécurité et de sécurité commune?*, Brussels, Larcier, 2014.

6 Working Group VIII, Working Document 38, WG VIII-WD 38, Brussels, 4 December 2002.

7 Council Decision 2014/415/EU of 24 June 2014 on the arrangements for the implementation by the Union of the Solidarity clause, [2014] *OJ* L192/53. See also A. Hamonic, Chronique 'L'action extérieure de l'Union européenne: les modalités de sa mise en œuvre par l'Union sont enfin adoptées, mais des incertitudes persistent', *RTDE*, 2015/1, 5 June 2015.

8 Commission/High Representative, Joint proposal for a Council decision on the arrangements for the implementation by the Union of the Solidarity clause, 21 December 2012, JOIN(2012) 39 final.

I. THE SOLIDARITY CLAUSE IN THE TREATY SYSTEM

The word solidarity is used many times in the European treaties.[9] The Court refers to the concept to the point, according to some, of making it a general principle of EU law.[10] A policy document such as the Strategic Compass of May 2022[11] mentions solidarity nineteen times. These various references do not, however, correspond to a single definition of solidarity, which would be enshrined in the Treaties and cover all EU areas or sectors of activity. We therefore need to turn to legal doctrine to establish a definition that can bring together the different forms of solidarity enshrined in the Treaties. Elsa Bernard sees solidarity as 'the duty and attitude resulting from an awareness of the close interdependence existing between States and which prompts them not only to unite, but also to provide mutual aid and assistance and to cooperate with each other as members of the same organisation'.[12] This definition unquestionably applies to the clause contained in Article 222 TFEU. The latter even appears to be a particularly concrete manifestation of mutual assistance and cooperation between Member States, admittedly limited to cases where one of them is the object of a terrorist attack or the victim of a natural or man-made disaster.

The solidarity clause is not a priori part of the CSDP, or even the CFSP, since it is provided for in Article 222 TFEU,[13] and is therefore outside the Treaty on European Union and its Title V. As a measure falling within the

---

9 E. Brosset, N. Rubio and R. Mehdi (eds.), *Solidarité et droit de l'Union européenne - Un principe à l'épreuve*, Confluences des Droits, Aix-en-Provence, DICE Éditions, 2021. And in particular: K. Abderemane, 'Le "mot" solidarité en droit de l'Union européenne', in E. Brosset, N. Rubio and R. Mehdi (eds.), *Solidarité et droit de l'Union européenne - Un principe à l'épreuve*, Aix-en-Provence, DICE Éditions, 2021, pp. 17–38. See also: A. Biondi, E. Dagilytė and E. Küçük (eds.), *Solidarity in EU Law: Legal Principle in the Making*, Cheltenham, Edward Elgar Publishing, 2018; I. Domurath, 'The three dimensions of solidarity in the EU legal order: Limits of the judicial and legal approach' (2013) 35(4) *Journal of European integration*, pp. 459–475; W.T. Eijsbouts and D. Nederlof, 'Rethinking Solidarity in the EU, from Fact to Social Contract' (2011) 7(2) *European Constitutional Law Review*, p. 169; J. Hayward and R. Wurzel (eds.), *European disunion: between sovereignty and solidarity*, Basingstoke, Palgrave McMillan, 2012; M. Ross and Y. Borgmann-Prebil, *Promoting Solidarity in the European Union*, Oxford, Oxford University Press, 2010.

10 A.-M. Oliva, 'Solidarité et construction européenne', in J.-C. Beguin, P. Charlot and Y. Laidié (dir.), *La solidarité en droit public*, Logiques juridiques, Paris, L'Harmattan, 2005, pp. 65–96.

11 Council of the European Union, 'A strategic compass for security and defence – For a European Union that protects its citizens, values and interests and contributes to international peace and security', 4 May 2022, 7371/22 COR 1.

12 E. Bernard, 'La solidarité, condition et corollaire d'une défense européenne', in M. Mezaguer, A. Millet-Devalle and N. Pigeon (eds.), *Union européenne et solidarités*, Bruxelles, Bruylant, forthcoming.

13 T. Konstadinides, 'Civil Protection Cooperation in EU law: Is there Room for Solidarity to wriggle past?' (2013) 19(2) *European Law Journal*, pp. 267–282. P. Hilpold, 'Filling a Buzzword with Life: The Implementation of the Solidarity Clause in Article 222 TFEU' (2015)

scope of the TFEU, it can also be read in conjunction with various articles of that Treaty, in particular those relating to terrorism (Articles 75, 83 and 88 TFEU) and civil protection (Articles 6(f) and 196 TFEU).

The link with terrorism is obvious, since the response to a terrorist attack is one of the grounds for invoking the solidarity clause. The solidarity clause therefore appears to be one of the facets of an action aimed at combating terrorism in a way that is both preventive and reactive.

The link with civil protection, defined as the protection of people, the environment and property against natural or man-made disasters (Art. 6(f) TFEU), is just as tight. Article 196 TFEU aims to 'a) support and complement Member States' action at national, regional and local level in risk prevention, in preparing their civil-protection personnel and in responding to natural or man-made disasters within the Union; b) promote swift, effective operational cooperation within the Union between national civil-protection services; c) promote consistency in international civil-protection work'. Articles 196 and 222 of the TFEU are both concerned with intervention 'in the event of natural or man-made disasters'. In operational terms, the solidarity clause can therefore draw on the EU civil protection mechanism (CPME), created by Decision 1313/2013/EU,[14] as well as on the RescEU reserve, a pool of European intervention capacities that can be deployed to assist Member States affected by a disaster.

While there is a close link between the solidarity clause on the one hand, and civil-protection as well as the fight against terrorism on the other hand, this link is far from exclusive and in no way prevents the connection between Article 222 TFEU and CSDP. As the CSDP is primarily envisaged as an operational tool of the EU, it is not surprising that it can be mobilised within the framework of Article 222 TFEU.

The relationship between the solidarity clause and the CSDP is embodied in Article 222 TFEU by one explicit and two more implicit references. The explicit reference appears in paragraph 3(2), which mentions 'the Political and Security Committee' (a CFSP-CSDP body), as well as 'support of the structures developed in the context of the common security and defence policy'. More implicitly, the CSDP is also present in Article 222(1), which states that the EU 'shall mobilise all the instruments at its disposal, including the military resources made available by the Member States', as well as in paragraph 3(1),

---

42(3) *Legal Issues of Economic Integration*; S. Blockmans, 'L'Union fait la Force: Making the Most of the Solidarity Clause Article 222 TFEU', in I. Govaere and S. Poli (eds.), *EU management of global emergencies*, Leiden, Brill Nijhoff, 2014, pp. 111–135.

[14] Decision 1313/2013/EU of the European Parliament and of the Council of 17 December 2013 on a Union Civil Protection Mechanism, [2024] OJ L347/924. This Decision was amended by Decision (EU) 2019/420 and Regulation (EU) 2021/836.

through the reference to the 'defence implications' that the implementation of Article 222 TFEU may have.

Since the CSDP may be mobilised in the framework of Article 222 TFEU, it follows that the solidarity clause interacts with the forms of solidarity provided for in the CSDP framework: the provision of capabilities in the framework of operations and missions, and the strengthening of those capabilities, as well as the mutual assistance clause in Article 42(7) TEU.[15] Indeed, by making capabilities available, the CSDP contributes both to the implementation of the solidarity clause and to the implementation of the solidarity objectives of the CFSP, set out in Article 24(2) TEU (the Union 'shall conduct, define and implement a common foreign and security policy, based on the development of mutual political solidarity among Member States'),[16] in Article 24(3) TEU (Member States 'shall support the Union's external and security policy actively and unreservedly in a spirit of loyalty and mutual solidarity and shall comply with the Union's action in this area') and in Article 32(1) TEU (Member States 'shall show mutual solidarity' in the context of systematic cooperation within the CFSP).[17] Consequently, CSDP capability enhancement constitutes a form of solidarity, whether through the European Defence Fund,[18] Permanent Structured Cooperation[19] or the European Peace Facility.[20] It offers external benefits (within the framework of the CFSP), or internal benefits (within the framework of the solidarity clause).

It is also logical to relate Article 222 TFEU to the other assistance clause, namely the mutual defence clause provided for in Article 42(7) TEU.[21] The two clauses provide for a mechanism of assistance between Member States in the

---

15 F. Terpan, 'Le Traité de Lisbonne a-t-il rendu la solidarité possible dans le domaine de la sécurité et de la défense', in E. Brosset, N. Rubio and R. Mehdi (eds.), *Solidarité et droit de l'Union européenne – Un principe à l'épreuve*, Confluences des Droits, Aix-en-Provence, DICE Éditions, 2021, pp. 151–166.

16 The same Article 24(2) TEU links 'mutual political solidarity' to 'the identification of questions of general interest' and 'the achievement of an ever-increasing degree of convergence of Member States' actions'.

17 Article 44 TEU provides for a particular form of joint action, whereby the Council may entrust a group of Member States with the implementation of a particular operation. To date, this provision has never been formally applied. See the commentary on this article by N. Clinchamps in this publication.

18 Regulation (EU) 2021/697 of the European Parliament and of the Council of 29 April 2021 establishing the European Defence Fund and repealing Regulation (EU) 2018/1092 ([2021] *OJ* L170/149). On this regulation, see the commentary by S. Rodrigues in this publication.

19 On Articles 42(7) and 46 TEU, see the commentary by Q. Loïez, in this publication.

20 On the FEP, see the commentary on Articles 23 to 40 TEU by C. Schneider, in this publication.

21 On this Article, see the commentary by J.-C. Martin in this publication. See also: M. Fischer, 'Article 42 (CSDP: Goals and Objectives; Mutual Defence)', in H.-J. Blanke and S. Mangianelli (eds.), *The Treaty on European Union – A Commentary*, Berlin, Springer, 2013, pp. 1201–1236; S. Biscop, 'The European Union and mutual assistance: more than defence' (2016) 51(2) *The International Spectator*, pp. 119–125.

event of one of them being threatened by an attack or disaster. Although these two clauses are distinct, it will be shown below that it is not easy to delimit their respective perimeters.

II. INVOKING THE SOLIDARITY CLAUSE

The solidarity clause can only be invoked in specific situations (A) and in accordance with specific procedures laid down in the Treaties and secondary legislation. These procedures specify how the clause can be invoked (B), and how the response can be handled (C).

A. SITUATIONS JUSTIFYING INVOCATION OF THE CLAUSE

Article 222 TFEU may be triggered if a Member State is 'the object of a terrorist attack or the victim of a natural or man-made disaster' (paragraphs 1 and 2). Article 3 of Decision 2014/415/EU clarifies these concepts, and therefore the scope of the clause. A disaster is defined as 'any situation which has or may have a severe impact on people, the environment or property, including cultural heritage'. Terrorist attacks are defined by reference to Council Framework Decision 2002/475/JHA,[22] which distinguishes between terrorist offences (Article 3) and offences linked to a terrorist group (Article 4).

The geographical scope of the clause is specified in Article 2 of Decision 2014/415/EU. The clause applies 'within the territory of Member States to which the Treaties apply, meaning land area, internal waters, territorial sea and airspace' (Article 2(1)). The scope of the clause does not prejudge the origin of the attacks and disasters, which may be on or outside EU territory. On the other hand, the Decision reflects a restrictive approach to the territory in which solidarity is implemented. Indeed, the geographical limits, as defined, exclude from the scope of the clause situations such as an attack on an embassy or any other building outside EU territory. An exception is provided for in Article 2(1)(b) of the Decision, which envisages extraterritorial application where 'infrastructure (such as off-shore oil or gas platforms) situated in the territorial sea, the exclusive economic zone or the continental shelf of a Member State' is affected. Furthermore, despite the clarifications made, the Decision has not removed all the ambiguities. For example, can an influx of migrants resulting from a shipwreck at sea be considered to fall within the scope of Article 222 TFEU, insofar as it would indeed be a 'disaster' with 'serious effects on persons'?

---

22 Council Framework Decision 2002/475/JHA of 13 June 2002 on combating terrorism ([2002] *OJ* L164/3).

The Decision appears more restrictive than the approach of the European Parliament in its resolution of 22 November 2012, which called for 'no significant threat, such as attacks in cyberspace, pandemics or energy shortages, [to be] overlooked' and noted 'that the clause could also cover serious incidents occurring outside the Union having a direct and strong impact on a Member State' (point 20).[23]

Decision 2014/415/EU also specifies that the Member State affected may invoke the solidarity clause 'if, after having exploited the possibilities offered by existing means and tools at national and Union level, it considers that the crisis clearly overwhelms the response capabilities available to it' (Art. 4). The clause must therefore be implemented in accordance with the principle of subsidiarity, which tends to make its use exceptional.

In practice, and contrary to what might have been expected, the solidarity clause competes with the mutual defence clause when it comes to a terrorist attack. This was seen when the Foreign Affairs Council of 17 November 2015 activated Article 42(7) TEU, at France's request, following the attacks on Paris and its surroundings on 13 November 2015.[24] For this to be possible, the Council had to consider these attacks as an 'armed aggression' falling within the scope of Article 42(7) TEU, whereas the factual situation did appear to be that of a 'terrorist attack' falling within the scope of Article 222 TFEU.

By circumventing the solidarity clause, France opted for an intergovernmental mode of operation whereas, by invoking Article 222 TFEU, it would have had to deal with the Commission and the High Representative and submit to a relatively cumbersome procedure.[25] Moreover, the solidarity clause commits the Union and its Member States, whereas the mutual defence clause mobilises the Member States alone. This choice undoubtedly enables faster, more flexible action that falls entirely within the scope of the CSDP, whereas Article 222 TFEU may include a military dimension (and therefore come under Article 31(1) TEU, i.e. the CFSP), but in a more limited way and among other dimensions that do not concern the CSDP and the implementation of resources. Article 42(7) TEU also allowed for a reaction outside the territory of the Union. For France, this was mainly a question of obtaining support for its operations in Iraq, Syria and other countries likely to be breeding grounds for terrorism.

---

23 European Parliament resolution on the European Union's mutual defence and solidarity clauses: political and operational dimensions, 22 November 2012, 2012/2223(INI).

24 N.I. Nováky, 'The Invocation of the European Union's Mutual Assistance Clause: A Call for Enforced Solidarity' (2017) 22(3) *European Foreign Affairs Review*, pp. 357–375. See the commentary by J.-C. Martin in this volume.

25 The European Parliament also seemed to fear this cumbersomeness when it stressed, in its resolution of 22 November 2012 (cited above), 'that a decision-making process within the Council triggered by a request for assistance under the solidarity clause must not undermine the Union's responsiveness' (para. 42).

In the final analysis, there is no clear dividing line between the two clauses, contrary to what one might think, insofar as a response to a terrorist attack may fall within the scope of one or the other, or even possibly both at the same time. This ambiguity is hardly surprising, given that the fight against terrorism is not an area clearly defined by the Treaties: it can concern both the CFSP and the CSDP, as well as the areas of freedom, security and justice.

B. HOW TO INVOKE THE CLAUSE

The clause is invoked at the request of the 'political authorities' of the Member State which is the object of a terrorist attack or the victim of a natural or man-made disaster (Article 222(2) TFEU, confirmed by points (a) and (b) of the first paragraph). Assistance from the Union and its Member States cannot be imposed on a Member State: the logic is that of a request for assistance in the name of the principle of solidarity. Article 4 of Decision 2014/415/EU sets out the procedures for requesting assistance: the request must be addressed to the President-in-Office of the Council and the President of the Commission via the Emergency Response Coordination Centre (ERCC). The same procedure applies to withdraw the invocation. The 'Member State having invoked the solidarity clause shall indicate as soon as it considers that there is no longer a need for the invocation to remain active' (Article 7). The duration of invocation of the clause is therefore entirely at the discretion of that State.

There is no provision for the invocation to be followed by a formal decision by which the Council (or any other institution) would actually activate the clause. Article 222 TFEU, in its entirety, simply states that invocation leads to a reaction on the part of the Union and its Member States. Once Article 222 TFEU has been activated, 'the Union and its Member States shall act jointly in a spirit of solidarity' (§ 1) in order to render assistance to a Member State in its territory, in the event of both a terrorist attack and a natural or man-made disaster. As far as the Union alone is concerned, two other objectives, broader in scope, are referred to in the first paragraph of Article 222: 'to prevent the terrorist threat on the territory of the Member States'; 'to protect democratic institutions and the civilian population against a possible terrorist attack'. As far as the Member States are concerned, Article 222(2) TFEU specifies that their reaction presupposes 'coordination within the Council': it is therefore understood that the Council will discuss the modalities of the reaction but not its principle, which is established as soon as it is invoked by the State affected.

C. REACTION METHODS

The modalities of the reaction concern both the mechanisms and the instruments of the reaction.

There is little mention of mechanisms in Article 222 TFEU. All we know is that 'the European Council shall regularly assess the threats facing the Union in order to enable the Union and its Member States to take effective action'. It is clear, however, that the Council's action will focus primarily on major decisions of principle. Article 5 of Council Decision 2014/415/EU therefore provides more details on the response mechanisms at the EU level (to which Member States may add their own response mechanisms). This involves the Council, the Commission and the EEAS collectively ensuring a balance between supranational and intergovernmental institutions.

The response is placed under the political and strategic direction of the Council, while respecting the competences of the Commission and the High Representative (Article 5(1)). It implies the immediate activation of the EU's integrated political crisis response (IPCR) mechanism for organising a political response to crisis situations.[26] This mechanism comprises several tools, including an informal round table,[27] a web platform for exchanging information and a 24/7 contact point (the ERCC), and it can be activated for both external and internal crises within the EU. The IPCR can therefore be mobilised not only under the solidarity clause. It should be noted that the decision was made to make the ERCC the point of contact 24 hours a day, a decision that benefits the Commission and its DG ECHO (which hosts and manages the ERCC), to the detriment of the EEAS, which could have played this role.

The Commission and the High Representative are entrusted with two main tasks. Firstly, a task of analysis (Article 5(2)), which consists of identifying the existing instruments for responding to a crisis, including military means, and indicating to the Council the extent to which these instruments are sufficient, as well as regularly producing integrated analysis and situation reports to inform the Council's coordination and political direction work. Secondly, the Commission and the High Representative are tasked with proposing exceptional measures, going beyond the mobilisation of existing instruments (Article 5(3)).

Assistance makes it possible to envisage a wide range of possible responses, in line with the comprehensive approach advocated by the Commission and

---

26 Council Implementing Decision (EU) 2018/1993 of 11 December 2018 on the EU Integrated Political Crisis Response Arrangements, [2018] *OJ* L320/28.

27 This informal round table consists of a crisis meeting attended by the Council Presidency, representatives of the Commission, the EEAS, the services of the President of the European Council, the relevant EU agencies, the Member States and experts.

the High Representative.[28] The Union 'shall mobilise all the instruments at its disposal, including the military resources made available by the Member States' (Article 222(1) TFEU). The approach adopted is that of mobilising existing instruments. In this respect, Recital 4 of Decision 2014/415/EU states that the implementation of the solidarity clause 'should rely on existing instruments to the extent possible, should increase effectiveness by enhancing coordination and avoiding duplication, and should function on the basis of no additional resources'.

These instruments include, for example, the Internal Security Strategy for the EU, the civil-protection mechanism created by Decision 1313/2013/EU of the European Parliament and of the Council,[29] the health measures provided for by Decision /EU of the European Parliament and of the Council,[30] and the structures of the European External Action Service (military expertise, intelligence, delegations insofar as they can identify the external origins of crises).

It is specifically stated that military resources may be used under Article 222 TFEU. They are not therefore covered by Article 42(7) TEU alone. But as we have seen, if the response has to be made on the territory of third States, as was the case in the aftermath of the Paris attacks in 2015, Article 222 TFEU is not the appropriate framework. Moreover, if the response does take place on European territory but involves traditional territorial defence assets, it can again be assumed that Article 42(7) TEU would be the appropriate legal framework, insofar as the implementation of the solidarity clause 'has no defence implications' (Article 2(2) of Decision 2014/415/EU). The military resources envisaged for the implementation of Article 222 TFEU would appear to be the resources usually involved in tasks with a civilian dimension.

The reference to a wide range of instruments that can be used should not be interpreted as restricting the freedom of Member States to choose the form of their support. Declaration No 37 annexed to the Treaties states that, '[w]ithout prejudice to the measures adopted by the Union to comply with its solidarity obligation towards a Member State', 'none of the provisions in Article 222 is intended to affect the right of another Member State to choose the most appropriate means to comply with its own solidarity obligation towards that Member State'. The duties of the Member States thus appear to

---

28 High Representative and Commission European, Joint Communication to the European Parliament and the Council, 'The EU's comprehensive approach to external crises and conflicts', JOIN(2013) 30 final, 11 December 2013.

29 Decision 1313/2013/EU of the European Parliament and of the Council of 17 December 2013 on a Union Civil Protection Mechanism, [2024] *OJ* L347/924 (amended by Decision (EU) 2019/420 and Regulation (EU) 2021/836).

30 Decision 1082/2013/EU of the European Parliament and of the Council of 22 October 2013 on serious cross-border threats to health and repealing Decision No 2119/98/EC, [2013] *OJ* L293/1.

be limited in relation to those of the Union. This may lead to differentiated implementation of Article 222 TFEU, with some States participating more than others in assistance. This is hardly surprising. We know, for example, that the participation of States in CSDP operations and missions depends on the capabilities and willingness of the various States. The solidarity clause is no different. But this differentiation is likely to hamper the Union's response, given that the Union's means of action are largely in the hands of the Member States.

Ultimately, the forms of assistance provided by the Union and the Member States must be consistent, to avoid duplication and aim for maximum effectiveness. Decision 2014/415/EU is intended to provide guarantees in this respect. More precisely, it set out how the Union coordinates its action within the Council, in accordance with Article 222(2) TFEU. However, it does not deal with aspects of assistance having defence implications (these being the subject of a Council decision taken following the decision-making procedures laid down in Article 31 TEU for the CFSP).[31]

III. LEGAL EFFECTS OF THE COMMITMENTS AND EFFECTIVENESS OF THE SOLIDARITY CLAUSE

Article 222 TFEU is drafted in such a way that solidarity is a legal obligation. In the event of a terrorist attack or disaster, the Union and its Member States 'shall act' (Art. 222(1)), and the Member States 'shall assist' (Art. 222(2)) the States affected: the use of the present indicative tense clearly indicates that assistance is not optional.

However, this obligation remains limited, when looking at the precise content of these provisions. As mentioned above, there is no obligation as to the choice of means used by States to provide assistance. These means remain at the discretion of the Member States. This safeguard may be of particular benefit to States that do not wish to mobilise military means. The obligation to provide assistance is therefore weakened by the absence of any obligation regarding the means of assistance.

The Court of Justice of the European Union (CJEU) could be called upon to specify the obligations incumbent on the Member States. While the CFSP is partly outside the jurisdiction of the European courts, by virtue of Article 275 TFEU,[32] Article 222 TFEU – which is external to the CFSP– is subject to judicial

---

31 See the commentary by C. Schneider in this publication.

32 On Article 275 TFEU, see the comments by C. Schneider and N. Gros-Verheyde in this publication. See also: M. Brkan, 'The Role of the European Court of Justice in the field of Common Foreign and Security Policy after the Treaty of Lisbon: New challenges for the future', in P.J. Cardwell (ed.), *EU External Relations Law and Policy in the Post-Lisbon Era*,

review. However, strict control by the European courts remains difficult to envisage. Admittedly, in theory, the CJEU could consider a Member State's refusal to provide assistance on the basis of Article 222 TFEU to be a failure to fulfil its obligations. The Court could also consider the fact that the Council does not respond (or does not respond positively) to a request for assistance as a failure to act. It could rule that the arrangements for such assistance (despite Declaration No 37) lead to a form of assistance that is in fact so symbolic or so limited as to constitute a breach of the obligation to provide assistance. The principle of loyal cooperation in Article 4(3) TEU would no doubt support its reasoning. Yet all this remains hypothetical in the absence of litigation.

For the time being, few judgments mention Article 222 TFEU, and generally only to specify its scope. Thus the Court has confined itself to stating that the principle of energy solidarity is distinct from the solidarity clause.[33] And the Court of First Instance dismissed the claim of an applicant alleging infringement of Article 222 TFEU against the Commission's refusal to accept a European Citizens' Initiative entitled 'One Million Signatures for a Europe of Solidarity'. According to the applicant, Greece's situation in the context of the economic and financial crisis could be considered to be the result of a man-made disaster and therefore fall within the scope of the solidarity clause. The Court pointed out that this clause 'clearly does not relate to the economic and monetary policy, or economic circumstances or the budgetary difficulties of the Member States'.[34] The lack of precision of the obligations under Article 222 TFEU does not prejudge their possible effects. It may prove difficult for the Member States to refuse a request for assistance from one of their own, despite the fact that the content of the solidarity clause is legally quite soft.[35] However, the clause would have to be used in the first place, which is not currently the case.

The solidarity clause had raised many hopes. Article 222 TFEU is one of the provisions of the Treaties that give substance to solidarity in the European Union. Even though solidarity remains rather vague, it is often referred to in the Treaties. Some have even seen Article 222 TFEU as a 'factor in the emergence of a supranational political community'.[36] The Parliament envisaged

---

The Hague, T.M.C. ASSER, Berlin, Springer, 2012, pp. 97–115; S. Griller, 'The Court of Justice and the Common Foreign and Security Policy', in A. Rosas, E. Levits and Y. Bot (eds.), *Court of Justice of the European Union. The Court of Justice and the Construction of Europe. Analyses and Perspectives on Sixty Years of Case-law. Analyses and Perspectives on Sixty Years of Case-law*, The Hague, T.M.C. Asser Press, 2013, pp. 675–92.

33 Case C-848/19 P, *Germany v Poland*, ECLI:EU:C:2021:598.

34 Case T-450/12, *Anagnostakis v Commission*, ECLI:EU:T:2015:739, para. 60.

35 F. Terpan, 'Soft Law in the European Union – The Changing Nature of EU Law' (2015) 21(1) *European Law Journal*, pp. 68–96.

36 P. Berthelet, 'Le principe de solidarité dans la lutte contreterroriste européenne: un facteur d'émergence d'une communauté politique supranationale', *Revue de l'Union européenne*, 2018/616, 8 March 2018. Our translation.

the clause as a means to 'provide the impetus for enhancing the EU's leverage among European citizens, offering tangible evidence of the benefits of increased EU cooperation in terms of crisis management and disaster response capabilities'.[37]

The lack of implementation has disappointed these expectations. As regards the response to a terrorist attack, Article 42(7) TEU was preferred, because it was more intergovernmental, more likely to involve a military dimension and less limited in territorial terms. For natural or man-made disasters, Member States have made extensive use of the Solidarity Fund, based on Article 175 TFEU[38] and Article 212(2) TFEU,[39] rather than the solidarity clause. The fund is less cumbersome and less intrusive than the clause. It does not give the Union a say in the internal affairs of a State and offers it (financial) support that fully respects its sovereignty. And when disasters affect all Member States, like the Covid-19 pandemic, for example, the solidarity clause loses its meaning, with activation of the IPCR being more appropriate.

In short, guarantees had been given that the solidarity clause would respect existing instruments and would only be used if other responses were not sufficient. Paradoxically, the subsidiarity approach that was favoured has resulted in the clause not being used.

---

37 Para. 23 of the resolution of 22 November 2012, see above.

38 On this article, see the commentary by S. Rodrigues in this publication.

39 Implemented by Council Regulation (EC) No 2012/2002 of 11 November 2022 establishing the European Union Solidarity Fund and Regulations (EU) No 661/2014 and (EU) 2020/461 of the European Parliament and of the Council amending Council Regulation (EC) No 2012/2002.

ARTICLE 270 TFEU: THE JURISDICTION OF THE COURT OF JUSTICE OF THE EUROPEAN UNION TO RULE ON DISPUTES BETWEEN THE UNION AND ITS SERVANTS IN THE FIELD OF DEFENCE

Nicolas GROS-VERHEYDE
Journalist, founder and editor-in-chief of the B2 website

Article 270 TFEU

The Court of Justice of the European Union shall have jurisdiction in any dispute between the Union and its servants within the limits and under the conditions laid down by the Staff Regulations of Officials and the Conditions of Employment of other servants of the Union.

The courts of the European Union (General Court and Court of Justice) do not, in principle, have the power to review the EU's Common Foreign and Security Policy (CFSP), including in the field of the Common Security and Defence Policy (CSDP), and civilian or military crisis management operations.

Nevertheless, under Article 270 TFEU, '[t]he Court of Justice of the European Union shall have jurisdiction in any dispute between the Union and its servants within the limits and under the conditions laid down by the Staff Regulations of Officials and the Conditions of Employment of other servants of the Union'.

This provision has undoubtedly given rise to the most extensive litigation before the European courts in defence matters. Since a turnaround in case law in 2016, CSDP mission staff whose contracts have not been renewed or who have been subject to disciplinary sanctions no longer hesitate to bring cases before the courts, notably on the basis of Article 270 TFEU.[1] However, it is important to distinguish between what falls within the jurisdiction of the EU courts (Section I) and what does not (Section II).

I. THE SCOPE OF JUDICIAL REVIEW UNDER ARTICLE 270 TFEU

Firstly, the CJEU has recognised that it has full jurisdiction to review and/or annul decisions taken by the High Representative concerning the appointment, promotion or discipline of European officials of the European External Action Service (EEAS). On 15 March 2015, the former EU Civil Service Tribunal (EUCST) annulled the failure to promote certain EEAS staff on the grounds that no 'consideration of comparative merits of all officials eligible for promotion had actually been carried out by the Promotion Board and then by the appointing authority'.[2]

Nevertheless, for staff seconded to CSDP missions or operations, case law until recently distinguished between staff seconded by an EU institution and staff seconded by their State. In the case of staff seconded by an EU institution, the EU judicature has 'jurisdiction, in accordance with Article 270 TFEU to rule on all actions brought by EU staff members having been seconded to the EUPM [EU Police Mission]. They remain subject to the Staff Regulations during the period of their secondment to the EUPM and, therefore, fall within the jurisdiction of the EU judicature, in accordance with Article 91 of those regulations'.[3] For staff seconded by their States, the case law was more mixed. The General Court of the European Union has found several appeals by seconded national experts to be inadmissible. This was the case for a staff member of the European Union Police Mission in Bosnia and Herzegovina (EUPM) challenging his reassignment to the post of prosecutor,[4] or for disciplinary measures taken against a Greek police officer seconded to EULEX Kosovo.[5]

The Court of Justice reviewed this distinction in a judgment delivered by the Grand Chamber in July 2016.[6] This reversal followed a scrupulous analysis of the

---

1 Articles 268 and 340 TFEU (liability actions) may also potentially be invoked.

2 Case F-51/14, *Monteiro and others*, ECLI:EU:F:2015:11, para. 65. This judgement is only available in French. Quotation translated by the author. It should not be considered as an official EU translation. The EU shall not be liable for any content or error in this translation.

3 Case C-455/14, *H. v Council and Others*, ECLI:EU:C:2016:569, para. 44.

4 Case T-271/10, *H. v Council and Others*, ECLI:EU:T:2014:702, para. 46.

5 Case T-383/13, *Chatzianagnostou v Council of the EU and Others*, ECLI:EU:T:2015:246.

6 Case C-455/14, *H. v Council and Others*, ECLI:EU:C:2016:569. See also, on reference: Case T-271/10 RENV, *H. v Council*, ECLI:EU:T:2018:180, which dismisses the appeal but which will be annulled by: Case C-413/18 P, ECLI:EU:C:2019:1044, leading to a second referral to

differences and similarities between staff seconded by Member States and those seconded by the European Union in a number of areas: command, discipline, payment of expenses and handling of complaints. For the Court, all seconded staff, regardless of their status of origin, 'are subject to the same rules so far as concerns the performance of their duties "at theatre level"'.[7] The 'national authorities have transferred operational control of their personnel, teams and units to the Civilian Operation Commander, who [...] exercises command and control of the EUPM [...] and, in that capacity, issues instructions to the Head of Mission'. The Head of Mission, as the person responsible for the mission '"at theatre level", [shall exercise] command and control over that mission, in particular over personnel, teams and units from "contributing States". He is 'entrusted with ensuring the coordination and day-to-day management of the EUPM in Bosnia and Herzegovina by giving all necessary instructions to 'all' staff for the effective conduct of the mission in that theatre'.[8] There is therefore no justification for differences between CSDP mission staff depending on their origin prior to secondment.[9] The Court concludes from this that 'the scope of the limitation, by way of derogation, on the Court's jurisdiction, which is laid down in the final sentence of the second subparagraph of Article 24(1) TEU and in the first paragraph of Article 275 TFEU, cannot be considered to be so extensive as to exclude the jurisdiction of the EU judicature to review acts of staff management relating to staff members seconded by the Member States the purpose of which is to meet the needs of that mission at theatre level, when the EU judicature has, in any event, jurisdiction to review such acts where they concern staff members seconded by the EU institutions'.[10]

---

the General Court: Case T-271/10 RENV II, ECLI:EU:T:2020:548, which this time annulled the contested reassignment decisions.

7 Case C-455/14, *H. v Council and Others*, ECLI:EU:C:2016:569, para. 50.

8 Ibid., paras. 50–53.

9 This position applies to staff seconded by Member States. *A priori*, it could also apply to staff seconded by third countries, unless we consider that secondments from these countries are not 'internal' secondments but international secondments, which are covered by secondment agreements.

10 Para. 55 of the aforementioned judgment of 19 July 2016. At the same time, the Court settled an inter-institutional dispute between the Council and the Commission. The Court found that 'the contested decisions are imputable to the Council'. The action is 'admissible only in so far as it is directed against the Council'. 'The Head of EUPM in Bosnia-Herzegovina, who adopted the contested decisions, is appointed by the PSC [Political and Security Committee of the EU]. He is under the authority of the Civilian Operation Commander, who [...] is himself placed under the control of the PSC and the overall authority of the High Representative'. '[T]he PSC exercises political control and strategic direction of EUPM under the responsibility of the Council'. The European Commission was in no way affected by this decision, the Court emphasised. '[It] was not involved in the chain of command of the EUPM in Bosnia and Herzegovina, and the contested decisions do not concern the implementation of the EUPM's budget'(see paras. 63 to 68 of the judgment).

In application of this new case law, we can cite a judgment by the General Court in 2018 which confirmed the jurisdiction of the Court of the European Union in relation to disciplinary measures taken by the Director of the EU Satellite Centre (EUSC) against a contract staff member.[11] The judgement was upheld by the Court of Justice on appeal, which noted that the EUSC's Staff Regulations expressly exclude any judicial review by the national courts or by the Court of the Union of the decisions of the Board of Appeal and, consequently, of the decisions of the Director of the EUSC which are the subject-matter thereof. Accordingly 'against such a background, if the Court and the General Court declined to exercise the jurisdiction conferred on them by Articles 263 and 268 TFEU, the result would be [...] that such decisions would be exempt from any judicial review, either by the EU courts or the national courts, without that decision to decline jurisdiction being justified by a concern to respect the allocation of jurisdiction between the EU courts and the national courts required by the FEU Treaty'.[12]

The European courts have gone even further, recognising a staff member's right to compensation. The EU court awarded compensation to an international magistrate working for EULEX Kosovo who had not had her contract renewed after several successive contracts between January 2014 and November 2016. It acknowledged a 'lack of impartiality, if not a conflict of interest' on the part of the superior, who chaired the internal examination committee and with whom the complainant had an ongoing dispute. The amount of compensation awarded was substantial: compensation equivalent to 19 months' gross salary, to which must be added daily allowances, the foreseeable 'increase in salary', and compensation for 'non-material' damage quantified at €50,000; this is virtually equivalent to the amount of the contract that could have been concluded and is at the top end of the range of amounts awarded in European civil service contractual disputes, and bears witness to the very serious fault recognised by the court.[13]

---

11 The EUSC, although it has legal personality, is a CFSP body under the control of the PSC referred to above.

12 Case C-14/19 P, *CSUE v KF*, ECLI:EU:C:2020:492, para. 84.

13 Case T-242/17 RENV, *SC v EULEX Kosovo*, ECLI:EU:T:2022:637. This judgment was the subject of an appeal dismissed Case C-785/22 P, *EULEX Kosovo v SC*, EU:C:2024:52. See also Case T-763/16, *PY v EUCAP Sahel Niger*, ECLI: ECLI:EU:T:2018:181, which ordered the Mission to pay the applicant the sum of EUR 10,000 in respect of non-material damage suffered (deterioration in his state of health) for having failed to open a preliminary investigation to examine the facts reported by the applicant as constituting harassment by one of his colleagues.

II. ISSUES STILL EXCLUDED FROM JUDICIAL REVIEW UNDER ARTICLE 270 TFEU

The European Court of Justice did not want to consider the reclassification of a succession of fixed-term contracts as contracts of indefinite duration when the matter was referred to it by Liam Jenkinson, an Irish citizen and a veteran of CSDP missions. He had been first recruited to the EUMM (the EU's monitoring mission in the former Yugoslavia), as head of telecoms in 1994. He then moved on to the police mission in Bosnia-Herzegovina EUPM and, finally, to the European 'rule of law' mission in Kosovo EULEX Kosovo from 2010 to 2014 in a series of eleven fixed-term contracts. On learning that his contract would not be extended, he lodged a complaint with the court, requesting that the various fixed-term contracts be reclassified as open-ended contracts and that various compensation payments be made. The General Court acknowledged the full legal capacity of EULEX Kosovo, which had 'legal personality and could be a defendant in proceedings before the EU courts, in accordance with the amendments inserted by Decision'. It therefore did have the status of an employer.[14] But the Court considered itself competent only for the last fixed-term contract, which contained an explicit clause conferring jurisdiction on the Court of Justice of the EU. For the other contracts, the Court considered it did not have jurisdiction because of the existence of a clause conferring jurisdiction on the Brussels court (Belgium) in the various contracts signed.

According to the General Court, the very existence of this jurisdictional clause did not render the previous jurisdiction clauses null and void and could not be 'be extended to previous contracts providing for other courts to have jurisdiction'. The judgement states that 'since the jurisdiction of the Court under Article 272 TFEU derogates from the ordinary rules of law, it must be given a restrictive interpretation'. '[T]he General Court can adjudicate on a contractual dispute only if the parties have expressed their will to confer that jurisdiction on the Court. [The] applicant voluntarily entered into the employment contracts with the missions on the terms proposed to him [and] he expressly accepted the terms and conditions set out therein, including the remedies provided and the clauses expressly giving jurisdiction to the Belgian courts'.[15] This decision was overturned in 2018 by the Court of Justice of the European Union, which considered that 'by declar[ing] that it manifestly lacks jurisdiction', the General Court had erred in law. In the light of European legislation on fixed-term contracts,[16] 'the General Court should have verified

---

14 Case T-602/15, *Jenkinson v Council and Others*, ECLI:EU:T:2016:660, paras. 36 and 37.

15 Ibid., paras. 25–27.

16 The Court thus held that the fact that the same clause did not appear in the previous contracts and that, as far as the first years were concerned, there were not even any written contracts, could not prevent the Court from taking account, in its assessment of the

whether and, if so, to what extent, it was entitled to take account of the previous employment contracts in assessing Mr Jenkinson's claims'.[17] On referral, the EU General Court again rejected 'the claim that the consecutive FTCs (fixed term contracts) should be re-categorised as a single CID (contract of indefinite duration)'.[18] Firstly, there were objective reasons, linked to the temporary and constantly changing nature of the mandate of the EULEX Kosovo mission, for concluding successive fixed-term contracts. Secondly, the applicant was 'well aware [...] that, in the light of the mission's restructuring and the ensuing abolition of the post he had hitherto held, there was no feasible prospect of his contract being renewed'.[19] This position was confirmed, on appeal, by the Court of Justice.[20]

Finally, it should be noted that the Court of Justice, acting on a question referred for a preliminary ruling by the Court of Brussels on behalf of various employees of the same EULEX Kosovo mission, confirmed that 'starting from 15 June 2014, it designates EULAX Kosovo as responsible and therefore as defendant in any action relating to the consequences of the implementation of the mission entrusted to it, irrespective of whether the facts underlying such an action occurred before 12 June 2014, the date when Decision 2014/349 entered into force'.[21] In other words, any dispute, even for old contracts, is now the responsibility of the CSDP mission.

Update by Athanase Popov, 15 November 2025

In *H v Council and Others*, the most decisive point in retaining the Court's jurisdiction in this action for damages was that the contested decisions constitute acts of staff management whose purpose was the redeployment of members of the mission at theatre level, and not acts concerning questions linked to the secondment.[22] Likewise, in *[Tartisai]*,[23] the most decisive element was that Article 7(3) of Council Decision 2010/279/CFSP 'is not directly related to the political or strategic choices made by the institutions, bodies, offices and agencies of the European Union in the context of the

relationship between the parties, of all the contracts concluded (Joined Cases C-109/81, C-110/81 and C-111/81, *Porta v Commission*, ECLI:EU:C:1982:253, para. 10).

17 Case C-43/17, *Jenkinson v Council and Others*, ECLI:EU:C:2018:531, para. 50.

18 Case T-602/15 RENV, *Jenkinson v Council and Others*, ECLI:EU:T:2021:764, para. 210.

19 Ibid., paras. 186 and 188.

20 Case C-46/22 P, *Jenkinson v Council and Others*, ECLI:EU:C:2024:50.

21 Case C-283/20, *EULEX Kosovo*, ECLI:EU:C:2022:126, para. 47.

22 Case C-455/14 P, *H v Council and Others*, ECLI:EU:C:2016:569, para. 59. That distinction wasn't yet raised to the level of an abstract statement of principle for the determination of the scope of the Court's jurisdiction in CFSP (CSDP) matters.

23 Case C-238/24, *[Tartisai]*, ECLI:EU:C:2025:258.

CFSP'. That provision determines the costs related to the seconded staff. Are the costs related to the seconded staff 'related to political or strategic issues concerning the definition and implementation of the CFSP'? If only the lack of appropriate personnel may be comprised in the broader definition of acts falling under the jurisdiction of the Court, to the exclusion of the inadequacy of resources, then it is striking that in *[Tartisai]*, the determination of the costs related to the seconded staff was ruled not to be related to political or strategic issues concerning the definition and implementation of the CFSP, of which CSDP is a component. It is difficult to identify a conceptual distinction between cost determination and the determination of the adequacy of resources. As a result, the *ratione materiae* scope of the Court's jurisdiction in CSDP matters is yet to be further clarified in future cases, including also staff cases.

ARTICLE 275 TFEU: LACK OF JURISDICTION OF THE COURT OF JUSTICE OF THE EUROPEAN UNION IN CFSP/CSDP MATTERS: PRINCIPLE AND EXCEPTIONS

Nicolas Gros-Verheyde (Part 1)
Journalist, founder and editor-in-chief of the B2 website

Catherine Schneider (Part 2)
Emeritus Professor at the University of Grenoble

and

Athanase Popov (update)
PhD in EU law and EU official

Art. 275 TFEU

The Court of Justice of the European Union shall not have jurisdiction with respect to the provisions relating to the common foreign and security policy nor with respect to acts adopted on the basis of those provisions.

However, the Court shall have jurisdiction to monitor compliance with Article 40 of the Treaty on European Union and to rule on proceedings, brought in accordance with the conditions laid down in the fourth paragraph of Article 263 of this Treaty, reviewing the legality of decisions providing for restrictive measures against natural or legal persons adopted by the Council on the basis of Chapter 2 of Title V of the Treaty on European Union.

Article 275 TFEU, resulting from the Treaty of Lisbon, has its source in Article 46 TEU, in the version of the Treaty of Amsterdam, which itself had its origins in Article L of the Treaty resulting from the Maastricht revision. The Maastricht Treaty already excluded provisions relating to the CFSP/CSDP from the jurisdiction of the Court of Justice of the European Union (CJEU).[1] In so doing, the first subparagraph of Article 275 TFEU confirms a principle that derives from the intergovernmental nature of this pillar: that of the exclusion of the jurisdiction of the EU judicature in the field of the Common Foreign and Security Policy (CFSP), including its defence component, the Common Security and Defence Policy (CSDP) (Section I). But the Article's second subparagraph now opens the way to two series of exceptions (Section II).

I. THE PRINCIPLE OF EXCLUSION OF THE JURISDICTION OF THE CJEU IN THE FIELD OF CFSP/CSDP

Article 275 TFEU echoes Article 24(1) TEU, which states that the Court 'shall not have jurisdiction with respect to these provisions'.[2] These are the specific CFSP provisions contained in Chapter 2 of Title V of the TEU of which Article 24 TEU forms part.[3] Immunity applies only to these provisions and to acts adopted on their basis. The first subparagraph of Article 275 TFEU establishes immunity by making an initial reference of a fairly general nature 'to the provisions relating to the common foreign and security policy' (CFSP). However, such a reference goes well beyond the specific provisions of the CFSP Chapter referred to in Article 24(1) TEU and could have opened the way to a broader interpretation of jurisdictional immunity, in particular to acts which, without having been taken within the framework of that Chapter, could have benefited from immunity because they 'related to the CFSP'. But the first paragraph of Article 275 TFEU lays down a second criterion of immunity for acts adopted on the legal basis of the CFSP. The question will soon arise as to whether the CFSP legal basis of an act is sufficient in itself to prevent the Court from reviewing it.

For the time being, the main purpose of the first subparagraph of Article 275 TFEU is to establish total immunity for CFSP decisions, motivated by the concern to avoid actions for annulment or liability for eminently political decisions. In the Court's view, insofar as these provisions 'introduce a derogation

[1] Essentially, insofar as the jurisdiction of the CJEU remains in cases where a CFSP measure involves a contribution from the EU budget: see A. Potteau's commentary on Article 41 TEU in this publication.

[2] See the commentary on Articles 23 to 40 TEU by C. Schneider in this publication.

[3] Arts. 23–46 TEU.

from the rule of general jurisdiction which Article 19 TEU confers on the Court to ensure that in the interpretation and application of the Treaties', they must 'therefore, be interpreted narrowly'.[4] This classic approach to interpreting an exception to a principle has led the European Court of Justice to establish, as far as possible, its jurisdiction independently of the exceptions arising from the second subparagraph of Article 275 TFEU. Five areas in particular illustrate this trend, dealing successively with agreements concluded under the CSDP (Section A), as well as contracts and public procurement contracts negotiated in this context (Section B), the regime under Article 346 TFEU (Section C), access to operational documents of CSDP missions (Section D) and liability for the acts of a CSDP mission (Section E).

A. PARLIAMENT'S 'RIGHT OF SCRUTINY' OVER CSDP AGREEMENTS

The Court has recognised that it has jurisdiction to ensure that the rights of the European Parliament to be informed, and even consulted, on agreements concluded at international level (Art. 218 TFEU) are properly safeguarded, even in the case of agreements fully linked to CSDP operations. For example, the Court has successively annulled the agreements concluded as part of the anti-piracy maritime operation EUNAVFOR Atalanta for the transfer of pirates to Mauritius[5] and Tanzania.[6]

The decision to sign an agreement with Mauritius, even though it was 'adopted on the basis of a single substantive legal basis falling within the CFSP, that is Article 37 TEU', also states in its 'preamble […] that its procedural legal basis is Article 218(5) and (6) TFEU'. This procedure has a 'general scope' and is intended to apply to 'all international agreements negotiated and concluded by the European Union'.[7]

---

4 Case C-658/11, *Parliament v Council*, ECLI:EU:C:2014:2025, para. 70; Case C-439/13 P, *Elitaliana v EULEX Kosovo*, ECLI:EU:C:2015:753, para. 42; and Case C-455/14, *H. v Council and Others*, ECLI:EU:C:2016:569, para. 40.

5 Case C-658/11, *Parliament v Council*, ECLI:EU:C:2014:2025. It should be noted that in this case, the European Parliament, supported by the Commission, considered that the EU-Mauritius Agreement, given its objectives and contents, related not only to the CFSP, but also to legal cooperation in criminal matters, police cooperation and development cooperation, areas covered by the ordinary legislative procedure. The Court however was not convinced.

6 Case C-263/14, *Parliament v Council*, ECLI:EU:C:2016:435. In this case too, the European Parliament argued that the EU-Tanzania agreement covered both the CFSP and the areas of legal cooperation in criminal matters and police cooperation. It was not followed by the Court on this point.

7 Case C-658/11, *Parliament v Council*, ECLI:EU:C:2014:2025, paras. 71 and 72.

The Court acknowledges that it has jurisdiction to examine the legal bases of the decision to verify that the Council, in particular, has not encroached on the powers of the other institutions. It also has jurisdiction to ensure that the Parliament is kept informed. The general obligation to inform Parliament of international agreements 'is not as such among the provisions of primary law relating to the CFSP [...] but applies across the board to all Union procedures for the conclusion of international agreements', explains Advocate General J. Kokott.[8]

Admittedly, the judges have emphasised that during the conclusion of a CFSP agreement by the European Union, the role of the Parliament 'remains limited'. It remains 'exclu[ded] from the procedure for negotiating and concluding an agreement relating exclusively to the CFSP'. However, it retains a 'right of scrutiny in respect of that EU policy'.[9] As specified in Article 218(10) TFEU, the Parliament 'shall be immediately and fully informed at all stages of the procedure' for negotiating and concluding international agreements. This right extends 'also to the stages preceding the conclusion' of an agreement and covers 'in particular the negotiation phase'. This concerns: (i) the authorisation to open negotiations; (ii) the definition of negotiating directives; (iii) the appointment of the Union negotiator or, where appropriate, the special committee; (iv) the closure of negotiations; (v) the authorisation to sign the agreement or, failing that, the decision on provisional application of the agreement before it enters into force; and (vi) the conclusion of the agreement.

Echoing the conclusions of Advocate General J. Kokott, the judges went very far in granting the Parliament this right of scrutiny. They therefore consider that it must extend to 'the interim results achieved by the negotiations'. The Parliament must also be provided with 'the text of the draft agreement and the text of the draft decision approved by the Council's Foreign Relations Counsellors who are responsible for the negotiations, when the text of those drafts was communicated to the Tanzanian authorities with a view to the conclusion of the agreement'.[10] For the Court, beyond the formalism of the information, this procedure is fundamental. 'That rule is an expression of the democratic principles on which the European Union is founded [...] the Parliament's involvement in the decision-making process is the reflection, at EU level, of the fundamental democratic principle that the people should

---

8 Opinion of Advocate General J. Kokott of 28 October 2015, Case C-263/14, *Parliament v Council*, ECLI:EU:C:2015:729, para. 44.

9 Case C-658/11, *Parliament v Council*, ECLI:EU:C:2014:2025, paras. 83 and 84; and Case C-263/14, *Parliament v Council*, ECLI:EU:C:2016:435, para. 69.

10 Case C-263/14, *Parliament v Council*, ECLI:EU:C:2016:435, para. 77.

participate in the exercise of power through the intermediary of a representative assembly'.[11] This principle had already been laid down in previous case law.[12]

Failure to comply with this provision will result in the annulment of the deed. The Court's finding is unequivocal. By only informing the Parliament when 'authorising the opening of negotiations and their conclusion', the Council was guilty of 'an infringement of an essential procedural requirement' preventing the Parliament from exercising its prerogatives.[13] As for the Council's argument that the Parliament was able to exercise its prerogatives when it became aware of the content of the texts adopted on the occasion of their publication in the *Official Journal of the European Union*, this was rejected by the Court: publication in the *OJ* is not sufficient, as it merely 'satisfies the publicity requirements to which an EU act is subject if it is to enter into force'; whereas the 'requirement to inform' the Parliament is intended to ensure 'that the Parliament is in a position to exercise democratic scrutiny of the European Union's external action and, more particularly, to verify that its powers are respected'.[14] However, despite the annulment, the Court went on to maintain the effects of the act until a new international agreement is signed, as it often does in such circumstances.[15]

B. CONTROL OF PUBLIC CONTRACTS AND PROCUREMENT OF THE CSDP

The Court has also asserted its jurisdiction over contracts and public procurement contracts that CSDP missions may award.[16] However, the Court has qualified its jurisdiction in terms of both form and substance. Contracts awarded by military forces are normally subject to the competition rules, subject to certain reservations due to their specific nature, as the Court's Advocate General, Yves Bot, noted in a case between the Italian Ministry of the

11 Case C-658/11, *Parliament v Council*, ECLI:EU:C:2014:2025, para. 81; and Case C-658/11, *Parliament v Council*, ECLI:EU:C:2014:2025, para. 70.

12 Case C-138/79, *Roquette Frères v Conseil*, ECLI:EU:C:1980:249, para. 33, and Case C-130/10, *Parlement v Conseil*, ECLI:EU:C:2012:472, para. 81.

13 Case C-658/11, *Parliament v Council*, ECLI:EU:C:2014:2025, para. 84.

14 Case C-658/11, *Parliament v Council*, ECLI:EU:C:2014:2025, paras. 79 and 80.

15 In this case, the cancellation of the agreement had virtually no operational effect. The net decrease in piracy – reduced to almost zero in the years 2014–2016 – led to a reduction in arrests and therefore in transfers to the countries concerned. Without having been cancelled, these agreements had become ineffective in practice.

16 In application in particular of the EU Financial Regulation: Regulation (EU, Euratom) 2018/1046 of the European Parliament and of the Council of 18 July 2018 on the financial rules applicable to the general budget of the Union, amending Regulations (EU) No 1296/2013, (EU) No 1301/2013, (EU) No 1303/2013, (EU) No 1304/2013, (EU) No 1309/2013, (EU) No 1316/2013, (EU) No 223/2014, (EU) No 283/2014 and Decision No 541/2014/EU, and repealing Regulation (EU, Euratom) No 966/2012, [2018] *OJ* L193/1.

Interior and a telecoms company for the equipment for Italy's Carabinieri.[17] It may 'be legitimate to refrain from applying certain provisions of procurement law, since some contracts are so sensitive that it would be inappropriate to publicise them and open them up to competition between economic operators beforehand'.[18] The magistrate went on to give four specific examples: 'contracts concluded by intelligence services or relating to counter-espionage activities, for example. It is also the case for particularly sensitive purchases, requiring an extremely high degree of confidentiality, such as those linked to anti-terrorism or related specifically to sensitive activities carried out by the forces of law and order'.

In a dispute concerning a public contract for helicopter transport launched by the 'Rule of Law in Kosovo' mission (EULEX Kosovo), contested by an unsuccessful competitor Elitaliania, the EU General Court accepted jurisdiction but dismissed the action on formal grounds.[19] It considered that by referring to EULEX Kosovo in its application, the applicant had committed a substantial error, as the mission had no legal personality according to the Court.[20] This position was confirmed by the Court.[21] The Court of Cassation[22] provided particularly elaborate reasoning about the role of the head of mission, the definition of a CSDP mission and the existence, or otherwise, of an autonomous legal personality for a CSDP mission. In particular, it analysed in detail the decision establishing the EULEX Kosovo mission, its organisation chart and its chain of command (from the High Representative and the PSC to the Head of Mission and the Civilian Operations Commander), and concluded that EULEX Kosovo had 'no legal personality'. It is not 'a body, office or agency of the EU' because it does not have legal personality. It cannot therefore 'be a party to proceedings before the European Union Courts'. It was 'a Mission [i.e. a simple action], of limited duration'.[23]

The real person responsible for the decision to award the contract was therefore the head of EULEX Kosovo, who 'exercises command and control of the staff as well as administrative and logistical responsibility', according to the Council Joint Action 2008/124/CFSP of 4 February 2008 on the European Union Rule of Law Mission in Kosovo, EULEX KOSOVO (see Article 8(2)). This is a responsibility that he assumes by delegation and on behalf of the

17 Conclusions Y. Bot, 10 April 2014, under Case C-19/13, *Fastweb*, ECLI:EU:C:2014:266, para. 110.

18 Yves Bot was particularly familiar with the security sector, having been a prosecutor in charge of anti-terrorism cases in France.

19 Case T-213/12, *Elitaliania v/ EULEX Kosovo*, ECLI:EU:T:2013:292.

20 This case law must be seen in the context of the time when the EU's civilian missions were not expressly recognised as having legal personality.

21 Case C-439/13 P, *Elitaliania v EULEX Kosovo*, ECLI:EU:C:2015:753, paras. 74 and 75.

22 The Court of Cassation is the highest court in France.

23 Case C-439/13 P, *Elitaliania v EULEX Kosovo*, ECLI:EU:C:2015:753, paras. 54–59.

European Commission, which controls the European budget. The measures taken as part of the procedure for awarding the public contract in question concern the EULEX Kosovo budget. And 'all expenditure shall be managed in accordance with the rules and procedures applicable to the general budget of the [European Union]' (see Article 16(2) of the Council Joint Action 2088/124/CFSP). In this case, the Commission 'delegated certain tasks for the implementation of the EULEX Kosovo budget to the Head of EULEX Kosovo'.

The fact that the Head of Mission 'represents EULEX Kosovo in the area of operation and ensures the proper visibility of EULEX Kosovo, may conclude technical agreements with Member States or participating third States and other international actors deployed in Kosovo relating to the provision of equipment, services and premises to EULEX Kosovo' does not affect that characterisation. The acts adopted by it 'in the context of the procedure for awarding the contract in question are attributable to the Commission, which has the status of defendant'. Indeed, as the Court has already recognised, 'measures adopted pursuant to delegated powers are normally attributed to the delegating institution, on which it falls to defend the measure in question before the courts'.[24] The judge rejected the admissibility of the application for a purely formal reason. It was directed against EULEX Kosovo and not against the European Commission. The missions' lack of legal personality has now been rectified. The new missions have been granted legal personality, and as older missions were extended, CSDP missions have been given legal personality.[25]

The Court has thus accepted that it has direct jurisdiction to review contracts awarded in the context of CSDP missions or operations. Argus Security won a case before the General Court of the European Union against the European Union for non-renewal of its contract to provide security services for the EU Border Assistance Mission in Libya, EUBAM Libya.[26]

C. REVIEW OF THE EXCEPTION FOR THE PROTECTION OF MEMBER STATES' ESSENTIAL SECURITY INTERESTS[27]

The Court has asserted its full jurisdiction in matters of the internal market and competition, thus daring to enter the closed circle of defence markets, and in particular to review the use made by Member States of the exception set

---

24 Case T-395/11, *Elti v Delegation of the Union to Montenegro*, ECLI:EU:T:2012:274, para. 62.

25 See in particular Council Decision 2014/349/CFSP of 12 June 2014 amending Joint Action 2008/124/CFSP on the European Union Rule of Law Mission in Kosovo, EULEX KOSOVO ([2014] *OJ* L174/42).

26 Case T-266/14, *Argus Security Projects v Council*, ECLI:EU:T:2016:415.

27 Art. 346 TFEU. See the commentary on this article by S. Rodrigues in this publication.

out in Article 346 TFEU. The latter allows them, in the name of their essential security interests, to escape certain rules of EU law. In response to a complaint lodged by the European Commission against Italy for concluding a contract with the national firm Agusta to equip various State forces (fire brigades, forest guards, coastguards, Guardia di Finança, and the Carabinieri) with helicopters without a competitive tendering procedure, the Court of Justice of the European Communities not only upheld the complaint but also took the opportunity to define the scope of the national security interest exception. The grounds for the ruling were rather harsh on the Italian government, as they considered illegal 'a long-standing practice of the Italian State of directly awarding contracts for the purchase of Agusta and Agusta Bell helicopters without any competitive tendering procedure at Community level'.[28]

In addition to the case in point, the courts have given a serious framework to the national interest requirement. The Court first recalled the principle that no measure is exempt from European supervision: 'measures adopted by the Member States in connection with the legitimate requirements of national interest are not excluded in their entirety from the application of Community law solely because they are taken in the interests of public security or national defence'.[29] The exception in the former Article 296 TEC (now Article 346 TFEU as amended by the Lisbon Treaty) only concerns products 'intended for specifically military purposes'. 'The purchase of equipment, the use of which for military purposes is hardly certain, must necessarily comply with the rules governing the award of public contracts'. The Court went on to find that since the purchase of these helicopters covered both civilian and military needs – 'they may serve both military and civilian purposes' – the tendering procedure was indeed applicable. The need to exchange confidential data was not really an excuse.[30] 'The requirement to impose an obligation of confidentiality in no way prevents the use of a competitive tendering procedure for the award of a contract'. The risk of awarding contracts to European companies was not proven from a security point of view, according to the judges.[31]

The Court of Justice has extended this judicial review to public undertakings operating in the defence sector, which must comply with the various rules on equality before the state. It ruled that the property tax exemption enjoyed by the Spanish shipbuilding company Navantia could constitute 'State aid' and

---

28 Case C-337/05, *Commission v Italy*, ECLI:EU:C:2008:203. The following quotations are taken from this judgment.

29 Ibid., para. 42.

30 See para. 52 of the judgment: 'the requirement to impose an obligation of confidentiality in no way prevents the use of a competitive tendering procedure for the award of a contract'.

31 See para. 51 of the judgment: 'the Italian Republic has not stated the reasons for which it submits that the confidentiality of the information communicated for the production of the helicopters manufactured by Agusta would be less well guaranteed were such production entrusted to other companies, be they established in Italy or in other Member States'.

be deemed unlawful under European regulations. The fact that the objectives pursued by this exemption 'relate to considerations of national defence [...] do not suffice to exclude the measure at the outset from being categorised as aid'. '[A]n exemption for immovable property owned by the State and used for the purposes of national defence does not appear to be directly related to the objectives of the property tax itself'.[32]

D. ACCESS TO OPERATIONAL DOCUMENTS FOR CSDP MISSIONS

The Court of Justice has also accepted jurisdiction over the fate of operational documents from CSDP missions. For the time being, however, it takes a fairly restrictive view of access to documents.

In the case of *Jurašinović v Council*, decided in 2012 by the General Court[33] and then on appeal in 2013,[34] the applicant (a former Yugoslav refugee in France) sought access to the reports of the European observers who were present as part of the European Commission Monitoring Mission (ECMM) in the former Yugoslavia during the Croatian counter-offensive (Operation Tempest) in the Knin area, in August 1995.[35] In a highly political assessment, both the General Court and the Court of Justice considered that access to documents of European security and defence missions must remain exceptional, especially when such access takes place in a sensitive area where peace is not yet assured.

The Court recalled that overriding European interest takes precedence over individual interests and confirmed the legitimacy of the refusal. 'The aim of the Union's policies in the Western Balkans region is to contribute to peace, stability and lasting regional reconciliation'; as a result, the 'disclosure of information or assessments contained in the reports could, at the date of the contested decision, undermine the pursuit of these objectives by revealing matters liable to give rise to or increase resentment or tension between the various communities' in former Yugoslavia.[36]

The judges thus accepted the arguments of the Council, which had refused to disclose most of the documents as it 'considered that the reports were still highly sensitive despite the fact that 14 years had passed since the events to which they referred'. The documents requested were likely to 'create further

32 Case C-522/13, *Ministerio de Defensa and Navantia*, ECLI:EU:C:2014:2262, paras. 28 and 44.

33 Case T-465/09, *Jurašinović v Council*, ECLI:EU:T:2012:515.

34 Case C-576/12 P, *Jurašinović v Council*, ECLI:EU:C:2013:777.

35 The offensive, led by the Croatian army with the support of Western advisers, led to the ultimate 'ethnic cleansing' of this 'Serb enclave' in Croatia and was the prelude to the Dayton-Paris peace agreements in Bosnia-Herzegovina.

36 See para. 39 of the judgment of the General Court.

difficulties in the European Union's relations with the different parties to the conflicts which had taken place in former Yugoslavia and with other countries concerned'. Finally, there were issues of 'public security, particularly the security and physical integrity of observers, witnesses and other sources of information, whose identity and assessments would be revealed by disclosure of the reports'. The climate was 'a particularly delicate political, military and human rights situation' at the time. And the interviews held with local players and witnesses were conducted 'on the basis of confidentiality'.

This argument was thus endorsed by the General Court and the Court of Justice without going into detail. The fact that the documents had not been classified as 'defence' did not affect the negative outcome of the judgment. For the Court, 'the fact that a document has not previously been classified' did not prevent 'an institution from refusing access' to it.[37]

Nonetheless, these cases provided an opportunity for the European Court of Justice to restate its jurisdiction to review the legality of decisions by the institutions refusing access to documents on the basis of the public interest exceptions provided for in Article 4(1)(a) of Regulation 1049/2001, including, therefore, those relating to international relations, and even if that review is limited to 'verifying whether the procedural rules and the duty to state reasons have been complied with, whether the facts have been accurately stated, and whether there has been a manifest error of assessment of the facts or a misuse of powers'.[38]

E. LIABILITY FOR THE ACTS OF A CSDP MISSION

A new development in case law is to be expected. In the case of two women against the EULEX Kosovo mission,[39] the Court's Advocate General, Tamara Ćapetais, is calling for a real turning point in a long-standing case challenging the action of the rule of law mission in Kosovo (EULEX).

Known by their initials KS and KD, these two women lost family members in 1999 during Kosovo's war of independence. Their murders and disappearances have never been solved, either by the UN mission (UNMIK), which had jurisdiction over these crimes until 2008, nor by the European mission EULEX Kosovo, which succeeded UNMIK and which was tasked with investigating the crimes and finding or identifying missing persons. The plaintiffs believed that the crimes were not properly investigated and were claiming compensation.

---

37 Para. 41 of the Court's judgment.

38 Para. 28 of the judgment of the General Court.

39 Opinion of AG Capeta on Joined Cases C-29/22 and C-44/22 *KS-KD v Council and Others* and *European Commission and Others v KS-KD*, ECLI:EU:C:2023:901. See also the commentary by A. Hamonic in this publication.

Their appeal was deemed inadmissible by the EU General Court, which declared that it lacked jurisdiction on two occasions in 2017 and 2021.[40]

The Court of Justice partially quashed the judgment. It recognised the principle that 'the basic principles of the EU legal order also apply in the context' of the Common Foreign and Security Policy (CFSP). This is included in the Treaty. But within the limits of the exceptions to jurisdiction recognised by the Treaty. It also extends jurisdiction to acts of day-to-day management of a CSDP mission that cannot be linked 'directly to the political or strategic choices made within the framework of the CFSP'. This is the case when 'the lack of adequate staff', 'whether or not to make the acts and omissions of that mission subject to a review mechanism' set up by the mission, or for the granting of legal aid to complainants before this same control committee are at issue. The case will have to be reheard by the General Court of the EU on both the admissibility of the action and on its merits.[41]

II. EXCEPTIONS TO THE PRINCIPLE OF EXCLUSION FROM THE JURISDICTION OF THE CJEU IN THE FIELD OF CFSP/CSDP

The second paragraph of Article 275 TFEU provides for two sets of exceptions to the principle of exclusion from the jurisdiction of the CJEU in the field of the CFSP/CSDP: on the one hand, the review of compliance with Article 40 TEU (Section A) and, on the other hand, the review of decisions providing for restrictive measures against natural or legal persons (Section B).

A. THE COURT OF JUSTICE'S REVIEW OF COMPLIANCE WITH ARTICLE 40 TEU

Please refer to the general commentary on Articles 23 to 40 TEU, by Catherine Schneider, in this publication.

40 Case T-771/20, *KS-KD v Council of the EU, European Commission and EEAS.*

41 Case C-29/22, *KS-KD v Council of the EU, European Commission and EEAS*, ECLI:EU:C:2024:725.

B. REVIEW OF DECISIONS PROVIDING FOR RESTRICTIVE MEASURES AGAINST NATURAL OR LEGAL PERSONS

The second exception to the Court's lack of jurisdiction in CFSP/CSDP matters provided for in the second paragraph of Article 275 TFEU concerns the review of the legality of restrictive measures, also known as 'sanctions', against third countries, entities or individuals.

The Court did not wait for the Treaty of Lisbon to recognise its jurisdiction to review restrictive measures, as the drama of the *Kadi* saga perfectly illustrated.[42] However, the wording of the Treaty expressly conferring this jurisdiction on the Court has not failed to raise questions.

The first of these relates to the reference in the second paragraph of Article 275 TFEU to actions 'brought in accordance with the conditions laid down in the fourth paragraph of Article 263' TFEU. Literally interpreted, this might have suggested that it was limited to actions for annulment. Such an interpretation 'of the exception to the exception' would obviously have reduced the jurisdiction of the Court of Justice. It was rejected by the Court in the *Rosneft* case,[43] in which the Court accepted jurisdiction to hear and determine a reference for a preliminary ruling on the validity of a CFSP decision and its implementing regulation relating to restrictive economic and financial measures against Russia, following the annexation of Crimea. The question of law thus put to the Court was different from that which it had already ruled on in the *Peftiev* case, where it had accepted jurisdiction to give a preliminary ruling on the interpretation of a regulation implementing a decision imposing targeted sanctions on Belarus.[44] Relying on the necessary restrictive interpretation of the rule of general jurisdiction in Article 19 TEU of the provisions on jurisdictional immunity of the CFSP, the Court held that to review the legality of the sanctions provided for in Article 24 TEU is not

---

42 Joined Cases C-402/05 P and C-415/05 P, *Kadi and Al Barakaat International Foundation v Council and Commission*, ECLI:EU:C:2008:461 and Joined Cases C-584/10 P, C-593/10 P and C-595/10 P, *Kadi II*, ECLI:EU:C:2013:518.

43 Case C-72/15, *Rosneft*, ECLI:EU:C:2017:236, on a question referred for a preliminary ruling to assess the validity of Council Decision 2014/512/CFSP of 31 July 2014 concerning restriction measures in view of Russia's actions destabilising the situation in Ukraine (export bans and restrictions on access to the European capital market for certain operators in those sectors, including Rosneft, a company about 70% owned by the Russian State). This Decision is the founding act of the legal regime of economic and financial sanctions against Russia for its destabilising actions and the situation in Ukraine, which must be distinguished from the legal regime of targeted sanctions of Council Decision 2014/145/CSFP of 17 March 2014 concerning restrictive measures in respect of actions undermining or threatening the territorial integrity, sovereignty and independence of Ukraine (entry bans on the territory of the Union and freezing of assets and economic resources in response to actions undermining the territorial integrity, independence and sovereignty of Ukraine and which do not concern only Russian personalities).

44 Case C-314/13, *Peftiev and Others*, ECLI:EU:C:2014:1645.

limited to actions for annulment alone, but also includes preliminary rulings on validity. Like such actions, this validity constitutes a means of reviewing the legality of acts by the EU institutions.

Thus, despite the jurisdictional immunity granted to the CFSP, the Court extended to the latter the scope of its Foto-Frost case law,[45] in which it had extended 'the review of legality' to the preliminary question on validity.

Lastly, and in addition to the development of preliminary rulings in cases relating to the CFSP, sanctions and CSDP operations and missions, it is also the action for annulment of Article 263(4) TFEU expressly referred to by the exception in Article 275(2) TFEU in favour of sanctions that has enabled the Court to 'consolidate' its jurisdiction.

This is the contribution of the important decision in *Venezuela v Council*,[46] in which the Court of its own volition raised the question 'whether a third State, [...] which cannot bring an action on the basis of the second paragraph of Article 263 TFEU, may be regarded as a '*legal person*' within the meaning of the fourth paragraph of that article'. The Court held that this was indeed the case, extending to the specific case of the third State its rejection of the restrictive interpretation of the concept of legal person developed in previous case law.[47] To do so, in the specific context of the interpretation of Article 263(4) TFEU, the Court explicitly relied on 'the contextual and teleological interpretation' in relation to the existence of effective judicial control and the rule of law resulting from Article 2 TEU and Articles 21 and 23 TEU and whose emblematic case law it recalls in other areas of its controls concerning both CSDP missions,[48] and restrictive measures.[49]

The Court's lack of jurisdiction over the CFSP has been extended to include actions for compensation for damage suffered as a result of restrictive measures following their annulment. The Court's jurisdiction, which had already been recognised for claims relating to damage suffered as a result of such measures provided for in a regulation,[50] has now been further extended to claims for compensation relating to damage suffered, this time, as a result of a CFSP decision, a different question from that raised in *Safa Nicu Sepahan*

---

[45] Case C-314/85, *Foto-Frost v Hauptzollamt Lübeck-Ost*, ECLI:EU:C:1987:452.

[46] Case C-872/19 P, *Venezuela v Council (brought by a third State)*, ECLI:EU:C:2021:507.

[47] See in particular the broad interpretation in favour of the regional or local entities of a Member State (Case C-444/08 P, *Região autonoma dos Açores v Council*, ECLI:EU:C:2009:733) or in favour of organisations which do not have legal personality but which exist sufficiently to be the subject of restrictive measures, which implies, from the point of view of consistency and justice, that they also exist sufficiently to challenge them before the courts (Case C-229/05 P, *PKK and KNK v Council*, ECLI:EU:C:2007:32).

[48] Case C-455/14 P, *H v Council and Others*, ECLI:EU:2016:569.

[49] See the above-mentioned judgments in the *Rosneft* and *Bank Refah Karagan* cases. See also, in the context of the war in Ukraine unleashed by Russia in February 2022: Case T-233/22, *Islentyeva v Council*, ECLI:EU:T:2023:828, which dismissed the action for annulment of a flight ban on Russian-controlled aircraft on the grounds that the applicant had not been directly affected.

[50] Case C-45/15 P, *Safa Nicu Sepahan v Council*, ECLI:EU:C:2017:402.

v Council.[51] This is the contribution of the judgment on appeal in *Bank Refah Kargaran v Council*,[52] in which the Court affirmed the need to assess it in the light of jurisdictional protection as a whole, following a veritable course on jurisdictional immunity of the CFSP and also on the action for damages, while recalling its autonomous nature in the system of remedies. It thus deduced that the necessary consistency of the system of judicial protection, with a view to avoiding a gap in the latter, should imply its jurisdiction to rule on actions for damages in respect of restrictive measures based on a CFSP/CFSP decision. Such considerations prevail over the absence of an express reference in Article 275 TFEU to the Court's jurisdiction to rule on the damage allegedly suffered as a result of restrictive measures provided for in CFSP decisions.[53] In addition, the Court emphasises the place of the action for damages in the overall system of judicial protection of individuals established by the Treaties, in that it contributes to the effectiveness of that protection.[54] Thus, the Court of Justice found that the General Court erred in law by holding (in the judgment under appeal)[55] that an action for damages seeking compensation for the loss allegedly suffered by a natural or legal person as a result of restrictive measures provided for in CFSP decisions fell outside its jurisdiction.[56]

Finally, in the *Neves 77 SRL* judgment, delivered by the Grand Chamber on 10 September 2024,[57] the Court of Justice considered that it has jurisdiction to interpret a general measure of a CFSP decision which should have been implemented in a regulation where that general measure serves as the basis for a national restrictive measure imposed on a natural or legal person.

The Court points out that 'as regards measures adopted on the basis of provisions relating to the CFSP, it is the individual nature of those measures which, in accordance with the second paragraph of Article 275 TFEU, permits access to the Courts of the European Union'.[58] Thus, a measure whose scope is defined by reference not to identified natural or legal persons but to objective criteria does not fall within the restrictive measures referred to in the second paragraph of Article 275 TFEU. However, the Court ensured that the Council, by not adopting the 'necessary measures' following a CFSP decision, as it is required

---

51 Ibid.

52 Case C-134/19 P, ECLI:EU:C:2020:793.

53 Ibid., para. 31.

54 Ibid., para. 34.

55 Case T-552/15, *Bank Refah Kargaran v Council*, ECLI:EU:T:2018:897, para. 30. The subject-matter of the action was a claim under Article 268 TFEU for compensation for the damage it allegedly suffered as a result of the adoption of restrictive measures against it, in the context of the war in Ukraine unleashed by Russia in February 2022.

56 The appeal was nevertheless dismissed because the error of law found had no impact on the operative part of the contested judgment, insofar as none of the grounds of appeal had led to the General Court's assessment of the merits of the claim for damages being overturned.

57 Case C-351/22, *Neves Solutions SRL*, ECLI:EU:C:2024:723.

58 Para. 37.

to do under Article 275 TFEU,[59] cannot circumvent the jurisdiction conferred on the Court by the Treaties with a view to ensuring the judicial protection of third parties. Consequently, 'the possibility provided for by the Treaties of making a reference to the Court for a preliminary ruling regarding a regulation adopted on the basis of Article 215(1) TFEU must be available in respect of all the provisions that the Council should have included in such a regulation'.

In the light of the developments described in the case law, it may be concluded that the principle of exclusion of the jurisdiction of the Union courts in the field of the CFSP is gradually and seriously limited in scope, to the benefit of greater consistency of jurisdictional protection within the Union.[60]

Update by Athanase Popov, 15 November 2025

In *Commission v KS and Others*, the Court considered that it has jurisdiction over CFSP (including CSDP) matters on certain occasions in a given case – presumably through the full range of existing in EU legal remedies – before the European Court of Human Rights rules on the same subject matter. The extent to which the Court's jurisdiction in CFSP matters is limited is now defined, it is excluded when the case is 'related to political or strategic issues concerning the definition and implementation of the CFSP'. There is no distinction as to the type of remedy: although *Commission v KS and Others* was about an action for damages, the scope of the Court's jurisdiction is merely defined *ratione materiae* also about actions for annulment and preliminary references on both interpretation and validity.

The final determination by the General Court regrettably led to the action for damages being dismissed due to a finding of non-attributability of the alleged omissions by EULEX Kosovo. In so doing, the General Court recalled that it does not have jurisdiction to rule on an action for damages seeking compensation for damage resulting from the alleged 'inadequacy of the resources' allocated to the EULEX Kosovo mission, in so far as the decisions taken in that regard are directly related to the political or strategic choices made in the framework of the CFSP.[61] The General Court would have had jurisdiction in relation to the 'lack of appropriate personnel' chosen with the

[59] For the Court, 'it is apparent from the clear wording of Article 215(1) TFEU, particularly the use of 'shall adopt', distinct from the terms 'may adopt' used in paragraph 2 of that article, that it falls to the Council to adopt the necessary measures referred to in paragraph 1 of that article to give effect to a CFSP decision setting out the European Union's position regarding the interruption or reduction of economic and financial relations with a third country. That institution therefore has, in the situation covered by that paragraph, circumscribed powers', para. 46.

[60] See I. Bosse-Platière, 'Le juge de l'Union, artisan de la cohérence du système de contrôle juridictionnel au sein de l'Union européenne, y compris en matière de PESC', *RTDE*, 2017, pp. 555–563.

[61] Case T-771/20 RENV, *KS and KD v Council and Others*, ECLI:EU:T:2025:923, para. 70.

resources allocated to EULEX Kosovo. Although the CSDP mission lacked appropriate personnel, the alleged failures in its 'day-to-day management' cannot be attributed to the Council, the Commission and the EEAS, in so far as they come within the implementation of the executive mandate of that mission and, as such, give rise to the exclusive responsibility of that mission, in accordance with the provisions of Article 16(5) of the Joint Action, as amended by Decision 2014/349.[62] Arguably (although it seems unlikely), if the defendant had been properly chosen, it would have been possible to obtain compensation for the lack of appropriate personnel without challenging the adequacy of the resources allocated to the CSDP mission.[63]
When applying the criteria set out in *Commission v KS and Others* on appeal to determine the scope of jurisdiction about a preliminary reference on interpretation, the Court reached a different conclusion in *[Tartisai]* from that reached by the General Court in the final determination of the case in *Commission v KS and Others*. Both rulings (the order and the judgment) refer to the same statement of principle, but in a different factual context in the sense that the EUPOL Afghanistan CSDP mission was staffed with seconded national and EU experts rather than with ad hoc EU staff, as was the case with EULEX Kosovo. Thus, each Member State or EU institution had to bear the costs related to any of the staff seconded by it, while all staff had to carry out their duties and act in the interests of the [EUPOL Afghanistan] mission.[64] The dispute in the main proceedings in *[Tartisai]* arose out of a difficulty with the interpretation of Article 7(3) of Council Decision 2010/279/CFSP, providing that: 'Each Member State or EU institution shall bear the costs related to any of the staff seconded by it, including travel expenses to and from the place of deployment, salaries, medical coverage, and allowances, other than applicable per diems as well as hardship and risk allowances.' The Court considered that it had jurisdiction to interpret that provision on the basis of the principle set out in *Commission v KS and Others* on appeal, as Article 7(3) of Decision 2010/279 concerns expenditure relating to staff seconded in the context of the EUPOL Afghanistan mission, with the result that that provision 'is not directly related to the political or strategic choices made by the institutions, bodies, offices and agencies of the European Union in the context of the CFSP'.[65]

62 Ibid., paras. 52 and 72.

63 See S. Notario, 'The Evolutionary Role of the Court of Justice in Defence Matters: Administrative or not Administrative, that is the Question', *EU Law Live*, 06/10/2025, https://eulawlive.com/op-ed-the-evolutionary-role-of-the-court-of-justice-in-defence-matters-administrative-or-not-administrative-that-is-the-question.

64 Article 7(3) and 7(5) of Council Decision 2010/279/CFSP of 18 May 2010 on the European Union Police Mission in Afghanistan (EUPOL AFGHANISTAN), [2010] *OJ* L123/4.

65 Case C-238/24, *[Tartisai]*, ECLI:EU:C:2025:258, para. 25.

Absent the reliance on *Commission v KS and Others* on appeal, the Court would have considered itself compelled to follow the prior case-law, according to which the derogatory limitation, on the Court of Justice 's jurisdiction (arising from the final sentence of the second subparagraph of Article 24(1) TEU and the first paragraph of Article 275 TFEU), cannot be construed so widely as to exclude judicial control over 'acts of staff management' adopted in respect of 'staff members seconded by the Member States' for the operational needs of missions such as EUPOL Afghanistan. In any event, EU judicial review indisputably applies to such acts where they concern staff members seconded by the EU institutions.[66]

Notwithstanding the fact that Article 7(3) of Council Decision 2010/279/CFSP is not an 'act of staff management', the fact remains that, on the same basis, it concerns staff members seconded *by the Member States* and *by the EU institutions* respectively as regards the defrayal of that expenditure. The Court held that it had jurisdiction to interpret this provision, in order to ensure a uniform interpretation of the provision and to avoid a situation in which decisions concerning staff seconded *by the Member States* are irreconcilable with those made by the EU judiciary concerning staff seconded *by the EU institutions*.[67]

[66] See, to that effect, Case C-455/14 P, *H v Council and Others*, ECLI:EU:C:2016:569, para. 55, referred to in *[Tartisai]*, ibid., para. 23.

[67] Case C-238/24, *[Tartisai]*, ECLI:EU:C:2025:258, para. 26.

ARTICLES 308 AND 309 TFEU: THE EUROPEAN INVESTMENT BANK AT THE SERVICE OF THE DEFENCE INDUSTRY?

Stéphane Rodrigues
Senior Lecturer at the Université Paris 1 Panthéon-Sorbonne
Member of the Sorbonne Institute for Research in International and European Law (IREDIES-EA 4536)
Member of the Brussels Bar

Article 308

The European Investment Bank shall have legal personality.

The members of the European Investment Bank shall be the Member States.

The Statute of the European Investment Bank is laid down in a Protocol annexed to the Treaties. The Council acting unanimously in accordance with a special legislative procedure, at the request of the European Investment Bank and after consulting the European Parliament and the Commission, or on a proposal from the Commission and after consulting the European Parliament and the European Investment Bank, may amend the Statute of the Bank.

Article 309

The task of the European Investment Bank shall be to contribute, by having recourse to the capital market and utilising its own resources, to the balanced and steady development of the internal market in the interest of the Union. For this purpose the Bank shall, operating on a non-profitmaking basis, grant loans and give guarantees which facilitate the financing of the following projects in all sectors of the economy:

a) projects for developing less-developed regions;

> b) projects for modernising or converting undertakings or for developing fresh activities called for by the establishment or functioning of the internal market, where these projects are of such a size or nature that they cannot be entirely financed by the various means available in the individual Member States;
>
> c) projects of common interest to several Member States which are of such a size or nature that they cannot be entirely financed by the various means available in the individual Member State.
>
> In carrying out its task, the Bank shall facilitate the financing of investment programmes in conjunction with assistance from the Structural Funds and other Union Financial Instruments.

Articles 308 and 309 TFEU make up Chapter 4 of the Treaty and are devoted to the European Investment Bank (hereinafter EIB) in Title I on institutional provisions of Part Five of the TFEU. Established by the 1957 Treaty of Rome, the EIB is not as such an 'institution' of the EU,[1] but according to the case law of the Court of Justice, 'a Community institution established and with legal personality by the Treaty', which is intended 'to contribute to the attainment of the objectives of the Community and therefore, by virtue of the Treaty, forms part of the Community framework'.[2] It has been described as an 'atypical, *sui generis* institution.[3] And it describes itself as 'the lending arm of the European Union'.[4]

In addition to Articles 308 and 309 of the TFEU, reference should also be made to Protocol No 5 annexed to the TEU and TFEU, on the EIB's Statute,[5] which states that the EIB is an independent public bank, even though its capital (approximately EUR 250 billion) is subscribed by the Member States.[6] It also has a reserve fund of at least 10% of its capital.

There is also a reference to Protocol No. 28 on economic, social and territorial cohesion, which emphasises the EIB's contribution to this EU policy.[7]

After outlining the EIB's mandate and means of action (Section I), this chapter examines the extent to which it can support the defence industry (Section II).

---

1 It is not included in the list of 'EU institutions' in Article 13 of the TEU.

2 See Case 85/86, *Commission v EIB*, ECLI:EU:C:1988:110, para. 29.

3 F. Peraldi Leneuf, 'Banque européenne d'investissement', *JurisClasseur Europe Traité*, fasc. 242, 2012, first key point.

4 See its public website: https://www.eib.org/en/about/index.htm (consulted on 31 May 2025).

5 See also the EIB's Rules of Procedure of 4 December 1958, which have been amended several times since then.

6 France's share is 16.3%.

7 See the commentary on Article 174 TFEU by S. Rodrigues in this publication.

I. THE EIB'S MANDATE AND MEANS OF ACTION

Article 309 TFEU mandates the EIB to 'contribute, by having recourse to the capital market and utilising its own resources, to the balanced and steady development of the internal market in the interest of the Union'. To this end, like any banking institution, the EIB mainly mobilises two types of financing: repayable loans and bank guarantees. It also makes equity investments (venture capital) and provides advisory services through one of its subsidiaries, the European Investment Fund (EIF).[8] Unlike a private bank, however, the EIB is not profit-oriented.

Three categories of project are eligible for EIB support.[9] They are defined relatively broadly by Article 309 TFEU: firstly, projects 'for developing less-developed regions'; secondly, projects for modernising or converting undertakings or for developing new activities brought about by the internal market which, by their scale or nature, cannot be entirely covered by the various means of financing available in each of the Member States; and lastly, 'projects of common interest to several Member States' which, again by their scale or nature, cannot be entirely covered by the various means of financing available in each of the Member States.

Total EIB financing has reached €1,000 billion since 1959, including €88.8 billion in 2024, including loans to non-EU countries such as Ukraine.[10]

II. THE EIB CALLED UPON TO HELP THE EUROPEAN DEFENCE INDUSTRY

The EIB is regularly called upon to provide support, particularly in times of crisis. For example, the aforementioned EIF was set up in 1994, following a call from the Edinburgh European Council (1992) as part of the European Growth Initiative. This is also how, in December 2014, the European Council called for 'the setting up a European Fund for Strategic Investments (EFSI) in the EIB

---

8 The EIF has been operational since 1994, and is 60% owned by the EIB. In 2023, NATO set up a multi-sovereign venture capital fund, the NATO Innovation Fund (NIF). Twenty-three NATO member states are sponsors. France is not one of them (and neither is the United States), officially because it is already involved in two specialised funds operated by BPI France: Definvest (dedicated to strategic SMEs) and the Defence Innovation Fund (dedicated to dual technologies).

9 See also the eligibility criteria in Article 18 of the EIB's Statute.

10 More than €8 billion since 2007 and a dedicated action, known as 'EU for Ukraine (EU4U)', since March 2023, in response to the war launched by Russia in February 2022.

Group with the view to mobilising €315 billion in new investments' by 2017, in response to the financial crisis.[11]

It is hardly surprising, then, that the EIB should be called upon once again to come to the rescue in the context of the crisis triggered by the Russian war in Ukraine. In March 2024, the European Council, stressing the need to 'improve the European defence industry's access to public and private finance', invited the EIB 'to adapt its policy for lending to the defence industry and its current definition of dual-use goods, while safe-guarding its financing capacity'.[12]

This is not the first time such an invitation has been made. The June 2017 European Council meeting conclusions had already suggested that the EIB 'examine further steps with a view to supporting investments in defence research and development activities'.[13] It is true that the Commission had just announced the launch of the European Defence Fund with increased EIB support but only for 'dual-use technologies' and investments 'ancillary' to security and defence activities.[14]

The war in Ukraine then increased the pressure on the EIB. The March 2022 European Council asked for measures to be taken, by the end of 2022, 'to promote and facilitate access to private funding for the defence industry, also by making best use of the possibilities offered by the European Investment Bank... '.[15] In May 2022, European Council asked the Council to examine 'an enhanced role for the European Investment Bank in support of European security and defence, in line with its recent Strategic European Security Initiative'.[16]

Reference was made here to the decision of the EIB's Board of Directors of 10 March 2022 approving an EIB Strategic European Security Initiative (SESI). The stated aim is to strengthen European security and defence by mobilising

---

[11] This led to the creation of the European Strategic Investment Fund (ESIF) managed by the EIB: see Regulation (EU) 2015/1017 of the European Parliament and of the Council of 25 June 2015 on the European Fund for Strategic Investments, the European Investment Advice Hub and the European Investment Project Portal and amending Regulations (EU) No 1291/2013 and (EU) No 1316/2013, [2015] *OJ* L169/1. The target was then raised to €500 billion of investment by 2020. This was even exceeded, with the fund reaching €547 billion, for an EIB contribution of €103 billion. As a result, the InvestEU programme was set up for 2021-2027 (see Regulation (EU) 2021/523 of the European Parliament and of the Council of 24 March 2021 establishing the InvestEU Programme and amending Regulation (EU) 2015/1017, [2021] *OJ* L107/30). On the ESIF and InvestEU: see the commentary on Article 174 TFEU by S. Rodrigues in this publication.

[12] See para. 15(b) of the conclusions adopted by the European Council meeting on 22 March 2024, EUCO 7/24.

[13] The same formula will be used in para. 14 of the Presidency Conclusions of the European Council of 19 October 2017, EUCO 14/17.

[14] See also COM (2017) 295 final of 7 June 2017, pp. 18–19.

[15] See para. 14 of the conclusions adopted by the European Council on 24–25 March, 2022, EUCO 1/22.

[16] See para. 24 of the conclusions adopted by the European Council on 30–31 May 2022, EUCO 21/22.

investment in research, development and innovation (RDI) projects, civil security infrastructure and cutting-edge technologies. A budget of €8 billion is available for 2022-2027.[17] However, the EIB's press release is clear: 'it 'will not change what is eligible for EIB or modify the definition of its excluded sectors' and it 'will not invest in weaponry and the EIB cannot finance investments in core defence', while stating its willingness 'to further strengthen institutional cooperation with the European Commission (DG DEFIS), the EU Space Programme Agency (EUSPA) and the European Defence Agency'.[18]

In May 2023, the Commission attempted to go even further by including a recital in the proposal for a regulation on the establishment of an '*Act in Support* of Ammunition Production' (ASAP); 'While pursuing in full its other economic development and public policy financing missions, including the twin transition and in line with Article 309 TFEU as well as its statute, the European Investment Bank (EIB) should enhance its support to the European defence industry and joint procurement beyond its ongoing support to dual use, where such investments would clearly serve to implement the Strategic Compass priorities'.[19] This wording was finally included in Recital (35) of the final ASAP regulation.[20]

Besides, in their joint communication of 5 March 2024 entitled 'A new European Defence Industrial Strategy: Achieving EU readiness through a responsive and resilient European Defence Industrial Strategy (EDIS), the European Commission and the High Representative for Foreign Affairs and Security Policy invited the EIB 'to adapt defence-related exclusions from the EIB Group's Lending Policies, in line with EU policy priorities and applicable law'.[21] The aim is to enable the EIB to support the production of military equipment and, more generally, the European defence industry, as also requested by the European Parliament in a February 2024 resolution.[22]

---

17 An example of a project supported by the SESI (EIB) is the development and launch of the first two Earth observation satellites in Poland, with a €300 million loan to Bank Gospodarstwa Krajowego. See EIB press release of 20 May 2024: https://www.eib.org/fr/press/all/2024-180-eib-backs-first-polish-satellite-programme-with-loan-to-bank-gospodarstwa-krajowego.

18 EIB, 'EIB approves Strategic European Security Initiative, confirms Ukraine disbursement and backs €543 million business and clean energy investment', press release, 10 March 2022: https://www.eib.org/en/press/all/2022-122-eib-approves-strategic-european-security-initiative-confirms-ukraine-disbursement-and-backs-eur543-million-business-and-clean-energy-investment. Since 2022, the European Defence Agency (EDA) has been hosting the *Hub for EU Defence Innovation* (HEDI).

19 See document COM(2023) 237 final of 3 May 2023, Recital 46.

20 Regulation (EU) 2023/1525 of the European Parliament and of the Council of 20 July 2023 on supporting ammunition production (ASAP), [2023] *OJ* L185/7. On this regulation: see the commentary by E. Bernard in this publication.

21 See p. 26 of JOIN(2024) 10 final.

22 European Parliament resolution of 28 February 2024 on Financial activities of the European Investment Bank – annual report 2023 (2023/2229(INI)).

Lastly, on 21 March 2025, the EIB's Board further expanded EIB Group eligibilities for financing Europe's security and defence industry and infrastructure, to ensure that excluded activities are as limited as possible in scope, in line with the proposals endorsed by EU leaders at the Special European Council on 6 March 2025. Therefore, the SESI will be integrated into a cross-cutting and permanent public policy goal, which will complement the existing public policy goals. There will be no predefined ceiling for financing in this area, which will be determined annually in the EIB Group Operational Plan. The list of areas concerned includes, notably, barracks and storage facilities, land and aerial vehicles, drones and helicopters, radars and satellites, advanced avionics, propulsion and optics, land border protection, military mobility, critical infrastructures, de-mining and de-contamination, space, cybersecurity, anti-jamming technologies, military equipment, seabed infrastructure protection and research.[23]

However, such a development does not seem to be self-evident, given the mandate of the EIB under Article 309 TFEU, namely to contribute to the EU's objective of economic, social and territorial cohesion. The European Economic and Social Committee (EESC) has taken the position that EIB investments can only 'serve non-military purposes'.[24] But the new EDIS strategy goes against this interpretation, pointing out that the defence industry is an integral part of the internal market and that the EIB must help to ensure the balanced and smooth development of the internal market in the interests of the Union.

Be that as it may, there are a number of concrete avenues that could be explored. The first is to make it easier to access and mobilise the SESI. Although €8 billion was available, only €2.2 billion were mobilised by 2022-2023.[25] In a joint letter addressed to the President of the EIB and made public on 17 March 2024, fourteen EU Member States called for the creation of a one-stop SESI.[26]

Expanding EIB military spending also involves developing EIB/Commission cooperation within existing financial instruments such as the European Defence

---

23 See EIB Press release of 21 March 2025: https://www.eib.org/en/press/all/2025-156-eib-steps-up-financing-for-european-security-and-defence-and-critical-raw-materials (consulted on 31 May 2025).

24 See EESC opinion on the 'European Defence Action Plan' of 31 May 2017, [2017] *OJ* C288/62, spec. para. 1.8, p. 62.

25 Examples include the CEGELOG project, launched in February 2022 to renovate and build several thousand homes across France for military and civilian personnel and their families (SISE budget: €484 million), and the SIREN project, named after an Irish company that was awarded €12 million in SISE support in February 2023 to improve its capabilities, particularly in cyber threat intelligence.

26 Available at: https://vnk.fi/documents/10616/334517/Joint+EU+leaders+letter+to+EIB+17+March+2024.pdf/50e3a2d7-f9c6-18e5-8f4a-180ade0ffb99?t=1710751672269 (accessed on 24 March 2024).

Fund (EDF).[27] An example of this was the launch in January 2024 of the *Defence Equity Facility* (DEF) which is co-managed by the Commission (participation of €100 million from the EDF) and the EIB (participation of €75 million from the EIF). The aim is to support private equity and venture capital funds over the period 2024-2027 with strategies covering technologies relevant to defence. The hoped-for leverage effect is to mobilise a total of €500 million.[28] A first step in this direction has been taken with the announcement by EIF of its first investment in defence-focused ventures in Europe, i.e. a €40 million investment in Keen's European Defence and Security Tech Fund, which aims to support companies that are pioneering solutions in areas such as information superiority, cyber defence, robotics, AI and autonomous systems, and space technologies such as securing satellite communications, satellite image analysis and defence of space assets. This initiative will be pan-European, since entities from the United Kingdom, Turkey and Norway will be involved.[29]

Finally, the EDIS strategy refers to the possibility of reaching an agreement between the Commission and the EIB on a common definition of 'dual-use technologies' in order to broaden their scope and adapt lending policy accordingly, and to invite all public financial players in the Member States to do likewise.[30]

As a result of these various political guidelines and incentives, on 12 April 2024 the President of the EIB presented an action plan to support the defence industry to the Council of Finance Ministers, which approved it.[31] Agreed to by the EIB's Board of Directors on 8 May 2024,[32] this plan includes the waiving of the criterion requiring dual-use projects to derive more than 50% of their expected revenues from civilian applications. These include reconnaissance, surveillance, spectrum protection and control, decontamination, R&D, equipment, military mobility, border control and the protection of other critical infrastructures, as well as drones.

---

27 Regulation (EU) 2021/697 of the European Parliament and of the Council of 29 April 2021 establishing the European Defence Fund and repealing Regulation (EU) 2018/1092, [2021] *OJ* L170/149177. On this regulation: see the commentary by S. Rodrigues in this volume.

28 The DEF Facility is part of a more general framework, the *EU Defence Innovation Scheme* (EUDIS) of the EDF, with a budget of €2 billion.

29 See EIF Press release of 22 May 2025: https://www.eif.org/InvestEU/news/2025/eif-announces-eur40-million-investment-in-keen-venture-partners-european-defence-and-security-tech-fund-under-investeu.htm (consulted on 31 May 2025).

30 See p. 26 of JOIN(2024) 10 final.

31 See the EIB press release of 12 April 2024: https://www.eib.org/fr/press/all/2024-143-eu-finance-ministers-set-in-motion-eib-group-action-plan-to-further-step-up-support-for-europe-s-security-and-defence-industry (consulted on 14 April 2024).

32 See the EIB press release of 8 May 2024: https://www.eib.org/fr/press/all/2024-174-eib-board-of-directors-steps-up-support-for-europe-s-security-and-defence-industry-and-approves-eur-4-5-billion-in-other-financing.

In addition, the rules governing the financing of SMEs in the security and defence sector will be revised to introduce dedicated credit lines, particularly for innovative start-ups in dual technologies.[33] Finally, in terms of administrative cooperation and simplification, the EIB Group is opening a one-stop security and defence shop and intends to update its memorandum of understanding with the European Defence Agency.

***

By way of conclusion, the question arises as to whether, beyond the announcement effect, the EIB is ready to take the plunge towards what might almost be called a change in corporate culture. The gap between the EIB's claim to become the 'European Climate Bank' from 2019 onwards, having mobilised and recruited staff for this cause,[34] and the prospect of becoming the 'European Defence Bank', might indeed seem wide, since in 2024, the EIB's support to security and defence projects was around €1 billion, out of a total of €88.8 billion in new financing. This trend was confirmed on 20 June 2025 by the EIB Board of Governors which endorsed a plan to increase new financing to a record €100 billion in 2025, with a revised ceiling for European security and defence of 3.5% out of this total.[35]

The debate on this new EIB endorsement is not unrelated to that on the classification of economic activities as sustainable for access to finance (the so-called taxonomy regulation).[36] It may be recalled in this respect that in

---

33 A first application of these new rules was announced by the EIB on 11 June 2025 with an increase of intermediated loans and guarantees available for SMEs in the defence sector to €3 billion from €1 billion and with the first agreement with Deutsche Bank to enable €1 billion financing for defence research, as well as military and police infrastructure. See EIB press release: https://www.eib.org/en/press/all/2025-236-eib-triples-financing-for-banks-to-provide-liquidity-to-smes-in-the-supply-chain-of-europe-s-defence-industry-signs-first-deal-with-deutsche-bank#:~:text=All%20releases-,EIB%20triples%20financing%20for%20banks%20to%20provide%20liquidity%20to%20SMEs,first%20deal%20with%20Deutsche%20Bank&text=EIB%20increases%20intermediated%20loans%20and,billion%20from%20%E2%82%AC1%20billion (consulted on 15 June 2025).

34 On 14 November 2019, the EIB's Board of Directors adopted a new energy lending policy and revised upwards its ambitions regarding climate action and environmental sustainability. This was followed by the adoption of a 'Roadmap for the EIB Group in its role as climate bank for the period 2021-2025', https://www.eib.org/fr/projects/topics/climate-action/cbr (accessed on 28 March 2024).

35 See EIB Press Release of 20 June 2025: https://www.eib.org/en/press/all/2025-247-eib-group-increases-2025-financing-ceiling-to-record-eur100-billion-to-step-up-investments-in-security-and-defence-energy-grids-and-europe-s-tech-leadership [accessed on 21 June 2025]. On the same day, the EIB approved a loan of €540 million for the Lithuanian military base in Rūdninkai to strengthen NATO's defence capabilities.

36 See Regulation (EU) 2020/852 of the European Parliament and of the Council of 18 June 2020 on the establishment of a framework for sustainable investment and amending Regulation (EU) 2019/2088, [2020] *OJ* L198/13. On its application to the defence industry: M. Bol, *La production d'armes comme ' activité socialement nuisible ': les limites d'une taxonomie sociale*

its 'contribution' to European defence 2022, the Commission stressed the importance of 'ensur[ing] that other horizontal policies, such as initiatives on sustainable finance, remain consistent with the European Union efforts to facilitate the European defence industry's sufficient access to finance and investment'.[37] And in one of its communications interpreting the EU taxonomy, the Commission acknowledges 'the need to ensure access to finance and investment including from the private sector for all strategic sectors, in particular the defence industry, which contributes to European citizens' security'.[38] The Council itself was keen to underscore that 'the sustainable finance framework does not impede financing the defence sector' and that 'the defence industry can also bring substantial economic benefits and jobs and stimulate innovation'.[39] It remains to be seen whether this approach will be shared by the EIB in its financing practice over the long term.

---

européenne mal engagée, Note d'analyse du Groupe de recherche et d'information sur la paix et la sécurité (GRIP), August 2023; A. Férey and L. de Roucy Rochegonde, '*Don't bank on the bombs'. L'industrie de défense face aux nouvelles normes européennes*, Briefings, Centre des études de sécurité, Institut français des relations internationales (IFRI), September 2022 and N. Lenoir, 'Industries et marché de l'armement contre le changement climatique', *Revue Défense Nationale*, no. 854, 2022, pp. 33–38.

37 Commission Communication COM(2022) 60 final of 15 February 2022, p. 6. This passage is said to have been inspired by France: see the reply from the Minister for Defence to a parliamentary question (No. 05887) on 'European taxonomy and the defence industry' (*JORF*, Sénat, 28 September 2023, p. 5613).

38 Commission Notice on the interpretation and implementation of certain legal provisions of the EU Taxonomy Climate Delegated Act establishing technical screening criteria for economic activities that contribute substantially to climate change mitigation or climate change adaptation and do no significant harm to other environmental objective, [2023] *OJ* C2023/6756, especially Section 11.

39 Council conclusions of 27 May 2024 on EU security and defence, document 9225/24, which also recall 'the invite of the European Council Conclusions of March 2024 to adapt its policy for lending to the defence industry and its current definition of dual-use goods, while safeguarding its financing capacity'.

Postscript December 2025

On 16 October 2025, in their joint communication entitled 'Preserving Peace – Defence Readiness Roadmap 2030',[40] the European Commission and the High Representative announced the creation, with EIB/EIF, of an up to 1 billion Fund of funds (equity) supporting the fast growth of defence-related scale-ups and defence-related projects, by first quarter of 2026. This has been confirmed by the Commission in its communication of 19 November 2025, on an EU Defence Industry Transformation Roadmap: Unleashing Disruptive Innovation for Defence Readiness – COM(2025) 845 final.

On 23 October 2025, the European Council welcomed the efforts made by the EIB 'to step up, simplify and accelerate its support for European security and defence capabilities' and has encouraged the EIB Group, one more time, 'to further explore ways to finance industries and companies, and help start-ups to scale up in the security and defence sector in Europe'.[41]

On 30 December 2025, the Commission has published a Notice on the application of the sustainable finance framework and the Corporate Sustainability Due Diligence Directive to the defence sector (see OJ C/2025/4950).

[40] JOIN(2025) 27 final.

[41] Conclusions of the European Council of 23 October 2025, point 25.

ARTICLES 346, 347 AND 348 TFEU: SAFEGUARD CLAUSES FOR THE BENEFIT OF MEMBER STATES' SECURITY, THE APPLICATION OF WHICH IS ONLY RELATIVELY REGULATED

Stéphane RODRIGUES[1]
Senior Lecturer at the Université Paris 1 Panthéon-Sorbonne
Member of the Sorbonn\e Institute for Research in International and European Law (IREDIES-EA 4536)
Member of the Brussels Bar

Article 346

1. The provisions of the Treaties shall not preclude the application of the following rules:

a) no Member State shall be obliged to supply information the disclosure of which it considers contrary to the essential interests of its security,

b) any Member State may take such measures as it considers necessary for the protection of the essential interests of its security which are connected with the production of or trade in arms, munitions and war material; such measures shall not adversely affect the conditions of competition in the internal market regarding products which are not intended for specifically military purposes.

---

1 Commentary based on the translated, amended and updated version of: S. RODRIGUES, 'Articles 346, 347 and 348 of the treaty on the functioning of the European Union', in J. BLANKE and R. BÖTTNER (eds.), *The Treaty on the Functioning of the European Union*, vol. IV, Springer, forthcoming 2026.

2. The Council may, acting unanimously on a proposal from the Commission, make changes to the list, which it drew up on 15 April 1958, of products to which the provisions of paragraph 1(b) apply.

Article 347

Member States shall consult each other with a view to taking together the steps needed to prevent the functioning of the internal market being affected by measures which a Member State may be called upon to take in the event of serious internal disturbances affecting the maintenance of law and order, in the event of war, serious international tension constituting a threat of war, or in order to carry out obligations it has accepted for the purpose of maintaining peace and international security.

Article 348

If measures taken in the circumstances referred to in Articles 346 and 347 have the effect of distorting the conditions of competition in the internal market, the Commission shall, together with the State concerned, examine how these measures can be adjusted to the rules laid down in the Treaties.

By way of derogation from the procedure laid down in Articles 258 and 259, the Commission or any Member State may bring the matter directly before the Court of Justice if it considers that another Member State is making improper use of the powers provided for in Articles 346 and 347. The Court of Justice shall give its ruling in camera.

Articles 346, 347 and 348 are all in the seventh and final part of the TFEU. They are part of the general and final provisions of the Treaty and are three interrelated provisions. While Article 346 TFEU corresponds to a safeguard clause which may be invoked, under certain conditions, by Member States failing to comply with the rules of the Treaty in circumstances challenging their essential security interests (Section I), Article 347 TFEU provides for a consultation procedure between Member States in the event of crisis situations, also disrupting their security (Section II). The use of these two provisions is subject to special scrutiny by the Commission and the Court of Justice under Article 348 TFEU (Section III).

I. THE SAFEGUARD CLAUSE OF ARTICLE 346 TFEU

Article 346 TFEU allows derogations from the rules of the Treaty in the name of protecting national security within the Member States (Section A). It applies to two distinct cases (Section B), for which strict conditions for implementation are defined (Section C).

A. GENESIS AND OBJECTIVES OF ARTICLE 346 TFEU

The safeguard clause, referred to by some authors as the 'security reserve'[2] or the 'defence exception',[3] introduced by Article 346 TFEU has its origins in the 1957 Treaty of Rome as Article 223 of the EEC Treaty, which subsequently became Article 296 of the EC Treaty.[4] In its current wording following the Treaty of Lisbon (2007), Article 346 TFEU results 'taking a political and subjective point of view [...] from the reluctance of some Member States to pursue European integration, for both strategic and economic reasons'.[5] From a more legal point of view, there is a clear link with Article 4.2 TEU, inserted by the Treaty of Lisbon, according to which the Union 'shall respect their essential State functions, including ensuring the territorial integrity of the State, maintaining law and order and safeguarding national security...' and according to which 'national security remains the sole responsibility of each Member State'.

As Advocate General Szpunar has pointed out, that link was confirmed by the explanatory note to Article 52 of the Charter of Fundamental Rights of the European Union (hereinafter 'the Charter' or 'the CFREU'), according to which the reference in that Article to 'objectives of general interest recognised by the Union'. These objectives 'cover, in addition to the objectives of the European Union listed in Article 3 TEU, the interests of Member States which the European Union is bound to respect'.[6]

---

2 P. Gilsdorf, 'Les réserves de sécurité du traité CEE, à la lumière du traité sur l'Union européenne', *Revue du Marché commun*, 1994, pp. 17–25, spec. p. 17.

3 E. Simon, *Rôles et fonctions du droit de l'Union européenne dans l'intégration des politiques d'acquisition d'armement*, PhD thesis, Paris, Université Paris 1 Panthéon-Sorbonne, defended on 13 July 2017, supervised by V. de Beaufort and S. Rodrigues, spec. pp. 137–155. The author evokes the 'defence exceptions' by referring to both Article 346 TFEU (qualified as a 'principal' defence exception) and Article 347 TFEU.

4 It should be noted that the Treaty establishing the European Atomic Energy Community (EAEC, Euratom) contains a similar provision, albeit worded differently, in Article 84: 'The safeguards [of security for which the Commission is responsible within the scope of the Treaty] may not extend to materials intended to meet defence requirements which are in the course of being specially processed for this purpose or which, after being processed, are, in accordance with an operational plan, placed or stored in a military establishment'. See A. Popov's commentary on the Euratom Treaty in this publication.

5 On this meaning, see N.B. Bernard, 'La procédure de remplacement des F-16: entre transparence et opacité', *Revue belge de droit constitutionnel*, 2019, pp. 161–200, spec. p. 184.

6 See Opinion AG Szpunar, 25 October 2018, in Case C-469/17, *Funke Medien NRW*, ECLI:EU:C:2018:870, para. 48 (see Case C-469/17, *Funke Medien NRW GmbH v Bundesrepublik Deutschland*, ECLI:EU:C:2019:623).

There have been two notable developments on the part of the Union's co-legislators: firstly, the tendency to place the protection of the essential security interests of the Member States and those of the EU on the same footing;[7] and, secondly, to associate these essential security interests with those of defence, more generally.[8]

In so doing, these approaches are consistent with the case law of the Court of Justice, according to which Article 346 TFEU is 'intended to preserve the freedom of action of the Member States in certain matters affecting national defence and security'.[9] Much more recently, the Court added that this objective of preserving national security 'corresponds to the primary interest in protecting the essential functions of the State and the fundamental interests of society through the prevention and punishment of activities capable of seriously destabilising the fundamental constitutional, political, economic or social structures of a country and, in particular, of directly threatening society, the population or the State itself, such as terrorist activities'.[10]

As to the scope of the derogation, case law has clarified that Article 346 TFEU confirms 'its position among the Treaty's general and final provisions [... so] it has, for the activities which it covers and on the conditions which it sets forth, a general effect, capable of affecting all the ordinary legal provisions of the Treaty, including those on competition rules'.[11] Furthermore, by providing

---

7 For example, Regulation (EU) 2021/697 of the European Parliament and of the Council of 29 April 2021 establishing the European Defence Fund and repealing Regulation (EU) 2018/1092 ([2021] *OJ* L170/149) provides that the participation of entities established in third States is possible only if guarantees provide assurances that such participation would not be 'contravene the security and defence interests of the Union and its Member States as established in the framework of the CFSP pursuant to Title V of the TEU, or the objectives set out in Article 3 of this Regulation' (see Article 9 of the Regulation). On this provision: see the commentary by S. Rodrigues in this publication.

8 For example, Regulation (EU) 2024/1252 of the European Parliament and of the Council of 11 April 2024 establishing a framework for the secure and sustainable supply of critical raw materials and amending Regulations (EU) No 168/2013, (EU) 2018/858, (EU) 2018/1724 and (EU) 2019/1020 ([2024] *OJ* L2024/1252) states, inter alia, that the information-sharing obligations it lays down do not apply to data which concern 'essential interests of the security or defence of Member States', without however making any explicit reference to Article 346 TFEU.

9 Case T-26/01, *Fiocchi munizioni SpA v Commission*, ECLI:EU:T:2003:248, para. 58.

10 See Case C-601/21, *Commission v Poland*, ECLI:EU:C:2023:629, para. 79, concerning Polish legislation providing for the direct award, without a prior competitive tendering procedure, to an undertaking of the contract for the production of national identity cards and other official documents. It should be noted that this conceptual approach was directly inspired by that used to interpret the concept of national security within the meaning of Directive 2002/58/EC of the European Parliament and of the Council of 12 July 2002 concerning the processing of personal data and the protection of privacy in the electronic communications sector (Directive on privacy and electronic communications), *OJ* L201/37; see in this regard: Joined Cases C-511/18, C-512/18 and C-520/18, *La Quadrature du Net and Others*, ECLI:EU:C:2020:791, para. 135, Case C-140/20, *Commissioner of An Garda Síochána and Others*, ECLI:EU:C:2022:258, para. 61, Joined Cases C-793/19 and C-794/19, *Germany v SpaceNet and Others*, ECLI:EU:C:2022:854, para. 92 and Case C-470/21, *La Quadrature du Net and Others*, ECLI:EU:C:2024:370, para. 66.

11 Case T-26/01, *Fiocchi munizioni SpA v Commission*, ECLI:EU:T:2003:248, para. 58.

that it does not preclude a Member State from taking such measures as it considers necessary for the protection of the essential interests of its security in respect of the activities concerned, this provision confers on Member States a particularly wide discretion in assessing the needs benefiting from such protection.[12] The use of the verb 'consider' seems to confirm this discretionary approach in favour of the Member States.[13]

The European Commission has confirmed this approach by stating that '[I] t is Member States' responsibility to define and protect their security interests. Article [346 TFEU] recognises this prerogative and provides for a derogation for cases where compliance with European law would undermine Member States' essential security interests'.[14]

It follows that Article 346 TFEU can be invoked against any provision of EU law. The reference to the phrase 'the provisions of the Treaties shall not preclude…' seems to us to support this interpretation, as regards both the TFEU and the TEU. However, the question remains whether Article 346 TFEU also applies to the provisions of the TEU relating to the CFSP, or whether its application is excluded by certain special provisions (for example, the unanimity principle in Article 31(1) TEU, constructive abstention in Article 31(1)(2) TEU or the reference to emergency measures in Article 28(4) TEU). The same question may arise with regard to the Euratom Treaty. Although this Treaty does not contain comparable provisions, can Article 346 TFEU and Articles 347 to 348 TFEU be applied by analogy to the Euratom Treaty? The Court of Justice seemed open to such an approach by analogy in Case C-61/03, although Advocate General Geelhoed was more explicit in his Opinion in 2004.[15]

In practice, however, Article 346 TFEU is often used against EU directives on public procurement,[16] harmonisation of customs and VAT rules,[17] competition rules[18] or free movement rules.[19]

---

12 Ibid.

13 N. Mackel, 'Article 296 of the EC Treaty', in P. Léger (ed.), *Commentaire article par article des traités UE et CE*, Bâle/Paris/Bruxelles, Helbing Lichtenhahn/Dalloz/Bruylant, 2000, spec. p. 1880.

14 European Commission, 'Interpretative Communication on the application of Article 296 of the Treaty in the field of defence procurement', COM(2006) 779 final, Section 2, p. 5. Hereinafter: the '2006 Interpretative Communication'.

15 Case C-61/03, *Commission v United Kingdom*, ECLI:EU:C:2005:210, para. 44, and Geelhoed conclusions of 2 December 2004, paras. 100 et seq.

16 For example: Case C-157/06, *Commission v Italy*, ECLI:EU:C:2008:530 and Case C-187/16, *Commission v Austria*, ECLI:EU:C:2018:194; and Case T-509/09, *Portugal v Commission*, ECLI:EU:T:2013:323.

17 For example: Case C-414/97, *Commission v Spain*, ECLI:EU:C:1999:417 and Case C-284/05, *Commission v Finland*, ECLI:EU:C:2009:778.

18 For example, Case T-26/01, *Fiocchi munizioni SpA v Commission*, ECLI:EU:T:2003:248, Case C-246/12, *Ellinika Nafpigeia AE*, ECLI:EU:C:2013:133 and Case C-93/17, *Commission v Greece*, ECLI:EU:C:2018:903.

19 Case C-474/12, *Schiebel Aircraft GmbH*, ECLI:EU:C:2014:2139.

A case in point is the Greek shipyards case, which applies to the control of State aid governed by Articles 107 to 109 TFEU.[20] Before coming under the control of ThyssenKrupp AG, Hellenic Shipyards SA (Ellinika Nafpigeia AE, hereinafter 'ENAE'), which specialises in the construction of naval vessels, benefited from numerous support measures from the Greek State between 1996 and 2003, in particular in the form of capital injections, guarantees and loans to ENAE. The Commission considered these measures to be aid incompatible with the internal market[21] and ordered their recovery from the civil part of ENAE's assets only, having found that they had benefited ENAE's civil activities exclusively. In view of ENAE's difficult economic situation, the Greek Government argued that full recovery of the aid in question could lead to ENAE's bankruptcy, thereby affecting its military activities, including the construction and modernisation of some of its submarines, in such a way that it was liable to undermine the essential security interests of the Greek State within the meaning of Article 346 TFEU. In response to this concern, the Commission proposed to regularise the situation by means of a series of commitments, leading ENAE in particular to cease its civil activities, to sell its assets linked to these same activities and to give up the concession of a dry dock the use of which was not necessary for the pursuit of its military activities. The Commission's approach was therefore based on a strict interpretation of Article 346 TFEU, which can only be applied to military activities in order to neutralise the application of the Treaty rules.[22]

It should be added that the defence exception may also be invoked by national authorities before their own courts, which may mean that the latter have to apply and interpret it.[23]

---

20 See commentary on Articles 101 to 109 TFEU.

21 See Decision 2009/610/EC of 2 July 2008 on the measures C 16/04 (ex NN 29/04, CP 71/02 and CP 133/05) implemented by Greece in favour of Hellenic Shipyards SA ([2009] *OJ* L225/104).

22 In the end, Greece did not comply with its commitments and was condemned for failure to comply with EU law by the Court of Justice (see Case C-485/10, *Commission v Greece*, ECLI:EU:C:2012:395) and subsequently fined €10 million, together with a half-yearly penalty payment of €7,294,000 for failing to comply with the Court's judgment (see Case C-93/17, *Commission v Greece*, ECLI:EU:C:2018:903).

23 Reference will be made here, by way of example, to litigation before the Belgian courts in two emblematic cases: the first relating to the purchase by the Belgian government of American F-16 fighter aircraft (see N.B. Bernard, 'La procédure de remplacement des F-16: entre transparence et opacité', *Revue belge de droit constitutionnel*, 2019, pp. 161–200) and the second, relating to the negotiated procedure without advertising launched by the Belgian Ministry of Defence to establish a strategic partnership with the company FN Herstal in the field of light weapons systems (see judgment no. 258.383 of 10 January 2024 of the Belgian Council of State, which rejected the request for suspension lodged by the competing German company, Heckler & Koch that invoked in particular the abusive use of Article 346 TFEU).

In addition to the litigation framework, the European legislator may also refer, in a specific legal act, to the possibility for Member States to invoke Article 346 TFEU, even if this is more of a confirmation than an extension of the scope of this derogation. Examples include Council Regulation 139/2004 on the control of concentrations between undertakings,[24] Council Regulation (EC) No 428/2009 setting up a Community regime for the control of exports, transfer, brokering and transit of dual-use items,[25] Directive 2014/24/EU of the European Parliament and of the Council on public procurement and repealing Directive 2004/18/EC,[26] or Regulation (EU) 2019/452 of the European Parliament and of the Council of 19 March 2019 establishing a framework for the screening foreign direct investment into the Union.[27]

However, according to the Court's settled case-law, 'it is for the Member States, which have to adopt appropriate measures to ensure their internal and external security, to take decisions on the organisation of their armed forces. It does not follow, however, that such decisions must fall entirely outside the scope of [EU]'.[28] In this respect, the Court has had occasion to stress that 'the only articles in which the Treaty provides for derogations applicable in situations which may affect public security are Article 30 EC [now Article 36 TFEU], 39 EC [now Article 45 TFEU], 46 EC [now Article 52 TFEU], 58 EC

24 [2004] *OJ* L24/1. Recital 19 of that Regulation states the following: 'Furthermore, the exclusive application of this Regulation to concentrations with a Community dimension is without prejudice to Article 296 of the Treaty, and does not prevent the Member States from taking appropriate measures to protect legitimate interests other than those pursued by this Regulation, provided that such measures are compatible with the general principles and other provisions of [EU] law'. However, use of this derogation by the Member States seems to have been sparing during the first years of implementation; see G. Arnoux, 'L'exception défense: réflexions sur le contrôle européen des concentrations', *Concurrences*, No. 2, 2011, pp. 1–8.

25 [2009] *OJ* L134/1. See Art. 26: 'This Regulation does not affect: the application of Article [346 TFEU...]'. Regulation (EC) No 429/2009 was part of the so-called 'defence package', which also included Directive 2009/81/EC on [public procurement] in the fields of defence and security, [2009] OJ L216/76, and Directive 2009/43/EC simplifying terms and conditions of transfers of defence-related products within the Community, [2009] *OJ* L146/1. See commentary under Article 114 TFEU.

26 [2014] OJ L94/65. Article 1(3) of this Directive states that '[t]he application of this Directive is subject to Article 346 of the TFEU'. See also Articles 15 to 17 of this Directive, relating to contracts involving defence or security aspects. On the link between EU public procurement directives and Article 346 TFEU, see N. Pourbaix, 'The future scope of application of Article 346 TFEU', *Public Procurement Law Review*, 2011, pp. 1–8.

27 [2019] OJ L79I/1. See Art. 1(2): 'This Regulation is without prejudice to each Member State having sole responsibility for its national security, as provided for in Article 4(2) TEU, and to the right of each Member State to protect its essential security interests in accordance with Article 346 TFEU'.

28 See Case C-273/97, *Sirdar*, ECLI:EU:C:1999:523, para. 15, and Case C-285/98, *Kreil*, ECLI:EU:C:2000:2, para. 15; confirmed by seven judgments of the Grand Chamber of the Court of 15 December 2009, cited above, in Joined Cases C-284/05, *Commission v Finland*, and others, ECLI:EU:C:2009:778, para. 47.

[now Article 65 TFEU], 64 EC [now Article 72 TFEU], 296 EC [now Article 346 TFEU] and 297 EC [now Article 348 TFEU], which deal with exceptional and clearly defined cases. It cannot be inferred from those articles that the Treaty contains an inherent general exception excluding all measures taken for reasons of public security from the scope of [now EU law]. To recognise the existence of such an exception, regardless of the specific requirements laid down by the Treaty, might impair the binding nature of Community law and its uniform application'.[29]

This is why the Treaty lays down strict conditions for the use of Article 346 TFEU as a derogation, 'balancing Member States' interests in the field of defence and security against the fundamental principles and objectives of [the EU]', since 'these conditions are intended to prevent possible abuses and to ensure that the derogation remains an exception limited to cases where Member States have no other choice than to protect their security interests nationally'.[30]

Consequently, the derogation provided for in Article 346 TFEU must 'be interpreted strictly',[31] in accordance with settled case law on derogations from fundamental freedoms, as regards both its scope and its conditions of application.

B. SCOPE OF ARTICLE 346 TFEU

In view of its 'power of derogation', to use the expression of one author,[32] the scope of application of Article 346 TFEU is restricted. It depends on two different situations set out successively in its first paragraph in point (a) and point (b). These two situations must be regarded as 'well-defined exceptional situations'.[33]

1. *Scope of Article 346(1)(a) TFEU*

The scope of Article 346(1)(a) TFEU is broader than that of Article 346(1)(b) TFEU. Indeed, the possibility for Member States to refrain from providing information the disclosure of which they consider 'contrary to the essential

---

29 See Case C-186/01, *Dory*, ECLI:EU:C:2003:146, para. 31.

30 European Commission, '2006 Interpretative Communication', COM(2006) 779, Section 2, p. 5.

31 See Case C-387/05, *Commission v Italy*, ECLI:EU:C:2009:781, para. 46.

32 G. Arnoux, *Le droit européen de la concurrence et l'industrie de la défense*, PhD thesis, under the supervision of L. Idot, Paris, Université Paris 1 Panthéon-Sorbonne, 2011, spec. p. 27.

33 In this regard: L. Weitzel, 'Art. 297 EC', in I. Pingel (ed.), *De Rome à Lisbonne. Commentaire article par article des traités UE et CE*, 2nd ed., Bâle/Paris/Bruxelles, Helbing Lichtenhahn/Dalloz/Bruylant, 2010, spec. p. 1827.

interests' of their security is not limited to a specific area, contrary to the wording of Article 346(1)(b) TFEU, which refers to measures 'connected with the production of or trade in arms, munitions and war material'. As the Commission pointed out in its 2006 Interpretative Communication, Article 346(1)(a) TFEU 'goes beyond defence, aiming in general at protecting information which Member States cannot disclose to anyone without undermining their essential security interests'.[34] Indeed, there are no restrictions or limitations on the scope of this provision. In other words, the scope is open. When a Member State has to comply with an obligation to provide information, it may refer to Article 346(1)(a) TFEU, regardless of the area concerned.

The interpretation of a broader scope for Article 346(1)(a) TFEU is confirmed by the fact that Article 346(2) TFEU refers to a list, drawn up by the Council on 15 April 1958, naming the products to which only the provisions of paragraph 1(b) apply.[35] There is no reference to an equivalent list for the first paragraph.

2. *Scope of Article 346(1)(b) TFEU*

The scope of Article 346(1)(b) TFEU is restrictive, as there is an explicit link with 'the production of or trade in arms, munitions and war material'; i.e. military products. This is confirmed by paragraph 2 of Article 346 TFEU which refers to the 1958 list in which only military equipment or material is included.

This 1958 list was kept secret until 2001, when the Council replied to a written parliamentary question asking for the contents of this list.[36] Fifteen product categories were defined as follows:

1. Portable and automatic firearms, such as rifles, carbines, revolvers, pistols, sub-machine guns and machine guns, except for hunting weapons, pistols and other low calibre weapons of the calibre less than 7 mm.
2. Artillery, and smoke, gas and flame throwing weapons such as:
   (a) cannon, howitzers, mortars, artillery, anti-tank guns, rocket launchers, flame throwers, recoilless guns;
   (b) military smoke and gas guns.
3. Ammunition for the weapons at 1 and 2 above.

---

34 European Commission, '2006 Interpretative Communication', COM(2006) 779, Section 1, p. 4.

35 Decision defining the list of products (arms, munitions and war material) to which the provisions of Article [346.1 lit. b TFEU] apply (Doc. 255/58), Minutes of 15 April 1958 (Doc. 368/58).

36 Council's answer to Written Question E-1324/01 by Bart Staes (Greens/EFA), [2001] *OJ* C364E/85.

4. Bombs, torpedoes, rockets and guided missiles:
   (a) bombs, torpedoes, grenades, including smoke grenades, smoke bombs, rockets, mines, guided missiles, underwater grenades, incendiary bombs;
   (b) military apparatus and components specially designed for the handling, assembly, dismantling, firing or detection of the articles at (a) above.
5. Military fire control equipment:
   (a) firing computers and guidance systems in infra-red and other night guidance devices;
   (b) telemeters, position indicators, altimeters;
   (c) electronic tracking components, gyroscopic, optical and acoustic;
   (d) bomb sights and gun sights, periscopes for the equipment specified in this list.
6. Tanks and specialist fighting vehicles:
   (a) tanks;
   (b) military type vehicles, armed or armoured, including amphibious vehicles;
   (c) armoured cars;
   (d) half-tracked military vehicles;
   (e) military vehicles with tank bodies;
   (f) trailers specially designed for the transportation of the ammunition specified at paragraphs 3 and 4.
7. Toxic or radioactive agents:
   (a) toxic, biological or chemical agents and radioactive agents adapted for destructive use in war against persons, animals or crops;
   (b) military apparatus for the propagation, detection and identification of substances at paragraph (a) above;
   (c) counter-measures material related to paragraph (a) above.
8. Powders, explosives and liquid or solid propellants:
   (a) powders and liquid or solid propellants specially designed and constructed for use with the material at paragraphs 3, 4 and 7 above;
   (b) military explosives;
   (c) incendiary and freezing agents for military use.
9. Warships and their specialist equipment:
   (a) warships of all kinds;
   (b) equipment specially designed for laying, detecting and sweeping mines;
   (c) underwater cables.
10. Aircraft and equipment for military use.
11. Military electronic equipment.
12. Cameras specially designed for military use.
13. Other equipment and material.

14. Specialised parts and items of material included in this list insofar as they are of a military nature.
15. Machines, equipment and items exclusively designed for the study, manufacture, testing and control of arms, munitions and apparatus of an exclusively military nature included in this list.

Such a list must be regarded as exhaustive. According to the Court's case-law, 'it is clear from [Article 346(1)(a) TFEU], read in conjunction with [Article 346(2) TFEU], that [those] rules [...are] not intended to apply to activities relating to products other than military products identified in the Council list of 15 April 1958'.[37] In other words, the material scope of Article 346(1)(b) TFEU is exhaustively regulated by the 1958 list.

However, as Advocate General Kokott has explained, 'this does not mean that the list cannot be given a contemporary interpretation and application in order to take account of current developments [...]. The list is thus applicable not only to the military products known in 1958, but also to those used today in the Member States' armed forces, provided they can be classified under the categories described in the list'.[38] This approach was confirmed by the Commission's 2006 Interpretative Communication, according to which the interpretation of Article 346(1)(b) TFEU and the definition of its scope 'must also take account of the evolving character of technology and procurement policies'. As far as technology is concerned, the list of 1958 seems sufficiently generic to cover recent and future developments. Similarly, '[Article 346(1)(b) TFEU] can also cover the procurement of services and works directly related to the goods included in the list, as well as modern, capability-based acquisition methods, provided always that the other conditions for applicability of [Article 346 TFEU] are met'.[39]

The European legislator also confirmed this possibility of evolutionary interpretation when it adopted Directive 2009/81/EC, cited above, on defence and security procurement. Recital 10 of this directive states that the 1958 list 'is generic and is to be interpreted in a broad way in the light of the evolving character of technology, procurement policies and military requirements which lead to the development of new types of equipment, for instance on the basis of the Common Military List of the Union'.

This flexibility is to be welcomed, given that although the list of 1958 can be amended by the Council, acting unanimously on a proposal from the Commission, no amendment has yet been adopted.

---

37 See Case T-26/01, *Fiocchi munizioni SpA v Commission*, ECLI:EU:T:2003:248, para. 61.

38 See the opinion of AG Kokott of 19 January 2012 in Case C-615/10 *Insinööritoimisto InsTiimi Oy*, ECLI:EU:C:2012:26, fn. 23.

39 European Commission, '2006 Interpretative Communication', COM(2006) 779, Section 3, p. 6.

A second consequence of the existence of the 1958 list is that only equipment of a purely military nature and purpose is included. According to the Commission, 'the nature of the products on the 1958 list and the explicit reference in [Article 346 TFEU] to "*specifically military purposes*" confirms that only [...] equipment which is designed, developed and produced for specifically military purposes can be exempted from [EU] rules on the basis of [Article 346(1)(b) TFEU]'.[40] The Court upheld this restrictive interpretation: first, a Member State cannot rely on Article 346(1)(b) TFEU to justify a derogating measure in respect of equipment 'which [is] certainly intended for civilian use and possibly for military use';[41] secondly, 'even if a product comes within one or other of the categories of materials included in the Council list of 15 April 1958, that product can, if it has technical applications for civilian use which are largely identical, be considered to be intended for specifically military purposes, within the terms of [Article 346 TFEU], only if such use is not solely that which the contracting authority intends to confer on it but also [...] that which results from the intrinsic characteristics of a piece of equipment specially designed, developed or modified significantly for those purposes'.[42] In this respect, the judge also noted that 'the word 'military' used in point 11 of that list and the words 'insofar as they are of a military nature' and 'exclusively designed' used respectively in points 14 and 15 of that list indicate that the products referred to in those points must, in objective terms, have a specifically military nature'.[43]

It is not always easy to draw such a distinction between 'specifically military objectives' and dual objectives. As the Commission has pointed out, 'security has become an increasingly complex concept, with new threats blurring the traditional dividing line between military and non-military, external and internal security dimension'.[44] This is perhaps why the European Parliament and the Council stated, in the tenth recital of Directive 2009/81/EC, cited above, that the term 'military equipment', as used in this Directive, should cover products which, although initially designed for civilian use, are subsequently adapted for military purposes to be used as weapons, munitions or war material.

In any event, the EU Court seems cautious and considers that it is up to national courts to determine whether products can be classified in one or other of the categories included in the 1958 list.[45] However, it does not

40 Ibid.

41 See Case C-337/05, *Commission v Italy*, ECLI:EU:C:2008:203, paras. 48 and 49.

42 See Case C-615/10, *Insinööritoimisto InsTiimi Oy*, ECLI:EU:C:2012:324, para. 40.

43 Ibid., para. 41.

44 European Commission, '2006 Interpretative Communication', COM(2006) 779, Section 3, p. 6.

45 Case C-615/10, *Insinööritoimisto InsTiimi Oy*, ECLI:EU:C:2012:324, para. 37.

hesitate to help national courts draw the line, by giving some guidelines, as is often the case in the context of preliminary rulings (see Art. 267 TFEU). Case C-615/10 provides an interesting illustration of this approach. This is a preliminary ruling on a dispute concerning the award by the Technical Research Centre of the Finnish Defence Forces, following a procedure different from those provided for in the public procurement directives, of a contract for the supply of equipment with a tilting turntable intended to be used to support objects subject to electromagnetic measurements. In examining the question of whether or not such equipment should be classified as military in nature, the Court developed a twofold reasoning: first, on the basis of the information provided, the Court assumed that such equipment was intended, in its view, 'to facilitate the carrying-out of electromagnetic measurements and the simulation of combat situations. It could, therefore, be characterised as a component of military equipment for the testing and control of arms, within the meaning of point 15 of the Council list of 15 April 1958, read together with points 11 and 14 of that list, this being a matter for the referring court to determine'.[46] However, in a second stage of the reasoning, the Court added that 'such tiltable turntable equipment, which the contracting authority intends to use only for military purposes, can be considered to be intended specifically for such purposes, within the terms of Article 296(1)(b) EC, only if it is established that, unlike the similar material intended for civilian uses invoked by the applicant in the main proceedings, that equipment, by virtue of its intrinsic characteristics, may be regarded as having been specially designed and developed, also as a result of substantial modifications, for such purposes, this also being a matter for the referring court to determine'.[47]

In other cases, however, the evidence in the file may be sufficient for the Court to decide whether or not to include the products concerned within the scope of Article 346(1)(b) TFEU. The so-called *Agusta* case illustrates such a scenario. In this case, the Commission asked the Court to declare that, by adopting a long-standing procedure for the direct award to Agusta SpA ('Agusta') of contracts for the purchase of Agusta and Agusta Bell helicopters to meet the needs of several military and civil corps of the Italian State, without any tendering procedure and, in particular, without complying with the procedures laid down by the EU Directives on public procurement, the Italian Republic had failed to fulfil its obligations under those Directives. Given the diversity of the bodies involved, including the Corpo dei Vigili del Fuoco (Fire Brigade), the Carabinieri, the Corpo Forestale dello Stato (State Forestry Corps), the Guardia Costiera (Coastguard), the Guardia di Finanza (Treasury Guard), the Polizia di Stato (State Police), the Carabinieri and the

46 Ibid., para. 43.
47 Ibid., para. 44.

Civil Protection Department of the Presidency of the Council of Ministers, the Court found that the helicopters in question were 'certainly for civilian use' and only 'possibly for military use',[48] and consequently held that '[Article 346(1)(b) TFEU] cannot be properly invoked by the Italian Republic to justify the recourse to the negotiated procedure for the purchase of those helicopters'.[49]

Finally, the interpretation of Article 346(1)(b) TFEU provides, by contrast, some keys for interpreting the scope of Article 346(1)(a) TFEU: the latter provision may cover both dual-use equipment for military and non-military security purposes,[50] provided that it can demonstrate that the disclosure of such information would be prejudicial to the essential interests of its security. This leads to an examination of the conditions for applying Article 346 TFEU.

3. *Conditions for Recourse to Article 346 TFEU*

The conditions for applying Article 346 TFEU must be distinguished with regard to the two situations covered by this provision, as they are different in nature and intensity.

a. – Conditions for Implementing Article 346(1)(a) TFEU

Under Article 346(1)(a) TFEU, 'no Member State shall be obliged to supply information the disclosure of which it considers contrary to the essential interests of its security'. Consequently, two elements must be identified: first, the existence of an obligation to provide information and, second, the existence of a conflict with the essential interests of national security.

i. *First Condition: The Existence of an Obligation to Provide Certain Information*

Article 346(1)(a) TFEU only applies where a Member State is faced with an obligation to provide information. This may be the case by reference to a general legal basis, such as the principle of loyal cooperation (Art. 4(3) of the EU Treaty) or the power conferred on the Commission under Article 337 of the TFEU to collect all the information and carry out all the checks necessary for the performance of the tasks entrusted to it; but also by complying with specific procedures, for example, the Court's rules of procedure,[51] or

---

48 Case C-337/05, *Commission v Italy*, ECLI:EU:C:2008:203, para. 48.

49 Ibid., para. 49.

50 Cf. European Commission, '2006 Interpretative Communication', COM(2006) 779, Section 3, p. 6.

51 See Order of the President of the Court of 13 September 2007, in Case C-294/05, *Commission v Sweden*, not published, paras. 11 to 13, concerning the protection of sensitive information in the context of an application to intervene in proceedings brought by another Member State.

EU customs procedures, as in Case C-372/05 where the Court was faced with an argument from the Federal Republic of Germany that these procedures were not capable of safeguarding its security in the light of the confidentiality requirements contained in the agreements concluded with the exporting States. The European Court of Justice held that 'the application of the [EU] customs system requires the active involvement of [EU] and national officials who are bound when necessary by an obligation of confidentiality, when dealing with sensitive data, which is capable of protecting the essential security interests of Member States'.[52] Consequently, 'in accordance with [former] Article 10 EC which obliges Member States to facilitate the achievement of the Commission's task of ensuring compliance with the Treaty, Member States are obliged to make available to the Commission the documents necessary to permit inspection to ensure that the transfer of the Community's own resources is correct. However [...] such an obligation does not mean that Member States may not, on a case-by-case basis and by way of exception, on the basis of [Article 346 TFEU], either restrict the information sent to certain parts of a document or withhold it completely'.[53]

ii. *Second Condition: Existence of a Conflict with the Essential Interests of National Security*

The second condition for the application of Article 346(1)(a) TFEU is also required for the use of Article 346(1)(b) TFEU: the existence of a conflict of interest with the essential security interests of a Member State. This is a key criterion which involves the difficult task of defining what the essential interests of national security are. The Commission and the EU courts have provided some guidance on this issue.

Firstly, as explained in the 2006 Interpretative Communication, '[t]he objective justifying the exemption is only the protection of a Member State's essential security interests. Other interests, in particular industrial and economic interests, although connected with the production of and trade in arms, munitions and war material, cannot justify by themselves an exemption on the basis of Article [Article 346(1)(b) TFEU]'.[54]

It is questionable whether these security interests should be interpreted solely in a national context. For the Commission, 'Member States' security interests should also be considered from a European perspective. They may

52 See Case C-372/05, *Commission v Germany*, ECLI:EU:C:2009:780, para. 74.

53 Ibid., para. 76.

54 European Commission, '2006 Interpretative Communication', COM (2006) 779, Section 4, p. 7, referring to the example of indirect non-military offsets which, because they do not serve specific security interests but general economic interests, are not covered by Article 346 TFEU, even if they are linked to a defence procurement contract exempted on the basis of this provision.

vary, e.g. for geographical or historical reasons. On the other hand, European integration has led to an ever-growing convergence of national interests among Member States. The development of the CFSP and the ESDP illustrate that this is increasingly the case in the field of security and defence as well. Member States share in particular the objective of developing a common Defence Equipment Market and a competitive Defence Industrial and Technological Base. They should take this into account when assessing whether the application of EU procurement rules, which are aimed at fostering intra-European competition, would undermine the essential interests of their security'.[55]

This approach was endorsed by Advocate General Ruiz-Jarabo Colomer in Cases C-284/05 and others: account must be taken of 'certain approximation of laws in the field of security (134) and the establishment of the European Defence Agency [...] There is clearly a certain anachronism when [the measures taken on the basis of Article 346 TFEU] are compared with the competence of the Union to frame progressively a common defence policy [Articles 24(1) and 42, (2) TEU] and with the solidarity clause, which provides for the mobilisation of military forces if one of the Member States is the object of a terrorist attack or the victim of a natural or man-made disaster [Article 222 TFEU]'.[56]

Secondly, according to the case law, 'the concept of public security within the meaning of [Article 346 TFEU] covers both a Member State's internal security [...], and its external security'.[57] Even if the Member States have a wide discretion in defining such a broad concept[58] and even if there is no precise definition at EU level,[59] it should be remembered that a narrow interpretation must prevail.[60]

Thirdly, Article 346 TFEU does not refer to security interests in general, but only to essential security interests. For the Commission, 'this specification underlines the exceptional character of the derogation and [...] the particularly strong wording ("essential") limits the possible exemptions to procurements which are of the highest importance for Member States' military capabilities'.[61] Consequently, the protection of essential security interests is the only reason

55 Ibid.

56 Opinion of AG Colomer of 10 February 2009 in Joined Cases C-284/05 and others, ECLI:EU:C:2009:67, paras. 182–183.

57 See Case C-273/97, *Sirdar*, ECLI:EU:C:1999:523, para. 17; confirmed by Case C-285/98, *Kreil*, ECLI:EU:C:2000:2, para. 17.

58 See European Parliament, Directorate-General for Internal Policies, *National security and secret evidence in legislation and the courts: exploring the challenges*, Study for the LIBE Committee, 2014.

59 See C. Chardigny, *Contrats et marchés publics de défense*, Brussels, Bruylant, 2013, p. 21.

60 See Case C-474/12, *Schiebel Aircraft GmbH*, ECLI:EU:C:2014:2139, para. 33.

61 European Commission, '2006 Interpretative Communication', COM(2006) 779, Section 4, p. 8.

that can justify a derogation.[62] However, there is no limited list of essential security interests defined at EU level, although in some areas the EU legislator tries to be more explicit. This is the case with Directive 2009/81/EC, cited above. Article 13 of this Directive establishes a list of 'specific exclusions' which may be regarded as a 'clarification of the hypotheses' falling within the scope of Article 346 of the TFEU.[63] Excluded in particular are contracts for which the application of the rules of this Directive would oblige a Member State to provide information the disclosure of which it considers contrary to the essential interests of its security (Art. 13(a)), which is clearly a copy and paste of Article 346(1)(a) TFEU); contracts concerning intelligence activities (Art. 13(b)); contracts awarded by one government to another for the supply of military equipment or sensitive equipment, works and services directly related to such equipment, or works and services specifically intended for military purposes, or sensitive works and services (Art. 13(f)). This last reference to 'sensitive' work or products is new and interesting. However, it is not yet clear whether it can be considered a key reference for the concept of essential national interests.

As the protection of essential national security interests is more or less identified, Article 346(1)(a) TFEU can only be invoked by a Member State if the disclosure of information can be considered to be 'contrary' to its essential security interests. In terms of procedural consequences, in particular as regards the burden of proof, 'it is for the Member State which seeks to take advantage of [Article 346 TFEU] to prove that it is necessary to have recourse to that derogation in order to protect the essential security interests'.[64] As the Commission points out, 'if a Member State intends to rely on Article 346, it must be able to demonstrate that the concrete measures in the military sector are necessary and proportionate for the protection of its essential security interests and that they do not go beyond what is strictly necessary for that purpose. The burden of proof that these conditions are fulfilled lies upon Member States'.[65] According to the EU courts, this provision cannot be read 'in such a way as to give Member States the power to depart from the provisions of the Treaty solely on the basis of those interests'.[66] This applies to both points (a) and (b) of Article 346(1) TFEU.

62 N. Cunha Rodrigues, 'Artigos 346-347-348 TFUE', in M. Lopes Porto and G. Anastácio, *Tratado de Lisboa anotado he comentado*, Lisbon, Almedina, 2012, p. 1218.

63 A. Cammilleri-Subrenat, *Le droit de la politique européenne de sécurité et de défense dans le cadre du traité de Lisbonne*, Paris/Cachan, Lavoisier/Éditions TEC & DOC, 2010, p. 158.

64 See Case C-387/05, *Commission v Italy*, ECLI:EU:C:2009:781, para. 49.

65 Communication from the Commission, 'Towards a more competitive and efficient defence and security sector', COM(2013) 542, Section 2.2, pp. 6–7.

66 See Case C-387/05, *Commission v Italy*, ECLI:EU:C:2009:781, para. 47.

b. – Conditions for Implementing Article 346(1)(b) TFEU

In addition to the condition of invoking the protection of the essential interests of national security in the same sense as for the application of Article 346(1)(a) TFEU, two other conditions must be demonstrated by a Member State invoking Article 346(1)(b) TFEU: the need for protection and the absence of effect on the conditions of competition in the internal market, as regards products which are not intended for specifically military purposes.

i. *First Condition: The Need to Protect Essential National Security Interests*

Under Article 346(1)(b) TFEU, Member States may take such measures as they deem necessary for the protection of their essential security interests. As mentioned above, this provision has been recognised as giving Member States a wide discretion in deciding how to protect their essential security interests.[67] However, as the 2006 Interpretative Communication points out, 'the text ("necessary for the protection…") also demonstrates that this discretion is not unfettered. The very existence of [Article 348 TFEU], which lays down a special procedure to be followed in the event of possible improper use of [Article 346 TFEU], confirms that Member States do not have absolute freedom in their decision to exempt a specific procurement contract from the rules of the Internal Market'.[68]

This approach has been confirmed by the Court: 'it is for the Member State which seeks to rely on [Article 346 TFEU] to supply evidence that the exemptions in question do not go beyond the limits of those [clearly defined] cases' and to demonstrate 'that the exemptions […] are necessary for the protection of the essential interests of its security'.[69]

To verify this condition of necessity, the EU courts use their traditional proportionality test. As the Commission points out, 'if a Member State intends to rely on Article 346, it must be able to demonstrate that the concrete measures in the military sector are necessary and proportionate for the protection of their essential security interests and that they do not go beyond what is strictly necessary for that purpose. The burden of proof that these conditions are fulfilled lies upon Member States'.[70]

Three examples can illustrate this approach of the General Court and the Court of Justice. In Case T-509/09, the question was, in essence, whether a

67 See Case T-26/01, *Fiocchi munizioni SpA v Commission*, ECLI:EU:T:2003:248, para. 58.
68 European Commission, '2006 Interpretative Communication', COM (2006) 779, Section 4, p. 7.
69 See Case C-414/97, *Commission v Spain*, ECLI:EU:C:1999:417, para. 22.
70 Communication from the Commission, 'Towards a more competitive and efficient defence and security sector', COM(2013) 542 final, Section 2.2.

Member State requesting assistance from the Union, under certain specific EU rules,[71] to acquire equipment for the control of fishing activities, may derogate from EU public procurement rules by invoking the military nature of the equipment concerned, by relying on Article 346(1)(b) TFEU. First the General Courd held that 'under Decision 2001/431, it is not permissible for a Member State to request, on the one hand, co-financing by the Union of the acquisition of vessels wholly or partly intended for the purposes control and surveillance of fishing activities which, in accordance with that decision, must comply with the rules on the award of public contracts and to decide, on the other hand, not to apply those rules on the basis of [Article 346(1)(b) TFEU], on account of the military nature of the equipment acquired'.[72] The Court then stated that on the basis of Article 346(1)(b) TFEU the Union 'does not prevent the Member States which intend to acquire military equipment falling within the scope of that provision from deciding nonetheless to comply with the common procedures for the award of public contracts and, accordingly, from being able to claim the financial contribution provided for in Decision 2001/431'.[73] Thus, the only possibility for a Member State not to comply with EU public procurement rules is to demonstrate the necessary protection of its essential security interests. However, the General Court noted that 'the Portuguese Republic merely relies on the confidentiality of sensitive information, relating to the development and installation of military communications software on the ocean patrol vessels, without providing any specific evidence with regard to the particular security measures needed for the supply of the ocean patrol vessels, or the reasons why it considered that the objective of protecting the confidentiality of particular data would be less well safeguarded if that production was entrusted to companies other than Estaleiros Navais de Viana do Castelo'.[74] Consequently, the invocation of derogatory processing 'seems to be disproportionate as regards the objective of preventing the disclosure of sensitive information relating to the production of those vessels'.[75]

Secondly, in Case C-474/12, the proportionality test is perhaps even more thorough. The Court of Justice was asked to reply to a reference for a preliminary ruling raising the question whether EU law, and in particular Articles 45 and 49 TFEU, read in conjunction with Article 346(1)(b) TFEU, preclude legislation of a Member State under which, in the case of undertakings wishing to trade in military arms and munitions and to act as intermediaries

71 Council Decision 2001/431/EC of 28 May 2001 on a financial contribution by the Community towards certain expenditure incurred by the Member States in implementing the control, inspection and surveillance systems applicable to the common fisheries policy, [2001] *OJ* L154/22.

72 See Case T-509/09, *Portugal v Commission*, ECLI:EU:T:2013:323, para. 42.

73 Ibid., para. 45.

74 Ibid., para. 50.

75 Ibid., para. 52.

for the sale and purchase of such goods, the members of their statutory representative bodies or the managing partners authorised to represent a partnership must be nationals of that Member State, with possession of the nationality of another EEA Member State not being sufficient. The application was made in the context of a dispute between Schiebel Aircraft GmbH and the Austrian Federal Minister for Economic Affairs, Family and Youth concerning the refusal to grant Schiebel Aircraft authorisation to carry on activities in the armaments sector. Firstly, the Court held that 'even assuming that it could be shown that the objectives [...] of ensuring the trustworthiness of persons authorised to trade in military weapons and munitions or to broker the sale and purchase of such goods, of ensuring security of supply as regards defence material and of preventing the disclosure of strategic information — constitute essential interests of the Republic of Austria's security, for the purposes of Article 346(1)(b) TFEU, the nationality condition would still, in accordance with the principle of proportionality, not have to go beyond what is appropriate and necessary for achieving those objectives'.[76] Consequently, the Court emphasised that 'even if the nationality condition were suitable for achieving the objectives referred to [...] above, such objectives can, in the circumstances, be achieved through the use of less restrictive measures, such as regular controls of the production of and trade in arms, or an obligation of confidentiality under administrative law, or even the imposition of penalties for the disclosure of strategic information, on the basis of criminal law'.[77] This leads to the following conclusion by the Court: Articles 45 TFEU and 49 TFEU must be interpreted as precluding the nationality requirement imposed by the Austrian legislation, but it is for the national court to ascertain whether the Member State which, in order to justify that legislation, relies on the derogation provided for in Article 346(1)(b) TFEU is able to demonstrate that that derogation is necessary for the protection of the essential interests of its security, taking into account, of course, the valuable guidance of the Court's preliminary ruling.[78]

As a third and final example, reference is made to the case already cited concerning Polish legislation authorising the direct award, without competition, of contracts relating to the production of official documents, printed matter and other stamps and markings. To justify this derogation, the Polish Government first invoked Article 15(3) of Directive 2014/24/EU on the award of public contracts, under which, '[w]here the procurement

---

76 See Case C-474/12, *Schiebel Aircraft GmbH*, ECLI:EU:C:2014:2139, para. 37, referring to Case 222/84, *Johnston*, ECLI:EU:C:1986:206, para. 38 and Case C-423/98, *Albore*, ECLI:EU:C:2000:401, para. 19.

77 See Case C-474/12, *Schiebel Aircraft GmbH*, ECLI:EU:C:2014:2139, para. 38.

78 E. Daniel, 'Exception de sécurité nationale (article 346 TFUE)', *Europe*, 2014, comm. 448, 23–24, spec. p. 24.

and performance of the public contract or design contest are declared to be secret or must be accompanied by special security measures in accordance with the laws, regulations or administrative provisions in force in a Member State, this Directive shall not apply provided that the Member State has determined that the essential interests concerned cannot be guaranteed by less intrusive measures…'. The Court will apply this in the light of the principle of proportionality, distinguishing between two categories of public documents concerned: for the first category, relating to the production of excise stamps, legal notices, control stickers, ballot papers, holographic signs on voting right certificates and microprocessor systems with software for managing public documents, computer systems and databases necessary for the use of public documents, the non-application of the public procurement procedures provided for in Directive 2014/24 'appears disproportionate in the light of the objectives on which the Republic of Poland relies',[79] principally the continuity of the supply of official documents, confidentiality and the security and safety of its citizens. It is true that, in this respect, Directive 2014/24/EU already provides sufficient safeguards to mitigate the risks invoked by that Member State with regard to its essential security interests, in particular by being authorised to impose an obligation of secrecy as well as compliance with appropriate technical specifications and selection criteria.

The second category of public documents must on the other hand be treated differently, including: the personal documents of military personnel and their identity cards, the service cards of police officers, border guards, State security agents, Internal Security Agency agents, Intelligence Agency agents, agents of the Military Counter-Intelligence Service and professional soldiers appointed to a post in that service, agents of the Military Intelligence Service and professional soldiers appointed to a post in that service, and members of the military police. In the Court's view, these 'documents present a direct and close link to the objective of protecting national security, with the result that these may justify additional confidentiality requirements' and 'can render indispensable a limitation on the disclosure of the characteristics of such documents and the information that they contain – including, in particular, the identity of those agents and officers – with the result that such documents must be regarded as having a particularly high level of sensitivity which requires greater protection against, inter alia, leaks and falsification'.[80] The derogation in Article 15(3) of Directive 2014/24/EU finds proportionate application in this case, in line with the Court's case law on Article 346 TFEU.[81]

---

[79] See Case C-601/21, *Commission v Poland*, ECLI:EU:C:2023:629para. 107.

[80] Ibid., para. 108.

[81] See D. Bouvier, 'Marchés publics. Exclusion en raison d'intérêts essentiels de la sécurité nationale', *Europe*, No. 11, November 2023, comm. 383, pp. 36–37.

ii. *Second Condition: That the Conditions of Competition in the Internal Market Are Not Affected as regards Products which Are Not Intended for Specifically Military Purposes*

As EU case law points out, 'two specific remedies are provided for by the Treaty in relation to measures adopted by the Member States under [Article 346(1)(b) TFEU] in favour of activities in connection with the products mentioned in the Council's list of 15 April 1958'.[82] The first refers to the last sentence of that provision and the second is prescribed by Article 348 TFEU (see below).

The last sentence of Article 346(1)(b) TFEU states that the measures referred to in the previous paragraph must not adversely affect the conditions of competition in the internal market in respect of 'products which are not intended for specifically military purposes'. This reference to the criteria for distortion of the conditions of competition is confirmed by Article 348(1) TFEU (see below). It follows from the case law, even if cases interpreting this criterion in the context of Article 346 TFEU are not so frequent, that a national measure (e.g. State aid) may be considered to be a source of such distortion if 'it benefits activities connected to products which are on the Council's list of 15 April 1958 but are capable of being put to civilian use as well (products called mixed use [products]) or products covered by the said list but intended for export'.[83] Another example can be given with regard to certain national measures in the field of defence procurement and, in particular, concerning economic compensation, especially indirect and non-military compensation.[84] As the Commission has consistently pointed out, 'requirements for economic compensation, no matter how they are labelled, stand in contrast to both EU Treaty and effective procurement methods'.[85] The Commission is therefore working to eliminate this practice quickly and to promote other non-discriminatory measures to facilitate SMEs' access to cross-border contracts, by invoking strict compliance with the demands of Article 346(1)(b) TFEU that 'measures shall not adversely affect the conditions of competition in the internal market'. In this respect, it may be useful and relevant to refer to the way in which the Commission and the Court of Justice interpret EU competition rules, namely Articles 101 and 102 TFEU, in order to ensure consistency in the interpretation of such a clause.[86]

---

82 See Case T-26/01, *Fiocchi munizioni SpA v Commission*, ECLI:EU:T:2003:248, para. 62.

83 *Ibid.*, para. 63.

84 On these offsets and the practice known as 'offsets', see D. Eisenhut, 'Offsets in defence procurement: a strange animal – at the brink of extinction?' (2013) 38(3) *European Law Review*, pp. 393–403.

85 Report from the Commission, 'A New Deal for European Defence Implementation Roadmap for Communication COM(2013) 542; Towards a more competitive and efficient defence and security sector, COM/2014/0387 final, 24 June 2014, Section 2.1.

86 See commentary on Articles 101 to 109 TFEU.

***

How the Commission intends to apply Article 346 TFEU is now constant: it is a case-by-case assessment, which must be 'particularly rigorous at the borderline of Article [346 TFEU] where the use of the exemption may be controversial'.[87] In particular, this means that Member States must assess: the essential security interest involved; the real link between this security interest and the specific national measure concerned; and why the non-application of EU rules in a specific case is necessary to protect this essential security interest. These issues must be analysed because the national measures concerned may be of a permanent nature, provided that the reasons for their adoption are still valid. This contrasts with other national measures adopted in different situations, for example, to comply with Article 347 TFEU, which must be temporary (see below).

Despite this clear standard of review, the use and abuse of Article 346 TFEU by Member States seems to be a constant practice, especially as its provisions do not require prior notification before it can be invoked. In the view of some authors, this is 'one of its major weaknesses'.[88]

This is why certain procedural safeguards have been introduced in Article 348 TFEU, with a special procedure for monitoring and consulting the European Commission and a derogation procedure in the event of an infringement of EU law (see below, Article 348 TFEU). However, the fact is that Article 346 TFEU is by no means obsolete, as Advocate General Ruiz-Jarabo Colomer has pointed out: it is a durable provision which 'has withstood the test of time since 1957 and was retained in the Treaty of Lisbon'.[89] Even today, 'there is a clear tension between the two interpretations of Article [346 TFEU]: the first is advanced by the Member States and concerns the notion of omnipresent sovereignty in matters relating to defence, while, in contrast, the other is more communitarian and restricts the scope of the article to a more narrowly defined sphere'.[90] Thus, as Article 346 TFEU 'is capable of giving rise to false expectations in both Member States and new accession States', while this provision 'remains in good health', the EU judge 'must not shirk their responsibility and must restrict its scope, as the uniformity of Community

87 European Commission, '2006 Interpretative Communication', COM(2006) 779, Section 5, p. 8.

88 See also G. Arnoux, *Le droit européen de la concurrence et l'industrie de la défense*, PhD thesis, under the supervision of L. Idot, Paris, Université Paris 1 Panthéon-Sorbonne, 2011, p. 38, who speaks of the 'paradox of invocation' and advocates a revision of Article 346 TFEU to introduce a pre-notification procedure.

89 See the opinion of AG Colomer of 10 February 2009 in Joined Cases C-284/05 and others, ECLI:EU:C:2009:67, para. 176.

90 Ibid., para. 177.

law is at stake'.[91] Standardisation has not yet been achieved in this area.[92] This is hardly surprising if we are to see in Article 346 TFEU a way of 'drawing a dividing line between the competence of the EU and that of the Member States when the regulation of the arms market is at stake'.[93]

Incidentally, this dilemma is neither new nor original in the context of relations between the European and national legal orders. But given the sensitive characteristics of the national security spectrum, only a change in primary law could lead Member States to reconsider the use of Article 346 TFEU for their own interests, which are more closely linked to the broader perspectives of the Union.

Finally, it should be added that the TFEU is not the only international treaty to provide a mechanism for protecting national security. The General Agreement on Tariffs and Trade (GATT), as incorporated into the Treaty establishing the World Trade Organisation (WTO), also contains a provision on security exceptions. Article XXI states that '[n]othing in this Agreement shall be construed: '(a) to require any contracting party to furnish any information the disclosure of which it considers contrary to its essential security interests; or; (b) to prevent any contracting party from taking any action which it considers necessary for the protection of its essential security interests: i) relating to fissionable materials or materials from which they are derived; ii) relating to the traffic in arms, ammunition and implements of war and to such traffic in other goods and materials as is carried on directly or indirectly for the purpose of supplying a military establishment; iii) taken in time of war or other emergency in international relations; or c) to prevent any contracting party from taking any action in pursuance of its obligations under the United Nations Charter for the maintenance of international peace and security'.[94] It should be noted that the European Court of Justice has already had occasion to refer to this.[95]

---

[91] Ibid., para. 186.

[92] Despite what some authors had predicted: D. Vincetelli-Meria, 'Vers une normalisation de l'application de l'article 296 du TCE dans le secteur des industries de l'armement', *RMCUE*, 2001, no. 445, pp. 96–101.

[93] See also E. Simon, *Rôles et fonctions du droit de l'Union européenne dans l'intégration des politiques d'acquisition d'armement*, PhD thesis, Paris, Université Paris 1 Panthéon-Sorbonne, defended on 13 July 2017, supervised by V. de Beaufort and S. Rodrigues, p. 139.

[94] These last two references seem to echo the provisions of Article 347 TFEU: see below.

[95] See the judgment of the General Court of 13 September 2018 in Case T-715/14, *Rosneft Oil Company and Others v Council of the EU*, ECLI:EU:T:2018:544, paras. 181–182 and aforementioned Opinion of Advocate General Szpunar of 25 October 2018, in Case C-469/17, para. 48.

The same approach inspired the drafting of Article 28.6 entitled 'National Security' of the Comprehensive Economic and Trade Agreement (CETA) between Canada and the European Union, as well as its Member States.[96]

II. THE CONSULTATION PROCEDURE UNDER ARTICLE 347 TFEU IN THE EVENT OF A CRISIS

Like Article 346 TFEU, Article 347 TFEU is a possible derogation clause from Union law (Section A). Its scope covers certain crisis situations (Section B) and its implementation by the Member States implies an obligation for them to consult each other (Section C).

A. ARTICLE 347 TFEU AS A CLAUSE DEROGATING FROM THE RULES OF THE TREATY

Described by some jurists as a 'safety valve for the protection of certain crucial interests of the Member States'[97] or an 'emergency clause',[98] Article 347 TFEU follows on from Article 224 of the Treaty of Rome (EEC), then Article 297 EC, before taking its current version resulting from the Treaty of Lisbon (2007).

It should be noted that, unlike other Treaty provisions which provide for Union competence in crisis situations, for example Article 215 TFEU in combination with the CFSP, Article 347 TFEU itself does not confer any competence on the Union. However, it may be assumed that in a crisis situation involving disturbances in the functioning of the internal market within the meaning of that provision, the Union might also consider using its

---

96 [2017] *OJ* L11/23. Article 28.6 of CETA reads as follows: 'Nothing in this Agreement shall be construed:(a) to require a Party to furnish or allow access to information if that Party determines that the disclosure of this information would be contrary to its essential security interests; or (b) to prevent a Party from taking an action that it considers necessary to protect its essential security interests: (i) connected to the production of or traffic in arms, ammunition and implements of war and to such traffic and transactions in other goods and materials, services and technology undertaken, and to economic activities, carried out directly or indirectly for the purpose of supplying a military or other security establishment (35); (ii) taken in time of war or other emergency in international relations; or (iii) relating to fissionable and fusionable materials or the materials from which they are derived; or (c) prevent a Party from taking any action in order to carry out its international obligations for the purpose of maintaining international peace and security'.

97 See the opinion of AG Cosmas, 23 March 2000, in Case C-423/98, *Albore*, ECLI:EU:C:2000:158, para. 23.

98 See the opinion of AG Kokott, 13 June 2014, para. 257, under Opinion 2/13 of the Court (Full Court), *Accession of the EU to the ECHR*, ECLI:EU:C:2014:2454.

specific powers to deal with such disturbances (for example, where the national measures in question have been adopted against a third country).

Like other derogations applicable in situations that may jeopardise national security, in particular Article 346 TFEU, the Court of Justice of the European Union considers that Article 347 TFEU concerns 'a wholly exceptional situation'[99] and therefore deals with 'exceptional and clearly defined cases'.[100] Consequently, it cannot be inferred from this article that 'the Treaty contains an inherent general exception excluding all measures taken for reasons of public security from the scope of [EU] law'. Recognition of the existence of such an exception, irrespective of the specific requirements laid down in the Treaty, 'might impair the binding nature of [EU] law and its uniform application'.[101] In this respect, 'it is for the Member State which seeks to rely on those exceptions to furnish evidence that the exemptions in question do not exceed the limits of such cases'.[102]

Another logical consequence of this approach is that, like other safeguard clauses accompanying EU rules, Article 347 TFEU 'must be construed strictly since it constitutes a derogation from the generally applicable regime created by those rules'.[103]

However, unlike other safeguard clauses, 'it does not appear to be capable of being implemented in "normal circumstances"; it is intended only for the extreme situations listed exhaustively in the article itself'.[104]This last consideration has led the Court to regard Article 347 TFEU as ancillary to other provisions of the Treaty: i.e. it applies only in the absence of special rules, such as those referred to in Articles 36, 45, 52, 65 or 72 TFEU.[105] In other words, Article 347 of the TFEU constitutes 'the ultima ratio to which recourse may be had only in the absence of any [EU] provision enabling the demands of the public order in question to be met'.[106] This is perhaps the main reason why this provision has not been applied to date in various cases.

It should be pointed out, however, that this interpretation of Article 347 TFEU as an ancillary provision has been challenged by some Advocates

---

99 See Case 222/84, *Johnston*, ECLI:EU:C:1986:206, para. 27.

100 See Case C-337/05, *Commission v Italy*, ECLI:EU:C:2008:203, para. 43.

101 See Case 222/84, *Johnston*, ECLI:EU:C:1986:206, para. 26, Case C-273/97, *Sirdar*, ECLI:EU:C:1999:523, para. 16 and Case C-285/98, *Kreil*, ECLI:EU:C:2000:2, para. 16.

102 Case C-414/97, *Commission v Spain*, ECLI:EU:C:1999:417, para. 22.

103 See the opinion of AG Cosmas, 23 March 2000, in Case C-423/98, *Albore*, ECLI:EU:C:2000:158, para. 23.

104 Ibid., para. 23.

105 See Case C-83/94, *Leifer and Others*, ECLI:EU:C:1995:329, paras. 14–15.

106 See the opinion of AG Cosmas, 23 March 2000, in Case C-423/98, *Albore*, ECLI:EU:C:2000:158, para. 4, who refers to the opinion of AG Darmon, 28 January 1986 in Case 222/84, *Johnston*, ECLI:EU:C:1986:44, para. 5. See also L. Weitzel, 'Art. 297 EC', in I. Pingel (ed.), *De Rome à Lisbonne. Commentaire article par article des traités UE et CE*, 2nd ed., Bâle/Paris/Bruxelles, Helbing Lichtenhahn/Dalloz/Bruylant, 2010, p. 1827.

General, notably Mr Cosmas, who considers that Article 347 TFEU 'is intended to fulfil an additional role in the system of Treaty provisions, beyond merely enabling Member States to take specific measures derogating from an [EU] rule, measures which could perhaps be justified by recourse to other provisions of primary [EU] law'. Article [347 TFEU] appears to be the dividing line between the normal circumstances in which national and EU institutions operate and the difficult situations of national danger which affect the more general relationship between the EU and the Member States. Since it significantly alters the nature, strength and extent of the links that bind a national legal order to the EU legal order, it is imperative to establish, in each particular case, whether the preconditions for its application are met. This explains why the [EU] legislature has not expressly made the exercise of the powers conferred by Article [347 TFEU] subject to the inadequacy of the other legal remedies which the Treaty makes available to the Member States for the purpose of safeguarding their interests'.[107]

Article 347 of the TFEU is therefore a safeguard clause of general application. This means that it 'permits a Member State in certain exceptional circumstances to derogate even from fundamental [EU] rules'.[108] Case law shows that this provision has already been invoked against the common commercial policy and the free movement of goods,[109] the principle of equal treatment for men and women,[110] the free movement of capital[111] and EU rules on public procurement.[112]

However, the question has been raised as to whether certain fundamental rights should prevail in all cases under Article 347 TFEU. The answer was affirmative in the *Kadi and Al Barakaat* cases. After acknowledging that Article 347 TFEU 'implicitly permits obstacles to the operation of the common market when they are caused by measures taken by a Member State to carry out the international obligations it has accepted for the purpose of maintaining international peace and security',[113] the Court held that such provisions 'cannot,

[107] See the opinion of AG Cosmas, 23 March 2000, in Case C-423/98, *Albore*, ECLI:EU:C:2000:158, para. 27.

[108] See Order of the Court of 29 June 1994, Case C-120/94 R, *Commission v Greece*, ECLI:EU:C:1994:275, para. 68.

[109] Ibid., para. 67.

[110] See Case C-273/97, *Sirdar*, ECLI:EU:C:1999:523, para. 19: '[T]here is no general reservation as regards the application of the principle of equal treatment for men and women to measures of organisation of the armed forces taken for reasons of protection of public security, with the exception of the possible application of Article 224 of the Treaty [EC, now Article 347 TFEU], which concerns a wholly exceptional situation'.

[111] See Case C-423/98, *Albore*, ECLI:EU:C:2000:401, para. 21.

[112] See the opinion of AG Stix-Hackl, of 12 April 2005, in Case C-231/03, *Co.Na.Me.*, ECLI:EU:C:2005:212, para. 62, for the judgment of the Court of 21 July 2005, Case C-231/03, *Co.Na.Me*, ECLI:EU:C:2005:487.

[113] See Joined Cases C-402/05 P and C-415/05 P, *Kadi and Al Barakaat*, ECLI:EU:C:2008:461, para. 302.

however, be understood as authorising any derogation from the principles of liberty, democracy and respect for human rights and fundamental freedoms enshrined in Article 6(1) EU as a foundation of the Union'.[114] However, it may be worth pointing out that other international instruments also contain similar provisions. The ECHR contains an emergency clause in Article 15, which allows the contracting parties, within certain limits, to take 'measures' derogating from their obligations under the Convention 'in time of war or other public emergency threatening the life of the nation'.[115] Similarly, Article XXI (b) (iii) of the aforementioned GATT provides that '[n]othing in this Agreement shall be construed [...] to prevent any contracting party from taking any action which it considers necessary for the protection of its essential security interests [...] taken in time of war or other public emergency in international relations'.[116]

B. THE SCOPE OF ARTICLE 347 OF THE TFEU LIMITED TO CERTAIN CRISIS SITUATIONS

Article 347 of the TFEU only authorises Member States to take certain measures in exceptional circumstances that can be considered as specific crisis situations. Four cases are described exhaustively at:[117] serious internal disturbances affecting the maintenance of law and order (Section 1); war (Section 2); serious international tension constituting a threat of war (Section 3); and the fulfilment of obligations which a Member State has accepted with a view to maintaining peace and international security (Section 4), for example by complying with NATO membership or with United Nations Security Council resolutions (see in particular Chapter VII of the United Nations Charter). The list should be

---

114 Ibid., para. 303.

115 See AG Kokott's aforementioned conclusion in Opinion 2/13, para. 258. This is why, in her view: 'There is thus no reason to be concerned that the proposed accession of the EU to the ECHR might in any way affect the situation of Member States in relation to Article 15 ECHR'.

116 See the aforementioned judgment of the General Court in Case T-715/14, in which the judge considered that this provision could cover certain 'actions by the Russian Federation undermining or threatening Ukraine's territorial integrity, sovereignty and independence' (see para. 182). This judgment was confirmed, on appeal, by Case C-732/18 P, *Rosneft a.o. v Council*, ECLI:EU:C:2020:727.

117 However, see L. Weitzel, 'Art. 297 EC', in I. Pingel (ed.), *De Rome à Lisbonne. Commentaire article par article des traités UE et CE*, 2nd ed., Bâle/Paris/Bruxelles, Helbing Lichtenhahn/Dalloz/Bruylant, 2010, p. 1827, who refers to three types of situation, considering both situations of war and the threat of war. Sharing the same approach: see opinion of M. Jacobs in Case C-120/94, *Commission v Greece*, ECLI:EU:C:1995:109, para. 44. But in favour of examining the '4 situations': N. Cunha Rodrigues, 'Artigos 346-347-348 TFUE', in M. Lopes Porto and G. Anastácio, *Tratado de Lisboa anotado he comentado*, Lisbon, Almedina, 2012, p. 1219.

seen as exhaustive, in accordance with the restrictive interpretation of any derogation provision.

These different situations are not always easy to identify, especially as regards the first, which concerns serious internal disturbances affecting the maintenance of public order. A number of questions remain unanswered, for example: are economic or social crises included among such situations, or do they involve cases of 'civil war' or civil unrest? It might be interesting to refer to ECJ case law requiring Member States to prove the existence of a 'danger to public order with which [a government] could not cope' or a 'threat of serious disturbance to public order' to justify a failure to correctly apply Community law, for example, concerning the rules on the free movement of goods.[118] Another question is whether terrorist attacks or natural or man-made disasters, within the meaning of Article 222 TFEU, are sufficient to meet the requirement of Article 347 TFEU or whether there must also be subsequent serious internal disturbances?

Further questions may also be asked regarding the other specific circumstances referred to in Article 347 TFEU, such as a war situation: should the definition of public international law be applied, namely an 'armed conflict' involving the 'resort to armed force between States or protracted armed violence between governmental authorities and organized armed groups or between such groups within a State'?[119] And does the Member State concerned have to be one of the parties to the war?

The difficulty of identifying accurately the types of crisis situations likely to be covered by Article 347 TFEU is therefore very real. Two concrete examples illustrate this. The first example was Argentina's invasion of the Falkland Islands in 1982, which was the subject of United Nations Security Council Resolution 502 and led the United Kingdom to take certain measures, including a ban on imports of products from Argentina. This situation was considered to be one of war (the 'Falklands War').

The second example has more to do with the international tensions that arose between Greece and the Former Yugoslav Republic of Macedonia (FYROM) after the latter declared its independence in 1991 using the name Macedonia, which was disputed by Greece. In 1994, Greece adopted unilateral measures prohibiting trade, in particular via the port of Thessaloniki, in products originating in, coming from or destined for FYROM and the import into Greece of products originating in or coming from FYROM.[120] In this case, Greece referred to serious internal disturbances affecting the maintenance of

---

118 See Case C-265/95, *Commission v France*, ECLI:EU:C:1997:595, paras. 54–58.

119 See judgment of 2 October 1995 of the International Criminal Tribunal for the former Yugoslavia, *Prosecutor v. Dusko Tadić*, case no. IT-94-1-AR72(70).

120 On this dispute see C. Stefanou and H. Xanthaki, *A Legal and Political Interpretation of Articles 224 and 225 of the Treaty of Rome. The FYROM Cases*, Dartmouth, Ashgate, 1997.

public order, as well as war and serious international tensions constituting a threat of war. This led Advocate General Jacobs to question the relationship between the reference in Article 30 TFEU to public security and the reference in Article 347 TFEU to serious internal disturbances affecting the maintenance of public order. Indeed, the Commission argued that the two provisions were analogous and that the Court's case law on the restrictive interpretation of Article 30 TFEU was therefore applicable to Article 347 TFEU. According to Advocate General Mr Jacobs, the analogy between these two provisions 'must not be taken too far' for the following reasons: 'In the first place, whereas the situations covered by Article [30] may be described as exceptional, those covered by Article [347 TFEU] are, as the Court recognized in paragraph 27 of the *Johnston* judgment, *wholly* exceptional. That is confirmed by the fact that Article [347 TFEU] has so rarely been invoked, while recourse to Article [30 TFEU] is relatively common. A second difference relates to the breadth of the possible derogations permitted by the two articles. Article [30 TFEU] permits derogations from one aspect of the common market (admittedly a fundamental one); Article [347 TFEU], on the other hand, permits derogations from the rules of the common market in general'.[121] Consequently, Mr Jacobs considered that when Article 347 TFEU speaks of 'serious internal disturbances affecting the maintenance of law and order', it must be read 'as envisaging a breakdown of public order on a scale much vaster than the type of civil unrest which might justify recourse to Article [30 TFEU]. What seems to be envisaged is a situation verging on a total collapse of internal security, for otherwise it would be difficult to justify recourse to a sweeping derogation which is capable of authorizing the suspension of all of the ordinary rules governing the common market'.[122]

In any event, the list referred to in Article 347 TFEU raises 'the fundamental issue of the scope of the Court's power to exercise judicial review in such situations',[123] in particular those involving the concept of 'war' or 'threat of war'. In such cases, 'the intensity of the review may be severely curtailed by the absence of any appropriate legal criteria capable of judicial application'.[124] Furthermore, Advocate General Jacobs pointed out that the scope for judicial review of possible misuse of powers 'is extremely limited [...] because of the nature of the subject-matter'.[125] Therefore, as Advocate General Cosmas pointed out, 'while the national perception of whether the circumstances meet the conditions of Article [347 TFEU] is not uncontrolled from the point of view

121 See the opinion of M. Jacobs in Case C-120/94, *Commission v Greece*, ECLI:EU:C:1995:109, para. 46.
122 Ibid., para. 47.
123 Ibid., para. 50.
124 Ibid., para. 51.
125 Ibid., para. 63.

of [EU] law it is not amenable to full judicial review as to the substance, such as the review of proportionality carried out in the context of [other provisions of EU law relating to public security]'.[126]

However, one may wonder whether the duration of the measures adopted by the Member States does not constitute another possibility for revision. The logical interpretation of a crisis situation is that, by its very nature, such a situation is not intended to last. Consequently, the national measures concerned must be temporary and not permanent in nature.[127] This is in clear contrast to the measures adopted in the context of the application of Article 346 TFEU (see above).

C. THE CONSULTATION PROCEDURE REQUIRED BY ARTICLE 347 TFEU

The only formal obligation imposed on a Member State wishing to adopt the measures referred to in Article 347 TFEU is to enter into consultations with the other Member States 'with a view to taking together the steps needed'. The objective of this consultation process is clearly defined: 'to prevent the functioning of the internal market being affected'.

It should be noted that this reference to the functioning of the internal market is broader than the reference to 'the conditions of competition in the internal market' used in Article 346(1)(b) TFEU (see above). Moreover, while there is an obligation to consult, there is no obligation to achieve results.[128] In other words, the Member State may not take the measures necessary to prevent the functioning of the internal market from being affected.

With regard to the outcome of this consultation process, it is interesting to note that while the English version of Article 347 TFEU refers to 'steps needed' the French version refers to 'dispositions nécessaires'. Be that as it may, the Member States enjoy broad discretion as to the nature and content of these common measures, within the limits of the EU's competences and in particular 'in the light of the provisions of the TEU concerning the CFSP'.[129] An example can be given in the context of the aforementioned Falklands War. Following the measures taken by the United Kingdom, the Member States consulted each

---

126 See the opinion of AG Cosmas, 23 March 2000, in Case C-423/98, *Albore*, ECLI:EU:C:2000:158, para. 29.

127 See in this regard: N. Mackel, 'Article 296 of the EC Treaty', in P. Léger (ed.), *Commentaire article par article des traités UE et CE*, Bâle/Paris/Bruxelles, Helbing Lichtenhahn/Dalloz/Bruylant, 2000, p. 1880 and N. Cunha Rodrigues, 'Artigos 346-347-348 TFUE', in M. Lopes Porto and G. Anastácio, *Tratado de Lisboa anotado he comentado*, Lisbon, Almedina, 2012, p. 1220.

128 See in this regard: N. Mackel, 'Article 296 of the EC Treaty', ibid, p. 1883.

129 Ibid., p. 1883.

other in accordance with ex-Article 224 of the EC Treaty (now Article 347 TFEU) and decided to adopt a Council Regulation suspending imports of all products originating in Argentina.[130]

III. THE CONTROL REGIME UNDER ARTICLE 348 TFEU

Article 348 TFEU also has its origins in the 1957 Treaty of Rome (Article 225 of the EEC Treaty). It subsequently became Article 298 of the EC Treaty, and its current wording is set out in the Treaty of Lisbon (2007), without changing its substance.

The objective assigned to Article 348 TFEU is clear: it is to control the use by Member States of the powers conferred on them in the circumstances referred to in Articles 346 and 347 TFEU and, consequently, to 'avoid the collateral effects which [these] Articles [...] may have on competition and the economy'.[131]

As Advocate General Stix-Hackl pointed out in *Co.Na.Me.*, cited above, 'as is apparent in particular from Article [348 TFEU], the Member States' powers in applying [Articles 346 and 347 TFEU] are not by any means unlimited and are in particular subject to scrutiny by the Commission and the Court of Justice'.[132] In other words, and in accordance with the case law, 'two specific legal remedies are prescribed by the Treaty in relation of measures adopted by the Member States under [Articles 346 and 347 TFEU]'.[133]

These two specific remedies are different in nature: the first, covered by the first paragraph of Article 348 TFEU, is administrative in nature (Section A); the second, covered by the second paragraph of Article 348 TFEU, is judicial in nature (Section B).

A. THE ADMINISTRATIVE PROCEDURE PROVIDED FOR IN ARTICLE 348(1) TFEU

The first paragraph of Article 348 TFEU requires the Commission to enter into bilateral discussions with Member States which have taken measures in the circumstances referred to in Articles 346 and 347 TFEU to examine how those

130 Council Regulation (EEC) No 877/82 suspending imports of all products originating in Argentina, [1982] *OJ* L102/1.

131 See the opinion of AG Colomer in Joined Cases C-284/05 et al, ECLI:EU:C:2009:67, para. 39.

132 See the opinion of AG Stix-Hackl in Case C-231/03, *Co.Na.Me.*, ECLI:EU:C:2005:212, para. 63.

133 See Case T-26/01, *Fiocchi munizioni SpA v Commission*, ECLI:EU:T:2003:248, para. 62.

measures can be adapted to the rules laid down by the Treaties if – and only if – those measures have the effect of distorting the conditions of competition in the internal market.

It should be added that Member States themselves may request the application of the review procedure provided for in Article 348(1) TFEU, provided that the national measures concerned actually fall within the scope of Article 346 TFEU or Article 347 TFEU.[134]

Thus, the obligation for the Commission to carry out a bilateral examination is subject to the existence of such a distortion of the conditions of competition in the internal market. A parallel can be drawn with the last sentence of Article 346(1)(b) TFEU, which stipulates that national measures must 'not adversely affect the conditions of competition in the internal market regarding products which are not intended for specifically military purposes' (see above). However, this is not the same criterion as that used in Article 347 TFEU, which refers to affecting the 'functioning of the internal market' (see above). Without further guidance, reference may be made to how EU competition rules, in particular Articles 101 and 102 TFEU, are applied and interpreted by the Commission and the Court, insofar as these provisions include as an essential criterion the fact of 'preventing, restricting or distorting competition within the internal market'.[135]

However, it should be made clear that the Commission's allegation or demonstration of the existence of a distortion of the conditions of competition in the internal market as defined by Article 348(1) TFEU is not in itself sufficient to consider that there has been an infringement by the Member States concerned in relation to their Community obligations. This is because, by definition, the use of Article 346 TFEU and/or Article 347 TFEU allows them to derogate from Community law, subject to certain conditions (see above).[136]

If such a distortion is identified, the Commission's only obligation is to examine, with the Member States concerned, the possibilities of adjusting their national measures to comply with Community law. However, there is no obligation other than this duty to examine. Indeed, there is no reference to the type of results or follow-up that may be obtained after the control exercise. As the case law confirms, 'the Commission is not required, at the conclusion of the examination provided for by the first paragraph of Article [348 TFEU], to adopt a decision concerning the measures in question. Furthermore, […] the

---

134 See Case C-246/12 P, *Ellinika Nafpigeia AE v European Commission*, ECLI:EU:C:2013:133, paras. 40–42.

135 See commentary on Arts. 101 to 109 TFEU.

136 See N. Mackel, 'Article 296 of the EC Treaty', in P. Léger (ed.), *Commentaire article par article des traités UE et CE*, Bâle/Paris/Bruxelles, Helbing Lichtenhahn/Dalloz/Bruylant, 2000, p. 1880.

first paragraph of Article [348 TFEU] does not state that the Commission shall, where necessary, address an appropriate directive or decision to the Member State concerned. Where it decides, as in this case, to have recourse to the special procedural regime established by Article [348 TFEU], the Commission therefore has no power to address a final decision or directive to the Member State concerned'.[137] Consequently, when the Commission decides to use the bilateral review provided for in Article 348(1) TFEU, it does not have the power to adopt 'any mandatory measure on the compliance of the measures at issue with [EU] law'.[138] This is an important difference from other remedies where the Commission must examine national measures and, if necessary, issue appropriate directives or decisions to the Member States, for example concerning State aid,[139] or national measures in favour of public undertakings and undertakings entrusted with the operation of services of general economic interest or having the character of a fiscal monopoly.[140]

Furthermore, Article 348(1) TFEU is silent on the legal nature of the indications or proposals for adjustments that the Commission may suggest to the Member States as part of its examination. The fact is that Member States are not obliged to comply with such suggestions, if they are made by the Commission.[141]

This leads some authors to conclude that the legal force of Article 348(1) TFEU is 'considerably limited'.[142] However, if the Commission is convinced that certain measures are necessary to neutralise the distortion of conditions of competition in the internal market, and that this distortion is therefore the result of an abuse by a Member State of Article 346 TFEU and/or Article 347 TFEU, then it is still possible (but not obligatory) for it to refer the matter directly to the Court of Justice, following Article 348(2) TFEU.

B. THE JUDICIAL PROCEDURE PROVIDED FOR IN ARTICLE 348(2) TFEU

Article 348(2) TFEU provides that the Commission (like any Member State) may, by way of derogation from the usual infringement procedure provided for

---

137 See Case T-26/01, *Fiocchi munizioni SpA v Commission*, ECLI:EU:T:2003:248, para. 74.

138 Ibid., para. 75.

139 See commentary on Art. 108 TFEU.

140 See commentary on Art. 106 TFEU.

141 In support of this view: N. Cunha Rodrigues, 'Artigos 346-347-348 TFUE ', in M. Lopes Porto and G. Anastácio, *Tratado de Lisboa anotado he comentado*, Lisbon, Almedina, 2012, p. 1221.

142 In this sense: E. Barbier de La Serre, 'Art. 298 EC', in I. Pingel (ed.), *De Rome à Lisbonne. Commentaire article par article des traités UE et CE*, 2nd ed., Bâle/Paris/Bruxelles, Helbing Lichtenhahn/Dalloz/Bruylant, 2010, p. 1830.

in Articles 258 and 259 TFEU, refer a case directly to the Court of Justice if it considers that a Member State is making improper use of the power provided for in Articles 346 and 347 TFEU. However, the control exercised by the Court is relatively limited.

1. *A Derogatory Referral to the Court of Justice*

Article 348(2) TFEU provides for a derogation in the way in which cases may be brought before the Court, by doing away with the pre-litigation phase provided for in Articles 258 and 259 TFEU. These arrangements are not new. It is found in Article 108(2) TFEU in the field of State aid.[143] Similarly, under Article 114(9) TFEU, '[b]y way of derogation from the procedure laid down in Articles 258 and 259, the Commission and any Member State may bring the matter directly before the Court of Justice of the European Union if it considers that another Member State is making improper use of the powers provided for in this Article': i.e. in respect of national provisions derogating from a Union harmonisation measure.[144]

The possibility of dispensing with the pre-litigation phase may seem logical in view of Article 348(1) of the TFEU, which provides for a bilateral examination procedure between the Commission and the Member State concerned, in the event of distortion of the conditions of competition in the internal market. This examination must be regarded as a pre-litigation procedure. However, this reasoning is only partially justified: the criterion for recourse to Article 348(2) TFEU is not necessarily the distortion of the conditions of competition in the internal market, but may also be misuse of the powers provided for in Articles 346 and 347 TFEU. While it is true that such misuse may lead to a distortion of the conditions of competition in the internal market, it is clearly a broader concept, even if it is not precisely defined by primary law.

The question remains as to whether and to what extent such misuse must be demonstrated by the Commission. According to the Commission, 'the burden of proof that an exemption is justified lies with the Member States'.[145] However, it should be emphasised that this burden of proof must be shared with the Commission, which must also explain how Article 346 TFEU and/or Article 347 TFEU has/have been misused in practice.

Apart from the important difference concerning the absence of a pre-litigation phase, the legal remedy provided for in Article 348(2) TFEU bears certain similarities to that provided for in Articles 258 and 259 TFEU: first, a Member State may also refer a case directly to the Court (without, however,

---

[143] See commentary on Art. 108 TFEU.

[144] See commentary on Art. 114 TFEU.

[145] European Commission, 'Interpretative Communication on the application of Article 296 of the Treaty in the field of defence procurement', COM(2006) 779 final, Section 6, p. 9.

being obliged to first ask the Commission to do so) and, second, the Commission is not obliged to refer a case to the Court, the use of the word 'may' being sufficient to confirm that interpretation. As Advocate General Colomer pointed out, '[i]t does not follow from any of the language versions of Article 298 EC that the Commission must use that special procedure. Thus, the Spanish ('*la Comisión o cualquier Estado miembro podrá recurrir directamente*'), French ('*la Commission ou tout État membre peut saisir directement la Cour de justice*'), English ('the Commission or any Member State may bring the matter directly before the Court of Justice') and German ('*verfahren kann die Kommission oder ein Mitgliedstaat den Gerichtshof unmittelbar anrufen*') versions do not connote obligation because the reference to that direct method of challenge is framed merely as a right'.[146]

If the option of referring the case to the Court is taken up, a particular procedural feature should be noted: the Court will rule *in camera*. This is an explicit derogation from the rule laid down in Article 31 of the Statute of the Court, according to which '[t]he hearing in court shall be public, unless the Court of Justice, of its own motion or on application by the parties, decides otherwise for serious reasons'. The Court has no discretion. The hearing must be secret.

Once again, recourse to secrecy seems justified by the subject matter of the dispute. The Member State concerned would not appreciate sensitive information becoming public, in particular information the disclosure of which it considers contrary to its essential security interests, within the meaning of Article 346(1)(a) TFEU (see above). On the other hand, as a counterpart to the *in camera* requirement, this latter provision may not be relied on against the Court during the written and oral phases of the proceedings.

2. *Limited Scope of Judicial Review*

In the event of a referral to the Court, the Court will confine itself 'to assessing whether the Member State concerned has made improper use of the powers conferred on it by [Articles 346 and 347 of the TFEU]'.[147]

The Court of the European Union will be faced with the same dilemma as the Commission in determining the extent to which there is misuse, which cannot, in our view, be limited to demonstrating a distortion of the conditions of competition in the internal market. However, this interpretation does not seem to be shared by Advocate General Colomer, for whom the procedure under Article 348(2) TFEU is 'a summary procedure, since it limits the

[146] See the opinion of AG Colomer in Joined Cases C-284/05 et al, ECLI:EU:C:2009:67, para. 34.

[147] See the opinion of AG Cosmas, 23 March 2000, in Case C-423/98, *Albore*, ECLI:EU:C:2000:158, para. 26.

jurisdiction of the Court to simply determining whether the market and trade are functioning properly'.[148]

In any event, the scope of judicial review is difficult to assess since, to our knowledge, there has been very little case law to date on the application of Article 348(2) TFEU. Suffice it to mention one case (already referred to) in which the Court made an order in response to a request by the Commission for interim measures ordering Greece to suspend measures it adopted in February 1994, pending the judgment in the main proceedings: these measures concerned the Former Yugoslav Republic of Macedonia (FYROM), and prohibited trade, in particular via the port of Thessaloniki, in products originating in, coming from or going to that Republic, as well as the importation into Greece of products originating in, or coming from the FYROM.[149]

In its appeal, the Commission acknowledged that the intensity of judicial review may be limited by the wide margin of discretion enjoyed by the Member State under Article 348 TFEU. However, it maintained that, apart from this reservation due to the nature of the subject-matter, the Court had, in cases brought under that provision, its normal powers to review the compatibility of a Member State's acts with EU law. For example, according to the Commission, the Court could examine not only whether an act constitutes a misuse of powers, but also whether it is vitiated by a manifest error of assessment or is contrary to general principles of law, such as the principles of equal treatment or proportionality. Greece argued, on the contrary, that the expression 'misuse' in Article 348 TFEU meant the same thing as 'misuse of powers' within the meaning of Article 263 TFEU, observing that the same expression is used in both articles in the Greek, German and Dutch versions of the Treaty, and deducing from this terminology that the Court's power of review under Article 348 TFEU was extremely limited and that the Member State can be regarded as having misused its powers only if it claims that its action is intended to achieve an objective included within the terms of Article 346 or 347 TFEU, whereas its real aim is to achieve a different objective.

In his Opinion in this case, Advocate General Jacobs stated that 'irrespective of the question whether the concept of improper use ('usage abusif', in French) of powers in Article [348 TFEU] is identical to the concept of misuse of powers ('détournement de pouvoir', in French) in Article [263 TFEU], it is clear that the scope of the judicial review to be exercised under Article 225 is extremely limited – not just because of the terminology of that and the preceding article

[148] See the opinion of the AG Colomer of 10 February 2009 in Joined Cases C-284/05 and others, ECLI:EU:C:2009:67, para. 41.

[149] See Order of the Court of 29 June 1994, Case C-120/94 R, *Commission v Greece*, ECLI:EU:C:1994:275.

but also because of the nature of the subject-matter'.[150] Consequently, '[i]f a Member State considers, rightly or wrongly, that the attitude of a third State threatens its vital interests, its territorial integrity or its very existence, then it is for the Member State to determine how to respond to that perceived threat: for example, by diplomatic pressure, by the severing of sporting and cultural links, by economic sanctions or even by military action. It is not for the Court of Justice to criticize the appropriateness of the Member State's response, and to say that the chosen course of action is unlikely to achieve the desired aim or that the Member State would have a better prospect of successfully defending its interests by other means. Once again there are no judicial criteria by which such matters may be measured. It is difficult to identify a precise legal test for determining whether a trade embargo is a suitable means of pursuing a political dispute between a Member State and a third State. The decision to take such action is essentially of a political nature'.[151] Consequently, 'the sole limit placed on the autonomy of the Member States is that they may not make improper use of their powers. Clearly a Member State would be using its powers improperly if its real purpose in imposing an embargo on trade with a third State was not to prosecute any political dispute with the third State but to protect its own economy or the interests of domestic traders'.[152]

Finally, the Court did not give judgment on the merits of the case, as the proceedings were discontinued at the Commission's request.[153] However, it is clear from the order on the application for interim measures that the Court seemed reluctant to exercise an extensive judicial review. First of all, the Court considered that 'the speedier nature of the procedure up until Article [348] and the difficult assessments and explanations the examination of which is called for under Articles [347 and 348] are arguments which may be taken into consideration when considering the actual circumstances which may make it necessary to prescribe interim measures'.[154] Next, with regard to the damage resulting from the exacerbation of tension in the Balkans and the risk of war, which would have been caused by the maintenance of the measures adopted by Greece against FYROM, the Court of the Union noted that 'even if the Court were competent to make the political judgments which would be

150 See the opinion of M. Jacobs in Case C-120/94, *Commission v Greece*, ECLI:EU:C:1995:109, para. 63.

151 Ibid., para. 65.

152 Ibid., para. 67.

153 The Commission informed the Court that it considered that it no longer had an interest in continuing the proceedings in view of the fact that a temporary agreement had been concluded between the Hellenic Republic and FYROM on certain matters, following which the former had lifted the trade restrictions imposed in February 1994. See Order of the President of the Court of 19 March 1996, Case C-120/94, *Commission v Greece*, ECLI:EU:C:1996:116, para. 5.

154 See Order of the Court of 29 June 1994, Case C-120/94 R, *Commission v Greece*, ECLI:EU:C:1994:275, para. 43.

indispensable in order to assess the existence of harm and, above all, of a link between that harm and the conduct of the Greek Government, it could not, in any event, form an opinion at this stage of the procedure for interim measures. The assessments it might make would inevitably encroach upon the powers of the Court in the context of Articles [347 and 348] of the Treaty [TFEU] and, therefore, prejudice the decision on the substance of the case'.[155]

In any event, because of the restrictive interpretation of Articles 346 and 347 TFEU to which Article 348 TFEU is linked, some authors consider that judicial review of the latter provision might not be limited to verifying compliance with the objective conditions for the application of those Articles (for example, is the product concerned included in the 1958 list referred to in Article 346 TFEU? Are the conditions of competition in the internal market affected within the meaning of Article 347 TFEU?). But judicial review could also cover the assessment of the measures themselves taken by the Member State,[156] although it remains difficult to strike the right balance, given the wide margin of discretion granted to Member States in this area.

The limited scope of the infringement procedure provided for in Article 348 TFEU is perhaps simply a reflection of the 'unfulfilled repressive function' of the defence exception in general, which means that the arms market is still 'very largely on the fringes of EU law'.[157]

---

155 Ibid., para. 94.

156 See in this regard: N. Cunha Rodrigues, 'Artigos 346-347-348 TFUE', in M. Lopes Porto and G. Anastácio, *Tratado de Lisboa anotado he comentado*, Lisbon, Almedina, 2012, p. 1121.

157 See E. Simon, *Rôles et fonctions du droit de l'Union européenne dans l'intégration des politiques d'acquisition d'armement*, PhD thesis, Paris, Université Paris 1 Panthéon-Sorbonne, defended on 13 July 2017, supervised by V. de Beaufort and S. Rodrigues, p. 151.

PART III

Nuclear Law within the scope of the common security and defence policy

NUCLEAR LAW WITHIN THE SCOPE OF THE COMMON SECURITY AND DEFENCE POLICY

Athanase Popov[1]
PhD in EU law and EU official

I. INTRODUCTION: THE EURATOM TREATY AND THE COMMON SECURITY AND DEFENCE POLICY

The commentary on certain provisions of the Treaty establishing the European Atomic Energy Community (hereinafter 'EAEC' or 'Euratom Treaty')[2] – principally Chapter 7 – may be relevant to the Common Security and Defence Policy (CSDP), given that security and defence are, in the author's view, intertwined, without of course being synonymous. This is all the more so in the nuclear sector. *De lege lata*, nuclear security has its own legal regime, but it is not impossible to reflect, *de lege ferenda*, on its inclusion in the general

---

1 This analysis is provided in a personal capacity and is the sole responsibility of the author. It does not necessarily reflect the official position of the European Commission.

2 Consolidated version, [2016] *OJ* C203/1. The Treaty was signed in Rome on 25 March 1957. Before the mergers of the executives in 1965, there was a Commission (the archives of the Euratom Commission, 1958–1965, are available from the central archives in Florence) and a Council for Euratom, the Court of Justice having always been common to the three Communities of the time. Unlike the Treaty establishing the ECSC, the Euratom Treaty never provided for the existence of a Parliamentary Assembly among the institutions of the Euratom Community, and at present the European Parliament can only be consulted on the adoption of Euratom acts, without being able to intervene as co-legislator. A first commentary, published the year the Euratom Treaty entered into force, is very useful but predates most current developments in nuclear law. It was written by J. Errera, E. Symon, J. Van der Meulen and I. Vernaeve: *Euratom, Analyse et Commentaires du Traité*, Bibliothèque de l'Institut belge de science politique, Brussels, Éditions de la librairie encyclopédique, 1958. A commentary in English, but chapter by chapter rather than article by article, is provided by R. Engstedt, *Handbook on European Nuclear Law: Competences of the Euratom Community under the Euratom Treaty*, Wolters Kluwer Law International, 2020.

regime of the Common Security Policy, the contours of which are not yet fully defined in positive law.

Article 42(1) TEU[3] defines the common security and defence policy as follows:

> The common security and defence policy shall be an integral part of the common foreign and security policy. It shall provide the Union with an operational capacity drawing on civilian and military assets. The Union may use them on missions outside the Union for peace-keeping, conflict prevention and strengthening international security in accordance with the principles of the United Nations Charter. The performance of these tasks shall be undertaken using capabilities provided by the Member States.

Chapter 7 of the Euratom Treaty on 'Safeguards' aims to establish controls that contribute to nuclear non-proliferation, which makes it possible to *prevent the use of nuclear weapons and thus to strengthen international security* (emphasis added). Another way of approaching the commentary on the Euratom Treaty as a treaty relevant to the common security and defence policy is to refer very specifically to the wording of the third paragraph of Article 84 of the EAEC, which states, with regard to safeguards:

> The safeguards may not extend to materials intended to meet defence requirements which are in the course of being specially processed for this purpose or which, after being so processed, are, in accordance with an operational plan, placed or stored in a military establishment.

On the other hand, safeguards should be able to extend to nuclear materials intended for defence purposes which are not being specially processed for defence purposes or which, after such processing, are not located or stored in a military establishment. Thus, military uses of nuclear energy are theoretically likely to fall within the scope of the Euratom Treaty. Nevertheless, the Court of Justice has taken the view that activities in the military field 'are outside the scope of that Treaty', expressed in a body of case-law that may seem at odds with the overall structure of the wording of the third paragraph of Article 84 EAEC (a provision to which the Court does not expressly refer), in particular in the judgment of 12 April 2005, Commission v United Kingdom.[4] Several subsequent judgments have reiterated and consolidated this position, in an even more general statement:

---

3 See, *mutatis mutandis*, J. Schmidt, *The European Union and the Use of Force*, Leiden, Brill/Nijhoff, 2020. See also the commentary on Article 42(1) TEU by A. Hamonic in this publication.

4 Case C-61/03, *Commission of the European Communities v United Kingdom of Great Britain and Northern Ireland* (Jason reactor decommissioning case), ECLI:EU:C:2005:210, para. 36.

> [T]he use of nuclear energy for military purposes falls outside the scope of *all the provisions of the EAEC Treaty*, and not just some of them.[5]

The considerations that led to the crystallisation of this case-law did not exist when the Euratom Treaty entered into force, since in 1958 no Member State had yet acquired nuclear weapons. The French nuclear test of France's first nuclear weapon took place on 13 February 1960 at Hammoudia, in the Saharan region of Reggane, which at the time was still French, while the Algerian war was ongoing.[6] The Euratom Treaty was not, therefore, conceived to completely exclude its application to a future common security and defence policy. It was signed five years after the signing of the second Treaty of Paris instituting the European Defence Community (EDC) on 27 May 1952, which as we know never entered into force.[7] These three Treaties (ECSC, EDC and Euratom) share a conspicuously federalist and supranational conception of common policies, contrasting with the current state of Union law as regards the Common Security and Defence Policy,[8] and other areas. Thus, Article 1 of the EDC Treaty was to provide (emphasis added):

> By the present Treaty the High Contracting Parties institute among themselves a European Defence Community, *supranational in character, consisting of common institutions, common armed Forces* and a common budget.

The European Atomic Energy Community[9] (hereinafter the 'Euratom Community'), described by Jacques Pertek as a 'sectoral Community which has long been discreet and now seems dormant',[10] has rarely met with

---

5 Case C-65/04, *Commission of the European Communities v United Kingdom of Great Britain and Northern Ireland*, ECLI:EU:C:2006:161, para. 26, emphasis added.

6 See the Wikipedia article '*Gerboise Bleue* (nuclear test)', at https://en.wikipedia.org/wiki/Gerboise_Bleue_(nuclear_test), consulted on 23 May 2025.

7 The text of the EDC Treaty is rarely reproduced in currently available works. It is little read and little known. It is available online in English at https://aei.pitt.edu/5201/1/5201.pdf. The only commentary on this Treaty ever published seems to be that by J. Legaret and E. Martin-Dumesnil, *La Communauté européenne de défense, Étude analytique du traité du 27 mai 1952*, Paris, Vrin, 1953.

8 However, even if the current state of the Union does not involve the same governance structure, see E. Bernard, 'La communautarisation de la défense européenne dans le contexte de la guerre en Ukraine', *RTDE*, 2023/3, on recent developments in certain aspects of European defence.

9 See in particular A. Södersten, *Euratom at the Crossroads*, Cheltenham, Edward Elgar Publishing, 2018; A. Popov, 'Euratom competence in the areas of nuclear security and nuclear safety: An impossible parallel?', OECD, Nuclear Energy Agency, *Nuclear Law Bulletin*, Volume 2018/2, pp. 63–70, at https://www.oecd.org/content/dam/oecd/en/publications/reports/2019/02/nuclear-law-bulletin-volume-2018-issue-2_5a272d43/92257d45-en.pdf.

10 J. Pertek, *Droit des institutions de l'Union européenne*, Thémis droit, 4th ed., Paris, PUF, 2014, p. 99.

unanimous approval, despite the initial enthusiasm for nuclear energy.[11] Academic commentators have referred to 'the dormancy of certain aspects of the Euratom Treaty', as well as 'the desire of certain Member States to confine the Community to a very limited role'.[12] However, when the two Treaties of Rome were signed in 1957, sectoral communitarianism was imposed against the logic of creating a general common market covering both coal and steel and nuclear energy. Initially, France opposed the creation of such a general common market, believing that it would be preferable to establish sectoral cooperation.[13] Indeed, 'all the delegations with the exception of the French delegation insisted on the principle of not separating the need to achieve economic integration of the nuclear market from that of achieving general economic integration'.[14] But it was the French point of view that eventually

---

[11] For J. Grunwald, 'arguing in defence of the Euratom Treaty means a constant uphill struggle': 'in the light of the opposition and sometimes even outright obstruction which the Treaty has encountered throughout its history, it is almost an understatement to say that the Treaty has few friends' ('From Challenge to Response: Dormant Powers in Euratom Law', in C. Raetzke (ed.), *Nuclear Law in the EU and Beyond*, Proceedings of the AIDN/INLA Regional Conference 2013 in Leipzig, Baden-Baden, Nomos, 2014, p. 21). Three years later, the same author reiterated this observation: 'Despite its economic weight and its undisputed standing in the nuclear world as a factor of stability, progress and inspiration for almost 60 years, EURATOM and the Treaty establishing it have not got the attention they deserve – neither inside nor outside Europe' (J. Grunwald, 'Peaceful Uses of Nuclear Energy under EURATOM Law', in J.L. Black-Branch, Fleck (eds.), *Nuclear Non-Proliferation in International Law*, Vol. III, Legal Aspects of the Use of Nuclear Energy for Peaceful Purposes, Asser, Springer, 2016, Chapter 6, p. 175).

[12] C. Blumann, 'Euratom', *Encyclopédie Dalloz* (undated, but prior to 1990), point 135. C. Blumann was probably thinking above all of France, whose position is still more sovereignist in nuclear matters than that of its neighbours, at least as far as nuclear security and armament are concerned. There is an emblematic passage from Charles de Gaulle's *Mémoires d'espoir*, which seems out of date only insofar as the situation has changed somewhat since then, in particular because other Member States have caught up their initial lag and because of the accession of new Member States, but which still essentially characterises the French position: 'As far as Euratom was concerned, there appeared to be an irreconcilable opposition between the situation of France, which had already had an active Atomic Energy Commission for some fifteen years, was equipped with numerous facilities and was committed to implementing precise and extensive research and development programmes, and that of the other countries which, having done nothing themselves, would like the appropriations in the common budget to be used to provide them with what they lacked by placing orders with American suppliers' (C. de Gaulle, *Mémoires d'espoir*, Paris, Plon, 1999 (reprint), p. 145, translated here from French).

[13] C. Deubner, 'The expansion of West German capital and the founding of Euratom' (1979) 33(2) *International Organization*, p. 207. See generally O. Pirotte and P. Girerd, fasc. 5010, 5020 and 5021 of the *Juris-Classeurs* devoted to the European Atomic Energy Community, Éditions Techniques, 1994.

[14] S. Neri and H. Sperl, *Treaty establishing the European Atomic Energy Community (Euratom), Preparatory Works, Interpretative Declarations by the Six Governments, Parliamentary Documents*, Court of Justice of the European Communities, Luxembourg, 1962, p. XIX. The statement by P. Pescatore, who wrote in 1982: 'No credit should be attached to the scraps of documents subsequently collected and reproduced in the form of "preparatory work". These elements are certainly authentic, but they have no meaning, given that the

prevailed, so much so that even today, with a few exceptions, nuclear energy is not part of the EU's general economic integration,[15] even though it was also France that subsequently adopted a more reserved stance towards the Euratom Community. Furthermore, the Euratom Treaty is the only regional sectoral treaty on nuclear energy still in force in the world.[16]

II. PREAMBLE TO THE EURATOM TREATY (EXTRACTS)

> RECOGNISING that nuclear energy represents an essential resource for the development and invigoration of industry and will permit the advancement of the cause of peace.[17]

The Euratom Community has specific objectives, set out in the Euratom Treaty. The first paragraph of its Preamble states that the constituent power is aware that 'nuclear energy represents an essential resource for the development and invigoration of industry and will permit *the advancement of the cause of peace*' (emphasis added). With regard to peace, the 'Union's aim [...] to promoting peace' set out in Article 3(1) TEU (introduced by the Treaty of Lisbon) does not apply to the Euratom Community, as there is no reference to this provision in the wording of Article 106a EAEC,[18] pending a possible ruling to the contrary by the Court of Justice, unless the two concepts are synonymous, which could well be the case. Consequently, 'furthering the works of peace' and 'promoting peace' could be seen as complementary. The first of these two formulations is taken from the preamble to the ECSC Treaty:

> DESIROUS of assisting through the expansion of their basic production in raising the standard of living and in furthering the works of peace;[19]

There is no legal definition of the concept of 'peace' in European law. European law does not lay down a general ban on military operations, any more than

essence lies in a purely oral discussion whose only reflection of legal value is [...] the final text of the [t]reaties' (P. Pescatore, 'Les travaux du "groupe juridique" dans la négociation des traités de Rome', *Hémecht, Revue d'histoire luxembourgeoise*, 1982, no. 2, 34, pp. 145–161, article reproduced on the website www.cvce.eu, p. 6: translated here from French).

15 See above, commentary on Article 106a EAEC.

16 J. Grunwald, 'Europäische Atomgemeinschaft', in A. Hatje und P.-C. Müller-Graff (eds.), *Enzyklopädie Europarecht, Band 1: Europäisches Organisations- und Verfassungsrecht*, Baden-Baden, Nomos, 2014, p. 856. The ECSC Treaty predated this, but regulated two sectors: coal and steel. While coal is part of energy law, this is not the case for metallurgy. The Energy Charter Treaty covers energy in its entirety, whatever the source.

17 First paragraph of the preamble to the Euratom Treaty.

18 See the commentary on this article below.

19 Fourth paragraph of the preamble to the ECSC Treaty.

public international law does, and still less on rearmament efforts. On the contrary, since the aborted European Defence Community project, peace has meant both the absence of war and military 'peace-keeping' operations, 'in the spirit of the United Nations Charter', 'particularly by ensuring the defence of Western Europe against any aggression [...], and in close liaison with organisations having the same purpose'.[20]

ANXIOUS to create the conditions of safety necessary to eliminate hazards to the life and health of the public[21]

With regard to 'the conditions of safety necessary to eliminate hazards to the life and health of the public', a distinction should be made between security in the broad sense, which encompasses collective security, security of energy supply, cybersecurity, etc., and security under international nuclear law, which includes physical protection and can be distinguished from 'nuclear safeguards'. Security and 'safeguards' should also be distinguished from nuclear safety. In nuclear law, security and safety can converge to a certain extent. Security and safety 'have in common the aim of protecting persons, property, society and the environment',[22] but in different ways. As explained by the International Atomic Energy Agency (IAEA), nuclear security deals with '[t]he protection and detection of, and response to, theft, *sabotage*, unauthorised access, illegal transfer or other *malicious* acts involving *nuclear material* and other *radioactive substances* or their *associated facilities*'.[23] Nuclear safety, on the other hand, focuses on 'the achievement of proper *operating conditions*, prevention of *accidents* or mitigating of *accident* consequences, resulting in *protection of workers*, the public and the environment from undue *radiation* hazards'.[24] The IAEA also explains that:

> There is not an exact distinction between the general terms safety and security. In general, security is concerned with malicious or negligent actions by humans that could cause or threaten harm to other humans; safety is concerned with the broader issue of harm to humans (or the environment) from radiation, whatever the cause.[25]

20 Extracts from the second paragraph of the preamble to the draft EDC Treaty.
21 Fourth paragraph of the preamble to the Euratom Treaty. See also the commentary on Article 2(e) EAEC below.
22 IAEA, *Objective and Essential Elements of a State's Nuclear Security Regime*, Nuclear Security Fundamentals, *IAEA Nuclear Security Series*, No. 20, Vienna, IAEA, 2013, p. 1.
23 IAEA, *IAEA Safety Glossary: Terminology used in nuclear safety and radiation protection*, 2007 edition, IAEA, Vienna, 2007, p. 133.
24 Ibid. See also the Convention on Nuclear Safety (1994), IAEA document 'INFCIRC/449', 1963 UNTS 293, which entered into force on 24 October 1996, Article 1, 'Objectives'.
25 Ibid., definition of 'nuclear safety'.

The links between safety and security stem in particular from certain language versions of the Euratom Treaty, as well as from the concepts used in national nuclear law. For example, in German – a language renowned for its many subtle conceptual distinctions – only the legal term *Sicherheit* is used to designate both safety and security, in the fourth paragraph of the preamble, as in the rest of the Euratom Treaty. Similarly, in Italian, *sicurezza* refers to both safety and security. The wording of the preamble itself brings together 'safety' and 'health of populations', in the knowledge that the latter comes under 'the broader issue of radiological damage to human beings'. French law regards nuclear law as deriving from nuclear security.[26] This does not reflect the greater precision of the English language, which distinguishes between *safeguards, security* and *safety*, but rather conceptual differences that reflect differences in the legal regime for nuclear security in national, European and international law.

> DESIRING to associate other countries with their work and to cooperate with international organisations concerned with the peaceful development of atomic energy[27]

What is most striking about reading the Euratom Treaty is the overriding importance given to international cooperation with third countries and other international organisations, whereas the ECSC and then EEC Treaties focused mainly on cooperation between Member States and the construction of a common market, the predecessor of the single market. As a result, the Euratom Community's external policy has been highly ambitious from the outset, even if it does not currently enjoy the visibility and public interest it deserves due to the hostility of part of European public opinion towards nuclear energy. The initial activism in external relations can be explained by the fact that American diplomacy very early on wanted to have a single interlocutor in Europe for nuclear policies.[28] As a little-known example, Euratom has a partnership with

---

26 See Article L 591-1 of the Environment Code, first and second paragraphs, which states: 'Nuclear security includes nuclear safety, radiation protection, the prevention of and fight against malicious acts as well as civil security actions in the event of an accident. Nuclear safety is the set of technical and organisational measures relating to the design, construction, operation, shutdown and decommissioning of basic nuclear installations and the transport of radioactive substances, taken with a view to preventing accidents or limiting their effects'.

27 Fifth paragraph of the preamble to the Euratom Treaty.

28 The United States even seems to have actively contributed to the establishment of the Euratom Community: 'Confronted by the determination of German industrialists and the French CEA to go their own way, the State Department clung to the hope that the American lead in the nuclear domain, though a wasting asset, if mobilized rapidly could draw these nations together in a supranational entity that would cohere with the foreign policy and security interests of the United States' (J. Krige, 'The peaceful atom as political weapon: Euratom and the American foreign policy in the late 1950s' (2008) 38(1) *Historical Studies in the Natural Sciences*, pp. 43–44.

the Korean Peninsula Energy Development Organisation (KEDO). KEDO was established under the Agreement of 9 March 1995 on the establishment of the Korean Peninsula Energy Development Organisation, as amended on 19 September 1997, between the Governments of the Republic of Korea, Japan and the United States of America. The eighth agreement between the Community and KEDO expired on 31 May 2021. Following its decision to terminate the KEDO light water nuclear reactor project and the 2007 decision to assume the responsibilities of the secretariat with a much-reduced staff and minimal premises, the KEDO Steering Committee decided in 2021 to maintain the organisation beyond 31 May 2021. Both the Community and KEDO have expressed the wish to continue their cooperation in order to bring the light water reactor project to an end and to wind up KEDO in due form. After 31 May 2021, the agreement has been automatically renewed each year. It is therefore necessary to apply the agreement retroactively. The agreement was to remain in force until at least 31 May 2024.[29]

The Euratom Community cooperates with several international organisations, sometimes in the absence of binding cooperation agreements. For example, it has observer status at the Nuclear Energy Agency (NEA), part of the Organisation for Economic Cooperation and Development (OECD) in Europe and based in Paris, which currently specialises mainly in the issue of civil nuclear liability. The Secretary-General of the OECD, to which the NEA reports, is in particular the depositary of the Paris Convention on Third Party Liability in the Field of Nuclear Energy, to which Euratom has not acceded, but which the Member States were authorised to sign and ratify in the interests of the EEC.[30]

---

[29] See also Council Decision (Euratom) 2023/2781 of 8 December 2023 approving the conclusion by the European Commission of the Agreement between the European Atomic Energy Community (Euratom) and the Korean Peninsula Energy Development Organisation (KEDO), [2023] OJ L223/2781.

[30] See Proposal for a Council Decision authorising the Member States which are Contracting Parties to the Paris Convention of 29 July 1960 on Third Party Liability in the Field of Nuclear Energy to sign, in the interest of the European Community, the Protocol amending that Convention; Proposal for a Council Decision authorising the Member States which are Contracting Parties to the Paris Convention of 29 July 1960 on Third Party Liability in the Field of Nuclear Energy to ratify, or accede to, in the interest of the European Community, the Protocol amending that Convention. The two proposed decisions were adopted on 8 March 2004 (https://www.senat.fr/ue/pac/E2346.html). It should be noted that although they concern nuclear energy, the two decisions were adopted by the EEC and not by Euratom, as their main purpose is to amend the rules on jurisdiction in application of the Brussels I Regulation.

III. ARTICLE 2 EAEC

TITLE I. THE TASKS OF THE COMMUNITY

Article 2 EAEC

In order to perform its task, the Community shall, as provided in this Treaty:

[...]

a) make certain, by appropriate supervision, that nuclear materials are not diverted to purposes other than those for which they are intended;

[...]

Article 2(e) EAEC sets out what is meant by 'safeguards', to which Chapter 7 is devoted. This provision also introduces the concept of 'safeguards', hence the term '*accord relatif à l'application de garanties*' used in French in multilateral agreements with the IAEA, in order to transpose the concept of 'safeguards' from international nuclear law.

h) establish with other countries and international organisations such relations as will foster progress in the peaceful uses of nuclear energy.

The Euratom Treaty has its own logic. As primary law, it takes precedence in principle over public international law in the domestic legal order.[31] However, nowadays, it is interpreted for the most part in light of the Treaty on the Non-Proliferation of Nuclear Weapons of 1970[32] (hereinafter NPT), even though the Euratom Community is not a party to the NPT. This Treaty was concluded during the Cold War, when several States had already acquired nuclear weapons, including France, a Member State of the Euratom Community. Article 1 of the NPT provides:

> Each nuclear-weapon State Party to the Treaty undertakes not to transfer to any recipient whatsoever nuclear weapons or other nuclear explosive devices or control over such weapons or explosive devices directly, or indirectly; and not in any way

[31] At least since Joined Cases C-584/10 P, C-593/10 P and C-595/10 P, *European Commission and Others v Yassin Abdullah Kadi*, ECLI:EU:C:2013:518.

[32] Reproduced as an IAEA document INFCIRC/140, 22 April 1970, 729 UNTS 169. The NPT entered into force on 5 March 1970. The depositaries of the NPT at the time were the governments of the United Kingdom of Great Britain and Northern Ireland, the United States of America and the Union of Soviet Socialist Republics (succeeded by the government of the Russian Federation). France only acceded to the NPT in 1992. Only four States have never signed the NPT: India, Israel, Pakistan and South Sudan (see https://treaties.unoda.org/t/npt/participants).

> to assist, encourage, or induce any non-nuclear-weapon State to manufacture or otherwise acquire nuclear weapons or other nuclear explosive devices, or control over such weapons or explosive devices.

It was legitimate to think that the purpose of the Euratom Treaty was to prevent Member States from acquiring nuclear weapons by encouraging cooperation in civil nuclear energy. Nowhere does the Euratom Treaty state that the manufacture or acquisition of nuclear weapons is left to the discretion of the Member States. Several States parties to the NPT had already acquired nuclear weapons when they joined or did so subsequently, as part of a strategy of 'nuclear deterrence' designed to promote peace rather than threaten it.[33] In the absence of a legal definition of 'peace', contradictory objectives can be assigned to it. The Euratom Treaty establishes a common regime for all Member States. To say that it merely acknowledges the existence of nuclear-weapon States and that it simply contributes to ensuring that other Member States do not acquire nuclear weapons by simply checking that the actual use of nuclear material complies with its declared use is an anachronism, and also a challenge of the equality of Member States, enshrined in Article 4(2) TEU, to which Article 106a EAEC, quite sensibly, does not refer.

Article 3(1) of the NPT provides:

> Each non-nuclear-weapon State Party to the Treaty undertakes to accept safeguards, as set forth in an agreement to be negotiated and concluded with the International Atomic Energy Agency in accordance with the Statute of the International Atomic Energy Agency and the Agency's safeguards system, for the exclusive purpose of verification of the fulfilment of its obligations assumed under this Treaty with a view to preventing diversion of nuclear energy from peaceful uses to nuclear weapons or other nuclear explosive devices. [...]

Thus, contrary to the principle of equality between Member States, only non-nuclear-weapon States undertake to accept the safeguards stipulated in an agreement negotiated and concluded with the IAEA, in accordance with the IAEA Statute and the IAEA safeguards system.

It cannot be denied that nuclear non-proliferation contributes to common security. Several international agreements and secondary legislation have been adopted jointly on the basis of Chapter 7 of the Euratom Treaty and the NPT.[34]

---

33 Nuclear deterrence may have worked during the Cold War, but it is now clear that it can no longer prevent a war involving nuclear-weapon states. This poses the question of whether the whole body of international law on which collective security is based needs to be rethought.

34 See the international agreements cited below under Articles 77–79 EAEC.

IV. CHAPTER 7 OF THE EURATOM TREATY

A. ARTICLES 77 AND 79 EAEC

CHAPTER 7. Safeguards

Article 77 EAEC

In accordance with the conditions laid down in this Chapter, the Commission shall ensure that it is present in the territories of the Member States:

a) that ores, source materials and special fissile materials are not diverted from the uses for which their users have declared them;

The safeguards defined in this way are carried out in two ways: by verifying the nuclear compatibility of nuclear operators and by physical verification through inspections by Euratom inspectors.

b) the provisions relating to supply and any particular safeguarding obligations assumed by the Community under an agreement concluded with a third State or an international organisation are complied with.

Whereas Article 77(a) EAEC refers to the non-diversion of nuclear material from its intended use, Article 77(b) EAEC refers to the numerous international commitments entered into by Euratom, which are binding on both States and nuclear operators.

These commitments are of two types. On the one hand, there are bilateral nuclear cooperation agreements in force between the Euratom Community and third countries (Section 1). On the other hand, the Community and its Member States have obligations under several multilateral agreements, in particular the three 'safeguards agreements' currently in force with the IAEA (Section 2).

1. *Bilateral Cooperation Agreements*

Bilateral agreements are nuclear cooperation agreements concluded by the Euratom Community with third countries. The Member States are represented by Euratom, as this is an exclusive competence of the Community under Article 77(b) of the EAEC. They do not have to be transposed into national law, as their implementation is the responsibility of the European Commission, which enters into direct relations with the operators of national nuclear installations for this purpose.

To date, the Euratom Community has concluded ten nuclear cooperation agreements, with the United States, Canada, Australia, Kazakhstan, Argentina,

Japan, South America, Ukraine, the United Kingdom and Uzbekistan. These agreements do not affect the unity of (Euratom) Community or European law, as they apply in each case to nuclear material covered by commitments with the third country in question. They therefore do not affect the equality between Member States, unlike the right granted to some Member States – but not to others – to acquire nuclear weapons.[35] The Commission's proposal for a new regulation on the application of Euratom safeguards (adopted in May 2025),[36] initially reflected the nuclear cooperation agreements in force between the Community and third countries,[37] which provided a better overview of all the applicable rules. If the Community's competences are extended to implicit competences, this is always due to the nuclear cooperation agreements approved by the Council and not because of a reminder of the obligations incumbent on nuclear operators under the said nuclear cooperation agreements in a Commission Regulation.

For example, the most recent nuclear cooperation agreement is the 'Agreement between the Government of the United Kingdom of Great Britain and Northern Ireland and the European Atomic Energy Community for the Safe and Peaceful Uses of Nuclear Energy'.[38] Like other similar agreements, it regulates the transfer of nuclear and non-nuclear materials, equipment and technology.[39] It is open to any Member State to consider that the competences of the Euratom Community exclude non-nuclear material, equipment and technology, but the Council has approved the inclusion of such provisions concerning nuclear material, but also non-nuclear material, equipment and technology covered by commitments with the third country in question. Finally, the nuclear cooperation agreements of this type extend Euratom's competence in physical protection matters to relations with the operators of the third country in question:

> Application of physical protection measures shall be at all times at levels which satisfy as a minimum the criteria set out in Annex C of the Guidelines for Nuclear Transfers. Supplementary to that document, the United Kingdom, the Community as represented by the European Commission where appropriate, and the Member States of the Community shall refer, when applying physical protection measures, to

35 See above, commentary on Article 2(h), EAEC.

36 COM(2023) 793: Proposal for a Council Decision approving a Commission Regulation (Euratom) on the application of Euratom safeguards, Non-legislative procedure 2023/0465/NLE; and Commission Regulation (Euratom) 2025/974 of 26 May 2025 on the application of Euratom safeguards, C/2025/3204, [2025] *OJ* L2025/974.

37 Ibid. Art. 39 ('International obligations'), para. 2: 'The provisions of this Regulation, and in particular Articles 19, 20, 23, 24 and 37 shall be applied in conformity with the NCAs in force between the Community and third countries and in such a way that the Commission can fulfil the obligations of the Community under such agreements'.

38 [2021] *OJ* L150/2.

39 See also Art. 9.

their obligations under the Amended CPPNM, including any further amendments to the Amended CPPNM that are in force for each Party, and the recommendations in IAEA INFCIRC/225/Rev.5 (Nuclear Security Recommendations on Physical Protection of Nuclear Material and Nuclear Facilities), including any revision unless mutually determined otherwise by the Parties after consultations in the Joint Committee.[40]

2. *Multilateral Agreements and 'Safeguards Agreements'*

The Convention on the Physical Protection of Nuclear Material (CPPNM)[41] negotiated under the auspices of the IAEA and amended in 2005, in particular so that it also covers nuclear installations,[42] is one of the main legal instruments extending Community competence to physical protection, which is an essential component of nuclear security.[43] Unlike competence under nuclear cooperation agreements,[44] this competence is enforceable vis-à-vis Member States, which are themselves the addressees of the obligations. This competence is little exercised by the Euratom Community, but cannot be completely denied, at least legally speaking. The 2005 amendment extended the scope of the protection required by the CPPNM: whereas the obligations imposed by the CPPNM concerning physical protection were aimed at nuclear materials during international transport, the 2005 amendment obliges the contracting parties to protect both *nuclear materials* and *nuclear installations* used for peaceful purposes during use, storage or transport. The amendment also extends cooperation between States to include prompt measures to be taken to locate and recover stolen or smuggled nuclear material; to mitigate any radiological consequences of an act of sabotage; and to prevent and combat related offences.

Thus, the CPPNM represents an important step in the international community's efforts to improve the physical protection of nuclear materials and facilities. As it is a mixed agreement, both Euratom and its Member States are competent to apply it,[45] although this joint competence cannot be included

---

40 See also Art. 7.

41 Convention on the Physical Protection of Nuclear Material (1980), doc. IAEA INFCIRC/274 Rev. 1, 1456 TRNU 125, entered into force on 8 February 1987 (CPPNM).

42 Amendment to the Convention on the Physical Protection of Nuclear Material (2005), IAEA document INFCIRC/274/Rev.1/Mod.1, entered into force on 8 May 2016.

43 See S. Drobysz, 'Nuclear security: Physical protection, illicit trafficking and nuclear terrorism', in K. Sexton Nick and S.G. Burns (eds.), *Principles and practice of international nuclear law*, NEA, No. 7599, OECD, 2022, pp. 339–355.

44 See subsection 1 above.

45 'Ruling' of the Court of Justice of 14 November 1978 pursuant to Article 103(3) of the EAEC Treaty – Draft Convention of the International Atomic Energy Agency on the Physical Protection of Nuclear Materials, Facilities and Transport, 1/78, ECLI:EU:C:1978:202, p. 02151.

in the definition of EU shared competence, which does not a priori apply to the Euratom Community.

According to the Court of Justice of the European Communities, the measures provided to ensure physical protection 'concern in part the sphere of competence of the Member States and in part that of the Community'.[46] It was able to reach this conclusion because 'the concept of 'safeguards ' under the [Euratom] Treaty is sufficiently comprehensive to encompass physical protection measures'.[47] To date, this competence has not been fully exercised by Euratom. However, according to the declaration made by the Euratom Community when it joined the CPPNM, 'Articles 8 to 13 and paragraphs 2 and 3 of Article 14 of the [CPPNM] do not apply to [Euratom]'.[48] Consequently, Articles 1, 2, 6, 7, 14(1) and 15 to 23 (i.e. most of the provisions of the CPPNM) are part of the Euratom Community's *acquis*. Thus, among the articles applicable to it, Euratom could take into account an important aspect of nuclear security under the new Article 2A(1)(c) and (d) introduced by the CPPNM, which requires each State Party to '(c) protect[...] nuclear material and nuclear facilities against sabotage; and (d) mitigate[e] or minimis[e] the radiological consequences of sabotage' under its jurisdiction.

The safeguards agreements currently in force include the 78/164/Euratom agreement,[49] which is the only one to have been formally concluded as a Euratom Community agreement. This probably means that the other two have never been the subject of discussions in the Council concerning their adoption, but only of trilateral discussions between the IAEA, France and the European Commission. The 78/164/Euratom agreement implements the NPT by taking note of the distinction, introduced in 1970, between nuclear-weapon States and non-nuclear-weapon States. Its contracting parties are the non-nuclear-weapon

---

46 Ibid., para. 31. On this ruling, see J.P. Puissochet, 'À propos d'une délibération de la Cour de justice des Communautés européennes – Le régime des matières nucléaires et la capacité de la Communauté de conclure des accords internationaux', *Annuaire français de droit international*, 1978, n° 24, pp. 977–988. The competence in question is not a 'shared competence' in the strict sense of the term, because pursuant to Article 106a(1) of the Euratom Treaty, Article 2(2) TFEU does not apply to Euratom. Indeed, under Article 2(2) TFEU:

When the Treaties confer on the Union a competence shared with the Member States in a specific area, the Union and the Member States may legislate and adopt legally binding acts in that area. The Member States shall exercise their competence to the extent that the Union has not exercised its competence. The Member States shall again exercise their competence to the extent that the Union has decided to cease exercising its competence.

Thus, the Euratom Community's competence in the field of physical protection can be defined as a joint competence, which does not prevent or preclude the Member States from exercising the same competence even if the Community has already exercised its own and has not decided to cease exercising its own.

47 Ruling 1/78, ibid., para. 21.

48 Available at: https://eur-lex.europa.eu/eli/dec/2007/513/oj/eng.

49 [1978] *OJ* L51/2.

Member States, the IAEA and the Euratom Community (which is not a party to the NPT). The fifth recital of its preamble states in particular:

> WHEREAS Article III (1) of the Treaty provides that each non-nuclear-weapon State party to the Treaty undertakes to accept safeguards, as set forth in an agreement to be negotiated and concluded with the International Atomic Energy Agency (hereinafter referred to as 'the Agency') in accordance with the Statute of the Agency (hereinafter referred to as 'the Statute') and the Agency's safeguards system, for the exclusive purpose of verification of the fulfilment of its obligations assumed under this Treaty with a view to preventing diversion of nuclear energy from peaceful uses to nuclear weapons or other nuclear explosive devices.

We can see how problematic this position is in terms of the uniform application of Community law and EU law, given that the 78/164/Euratom agreement is part of the *acquis communautaire*: the majority of Member States are prohibited from doing what a minority (currently only France) has already done.

Moreover, according to the seventh recital, it is the European Commission, guardian of the uniform application of the Treaties, which must ensure that this state of positive law is respected:

> WHEREAS the States are members of the European Atomic Energy Community (Euratom) (hereinafter referred to as 'the Community') and have assigned to institutions common to the European Communities regulatory, executive and judicial powers which these institutions exercise in their own right in those areas for which they are competent and which may take effect directly within the legal systems of the Member States.

In practice, the Council is only informed of the implementation of the safeguards agreement by the Commission. This agreement introduces a system of joint inspections by the IAEA and Euratom within the Member States, except in France, the only nuclear-weapon Member State, where inspections are not joint. According to the last recital of the safeguards agreement, it is 'the desire of the Agency, the Community and the States to avoid unnecessary duplication of safeguard activities', which is reiterated in Article 4:

> The Agency, the Community and the States shall cooperate, in so far as each Party is concerned, to facilitate the implementation of the safeguards provided for in this Agreement and shall avoid unnecessary duplication of safeguards activities.

This provision is fundamental, as in practice the duplication of work is common. Euratom and IAEA inspectors try to complement each other as far as possible, while verifying the work carried out by the inspector from the other organisation. However, legally, such verification is not always necessary, so inspections can sometimes take place in the absence of an inspector from either organisation.

The 78/164/Euratom agreement must be read in conjunction with its additional 1999/188/Euratom protocol,[50] which entered into force on 30 April 2004. This introduces provisions which allow the IAEA to have certain direct exchanges with the Member States, thereby weakening the Community dimension of nuclear policies.[51] The absence of a consolidated agreement[52] makes it difficult to handle the two texts – the basic agreement and the additional protocol – together. This is all the more so since the *subsidiary arrangements* adopted under Article 39[53] of the 78/164/Euratom Agreement are common to the Agreement and its Additional Protocol. These subsidiary arrangements, which constitute a more detailed implementation of the Safeguards Agreement, have unfortunately never been published, which undoubtedly goes against current rules on transparency. Sensitive data could be redacted from a public version, which would then contain only the detailed legal rules.

Under the terms of Articles 4 and 5 of the 'Protocol' to the 78/164/Euratom Agreement (not to be confused with the 'Additional Protocol'), the IAEA and the Community periodically supplement the 'subsidiary arrangements' with 'facility attachments' relating to 'arrangements for facilities and material balance areas outside facilities'. These facility attachments constitute a concrete implementation of the safeguards agreement by the facility or material balance area outside the facilities and form an integral part of the subsidiary arrangements.

France applies the *Agreement of 27 July 1978 Between France, the European Atomic Energy Community and the International Atomic Energy Agency for the Application of Safeguards in France*,[54] which came into force on 12 September

50 Additional Protocol to the Agreement between the Republic of Austria, the Kingdom of Belgium, the Kingdom of Denmark, the Republic of Finland, the Federal Republic of Germany, the Hellenic Republic, Ireland, the Italian Republic, the Grand Duchy of Luxembourg, the Kingdom of the Netherlands, the Portuguese Republic, the Kingdom of Spain, the Kingdom of Sweden, the European Atomic Energy Community and the International Atomic Energy Agency in implementation of Article III(1) and (4) of the Treaty on the Non-proliferation of Nuclear weapons (notified under document number COM(1998) 314), [1999] *OJ* L67/1.

51 For example, Article 2 provides for a certain number of cases in which States provide the IAEA with a whole range of information directly, without going through the European Commission.

52 The consolidation of any legal instrument is a service provided by the Publications Office at the request of the department concerned.

53 'The Community shall make subsidiary arrangements with the Agency which shall specify in detail, to the extent necessary to permit the Agency to fulfil its responsibilities under this Agreement in an effective and efficient manner, how the procedures laid down in this Agreement are to be applied. The subsidiary arrangements may be extended or changed by agreement between the Agency and the Community without amendment of this Agreement'.

54 For the IAEA, INFCIRC ('*Information circular*')/290.

1981. This agreement was supplemented by an additional protocol dated 22 September 1998. The logic of this tripartite agreement is different from that of the 78/164/Euratom agreement: under the terms of Article 1, subparagraph a):

> France shall accept the application of safeguards, in accordance with the terms of this Agreement, on source or special fissionable material to be designated by France, in facilities or parts thereof within France, with a view to enabling the Agency to verify that such material is not withdrawn from civil activities, except as provided for in this Agreement.

This means that France itself designates the material that is subject to IAEA safeguards, without any Community or EU controls. Nevertheless, for civilian uses of source materials or special fissile products, France remains subject to safeguards like any other Member State of the Euratom Community.

France also applies the *Agreement between the French Republic, the European Atomic Energy Community and the International Atomic Energy Agency for the application of safeguards in connection with the Treaty for the Prohibition of Nuclear Weapons in Latin America and the Caribbean.*[55] Article 1 of this Agreement states:

> France undertakes to accept safeguards, in accordance with the terms of this Agreement, on all source or special fissionable material in all peaceful nuclear activities within French Protocol I territories for the exclusive purpose of verifying that such material is not diverted to nuclear weapons or other nuclear explosive devices.

France itself applies the objective of non-proliferation of nuclear weapons, including in its relations with the IAEA, but only on part of its territory.

Article 79 EAEC

The Commission shall require that operating records be kept and produced in order to permit accounting for ores, source materials and special fissile materials used or produced. The same requirement shall apply in the case of the transport of source materials and special fissile materials.

The first paragraph of Article 79 EAEC sets out a general obligation to keep nuclear accounts. The explicit reference to 'ores, source materials and special fissile materials used or produced' obviously does not exhaust all the powers implicit in safeguards. The article's second paragraph states:

[55] For the IAEA, INFCIRC/718 of 12 February 2008.

> Those subject to such requirements shall notify the authorities of the Member State concerned of any communications they make to the Commission pursuant to Article 78 and to the first paragraph of this Article.

'Those subject to such requirements' are the operators of nuclear installations, and their interlocutors are the relevant departments of the European Commission, as well as the national authorities. It should be noted that the existence of an independent national regulator responsible for nuclear safeguards is not a legal requirement under Euratom law. In some countries, such as France, regulators such as the French Nuclear Safety and Radiation Protection Authority (ASNR) do not intervene on nuclear safeguards.

Article 79(3) EAEC further provides:

> The nature and the extent of the requirements referred to in the first paragraph of this Article shall be defined in a regulation made by the Commission and approved by the Council.

The regulation 'made by the Commission and approved by the Council' is closer to the concept of regulation in national law than to that of regulations adopted by the Council or jointly by the Parliament and the Council. It is not an autonomous regulation similar to those under Article 37 of the French Constitution, for example, but the comparison with ordinances under Article 38 of the French Constitution is more apt. Whereas the French National Assembly may amend the provisions of an ordinance that has entered into force,[56] the Council may amend the Commission's proposal for a regulation before it is adopted.

Commission Regulation (Euratom) 2025/974, which entered into force in July 2025, merits a detailed commentary in its own right.[57] It is based on Articles 77, 78, 79 and 81 of the EAEC Treaty and is the successor to Regulations (Euratom) No 3227/76 and No 302/2005.[58] The first subparagraph of Article 8(1) of Regulation 2025/974 provides that 'the Commission adopts *particular safeguard provisions*' (emphasis added), which in practice are mostly aligned with the facility attachments under Agreement 78/164/Euratom.[59] The same article provides that 'the particular safeguard provisions shall be drawn

---

56 See Constitutional Council decision of 12 February 2015, no. 2015-710 DC, para. 7.

57 Commission Regulation (Euratom) 2025/974 of 26 May 2025 on the application of Euratom safeguards, C/2025/3204, [2025] *OJ* L2025/974.

58 Commission Regulation (Euratom) No 3227/76 of 19 October 1976 concerning the application of the provisions on Euratom safeguards, [1976] *OJ* L363/1; Commission Regulation (Euratom) No 302/2005 of 8 February 2005 on the application of Euratom Safeguards, [2005] *OJ* L54/1.

59 See above, commentary on Art. 77(b) EAEC.

up by means of a Commission decision addressed to the operator concerned, taking account of operational and technical constraints and after close consultation with the operator concerned and the relevant Member State'. In addition, the fifth subparagraph of Article 8(1) provides that '[t]he operator to whom a decision of the Commission is addressed shall be notified thereof, and a copy of such notification shall be transmitted to the relevant Member State'. Where there are particular safeguard provisions, these constitute a *lex specialis* which takes precedence over the general provisions.

The new Regulation, which repeals Regulation (Euratom) No 302/2005, is intended to update the nature and scope of the obligations referred to in Article 79 EAEC, 'in the light of developments, particularly in the fields of nuclear and information technology'.[60] Recital 17 specifies that up-to-date particular safeguard provisions at relevant installations are important for the implementation of safeguards. From this point of view, 'the Commission should continue to adopt particular safeguard provisions after close consultation with the operators and Member States concerned, paying particular attention to ensuring that they are up-to-date'. Recital 17 specifies *in fine* that 'to the extent possible, the Commission should strive to have particular safeguard provisions adopted before the installation is foreseen to start its operations'.

The new Regulation includes new definitions. For example, 'pool accounting' is defined for the first time as a 'specific accounting method whereby a unique obligation code (pool code) is used to declare book inventories and physical inventory listings to the Commission pursuant to Articles 14 and 15 of this Regulation, although the nuclear material may be subject to various specific safeguard obligations'.[61] Among the notable innovations is the provision in the fourth subparagraph of Article 3(1): 'for new installations [...], a preliminary declaration shall be provided to the Commission and the Member State concerned as soon as the main design options are defined to enable the inclusion of safeguards considerations early in the installation's planning stage'.

60 Recital 2 of the new Commission Regulation on the application of Euratom safeguards.
61 Art. 2, para. 38.

B. ARTICLE 78 EAEC

> Anyone setting up or operating an installation for the production, separation or other use of source materials or special fissile materials or for the processing of irradiated nuclear fuels shall declare to the Commission the basic technical characteristics of the installations, to the extent that knowledge of these characteristics is necessary for the attainment of the objectives set out in Article 77.
> The Commission must approve the techniques to be used for the chemical processing of irradiated materials, to the extent necessary to attain the objectives set out in Article 77.

The first paragraph introduces an obligation to declare the basic technical characteristics of each installation and, implicitly, to update them, at least on request. Unlike the fundamental technical characteristics of each facility, the processes to be used for the chemical treatment of irradiated materials are no longer simply declared, but approved by the Commission.

C. ARTICLES 81 TO 83 EAEC

> **Article 81**
>
> The Commission may send inspectors into the territories of Member States. Before sending an inspector on his first assignment in the territory of a Member State, the Commission shall consult the State concerned; such consultation shall suffice to cover all future assignments of this inspector.

There is no need to adopt secondary legislation concerning the conduct of Euratom inspections, as primary legislation is sufficiently detailed. For example, Member States approve the appointment of each inspector, ensuring in particular that their security clearance is in order.

> On presentation of a document establishing their authority, inspectors shall at all times have access to all places and data and to all persons who, by reason of their occupation, deal with materials, equipment or installations subject to the safeguards provided for in this Chapter, to the extent necessary in order to apply such safeguards to ores, source materials and special fissile materials and to ensure compliance with the provisions of Article 77. Should the State concerned so request, inspectors appointed by the Commission shall be accompanied by representatives of the authorities of that State; however, the inspectors shall not thereby be delayed or otherwise impeded in the performance of their duties.

Under the terms of the second paragraph of Article 81 of the Euratom Convention, Euratom inspectors 'shall at all times have access to all places and data and to all persons who, by reason of their occupation, deal with materials, equipment or installations subject to the safeguards provided for in this Chapter'. Their mission is not defined in detail, so each inspector can define it themself, in agreement with their superiors and the operator of the installation.

> If the carrying out of an inspection is opposed, the Commission shall apply to the President of the Court of Justice of the European Union for an order to ensure that the inspection be carried out compulsorily. The President of the Court of Justice of the European Union shall give a decision within three days.

It is clear that, since 1958, there have already been cases of opposition to the performance of a security check, yet the Commission has never requested an 'order' from the President of the Court of Justice. It would be interesting to test the possibility of the President of the Court of Justice issuing such an order within three days.

> If there is danger in delay, the Commission may itself issue a written order, in the form of a decision, to proceed with the inspection. This order shall be submitted without delay to the President of the Court of Justice of the European Union for subsequent approval.

The Commission has never made use of this possibility. It is a power that has never been exercised.

> After the order or decision has been issued, the authorities of the State concerned shall ensure that the inspectors have access to the places specified in the order or decision

The last paragraph of Article 81 EAEC sets out the procedures for the execution of such mandates or decisions.

> **Article 82 EAEC**
>
> Inspectors shall be recruited by the Commission.
>
> They shall be responsible for obtaining and verifying the records referred to in Article 79. They shall report any infringement to the Commission.

Euratom inspectors have several means at their disposal to carry out their tasks, one of the main ones being the control of nuclear accounting.

> The Commission may issue a directive calling upon the Member State concerned to take, by a time limit set by the Commission, all measures necessary to bring such infringement to an end; it shall inform the Council thereof.
>
> If the Member State does not comply with the Commission directive by the time limit set, the Commission or any Member State concerned may, in derogation from Articles 258 and 259 of the Treaty on the Functioning of the European Union, refer the matter to the Court of Justice of the European Union direct

This power is not exercised by the Commission either, which prefers to make use of the *lex generalis* of Articles 258 and 259 TFEU, by means of administrative exchanges, possibly a letter of formal notice, followed by a reasoned opinion, prior to the introduction of any action for failure to fulfil obligations. But these measures are used more in relation to the nuclear safety *acquis*. With regard to nuclear safeguards, the Commission has always managed to resolve disputes amicably over the last few decades.

> **Article 83 EAEC**
>
> **1.** In the event of an infringement on the part of persons or undertakings of the obligations imposed on them by this Chapter, the Commission may impose sanctions on such persons or undertakings.
>
> These sanctions shall be in order of severity:
>
> **a)** a warning;
>
> **b)** the withdrawal of special benefits such as financial or technical assistance;
>
> **c)** the placing of the undertaking for a period not exceeding four months under the administration of a person or board appointed by common accord of the Commission and the State having jurisdiction over the undertaking;
>
> **d)** total or partial withdrawal of source materials or special fissile materials

The main difference in terms of the safeguards carried out by the IAEA and Euratom[62] in non-nuclear-weapon States lies in the powers that enable

[62] The only other supra-state regional organisation of the same type as Euratom in the world is the Argentine-Brazilian Agency for Accounting and Control of Nuclear Materials. However, the IAEA enjoys greater political support than Euratom, which does not send nuclear inspectors to third countries due to the lack of international agreements allowing it to do so.

Euratom, represented by the Commission, to have direct dealings with the operators of nuclear installations and, where appropriate, to impose sanctions. However, Commission decisions imposing penalties under Article 83(1) EAEC are not always published because of the sensitive or even classified information they contain. They have rarely been commented on by legal writers.

> **2.** Decisions taken by the Commission in implementation of paragraph 1 and requiring the surrender of materials shall be enforceable. They may be enforced in the territories of Member States in accordance with Article 164.
>
> By way of derogation from Article 157, appeals brought before the Court of Justice of the European Union against decisions of the Commission which impose any of the sanctions provided for in paragraph 1 shall have suspensory effect. The Court of Justice of the European Union may, however, on application by the Commission or by any Member State concerned, order that the decision be enforced forthwith.
>
> There shall be an appropriate legal procedure to ensure the protection of interests that have been prejudiced.
>
> **3.** The Commission may make any recommendations to Member States concerning laws or regulations which are designed to ensure compliance in their territories with the obligations arising under this Chapter.
>
> **4.** Member States shall ensure that sanctions are enforced and, where necessary, that the infringements are remedied by those committing them.

Article 83(2) EAEC is also little used in practice. Almost every time sanctions have been imposed on nuclear operators, it has not been necessary to ask the Member State concerned to enforce them, as they have quickly proved effective and dissuasive.

D. ARTICLE 84 EAEC

> **Article 84 EAEC**
>
> In the application of the safeguards, no discrimination shall be made on grounds of the use for which ores, source materials and special fissile materials are intended.
>
> The scope of and procedure for the safeguards and the powers of the bodies responsible for their application shall be confined to the attainment of the objectives set out in this Chapter.

The safeguards may not extend to materials intended to meet defence requirements which are in the course of being specially processed for this purpose or which, after being so processed, are, in accordance with an operational plan, placed or stored in a military establishment.

As already stated in the introduction, safeguards should have been able to extend to nuclear materials intended for defence purposes which are not being specially processed for such purposes or which, after such processing, are not located or stored in a military establishment. In other words, according to the wording of Article 84 EAEC, as long as the manufacture of nuclear weapons has not begun in earnest, it could be prohibited; similarly, any nuclear weapon which, once manufactured, is not located or stored in a military establishment (which, so to speak, 'is wandering in the wildness', is the subject of trafficking or is intended for export) could fall under the scope of safeguards. Thus, 'all routine operations for the preparation of special fissile materials (the essential material of nuclear weapons), from the extraction of the ore to the isotopic separation of uranium 235, or the chemical separation of plutonium or uranium 233, as the case may be',[63] are subject to safeguards. Early commentators on this provision have further stated:

> On the other hand, all operations involving details of the design and manufacture of weapons are exempt from control. It should also be noted that if materials – thus exempted from control – ceased at any given time to be used in military devices or stored in a military establishment, they would fall back under the application of the Euratom control provisions'.[64]

It is true that the Court of Justice held, notably in the judgment of 12 April 2005, *Commission v. United Kingdom*, cited above, that military activities 'fall outside the scope of this Treaty'.[65] Subsequent judgments have reiterated and consolidated this position, in even more general terms:

---

63 J. Errera, E. Symon, J. Van der Meulen, I. Vernaeve: *Euratom, Analyse et Commentaires du Traité*, Bibliothèque de l'Institut belge de science politique, Brussels, Éditions de la Librairie encyclopédique, 1958, p. 161. Translated here.

64 Ibid.

65 Case C-61/03, *Commission of the European Communities v United Kingdom of Great Britain and Northern Ireland* (Jason Decommissioning Case), ECLI:EU:C:2005:210, para. 36. It should be noted that the justification proposed by the Court in the same point of the judgment bears the stamp of considerations of expediency: 'it is clear that the application of such provisions [of Chapters 1 and 3 of the Euratom Treaty] to military installations, research programmes and other activities *might be such as to compromise essential national defence interests of the Member States. Consequently*, as the United Kingdom and the French Republic have rightly argued, *the absence in the Treaty of any derogation laying down the*

the use of nuclear energy for military purposes falls outside the scope of all the provisions of the EAEC Treaty, not just some of them.[66]

However, this case law could gradually evolve, especially based on Article 106a(3) EAEC.[67]

V. ARTICLES 101 TO 103 EAEC

CHAPTER 10. External relations

Article 101 EAEC

The Community may, within the limits of its powers and jurisdiction, enter into obligations by concluding agreements or contracts with a third State, an international organisation or a national of a third State.

Under the Euratom Treaty, which innovates in this respect concerning the ECSC and TEC Treaties, the AETR case law[68] is partly unnecessary because the external competences implicit in the TFEU are explicit in the Euratom Treaty.[69]

Such agreements or contracts shall be negotiated by the Commission in accordance with the directives of the Council; they shall be concluded by the Commission with the approval of the Council, which shall act by a qualified majority.

In the field of external relations, the European Commission has more powers as an institution of the Euratom Community than as an institution of the Union, since it is especially the Commission which concludes agreements

detailed rules according to which the Member States would be authorised to rely on and protect those essential interests leads to the conclusion that activities falling within the military sphere are outside the scope of that Treaty'. (Emphasis added.)

66 Case C-65/04, *Commission of the European Communities v United Kingdom of Great Britain and Northern Ireland*, ECLI:EU:C:2006:161, para. 26.

67 See the commentary on this article below.

68 Case 22/70, *Commission of the European Communities v Council of the European Communities, European Agreement on Road Transport*, ECLI:EU:C:1971:32. See M. Dony, 'Retour sur les compétences externes implicites de l'Union', *Cahiers de droit européen*, no. 1/2018, pp. 109–176.

69 See P. Koutrakos, 'Case C-29/99 *Commission v. Council (re: Nuclear Safety Convention)*' (2004) 41(1) *Common Market Law Review*, pp. 191–208, p. 192: 'It was precisely the absence of a provision such as Article 101(1) of the Euratom Treaty in the EC Treaty that led the Court of Justice to the introduction of the principle of implied powers in *ERTA*, which then gave rise to a considerable body of case-law and an even more considerable volume of academic debate'.

or conventions with third States, international organisations or with citizens of third States, simply with the approval of the Council (Article 101, second paragraph, EAEC), whereas it is the Council which adopts a decision concluding the agreement under the TFEU (Article 218(6)).

> Agreements or contracts whose implementation does not require action by the Council and can be effected within the limits of the relevant budget shall, however, be negotiated and concluded solely by the Commission; the Commission shall keep the Council informed

The third subparagraph allows the Commission to negotiate and conclude agreements or conventions binding the Community, simply by informing the Council, but without its formal approval, provided that their implementation can be ensured within the limits of the budget concerned. This does not usually happen, of course, as most international agreements have budgetary implications. Nevertheless, this provision enshrines a kind of autonomous regulatory power for the Commission in the Community's external relations: the comparison with this concept in national law is enlightening here.

Article 101 EAEC is the essential complement to Article 77(b) EAEC concerning the Euratom Community's international undertakings on safeguards.

VI. ARTICLE 106A EAEC

> **TITLE III. INSTITUTIONAL AND FINANCIAL PROVISIONS**
>
> **CHAPTER 1. Application of certain provisions of the Treaty on European Union and the Treaty on the Functioning of the European Union**
>
> **Article 106a EAEC**
>
> **1.** Article 7, Articles 13 to 19, Article 48(2) to (5), and Articles 49 and 50 of the Treaty on European Union, and Article 15, Articles 223 to 236, Articles 237 to 244, Article 245, Articles 246 to 270, Article 272, 273 and 274, Articles 277 to 281, Articles 285 to 304, Articles 310 to 320, Articles 322 to 325 and Articles 336, 342 and 344 of the Treaty on the Functioning of the European Union, and the Protocol on Transitional Provisions, shall apply to this Treaty.

> **2.** Within the framework of this Treaty, the references to the Union, to the 'Treaty on European Union', to the 'Treaty on the Functioning of the European Union' or to the 'Treaties' in the provisions referred to in paragraph 1 and those in the protocols annexed both to those Treaties and to this Treaty shall be taken, respectively, as references to the European Atomic Energy Community and to this Treaty.
> **3.** The provisions of the Treaty on European Union and of the Treaty on the Functioning of the European Union shall not derogate from the provisions of this Treaty.

From a legislative point of view, Article 106a EAEC, introduced by the Treaty of Lisbon, is an enigma. Its first two paragraphs enshrine the will of the constituent power to indicate clearly which provisions of the TEU and TFEU apply to the Euratom Community. However, if this list of provisions was supposed to be exhaustive to clarify the case law prior to the Treaty of Lisbon, it is difficult to explain why it was necessary to repeat, in the third and last paragraph of Article 106a EAEC, the wording of Article 305(2) TEC.[70] It should be remembered that Article 305 TEC, repealed by the Treaty of Lisbon, governed the relationship between the general EC Treaty and the sectoral Treaties establishing the other two Communities. However, according to Article 305 TEC, the provisions of the EC Treaty were not to 'amend' those of the ECSC Treaty, while the provisions of the EC Treaty (now the TEU and TFEU) were not to 'derogate' from the provisions of the Euratom Treaty.[71] The first wording can be explained by the fact that the ECSC Treaty predates the two Treaties of Rome (consequently, the ECSC Treaty was not to be amended by the Treaty of Rome). The fact remains that 'amend' and 'derogate' do not mean the same thing, so that the application, by analogy, of the case law on relations between the ECSC and the EEC to those between the Union and the Euratom Community would be marred by a methodological difficulty.[72]

---

70 It has to be said that, in the absence of unambiguous interpretations in the case law, Article 106a EAEC does not allow a decision to be taken between the application of the maxim *expressio unius est exclusio alterius* and the application of the case law prior to the entry into force of the Treaty of Lisbon (see J. Grunwald, 'Der Euratom-Vertrag nach Lissabon', in C. Calliess (ed.), *Herausforderungen an Staat und Verfassung*, Baden-Baden, Nomos, 2015, pp. 543–559).

71 Art. 305 TEC (former Art. 232): 1. The provisions of this Treaty shall not affect those of the Treaty establishing the European Coal and Steel Community, in particular as regards the rights and obligations of Member States, the powers of the institutions of that Community and the rules laid down by that Treaty for the functioning of the common market in coal and steel. 2. The provisions of this Treaty shall not derogate from the provisions of the Treaty establishing the European Atomic Energy Community.

72 See Case T-6/99, *ESF Elbe-Stahlwerke Feralpi GmbH v Commission of the European Communities*, ECLI:EU:T:2001:145, para. 102: 'the ECSC Treaty constitutes a *lex specialis* derogating from the *lex generalis* which is the EC Treaty'. The analogy is tempting because of

Paragraph 3 of Article 106a EAEC states: 'The provisions of the Treaty on European Union and of the Treaty on the Functioning of the European Union shall not derogate from the provisions of this Treaty'. Even if 'derogate' here means 'to make an exception to the principle' or 'to set aside the application of a rule in a particular case', the current case law seems to be based on the wording of the Euratom Treaty,[73] the jurisprudence seems to be inspired by the wording of the Euratom Treaty in German, which reads (in Article 106a(2) EAEC): '*beinträchtigen nicht die Vorschriften dieses Vertrags*'. In other words, derogations 'do not compromise' the provisions of the Euratom Treaty. This raises the question of how the TFEU could compromise the useful effect of the Euratom Treaty. The implicit understanding is that even if a provision of the TEU or the TFEU is not listed in Article 106a EAEC, it can still be applied to the nuclear sector, on a case-by-case basis, if the Court of Justice so decides, because this would hardly compromise or undermine the useful effect of the provisions of the Euratom Treaty. This is what should be retained from the judgment in *Austria v. Commission* judgment of 22 September 2020:

> First, the Euratom Treaty and the FEU Treaty have the same legal value, as illustrated by Article 106a(3) of the Euratom Treaty, according to which the provisions of the EU Treaty and the FEU Treaty are not to derogate from the provisions of the Euratom Treaty. As the Advocate General has observed in points 37 and 38 of his Opinion, since the Euratom Treaty is a sectoral treaty directed at the development of nuclear energy, whereas the FEU Treaty has much more far-reaching aims and confers upon the European Union extensive competences in numerous areas and sectors, *the rules of the FEU Treaty apply in the nuclear energy sector when the Euratom Treaty does not contain specific rules. Accordingly, since the Euratom Treaty does not contain rules concerning State aid, Article 107 TFEU may be applied in that sector* [...].[74] (Emphasis added.)

If Article 107 TFEU can be applied to the nuclear sector, even though it does not appear in the provisions listed in Article 106a EAEC, it may be asked if Article 42(1) TEU may not also be applied.

Similarly, a number of legislative acts already apply to the nuclear sector even though their legal basis is the TFEU. For example, Regulation (EU) 2021/821 of 'dual-use items', an instrument of Union law and not of the Euratom Community based on Article 207(2) TFEU, makes it possible to prevent nuclear proliferation directly by controlling exports of so-called

---

the CFI's use of the verb 'derogate' in relation to the relationship between the EC and ECSC Treaties, instead of 'not amend', as it should have done in accordance with the wording of Article 305(1) TEC.

[73] See G. Cornu, *Vocabulaire juridique*, Paris, PUF, 2000.

[74] Case C-594/18 P, *Republic of Austria v European Commission*, ECLI:EU:C:2020:742, para. 32.

'dual-use' items, i.e. items that can be used for both civilian and military purposes.[75] This instrument makes the export of certain dual-use goods subject to authorisation. Refusal of authorisation makes it possible to effectively combat nuclear proliferation in third countries. The definition of dual-use items in Article 2(1) of Regulation (EU) 2021/821 explicitly refers to nuclear weapons (emphasis added):

> For the purposes of this Regulation [...], 'dual-use items' means items, including software and technology, which can be used for both civil and military purposes, and includes items which can be used for the design, development, production or use of *nuclear*, chemical or biological *weapons* or their means of delivery, including all items which can be used for both non-explosive uses and assisting in any way in the manufacture of *nuclear weapons or other nuclear explosive devices*.[76]

VII. CONCLUSION

When the Treaty of Lisbon came into force in 2009, the EU absorbed the European Community (the successor to the European Economic Community). Nevertheless, the Euratom Treaty has been maintained outside the *acquis* of the Union, with the repeal of certain institutional provisions, the removal of the possibility of simple majority voting in the Council and the addition of a new Article 106a EAEC, the third paragraph of which reproduces the wording of Article 305(2) TEC.

Olivier Dupéré believes that the Treaty of Lisbon has 'strengthened the potential for complementarity' between the Euratom Treaty and the TFEU by virtue of the fact that Article 305(2) TEC is not included in the TFEU (but in the Euratom Treaty), which would be tantamount to a repeal.[77] This potential for complementarity is to be found everywhere, including in the Common Security and Defence Policy. For example, there is no legal obstacle to the

---

75 Regulation (EU) 2021/821 of the European Parliament and of the Council of 20 May 2021 setting up a Union regime for the control of exports, brokering, technical assistance, transit and transfers of dual-use items (recast), [2021] *OJ* L206/1. See the commentaries on this Regulation by A. Millet-Devalle and on Article 207 TFEU by S. Robert-Cuendet in this publication.

76 See also Category 0 relating to 'nuclear materials, facilities and equipment' in Annex I, which lists the DUIs covered by the regulation. For an analysis of Regulation (EU) 2021/821, see A. Millet-Devalle in this publication.

77 O. Dupéré, 'Cinquante ans de jurisprudence pour un traité sexagénaire: le façonnage de la structure du traité Euratom par la Cour de Justice', *Revue de l'Union européenne*, 2018, pp. 326 et seq. Keeping a provision not in the TFEU, which incorporates most of the provisions of the EC Treaty, but in another treaty (the Euratom Treaty), is tantamount to repealing that provision and modifying the structure of that other treaty.

communitarianism of nuclear deterrence: even if France is the only nuclear-weapon Member State, control of the French nuclear arsenal could be exercised jointly with France's European partners. This is essentially what the first commentators on the Euratom Treaty invited us to do – before any Member State had nuclear weapons – namely to develop more in-depth international cooperation on the control of the European and international nuclear arsenal:

> Euratom control therefore makes it possible to know at any time which nuclear materials are used for peaceful purposes and which are used for military purposes. To extend this, i.e. to know in the latter case for which type of weapons the materials are being used, and what stock levels of these weapons are, is not within the remit of a treaty such as this, which is not intended to restrict the sovereignty of Member States as regards their national defence. But another international agreement, dealing not with nuclear materials in general, but with armaments and their limitations, could provide for a separate organisation exercising control in military establishments and, in short, taking over from Euratom control where the latter stops'.[78]

This new international agreement, which allows for the establishment of a separate body (perhaps a new European agency?) to exercise control over military establishments, could, all things considered, require the adoption of a new secondary legal instrument, the Treaty on European Union, which did not exist when the aforementioned commentary on the Euratom Treaty was published.

[78] J. Errera, E. Symon, J. Van der Meulen and I. Vernaeve: *Euratom, Analyse et Commentaires du Traité*, Bibliothèque de l'Institut belge de science politique, Brussels, Éditions de la Librairie encyclopédique, 1958, pp. 161–162.

ALPHABETICAL INDEX

The index entries refer to page numbers.

EU LAW TABLE

I. TEU

II. TFEU

III. DECLARATIONS AND PROTOCOLS

IV. EURATOM TREATY

V. DIRECTIVES

VI. REGULATIONS

VII. DECISIONS

LIST OF CASES

I. COURT OF JUSTICE OF THE EUROPEAN UNION (CJEU)

II. GENERAL COURT OF THE EUROPEAN UNION (GC)

III. INTERNATIONAL COURT OF JUSTICE

www.ingramcontent.com/pod-product-compliance
Ingram Content Group UK Ltd.
Pitfield, Milton Keynes, MK11 3LW, UK
UKHW051905290926
8980IPUK00017B/1778

9 781839 705755